CASES AND MATERIALS ON
CRIMINAL LAW

By

Joshua Dressler
Professor of Law
McGeorge School of Law
University of the Pacific

AMERICAN CASEBOOK SERIES®

WEST GROUP

Bancroft-Whitney • Banks-Baldwin • Clark Boardman Callaghan
Lawyers Cooperative Publishing • WESTLAW • West Publishing

ISBN 0–314–03791–8

3rd Reprint–1998

*But the student should not imagine, that enough is done, if he has so far mastered the general doctrines of the common law, that he may enter with some confidence into practice. There are other studies, which demand his attention. He should addict himself to the study of philosophy, of rhetoric, of history, and of human nature. It is from the want of this enlarged view of duty, that the profession has sometimes been reproached *** with a deficiency in liberal and enlightened policy.*

Joseph Story, "The Value and Importance of Legal Studies,"
in Miscellaneous Writings of Joseph Story 527
(William W. Story ed. 1852)

*

Preface

This casebook was prepared for use in a basic course on criminal law. Although it is designed for a three- or four-unit semester-long class, the casebook will also work well in a shorter course, with deletions, some lecturing, and/or use of outside readings.

As its "author" I bring to this casebook my own experiences and philosophies, but ultimately the book is intended for *your* use, and not simply to please me. Therefore, the cases and readings were selected, the Notes and Questions formulated, and the casebook organized, so that it can comfortably be used by teachers who do not share all, or even most, of my pedagogical goals.

My goals in teaching criminal law. I have taught Criminal Law for nearly twenty years, in five different law schools, to students with widely varied academic backgrounds and capacities, life experiences, and levels of interest in the subject. But, I have always been guided in my teaching by certain general principles:

—Doctrine matters. I use the term "doctrine" here broadly to mean that students ought to leave a course in Criminal Law with a substantial body of knowledge. In the context of this casebook, this means that students will become familiar with the general and the specific: primary attention is directed to the "general part" of the criminal law, i.e., the common law principles of criminal responsibility that serve even today as the core of Anglo-American criminal law; but, as the general cannot be understood except in the context of the specific, some of the most important crimes against persons and property are covered in detail, both in their common law and modern statutory forms.

—In understanding doctrine, penal theory matters. A course in Criminal Law offers students an opportunity to consider jurisprudential concerns more forthrightly than in other first-year courses. Therefore, I want students to put the criminal law in its philosophical context, in particular, to test the rules of criminal responsibility by the standards of retributivism and utilitarianism, in order to see if the criminal law is fair, rational, or even intellectually consistent. I teach my class, and this casebook is written, with the view that these principles of punishment can inform our understanding of the law and guide us in our efforts to reform it.

—In understanding doctrine, other things matter, too. Since the criminal law seeks to affect and to render judgments about human behavior, it seems prudent to take some note of the findings of the behavioral sciences, e.g., psychology, anthropology, and sociology. Students should also see that social, economic, and political forces inevitably shape

the law. Often these forces are noncontroversial, but not always. Therefore, the materials in the casebook invite discussion regarding social
attitudes about such matters as race, gender, and sexual orientation,
where they may have had a substantial impact on the development or
application of the criminal law (e.g., rape law, self-defense, provocation,
the death penalty).

    —Statutes matter. Students start law school bewildered by the case
method of study, yet they so quickly grow accustomed to it that many
of them lose interest in statutes, even when good lawyering requires
their attention. Consequently, I have selected materials that help students understand the rules of statutory construction and appreciate the
lawyering skills relating to statutory interpretation. Also, the casebook
emphasizes the Model Penal Code, in part so that students have ample
opportunity to work with an integrated criminal code.

    —Professional ethics matter. Even before they take courses on crim-
inal procedure and professional responsibility, students should be sensi-
tized to some of the ethical issues confronting criminal defense lawyers
and prosecutors. I have selected various cases in part because they lend
themselves to discussion of professional ethics, in case the teacher wishes
to follow this route.

    —Controversy in the classroom is good if discussion of it is thought-
ful, wide-open, and relevant. I want students to be angry—or pleased—
with where the law may be going, because this means that they understand that the criminal law matters deeply in everyones' lives. Consequently, I want students to be aware of the "cutting edge" controversies
in the criminal law. In support of this, the casebook is attentive to the
Model Penal Code, since virtually all recently drafted penal codes are
based, at least in part, on it, and because it provides a thoughtful alternative to the common law. The casebook also brings to the forefront—it
does not shy away from—many present-day controversies, such as the
death penalty, subjectivization of the objective "reasonable man" standard, "battered woman/child self-defense," suicide assistance and euthanasia, and acquaintance rape.

    As I stated earlier, although this casebook is shaped by the preced-
ing principles, it was prepared for use by teachers whose pedagogical
goals may differ from mine. I do expect, however, that there will be at
least one common link among adopters of this book: A belief that Criminal Law is an exciting subject to teach, in large part because it allows
students to confront some of the Big Questions—questions about human
nature, personal and social responsibility, and "right and wrong"—that
philosophers, theologians, scientists, and poets, as well as lawyers, have
grappled with for centuries.

    Editing policies. I prefer students to read judicial opinions in largely
intact form. Nonetheless, deletions are necessary. Because this book is
intended for pedagogical use, rather than for serious scholarly pursuits,
I have not followed all scholarly conventions in identifying omissions
from the extracted materials. Therefore, users of the book should not

quote directly from the extracts in legal or scholarly documents, but should instead go to the primary sources. Specifically, I have applied the following rules of thumb to extracted materials:

1. Footnotes and citations have been omitted, unless there was a sound pedagogical reason for their retention. Neither ellipses nor other signals have been used to indicate their omission. Asterisks or brackets have been used, however, to indicate deletions of other textual material.

2. Numbered footnotes are from the original materials and retain their original numbering. My own footnotes are designated by letters.

Outside reading materials. Students who wish to go beyond the casebook for additional study will find excellent references in various forms. Among "hornbooks," I recommend the following, in alphabetical order:

Joshua Dressler, Understanding Criminal Law (Matthew Bender & Co. 1987). This book, addressed to law students, focuses on the issues most commonly covered in criminal law casebooks. Obviously, it is especially suited for use with this casebook. A second edition will be published in the near future.

Wayne LaFave and Austin Scott, Jr., Criminal Law (West Publishing Co. 2d ed. 1986). The student edition is an abridgement of the authors' two-volume lawyers' treatise. Widely cited by courts and lucidly written, it emphasizes modern law and the Model Penal Code.

Rollin M. Perkins and Ronald N. Boyce, Criminal Law (Foundation Press 3d ed. 1982). The late Professor Perkins, one of the foremost scholars of the common law of crimes, originated this treatise. It remains strong in setting out the common law definitions of crimes. There is no special student edition.

Glanville Williams, Criminal Law: The General Part (Stevens & Sons 2d ed. 1961). Written by one of England's paramount scholars, this is the classic English treatise on the general principles of the criminal law.

By far the best reference source regarding the Model Penal Code is:

American Law Institute, Model Penal Code and Commentaries (1980 and 1985). This six-volume reference contains all of the sections of the Model Penal Code and their supporting Commentaries. The Commentaries are exceedingly helpful in explaining pre-Code law and the method and rationale of Code provisions.

Among the best books dealing with the underlying theories of the criminal law are:

George P. Fletcher, Rethinking Criminal Law (Little Brown & Co. 1978). Building heavily on common law traditions and the views of Continental, especially German, legal theorists, the author has written "neither a hornbook nor a treatise, but a reformist, critical work." (Preface, xxiii.) This book has deservedly received substantial scholarly attention since its publication.

Jerome Hall, General Principles of Criminal Law (Bobbs Merrill 2d ed. 1960). Now a classic in the field, the author states as his goal, "to elucidate the basic ideas of criminal law in light of current knowledge and to organize the law in terms of definite theory." (Preface, v.) The book centers on the general part of the criminal law.

H.L.A. Hart, Punishment and Responsibility (Oxford University Press 1968). This book contains previously published essays by the author, then Professor of Jurisprudence at Oxford University, regarding theories of punishment and legal standards of responsibility. These writings have greatly influenced thinking on the subjects.

Leo Katz, Bad Acts and Guilty Minds: Conundrums of the Criminal Law (University of Chicago Press 1987). Katz draws on insights from philosophy, psychology, and anthropology, as well as on well-known fictional incidents, to reflect on the basic concepts of the criminal law. Written for a general audience, the book provides considerable "food for thought."

Personal acknowledgements.[a] Many people assisted me in producing this book. Various colleagues offered useful advice and specific suggestions (many of which found their way into the book), including: Peter Arenella (UCLA); Pamela Bucy (Alabama); Linda Carter (McGeorge); Deborah Denno (Fordham); Catherine Hancock (Tulane); Yale Kamisar (Michigan); Leo Katz (Pennsylvania); Larry Levine (McGeorge); Fred Lawrence (Boston University); Steve Morse (Pennsylvania); Michael Perlin (New York); Michael Vitiello (McGeorge); and David Yellen (Hofstra). Especially generous with their time were two of my colleagues from Wayne State University: Lee Lamborn, who gave me many leads on materials to include in the text; and Jessica Litman, who was amazingly patient as I hounded her with copyright law questions.

My student research assistants helped me search for cases, commented on early drafts of the manuscript, and did critical cite checking. From Wayne State, I thank Joseph Hart, Sarah Resnick, Ted Tow and Michael Zousmer; from McGeorge, my thanks go to Sidonie Christian, Debra Larson, and Barry deWalt.

Thanks also go to June Frierson (Wayne State), on whom I called often for assistance in typing and reproduction of the manuscript. She did this work for me promptly, well, and with good humor.

I must also mention a few people who have helped me in very special ways. John Dolan and Lee Lamborn (Wayne State) are, quite simply, mensches. No matter how busy they were, their office doors were open to me when my work on the casebook—or life in general—temporarily got me down. They were and are true friends.

Nobody has provided me with greater support and love over the years than my partner in life, Dottie Kridler Dressler. I am not exagger-

---

a Copyright acknowledgements are separately listed.

ating when I say that this casebook would not have been born without her presence by my side.

Finally, I want to acknowledge two other persons who have influenced me. The first is David Dressler, who during his too-short life was Chief of Parole for New York State, a professor of both sociology and criminology, a scholar and talented writer (many of us are the former, but few are the latter), and, most importantly, was my father. He never said, "Be as I am" or "Look at me," but nobody has been a more powerful role model in my life than he.

The other person whose influence cannot be understated is Sandy Kadish, one of this country's most thoughtful criminal law scholars and legal educators. Nobody can look at this casebook without realizing his influence on it. And, how could it be otherwise? I studied criminal law from his casebook (Paulsen and Kadish; and then Kadish and Paulsen) and, for fifteen years, I taught the subject from his book (now, Kadish and Schulhofer). With the publication of my own casebook comes my professional *bar mitzvah*, but I can think of no higher accolade than if someone were to say of this book, "Why, it is a son-of-Kadish (and Schulhofer)."

JOSHUA DRESSLER

April, 1994

*

Acknowledgements

I am grateful to the copyright holders for permission to reproduce portions of the following materials:

Susan Ager, "The Incident," *Detroit Free Press Magazine*, March 22, 1992, p. 17. Copyright © 1992, Susan Ager. Reprinted by permission of the author.

Ralph B. Allison, *The Possession Syndrome On Trial*, 6 American Journal of Forensic Psychiatry 46 (1985). Copyright © 1985, The American Journal of Forensic Psychiatry. This article is reprinted from the *American Journal of Forensic Psychiatry*, Volume 6, issue 1, 1985. The Journal is a publication of the American College of Forensic Psychiatry, 26701 Quail Creek, #295, Laguna Hills, CA 92656. Reprinted with permission.

American Law Institute, Model Penal Code and Commentaries, copyright © 1962, 1980, and 1985 by The American Law Institute. Reprinted with the permission of The American Law Institute.

Peter Arenella, *Convicting the Morally Blameless: Reassessing the Relationship Between Legal and Moral Accountability*, 39 UCLA L. Rev. 1511 (1992). Copyright © 1992, Peter Arenella. Reprinted by permission.

Peter Arenella, *The Diminished Capacity and Diminished Responsibility Defenses: Two Children of a Doomed Marriage*, 77 Columbia Law Review 827 (1977). Copyright © 1977 by the Directors of the Columbia Law Review Association, Inc. All Rights Reserved. This article originally appeared at 77 Colum. L. Rev. 827 (1977). Reprinted by permission.

Andrew Ashworth, *Criminal Attempts and the Role of Resulting Harm Under the Code, and in the Common Law*, 19 Rutgers Law Journal 725 (1988). Copyright © 1988, Rutgers School of Law, Camden. Reprinted by permission of *Rutgers Law Journal* and the author.

Steve M. Bauer & Peter J. Eckerstrom, *The State Made Me Do It: The Applicability of the Necessity Defense to Civil Disobedience*, 39 Stanford Law Review 1173 (1987). Copyright © 1987 by the Board of Trustees of the Leland Stanford Junior University. Reprinted by permission of *Stanford Law Review* and Fred B. Rothman & Co.

Vivian Berger, *Not So Simple Rape*, Criminal Justice Ethics, Vol. 7, No. 1 (Winter/Spring 1988) pp. 75–77. Copyright © 1988, Criminal Justice Ethics. Reprinted by permission of the Institute for Criminal Justice Ethics and the author.

Joshua Dressler, *Exegesis of the Law of Duress: Justifying the Excuse and Searching for its Proper Limits*, 62 Southern California Law Review 1331–1386 (1989). Copyright © 1989, University of Southern California. Reprinted with the permission of the *Southern California Law Review*.

Joshua Dressler, *Reflections on Excusing Wrongdoers: Moral Theory, New Excuses, and the Model Penal Code*, 19 Rutgers Law Journal 671 (1988). Copyright © 1988, Rutgers School of Law, Camden. Reprinted by permission.

Joshua Dressler, *Justifications and Excuses: A Brief Review of the Concepts and the Literature*, 33 Wayne Law Review 1155 (1987). Copyright © 1987, Wayne State University. Reprinted by permission.

Joshua Dressler, *Reassessing the Theoretical Underpinnings of Accomplice Liability: New Solutions to an Old Problem*, 37 Hastings Law Journal 91 (1985). Copyright © 1985, Hastings College of the Law, reprinted from 37 Hastings L.J. 91 by permission.

Joshua Dressler, *Reaffirming the Moral Legitimacy of the Doctrine of Diminished Capacity: A Brief Reply to Professor Morse*, 75 Journal of Criminal Law & Criminology 953 (1984). Copyright © 1984, Joshua Dressler.

Joshua Dressler, *Rethinking Heat of Passion: A Defense In Search of a Rationale*, 73 Journal of Criminal Law & Criminology 421 (1982). Copyright © 1982, Northwestern University School of Law. Reprinted by special permission of Northwestern University School of Law, *Journal of Criminal Law and Criminology*, Volume 73, pp. 421 (1982).

Joshua Dressler, *Professor Delgado's "Brainwashing" Defense: Courting a Determinist Legal System*, 63 Minnesota Law Review 335 (1979). Copyright © 1979, Minnesota Law Review Foundation. Reprinted with the permission of *Minnesota Law Review*.

Arnold N. Enker, *Impossibility in Criminal Attempts—Legality and the Legal Process*, 53 Minnesota Law Review 665 (1969). Copyright © 1969, Minnesota Law Review Foundation. Reprinted by permission.

Albin Eser, *The Principle of "Harm" in the Concept of Crime: A Comparative Analysis of the Criminally Protected Legal Interests*, 4 Duquesne Law Review 345 (1965). Copyright © 1965, Duquesne University. Reprinted by permission.

Susan Estrich, *Defending Women*, 88 Michigan Law Review 1430 (1990). Copyright © 1990 by The Michigan Law Review Association. Reprinted by permission of *Michigan Law Review* and the author.

Susan Estrich, *Rape*, 95 Yale Law Journal 1087 (1986). Copyright © 1986, by Susan Estrich. Reprinted by permission of the author.

George P. Fletcher, *Should Intolerable Prison Conditions Generate a Justification or an Excuse for Escape?*, originally published in 26 UCLA L. Rev. 1355 (1979). Copyright © 1979, The Regents of the

Phillip E. Johnson, *The Unnecessary Crime of Conspiracy*, 61 California Law Review 1137 (1973). Copyright © 1973 by California Law Review, Inc. Reprinted by permission of University of California Press Journals and the author.

Sanford H. Kadish, *Excusing Crime*, 75 California Law Review 257 (1987). Copyright © 1987 by California Law Review, Inc. Reprinted from *California Law Review*, Vol. 75, No. 1 (January 1987), pp. 263–65, by permission of the University of California Press Journals and the author.

Sanford H. Kadish, *Complicity, Cause and Blame: A Study in the Interpretation of Doctrine*, 73 California Law Review 323 (1985). Copyright © 1985 by California Law Review, Inc. Reprinted from California Law Review, Vol. 73, No. 2, Mar. 1985, pp. 323–410, by permission of University of California Press Journals and the author.

Yale Kamisar, *Some Non-Religious Views Against Proposed "Mercy-Killing" Legislation*, 42 Minnesota Law Review 969 (1958). Copyright © 1958, Minnesota Law Review Foundation. Reprinted by permission.

John Kaplan, *The Problem of Capital Punishment*, 1983 University of Illinois Law Review 555. Copyright © 1983, by the Board of Trustees of the University of Illinois. Reprinted by permission.

Deborah Kochan, *Beyond the Battered Woman Syndrome: An Argument for the Development of New Standards and the Incorporation of a Feminine Approach to Ethics*, 1 Hastings Women's Law Journal 89 (1989). Copyright © 1989 by Deborah Kochan. Reprinted by permission of the author.

Arthur Leavens, *A Causation Approach to Criminal Omissions*, 76 California Law Review 547 (1988). Copyright © 1988, California Law Review, Inc. Reprinted from *California Law Review*, Vol. 76, No. 3, May 1988, pp. 547–92. Reprinted by permission.

Gerald E. Lynch, *RICO: The Crime of Being a Criminal, Parts III and IV*, 87 Columbia Law Review 920 (1987) Copyright © 1987 by the Directors of the Columbia Law Review Association, Inc. All Rights Reserved. This article originally appeared at 87 Colum. L. Rev. 920 (1987). Reprinted by permission.

Gerald E. Lynch, *RICO: The Crime of Being a Criminal, Parts I and II*, 87 Columbia Law Review 661 (1987). Copyright © 1987 by the Directors of the Columbia Law Review Association, Inc. All Rights Reserved. This article originally appeared at 87 Colum. L. Rev. 661 (1987). Reprinted by permission.

Norman Mailer, The Executioner's Song (1979). Copyright © 1979, by Norman Mailer, Lawrence Schiller, and the New Ingot Company, Inc. Reprinted by permission of the author and the author's agents, Scott Meredith Literary Agency, Inc., 845 Third Avenue, New York, New York 10022.

Rollin M. Perkins, *An Analysis of Assault and Attempts to Assault*, 47 Minnesota Law Review 71 (1962). Copyright © 1962, Minnesota Law Review Foundation. Reprinted by permission.

Philip G. Peters, Jr., *The State's Interest in the Preservation of Life: From Quinlan to Cruzan*, 50 Ohio State Law Journal 891 (1989). Copyright © 1989, Philip G. Peters, Jr. Reprinted by permission.

Samuel H. Pillsbury, *The Meaning of Deserved Punishment: An Essay on Choice, Character, and Responsibility*, 67 Indiana Law Journal 719 (1992). Copyright © 1992, Samuel H. Pillsbury. Reprinted by permission.

Samuel H. Pillsbury, *Evil and the Law of Murder*, 24 University of California Davis Law Review 437 (1990). Copyright © 1991 by the Regents of the University of California. Reprinted with permission of *U.C. Davis Law Review* and the author.

Samuel H. Pillsbury, *Emotional Justice: Moralizing the Passions of Criminal Punishment*, 74 Cornell Law Review 655 (1989). Copyright © 1989 by Cornell University. All Rights Reserved. Reprinted with the permission of *Cornell Law Review*, Fred B. Rothman & Co., and the author. This article orginally appeared in Volume 74, Number 4, May 1989, of *Cornell Law Review*.

Ira P. Robbins, *Double Inchoate Crimes*, 26 Harvard Journal on Legislation 1 (1989). Copyright © 1989, Ira P. Robbins. Reprinted by permission.

Paul H. Robinson, 1 CRIMINAL LAW DEFENSES (1984). Reprinted from CRIMINAL LAW DEFENSES, Paul H. Robinson, Copyright © 1984, West Publishing Company, with permission of the West Publishing Company.

Paul H. Robinson, *Criminal Law Defenses: A Systematic Analysis*, 82 Columbia Law Review 199 (1982). Copyright © 1982, Paul H. Robinson. Reprinted with permission.

Paul H. Robinson, *A Theory of Justification: Societal Harm as a Prerequisite for Criminal Liability*, 23 UCLA L. Rev. 266 (1975). Originally published in 23 *UCLA L. Rev.* 266. Copyright © 1975, The Regents of the University of California. All Rights Reserved. Reprinted with permission of *UCLA Law Review* and the author.

Nelson E. Roth & Scott E. Sundby, *The Felony-Murder Rule: A Doctrine at Constitutional Crossroads*, 70 Cornell Law Review 446 (1985). Copyright © 1985 by Cornell University. All Rights Reserved. Reprinted with the permission of *Cornell Law Review*, Fred B. Rothman & Co., and the authors. This article originally appeared in Volume 70, Number 3, March 1985 of *Cornell Law Review*.

Richard G. Singer, *The Resurgence of Mens Rea: III—The Rise and Fall of Strict Criminal Liability*, 30 Boston College Law Review 337 (1989). Copyright © 1989, Richard Singer. Reprinted by permission.

Richard Singer, *The Resurgence of Mens Rea: II—Honest But Unreasonable Mistake of Fact in Self Defense*, 28 Boston College Law Review 459 (1987). Copyright © 1987 by Richard Singer. Reprinted by permission.

Laurie J. Taylor, Comment, *Provoked Reason in Men and Women: Heat-of-Passion Manslaughter and Imperfect Self-Defense*, 33 UCLA Law Review 1679 (1986). Copyright © 1986, The Regents of the University of California. All Rights Reserved. Permission granted by *UCLA Law Review* and Fred B. Rothman & Co.

Ernest van den Haag, *In Defense of the Death Penalty: A Legal-Practical-Moral Analysis*, 14 Criminal Law Bulletin 51 (1978). Reprinted with permission from *Criminal Law Bulletin*, Copyright © 1978, Research Institute of America, Inc., Warren, Gorham & Lamont Professional Publishing Division, 210 South Street, Boston, MA 02111. 1–800–950–1205. All Rights Reserved.

Andrew von Hirsch, *Lifeboat Law*, 4 Criminal Justice Ethics (Summer/Fall 1985), at 88. Copyright © 1985, Criminal Justice Ethics. Reprinted by permission of the Institute for Criminal Justice Ethics and the author.

Richard A. Wasserstrom, *Strict Liability in the Criminal Law*, 12 Stanford Law Review 731 (1960). Copyright © 1960 by the Board of Trustees of the Leland Stanford Junior University. Reprinted by permission of *Stanford Law Review* and Fred B. Rothman & Co.

Glanville Williams, *"Mercy-Killing" Legislation: A Rejoinder*, 43 Minnesota Law Review 1 (1958). Copyright © 1958, Minnesota Law Review Foundation. Reprinted by permission.

Summary of Contents

———

*

Table of Contents

Table of Cases

The principal cases are in bold type. Cases cited or discussed in the text are roman type. References are to pages. Cases cited in principal cases and within other quoted materials are not included.

Table of Model Penal Code Sections

*

xliii

CASES AND MATERIALS ON
CRIMINAL LAW

*

Chapter 1

INTRODUCTION

A. NATURE, SOURCES, AND LIMITS OF THE CRIMINAL LAW

HENRY M. HART, JR.—THE AIMS OF THE CRIMINAL LAW

23 Law and Contemporary Problems 401 (1958), 402–406

* * * What do we mean by "crime" and "criminal"? Or, put more accurately, what should we understand to be "the method of the criminal law," the use of which is in question? This latter way of formulating the preliminary inquiry is more accurate, because it pictures the criminal law as a process, a way of doing something, which is what it is. * * *

What then are the characteristics of this method?

1. The method operates by means of a series of directions, or commands, formulated in general terms, telling people what they must or must not do. Mostly, the commands of the criminal law are "must-nots," or prohibitions, which can be satisfied by inaction. "Do not murder, rape, or rob." But some of them are "musts," or affirmative requirements, which can be satisfied only by taking a specifically, or relatively specifically, described kind of action. "Support your wife and children," and "File your income tax return."

2. The commands are taken as valid and binding upon all those who fall within their terms when the time comes for complying with them, whether or not they have been formulated in advance in a single authoritative set of words. They speak to members of the community, in other words, in the community's behalf, with all the power and prestige of the community behind them.

3. The commands are subject to one or more sanctions for disobedience which the community is prepared to enforce.

Thus far, it will be noticed, nothing has been said about the criminal law which is not true also of a large part of the noncriminal, or civil, law.

The law of torts, the law of contracts, and almost every other branch of private law that can be mentioned operate, too, with general directions prohibiting or requiring described types of conduct, and the community's tribunals enforce these commands. What, then, is distinctive about the method of the criminal law? .

Can crimes be distinguished from civil wrongs on the ground that they constitute injuries to society generally which society is interested in preventing? The difficulty is that society is interested also in the due fulfillment of contracts and the avoidance of traffic accidents and most of the other stuff of civil litigation. The civil law is framed and interpreted and enforced with a constant eye to these social interests. Does the distinction lie in the fact that proceedings to enforce the criminal law are instituted by public officials rather than private complainants? The difficulty is that public officers may also bring many kinds of "civil" enforcement actions—for an injunction, for the recovery of a "civil" penalty, or even for the detention of the defendant by public authority. Is the distinction, then, in the peculiar character of what is done to people who are adjudged to be criminals? The difficulty is that, with the possible exception of death, exactly the same kinds of unpleasant consequences, objectively considered, can be and are visited upon unsuccessful defendants in civil proceedings.

If one were to judge from the notions apparently underlying many judicial opinions, and the overt language even of some of them, the solution of the puzzle is simply that a crime is anything which is *called* a crime, and a criminal penalty is simply the penalty provided for doing anything which has been given that name. So vacant a concept is a betrayal of intellectual bankruptcy. * * * [A] conviction for crime is a distinctive and serious matter—a something, and not a nothing. What is that something?

4. What distinguishes a criminal from a civil sanction and all that distinguishes it, it is ventured, is the judgment of community condemnation which accompanies and justifies its imposition. As Professor Gardner wrote not long ago, in a distinct but cognate connection: [13]

> The essence of punishment for moral delinquency lies in the criminal conviction itself. One may lose more money on the stock market than in a court-room; a prisoner of war camp may well provide a harsher environment than a state prison; death on the field of battle has the same physical characteristics as death by sentence of law. It is the expression of the community's hatred, fear, or contempt for the convict which alone characterizes physical hardship as punishment.

If this is what a "criminal" penalty is, then we can say readily enough what a "crime" is. It is not simply anything which a legislature chooses to call a "crime." It is not simply antisocial conduct which

---

13. Gardner, *Bailey v. Richardson and the Constitution of the United States,* 33   B.U.L.Rev. 176, 193 (1953). * * *

public officers are given a responsibility to suppress. It is not simply any conduct to which a legislature chooses to attach a "criminal" penalty. It is conduct which, if duly shown to have taken place, will incur a formal and solemn pronouncement of the moral condemnation of the community.

5. The method of the criminal law, of course, involves something more than the threat (and, on due occasion, the expression) of community condemnation of antisocial conduct. It involves, in addition, the threat (and, on due occasion, the imposition) of unpleasant physical consequences, commonly called punishment. But if Professor Gardner is right, these added consequences take their character as punishment from the condemnation which precedes them and serves as the warrant for their infliction. Indeed, the condemnation plus the added consequences may well be considered, compendiously, as constituting the punishment. Otherwise, it would be necessary to think of a convicted criminal as going unpunished if the imposition or execution of his sentence is suspended.

In traditional thought and speech, the ideas of crime and punishment have been inseparable; the consequences of conviction for crime have been described as a matter of course as "punishment." The Constitution of the United States and its amendments, for example, use this word or its verb form in relation to criminal offenses no less than six times. Today, "treatment" has become a fashionable euphemism for the older, ugly word. * * * [T]o the extent that it dissociates the treatment of criminals from the social condemnation of their conduct which is implicit in their conviction, there is danger that it will confuse thought and do a disservice.

At least under existing law, there is a vital difference between the situation of a patient who has been committed to a mental hospital and the situation of an inmate of a state penitentiary. The core of the difference is precisely that the patient has not incurred the moral condemnation of his community, whereas the convict has.

Notes and Questions

1. *Sources of American criminal law.* The roots of American criminal law can be found in English soil. The early colonists brought to this country, and in large part accepted as their own, the judge-made law, i.e., common law, of England. Over time, however, the American common law of crimes diverged in key respects from the English version.

Beginning in the late nineteenth century, many state legislatures claimed authority to enact criminal statutes. At first, they used their power to supplement the common law, but eventually they replaced it by legislation. Today, in every state and in the federal system, legislators, rather than judges, exercise primary responsibility for defining criminal conduct and for devising the rules of criminal responsibility.

2. *Model Penal Code.* Until recently, most state criminal codes were little more than a collection of statutes, enacted by legislators in piecemeal

fashion over many decades, defining various crimes and the punishments therefor.

These penal codes left much to be desired. First, not all common law crimes and defenses were codified, thereby leaving to the courts the determination of whether these gaps were intended or inadvertent. Second, many statutory systems were silent regarding important criminal law doctrines, such as accomplice liability. Third, state criminal codes typically included overlapping, even conflicting, penal statutes. Finally, many penal codes applied internally inconsistent principles of criminal punishment.

In order to bring coherence to the criminal law, the American Law Institute, an organization composed of eminent judges, lawyers, and law professors, set out in 1952 to develop a model code. Ten years later, the Institute adopted and published the Model Penal Code and Commentaries thereto. Key portions of the Code are set out in the appendix to this casebook.

The Model Penal Code has substantially influenced the reform of American criminal law. Some states have adopted it in whole or in substantial part. In other states, courts look to the Model Code for guidance in filling holes in their own statutory systems. Perhaps most usefully, the Commentaries to the specific provisions of the Model Penal Code have shaped the reform debate in many state legislatures. For a fuller discussion of the status of the criminal law before the adoption of the Model Penal Code, see Sanford H. Kadish, *The Model Penal Code's Historical Antecedents,* 19 Rutgers L.J. 521 (1988).

3. *Limitations on the criminal law.* Legislatures do not have unlimited lawmaking power. Their actions are subject to federal and state constitutional provisions. For example, the United States Constitution prohibits *ex post facto* legislation (Article 1, §§ 9 and 10) and cruel and unusual punishment (Eighth Amendment), and provides that persons may not be deprived of life, liberty or property without due process of law (Fifth and Fourteenth Amendments). The study of the criminal law necessarily includes, therefore, consideration of these and other constitutional provisions.

In thinking about constitutional law issues, it is important to be sensitive to competing policy concerns. On the one hand, the doctrine of *federalism* teaches that each state has sovereign authority to promulgate and enforce its own criminal laws; and, under the doctrine of *separation of powers,* the legislative branch of government, rather than the judiciary, is now considered the appropriate lawmaking body.[a] Therefore, when a federal court declares that a state statute is unconstitutional, it runs the risk of violating the principle of federalism and of usurping the authority of the legislative body. In that vein, the Supreme Court has instructed federal courts not to interpret the Constitution so as to make the federal judiciary "the ultimate arbiter of the standards of criminal responsibility, in diverse areas of the criminal law, throughout the country." Powell v. Texas, 392 U.S. 514, 533, 88 S.Ct. 2145, 2154, 20 L.Ed.2d 1254, 1268 (1968).

On the other hand, as President (later Chief Justice) William Howard Taft once stated, "[c]onstitutions are checks upon the hasty action of the

---

a. Why would this be?

majority. They are self-imposed restraints of a whole people upon a majority of them to secure sober action and a respect for the rights of the minority." H.R.J.Res. 4, 62nd Cong., 1st Sess., 47 Cong.Rec. 4 (1911). With the adoption of the Bill of Rights, which serves as a "check upon the hasty action of the majority," James Madison predicted in an address to the First Congress on June 8, 1789, that "independent tribunals of justice"—the judiciary—would serve as "the guardians of those rights." 1 Annals of Cong. 439 (1789). Consequently, if courts defer too readily to legislatures, they run the risk of abdicating their responsibility for enforcing the Constitution.

The question that must often be asked in the criminal law context, therefore, is this: At what point does the virtue of judicial deference to legislative action turn into the vice of judicial abdication of constitutional responsibilities?

B. CRIMINAL LAW IN A PROCEDURAL CONTEXT: PRE–TRIAL

Criminal law casebooks, including this one, use judicial opinions, mainly those of appellate courts, as the primary tool for exposing students to the general principles of the criminal law. This process can be misleading. It is easy to think that the commission of a crime inevitably results in a prosecution, culminating in a trial, conviction, and appeal of the conviction by the defendant. In fact, however, trials are the exception, not the rule, in the criminal justice system. A great deal of the criminal process is barely visible in a criminal law course, although it is the focus of attention in courses relating to criminal procedure.

Some crimes—we have no way of knowing with certainty how many—go unreported. Recent government data suggest, however, that approximately one-fourth of the 95 million households in the United States in 1989 were victimized by a crime of violence or theft. U.S. Department of Justice, Bureau of Justice Statistics, Crime and the Nation's Households, 1989 (NCJ–124544, 1990).[b]

Even if a crime is reported, an arrest might not be made. The police might not investigate the report with vigor because they doubt (rightly or wrongly) the authenticity of the claim. Or, they may give the investigation low priority, as police departments, especially in urban areas, have inadequate resources to investigate every reported offense.

Even if the police investigate a crime report thoroughly, insufficient evidence may exist to make an arrest. The United States Constitution prohibits the police from arresting a suspect (a *seizure* of the person, in the nomenclature of the Fourth Amendment, which prohibits "unrea-

---

b. A relationship exists between certain demographic characteristics and risk of crime victimization. Males, younger persons (especially those under the age of 25), African–Americans and Hispanics, residents of central cities, and poor persons tend to have higher rates of victimization than others. U.S. Department of Justice, Bureau of Justice Statistics, *Criminal Victimization 1991* 6 (October, 1992).

sonable searches and seizures") unless they have *probable cause* to believe that the individual committed an offense. The concept of "probable cause" is a fluid one, not quantifiable in percentage terms, but it is not satisfied unless there is a substantial chance that the suspected party committed the offense under investigation. See Illinois v. Gates, 462 U.S. 213, 103 S.Ct. 2317, 76 L.Ed.2d 527 (1983).

If a suspect is arrested, the prosecutor must still overcome various hurdles before a trial may be held. In most states, the defendant is entitled to a *preliminary hearing* within two weeks after arrest, at which proceeding a judge must determine whether the arrest was justified. If the arrest was unjustified, the accused is set free. If the judge rules that there is probable cause to proceed with the prosecution, the prosecutor is permitted in some states to file an *information* in the trial court and to proceed to trial. An information is a document that sets out the formal charges against the defendant and the basic facts relating to them.

In most states and in the federal system, however, even if a preliminary hearing judge rules that the arrest was justified, the accused may not be brought to trial unless she is indicted by a grand jury. A grand jury consists of lay members of the community who listen to evidence presented by a prosecutor, after which they deliberate privately, and determine whether adequate evidence exists to prosecute the accused. If sufficient evidence exists, the grand jury issues an *indictment,* a document similar to an information.

Even if an indictment is issued by the grand jury or an information is filed by the prosecutor, a trial might still not be held. First, the accused is entitled to make various pretrial motions which, if successful, sometimes require the dismissal of charges. For example, if evidence to be used by the government was secured in violation of the Constitution, the tainted evidence may not be introduced at trial. Occasionally, the suppression of such evidence so weakens the prosecutor's case that charges must be dismissed.

Second, a defendant may plead guilty rather than proceed to trial. Nearly always, a guilty plea is the result of bargaining between the prosecutor and the defendant's lawyer. Typically, in exchange for a guilty plea, a prosecutor agrees to dismiss certain charges, reduce the severity of a charge, or agrees to recommend a more lenient sentence upon conviction. Guilty plea rates vary by jurisdiction, by offense, and by year, but the conviction rate obtained by guilty pleas sometimes exceeds ninety percent.

C. CRIMINAL LAW IN A PROCEDURAL CONTEXT: TRIAL BY JURY

1. RIGHT TO A JURY TRIAL

The Sixth Amendment to the United States Constitution provides that "in all criminal prosecutions, the accused shall enjoy the right to a speedy and public trial, by an impartial jury." The right to trial by jury includes, "as its most important element, the right to have the jury, rather than the judge, reach the requisite finding of 'guilty'" in all prosecutions for which the maximum potential punishment exceeds incarceration of six months. Sullivan v. Louisiana, 508 U.S. ___, ___, 113 S.Ct. 2078, 2080, 124 L.Ed.2d 182, 188 (1993).

In Duncan v. Louisiana, 391 U.S. 145, 155–56, 88 S.Ct. 1444, 1451, 20 L.Ed.2d 491, 499–50 (1968), the Supreme Court explained the history and rationale of the right to trial by jury this way:

> The guarantees of jury trial in the Federal and State Constitutions reflect a profound judgment about the way in which law should be enforced and justice administered. A right to jury trial is granted to criminal defendants in order to prevent oppression by the Government. Those who wrote our constitutions knew from history and experience that it was necessary to protect against unfounded criminal charges brought to eliminate enemies and against judges too responsive to the voice of higher authority. Providing an accused with the right to be tried by a jury of his peers gave him an inestimable safeguard against the corrupt or overzealous prosecutor and against the compliant, biased, or eccentric judge. If the defendant preferred the common-sense judgment of a jury to the more tutored but perhaps less sympathetic reactions of the single judge, he was to have it.

2. SCOPE OF THE "JURY TRIAL" RIGHT

In the federal system and in most states, a jury in a criminal trial is composed of 12 persons, who must reach a unanimous verdict to acquit or to convict. However, juries as small as six in number are constitutionally permissible. Williams v. Florida, 399 U.S. 78, 90 S.Ct. 1893, 26 L.Ed.2d 446 (1970) (jury of six is allowed); Ballew v. Georgia, 435 U.S. 223, 98 S.Ct. 1029, 55 L.Ed.2d 234 (1978) (jury of five is not allowed). Furthermore, state laws permitting non-unanimous verdicts by 12–person juries are permissible, as long as the vote to convict constitutes a "substantial majority" of the jurors. Johnson v. Louisiana, 406 U.S. 356, 92 S.Ct. 1620, 32 L.Ed.2d 152 (1972) (upholding a 9–3 guilty verdict).

The Sixth Amendment provides that "the accused shall enjoy the right to * * * an impartial jury * * *." A juror is not impartial if her state of mind in reference to the issues or parties involved in the case would substantially impair her performance as a juror in accordance with the court's instructions on the law. See Adams v. Texas, 448 U.S. 38, 100 S.Ct. 2521, 65 L.Ed.2d 581 (1980).

In order to discover possible bias prior to trial, the judge and the attorneys examine prospective jurors ("venirepersons") regarding their attitudes and beliefs. The examination is called a *"voir dire."* If a venireperson's responses demonstrate partiality, the judge must, upon the motion of one of the parties, excuse the juror "for cause."

The defense and the prosecutor are also entitled to exercise a limited number of "peremptory" challenges, i.e., challenges not based on cause. The primary purpose of peremptory challenges is to allow the parties to exclude persons from the jury whom they believe (often intuitively, or as the result of subjective factors, such as "body language") are biased, but whose partiality was not adequately proven through the *voir dire*. Although the tradition of peremptory challenges is a venerable one, the Supreme Court ruled in Batson v. Kentucky, 476 U.S. 79, 106 S.Ct. 1712, 90 L.Ed.2d 69 (1986), that the Fourteenth Amendment equal protection clause is violated if a prosecutor exercises such a challenge solely on the basis of the venireperson's race. The same rule applies to the defense. Georgia v. McCollum, 505 U.S. ___, 112 S.Ct. 2348, 120 L.Ed.2d 33 (1992).

Because the purpose of the jury system is to defend against exercises of arbitrary power by the government and to make available to defendants the common-sense judgment of the community, the accused is entitled to a jury drawn from a pool of persons constituting a fair cross-section of the community. Taylor v. Louisiana, 419 U.S. 522, 95 S.Ct. 692, 42 L.Ed.2d 690 (1975). This right is violated if large distinctive groups of persons, such as women or members of a racial or religious group, are systematically excluded from the jury pool for illegitimate reasons.

D. PROOF OF GUILT AT TRIAL

1. "PROOF BEYOND A REASONABLE DOUBT"

The Supreme Court ruled in In re Winship, 397 U.S. 358, 363–64, 90 S.Ct. 1068, 1072–73, 25 L.Ed.2d 368, 375 (1970), that in order to provide "concrete substance for the presumption of innocence—that bedrock 'axiomatic and elementary' principle whose 'enforcement lies at the foundation of our criminal law' "—the due process clause of the United States Constitution requires the prosecutor to persuade the factfinder "beyond a reasonable doubt of every fact necessary to constitute the crime charged." (The meaning of the word "fact" in this context is considered at p. 395 infra.)

How onerous a burden is "proof beyond a reasonable doubt"? Trial courts often instruct juries regarding the meaning of "reasonable doubt" by using language that originated in Commonwealth v. Webster, 59 Mass. (5 Cush.) 295, 320 (1850):

[Reasonable doubt] is not merely possible doubt; because every thing relating to human affairs, and depending on moral evidence, is open to some possible or imaginary doubt. It is that state of the case, which, after the entire comparison and consideration of all the evidence, leaves the minds of jurors in that condition that they cannot say they feel an abiding conviction, to a moral certainty, of the truth of the charge * * *.

Why do we demand that jurors have an "abiding conviction, to a moral certainty" of the defendant's guilt in order to convict? Won't this rule result in more guilty people going free than in innocent persons avoiding unjust conviction? The Supreme Court in *Winship* (397 U.S. at 363–64, 90 S.Ct. at 1072–73, 25 L.Ed.2d at 375) justified the reasonable-doubt standard this way:

> The reasonable-doubt standard plays a vital role in the American scheme of criminal procedure. It is a prime instrument for reducing the risk of convictions resting on factual error. * * *

> * * * The accused during a criminal prosecution has at stake interests of immense importance, both because of the possibility that he may lose his liberty upon conviction and because of the certainty that he would be stigmatized by the conviction. Accordingly, a society that values the good name and freedom of every individual should not condemn a man for commission of a crime when there is reasonable doubt about his guilt. * * *

> Moreover, use of the reasonable-doubt standard is indispensable to command the respect and confidence of the community in applications of the criminal law. It is critical that the moral force of the criminal law not be diluted by a standard of proof that leaves people in doubt whether innocent men are being condemned.

Justice Harlan, who concurred in *Winship,* conceded that the practical effect of the reasonable-doubt standard is to enhance the risk that factually guilty people will be set free. But, he stated (id. at 372, 90 S.Ct. at 1076–77, 25 L.Ed.2d at 380):

> In a criminal case, * * * we do not view the social disutility of convicting an innocent man as equivalent to the disutility of acquitting someone who is guilty. * * * In this context, I view the requirement of proof beyond a reasonable doubt in a criminal case as bottomed on the fundamental value determination of our society that it is far worse to convict an innocent man than to let a guilty man go free.

2. ENFORCEMENT OF THE BURDEN OF PROOF AT TRIAL AND ON APPEAL

OWENS v. STATE

Court of Special Appeals of Maryland, 1992.
93 Md.App. 162, 611 A.2d 1043.

MOYLAN, JUDGE.

This appeal presents us with a small gem of a problem from the borderland of legal sufficiency. It is one of those few occasions when some frequently invoked but rarely appropriate language is actually pertinent. Ironically, in this case it was not invoked. The language is, "[A] conviction upon circumstantial evidence *alone* is not to be sustained unless the circumstances are inconsistent with any reasonable hypothesis of innocence."

We have here a conviction based upon circumstantial evidence alone. The circumstance is that a suspect was found behind the wheel of an automobile parked on a private driveway at night with the lights on and with the motor running. Although there are many far-fetched and speculative hypotheses that might be conjured up (but which require no affirmative elimination), there are only two unstrained and likely inferences that could reasonably arise. One is that the vehicle and its driver had arrived at the driveway from somewhere else. The other is that the driver had gotten into and started up the vehicle and was about to depart for somewhere else.

The first hypothesis, combined with the added factor that the likely driver was intoxicated, is consistent with guilt. The second hypothesis, because the law intervened before the forbidden deed could be done, is consistent with innocence. With either inference equally likely, a fact finder could not fairly draw the guilty inference and reject the innocent with the requisite certainty beyond a reasonable doubt. We are called upon, therefore, to examine the circumstantial predicate more closely and to ascertain whether there were any attendant and ancillary circumstances to render less likely, and therefore less reasonable, the hypothesis of innocence. Thereon hangs the decision.

The appellant, Christopher Columbus Owens, Jr., was convicted * * * by Judge D. William Simpson, sitting without a jury, of driving while intoxicated. Upon this appeal, he raises the single contention that Judge Simpson was clearly erroneous in finding him guilty because the evidence was not legally sufficient to support such finding.

The evidence, to be sure, was meager. The State's only witness was Trooper Samuel Cottman, who testified that at approximately 11 P.M. on March 17, 1991, he drove to the area of Sackertown Road in Crisfield in response to a complaint that had been called in about a suspicious vehicle. He spotted a truck matching the description of the "suspicious vehicle." It was parked in the driveway of a private residence.

The truck's engine was running and its lights were on. The appellant was asleep in the driver's seat, with an open can of Budweiser clasped between his legs. Two more empty beer cans were inside the vehicle. As Trooper Cottman awakened him, the appellant appeared confused and did not know where he was. He stumbled out of the vehicle. There was a strong odor of alcohol on his breath. His face was flushed and his eyes were red. When asked to recite the alphabet, the appellant "mumbled through the letters, didn't state any of the letters clearly and failed to say them in the correct order." His speech generally was "slurred and very unclear." * * * A check with the Motor Vehicles Administration revealed, moreover, that the appellant had an alcohol restriction on his license. The appellant declined to submit to a blood test for alcohol.

After the brief direct examination of Trooper Cottman (consuming but 3½ pages of transcript), defense counsel asked only two questions, establishing that the driveway was private property and that the vehicle was sitting on that private driveway. The appellant did not take the stand and no defense witnesses were called. The appellant's argument as to legal insufficiency is clever. He chooses to fight not over the fact of drunkenness but over the place of drunkenness. He points out that his conviction was under the Transportation Article, which is limited in its coverage to the driving of vehicles on "highways" and does not extend to driving on a "private road or driveway."

We agree with the appellant that he could not properly have been convicted for driving, no matter how intoxicated, back and forth along the short span of a private driveway. The theory of the State's case, however, rests upon the almost Newtonian principle that present stasis on the driveway implies earlier motion on the highway. The appellant was not convicted of drunken driving on the private driveway, but of drunken driving on the public highway before coming to rest on the private driveway.

It is a classic case of circumstantial evidence. From his presence behind the wheel of a vehicle on a private driveway with the lights on and the motor running, it can reasonably be inferred that such individual either 1) had just arrived by way of the public highway or 2) was just about to set forth upon the public highway. The binary nature of the probabilities—that a vehicular odyssey had just concluded or was just about to begin—is strengthened by the lack of evidence of any third reasonable explanation, such as the presence beside him of an inamorata or of a baseball game blaring forth on the car radio. Either he was coming or he was going.

The first inference would render the appellant guilty; the second would not. * * * For the State to prevail, there has to be some other factor to enhance the likelihood of the first inference and to diminish the likelihood of the second. We must look for a tiebreaker. * * *

In trying to resolve whether the appellant 1) had just been driving or 2) was just about to drive, it would have been helpful to know whether the driveway in which he was found was that of his own residence or that of some other residence. If he were parked in someone else's driveway with the motor still running, it would be more likely that he had just driven there a short time before. If parked in his own driveway at home, on the other hand, the relative strength of the inbound inference over the outbound inference would diminish.

The driveway where the arrest took place was on Sackertown Road. The charging document (which, of course, is not evidence) listed the appellant's address as 112 Cove Second Street. When the appellant was arrested, presumably his driver's license was taken from him. Since one of the charges against the appellant was that of driving in violation of an alcohol restriction on his license, it would have been routine procedure to have offered the license, showing the restriction, into evidence. In terms of our present legal sufficiency exercise, the license would fortuitously have shown the appellant's residence as well. Because of the summary nature of the trial, however, the license was never offered in evidence. For purposes of the present analysis, therefore, the appellant's home address is not in the case. We must continue to look for a tiebreaker elsewhere.

Three beer cans were in evidence. The presence of a partially consumed can of beer between the appellant's legs and two other empty cans in the back seat would give rise to a reasonable inference that the appellant's drinking spree was on the downslope rather than at an early stage. At least a partial venue of the spree, moreover, would reasonably appear to have been the automobile. One does not typically drink in the house and then carry the empties out to the car. Some significant drinking, it may be inferred, had taken place while the appellant was in the car. The appellant's state of unconsciousness, moreover, enforces that inference. One passes out on the steering wheel after one has been drinking for some time, not as one only begins to drink. It is not a reasonable hypothesis that one would leave the house, get in the car, turn on the lights, turn on the motor, and then, before putting the car in gear and driving off, consume enough alcohol to pass out on the steering wheel. Whatever had been going on (driving and drinking) would seem more likely to have been at a terminal stage than at an incipient one.

Yet another factor would have sufficed, we conclude, to break the tie between whether the appellant had not yet left home or was already abroad upon the town. Without anything further as to its contents being revealed, it was nonetheless in evidence that the thing that had brought Trooper Cottman to the scene was a complaint about a suspicious vehicle. The inference is reasonable that the vehicle had been observed driving in some sort of erratic fashion. Had the appellant simply been sitting, with his motor idling, on the driveway of his own residence, it is not likely that someone from the immediate vicinity would have found suspicious the presence of a familiar neighbor in a familiar car sitting in his own driveway. The call to the police, even without more being shown, inferentially augurs more than that. It does not prove guilt in and of itself. It simply makes one of two alternative inferences less reasonable and its alternative inference thereby more reasonable.

The totality of the circumstances are, in the last analysis, inconsistent with a *reasonable* hypothesis of innocence. They do not, of course, foreclose the hypothesis but such has never been required. They do make the hypothesis more strained and less likely. By an inverse proportion, the diminishing force of one inference enhances the force of its alternative. It makes the drawing of the inference of guilt more than a mere flip of a coin between guilt and innocence. It makes it rational and therefore within the proper purview of the factfinder. We affirm.

Notes and Questions

1. In *Owens,* the trial judge served as factfinder, the role ordinarily reserved for a jury. If you had been a member of a jury hearing this case, would you have voted to convict Owens? Are you convinced of his guilt beyond a reasonable doubt?

At the conclusion of the opinion, the Court of Special Appeals stated that the drawing of the inference of guilt in this case involved "more than a flip of a coin between guilt and innocence" and that a finding of guilt was "rational and therefore within the proper purview of the factfinder." Is that enough to meet the proof-beyond-a-reasonable-doubt standard?

2. *The roles of judge, jury, and the appellate court in determining guilt.* In a criminal trial, the prosecutor ordinarily makes an opening statement to the factfinder, ordinarily the jury, in which she outlines the evidence she plans to present at trial. Afterward, she calls her witnesses. When she completes her presentation of the state's evidence, the defense may make a motion for directed verdict of acquittal. In doing so, the defense asserts the presumption of innocence and claims by the motion that the prosecutor has failed to overcome the presumption in her presentation of the state's case. The effect of such a motion, if granted, is to terminate the trial in defendant's favor.

If the motion for directed verdict is denied (or if no motion is made), the defense puts on its case, after which the prosecutor is permitted to present rebuttal testimony. At the conclusion, the defense may again move for a directed verdict for acquittal. If granted, the judge either takes the case from the jury and renders the not-guilty verdict, or she directs the jury to find the defendant not guilty. If the motion is denied (or is not made), the judge (after consultation with the parties) instructs the jury on the principles of law relevant to the case, including the constitutional presumption of innocence.

In *Owens,* by putting on no evidence in his defense, the defendant essentially stood on the presumption of innocence. Presumably, if this case had been heard by a jury, the defendant would have moved for a directed verdict of acquittal at the conclusion of the prosecutor's case.

How does a judge decide whether to grant such a motion and thereby strip the jury of its factfinding role?[c] The following explanation may be helpful:

> The principal point made by appellant * * * is that the trial court erred in refusing to direct a verdict of acquittal as to him. It is not disputed that upon a motion for a directed verdict, the judge must assume the truth of the Government's evidence and give the Government the benefit of all legitimate inferences to be drawn therefrom. Appellant relies upon statements of this and other courts concerning the tests by which a trial judge must determine the proper action upon the motion. For example, in Hammond v. United States, 1942, 75 U.S.App.

---

c. Because the defendant has a constitutional right to trial by jury, which includes the right to have the jury reach the requisite finding of guilt, a trial judge may not direct a verdict for conviction, no matter how overwhelming the evidence. Sullivan v. Louisiana, 508 U.S. ___, 113 S.Ct. 2078, 124 L.Ed.2d 182 (1993).

D.C. 397, 127 F.2d 752, 753, this court [stated] * * * as follows: "Unless there is substantial evidence of facts which exclude every other hypothesis but that of guilt it is the duty of the trial judge to instruct the jury to return a verdict for the accused, and where all the substantial evidence is as consistent with innocence as with guilt it is the duty of the appellate court to reverse a judgment against him."

It is true that the quoted statement seems to say that unless the evidence excludes the hypothesis of innocence, the judge must direct a verdict. And it also seems to say that if the evidence is such that a reasonable mind might fairly conclude either innocence or guilt, a verdict of guilt must be reversed on appeal. But obviously neither of those translations is the law. Logically, the ultimate premise of that thesis is that if a reasonable mind might have a reasonable doubt, there is, therefore, a reasonable doubt. That is not true. Like many another rule become trite by repetition, the quoted statement is misleading and has become confused in application.

The functions of the jury include the determination of the credibility of witnesses, the weighing of the evidence, and the drawing of justifiable inferences of fact from proven facts. It is the function of the judge to deny the jury any opportunity to operate beyond its province. The jury may not be permitted to conjecture merely, or to conclude upon pure speculation or from passion, prejudice or sympathy. The critical point in this boundary is the existence or non-existence of a reasonable doubt as to guilt. If the evidence is such that reasonable jurymen must necessarily have such a doubt, the judge must require acquittal, because no other result is permissible within the fixed bounds of jury consideration. But if a reasonable mind might fairly have a reasonable doubt or might fairly not have one, the case is for the jury, and the decision is for the jurors to make. * * * Both innocence and guilt beyond reasonable doubt may lie fairly within the limits of reasonable conclusion from given facts. The judge's function is exhausted when he determines that the evidence does or does not permit the conclusion of guilt beyond reasonable doubt within the fair operation of a reasonable mind.

The true rule, therefore, is that a trial judge, in passing upon a motion for directed verdict of acquittal, must determine whether upon the evidence, giving full play to the right of the jury to determine credibility, weigh the evidence, and draw justifiable inferences of fact, a reasonable mind might fairly conclude guilt beyond a reasonable doubt. If he concludes that upon the evidence there must be such a doubt in a reasonable mind, he must grant the motion; or, to state it another way, if there is no evidence upon which a reasonable mind might fairly conclude guilt beyond reasonable doubt, the motion must be granted. If he concludes that either of the two results, a reasonable doubt or no reasonable doubt, is fairly possible, he must let the jury decide the matter.

Curley v. United States, 160 F.2d 229, 232–33 (D.C.Cir.1947).

In *Owens,* the defendant appealed his conviction on the ground of "insufficiency of the evidence," a shorthand way of claiming that the prosecutor did not overcome the presumption of innocence or that the judge should have granted a motion for acquittal, if made. An appellate court's role in such circumstances is similar to that of the trial judge in a jury trial, namely, to determine whether the factfinder *could* properly have reached the result that it did (to convict the defendant).

E. JURY NULLIFICATION
INTRODUCTORY COMMENT

Suppose that a prosecutor proves beyond a reasonable doubt every fact necessary to constitute the crime charged, but the jury—the community's representative—does not want to convict the defendant. Perhaps the jurors believe that the defendant's conduct should not constitute a crime (although it does), or that she was morally (but not legally) justified in violating the law. Or, perhaps, the jurors simply feel compassion for the accused. May the jury ignore the facts and the law and acquit the defendant, i.e., may the jury "nullify" the law?

The Fifth Amendment double jeopardy clause ("No person shall * * * be subject for the same offense to be twice put in jeopardy") bars the government from reprosecuting a defendant after an acquittal. Therefore, ultimately, the factfinder in a criminal trial has the raw power irrevocably to acquit a defendant for any reason whatsoever. But, *should* juries nullify the law? And, since they have the power to do so, should they be informed of their "right" of nullification? These questions are considered in the next case.

STATE v. RAGLAND

Supreme Court of New Jersey, 1986.
105 N.J. 189, 519 A.2d 1361.

WILENTZ, C.J. * * *

[Defendant Ragland, a previously convicted felon, was prosecuted for various offenses, including armed robbery and possession of a weapon by a convicted felon. At the conclusion of the trial of the latter offense, the judge instructed the jury that if it found that the defendant was in possession of a weapon during the commission of the robbery, "you must find him guilty of the [possession] charge."

On appeal, the defendant argued that the judge's use of the word "must" in the instruction conflicted with the jury's nullification power, which he claimed was an essential attribute of his constitutional right to a jury trial. He also contended that the judge should have informed the jury regarding its power of nullification, as follows:

"You are here as representatives of your community. Accordingly you are entitled to act upon your conscientious feeling about what is a fair result in this case and acquit the defendant, even if the State has proven its case, if you believe that justice requires such a result."]

The defendant would require a charge that states, in effect, that if the jury does not find a, b and c beyond a reasonable doubt, it must find defendant not guilty, but that if it does find a, b and c beyond a reasonable doubt, then it may find defendant guilty. In support of this change in present practice, defendant contends that the jury's power of nullification—the unquestioned power of the jury to acquit with finality no matter how overwhelming the proof of guilt—is an essential attribute of a defendant's right to trial by jury; that use of the word "must" conflicts with that attribute, for it incorrectly advises the jury that if it finds the proof of guilt beyond a reasonable doubt it *must* convict, whereas the truth is that it need not do so, it may, in fact, acquit; that "must" convict, therefore, should never be used. * * *

While defendant's arguments suggest that the ultimate object is to assure that the jury is not impeded by this coercive language from performing its proper role, the effect of the change is somewhat different. Its only effect, its only tendency, is to make it more likely that juries will nullify the law, more likely, in other words, that no matter how overwhelming the proof of guilt, no matter how convinced the jury is beyond any reasonable doubt of defendant's guilt, despite the law, it will acquit. Even without an explicit charge on the power of nullification, the jury must understand from this contrasting language (*must* acquit but *may* convict) that it is quite properly free, and quite legally free (since it is the court who is telling it "may") to acquit even if it is convinced beyond a reasonable doubt of defendant's guilt. * * *

* * * We have been able to find but one federal case that supports the defendant's argument, *United States v. Hayward,* 420 F.2d 142 (D.C.Cir.1969). This seventeen-year-old case has not been followed in other federal courts on this proposition. The overwhelming weight of authority is to the contrary, namely, even in those cases where the use of the word "must" is discouraged, it is not as a result of a constitutional command. * * *

We conclude that the power of the jury to acquit despite not only overwhelming proof of guilt but despite the jury's belief, beyond a reasonable doubt, in guilt, is not one of the precious attributes of the right to trial by jury. It is nothing more than a power. By virtue of the finality of a verdict of acquittal, the jury simply has the *power* to nullify the law by acquitting those believed by the jury to be guilty. We believe that the exercise of that power, while unavoidable, is undesirable and that judicial attempts to strengthen the power of nullification are not only contrary to settled practice in this state, but unwise both as a matter of governmental policy and as a matter of sound administration of criminal justice.

It is only relatively recently that some scholars have characterized this power as part of defendant's right to trial by jury and have defended it as sound policy. *See, e.g.,* Scheflin, *Jury Nullification: The Right to Say No,* 45 S.Cal.L.Rev. 168 (1972); Kaufman, *The Right of Self-Representation and the Power of Jury Nullification,* 28 Case.W.Res. 269 (1978). Like defendant, they take the position that the exercise of the power is essential to preserve the jury's role as the "conscience of the community."

There are various elements in this view of the jury as the "conscience of the community." Some laws are said to be unfair. Only the jury, it is thought, is capable of correcting that unfairness—through its nullification power. Other laws, necessarily general, have the capacity of doing injustice in specific applications. Again, only the jury can evaluate these specific applications and thereby prevent injustice through its nullification power. Cast aside is our basic belief that only our elected representatives may determine what is a crime and what is not, and only they may revise that law if it is found to be unfair or imprecise; only they and not twelve people whose names are picked at random from the box.

Finally, there is an almost mystical element to this contention about the "conscience of the community": before anyone is imprisoned, that person is entitled to *more* than a fair trial even when such a trial is pursuant to a fair law. He is entitled to the benefit of the wisdom and compassion of his peers, entitled to the right to have them conclude that he is guilty beyond any doubt, but that he shall be acquitted and go free because of some irrational, inarticulable instinct, some belief, some observation, some value, or some other notion of that jury.

If the argument is that jury nullification has proven to serve society well, that proof has been kept a deep secret. It is no answer to point to the occasions when laws that are deemed unjust have, in effect, been nullified by the jury. That proves only that the power may have done justice in those limited instances, without reflecting on whether, even in those instances, the cost of that justice exceeded its benefit, or whether in other instances it has done more harm, on balance, than the good. We know so little about this power that it is impossible to evaluate it in terms of results.

Since there is neither constitutional nor other legal authority mandating the proposed change in jury instructions, its ultimate justification must be that this new formulation of the proper charge is desirable; desirable that a jury should *not* be compelled to follow the law, for compulsion to follow the law is the natural tendency of the use of the word "must"; desirable that a jury should be left free to ignore the law, for that is the obvious tendency of telling the jury simply that it "may," or is "authorized" to, bring in a verdict of guilty, after saying it "must" find defendant not guilty. If indeed this is a desirable state of affairs, then the jury should be told of its power, so as to leave no doubt that the jury *knows* it is not compelled to bring back a guilty verdict despite its finding beyond a reasonable doubt that the defendant has committed the crime. The point here is different from that of those who say they are not sure whether the nullification power is desirable or undesirable, but since it exists, the jury should be told about it * * *. Defendant's position is that the nullification power is one of the essential attributes of his right to trial by jury, and that it is desirable. Given that premise, the conclusion is inescapable—the jury should be told.

Other consequences should follow a conclusion that the nullification power is desirable. Counsel should be told that they may address that point in summation, that defense counsel should be allowed to argue to the jury that it should *not* apply the law given by the court, but rather should follow its own conscience, along with whatever argument counsel deems persuasive, and the prosecutor similarly should address these otherwise irrelevant issues, presumably including an encomium on law and order. If the court makes introductory remarks to give the jury some idea of its role (as is customary), it should add to the usual explanation—that the jury is the finder of the facts and the judge is the finder of the law—the qualification that ultimately, regardless of the facts and regardless of the law, the jury, and only the jury, will determine guilt or innocence. On voir dire, potential jurors, in addition to being asked whether they believe they will be able to obey the court's charge, should also be asked if they believe they will be able to ignore the court's charge. If the nullification power is desirable, then, obviously, juries should include only those people who are capable of exercising it.[7]

If we are correct, that is, if such a change in the charge given to the jury is not compelled either by constitution, by statute, or by common law, then the question boils down to one of policy and the power of this Court. In deciding that question, it is essential to recognize precisely what we are talking about. There is no mystery about the power of nullification. It is the power to act against the law, against the Legislature and the Governor who made the law. In its immediate application, it transforms the jury, the body thought to provide the ultimate assurance of fairness, into the only element of the system that is permissibly arbitrary. And in its immediate application, it would confuse any conscientious citizen serving on a jury by advising that person, after the meticulous definition of the elements of the crime, the careful description of the burden of proof, and the importance of the conscientious discharge of that person's duties, that, after all is said and done, he can do whatever he pleases. Spectators, formerly amazed at verdicts that clearly violated the law (namely, verdicts that suggested that the jury had nullified the law), will be comforted to know that there is nothing to be amazed about, that juries are not required to follow the law, that they are advised that one of their important functions is *not* to follow the law, and that this advice is given by the ultimate symbol of lawfulness, the judge. It is difficult to imagine a system more likely to lead to cynicism.
* * *

The fundamental defect in jury nullification is obvious. It is a power that is absolutely inconsistent with the most important value of

---

7. Our review of recent jury instructions in criminal cases shows that the trial court invariably instructs the jury that it, and not the judge, is the final arbiter of the facts but that the judge determines the law, and that the jury is controlled by that law and *must* follow it. Defendant claims that this settled charge is also impermissible. * * *

Western democracy, that we should live under a government of laws and not of men. * * *

Jury nullification is an unfortunate but unavoidable power. It should not be advertised, and, to the extent constitutionally permissible, it should be limited. Efforts to protect and expand it are inconsistent with the real values of our system of criminal justice. * * *

[The conviction was reversed, and a new trial ordered, on other grounds.]

Notes and Questions

1. Perhaps the most famous example of jury nullification in this country arose during the colonial era, when John Peter Zenger, a New York printer, was prosecuted for criminal sedition under a British law that required prior government authorization to publish certain materials (in this case, the publication of an anti-British tract). Zenger's attorney told the jury that they "ha[d] the right * * * to determine both the law and the fact[s]." A Brief Narration of the Case and Trial of John Paul Zenger 78 (J. Alexander ed. 1963). The jury acquitted Zenger.

In the nineteenth century, as well, juries in Northern states occasionally acquitted persons prosecuted under the Fugitive Slave Act, ch. 113, § 4, 3 Stat. 600 (1820), which made it a felony to assist slaves to escape their servitude.

Were the juries wrong to acquit in such circumstances? If so, why? If not, how do you answer *Ragland?* If you personally would nullify the law in some circumstances, are you unqualified to sit on a jury because you would not respect your oath as a juror to act in accordance with the law, as instructed by the judge?

2. In 1990, voters in the State of Oregon rejected an initiative measure that would have enshrined the concept of jury nullification in that state's constitution. The initiative would have amended the state charter to read, in part:

> It is the natural right of every citizen of the state of Oregon, when serving on a criminal-trial jury, to judge both the law and the facts pertaining to the case before the jury, in order to determine whether justice will be served by applying the law to the defendant.

The proposed amendment would have required the judge to inform the jury of this "natural right" in the following words:

> If you decide that the prosecution has proven beyond reasonable doubt every element of the criminal charge but * * * you cannot in good conscience support a guilty verdict, you are not required to do so. To reach a verdict which you believe is just, each of you has the right to consider to what extent the defendant's actions have actually caused harm or otherwise violated your sense of right and wrong. If you believe justice requires it, you may also judge both the merits of the law under which the defendant has been charged and the wisdom of applying that law to the defendant. * * * The court cautions that with the

exercise of this right comes the full moral responsibility for the verdict you bring in.

See Fauvre v. Roberts, 309 Or. 691, 693–94, 791 P.2d 128, 129–30 (1990).

Would you have voted for the initiative?

3.   In a classic study of American jury behavior, Harry Kalven, Jr. and Hans Zeisel observed that "[i]n many ways the jury is the law's most interesting critic." Harry Kalven, Jr. & Hans Zeisel, The American Jury 219 (1966). According to them, among the factors jurors consider in determining whether to acquit a defendant are: (1) the personal characteristics of the defendant; (2) the degree of harm caused by the defendant; (3) the jurors' belief that the victim was partially at fault for the offense; (4) their view of the morality or wisdom of the law that the defendant violated; (5) their belief that the defendant has been punished enough or that violation of the offense carries too harsh a penalty; and (6) their perception that the police or prosecutor acted improperly in bringing the case. Do you believe that any or all of these reasons should serve as a basis for acquitting a factually guilty defendant?

4.   Should a judge, sitting without a jury, nullify the law if she believes that the law is unjust or that punishment of the defendant would be morally wrong under the circumstances? Is judicial nullification more—or less—troubling than jury nullification?

Chapter 2

PRINCIPLES OF PUNISHMENT

A. JUSTIFICATIONS OF PUNISHMENT: IN GENERAL

KENT GREENAWALT—PUNISHMENT

4 Encyclopedia of Crime and Justice 1336 (Sanford
H. Kadish, Editor in Chief 1983), 1336–1338

Although punishment has been a crucial feature of every legal system, widespread disagreement exists over the moral principles that can justify its imposition. One fundamental question is why (and whether) the social institution of punishment is warranted. A second question concerns the necessary conditions for punishment in particular cases. A third relates to the degree of severity that is appropriate for particular offenses and offenders. * * *

Since punishment involves pain or deprivation that people wish to avoid, its intentional imposition by the state requires justification. The difficulties of justification cannot be avoided by the view that punishment is an inevitable adjunct of a system of criminal law. If *criminal law* is defined to include punishment, the central question remains whether society should have a system of mandatory rules enforced by penalties. Relatively small associations of like-minded people may be able to operate with rules that are not backed by sanctions, and a choice by the larger society against authorizing legal punishment is at least theoretically possible. Moreover, actual infliction of penalties is not inextricably tied to authorization. A father who has threatened punishment if two daughters do not stop fighting must decide whether to follow through if the fight continues. Congruence between threat and actual performance on the scene does constitute one good reason for punishing. Future threats will be taken less seriously if past threats are not fulfilled, and parents usually wish to avoid the impression that they will not do what they say. Nevertheless, because he now sees that the punishment threatened is too severe, or understands better the children's reasons for fighting, the father may fail to carry out his threat.

In the broader society also, threatened punishments are not always inflicted on persons who have unquestionably committed crimes. The police or prosecutor may decide not to proceed, a jury may acquit in the face of unmistakable evidence of guilt, or a judge may decide after conviction not to impose punishment. A judge with legal authority to make such a decision must determine if punishment is appropriate; even if he is legally required to inflict it, he may find the countervailing reasons so powerful that he will not do so.

If actual punishment never or very rarely followed threatened punishment, the threat would lose significance. Thus, punishment in some cases is a practical necessity for any system in which threats of punishment are to be taken seriously; and to that extent, the justification of punishment is inseparable from the justification of threats of punishment.

The dominant approaches to justification are retributive and utilitarian. Briefly stated, a retributivist claims that punishment is justified because people deserve it; a utilitarian believes that justification lies in the useful purposes that punishment serves. Many actual theories of punishment do not fit unambiguously and exclusively into one of these two categories. Satisfying both retributive and utilitarian criteria may be thought necessary to warrant punishment; or utilitarian criteria may be thought crucial for one question (for example, whether there should be a system of punishment) and retributive criteria for another (for example, who should be punished); or the use of retributive sorts of approaches may be thought appropriate on utilitarian grounds. Beginning from rather straightforward versions of retributive and utilitarian theory, the analysis proceeds to positions that are more complex.

Notes and Questions

1. Professor Greenawalt notes three "punishment" questions that retributivists and utilitarians seek to answer. As explained more fully in H.L.A. Hart, Punishment and Responsibility 1–27 (1968), the first question may be stated as follows: "What is the general justifying aim of the criminal justice system?" That is, why do we enact laws that define specified conduct as criminal and impose punishment for violation of those laws?

The remaining questions involve the distribution of punishment: "To whom may punishment be applied and in what amount?" Many scholars and lawmakers apply one penal theory—retribution or utilitarianism—to answer both questions, but others invoke one principle to answer the "general justifying aim" question and the second to resolve "distribution" problems. As you study criminal law this semester, consider whether you believe one principle resolves both issues. If not, how does your mixed theory work?

2. Retributivism is based on the principle that people who commit crimes deserve punishment. In that sense, the theory is backward looking: the justification for punishment is found in the prior wrongdoing. In contrast, utilitarianism is forward looking because it is justified on the basis

of the supposed benefits that will accrue from its imposition. In the materials that follow, these two philosophies are considered in greater depth.

B. UTILITARIAN JUSTIFICATIONS

JEREMY BENTHAM—AN INTRODUCTION TO THE PRINCIPLES OF MORALS AND LEGISLATION

(John Bowring edition 1843), 1, 15–16, 83–84

[Chapter 1] I. Nature has placed mankind under the governance of two sovereign masters, *pain* and *pleasure*. It is for them alone to point out what we ought to do, as well as to determine what we shall do. * * * They govern us in all we do, in all we say, in all we think: every effort we can make to throw off our subjection, will serve but to demonstrate and confirm it. In words a man may pretend to abjure their empire: but in reality he will remain subject to it all the while. The *principle of utility* recognises this subjection, and assumes it for the foundation of that system, the object of which is to rear the fabric of felicity by the hands of reason and of law. Systems which attempt to question it, deal in sounds instead of sense, in caprice instead of reason, in darkness instead of light. * * *

II. * * * By the principle of utility is meant that principle which approves or disapproves of every action whatsoever, according to the tendency which it appears to have to augment or diminish the happiness of the party whose interest is in question: or, what is the same thing in other words, to promote or to oppose that happiness. I say of every action whatsoever; and therefore not only of every action of a private individual, but of every measure of government. * * *

[Chapter IV] I. Pleasures then, and the avoidance of pains, are the *ends* which the legislator has in view: it behoves him therefore to understand their *value*. Pleasures and pains are the *instruments* he has to work with: it behoves him therefore to understand their force, which is again, in other words, their value.

II. To a person considered *by himself,* the value of a pleasure or pain considered *by itself,* will be greater or less, according to the four following circumstances:

1. Its *intensity.*

2. Its *duration.*

3. Its *certainty or uncertainty.*

4. Its *propinquity or remoteness.* * * *

[Chapter XV] I. The general object which all laws have, or ought to have, in common, is to augment the total happiness of the community; and therefore, in the first place, to exclude, as far as may be, every thing that tends to subtract from the happiness: in other words, to exclude mischief.

II. But all punishment is mischief: all punishment in itself is evil. Upon the principle of utility, if it ought at all to be admitted, it ought only to be admitted in as far as it promises to exclude some greater evil.

III. It is plain, therefore, that in the following cases punishment ought not to be inflicted.

1. Where it is *groundless:* where there is no mischief for it to prevent; the act not being mischievous upon the whole.

2. Where it must be *inefficacious:* where it cannot act so as to prevent the mischief.

3. Where it is *unprofitable,* or too *expensive:* where the mischief it would produce would be greater than what it prevented.

4. Where it is *needless:* where the mischief may be prevented, or cease of itself, without it: that is, at a cheaper rate.

KENT GREENAWALT—PUNISHMENT

4 Encyclopedia of Crime and Justice 1336 (Sanford
H. Kadish, Editor in Chief 1983), 1340–1341

Utilitarian theories of punishment have dominated American jurisprudence during most of the twentieth century. According to Jeremy Bentham's classical utilitarianism, whether an act or social practice is morally desirable depends upon whether it promotes human happiness better than possible alternatives. Since punishment involves pain, it can be justified only if it accomplishes enough good consequences to outweigh this harm. A theory of punishment may make the balance of likely consequences central to justification without asserting, as Bentham did, that all relevant consequences are reducible to happiness and unhappiness. It may even claim that reducing future instances of immoral violations of right is itself an appropriate goal independent of the effect of those violations on the people involved. In modern usage, *utilitarianism* is often employed to refer broadly to theories that likely consequences determine the morality of action, and this usage is followed here.

The catalogs of beneficial consequences that utilitarians have thought can be realized by punishment have varied, but the following have generally been regarded as most important.

1. *General deterrence.* Knowledge that punishment will follow crime deters people from committing crimes, thus reducing future violations of right and the unhappiness and insecurity they would cause. The person who has already committed a crime cannot, of course, be deterred from committing that crime, but his punishment may help to deter others. In Bentham's view, general deterrence was very much a matter of affording rational self-interested persons good reasons not to commit crimes. With a properly developed penal code, the benefits to be gained from criminal activity would be outweighed by the harms of punishment, even when those harms were discounted by the probability of avoiding detection. Accordingly, the greater the temptation to com-

mit a particular crime and the smaller the chance of detection, the more severe the penalty should be.

Punishment can also deter in ways more subtle than adding a relevant negative factor for cool calculation. Seeing others punished for certain behavior can create in people a sense of association between punishment and act that may constrain them even when they are sure they will not get caught. Adults, as well as children, may subconsciously fear punishment even though rationally they are confident it will not occur. * * *

[2.] *Individual deterrence.* The actual imposition of punishment creates fear in the offender that if he repeats his act, he will be punished again. Adults are more able than small children to draw conclusions from the punishment of others, but having a harm befall oneself is almost always a sharper lesson than seeing the same harm occur to others. To deter an offender from repeating his actions, a penalty should be severe enough to outweigh in his mind the benefits of the crime. For the utilitarian, more severe punishment of repeat offenders is warranted partly because the first penalty has shown itself ineffective from the standpoint of individual deterrence.

[3.] *Incapacitation.* Imprisonment puts convicted criminals out of general circulation temporarily, and the death penalty does so permanently. These punishments physically prevent persons of dangerous disposition from acting upon their destructive tendencies.

[4.] *Reform.* Punishment may help to reform the criminal so that his wish to commit crimes will be lessened, and perhaps so that he can be a happier, more useful person. Conviction and simple imposition of a penalty might themselves be thought to contribute to reform if they help an offender become aware that he has acted wrongly. However, reform is usually conceived as involving more positive steps to alter basic character or improve skills, in order to make offenders less antisocial. Various psychological therapies, and more drastic interventions such as psychosurgery, are designed to curb destructive tendencies. Educational and training programs can render legitimate employment a more attractive alternative to criminal endeavors. These may indirectly help enhance self-respect, but their primary purpose is to alter the options that the released convict will face.

Notes and Questions

1. Does punishment deter? Do prisons rehabilitate? These simple questions do not yield simple answers. Regarding the deterrent value of punishment, research indicates that the benefit of punishment depends on various factors, including: the nature of the offense; the type of offender involved; the perceived risk of detection, arrest, and conviction; and the nature and severity of the penalties threatened or imposed. In general, an increase in the detection, arrest and conviction rate is of greater deterrent consequence than an increase in the severity of the penalty upon conviction. Johannes Andenaes, Punishment and Deterrence 54 (1974).

Incapacitation by imprisonment has deterrent value in the straightforward sense that, during incarceration, an inmate cannot commit an offense in the outside society. Because utilitarians believe that punishment is a mischief that should not be imposed unless it will result in a net benefit to society, punishment based on this principle is only justifiable to the extent that the sentencing authority can reliably predict the future dangerousness of the offender. Criminological studies do not provide an optimistic appraisal of our predictive capacities in this regard. For a discussion of the subject, see Prediction and Classification: Criminal Justice Decision Making (Don Gottfredson & Michael Tonry eds., 1987).

Incarceration rarely is imposed today for reform, or rehabilitative, purposes. Serious rehabilitative efforts in the past were only occasionally successful. Moreover, reform efforts are costly; in these days of serious budgetary constraints, legislators are often hesitant to appropriate large sums of money for what some taxpayers consider "coddling" of criminals. For a survey of the failures and successes of reformative efforts, see Robert Martinson, *New Findings, New Views: A Note of Caution Regarding Sentencing Reform,* 7 Hofstra L.Rev. 243 (1979); Robert Martinson, *What Works?—Questions and Answers About Prison Reform,* 36 Pub.Interest 22 (1974). For a survey of the philosophical attacks on rehabilitation as a justification for punishment and the effort to "rehabilitate rehabilitation," see Michael Vitiello, *Reconsidering Rehabilitation,* 65 Tul.L.Rev. 1011 (1991).

2. Utilitarians and retributivists speak in distinct languages when they discuss punishment. A retributivist is likely to talk about whether punishment is (or is not) "deserved" (see subsection C. infra), whereas utilitarians worry about whether punishment is "rational," "efficacious," or "profitable." As a consequence, utilitarians and retributivists can both be correct in their factual assertions, even though they reach conflicting conclusions regarding the justifiability of punishment in a particular case. For example, punishment might be "deserved" (in the retributivist sense that the person voluntarily committed a crime), and yet such punishment might not be "profitable," because it will have no deterrent value.

What about the converse situation? That is, could "undeserved" punishment of an innocent person be rational, efficacious or profitable? Consider the following scenario: An especially violent murder occurs in a small, racially divided community. The victim is white and, although there is no hard evidence to prove it, a rumor quickly spreads that the killer was black. As the result of racist activity by white supremacist groups, a white mob threatens to enter the black community and kill innocent African–Americans and burn down their homes in order to exact vengeance. The town sheriff realizes that she lacks adequate personnel to stop the mob. She is convinced, however, that if she arrests an African–American for the crime and promises a quick trial, the mob will be satisfied. Therefore, she arrests and frames a homeless black man with a prior record of violent criminal activity. As predicted, the mob is satisfied; the man is subsequently tried, convicted, and punished for the crime.

Could a utilitarian justify the sheriff's actions? If not, why not? Compare H.J. McCloskey, *A Non–Utilitarian Approach to Punishment* in

Contemporary Utilitarianism 239–259 (Michael D. Bayles, ed. 1968) (contending that a utilitarian would punish an innocent person in similar circumstances) with T.L.S. Sprigge, *A Utilitarian Reply to Dr. McCloskey,* in Contemporary Utilitarianism, supra, at 261–299 (disagreeing with McCloskey).

C. RETRIBUTIVE JUSTIFICATIONS

IMMANUEL KANT—THE PHILOSOPHY OF LAW

(W. Hastie translation 1887), 194–198

The right of administering punishment is the right of the sovereign as the supreme power to inflict pain upon a subject on account of a crime committed by him. * * *

Judicial or juridical punishment (*poena forensis*) is to be distinguished from natural punishment (*poena naturalis*), in which crime as vice punishes itself, and does not as such come within the cognizance of the legislator. Juridical punishment can never be administered merely as a means for promoting another good either with regard to the criminal himself or to civil society, but must in all cases be imposed only because the individual on whom it is inflicted *has committed a crime.* For one man ought never to be dealt with merely as a means subservient to the purpose of another, nor be mixed up with the subjects of real right. Against such treatment his inborn personality has a right to protect him, even although he may be condemned to lose his civil personality. He must first be found guilty and *punishable,* before there can be any thought of drawing from his punishment any benefit for himself or his fellow-citizens. The penal law is a categorical imperative; and woe to him who creeps through the serpent-windings of utilitarianism to discover some advantage that may discharge him from the justice of punishment, or even from the due measure of it, according to the Pharisaic maxim: "It is better that *one* man should die than that the whole people should perish." For if justice and righteousness perish, human life would no longer have any value in the world. What, then, is to be said of such a proposal as to keep a criminal alive who has been condemned to death, on his being given to understand that, if he agreed to certain dangerous experiments being performed upon him, he would be allowed to survive if he came happily through them? It is argued that physicians might thus obtain new information that would be of value to the commonweal. But a court of justice would repudiate with scorn any proposal of this kind if made to it by the medical faculty; for justice would cease to be justice, if it were bartered away for any consideration whatever.

* * * Even if a civil society resolved to dissolve itself with the consent of all its members—as might be supposed in the case of a people inhabiting an island resolving to separate and scatter themselves throughout the whole world—the last murderer lying in the prison ought to be executed before the resolution was carried out. This ought to be done in order that every one may realize the desert of his deeds, and that blood-guiltiness may not remain upon the people; for otherwise they might all be regarded as participators in the murder as a public violation of justice.

Notes and Questions

1. Should punishment that is deserved be imposed, even if it will not be beneficial in a utilitarian sense? Reflect on the following case: *D* kidnapped and, over a 12–hour period, repeatedly raped *V,* a young woman who had stopped on the freeway because of a flat tire. During her ordeal, *V* begged *D* to kill her in order to end her agony. He responded, "You'll die when I tell you." *V* survived. *D* was arrested, convicted, and sentenced to imprisonment for life. Nine years later, *D* asked the victim for forgiveness. See Patricia Chargot, *Freeway Rape Still Twists Victim's Life,* Detroit Free Press, Mar. 31, 1985, at A1; Jack Kresnak, *Rapist Asks for "Forgiveness",* id.

Assume that the following facts were conclusively proved: *D*'s plea for forgiveness is genuine, as the result of a change of character; because of his repentance and successful rehabilitative measures in prison, he would no longer constitute a threat to the safety of others if he were released; indeed, if released, he would voluntarily work in the community in anti-crime programs; and *D* could quietly be set free, so that other criminals would not be emboldened by the state's leniency to commit an offense.

Under these circumstances, would you favor early release of *D*? If not, why not?

2 JAMES FITZJAMES STEPHEN—A HISTORY OF THE CRIMINAL LAW OF ENGLAND

(1883), 80–82

* * * Whatever may be the nature or extent of the differences which exist as to the nature of morals, no one in this country regards murder, rape, arson, robbery, theft, or the like, with any feeling but detestation. I do not think it admits of any doubt that law and morals powerfully support and greatly intensify each other in this matter. Everything which is regarded as enhancing the moral guilt of a particular offence is recognised as a reason for increasing the severity of the punishment awarded to it. On the other hand, the sentence of the law is to the moral sentiment of the public in relation to any offence what a seal is to hot wax. It converts into a permanent final judgment what might otherwise be a transient sentiment. The mere general suspicion or knowledge that a man has done something dishonest may never be brought to a point, and the disapprobation excited by it may in time pass away, but the fact that he has been convicted and punished as a thief stamps a mark upon him for life. In short, the infliction of punishment by law gives definite expression and a solemn ratification and justification to the hatred which is excited by the commission of the offence, and which constitutes the moral or popular as distinguished from the conscientious sanction of that part of morality which is also sanctioned by the criminal law. The criminal law thus proceeds upon the principle that it

is morally right to hate criminals, and it confirms and justifies that sentiment by inflicting upon criminals punishments which express it.

* * * I am * * * of opinion that this close alliance between criminal law and moral sentiment is in all ways healthy and advantageous to the community. I think it highly desirable that criminals should be hated, that the punishments inflicted upon them should be so contrived as to give expression to that hatred, and to justify it so far as the public provision of means for expressing and gratifying a healthy natural sentiment can justify and encourage it.

These views are regarded by many persons as being wicked, because it is supposed that we never ought to hate, or wish to be revenged upon, any one. The doctrine that hatred and vengeance are wicked in themselves appears to me to contradict plain facts, and to be unsupported by any argument deserving of attention. Love and hatred, gratitude for benefits, and the desire of vengeance for injuries, imply each other as much as convex and concave.

JOSHUA DRESSLER—HATING CRIMINALS: HOW CAN SOMETHING THAT FEELS SO GOOD BE WRONG?

88 Michigan Law Review 1448 (1990), 1451–1453

I. STAKING OUT THE ISSUES * * *

The theory of retributivism is divisible into "negative" and "positive" variants. Negative retributivism, accepted by many or perhaps most scholars, holds only that it is morally wrong to punish an innocent person even if society might benefit from the action, *i.e.,* that the retributive principle of just deserts is a necessary condition of punishment. A person can accept this retributive limitation on utilitarian goals without being a full-blown retributivist.

Positive retributivism is more controversial. It takes the stronger position that not only must an innocent person never be punished; but, affirmatively, one who is guilty of an offense must be punished, *i.e.,* retributive justice is a necessary and sufficient condition of punishment. * * *

Positive retributivism is * * * divisible into two categories, "assaultive" and "protective" retribution.[19] The most famous exponent of the assaultive variety is James Stephen, who claimed that "it is morally right to hate criminals." Under Stephen's view, punishment is justified without any consideration of the criminal's rights or best interests * * *.

The difficulty with this thesis * * * is that * * * [it] is based in significant part on revenge-utilitarianism rather than on retribution. In other words, Stephen's assaultive retribution justifies punishment of criminals because it deters private vengeance and sends a useful denunciatory message to would-be offenders that such conduct is wrongful. What [Jeffrie] Murphy seeks to do in *Forgiveness and Mercy* [excerpted

---

19. The terms were coined by Radin, *Cruel Punishment and Respect for Persons:* *Super Due Process for Death,* 53 S.Cal. L.Rev. 1143, 1168–69 (1980).

below] is to provide a nonutilitarian justification of Stephen's assaultive "hate-the-criminal" ethic.

However, there is another way to justify positive retribution without accepting the principle that criminals should be hated. In stark contrast to assaultive retribution is protective retribution, an idea eloquently defined on recent years by Herbert Morris. Protective retribution is based on the proposition that not only does a just society [23] have a right to punish voluntary wrongdoers, but that criminals also have a right to be punished.

Morris' defense of this theory [excerpted below] is based on a principle of reciprocal benefits and burdens. * * *

[Jean] Hampton rejects both Murphy's hate-the-criminal defense of retribution and Morris' benefits-and-burdens conception. * * * [H]er goal in *Forgiveness and Mercy* [excerpted below] * * * is to develop an alternative retributive justification that is not based, even in part, on the criminal's interests, but which also does not fall back on the hatred that Stephen glorifies and Murphy qualifiedly justifies.

JEFFRIE G. MURPHY & JEAN HAMPTON— FORGIVENESS AND MERCY

(1988), 16, 91–95 [a]

* * * If a total case is to be made against hatred, it must be made against examples where the hatred appears at its best and most *prima facie* justified—examples where a person has in fact been treated very immorally, has been hurt badly by the immoral treatment, reasonably believes that the wrongdoer is totally unrepentant of the wrongdoing and is in fact living a life of freedom and contentment, and—*given all that*—hates the wrongdoer and desires that the wrongdoer suffer. Such cases may be rare, but—confessing that I firmly hold the unmodern view that there is such a thing as evil in this world—I believe that they do exist. For example, when the victims in a recent series of vicious rapes in Phoenix testified that they wanted the "Camelback rapist," who had utterly trashed the lives of some of them, to be sentenced to the maximum term that the law allowed, many of them openly admitted that they were acting out of anger and hatred. These women were outraged at the thought that this vicious man, utterly unrepentant, could soon continue to lead a free life, given what he had done to their lives. I sympathized with their anger and hatred, having no inclination at all to call them petty or spiteful. * * * *This* is the kind of case that must be discussed and made central in any comprehensive attack on the nature and justification of hatred, the kind of hatred I have called retributive in nature.

---

23. The theory will not hold in an unjust society, such as one based on apartheid, in which the benefits and burdens of society are not fairly apportioned.

a. The book is written in the form of a dialogue between the two authors. Professor Jeffrie Murphy wrote this excerpt.

Resentment, I have previously argued, is essentially tied to self-respect. It is an emotional defense against attacks on self-esteem * * *.[b]

Even supposing that what I have said about resentment is correct, however, it may not seem that it will help very much in mounting a case for the justification of hatred—even retributive hatred. For the hater, unlike the resenter, is not simply engaged in protest and self-assertion. He also desires that the object of his hate be *hurt*. If hate is sometimes justified, then the desire to hurt another must sometimes be justified. But how can this be?

This is how: If it is morally permissible intentionally to do *X* (under a certain description), then it is surely permissible to *desire* to do *X* (under the same description). If there is any truth at all in retributive theories of punishment, then it is sometimes permissible that persons be hurt (punishment hurts) in response to their wrongdoing. It is thus sometimes permissible to hurt people for retributive reasons. Given this, it is sometimes permissible to desire to hurt people for retributive reasons. * * * [W]e may say that retributive hatred is a strategy designed to see (and to let the victim see) that people get their just deserts; as such it is neither irrational nor immoral. The wrongdoer gets his just deserts (and what is wrong with that?), and the victim gets some personal satisfaction from seeing the justice done (and what is wrong with that?). * * * Retributive hatred is thus in principle vindicated as a permissible, if not mandatory, response of a victim to wrongdoing.

HERBERT MORRIS—PERSONS AND PUNISHMENT
52 Monist 475 (1968), 476–479

My aim is to argue for four propositions concerning rights that will certainly strike some as not only false but preposterous: first, that we have a right to punishment; second, that this right derives from a fundamental human right to be treated as a person; third, that this fundamental right is a natural, inalienable, and absolute right; and, fourth, that the denial of this right implies the denial of all moral rights and duties. Showing the truth of one, let alone all, of these large and

---

b. "In my view, resentment (in its range from righteous anger to righteous hatred) functions primarily in defense, not of *all* moral values and norms, but rather of certain *values of the self*. Resentment is a response not to general wrongs but to wrongs against oneself; and these resented wrongs can be of two sorts: resentment of direct violations of one's rights (as in assault) *or* resentment that another has taken unfair advantage of one's sacrifices by free riding on a mutually beneficial scheme of reciprocal cooperation. Only the immediate victim of crime is in a position to resent a criminal in the first way; all the law-abiding citizens, however, may be in a position to resent the criminal (and thus be secondary victims) in the second way * * *.

"I am, in short, suggesting that the primary value defended by the passion of resentment is *self-respect*, that proper self-respect is essentially tied to the passion of resentment, and that a person who does not resent moral injuries done to him * * * is almost necessarily a person lacking in self-respect. * * * In some limited sense, then, I side with Stephen: Resentment (perhaps even some hatred) is a good thing, for it is essentially tied to a non-controversially good thing—self respect."

questionable claims, is a tall order. The attempt or, more properly speaking, the first steps in an attempt, follow. * * *

Let us first turn attention to the institutions in which punishment is involved. The institutions I describe will resemble those we ordinarily think of as institutions of punishment; they will have, however, additional features we associate with a system of just punishment.

Let us suppose that men are constituted roughly as they now are, with a rough equivalence in strength and abilities, a capacity to be injured by each other and to make judgments that such injury is undesirable, a limited strength of will, and a capacity to reason and to conform conduct to rules. Applying to the conduct of these men are a group of rules, ones I shall label "primary," which closely resemble the core rules of our criminal law, rules that prohibit violence and deception and compliance with which provides benefits for all persons. These benefits consist of noninterference by others with what each person values, such matters as continuance of life and bodily security. The rules define a sphere for each person then, which is immune from interference by others. Making possible this mutual benefit is the assumption by individuals of a burden. The burden consists in the exercise of self-restraint by individuals over inclinations that would, if satisfied, directly interfere or create a substantial risk of interference with others in proscribed ways. If a person fails to exercise self-restraint even though he might have and gives in to such inclinations, he renounces a burden which others have voluntarily assumed and thus gains an advantage which others, who have restrained themselves, do not possess. This system, then, is one in which the rules establish a mutuality of benefit and burden and in which the benefits of noninterference are conditional upon the assumption of burdens.

Connecting punishment with the violation of these primary rules, and making public the provision for punishment, is both reasonable and just. First, it is only reasonable that those who voluntarily comply with the rules be provided some assurance that they will not be assuming burdens which others are unprepared to assume. * * * Second, fairness dictates that a system in which benefits and burdens are equally distributed have a mechanism designed to prevent a maldistribution in the benefits and burdens. * * *

Third, it is just to punish those who have violated the rules and caused the unfair distribution of benefits and burdens. A person who violates the rules has something others have—the benefits of the system—but by renouncing what others have assumed, the burdens of self-restraint, he has acquired an unfair advantage. Matters are not even until this advantage is in some way erased. Another way of putting it is that he owes something to others, for he has something that does not rightfully belong to him. Justice—that is punishing such individuals— restores the equilibrium of benefits and burdens by taking from the individual what he owes, that is, exacting the debt. * * *

There are also in this system we are considering a variety of operative principles compliance with which provides some guarantee that the system of punishment does not itself promote an unfair distribution of benefits and burdens. For one thing, provision is made for a variety of defenses, each one of which can be said to have as its object diminishing the chances of forcibly depriving a person of benefits others have if that person has not derived an unfair advantage. A person has not derived an unfair advantage if he could not have restrained himself or if it is unreasonable to expect him to behave otherwise than he did. Sometimes the rules preclude punishment of classes of persons such as children. Sometimes they provide a defense if on a particular occasion a person lacked the capacity to conform his conduct to the rules. Thus, someone who in an epileptic seizure strikes another is excused. Punishment in these cases would be punishment of the innocent, punishment of those who do not voluntarily renounce a burden others have assumed. Punishment in such cases, then, would not equalize but rather cause an unfair distribution in benefits and burdens.

JEFFRIE G. MURPHY & JEAN HAMPTON— FORGIVENESS AND MERCY

(1988), 124–128, 130 [c]

Retributive idea 1: punishment as a defeat. Those who wrong others * * * objectively demean them. They incorrectly believe or else fail to realize that others' value rules out the treatment their actions have accorded the others, and they incorrectly believe or implicitly assume that their own value is high enough to make this treatment permissible. So, implicit in their wrongdoings is a message about their value relative to that of their victims. * * *

* * * A retributivist's commitment to punishment is not merely a commitment to taking hubristic wrongdoers down a peg or two; it is also a commitment to asserting moral truth in the face of its denial. If I have value equal to that of my assailant, then that must be made manifest after I have been victimized. By victimizing me, the wrongdoer has declared himself elevated with respect to me, acting as a superior who is permitted to use me for his purposes. A false moral claim has been made. Moral reality has been denied. The retributivist demands that the false claim be corrected. The lord must be humbled to show that he isn't the lord of the victim. If I cause the wrongdoer to suffer in proportion to my suffering at his hands, his elevation over me is denied, and moral reality is reaffirmed. I master the purported master, showing that he is my peer.

So I am proposing that retributive punishment is the defeat of the wrongdoer at the hands of the victim (either directly or indirectly through an agent of the victim's, e.g., the state) that symbolizes the correct relative value of wrongdoer and victim. It is a symbol that is

c. Professor Jean Hampton wrote this excerpt.

conceptually required to reaffirm a victim's equal worth in the face of a challenge to it. * * *

But exactly how does punishment make this assertion? Consider that retributivists typically endorse the *lex talionis* as a punishment formula, or (as I would reinterpret it) as a formula for determining the extent to which the wrongdoer must be mastered. That formula calls for a wrongdoer to suffer something like what his victim suffered * * *.
* * * To inflict on a wrongdoer something comparable to what he inflicted on the victim is to master him in the way that he mastered the victim. The score is even. Whatever mastery he can claim, she can also claim. If her victimization is taken as evidence of her inferiority relative to the wrongdoer, then his defeat at her hands negates that evidence. Hence the *lex talionis* calls for a wrongdoer to be subjugated in a way that symbolizes his being the victim's equal. The punishment is a second act of mastery that denies the lordship asserted in the first act of mastery. * * *

* * * [T]he *retributive* motive for inflicting suffering is to annul or counter the appearance of the wrongdoer's superiority and thus affirm the victim's real value. So even in a situation where neither the wrongdoer nor society will either listen to or believe the message about the victim's worth which the "punitive defeat" is meant to carry, and where the victim doesn't need to hear (or will not believe) that message in order to allay any personal fears of diminishment, the retributivist will insist on the infliction of punishment insofar as it is a way of "striking a blow for morality" or (to use a phrase of C.S. Lewis's) a way to "plant the flag" of morality.

Notes and Questions

1. *Assaultive versus protective retribution.* Death is a justifiable penalty for various offenses under James Stephen's version of assaultive retribution. Capital punishment is a much more complicated issue for *protective* retributivists, many of whom mount anti-death-penalty arguments. Nonetheless, the difference between assaultive and protective retribution is evident in following statements regarding capital punishment.

First, consider the purported remarks of a federal judge in the New Mexico Territory at the 1881 sentencing of a malefactor.[d]

Jose Manuel Miguel Xavier Gonzales, in a few short weeks it will be spring. The snows of winter will flee away, the ice will vanish, and the air will become soft and balmy. In short, Jose Manuel Miguel Xavier Gonzales, the annual miracle of the years will awaken and come to pass, but you won't be there.

The rivulet will run its soaring course to the sea, the timid desert flowers will put forth their tender shoots, the glorious valleys of this

---

d. The statement, which I have not discovered in any official legal report relating to the territory, may be apocryphal. An excerpt of the remarks may be found in Jack Smith, *Page Out of the Old West and a* *Poetic Hanging Judge,* Los Angeles Times, Oct. 18, 1990, at E1. I thank Mr. Lee Cannon of Marshall, Texas for providing me with a copy of the full statement.

imperial domain will blossom as the rose. Still, you won't be here to see.

From every treetop some wild woods songster will carol his mating song; butterflies will sport in the sunshine, the busy bee will hum happy as it pursues its accustomed vacation; the gentle breeze will tease the tassels of the wild grasses, and all nature will be glad, but you. You won't be here to enjoy it because I command the sheriff or some other officers of the country [sic] to lead you out to some remote spot, swing you by the neck from a knotting bough of some sturdy oak, and let you hang until you are dead.

And then, Jose Manuel Miguel Xavier Gonzales, I further command that such officer or officers retire quickly from your dangling corpse, so that vultures may descend from the heavens upon your filthy body until nothing shall remain but bare, bleached bones of a cold-blooded, * * * bloodthirsty, throat-cutting, murdering son of a bitch.

In contrast to these expressions of assaultive retribution are the thoughts of Gary Gilmore, a murderer awaiting execution on Utah's Death Row, expressed in a letter to his friend, Nicole:

Recently it has begun to make a little sense. I owe a debt, from a long time ago. * * * I'm on the verge of knowing something very personal, something about myself. Something that somehow wasn't completed and made me different. Something I owe, I guess. Wish I knew.

Once you asked me if I was the devil, remember? I'm not. The devil would be far more clever than I, would operate on a much larger scale and of course would feel no remorse. * * * And I know the devil can't feel love. But I might be further from God than I am from the devil. Which is not a good thing. It seems that I know evil more intimately than I know goodness and that's not a good thing either. I want to get even, to be made even, whole, my debts paid (whatever it may take!) to have no blemish, no reason to feel guilt or fears. I hope this ain't corny, but I'd like to stand in the sight of God. To know that I'm just and right and clean.

Norman Mailer, The Executioner's Song 305–06 (1979).

D.   THE PENAL THEORIES IN ACTION
THE QUEEN v. DUDLEY AND STEPHENS

Queen's Bench Division, 1884.
14 Q.B.D. 273.

LORD COLERIDGE, C.J. The two prisoners, Thomas Dudley and Edwin Stephens, were indicted for the murder of Richard Parker on the high seas on the 25th day of July in the present year. They were tried before my Brother Huddleston at Exeter on the 6th of November, and, under the direction of my learned Brother, the jury returned a special verdict, the legal effect of which has been argued before us, and on which we are now to pronounce judgment.

The special verdict as * * * it is finally settled before us is as follows.

[T]hat on July 5, 1884, the prisoners, Thomas Dudley and Edward Stephens, with one Brooks, all able-bodied English seamen, and the deceased also an English boy, between seventeen and eighteen years of age, the crew of an English yacht, a registered English vessel, were cast away in a storm on the high seas 1600 miles from the Cape of Good Hope, and were compelled to put into an open boat belonging to the said yacht. That in this boat they had no supply of water and no supply of food, except two 1lb. tins of turnips, and for three days they had nothing else to subsist upon. That on the fourth day they caught a small turtle, upon which they subsisted for a few days, and this was the only food they had up to the twentieth day when the act now in question was committed. That on the twelfth day the remains of the turtle were entirely consumed, and for the next eight days they had nothing to eat. That they had no fresh water, except such rain as they from time to time caught in their oilskin capes. That the boat was drifting on the ocean, and was probably more than 1000 miles away from land. That on the eighteenth day, when they had been seven days without food and five without water, the prisoners spoke to Brooks as to what should be done if no succour came, and suggested that some one should be sacrificed to save the rest, but Brooks dissented, and the boy, to whom they were understood to refer, was not consulted. That on the 24th of July, the day before the act now in question, the prisoner Dudley proposed to Stephens and Brooks that lots should be cast who should be put to death to save the rest, but Brooks refused to consent, and it was not put to the boy, and in point of fact there was no drawing of lots. That on that day the prisoners spoke of their having families, and suggested it would be better to kill the boy that their lives should be saved, and Dudley proposed that if there was no vessel in sight by the morrow morning the boy should be killed. That next day, the 25th of July, no vessel appearing, Dudley told Brooks that he had better go and have a sleep, and made signs to Stephens and Brooks that the boy had better be killed. The prisoner Stephens agreed to the act, but Brooks dissented from it. That the boy was then lying at the bottom of the boat quite helpless, and extremely weakened by famine and by drinking sea water, and unable to make any resistance, nor did he ever assent to his being killed. The prisoner Dudley offered a prayer asking forgiveness for them all if either of them should be tempted to commit a rash act, and that their souls might be saved. That Dudley, with the assent of Stephens, went to the boy, and telling him that his time was come, put a knife into his throat and killed him then and there; that the three men fed upon the body and blood of the boy for four days; that on the fourth day after the act had been committed the boat was picked up by a passing vessel, and the prisoners were rescued, still alive, but in the lowest state of prostration. That they were carried to the port of Falmouth, and committed for trial at Exeter. That if the men had not fed upon the body of the boy they would probably not have survived to be so picked up and rescued, but would within the four days have died of famine. That the boy, being in a much weaker condition, was likely to have died before them. That at the time of the act in question there was no sail in sight, nor any reasonable prospect of relief. That under these circumstances there appeared to the prisoners every probability that unless they then fed or very soon fed upon the boy or one of themselves they would die of starvation. That there was no appreciable chance of saving life except by killing some one for the others to eat. That assuming any necessity to kill anybody, there was no greater necessity for killing the boy than any of the other three men. But whether upon the whole matter by the jurors found the killing of Richard Parker by Dudley and Stephens be felony and murder the jurors are ignorant, and pray the advice of the Court thereupon, and if upon the whole matter the Court shall be of opinion that the killing of Richard Parker be felony and murder, then the jurors say that Dudley and Stephens were each guilty of felony and murder as alleged in the indictment.

Notes and Questions

1. The court unanimously held "that the facts as stated in the verdict are no legal justification of the homicide," after which Lord Coleridge pronounced the sentence of death. The sentence was commuted by the Crown to six months' imprisonment.

Should Dudley and Stephens have been punished for their conduct? If so, was a severe sentence appropriate, or was the Crown's lenient response preferable? Was the latter solution an unjustifiable compromise, in that it treated the killing as wrongful, but only minimally so?

2. A fuller picture of the events relating to the *Dudley and Stephens* affair is set out brilliantly in A.W. Brian Simpson, Cannibalism and the Common Law (1984). According to Professor Simpson, Dudley, captain of the ill-fated Mignonette, was an experienced yachtsman. He was married and the father of three children. Devoutly religious, he took prayer books to sea and conducted regular religious services on board. Dudley acted decisively and courageously throughout the crisis and was largely responsible for the seamen's survival during the early period in the dinghy.

Stephens was a devoted husband, father of five, and respected local figure. His impeccable career as a seaman was sullied as the result of the wreck of a vessel of which he was junior officer. Although he was not culpable for the loss, Stephens found it difficult to find employment until Dudley hired him to serve on the Mignonette.

Brooks's background is less clear. He claimed to be a bachelor, but there is evidence to suggest that he was married, deserted his wife, and accepted a position on the Mignonette in order to escape his wife, who may have been on his trail.

Parker was a wild-living illiterate youth. He signed on to the Mignonette in order to travel abroad, as a rite of passage into manhood.

Does this information regarding the parties affect your views regarding the sentence imposed?

UNITED STATES v. JACKSON

United States Court of Appeals, Seventh Circuit, 1987.
835 F.2d 1195.

EASTERBROOK, CIRCUIT JUDGE.

Thirty minutes after being released from prison, to which he had been sent on conviction of two bank robberies, Dwight Jackson robbed another bank. He was let out as part of a "work release program" and returned to his old line of work. Told to get a job, he decided to do a bank job. A passer-by saw a suspicious person flee the bank and noted the license plate of the car. * * * Jackson was back in prison before the sun set on the day of his release. His principal sentence—life in prison without possibility of parole—came under a statute forbidding possession of weapons by career criminals, 18 U.S.C.App. § 1202. * * *

Section 1202 * * * provided that anyone "who . . . possesses . . . any firearm and who has three previous [felony] convictions for robbery or burglary, or both, . . . shall be fined not more than $25,000 and imprisoned not less than fifteen years, and, notwithstanding any other provision of law, * * * such person shall not be eligible for parole with respect to the sentence imposed under this subsection." Jackson, who had been convicted of four armed bank robberies and one armed robbery, brandished his revolver and robbed the Continental Bank of Oakbrook Terrace, Illinois, on May 30, 1986, while this statute was in force. * * *

Jackson received a life sentence under § 1202, which forbade release on parole. He concedes that the statute permitted the imposition of any term of years but insists that it allowed only determinate numbers of years and therefore did not authorize a life sentence. When parole is forbidden, however, a judge may use either method to reach the same result. Jackson was 35 when he committed the crime. Unless there are startling advances in geriatric medicine, a long term of imprisonment (say, 60 years) and life are the same sentence; it would be silly to read the statute as authorizing one but not the other. Other statutes without stated maxima have been treated as authorizing life sentences. * * *

The imposition of life in prison on Jackson was permissible. * * * Armed bank robbery on the day of release—following earlier armed robbery convictions back to 1973—marked Jackson as a career criminal. Specific deterrence had failed. The court was entitled to consider general deterrence and incapacitation. Although life without possibility of parole is the upper end of the scale of sanctions (short of capital punishment), the statute reflects a judgment that career criminals who persist in possessing weapons should be dealt with most severely. * * * If this sentence is unduly harsh, the holder of the clemency power may supply a remedy. * * *

Affirmed

POSNER, CIRCUIT JUDGE, concurring.

I join the opinion and judgment of the court; but I think the sentence Jackson received is too harsh and I think it appropriate to point this out even though he presents no ground on which we are authorized to set aside an excessively severe sentence.

Jackson is unquestionably a dangerous and hardened criminal. He has been convicted of armed robbery four times (three were bank robberies—all of the same bank!); in each robbery he was carrying a loaded gun. I do not mean to denigrate the gravity of his offenses by pointing out that he has never inflicted a physical injury; but that fact is relevant to deciding whether the sheer enormity of his conduct warrants imprisonment for the rest of his life as a matter of retributive justice. It does not. Few murderers, traitors, or rapists are punished so severely * * *. The grounds for the sentence in this case must be sought elsewhere.

One ground, the one articulated by the district judge, is the need to prevent Jackson from committing further crimes. There is little doubt that if he were released tomorrow he would commit a bank robbery, perhaps on the same day. But it is extremely unlikely that if he were released 25 or 30 years from now (he is 35 years old) he would resume his career as a bank robber. We know that criminal careers taper off with age, although with the aging of the population and the improvements in the health of the aged the fraction of crimes committed by the elderly is rising. Crimes that involve a risk of physical injury to the criminal are especially a young man's game. In 1986 more than 62 percent of all persons arrested for robbery (any sort of robbery—I can find no breakdown by type of robbery) were below the age of 25, and only 3.4 percent were 60 years old or older. FBI, Uniform Crime Reports 20, 174–75, 180 (1986). * * * Bank robbery in particular, I suspect, is a young man's crime. A bank robber must be willing to confront armed guards and able to make a quick getaway. To suppose that if Jackson is fortunate enough to live on in prison into his seventies or eighties it would still be necessary to detain him lest he resume his life of crime after almost a lifetime in prison is too speculative to warrant imprisoning him until he dies of old age. The probation officer who conducted the presentence investigation of Jackson and compiled a meticulous 16–page single-spaced presentence report covering every facet of Jackson's history, personality, and criminal activity recommended a 10–year sentence. This may well be too short, but it is some indication that imprisonment for the rest of Jackson's life is too long if the only concern is with the crimes he might commit if he were ever released.

The remaining possibility is that this savage sentence is proper *pour encourager les autres*. Indeed, deterrence is the surest ground for punishment, since retributive norms are so unsettled and since incapacitation may, by removing one offender from the pool of offenders, simply make a career in crime more attractive to someone else, who is balanced on the razor's edge between criminal and legitimate activity and who now faces reduced competition in the crime "market." Thus, even if one were sure that Jackson would be as harmless as a mouse in the last

10, or 15, or 20 years of his life, his sentence might be justified if the example of it were likely to deter other people, similarly situated, from committing such crimes. This is possible, but speculative; it was not mentioned by the district judge.

We should ask how many 35 years olds would rob a bank if they knew that if they were caught it would mean 20 years in prison with no possibility of parole (the sentence I would have given Jackson if I had been the sentencing judge), compared to the number who would do so if it would mean life in prison. Probably very few would be deterred by the incremental sentence. Bank robbery is a crime of acquisition, not of passion; the only gains are financial—and are slight (in 1986 the average "take" from a bank robbery was $2,664, see Uniform Crime Reports, *supra,* at 18). The net gains, when the expected cost of punishment is figured in, must be very small indeed. Clearance rates for bank robbery are very high; of all bank robberies investigated by the FBI during 1978 and 1979 (and virtually all bank robberies are reported and therefore investigated), 69 percent had been cleared by arrest by 1982. Conviction rates are high (90 percent in federal prosecutions for bank robbery) and average punishments severe (more than 13 years for federal defendants). It's a losers' game at best. Persons who would go ahead and rob a bank in the face of my hypothetical 20–year sentence are unlikely to be deterred by tightening the punishment screws still further. A civilized society locks up such people until age makes them harmless but it does not keep them in prison until they die.

Notes and Questions

1. What penalty would you have imposed, and why?

UNITED STATES v. JACKSON

United States District Court, N.D. Illinois, E.D., 1991.
780 F.Supp. 1508.

Brian Barnett Duff, District Judge.

Dwight Eugene Jackson moves for reduction of sentence.   * * *

The majority opinion written by Judge Easterbrook does not say that the sentence is unduly harsh, but speculates that if it is, "the holder of the clemency power may supply a remedy." The instant motion calls upon this court * * * to make that determination under judicial authority, which it has, and not under clemency power, which it has not. For fifteen years, since 1976, this court has had, in one venue or another, the awesome responsibility of sentencing, and of frequently depriving of freedom, fellow citizens. Through that period of time, the court estimates it has dealt with the conviction and sentencing of over 2,000 persons. There is no responsibility in this life which this court throughout this experience has considered more carefully, even more prayerfully. * * *

In ruling on the motion the court reviews the sentence with the utmost seriousness in light of the fact that it is a most severe sentence, the most severe ever administered by this court. Because serious examination is required, even unavoidable, in light of the harsh approbation of the concurrence to the Seventh Circuit opinion affirming the sentence imposed on Mr. Jackson. Mr. Jackson relies heavily upon that concurrence in his motion. The court's respect for the opinions of Judge Posner is real; it feels constrained to give full consideration to his criticism of the court's "savage[ry]" and of the court's affront to the norms of a "civilized society". * * *

The concurring opinion cites the confidential sentencing recommendation of the probation officer (which was not a part of the court record, and was given to the higher court in violation of the local court rule * * *). * * *

It is worth noting that the non-confidential parts of this recommendation which Judge Posner ordered to be delivered to him also include a number of relevant comments including:

1. The defendant continued to deny his guilt to the probation officer even after his conviction, arguing that the charges were trumped up and federal officials in charge of his case were conspiring against him.

2. In addition to his seven armed robbery convictions, he had attempted to murder his army colonel in Vietnam, and assaulted a sergeant. He had been convicted in the army of possession of drugs. He admitted to additional possession of drugs, and he was charged with an additional armed bank robbery which charge was dismissed.

3. The report supplements a finding by Judge Grady in a prior sentencing and notes that the Judge's comments were extremely important when he wrote: "It is entirely fortuitous that no one other than the defendant was injured in this escapade.... He shows no remorse.... The odds of his succeeding on parole are obviously poor. I would recommend against parole unless there is some fairly objective evidence of it and it is difficult to foresee what that evidence would be."

4. The defendant was unable to clearly respond when asked what he would have done if he was confronted by a bank guard with his pistol drawn.

5. His record reflects the use of violence and force in perpetrating criminal acts.

6. * * * If the defendant is given his freedom anytime soon, there is a distinct possibility that further involvement in illegal activity *might result in severe injury or death to some individual* * * *.

The concurring opinion agrees with this court that "Jackson is unquestionably a dangerous and hardened criminal." * * * This court respectfully agrees * * * and recognizes the thesis that Mr. Jackson's conduct does not warrant life imprisonment solely as a matter of retributive justice.   * * *

* * * Judge Posner suggests that this criminal defendant would probably not commit a bank robbery at age 55 after completion of Judge Posner's suggested sentence of twenty years.   * * *

Judge Posner does not consider whether strong arm robberies are more frequent than armed robberies, or whether older persons more frequently 'snatch and run', or physically roll their victims, or beat them, etc. than do younger, stronger, quicker men. Nor do the statistics offered suggest whether there are fewer recidivists on the streets because more of them are in jail in their later years. The Judge suspects that bank robbery is more of a young man's crime than an old man's crime because a bank robber must be willing to confront armed guards and able to make a quick getaway. Well, a gun helps any robber, young or old, and a car helps any robber, young or old, but either a gun or a car tolerates the strong possibility of victims. It would appear that the Judge has never heard of the most famous bank robber of our time, the nefarious Willie Sutton, who when asked, in his seventies, why he continued to rob banks, replied "Because that's where the money is."

The concurring opinion suggests that the risk that Mr. Jackson will commit another robbery in his 70's or 80's is too speculative here to warrant imprisonment until the defendant dies of old age. One wonders whether, in true justice, we should speculate equally whether, if released, the man would eventually kill somebody. Which of these speculations on these facts is the wiser course? We cannot make this choice without conscience, and we certainly cannot do it savagely.

The concurring opinion amazingly brings Law and Economics into the equation and suggests, apparently with careful thought, * * * that incapacitation may, by imprisoning Mr. Jackson, "simply make a career in crime more attractive to someone else.... who now faces reduced competition in the crime 'market.'" Unless, of course, deterrence works, a proposition the concurring opinion finds possible but speculative. Taking the suggestion to heart, the court is deeply concerned that by sentencing Mr. Jackson to prison it may have seduced some irresolute person into the bank robbery "market."   * * *

In concentrating on the issue of bank robberies from an economic standpoint, the concurring opinion notes that the gains from such crimes are slight. The concurring opinion points out that in 1986 the average "take" from a bank robbery was $2,664. It doesn't point out that bank robberies were ten times more lucrative that year than other robberies, or that the successive "takes" of this defendant were many thousands more than the average. Many bank robbers are 'green' and scared notepassers—Mr. Jackson was neither.

If, as the concurring opinion points out, the average punishment for bank robbery (without enhancement) is something more than 13 years, then one wonders why 20 * * * would be the right number of years for this incorrigible and hostile recidivist.

The concurring opinion never touches the problem of the possession of guns by violent felons although that is what underlies this sentence. * * *

No one disagrees that the law authorized this court to impose the sentence it did. But the court must also ask itself, in light of the severity of the sentence, did justice require it? After long, careful and thorough consideration, this court has concluded that it did.

Mr. Jackson is a criminal who has shown no desire to amend his ways. Indeed, it is relevant to note (again) that the crime for which this sentence was imposed was committed just *half an hour* after he was released from prison for two prior bank robberies. A severe sentence is thus mandated both as retribution for his crime and, perhaps even more so, because of his recidivism.

Retribution and the prevention of his recidivism, of course, are not the only considerations which have guided this court in imposing Mr. Jackson's sentence. The court has also carefully considered the potential deterrent effect that a harsh sentence will have on other would-be bankrobbers. Judge Posner is correct; no one knows the true deterrent effect of any particular sentence. However, the likelihood that a particular sentence will deter others from committing similar crimes is a consideration which is well established in both the law and literature relating to sentencing.

Finally, the court has considered whether Mr. Jackson has the ability to function outside of prison. He has not demonstrated that ability to date (Mr. Jackson has been in trouble of one kind or another almost constantly since he was 18 years old). * * *

* * * Accordingly, the court denies Mr. Jackson's motion for reduction of his sentence. The court also notes, however, that if Mr. Jackson maintains a good record in prison, he may at some later date be able to press a successful petition to the true holder of clemency power—the President of the United States. * * *

Notes and Questions

1. In light of everything you now know about Dwight Jackson, what penalty would you have imposed? Should a judge consider a convicted defendant's remorse or lack thereof in setting the penalty? Would a retributivist consider it relevant that Jackson committed the robbery on the day of his release from prison?

2. *Sentencing procedures.* Until comparatively recently, most state trial judges and federal district judges had broad sentencing discretion. Typically, a judge could impose a sentence from a range of penalties set by the legislature. As long as the sentence fell within the parameters laid out by the legislature, it was largely unreviewable. Among the options ordinarily available to the judge were to impose a specific term of years, for example, five years' imprisonment, or to set the minimum and maximum lengths of incarceration, for example, "from two to ten years." In the latter case, once the inmate served the minimum sentence, she became eligible for conditional

release ("parole"). Typically in such a sentencing design, the inmate was entitled to periodic hearings before a parole board, which had discretion to set an early release date.

Beginning in the 1970s, the traditional sentencing system came under attack. The primary objection was that judges were imposing grossly disparate sentences for largely similar offenses. In response to the criticism, Congress passed the Federal Crime Control Act of 1984, which established new sentencing procedures for the federal courts, created a United States Sentencing Commission charged with the responsibility for devising sentencing guidelines, and abolished parole. See 28 U.S.C. §§ 991–998. Many states have followed a similar course.

The Federal Sentencing Commission sent its initial guidelines to Congress in April, 1987, although they have been amended by the Commission regularly since then. The outcome was a complex, more–than–200–page, document consisting of guidelines, policy statements and commentaries. A federal judge must now proceed through a seven-step process in order to determine a convictee's sentence, and may not impose a sentence outside the guidelines unless the case involves an aggravating or mitigating circumstance not considered by the Sentencing Commission.[e] Sentences outside the guidelines are reviewable on appeal. See generally Stephen Breyer, *The Federal Sentencing Guidelines and the Key Compromises Upon Which They Rest*, 17 Hofstra L.Rev. 1 (1988).

The federal sentencing guidelines have been the subject of considerable analysis and criticism since their adoption. See, e.g., Daniel J. Freed, *Federal Sentencing in the Wake of Guidelines: Unacceptable Limits on the Discretion of Sentencers*, 101 Yale L.J. 1681 (1992); Kate Smith & Steve Y. Koh, *The Politics of Sentencing Reform: The Legislative History of the Federal Sentencing Guidelines*, 28 Wake Forest L.Rev. 223 (1993); Andrew von Hirsch, *Federal Sentencing Guidelines: Do They Provide Principled Guidance?*, 27 Am.Crim.L.Rev. 367 (1989); Stanley A. Weigel, *The Sentencing Reform Act of 1984: A Practical Appraisal*, 36 UCLA L.Rev. 83 (1988).

3. One nineteenth century observer equated prisons to sewers, from which a "constant flow of poison and contagious germs of a physiological and moral nature are poured into society. [A prison] poisons, stupifies [sic], depresses and ruins [its confinees]." Paul Reiwald, Society and Its Criminals 172 (1949) (quoting Gauthier). If this description remains accurate, at least regarding some prisons in the United States, does this mean that punishment, although morally justified in theory, is unjustified in practice?

It is easy to lose sight of the fact that incarceration is not the only form of punishment available for violations of criminal laws. For example, fines, compelled victim restitution, house arrest, and work-furlough programs constitute punishment.

Occasionally, judges and lawmakers devise other means to punish criminals. For example, in Nevada, persons convicted of driving while intoxicated may choose, in lieu of a jail sentence, to perform community service while

e. If the guidelines had applied to Dwight Jackson, he apparently would have received a sentence of imprisonment of no less than 30 years. United States v. Jackson, 780 F.Supp. 1508, 1514 (N.D.Ill.1991).

dressed in clothing that identifies them as drunk drivers. Nev.Rev.Stat. 484.3792(1)(a)(2) (1990 & Supp.1991). In Newport, Oregon, a judge required some offenders to write and pay for a newspaper advertisement in which they apologized to the community for their criminal conduct. For discussion of these and other shaming techniques as a means of punishment, see Toni M. Massaro, *Shame, Culture, and American Criminal Law,* 89 Mich.L.Rev. 1880 (1991).

Despite the alternatives to imprisonment, incarceration is the punishment-of-choice of most legislators and trial judges in the United States. During the fifty-year period from the mid–1920s to the mid–1970s, the incarceration rate was remarkably stable, averaging approximately 110 prisoners per 100,000 population. Alfred Blumenstein, *Racial Disproportionality of U.S. Prison Populations Revisited,* 64 U.Colo.L.Rev. 743, 743–45 (1993). Over the past two decades, however, the prison population rate has grown dramatically. In 1991, 823,414 persons were incarcerated in federal or state correctional facilities, an increase of 150% in eleven years, or 310 sentenced prisoners per 100,000 residents, a new record. Bureau of Justice Statistics, U.S. Dept. of Justice, Bureau of Justice Statistics Bulletin, *Prisoners in 1991* (May 1992).

E. PROPORTIONALITY OF PUNISHMENT

1. GENERAL PRINCIPLES

IMMANUEL KANT—THE PHILOSOPHY OF LAW
(W. Hastie translation 1887), 447–448

But what is the mode and measure of punishment which public justice takes as its principle and standard? It is just the principle of equality, by which the pointer of the scale of justice is made to incline no more to one side than the other. It may be rendered by saying that the undeserved evil which any one commits on another is to be regarded as perpetrated on himself. Hence it may be said: "If you slander another, you slander yourself; if you strike another, you strike yourself; if you kill another, you kill yourself." This is the right of retaliation (*jus talionis*); and, properly understood, it is the only principle which in regulating a public court, as distinguished from a private judgement, can definitely assign both the quality and the quantity of a just penalty. * * * But how then would we render the statement: "If you *steal* from another, you steal from yourself?" In this way, whoever steals anything makes the property of all insecure; he therefore robs himself of all security in property, according to the right of retaliation. Such a one has nothing, and can acquire nothing * * *. But whoever has committed murder, must *die*. There is, in this case, no juridical substitute or surrogate, that can be given or taken for the satisfaction of justice. There is no *likeness* or proportion between life, however painful, and death; and therefore there is no equality between the crime of murder and the retaliation of it but what is judicially accomplished by the execution of the criminal. His death, however, must be kept free from all maltreatment that would make the humanity suffering in his person loathsome or abominable.

JEREMY BENTHAM—AN INTRODUCTION TO THE PRINCIPLES OF MORALS AND LEGISLATION
(John Bowring ed. 1843), 86–88

[Chapter XIV] I. We have seen that the general object of all laws is to prevent mischief; that is to say, when it is worth while; but that, where there are no other means of doing this than punishment, there are four cases in which it is not worth while.

II. When it *is* worth while, there are four subordinate designs or objects, which, in the course of his endeavours to compass, as far as may be, that one general object, a legislator, whose views are governed by the principle of utility, comes naturally to propose to himself.

III. 1. His first, most extensive, and most eligible object, is to prevent, in as far as it is possible, and worth while, all sorts of offences whatsoever: in other words, so to manage, that no offence whatsoever may be committed.

IV. 2. But if a man must needs commit an offence of some kind or other, the next object is to induce him to commit an offence *less* mischievous, *rather* than one *more* mischievous: in other words, to choose always the *least* mischievous, of two offences that will either of them suit his purpose.

V. 3. When a man has resolved upon a particular offence, the next object is to dispose him to do *no more* mischief than is *necessary* to his purpose: in other words, to do as little mischief as is consistent with the benefit he has in view.

VI. 4. The last object is, whatever the mischief be, which it is proposed to prevent, to prevent it at as *cheap* a rate as possible.

VII. Subservient to these four objects, or purposes, must be the rules or canons by which the proportion of punishments to offences is to be governed.

VIII. Rule 1. The first object, it has been seen, is to prevent, in as far as it is worth while, all sorts of offences: therefore,

The value of the punishment must not be less in any case than what is sufficient to outweigh that of the profit of the offence. * * *

X. Rule 2. But whether a given offence shall be prevented in a given degree by a given quantity of punishment, is never any thing better than a chance; for the purchasing of which, whatever punishment is employed, is so much expended in advance. However, for the sake of giving it the better chance of outweighing the profit of the offence,

The greater the mischief of the offence, the greater is the expense, which it may be worth while to be at, in the way of punishment.

XI. Rule 3. The next object is, to induce a man to choose always the least mischievous of two offences: therefore

Where two offences come in competition, the punishment for the greater offence must be sufficient to induce a man to prefer the less.

XII. Rule 4. When a man has resolved upon a particular offence, the next object is, to induce him to do no more mischief than what is necessary for his purpose: therefore

The punishment should be adjusted in such manner to each particular offence, that for every part of the mischief there may be a motive to restrain the offender from giving birth to it.

XIII. Rule 5. The last object is, whatever mischief is guarded against, to guard against it at as cheap a rate as possible: therefore

The punishment ought in no case to be more than what is necessary to bring it into conformity with the rules here given. * * *

XV. Of the above rules of proportion, the four first, we may perceive, serve to mark out the limits on the side of diminution; the limits *below* which a punishment ought not to be *diminished;* the fifth, the limits on the side of *increase;* the limits *above* which it ought not to be *increased.* The five * * * are calculated to serve as guides to the legislator * * *.

Notes and Questions

1. If you were a legislator setting the penalty or range of penalties for the offense of "driving a motor vehicle under the influence of alcohol," what factors would you consider under Bentham's analysis? Suppose you were seeking a retributivist solution?

2. Recidivist statutes permit or require a judge to sentence a repeat offender to a longer prison term than may be imposed on a first-time offender. For example, the maximum penalty for larceny might be five years' imprisonment, but for a third-time thief, the requisite punishment could be life imprisonment.

Are habitual offender laws justifiable under utilitarian principles? On what basis? Can a retributivist defend enhanced punishment of a recidivist, assuming that the offender has already paid her debt to society for the earlier crimes? See Michael Davis, *Just Deserts for Recidivists,* Crim.Just.Ethics, Summer/Fall 1985, at 29; George P. Fletcher, *The Recidivist Premium,* Crim.Just.Ethics, Summer/Fall 1982, at 54; Andrew von Hirsch, *Desert and Previous Convictions in Sentencing,* 65 Minn.L.Rev. 591 (1981).

2. CONSTITUTIONAL PRINCIPLES

INTRODUCTORY COMMENT

The Eighth Amendment to the United States Constitution provides: "Excessive bail shall not be required, nor excessive fines imposed, nor cruel and unusual punishment inflicted." In 1910, the United States

Supreme Court ruled that the cruel and unusual punishment clause "was directed, not only against punishments which inflict torture, 'but against all punishments which by their excessive length or severity are greatly disproportioned to the offense charged.'" Weems v. United States, 217 U.S. 349, 371, 30 S.Ct. 544, 551, 54 L.Ed. 793, 800 (1910), quoting O'Neil v. Vermont, 144 U.S. 323, 339–40, 12 S.Ct. 693, 699–700, 36 L.Ed. 450, 458 (1892) (Field, J., dissenting).

As the two cases that follow demonstrate, the Supreme Court has struggled with the question of what constitutes "grossly disproportional" punishment and, especially in the non-death penalty context, is deeply divided on the question of whether the federal judiciary should become involved at all in proportionality overview.

COKER v. GEORGIA

Supreme Court of the United States, 1977.
433 U.S. 584, 97 S.Ct. 2861, 53 L.Ed.2d 982.

Mr. Justice White announced the judgment of the Court and filed an opinion in which Mr. Justice Stewart, Mr. Justice Blackmun, and Mr. Justice Stevens, joined.

Georgia Code Ann. § 26–2001 (1972) provides that "[a] person convicted of rape shall be punished by death or by imprisonment for life, or by imprisonment for not less than one nor more than 20 years." [1] Punishment is determined by a jury in a separate sentencing proceeding in which at least one * * * statutory aggravating circumstances must be found before the death penalty may be imposed. Petitioner Coker was convicted of rape and sentenced to death. Both the conviction and the sentence were affirmed by the Georgia Supreme Court. Coker was granted a writ of certiorari, limited to the single claim, rejected by the Georgia court, that the punishment of death for rape violates the Eighth Amendment, which proscribes "cruel and unusual punishments" and which must be observed by the States as well as the Federal Government.

I

While serving various sentences for murder, rape, kidnaping, and aggravated assault, petitioner escaped from the Ware Correctional Institution near Waycross, Ga., on September 2, 1974. At approximately 11 o'clock that night, petitioner entered the house of Allen and Elnita Carver through an unlocked kitchen door. Threatening the couple with a "board," he tied up Mr. Carver in the bathroom, obtained a knife from the kitchen, and took Mr. Carver's money and the keys to the family car. Brandishing the knife and saying "you know what's going to happen to you if you try anything, don't you," Coker then raped Mrs. Carver. Soon thereafter, petitioner drove away in the Carver car, taking Mrs.

---

1. The section defines rape as having "carnal knowledge of a female, forcibly and against her will. Carnal knowledge in rape occurs when there is any penetration of the female sex organ by the male sex organ."

Carver with him. Mr. Carver, freeing himself, notified the police; and not long thereafter petitioner was apprehended. Mrs. Carver was unharmed.

Petitioner was charged with escape, armed robbery, motor vehicle theft, kidnaping, and rape. * * * The jury returned a verdict of guilty, rejecting his general plea of insanity. A sentencing hearing was then conducted. * * * The jury was instructed that it could consider as aggravating circumstances whether the rape had been committed by a person with a prior record of conviction for a capital felony and whether the rape had been committed in the course of committing another capital felony, namely, the armed robbery of Allen Carver. The court also instructed, pursuant to statute, that even if aggravating circumstances were present, the death penalty need not be imposed if the jury found they were outweighed by mitigating circumstances, that is, circumstances not constituting justification or excuse for the offense in question, "but which, in fairness and mercy, may be considered as extenuating or reducing the degree" of moral culpability or punishment. The jury's verdict on the rape count was death by electrocution. Both aggravating circumstances on which the court instructed were found to be present by the jury.

II

* * * It is now settled that the death penalty is not invariably cruel and unusual punishment within the meaning of the Eighth Amendment; it is not inherently barbaric or an unacceptable mode of punishment for crime; neither is it always disproportionate to the crime for which it is imposed. * * *

In sustaining the imposition of the death penalty * * *, however, the Court firmly embraced the holdings and dicta from prior cases to the effect that the Eighth Amendment bars not only those punishments that are "barbaric" but also those that are "excessive" in relation to the crime committed. * * * [A] punishment is "excessive" and unconstitutional if it (1) makes no measurable contribution to acceptable goals of punishment and hence is nothing more than the purposeless and needless imposition of pain and suffering; or (2) is grossly out of proportion to the severity of the crime. A punishment might fail the test on either ground. Furthermore, these Eighth Amendment judgments should not be, or appear to be, merely the subjective views of individual Justices; judgment should be informed by objective factors to the maximum possible extent. To this end, attention must be given to the public attitudes concerning a particular sentence—history and precedent, legislative attitudes, and the response of juries reflected in their sentencing decisions are to be consulted. * * *

III

That question, with respect to rape of an adult woman, is now before us. We have concluded that a sentence of death is grossly disproportionate and excessive punishment for the crime of rape and is therefore forbidden by the Eighth Amendment as cruel and unusual punishment.[4] * * *

[Justice White considered objective indicia of public attitudes concerning the acceptability of death as a penalty for the rape of an adult woman. He recounted that in 1925, 18 states, the District of Columbia, and the federal government authorized capital punishment in such circumstances. By 1977, however, Georgia was the sole jurisdiction authorizing death for the rape of an adult woman, and only two other states allowed capital punishment for the rape of a child.

Also, since 1973, Georgia juries had sentenced rapists to death only six times in 63 rape convictions appealed to the state supreme court. Justice White observed that "[t]his obviously is not a negligible number * * *. Nevertheless, it is true that in the vast majority of cases, at least 9 out of 10, juries have not imposed the death sentence."]

IV

These recent events evidencing the attitude of state legislatures and sentencing juries do not wholly determine this controversy, for the Constitution contemplates that in the end our own judgment will be brought to bear on the question of the acceptability of the death penalty under the Eighth Amendment. Nevertheless, the legislative rejection of capital punishment for rape strongly confirms our own judgment, which is that death is indeed a disproportionate penalty for the crime of raping an adult woman.

We do not discount the seriousness of rape as a crime. It is highly reprehensible, both in a moral sense and in its almost total contempt for the personal integrity and autonomy of the female victim and for the latter's privilege of choosing those with whom intimate relationships are to be established. Short of homicide, it is the "ultimate violation of self." It is also a violent crime because it normally involves force, or the threat of force or intimidation, to overcome the will and the capacity of the victim to resist. Rape is very often accompanied by physical injury to the female and can also inflict mental and psychological damage. Because it undermines the community's sense of security, there is public injury as well.

Rape is without doubt deserving of serious punishment; but in terms of moral depravity and of the injury to the person and to the public, it does not compare with murder, which does involve the unjustified taking of human life. Although it may be accompanied by another crime, rape by definition does not include the death of or even the

---

4. Because the death sentence is a disproportionate punishment for rape, it is cruel and unusual punishment within the meaning of the Eighth Amendment even though it may measurably serve the legitimate ends of punishment and therefore is not invalid for its failure to do so. We observe that in the light of the legislative decisions in almost all of the States and in most of the countries around the world, it would be difficult to support a claim that the death penalty for rape is an indispensable part of the States' criminal justice system.

serious injury to another person.[13] The murderer kills; the rapist, if no more than that, does not. Life is over for the victim of the murderer; for the rape victim, life may not be nearly so happy as it was, but it is not over and normally is not beyond repair. We have the abiding conviction that the death penalty, which "is unique in its severity and irrevocability," is an excessive penalty for the rapist who, as such, does not take human life.

This does not end the matter; for under Georgia law, death may not be imposed for any capital offense, including rape, unless the jury or judge finds one of the statutory aggravating circumstances and then elects to impose that sentence. For the rapist to be executed in Georgia, it must therefore be found not only that he committed rape but also that one or more of the following aggravating circumstances were present: (1) that the rape was committed by a person with a prior record of conviction for a capital felony; (2) that the rape was committed while the offender was engaged in the commission of another capital felony, or aggravated battery; or (3) the rape "was outrageously or wantonly vile, horrible or inhuman in that it involved torture, depravity of mind, or aggravated battery to the victim." Here, the first two of these aggravating circumstances were alleged and found by the jury.

Neither of these circumstances, nor both of them together, change our conclusion that the death sentence imposed on Coker is a disproportionate punishment for rape. Coker had prior convictions for capital felonies—rape, murder, and kidnaping—but these prior convictions do not change the fact that the instant crime being punished is a rape not involving the taking of life. * * *

* * * The judgment of the Georgia Supreme Court upholding the death sentence is reversed * * *.

Mr. Justice Powell, concurring in the judgment in part and dissenting in part.

I concur in the judgment of the Court on the facts of this case, and also in the plurality's reasoning supporting the view that ordinarily death is disproportionate punishment for the crime of raping an adult woman. Although rape invariably is a reprehensible crime, there is no indication that petitioner's offense was committed with excessive brutality or that the victim sustained serious or lasting injury. The plurality, however, does not limit its holding to the case before us or to similar cases. Rather, in an opinion that ranges well beyond what is necessary, it holds that capital punishment *always*—regardless of the circumstances—is a disproportionate penalty for the crime of rape.

* * * It is * * * quite unnecessary for the plurality to write in terms so sweeping as to foreclose each of the 50 state legislatures from creating a narrowly defined substantive crime of aggravated rape punishable by death.[1] * * *

---

13. See n. 1, *supra,* for the Georgia definition of rape.

1. It is not this Court's function to formulate the relevant criteria that might dis-

Mr. Chief Justice Burger, with whom Mr. Justice Rehnquist joins, dissenting.

* * * I accept that the Eighth Amendment's concept of disproportionality bars the death penalty for minor crimes. But rape is not a minor crime; hence the Cruel and Unusual Punishments Clause does not give the Members of this Court license to engraft their conceptions of proper public policy onto the considered legislative judgments of the States. Since I cannot agree that Georgia lacked the constitutional power to impose the penalty of death for rape, I dissent from the Court's judgment. * * *

Unlike the plurality, I would narrow the inquiry in this case to the question actually presented: Does the Eighth Amendment's ban against cruel and unusual punishment prohibit the State of Georgia from executing a person who has, within the space of three years, raped three separate women, killing one and attempting to kill another, who is serving prison terms exceeding his probable lifetime and who has not hesitated to escape confinement at the first available opportunity? Whatever one's view may be as to the State's constitutional power to impose the death penalty upon a rapist who stands before a court convicted for the first time, this case reveals a chronic rapist whose continuing danger to the community is abundantly clear. * * *

In my view, the Eighth Amendment does not prevent the State from taking an individual's "well-demonstrated propensity for life-endangering behavior" into account in devising punitive measures which will prevent inflicting further harm upon innocent victims. * * *

The plurality acknowledges the gross nature of the crime of rape. A rapist not only violates a victim's privacy and personal integrity, but inevitably causes serious psychological as well as physical harm in the process. The long-range effect upon the victim's life and health is likely to be irreparable; it is impossible to measure the harm which results. Volumes have been written by victims, physicians, and psychiatric specialists on the lasting injury suffered by rape victims. Rape is not a mere physical attack—it is destructive of the human personality. The remainder of the victim's life may be gravely affected, and this in turn may have a serious detrimental effect upon her husband and any children she may have. * * * Victims may recover from the physical damage of knife or bullet wounds, or a beating with fists or a club, but recovery from such a gross assault on the human personality is not healed by medicine or surgery. To speak blandly, as the plurality does, of rape victims who are "unharmed," * * * takes too little account of the profound suffering the crime imposes upon the victims and their loved ones. * * *

tinguish aggravated rape from the more usual case, but perhaps a workable test would embrace the factors identified by Georgia: the cruelty or viciousness of the offender, the circumstances and manner in which the offense was committed, and the consequences suffered by the victim. * * *

* * * The plurality's conclusion * * * is based upon the bare fact that murder necessarily results in the physical death of the victim, while rape does not. However, no Member of the Court explains why this distinction has relevance, much less constitutional significance. It is, after all, not irrational—nor constitutionally impermissible—for a legislature to make the penalty more severe than the criminal act it punishes [16] in the hope it would deter wrongdoing * * *.

As a matter of constitutional principle, th[e] test cannot have the primitive simplicity of "life for life, eye for eye, tooth for tooth." Rather States must be permitted to engage in a more sophisticated weighing of values in dealing with criminal activity which consistently poses serious danger of death or grave bodily harm. If innocent life and limb are to be preserved I see no constitutional barrier in punishing by death all who engage in such activity, regardless of whether the risk comes to fruition in any particular instance. * * *

Notes and Questions

1. Justices Brennan and Marshall concurred in the judgment, based on their shared view that the death penalty, in all circumstances, constitutes cruel and unusual punishment.

2. The dissent provided a fuller account than is set out in Justice White's opinion of Coker's criminal history and of the rape for which he was sentenced to death. In 1971, Coker raped and stabbed to death a young woman. Still free eight months later, he kidnapped and twice raped a second victim, sixteen years old, and then beat her severely with a club, after which he dragged her into a wooded area where he left her for dead. After the latter incident, Coker was arrested, prosecuted for his crimes, and sentenced to three life terms, two 20–year terms, and one eight-year term of imprisonment.

Less than two years later, Coker escaped from prison and raped the victim here, "Mrs. Carver," who was also sixteen years old. After the rape, Coker took the victim with him in the Carver family automobile. Before he left, the defendant told Mr. Carver, whom he had tied up and gagged, that he would kill his wife if the police caught him, because "[I] don't have nothing to lose—[I am in] prison for the rest of [my] life, anyway."

Do these additional facts change your view of the proper outcome?

3. Does Justice White's constitutional analysis conform to utilitarian or retributive conceptions of proportionality? What about Chief Justice Burger's dissent? Is Justice Powell correct in concluding that, as a matter of proportional punishment, aggravated rapes that do not result in death may merit capital punishment? If so, do you agree with the criteria that he set out for distinguishing simple from aggravated rapes?

4. Consider footnote 16 of the dissent: Is it likely that either a retributivist or utilitarian would believe that restitution is proportional punishment for theft?

16. For example, hardly any thief would be deterred from stealing if the only punishment upon being caught were return of the money stolen.

5. In a state that permits executions of murderers, is death grossly disproportional punishment for *attempted* murder?

6. "The death penalty for rape has been reserved overwhelmingly for black defendants, especially those convicted of raping white woman." James R. Acker, *Social Science in Supreme Court Death Penalty Cases: Citation Practices and Their Implications,* 8 Just.Quarterly 421, 431 (1991). The briefs filed on behalf of Coker cited statistical studies informing the Supreme Court of this fact. Although none of the Justices in *Coker* referred to these studies, their knowledge of the discriminatory application of the death penalty for this crime may have affected the outcome.

HARMELIN v. MICHIGAN

Supreme Court of the United States, 1991.
501 U.S. ___, 111 S.Ct. 2680, 115 L.Ed.2d 836.

JUSTICE SCALIA announced the judgment of the Court and delivered * * * an opinion with respect to Parts I, II, III, and IV, in which THE CHIEF JUSTICE joins.

Petitioner was convicted of possessing 672 grams of cocaine and sentenced to a mandatory term of life in prison without possibility of parole.[1] The Michigan Court of Appeals * * * affirmed petitioner's sentence, rejecting his argument that the sentence was "cruel and unusual" within the meaning of the Eighth Amendment. * * *

Petitioner claims that his sentence is unconstitutionally "cruel and unusual" * * * because it is "significantly disproportionate" to the crime he committed. * * *

I

A

* * * In *Rummel v. Estelle,* 445 U.S. 263, 100 S.Ct. 1133, 63 L.Ed.2d 382 (1980), we held that it did not constitute "cruel and unusual punishment" to impose a life sentence, under a recidivist statute, upon a defendant who had been convicted, successively, of fraudulent use of a credit card to obtain $80 worth of goods or services, passing a forged check in the amount of $28.36, and obtaining $120.75 by false pretenses. We said that "one could argue without fear of contradiction by any decision of this Court that for crimes concededly classified and classifiable as felonies, that is, as punishable by significant terms of imprisonment in a state penitentiary, the length of the sentence actually imposed is purely a matter of legislative prerogative." We specifically rejected the proposition asserted by the dissent [in *Rummel*] that unconstitutional disproportionality could be established by weighing three factors: (1) gravity of the offense compared to severity of the penalty, (2)

---

1. Mich.Comp.Laws Ann. § 333.-7403(2)(a)(i) (Supp.1990–1991) provides a mandatory sentence of life in prison for possession of 650 grams or more of "any mixture containing [a schedule 2] controlled substance"; § 333.7214(a)(iv) defines cocaine as a schedule 2 controlled substance. * * *

penalties imposed within the same jurisdiction for similar crimes, and (3) penalties imposed in other jurisdictions for the same offense. * * *

Two years later, in *Hutto v. Davis,* 454 U.S. 370, 102 S.Ct. 703, 70 L.Ed.2d 556 (1982), we similarly rejected an Eighth Amendment challenge to a prison term of 40 years and fine of $20,000 for possession and distribution of approximately nine ounces of marijuana. We thought that result * * * clear in light of *Rummel* * * *.

A year and a half after *Davis* we uttered what has been our last word on this subject to date. *Solem v. Helm,* 463 U.S. 277, 103 S.Ct. 3001, 77 L.Ed.2d 637 (1983), set aside under the Eighth Amendment, because it was disproportionate, a sentence of life imprisonment without possibility of parole, imposed under a South Dakota recidivist statute for successive offenses that included three convictions of third-degree burglary, one of obtaining money by false pretenses, one of grand larceny, one of third-offense driving while intoxicated, and one of writing a "no account" check with intent to defraud. * * * As for the statement in *Rummel* that "one could argue without fear of contradiction by any decision of this Court that for crimes concededly classified and classifiable as felonies ... the length of the sentence actually imposed is purely a matter of legislative prerogative," according to *Solem,* the really important words in that passage were " *'one could argue.' '' "The Court [in *Rummel*] ... merely recognized that the argument was possible. To the extent that the State ... makes the argument here, we find it meritless." * * * Having decreed that a general principle of disproportionality exists, the Court used as the criterion for its application the three-factor test that had been explicitly rejected in both *Rummel* and *Davis.* * * *

It should be apparent from the above discussion that our 5–to–4 decision eight years ago in *Solem* was scarcely the expression of clear and well accepted constitutional law. * * * Accordingly, we have addressed anew, and in greater detail, the question whether the Eighth Amendment contains a proportionality guarantee—with particular attention to the background of the Eighth Amendment * * * and to the understanding of the Eighth Amendment before the end of the 19th century * * *. We conclude from this examination that *Solem* was simply wrong; the Eighth Amendment contains no proportionality guarantee.

B

Solem based its conclusion principally upon the proposition that a right to be free from disproportionate punishments was embodied within the "cruell and unusuall Punishments" provision of the English Declaration of Rights of 1689, and was incorporated, with that language, in the Eighth Amendment. * * *

[Justice Scalia surveyed the historical literature relating to the English Declaration of Rights, from which study he concluded that it did not forbid disproportionate punishments. He also concluded from debates at the state ratifying conventions and in the floor debates of the First Congress, which proposed the cruel and unusual punishment clause, that the Eighth Amendment provision was directed only at certain methods of torturous punishment, and not at excessive punishment.]

III

We think it enough that those who framed and approved the Federal Constitution chose, for whatever reason, not to include within it the guarantee against disproportionate sentences that some State Constitutions contained. It is worth noting, however, that there was good reason for that choice—a reason that reinforces the necessity of overruling *Solem*. While there are relatively clear historical guidelines and accepted practices that enable judges to determine which *modes* of punishment are "cruel and unusual," *proportionality* does not lend itself to such analysis. Neither Congress nor any state legislature has ever set out with the objective of crafting a penalty that is "disproportionate," yet * * * many enacted dispositions seem to be so—because they were made for other times or other places, with different social attitudes, different criminal epidemics, different public fears, and different prevailing theories of penology. This is not to say that there are no absolutes; one can imagine extreme examples that no rational person, in no time or place, could accept. But for the same reason these examples are easy to decide, they are certain never to occur.[11] The real function of a constitutional proportionality principle, if it exists, is to enable judges to evaluate a penalty that *some* assemblage of men and women *has* considered proportionate—and to say that it is not. For that real-world enterprise, the standards seem so inadequate that the proportionality principle becomes an invitation to imposition of subjective values.

This becomes clear, we think, from a consideration of the three factors that *Solem* found relevant to the proportionality determination: (1) the inherent gravity of the offense, (2) the sentences imposed for similarly grave offenses in the same jurisdiction, and (3) sentences imposed for the same crime in other jurisdictions. As to the first factor: Of course some offenses, involving violent harm to human beings, will always and everywhere be regarded as serious, but that is only half the equation. The issue is *what else* should be regarded to be *as serious* as these offenses, or even to be *more serious* than some of them. On that point, judging by the statutes that Americans have enacted, there is

---

11. Justice White argues that the Eighth Amendment must contain a proportionality principle because otherwise legislatures could "mak[e] overtime parking a felony punishable by life imprisonment." * * * Justice White's argument has force only for those who believe that the Constitution prohibited everything that is intensely undesirable—which is an obvious fallacy, see Art. I, § 9 (implicitly permitting slavery). Nor is it likely that the horrible example imagined would ever in fact occur, unless, of course, overtime parking should one day become an arguably major threat to the common good, and the need to deter it arguably critical—at which time the members of this Court would probably disagree as to whether the punishment really *is* "disproportionate," even as they disagree regarding the punishment for possession of cocaine today. * * *

enormous variation—even within a given age, not to mention across the many generations ruled by the Bill of Rights. The State of Massachusetts punishes sodomy more severely than assault and battery, * * * whereas in several States, sodomy is not unlawful *at all*. In Louisiana, one who assaults another with a dangerous weapon faces the same maximum prison term as one who removes a shopping basket "from the parking area or grounds of any store ... without authorization." * * *

The difficulty of assessing gravity is demonstrated in the very context of the present case * * *. [S]urely whether it is a "grave" offense merely to possess a significant quantity of drugs—thereby facilitating distribution, subjecting the holder to the temptation of distribution, and raising the possibility of theft by others who might distribute— depends entirely upon how odious and socially threatening one believes drug use to be. Would it be "grossly excessive" to provide life imprisonment for "mere possession" of a certain quantity of heavy weaponry? If not, then the only issue is whether the possible dissemination of drugs can be as "grave" as the possible dissemination of heavy weapons. Who are we to say no? The Members of the Michigan Legislature, and not we, know the situation on the streets of Detroit.

The second factor suggested in *Solem* fails for the same reason. One cannot compare the sentences imposed by the jurisdiction for "similarly grave" offenses if there is no 'objective standard of gravity. * * * Moreover, even if "similarly grave" crimes could be identified, the penalties for them would not necessarily be comparable, since there are many other justifications for a difference. For example, since deterrent effect depends not only upon the amount of the penalty but upon its certainty, crimes that are less grave but significantly more difficult to detect may warrant substantially higher penalties. * * * In fact, it becomes difficult even to speak intelligently of "proportionality," once deterrence and rehabilitation are given significant weight. Proportionality is inherently a retributive concept, and perfect proportionality is the talionic law.

As for the third factor mentioned by *Solem*—the character of the sentences imposed by other States for the same crime—it must be acknowledged that that can be applied with clarity and ease. The only difficulty is that it has no conceivable relevance to the Eighth Amendment. That a State is entitled to treat with stern disapproval an act that other States punish with the mildest of sanctions follows *a fortiori* from the undoubted fact that a State may criminalize an act that other States do not criminalize *at all*. Indeed, a State may criminalize an act that other States choose to *reward* —punishing, for example, the killing of endangered wild animals for which other States are offering a bounty. What greater disproportion could there be than that? * * *

IV * * *

* * * In *Coker v. Georgia,* the Court held that, because of the disproportionality, it was a violation of the Cruel and Unusual Punishments Clause to impose capital punishment for rape of an adult woman.

* * * *Rummel* treated this * * * authority as an aspect of our death penalty jurisprudence, rather than a generalizable aspect of Eighth Amendment law. We think that is an accurate explanation, and we reassert it. Proportionality review is one of several respects in which we have held that "death is different," and have imposed protections that the Constitution nowhere else provides. We would leave it there, but will not extend it further. * * *

JUSTICE KENNEDY, with whom JUSTICE O'CONNOR and JUSTICE SOUTER join, * * * concurring in the judgment.

I concur * * * in the judgment. I write this separate opinion because my approach to the Eighth Amendment proportionality analysis differs from Justice Scalia's. Regardless of whether Justice Scalia or the dissent has the best of the historical argument, *stare decisis* counsels our adherence to the narrow proportionality principle that has existed in our Eighth Amendment jurisprudence for 80 years. Although our proportionality decisions have not been clear or consistent in all respects, they can be reconciled, and they require us to uphold petitioner's sentence.

I * * *

Though our decisions recognize a proportionality principle, its precise contours are unclear. * * * Our most recent pronouncement on the subject in *Solem,* furthermore, appeared to apply a different analysis than in *Rummel* and *Davis.* * * * Despite these tensions, close analysis of our decisions yields some common principles that give content to the uses and limits of proportionality review.

The first of these principles is that the fixing of prison terms for specific crimes involves a substantive penological judgment that, as a general matter, is "properly within the province of legislatures, not courts." * * * The efficacy of any sentencing system cannot be assessed absent agreement on the purposes and objectives of the penal system. And the responsibility for making these fundamental choices and implementing them lies with the legislature. * * *

The second principle is that the Eighth Amendment does not mandate adoption of any one penological theory. * * *

Third, marked divergences both in underlying theories of sentencing and in the length of prescribed prison terms are the inevitable, often beneficial, result of the federal structure. * * * And even assuming identical philosophies, differing attitudes and perceptions of local conditions may yield different, yet rational, conclusions regarding the appropriate length of prison terms for particular crimes. Thus, the circumstance that a State has the most severe punishment for a particular crime does not by itself render the punishment grossly disproportionate. * * *

The fourth principle at work in our cases is that proportionality review by federal courts should be informed by " 'objective factors to the maximum possible extent.' " * * *

All of these principles—the primacy of the legislature, the variety of legitimate penological schemes, the nature of our federal system, and the requirement that proportionality review be guided by objective factors—inform the final one: the Eighth Amendment does not require strict proportionality between crime and sentence. Rather, it forbids only extreme sentences that are "grossly disproportionate" to the crime. * * *

II

With these considerations stated, it is necessary to examine the challenged aspects of petitioner's sentence * * *.

Petitioner's life sentence without parole is the second most severe penalty permitted by law. It is the same sentence received by the petitioner in *Solem*. Petitioner's crime, however, was far more grave than the crime at issue in *Solem*.

The crime of uttering a no account check at issue in *Solem* was " 'one of the most passive felonies a person could commit.' " It "involved neither violence nor threat of violence to any person," and was "viewed by society as among the less serious offenses." The felonies underlying the defendant's recidivism conviction, moreover, were "all relatively minor." * * *

Petitioner was convicted of possession of more than 650 grams (over 1.5 pounds) of cocaine. This amount of pure cocaine has a potential yield of between 32,500 and 65,000 doses. From any standpoint, this crime falls in a different category from the relatively minor, nonviolent crime at issue in *Solem*. Possession, use, and distribution of illegal drugs represents "one of the greatest problems affecting the health and welfare of our population." Petitioner's suggestion that his crime was nonviolent and victimless, * * * is false to the point of absurdity. To the contrary, petitioner's crime threatened to cause grave harm to society. * * *

Petitioner and *amici* contend that our proportionality decisions require a comparative analysis between petitioner's sentence and sentences imposed for other crimes in Michigan and sentences imposed for the same crime in other jurisdictions. Given the serious nature of petitioner's crime, no such comparative analysis is necessary. Although *Solem* considered these comparative factors after analyzing "the gravity of the offense and the harshness of the penalty," it did not announce a rigid three-part test. In fact, *Solem* stated that in determining unconstitutional disproportionality, "no one factor will be dispositive in a given case." * * *

A better reading of our cases leads to the conclusion that intra- and inter-jurisdictional analyses are appropriate only in the rare case in which a threshold comparison of the crime committed and the sentence imposed leads to an inference of gross disproportionality. * * *

The proper role for comparative analysis of sentences, then, is to validate an initial judgment that a sentence is grossly disproportionate to a crime. * * * In light of the gravity of petitioner's offense, a comparison of his crime with his sentence does not give rise to an inference of gross disproportionality, and comparative analysis of his sentence with others in Michigan and across the Nation need not be performed. * * *

Justice White, with whom Justice Blackmun and Justice Stevens join, dissenting.

* * * Justice Scalia concludes that "the Eighth Amendment contains no proportionality guarantee." * * * Justice Kennedy, on the other hand, asserts that the Eighth Amendment's proportionality principle is so "narrow," that *Solem's* analysis should be reduced from three factors to one. With all due respect, I dissent.

The language of the Amendment does not refer to proportionality in so many words, but it does forbid "excessive" fines, a restraint that suggests that a determination of excessiveness should be based at least in part on whether the fine imposed is disproportionate to the crime committed. Nor would it be unreasonable to conclude that it would be both cruel and unusual to punish overtime parking by life imprisonment, or, more generally, to impose any punishment that is grossly disproportionate to the offense for which the defendant has been convicted. * * *

* * * Justice Scalia argues that all of the available evidence of the day indicated that those who drafted and approved the Amendment "chose ... not to include within it the guarantee against disproportionate sentences that some State Constitutions contained." Even if one were to accept the argument that the First Congress did not have in mind the proportionality issue, the evidence would hardly be strong enough to come close to proving an affirmative decision against the proportionality component. Had there been an intention to exclude it from the reach of the words that otherwise could reasonably be construed to include it, perhaps as plain-speaking Americans, the Members of the First Congress would have said so. And who can say with confidence what the members of the state ratifying conventions had in mind when they voted in favor of the Amendment? * * *

In any event, the Amendment as ratified contained the words "cruel and unusual," and there can be no doubt that prior decisions of this Court have construed these words to include a proportionality principle. * * *

Contrary to Justice Scalia's suggestion, the *Solem* analysis has worked well in practice. Courts appear to have had little difficulty applying the analysis to a given sentence, and application of the test by numerous state and federal appellate courts has resulted in a mere handful of sentences being declared unconstitutional. Thus, it is clear that reviewing courts have not baldly substituted their own subjective moral values for those of the legislature. * * * *Solem* * * * analysis affords "substantial deference to the broad authority that legislatures necessarily possess in determining the types and limits of punishments for crimes, as well as to the discretion that trial courts possess in sentencing convicted criminals," and will only rarely result in a sentence failing constitutional muster. The fact that this is one of those rare instances is no reason to abandon the analysis. * * *

* * * [D]angers lurk in Justice Scalia's analysis. * * * [H]e provides no mechanism for addressing a situation such as that proposed in *Rummel,* in which a legislature makes overtime parking a felony punishable by life imprisonment. He concedes that "one can imagine extreme examples"—perhaps such as the one described in *Rummel*—"that no rational person, in no time or place, could accept," but attempts to offer reassurance by claiming that "for the same reason these examples are easy to decide, they are certain never to occur." This is cold comfort indeed, for absent a proportionality guarantee, there would be no basis for deciding such cases should they arise. * * *

While Justice Scalia seeks to deliver a swift death sentence to *Solem,* Justice Kennedy prefers to eviscerate it, leaving only an empty shell. * * *

Justice Kennedy's abandonment on the second and third factors set forth in *Solem* makes any attempt at an objective proportionality analysis futile. The first prong of *Solem* requires a court to consider two discrete factors—the gravity of the offense and the severity of the punishment. * * * Were a court to attempt such an assessment, it would have no basis for its determination that a sentence was—or was not—disproportionate, other than the "subjective views of individual [judges]," which is the very sort of analysis our Eighth Amendment jurisprudence has shunned. * * *

Because there is no justification for overruling or limiting *Solem,* it remains to apply that case's proportionality analysis to the sentence imposed on petitioner. Application of the *Solem* factors to the statutorily mandated punishment at issue here reveals that the punishment fails muster under *Solem* and, consequently, under the Eighth Amendment to the Constitution. * * *

The first *Solem* factor requires a reviewing court to assess the gravity of the offense and the harshness of the penalty. The mandatory sentence of life imprisonment without possibility of parole "is the most severe punishment that the State could have imposed on any criminal for any crime," for Michigan has no death penalty.

Although these factors are "by no means exhaustive," in evaluating the gravity of the offense, it is appropriate to consider "the harm caused or threatened to the victim or society," based on such things as the degree of violence involved in the crime and "[t]he absolute magnitude of the crime," and "the culpability of the offender," including the degree of requisite intent and the offender's motive in committing the crime.

Drugs are without doubt a serious societal problem. To justify such a harsh mandatory penalty as that imposed here, however, the offense should be one which will *always* warrant that punishment. Mere possession of drugs—even in such a large quantity—is not so serious an offense that it will always warrant, much less mandate, life imprisonment without possibility of parole. Unlike crimes directed against the persons and property of others, possession of drugs affects the criminal who uses the drugs most directly. The ripple effect on society caused by possession of drugs, through related crimes, lost productivity, health problems, and the like, is often not the direct consequence of possession, but of the resulting addiction, something which this Court held in *Robinson v. California,* 370 U.S., at 660–667, 82 S.Ct., at 1417–1420, cannot be made a crime. * * *

The second prong of the *Solem* analysis is an examination of "the sentences imposed on other criminals in the same jurisdiction." As noted above, there is no death penalty in Michigan; consequently, life without parole, the punishment mandated here, is the harshest penalty available. It is reserved for three crimes: first-degree murder; manufacture, distribution, or possession with intent to manufacture or distribute 650 grams or more of narcotics; and possession of 650 grams or more of narcotics. Crimes directed against the persons and property of others—such as second-degree murder, rape, and armed robbery—do not carry such a harsh mandatory sentence, although they do provide for the possibility of a life sentence in the exercise of judicial discretion. It is clear that petitioner "has been treated in the same manner as, or more severely than, criminals who have committed far more serious crimes."

The third factor set forth in *Solem* examines "the sentences imposed for commission of the same crime in other jurisdictions." No other jurisdiction imposes a punishment nearly as severe as Michigan's for possession of the amount of drugs at issue here. * * *

Application of *Solem*'s proportionality analysis leaves no doubt that the Michigan statute at issue fails constitutional muster. * * *

JUSTICE MARSHALL, dissenting.

* * * I adhere to my view that capital punishment is in all instances unconstitutional. * * *

Notes and Questions

1. Count the votes in *Harmelin.* Is there still an Eighth Amendment proportionality doctrine in non-capital cases? If so, whose approach to proportionality has prevailed?

2. Justice Kennedy states that the proportionality cases (e.g., *Coker, Rummel,* and *Solem*) yield as one of their principles that the "Eighth Amendment does not mandate adoption of any one penological theory." Is he correct?

Justice Scalia states that "it becomes difficult" to discuss proportionality, "inherently a retributive concept," in a utilitarian context. Is he correct? If so, and if Justice Kennedy's observation is also correct, does that mean that Justice Scalia is right in rejecting the proportionality principle in non-capital cases?

3. Consider these pairs of offenses: (1) forcible rape of a stranger in a park; and an impulsive killing of one spouse's paramour; (2) embezzlement

of one million dollars from a union pension fund; and armed robbery of $10; and (3) international drug smuggling; and sexual contact with a young child. In each pair, which offense deserves greater punishment? Among all six, how would you rank them? If you were a legislator, how would you go about imposing proportional punishment for each offense?

4. In setting and imposing terms of imprisonment, should legislatures and judges consider factors beyond the quantity of time that the convicted defendant will be incarcerated? For example, should five years' imprisonment in a maximum security prison count for more punishment than ten years' imprisonment in a low security ("prison without walls") institution? Do you agree with one commentator who suggests that "the reality of each criminal's punishment consists in the experience of that punishment. What actually happens to prisoners—their daily pain and suffering inside prison— is the only true measure of whether the traditional concepts have meaning * * *"? Robert Blecker, *Haven or Hell? Inside Lorton Central Prison: Experiences of Punishment Justified,* 42 Stan.L.Rev. 1149, 1152 (1990) (emphasis deleted).

5. In 1992, the Michigan Supreme Court ruled that the drug statute considered in *Harmelin* was unconstitutional under that state's constitution, which bars "cruel *or* unusual" punishment. People v. Bullock, 440 Mich. 15, 485 N.W.2d 866 (1992). Should the substitution of "or" for "and" change the analysis?

6. *Problem. B,* a 23–year–old man (described in the record as "immature") suffering from various emotional insecurities, including a pending divorce, had sexual intercourse (described by the court as "entirely consensual") with two 15–year–old girls. *B* was convicted of two counts of sexual conduct with a minor and sentenced to two consecutive twenty-year prison terms. What result under *Harmelin?* State v. Bartlett, 171 Ariz. 302, 830 P.2d 823 (1992).

What about life imprisonment without the possibility of parole, imposed upon a 13–year–old defendant, for premeditated murder? Naovarath v. State, 105 Nev. 525, 779 P.2d 944 (1989).

Chapter 3

LEGALITY

INTRODUCTORY COMMENT

"Nullum crimen sine lege; nulla poena sine lege" ("no crime without (pre-existent) law, no punishment without (pre-existent) law")—the so-called principle of legality—has been described as *"the* first principle" of the American criminal law. Herbert L. Packer, The Limits of the Criminal Sanction 79–80 (1968). This chapter considers this first principle. Also considered is the "void for vagueness" doctrine, its "operational arm," John C. Jeffries, Jr., *Legality, Vagueness, and the Construction of Penal Statutes,* 71 Va.L.Rev. 189, 196 (1985), and related concepts, including the doctrines of strict construction (or "lenity") and statutory overbreadth.

A. THE REQUIREMENT OF PREVIOUSLY DEFINED CONDUCT

COMMONWEALTH v. MOCHAN

Superior Court of Pennsylvania, 1955.
117 Pa.Super. 454, 110 A.2d 788.

HIRT, JUDGE.

[Mochan was charged in separate indictments with intending "to debauch and corrupt, and further devising and intending to harass, embarrass and villify [sic] ... one Louise Zivkovich and the members of [her] family" by telephoning her various times, during which he

> did wickedly and maliciously refer to the said Louise Zivkovich as a lewd, immoral and lascivious woman of an indecent and lewd character, and [made] other scurrilous, opprobrious, filthy, disgusting, and indecent [comments] ... intending as aforesaid to blacken the character and reputation of the said Louise Zivkovich ... to the great damage, injury and oppression of the said Louise Zivkovich and other good citizens of this Commonwealth to the evil example of all other in like case offending, and against the peace and dignity of the Commonwealth of Pennsylvania.

The conduct alleged in the indictments was not prohibited by any state criminal statute. However, under Section 1101 of the Pennsylvania Penal Code of 1939, "[e]very offense * * * punishable either by the statutes or common law of this Commonwealth and not specifically provided for by this Act, * * * shall continue to be an offense punishable as heretofore." The prosecutor contended that Mochan's conduct was unlawful under Pennsylvania common law.]

* * * Defendant was tried before a judge without a jury and was convicted on both charges and was sentenced. He has appealed * * * on the ground * * * that the conduct charged in the indictments, concededly not a criminal offense in this State by any statute, does not constitute a misdemeanor at common law. * * *

It is established by the testimony that the defendant * * * on numerous occasions and on the specific dates laid in the indictments, telephoned one Louise Zivkovich, a stranger to him and a married woman of the highest character and repute. He called as often as three times each week and at any hour of the day or night. His language on these calls was obscene, lewd and filthy. He not only suggested intercourse with her but talked of sodomy as well, in the loathsome language of that criminal act, on a number of occasions. * * *

It is of little importance that there is no precedent in our reports which decides the precise question here involved. ⌠The test is not whether precedents can be found in the books but whether the alleged crimes could have been prosecuted and the offenders punished under the common law.⌡ In Commonwealth v. Miller, 94 Pa.Super. 499, 507, the controlling principles are thus stated: "The common law is sufficiently broad to punish as a misdemeanor, although there may be no exact precedent, any act which directly injures or tends to injure the public to such an extent as to require the state to interfere and punish the wrongdoer, as in the case of acts which injuriously affect public morality, or obstruct, or pervert public justice, or the administration of government." * * * Any act is indictable at common law which from its nature scandalously affects the morals or health of the community. * * * And as early as Updegraph v. Commonwealth, 11 Serg. & R. 394, it was held that Christianity is a part of the common law and maliciously to vilify the Christian religion is an indictable offense.

To endeavor merely to persuade a married woman to commit adultery is not indictable. Smith v. Commonwealth, 54 Pa. 209. The present defendant's criminal intent was evidenced by a number of overt acts beyond the mere oral solicitation of adultery. The vile and disgusting suggestions of sodomy alone and the otherwise persistent lewd, immoral and filthy language used by the defendant, take these cases out of the principle of the Smith case. Moreover potentially at least, defendant's acts injuriously affected public morality. The operator or any one on defendant's four-party telephone line could have listened in on the conversations, and at least two other persons in Mrs. Zivkovich's household heard some of defendant's immoral and obscene language over the telephone.

* * * [T]he factual charges in the body of the indictments identify the offense as a common law misdemeanor and the testimony established the guilt of the defendant.

Judgments and sentences affirmed.

WOODSIDE, JUDGE (dissenting).

Not unmindful of the reprehensible conduct of the appellant, I nevertheless cannot agree with the majority that what he did was a crime punishable under the laws of this Commonwealth.

The majority is declaring something to be a crime which was never before known to be a crime in this Commonwealth. They have done this by the application of such general principles as "it is a crime to do anything which injures or tends to injure the public to such an extent as to require the state to interfere and punish the wrongdoer;" and "whatever openly outrages decency and is injurious to public morals is a misdemeanor."

Not only have they declared it to be a crime to do an act "injuriously affecting public morality," but they have declared it to be a crime to do any act which has a "potentially" injurious effect on public morality.

Under the division of powers in our constitution it is for the legislature to determine what "injures or tends to injure the public."

One of the most important functions of a legislature is to determine what acts "require the state to interfere and punish the wrongdoer." There is no reason for the legislature to enact any criminal laws if the courts delegate to themselves the power to apply such general principles as are here applied to whatever conduct may seem to the courts to be injurious to the public.

There is no doubt that the common law is a part of the law of this Commonwealth, and we punish many acts under the common law. But after nearly two hundred years of constitutional government in which the legislature and not the courts have been charged by the people with the responsibility of deciding which acts do and which do not injure the public to the extent which requires punishment, it seems to me we are making an unwarranted invasion of the legislative field when we arrogate that responsibility to ourselves by declaring now, for the first time, that certain acts are a crime.

When the legislature invades either the judicial or the executive fields, or the executive invades either the judicial or legislative fields, the courts stand ready to stop them. But in matters of this type there is nothing to prevent our invasion of the legislative field except our own self restraint. * * *

Until the legislature says that what the defendant did is a crime, I think the courts should not declare it to be such.

I would therefore reverse the lower court and discharge the appellant.

Notes and Questions

1.   Is the court saying that Mochan's conduct fell within the scope of an existing common law offense, or is the court creating a new common law crime?

2.   What, if anything, troubles you about this case? Do you agree with the dissent that the court "invaded" the legislative province? If so, what is wrong with that? Aren't judges at least as qualified as legislators, many of whom are not lawyers, to formulate new criminal offenses?

Suppose that prior to Mochan's telephone calls the legislature had enacted a statute making it a crime "to do anything which injures or tends to injure the public or which openly outrages decency." Would that resolve your concerns about *Mochan?*

3.   Why is solicitation to commit sodomy punishable, but solicitation to commit adultery is not?

4.   Most states have abolished common law offenses, including now Pennsylvania. 18 Pa.Cons.Stat.Ann. § 107(b) (West 1983). Nonetheless, as the following materials suggest, even in states that have abolished common law offenses, common law doctrine remains important.

KEELER v. SUPERIOR COURT

Supreme Court of California, 1970.
2 Cal.3d 619, 87 Cal.Rptr. 481, 470 P.2d 617.

Mosk, Justice.

In this proceeding * * * we are called upon to decide whether an unborn but viable fetus is a "human being" within the meaning of the California statute defining murder (Pen.Code, § 187). We conclude that the Legislature did not intend such a meaning, and that for us to construe the statute to the contrary and apply it to this petitioner would exceed our judicial power and deny petitioner due process of law.

The evidence received at the preliminary examination may be summarized as follows: Petitioner and Teresa Keeler obtained an interlocutory decree of divorce on September 27, 1968. They had been married for 16 years. Unknown to petitioner, Mrs. Keeler was then pregnant by one Ernest Vogt, whom she had met earlier that summer. She subsequently began living with Vogt in Stockton, but concealed the fact from petitioner. * * *

On February 23, 1969, Mrs. Keeler was driving on a narrow mountain road * * *. She met petitioner driving in the opposite direction; he blocked the road with his car, and she pulled over to the side. He walked to her vehicle and began speaking to her. He seemed calm, and she rolled down her window to hear him. He said, "I hear you're pregnant. If you are you had better stay away * * * from here." She did not reply, and he opened the car door; as she later testified, "He

assisted me out of the car. * * * [I]t wasn't roughly at this time."
Petitioner then looked at her abdomen and became "extremely upset."
He said, "You sure are. I'm going to stomp it out of you." He pushed
her against the car, shoved his knee into her abdomen, and struck her in
the face with several blows. She fainted, and when she regained
consciousness petitioner had departed.

Mrs. Keeler drove back to Stockton, and the police and medical
assistance were summoned. She had suffered substantial facial injuries,
as well as extensive bruising of the abdominal wall. A Caesarian section
was performed and the fetus was examined *in utero*. Its head was found
to be severely fractured, and it was delivered stillborn. The pathologist
gave as his opinion that the cause of death was skull fracture with
consequent cerebral hemorrhaging, that death would have been immediate, and that the injury could have been the result of force applied to the
mother's abdomen. There was no air in the fetus' lungs, and the
umbilical cord was intact.

Upon delivery the fetus weighed five pounds and was 18 inches in
length. Both Mrs. Keeler and her obstetrician testified that fetal movements had been observed prior to February 23, 1969. The evidence was
in conflict as to the estimated age of the fetus; the expert testimony on
the point, however, concluded "with reasonable medical certainty" that
the fetus had developed to the stage of viability, i.e., that in the event of
premature birth on the date in question it would have had a 75 percent
to 96 percent chance of survival.

An information was filed charging petitioner, in Count I, with
committing the crime of murder (Pen.Code, § 187) in that he did
"unlawfully kill a human being, to wit Baby Girl VOGT, with malice
aforethought." In Count II petitioner was charged with wilful infliction
of traumatic injury upon his wife, and in Count III, with assault on Mrs.
Keeler by means of force likely to produce great bodily injury. * * *
[O]nly the murder count is actually in issue.

I

Penal Code section 187 provides: "Murder is the unlawful killing of
a human being, with malice aforethought." The dispositive question is
whether the fetus which petitioner is accused of killing was, on February
23, 1969, a "human being" within the meaning of this statute. If it was
not, petitioner cannot be charged with its "murder" * * *.

Section 187 was enacted as part of the Penal Code of 1872. Inasmuch as the provision has not been amended since that date, we must
determine the intent of the Legislature at the time of its enactment.
But section 187 was, in turn, taken verbatim from the first California
statute defining murder, part of the Crimes and Punishments Act of
1850. Penal Code section 5 (also enacted in 1872) declares: "The
provisions of this Code, so far as they are substantially the same as
existing statutes, must be construed as continuations thereof, and not as
new enactments." We begin, accordingly, by inquiring into the intent of

the Legislature in 1850 when it first defined murder as the unlawful and malicious killing of a "human being."

It will be presumed, of course, that in enacting a statute the Legislature was familiar with the relevant rules of the common law, and, when it couches its enactment in common law language, that its intent was to continue those rules in statutory form. * * *

We therefore undertake a brief review of the origins and development of the common law of abortional homicide. From that inquiry it appears that by the year 1850—the date with which we are concerned— an infant could not be the subject of homicide at common law *unless it had been born alive*. Perhaps the most influential statement of the "born alive" rule is that of Coke, in mid–17th century: "If a woman be quick with childe,[5] and by a potion or otherwise killeth it in her wombe, or if a man beat her, whereby the childe dyeth in her body, and she is delivered of a dead childe, this is a great misprision [i.e., misdemeanor], and no murder; but if the childe be born alive and dyeth of the potion, battery, or other cause, this is murder; for in law it is accounted a reasonable creature, *in rerum natura,* when it is born alive." (3 Coke, Institutes *58 (1648).) * * * In the 18th century * * * Coke's requirement that an infant be born alive in order to be the subject of homicide was reiterated * * * by both Blackstone and Hale. * * *

By the year 1850 this rule of the common law had long been accepted in the United States. As early as 1797 it was held that proof the child was born alive is necessary to support an indictment for murder, and the same rule was reiterated on the eve of the first session of our Legislature. * * *

We conclude that in declaring murder to be the unlawful and malicious killing of a "human being" the Legislature of 1850 intended that term to have the settled common law meaning of a person who had been born alive, and did not intend the act of feticide * * * to be an offense under the laws of California.

Nothing occurred between the years 1850 and 1872 to suggest that in adopting the new Penal Code on the latter date the Legislature entertained any different intent. * * *

It is the policy of this state to construe a penal statute as favorably to the defendant as its language and the circumstances of its application may reasonably permit; just as in the case of a question of fact, the defendant is entitled to the benefit of every reasonable doubt as to the true interpretation of words or the construction of language used in a statute. We hold that in adopting the definition of murder in Penal Code section 187 the Legislature intended to exclude from its reach the act of killing an unborn fetus.

---

5. "Quickening" is said to occur when movements of the fetus are first sensed or observed, and ordinarily takes place be-tween the 16th and 18th week of pregnancy. * * *

II

The People urge, however, that the sciences of obstetrics and pediatrics have greatly progressed since 1872, to the point where with proper medical care a normally developed fetus prematurely born at 28 weeks or more has an excellent chance of survival, i.e., is "viable"; that the common law requirement of live birth to prove the fetus had become a "human being" who may be the victim of murder is no longer in accord with scientific fact, since an unborn but viable fetus is now fully capable of independent life; and that one who unlawfully and maliciously terminates such a life should therefore be liable to prosecution for murder under section 187. We may grant the premises of this argument; indeed, we neither deny nor denigrate the vast progress of medicine in the century since the enactment of the Penal Code. But we cannot join in the conclusion sought to be deduced: we cannot hold this petitioner to answer for murder by reason of his alleged act of killing an unborn—even though viable—fetus. To such a charge there are two insuperable obstacles, one "jurisdictional" and the other constitutional.

Penal Code section 6 declares in relevant part that "No act or omission" accomplished after the code has taken effect "is criminal or punishable, except as prescribed or authorized by this Code, or by some of the statutes which it specifies as continuing in force and as not affected by its provisions, or by some ordinance, municipal, county, or township regulation * * *." This section embodies a fundamental principle of our tripartite form of government, i.e., that subject to the constitutional prohibition against cruel and unusual punishment, the power to define crimes and fix penalties is vested exclusively in the legislative branch. Stated differently, there are no common law crimes in California. * * *

Settled rules of construction implement this principle. Although the Penal Code commands us to construe its provisions "according to the fair import of their terms, with a view to effect its objects and to promote justice" (Pen.Code, § 4), it is clear the courts cannot go so far as to create an offense by enlarging a statute, by inserting or deleting words, or by giving the terms used false or unusual meanings. Penal statutes will not be made to reach beyond their plain intent; they include only those offenses coming clearly within the import of their language. * * *

Applying these rules to the case at bar, we would undoubtedly act in excess of the judicial power if we were to adopt the People's proposed construction of section 187. * * * We recognize that the killing of an unborn but viable fetus may be deemed by some to be an offense of similar nature and gravity; but as Chief Justice Marshall warned long ago, "It would be dangerous, indeed, to carry the principle, that a case which is within the reason or mischief of a statute, is within its provisions, so far as to punish a crime not enumerated in the statute, because it is of equal atrocity, or of kindred character, with those which are enumerated." (United States v. Wiltberger (1820) 18 U.S. (5 Wheat.) 76, 96, 5 L.Ed. 37.) Whether to thus extend liability for murder in California is a determination solely within the province of the Legislature. For a court to simply declare, by judicial fiat, that the time has now come to prosecute under section 187 one who kills an unborn but viable fetus would indeed be to rewrite the statute under the guise of construing it. Nor does a need to fill an asserted "gap" in the law * * * justify judicial legislation of this nature: to make it "a judicial function 'to explore such new fields of crime as they may appear from time to time' is wholly foreign to the American concept of criminal justice" and "raises very serious questions concerning the principle of separation of powers."

The second obstacle to the proposed judicial enlargement of section 187 is the guarantee of due process of law. Assuming *arguendo* that we have the power to adopt the new construction of this statute as the law of California, such a ruling, by constitutional command, could operate only prospectively, and thus could not in any event reach the conduct of petitioner on February 23, 1969.

The first essential of due process is fair warning of the act which is made punishable as a crime. "That the terms of a penal statute creating a new offense must be sufficiently explicit to inform those who are subject to it what conduct on their part will render them liable to its penalties, is a well-recognized requirement, consonant alike with ordinary notions of fair play and the settled rules of law." (Connally v. General Constr. Co. (1926) 269 U.S. 385, 391, 46 S.Ct. 126, 127, 70 L.Ed. 322.) "No one may be required at peril of life, liberty or property to speculate as to the meaning of penal statutes. All are entitled to be informed as to what the State commands or forbids." (Lanzetta v. New Jersey (1939) 306 U.S. 451, 453, 59 S.Ct. 618, 619, 83 L.Ed. 888.) * * *

This requirement of fair warning is reflected in the constitutional prohibition against the enactment of ex post facto laws (U.S. Const., art. I, §§ 9, 10; Cal. Const., art. I, § 16). When a new penal statute is applied retrospectively to make punishable an act which was not criminal at the time it was performed, the defendant has been given no advance notice consistent with due process. And precisely the same effect occurs when such an act is made punishable under a preexisting statute but by means of an unforeseeable *judicial* enlargement thereof. (Bouie v. City of Columbia (1964) 378 U.S. 347, 84 S.Ct. 1697, 12 L.Ed.2d 894.)

In *Bouie* two Negroes took seats in the restaurant section of a South Carolina drugstore; no notices were posted restricting the area to whites only. When the defendants refused to leave upon demand, they were arrested and convicted of violating a criminal trespass statute which prohibited entry on the property of another "after notice" forbidding such conduct. Prior South Carolina decisions had emphasized the necessity of proving such notice to support a conviction under the statute. The South Carolina Supreme Court nevertheless affirmed the convictions, construing the statute to prohibit not only the act of entering after notice not to do so but also the wholly different act of remaining on the property after receiving notice to leave.

The United States Supreme Court reversed the convictions, holding that the South Carolina court's ruling was "unforeseeable" and when an "unforeseeable state-court construction of a criminal statute is applied retroactively to subject a person to criminal liability for past conduct, the effect is to deprive him of due process of law in the sense of fair warning that his contemplated conduct constitutes a crime." Analogizing to the prohibition against retrospective penal legislation, the high court reasoned "Indeed, an unforeseeable judicial enlargement of a criminal statute, applied retroactively, operates precisely like an *ex post facto* law, such as Art. I, § 10, of the Constitution forbids. An *ex post facto* law has been defined by this Court as one 'that makes an action done before the passing of the law, and which was *innocent* when done, criminal; and punishes such action,' or 'that *aggravates* a *crime,* or makes it *greater* than it was, when committed.' Calder v. Bull, 3 Dall. 386, 390, 1 L.Ed. 648. If a state legislature is barred by the *Ex Post Facto* Clause from passing such a law, it must follow that a State Supreme Court is barred by the Due Process Clause from achieving precisely the same result by judicial construction. * * * If a judicial construction of a criminal statute is 'unexpected and indefensible by reference to the law which had been expressed prior to the conduct in issue,' it must not be given retroactive effect."

The court remarked in conclusion that "Application of this rule is particularly compelling where, as here, the petitioners' conduct cannot be deemed improper or immoral." In the case at bar the conduct with which petitioner is charged is certainly "improper" and "immoral," and it is not contended he was exercising a constitutionally favored right. But the matter is simply one of degree, and it cannot be denied that the guarantee of due process extends to violent as well as peaceful men. The issue remains, would the judicial enlargement of section 187 now proposed have been foreseeable to this petitioner? * * *

Turning to the case law, we find no reported decision of the California courts which should have given petitioner notice that the killing of an unborn but viable fetus was prohibited by section 187. * * * [Discussion omitted.]

Finally, although a defendant is not bound to know the decisional law of other states, * * * the cases decided in our sister states * * * are unanimous in requiring proof that the child was born alive before a charge of homicide can be sustained. And the text writers of the same period are no less unanimous on the point.

We conclude that the judicial enlargement of section 187 now urged upon us by the People would not have been foreseeable to this petitioner, and hence that its adoption at this time would deny him due process of law. * * *

BURKE, ACTING CHIEF JUSTICE (dissenting).

The majority hold that "Baby Girl" Vogt, who, according to medical testimony, had reached the 35th week of development, had a 96 percent chance of survival, and was "definitely" alive and viable at the time of her death, nevertheless was not a "human being" under California's homicide statutes. In my view, in so holding, the majority ignore significant common law precedents, frustrate the express intent of the Legislature, and defy reason, logic and common sense.

Penal Code section 187 defines murder as "the unlawful killing of a human being, with malice aforethought." * * * The majority pursue the meaning of the term "human being" down the ancient hallways of the common law, citing Coke, Blackstone and Hale to the effect that the slaying of a "quickened" * * * child constituted "a great misprision," but not murder. * * *

The majority cast a passing glance at the common law concept of quickening, but fail to explain the significance of that concept: At common law, the quickened fetus *was* considered to be a human being, a second life separate and apart from its mother. As stated by Blackstone, * * * "Life is the immediate gift of God, a right inherent by nature in every individual; *and it begins in contemplation of law as soon as an infant is able to stir in the mother's womb.*" * * *

This reasoning explains why the killing of a quickened child was considered "a great misprision," although the killing of an unquickened child was no crime at all at common law. Moreover, although the common law did not apply the labels of "murder" or "manslaughter" to the killing of a quickened fetus, it appears that at common law this "great misprision" was severely punished. * * *

Thus, at common law, the killing of a quickened child was severely punished, since that child was considered to be a human being. The majority would have us assume that the Legislature in 1850 and 1872 simply overlooked this "great misprision" in codifying and classifying criminal offenses in California, or reduced that offense to the lesser offense of illegal abortion with its relatively lenient penalties. * * *

Of course, I do not suggest that we should interpret the term "human being" in our homicide statutes in terms of the common law concept of quickening. At one time, that concept had a value in differentiating, as accurately as was then scientifically possible, between life and nonlife. The analogous concept of viability is clearly more satisfactory, for it has a well defined and medically determinable meaning denoting the ability of the fetus to live or survive apart from its mother.

The majority opinion suggests that we are confined to common law concepts, and to the common law definition of murder or manslaughter. However, the Legislature, in Penal Code sections 187 and 192, has defined those offenses for us: homicide is the unlawful killing of a "human being." Those words need not be frozen in place as of any particular time, but must be fairly and reasonably interpreted by this court to promote justice and to carry out the evident purposes of the Legislature in adopting a homicide statute. * * *

We commonly conceive of human existence as a spectrum stretching from birth to death. However, if this court properly might expand the definition of "human being" at one end of that spectrum, we may do so at the other end. Consider the following example: All would agree that "Shooting or otherwise damaging a corpse is not homicide. * * *" (Perkins, Criminal Law (2d ed. 1969) ch. 2, § 1, p. 31.) In other words, a corpse is not considered to be a "human being" and thus cannot be the subject of a "killing" as those terms are used in homicide statutes. However, it is readily apparent that our concepts of what constitutes a "corpse" have been and are being continually modified by advances in the field of medicine, including new techniques for life revival, restoration and resuscitation * * *. Would this court ignore these developments and exonerate the killer of an apparently "drowned" child merely because that child would have been pronounced dead in 1648 or 1850? Obviously not. Whether a homicide occurred in that case would be determined by medical testimony regarding the capability of the child to have survived prior to the defendant's act. And that is precisely the test which this court should adopt in the instant case.

The common law reluctance to characterize the killing of a quickened fetus as a homicide was based solely upon a presumption that the fetus would have been born dead. * * * Based upon the state of the medical art in the 17th, 18th and 19th centuries, that presumption may have been well-founded. However, as we approach the 21st century, it has become apparent that "This presumption is not only contrary to common experience and the ordinary course of nature, but it is contrary to the usual rule with respect to presumptions followed in this state." (People v. Chavez (1947) 77 Cal.App.2d 621, 626, 176 P.2d 92, 95.)

* * * If, as I have contended, the term "human being" in our homicide statutes is a fluid concept to be defined in accordance with present conditions, then there can be no question that the term should include the fully viable fetus.

The majority suggest that to do so would improperly create some new offense. However, the offense of murder is no new offense. Contrary to the majority opinion, the Legislature has not "defined the crime of murder in California to apply only to the unlawful and malicious killing of one who has been born alive." Instead, the Legislature simply used the broad term "human being" and directed the courts to construe that term according to its "fair import" with a view to effect the objects of the homicide statutes and promote justice. What justice will be promoted, what objects effectuated, by construing "human being" as excluding Baby Girl Vogt and her unfortunate successors? Was defendant's brutal act of stomping her to death any less an act of homicide than the murder of a newly born baby? No one doubts that the term "human being" would include the elderly or dying persons whose potential for life has nearly lapsed; their proximity to death is deemed immaterial. There is no sound reason for denying the viable fetus, with its unbounded potential for life, the same status.

The majority also suggest that such an interpretation of our homicide statutes would deny defendant "fair warning" that his act was punishable as a crime. Aside from the absurdity of the underlying premise that defendant consulted Coke, Blackstone or Hale before kicking Baby Girl Vogt to death, it is clear that defendant had adequate notice that his act could constitute homicide. * * *

Our homicide statutes have been in effect in this state since 1850. The fact that the California courts have not been called upon to determine the precise question before us does not render "unforeseeable" a decision which determines that a viable fetus is a "human being" under those statutes. Can defendant really claim surprise that a 5–pound, 18–inch, 34–week–old, living, viable child is considered to be a human being? * * *

Notes and Questions

1. In response to *Keeler,* the California legislature amended the definition of murder to read: "Murder is the unlawful killing of a human being, or a fetus, with malice aforethought." Cal.Penal Code § 187(a) (West 1988). (Therapeutic abortions, as defined by state law, are expressly excluded from the scope of the statute. Section 187(b).) Is the amended statute in accord with Justice Burke's dissent?

2. *Problem.* On January 1, Arnold kills Bob in self-defense. On the same day, Carla, who is insane, kills Donna. On January 2, the state legislature abolishes the defenses of self-defense and insanity. May the state now convict Arnold and Carla for their conduct? Is there a plausible argument for the position that Carla may be convicted, but that Arnold may not be? See Peter Alldridge, *Rules for Courts and Rules for Citizens,* 10 Oxford J. of Legal Studies 487 (1990); George P. Fletcher, *Rights and Excuses,* Crim. Just. Ethics, Summer/Fall, 1984, at 17.

3. According to *Keeler,* "a defendant is not bound to know the decisional law of other states." Why not? If a law-abiding person in Keeler's situation is expected to study Coke and Blackstone, why not expect him to check out the law of other states?

B. VAGUENESS, OVERBREADTH, AND LENITY DOCTRINES

IN RE BANKS

Supreme Court of North Carolina, 1978.
295 N.C. 236, 244 S.E.2d 386.

MOORE, JUSTICE.

The State argues that the trial court erred in ruling that G.S. 14–202, the so-called "Peeping Tom" statute, is unconstitutional. Respondent, however, contends that this statute is * * * unconstitutionally vague, because "men of common intelligence must necessarily guess at its meaning and differ as to its application...." *Connally v. General Construction Co.,* 269 U.S. 385, 46 S.Ct. 126, 70 L.Ed. 322 (1926).

G.S. 14–202 provides:

Penal code

> *"Secretly peeping into room occupied by female person.*—Any person who shall peep secretly into any room occupied by a female person shall be guilty of a misdemeanor and upon conviction shall be fined or imprisoned in the discretion of the court."

The requirement that a statute be couched in terms of appropriate definiteness has been referred to as a fundamental common law concept. * * *

This requirement of definiteness has in this century been declared an essential element of due process of law. *See Connally v. General Construction Co., supra.* Several United States Supreme Court cases indicate that the evils remedied by the definiteness requirement are the lack of fair notice of the conduct prohibited and the failure to define a reasonably ascertainable standard of guilt. * * *

Criminal statutes must be strictly construed. But, while a criminal statute must be strictly construed, the courts must nevertheless construe it with regard to the evil which it is intended to suppress. The intent of the legislature controls the interpretation of a statute. * * *

On the subject of the constitutional challenge of a statute for indefiniteness, the United States Supreme Court has said, in *Boyce Motor Lines v. United States,* 342 U.S. 337, 72 S.Ct. 329, 96 L.Ed. 367 (1952):

> "A criminal statute must be sufficiently definite to give notice of the required conduct to one who would avoid its penalties, and to guide the judge in its application and the lawyer in defending one charged with its violation. But few words possess the precision of mathematical symbols, most statutes must deal with untold and unforeseen variations in factual situations, and the practical necessities of discharging the business of government inevitably limit the specificity with which legislators can spell out prohibitions. Consequently, no more than a reasonable degree of certainty can be demanded. Nor is it unfair to require that one who deliberately goes perilously close to an area of proscribed conduct shall take the risk that he may cross the line."

In *Wainwright v. Stone,* [414 U.S. 21, 94 S.Ct. 190, 38 L.Ed.2d 179 (1973)], where defendant challenged the Florida "Crime Against Nature" statute on grounds of vagueness, the United States Supreme Court, in upholding the constitutionality of the statute, held that the judgment of federal courts as to the vagueness of a state statute must be made in the light of prior state constructions of the statute. This holding implies that a statute challenged on the grounds of impermissible vagueness should not be tested for constitutional specificity in a vacuum, but should be judged in the light of its common law meaning, its statutory history and the prior judicial interpretation of its particular terms.

Applying the foregoing principles, we now turn to an examination of G.S. 14–202, commonly known as the "Peeping Tom" statute. The statute apparently was derived from the common law crimes of common nuisance and eavesdropping. The words "Peeping Tom" have a commonly understood meaning in this country as being one who sneaks up to a window and peeps in for the purpose of spying on and invading the privacy of the inhabitants. * * *

Our statute, passed by the General Assembly in 1923, makes it a crime to "peep secretly." This Court has had the occasion to deal with this statute in * * * prior cases: *State v. Banks,* 263 N.C. 784, 140 S.E.2d 318 (1965); *State v. Bivins,* 262 N.C. 93, 136 S.E.2d 250 (1964). * * * [T]hese cases involved conduct within the purview of the common usage of the term "Peeping Tom." In *State v. Bivins, supra,* the Court interpreted the word "peep" in a manner so as to convey the idea of a "Peeping Tom." The Court said that "to peep" means "to look cautiously or slyly—as if through a crevice—out from chinks and knotholes." * * *

In *State v. Banks, supra,* the Court * * * indicated that the word "secretly" as used in G.S. 14–202 conveys the definite idea of spying upon another with the intention of invading her privacy. Hence, giving the language of the statute its meaning as interpreted by this Court, G.S. 14–202 prohibits the wrongful spying into a room upon a female with the intent of violating the female's legitimate expectation of privacy. This is sufficient to inform a person of ordinary intelligence, with reasonable precision, of those acts the statute intends to prohibit, so that he may know what acts he should avoid in order that he may not bring himself within its provisions. * * *

We hold, therefore, that G.S. 14–202 is sufficiently definite to give an individual fair notice of the conduct prohibited, and to guide a judge in its application and a lawyer in defending one charged with its violation * * *.

Respondent next argues that G.S. 14–202 is unconstitutional because it prohibits innocent conduct, and is therefore overly broad. In speaking to a similar contention, Mr. Justice Brennan, for the Supreme Court of the United States, in *Zwickler v. Koota,* 389 U.S. 241, 88 S.Ct. 391, 19 L.Ed.2d 444 (1967), stated:

> "[H]is constitutional attack is that the statute, although lacking neither clarity nor precision, is void for 'overbreadth,' that is, that it offends the constitutional principle that 'a governmental purpose to control or prevent activities constitutionally subject to state regulation may not be achieved by means which sweep unnecessarily broadly and thereby invade the area of protected freedoms.' [Citations omitted.]" * * *

* * * [T]he Court indicated that the doctrine of overbreadth has not and will not be invoked when a limiting construction has been or could be placed on the challenged statute.

In *Lemon v. State*, 235 Ga. 74, 218 S.E.2d 818 (1975), the Supreme Court of Georgia upheld the validity of their "Peeping Tom" statute. There, as here, defendant argued that the Georgia statute was overbroad and hence unconstitutional. In answer to this argument, that court stated:

> "[T]he statute is not so overbroad as to proscribe legitimate conduct. The statute is sufficiently narrowed by the requirement that the defendant act with wrongful intent, thereby omitting from its scope those persons who have a legitimate purpose upon another's property, or those who only inadvertently glance in the window of another."

Likewise, our statute, G.S. 14–202, is sufficiently narrowed by judicial interpretation to require that the act condemned must be a spying for the wrongful purpose of invading the privacy of the female occupant of the room, thereby omitting from its scope those persons who have a legitimate purpose upon another's property and those who only inadvertently glance in the window of another. Thus, the statute is not so overbroad as to proscribe legitimate conduct. * * *

Notes and Questions

1. What is the rationale of the vagueness doctrine? Does enforcement of the doctrine have a counter-utilitarian effect, i.e., does it frustrate legitimate efforts to deter injurious conduct?

2. Suppose that Banks had fantasized that the victim liked being spied upon. Would he be guilty of violation of Section 14–202, as it is drafted? Is he guilty, as the court has interpreted the statute?

3. Does *Banks* adequately clarify the meaning of the statute? For example, what does the court mean when it states that the wrongful spying must violate "the female's legitimate expectation of privacy"?

The phrase "legitimate expectation of privacy" is a term of art, introduced by the United States Supreme Court in Katz v. United States, 389 U.S. 347, 88 S.Ct. 507, 19 L.Ed.2d 576 (1967). Under *Katz* and subsequent court decisions construing it, only police surveillance that intrudes upon a person's "legitimate expectation of privacy" constitutes a "search" within the meaning of the Fourth Amendment, which prohibits "unreasonable searches and seizures."

Does—and should—the North Carolina court's use of this phrase mean that a would-be peeper is expected to investigate the tens of thousands of judicial opinions that have given meaning to this phrase?

4. In *Wainwright v. Stone,* cited in *Banks,* the Supreme Court upheld against a void-for-vagueness attack a Florida statute that prohibited, without defining, "the abominable and detestable crime against nature, either with mankind or beast * * *." If no Florida court had previously construed the statute, would it have been susceptible to constitutional attack on vagueness

grounds? Suppose that courts in other states with a similar statute had clarified its meaning. Should a Floridian be expected to look beyond the confines of her own state in order to determine the meaning of the law? Beyond researching case law on the subject, are there other ways in which a person of common intelligence might ascertain the meaning of this Florida statute?

5. As a matter of constitutional law, can a statute be too *specific?* Suppose that Eunice is arrested for violation of a statute that prohibits the operation of a motor vehicle by a person "who has a blood alcohol concentration of .10% or more"? Is it unrealistic to expect her to determine by her own senses whether her blood alcohol concentration is a "legal" .09% or an "illegal" .10%? See State v. Muehlenberg, 118 Wis.2d 502, 347 N.W.2d 914 (App.1984); Burg v. Municipal Court, 35 Cal.3d 257, 198 Cal.Rptr. 145, 673 P.2d 732 (1983).

6. *Overbreadth doctrine.* A statute is subject to attack on the independent ground that it is overly broad, in that it prohibits constitutionally protected conduct, such as freedom of speech, or that it bars other innocent behavior. Sometimes the overbreadth doctrine overlaps the vagueness claim, i.e., the statute is so imprecise that it plausibly can be interpreted to prohibit innocent conduct. When a law seems to intrude on constitutionally protected rights, especially freedom of speech, courts are particularly inclined to invalidate it.

7. In regard to the dangers—and benefits—of imprecise statutes, consider a Jacksonville, Florida ordinance declared violative of the due process clause in Papachristou v. City of Jacksonville, 405 U.S. 156, 92 S.Ct. 839, 31 L.Ed.2d 110 (1972).

The ordinance prohibited vagrancy. "Vagrants" were defined to include "rogues," "vagabonds," "dissolute persons who go about begging," "common drunkards," "common night walkers," "lewd, wanton [or] lascivious persons," "disorderly persons," "persons habitually spending their time by frequenting houses of ill fame," "persons able to work but habitually living upon the earnings of their wives or minor children," as well as those people found "wandering or strolling around from place to place without any lawful purpose."

The Court ruled that the ordinance was fatally defective not only on traditional fair notice grounds, but because its vagueness "encourage[d] arbitrary and erratic arrests and convictions." Id. at 162, 92 S.Ct. at 843, 31 L.Ed.2d at 115. What do you think the Court had in mind by this remark?

The Court also criticized the ordinance because it criminalized "activities which by modern standards are normally innocent." For example, the Court observed, "Luis Munoz–Marin, former Governor of Puerto Rico, commented once that 'loafing' was a national virtue in his Commonwealth and that it should be encouraged. It is, however, a crime in Jacksonville." Id. at 163, 92 S.Ct. at 844, 31 L.Ed.2d at 116.

All of this said, do vagrancy laws have a legitimate purpose? What is it? Can you think of a way to redraft the Jacksonville ordinance, consistent with due process, to further that interest? In this regard, consider Model Penal

Code § 250.6. Does this section, adopted before *Papachristou,* withstand constitutional scrutiny?

8. *Lenity.* In *Keeler,* the court stated that its policy was "to construe a penal statute as favorably to the defendant as its language and the circumstances of its application may **reasonably permit**." In *Banks,* as well, the court noted that criminal statutes must be strictly construed. These are expressions of the doctrine of lenity, another tool for implementing the legality principle.

The "touchstone" of the rule of lenity is statutory ambiguity. Moskal v. United States, 498 U.S. 103, 107, 111 S.Ct. 461, 465, 112 L.Ed.2d 449, 458 (1990). That is, the lenity doctrine does not come into play unless the statute is reasonably susceptible to multiple interpretations, one of which would result in more lenient treatment of the defendant.

Assuming that a statute is ambiguous, in what ways does lenity further the legality principle? Consider the following explanation by Professor John Jeffries:

> Just as the concern for notice would require invalidation of laws that give no fair warning, it would also imply that remaining ambiguities be resolved against the state. Otherwise, the interpretation of penal statutes would threaten that same unfair surprise against which the vagueness doctrine more generally guards. In effect, strict construction strips away from the criminal law those potential applications for which fair warning was not clearly given. In this respect, the rule of strict construction is thought to implement the principle of legality and to reinforce the prohibitions against indefinite laws.

John C. Jeffries, Jr., *Legality, Vagueness, and the Construction of Penal Statutes,* 71 Va.L.Rev. 189, 210 (1985). According to the author, the doctrine "no longer commands the allegiance of the courts" and is followed only "variously and unpredictably."

Chapter 4

ACTUS REUS

INTRODUCTORY COMMENT

In general, a crime contains two components: an *"actus reus"* and the *"mens rea."* The *"actus reus"* is the physical, or external, part of the crime; the *"mens rea"* is the mental, or internal, ingredient.

The term *"actus reus"* has no universally accepted meaning. It is sometimes used to describe the actions that result in criminal harm. For example, if *A* aims a gun at *B* and pulls the trigger, killing *B,* the *"actus reus"* in this sense consists of the acts of aiming the gun and pulling the trigger. For other courts and commentators, however, *"actus reus"* signifies the resulting harm, in this case *B*'s death. Another view, perhaps the most common one, is that the term *"actus reus"* includes both the actions and the criminal result:

> [A]ctus reus is to be interpreted as the comprehensive notion of act, harm, and its connecting link, causation, with *actus* expressing the voluntary physical movement in the sense of conduct and *reus* expressing the fact that this conduct results in a certain proscribed harm, i.e., that it "causes" an injury to the legal interest protected in that crime.

Albin Eser, *The Principle of "Harm" in the Concept of Crime: A Comparative Analysis of the Criminally Protected Legal Interests,* 4 Duq.L.Rev. 345, 386 (1965).

This chapter considers two ingredients of the *"actus reus"*: (1) the requirement of voluntary physical movement by the actor (or, alternatively, the omission of a voluntary act when such inaction involves a breach of duty to act); and (2) the harm (or, more accurately, "social harm") resulting from the voluntary act. The causal link between these two elements is considered in Chapter 6.

A. VOLUNTARY ACT

MARTIN v. STATE

Alabama Court of Appeals, 1944.
31 Ala.App. 334, 17 So.2d 427.

SIMPSON, JUDGE.

Appellant was convicted of being drunk on a public highway, and appeals. Officers of the law arrested him at his home and took him onto the highway, where he allegedly committed the proscribed acts, viz., manifested a drunken condition by using loud and profane language.

The pertinent provisions of our statute are: "Any person who, while intoxicated or drunk, appears in any public place where one or more persons are present, * * * and manifests a drunken condition by boisterous or indecent conduct, or loud and profane discourse, shall, on conviction, be fined", etc. Code 1940, Title 14, Section 120.

Under the plain terms of this statute, a voluntary appearance is presupposed. The rule has been declared, and we think it sound, that an accusation of drunkenness in a designated public place cannot be established by proof that the accused, while in an intoxicated condition, was involuntarily and forcibly carried to that place by the arresting officer.

Conviction of appellant was contrary to this announced principle and, in our view, erroneous. * * *

Reversed and rendered.

Notes and Questions

1. *Punishing thoughts.* Would it be objectionable for Congress to make it a crime "to intend to assassinate the President of the United States"?

Punishment for mere thoughts is condemned on various grounds:

> Rooted in skepticism about the ability either to know what passes through the minds of men or to predict whether antisocial behavior will follow from antisocial thoughts, the act requirement serves a number of closely-related objectives: it seeks to assure that the evil intent of the man branded a criminal has been expressed in a manner signifying harm to society; that there is no longer any substantial likelihood that he will be deterred by the threat of sanction; and that there has been an identifiable occurrence so that multiple prosecution and punishment may be minimized.

Abraham S. Goldstein, *Conspiracy to Defraud the United States,* 68 Yale L.J. 405, 405–06 (1959).

Do these objections withstand scrutiny? Suppose that a person charged with intending to assassinate the President freely confesses to the crime? Is it still wrong to punish for thoughts alone? Is the truer explanation that there is no way to distinguish "between desires of the day-dream variety and fixed intentions that may pose a real threat to society"? Powell v. Texas, 392 U.S. 514, 543–44, 88 S.Ct. 2145, 2160, 20 L.Ed.2d 1254, 1274 (1968) (Black and Harlan, JJ., concurring). Or, is the reason for the rule that if we did punish for mere thoughts of wrongdoing we would all be subject to prosecution?

2. *Voluntary versus involuntary actions.* Influenced by Model Penal Code § 2.01(1), many modern criminal codes provide that a person is not guilty of an offense unless his conduct "includes a voluntary act or the omission to perform an act of which he is physically capable." This provision not only excludes punishment for mere thoughts, but it bars criminal liability for purely involuntary conduct. Do you find the following justification of the latter provision persuasive?

> It is fundamental that a civilized society does not punish for thoughts alone. Beyond this, the law cannot hope to deter involuntary movement * * *; the sense of personal security would be undermined in a society where such movement * * * could lead to formal social condemnation of the sort that a conviction necessarily entails. Persons whose involuntary movements threaten harm to others may present a public health or safety problem, calling for therapy or even for custodial commitment; they do not present a problem of correction.

American Law Institute, Model Penal Code and Commentaries, Comment to § 2.01 at 214–15 (1985). See, also, Michael Corrado, *Automatism and the Theory of Action,* 39 Emory L.J. 1191 (1990); Kevin W. Saunders, *Voluntary Acts and the Criminal Law: Justifying Culpability Based on the Existence of Volition,* 49 U.Pitt.L.Rev. 443 (1988).

3. What constitutes a "voluntary act"? In reading the remaining materials in this subsection, consider Michael S. Moore, *Responsibility and the Unconscious,* 53 S.Cal.L.Rev. 1563, 1567–68 (1980):

> In law, no less than in morals, the idea of human action lies at the heart of ascriptions of responsibility. One is responsible only for those consequences that are caused by his actions, and not for those things in which his body, but not his acting self, is causally implicated. One is responsible if he hits another with a stick, but is not responsible if his arm-with-stick is caused by the wind to strike another. On what basis does one distinguish those bodily motions that are actions from those that are not? * * *
>
> What one seeks is an answer to Wittgenstein's famous question, "[W]hat is left over if I subtract the fact that my arm goes up from the fact that I raise my arm?"[4] Seemingly "something" is left over, as is shown by the relationship between the following statements:
>
> (1) *X* raised his arm.
>
> (2) *X*'s arm went up.

(1) implies (2), but (2) does not imply (1). *X*'s arm may go up because, for example, the wind blows it, someone grabs it, or a reflex occurs. Hence (1)

---

4. L. Wittgenstein, Philosophical Inves-   1958).
tigations 161 (3d ed. G. Anscombe trans.

and (2) are not equivalent statements. To say that *X* raised his arm is to say *more* than merely that certain motions of his body took place.

STATE v. UTTER

Court of Appeals of Washington, 1971.
4 Wash.App. 137, 479 P.2d 946.

FARRIS, JUDGE.

Claude Gilbert Utter was charged * * * with the crime of murder in the second degree. He was convicted by a jury of the crime of manslaughter. He appeals from that conviction.

Appellant and the decedent, his son, were living together at the time of the latter's death. The son was seen to enter his father's apartment and shortly after was heard to say, "Dad, don't." Shortly thereafter he was seen stumbling in the hallway of the apartment building where he collapsed, having been stabbed in the chest. He stated, "Dad stabbed me" and died before he could be moved or questioned further.

Mr. Utter entered the armed services in December of 1942 and was honorably discharged in October of 1946. He was a combat infantryman. As a result of his service, he was awarded a 60 per cent disability pension.

Appellant testified that on the date of his son's death he began drinking during the morning hours. He was at the liquor store at 9 a.m. and purchased a quart of Thunderbird wine and a quart of port wine and drank the bottle of port wine with the exception of two drinks. Mr. Utter went for more liquor around noon. At that time he purchased 2 quarts of whiskey and 4 quarts of wine. Upon his return from the liquor store, he and another resident of the apartment "sat around drinking whiskey out of water glasses." Appellant remembers drinking with his friend and the next thing he remembers was being in jail subsequent to the death of his son. He has no recollection of any intervening events.

Appellant introduced evidence on "conditioned response" during the trial. Conditioned response was defined by Dr. Jarvis, a psychiatrist, as "an act or a pattern of activity occurring so rapidly, so uniformly as to be automatic in response to a certain stimulus." Mr. Utter testified that as a result of his jungle warfare training and experiences in World War II, he had on two occasions in the 1950's reacted violently towards people approaching him unexpectedly from the rear.

The trial court ruled that conditioned response was not a defense in Washington and instructed the jury to disregard all evidence introduced on this subject. * * *

The major issue presented on appeal is whether it was error for the trial court to instruct the jury to disregard the evidence on conditioned response. * * *

In the present case, the appellant was charged with second degree murder and found guilty of manslaughter. The actus reus of both is the same—homicide. Thus, in order to establish either, the fact of homicide must first be established.

Appellant contends that his evidence was presented for the purpose of determining whether in fact a homicide had been committed. He argues that his evidence, if believed, establishes that no "act" was committed within the definition of homicide (RCW 9.48.010):

> Homicide is the killing of a human being by the act, procurement or omission of another and is either (1) murder, (2) manslaughter, (3) excusable homicide or (4) justifiable homicide.

What is the meaning of the word "act" as used in this statute?

> It is sometimes said that no crime has been committed unless the harmful result was brought about by a "voluntary act." Analysis of such a statement will disclose, however, that as so used the phrase "voluntary act" means no more than the mere word "act." An act must be a willed movement or the omission of a possible and legally-required performance. This is essential to the *actus reus* rather than to the mens rea. "A spasm is not an act."

R. Perkins, Criminal Law 660 (1957).

> [A]n "act" involves an exercise of the will. It signifies something done voluntarily. * * * We find these statements abundantly sustained by the text-writers and decisions of our courts.

Heiman v. Pan American Life Ins. Co., 183 La. 1045, 1061, 165 So. 195 (1935).

Thus, to invert the statement of Perkins, the word "act" technically means a "voluntary act."

It is the appellant's contention that any of the alleged "acts" he committed were not those which involved mental processes, but rather were learned physical reactions to external stimuli which operated automatically on his autonomic nervous system. * * *

Appellant contends that a person in an automatistic or unconscious state is incapable of committing a culpable act—in this case, a homicidal act.

The question is not one of mental incapacity. "Criminal responsibility must be judged at the level of the conscious." State v. Sikora, 44 N.J. 453, 470, 210 A.2d 193 (1965).

There is authority to support the proposition of the appellant. * * *

> If a person is in fact unconscious at the time he commits an act which would otherwise be criminal, he is not responsible therefor.

> The absence of consciousness not only precludes the existence of any specific mental state, but also excludes the possibility of a voluntary act without which there can be no criminal liability.

R. Anderson, 1 Wharton's Criminal Law and Procedure § 50 (1957).
* * *

In State v. Strasburg, 60 Wash. 106, 110 P. 1020 (1910) the Washington Supreme Court * * * made an extensive review of basic tenets of criminal law and noted in part as follows:

> "All of the several pleas and excuses which protect the committer of a forbidden act from the punishment which is otherwise annexed thereto may be reduced to this single consideration, the want or defect of *will*. An involuntary act, as it has no claim to merit, so neither can it induce any guilt; the concurrence of the will, when it has its choice either to do or to avoid the fact in question, being the only thing that renders human actions either praiseworthy or culpable.

> * * *

> "Without the consent of the *will*, human actions cannot be considered as culpable; nor where there is no will to commit an offense is there any just reason why a party should incur the penalties of a law made for the punishment of crimes and offenses."

An "act" committed while one is unconscious is in reality no act at all. It is merely a physical event or occurrence for which there can be no criminal liability. However, unconsciousness does not, in all cases, provide a defense to a crime. When the state of unconsciousness is voluntarily induced through the use and consumption of alcohol or drugs, then that state of unconsciousness does not attain the stature of a complete defense. Thus, in a case such as the present one where there is evidence that the accused has consumed alcohol or drugs, the trial court should give a cautionary instruction with respect to voluntarily induced unconsciousness.

The issue of whether or not the appellant was in an unconscious or automatistic state at the time he allegedly committed the criminal acts charged is a question of fact. Appellant's theory of the case should have been presented to the jury if there was substantial evidence in the record to support it. * * *

We find that the evidence presented was insufficient to present the issue of defendant's unconscious or automatistic state at the time of the act to the jury. There is no evidence, circumstantial or otherwise from which the jury could determine or reasonably infer what happened in the room at the time of the stabbing; the jury could only speculate on the existence of the triggering stimulus. * * *

Notes and Questions

1. What is the Wittgenstein/Moore "something" (Note 3, p. 83 supra) that distinguishes voluntary acts from involuntary ones? How does the Model Penal Code define "voluntary act"?

2. Utter may have suffered from what is now termed "post-traumatic stress disorder" (PTSD), a condition experienced by some persons "following

a psychologically distressing event that is outside the range of usual human experience," such as a rape, military combat, or a natural disaster. American Psychiatric Association, Diagnostic and Statistical Manual of Mental Disorders 247 (3d ed. Rev.1987).

When an everyday event triggers a memory of the traumatic experience, the PTSD victim may suffer "dissociative" or "flashback" episodes, hallucinations, or illusions. Although a claim of unconsciousness under such circumstances is sometimes successful, the disorder is usually raised in the context of an insanity plea. As a practical matter, why might a defendant prefer acquittal on the basis of unconsciousness? See Fulcher v. State, 633 P.2d 142 (Wyo.1981). w/ insanity he could be committed ~ unconscious means ← he is simply free ~ no state intervention

3. *Different meanings of "involuntary."* You should be alert to the fact that the term "involuntary" has multiple meanings in the criminal law. For example, if Jill points a loaded gun at Jack's head and threatens to kill him immediately unless he helps her rob a bank, Jack's decision to accede to her threat is "involuntary" in the sense that his actions were coerced, but are his actions "involuntary" in the sense described in *Utter?*

4. *"Voluntary act" versus "mens rea."* The doctrines of "voluntary act" and *"mens rea"* should not be confused. As developed more fully in the next chapter, the term *"mens rea"* signifies the actor's state of mind regarding the *social harm* of the offense, whereas the element of voluntariness applies to the *act* that caused the social harm.

For example, suppose that Carl, standing on a target range, aims his gun at the target and pulls the trigger, at which instant Dorothy unforeseeably walks in front of the target, is struck by a bullet from Carl's gun, and dies. On these facts, Carl lacks any blameworthy state of mind (*mens rea*) as to Dorothy's death (the social harm of "criminal homicide"), i.e., Carl did not intentionally, recklessly, or negligently kill Dorothy. Nonetheless, Carl's act of pulling the trigger was voluntary.

Even when an offense does not contain a *mens rea* component, as is occasionally the case, a voluntary act may still be required for conviction. See State v. Baker, 1 Kan.App.2d 568, 571 P.2d 65 (1977); but see Model Penal Code § 2.05.

5. In People v. Decina, 2 N.Y.2d 133, 157 N.Y.S.2d 558, 138 N.E.2d 799 (1956), *D,* who knew he was subject to epileptic seizures, suffered an attack while driving his automobile. During the seizure, his car struck and killed four children. *D* was charged with "operating a vehicle in a reckless or culpably negligent manner, causing the death of four persons." The court allowed the prosecution to proceed.

Isn't conduct during an epileptic seizure "involuntary"? If so, was *Decina* wrongly decided? Would the prosecution have been permitted under the Model Penal Code?

6. Suppose that a state legislature enacted a law making it a criminal offense "to be an epileptic." Is this legislation objectionable? On what ground? Would your objections be satisfied if the legislature redrafted the law to make it an offense for a person "to have an epileptic seizure"? The constitutionality of such statutes are considered at p. 539 infra.

7. Should a person who commits a crime as the result of hypnotic suggestion be exculpated on the ground that her actions were involuntary? Yes, according to the drafters of the Model Penal Code:

The case of hypnotic suggestion * * * seems to warrant explicit treatment [in Section 2.01(2)(c)]. Hypnosis differs from both sleep and fugue, but as it is characterized by the subject's dependence on the hypnotist, it does not seem politic to treat conduct resulting from hypnotic suggestion as voluntary, despite the state of consciousness involved. The widely held view that the hypnotized subject will not follow suggestions that are repugnant to him was deemed insufficient to warrant treating his conduct while hypnotized as voluntary; his dependence and helplessness are too pronounced.

American Law Institute, Model Penal Code and Commentaries, Comment to § 2.01 at 221 (1985).

Not all commentators agree with the Model Code in this regard:

There is good reason why such a defense is accepted by so few jurisdictions. * * * [S]cientific understanding of hypnosis is * * * still seriously incomplete. In 1961, experts were found to be undecided on the extent to which people could be convinced by hypnosis to commit criminal acts. A recent survey of 215 scientific studies indicated that although some "enhancement of hypnotic-like behavior as a consequence of induction" may exist, such enhancement is minimal, and "this is the least resolved of the [various] issues." This survey supports the belief that personal traits are much more important than hypnotic induction in making one suggestible.

As a result, it is difficult to distinguish between hypnosis cases and countless other examples of suggestiveness: *A* yawns, *B* follows; likewise, some people simply follow other people's leads, almost unthinkingly, because of friendship or other psychological or sociological dynamics. In such cases, either we say that choice is present—one chooses to follow, or chooses not to think for oneself—or we admit that due to personal or sociological factors beyond the person's control, many or all people are so suggestible as to lack real free will. This, however, is a determinist argument, and is therefore antithetical to current legal values.

Joshua Dressler, *Professor Delgado's "Brainwashing" Defense: Courting a Determinist Legal System*, 63 Minn.L.Rev. 335, 350–51 (1979).

B. OMISSIONS ("NEGATIVE ACTS")

1. GENERAL PRINCIPLES

PEOPLE v. BEARDSLEY

Supreme Court of Michigan, 1907.
150 Mich. 206, 113 N.W. 1128.

McAlvay, C.J. Respondent was convicted of manslaughter * * * and was sentenced to the state prison * * * for a minimum term of one year and a maximum term not to exceed five years.

He was a married man living at Pontiac, and at the time the facts herein narrated occurred, he was working as a bartender and clerk at the Columbia Hotel. He lived with his wife in Pontiac, occupying two rooms on the ground floor of a house. Other rooms were rented to tenants, as was also one living room in the basement. His wife being temporarily absent from the city, respondent arranged with a woman named Blanche Burns, who at the time was working at another hotel, to go to his apartments with him. He had been acquainted with her for some time. They knew each other's habits and character. They had drunk liquor together, and had on two occasions been in Detroit and spent the night together in houses of assignation. On the evening of Saturday, March 18, 1905, he met her at the place where she worked, and they went together to his place of residence. They at once began to drink and continued to drink steadily, and remained together, day and night, from that time until the afternoon of the Monday following, except when respondent went to his work on Sunday afternoon. There was liquor at these rooms, and when it was all used they were served with bottles of whiskey and beer by a young man who worked at the Columbia Hotel * * *. He was the only person who saw them in the house during the time they were there together. Respondent gave orders for liquor by telephone. On Monday afternoon, about 1 o'clock, the young man went to the house to see if anything was wanted. At this time he heard respondent say they must fix up the rooms, and the woman must not be found there by his wife, who was likely to return at any time. During this visit to the house the woman sent the young man to a drug store to purchase, with money she gave him, camphor and morphine tablets. He procured both articles. There were six grains of morphine in quarter-grain tablets. She concealed the morphine from respondent's notice, and was discovered putting something into her mouth by him and the young man as they were returning from the other room after taking a drink of beer. She in fact was taking morphine. Respondent struck the box from her hand. Some of the tablets fell on the floor, and of these, respondent crushed several with his foot. She picked up and swallowed two of them, and the young man put two of them in the spittoon. Altogether it is probable she took from three to four grains of morphine. The young man went away soon after this. Respondent called him by telephone about an hour later, and after he came to the house requested him to take the woman into the room in the basement which was occupied by a Mr. Skoba. She was in a stupor, and did not rouse when spoken to. Respondent was too intoxicated to be of any assistance and the young man proceeded to take her downstairs. While doing this, Skoba arrived, and together they put her in his room on the bed. Respondent requested Skoba to look after her, and let her out the back way when she waked up. Between 9 and 10 o'clock in the evening, Skoba became alarmed at her condition. He at once called the city marshal and a doctor. An examination by them disclosed that she was dead.

* * * In the brief of the prosecutor, his position is stated as follows: "It is the theory of the prosecution that the facts and circumstances attending the death of Blanche Burns in the house of respondent were such as to lay upon him a duty to care for her, and the duty to take steps for her protection, the failure to take which, was sufficient to constitute such an omission as would render him legally responsible for her death. * * * There is no claim on the part of the people that the respondent was in any way an active agent in bringing about the death of Blanche Burns, but simply that he owed her a duty which he failed to perform, and that in consequence of such failure on his part she came to her death." Upon this theory a conviction was asked and secured.

The law recognizes that under some circumstances the omission of a duty owed by one individual to another, where such omission results in the death of the one to whom the duty is owing, will make the other chargeable with manslaughter. (This rule of law is always based upon the proposition that the duty neglected must be a legal duty, and not a mere moral obligation.) It must be a duty imposed by law or by contract, and the omission to perform the duty must be the immediate and direct cause of death. Although the literature upon the subject is quite meager and the cases few, nevertheless the authorities are in harmony as to the relationship which must exist between the parties to create the duty, the omission of which establishes legal responsibility. One authority has briefly and correctly stated the rule, which the prosecution claims should be applied to the case at bar, as follows: "If a person who sustains to another the legal relation of protector, as husband to wife, parent to child, master to seaman, etc., knowing such person to be in peril of life, willfully or negligently fails to make such reasonable and proper efforts to rescue him as he might have done without jeopardizing his own life or the lives of others, he is guilty of manslaughter at least, if by reason of his omission of duty the dependent person dies." "So one who from domestic relationship, public duty, voluntary choice, or otherwise, has the custody and care of a human being, helpless either from imprisonment, infancy, sickness, age, imbecility, or other incapacity of mind or body, is bound to execute the charge with proper diligence and will be held guilty of manslaughter, if by culpable negligence he lets the helpless creature die." * * *

* * * Seeking for a proper determination of the case at bar by the application of the legal principles involved, we must eliminate from the case all consideration of mere moral obligation, and discover whether respondent was under a legal duty towards Blanche Burns at the time of her death, knowing her to be in peril of her life, which required him to make all reasonable and proper effort to save her, the omission to perform which duty would make him responsible for her death. This is the important and determining question in this case. If we hold that such legal duty rested upon respondent it must arise by implication from the facts and circumstances already recited. The record in this case discloses that the deceased was a woman past 30 years of age. She had been twice married. She was accustomed to visiting saloons and to the

use of intoxicants. She previously had made assignations with this man in Detroit at least twice. There is no evidence or claim from this record that any duress, fraud, or deceit had been practiced upon her. On the contrary it appears that she went upon this carouse with respondent voluntarily and so continued to remain with him. Her entire conduct indicates that she had ample experience in such affairs.

It is urged by the prosecutor that the respondent "stood towards this woman for the time being in the place of her natural guardian and protector, and as such owed her a clear legal duty which he completely failed to perform." The cases cited and digested establish that no such legal duty is created based upon a mere moral obligation. The fact that this woman was in his house created no such legal duty as exists in law and is due from a husband towards his wife, as seems to be intimated by the prosecutor's brief. Such an inference would be very repugnant to our moral sense. Respondent had assumed either in fact or by implication no care or control over his companion. Had this been a case where two men under like circumstances had voluntarily gone on a debauch together and one had attempted suicide, no one would claim that this doctrine of legal duty could be invoked to hold the other criminally responsible for omitting to make effort to rescue his companion. How can the fact that in this case one of the parties was a woman change the principle of law applicable to it? * * * We find no more apt words to apply to this case than those used by Mr. Justice Field, in United States v. Knowles [4 Sawy. (U.S.) 517, Fed.Cas. No. 15,540]: "In the absence of such obligations, it is undoubtedly the moral duty of every person to extend to others assistance when in danger, * * * and, if such efforts should be omitted by any one when they could be made without imperiling his own life, he would by his conduct draw upon himself the just censure and reproach of good men; but this is the only punishment to which he would be subjected by society." * * *

The conviction is set aside, and respondent is ordered discharged.

Notes and Questions

1. Graham Hughes, *Criminal Omissions,* 67 Yale L.J. 590, 624 (1958):

To be temperate about such a decision is difficult. In its savage proclamation that the wages of sin is death, it ignores any impulse of charity and compassion. It proclaims a morality which is smug, ignorant and vindictive. In a civilized society, a man who finds himself with a helplessly ill person who has no other source of aid should be under a duty to summon help, whether the person is his wife, his mistress, a prostitute or a Chief Justice. The *Beardsley* decision deserves emphatic repudiation by the jurisdiction which was responsible.

Do you agree with Professor Hughes? Is the Michigan court correct that, if Beardsley were legally responsible for Blanche Burns's death, he would also have to be held accountable for failing to come to the aid of a *male* drinking partner who attempted to commit suicide?

2. Jones v. United States, 308 F.2d 307, 310 (D.C.Cir.1962):

[handwritten margin note: 4 scenarios creating legal duty]

There are at least four situations in which the failure to act may constitute breach of a legal duty. One can be held criminally liable: first, where a statute imposes a duty * * *; second, where one stands in a certain status relationship to another; third, where one has assumed a contractual duty to care for another; and fourth, where one has voluntarily assumed the care of another and so secluded the helpless person as to prevent others from rendering aid.

Failure to act may also constitute a breach of a legal duty in a fifth situation: when a person creates a risk of harm to another. For example, if an automobile driver, by negligence (or, perhaps, even innocently), strikes and seriously injures a pedestrian, the driver has a legal duty to make sure that the injured party receives medical care. If the driver fails to assist, she may be held criminally responsible for the resulting harm, such as the pedestrian's death.

3. *Problem.* *I* lived with *V,* her elderly aunt, in the aunt's home. During *I* 's stay, *V* suffered gangrene in one leg, which made it impossible for her to attend to herself or to procure outside assistance. *I* did not inform others of her aunt's condition, although she had many opportunities to do so, nor did she obtain medical care for *V,* who died ten days later. Is *I* criminally responsible for *V* 's death? See Regina v. Instan, [1893] 1 Q.B. 450. *[handwritten: once you start to care for someone you have a duty to continue.]*

4. *Problem.* Robert Hogans stole Pam Bandy's car, kidnapped Bandy, and placed her in the car trunk. For five days, he drove the car while Bandy pounded on the inside of the trunk and begged for help. During some of this time, Teressa Nix, Hogans's 25–year–old girlfriend, was a passenger in the stolen car, and once was in it alone for a few minutes, during which time she did nothing to help Bandy, although she heard the cries for help. Bandy eventually died from drinking window washer fluid to quench her thirst. Is Nix criminally responsible for Bandy's death, on the basis of her omission? See Sandy McClure, *Pontiac Woman Is Cleared of Murder in Trunk Death,* Detroit Free Press, July 19, 1991, at 2B; Robin Fornoff, *Murder Charge Revived in Car Trunk Death Case,* id., Aug. 3, 1991, at 3A; Sandy McClure, *High Court May Decide on Resuming Trunk Death Trial,* id., Aug. 6, 1991, at 10A.

5. No discussion of the omission rule seems complete without consideration of the tragic 1964 murder of Katherine ("Kitty") Genovese, which occurred just outside her apartment building in Queens, New York. The events were described years later this way in Hughes v. State, 719 S.W.2d 560, 565 (Tex.Cr.App.1986) (Teague, J., concurring):

> [R]eference [should be made] to the well known case involving Katherine "Kitty" Genovese, whose screams and cries for help went unheard one night * * * because [38] persons in the neighborhood where she was assaulted and later murdered chose not to get involved, or intervene on Kitty's behalf, but chose, instead, to pull their window shades, blinds, or curtains, and shut their windows and doors, in order not to see or hear the butchery that was then taking place. Why did those good persons not come forth to aid Kitty, a fellow human being, who was then being mauled by nothing less than a rabies-infected animal, who was then disguised as a human being?

In the incident, Genovese's cries for help ("Oh, my God, he stabbed me! Please help me! Please help me!") continued for many minutes, as her assailant attacked her, fled when she cried for help, and then returned when nobody came to her aid. Over this time, any one of the 38 persons who woke up to her screams could have called the police, perhaps saving her life. Her murderer was arrested six days later and received a term of life imprisonment for the crime. In view of the common law omission rule, however, none of the onlookers was prosecuted. Should they have been held criminally responsible? The incident is described in detail in Abraham M. Rosenthal, Thirty–Eight Witnesses (1964).

The usual answer to the question asked in *Hughes* ("Why did those good persons not come forth to aid Kitty?") is that her neighbors were guilty of typical urban indifference to the needs of others. But, this may not have been the case. Intrigued by the Genovese case, social scientists conducted various studies of bystander behavior in emergency circumstances. In the first such examination, New York University undergraduates (the "subjects") were invited by the experimenters to participate in what the subjects were led to believe would be discussions of personal problems confronting college students.

The subjects were told that they would be part of either two-person, three-person, or six-person discussion groups, in which each discussant would be placed alone in a cubicle where he or she could talk to the other discussion group member(s) by intercom, to avoid embarrassment. The experimenters then played a tape, in which it sounded as if another student (really, an experimenter feigning illness) was suffering a life-threatening epileptic seizure in another cubicle.

The results of the study, replicated in subsequent experiments, suggest the existence of a so-called "bystander effect." That is, in 81 percent of the cases in which a subject believed that he or she was the only person who could hear the victim suffering the attack, the seizure was reported in a timely manner. Only 31 percent of the subjects acted promptly, however, when they thought that four other persons had heard the attack. Bibb Latane & John M. Darley, The Unresponsive Bystander: Why Doesn't He Help? 90–96 (1970); see also Morton M. Hunt, The Compassionate Beast 128–57 (1990). As Professor Leo Katz has explained the results, "[i]f Kitty Genovese failed to receive help, it was because, being part of a large group, nobody felt responsible. For Kitty Genovese, then, there was no safety in numbers." Leo Katz, Bad Acts and Guilty Minds 150 (1987).

6. Why does the common law permit people to stand by and allow harm to come to others, even when they could prevent it at no significant risk to themselves? Consider the following justifications. Are you persuaded by any of them? Can you suggest a better justification for the no-duty rule?

First, an omission is more ambiguous than an act. It is harder, therefore, to determine the motives—and, thus, the culpability—of the omitter. If Alice points a gun at Betty's head and voluntarily pulls the trigger, it is reasonable to infer that she intended to kill (or, at least, seriously harm) Betty. But, when Carole fails to help David, who is drowning in a pool, there are various non-exculpatory plausible explanations for Carole's omission, e.g., she did not appreciate the seriousness of David's predicament or was paralyzed with fear.

Second, difficult line-drawing problems arise in omission cases. For example, in the Kitty Genovese case (Note 5 supra), if punishment for omissions were appropriate, who besides the assailant would be responsible for Genovese's death? All 38 persons who awakened to her cries for help? Only those who realized the seriousness of her plight? Only those whose inaction was the result of moral indifference?

Third, the legal system should maximize individual freedom, rather than to curtail it. People should only be restrained by the state when they threaten to cause harm to others. The critical difference between an act and an omission is that, although an act may cause positive harm to others, a bystander's failure to act constitutes only the withholding of a benefit.

2. DISTINGUISHING ACTS FROM OMISSIONS

BARBER v. SUPERIOR COURT

California Court of Appeal, Second District, 1983.
147 Cal.App.3d 1006, 195 Cal.Rptr. 484.

COMPTON, ASSOCIATE JUSTICE.   * * *

Deceased Clarence Herbert underwent surgery for closure of an ileostomy. Petitioner Robert Nejdl, M.D., was Mr. Herbert's surgeon and petitioner Neil Barber, M.D. was his attending internist. Shortly after the successful completion of the surgery, and while in the recovery room, Mr. Herbert suffered a cardio-respiratory arrest. He was revived by a team of physicians and nurses and immediately placed on life support equipment.

Within the following three days, it was determined that Mr. Herbert was in a deeply comatose state from which he was not likely to recover. Tests and examinations performed by several physicians, including petitioners herein, each specializing in relevant fields of medicine indicated that Mr. Herbert had suffered severe brain damage, leaving him in a vegetative state, which was likely to be permanent.

At that time petitioners informed Mr. Herbert's family of their opinion as to his condition and chances for recovery. While there is some dispute as to the precise terminology used by the doctors, it is clear that they communicated to the family that the prognosis for recovery was extremely poor. At that point, the family convened and drafted a written request to the hospital personnel stating that they wanted "all machines taken off that are sustaining life" (sic). As a result, petitioners, either directly or as a result of orders given by them, caused the respirator and other life-sustaining equipment to be removed. Mr. Herbert continued to breathe without the equipment but showed no signs of improvement.   * * *

After two more days had elapsed, petitioners, after consulting with the family, ordered removal of the intravenous tubes which provided hydration and nourishment. From that point until his death, Mr. Herbert received nursing care which preserved his dignity and provided a clean and hygienic environment.

The precise issue for determination by this court is whether the evidence presented before the magistrate was sufficient to support his determination that petitioners should not be held to answer to the charges of murder and conspiracy to commit murder. * * *

Murder is "the *unlawful* killing of a human being, ... with malice aforethought." (Pen.Code, § 187, emphasis added.) Malice may be express or implied. It is express when there is an intent *unlawfully* to take any life. It is implied when the circumstances show an abandoned and malignant heart. (Pen.Code, § 188.) * * *

The use of the term "unlawful" in defining a criminal homicide is generally to distinguish a criminal homicide from those homicides which society has determined to be "justifiable" or "excusable." Euthanasia, of course, is neither justifiable nor excusable in California. * * *

Obviously the [legal doctrines relating to criminal homicide] evolved and were codified at a time well prior to the development of the modern medical technology which is involved here, which technology has caused our society to rethink its concepts of what constitutes "life" and "death."

This gap between the statutory law and recent medical developments has resulted in the instant prosecution and its attendant legal dispute. That dispute in order to be resolved within the framework of existing criminal law must be narrowed to a determination of whether petitioners' conduct was unlawful. * * *

Historically, death has been defined in terms of cessation of heart and respiratory function. Health and Safety Code section 7180(a)(2) [1] now provides for an alternative definition in terms of irreversible cessation of all brain function.

This is a clear recognition of the fact that the real seat of "life" is brain function rather than mere metabolic processes which result from respiration and circulation.

Of course it is conceded by all that at the time petitioners terminated further treatment, Mr. Herbert was not "dead" by either statutory or historical standards since there was still some minimal brain activity. If Mr. Herbert had in fact been "brain dead," this prosecution could not have been instituted because one cannot be charged with killing another person who is already dead.

---

1. Health and Safety Code section 7180 provides:

"(a) An individual who has sustained either (1) irreversible cessation of circulatory and respiratory functions, or (2) irreversible cessation of all functions of the entire brain, including the brain stem, is dead. A determination of death must be made in accordance with accepted medical standards. * * *." * * *

We deal here with the physician's responsibility in a case of a patient who, though not "brain dead," faces an indefinite vegetative existence without any of the higher cognitive brain functions. * * *

As a predicate to our analysis of whether the petitioners' conduct amounted to an "unlawful killing," we conclude that the cessation of "heroic" life support measures is not an affirmative act but rather a withdrawal or omission of further treatment.

Even though these life support devices are, to a degree, "self-propelled," each pulsation of the respirator or each drop of fluid introduced into the patient's body by intravenous feeding devices is comparable to a manually administered injection or item of medication. Hence "disconnecting" of the mechanical devices is comparable to withholding the manually administered injection or medication.

Further we view the use of an intravenous administration of nourishment and fluid, under the circumstances, as being the same as the use of the respirator or other form of life support equipment.

The prosecution would have us draw a distinction between the use of mechanical breathing devices such as respirators and mechanical feeding devices such as intravenous tubes. The distinction urged seems to be based more on the emotional symbolism of providing food and water to those incapable of providing for themselves rather than on any rational difference in cases such as the one at bench.

* * * Medical procedures to provide nutrition and hydration are more similar to other medical procedures than to typical human ways of providing nutrition and hydration. Their benefits and burdens ought to be evaluated in the same manner as any other medical procedure.

The authority cited by the People for the holding that a murder charge may be supported by the failure to feed an infant is easily distinguishable. The parent in that case had a clear duty to feed an otherwise healthy child. As we will discuss, *infra,* the duty of a physician under the circumstances of the case at bench is markedly different.

In the final analysis, since we view petitioners' conduct as that of omission rather than affirmative action, the resolution of this case turns on whether petitioners had a duty to continue to provide life sustaining treatment.

There is no criminal liability for failure to act unless there is a legal duty to act. Thus the critical issue becomes one of determining the duties owed by a physician to a patient who has been reliably diagnosed as in a comatose state from which any meaningful recovery of cognitive brain function is exceedingly unlikely. * * *

In examining this issue we must keep in mind that the life-sustaining technology involved in this case is not traditional treatment in that it is not being used to directly cure or even address the pathological condition. It merely sustains biological functions in order to gain time to permit other processes to address the pathology. * * *

A physician has no duty to continue treatment, once it has proved to be ineffective. Although there may be a duty to provide life-sustaining machinery in the *immediate* aftermath of a cardio-respiratory arrest, there is no duty to continue its use once it has become futile in the opinion of qualified medical personnel. * * *

Of course, the difficult determinations that must be made under these principles is the point at which further treatment will be of no reasonable benefit to the patient, who should have the power to make that decision and who should have the authority to direct termination of treatment.

No precise guidelines as to when or how these decisions should be made can be provided by this court since this determination is essentially a medical one to be made at a time and on the basis of facts which will be unique to each case. * * *

Several authorities have discussed the issue of which life-sustaining procedures must be used and for how long their use must be maintained in terms of "ordinary" and "extraordinary" means of treatment. The use of these terms begs the question. A more rational approach involves the determination of whether the proposed treatment is proportionate or disproportionate in terms of the benefits to be gained versus the burdens caused.

Under this approach, proportionate treatment is that which, in the view of the patient, has at least a reasonable chance of providing benefits to the patient, which benefits outweigh the burdens attendant to the treatment. Thus, even if a proposed course of treatment might be extremely painful or intrusive, it would still be proportionate treatment if the prognosis was for complete cure or significant improvement in the patient's condition. On the other hand, a treatment course which is only minimally painful or intrusive may nonetheless be considered disproportionate to the potential benefits if the prognosis is virtually hopeless for any significant improvement in condition. * * *

Of course the patient's interests and desires are the key ingredients of the decision making process. * * *

When the patient, however, is incapable of deciding for himself, because of his medical condition or for other reasons, there is no clear authority on the issue of who and under what procedure is to make the final decision. * * *

Under the circumstances of this case, the wife was the proper person to act as a surrogate for the patient with the authority to decide issues regarding further treatment, and would have so qualified had judicial approval been sought. There is no evidence that there was any disagreement among the wife and children. Nor was there any evidence that they were motivated in their decision by anything other than love and concern for the dignity of their husband and father.

Furthermore, in the absence of legislative guidance, we find no legal requirement that prior judicial approval is necessary before any decision to withdraw treatment can be made. * * *

In summary we conclude that the petitioners' omission to continue treatment under the circumstances, though intentional and with knowledge that the patient would die, was not an unlawful failure to perform a legal duty. In view of our decision on that issue, it becomes unnecessary to deal with the further issue of whether petitioners' conduct was in fact the proximate cause of Mr. Herbert's ultimate death.

* * * The superior court erred in determining that as a matter of law the evidence required the magistrate to hold petitioners to answer [to the charges of murder]. * * *

Notes and Questions

1. Arthur Leavens, *A Causation Approach to Criminal Omissions,* 76 Cal.L.Rev. 547, 586–87 (1988):

> Since the patient in *Barber,* even in his comatose state, was by California law alive and in no imminent danger of death when the doctors cut off his nutrition and hydration, it is difficult to avoid concluding that the doctors caused his death. Given that euthanasia is not legally justified in California, such intentional conduct seems unavoidably to constitute criminal homicide.

Kuorkian example

2. Suppose the doctors in *Barber* had injected Herbert with a lethal drug in order that he would die painlessly. Would this be an omission, according to the court's analysis? If not, would the doctors be guilty of murder?   voluntary act

What if a doctor fails to provide needed insulin to her diabetic patient, who dies as a result? Is this an omission or an act? If it is an omission, does the doctor escape potential criminal liability for her patient's death? duty to act

Assuming that the doctors in these hypotheticals could be convicted of criminal homicide, is there any principled reason why the doctors in *Barber* should escape liability? In what way, if at all, was their behavior morally different?

3. A child is chased down the street by a pit bull. She runs toward an open door of a stranger's house. The homeowner, aware of her plight, slams the door in the child's face. See Leo Katz, Bad Acts and Guilty Minds 140 (1987). Did the homeowner act by closing the door, or did he omit an act by failing to protect the child? As a matter of moral intuitions, does the answer to the question matter? In determining legal responsibility, should it matter whether the homeowner, aware of the child's situation, closed an open door or simply failed to open a closed one?

In this context, consider as well the following scenario: A machine contains two children, John and Mary. A button is attached to the machine. If Aaron, who is unrelated to either child, pushes the button, John will be killed, but Mary will emerge from the machine unscathed. If he does not push the button within one minute, John will emerge unhurt, but Mary will be killed. See Michael Tooley, *An Irrelevant Consideration: Killing versus*

Letting Die, in Killing and Letting Die 60 (Bonnie Steinbock ed. 1980). Are Aaron's choices morally equivalent? Would he have "more explaining to do" to the children's parents if he pushed the button than if he did nothing?

4. Do you think the *Barber* court's treatment of the act-omission issue was colored by the fact that euthanasia is not a criminal defense? If euthanasia were a defense, might they have concluded that the defendants committed a voluntary act?

There is also a lurking constitutional issue in *Barber:* Does a patient have a constitutional right to compel medical personnel to withhold life-sustaining treatment or, even, to assist the patient to commit suicide? These issues are considered at p. 842 infra.

C. SOCIAL HARM

INTRODUCTORY COMMENT

The law does not punish people for their thoughts or even for their voluntary acts (or omissions). It punishes people for the harm that results from their voluntary acts or omissions. "[H]arm is the very essence" of crime. Albin Eser, *The Principle of "Harm" in the Concept of Crime: A Comparative Analysis of the Criminally Protected Legal Interests,* 4 Duq.L.Rev. 345, 345 (1965). It is the "focal point between criminal conduct on the one side, and the punitive sanction, on the other." Jerome Hall, General Principles of Criminal Law 213 (2d ed. 1960).

Because crimes are wrongs against the society and do not simply involve injuries to private individuals, the harm that constitutes the "reus" in *"actus reus"* may be described as "social harm," or the "negation, endangering, or destruction of an individual, group, or state interest, which [is] deemed socially valuable." Eser, supra, at 413. Notice that by this definition it is possible to say that "social harm" occurs not only when, for example, *A* kills *B,* but also when *C* attempts to kill *D* with an unloaded gun, or when *E* drives on a public road in an intoxicated condition.

COMMONWEALTH v. TROWBRIDGE

Superior Court of Pennsylvania, 1978.
261 Pa.Super. 109, 395 A.2d 1337.

PER CURIAM:

Appellant contends that there was insufficient evidence to convict her of recklessly endangering another person [1] because she had no actual present ability to place others in danger of death or serious bodily injury. Because we agree, we reverse the judgment of sentence and discharge the appellant.

Appellant Mary Trowbridge lived * * * with her three children and six dogs. Her ex-husband John Trowbridge was also in the house during the events in question. * * *

---

1. 18 Pa.C.S.A. § 2705.

Around 2:30 in the morning of June 26, 1976, Officer John Schwemmer * * * was cruising on routine patrol on Main Street. As he approached the turn onto Zieglerville Road, a dog ran out in front of his car, forcing him to stop. Several other dogs then surrounded his vehicle. Concerned for his safety, Schwemmer radioed for assistance. Officer Harold J. Smith responded to the call and arrived in a few minutes. Using his nightstick, he dispersed the dogs, which ran back in the direction of appellant's house.

When appellant heard one of her dogs start to bark, she went outside to investigate the presence of the two police cars parked on Main Street near her driveway. An angry confrontation developed between appellant and Smith. The officers warned her that she could be cited for disorderly conduct and letting her dogs run loose. Appellant resisted an attempt by Officer Smith to arrest her and returned to the house. John Trowbridge observed his ex-wife grab their oldest son's unloaded "Daisy" BB gun from the kitchen.[2] He followed her back outside and waited on the porch while appellant walked onto her driveway, stopped behind her car, raised the gun to her shoulder, and pointed it at the officers in the street. The officers took cover behind their cars and drew their guns. After a tense half minute or so, appellant returned to her house. The officers left the scene, returning the next day to arrest her.

The Commonwealth charged appellant with recklessly endangering another person, making terroristic threats, and possession of instruments of crime. The jury acquitted appellant of the latter two charges but found her guilty of recklessly endangering another person. The lower court denied appellant's motion for arrest of judgment raising the issue of insufficient evidence. This appeal followed.

Recklessly endangering another person is a crime of assault under * * * the Crimes Code. The common law of criminal assault required that the defendant have the actual present ability to inflict a battery or otherwise cause injury. * * *

The present recklessly endangering statute, under which appellant was convicted, reads as follows: "A person commits a misdemeanor of the second degree if he recklessly engages in conduct which places or may place another person in danger of death or serious bodily injury." Thus, the crime requires (1) a mens rea—recklessness, (2) an actus reus—some "conduct," (3) causation—"which places," and (4) the achievement of a particular result—"danger," to another person, of death or serious bodily injury. By requiring the creation of danger, we think it is plain under § 2705 that the mere apparent ability to inflict

2. On the issue of whether the gun was loaded, both appellant and John Trowbridge testified that their son was not allowed to leave the gun in the house while it was loaded and had never before done so. Mr. Trowbridge further testified that when appellant picked up the BB gun, it made no noise. If the gun had been loaded, he testi-fied, he would have heard the sound of BB pellets rattling around inside the gun. * * *

* * * [T]he Commonwealth failed to present any evidence that the gun was loaded * * *. Under these circumstances, we must conclude that the weapon used by appellant was an unloaded BB gun * * *.

harm is not sufficient. Danger, and not merely the apprehension of danger, must be created. Therefore, we think that § 2705 retains the common law assault requirement of actual present ability to inflict harm. * * *

We now turn to an application of these principles to the facts of the case at bar. When appellant pointed her BB gun at officers Smith and Schwemmer, it was unloaded. As we have indicated, this in itself does not create a danger of death or serious bodily harm, and thus no violation of § 2705. * * * Because appellant did not place the police officers in danger of death or serious bodily harm, the Commonwealth failed to prove an essential element of the recklessly endangering statute. Therefore, we reverse the judgment of sentence and discharge the appellant.

Notes and Questions

1. Did the court apply the term *"actus reus"* correctly? Reconsider the definition of the term set out at p. 81 supra. As you read the reckless endangerment statute, which words constitute the *"mens rea"* and which words constitute the *"actus reus"* of this offense? Which words in particular identify the "social harm" of the crime?

2. The reckless endangerment statute includes the words "may place." Do these words have independent significance? Are they relevant to the determination of this case?

3. In People v. Decina, 2 N.Y.2d 133, 157 N.Y.S.2d 558, 138 N.E.2d 799 (1956) (Note 5, p. 87 supra), *D* was charged with the offense of "operating a vehicle in a reckless or culpably negligent manner, causing the death of another person." Notice that the *actus reus* of this offense includes a conduct (or "nature of conduct") element ("operating a vehicle") and a result (or "result of conduct") element ("causing the death of another person"). Sometimes a statute includes only conduct elements (e.g., "It is an offense to drive an automobile in an intoxicated condition"). Such crimes may be termed, for short, "conduct offenses."

Most offenses contain "attendant circumstance" elements. An attendant circumstance is a condition that must be present along with the prohibited conduct or result thereof in order to constitute the *actus reus* of the offense. For example, in the drunk-driving statute in the preceding paragraph, the words "in an intoxicated condition" represent an attendant circumstance: the social harm prohibited by this offense does not occur unless the actor drives her car (the conduct) while intoxicated (the circumstance that must be present at the time of the conduct). "In an intoxicated condition" is not a conduct element because the offense, as defined, does not prohibit a person from becoming intoxicated, only that, in such a condition, she not drive her automobile.

It is sometimes necessary for a lawyer to be able to distinguish between these various components of the *actus reus*, so familiarity with them is helpful. Consider, for example, Model Penal Code § 210.1, which provides that a person is guilty of criminal homicide if "he purposely, knowingly,

recklessly, or negligently causes the death of another human being." What
is the *actus reus* of this offense? What is the *mens rea?* Break down the
actus reus into its conduct, result and/or attendant circumstance elements.

Do the same with the common law offense of burglary: "Breaking and
entering a dwelling house of another at nighttime with the intent to commit
a felony therein."

Chapter 5

MENS REA

A. NATURE OF "MENS REA"

REGINA v. CUNNINGHAM

Court of Criminal Appeal, 1957.
41 Crim.App. 155, 2 Q.B. 396, 2 All.Eng.Rep. 412.

BYRNE J. read the following judgment. The appellant was convicted * * * upon an indictment framed under section 23 of the Offences against the Person Act, 1861, which charged that he unlawfully and maliciously caused to be taken by Sarah Wade a certain noxious thing, namely, coal gas, so as thereby to endanger the life of the said Sarah Wade. * * *

[Cunningham entered the cellar of a building, wrenched the gas meter from the gas pipes, and stole the meter and its contents. As a consequence, gas escaped from the pipes, some of which seeped through the wall of the cellar and partially asphyxiated the victim, Sarah Wade. Cunningham pleaded guilty to larceny of the meter and its contents. He was also charged with violation of Section 23 of the Offences against the Person Act, which provided that:

> Whosoever shall unlawfully and maliciously administer to or cause to be administered to or taken by any other person any poison or other destructive or noxious thing, so as thereby to endanger the life of such person, or so as thereby to inflict upon such person any grievous bodily harm, shall be guilty of [a] felony * * *.

At the conclusion of the trial, the judge instructed the jury that it could convict Cunningham, even if it were satisfied that he did not intend to poison the victim, as long as he acted "unlawfully and maliciously." In defining these terms, the judge stated:

> "Unlawful" does not need any definition. It is something forbidden by law. What about "malicious"? "Malicious" for this purpose means wicked—something which he has no business to do and perfectly well knows it. "Wicked" is as good a definition as any other which you would get.]

At the close of the case for the prosecution, Mr. Brodie, who appeared for the appellant at the trial and who has appeared for him again in this court, submitted that there was no case to go to the jury, but the learned judge, quite rightly in our opinion, rejected this submission. * * *

The act of the appellant was clearly unlawful and, therefore, the real question for the jury was whether it was also malicious within the meaning of section 23 of the Offences against the Person Act, 1861. * * *

Mr. Brodie argued * * * that the learned judge misdirected the jury as to the meaning of the word "maliciously". * * *

* * * [T]he following principle * * * was propounded by the late Professor C.S. Kenny in the first edition of his Outlines of Criminal Law published in 1902 * * *: "In any statutory definition of a crime, malice must be taken not in the old vague sense of wickedness in general, but as requiring either (1) An actual intention to do the particular kind of harm that in fact was done; or (2) recklessness as to whether such harm should occur or not (i.e. the accused has foreseen that the particular kind of harm might be done, and yet has gone on to take the risk of it). * * *." * * *

We think that this is an accurate statement of the law. * * *

With the utmost respect to the learned [trial] judge, we think it is incorrect to say that the word "malicious" in a statutory offence merely means wicked. We think the judge was, in effect, telling the jury that if they were satisfied that the appellant acted wickedly—and he had clearly acted wickedly in stealing the gas meter and its contents—they ought to find that he had acted maliciously in causing the gas to be taken by Mrs. Wade so as thereby to endanger her life.

In our view, it should have been left to the jury to decide whether, even if the appellant did not intend the injury to Mrs. Wade, he foresaw that the removal of the gas meter might cause injury to someone but nevertheless removed it. We are unable to say that a reasonable jury, properly directed as to the meaning of the word "maliciously" in the context of section 23, would, without doubt, have convicted. * * *

Appeal allowed.

Notes and Questions

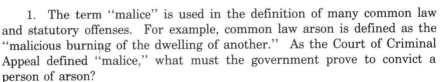

1. The term "malice" is used in the definition of many common law and statutory offenses. For example, common law arson is defined as the "malicious burning of the dwelling of another." As the Court of Criminal Appeal defined "malice," what must the government prove to convict a person of arson?

2. Oliver Wendell Holmes observed that, "I have always thought that most of the difficulties as to the *mens rea* was due to having no precise understanding what the *mens rea* is." 1 Holmes–Laski Letters 4 (M. Wolfe, ed. 1953) (letter of July 14, 1916). Part of the difficulty in understanding

"what the *mens rea* is" stems from the fact that the term has both a broad and a narrow meaning. Although the modern trend is to use the term in its narrow context, both meanings retain significance.

Broadly speaking, *"mens rea"* means "guilty mind," "vicious will," "immorality of motive," or, simply, "morally culpable state of mind." See Joshua Dressler, Understanding Criminal Law § 10.02[B] (1987). In this sense, a defendant is guilty of a crime if she commits the *actus reus* of the offense with a morally blameworthy state of mind; it is not significant whether she caused the social harm intentionally or with some other blameworthy mental state. This is the "culpability" meaning of *"mens rea."*

More narrowly, *"mens rea"* refers to the mental state specifically required in the definition of the offense. Under this "elemental" approach, a defendant is not guilty of an offense, even if she has a culpable frame of mind, if she lacks the mental state specified in the definition of the crime.

For example, an offense may definitionally be structured as follows: "A person is guilty of [name of offense] if she *intentionally* does X [e.g., robs a bank, takes a human life, injures another]." Under this definition, a defendant is not guilty of the offense if she does X recklessly, even though recklessness is a morally blameworthy state of mind (and, thus, the defendant has a *"mens rea"* in the broad sense of the term), because she does not have the specific state of mind required for this offense ("to do X intentionally").

In *Cunningham,* did the trial court use the culpability or elemental approach to the *mens rea* issue? What about the Court of Criminal Appeal?

3. "The existence of a *mens rea* is the rule of, rather than the exception to, the principles of Anglo–American criminal jurisprudence." Dennis v. United States, 341 U.S. 494, 500, 71 S.Ct. 857, 862, 95 L.Ed. 1137, 1147 (1951). Why? Is the requirement of culpability justifiable from a utilitarian perspective? Is *mens rea* a retributive-based concept?

Arguments for permitting criminal convictions in the absence of *mens rea*—"strict liability"—are considered in detail in Section C. of this chapter. For discussion of the nature and rationale of *mens rea,* see Gerhard O.W. Mueller, *On Common Law Mens Rea,* 42 Minn.L.Rev. 1043 (1958); Herbert L. Packer, *Mens Rea and the Supreme Court,* 1962 Sup.Ct.Rev. 107; Francis Bowes Sayre, *Mens Rea,* 45 Harv.L.Rev. 974 (1932); Richard A. Wasserstrom, *H.L.A. Hart and the Doctrines of Mens Rea and Criminal Responsibility,* 35 U.Chi.L.Rev. 92 (1967).

B. GENERAL ISSUES IN PROVING CULPABILITY

1. "INTENT"

PEOPLE v. CONLEY

Illinois Appellate Court, 1989.
187 Ill.App.3d 234, 134 Ill.Dec. 855, 543 N.E.2d 138.

Justice Cerda delivered the opinion of the court:

The defendant, William J. Conley, was charged with two counts of aggravated battery based on permanent disability and great bodily harm. (Ill.Rev.Stat.1983, ch. 38, par. 12–4(a).) He was found guilty * * * of aggravated battery based solely on permanent disability * * *. On appeal, it is contended that * * * the State failed to prove beyond a reasonable doubt that the victim incurred a permanent disability and that the defendant intended to inflict a permanent disability * * *. * * * For the following reasons, we affirm.

The defendant was charged with aggravated battery in connection with a fight which occurred at a party * * *. Approximately two hundred high school students attended the party and paid admission to drink unlimited beer. One of those students, Sean O'Connell, attended the party with several friends. At some point during the party, Sean's group was approached by a group of twenty boys who apparently thought that someone in Sean's group had said something derogatory. Sean's group denied making a statement and said they did not want any trouble. Shortly thereafter, Sean and his friends decided to leave and began walking toward their car which was parked a half block south of the party.

A group of people were walking toward the party from across the street when someone from that group shouted "There's those guys from the party." Someone emerged from that group and approached Sean who had been walking with his friend Marty Carroll * * *. That individual demanded that Marty give him a can of beer from his six-pack. Marty refused, and the individual struck Sean in the face with a wine bottle causing Sean to fall to the ground. The offender attempted to hit Marty, but missed as Marty was able to duck. Sean had sustained broken upper and lower jaws and four broken bones in the area between the bridge of his nose and the lower left cheek. Sean lost one tooth and had root canal surgery to reposition ten teeth that had been damaged. Expert testimony revealed that Sean has a permanent condition called mucosal mouth and permanent partial numbness in one lip. The expert also testified that the life expectancy of the damaged teeth might be diminished by a third or a half.

At trial, * * * Marty Carroll identified Conley as the offender. * * *

The defendant initially contends on appeal that the State failed to prove beyond a reasonable doubt that Sean O'Connell incurred a permanent disability. Section 12–4(a) of the Criminal Code of 1961 provides that: "[a] person who, in committing a battery, intentionally or knowingly causes great bodily harm, or permanent disability or disfigurement commits aggravated battery." The defendant contends there must be some disabling effect for an aggravated battery conviction based on permanent disability. The defendant does not dispute that Sean lost a tooth or that surgery was required to repair damaged teeth. The defendant also does not dispute that Sean will have permanent partial numbness in one lip or suffer from a condition called mucosal mouth.

The defendant maintains, however, that there is no evidence as to how these injuries are disabling because there was no testimony of any tasks that can no longer be performed as a result of these injuries.   * * *

The function of the courts in construing statutes is to ascertain and give effect to the intent of the legislature. The starting point for this task is the language itself, and the language should be given its plain and ordinary meaning. The defendant urges the court to adopt the definition found in Webster's Third New International Dictionary which defines disability as an "inability to do something." The State refers to additional language from the same source that a disability is a "physical or mental illness, injury or condition that incapacitates in any way." * * *

In arriving at a definition, however, it is also proper to consider the statute's purpose and the evils sought to be remedied. The Committee Comment explains that section 12–4(a) incorporates the old offense of mayhem. At common law the offense of mayhem required the dismemberment or disablement of some bodily part. Initially, the law sought to protect the King's right to the military services of his subjects. However, modern criminal codes have expanded their protection against a wider range of injuries. As one court explained:

> "What, then, originated as the narrow common law offense of mayhem is generally today a statutory offense of considerably larger dimensions. The transition has been accompanied, if not induced, by a shift in emphasis from the military and combative effects of the injury to the preservation of the human body in normal functioning. The statutory counterparts of nonstatutory mayhem doubtless include all that the common law proscribed. But what is important now is not the victim's capacity for attack or defense, but the *integrity of his person*." (*United States v. Cook* (1972), 462 F.2d 301, 303.) (Emphasis added.)

Under this view, it seems apparent that for an injury to be deemed disabling, all that must be shown is that the victim is no longer whole such that the injured bodily portion or part no longer serves the body in the same manner as it did before the injury. Applying this standard to the case at hand, the injuries Sean O'Connell suffered are sufficient to constitute a permanent disability. Sean will endure permanent partial numbness in one lip and mucosal mouth.[1] He lost one tooth and there is also a chance he may loose some teeth before attaining the age of seventy.

The defendant further argues that the State failed to prove beyond a reasonable doubt that he intended to inflict any permanent disability. The thrust of defendant's argument is that under section 12–4(a), a person must intend to bring about the particular harm defined in the statute. The defendant asserts that while it may be inferred from his

---

1. The State's expert witness never defined mucosal mouth and its meaning cannot be gleaned from the record. The defendant, however, never challenged the expert's testimony.

conduct that he intended to cause harm, it does not follow that he intended to cause permanent disability. The State contends it is not necessary that the defendant intended to bring about the particular injuries that resulted. The State maintains it met its burden by showing that the defendant intentionally struck Sean. * * *

For proper resolution of this issue, it is best to return to the statutory language. Section 12–4(a) employs the terms "intentionally or knowingly" to describe the required mental state. The relevant statutes state:

> "4–4. Intent. A person intends, or acts intentionally or with intent, to accomplish a result or engage in conduct described by the statute defining the offense, when his conscious objective or purpose is to accomplish that result or engage in that conduct."

> "4–5. Knowledge. A person knows or acts knowingly or with knowledge of: (b) The result of his conduct, described by the statute defining the offense, when he is consciously aware that such result is practically certain to be caused by his conduct."

Section 12–4(a) defines aggravated battery as the commission of a battery where the offender intentionally or knowingly causes great bodily harm, or permanent disability or disfigurement. Because the offense is defined in terms of result, the State has the burden of proving beyond a reasonable doubt that the defendant either had a "conscious objective" to achieve the harm defined, or that the defendant was "consciously aware" that the harm defined was "practically certain to be caused by his conduct." * * *

Although the State must establish the specific intent to bring about great bodily harm, or permanent disability or disfigurement under section 12–4(a), problems of proof are alleviated [by] the ordinary presumption that one intends the natural and probable consequences of his actions * * *. * * * Intent can be inferred from the surrounding circumstances, the offender's words, the weapon used, and the force of the blow. As the defendant's theory of the case was mistaken identity, there was no evidence introduced negating the presumption of intent. However, even if Conley had denied any intention to inflict permanent disability, the surrounding circumstances, the use of a bottle, the absence of warning and the force of the blow are facts from which the jury could reasonably infer the intent to cause permanent disability. Therefore, we find the evidence sufficient to support a finding of intent to cause permanent disability beyond a reasonable doubt. * * *

Notes and Questions

1. *Battery.* A criminal battery at common law is an unlawful application of force to the person of another. Even the slightest unlawful touching, if offensive, satisfies the *actus reus* component of the offense. Commonwealth v. McCan, 277 Mass. 199, 178 N.E. 633 (1931). The requisite mental state is less clear. Some courts and statutes, applying tort doctrine, require that the unlawful touching be intentional, but there is support for the

proposition that criminal negligence is sufficient. Rollin M. Perkins & Ronald N. Boyce, Criminal Law 156–57 (3d ed. 1982); see generally Lamb v. State, 93 Md.App. 422, 613 A.2d 402 (1992).

A common law battery was a misdemeanor. However, when the battery is aggravated, as in *Conley,* it is usually classified as a statutory felony.

2. In determining whether Conley acted intentionally, the court mentioned the "ordinary presumption" that a person "intends the natural and probable consequences of his actions." This "presumption" is really an inference. That is, the natural-and-probable-consequences doctrine simply states the obvious, i.e., that it is reasonable for a juror, like anyone else, to infer that a person ordinarily intends the foreseeable consequences of his actions. For example, if a person points a loaded gun at another's head and voluntarily pulls the trigger, a juror may reasonably infer that the actor intended to kill or seriously hurt the victim, because our common experience tells us that this is the "natural and probable" outcome of such behavior.

In Sandstrom v. Montana, 442 U.S. 510, 99 S.Ct. 2450, 61 L.Ed.2d 39 (1979), the Supreme Court ruled that it is unconstitutional for a judge to instruct the jury that "the law presumes that a person intends the ordinary consequences of his voluntary acts." As discussed at p. 395 infra, the prosecutor is required to prove every element of an offense beyond a reasonable doubt. The due process clause is violated, therefore, if the element of intent is presumed and the defendant is required to disprove that he intended the ordinary consequences of his voluntary acts. The Constitution is not violated, however, if the jury simply applies its common sense in such circumstances; and a judge is allowed to inform the jurors that they may, but need not, draw such an inference.

3. *Common law "intent."* In the context of "result" crimes, i.e., offenses such as battery and murder that are defined in terms of harmful results, the term "intent" ordinarily is defined to include not only those results that are the conscious object of the actor, but also those results that the actor knows are virtually certain to occur from his conduct ("knowledge" under the Illinois law).

For example, if Roger, wishing to kill Zachary, blows up a building occupied, as Roger knows, by Zachary and his wife, Roger may be said to "intend" the deaths of both Zachary (because it is his conscious object to kill him) and Zachary's wife (because Roger knows that she will almost certainly die in the same explosion).

4. In *Conley,* the defendant sought to strike one person (Marty), but hit another (Sean) instead. Even if we grant that Conley intended to hurt Marty, he did not intend to hurt Sean. The following case addresses this "intent" problem.

PEOPLE v. CZAHARA

Court of Appeal, First District, 1988.
203 Cal.App.3d 1468, 250 Cal.Rptr. 836.

Low, Presiding Justice. * * *

Michael Andrew Czahara appeals his convictions for the attempted murders of Carole Christie and Ronald Johnson. We * * * reverse the conviction for attempted murder of Johnson, but affirm the conviction for attempted murder of Christie. * * *

[Czahara was angry at Carole Christie, whom he previously had been dating, because she was seeing Ronald Johnson. On the day in question, the defendant encountered Christie sitting next to Johnson in the front passenger's seat of Johnson's car. Czahara walked to the driver's side of the car, pointed a handgun directly at Christie and, from a distance of five or six feet, pulled the trigger of the weapon at least twice. One bullet struck Christie and another hit Johnson, causing great bodily injury to both.]

Over defense objection the court gave jury instruction number 2, which read: "When one attempts to kill a certain person, but by mistake or inadvertence injures a different person, the crime, if any, so committed is the same as though the person originally intended to be killed had been injured." The instruction * * * states the principle of transferred intent for homicide. Czahara contends that the transferred intent rule was inapplicable here because the intended victim, Carole Christie, was injured in the attempt.

The California Supreme Court has on several occasions approved the rule of transferred intent in homicide cases. The high court has not, however, considered application of the doctrine to homicides in which the intended victim was also killed or to attempted homicides in which the intended victim was injured in the attempt. * * *

The transferred intent rule for homicide was adopted in this state in *People v. Suesser,* [1904] 142 Cal. 354, 75 P. 1093. The court quoted from an encyclopedia which, examining the conflicting authorities regarding a victim who is killed "instead" of the one intended, stated, "The better doctrine is that a homicide so committed is as much murder * * * as it would have been had the fatal blow reached the person for whom intended...." The court then approved an instruction quoted from a Washington state case: "[W]here a person * * * attempts to kill one person, but by mistake or inadventure kills another instead, the law transfers the felonious intent from the object of his assault, and the homicide so committed is murder * * *." As the use of "instead" and the references to "homicide" in the singular indicate, the *Suesser* court, like the authorities it drew on, had in mind the assailant who misses the intended victim, and therefore can not be prosecuted for the killing he intended. The transferred intent rule serves to ensure that he is punished to the full extent of his culpability.

Transferred intent is a legal fiction, used to reach what is regarded with virtual unanimity as a just result: when an assailant, through "bad aim" or other mistake, kills the wrong person, he is just as culpable, and should be punished to the same extent, as if he had hit the intended mark. * * *

The purpose of the transferred intent rule—to ensure that prosecution and punishment accord with culpability—would not be served by convicting a defendant of two or more attempted murders for a single act by which he intended to kill only one person. * * * [T]here is a difference in culpability between an assailant who deliberately sets out to kill one person and in addition kills another accidentally, and one who deliberately kills two victims. Application of the transferred intent rule to the former would wipe out that distinction. Similarly, the attacker who shoots at two or more victims, with the intent of killing all, is more culpable than the one who aims at a single individual, even when the latter also injures a bystander. In the circumstances of this case, the transferred intent instruction obscured that difference. * * *

We conclude that it was error to instruct the jury on transferred intent in this case. If Czahara aimed only at Christie, intending to kill only her, then he was attempting to kill only her. He was prosecuted and convicted of that attempt. There was no need to employ the legal fiction of transferred intent in order to fully punish him for the attempt. Again assuming that he had no intent to shoot Johnson, that shooting should be punished according to the culpability which the law assigns it, but no more. * * *

Notes and Questions

1. Some scholars contend that "transferred intent" is a false or, at least, misleading, doctrine. E.g., Rollin M. Perkins & Ronald N. Boyce, Criminal Law 925 (3d ed. 1982). Professors Perkins and Boyce point out that no intent "transfers" in the typical case in which the doctrine is applied.

For example, the *actus reus* of common law murder is "the killing of a human being by another human being." Assume that the *mens rea* of the offense is "intent to kill." In this context, the latter phrase means that the defendant must "intend to kill *a human being*." The identity of the intended victim, however, is immaterial. Therefore, if the prosecutor shows that D intended to kill X, a human being, but accidentally killed Y, another human being, the crime of murder has been proven: the *actus reus* of the offense (the killing of a human being, Y) has occurred; and D possessed the required *mens rea* (D intended to kill a human being, X). There is no need to transfer the intent to kill from X to Y.

Confusion can arise if the prosecutor seeks to transfer the intent to commit one type of social harm to a different harm, rather than merely to transfer the intent from one victim to another. For example, in Regina v. Pembliton, 12 Cox Crim.Cas. 607 (1874), P threw a rock at X, intending to strike him with it. Instead, the rock hit a window in a building behind X. P was charged with "malicious injury to property." Does P have the requisite *mens rea*? May the prosecutor prove malice by transferring P's intent to hit X to the window behind him?

2. *"Specific intent" and "general intent" offenses.* Courts frequently use the terms "specific intent" and "general intent" to distinguish between two types of crimes. The concepts are "notoriously difficult * * * to define and apply, and a number of text writers [have] recommended that they be abandoned altogether." People v. Hood, 1 Cal.3d 444, 456, 82 Cal.Rptr. 618, 625, 462 P.2d 370, 377 (1969). In fact, in jurisdictions that apply the Model

Penal Code, no rules of law depend on whether an offense is labelled as "general intent" or "specific intent." However, many states persist in using the terms and drawing distinctions between them, so familiarity with the doctrines is necessary.

The terms "specific intent" and "general intent" do not have universally accepted definitions. In some circumstances, a crime is denominated as "specific intent" if any mental state is set out expressly in the definition of the offense; an offense is one of "general intent" if no particular mental state is required, i.e., if the prosecutor need only prove that the *actus reus* of the offense was performed in a morally blameworthy manner. (See Note 2, p. 104 supra.)

Sometimes the term "specific intent" is used to denote an offense that includes the *mens rea* element of "intent" or, perhaps, "knowledge"; "general intent" is reserved for crimes that permit conviction on the basis of a less culpable mental state, such as "recklessness" or "negligence."

Probably the most common usage of the term "general intent," however, is to designate any mental state, whether expressed or implied, that relates solely to the acts that constitute the criminal offense. For example, if battery is defined by state law as "an intentional application of force upon another," this offense would be considered "general intent" because the mental state required in the definition ("intentional") relates exclusively to the commission of the *actus reus* of the offense (the "application of force upon another").

In contrast, "specific intent" designates "a special mental element which is required above and beyond any mental state required with respect to the actus reus of the crime." State v. Bridgeforth, 156 Ariz. 60, 62, 750 P.2d 3, 5 (1988) (quoting W. LaFave & A. Scott, Handbook on Criminal Law § 28 at 201–02 (1972)).

Three types of special mental elements are typically found in specific intent offenses. First, to be guilty of some offenses, the state must prove an intention by the actor to commit some future act, separate from the *actus reus* of the offense ("assault *with the intent to rape* "). Second, an offense may require proof of a special motive or purpose for committing the *actus reus* ("offensive contact upon another *with the intent to cause humiliation* "). Third, some offenses require proof of the actor's awareness of an attendant circumstance ("the intentional sale of obscene literature to a person *known to be under the age of 18 years* "). If any of these special mental elements are part of the definition of an offense, the crime is described as "specific intent," even if the offense also contains a "general intent."

In view of the latter explanation, are the following offenses "general intent" or "specific intent"?

A. "Trespassory taking and carrying away of the personal property of another with the intent to steal."

B. "Sexual intercourse by a male with a female not his wife, without her consent."

C. "Intentional receipt of stolen property, with knowledge that it is stolen."

D.   "Breaking and entering the dwelling house of another at night with the intent to commit a felony therein."

2.   THE MODEL PENAL CODE APPROACH

Introductory Comment

Section 2.02 of the Model Penal Code ("General Requirements of Culpability") probably has been the most influential section of the Model Code. By statute or judicial action, many states have adopted this section's systematic approach to the issue of *mens rea.*

Section 2.02 is significant in various respects. First, the Code consistently applies an "elemental" approach (Note 2, p. 104 supra) to the issue of *mens rea.* That is, the prosecutor must prove that the defendant committed each material element of the offense with the particular state of mind required in the definition of the crime. Guilt cannot be based simply on proof that the defendant committed the *actus reus* of the offense in a morally blameworthy manner.

Second, the Code abandons the countless common law and pre-Code statutory *mens rea* terms and replaces them with just four terms of culpability, "purposely," "knowingly," "recklessly," and "negligently." Third, principles of statutory construction set out in Section 2.02 assist in resolving many of the *mens rea* issues that have plagued courts over the years.

You should read Section 2.02 (in the appendix) with great care in conjunction with the following excerpt from the Commentary to it. For a thorough survey of the Code's approach to matters concerning culpability, see Paul H. Robinson & Jane A. Grall, *Element Analysis in Defining Criminal Liability: The Model Penal Code and Beyond,* 35 Stan.L.Rev. 681 (1983); see, also, Ronald L. Gainer, *The Culpability Provisions of the Model Penal Code,* 19 Rutgers L.J. 575 (1988).

AMERICAN LAW INSTITUTE, MODEL PENAL CODE AND COMMENTARIES, COMMENT TO § 2.02

(1985), 229–30, 233–34, 236–38, 240–41, 244

1. *Objective.* This section expresses the Code's basic requirement that unless some element of mental culpability is proved with respect to each material element of the offense, no valid criminal conviction may be obtained. This requirement is subordinated only to the provision of Section 2.05 for a narrow class of strict liability offenses that are limited to those for which no severer sentence than a fine may be imposed.

The section further attempts the extremely difficult task of articulating the kinds of culpability that may be required for the establishment of liability. It delineates four levels of culpability: purpose, knowledge, recklessness and negligence. It requires that one of these levels of culpability must be proved with respect to each "material element" of the offense, which may involve (1) the nature of the forbidden conduct, (2) the attendant circumstances, or (3) the result of conduct.[1] The question of which level of culpability suffices to establish liability must be addressed separately with respect to each material element, and will be resolved either by the particular definition of the offense or the general provisions of this section.

The purpose of articulating these distinctions in detail is to advance the clarity of draftsmanship in the delineation of the definitions of specific crimes, to provide a distinct framework against which those definitions may be tested, and to dispel the obscurity with which the culpability requirement is often treated when such concepts as "general criminal intent," "mens rea," "presumed intent," "malice," "wilfulness," "scienter" and the like have been employed. What Justice Jackson called "the variety, disparity and confusion" of judicial definitions of "the requisite but elusive mental element"[2] in crime should, insofar as possible, be rationalized by a criminal code. * * *

2. *Purpose and Knowledge.* In defining the kinds of culpability, the Code draws a narrow distinction between acting purposely and knowingly, one of the elements of ambiguity in legal usage of the term "intent." Knowledge that the requisite external circumstances exist is a common element in both conceptions. But action is not purposive with respect to the nature or result of the actor's conduct unless it was his conscious object to perform an action of that nature or to cause such a result. It is meaningful to think of the actor's attitude as different if he is simply aware that his conduct is of the required nature or that the prohibited result is practically certain to follow from his conduct.

* * * Although in most instances either knowledge or purpose should suffice for criminal liability, articulating the distinction puts to the test the issue whether an actual purpose is required and enhances clarity in drafting. * * *

3. *Recklessness.* An important discrimination is drawn between acting either purposely or knowingly and acting recklessly. As the Code uses the term, recklessness involves conscious risk creation. It resembles acting knowingly in that a state of awareness is involved, but the awareness is of risk, that is of a probability less than substantial certainty; the matter is contingent from the actor's point of view. Whether the risk relates to the nature of the actor's conduct, or to the existence of the requisite attendant circumstances, or to the result that may ensue, is immaterial; the concept is the same, and is thus defined to apply to any material element.

---

1. * * * Section 1.13(10) defines the concept of "material element" to include all elements except those that relate exclusively to statutes of limitation, jurisdiction, venue, and the like. The "material elements" of offenses are thus those characteristics (conduct, circumstances, result) of the actor's behavior that, when combined with the appropriate level of culpability, will constitute the offense.

2. Morissette v. United States, 342 U.S. 246, 252 (1952).

The risk of which the actor is aware must of course be substantial in order for the recklessness judgment to be made. The risk must also be unjustifiable. Even substantial risks, it is clear, may be created without recklessness when the actor is seeking to serve a proper purpose, as when a surgeon performs an operation that he knows is very likely to be fatal but reasonably thinks to be necessary because the patient has no other, safer chance. Some principle must, therefore, be articulated to indicate the nature of the final judgment to be made after everything has been weighed. Describing the risk as "substantial" and "unjustifiable" is useful but not sufficient, for these are terms of degree, and the acceptability of a risk in a given case depends on a great many variables. Some standard is needed for determining *how* substantial and *how* unjustifiable the risk must be in order to warrant a finding of culpability. There is no way to state this value judgment that does not beg the question in the last analysis; the point is that the jury must evaluate the actor's conduct and determine whether it should be condemned. The Code proposes, therefore, that this difficulty be accepted frankly, and that the jury be asked to measure the substantiality and unjustifiability of the risk by asking whether its disregard, given the actor's perceptions, involved a gross deviation from the standard of conduct that a law-abiding person in the actor's situation would observe.

Ultimately, then, the jury is asked to perform two distinct functions. First, it is to examine the risk and the factors that are relevant to how substantial it was and to the justifications for taking it. In each instance, the question is asked from the point of view of the actor's perceptions, i.e., to what extent he was aware of risk, of factors relating to its substantiality and of factors relating to its unjustifiability. Second, the jury is to make the culpability judgment in terms of whether the defendant's conscious disregard of the risk justifies condemnation. Considering the nature and purpose of his conduct and the circumstances known to him, the question is whether the defendant's disregard of the risk involved a gross deviation from the standards of conduct that a law-abiding person would have observed in the actor's situation. * * *

4. *Negligence.* The fourth kind of culpability is negligence. It is distinguished from purposeful, knowing or reckless action in that it does not involve a state of awareness. A person acts negligently under this subsection when he inadvertently creates a substantial and unjustifiable risk of which he ought to be aware. He is liable if given the nature and degree of the risk, his failure to perceive it is, considering the nature and purpose of the actor's conduct and the circumstances known to him, a gross deviation from the care that would be exercised by a reasonable person in his situation. As in the case of recklessness, both the substantiality of the risk and the elements of justification in the situation form the relevant standards of judgment. And again it is quite impossible to avoid tautological articulation of the final question. The tribunal must evaluate the actor's failure of perception and determine whether, under all the circumstances, it was serious enough to be condemned. The jury

must find fault, and must find that it was substantial and unjustified; that is the heart of what can be said in legislative terms.

As with recklessness, the jury is asked to perform two distinct functions. First, it is to examine the risk and the factors that are relevant to its substantiality and justifiability. In the case of negligence, these questions are asked not in terms of what the actor's perceptions actually were, but in terms of an objective view of the situation as it actually existed. Second, the jury is to make the culpability judgment, this time in terms of whether the failure of the defendant to perceive the risk justifies condemnation. * * *

5. *Offense Silent as to Culpability.* Subsection (3) provides that unless the kind of culpability sufficient to establish a material element of an offense has been prescribed by law, it is established if a person acted purposely, knowingly or recklessly with respect thereto. This accepts as the basic norm what usually is regarded as the common law position. More importantly, it represents the most convenient norm for drafting purposes. When purpose or knowledge is required, it is conventional to be explicit. And since negligence is an exceptional basis of liability, it should be excluded as a basis unless explicitly prescribed.

Notes and Questions

1. *Problems*

A. Jacob wants to kill Vanessa, his wife, because she is having an affair. Consequently, he drives his car at a high rate of speed into Vanessa, while she is holding Xavier, their infant son. Jacob fervently hopes that Xavier will survive the collision. The car strikes Vanessa and Xavier, killing both instantly. Under the Model Penal Code, with what mental states (i.e., "purposely," "knowingly," "recklessly," or "negligently") did Jacob kill Vanessa and Xavier? At common law, what is Jacob's *mens rea* as to each victim?

B. The same as A. but assume that Jacob did not see Xavier in Vanessa's arms, although the child's presence was obvious.

C. The same as A., but assume that when Jacob struck Vanessa with his car, he did not want to kill either of them, but he did want to injure Vanessa. Therefore, he drove his car into her at a low rate of speed. As Jacob hoped, Vanessa was not killed. However, due to the impact, Vanessa dropped Xavier, who died from the fall. With what mental state did Jacob kill Xavier?

2. Model Penal Code § 222.1(1) defines robbery, in part, as follows: "A person is guilty of robbery if, in the course of committing a theft, he: (a) inflicts serious bodily injury upon another * * *." Under this provision, is Roberta guilty of robbery if, while committing a theft, she negligently inflicts serious bodily injury upon Sam?

3. "KNOWLEDGE" OF ATTENDANT CIRCUMSTANCES

UNITED STATES v. JEWELL

United States Court of Appeals, Ninth Circuit, 1976.
532 F.2d 697.

BROWNING, CIRCUIT JUDGE:

[Defendant Jewell was prosecuted for violation of two federal drug offenses. Count I, 21 U.S.C. § 952(a), proscribed the "knowing" transportation of a controlled substance into the United States. Count II, 21 U.S.C. § 841(a), barred the "knowing or intentional" possession of a controlled substance "with intent to manufacture, distribute, or dispense" it.]

It is undisputed that appellant entered the United States driving an automobile in which 110 pounds of marihuana worth $6,250 had been concealed in a secret compartment between the trunk and rear seat. Appellant testified that he did not know the marihuana was present. There was circumstantial evidence from which the jury could infer that appellant had positive knowledge of the presence of the marihuana, and that his contrary testimony was false.[1] On the other hand there was evidence from which the jury could conclude that appellant spoke the truth—that although appellant knew of the presence of the secret compartment and had knowledge of facts indicating that it contained marihuana, he deliberately avoided positive knowledge of the presence of the contraband to avoid responsibility in the event of discovery.[2] If the jury concluded the latter was indeed the situation, and if positive

---

1. Appellant testified that a week before the incident in question he sold his car for $100 to obtain funds "to have a good time." He then rented a car for about $100, and he and a friend drove the rented car to Mexico. Appellant and his friend were unable to adequately explain their whereabouts during the period of about 11 hours between the time they left Los Angeles and the time they admitted arriving in Mexico.

Their testimony regarding acquisition of the load car follows a pattern common in these cases: they were approached in a Tijuana bar by a stranger who identified himself only by his first name—"Ray." He asked them if they wanted to buy marihuana, and offered to pay them $100 for driving a car north across the border. Appellant accepted the offer and drove the load car back, alone. Appellant's friend drove appellant's rented car back to Los Angeles.

Appellant testified that the stranger instructed him to leave the load car at the address on the car registration slip with the keys in the ashtray. The person living at that address testified that he had sold the car a year earlier and had not seen it since. When the Customs agent asked appellant

about the secret compartment in the car, appellant did not deny knowledge of its existence, but stated that it was in the car when he got it.

There were many discrepancies and inconsistencies in the evidence reflecting upon appellant's credibility. Taking the record as a whole, the jury could have concluded that the evidence established an abortive scheme, concocted and carried out by appellant from the beginning, to acquire a load of marihuana in Mexico and return it to Los Angeles for distribution for profit.

2. Both appellant and his companion testified that the stranger identified as "Ray" offered to sell them marihuana and, when they declined, asked if they wanted to drive a car back to Los Angeles for $100. Appellant's companion "wanted no part of driving the vehicle." He testified, "It didn't sound right to me." Appellant accepted the offer. The Drug Enforcement Administration agent testified that appellant stated "he thought there was probably something wrong and something illegal in the vehicle, but that he checked it over. He looked in the glove box and under the front

knowledge is required to convict, the jury would have no choice consistent with its oath but to find appellant not guilty even though he deliberately contrived his lack of positive knowledge. Appellant urges this view. The trial court rejected the premise that only positive knowledge would suffice, and properly so.

Appellant tendered an instruction that to return a guilty verdict the jury must find that the defendant knew he was in possession of marihuana. The trial judge rejected the instruction because it suggested that "absolutely, positively, he has to know that it's there." * * *

The court instructed the jury that * * * the government must prove beyond a reasonable doubt that the defendant "knowingly" brought the marihuana into the United States (count 1: 21 U.S.C. § 952(a)), and that he "knowingly" possessed the marihuana (count 2: 21 U.S.C. § 841(a)(1)). The court continued:

> The Government can complete their burden of proof by proving, beyond a reasonable doubt, that if the defendant was not actually aware that there was marihuana in the vehicle he was driving when he entered the United States his ignorance in that regard was solely and entirely a result of his having made a conscious purpose to disregard the nature of that which was in the vehicle, with a conscious purpose to avoid learning the truth.

The legal premise of these instructions is firmly supported by leading commentators here and in England. Professor Rollin M. Perkins writes, "One with a deliberate anti-social purpose in mind ... may deliberately 'shut his eyes' to avoid knowing what would otherwise be obvious to view. In such cases, so far as criminal law is concerned, the person acts at his peril in this regard, and is treated as having 'knowledge' of the facts as they are ultimately discovered to be."[4] * * * Professor Glanville Williams states, on the basis [of] both English and American authorities, "To the requirement of actual knowledge there is one strictly limited exception.... [T]he rule is that if a party has his suspicion aroused but then deliberately omits to make further enquiries, because he wishes to remain in ignorance, he is deemed to have knowledge."[6] Professor Williams concludes, "The rule that wilful blindness is

---

seat and in the trunk, prior to driving it. *He didn't find anything, and, therefore, he assumed that the people at the border wouldn't find anything either* " (emphasis added). Appellant was asked at trial whether he had seen the special compartment when he opened the trunk. He responded, "Well, you know, I saw a void there, but I didn't know what it was." He testified that he did not investigate further. The Customs agent testified that when he opened the trunk and saw the partition he asked appellant "when he had that put in." Appellant told the agent "that it was in the car when he got it."

The jury would have been justified in accepting all of the testimony as true and concluding that although appellant was aware of facts making it virtually certain that the secret compartment concealed marihuana, he deliberately refrained from acquiring positive knowledge of the fact.

4. R. Perkins, Criminal Law 776 (2d ed. 1969).

6. G. Williams, Criminal Law: The General Part, § 57 at 157 (2d ed. 1961).

equivalent to knowledge is essential, and is found throughout the criminal law." [7]

The substantive justification for the rule is that deliberate ignorance and positive knowledge are equally culpable. The textual justification is that in common understanding one "knows" facts of which he is less than absolutely certain. To act "knowingly," therefore, is not necessarily to act only with positive knowledge, but also to act with an awareness of the high probability of the existence of the fact in question. When such awareness is present, "positive" knowledge is not required.

This is the analysis adopted in the Model Penal Code. Section 2.02(7) states: "When knowledge of the existence of a particular fact is an element of an offense, such knowledge is established if a person is aware of a high probability of its existence, unless he actually believes that it does not exist." As the Comment to this provision explains, "Paragraph (7) deals with the situation British commentators have denominated 'wilful blindness' or 'connivance,' the case of the actor who is aware of the probable existence of a material fact but does not satisfy himself that it does not in fact exist." [9] * * *

* * * Courts of Appeals reviewing the sufficiency of evidence have approved the premise that "knowingly" in criminal statutes is not limited to positive knowledge, but includes the state of mind of one who does not possess positive knowledge only because he consciously avoided it. These lines of authority appear unbroken. Neither the dissent nor the briefs of either party has cited a case holding that such an instruction is error or that such evidence is not sufficient to establish "knowledge."

There is no reason to reach a different result under the statute involved in this case. * * * Nothing is cited from the legislative history of the Drug Control Act indicating that Congress used the term "knowingly" in a sense at odds with prior authority. Rather, Congress is presumed to have known and adopted the "cluster of ideas" attached to such a familiar term of art. * * *

Appellant's narrow interpretation of "knowingly" is inconsistent with the Drug Control Act's general purpose to deal more effectively "with the growing menace of drug abuse in the United States." Holding that this term introduces a requirement of positive knowledge would make deliberate ignorance a defense. It cannot be doubted that those who traffic in drugs would make the most of it. * * *

---

7. *Id.* at 159. Mr. Williams' concluding paragraph reads * * *:

The rule that wilful blindness is equivalent to knowledge is essential, and is found throughout the criminal law. * * * A court can properly find wilful blindness only where it can almost be said that the defendant actually knew. He suspected the fact; he realised its probability; but he refrained from obtaining the final confirmation because he wanted in the event to be able to deny knowledge. This, and this alone, is wilful blindness. It requires in effect a finding that the defendant intended to cheat the administration of justice. Any wider definition would make the doctrine of wilful blindness indistinguishable from the civil doctrine of negligence in not obtaining knowledge.

9. Model Penal Code 129–30 (Tent. Draft No. 4, 1955). * * *

It is worth emphasizing that the required state of mind differs from positive knowledge only so far as necessary to encompass a calculated effort to avoid the sanctions of the statute while violating its substance. "A court can properly find wilful blindness only where it can almost be said that the defendant actually knew." [20] In the language of the instruction in this case, the government must prove, "beyond a reasonable doubt, that if the defendant was not actually aware ... his ignorance in that regard was *solely* and *entirely* a result of ... a conscious purpose to avoid learning the truth." [21]

No legitimate interest of an accused is prejudiced by such a standard, and society's interest in a system of criminal law that is enforceable and that imposes sanctions upon all who are equally culpable requires it.

The conviction is affirmed.

ANTHONY M. KENNEDY, CIRCUIT JUDGE, * * * dissenting. * * *

At the outset, it is arguable that the "conscious purpose to avoid learning the truth" instruction is inherently inconsistent with the additional mens rea required for count two—intent to distribute. It is difficult to explain that a defendant can specifically intend to distribute a substance unless he knows that he possesses it. In any event, we would not approve the conscious purpose instruction in this case, because it falls short of the scienter independently required under both counts.

The majority opinion justifies the conscious purpose jury instruction as an application of the wilful blindness doctrine recognized primarily by English authorities. A classic illustration of this doctrine is the connivance of an innkeeper who deliberately arranges not to go into his back room and thus avoids visual confirmation of the gambling he believes is taking place. The doctrine is commonly said to apply in deciding whether one who acquires property under suspicious circumstances should be charged with knowledge that it was stolen.

One problem with the wilful blindness doctrine is its bias towards visual means of acquiring knowledge. We may know facts from direct impressions of the other senses or by deduction from circumstantial evidence, and such knowledge is nonetheless "actual." Moreover, visual sense impressions do not consistently provide complete certainty.

Another problem is that the English authorities seem to consider wilful blindness a state of mind distinct from, but equally culpable as, "actual" knowledge. When a statute specifically requires knowledge as

---

20. G. Williams, *supra* note 6, at 159.

21. We do not suggest that the instruction given in this case was a model in all respects. The jury should have been instructed more directly (1) that the required knowledge is established if the accused is aware of a high probability of the existence of the fact in question, (2) unless he actually believes it does not exist.

The deficiency in the instruction does not require reversal, however. Appellant did not object to the instruction on this ground either below or in this court. Since both of the elements referred to are implied in the instruction, the deficiency in the instructions is not so substantial as to justify reversal for plain error. * * *

an element of a crime, however, the substitution of some other state of mind cannot be justified even if the court deems that both are equally blameworthy.

Finally, the wilful blindness doctrine is uncertain in scope. There is disagreement as to whether reckless disregard for the existence of a fact constitutes wilful blindness or some lesser degree of culpability. Some cases have held that a statute's scienter requirement is satisfied by the constructive knowledge imputed to one who simply fails to discharge a duty to inform himself. There is also the question of whether to use an "objective" test based on the reasonable man, or to consider the defendant's subjective belief as dispositive.

The approach adopted in section 2.02(7) of the Model Penal Code clarifies, and, in important ways restricts, the English doctrine * * *.

This provision requires an awareness of a high probability that a fact exists, not merely a reckless disregard, or a suspicion followed by a failure to make further inquiry. It also establishes knowledge as a matter of subjective belief, an important safeguard against diluting the guilty state of mind required for conviction. It is important to note that section 2.02(7) is a *definition* of knowledge, not a substitute for it * * *.

In light of the Model Penal Code's definition, the "conscious purpose" jury instruction is defective in three respects. First, it fails to mention the requirement that Jewell have been aware of a high probability that a controlled substance was in the car. It is not culpable to form "a conscious purpose to avoid learning the truth" unless one is aware of facts indicating a high probability of that truth. To illustrate, a child given a gift-wrapped package by his mother while on vacation in Mexico may form a conscious purpose to take it home without learning what is inside; yet his state of mind is totally innocent unless he is aware of a high probability that the package contains a controlled substance. Thus, a conscious purpose instruction is only proper when coupled with a requirement that one be aware of a high probability of the truth.

The second defect in the instruction as given is that it did not alert the jury that Jewell could not be convicted if he "actually believed" there was no controlled substance in the car. The failure to emphasize, as does the Model Penal Code, that subjective belief is the determinative factor, may allow a jury to convict on an objective theory of knowledge— that a reasonable man should have inspected the car and would have discovered what was hidden inside. * * *

Third, the jury instruction clearly states that Jewell could have been convicted even if found ignorant or "not actually aware" that the car contained a controlled substance. This is unacceptable because true ignorance, no matter how unreasonable, cannot provide a basis for criminal liability when the statute requires knowledge. A proper jury instruction based on the Model Penal Code would be presented as a way of defining knowledge, and not as an alternative to it. * * *

We do not question the sufficiency of the evidence in this case to support conviction by a properly-instructed jury. As with all states of mind, knowledge must normally be proven by circumstantial evidence. There is evidence which could support a conclusion that Jewell was aware of a high probability that the car contained a controlled substance and that he had no belief to the contrary. However, we cannot say that the evidence was so overwhelming that the erroneous jury instruction was harmless. Accordingly, we would reverse the judgment on this appeal.

Notes and Questions

1. The jury instruction approved in *Jewell* is sometimes termed the "ostrich" instruction. For a critical survey of the law relating to it, see Ira P. Robbins, *The Ostrich Instruction: Deliberate Ignorance as a Criminal Mens Rea,* 81 J.Crim.L. & Criminology 191 (1990).

2. Does the frame of mind that satisfies the "wilful blindness" test of Model Penal Code § 2.02(7) truly comport with the concept of knowledge? If you are aware that there is a high probability that X is the case, and you do not affirmatively believe that X is *not* the case, do you have "knowledge" of X, or would you describe your state of mind as a "belief"? For example, if you walk by a house totally engulfed in flames, but you continue on your journey without observing the outcome, do you know that the house burned down, or do you simply believe that it did? Does the answer depend on whether you harbor some doubt? If so, does that mean that cautious people virtually never "know" anything, but only "believe" many things?

Canvassing the literature on theories of knowledge, Professor Ira Robbins concludes that a person lacks knowledge of a fact "if he entertains any doubts concerning the validity of his judgment, and even when one is certain that he is correct * * * [he lacks knowledge] if additional evidence is available to confirm or refute his conclusion." Robbins, supra, at 220. Under this test, do you "know" that the house you saw engulfed in flames burned down?

Is Professor Robbins's standard too stringent? In any case, is there any reason why a person who believes that X is so, and avoids confirming her beliefs, should not be convicted of an offense that requires knowledge of X? Professor Robbins contends that the state of mind described in Section 2.02(7), more properly should be described as "recklessness," a less culpable state of mind than "knowledge." (See Model Code § 2.02(2)(c).) Circuit Judge Richard Posner, however, defends the treatment of wilful blindness as a form of "knowledge":

> The most powerful criticism of the * * * instruction is, precisely, that its tendency is to allow juries to convict upon a finding of negligence [or recklessness] for crimes that require [knowledge]. The criticism can be deflected by thinking carefully about just what it is that real ostriches do (or at least are popularly supposed to do). They do not just fail to follow through on their suspicions of bad things. They are not merely *careless* birds. They bury their heads in the sand so that they will not see or hear bad things. They *deliberately* avoid acquiring unpleasant

knowledge. * * * A deliberate effort to avoid guilty knowledge is all the guilty knowledge the law requires.

United States v. Giovannetti, 919 F.2d 1223, 1228 (7th Cir.1990).

3. *"Wilful."* "Wilful" (or "willful") is a term frequently used in non-Model Penal Code statutes. The word has "defied any consistent interpretation by the courts." United States v. Granda, 565 F.2d 922, 924 (5th Cir.1978).

"Wilful" can simply mean that the actor intentionally or knowingly committed the prohibited act. Trice v. United States, 525 A.2d 176, 181 (D.C.App.1987). Sometimes, however, the term implies more: namely, that the actor intentionally or knowingly performed the prohibited act in bad faith, with a wrongful motive, or in violation of a known legal duty. See generally Michael Tigar, *"Willfulness" and "Ignorance" in Federal Criminal Law,* 37 Clev.St.L.Rev. 525 (1989). In the latter sense of the term, an offense that requires a "wilful" state of mind is a specific intent crime. Do you see why?

Because the term "wilful" is used in many modern statutes, the drafters of the Model Code concluded that a general provision regarding the term would be useful. See Section 2.02(8).

4. PROBLEMS IN STATUTORY INTERPRETATION

UNITED STATES v. MORRIS

United States Court of Appeals, Second Circuit, 1991.
928 F.2d 504.

JON O. NEWMAN, CIRCUIT JUDGE:

This appeal presents two narrow issues of statutory construction concerning a provision Congress recently adopted to strengthen protection against computer crimes. Section 2(d) of the Computer Fraud and Abuse Act of 1986, 18 U.S.C. § 1030(a)(5)(A) (1988), punishes anyone who intentionally accesses without authorization a category of computers known as "[f]ederal interest computers" and damages or prevents authorized use of information in such computers, causing loss of $1,000 or more. The issue[ ] raised * * * [is] whether the Government must prove not only that the defendant intended to access a federal interest computer, but also that the defendant intended to prevent authorized use of the computer's information and thereby cause loss * * *.

FACTS

In the fall of 1988, Morris was a first-year graduate student in Cornell University's computer science Ph.D. program. Through undergraduate work at Harvard and in various jobs he had acquired significant computer experience and expertise. When Morris entered Cornell, he was given an account on the computer at the Computer Science Division. This account gave him explicit authorization to use computers at Cornell. Morris engaged in various discussions with fellow graduate students about the security of computer networks and his ability to penetrate it.

In October 1988, Morris began work on a computer program, later known as the INTERNET "worm" or "virus." [1] The goal of this program was to demonstrate the inadequacies of current security measures on computer networks by exploiting the security defects that Morris had discovered. The tactic he selected was release of a worm into network computers. Morris designed the program to spread across a national network of computers after being inserted at one computer location connected to the network. Morris released the worm into INTERNET, which is a group of national networks that connect university, governmental, and military computers around the country. The network permits communication and transfer of information between computers on the network.

Morris sought to program the INTERNET worm to spread widely without drawing attention to itself. The worm was supposed to occupy little computer operation time, and thus not interfere with normal use of the computers. Morris programmed the worm to make it difficult to detect and read, so that other programmers would not be able to "kill" the worm easily.

Morris also wanted to ensure that the worm did not copy itself onto a computer that already had a copy. Multiple copies of the worm on a computer would make the worm easier to detect and would bog down the system and ultimately cause the computer to crash. Therefore, Morris designed the worm to "ask" each computer whether it already had a copy of the worm. If it responded "no," then the worm would copy onto the computer; if it responded "yes," the worm would not duplicate. However, Morris was concerned that other programmers could kill the worm by programming their own computers to falsely respond "yes" to the question. To circumvent this protection, Morris programmed the worm to duplicate itself every seventh time it received a "yes" response. As it turned out, Morris underestimated the number of times a computer would be asked the question, and his one-out-of-seven ratio resulted in far more copying than he had anticipated. The worm was also designed so that it would be killed when a computer was shut down, an event that typically occurs once every week or two. This would have prevented the worm from accumulating on one computer, had Morris correctly estimated the likely rate of reinfection. * * *

On November 2, 1988, Morris released the worm from a computer at the Massachusetts Institute of Technology. MIT was selected to disguise the fact that the worm came from Morris at Cornell. Morris soon discovered that the worm was replicating and reinfecting machines at a much faster rate than he had anticipated. Ultimately, many machines

---

1. In the colorful argot of computers, a "worm" is a program that travels from one computer to another but does not attach itself to the operating system of the computer it "infects." It differs from a "vi-rus," which is also a migrating program, but one that attaches itself to the operating system of any computer it enters and can infect any other computer that uses files from the infected computer.

at locations around the country either crashed or became "catatonic." When Morris realized what was happening, he contacted a friend at Harvard to discuss a solution. Eventually, they sent an anonymous message from Harvard over the network, instructing programmers how to kill the worm and prevent reinfection. However, because the network route was clogged, this message did not get through until it was too late. Computers were affected at numerous installations, including leading universities, military sites, and medical research facilities. The estimated cost of dealing with the worm at each installation ranged from $200 to more than $53,000.

Morris was found guilty, following a jury trial, of violating 18 U.S.C. § 1030(a)(5)(A). He was sentenced to three years of probation, 400 hours of community service, a fine of $10,050, and the costs of his supervision.

DISCUSSION

I. The intent requirement in section 1030(a)(5)(A)

Section 1030(a)(5)(A), covers anyone who

> (5) *intentionally accesses* a Federal interest computer without authorization, *and* by means of one or more instances of such conduct alters, damages, or destroys information in any such Federal interest computer, or *prevents authorized use* of any such computer or information, *and thereby*

> (A) *causes loss* to one or more others of a value aggregating $1,000 or more during any one year period; ... [emphasis added].

The District Court concluded that the intent requirement applied only to the accessing and not to the resulting damage. Judge Munson found recourse to legislative history unnecessary because he considered the statute clear and unambiguous. However, the Court observed that the legislative history supported its reading of section 1030(a)(5)(A).

Morris argues that the Government had to prove not only that he intended the unauthorized access of a federal interest computer, but also that he intended to prevent others from using it, and thus cause a loss. The adverb "intentionally," he contends, modifies both verb phrases of the section. The Government urges that since punctuation sets the "accesses" phrase off from the subsequent "damages" phrase, the provision unambiguously shows that "intentionally" modifies only "accesses." Absent textual ambiguity, the Government asserts that recourse to legislative history is not appropriate.

With some statutes, punctuation has been relied upon to indicate that a phrase set off by commas is independent of the language that followed. However, we have been advised that punctuation is not necessarily decisive in construing statutes, and with many statutes, a mental state adverb adjacent to initial words has been applied to phrases or clauses appearing later in the statute without regard to the punctuation or structure of the statute. In the present case, we do not believe the comma after "authorization" renders the text so clear as to preclude review of the legislative history.

The first federal statute dealing with computer crimes was passed in 1984, codified at 18 U.S.C. § 1030 (Supp. II 1984). The specific provision under which Morris was convicted was added in 1986, along with some other changes. The 1986 amendments made several changes relevant to our analysis.

First, the 1986 amendments changed the scienter requirement in section 1030(a)(2) from "knowingly" to "intentionally." The subsection now covers anyone who

> (2) intentionally accesses a computer without authorization or exceeds authorized access, and thereby obtains information contained in a financial record of a financial institution, or of a card issuer as defined in section 1602(n) of title 15, or contained in a file of a consumer reporting agency on a consumer, as such terms are defined in the Fair Credit Reporting Act (15 U.S.C. 1681 et seq.).

According to the Senate Judiciary Committee, Congress changed the mental state requirement in section 1030(a)(2) for two reasons. Congress sought only to proscribe intentional acts of unauthorized access, not "mistaken, inadvertent, or careless" acts of unauthorized access.

Also, Congress expressed concern that the "knowingly" standard "might be inappropriate for cases involving computer technology." The concern was that a scienter requirement of "knowingly" might encompass the acts of an individual "who inadvertently 'stumble[d] into' someone else's computer file or computer data," especially where such individual was authorized to use a particular computer. The Senate Report concluded that "[t]he substitution of an 'intentional' standard is designed to focus Federal criminal prosecutions on those whose conduct evinces a clear intent to enter, without proper authorization, computer files or data belonging to another." Congress retained the "knowingly" standard in other subsections of section 1030. *See* 18 U.S.C. § 1030(a)(1), (a)(4).

This use of a *mens rea* standard to make sure that inadvertent accessing was not covered is also emphasized in the Senate Report's discussion of section 1030(a)(3) and section 1030(a)(5), under which Morris was convicted. Both subsections were designed to target "outsiders," individuals without authorization to access any federal interest computer. The rationale for the *mens rea* requirement suggests that it modifies only the "accesses" phrase, which was the focus of Congress's concern in strengthening the scienter requirement.

The other relevant change in the 1986 amendments was the introduction of subsection (a)(5) to replace its earlier version, subsection (a)(3) of the 1984 act, 18 U.S.C. § 1030(a)(3) (Supp. II 1984). The predecessor subsection covered anyone who

> knowingly accesses a computer without authorization, or having accessed a computer with authorization, uses the opportunity such

access provides for purposes to which such authorization does not extend, and by means of such conduct knowingly uses, modifies, destroys, or discloses information in, or prevents authorized use of, such computer, if such computer is operated for or on behalf of the Government of United States and such conduct affects such operation.

The 1986 version changed the mental state requirement from "knowingly" to "intentionally," and did not repeat it after the "accesses" phrase, as had the 1984 version. By contrast, other subsections of section 1030 have retained "dual intent" language, placing the scienter requirement at the beginning of both the "accesses" phrase and the "damages" phrase. *See, e.g.,* 18 U.S.C. § 1030(a)(1). * * *

The Government's argument that the scienter requirement in section 1030(a)(5)(A) applies only to the "accesses" phrase is premised primarily upon the difference between subsection (a)(5)(A) and its predecessor in the 1984 statute. The decision to state the scienter requirement only once in subsection (a)(5)(A), along with the decision to change it from "knowingly" to "intentionally," are claimed to evince a clear intent upon the part of Congress to apply the scienter requirement only to the "accesses" phrase, though making that requirement more difficult to satisfy. This reading would carry out the Congressional objective of protecting the individual who "inadvertently 'stumble[s] into' someone else's computer file."

The Government also suggests that the fact that other subsections of section 1030 continue to repeat the scienter requirement before both phrases of a subsection is evidence that Congress selectively decided within the various subsections of section 1030 where the scienter requirement was and was not intended to apply. * * *

Despite some isolated language in the legislative history that arguably suggests a scienter component for the "damages" phrase of section 1030(a)(5)(A), the wording, structure, and purpose of the subsection, examined in comparison with its departure from the format of its predecessor provision persuade us that the "intentionally" standard applies only to the "accesses" phrase of section 1030(a)(5)(A), and not to its "damages" phrase. * * *

CONCLUSION

For the foregoing reasons, the judgment [of conviction] of the District Court is affirmed.

Notes and Questions

1. *Problem.* Y, an employee of a company doing business with the federal government, supplied false information to his employer in connection with a Department of Defense security clearance questionnaire. Y's employer routinely sent the questionnaire, containing Y's false statements, to a federal agency concerned with security clearances. When the falsehoods

were discovered, *Y* was prosecuted for violation of 18 U.S.C. § 1001, which provides in pertinent part:

> Whoever, in any matter within the jurisdiction of any department or agency of the United States knowingly * * * makes any false, fictitious or fraudulent statements * * * [is guilty of a felony].

At his trial, *Y* admitted that his statements were inaccurate, but he requested a jury instruction requiring the government to prove not only that he had actual knowledge of their falsity, but also that he had knowledge that the statements were made in a matter within the jurisdiction of a federal agency. The trial judge rejected his request and instead instructed the jury that the government had to prove that *Y* "knew or should have known" that the information would be submitted to a federal agency. United States v. Yermian, 468 U.S. 63, 104 S.Ct. 2936, 82 L.Ed.2d 53 (1984).

Should the trial court have instructed the jury as *Y* requested? Was the trial judge's instruction proper? How would a court go about answering these questions under *Morris* ? Under Model Penal Code § 2.02?

C. STRICT LIABILITY OFFENSES

1. IN GENERAL

UNITED STATES v. UNITED STATES GYPSUM CO.

Supreme Court of the United States, 1978.
438 U.S. 422, 98 S.Ct. 2864, 57 L.Ed.2d 854.

MR. CHIEF JUSTICE BURGER delivered the opinion of the Court. * * *

We start with the familiar proposition that "[t]he existence of a *mens rea* is the rule of, rather than the exception to, the principles of Anglo–American criminal jurisprudence." Dennis v. United States, 341 U.S. 494, 500, 71 S.Ct. 857, 862, 95 L.Ed. 1137 (1951). In a much-cited passage in Morissette v. United States, [342 U.S. 246, 250–51, 72 S.Ct. 240, 243, 96 L.Ed. 288, 293–94 (1952)], Mr. Justice Jackson speaking for the Court observed:

> "The contention that an injury can amount to a crime only when inflicted by intention is no provincial or transient notion. It is as universal and persistent in mature systems of law as belief in freedom of the human will and a consequent ability and duty of the normal individual to choose between good and evil. A relation between some mental element and punishment for a harmful act is almost as instinctive as the child's familiar exculpatory 'But I didn't mean to,' and has afforded the rational basis for a tardy and unfinished substitution of deterrence and reformation in place of retaliation and vengeance as the motivation for public prosecution. Unqualified acceptance of this doctrine by English common law in the Eighteenth Century was indicated by Blackstone's sweeping statement that to constitute any crime there must first be a 'vicious will.' " (Footnotes omitted.)

Although Blackstone's requisite "vicious will" has been replaced by more sophisticated and less colorful characterizations of the mental state required to support criminality, intent generally remains an indispensable element of a criminal offense. * * *

This Court, in keeping with the common-law tradition and with the general injunction that "ambiguity concerning the ambit of criminal statutes should be resolved in favor of lenity," has on a number of occasions read a state-of-mind component into an offense even when the statutory definition did not in terms so provide. Indeed, the holding in *Morissette* can be fairly read as establishing, at least with regard to crimes having their origin in the common law, an interpretative presumption that *mens rea* is required. "[M]ere omission . . . of intent [in the statute] will not be construed as eliminating that element from the crimes denounced"; instead Congress will be presumed to have legislated against the background of our traditional legal concepts which render intent a critical factor, and "absence of contrary direction [will] be taken as satisfaction with widely accepted definitions, not as a departure from them."

While strict-liability offenses are not unknown to the criminal law and do not invariably offend constitutional requirements, see Shevlin–Carpenter Co. v. Minnesota, 218 U.S. 57, 30 S.Ct. 663, 54 L.Ed. 930 (1910), the limited circumstances in which Congress has created and this Court has recognized such offenses, attest to their generally disfavored status. Certainly far more than the simple omission of the appropriate phrase from the statutory definition is necessary to justify dispensing with an intent requirement. * * *

Notes and Questions

1. The term "strict liability" is used by courts in various contexts. Sometimes an offense expressly contains a *mens rea* element, but the question of strict liability arises because the actor's conduct, although intentional, was morally innocent, for example, because she acted due to a reasonable mistake of fact or of law. If she is punished in such circumstances, then she is being held "strictly liable" in the sense that she lacked culpability for her actions.

However, a crime may be strict liability as defined: the offense contains no *mens rea* element; the crime is complete upon proof of commission of the prohibited acts that constitute the *actus reus* of the crime. These offenses are the topic of consideration here.

2. *Strict liability and the Constitution.* Notice the ambivalence of the Supreme Court in speaking about *mens rea*. On the one hand, per *Morissette* (quoted in *United States Gypsum Co.*), *mens rea* is "no provincial or transient notion" and is "universal and persistent in mature systems of law." Yet, intent only *"generally* remains an indispensable element of a criminal offense" (emphasis added). And, although strict liability offenses have a *"generally* disfavored status," they "do not *invariably* offend constitutional requirements" (emphasis added).

More than three decades ago, Professor Herbert Packer exasperatedly described the Court's *mens rea* jurisprudence this way: "*Mens rea* is an important requirement, but it is not a constitutional requirement, except sometimes." Herbert L. Packer, *Mens Rea and the Supreme Court,* 1962 Sup.Ct.Rev. 107, 107. This description remains true today, although the "except sometimes" might be replaced by "except rarely."

The Supreme Court has frequently stated, albeit nearly always in dictum, that the absence of a mental-state term in a criminal offense does not in itself violate the due process clause. Is there any other constitutional basis for objecting to strict liability?

2. DETERMINING LEGISLATIVE INTENT TO IMPOSE STRICT LIABILITY

UNITED STATES v. FLUM

United States Court of Appeals, Eighth Circuit, 1975.
518 F.2d 39.

WEBSTER, CIRCUIT JUDGE.

Thomas Lawrence Flum was convicted in a jury-waived trial of attempting to board an aircraft while having about his person a concealed dangerous and deadly weapon, in violation of the Federal Aviation Act of 1958, as amended, 49 U.S.C. § 1472(*l*).[1] In this appeal Flum contends that he was convicted upon insufficient evidence since there was no evidence tending to establish that he intended to conceal the knives which were discovered during a preboarding search of his carry-on luggage and personal belongings. The government, while arguing in the alternative that there was sufficient evidence of intent to conceal, first contends that the statute does not require proof of such intent. The District Court so held and we agree.

The objective facts of the case are well established by the evidence. On July 20, 1973, defendant Flum, accompanied by some friends, arrived at the Lincoln Municipal Airport at approximately 5:20 p.m. He first went to the ticket counter and purchased a ticket. The agent instructed him to proceed immediately to the gate where the passengers on his flight were already boarding. The defendant proceeded to a security post through which passengers must pass before reaching the departure gate. During the security inspection which followed, guards discovered a switchblade knife with a 3¾ inch blade and a butcher knife with a 7⅞ inch blade. The butcher knife was found in a suitcase, wrapped in loose clothing. The switchblade knife was found inside a small gray box which was on the counter with other belongings.

---

1. At the time of the incident in question, the statute provided in relevant part:

[W]hoever, while aboard an aircraft being operated by an air carrier in air transportation, has on or about his person a concealed deadly or dangerous weapon, or whoever attempts to board such an aircraft while having on or about his person a concealed deadly or dangerous weapon, shall be fined not more than $1,000 or imprisoned not more than one year, or both. * * *

The essential elements of the relevant offense prohibited by 49 U.S.C. § 1472(*l*) are (1) attempting to board an aircraft (2) while carrying a deadly or dangerous weapon (3) which was concealed on or about the defendant's person. Flum was clearly attempting to board an aircraft, and the deadly and dangerous character of the knives is likewise not disputed. What is disputed is whether the evidence showed beyond reasonable doubt that the weapons were "concealed" within the meaning of the statute.

SPECIFIC INTENT

The defendant contends that the statute takes as its source the common law crime of carrying a concealed weapon and therefore requires the same proof of *mens rea,* that is, a specific intent to conceal. Flum testified that he had intended to check his bags in advance of boarding but lacked time to do so because he had arrived at the airport only five minutes prior to take-off time. Since no one inquired whether he had any weapons in his possession, he argues, his act of presenting his belongings for inspection negated any intent to conceal. If intent to conceal were an essential element of the offense, this would be a compelling argument.

In *Morissette v. United States,* 342 U.S. 246, 72 S.Ct. 240, 96 L.Ed. 288 (1952), the defendant had been convicted of converting government bomb casings which he had found on a government target range while deer hunting. The district court had refused to instruct on the issue of intent, holding no intent to be required by the statute * * *. On certiorari the Supreme Court reversed, holding that the statute, 18 U.S.C. § 641, made the offense a felony if the value of the property exceeded $100, that conviction would gravely besmirch the defendant as a thief, and that the offense was taken over from the common law, which required proof of intent. However, in distinguishing that case from cases based upon regulatory or "public welfare offenses," which do not require proof of intent, Justice Jackson explained the basis for the latter as follows:

> These cases do not fit neatly into any of such accepted classifications of common-law offenses, such as those against the state, the person, property, or public morals. Many of these offenses are not in the nature of positive aggressions or invasions, with which the common law so often dealt, but are in the nature of neglect where the law requires care, or inaction where it imposes a duty. Many violations of such regulations result in no direct or immediate injury to person or property but merely create the danger or probability of it which the law seeks to minimize. While such offenses do not threaten the security of the state in the manner of treason, they may be regarded as offenses against its authority, for their occurrence impairs the efficiency of controls deemed essential to the social order as presently constituted. In this respect, whatever the intent of the violator, the injury is the same, and the consequences are injurious or not according to fortuity. Hence, legislation applicable to such offenses,

as a matter of policy, does not specify intent as a necessary element. The accused, if he does not will the violation, usually is in a position to prevent it with no more care than society might reasonably expect and no more exertion than it might reasonably exact from one who assumed his responsibilities.

The provision of the statute applicable to the instant case makes no reference to intent. In order then to determine whether the requirement of specific intent is nonetheless implied from the nature of the statute, we turn again to the classic test which Judge (now Justice) Blackmun announced for our court in *Holdridge v. United States*, 282 F.2d 302, 310 (8th Cir.1960):

> From these cases emerges the proposition that where a federal criminal statute omits mention of intent and where it seems to involve what is basically a matter of policy, where the standard imposed is, under the circumstances, reasonable and adherence thereto properly expected of a person, where the penalty is relatively small, where conviction does not gravely besmirch, where the statutory crime is not one taken over from the common law, and where congressional purpose is supporting, the statute can be construed as one not requiring criminal intent. The elimination of this element is then not violative of the due process clause.

1. *Policy.* In 1961 Congress adopted certain amendments to the Federal Aviation Act of 1958, for the purpose of "extend[ing] Federal criminal laws to certain acts committed on board aircraft—in particular, such acts as aircraft 'hijacking', murder, manslaughter, assault, maiming, carrying concealed deadly or dangerous weapons, and stealing personal property." H.R. Report No. 958, 87th Cong., 1st Sess. (1961), 1961 U.S.Code Cong. & Admin.News, p. 2563. The report continues:

> A series of acts of a criminal nature recently committed aboard aircraft has dramatically underscored the gaps in existing law which can operate to provide criminals with a haven from prosecution.

* * *

> * * * The committee feels that it is necessary and appropriate for the legislation to have this broad coverage if it is to operate as an effective deterrent to crime and promote safety in air commerce. While the legislation is intended to be as broad in its coverage, geographic and otherwise, as its plain meaning indicates, it is not intended—and, of course, it cannot—extend beyond such limitations as may be imposed by the Constitution. * * *

* * *

> Broad, stringent legislation such as is proposed here cannot, of course, prevent piracy of aircraft, but it is to be hoped that the enactment of laws providing stiff penalties for various crimes in air commerce will deter all except the hopelessly unbalanced from risking life and liberty in such undertakings.

* * * Nowhere in the report is found any inference of a congressional purpose or policy that intent to conceal must be demonstrated in order to prove the fact of concealment. Instead, a clear legislative intent is expressed that the reach of the legislation be "as broad in its coverage * * * as its plain meaning indicates," subject only to constitutional limitations, none of which are in question here.

2. *Standard.* We cannot say that the standard expressed in the plain meaning of subsection (*l*) is unreasonable. A demonstrated need to halt the flow of weapons on board aircraft, which had exposed to peril large numbers of passengers and jeopardized the integrity of commercial travel, justified a stringent rule, adherence to which was properly expected of all persons traveling by air, for their mutual safety.

3. *Penalty.* The statutory penalty, a maximum fine of $1000 or imprisonment for not more than one year, or both, makes the offense a misdemeanor, and is thus "relatively small." Moreover, other amendments to the Act which were adopted at the same time as subsection (*l*) both require evidence of wilfulness and provide for more stringent penalties,[7] adding weight to the inference that the penalty here was a further manifestation of a congressional purpose that subsection (*l*) should define a no-intent offense.

4. *Effect of Conviction.* Little need be said of the fourth requirement. Conviction of this offense does not gravely besmirch; it does not brand the guilty person as a felon or subject him to any burden beyond the sentence imposed.

5. *Source of Statute.* It is argued that the statute makes into a federal offense that which was an offense at common law: carrying a concealed weapon. The common law offense required proof of an intent to conceal; hence, defendant argues, the statute impliedly contains the same requirement. We find sufficient differences in the offense defined by subsection (*l*), along with the other factors considered herein, to conclude that Congress did not intend to adopt *in toto* the "cluster of ideas" associated with the words "concealed weapons." The conventional common law concealed-weapons offense makes it a crime to carry a weapon upon one's person with the specific intent to conceal it. The thrust of the federal statute, a misdemeanor, is to prohibit entry of an airplane with such weapon concealed upon one's person. The offense is not simply carrying the concealed weapon about one's person, but in boarding or attempting to board an aircraft with it.

6. *Congressional Purpose Supporting.* The Congress, as demonstrated *supra,* sought to promote safety in aircraft by extending the federal criminal laws to aircraft-related acts as a deterrent to crime. This purpose supports the conclusion that Congress did not intend to impede the deterrent effect of its statute by imposing upon the government prosecutor the added burden of showing the state of mind of the

7. Both before and after the 1974 amendments, 49 U.S.C. § 1472(i) authorized a minimum penalty of 20 years imprisonment for aircraft piracy, defined to include an element of "wrongful intent."

person found attempting to board an aircraft with a deadly or dangerous concealed weapon. If conviction depended upon proof of misrepresentation at the security gate or some other furtive act inconsistent with innocence, then the congressional purpose to keep weapons out of the passenger section of aircraft would depend entirely upon the thoroughness of the inspection, since in almost every case a person who presented his bags for inspection would thereby have rebutted in advance a claim that he possessed a specific criminal intent to conceal. To the contrary, we think the congressional purpose of keeping weapons from being taken on board airplanes by passengers fully supports the conclusion that intent to conceal is not an essential element of the offense. * * *

It will be argued that the statute thus construed may operate harshly upon passengers boarding aircraft with articles which potentially are deadly or dangerous weapons. Balanced against the heavy risks to large numbers of passengers, including those who would carry such weapons on board with no evil purpose, we cannot say that the resulting effect is too severe. It requires no recitation of recent history to remind us that such risks are real, and in comparison, the statute—broad though its reach may be—is a reasoned response to a demonstrated need.

Affirmed.

HEANEY, CIRCUIT JUDGE (dissenting).

I respectfully dissent. It is my view that an essential element of the crime embodied in 49 U.S.C. § 1472(*l*) is intent to conceal. * * *

I start from principles fundamental to our system of criminal justice:

> The contention that an injury can amount to a crime only when inflicted by intention is no provincial or transient notion. It is as universal and persistent in mature systems of law as belief in freedom of the human will and a consequent ability and duty of the normal individual to choose between good and evil. * * *

> Crime, as a compound concept, generally constituted only from concurrence of an evil-meaning mind with an evil-doing hand, was congenial to an intense individualism and took deep and early root in American soil. As the states codified the common law of crimes, even if their enactments were silent on the subject, their courts assumed that the omission did not signify disapproval of the principle but merely recognized that intent was so inherent in the idea of the offense that it required no statutory affirmation. * * *

* * *

> * * * The purpose and obvious effect of doing away with the requirement of a guilty intent is to ease the prosecution's path to conviction, to strip the defendant of such benefit as he derived at common law from innocence of evil purpose, and to circumscribe the freedom heretofore allowed juries. Such a manifest impairment of the immunities of the individual should not be extended to common-law crimes on judicial initiative.

The spirit of the doctrine which denies to the federal judiciary power to create crimes forthrightly admonishes that we should not enlarge the reach of enacted crimes by constituting them from anything less than the incriminating components contemplated by the words used in the statute. And where Congress borrows terms of art in which are accumulated the legal tradition and meaning of centuries of practice, it presumably knows and adopts the cluster of ideas that were attached to each borrowed word in the body of learning from which it was taken and the meaning its use will convey to the judicial mind unless otherwise instructed. In such case, absence of contrary direction may be taken as satisfaction with widely accepted definitions, not as a departure from them.

Morissette v. United States, 342 U.S. 246, 250–252, 263, 72 S.Ct. 240, 243, 96 L.Ed. 288 (1952).

My interpretation of 49 U.S.C. § 1472(l) is consistent with those principles. When Congress enacted this statute, using language similar or identical to that employed by the states in prohibiting the carrying of concealed weapons, it can only be presumed that it meant to retain the common law meaning that universally required intent to conceal. At common law, the carrying of a concealed weapon was not a crime unless the weapon was concealed "knowingly," "intentionally" and/or "consciously." These words connote that the actor committed the prohibited acts either with the purpose of concealing the weapon or knowing that the weapon would be concealed. Culpability, in addition to the prohibited act, was required before the actor could be labeled a criminal. * * *

The decision of the majority of this Court that imposes criminal liability without regard to the intent of the actor, strict criminal liability, is not only contrary to the common law but is unnecessary for the fulfillment of the Congressional purpose.[3] The stated purpose of the statute is deterrence * * *. This policy of deterrence, as recognized by Congress, will have no effect upon the "hopelessly unbalanced;" it will also have no effect upon those who act innocently, without the intent to conceal.

The justification for imposing criminal liability where there is no fault has been that enforcement of society's demands requires it. * * * If a person's conduct has been truly without fault, however, the threat of punishment will not favorably affect his conduct. The imposition of punishment is not needed to "reform" or "rehabilitate" him; no fault requiring correction has been identified. Punishment, if it takes the form of detention, will prevent him from

---

3. * * * In the absence of an overriding policy objective which requires the use of criminal sanctions where moral blame does not attach, it is surely preferable to make criminal law conform to moral judgment. Working Papers of the National Commission on Reform of Federal Criminal Laws (Vol. I 1970) at 130.

engaging in the conduct while he is detained. It may also satisfy the community's (irrational) demand for retribution for the harm which the conduct caused.

These slight functions which can be served are manifestly inadequate justifications for criminal liability without fault. Preventive detention of the kind involved here has no place in the criminal law. It is unlikely that the community will feel strongly about offenses of this kind (although it may strongly support regulation of the activity involved), particularly when there is no culpability, and unlikelier still that, if the community has such feelings, they will be so strong that they should be recognized for the sake of the community, despite their irrationality.

Working papers, *supra* at 129.

The decision of the majority permits imposition of criminal liability upon the housewife who carries scissors in her sewing bag; the fisherman who carries a scaling knife in his tackle box; the professional who carries a letter opener in his briefcase; the doctor who carries scalpels in his medical bag; and the tradesman who carries a hammer in his took kit.
* * *

It is not the imposition of criminal liability upon those who innocently carry weapons in their hand luggage but the preflight boarding searches that will "halt the flow of weapons on board aircraft." This extraordinary procedure is the practical method Congress has chosen to insure flight safety. The requirement of intent as an essential element of 49 U.S.C. § 1472(*l*) will not undermine that procedure or its purpose. The intent requirement will only insure that prosecutions under the statute will be limited to those persons who would be deterred thereby. The statute should not be construed to serve a purpose it cannot achieve.

The troublesome problem of selective enforcement is also aggravated by the majority's decision. As revealed in the Federal Aviation Administration's First Semi–Annual Report to Congress on the Effectiveness of Passenger Screening Procedures, 67,710 weapons were detected in 1974. As a result thereof, however, only 1,147 arrests for weapons related offenses were made. The percentage of arrests made to weapons detected was 1.69%. It is apparent that the security officer possesses an enormous amount of unreviewable discretion. The decision of a majority of this Court increases that discretionary power and places the determination of innocence in the hands of the police. * * *

Notes and Questions

1. Is there any argument related to the *actus reus* of 49 U.S.C. § 1472(*l*) that should have made in Flum's defense?

2. Suppose that the knives had been planted in Flum's belongings by a stranger, without his knowledge. Would he be guilty? Suppose that Flum had placed the knives in his baggage the night before the flight and had forgotten that they were there? See United States v. Garrett, 984 F.2d 1402 (5th Cir.1993); United States v. Lee, 539 F.2d 606 (6th Cir.1976).

3. Suppose that a mother and son try to board an airplane with the child's authentic-looking toy gun in the parent's on-board luggage. If you represented her, what argument would you make in her defense?

3. SHOULD WE HAVE STRICT LIABILITY OFFENSES?

REGINA v. CITY OF SAULT STE. MARIE

Supreme Court of Canada, 1978.
85 Dominion Law.Rep. (3d) 161.

DICKSON, J.:

[The accused City entered into an agreement with a private company for garbage disposal. The private company disposed of the City's refuse in a manner that polluted nearby waters. The City was charged with violation of the Ontario Water Resources Act, which provided that it is an offense to "discharge, or cause to be discharged, or permit to be discharged or deposited," materials that "might impair the quality of the water." The City argued that the offense, although one of strict liability on its face, required proof of *mens rea*.]

The distinction between the true criminal offence and the public welfare offence is one of prime importance. Where the offence is criminal, the Crown must establish a mental element, namely, that the accused who committed the prohibited act did so intentionally or recklessly, with knowledge of the facts constituting the offence, or with wilful blindness toward them. * * *

In sharp contrast, "absolute liability" entails conviction on proof merely that the defendant committed the prohibited act constituting the *actus reus* of the offence. There is no relevant mental element. It is no defence that the accused was entirely without fault. He may be morally innocent in every sense, yet be branded as a malefactor and punished as such.

Public welfare offences obviously lie in a field of conflicting values. It is essential for society to maintain, through effective enforcement, high standards of public health and safety. Potential victims of those who carry on latently pernicious activities have a strong claim to consideration. On the other hand, there is a generally held revulsion against punishment of the morally innocent.

Public welfare offences evolved in mid–19th century Britain as a means of doing away with the requirement of *mens rea* for petty police offences. The concept was a judicial creation, founded on expediency. That concept is now firmly embedded in the concrete of Anglo–American and Canadian jurisprudence, its importance heightened by the ever-increasing complexities of modern society.

Various arguments are advanced in justification of absolute liability in public welfare offences. Two predominate. Firstly, it is argued that the protection of social interests requires a high standard of care and attention on the part of those who follow certain pursuits and such persons are more likely to be stimulated to maintain those standards if they know that ignorance or mistake will not excuse them. The removal of any possible loophole acts, it is said, as an incentive to take precautionary measures beyond what would otherwise be taken, in order that mistakes and mishaps be avoided. The second main argument is one based on administrative efficiency. Having regard to both the difficulty of proving mental culpability and the number of petty cases which daily come before the Courts, proof of fault is just too great a burden in time and money to place upon the prosecution. To require proof of each person's individual intent would allow almost every violator to escape. This, together with the glut of work entailed in proving *mens rea* in every case would clutter the docket and impede adequate enforcement as virtually to nullify the regulatory statutes. In short, absolute liability, it is contended, is the most efficient and effective way of ensuring compliance with minor regulatory legislation and the social ends to be achieved are of such importance as to override the unfortunate by-product of punishing those who may be free of moral turpitude. In further justification, it is urged that slight penalties are usually imposed and that conviction for breach of a public welfare offence does not carry the stigma associated with conviction for a criminal offence.

Arguments of greater force are advanced against absolute liability. The most telling is that it violates fundamental principles of penal liability. It also rests upon assumptions which have not been, and cannot be, empirically established. There is no evidence that a higher standard of care results from absolute liability. If a person is already taking every reasonable precautionary measure, is he likely to take additional measures, knowing that however much care he takes, it will not serve as a defence in the event of breach? If he has exercised care and skill, will conviction have a deterrent effect upon him or others? Will the injustice of conviction lead to cynicism and disrespect for the law, on his part and on the part of others? These are among the questions asked. The argument that no stigma attaches does not withstand analysis, for the accused will have suffered loss of time, legal costs, exposure to the processes of the criminal law at trial and, however one may downplay it, the opprobrium of conviction. It is not sufficient to say that the public interest is engaged and, therefore, liability may be imposed without fault. In serious crimes, the public interest is involved and *mens rea* must be proven. The administrative argument has little force. In sentencing, evidence of due diligence is admissible and therefore the evidence might just as well be heard when considering guilt. * * *

Public welfare offences involve a shift of emphasis from the protection of individual interests to the protection of public and social interests. The unfortunate tendency in many past cases has been to see the choice as between two stark alternatives: (i) full *mens rea;* or (ii) absolute liability. In respect of public welfare offences where full *mens rea* is not required, absolute liability has often been imposed. * * * There has, however, been an attempt in Australia, in many Canadian

Courts, and indeed in England, to seek a middle position, fulfilling the goals of public welfare offences while still not punishing the entirely blameless. There is an increasing and impressive stream of authority which holds that where an offence does not require full *mens rea,* it is nevertheless a good defence for the defendant to prove that he was not negligent.

Dr. Glanville Williams has written: "There is a half-way house between *mens rea* and strict responsibility which has not yet been properly utilized, and that is responsibility for negligence" (*Criminal Law: General Part,* 2nd ed. (1961), p. 262). Morris and Howard, in *Studies in Criminal Law* (1964), p. 200, suggest that strict responsibility might with advantage be replaced by a doctrine of responsibility for negligence strengthened by a shift in the burden of proof. The defendant would be allowed to exculpate himself by proving affirmatively that he was not negligent. * * *

I conclude * * * that there are compelling grounds for the recognition of three categories of offenses rather than the traditional two:

1.   Offences in which *mens rea,* consisting of some positive state of mind such as intent, knowledge, or recklessness, must be proved by the prosecution either as an inference from the nature of the act committed, or by additional evidence.

2.   Offences in which there is no necessity for the prosecution to prove the existence of *mens rea;* the doing of the prohibited act *prima facie* imports the offence, leaving it open to the accused to avoid liability by proving that he took all reasonable care. This involves consideration of what a reasonable man would have done in the circumstances. The defence will be available if the accused reasonably believed in a mistaken set of facts which, if true, would render the act or omission innocent, or if he took all reasonable steps to avoid the particular event. These offences may properly be called offences of strict liability. * * *

3.   Offences of absolute liability where it is not open to the accused to exculpate himself by showing that he was free of fault.

Offences which are criminal in the true sense fall in the first category. Public welfare offences would, *prima facie,* be in the second category. They are not subject to the presumption of full *mens rea.* * * * On the other hand, the principle that punishment should in general not be inflicted on those without fault applies. Offences of absolute liability would be those in respect of which the Legislature had made it clear that guilt would follow proof merely of the proscribed act. The over-all regulatory pattern adopted by the Legislature, the subject-matter of the legislation, the importance of the penalty, and the precision of the language used will be primary considerations in determining whether the offence falls into the third category. * * *

[The Supreme Court determined that the Ontario Water Resources Act was a strict (but not absolute) liability offense.]

Notes and Questions

1. From the City's perspective, beyond the matter of strict liability, is there another objectionable feature of the Ontario Water Resources Act, as drafted?

RICHARD G. SINGER—THE RESURGENCE OF *MENS REA:* III—THE RISE AND FALL OF STRICT CRIMINAL LIABILITY

30 Boston College Law Review 337 (1989), 389–90, 393–96

The discussions of the purported justifications for strict liability, and the repudiation of those justifications, are legion. Briefly, the defense of strict liability crimes rests on several grounds: (1) only strict criminal liability can deter profit-driven manufacturers and capitalists from ignoring the well-being of the consuming public; (2) the inquiry into *mens rea* would exhaust courts, which have to deal with thousands of "minor" infractions every day; [and] (3) the imposition of strict liability is not inconsistent with the moral underpinnings of the criminal law generally because the penalties are small, and conviction carries no social stigma

* * * * * *

1. THE ARGUMENT FROM DETERRENCE

The argument that only strict criminal liability can effect true safety in an industrial society, or at least motivate highly regulated businesses to act responsibly, may have been the moving force behind English statutes and decisions embracing "strict liability" in the nineteenth century. * * * Howard repudiates the argument from deterrence by noting:

> The assertion that a potentially inefficient or thoughtless member of society will more effectively mend his ways if he knows that no excuse will be allowed ... is no more than an assumption for which no evidence can be produced in support.... It is scarcely maintainable that the vast majority of regulatory offense defendants have any thoughts on the matter at all until they are prosecuted.[252]

Sanford Kadish similarly argues that strict criminal liability for the purposes of regulating business is not merely undesirable, but also self-defeating, and urges that civil sanctions be employed instead: "Civil fines, punitive damages, injunctions, profit divestiture programs or other varieties of non-criminal sanctions would thus appear to offer equivalent possibilities of enforcing the regulatory scheme. Indeed, these alternatives might enhance the possibilities, since proof and evidentiary, requirements are more onerous in criminal prosecutions than in civil suits."[253]

252. Howard, [Strict Responsibility] 24–26 [1962].

253. Kadish, *Some Observations on the Use of Criminal Sanctions in Enforcing Economic Regulations,* 30 U.Chi.L.Rev. 423, 442 (1963).

Moreover, to the extent that the deterrence arguments may have carried some weight during the early part of this century, they clearly are inapplicable now. Extensive government regulation of virtually every business generally protects the public as well as can reasonably be expected. To the extent that this is not true, strict tort liability allows private suit. In this light, then, the marginal deterrence gained by strict criminal liability, particularly when the penalties are light and do not generally entail imprisonment, seems minimal indeed. * * *

2. THE ARGUMENT FROM EXPEDITION

The second argument for strict criminal liability is efficiency—that it would simply take those courts faced with the areas in which strict criminal liability is now imposed too much time to inquire into *mens rea,* even into negligence, in every case. Thus, proponents point to the overwhelming numbers of regulatory offenses, including traffic and parking offenses, that face the courts daily and in which there is rarely if ever time for a substantial concern with *mens rea.* Perkins, for example, says that:

> [t]wo assumptions have been made, both seemingly correct: (1) The impressive group of governmental regulations, federal, state and local, cannot be effectively enforced without the aid of penalties; (2) because of important differences between violations of these penalty-clauses on the one hand, and true crimes on the other, the former require greater strictness in their enforcement.[270]

And another commentator has declared: "Because of the nature of these offenses, it would be almost impossible to secure conviction if the state were required to prove the criminal intent of persons who violated the law." [271] But Lord Brett has responded:

> The argument ... must be based on speculation rather than established fact, for the alternative has not, so far as I know, been tried. But in any event, it is an argument of expediency, akin to that on which the rulers of totalitarian states base their Draconian practices. I believe that we should base our practices on considerations of justice, morality and humanity.[272]

Brett is clearly right. The Perkins position that strict liability is desirable because it is more efficient fails to note that (1) courts often look to *mens rea* in assessing the penalty to be imposed, and (2) if the situation clearly requires a failure to make such an inquiry, the solution is not to distort the criminal process, but to label such offenses by some other nomenclature, thereby removing any notion that the offense is criminal. This latter path, of course, is the one taken by the Model

270. Perkins, [*Alignment of Sanction with Culpable Conduct,* 49 Iowa L.Rev. 325, 332 (1964)].

271. Note, *The Development of Crimes Requiring No Criminal Intent,* 26 Marq. L.Rev. 92, 93 (1942).

272. Brett, [*Strict Responsibility: Possible Solutions,* 37 Mod.L.Rev. 417, 438 (1974)].

Penal Code. The suggestion, often found in the literature, of making these offenses "regulatory" or "administrative," echoes this concern.

3. THE ARGUMENT FROM TRIVIALITY

A third argument for supporting strict criminal liability is that the penalties imposed * * * are so small that they can be ignored as criminal punishments. This argument attempts to gain strength by noting that such small penalties do not carry with them the usual criteria of criminal penalties, such as social stigma.

Two responses are possible. First, it is not clear that even small penalties will not carry the social stigma that "true crimes" carry. * * * [T]he stigmatic effect of a finding of guilty on the defendant is a substantial penalty, even if no loss of freedom is actually imposed. * * *

More importantly, that proponents of strict liability criminality must, in effect, resort to arguing that no one "really" considers these offenses as "crimes" demonstrates the weakness of the position. There is, of course, always the question of whether the defendant can in fact spread the loss. But Professor Fisse argues that "even if [the defendant] is in such a position clearly there should be no conviction since the distribution of fines to consumers would be quite contrary to the public interest, and would nullify the deterrent effect upon [the defendant] which conviction is designed to achieve." [278] * * * Thus, the argument from triviality is suspect both because it ignores justice and because it can be turned back upon itself: If the penalties are so trivial, they will be inefficacious.

RICHARD A. WASSERSTROM—STRICT LIABILITY IN THE CRIMINAL LAW

12 Stanford Law Review 731 (1960), 734–41

Critics of strict criminal liability usually argue that the punishment of persons in accordance with the minimum requirements of strict liability (1) is inconsistent with any or all of the commonly avowed aims of the criminal law; and (2) runs counter to the accepted standards of criminal culpability which prevail in the community. They assert that the imposition of criminal sanctions in a case in which—conceivably— the defendant acted both reasonably and with no intention to produce the proscribed events cannot be justified by an appeal to the deterrent, the rehabilitative, or the incarcerative functions of punishment. And, in fact, they assert the practical effect of strict liability offenses is simply to create that anomalous situation in which persons not morally blamed by the community are nevertheless branded criminal. Although the two lines of criticism are intimately related, for purposes of discussion they will be treated somewhat separately.

The notion that strict liability statutes can be defended as efficacious deterrents has been consistently rejected. * * *

278. Fisse, [*The Elimination of Vicarious Responsibility in Regulatory Offenses,* 42 Austl.L.J. 199, 206 (1968)].

* * * [R]easons for rejecting the deterrent quality of strict liability offenses are offered by Jerome Hall, among others. He rejects the argument that a *strict* liability statute is a more efficacious deterrent than an ordinary criminal statute for at least two reasons: (a) It is not plausible to suppose that the "strictness" of the liability renders it more of a deterrent than the liability of ordinary criminal statutes; and (b) persons are not, as a matter of fact, deterred by those penalties usually imposed for the violation of a strict liability offense.

The first of these objections is, it is submitted, inconclusive. For there seem to be at least two respects in which strict liability statutes might have a greater deterrent effect than "usual" criminal statutes. In the first place, it should be noted that Hall's first proposition is just as apt to be false as to be true. That is to say, it might be the case that a person engaged in a certain kind of activity would be more careful precisely because he knew that this kind of activity was governed by a strict liability statute. It is at least plausible to suppose that the knowledge that certain criminal sanctions will be imposed if certain consequences ensue might induce a person to engage in that activity with much greater caution than would be the case if some lesser standard prevailed.

In the second place (and this calls Hall's second premise into question as well), it seems reasonable to believe that the presence of strict liability offenses might have the added effect of keeping a relatively large class of persons from engaging in certain kinds of activity. A person who did not regard himself as capable of conducting an enterprise in such a way so as not to produce the deleterious consequences proscribed by the statute might well refuse to engage in that activity at all. Of course, if the penalties for violation of the statute are minimal—if payment of fines is treated merely as a license to continue in operation—then unscrupulous persons will not be deterred by the imposition of this sanction. But this does not imply that unscrupulous persons would be quite so willing to engage in these activities if the penalties for violation were appreciably more severe. In effect, Hall's second argument, if it proves anything, shows only that stronger penalties are needed if strict liability statutes are to be effective. * * *

To the extent to which the function of the criminal law is conceived to be that of regulating various kinds of conduct, it becomes relevant to ask whether this particular way of regulating conduct leads to more desirable results than possible alternative procedures. The problem is not peculiar to strict liability statutes but is endemic to the legal system as a whole. Consider, for instance, one such justification of the present jury system. In order to prevent the conviction of persons who did not in fact commit the crimes of which they are accused, it is required that a unanimous jury of twelve persons find, among other things, that they believe the accused did the act in question. Perhaps if the concern were solely with guaranteeing that no innocent man be convicted, a twenty or thirty man jury in which unanimous consent was required for conviction would do a better job. But such is not the sole concern of the criminal law; there is also the need to prevent too many guilty persons from going free. Here, a twelve man jury is doubtless more effective than a thirty man jury. Requiring unanimous vote for acquittal would be a still more efficacious means of insuring that every guilty man be convicted. The decision to have a twelve man jury which must be unanimous for conviction can be justified, in other words, as an attempt to devise an adjudicatory procedure (perhaps it is unsuccessful) which will yield a greater quantity of desirable results than would any of the alternatives.

Precisely the same kind of analysis can be made of strict liability offenses. One of the ways to prevent the occurrence of certain kinds of consequences is to enact strict liability offenses, since, *ex hypothesi,* these will be an added deterrent. One of the deleterious consequences of strict liability offenses is the possibility that certain socially desirable institutions will be weakened or will disappear. The problem is twofold: first one must decide whether the additional deterrent effect of the strict liability statutes will markedly reduce the occurrence of those events which the statute seeks quite properly to prevent. And second, one must decide whether this additional reduction in undesirable occurrences is more beneficial to society than the possible deleterious effects upon otherwise desirable activities such as banking or drug distribution. For even if it be conceded that strict liability offenses may have the additionally undesirable effect of holding as criminal some persons who would not on other grounds be so regarded, strict liability could be supported on the theory that the need to prevent certain kinds of occurrences is sufficiently great so as to override the undesirable effect of punishing those who might in some other sense be "innocent."

I do not urge that either or both of these arguments for strict liability offenses are either irrefutable or even particularly convincing. But I do submit that this is a perfectly plausible kind of argument which cannot be met simply by insisting either that strict liability is an inherently unintelligible concept or that the legislative judgment of the desirability of strict criminal liability is necessarily irrational. It is one thing to attack particular legislative evaluations on the grounds that they have misconstrued either the beneficial effects of strict liability or its attendant deleterious consequences, but it is quite another thing to attack the possible rationality of any such comparative determination.

As was observed earlier, the second of the two major kinds of criticism directed against strict criminal liability is that punishment of persons in accordance with the minimal requirements of strict liability— the punishment of persons in the absence of *mens rea*—is irreconcilable with those fundamental, long extant standards of criminal culpability which prevail in the community. As usually propounded the thesis is a complex one; it is also considerably more ambiguous than many of its proponents appear to have noted. One possible, although less interesting, implication concerns the notion of criminal culpability. The claim is made that the imposition of strict liability is inconsistent with the concept of criminal culpability—criminal culpability being defined to mean "requiring *mens rea.*" But unless the argument is to be vacuous it must be demonstrated that independent reasons exist for selecting just this definition which precludes strict liability offenses from the class of actions to which the criminal sanctions are to attach.

A more troublesome and related question is whether the proposition is presented as a *descriptive* or *prescriptive* assertion. It is not clear whether the imposition of strict liability is thought to be incompatible with the accepted values of society or whether the prevalence of strict liability is inconsistent with what ought to be accepted values.

As an empirical assertion the protest against strict liability on the grounds that it contravenes public sentiment is, again, at best an open hypothesis. Those who seek to substantiate its correctness turn to the fact that minimal penalties are often imposed. They construe this as indicative of the felt revulsion against the concept of strict criminal liability. That judges and juries often refuse to impose those sanctions which would be imposed in the comparable cases involving the presence of *mens rea,* is taken as additional evidence of community antipathy.

The evidence is, however, no less (and probably no more) persuasive on the other side. The fact that most strict liability offenses are creatures of statute has already been alluded to. While few persons would seriously wish to maintain that the legislature is either omniscient or a wholly adequate reflection of general or popular sentiment, the fact that so many legislatures have felt such apparently little compunction over enacting such statutes is surely indicative of the presence of a comparable community conviction. Strict liability offenses, as the critics so persistently note, are not mere sports, mere sporadic legislative oversights or anomalies. They are, again as the critics note, increasing in both number and scope. It may very well be the case that strict liability offenses ought to be condemned by the community; it is much more doubtful that they are presently held in such contumely. * * *

Notes and Questions

1. The position of the Model Penal Code regarding strict liability is set out in Section 2.05. The Commentary explains the American Law Institute's view on the subject:

> This section makes a frontal attack on absolute or strict liability in the penal law * * *. The method used is not to abrogate strict liability completely, but to provide that when conviction rests upon that basis the grade of the offense is reduced to a violation, which is not a "crime" [under Section 1.04] and under Sections 1.04(5) and 6.02(4) may result in no sentence other than a fine, or a fine and forfeiture or other authorized civil penalty. * * *

> * * * It has been argued, and the argument undoubtedly will be repeated, that strict liability is necessary for enforcement in a number of the areas where it obtains. But if practical enforcement precludes litigation of the culpability of alleged deviation from legal requirements, the enforcers cannot rightly demand the use of penal sanctions for the purpose. Crime does and should mean condemnation and no court

should have to pass that judgment unless it can declare that the defendant's act was culpable. This is too fundamental to be compromised.

American Law Institute, Model Penal Code and Commentaries, Comment to § 2.05 at 282–83 (1985).

D. MISTAKE OF FACT

INTRODUCTORY COMMENT

The Model Penal Code Commentary observes that "ignorance or mistake [of a matter of fact or of law] has * * * evidential import; it is significant whenever it is logically relevant, and it may be logically relevant to negate the required mode of culpability * * *." American Law Institute, Model Penal Code and Commentaries, Comment to § 2.04 at 269 (1985). In short, a mistake of fact or of law is relevant in a criminal prosecution when it potentially negatives the element of *mens rea* in the offense charged.

Unfortunately, as straightforward as the preceding statement is, the common law of mistake is far more complex. In part, the intricacy of the common law stems from the distinction between the "culpability" and "elemental" meanings of the term *"mens rea"* (Note 2, p. 104 supra), and the related distinction between "general intent" and "specific intent" crimes (Note 2, p. 111 supra). The common law and the comparatively simple approach of the Model Penal Code are considered in the remaining materials in this chapter.

PEOPLE v. NAVARRO

Appellate Department, Los Angeles County Superior Court, 1979.
99 Cal.App.3d Supp. 1, 160 Cal.Rptr. 692.

Dowds, Judge.

[Defendant was charged with a violation of California Penal Code § 487.1, grand theft, and was convicted of petty theft, a lesser offense. Under state law, "[e]very person who shall feloniously steal * * * the personal property of another * * * is guilty of theft." Cal.Pen.Code § 484(a). This statute codified the common law definition of larceny, i.e., "the trespassory taking and carrying away of the personal property of another with the intent to steal the property."]

* * * [Defendant's] contention on appeal is that the jury was improperly instructed. The only facts set forth in the record on appeal are that defendant was charged with stealing four wooden beams from a construction site and that the state of the evidence was such that the jury could have found that the defendant believed either (1) that the beams had been abandoned as worthless and the owner had no objection to his taking them or (2) that they had substantial value, had not been abandoned and he had no right to take them.

The court refused two jury instructions proposed by defendant reading as follows:

DEFENDANT'S A

"If one takes personal property with the good faith belief that the property has been abandoned or discarded by the true owner, he is not guilty of theft. This is the case even if such good faith belief is unreasonable.

The prosecutor must prove beyond a reasonable doubt that the defendant did not so believe for you to convict a defendant of theft."

DEFENDANT'S B

"If one takes personal property with the good faith belief that he has permission to take the property, he is not guilty of theft. This is the case even if such good faith belief is unreasonable.

The prosecutor must prove beyond a reasonable doubt that the defendant did not so believe for you to convict a defendant of theft."

Instead, the court instructed the jury in the words of the following modified instructions:

MODIFIED—DEFENDANT'S A

"If one takes personal property in the reasonable and good faith belief that the property has been abandoned or discarded by the true owner, he is not guilty of theft."

MODIFIED—DEFENDANT'S B

"If one takes personal property in the reasonable and good faith belief that he has the consent or permission of the owner to take the property, he is not guilty of theft.

If you have a reasonable doubt that the defendant had the required criminal intent as specified in these instructions, the defendant is entitled to an acquittal."

Accordingly, the question for determination on appeal is whether the defendant should be acquitted if there is a reasonable doubt that he had a good faith belief that the property had been abandoned or that he had the permission of the owner to take the property or whether that belief must be a reasonable one as well as being held in good faith.

A recent decision by the California Supreme Court throws light on this question. In *People v. Wetmore* (1978) 22 Cal.3d 318, 149 Cal.Rptr. 265, 583 P.2d 1308, defendant was charged with burglary, like theft a specific intent crime. The Supreme Court held that the trial court had erroneously refused to consider the * * * evidence that, because of mental illness, defendant was incapable of forming the specific intent required for conviction of the crime * * *. * * *

The instant case, does not, of course, involve evidence of mental illness. Evidence was presented, however, from which the jury could have concluded that defendant believed that the wooden beams had been abandoned and that the owner had no objection to his taking them, i.e., that he lacked the specific criminal intent required to commit the crime of theft (intent permanently to deprive an owner of his property). * * *

* * * In *People v. Devine* (1892) 95 Cal. 227, 30 P. 378, defendant's conviction of larceny was reversed. He had driven away in a wagon, without any attempt at secrecy, a number of hogs, his own and three bearing another's mark or brand. The Supreme Court pointed out: "There are cases in which all the knowledge which a person might have acquired by due diligence is to be imputed to him. But where a felonious intent must be proven it can be done only by proving what the accused knew. One cannot intend to steal property which he believes to be his own. He may be careless, and omit to make an effort to ascertain that the property which he thinks his own belongs to another; but so long as he believes it to be his own he cannot feloniously steal it...." (Id. at pp. 230–231, 30 P. at p. 379.) * * *

Cases in other jurisdictions also hold that where the law requires a specific criminal intent, it is not enough merely to prove that a reasonable man would have had that intent, without meeting the burden of proof that the defendant himself also entertained it. * * *

* * * The proper rule, it seems to us, is set forth in Perkins on Criminal Law (2d ed. 1969) at pages 940–941: "If no specific intent or other special mental element is required for guilt of the offense charged, a mistake of fact will not be recognized as an excuse unless it was based upon reasonable grounds ...   [On the other hand, B]ecause of the requirement of a specific intent to steal there is no such thing as larceny by negligence. One does not commit this offense by carrying away the chattel of another in the mistaken belief that it is his own, no matter how great may have been the fault leading to this belief, if the belief itself is genuine."

La Fave and Scott, Handbook on Criminal Law (1972) sets forth at page 357 what the authors call the "... rather simple rule that an honest mistake of fact or law is a defense when it negates a required mental element of the crime...." As an example they refer to the crime of receiving stolen property, stating "... if the defendant by a mistake of either fact or law did not know the goods were stolen, even though the circumstances would have led a prudent man to believe they were stolen, he does not have the required mental state and thus may not be convicted of the crime."

In the instant case the trial court in effect instructed the jury that even though defendant in good faith believed he had the right to take the beams, and thus lacked the specific intent required for the crime of theft, he should be convicted unless such belief was reasonable. In doing so it erred. It is true that if the jury thought the defendant's belief to be unreasonable, it might infer that he did not in good faith hold such belief. If, however, it concluded that defendant in good faith believed that he had the right to take the beams, even though such belief was unreasonable as measured by the objective standard of a hypothetical reasonable man, defendant was entitled to an acquittal since the specific intent required to be proved as an element of the offense had not been established.[3]

Notes and Questions

1. If Navarro's belief that the beams were abandoned as worthless was unreasonable, does this mean that he acted in a morally culpable manner? If so, why does he not have the requisite *mens rea* to be convicted of theft?

2. How would *Navarro* be analyzed under Model Penal Code § 2.04? For general discussion of the Code's treatment of mistake, see George P. Fletcher, *Mistake in the Model Penal Code: A False False Problem,* 19 Rutgers L.J. 649 (1988); Peter W. Low, *The Model Penal Code, The Common Law, and Mistakes of Fact: Recklessness, Negligence, or Strict Liability?,* 19 Rutgers L.J. 539 (1988).

3. Footnote 3 of *Navarro* makes mention of instructions found in a California jury instruction manual. In many states, a committee founded by the state bar association or by the state supreme court produces a set of model jury instructions that are intended to reflect, and to express in a fashion understandable to jurors, the relevant criminal and civil law of the jurisdiction. Trial judges often use the forms to instruct juries.

4. The *Navarro* court apparently accepted the common law mistake rule set out by Professor Perkins, which distinguishes between mistakes relating to specific intent offenses and those concerning general intent crimes. What is that distinction? Is there any good reason for it? Is Professor Perkins's statement of the law consistent with the "rather simple rule" set forth by Professors LaFave and Scott, quoted immediately thereafter?

STATE v. STIFFLER

Court of Appeals of Idaho, 1988.
114 Idaho 935, 763 P.2d 308.

Swanstrom, Judge.

Jason Stiffler entered a conditional plea of guilty to statutory rape, reserving his right to challenge on appeal the district court's refusal of his proposed jury instruction on a defense to the crime charged. The sole issue is whether an honest and reasonable mistake of fact as to the victim's age is a defense to the charge of statutory rape. We hold it is not.

3. Instruction No. 4.35 in the fourth edition of California Jury Instructions—Criminal, relating to ignorance or mistake of fact, reads as follows:

"An act committed or an omission made under an ignorance or mistake of fact which disproves any criminal intent is not a crime.

"Thus a person is not guilty of a crime if he commits an act or omits to act under an honest and reasonable belief in the existence of certain facts and circum-

stances which, if true, would make such act or omission lawful."

The use note for this instruction omits the caveat found under instruction No. 4.36, relating to ignorance or mistake of law, to the effect that the instruction would be inappropriate if the mistake may negative a specific intent or other mental state which the crime requires. We think trial judges would be well advised also to eschew or modify instruction No. 4.35 in cases involving crimes requiring a specific intent or mental state.

[Idaho Code § 18–6101 defined rape, punishable by a term of imprisonment of from one year to life, as "an act of sexual intercourse accomplished with a female under either of the following circumstances: [1.] Where the female is under the age of eighteen (18) years * * *." Subsections (2)–(6) listed various other forms of nonconsensual intercourse constituting rape.]

The underlying premise of rape laws is the lack of a female's consent to an invasion of her bodily privacy. The prohibition against sexual intercourse with a female minor, I.C. § 18–6101(1), is an attempt to prevent the sexual exploitation of persons deemed legally incapable of giving consent. Notwithstanding this deemed lack of consent in statutory rape, Stiffler contends that a reasonable mistake of fact as to the victim's age should be a defense because it would disprove any criminal intent to engage in non-consensual sexual activity.

The argument for the reasonable mistake defense is based upon I.C. §§ 18–114 and 18–201(1). Section 18–114 provides: "In every crime or public offense there must exist a union, or joint operation, of act and intent, or criminal negligence." Section 18–201(1) provides: "All persons are capable of committing crimes, except those ... [p]ersons who committed the act ... under an ignorance or mistake of fact which disproves any criminal intent." Stiffler contends that under section 18–114 criminal intent is a necessary element of statutory rape, which intent may be disproved under section 18–201(1) through evidence showing a reasonable mistake of fact. * * * He urges us to adopt the reasoning of *People v. Hernandez*, 61 Cal.2d 529, 39 Cal.Rptr. 361, 393 P.2d 673 (1964), which judicially recognized the reasonable mistake defense to statutory rape. * * *

We now examine the effect of sections 18–114 and 18–201(1) on the offense of statutory rape. The "intent" mentioned in section 18–114 is merely the knowing or conscious performance of an act, not an evil motive or criminal intent. A reasonable mistake of fact will be a defense only for those persons charged with an offense having criminal intent as an ingredient of the crime. Whether a criminal intent is a necessary element of an offense is a matter of statutory construction. Where such intent is not made an ingredient of an offense, the lack of criminal intent is immaterial.

Under I.C. § 18–6101(1), criminal intent is not a necessary element of statutory rape. The only elements the state must prove are: (1) the conscious performance of sexual intercourse, accomplished with (2) a female under the age of eighteen. Statutory rape is a strict liability offense. Therefore, it is immaterial whether an accused reasonably believes the victim is eighteen years of age or older. Accordingly, we hold that a reasonable mistake of fact as to the victim's age is no defense to statutory rape. * * *

The *Hernandez* Court judicially approved the defense based, in part, on the doubtful validity of a public policy against the defense because of

sexually active adolescents who may not need the law's protection. * * *

We do not find the reasoning in *Hernandez* to be compelling. We believe the public policy exception is better expressed, at least in Idaho, as a recognition that the accused's intent is immaterial to a charge of statutory rape. Furthermore, the Legislature is the proper forum for considering the merits of a "reasonable mistake" defense to statutory rape. * * * If the Legislature wanted to retain the defense, it could easily have done so. The absence of specific legislation on the matter is not an invitation to the courts to create a defense. * * *

We affirm the * * * judgment of conviction.

BURNETT, JUDGE, dissenting.

Rape is punishable by imprisonment for life. Today the majority holds that this serious felony has been committed when two persons engage in consensual intercourse and the male is reasonably mistaken in an honest belief that the female is eighteen years of age or older. To the majority, such a reasonable mistake of fact is irrelevant. I respectfully disagree.

The majority opinion invokes a policy of protecting young women from sexual exploitation. I emphatically support that policy. Indeed, the public policy of our state should be to protect all persons from sexual exploitation, regardless of age or gender. But today's case does not present a question of policy. It presents a question of statutory application.

Idaho Code § 18–114 provides that "[i]n *every* crime or public offense there must exist a union, or joint operation, of act and intent, or criminal negligence." Idaho Code § 18–201(1) further provides that no criminal responsibility shall attach to "[p]ersons who committed the act ... charged, under an ignorance or mistake of fact which disproves any criminal intent." These statutes are plain and unambiguous. They make no exception for rape. Neither does any subsection of the rape statute, I.C. § 18–6101, enunciate such an exception. Consequently, the crime of rape under I.C. § 18–6101(1) requires "a union ... of ... intent, or criminal negligence[,]" and the act of having sexual intercourse with a woman less than eighteen years old. A reasonable mistake of fact concerning the woman's age may "[disprove] any criminal intent" or criminal negligence.

Nevertheless, my colleagues refuse to recognize a defense based on reasonable mistake in a statutory rape case. * * * They suggest that if the Legislature had desired to establish a reasonable mistake defense, it could have done so at that time. This suggestion begs the underlying question of whether a reasonable mistake defense was already available under I.C. §§ 18–114 and 18–201(1). * * *

* * * The issue should be tendered to the jury upon a proper instruction. The jury should decide, in light of all the circumstances, whether the defendant's alleged mistake was subjectively honest and

objectively reasonable.[2] I have faith in the ability of jurors to make this determination. Today's majority, however, takes the issue away from Idaho juries.

My colleagues offer two additional rationales for their unfortunate decision. They contend that I.C. §§ 18–114 and 18–201(1) do not require criminal "intent" and that, regardless of these statutes, statutory rape is a "strict liability" offense. I am unable to accept either of these contentions.

On the question of intent, the majority declares that the Idaho statutes require only the "knowing or conscious performance of an act." Although there is some authority for this proposition, the better view, I submit, is that Idaho criminal law requires the union of an act and a culpable state of mind—a mens rea. It requires a criminal intent rather than the mere intent to do a particular act. * * *

On the question of "strict liability," I would simply note that the application of this doctrine in criminal law is ordinarily limited to statutes imposing mandatory duties in such areas as economic regulation and social welfare. Examples include statutes prescribing, or authorizing administrative agencies to prescribe, standards for job safety and pollution control. These statutes create new duties; they do not deal with intrinsically bad acts that have long been prohibited as felonies. Rape, including so-called "statutory rape," falls in the latter category. It is an intrinsically bad act condemned throughout history as a felony. Moreover, Idaho's rape statute, I.C. § 18–6101, has been held to establish a single felony which may take various forms depending on the age of the victim, the use of force or threats, and other factors. It is conceptually unsound to isolate one form of this unified felony and to characterize it as a crime of "strict liability," for which no criminal intent is required.

In the present case, I would allow the defendant to make his claim of a reasonable mistake regarding the age of the young woman with whom he had consensual intercourse. * * * If a jury accepted the defendant's claim, he would not be guilty of rape. However, he still might be found guilty of the lesser crime of fornication. I.C. § 18–6603.[a] Such a finding would achieve a rational correlation between crime and culpability. * * *

Notes and Questions

1. Most states treat statutory rape as a strict liability offense. The rule announced in *Hernandez* (discussed in *Stiffler*) is followed by few

2. To state the obvious, an issue of *reasonable* mistake is unlikely to arise unless the female is old enough, and mature enough, to appear eighteen years of age. In the instant case, for example, the magistrate who conducted the preliminary hearing expressed "surprise" at the victim's actual age. If Idaho's age of consent were lower than eighteen, as it is in many other states, the issue of reasonable mistake would arise less frequently.

a. "Any unmarried person who shall have intercourse with an unmarried person of the opposite sex shall be deemed guilty of fornication and, upon conviction thereof, shall be punished by a fine of not more than $300 or by imprisonment for not more than six months * * *."

jurisdictions. E.g., State v. Guest, 583 P.2d 836 (Alaska 1978); Perez v. State, 111 N.M. 160, 803 P.2d 249 (1990). Model Penal Code § 213.6(1) takes an intermediate position: when criminality for a sexual offense depends on the age of the victim, it imposes strict liability if the female is under the age of 10, but permits a defense of reasonable mistake where the critical age is above ten.

If the premise of *Stiffler* is correct—that statutory rape is a strict liability offense—then the court's conclusion that a reasonable mistake of fact will not exculpate the actor—is irrefutable: a crime that requires no *mens rea* has no element of culpability that can be negated by a mistake.

But, is the premise correct? Does the majority or the dissent have the better side of the argument regarding the meaning of Sections 18–114 and 18–201(1)? If the dissent is correct, why must the defendant's mistake even be reasonable? Doesn't an honest but *unreasonable* mistake regarding the female's age also disprove criminal intent, as in *Navarro* (p. 146 supra)?

2. *Statutory rape.*[b] Idaho's statutory rape provision is unusual in setting the age of valid consent at eighteen. Most modern statutes draw the line at age 16 or lower. The statute is typical, however, in its gender-specificity. Should it be an offense of equal severity for a female to have sexual intercourse with an underage male?

The Supreme Court has rejected a Fourteenth Amendment equal protection clause attack on California's gender-specific statutory rape law. Michael M. v. Superior Court, 450 U.S. 464, 101 S.Ct. 1200, 67 L.Ed.2d 437 (1981) (plurality opinion). The plurality concluded that states have a legitimate and strong interest in preventing teenage pregnancies, which interest justifies singling out females for protection. For a feminist analysis of statutory rape laws, see Frances Olsen, *Statutory Rape: A Feminist Critique of Rights Analysis,* 63 Tex.L.Rev. 387 (1984).

3. *The "moral wrong"/"legal wrong" doctrines.* In State v. Guest, 583 P.2d 836 (Alaska 1978), the defendant had sexual intercourse with an underage female whom he reasonably believed was above the age of consent. In adopting the minority view that a reasonable mistake of fact is a defense in a statutory rape prosecution, the court also rejected the argument urged upon it by the prosecutor that "where an offender is aware he is committing an act of fornication he therefore has sufficient criminal intent to justify a conviction for statutory rape because what was done would have been *unlawful* under the facts as he thought them to be." Id. at 839 (emphasis added).

Depending on what the prosecutor meant by the word "unlawful" in the preceding statement, he was asserting either the "moral wrong" or the "legal wrong" doctrine. Under the moral wrong doctrine, the term "unlawful," as used by the prosecutor, means "immoral." That is, under this view,

---

b. The term "statutory rape," although regularly used in judicial opinions and legal commentaries, is a misnomer. The offense—so-called because of an ancient English statute that prohibited unlawful intercourse with a female under the age of ten years—is old enough to be considered part of the common law of the United States. Rollin M. Perkins & Ronald N. Boyce, Criminal Law 198 (3d ed. 1982). In any case, rape in *all* forms (e.g., by force, fraud, or with an underage female) is now a statutory offense.

even if an actor's mistake of fact is reasonable (and, thus, no moral culpability can be found on the basis of the error), his intentional commission of an immoral act serves as the requisite blameworthiness to justify conviction (assuming, of course, that the *actus reus* of the offense was committed).

To apply the moral wrong doctrine, a court looks at the defendant's conduct through the accused's eyes, i.e., in *Guest,* this means that the defendant was having sexual relations with an unmarried female *above* the age of consent (because that is what he reasonably believed he was doing). If *that* conduct is considered immoral, the defendant must assume the risk that, unbeknownst to him, the attendant circumstances are not as he believes them to be and, therefore, that his conduct is not only immoral but also illegal, e.g., that the female is actually underage.

The legal wrong doctrine works in the same manner, except that the term "unlawful" means "illegal." Thus, if the defendant's conduct, based on the facts as he believes them to be, constitutes a criminal offense, he may be convicted of the greater offense of which he is factually guilty. For example, in *Guest,* if fornication is a lesser criminal offense than statutory rape, the defendant's intentional acts of fornication would justify his conviction of statutory rape. If fornication is not a criminal offense in the jurisdiction, however, the defendant would not be guilty of any offense.

Are these doctrines objectionable? How would *Stiffler* be handled under Model Penal Code § 2.04(2)?

4. *Problem.* *P* took an unmarried, 14–year–old, girl out of the possession and against the will of her parents, in violation of a statute that provided:

> Whosoever shall unlawfully take or cause to be taken an unmarried girl, being under the age of sixteen years, out of the possession and against the will of her father or mother * * * shall be guilty of a misdemeanor.

P reasonably believed that the female was eighteen years old. Under common law principles, is he guilty of the offense charged? Regina v. Prince, L.R. 2 Crim.Cas.Res. 154 (1875).

Suppose that *P* knew that the girl was under the age of sixteen, but he reasonably believed that she had no family. Would he be guilty of the offense?

5. *Problem.* In People v. Olsen, 36 Cal.3d 638, 205 Cal.Rptr. 492, 685 P.2d 52 (1984), *O* committed a lewd act upon *V,* a female of 13 years and 10 months. *O* believed that *V* was over the age of fourteen. He was prosecuted for violation of California Penal Code § 288, subdivision (a):

> Any person who shall willfully and lewdly commit any lewd or lascivious act * * * upon or with the body * * * of a child under the age of 14 years, with the intent of arousing * * * the * * * sexual desire of such person * * * shall be guilty of a felony and shall be imprisoned in the state prison for a term of three, six, or eight years * * *.

On the face of it, is this a strict liability offense, one of general intent, or is it a specific intent crime? Under common law principles, should *O* be acquitted on the basis of his mistake of fact?

6. *The "Morgan controversy."* Common law rape (as distinguished from "statutory rape") is generally regarded as a general intent offense. Therefore, the usual common law rule is that even if the *actus reus* of rape occurred—a male had sexual intercourse with a female, not his wife, without her consent—the man is not guilty of the offense if he reasonably believed that he had the victim's consent when the intercourse occurred. An unreasonable mistake of fact, however, does not exculpate the actor.

In view of this general rule, is there any principled way to explain Director of Public Prosecutions v. Morgan, [1976] App.Cas. 182, in which the House of Lords answered in the negative the question certified to it for consideration: "Whether in rape the defendant can properly be convicted notwithstanding that he in fact believed that the woman consented, if such a belief was not based on reasonable grounds?" At the time, Section 1 of the Sexual Offenses Act of 1956 provided that it was an offense "for a man to rape a woman." The word "rape" was not defined.

Morgan involved lurid facts. A husband invited three of his friends, fellow members of the Royal Air Force, to his home in order to have intercourse with his wife. According to the men, the husband falsely told them that his wife was "kinky" and could not "be turned on" except by the use of force. Therefore, with his assistance, they each had forcible nonconsensual intercourse with the victim. At their trial, the defendants asserted that, based on the husband's representations, they believed that the victim was feigning non-consent when she unsuccessfully fought off their advances.

Lord Cross of Chelsea explained why he believed that a negligent mistake of fact should exculpate a person in the defendants' circumstances:

> But, as I have said, Section 1 of the 1956 Act does not say that a man who has sexual intercourse with a woman who does not consent to it commits an offence; it says that a man who rapes a woman commits an offence. Rape is not a word in the use of which lawyers have a monopoly and the question to be answered in this case, as I see it, is whether according to the ordinary use of the English language a man can be said to have committed rape if he believed that the woman was consenting to the intercourse and would not have attempted to have it but for his belief, whatever his grounds for so believing. I do not think that he can. Rape, to my mind, imports at least indifference as to the woman's consent.

Lord Hailsham of St. Marylebone explained his position this way:

> The prohibited act in rape is to have intercourse without the victim's consent. The minimum mens rea or guilty mind in most common law offences, including rape, is the intention to do the prohibited act * * *.
>
> Once one has accepted, what seems to me to be abundantly clear, that the prohibited act in rape is non-consensual sexual intercourse, and that the guilty state of mind is an intention to commit it, it seems to me to follow as a matter of inexorable logic that there is no room either for a "defence" of honest belief or mistake, or of a defence of honest and reasonable belief and mistake. Either the prosecution proves that the accused had the requisite intent, or it does not.

In contrast, Lord Simon of Glaisdale would have answered the certified question in the affirmative:

> The answer to [the] question, in my view, depends on the * * * distinction between crimes of basic and of ulterior intent * * *. By "crimes of basic intent" I mean those crimes whose definition expresses (or, more often, implies) a mens rea which does not go beyond the actus reus. * * *

> On the other hand, there are crimes of ulterior intent—"ulterior" because the mens rea goes beyond contemplation of the actus reus. For example, in the crime of wounding with intent to cause grievous bodily harm, the actus reus is the wounding. The prosecution must prove a corresponding mens rea * * *, but the prosecution must go further: it must show that the accused foresaw that serious physical injury would probably be a consequence of his act * * *. The crime of wounding with intent to cause grievous bodily harm can be committed without any serious physical injury being caused to the victim. This is because there is no actus reus corresponding to the ulterior intent. * * *

> This brings me to the * * * question, namely whether rape is a crime of basic or ulterior intent. Does it involve an intent going beyond the actus reus? [English treatise authors] say No. I respectfully agree. * * * [B]ut I think there is also another reason. The policy of the law in this regard could well derive from its concern to hold a fair balance between victim and accused. * * * A respectable woman who has been ravished would hardly feel that she was vindicated by being told that her assailant must go unpunished because he believed, quite unreasonably, that she was consenting to sexual intercourse with him.

As a matter of *mens rea* doctrine, who analyzed the issue correctly, Lords Cross and Hailsham, on the one hand, or Lord Simon, on the other?

In response to negative public reaction to *Morgan,* the Parliament enacted the Sexual Offences (Amendment) Act of 1976, which provided in part:

> A man commits rape if (a) he has unlawful sexual intercourse with a woman who at the time of the intercourse does not consent to it; and (b) at that time he knows that she does not consent to the intercourse or he is reckless as to whether she consents to it.

How would the Model Penal Code resolve the *Morgan* controversy under its definition of rape? Consider the conjunction of Sections 213.1(1) and 2.04.

E. MISTAKE OR IGNORANCE OF LAW

1. MISTAKE OF LAW

PEOPLE v. MARRERO

Court of Appeals of New York, 1987.
69 N.Y.2d 382, 515 N.Y.S.2d 212, 507 N.E.2d 1068.

BELLACOSA, JUDGE. * * *

[Marrero, a federal corrections officer, was arrested in a social club for unlicensed possession of a loaded .38 caliber automatic pistol, in violation of New York Penal Law § 265.02.

Prior to trial, Marrero moved to dismiss his indictment on the ground that, under New York Penal Law § 265.20(a)(1), peace officers were exempt from criminal liability under the firearm possession statute. The term "peace officer," as defined in Criminal Procedure Law (CPL) §§ 1.20 and 2.10, included "correction officers of any state correctional facility or of any penal correctional institution." Marrero argued that as a federal corrections officer, he was a "peace officer" by virtue of the statutory language, "any penal correctional institution."

The trial judge agreed with Marrero's interpretation of the law, and granted the motion to dismiss the indictment. The state appealed. By a 3–2 vote, an appellate court reversed the trial court's ruling—holding that federal correctional officers were not peace officers within the meaning of Penal Law § 265.20—and reinstated the indictment. At his subsequent trial, Marrero was convicted of violation of Penal Law § 265.02, from which this appeal followed.]

On the trial of the case, the court rejected the defendant's argument that his personal misunderstanding of the statutory definition of a peace officer is enough to excuse him from criminal liability under New York's mistake of law statute (Penal Law § 15.20). The court refused to charge the jury on this issue and defendant was convicted of criminal possession of a weapon in the third degree. We affirm the Appellate Division order upholding the conviction. * * *

The starting point for our analysis is the New York mistake statute as an outgrowth of the dogmatic common-law maxim that ignorance of the law is no excuse. The central issue is whether defendant's personal misreading or misunderstanding of a statute may excuse criminal conduct in the circumstances of this case.

The common-law rule on mistake of law was clearly articulated in *Gardner v. People,* (62 N.Y. 299). In *Gardner,* the defendants misread a statute and mistakenly believed that their conduct was legal. The court insisted, however, that the "mistake of law" did not relieve the defendants of criminal liability. * * *

* * * This is to be contrasted with *People v. Weiss,* 276 N.Y. 384, 12 N.E.2d 514 where, in a kidnapping case, the trial court precluded testimony that the defendants acted with the honest belief that seizing and confining the child was done with "authority of law." We held it was error to exclude such testimony since a good-faith belief in the legality of the conduct would negate an express and necessary element of the crime of kidnapping, i.e., intent, without authority of law, to confine or imprison another.[c] Subject to the mistake statute, the instant case, of course, falls within the *Gardner* rationale because the weapons posses-

---

c. *Weiss* is considered in greater detail in Note 3 infra.

sion statute violated by this defendant imposes liability irrespective of one's intent.

The desirability of the *Gardner* -type outcome, which was to encourage the societal benefit of individuals' knowledge of and respect for the law, is underscored by Justice Holmes' statement: "It is no doubt true that there are many cases in which the criminal could not have known that he was breaking the law, but to admit the excuse at all would be to encourage ignorance where the law-maker has determined to make men know and obey, and justice to the individual is rightly outweighed by the larger interests on the other side of the scales" (Holmes, The Common Law, at 48 [1881]).

The revisors of New York's Penal Law intended no fundamental departure from this common-law rule in Penal Law § 15.20, which provides in pertinent part:

"§ 15.20. *Effect of ignorance or mistake upon liability.*

* * *

"2. A person is not relieved of criminal liability for conduct because he engages in such conduct under a mistaken belief that it does not, as a matter of law, constitute an offense, unless such mistaken belief is founded upon an official statement of the law contained in (a) a statute or other enactment * * * (d) an interpretation of the statute or law relating to the offense, officially made or issued by a public servant, agency, or body legally charged or empowered with the responsibility or privilege of administering, enforcing or interpreting such statute or law." * * *

The defendant claims as a first prong of his defense that he is entitled to raise the defense of mistake of law under section 15.20(2)(a) because his mistaken belief that his conduct was legal was founded upon an official statement of the law contained in the statute itself. Defendant argues that his mistaken interpretation of the statute was reasonable in view of the alleged ambiguous wording of the peace officer exemption statute, and that his "reasonable" interpretation of an "official statement" is enough to satisfy the requirements of subdivision (2)(a). * * *

The prosecution * * * counters defendant's argument by asserting that one cannot claim the protection of mistake of law under section 15.20(2)(a) simply by misconstruing the meaning of a statute but must instead establish that the statute relied on actually permitted the conduct in question and was only later found to be erroneous. To buttress that argument, the People analogize New York's official statement defense to the approach taken by the Model Penal Code (MPC). Section 2.04 of the MPC provides:

"Section 2.04. *Ignorance or Mistake.*

* * *

"(3) A belief that conduct does not legally constitute an offense is a defense to a prosecution for that offense based upon such conduct when * * * (b) he acts in reasonable reliance upon an official statement of the law, *afterward determined to be invalid or erroneous,* contained in (i) a statute or other enactment" (emphasis added).

Although the drafters of the New York statute did not adopt the precise language of the Model Penal Code provision with the emphasized clause, it is evident and has long been believed that the Legislature intended the New York statute to be similarly construed. In fact, the legislative history of section 15.20 is replete with references to the influence of the Model Penal Code provision * * *

It was early recognized that the "official statement" mistake of law defense was a statutory protection against prosecution based on reliance of a statute that did *in fact* authorize certain conduct. "It seems obvious that society must rely on some statement of the law, and that conduct which *is in fact* 'authorized' * * * should not be subsequently condemned. The threat of punishment under these circumstances can have no deterrent effect unless the actor doubts the validity of the official pronouncement—*a questioning of authority that is itself undesirable*" (Note, *Proposed Penal Law of New York,* 64 Colum.L.Rev. 1469, 1486 [emphasis added]). While providing a narrow escape hatch, the idea was simultaneously to encourage the public to read and rely on official statements of the law, not to have individuals conveniently and personally question the validity and interpretation of the law and act on that basis. If later the statute was invalidated, one who mistakenly acted in reliance on the authorizing statute would be relieved of criminal liability. That makes sense and is fair. To go further does not make sense and would create a legal chaos based on individual selectivity.

In the case before us, the underlying statute never *in fact authorized* the defendant's conduct; the defendant only thought that the statutory exemptions permitted his conduct when, in fact, the primary statute clearly forbade his conduct. * * *

We recognize that some legal scholars urge that the mistake of law defense should be available more broadly where a defendant misinterprets a potentially ambiguous statute not previously clarified by judicial decision and reasonably believes in good faith that the acts were legal. * * *

We conclude that the better and correctly construed view is that the defense should not be recognized, except where specific intent is an element of the offense or where the misrelied-upon law has later been properly adjudicated as wrong. Any broader view fosters lawlessness. * * *

* * * If defendant's argument were accepted, the exception would swallow the rule. Mistakes about the law would be encouraged, rather than respect for and adherence to law. There would be an infinite number of mistake of law defenses which could be devised from a good-

faith, perhaps reasonable but mistaken, interpretation of criminal statutes, many of which are concededly complex. Even more troublesome are the opportunities for wrong-minded individuals to contrive in bad faith solely to get an exculpatory notion before the jury. These are not in terrorem arguments disrespectful of appropriate adjudicative procedures; rather, they are the realistic and practical consequences were the dissenters' views to prevail. Our holding comports with a statutory scheme which was not designed to allow false and diversionary stratagems to be provided for many more cases than the statutes contemplated. This would not serve the ends of justice but rather would serve game playing and evasion from properly imposed criminal responsibility.

Accordingly, the order of the Appellate Division should be affirmed.

HANCOCK, JUDGE (dissenting). * * *

The basic difference which divides the court may be simply put. Suppose the case of a man who has committed an act which is criminal not because it is inherently wrong or immoral but solely because it violates a criminal statute. He has committed the act in complete good faith under the mistaken but entirely reasonable assumption that the act does not constitute an offense because it is permitted by the wording of the statute. Does the law require that this man be punished? The majority says that it does and holds that (1) Penal Law § 15.20(2)(a) must be construed so that the man is precluded from offering a defense based on his mistake of law and (2) such construction is compelled by prevailing considerations of public policy and criminal jurisprudence. We take issue with the majority on both propositions.

There can be no question that under the view that the purpose of the criminal justice system is to punish blameworthiness or "choosing freely to do wrong," our supposed man who has acted innocently and without any intent to do wrong should not be punished. * * * Since he has not knowingly committed a wrong there can be no reason for society to exact retribution. Because the man is law-abiding and would not have acted but for his mistaken assumption as to the law, there is no need for punishment to deter him from further unlawful conduct. Traditionally, however, under the ancient rule of Anglo–American common law that ignorance or mistake of law is no excuse, our supposed man would be punished.

The maxim *"ignorantia legis neminem excusat"* finds its roots in Medieval law when the "actor's intent was irrelevant since the law punished the *act itself.*" * * * Although the common law has gradually evolved from its origins in Anglo–Germanic tribal law (adding the element of intent *[mens rea]* and recognizing defenses based on the actor's mental state * * *) the dogmatic rule that ignorance or mistake of law is no excuse has remained unaltered. Various justifications have been offered for the rule, but all are frankly pragmatic and utilitarian— preferring the interests of society (e.g., in deterring criminal conduct, fostering orderly judicial administration, and preserving the primacy of the rule of law) to the interest of the individual in being free from punishment except for intentionally engaging in conduct which he knows is criminal.

Today there is widespread criticism of the common-law rule mandating categorical preclusion of the mistake of law defense. The utilitarian arguments for retaining the rule have been drawn into serious question; but the fundamental objection is that it is simply wrong to punish someone who, in good-faith reliance on the wording of a statute, believed that what he was doing was lawful. It is contrary to "the notion that punishment should be conditioned on a showing of subjective moral blameworthiness." This basic objection to the maxim *"ignorantia legis neminem excusat"* may have had less force in ancient times when most crimes consisted of acts which by their very nature were recognized as evil *(malum in se)*. In modern times, however, with the profusion of legislation making otherwise lawful conduct criminal *(malum prohibitum)*, the "common law fiction that every man is presumed to know the law has become indefensible in fact or logic."

With this background we proceed to a discussion of our disagreement with the majority's construction of Penal Law § 15.20(2)(a) and the policy and jurisprudential arguments made in support of that construction.   * * *

It is difficult to imagine a case more squarely within the wording of Penal Law § 15.20(2)(a) or one more fitted to what appears clearly to be the intended purpose of the statute than the one before us.   * * *

Defendant's mistaken belief that, as a Federal corrections officer, he could legally carry a loaded weapon without a license was based on the express exemption from criminal liability under Penal Law § 265.02 accorded * * * to "peace officers" as defined in the Criminal Procedure Law and on his reading of the statutory definition for "peace officer" * * * as meaning a correction officer "of *any* penal correctional institution" (emphasis added), including an institution not operated by New York State. Thus, he concluded erroneously that, as a corrections officer in a Federal prison, he was a "peace officer" and, as such, exempt by the express terms of Penal Law § 265.–20(a)(1)(a). This mistaken belief, based in good faith on the statute defining "peace officer," is, defendant contends, the precise sort of "mistaken belief * * * founded upon an official statement of the law contained in * * * a statute or other enactment" which gives rise to a mistake of law defense under Penal Law § 15.20(2)(a). He points out, of course, that when he acted in reliance on his belief he had no way of foreseeing that a court would eventually resolve the question of the statute's meaning against him and rule that his belief had been mistaken, as three of the five-member panel at the Appellate Division ultimately did in the first appeal.

The majority, however, has accepted the People's argument that to have a defense under Penal Law § 15.20(2)(a) "a defendant must show that the statute *permitted his conduct*, not merely that he believed it did."   * * *

Nothing in the statutory language suggests the interpretation urged by the People and adopted by the majority: that Penal Law § 15.20(2)(a) is available to a defendant *not* when he has mistakenly read a statute *but only* when he has correctly read and relied on a statute which is later invalidated.   Such a construction contravenes the general rule that penal statutes should be construed against the State and in favor of the accused * * *.

More importantly, the construction leads to an anomaly: only a defendant who is *not mistaken* about the law when he acts has a mistake of law defense.   * * * Such construction is obviously illogical; it strips the statute of the very effect intended by the Legislature in adopting the mistake of law defense.   The statute is of no benefit to a defendant who has proceeded in good faith on an erroneous but concededly reasonable interpretation of a statute, as defendant presumably has.   * * *

* * * It is self-evident that in enacting Penal Law §. 15.20(2) as part of the revision and modernization of the Penal Law the Legislature intended to effect a needed reform by abolishing what had long been considered the unjust archaic common-law rule totally prohibiting mistake of law as a defense.   * * *

The majority construes the statute, however, so as to rule out *any* defense based on mistake of law.   In so doing, it defeats the only possible purpose for the statute's enactment and resurrects the very rule which the Legislature rejected in enacting Penal Law § 15.20(2)(a) as part of its modernization and reform of the Penal Law.   * * *

Instead, the majority bases its decision on an analogous provision in the Model Penal Code and concludes that despite its totally different wording and meaning Penal Law § 15.20(2)(a) should be read as if it were Model Penal Code § 2.04(3)(b)(i).   But New York in revising the Penal Law did not adopt the Model Penal Code.   * * * New York followed parts of the Model Penal Code provisions and rejected others. * * *

While Penal Law § 15.20(2) and Model Penal Code § 2.04 are alike in their rejection of the strict common-law rule, they are not alike in wording and differ significantly in substance.   * * *

Thus, the precise phrase in the Model Penal Code limiting the defense under section 2.04(3)(b)(i) to reliance on a statute "afterward determined to be invalid or erroneous" which, if present, would support the majority's narrow construction of the New York statute, is omitted from Penal Law § 15.20(2)(a).   How the Legislature can be assumed to have enacted the very language which it has specifically rejected is not explained.   * * *

Any fair reading of the majority opinion, we submit, demonstrates that the decision to reject a mistake of law defense is based on considerations of public policy and on the conviction that such a defense would be bad, rather than on an analysis of CPL 15.20(2)(a) under the usual principles of statutory construction.   * * *

These * * * are the very considerations which have been consistently offered as justifications for the maxim *"ignorantia legis."* That these justifications are unabashedly utilitarian cannot be questioned. * * * [T]he fact remains that the Legislature in abandoning the strict *"ignorantia legis"* maxim must be deemed to have rejected them.

* * * [A] statute which recognizes a defense based on a man's good-faith mistaken belief founded on a well-grounded interpretation of an official statement of the law contained in a statute is a just law. The law embodies the ideal of contemporary criminal jurisprudence "that punishment should be conditioned on a showing of subjective moral blameworthiness." * * *

If defendant's offer of proof is true, his is not the case of a "free agent confronted with a choice between doing right and doing wrong and choosing freely to do wrong." He carried the gun in the good-faith belief that, as a Federal corrections officer, it was lawful for him to do so under the words of the statute. * * *

We do not believe that permitting a defense in this case will produce the grievous consequences the majority predicts. The unusual facts of this case seem unlikely to be repeated. Indeed, although the majority foresees "an infinite number of mistake of law defenses," New Jersey, which adopted a more liberal mistake of law statute in 1978, has apparently experienced no such adversity (no case construing that law is mentioned in the most recent annotation of the statute). Nor is there any reason to believe that courts will have more difficulty separating valid claims from "diversionary stratagem[s]" in making preliminary legal determinations as to the validity of the mistake of law defense than of justification or any other defense. * * *

There should be a reversal and defendant should have a new trial in which he is permitted to assert a defense of mistake of law under Penal Law § 15.20(2)(a).

Notes and Questions

1. Who has the better side of the arguments regarding the meaning of Section 15.20(2), New York's mistake-of-law statute? Who has the better side of the policy arguments? According to the dissent, is a good faith, but *unreasonable,* mistake of law a defense? If so, is such a position defensible? If a mistake of law must be reasonable, where is that requirement found in the statute?

2. If a person may not claim mistake-of-law based on her personal (mis)reading of a statute, on what or on whom may she rely for an official interpretation of the law? What would the results be in the following cases under the Model Penal Code?

A. *A* was convicted of distributing political leaflets outside the gate of a military base. On appeal, a federal circuit court overturned the conviction on the ground that the statute violated the First Amendment (Case 1). The government petitioned the Supreme Court to hear its appeal of the case. Meanwhile, *A* leafletted again, once before the government petitioned the

Supreme Court, and once after, but before the Supreme Court decided whether to hear the appeal. *A* was arrested again (Case 2). Subsequently, the Supreme Court heard the appeal in Case 1, reversed the circuit court, and upheld *A*'s conviction. In Case 2, may *A* defend his actions on the basis of mistake of law? United States v. Albertini, 830 F.2d 985 (9th Cir.1987).

B. *O,* a commercial fisherman opposed to a new law requiring him to obtain a permit to possess fish for commercial purposes, protested the statute by openly fishing without a permit and inviting arrest. Upon arrest and conviction, *O* sought and obtained post-conviction relief in the form of a ruling by a trial judge declaring the permit law unconstitutional and throwing out *O* 's conviction. The government applied to the state supreme court for an emergency stay of the trial judge's ruling, which was granted pending appeal. Thereafter, *O* went fishing again without a permit and was arrested. A few days later the state supreme court reversed the trial judge's ruling and upheld the statute. May *O* claim mistake of law? Ostrosky v. State of Alaska, 913 F.2d 590 (9th Cir.1990).

C. *H,* a minister, was convicted of violation of a statute making it unlawful to erect or maintain any sign intended to aid in the solicitation or performance of marriages. On appeal, *H* argued that his conviction was invalid because the court refused to permit him to introduce evidence that he did not erect the signs until the State's Attorney (the prosecutor) advised him that his intended actions were lawful. Should *H* have been permitted to introduce this evidence? Hopkins v. State, 193 Md. 489, 69 A.2d 456 (1949).

D. Prior to obtaining a divorce in Arkansas and moving to Delaware and remarrying, *L* hired a reputable divorce attorney from Delaware who advised him that an Arkansas divorce was "just as good as if obtained in Delaware." Based on this advice, *L* obtained a divorce in Arkansas from his first wife, and then remarried in Delaware, where he and his second wife cohabited. The attorney's advice regarding Delaware's acceptance of the Arkansas divorce proved to be incorrect, and *L* was prosecuted in Delaware for bigamy (a strict liability offense). May *L* validly assert a mistake-of-law defense? See Long v. State, 44 Del. 262, 65 A.2d 489 (1949).

3. If ignorance of the law is not an excuse, why did the Court of Appeal in *People v. Weiss,* cited in *Marrero,* permit the defendant there to claim a good faith (but erroneous) belief in the legality of his conduct? In *Weiss, W* was charged under the following statute:

> A person who wilfully: 1. seizes, confines, inveigles, or kidnaps another, with intent to cause him, without authority of law, to be confined or imprisoned within this state * * * against his will * * * is guilty of kidnapping * * *.

At trial, *W* was not permitted to introduce evidence that *X* requested his assistance in arresting *V,* a suspect in a criminal investigation. In order to ensure *W* of his authority to assist in the seizure, *X* "deputized" *W* by handing him a state Secret Service badge. In actuality, these actions did not provide *W* with legal authority to assist in the arrest.

The Court of Appeals reversed *W* 's conviction on the ground that he was entitled to have the jury consider his claim that he believed, *even unreasonably,* that he had legal authority to assist in the seizure. How does this mistake claim differ in character from that in *Marrero* ?

CHEEK v. UNITED STATES

Supreme Court of the United States, 1991.
498 U.S. 192, 111 S.Ct. 604, 112 L.Ed.2d 617.

JUSTICE WHITE delivered the opinion of the Court.

Title 26, § 7201 of the United States Code provides that any person "who willfully attempts in any manner to evade or defeat any tax imposed by this title or the payment thereof" shall be guilty of a felony. Under 26 U.S.C. § 7203, "[a]ny person required under this title ... or by regulations made under authority thereof to make a return ... who willfully fails to ... make such return" shall be guilty of a misdemeanor. This case turns on the meaning of the word "willfully" as used in §§ 7201 and 7203.

I

Petitioner John L. Cheek has been a pilot for American Airlines since 1973. He filed federal income tax returns through 1979 but thereafter ceased to file returns. He also claimed an increasing number of withholding allowances—eventually claiming 60 allowances by mid–1980—and for the years 1981 to 1984 indicated on his W–4 forms that he was exempt from federal income taxes. In 1983, petitioner unsuccessfully sought a refund of all tax withheld by his employer in 1982. Petitioner's income during this period at all times far exceeded the minimum necessary to trigger the statutory filing requirement.

As a result of his activities, petitioner was indicted for 10 violations of federal law. He was charged with six counts of willfully failing to file a federal income tax return for the years 1980, 1981, and 1983 through 1986, in violation of 26 U.S.C. § 7203. He was further charged with three counts of willfully attempting to evade his income taxes for the years 1980, 1981, and 1983 in violation of 26 U.S.C. § 7201. In those years, American Airlines withheld substantially less than the amount of tax petitioner owed because of the numerous allowances and exempt status he claimed on his W–4 forms. The tax offenses with which petitioner was charged are specific intent crimes that require the defendant to have acted willfully.

At trial, the evidence established that between 1982 and 1986, petitioner was involved in at least four civil cases that challenged various aspects of the federal income tax system. In all four of those cases, the plaintiffs were informed by the courts that many of their arguments, including that they were not taxpayers within the meaning of the tax laws, that wages are not income, that the Sixteenth Amendment does not authorize the imposition of an income tax on individuals, and that the Sixteenth Amendment is unenforceable, were frivolous or had been repeatedly rejected by the courts. During this time period, petitioner also attended at least two criminal trials of persons charged with tax offenses. In addition, there was evidence that in 1980 or 1981 an attorney had advised Cheek that the courts had rejected as frivolous the claim that wages are not income.

Cheek represented himself at trial and testified in his defense. He admitted that he had not filed personal income tax returns during the years in question. He testified that as early as 1978, he had begun attending seminars sponsored by, and following the advice of, a group that believes, among other things, that the federal tax system is unconstitutional. Some of the speakers at these meetings were lawyers who purported to give professional opinions about the invalidity of the federal income tax laws. Cheek produced a letter from an attorney stating that the Sixteenth Amendment did not authorize a tax on wages and salaries but only on gain or profit. Petitioner's defense was that, based on the indoctrination he received from this group and from his own study, he sincerely believed that the tax laws were being unconstitutionally enforced and that his actions during the 1980–1986 period were lawful. He therefore argued that he had acted without the willfulness required for conviction of the various offenses with which he was charged.

In the course of its instructions, the trial court advised the jury that to prove "willfulness" the Government must prove the voluntary and intentional violation of a known legal duty, a burden that could not be proved by showing mistake, ignorance, or negligence. The court further advised the jury that an objectively reasonable good-faith misunderstanding of the law would negate willfulness but mere disagreement with the law would not. The court described Cheek's beliefs about the income tax system and instructed the jury that if it found that Cheek "honestly and reasonably believed that he was not required to pay income taxes or to file tax returns," a not guilty verdict should be returned. * * *

At the end of the first day of deliberation, the jury sent out [a] note saying that it * * * could not reach a verdict because " '[w]e are divided on the issue as to if Mr. Cheek honestly & reasonably believed that he was not required to pay income tax.' " When the jury resumed its deliberations, the District Judge gave the jury an additional instruction. This instruction stated in part that "[a]n honest but unreasonable belief is not a defense and does not negate willfulness." * * * Approximately two hours later, the jury returned a verdict finding petitioner guilty on all counts.

Petitioner appealed his convictions, arguing that the District Court erred by instructing the jury that only an objectively reasonable misunderstanding of the law negates the statutory willfulness requirement. The United States Court of Appeals for the Seventh Circuit rejected that contention and affirmed the convictions. * * *

II

The general rule that ignorance of the law or a mistake of law is no defense to criminal prosecution is deeply rooted in the American legal system. Based on the notion that the law is definite and knowable, the common law presumed that every person knew the law. This common-law rule has been applied by the Court in numerous cases construing criminal statutes.

The proliferation of statutes and regulations has sometimes made it difficult for the average citizen to know and comprehend the extent of the duties and obligations imposed by the tax laws. Congress has accordingly softened the impact of the common-law presumption by making specific intent to violate the law an element of certain federal criminal tax offenses. Thus, the Court almost 60 years ago interpreted the statutory term "willfully" as used in the federal criminal tax statutes as carving out an exception to the traditional rule. This special treatment of criminal tax offenses is largely due to the complexity of the tax laws. In *United States v. Murdock,* 290 U.S. 389, 54 S.Ct. 223, 78 L.Ed. 381 (1933), the Court recognized that:

> "Congress did not intend that a person, by reason of a bona fide misunderstanding as to his liability for the tax, as to his duty to make a return, or as to the adequacy of the records he maintained, should become a criminal by his mere failure to measure up to the prescribed standard of conduct."

The Court held that the defendant was entitled to an instruction with respect to whether he acted in good faith based on his actual belief. In *Murdock,* the Court interpreted the term "willfully" as used in the criminal tax statutes generally to mean "an act done with a bad purpose," or with "an evil motive."

Subsequent decisions have refined this proposition. In *United States v. Bishop,* 412 U.S. 346, 93 S.Ct. 2008, 36 L.Ed.2d 941 (1973), we described the term "willfully" as connoting "a voluntary, intentional violation of a known legal duty," and did so with specific reference to the "bad faith or evil intent" language employed in *Murdock.* * * *

* * * Taken together, [these cases] conclusively establish that the standard for the statutory willfulness requirement is the "voluntary, intentional violation of a known legal duty."

* * *

III

A

Willfulness, as construed by our prior decisions in criminal tax cases, requires the Government to prove that the law imposed a duty on the defendant, that the defendant knew of this duty, and that he voluntarily and intentionally violated that duty. We deal first with the case where the issue is whether the defendant knew of the duty purportedly imposed by the provision of the statute or regulation he is accused of violating, a case in which there is no claim that the provision at issue is invalid. In such a case, if the Government proves actual knowledge of the pertinent legal duty, the prosecution, without more, has satisfied the knowledge component of the willfulness requirement. But carrying this burden requires negating a defendant's claim of ignorance of the law or a claim that because of a misunderstanding of the law, he had a good-faith belief that he was not violating any of the provisions of the tax laws. This is so because one cannot be aware that the law imposes a duty upon him and yet be ignorant of it, misunderstand the law, or believe that the duty does not exist. In the end, the issue is whether, based on all the evidence, the Government has proved that the defendant was aware of the duty at issue, which cannot be true if the jury credits a good-faith misunderstanding and belief submission, whether or not the claimed belief or misunderstanding is objectively reasonable.

In this case, if Cheek asserted that he truly believed that the Internal Revenue Code did not purport to treat wages as income, and the jury believed him, the Government would not have carried its burden to prove willfulness, however unreasonable a court might deem such a belief. Of course, in deciding whether to credit Cheek's good-faith belief claim, the jury would be free to consider any admissible evidence from any source showing that Cheek was aware of his duty to file a return and to treat wages as income, including evidence showing his awareness of the relevant provisions of the Code or regulations, of court decisions rejecting his interpretation of the tax law, of authoritative rulings of the Internal Revenue Service, or of any contents of the personal income tax return forms and accompanying instructions that made it plain that wages should be returned as income.

We thus disagree with the Court of Appeals' requirement that a claimed good-faith belief must be objectively reasonable if it is to be considered as possibly negating the Government's evidence purporting to show a defendant's awareness of the legal duty at issue. * * *

B

Cheek asserted in the trial court that he should be acquitted because he believed in good faith that the income tax law is unconstitutional as applied to him and thus could not legally impose any duty upon him of which he should have been aware. Such a submission is unsound, not because Cheek's constitutional arguments are not objectively reasonable or frivolous, which they surely are, but because the *Murdock* * * * line of cases does not support such a position. Those cases construed the willfulness requirement in the criminal provisions of the Internal Revenue Code to require proof of knowledge of the law. This was because in "our complex tax system, uncertainty often arises even among taxpayers who earnestly wish to follow the law" and "[i]t is not the purpose of the law to penalize frank difference of opinion or innocent errors made despite the exercise of reasonable care."

Claims that some of the provisions of the tax code are unconstitutional are submissions of a different order. They do not arise from innocent mistakes caused by the complexity of the Internal Revenue Code. Rather, they reveal full knowledge of the provisions at issue and a studied conclusion, however wrong, that those provisions are invalid and unenforceable. Thus in this case, Cheek paid his taxes for years, but after attending various seminars and based on his own study, he concluded that the income tax laws could not constitutionally require him to pay a tax.

We do not believe that Congress contemplated that such a taxpayer, without risking criminal prosecution, could ignore the duties imposed upon him by the Internal Revenue Code and refuse to utilize the mechanisms provided by Congress to present his claims of invalidity to the courts and to abide by their decisions. * * *

We thus hold that in a case like this, a defendant's views about the validity of the tax statutes are irrelevant to the issue of willfulness, need not be heard by the jury, and if they are, an instruction to disregard them would be proper. For this purpose, it makes no difference whether the claims of invalidity are frivolous or have substance. It was therefore not error in this case for the District Judge to instruct the jury not to consider Cheek's claims that the tax laws were unconstitutional. * * *

JUSTICE BLACKMUN, with whom JUSTICE MARSHALL joins, dissenting.

It seems to me that we are concerned in this case not with "the complexity of the tax laws," but with the income tax law in its most elementary and basic aspect: Is a wage earner a taxpayer and are wages income?

The Court acknowledges that the conclusively established standard for willfulness under the applicable statutes is the "voluntary, intentional violation of a known legal duty." That being so, it is incomprehensible to me how, in this day, more than 70 years after the institution of our present federal income tax system with the passage of the Revenue Act of 1913, any taxpayer of competent mentality can assert as his defense to charges of statutory willfulness the proposition that the wage he receives for his labor is not income, irrespective of a cult that says otherwise and advises the gullible to resist income tax collections. One might note in passing that this particular taxpayer, after all, was a licensed pilot for one of our major commercial airlines; he presumably was a person of at least minimum intellectual competence.

The District Court's instruction that an objectively reasonable and good faith misunderstanding of the law negates willfulness lends further, rather than less, protection to this defendant, for it added an additional hurdle for the prosecution to overcome. Petitioner should be grateful for this further protection, rather than be opposed to it.

This Court's opinion today, I fear, will encourage taxpayers to cling to frivolous views of the law in the hope of convincing a jury of their sincerity. If that ensues, I suspect we have gone beyond the limits of common sense. * * *

Notes and Questions

1. In what way is the claim of mistake of law raised in *Cheek* different in character from that in *Marrero* (p. 156, supra)? How is it similar in character to the mistake raised in *Weiss* (Note 3, p. 164 supra)?

In light of *Cheek*, reconsider *Weiss:* Was the case rightly decided?

2. Is Justice White correct in refusing to permit Cheek to raise a mistake-of-law claim relating to the constitutionality of the income tax laws? Did Cheek "intentionally violate a known legal duty," i.e., act wilfully, if he believed that the statute that created the duty to pay taxes is unconstitutional?

2. IGNORANCE OF LAW

LAMBERT v. CALIFORNIA

Supreme Court of the United States, 1957.
355 U.S. 225, 78 S.Ct. 240, 2 L.Ed.2d 228.

MR. JUSTICE DOUGLAS delivered the opinion of the Court.

Section 52.38(a) of the Los Angeles Municipal Code defines "convicted person" as follows:

"Any person who, subsequent to January 1, 1921, has been or hereafter is convicted of an offense punishable as a felony in the State of California, or who has been or who is hereafter convicted of any offense in any place other than the State of California, which offense, if committed in the State of California, would have been punishable as a felony."

Section 52.39 provides that it shall be unlawful for "any convicted person" to be or remain in Los Angeles for a period of more than five days without registering; it requires any person having a place of abode outside the city to register if he comes into the city on five occasions or more during a 30–day period; and it prescribes the information to be furnished the Chief of Police on registering.

Section 52.43(b) makes the failure to register a continuing offense, each day's failure constituting a separate offense.

Appellant, arrested on suspicion of another offense, was charged with a violation of this registration law. The evidence showed that she had been at the time of her arrest a resident of Los Angeles for over seven years. Within that period she had been convicted in Los Angeles of the crime of forgery, an offense which California punishes as a felony. Though convicted of a crime punishable as a felony, she had not at the time of her arrest registered under the Municipal Code. At the trial, appellant asserted that § 52.39 of the Code denies her due process of law * * * under the Federal Constitution * * *. The trial court denied this objection. The case was tried to a jury which found appellant guilty. The court fined her $250 and placed her on probation for three years. * * * [W]e now hold that the registration provisions of the Code as sought to be applied here violate the Due Process requirement of the Fourteenth Amendment.

The registration provision, carrying criminal penalties, applies if a person has been convicted "of an offense punishable as a felony in the State of California" or, in case he has been convicted in another State, if the offense "would have been punishable as a felony" had it been committed in California. No element of willfulness is by terms included in the ordinance nor read into it by the California court as a condition necessary for a conviction.

We must assume that appellant had no actual knowledge of the requirement that she register under this ordinance, as she offered proof of this defense which was refused. The question is whether a registration act of this character violates due process where it is applied to a person who has no actual knowledge of his duty to register, and where no showing is made of the probability of such knowledge.

We do not go with Blackstone in saying that "a vicious will" is necessary to constitute a crime, for conduct alone without regard to the intent of the doer is often sufficient. There is wide latitude in the lawmakers to declare an offense and to exclude elements of knowledge and diligence from its definition. But we deal here with conduct that is wholly passive—mere failure to register. It is unlike the commission of acts, or the failure to act under circumstances that should alert the doer to the consequences of his deed. The rule that "ignorance of the law will not excuse" is deep in our law * * *. On the other hand, due process places some limits on its exercise. Engrained in our concept of due process is the requirement of notice. Notice is required in a myriad of situations where a penalty or forfeiture might be suffered for mere failure to act. Recent cases illustrating the point * * * involved only property interests in civil litigation. But the principle is equally appropriate where a person, wholly passive and unaware of any wrongdoing, is brought to the bar of justice for condemnation in a criminal case.

Registration laws are common and their range is wide. Many such laws are akin to licensing statutes in that they pertain to the regulation of business activities. But the present ordinance is entirely different. Violation of its provisions is unaccompanied by any activity whatever, mere presence in the city being the test. Moreover, circumstances which might move one to inquire as to the necessity of registration are completely lacking. At most the ordinance is but a law enforcement technique designed for the convenience of law enforcement agencies through which a list of the names and addresses of felons then residing in a given community is compiled. * * * Nevertheless, this appellant on first becoming aware of her duty to register was given no opportunity to comply with the law and avoid its penalty, even though her default was entirely innocent. She could but suffer the consequences of the ordinance, namely, conviction with the imposition of heavy criminal penalties thereunder. We believe that actual knowledge of the duty to register or proof of the probability of such knowledge and subsequent failure to comply are necessary before a conviction under the ordinance can stand. As Holmes wrote in The Common Law [1881], "A law which punished conduct which would not be blameworthy in the average member of the community would be too severe for that community to bear." Id., at 50. * * * Where a person did not know of the duty to register and where there was no proof of the probability of such knowledge, he may not be convicted consistently with due process. Were it otherwise, the evil would be as great as it is when the law is written in print too fine to read or in a language foreign to the community. * * *

Reversed. * * *

MR. JUSTICE FRANKFURTER, * * * dissenting.

The present laws of the United States and of the forty-eight States are thick with provisions that command that some things not be done and others be done, although persons convicted under such provisions may have had no awareness of what the law required or that what they did was wrongdoing. The body of decisions sustaining such legislation, including innumerable registration laws, is almost as voluminous as the legislation itself. * * *

* * * Considerations of hardship often lead courts, naturally enough, to attribute to a statute the requirement of a certain mental element—some consciousness of wrongdoing and knowledge of the law's command—as a matter of statutory construction. Then, too, a cruelly disproportionate relation between what the law requires and the sanction for its disobedience may constitute a violation of the Eighth Amendment as a cruel and unusual punishment * * *.

But what the Court here does is to draw a constitutional line between a State's requirement of doing and not doing. What is this but a return to Year Book distinctions between feasance and nonfeasance—a distinction that may have significance in the evolution of common-law notions of liability, but is inadmissible as a line between constitutionality and unconstitutionality. * * *

If the generalization that underlies, and alone can justify, this decision were to be given its relevant scope, a whole volume of the United States Reports would be required to document in detail the legislation in this country that would fall or be impaired. I abstain from entering upon a consideration of such legislation, and adjudications upon it, because I feel confident that the present decision will turn out to be an isolated deviation from the strong current of precedents—a derelict on the waters of the law. Accordingly, I content myself with dissenting.

Notes and Questions

1. *Problems.* Do the defendants in the following hypothetical cases have valid due process claims under *Lambert*?

A. Whitney Houston, invited to sing the National Anthem at a Detroit Tigers baseball game, sings it as part of a medley of patriotic songs. She is charged with violation of Mich.Comp.Laws Ann. § 750.542 (1991), which prohibits the singing of the National Anthem

> in any public place * * * except as an entire and separate composition * * * and without embellishments of * * * other melodies; nor shall "The Star Spangled Banner" or any part thereof * * * be played as a part or selection of a medley of any kind * * *.

B. On January 1 a law takes effect requiring pharmacists to compile records of the names and addresses of all purchasers of prescription extra-strength aspirin. A pharmacist, unaware of the law until January 8, is prosecuted for her week-long recordkeeping omissions.

2. Does *Lambert* provide a broader defense than Model Penal Code § 2.04(3)(a)?

3. *"Cultural defense."* To what extent should a person's culturally-based belief that conduct is lawful serve as the relevant measure of culpability for criminal conduct? For example, on January 29, 1985, Mrs. Fumiko Kimura, a Japanese–American woman, attempted to commit *oyako-shinju* (parent-child suicide), by wading into the Pacific Ocean with her two young children, after learning that her husband was keeping a mistress. She survived, but the children drowned. Kimura was prosecuted for murder. People v. Kimura, No. A–091133 (L.A.Super.Ct.1985). Her "defense" was based upon the purported Japanese acceptance of *oyako-shinju* under such "shameful" circumstances.

Is Kimura's belief that she acted honorably relevant to her guilt? Suppose she were a recent arrival from Japan: Should she be permitted to prove that she was unaware that her conduct in this country was illegal? If not, why not? Do you believe that punishment would have a beneficial effect on her? On others? Do you believe Kimura is morally blameworthy? Should the answer to the latter question be measured by the standard of the "reasonable traditional Japanese woman"? If so, at what point should the law treat a person as sufficiently assimilated to be held to the standard of a "reasonable American"?

This case and the broader issues it raises are considered in Julia P. Sams, Note, *The Availability of the "Cultural Defense" As An Excuse for Criminal Behavior,* 16 Ga.J. Int'l & Comp.L. 335 (1986); Malek–Mithra Sheybani, Comment, *Cultural Defense: One Person's Culture Is Another's Crime,* 9 Loy.L.A. Int'l & Comp.L.J. 751 (1987); Note, *The Cultural Defense in the Criminal Law,* 99 Harv.L.Rev. 1293 (1986).

Chapter 6

CAUSATION

A. INTRODUCTION

VELAZQUEZ v. STATE

District Court of Appeal of Florida, 1990.
561 So.2d 347.

HUBBART, J. * * *

[Velazquez participated with the victim in a "drag race" on a public road. After they finished driving the course of the race, the victim unexpectedly turned his car around and drove at a speed estimated at 123 miles per hour toward the starting line, with the defendant following behind at similar speeds. As both drivers reached the starting point, which was at the end of a road, the victim was unable to stop his car. He died when his car hurtled through a guardrail. Velazquez was prosecuted for vehicular homicide. In the excerpt that follows, the court discusses the doctrine of causation in the context of the prosecution.]

The vehicular homicide statute, under which the defendant was charged and convicted, provides as follows:

"Vehicular homicide" is the killing of a human being by the operation of a motor vehicle by another in a reckless manner likely to cause the death of, or great bodily harm to, another. * * *

§ 782.071(1), Fla.Stat. (1987). There are two statutory elements to vehicular homicide: (1) the defendant must operate a motor vehicle in a reckless manner likely to cause the death of, or great bodily harm to, another, and (2) this reckless operation of a motor vehicle must be the proximate cause of the death of a human being. * * *

At the outset, it seems clear that the proximate cause element of vehicular homicide * * * embraces, at the very least, a causation-in-fact test; that is, the defendant's reckless operation of a motor vehicle must be a cause-in-fact of the death of a human being. In this respect, vehicular homicide is no different than any other criminal offense in which the occurrence of a specified result, caused by a defendant's conduct, is an essential element of the offense—such as murder, manslaughter, aggravated battery, and arson.   Clearly there can be no criminal liability for such result-type offenses unless it can be shown that the defendant's conduct was a cause-in-fact of the prohibited result, whether the result be the death of a human being, personal injury to another, or injury to another's property.   To be sure, this cause-in-fact showing is insufficient in itself to establish the aforesaid "proximate cause" element * * * but it is clearly a sine qua non ingredient thereof.

Courts throughout the country have uniformly followed the traditional "but for" test in determining whether the defendant's conduct was a cause-in-fact of a prohibited consequence in result-type offenses such as vehicular homicide.   Under this test, a defendant's conduct is a cause-in-fact of the prohibited result if the said result would *not* have occurred "but for" the defendant's conduct;   stated differently, the defendant's conduct is a cause-in-fact of a particular result if the result would *not* have happened in the absence of the defendant's conduct. Thus, a defendant's reckless operation of a motor vehicle is cause-in-fact of the death of a human being under Florida's vehicular homicide statute if the subject death would *not* have occurred "but for" the defendant's reckless driving or would not have happened in the absence of such driving.

In relatively rare cases, however, the "but for" test for causation-in-fact fails and has been abandoned in favor of the "substantial factor" test.   This anomaly occurs when two defendants, acting independently and not in concert with one another, commit two separate acts, each of which alone is sufficient to bring about the prohibited result—as when two defendants concurrently inflict mortal wounds upon a human being, each of which is sufficient to cause death.   In such case, each defendant's action was not a "but for" cause of death because the deceased would have died even in the absence of each defendant's conduct— although obviously not in the absence of both defendants' conduct considered together.   In these rare cases, the courts have followed a "substantial factor" test, namely, the defendant's conduct is a cause-in-fact of a prohibited result if the subject conduct was a "substantial factor" in bringing about the said result.   Thus, each defendant's conduct in independently and concurrently inflicting mortal wounds on a deceased clearly constitutes a "substantial factor" in bringing about the deceased's death, and, consequently, is a cause-in-fact of the deceased's death.

The "proximate cause" element * * * embraces more, however, than the aforesaid "but for" causation-in-fact test as modified by the "substantial factor" exception.   Even where a defendant's conduct is a cause-in-fact of a prohibited result, as where a defendant's reckless operation of a motor vehicle is a cause-in-fact of the death of a human being, * * * courts throughout the country have for good reason declined to impose criminal liability (1) where the prohibited result of the defendant's conduct is beyond the scope of any fair assessment of the danger created by the defendant's conduct, or [(2)] where it would otherwise be unjust, based on fairness and policy considerations, to hold the defendant criminally responsible for the prohibited result. * * *

Notes and Questions

1. Theoretically, a causal link between a defendant's voluntary act (or omission, when a duty to act arises) and the social harm of the offense is an element of every crime. Practically speaking, however, questions of causation only arise in the prosecution of "result" crimes, particularly criminal homicide.

2. Suppose that Elmer, a pedestrian, is struck by an automobile and killed. Through careful investigation the police determine that four cars, driven by Arthur, Betty, Carl, and Dorene respectively, were the only vehicles in the vicinity at the time of the accident, and that each of them drove at an unsafe and negligent rate of speed. However, the police cannot identify the one car and driver that struck Elmer. Since all four drivers were equally dangerous and equally negligent, why should the three drivers who did not cause the death be treated differently than the one who did?

B. ACTUAL CAUSE (CAUSE–IN–FACT)

OXENDINE v. STATE

Supreme Court of Delaware, 1987.
528 A.2d 870.

HORSEY, JUSTICE:

Defendant, Jeffrey Oxendine, Sr., appeals his conviction * * * of manslaughter (11 *Del.C.* § 632(1))[1] in the beating death of his six-year-old son, Jeffrey Oxendine, Jr. Oxendine was sentenced to twelve years' imprisonment.[2] On appeal, Oxendine's principal argument is that the Trial Court committed reversible error by denying his motion for a judgment of acquittal on the issue of causation. Specifically, he argues that the State's medical testimony, relating to which of the codefendants' admittedly repeated beatings of the child was the cause of death, was so vague and uncertain as to preclude his conviction of any criminal offense.

We conclude that the evidence upon causation was insufficient to sustain Oxendine's conviction of manslaughter, but that the evidence was sufficient to sustain his conviction of the lesser included offense of assault in the second degree (11 *Del.C.* § 612(1)).[3] * * *

---

1. 11 *Del.C.* § 632(1) states:

"A person is guilty of manslaughter when: (1) He recklessly causes the death of another person."

2. Codefendant, Leotha Tyree, was also convicted in the same trial of manslaughter in the death of Jeffrey Oxendine, Jr. and was sentenced to nine years' imprisonment. On direct appeal, this Court has affirmed her conviction.

3. 11 *Del.C.* § 612(1) states:

"A person is guilty of assault in the second degree when: (1) He intentionally causes serious physical injury to another person."

Assault in the Second Degree is a Class C felony for which the range of punishment is 2 to 20 years.

The facts may be summarized as follows: On the morning of January 18, 1984, Leotha Tyree, Oxendine's girlfriend, who lived with him, pushed Jeffrey into the bathtub causing microscopic tears in his intestines which led to peritonitis. During a break at work that evening, Oxendine telephoned home and talked to Jeffrey, who complained of stomach pains. When Oxendine returned home from work, he saw bruises on Jeffrey and knew that Tyree had beaten the child during the day. * * *

The next morning at approximately 7:30 a.m., Oxendine went into Jeffrey's bedroom and began screaming at him to get up. A neighbor in the same apartment building testified to hearing sounds coming from the room of blows being struck, obscenities uttered by a male voice, and cries from a child saying, "Please stop, Daddy, it hurts." After hearing these sounds continue for what seemed like five to ten minutes, the witness heard a final noise consisting of a loud thump, as if someone had been kicked or punched "with a great blow."

Later that day, Jeffrey's abdomen became swollen. When Oxendine arrived home from work at about 5:00 p.m., Tyree told him of Jeffrey's condition and urged him to take Jeffrey to the hospital. Oxendine, apparently believing that Jeffrey was exaggerating his discomfort, went out, bought a newspaper, and returned home to read it. Upon his return, Tyree had prepared to take Jeffrey to the hospital. En route, Jeffrey stopped breathing; and was pronounced dead shortly after his arrival at the hospital.

I

In order to convict Oxendine of manslaughter, the State had to show that his conduct caused Jeffrey's death. 11 *Del.C.* § 261 defines causation as the "antecedent but for which the result in question would not have occurred." * * *

During its case-in-chief, the State called medical examiners Dr. Inguito and Dr. Hameli, who both testified that Jeffrey's death was caused by intra-abdominal hemorrhage and acute peritonitis, occurring as a result of blunt force trauma to the front of the abdomen. Similarly, each pathologist identified two distinct injuries, one caused more than twenty-four hours before death, and one inflicted less than twenty-four hours before death.

Dr. Inguito could not separate the effects of the two injuries. In his view, it was possible that both the older and more recent hemorrhage could have contributed to the death of the child, but he was unable to tell which of the hemorrhages caused the death of the child. Dr. Inguito could not place any quantitative value on either of the hemorrhages nor could he state whether the fresh hemorrhage or the older hemorrhage caused the death. The prosecutor never asked, nor did Dr. Inguito give, an opinion on whether the second hemorrhage accelerated Jeffrey's death.

Dr. Hameli, on the other hand, was of the opinion that the earlier injury was the underlying cause of death. According to him, the later injury, *i.e.*, the second hemorrhage, "was an aggravating, and probably some factors [sic] contributing," but it was the earlier injury that was the plain underlying cause of death.

The prosecutor, however, did explicitly ask Dr. Hameli if the second injury accelerated Jeffrey's death. The relevant portion of the testimony is as follows:

Prosecutor: Dr. Hameli, within a reasonable degree of medical certainty and in your expert opinion, did the second hemorrhage accelerate this child's death?

Hameli: I do not know. If you are talking about timewise—I assume that's what you are talking about, exploration.

Prosecutor: You cannot give an opinion of that area; is that correct?

Hameli: No.

Oxendine moved for judgment of acquittal at the end of the State's case-in-chief. The Trial Court, however, denied his motion.

As part of her case, codefendant Tyree called Dr. Hofman, a medical examiner, who disagreed about the number of injuries. He perceived only one injury inflicted about twelve hours before death. Subsequently, the prosecutor asked Hofman the following hypothetical question that assumed two blows when Hofman only testified as to one blow:

Prosecutor: In your expert medical opinion within a reasonable degree of medical certainty, if this child, given his weakened state as a result of the significant trauma to his abdominal cavity, suffered subsequently another blunt force trauma to the same area, would it accelerate this child's death?   * * *

Hofman: My opinion, as in a general statement, not knowing this child, it certainly would have an impact on shortening this child's life.

Prosecutor: Is then, therefore, your answer yes?

Hofman: Yes.

At the end of trial, Oxendine again moved for judgment of acquittal. The Trial Court denied the motion and instructed the jury on the elements of recklessness, causation and on various lesser included offenses. The ultimate and only theory of causation on which the jury was charged was based on "acceleration." The Trial Court instructed the jury that "[a] defendant who causes the death of another ... is not relieved of responsibility for causing the death if another later injury accelerates, that is, hastens the death of the other person. Contribution without acceleration is not sufficient." As previously noted, the jury returned verdicts of manslaughter against Oxendine and Tyree.

II

In this case, the evidence established that Oxendine inflicted a nonlethal injury upon Jeffrey after his son had, twenty-four hours earlier, sustained a lethal injury from a previous beating inflicted by Tyree.   Thus, for Oxendine to be convicted of manslaughter in this factual context, the State was required to show for purposes of causation under 11 *Del.C.* § 261 that Oxendine's conduct hastened or accelerated the child's death.   The Superior Court correctly instructed the jury that "[c]ontribution [or aggravation] without acceleration is insufficient to establish causation."   We do not equate aggravation with acceleration. It is possible to make the victim's pain more intense, *i.e.,* aggravate the injury, without accelerating the time of the victim's death.   Thus, in terms of section 261, and as applied to defendant, the relevant inquiry is: but for his infliction of the second injury, would the victim have died when he died?   If the second injury caused his son to die *any* sooner, then defendant, who inflicted the second injury, would be deemed to have caused his son's death within the definition of section 261.

A finding of medical causation may not be based on speculation or conjecture.   A doctor's testimony that a certain thing is possible is no evidence at all.   His opinion as to what is possible is no more valid than the jury's own speculation as to what is or is not possible.   Almost anything is possible, and it is improper to allow a jury to consider and base a verdict upon a "possible" cause of death.   Therefore, a doctor's testimony can only be considered evidence when his conclusions are based on reasonable medical certainty that a fact is true or untrue.

The State's expert medical testimony, even when viewed in the light most favorable to the State, was * * * insufficient to sustain the State's ultimate theory of causation ("acceleration") on which the court instructed the jury.   Both of the State's expert witnesses, Dr. Inguito and Dr. Hameli, were unable to state with any degree of medical certainty that the second injury contributed to the death of the child.   Dr. Inguito could only testify that it was possible that both the older and more recent hemorrhage could have contributed to the death of the child.   As for Dr. Hameli, he testified that the second injury independent of the first injury could have caused death but probably would not cause death. Furthermore, Dr. Hameli explicitly stated that he could not give an opinion as to whether the second injury accelerated Jeffrey's death. Similarly, Dr. Inguito was neither asked nor did he offer an opinion about acceleration.

The record establishes that the only theory of causation under which the State submitted the case to the jury was the acceleration theory. The State apparently abandoned its initial theories of causation and adopted the acceleration theory as the cause of death * * *.   * * *

It is extremely "difficult to be objective about the death of a child. . . .   Those responsible ought to be punished.   Nevertheless, there must be proof as to who, if anyone, inflicted the injuries that resulted in death."   *State v. Lynn,* Wash.Supr., 73 Wash.2d 117, 436 P.2d 463, 466

(1968) (en banc). "Reprehensible and repulsive as the conduct of the defendant is, nevertheless it is not proof of manslaughter." *State v. Guiles*, Wash.Supr., 53 Wash.2d 386, 333 P.2d 923, 924 (1959).

The Trial Court, however, properly denied Oxendine's motion for judgment of acquittal at the close of the State's case because its medical testimony was sufficient for a rational trier of fact to conclude beyond a reasonable doubt that Oxendine was guilty of the lesser included offense of assault in the second degree, 11 *Del.C.* § 612(1). Therefore, we reverse Oxendine's conviction of manslaughter and remand the case to Superior Court for entry of a judgment of conviction and resentence of defendant for the lesser included offense of assault in the second degree.

Notes and Questions

1. The court observed that the prosecution abandoned its initial theories of causation in favor of the acceleration theory. What other theories might the prosecution have had in mind?

2. Why was Dr. Hofman's testimony insufficient to justify Oxendine's conviction for manslaughter?

3. Who is the actual cause of *V*'s death in the following hypotheticals? (Assume that *D* and *X* did not act in concert.) How would these cases be resolved under Model Penal Code § 2.03?

A. *X* intentionally stabs *V* in the chest. *V* will die from loss of blood in 15 minutes. Simultaneously, *D* intentionally shoots *V* in the leg. *V* would not die from this wound by itself. *V* dies in 10 minutes.

B. The same as A., except that *D* *un*intentionally shoots *V*.

C. The same as A., except that *V* dies in 15 minutes.

D. *X* stabs *V*. Simultaneously, *D* stabs *V*. Neither wound by itself would kill *V*. *V* dies from loss of blood from the two wounds.

E. *X* shoots *V* in the heart. Simultaneously, *D* shoots *V* in the head. *V* would die instantly from either wound. *V* dies instantly.

4. Nancy, a hiker, enters the desert with a canteen filled with sufficient water to survive. Unbeknownst to her, Oscar, intending to kill her, places a fatal dose of a fast-acting poison in the canteen. While in the desert, Petunia steals the canteen, believing that it contains pure water. Nancy, without water, dies of thirst in the desert. Who caused her death? See H.L.A. Hart & Tony Honoré, Causation in the Law 239–41 (2d ed. 1985).

C. PROXIMATE CAUSE ("LEGAL" CAUSE)
INTRODUCTORY COMMENT

The but-for test is too imprecise a standard for determining causal accountability for harm because it fails to exclude remote candidates for legal responsibility. "Mankind might still be in Eden, but for Adam's biting an apple." Welch v. State, 45 Ala.App. 657, 659, 235 So.2d 906, 907 (1970). Although Adam's conduct satisfies the but-for test of responsibility for today's wrongdoing, we do not follow the causal chain as far back as it may lead us.

The doctrine of "proximate" or "legal" causation serves the purpose of determining who or what events among those that satisfy the but-for standard should be held accountable for resulting harm. (Thus, it should be noticed, a person or event cannot be a proximate cause of harm unless she or it is an actual cause, but a person or event can be an actual cause without being the proximate cause.)

Issues of proximate causation generally arise when an intervening force exists, i.e., when some but-for causal agent comes into play *after* the defendant's voluntary act or omission and *before* the social harm occurs. Typically, an intervening cause will be: (1) "an act of God," i.e., an event that cannot be traced back to any human intermediary; (2) an act of an independent third party, which accelerates or aggravates the harm caused by the defendant, or which causes it to occur in an unexpected manner; or (3) an act or omission of the victim that assists in bringing about the outcome.

Proximate causation analysis is less a matter of applying hard and fast rules than it is an effort by the factfinder to determine, for reasons of social policy or out of a conception of justice, on whom to impose criminal penalties. Consequently, although courts sometimes act as if there is a foolproof way of identifying the proximate cause of social harm, it is more accurate to think in terms of factors relating to causal responsibility that help lawyers predict and effect outcomes. The materials that follow relate to those factors.

In considering the factors, ask yourself whether the law inappropriately applies an "individualist ideology of law." Alan Norrie, *A Critique of Criminal Causation,* 54 Modern L.Rev. 685, 701 (1991). That is, does Anglo–American law locate responsibility for harm in individuals, "in abstraction from their place in social relations, structures, and belief systems," thereby ignoring "deeper causes" of criminal wrongdoing, such as racial discrimination, economic disparity, and similar institutional factors?

KIBBE v. HENDERSON

United States Court of Appeals, Second Circuit, 1976.
534 F.2d 493.

LUMBARD, CIRCUIT JUDGE:

* * * Barry Warren Kibbe was found guilty * * * of murder, robbery in the second degree and grand larceny in the third degree. He brings this appeal from an order of the Northern District denying his petition for habeas corpus which was sought, in part, because the trial judge failed to charge the jury with respect to causation of death on the murder count. * * * We hold that the trial judge's instructions permitted the jury, in its fact-finding process to disregard Kibbe's colorable claim that, as to the murder charge, his actions had not caused the death of a decedent and thus violated Kibbe's constitutional right to have every element of the crime with which he was charged proven beyond a

reasonable doubt. We therefore grant the writ with respect to the murder count.

Kibbe and his codefendant, Roy Krall, met the decedent, George Stafford, at a bar in Rochester, New York on the evening of December 30, 1970. Stafford had been drinking heavily and by about 9:00 p.m. he was so intoxicated that the bartender refused to serve him further. Apparently the defendants saw Stafford offer a one hundred dollar bill for payment, which the bartender refused. At some point during the evening, Stafford began soliciting a ride to Canandaigua from the other patrons in the bar. Kibbe and Krall, who confessed to having already decided to rob Stafford, offered a ride and the three men left the bar together. Before starting out for Canandaigua, the three visited a second bar. When the bartender at this bar also refused to serve Stafford because of his inebriated condition, the three proceeded to a third bar, where each was served additional drinks.

Kibbe, Krall and Stafford left for Canandaigua in Kibbe's car about 9:30 that evening. According to statements of the defendants, as Krall was driving the car, Kibbe demanded Stafford's money and, upon receiving it, forced Stafford to lower his trousers and remove his boots to prove he had no more. At some time between 9:30 and 9:40 p.m., Stafford was abandoned on the side of an unlit, rural two-lane highway. His boots and jacket were also placed on the shoulder of the highway; Stafford's eyeglasses, however, remained in the car. There was testimony that it was "very cold" that night and that strong winds were blowing recently fallen snow across the highway, although the night was clear and the pavement was dry. There was an open and lighted service station in the general vicinity, but testimony varied as to its precise distance from the place where Stafford was abandoned. In any case, the station was no more than one-quarter of a mile away.

About half an hour after Kibbe and Krall had abandoned Stafford, Michael Blake, a college student, was driving his pickup truck northbound on the highway at 50 miles an hour, ten miles per hour in excess of the posted speed limit. A car passed Blake in a southbound direction and the driver flashed his headlights at Blake. Immediately thereafter, Blake saw Stafford sitting in the middle of the northbound lane with his hands in the air. Blake testified that he "went into a kind of shock" as soon as he saw Stafford, and that he did not apply his brakes. Blake further testified that he did not attempt to avoid hitting Stafford because he "didn't have time to react." After the collision, Blake stopped his truck and returned to assist Stafford, whereupon he found the decedent's trousers were around his ankles and his shirt was up to his chest. Stafford was wearing neither his jacket nor his boots.

Stafford suffered massive head and body injuries as a result of the collision and died shortly thereafter. An autopsy revealed a high alcohol concentration of .25% in his blood. The Medical Examiner testified that these injuries were the direct cause of death.

Kibbe and Krall were * * * tried for * * * the murder of Stafford under New York Penal Law § 125.25(2) which provides:

A person is guilty of murder in the second degree when:

* * *

(2) Under circumstances evincing a depraved indifference to human life, he recklessly engages in conduct which creates a grave risk of death to another person, and thereby causes the death of another person.[2]

In his charge to the jury, the judge failed to define or explain the issue of causation as that term is used in § 125.25(2). No mention was made of the legal effect of intervening or supervening cause. * * * The jury returned guilty verdicts on the charges of second degree murder * * *.

The Appellate Division affirmed the conviction on finding that there was sufficient evidence that Stafford's death was caused by appellant's acts "as well as by the acts of Blake." * * *

Kibbe * * * contends that the question of causation was a pivotal issue at trial and that the judge's failure to instruct the jury with respect to that issue allowed the jury to convict without finding that every element of the crime had been proven beyond a reasonable doubt. On the limited and singular facts of this case, we agree. * * *

In this case, by the language of the statute, the state was bound to prove to the jury beyond a reasonable doubt that appellant evinced a depraved indifference to Stafford's life, recklessly engaged in conduct that created a grave risk of Stafford's death, and thereby caused Stafford's death. The court scrupulously instructed the jury with respect to the meaning of "recklessly", "depraved", "grave", and "indifferent" as used in Penal Law § 125.25(2). The omission of any definition of causation, however, permitted the jury to conclude that the issue was not before them or that causation could be inferred merely from the fact that Stafford's death succeeded his abandonment by Kibbe and Krall.

Even if the jury were aware of the need to determine causation, the court's instruction did not provide the tools necessary to that task. * * * Error in the omission of an instruction is compounded where the legal standard is complex and requires that fine distinctions be made. That is most assuredly the situation in this case. It has been held that where death is produced by an intervening force, such as Blake's operation of his truck, the liability of one who put an antecedent force into action will depend on the difficult determination of whether the intervening force was a sufficiently independent or supervening cause of death. See W. LaFave & A. Scott, Criminal Law 257–63 (1972) (collecting cases).[6] The few cases that provide similar factual circumstances

---

2. Intent to kill is not a requirement under the statute.

6. The complexity of the definition of legal causation in LaFave and Scott, supra, demonstrates that an explanation of the

suggest that the controlling questions are whether the ultimate result was foreseeable to the original actor and whether the victim failed to do something easily within his grasp that would have extricated him from danger.[7] * * *

We are convinced that the trial judge's incomplete instructions took a necessary determination of causation of death from the jury and thereby deprived appellant of his right to due process. * * *

Notes and Questions

1. What was Kibbe, a defendant in a state criminal trial, doing in a federal court attacking his conviction? The answer is that after a convicted defendant exhausts his state appeals, he may file a petition for a writ of *habeas corpus* in a federal district court if he believes that his continued imprisonment violates federal law or the United States Constitution.

The purpose of a *habeas* petition is to convince the federal court that it should compel the warden of the prison (Henderson, in this case) to bring the petitioner (Kibbe) before the court so that it can determine whether the prisoner is being unlawfully or unconstitutionally incarcerated. Thus, the discussion in this case was couched in terms of whether the state court's failure to instruct the jury regarding causation violated Kibbe's federal constitutional right to due process.

concept of intervening and supervening cause would have been not merely helpful * * * but essential to the jury's determination here. Given the proper standard for causation, the jury could have found that Blake had been so reckless as to absolve defendants of legal responsibility for Stafford's death:

As might be expected, courts have tended to distinguish cases in which the intervening act was a *coincidence* from those in which it was a *response* to the defendant's prior action. An intervening act is a *coincidence* when the defendant's act merely put the victim at a certain place at a certain time, and because the victim was so located it was possible for him to be acted upon by the intervening cause. The case put earlier in which B, after being fired upon by A, changed his route and then was struck by lightning is an illustration of a coincidence. However, it is important to note that there may be a coincidence even when the subsequent act is that of a human agency, as where A shoots B and leaves him lying in the roadway, resulting in B being struck by C's car; or where A shoots at B and causes him to take refuge in a park, where B is then attacked and killed by a gang of hoodlums.

By contrast, an intervening act may be said to be a *response* to the prior actions of the defendant when it involves a reac-

tion to the conditions created by the defendant.

Thus—though the distinction is not carefully developed in many of the decided cases—it may be said that a coincidence will break the chain of legal cause unless it was foreseeable, while a response will do so only if it is abnormal (and, if abnormal, also unforeseeable). * * *

This kind of accident must be distinguished from a somewhat different situation, as where A, with intent to kill B, only wounds B, leaving him lying unconscious in the unlighted road on a dark night, and then C, driving along the road, runs over and kills B. Here C's act is a matter of coincidence rather than a response to what A has done, and thus the question is whether the subsequent events were foreseeable, as they undoubtedly were in the above illustration.

Without a proper definition of causation, the jury, if it considered causation at all, could have found that Blake's conduct, no matter how reckless, could merely supplement and not supervene defendants' culpability.

7. See *State v. Preslar*, 48 N.C.Rep. 421 (1856) (deliberate choice of victim to forego place of safety exonerates defendant of liability for victim's subsequent death from exposure).

After the Court of Appeals granted Kibbe's petition, the state appealed to the United States Supreme Court. The Supreme Court unanimously reversed the judgment of the Court of Appeals, holding that the trial court's failure to instruct the jury on causation, although erroneous, did not so infect the trial process as to violate Kibbe's constitutional rights. Henderson v. Kibbe, 431 U.S. 145, 97 S.Ct. 1730, 52 L.Ed.2d 203 (1977).

2. How should the trial court have instructed the jury? Should it have read to it the excerpt from the LaFave and Scott treatise? If not, how would you explain to the jury the doctrine of proximate causation?

3. Suppose that Stafford had been killed by an airplane making an emergency landing on the highway, rather than by Blake, the passing motorist. Should that difference matter to the defendants' liability?

4. Is *D* the proximate cause of *V*'s death in the following cases?

A. *X* and *V* steal property from *D*'s riverfront home. The thieves flee in a boat. *D* fires two shots at the boat, seeking (unlawfully) to kill the miscreants, but the bullets fail to hit their marks. *X*, fearful of another shot, dives into the water, causing it to capsize. *V* drowns. Letner v. State, 156 Tenn. 68, 299 S.W. 1049 (1927). Suppose that after the boat capsized, it floated miles down the river and over a waterfall, falling on the head of *V2*, another boater, killing her. Is *D* liable for *V2*'s death? *coincidental intervening event?* [handwritten marginalia]

B. *D* stabs *X* eleven times, drops the knife, and flees. *X*, mortally wounded, grabs the knife and staggers up a flight of stairs in search of *D*. On the second floor, *X* encounters *V*, an innocent party who tries to take the knife from him. *X* stabs and kills *V*. Medical testimony will indicate that at the time of this stabbing, *X* was in a state of shock from massive loss of blood from the initial wound. People v. Roberts, 2 Cal.4th 271, 6 Cal. Rptr.2d 276, 826 P.2d 274 (1992).

5. Consider People v. Acosta, 232 Cal.App.3d 1375, 284 Cal.Rptr. 117 (1991): The police pursued *A*, a car thief, on a 48 mile, high-speed (60–90 m.p.h.) car chase along numerous surface streets and freeways. According to the court, *A* "engaged in some of the most egregious driving tactics imaginable," such as failing to stop at red lights, driving on the wrong side of the road, and using a dirt shoulder to circumvent stationary vehicles. Before the chase ended, two police helicopters called into the pursuit collided in mid-air, killing the occupants. Was *A* the proximate cause of these deaths?

STATE v. CUMMINGS

Court of Appeals of North Carolina, 1980.
46 N.C.App. 680, 265 S.E.2d 923.

HARRY C. MARTIN, JUDGE.

[The defendants, John and Willie Mae Cummings, got into a verbal argument with the decedent, Oscar Melvin. The argument escalated into a physical altercation on the street when John, holding a thick board in his hands, and Willie Mae chased Melvin down the street. As Melvin ran backwards with his hands up in the air, John struck him various times with the board. The defendants finally cornered Melvin outside a grocery store, where Willie Mae stabbed him and John hit him again with the board. Melvin fell to the sidewalk, and the defendants fled. A police officer later discovered Melvin lying flat on his back, with his head in a puddle of blood. Melvin gasped a few breaths and died.

The pathologist who performed the autopsy on Melvin testified that he discovered a number of wounds on the decedent's body. He also found that Melvin's lungs and air passage system were congested with vomitus, which indicated that the immediate cause of death was asphyxiation.

The autopsy also showed that Melvin had .35 percent alcohol content in his bloodstream at the time of death. According to the pathologist, a person that severely intoxicated would likely become stuporous or unconscious, thereby impairing his "gag reflexes," and causing him to "drown" in his vomit. He further testified that such an outcome is more likely when a person is in a prone position, as Melvin was found.

The defendants were convicted of involuntary manslaughter.]

Defendants' principal assignment of error is directed to the court's refusal to grant their motions for dismissal at the close of all the evidence. Their argument is centered on the lack of a showing that the assault by defendants was a proximate cause of Melvin's death. * * *

The state's evidence * * * shows Melvin was highly intoxicated and that this affected his ability to expel vomitus from his mouth; his "gag reflexes" were inoperative. He was more likely to inhale vomitus into his airway system if in a prone position. Prior to the assault by defendants, he was in an upright position, running backwards and moving about freely, and a logical inference from the evidence is that he was not vomiting prior to being knocked down. Defendants struck Melvin about the head and body with a board * * * several times and knocked him to the sidewalk, flat on his back. Defendants made no effort to aid him but left him and ran [away] * * *. When Officer Burgess got to Melvin, he was still on his back, with his eyes glassed over, taking deep gasping breaths.

The state must produce evidence sufficient to establish beyond a reasonable doubt that the death proximately resulted from defendants' unlawful acts. The act complained of does not have to be the sole proximate cause of the death, nor the last act in sequence of time. There may be more than one proximate cause of the death in question. It is enough if defendants' unlawful acts join and concur with other causes in producing the result. * * *

The jury could reasonably find from the evidence that Melvin's death resulted not from the injuries themselves, inflicted upon him in the unlawful battery by defendants, but from being knocked to the sidewalk upon his back where, because of his intoxicated condition, he was unable to expel the vomitus from his mouth and thereby "drowned," and that Melvin would not have died but for defendants' unlawful assault upon him. The direct cause of Melvin's death, the aspiration of vomitus, was the natural result of defendants' assault upon him.

The defendant must accept his victim in the condition that he finds him. We hold defendants' motions for dismissal were properly overruled. Further, we hold the evidence is sufficient for a rational trier of fact to find defendants guilty beyond a reasonable doubt of involuntary manslaughter under the laws of North Carolina. * * *

CLARK, JUDGE, dissents:

* * * I dissent from the majority opinion because I believe that, as a matter of law, the death of Oscar M. Melvin was not proximately caused by the defendants' actions. "[I]f defendant did not cause the death of decedent, within the rules of legally-recognized causation, he cannot be convicted of homicide even if he committed an assault and battery upon that person and is subject to conviction upon a charge of this lesser offense." Perkins, *Criminal Law* (2d ed. 1969) at 727.

First, as explained by Professor Perkins, " * * * [S]ince the degree of moral obliquity exhibited by the act, and the extent of the social menace involved[ ] are factors to be considered, the result will not necessarily be the same for all offenses. *In particular, the legal eye reaches further in the examination of intentional crimes than in those in which this element is wanting, such as involuntary manslaughter.*" (Emphasis supplied.) *Perkins, supra,* at 693. * * *

[Second], when the force which was set in motion by defendants has come to a position of apparent safety or when the victim has reached a place of apparent safety, and death results from another cause, the acts of the defendants will not be the proximate cause of the decedent's death. *See, State v. Preslar,* 48 N.C. 421 (1856); *Perkins, supra,* at 696–97. *See, also, People v. Elder,* 100 Mich. 515, 59 N.W. 237 (1894) in which it was held that one who knocks another down is not the proximate cause of death, which resulted when another bystander took advantage of the helpless situation of the victim to administer a fatal kick.

Finally, * * * [t]he medical doctor could not state that the vomiting was a response to defendant's blows. The vomiting was, rather, coincidental to the defendant's act and was therefore not the proximate cause of the decedent's death.

Notes and Questions

1. Who has the better side of the argument, the majority or the dissent? Do the principles articulated by Judge Clark support his conclusion? Can you think of a different explanation for the result in *Elder*, which the dissent cites and explains by way of the apparent safety doctrine?

2. *Omissions.* Although an omission may be an actual cause of harm—and, thus, an omitter may be criminally responsible for her inaction—can an omission ever function as a superseding intervening cause, so as to relieve an earlier wrongdoer of criminal responsibility? According to

one treatise, Rollin M. Perkins & Ronald N. Boyce, Criminal Law 819–21 (3d ed. 1982), the answer is no: no matter how unforeseeable the omission may be, this "negative act" will not cut off liability of an earlier "positive act." In essence, "nothing" can never supersede "something."

Should this be? For example, suppose that in *Kibbe* (p. 181 supra) Stafford had been lying unconscious next to the road, freezing to death. If the lone driver to observe him realized Stafford's predicament, and yet drove on without helping, should his failure to act relieve the defendants of their liability for Stafford's death? Suppose that the driver was Stafford's brother, who wanted him dead in order to inherit the decedent's large estate?

3. *Intended consequences.* The dissent, quoting Professor Perkins, claims that a defendant's *mens rea* is relevant in determining proximate causation. Indeed, Professors Perkins and Boyce state that "any intended consequence of an act is proximate." Rollin M. Perkins & Ronald N. Boyce, Criminal Law 818 (3d ed. 1982) (quoting Henry T. Terry, *Proximate Consequence in the Law of Torts,* 28 Harv.L.Rev. 10, 17 (1914)). Should this always be so? Consider the following cases.

A. *M,* wishing to kill *V,* her young son, obtains poison, which she furnishes to *N, V*'s nurse, in the guise of medicine. *M* instructs *N* to give *V* a teaspoonful (a lethal dose) of the "medicine" later that day. *N* does not do so because she believes that the medication is unnecessary, but she negligently leaves the potion nearby. A few days later *Y,* a five-year-old youth, picks it up and innocently administers the poison to *V,* who dies. Regina v. Michael, 9 Car. & P. 356, 169 Eng.Rep. 48 (1840). Is *M* the proximate cause of *V*'s death?

Suppose that *N* had realized that the medicine was poison, yet she went ahead and administered it? Or, suppose that *Y* had found a gun, kept for self-defense, hidden under *M*'s bed, and had innocently shot and killed *V*? Should *M* escape criminal liability for the death of *V* in either of these circumstances?

B. *B* shoots *V,* with the intent to kill. *V*'s wound is not mortal, but he requires hospitalization. In the hospital, *V* is treated by a physician still recovering from scarlet fever. *V* contracts the disease and dies from it. Bush v. Commonwealth, 78 Ky. 268 (1880). Is *B* the proximate cause of *V*'s death?

4. *"Apparent safety" doctrine.* The dissent in *Cummings* cites *State v. Preslar* in support of the "apparent safety" doctrine. (*Preslar* is also cited in footnote 7 of *Kibbe.*) In *Preslar, P, V*'s husband, struck *V* and threatened to kill her. As a result, *V* left their house on a freezing night and travelled by foot to her father's home. Because it was late and she did not want to disturb her father, *V* slept outside under a blanket, where she died from the cold. The court concluded that *P* was not responsible for *V*'s death.

Do you agree? Suppose that *V* had died from the cold before she reached her father's house, but she would have received lodging from good samaritans living along the way if she had only requested help. Should *P* escape liability in such circumstances?

5. *"Free, deliberate and informed human intervention."* According to Professors H.L.A. Hart & Tony Honoré in their influential treatise, *Causa-*

tion in the Law (2d ed. 1985), the criminal law does not hold a person responsible for resulting harm if there is an intervening cause that springs from "free, deliberate and informed" human action. That is, once a voluntary human act is discovered, the law will not trace back the causal chain any further. How would *Preslar* (Note 4) be decided under this doctrine? What is the justification for this principle?

6. In view of all of the factors discussed above, how would you resolve the following cases?

A. In the early morning hours, *Ds,* three white youths, wielding bats and clubs and uttering racial epithets and threatening remarks, chased *V* and other African–American youths through the streets. In order to escape, the black youths ran onto a highway, where *V* was struck by a motorist who did not see him in the dark. Are *Ds* the proximate cause of *V*'s death? People v. Kern, 149 A.D.2d 187, 545 N.Y.S.2d 4 (1989), affirmed, 75 N.Y.2d 638, 555 N.Y.S.2d 647, 554 N.E.2d 1235 (1990).

B. *D1* stabbed *V* multiple times. *V* was taken to a hospital where, after numerous medical procedures, she lapsed into multiple-organ failure and was placed on life support machinery. *D2,* a nurse, aware that her actions would cause *V*'s rapid death, turned off the ventilator, "because someone had to have the balls to do it." *V* died. The prosecutor sought a murder prosecution of *D2*. If such a prosecution proceeds, does this preclude prosecution of *D1* for *V*'s death? People v. Vaughn, 152 Misc.2d 731, 579 N.Y.S.2d 839 (1991);[a] see also State v. Scates, 50 N.C. 420 (1858); People v. Lewis, 124 Cal. 551, 57 P. 470 (1899).

D1 was responsible

C. *The "drag race" cases.* Reconsider the facts in *Velazquez* (p. 174 supra). Should the victim's decision to turn his car around and continue the race constitute a superseding intervening cause? If your answer is yes, would your analysis be different if his car, when it struck the guardrail, killed an innocent bystander as well? Should Velazquez be held responsible for *that* death? See State v. McFadden, 320 N.W.2d 608 (Iowa 1982); Commonwealth v. Root, 403 Pa. 571, 170 A.2d 310 (1961).

free deliberate choice theory

D. *Victims with hidden "defects."* *B* stabbed *V,* an 18–year–old Jehovah's Witness, after she refused *B*'s sexual advances. *V*'s lung was pierced in the attack. She was taken to a hospital where a doctor decided that she required a blood transfusion to survive. *V* refused to consent to the transfusion, although she realized that she would die without the blood, based on her religious belief that to accept the transfusion constituted a sin. Is *B* the proximate cause of *V*'s death? Regina v. Blaue, [1975] 1 W.L.R. 1411, [1975] 3 All Eng.Rep. 446 (C.A.). Can *Blaue* properly be distinguished from a case in which the victim, unknown to the assailant, has a heart ailment and dies from a heart attack brought on by the assault?

E. *Suicidal acts by the victim.* *M* and his girl friend, *V,* spent an afternoon drinking together. *V,* who was depressed because she had lost custody of her children from a prior marriage, told *M* that her life was not worth living and that she might kill herself. Later that day, *V* picked up a

a. The court described the issue this way: "[F]or the purpose of assessing criminal responsibility, may a person be found to have been killed twice?" Is this a fair description of the issue?

gun and attempted to load it. Because she was too drunk to do so, *V* asked *M* to load the weapon, which he did. *V* picked up the gun and killed herself. Is *M* the proximate cause of *V*'s death? State v. Marti, 290 N.W.2d 570 (Iowa 1980).

7. *Model Penal Code.* Section 2.03 of the Model Penal Code takes "a fresh approach" to the issues discussed in this chapter section:

> Subsections (2) and (3) are based on the theory that but-for causation is the only strictly causal requirement that should be imposed generally, and that the remaining issue is the proper scope of liability in light of the actor's culpability. These subsections assume that liability requires purpose, knowledge, recklessness, or negligence with respect to the result that is an element of the offense, and deal explicitly with variations between the actual result and the intended, contemplated or foreseeable result. Criteria are provided for determining the materiality or immateriality of such variations.
>
> Subsection (2) addresses cases in which the culpability requirement with respect to the result is purpose or knowledge, i.e., cases in which purposely or knowingly causing a specified result is a material element of the offense. If the actual result is not within the purpose or contemplation of the actor, the culpability requirement is not satisfied, except in the circumstances set out in Subsections (2)(a) and (2)(b).
>
> Subsection (2)(a) deals with situations in which the actual result differs from the result designed or contemplated only in that a different person or property was injured or affected,[14] or in that the injury or harm designed or contemplated would have been more serious or extensive than that which actually occurred.[15] Following existing law, the Code makes such differences immaterial.
>
> Subsection (2)(b) deals with situations in which the actual result involves the same kind of injury or harm as that designed or contemplated, but in which the precise injury inflicted was different or occurred in a different way. Here the Code makes no attempt to catalogue the possibilities—intervening or concurrent causes, natural or human; unexpected physical conditions; distinctions between mortal and nonmortal wounds; and so on. It deals only with the ultimate criterion by which the significance of such factors ought to be judged—whether the actual result is too remote or accidental in its occurrence to have a

14. For example, if a bullet misses its intended victim and kills an unseen bystander, the actor's lack of purpose to kill the bystander does not bar liability for murder under Section 210.2(1)(a) so long as there was an intention to kill the original target.

15. For example, a person would not escape liability for causing (nonfatal) bodily injury under Section 211.1(1)(a) [assault] on the grounds that he intended to cause death. If the reverse is true, and the harm caused is more extensive or serious than the harm designed or contemplated (or, in the case of Section 2.03(3), the probable harm), then liability for the excess would be prohibited by application of the normal principles of culpability stated in Section 2.02. E.g., an attack that results in death, though only intended to cause injury, would not support a conviction for murder under Section 210.2(1)(a) [murder]. The actor might well be liable, however, for recklessly or negligently causing death (Sections 210.-2(1)(b), 210.3, and 210.4) if he intended to cause serious bodily harm.

[just] [16] bearing on the actor's liability or the gravity of his offense.
* * *

Subsection (3) deals with offenses in which recklessness or negligence is the required culpability and in which the actual result is not within the risk of which the actor was aware or, in the case of negligence, of which he should have been aware. The governing principles are the same as in the case of crimes requiring purpose or knowledge.

American Law Institute, Model Penal Code and Commentaries, Comment to § 2.03 at 260–61, 263 (1985).

D. CONCURRENCE OF THE ELEMENTS

STATE v. ROSE

Supreme Court of Rhode Island, 1973.
112 R.I. 402, 311 A.2d 281.

ROBERTS, CHIEF JUSTICE.

These are two indictments, one (No. 70–573) charging the defendant, Henry Rose, with leaving the scene of an accident, death resulting, in violation of G.L.1956 § 31–26–1 [1] and the other (No. 70–572) charging the defendant with [negligent] manslaughter. The defendant was tried on both indictments * * *, and a verdict of guilty was returned in each case. Thereafter the defendant's motions for a new trial were denied * * *.

These indictments followed the death of David J. McEnery, who was struck by defendant's motor vehicle at the intersection of Broad and Summer Streets in Providence at about 6:30 p.m. on April 1, 1970. According to the testimony of a bus driver, he had been operating his vehicle north on Broad Street and had stopped at a traffic light at the intersection of Summer Street. While the bus was standing there, he observed a pedestrian starting to cross Broad Street, and as the pedestrian reached the middle of the southbound lane he was struck by a "dirty, white station wagon" that was proceeding southerly on Broad Street. The pedestrian's body was thrown up on the hood of the car. The bus

---

16. The word "just" is in brackets because of disagreement within the Institute over whether it is wise to put undefined questions of justice to the jury. The inclusion of the term has the merit of putting it clearly to the jury that the issue it must decide is whether in light of the remoteness or accidental quality of the occurrence of the actual result, it would be just to accord it significance in determining the actor's liability or the gravity of his offense. Submitting explicit questions involving a broad moral concept like "justice" to the jury is not so different from submitting questions of "unjustifiable risk" and "gross deviation" required by the Code's definition of

recklessness and negligence. Section 2.02.
* * *

1. General Laws 1956 § 31–26–1 reads, in part, as follows: "Duty to stop in accidents resulting in personal injury.—(a) The driver of any vehicle knowingly involved in an accident resulting in injury to or death of any person shall immediately stop such vehicle at the scene of such accident or as close thereto as possible but shall then forthwith return to and in every event shall remain at the scene of the accident until he has fulfilled the requirements of § 31–26–3. Every such stop shall be made without obstructing traffic more than is necessary. * * * "

driver further testified that the station wagon stopped momentarily, the body of the pedestrian rolled off the hood, and the car immediately drove off along Broad Street in a southerly direction. The bus operator testified that he had alighted from his bus, intending to attempt to assist the victim, but was unable to locate the body.

Subsequently, it appears from the testimony of a police officer, about 6:40 p.m. the police located a white station wagon on Haskins Street, a distance of some 610 feet from the scene of the accident. The police further testified that a body later identified as that of David J. McEnery was wedged beneath the vehicle when it was found and that the vehicle had been registered to defendant.   * * *

We turn, first, to defendant's contention that the trial court erred in denying his motion for a directed verdict of acquittal in each case.   * * * In a criminal case the trial justice, in passing on such a motion, is required to give full credibility to the state's evidence, view it in a light most favorable to the state, and draw therefrom every reasonable inference consistent with guilt. However, where the evidence adduced by the state and the reasonable inferences to be drawn therefrom, even when viewed in a light most favorable to the state, are insufficient to establish guilt beyond a reasonable doubt, the court must grant the defendant's motion for a directed verdict.   * * *

The defendant here argues that in neither case did the evidence exclude any reasonable hypothesis or theory of the innocence of defendant. In so arguing in case No. 70–572, charging defendant with manslaughter, defendant directs our attention to the fact that the court charged the jury that there was no evidence in the case of culpable negligence on the part of defendant up to and including the time at which Mr. McEnery was struck by the station wagon. He further charged the jury that, in order to find defendant guilty of manslaughter, it would be necessary to find that McEnery was alive immediately after the impact and that the conduct of defendant following the impact constituted culpable negligence.

The defendant is contending that if the evidence is susceptible of a finding that McEnery was killed upon impact, he was not alive at the time he was being dragged under defendant's vehicle and defendant could not be found guilty of manslaughter. An examination of the testimony of the only medical witness makes it clear that, in his opinion, death could have resulted immediately upon impact by reason of a massive fracture of the skull. The medical witness also testified that death could have resulted a few minutes after the impact but conceded that he was not sure when it did occur.

We are inclined to agree with defendant's contention in this respect. Obviously, the evidence is such that death could have occurred after defendant had driven away with McEnery's body lodged under his car and, therefore, be consistent with guilt. On the other hand, the medical testimony is equally consistent with a finding that McEnery could have died instantly upon impact and, therefore, be consistent with a reasonable conclusion other than the guilt of defendant. It is clear, then, that, the testimony of the medical examiner lacking any reasonable medical certainty as to the time of the death of McEnery, we are unable to conclude that on such evidence defendant was guilty of manslaughter beyond a reasonable doubt. Therefore, we conclude, with respect to Indictment No. 70–572, that it was error to deny defendant's motion for a directed verdict of acquittal.

We are unable, however, to reach the same conclusion concerning the denial of the motion for a directed verdict of acquittal with respect to Indictment No. 70–573, in which defendant was charged with leaving the scene of an accident. * * *

Notes and Questions

1. *D* poisons *V*, intending to kill *V*. The poison renders *V* unconscious, but does not kill her. *D*, believing that *V* is dead, decapitates her, in order to make identification of the body more difficult. *V* dies instantly. Is *D* guilty of intent-to-kill murder? See Jackson v. Commonwealth, 100 Ky. 239, 38 S.W. 422 (1896); Thabo Meli v. Regina, [1954] 1 W.L.R. 228, [1954] 1 All Eng.Rep. 373.

Chapter 7

CRIMINAL HOMICIDE

A. OVERVIEW

1. COMMON LAW ORIGINS AND STATUTORY REFORM

AMERICAN LAW INSTITUTE, MODEL PENAL CODE AND COMMENTARIES, COMMENT TO § 210.2
(1980), 13–16

1. *Common–Law Background*. At common law, murder was defined as the unlawful killing of another human being with "malice aforethought."[1] Whatever the original meaning of that phrase, it became over time an "arbitrary symbol" used by judges to signify any of a number of mental states deemed sufficient to support liability for murder. Successive generations added new content to "malice aforethought" until it encompassed a variety of mental attitudes bearing no predictable relation to the ordinary sense of the two words. Even today, judges find in the elasticity of this ancient formula a convenient vehicle for announcing new departures in the law of homicide.

Various authorities have given different summaries of the several meanings of "malice aforethought." Generally, these definitions converge on four constituent states of mind. First and foremost, there was intent to kill. Common-law authorities included in the notion of intent to kill awareness that the death of another would result from one's actions, even if the actor had no particular desire to achieve such a consequence. Thus, intentional or knowing homicide was murder unless the actor killed in the heat of passion engendered by adequate provocation, in which case the crime was manslaughter. A second species of murder involved intent to cause grievous bodily harm. Again, knowl-

---

1. The traditional definition of murder was given by Coke in the seventeenth century: "When a man of sound memory and of the age of discretion unlawfully kills any reasonable creature in being, and under the King's peace, with malice aforethought, either express or implied by the law, the death taking place within a year and a day." Quoted in Royal Comm'n on Capital Punishment, Report, CMD. No. 8932, at 26 (1953).

edge that conduct would cause serious bodily injury was generally assimilated to intent and was deemed sufficient for murder if death of another actually resulted. A third category of murder was sometimes called depraved-heart murder. This label derived from decisions and statutes condemning as murder unintentional homicide under circumstances evincing a "depraved mind" or an "abandoned and malignant heart." Older authorities may have described such circumstances as giving rise to an "implied" or "presumed" intent to kill or injure, but the essential concept was one of extreme recklessness regarding homicidal risk. Thus, a person might be liable for murder absent any actual intent to kill or injure if he caused the death of another in a manner exhibiting a "wanton and wilful disregard of an unreasonable human risk" or, in confusing elaboration, a "wickedness of disposition, hardness of heart, cruelty, recklessness of consequences, and a mind regardless of social duty." The fourth kind of murder was based on intent to commit a felony. This is the origin of the felony-murder rule, which assigns strict liability for homicide committed during the commission of a felony. These four states of mind exhausted the meaning of "malice aforethought"; the phrase had no residual content.[13]

2. *Antecedent Statutory Variations.* Prior to the recodification effort begun by the Model Penal Code, most American jurisdictions maintained a law of murder built around these common-law classifications. The most significant departure was the division of murder into degrees, a change initiated by the Pennsylvania legislation of 1794. That statute provided that "all murder, which shall be perpetrated by means of poison, or by lying in wait, or by any other kind of willful, deliberate or premeditated killing, or which shall be committed in the perpetration, or attempt to perpetrate any arson, rape, robbery or burglary shall be deemed murder in the first degree; and all other kinds of murder shall be deemed murder in the second degree." The thrust of this reform was to confine the death penalty, which was then mandatory on conviction of any common-law murder, to homicides judged particularly heinous. Other states followed the Pennsylvania practice until at one time the vast majority of American jurisdictions differentiated degrees of murder and the term "first-degree murder" passed into common parlance.

Leaving the question of felony murder aside, the extent to which the common law had been modified in other ways prior to the drafting of the Model Penal Code varied considerably from jurisdiction to jurisdiction.

---

13. Some early writers asserted a fifth distinct species of "malice aforethought" based on intent to oppose lawful arrest. Under this rule, causing the death of another while resisting lawful arrest would be murder even if the facts did not show an intent to kill or injure or any form of extreme recklessness. Modern authorities agree, however, that resisting arrest is not an independently sufficient basis of liability for murder. * * *

AMERICAN LAW INSTITUTE, MODEL PENAL CODE AND COMMENTARIES, COMMENT TO § 210.3

(1980), 44–46

1. *Common–Law Background.* Initially, the common law did not distinguish murder from manslaughter. Early statutes, however, sought to differentiate among criminal homicides for the purpose of withdrawing benefit of clergy from the more heinous killings. This initiative led to the division of criminal homicides into murder, which retained its status as a capital crime, and the lesser offense of manslaughter. The courts defined murder in terms of the evolving concept of "malice aforethought" and treated manslaughter as a residual category for all other criminal homicides. Thus, in its classic formulation, manslaughter consisted of homicide without malice aforethought on the one hand and without justification or excuse on the other.

Traditional statements of the English law as it further evolved divided the offense into two types. First, homicide, even if intentional, was said to be without malice and hence manslaughter if committed in the heat of passion upon adequate provocation. Second, homicide was also manslaughter if it resulted from an act that was regarded as unduly dangerous to life or limb or from an act that was otherwise unlawful. This category thus encompassed conduct that was insufficiently reckless or negligent to constitute "depraved-heart" murder but at the same time exhibited culpability greater than needed for ordinary conceptions of civil negligence. It also included cases where the actor caused the death of another in the commission of an unlawful act, sometimes described as the misdemeanor-manslaughter analogue to the felony-murder rule. Courts commonly referred to the first category as voluntary manslaughter and the second as involuntary manslaughter, although the distinction had no grading significance at common law.

2. *Antecedent Statutory Variations.* Virtually every state recognized the crime of manslaughter at the time the Model Penal Code was drafted. The largest number contained no explicit definition of the offense and hence determined its content by reference to the common law. There were also a few states, typified by Florida, that carried forward the substance of the common-law offense by defining manslaughter as "the killing of a human being by the act, procurement or culpable negligence of another where such killing shall not be justifiable or excusable homicide nor murder." A more common variation was reflected in the federal manslaughter provision:

> Manslaughter is the unlawful killing of a human being without malice. It is of two kinds:
>
> > Voluntary—Upon a sudden quarrel or heat of passion.
> >
> > Involuntary—In the commission of an unlawful act not amounting to a felony, or in the commission in an unlawful manner, or without due caution and circumspection, of a lawful act which might produce death.[9]

9. 18 U.S.C. § 1112. * * *

Statutes that followed this pattern typically departed from the common law by providing a grading differential between voluntary and involuntary manslaughter.

2. VARIATIONS ON THE THEME: SOME HOMICIDE STATUTES

CALIFORNIA PENAL CODE

§ 187. Murder defined; death of fetus

(a) Murder is the unlawful killing of a human being, or a fetus [except during a lawful abortion or when consented to by the mother], with malice aforethought. * * *

§ 188. Malice * * * defined

Such malice may be express or implied. It is express when there is manifested a deliberate intention unlawfully to take away the life of a fellow creature. It is implied, when no considerable provocation appears, or when the circumstances attending the killing show an abandoned and malignant heart.

When it is shown that the killing resulted from the intentional doing of an act with express or implied malice as defined above, no other mental state need be shown to establish the mental state of malice aforethought. * * *

§ 189. Murder; degrees

All murder which is perpetrated by means of a destructive device or explosive, knowing use of ammunition designed primarily to penetrate metal or armor, poison, lying in wait, torture, or by any other kind of willful, deliberate, and premeditated killing, or which is committed in the perpetration of, or attempt to perpetrate, arson, rape, robbery, burglary, mayhem, kidnapping, train wrecking, or any act punishable under [various enumerated Penal Code sections, prohibiting various forms of criminal sexual conduct], is murder in the first degree [punishable by death, life imprisonment without possibility of parole, or imprisonment for 25 years to life]; and all other kinds of murder are of the second degree [generally punishable by imprisonment for 15 years to life]. * * *

To prove the killing was "deliberate and premeditated," it shall not be necessary to prove the defendant maturely and meaningfully reflected upon the gravity of his or her act.

§ 192 Manslaughter * * *

Manslaughter is the unlawful killing of a human being without malice. It is of three kinds:

(a) Voluntary—upon a sudden quarrel or heat of passion. [Punishable by imprisonment for 3, 6, or 11 years.]

(b) Involuntary—in the commission of an unlawful act, not amounting to felony; or in the commission of a lawful act which might produce death, in an unlawful manner, or without due caution and circumspection. This subdivision shall not apply to acts committed in the driving of a vehicle. [Punishable by imprisonment for 2, 3, or 4 years.]

(c) Vehicular—

(1) * * * driving a vehicle in the commission of an unlawful act, not amounting to a felony, and with gross negligence; or driving a vehicle in the commission of a lawful act which might produce death, in an unlawful manner, and with gross negligence. [Punishable by up to one year in county jail, or imprisonment for 2, 4, or 6 years.]

(2) * * * driving a vehicle in the commission of an unlawful act, not amounting to a felony, but without gross negligence, or driving a vehicle in the commission of a lawful act, which might produce death, in an unlawful manner, but without gross negligence. [Punishable by up to one year in a county jail.] * * *

"Gross negligence," as used in this section, shall not be construed as prohibiting or precluding a charge of murder under Section 188 upon facts exhibiting wantonness and a conscious disregard for life to support a finding of implied malice * * *.

§ 194. Murder and manslaughter; time of death; computation

To make the killing either murder or manslaughter, it is requisite that the party die within three years and a day after the stroke received or the cause of death administered. In the computation of such time, the whole of the day on which the act was done shall be reckoned the first.

MICHIGAN PENAL CODE

§ 750.316. First degree murder

Murder which is perpetrated by means of poison, lying in wait, or other wilful, deliberate, and premeditated killing, or which is committed in the perpetration, or attempt to perpetrate arson, criminal sexual conduct * * *, robbery, breaking and entering a dwelling, larceny of any kind, extortion, or kidnapping, is murder of the first degree, and shall be punished by imprisonment for life [without the possibility of parole].

§ 750.317. Second degree murder

All other kinds of murder shall be murder of the second degree, and shall be punished by imprisonment in the state prison for life [with the possibility of parole], or any terms of years, in the discretion of the court trying the same.

§ 750.321. Manslaughter

Any person who shall commit the crime of manslaughter shall be guilty of a felony punishable by imprisonment in the state prison, not more than 15 years or by fine of not more than 7,500 dollars, or both, at the discretion of the court.

§ 750.322. Manslaughter; wilful killing of unborn quick child

The wilful killing of an unborn quick child by any injury to the mother of such child, which would be murder if it resulted in the death of such mother, shall be deemed manslaughter.

NEW YORK PENAL LAW

§ 125.10 Criminally negligent homicide

A person is guilty of criminally negligent homicide [a Class E felony, punishable by imprisonment of from one to four years] when, with criminal negligence, he causes the death of another person.

§ 125.15 Manslaughter in the second degree

A person is guilty of manslaughter in the second degree [a Class C felony, punishable by imprisonment of from one to fifteen years] when:

(1) He recklessly causes the death of another person; or

(2) He commits upon a female an abortional act which causes her death, unless such abortional act is justifiable [under the state abortion law]; or

(3) He intentionally causes or aids another person to commit suicide.

§ 125.20 Manslaughter in the first degree

A person is guilty of manslaughter in the first degree [a Class B felony, punishable by imprisonment of from 1 to 25 years] when:

(1) With intent to cause serious physical injury to another person, he causes the death of such person or of a third person; or

(2) With intent to cause the death of another person, he causes the death of such person or of a third person under circumstances which do not constitute murder because he acts under the influence of extreme emotional disturbance, as defined in paragraph (a) of subdivision one of section 125.25. The fact that homicide was committed under the influence of extreme emotional disturbance constitutes a mitigating circumstance reducing murder to manslaughter in the first degree and need not be proved in any prosecution initiated under this subdivision; or

(3) He commits upon a female pregnant for more than twenty-four weeks an abortional act which causes her death, unless such abortional act is justifiable [under the state abortion law]; or

(4) Being eighteen years old or more and with intent to cause physical injury to a person less than eleven years old, the defendant recklessly engages in conduct which creates a grave risk of a serious

physical injury to such person and thereby causes the death of such person.

§ 125.25 Murder in the second degree

A person is guilty of murder in the second degree [a Class A–I felony, punishable by imprisonment of from 15 years to life] when:

(1) With intent to cause the death of another person, he causes the death of such person or of a third person; except that in any prosecution under this subdivision, it is an affirmative defense that:

> (a) The defendant acted under the influence of extreme emotional disturbance for which there was a reasonable explanation or excuse, the reasonableness of which is to be determined from the viewpoint of a person in the defendant's situation under the circumstances as the defendant believed them to be * * *; or

> (b) The defendant's conduct consisted of causing or aiding, without the use of duress or deception, another person to commit suicide * * *; or

(2) Under circumstances evincing a depraved indifference to human life, he recklessly engages in conduct which creates a grave risk of death to another person, and thereby causes the death of another person; or

(3) Acting either alone or with one or more persons, he commits or attempts to commit robbery, burglary, kidnapping, arson, rape * * *, sodomy * * *, or [prison] escape * * *, and, in the course of and in furtherance of such crime or of immediate flight therefrom he, or another participant, if there be any, causes the death of a person other than one of the participants * * *; or

(4) Under circumstances evincing a depraved indifference to human life, and being eighteen years old or more the defendant recklessly engages in conduct which creates a grave risk of serious physical injury or death to another person less than eleven years old and thereby causes the death of such person.

§ 125.27 Murder in the first degree

A person is guilty of murder in the first degree [a Class A–I felony, for which the maximum statutory penalty is death] when:

(1) With intent to cause the death of another person, he causes the death of such person; and

> (a) Either:

>> (i) the victim was a police officer * * * performing his official duties, and the defendant knew or reasonably should have known that the victim was a police officer; or

>> (ii) the victim was an employee of a * * * correctional institution * * * performing his official duties, and the defendant knew or reasonably should have known that the victim was a [correctional employee]; or

(iii) at the time of the commission of the crime, the defendant was confined in a state correctional institution [or had escaped from such confinement] or was otherwise in custody upon a sentence for the term of his natural life, or upon a sentence commuted to one of natural life, or upon a sentence for an indeterminate term the minimum of which was at least fifteen years and the maximum of which was natural life * * *; and

(b) The defendant was more than eighteen years old at the time of the commission of the crime. * * *

Notes and Questions

1. The Model Penal Code divides criminal homicide into three, rather than the traditional two, categories: murder, manslaughter, and negligent homicide. These offenses differ in key respects from the common law and antecedent statutory law, as explained infra.

3. THE PROTECTED INTEREST: "HUMAN BEING"

PEOPLE v. EULO

Court of Appeals of New York, 1984.
63 N.Y.2d 341, 482 N.Y.S.2d 436, 472 N.E.2d 286.

COOKE, CHIEF JUDGE.

These appeals involve a question of criminal responsibility in which defendants, charged with homicide, contend that their conduct did not cause death. * * *

I

[Defendants Eulo and Bonilla were convicted of manslaughter in separate prosecutions based on similar facts. In each case the accused shot his victim in the head, the victim was brought to a hospital in an unconscious state, after which the patient was placed on a respirator to enable breathing. Medical tests determined in each case that the victim's brain had irreversibly ceased to function, as evidenced in part by "flat" or "isoelectric" readings on an electroencephalogram (EEG). With the consent of the families, the patients in both cases were declared dead, artificial respiration terminated, and organs from the bodies removed for transplantation purposes.]

II

Defendants' principal point in each of these appeals is that the respective Trial Judges failed to adequately instruct the juries as to what constitutes a person's death, the time at which criminal liability for a homicide would attach. It is claimed that in New York, the time of death has always been set by reference to the functioning of the heart and the lungs; that death does not occur until there has been an irreversible cessation of breathing and heartbeat.

There having been extensive testimony at both trials concerning each victim's diagnosis as "brain dead," defendants argue that, in the absence of clear instruction, the juries may have erroneously concluded that defendants would be guilty of homicide if their conduct was the legal cause of the victims' "brain death" rather than the victims' ultimate state of cardiorespiratory failure. In evaluating defendants' contentions, it is first necessary to review: how death has traditionally been determined by the law; how the principle of "brain death" is now sought to be infused into our jurisprudence; and, whether, if at all, this court may recognize a principle of "brain death" without infringing upon a legislative power or prerogative.

A person's passing from life has long been an event marked with a variety of legal consequences. * * * In the immediate context, * * * determination of a person's "death" is relevant because our Penal Law defines homicide in terms of "conduct which causes the *death* of a person" (Penal Law, § 125.00 [emphasis added]).

Death has been conceptualized by the law as, simply, the absence of life * * *. But, while erecting death as a critical milepost in a person's legal life, the law has had little occasion to consider the precise point at which a person ceases to live. * * *

Within the past two decades, machines that artificially maintain cardiorespiratory functions have come into widespread use. This technical accomplishment has called into question the universal applicability of the traditional legal and medical criteria for determining when a person has died.

These criteria were cast into flux as the medical community gained a better understanding of human physiology. It is widely understood that the human brain may be anatomically divided, generally, into three parts: the cerebrum, the cerebellum, and the brain stem. The cerebrum, known also as the "higher brain," is deemed largely to control cognitive functions such as thought, memory, and consciousness. The cerebellum primarily controls motor coordination. The brain stem, or "lower brain," which itself has three parts known as the midbrain, pons, and medulla, controls reflexive or spontaneous functions such as breathing, swallowing, and "sleep-wake" cycles.

* * * Within a relatively short period after being deprived of oxygen, the brain will irreversibly stop functioning. With the suffocation of the higher brain all cognitive powers are lost and a cessation of lower brain functions will ultimately end all spontaneous bodily functions.

Notwithstanding a total irreversible loss of the entire brain's functioning, contemporary medical techniques can maintain, for a limited period, the operation of the heart and the lungs. Respirators or ventilators can substitute for the lower brain's failure to maintain breathing. This artificial respiration, when combined with a chemical regimen, can support the continued operation of the heart. This is so because, unlike respiration, the physical contracting or "beating" of the heart occurs independently of impulses from the brain: so long as blood containing oxygen circulates to the heart, it may continue to beat and medication can take over the lower brain's limited role in regulating the rate and force of the heartbeat.

It became clear in medical practice that the traditional "vital signs"—breathing and heartbeat—are not independent indicia of life, but are, instead, part of an integration of functions in which the brain is dominant. As a result, the medical community began to consider the cessation of brain activity as a measure of death.[15]

The movement in law towards recognizing cessation of brain functions as criteria for death followed this medical trend. The immediate motive for adopting this position was to ease and make more efficient the transfer of donated organs. Organ transfers, to be successful, require a "viable, intact organ." Once all of a person's vital functions have ceased, transferable organs swiftly deteriorate and lose their transplant value. * * *

* * * [T]he first legal recognition of cessation of brain functions as a criterion for determining death came in the form of a Kansas statute enacted in 1970.[20] Denominated "[an] Act relating to and defining death," the statute states, in part, that death will be deemed to have occurred when a physician applying ordinary medical standards determines that there is an "absence of spontaneous respiratory and cardiac functions and * * * attempts at resuscitation are considered hopeless * * * *or* * * * there is the absence of spontaneous brain function."

In the years following enactment of this statute, a growing number of sister States enacted statutes of their own. Some opted for the Kansas approach. Others defined death solely in terms of brain-based criteria as determined by accepted methods of medical practice. And still others retain the cardiorespiratory yardstick, but provide that when artificial means of sustaining respiration and heartbeat preclude application of the traditional criteria, death may be determined according to brain-based criteria * * *. In the absence of any statute defining death, some jurisdictions have judicially adopted brain-based criteria for determining death. * * *

In New York, the term "death," although used in many statutes, has not been expressly defined by the Legislature. This raises the

15. The initial problem for doctors was to devise a technical means of verifying when the entire brain ceases to function. Unlike tests for determining the cessation of breathing and heartbeat, more sophisticated means were necessary to measure the less obvious functioning of the brain. A seminal study was issued in 1968, under the auspices of Harvard Medical School, setting forth a multistep test designed to identify the existence of physical indicia of brain activity. Under it, responsiveness to painful stimuli is to be tested. The subject is also to be observed for any spontaneous movement or respiration and any operation of various bodily reflexes. The absence of brain activity, when demonstrated under these tests, is then sought to be confirmed by reapplication of the tests at least 24 hours later and through the reading of an EEG, which when "flat" has confirmatory value. This test has served as the foundation for currently applied tests for determining when the brain has ceased to function.

20. See L.1970, ch. 348, Kan.Laws 994, codified at Kan.Stats.Ann., § 77–202.

question of how this court may construe these expressions of the term "death" in the absence of clarification by the Legislature. * * *

It has been called to this court's attention that the Legislature has, on a number of occasions, had bills before it that would expressly recognize brain-based criteria for determining death and has taken no affirmative action. This legislative void in no way impedes this court from fulfilling its obligation to construe laws of the State. * * * It is incumbent upon this court to instill certainty and uniformity in these important areas.

We hold that a recognition of brain-based criteria for determining death is not unfaithful to prior judicial definitions of "death," as presumptively adopted in the many statutes using that term. Close examination of the common-law conception of death and the traditional criteria used to determine when death has occurred leads inexorably to this conclusion. * * *

* * * Ordinarily, death will be determined according to the traditional criteria of irreversible cardiorespiratory repose. When, however, the respiratory and circulatory functions are maintained by mechanical means, their significance, as signs of life, is at best ambiguous. Under such circumstances, death may nevertheless be deemed to occur when, according to accepted medical practice, it is determined that the entire brain's function has irreversibly ceased. * * *

This court searches in vain for evidence that * * * the Legislature intended to render immutable the criteria used to determine death. By extension, to hold to the contrary would be to say that the law could not recognize diagnostic equipment such as the stethoscope or more sensitive equipment even when it became clear that these instruments more accurately measured the presence of signs of life. * * *

Moreover, the Legislature has consistently declared, from the time it adopted the * * * Penal Code in 1881 through several recodifications, that our Penal Law should be construed "according to the fair import of [its] terms to promote justice and effect the objects of the law" (Penal Law, § 5.00). It is the first object of our Penal Law "[to] proscribe conduct which unjustifiably and inexcusably causes or threatens substantial harm to individual or public interests (Penal Law, § 1.05, subd. 1). Therefore, in the instant matters, to construe our homicide statute to provide for criminal responsibility for homicide when a defendant's conduct causes injury leading to the victim's total loss of brain functions, is entirely consistent with the Legislature's concept of death. * * *

III

Each defendant correctly notes that the respective Trial Judges did not expressly instruct the juries concerning the criteria to be applied in determining when death occurred. Whether medically accepted brain-based criteria are legally cognizable became an issue in these cases when the respective juries heard testimony concerning the victims being pronounced medically dead while their hearts were beating and before artificial maintenance of the cardiorespiratory systems was discontinued. To properly evaluate whether these diagnoses of death were legally and medically premature and, therefore, whether the subsequent activities were possibly superseding causes of the deaths, the juries had to have been instructed as to the appropriate criteria for determining death: irreversible cessation of breathing and heartbeat or irreversible cessation of the entire brain's functioning.

The courts here adequately conveyed to the juries their obligation to determine the fact and causation of death. The courts defined the criteria of death in relation to the chain of causation. By specifically charging the juries that they might consider the surgical [transplantation] procedures as superseding causes of death, the courts made clear by ready implication that death should be deemed to have occurred after all medical procedures had ended.

The trial courts could have given express instructions that death may be deemed to have occurred when the victims' entire brain, including the brain stem, had irreversibly ceased to function. On the facts of these cases, that would have been the better practice. But, as mentioned, the brain-based criteria are supplemental to the traditional criteria, each describing the same phenomenon of death. In the context of a criminal case for homicide, there is no theoretical or practical impediment to the People's proceeding under a theory that the defendant "[caused] the death" of a person, with death determined by either criteria.

Even though each of these cases was presented to a jury which had been charged that death should be deemed to have occurred after the medical intervention had ended, testimony concerning the attending physicians' diagnoses of the victims as dead, according to brain-based criteria, was nonetheless highly relevant. It was these medical pronouncements that caused the victims to be removed from the medical systems that maintained their breathing and heartbeat. If the victims were properly diagnosed as dead, of course, no subsequent medical procedure such as the organ removals would be deemed a cause of death. If victims' deaths were prematurely pronounced due to a doctor's negligence, the subsequent procedures may have been a cause of death, but that negligence would not constitute a superseding cause of death relieving defendants of liability. If, however, the pronouncements of death were premature due to the gross negligence or the intentional wrongdoing of doctors, as determined by a grave deviation from accepted medical practices or disregard for legally cognizable criteria for determining death, the intervening medical procedure would interrupt the chain of causation and become the legal cause of death. Thus, the propriety of the medical procedures is integral to the question of causation.

A review of the records, viewed in a light most favorable to the People, indicates that there was sufficient evidence for a rational juror to have concluded beyond a reasonable doubt that each defendant's conduct caused the victim's death and that the medical procedures were not superseding causes of death * * *.

Notes and Questions

1. Did the court overstep its authority by recognizing brain-based criteria for determining "death" for criminal law purposes? Isn't this a matter for legislative judgment? Whichever branch of government makes the determination, what factors ought to be considered? Is the need for viable organs for transplantation purposes a valid criterion?

2. *Fetuses as "human beings."* At the other end of life's continuum, the common law requirement of live birth to prove that a fetus is a "human being" (see Keeler v. Superior Court, 2 Cal.3d 619, 87 Cal.Rptr. 481, 470 P.2d 617 (1970), p. 67 supra) has been abrogated by some state legislatures. For example, consider the California and Michigan homicide codes (Section A., subsection 2. supra). In these states, assuming the death of a fetus, of what offense is a person guilty if he strikes a pregnant woman in the abdomen, with the intent of killing the fetus?

In contrast to these statutes, consider Minn.Stat.Ann. § 609.2661 (1988), which provides that a person is guilty of first degree murder, and must be sentenced to imprisonment for life, if he "causes the death of an unborn child * * * with intent to effect the death of the unborn child or of another." Suppose that Alice, intending to kill Barbara, shoots Barbara in the abdomen, unaware that she is pregnant with a 28-day-old embryo. Barbara and the embryo die. Is Alice guilty of first degree murder of the embryo? See State v. Merrill, 450 N.W.2d 318 (Minn.1990).

3. *"Year and a day rule."* The advent of modern medical technology has compelled courts and legislators to consider the present-day vitality of the "year and a day rule" in homicide law:

> The year and a day rule has roots deep in the soil of our common law. Its origins have been traced back to the thirteenth century. See * * * the antique Statute of Glouster, 6 Edw. 1, c. 9 (1278), which provided that a private prosecution for homicide shall not abate if brought within a year and a day of the death. By the 18th century, the assumption was that a homicide prosecution could be brought only if the victim had died within a year and a day of the injury. This doctrine, quite separate from earlier statues [sic] of limitation, was discussed by Lord Coke, and also by the eighteenth century commentators Hawkins and Blackstone. * * * The application of the rule to criminal prosecutions has been acknowledged by the Supreme Court * * *.

United States v. Jackson, 528 A.2d 1211, 1214 (D.C.App.1987).

In *Jackson,* the defendant shot the victim in the head on January 2, 1982. The victim was taken to a nearby hospital, where he remained until his death fourteen months after the assault. Under the year-and-a-day rule, the defendant could not be prosecuted for the death.

What do you think is the rationale of the rule? Is the rule anachronistic, as its critics claim? Should there be some time limitation, but a longer one? See, e.g., West's Ann.Cal.Penal Code § 194 (1985) ("[I]t is requisite that the party die within three years and a day after the stroke received or the cause of death administered.'').

The *Jackson* court abolished the year-and-a-day rule in the District of Columbia, but it concluded that prosecution of the defendant in that case would violate the *ex post facto* clause. Was the court correct in the latter regard? For the contrary position, see People v. Snipe, 25 Cal.App.3d 742, 102 Cal.Rptr. 6 (1972).

B. INTENTIONAL KILLINGS

1. DEGREES OF MURDER: THE DELIBERATION–PREMEDITATION FORMULA

STATE v. SCHRADER

Supreme Court of Appeals of West Virginia, 1982.
172 W.Va. 1, 302 S.E.2d 70.

NEELY, JUSTICE.

The appellant, William Schrader, Jr. was found guilty of murder in the first degree without a recommendation of mercy after a jury trial * * *. The circuit court then sentenced the appellant to life imprisonment * * *.

On the morning of 14 December 1977, the appellant went to Frank Millione's Gun and Coin Shop in Marion County to purchase and trade war souvenirs. The appellant asserts that an argument developed between the appellant and the victim after the appellant questioned the authenticity of a German sword that he had previously purchased. During the course of the argument, the appellant stabbed Frank Millione fifty-one times with a hunting knife. At trial the appellant claimed that he had acted in self-defense. He maintained that the victim was known by him to carry weapons and that the victim had reached into his pocket to draw a gun during the course of the argument. The appellant did testify, however, that Mr. Millione never produced any gun from his pocket. Stab wounds were found on the victim's face, head, neck, back, and chest. * * *

The appellant objects to the portion of the jury charge that read:

> I would advise you that to constitute a willful, deliberate and premeditated killing, it is not necessary that the intention to kill should exist for any set length of time prior to the actual killing; it is only necessary that such intention should have come into existence for the first time at the time of such killing, or at any time previously.

The appellant contends that such an instruction takes the "pre" out of "premeditation" and is therefore an inaccurate statement of law. We disagree.

The appellant assumes that premeditation as used in a murder statute has the same meaning as that found in a dictionary. While the meanings of words in a statute are often congruent with their dictionary definitions, this is not necessarily the case when the statute is very old, the language has been unchanged for almost two centuries, and specific words have taken on a particular meaning which is as well known and as much a part of the law as the statute itself. Today we must decide what the Legislature meant when it used the word "premeditated" to describe first degree murder.

The crime of murder was first divided into degrees in the statute passed by the Pennsylvania Assembly in 1794. That statute used the phrase "willful, deliberate and premeditated" to describe one class of first degree murder. * * * Virginia adopted a similar statute in 1796.

By the time the West Virginia Legislature adopted the Virginia statute in 1868, the law was settled that in order to constitute a "premeditated" murder an intent to kill need exist only for an instant. * * *

The first case to construe the meaning of "premeditated" in such a statute was *Commonwealth v. Mullato Bob,* 4 Dall. 145 (Pa.1795). In that case, Pennsylvania Chief Justice M'Kean noted:

> It has been objected, however, that the amendment of our Penal Code renders premeditation an indispensable ingredient, to constitute murder of the first degree. But still, it must be allowed, that the intention remains as much as ever, the true criterion of the crimes, in Law as well as in Ethics; and the intention of the party can only be collected from his words and actions.... But, let it be supposed, that a man, without uttering a word, should strike another on the head with an ax, it must, on every principle by which we can judge human actions, be deemed a premeditated violence.

This holding became the foundation for Virginia's law on the issue of premeditation. * * * *Commonwealth v. King,* 2 Va.Cas. 78 (1826) discussed with approval *Mulatto Bob's Case* and a host of other Pennsylvania cases which held essentially that * * * "no time is too short for a wicked man to frame in his mind a scheme for murder, and to contrive the means of accomplishing it." 2 Va.Cas. at 85. * * *

Hence, when the West Virginia Legislature adopted the Virginia murder statute in 1868, the meaning of "premeditated" as used in the statute was essentially "knowing" and "intentional." Since then, courts have consistently recognized that the mental process necessary to constitute "willful, deliberate and premeditated" murder can be accomplished very quickly or even in the proverbial "twinkling of an eye." In fact, Justice Cardozo recommended that the mere exercise of choice by a defendant would justify the inference of deliberation and premeditation necessary to constitute first degree murder. * * *

In a homicide trial the jury is usually presented with a smorgasbord of verdicts with their statutorily prescribed punishments. These various verdicts correspond to different levels of culpability. The lines between the verdicts are thin and hard to distinguish even after centuries of legal scholarship. They are all the more difficult to explain to a jury in one set of instructions. As Justice Cardozo explained while discussing a New York statute similar to the West Virginia homicide statute: "What we have is merely a privilege offered to the jury to find the lesser degree when the suddenness of the intent, the vehemence of the passion, seems to call irresistibly for the exercise of mercy." Cardozo, "What Medicine Can Do for Law" in *Law and Literature,* 70, 100 (1931).

Unfortunately, all of the considerations to which Justice Cardozo alluded that can be subsumed under the category of "culpability" cannot be reduced to neat, prepackaged, jury instructions. The traditional instructions on the subject of murder are continually repeated not because they succeed in converting subjective considerations to objective considerations, but rather because they have always been given and they do about as well in this regard as any other attempt. The instruction objected to in this case has been given for years and has withstood our scrutiny before.

Since the instruction to which the appellant objects is a correct statement of law, * * * we find that the court did not err by giving this instruction. * * *

Notes and Questions

1. Not all courts apply the deliberation-premeditation formula as the West Virginia tribunal did in *Schrader.* Consider People v. Morrin, 31 Mich.App. 301, 325–26, 329–30, 187 N.W.2d 434, 447, 449 (1971):

[T]he division of murder into degrees was prompted by a feeling that not all murders reflected the same quantum of culpability on the part of the wrongdoer. * * *

The clarity of the policy underlying the statutory division of murder into degrees contrasts sharply with the lack of precise standards for determining what constitutes premeditation and deliberation sufficient to establish first-degree murder. Since premeditation and deliberation are all that distinguish first-degree from second-degree murder, imprecise definition of these elements tends to erode the distinction between the two offenses.

A number of jurisdictions have all but obliterated this distinction by observing the rule that premeditation and deliberation need precede the homicidal act only momentarily. * * * The rule prevalent in those jurisdictions grants the jury an unstructured discretion to find [first-degree murder].

Michigan adheres to a more meaningful standard. * * * Accordingly, it underscores the difference between the statutory degrees of murder to emphasize that premeditation and deliberation must be given independent meaning in a prosecution for first-degree murder. The ordinary meaning of the terms will suffice. To premeditate is to think about beforehand; to deliberate is to measure and evaluate the major facets of a choice or problem. As a number of courts have pointed out, premeditation and deliberation characterize a thought process undisturbed by hot blood. While the minimum time necessary to exercise this process is incapable of exact determination, the interval between initial thought and ultimate actions should be long enough to afford a reasonable man time to subject the nature of his response to a "second look."

Under *Morrin*, is it possible for a person to deliberate without premeditating? Can she premeditate without deliberating? Can a person kill wilfully without premeditating *or* deliberating? Of what degree of murder would Schrader be guilty under *Morrin?*

2. *Schrader* and *Morrin* agree on one matter: the purpose of the deliberation-premeditation formula is to distinguish between more and less culpable murders. In view of this, which version of the formula is preferable? In reading the next two cases, reflect as well on whether the formula (in either version) properly separates the more culpable killers from the lesser ones.

MIDGETT v. STATE

Supreme Court of Arkansas, 1987.
292 Ark. 278, 729 S.W.2d 410.

NEWBERN, JUSTICE.

This child abuse case resulted in the appellant's conviction of first degree murder. The sole issue on appeal is whether the state's evidence was sufficient to sustain the conviction. We hold there was no evidence of the "... premeditated and deliberated purpose of causing the death of another person ..." required for conviction of first degree murder * * *. However, we find the evidence was sufficient to sustain a conviction of second degree murder, described in Ark.Stat.Ann. § 41–1503(1)(c) (Repl. 1977), as the appellant was shown to have caused his son's death by delivering a blow to his abdomen or chest "... with the purpose of causing serious physical injury...." The conviction is thus modified from one of first degree murder to one of second degree murder and affirmed.

The facts of this case are as heart-rending as any we are likely to see. The appellant is six feet two inches tall and weighs 300 pounds. His son, Ronnie Midgett, Jr., was eight years old and weighed between thirty-eight and forty-five pounds. The evidence showed that Ronnie Jr. had been abused by brutal beatings over a substantial period of time. Typically, as in other child abuse cases, the bruises had been noticed by school personnel, and a school counselor * * * had gone to the Midgett home to inquire. Ronnie Jr. would not say how he had obtained the bruises or why he was so lethargic at school except to blame it all, vaguely, on a rough playing little brother. He did not even complain to his siblings about the treatment he was receiving from the appellant. His mother, the wife of the appellant, was not living in the home. The other children apparently were not being physically abused by the appellant.

Ronnie Jr.'s sister, Sherry, aged ten, testified that on the Saturday preceding the Wednesday of Ronnie Jr.'s death their father, the appellant, was drinking whiskey (two to three quarts that day) and beating on Ronnie Jr. She testified that the appellant would "bundle up his fist" and hit Ronnie Jr. in the stomach and in the back. On direct examination she said that she had not previously seen the appellant beat Ronnie Jr., but she had seen the appellant choke him for no particular reason on Sunday nights after she and Ronnie Jr. returned from church. * * * She said the bruises on Ronnie Jr.'s body noticed over the preceding six months had been caused by the appellant. She said the beating administered on the Saturday in question consisted of four blows, two to the stomach and two to the back.

On the Wednesday Ronnie Jr. died, the appellant appeared at a hospital carrying the body. He told hospital personnel something was wrong with the child. An autopsy was performed, and it showed Ronnie Jr. was a very poorly nourished and under-developed eight-year-old. There were recently caused bruises on the lips, center of the chest plate, and forehead as well as on the back part of the lateral chest wall, the soft tissue near the spine, and the buttocks. There was discoloration of the abdominal wall and prominent bruising on the palms of the hands. Older bruises were found on the right temple, under the chin, and on the left mandible. Recent as well as older, healed, rib fractures were found.

The conclusion of the medical examiner who performed the autopsy was that Ronnie Jr. died as the result of intra-abdominal hemorrhage caused by a blunt force trauma consistent with having been delivered by a human fist. The appellant argues that in spite of all this evidence of child abuse, there is no evidence that he killed Ronnie Jr. having premeditated and deliberated causing his death. We must agree. * * *

* * * The evidence in this case supports only the conclusion that the appellant intended not to kill his son but to further abuse him or that his intent, if it was to kill the child, was developed in a drunken, heated, rage while disciplining the child. Neither of those supports a finding of premeditation or deliberation.

Perhaps because they wish to punish more severely child abusers who kill their children, other states' legislatures have created laws permitting them to go beyond second degree murder. For example, Illinois has made aggravated battery one of the felonies qualifying for "felony murder," and a child abuser can be convicted of murder if the child dies as a result of aggravated battery. * * * California has also adopted a murder by torture statute making the offense murder in the first degree without regard to the intent to kill. * * *

All of this goes to show that there remains a difference between first and second degree murder, not only under our statute, but generally. Unless our law is changed to permit conviction of first degree murder for something like child abuse or torture resulting in death, our duty is to give those accused of first degree murder the benefit of the requirement that they be shown by substantial evidence to have premeditated and deliberated the killing, no matter how heinous the facts may otherwise be. * * *

* * * The dissenting opinion's conclusion that the appellant starved Ronnie Jr., must be based solely on the child's underdeveloped condition which could, presumably, have been caused by any number of physical malfunctions. There is no evidence the appellant starved the child. The dissenting opinion says it is for the jury to determine the degree of murder of which the appellant is guilty. That is true so long as there is substantial evidence to support the jury's choice. The point of this opinion is to note that there was no evidence of premeditation or deliberation which are required elements of the crime of first degree murder. * * *

HICKMAN, JUSTICE, dissenting.

Simply put, if a parent deliberately starves and beats a child to death, he cannot be convicted of the child's murder. In reaching this decision, the majority * * * substitutes its judgment for that of the jury. The majority has decided it cannot come to grips with the question of the battered child who dies as a result of deliberate, methodical, intentional and severe abuse. A death caused by such acts is murder by any legal standard, and that fact cannot be changed—not even by the majority. The degree of murder committed is for the jury to decide—not us. * * *

In this case the majority, with clairvoyance, decides that this parent did not intend to kill his child, but rather to keep him alive for further abuse. This is not a child neglect case. The state proved Midgett starved the boy, choked him, and struck him several times in the stomach and back. The jury could easily conclude that such repeated treatment was intended to kill the child. * * *

I cannot fathom how this father could have done what he did; but it is not my place to sit in judgment of his mental state, nor allow my human feelings to color my judgment of his accountability to the law. The law has an objective standard of accountability for all who take human life. If one does certain acts and the result is murder, one must pay. The jury found Midgett guilty and, according to the law, there is substantial evidence to support that verdict. That should end the matter for us. He is guilty of first degree murder in the eyes of the law. His moral crime as a father is another matter, and it is not for us to speculate why he did it.

I would affirm the judgment.

STATE v. FORREST

Supreme Court of North Carolina, 1987.
321 N.C. 186, 362 S.E.2d 252.

MEYER, JUSTICE.

Defendant was convicted of the first-degree murder of his father, Clyde Forrest. * * * [T]he case was tried as a noncapital case, and defendant was sentenced accordingly to life imprisonment. * * *

The facts of this case are essentially uncontested, and the evidence presented at trial tended to show the following series of events. On 22

December 1985, defendant John Forrest admitted his critically ill father, Clyde Forrest, Sr., to Moore Memorial Hospital. Defendant's father, who had previously been hospitalized, was suffering from numerous serious ailments, including severe heart disease, hypertension, a thoracic aneurysm, numerous pulmonary emboli, and a peptic ulcer. By the morning of 23 December 1985, his medical condition was determined to be untreatable and terminal. Accordingly, he was classified as "No Code," meaning that no extraordinary measures would be used to save his life, and he was moved to a more comfortable room.

On 24 December 1985, defendant went to the hospital to visit his ailing father. No other family members were present in his father's room when he arrived. While one of the nurse's assistants was tending to his father, defendant told her, "There is no need in doing that. He's dying." She responded, "Well, I think he's better." The nurse's assistant noticed that defendant was sniffling as though crying and that he kept his hand in his pocket during their conversation. She subsequently went to get the nurse.

When the nurse's assistant returned with the nurse, defendant once again stated his belief that his father was dying. The nurse tried to comfort defendant, telling him, "I don't think your father is as sick as you think he is." Defendant, very upset, responded, "Go to hell. I've been taking care of him for years. I'll take care of him." Defendant was then left alone in the room with his father.

Alone at his father's bedside, defendant began to cry and to tell his father how much he loved him. His father began to cough, emitting a gurgling and rattling noise. Extremely upset, defendant pulled a small pistol from his pants pocket, put it to his father's temple, and fired. He subsequently fired three more times and walked out into the hospital corridor, dropping the gun to the floor just outside his father's room.

Following the shooting, defendant, who was crying and upset, neither ran nor threatened anyone. Moreover, he never denied shooting his father and talked openly with law enforcement officials. Specifically, defendant made the following oral statements: "You can't do anything to him now. He's out of his suffering." "I killed my daddy." "He won't have to suffer anymore." "I know they can burn me for it, but my dad will not have to suffer anymore." "I know the doctors couldn't do it, but I could." "I promised my dad I wouldn't let him suffer."
* * *

* * * Though defendant's father had been near death as a result of his medical condition, the exact cause of the deceased's death was determined to be the four point-blank bullet wounds to his head. Defendant's pistol was a single-action .22–calibre five-shot revolver. The weapon, which had to be cocked each time it was fired, contained four empty shells and one live round.

At the close of the evidence, defendant's case was submitted to the jury for one of four possible verdicts: first-degree murder, second-degree murder, voluntary manslaughter, or not guilty. After a lengthy deliberation, the jury found defendant guilty of first-degree murder. * * *

In his * * * assignment of error, defendant asserts that the trial court committed reversible error in denying his motion for directed verdict as to the first-degree murder charge. Specifically, defendant argues that the trial court's submission of the first-degree murder charge was improper because there was insufficient evidence of premeditation and deliberation presented at trial. We do not agree * * *.

We recently addressed this very issue in the case of *State v. Jackson*, 317 N.C. 1, 343 S.E.2d 814 (1986). Our analysis of the relevant law in that case is instructive in the case at bar:

> Before the issue of a defendant's guilt may be submitted to the jury, the trial court must be satisfied that substantial evidence has been introduced tending to prove each essential element of the offense charged * * *.

> First-degree murder is the intentional and unlawful killing of a human being with malice and with premeditation and deliberation. * * *

> Premeditation and deliberation relate to mental processes and ordinarily are not readily susceptible to proof by direct evidence. Instead, they usually must be proved by circumstantial evidence. Among other circumstances to be considered in determining whether a killing was with premeditation and deliberation are: (1) want of provocation on the part of the deceased; (2) the conduct and statements of the defendant before and after the killing; (3) threats and declarations of the defendant before and during the course of the occurrence giving rise to the death of the deceased; (4) ill-will or previous difficulty between the parties; (5) the dealing of lethal blows after the deceased has been felled and rendered helpless; and (6) evidence that the killing was done in a brutal manner. We have also held that the nature and number of the victim's wounds is a circumstance from which premeditation and deliberation can be inferred.

As in *Jackson*, we hold in the present case that there was substantial evidence that the killing was premeditated and deliberate * * *. Here, many of the circumstances that we have held to establish a factual basis for a finding of premeditation and deliberation are present. It is clear, for example, that the seriously ill deceased did nothing to provoke defendant's action. Moreover, the deceased was lying helpless in a hospital bed when defendant shot him four separate times. In addition, defendant's revolver was a five-shot single-action gun which had to be cocked each time before it could be fired. Interestingly, although defendant testified that he always carried the gun in his job as a truck driver, he was not working on the day in question but carried the gun to the hospital nonetheless.

Most persuasive of all on the issue of premeditation and deliberation, however, are defendant's own statements following the incident. Among other things, defendant stated that he had thought about putting his father out of his misery because he knew he was suffering. He stated further that he had promised his father that he would not let him suffer and that, though he did not think he could do it, he just could not stand to see his father suffer any more. These statements, together with the other circumstances mentioned above, make it clear that the trial court did not err in submitting to the jury the issue of first-degree murder based upon premeditation and deliberation. * * *

Notes and Questions

1. In your view, who was more culpable, Midgett or Forrest? Is your answer consistent with the results in these cases? If not, is it because one (or both) of the courts misapplied the deliberation-premeditation formula? In this regard, consider the following observation about the deliberation-premeditation formula:

> In many jurisdictions the judicial deconstruction of premeditation has made the first-degree murder category over-inclusive. Offenses which do not involve the highest degree of rational choice-making are treated the same as those that do. More seriously, offenses where the motive for the killing might provide grounds for mitigation are treated the same as those where the motive argues for greatest culpability.

Samuel H. Pillsbury, *Evil and the Law of Murder,* 24 U.C.Davis L.Rev. 437, 454 (1990).

Is the author correct? If so, is the solution to apply the deliberation-premeditation formula differently, or is it to abandon it as inherently flawed, on the ground that it does not accurately distinguish between murderers who deserve the maximum punishment and those who do not? Are the drafters of the Model Penal Code correct when they suggest that the premise of the distinction, "that the person who plans ahead is worse than the person who kills on sudden impulse[,] * * * does not * * * survive analysis"? American Law Institute, Model Penal Code and Commentaries, Comment to § 210.6 at 127 (1980).

If you would abandon the distinction, how would you draw the line? Or should all intentional killings be treated alike?

2. According to *Forrest,* proof of brutality, including the existence of many wounds on the victim, is circumstantial evidence of deliberation and premeditation. However, in People v. Anderson, 70 Cal.2d 15, 73 Cal.Rptr. 550, 447 P.2d 942 (1968), the California Supreme Court took the opposite position, suggesting that the inference of deliberation and premeditation is stronger when the defendant inflicts a single, lethal wound. What is the basis for the latter argument? Which approach makes more sense?

3. *Diminished capacity.* In People v. Wolff, 61 Cal.2d 795, 40 Cal.Rptr. 271, 394 P.2d 959 (1964), the defendant, a 15–year–old mentally ill (but legally sane) youth, killed his mother with an axe after careful planning. The jury convicted him of first degree murder, but the state supreme court reversed the conviction on the ground that "the true test [of deliberation

and premeditation] must include consideration of the somewhat limited extent to which the defendant *could maturely and meaningfully reflect upon the gravity of his contemplated act.*" Id. at 821, 40 Cal.Rptr. at 287, 394 P.2d at 975 (emphasis added). Applying this standard, the court concluded that the youth could only be convicted of second degree murder.

The italicized words in *Wolff* represent a "shorthand way of applying the concept of diminished capacity to the elements of deliberation and premeditation." People v. Stress, 205 Cal.App.3d 1259, 1270, 252 Cal.Rptr. 913, 920 (1988). "Diminished capacity" is a much misunderstood and often misused term (see p. 632 infra), but in the context of this case it means that, as a result of a mental condition, the youth did not form the mental state required in the definition of the offense, in this case, the elements of deliberation and premeditation.

The *Wolff* standard for distinguishing between degrees of murder was eliminated by statute in 1981 and, again, by the California electorate through the initiative process a year later. See West's Ann.Cal.Penal Code § 189 (p. 197 supra). Is the now-abandoned language from *Wolff* "so vague as to escape understanding, so complex as to prevent workable application, and so ambiguous as to allow for capricious results"? People v. Stress, 205 Cal.App.3d at 1270, 252 Cal.Rptr. at 920. Is it any more vague or unworkable than the traditional deliberation-premeditation formula? Was the conclusion in *Wolff*—that the youth was not guilty of first degree murder—more counter-intuitive than the results in *Midgett* or *Forrest?*

2. MANSLAUGHTER: "HEAT OF PASSION" KILLINGS

a. *Common Law Principles*

GIROUARD v. STATE

Court of Appeals of Maryland, 1991.
321 Md. 532, 583 A.2d 718.

COLE, JUDGE.

In this case we are asked to reconsider whether the types of provocation sufficient to mitigate the crime of murder to manslaughter should be limited to the categories we have heretofore recognized, or whether the sufficiency of the provocation should be decided by the factfinder on a case-by-case basis. Specifically, we must determine whether words alone are provocation adequate to justify a conviction of manslaughter rather than one of second degree murder.

The Petitioner, Steven S. Girouard, and the deceased, Joyce M. Girouard, had been married for about two months on October 28, 1987, the night of Joyce's death. Both parties, who met while working in the same building, were in the army. They married after having known each other for approximately three months. The evidence at trial indicated that the marriage was often tense and strained, and there was some evidence that after marrying Steven, Joyce had resumed a relationship with her old boyfriend. * * *

On the night of Joyce's death, Steven overheard her talking on the telephone to her friend, whereupon she told the friend that she had asked her first sergeant for a hardship discharge because her husband did not love her anymore. Steven went into the living room where Joyce was on the phone and asked her what she meant by her comments; she responded, "nothing." Angered by her lack of response, Steven kicked away the plate of food Joyce had in front of her. He then went to lie down in the bedroom.

Joyce followed him into the bedroom, stepped up onto the bed and onto Steven's back, pulled his hair and said, "What are you going to do, hit me?" She continued to taunt him by saying, "I never did want to marry you and you are a lousy fuck and you remind me of my dad." [1] The barrage of insults continued with her telling Steven that she wanted a divorce, that the marriage had been a mistake and that she had never wanted to marry him. She also told him she had seen his commanding officer and filed charges against him for abuse. She then asked Steven, "What are you going to do?" Receiving no response, she continued her verbal attack. She added that she had filed charges against him in the Judge Advocate General's Office (JAG) and that he would probably be court martialed. [2]

When she was through, Steven asked her if she had really done all those things, and she responded in the affirmative. He left the bedroom with his pillow in his arms and proceeded to the kitchen where he procured a long handled kitchen knife. He returned to Joyce in the bedroom with the knife behind the pillow. He testified that he was enraged and that he kept waiting for Joyce to say she was kidding, but Joyce continued talking. She said she had learned a lot from the marriage and that it had been a mistake. She also told him she would remain in their apartment after he moved out. When he questioned how she would afford it, she told him she would claim her brain-damaged sister as a dependent and have the sister move in. Joyce reiterated that the marriage was a big mistake, that she did not love him and that the divorce would be better for her.

After pausing for a moment, Joyce asked what Steven was going to do. What he did was lunge at her with the kitchen knife he had hidden behind the pillow and stab her 19 times. Realizing what he had done, he dropped the knife and went to the bathroom to shower off Joyce's blood. Feeling like he wanted to die, Steven went back to the kitchen and found two steak knives with which he slit his own wrists. He lay down on the bed waiting to die, but when he realized that he would not die from his self-inflicted wounds, he got up and called the police, telling the dispatcher that he had just murdered his wife.

1. There was some testimony presented at trial to the effect that Joyce had never gotten along with her father, at least in part because he had impregnated her when she was fourteen, the result of which was an abortion. Joyce's aunt, however, denied that Joyce's father was the father of Joyce's child.

2. Joyce lied about filing the charges against her husband.

When the police arrived they found Steven wandering around outside his apartment building. Steven was despondent and tearful and seemed detached, according to police officers who had been at the scene. He was unconcerned about his own wounds, talking only about how much he loved his wife and how he could not believe what he had done. Joyce Girouard was pronounced dead at the scene.

At trial, defense witness, psychologist, Dr. William Stejskal, testified that Steven was out of touch with his own capacity to experience anger or express hostility. He stated that the events of October 28, 1987, were entirely consistent with Steven's personality, that Steven had "basically reach[ed] the limit of his ability to swallow his anger, to rationalize his wife's behavior, to tolerate, or actually to remain in a passive mode with that. He essentially went over the limit of his ability to bottle up those strong emotions. What ensued was a very extreme explosion of rage that was intermingled with a great deal of panic." Another defense witness, psychiatrist, Thomas Goldman, testified that Joyce had a "compulsive need to provoke jealousy so that she's always asking for love and at the same time destroying and undermining any chance that she really might have to establish any kind of mature love with anybody."

Steven Girouard was convicted * * * of second degree murder and was sentenced to 22 years incarceration, 10 of which were suspended. * * *

Petitioner relies primarily on out of state cases to provide support for his argument that the provocation to mitigate murder to manslaughter should not be limited only to the traditional circumstances of: extreme assault or battery upon the defendant; mutual combat; defendant's illegal arrest; injury or serious abuse of a close relative of the defendant's; or the sudden discovery of a spouse's adultery. Petitioner argues that manslaughter is a catchall for homicides which are criminal but that lack the malice essential for a conviction of murder. Steven argues that the trial judge did find provocation (although he held it inadequate to mitigate murder) and that the categories of provocation adequate to mitigate should be broadened to include factual situations such as this one.

The State counters by stating that although there is no finite list of legally adequate provocations, the common law has developed to a point at which it may be said there are some concededly provocative acts that society is not prepared to recognize as reasonable. Words spoken by the victim, no matter how abusive or taunting, fall into a category society should not accept as adequate provocation. According to the State, if abusive words alone could mitigate murder to manslaughter, nearly every domestic argument ending in the death of one party could be mitigated to manslaughter. This, the State avers, is not an acceptable outcome. Thus, the State argues that the courts below were correct in holding that the taunting words by Joyce Girouard were not provocation adequate to reduce Steven's second degree murder charge to voluntary manslaughter.

Initially, we note that the difference between murder and manslaughter is the presence or absence of malice. Voluntary manslaughter has been defined as "an *intentional* homicide, done in a sudden heat of passion, caused by adequate provocation, before there has been a reasonable opportunity for the passion to cool" (Emphasis in original). *Cox v. State,* 311 Md. 326, 331, 534 A.2d 1333 (1988).

There are certain facts that may mitigate what would normally be murder to manslaughter. For example, we have recognized as falling into that group: (1) discovering one's spouse in the act of sexual intercourse with another; (2) mutual combat; (3) assault and battery. There is also authority recognizing injury to one of the defendant's relatives or to a third party, and death resulting from resistance of an illegal arrest as adequate provocation for mitigation to manslaughter. Those acts mitigate homicide to manslaughter because they create passion in the defendant and are not considered the product of free will.

In order to determine whether murder should be mitigated to manslaughter we look to the circumstances surrounding the homicide and try to discover if it was provoked by the victim. Over the facts of the case we lay the template of the so-called "Rule of Provocation." The courts of this State have repeatedly set forth the requirements of the Rule of Provocation:

1. There must have been adequate provocation;

2. The killing must have been in the heat of passion;

3. It must have been a sudden heat of passion—that is, the killing must have followed the provocation before there had been a reasonable opportunity for the passion to cool;

4. There must have been a causal connection between the provocation, the passion, and the fatal act.

We shall assume without deciding that the second, third, and fourth of the criteria listed above were met in this case. We focus our attention on an examination of the ultimate issue in this case, that is, whether the provocation of Steven by Joyce was enough in the eyes of the law so that the murder charge against Steven should have been mitigated to voluntary manslaughter. For provocation to be "adequate," it must be " 'calculated to inflame the passion of a reasonable man and tend to cause him to act for the moment from passion rather than reason.' " *Carter v. State,* 66 Md.App. [567,] 572, 505 A.2d 545 [(1986)] quoting R. Perkins, *Perkins on Criminal Law* at p. 56 (2d ed. 1969). The issue we must resolve, then, is whether the taunting words uttered by Joyce were enough to inflame the passion of a *reasonable* man so that that man would be sufficiently infuriated so as to strike out in hot-blooded blind passion to kill her. Although we agree with the trial judge that there was needless provocation by Joyce, we also agree with him that the provocation was not adequate to mitigate second degree murder to voluntary manslaughter.

Although there are few Maryland cases discussing the issue at bar, those that do hold that words alone are not adequate provocation. * * *

* * * [W]ords can constitute adequate provocation if they are accompanied by conduct indicating a present intention and ability to cause the defendant bodily harm. Clearly, no such conduct was exhibited by Joyce in this case. While Joyce did step on Steven's back and pull his hair, he could not reasonably have feared bodily harm at her hands. This, to us, is certain based on Steven's testimony at trial that Joyce was about 5′1″ tall and weighed 115 pounds, while he was 6′2″ tall, weighing over 200 pounds. Joyce simply did not have the size or strength to cause Steven to fear for his bodily safety. Thus, since there was no ability on the part of Joyce to cause Steven harm, the words she hurled at him could not * * * constitute legally sufficient provocation.

Other jurisdictions overwhelmingly agree with our cases and hold that words alone are not adequate provocation. * * *

Thus, with no reservation, we hold that the provocation in this case was not enough to cause a reasonable man to stab his provoker 19 times. Although a psychologist testified to Steven's mental problems and his need for acceptance and love, we agree with the Court of Special Appeals * * * that "there must be not simply provocation in psychological fact, but one of certain fairly well-defined classes of provocation recognized as being adequate as a matter of law." *Tripp v. State,* 36 Md.App. [459,] 473, 374 A.2d 384 [(1977)]. The standard is one of reasonableness; it does not and should not focus on the peculiar frailties of mind of the Petitioner. That standard of reasonableness has not been met here. We cannot in good conscience countenance holding that a verbal domestic argument ending in the death of one spouse can result in a conviction of manslaughter. We agree with the trial judge that social necessity dictates our holding. Domestic arguments easily escalate into furious fights. We perceive no reason for a holding in favor of those who find the easiest way to end a domestic dispute is by killing the offending spouse. * * *

Notes and Comments

1. According to *Girouard,* what constitutes "adequate provocation"? One of the most commonly quoted definitions of the term was crafted by Judge Christiancy of the Michigan Supreme Court in the nineteenth century:

> The principle involved in the question [of what constitutes "adequate provocation"], and which I think clearly deducible from the majority of well considered cases, would seem to suggest as the true general rule, that reason should, at the time of the act, be disturbed or obscured by passion to an extent which *might render* ordinary men, of fair average disposition, *liable* to act rashly or without due deliberation or reflection, and from passion, rather than judgment.

Maher v. People, 10 Mich. 212, 220 (1862). If this standard had been applied in *Girouard,* would the result have been different?

2. Why do words alone not constitute adequate provocation? Is the reason that ordinary people do not act violently in response to verbal assaults?

Should the law distinguish between insulting words and informational ones (e.g., "Your husband is having an affair with Zelda")? Some courts consider informational words more provocative. See People v. Pouncey, 437 Mich. 382, 391, 471 N.W.2d 346, 351 (1991); Raines v. State, 247 Ga. 504, 277 S.E.2d 47 (1981). Do you agree?

At a minimum, should the law recognize an exception to the "mere words" rule when one spouse admits her prior infidelity to the other spouse? The Ohio Supreme Court rejected such a special rule:

> This exception to the general rule has its foundation in the ancient common-law concept that a wife is the property of the husband. * * * This archaic rule has no place in modern society. * * * The killing of a spouse (usually a wife) by a spouse (usually a husband) who has just been made aware of the victim spouse's adultery simply is not an acceptable response to the confession of infidelity.

State v. Shane, 63 Ohio St.3d 630, 637, 590 N.E.2d 272, 278 (1992). Has the court missed the point as to why informational words about adultery might serve as a legitimate basis for partial exculpation?

3. As a general matter, who should decide what constitutes adequate provocation, courts or juries? The answer to this question has changed over time:

> Under the common law, the doctrine of provocation developed along the lines of fixed categories of conduct by the victim, paradigms of misbehavior, which the law recognized as sufficiently provocative to mitigate what would otherwise be malicious conduct by the defendant. * * * Traditionally, a defendant seeking to negate the malice element * * * would have to present some evidence of provocative behavior by the victim. However, such evidence would not automatically entitle the defendant to an instruction on [voluntary manslaughter] * * *. First, the court would have to determine that the victim's conduct constituted legally adequate provocation, i.e., that it fit within one of the tried and true categories of provocative conduct like adultery or assault. Thus, in order to have the jury consider such evidence, the defendant either would have to present it in a form recognized as legally adequate by the court, or ask the court to recognize a new category of provocative conduct. * * * Thus, under the common law, there grew up a process of pigeon-holing provocative conduct. * * *
>
> Over the years this traditional view of provocation as a set of rigid categories of recognized conduct has been abandoned by a growing number of state legislatures, courts, and commentators, with the result that the emerging "modern" view of provocation * * * has now swung around to the view [that the matter should be left to the jury].
>
> The rationale offered for the modern view is strikingly similar to that offered by Judge Christiancy, who, writing for the *Maher* court [10 Mich. 212 (1862)], said: "[t]he law can not with justice assume by the light of past decisions to catalogue all the various facts and combinations

of facts which shall be held to constitute reasonable or adequate provocation." The Pennsylvania Supreme Court [Commonwealth v. Pease, 220 Pa. 371, 373, 69 A. 891, 892 (1908)] came to the same conclusion * * *: "What is sufficient provocation * * * has not been exactly defined, and is probably incapable of exact definition, for it must vary with the myriad shifting circumstances of men's temper and quarrels. It is a concession to the infirmity of human nature, not an excuse for undue or abnormal irascibility, and, therefore to be considered in view of all circumstances."

Brown v. United States, 584 A.2d 537, 540–42 (D.C.Cir.1990).

4. Although heat-of-passion cases typically involve a killing committed in rage, most courts permit the defendant to raise the defense if, as the result of adequate provocation, the killer experiences virtually *any* intense emotion, such as fear, LaPierre v. State, 734 P.2d 997 (Alaska App.1987), or jealousy, People v. Berry, 18 Cal.3d 509, 134 Cal.Rptr. 415, 556 P.2d 777 (1976).

5. *"Cooling off time."* The provocation defense is unavailable to a defendant who kills the victim after she has a "reasonable opportunity for the passion to cool," i.e., after a reasonable person in the defendant's situation would have calmed down. Originally, this element of the defense was determined by the judge, rather than by the jury. Again, Judge Christiancy, in Maher v. People, 10 Mich. 212, 223–24 (1862), led the way for change:

> The same principles which govern, as to the extent to which the passions must be excited and reason disturbed, apply with equal force to the time during which its continuance may be recognized as a ground for mitigating the homicide to the degree of manslaughter, or, in other words, to the question of cooling time. This, like the provocation itself, must depend upon the nature of man and the laws of the human mind, as well as upon the nature and circumstances of the provocation, the extent to which the passions have been aroused, and the fact, whether the injury inflicted by the provocation is more or less permanent or irreparable. The passion excited by a blow received in a sudden quarrel, though perhaps equally violent for the moment, would be likely much sooner to subside than if aroused by a rape committed upon a sister or daughter, or the discovery of an adulterous intercourse with a wife; and no two cases of the latter kind would be likely to be identical in all their circumstances of provocation. No precise time, therefore, *in hours or minutes,* can be laid down by the court, as a rule of law, within which the passions *must be held* to have subsided and reason to have resumed its control * * *. The question is one of reasonable time * * *. [Ordinarily,] the question of such reasonable time * * * is a question of fact for the jury; and the court can not take it from the jury by assuming to decide it as a question of law, without confounding the respective provinces of the court and jury.

THIBODEAUX v. STATE

Court of Appeals of Texas, 1987.
733 S.W.2d 668.

POWERS, JUSTICE.

Paul Thibodeaux appeals a judgment of conviction for murder. The jury found him guilty and assessed punishment at ninety-nine years imprisonment. We will affirm the judgment.

* * * Thibodeaux and Elizabeth Harris lived together for several years. During that time, Harris had four children and Thibodeaux believed he was the father of all four. According to Thibodeaux, on April 7, 1986, he and Harris argued heatedly and Harris told him that he was not the father of her youngest child, a two-month old baby girl. The revelation devastated Thibodeaux, and angered him to the point that he took the baby, walked with her 1.1 miles, and then killed her. Harris saw Thibodeaux again about 30 minutes later when he returned to the apartment crying, saying that he had killed the baby. Police apprehended Thibodeaux at a nearby church where he wandered after leaving Harris. The baby's body was discovered about five days later after an extensive search. * * *

* * * Thibodeaux complains the trial court erred in refusing to charge the jury on the lesser-included offense of voluntary manslaughter. An issue on a lesser-included offense must be submitted to the jury where evidence from any source, including the testimony of the defendant, raised the issue. Thibodeaux argues his own testimony constitutes some evidence of voluntary manslaughter sufficient to require submission of the issue to the jury. He refers to the following:

> I felt like—when she had gave me the thought that the baby wasn't mines [sic], I thought it was just play—she was playing. And then she was really serious and looking in my eyes and things, telling me the baby wasn't mines [sic]. And I felt like I lost everything in life. I got so angry, I just lost it.

In Tex.Pen.Code Ann. § 19.04(a) (1974), voluntary manslaughter is defined as murder, except that the death was caused while the defendant was "under the immediate influence of sudden passion arising from adequate cause." "Sudden passion" is defined in § 19.04(b):

> ... passion directly caused by and arising out of provocation by the individual killed or *another acting with the person killed* which arises at the time of the offense ... [emphasis added].

The emphasized language points out the most obvious defect in Thibodeaux's theory * * *. Under the evidence, the provocation came from Harris while the "person killed" was a two-month-old baby whose only "action" was to lie on a blanket in the apartment. Thus, the * * * question which must be answered is whether Harris was shown to be "acting with" the infant victim within the meaning of § 19.04(b). * * *

We fail to see how Harris was "acting with" the infant to provoke the defendant. * * * [T]he sole *actor* in the present case, under Thibodeaux's testimony, was Harris. The child under that testimony was no more than the *object* of her remarks. We overrule appellant's * * * point of error. * * *

Notes and Questions

1. *Problem.* Suppose that Aaron is lawfully walking along the road with his daughter Sarah when a car recklessly driven by Ben strikes and kills Sarah. Ben's car hits a tree, immobilizing him. Aaron, emotionally overwrought, pulls out a knife that he was carrying and moves toward the car, intending to kill Ben. Ruth, a bystander, blocks Aaron's path to the car. Aaron intentionally kills Ruth. Prosecuted for Ruth's death, should Aaron be allowed to assert the defense of heat-of-passion? See Regina v. Scriva (No. 2), [1951] Vict.L.R. 298.

JOSHUA DRESSLER—RETHINKING HEAT OF PASSION: A DEFENSE IN SEARCH OF A RATIONALE

73 Journal of Criminal Law and Criminology 421 (1982), 436–43

Ordinarily, * * * a person is punishable for a crime if it is shown that the actor voluntarily caused the social harm with the * * * mental state, or mens rea, deemed serious enough to make the harm punishable. If the government proves beyond a reasonable doubt, for example, that the actor intentionally killed a human being by a voluntary act, the government has proven murder. * * *

Such proof only fulfills the prima facie case of the crime of murder. The defendant may raise a * * * defense. It is here that the concepts of "justification" and "excuse" materialize. * * * The theories underlying the two defenses differ substantially * * *. With a justification, society indicates its approval of the actor's conduct * * *. With homicide, for example, the existence of a justification [such as self-defense] implies that under the circumstances * * * society either does not believe that the death of the human being was undesirable, or that it at least represents a lesser harm than if the defendant had not acted as he did. * * *

A defendant asserting an excuse admits to wrongdoing, but asserts that he should not be punished because he is not morally blameworthy for the harm. Thus, excuses focus on the actor, not on the act. * * * The insane killer, for example, avoids punishment, not because there was no harm in the killing, but because his mental disease renders his conduct in some fashion morally blameless. * * *

A careful analysis of the language and of the results of common law heat of passion cases demonstrates that there is uncertainty whether the defense is a sub-species of justification or of excuse. The uncertainty is well expressed by Austin.

Is [the provoker] partly responsible because he roused a violent impulse or passion in me so that it wasn't truly or merely me "acting of my own accord" [excuse]? Or is it rather that he having done me such injury, I was entitled to retaliate [justification]? [157]

* * *

Unfortunately, courts have often failed to coherently state which doctrinal path is involved; or worse, they have rationalized the doctrine under both theories. * * *

A reasonable interpretation of some common law precedent can support the thesis that heat of passion is a partial justification. All of the common law forms of "adequate provocation" have one thing in common; they all involve unlawful conduct by the provoker. Lawful conduct, no matter how provocative, is never adequate provocation. It is possible, of course, to defend this rule with excusing language,[166] but it is far easier to explain it as justification based, by contending that it is the unlawfulness of the provocation which makes the response (killing) less socially undesirable. As Aristotle said, "it is apparent injustice that occasions rage." The typical victim in a heat of passion case is someone who has "asked for it." The attacker is, in a way, only "restor[ing] the balance of justice." * * *

Specifically, the [common law] "sight of adultery" cases add support to the justification thesis. * * * [A] married person who kills upon sight of adultery commits manslaughter, but an unmarried individual who kills upon sight of unfaithfulness by one's lover or fiancé is a murderer. Only a highly unrealistic belief about passion can explain this rule in terms of excusing conduct. It is implausible to believe that when an actor observes his or her loved one in an act of sexual disloyalty, that actor will suffer from less anger simply because the disloyal partner is not the actor's spouse. Instead, this rule is really a judgment by courts that adultery is a form of injustice perpetrated upon the killer which merits a violent response, whereas "mere" sexual unfaithfulness out of wedlock does not. Thus, it has been said that adultery is the "highest invasion of [a husband's] property," whereas in the unmarried situation the defendant "has no such control" over his faithless lover.

Another justification-oriented rule is the misdirected retaliation doctrine, wherein it is said that the defense is only applicable when it is an "act ... by the dead man," not a third person, which provokes the accused. Although the character of the dead person may be irrelevant, his blame as it relates to the final act, is not only pertinent, but usually necessary. Assume, for example, that a father observes his daughter being seriously injured by a reckless driver. If the enraged parent then kills the driver, the homicide may be manslaughter; but if the father kills an innocent bystander who tries to protect the driver, that homicide

---

157. J.L. Austin, [A Plea for Excuses, "The Presidential Address to the Aristotelian Society, 1956," "Proceedings of the Aristotelian Society, 1956–1957," Vol. LVIV, *re-printed in* Ordinary Language 42 (V. Chappel ed. 1965)], at 43.

166. *E.g.,* reasonable, blameless actors never become enraged by lawful conduct.

is murder, even though the killing was committed as a result of the same rage.

Similarly, when an emotionally over-wrought father kills his sleeping, terminally ill child after the father [has] learned that his wife has been unfaithful to him, the father is not entitled to a manslaughter claim.[176] In both cases the provocation is great, the rage or similar emotion is understandable, but the victim of the killing is wholly innocent of bringing on the rage. Under an excuse theory, * * * the father could argue that he is less blameworthy than the usual calm killer, because his anger was understandable, and his inability to completely separate innocent from guilty victims was similarly less blameworthy under such circumstances. A manslaughter conviction seems plausible, therefore, by application of an excusing theory. The homicide of any entirely innocent person, however, is not capable of mitigation under any rational theory of * * * justification, so the "dead man" rule is necessarily justificatory based.

There is substantial basis, then, for the claim that heat of passion is, at least at times, viewed as a partial justification, although the precise reason why it is so remains undeveloped. There is also substantial support, however, for the assertion that the defense is based on a theory that the harm is the same as with murder, but that the accused's personal blameworthiness is less than that of the murderer. The language, if not always the result, in provocation cases is usually excuse oriented. The problem, however, is that court opinions vary in their excuse reasoning. * * *

First, it has been said often that the passion serves to mitigate the punishment because the actor is "so dethroned of reason" that he either cannot premeditate or form the specific intent to kill. In essence, heat of passion negates the required mens rea of murder, thereby lessening the actor's blameworthiness.

Second, the language of many opinions implies that the blameworthiness of the actor is reduced because the killing is largely involuntary. Moreover, the requirement that the killing be sudden, before the actor can reasonably calm down, supports this voluntariness thesis, because if the defense were predicated on the injustice that initiated it, or on the mental state of the actor at the time of the killing, then the timing of the killing would seem largely irrelevant.

A third * * * reason given for the defense is that it represents a concession to human weakness. Of course, this may merely be a preface to a voluntarism theory, but at times there appears to be a different idea in mind. It is that the killing, although perhaps voluntary, does not stem from a "bad or corrupt heart, but from infirmity of passion to which even good men are subject." In essence, it may be reasoned that

176. Rex v. Simpson, [1915] 11 Crim. App. 218. *See also* State v. Speyer, 182 Mo. 77, 81 S.W. 430 (1904) (*D*, in fit of emotion, killed his sleeping son because he was arrested for a crime, and he feared for this child's well-being).

the character of the defendant is not as bad as that of a murderer, so the actor's guilt should be reduced.

Finally, there are courts which use all of the above theories, and the kitchen sink, to explain the defense.

Notes and Questions

1. *Should* the provocation defense be considered a (partial) justification or a (partial) excuse? For scholars' views on the issue, compare id. at 450–67 and Joshua Dressler, *Provocation: Partial Justification or Partial Excuse?*, 51 Mod.L.Rev. 467 (1988) (defending an excuse rationale) with Finbarr McAuley, *Anticipating the Past: The Defence of Provocation in Irish Law,* 50 Mod.L.Rev. 133 (1987) (defending the defense on justificatory terms) and Andrew von Hirsch and Nils Jareborg, *Provocation and Culpability* in Responsibility, Character, and the Emotions: New Essays in Moral Psychology 241 (Ferdinand Schoeman ed. 1987) (contending that a provoked person's anger may be justified, but the homicidal response must be defended as an excuse).

2. Reconsider Note 3 (p. 221 supra): Does the answer depend on whether provocation is a partial justification or a partial excuse?

b. The Objective Standard: Who is the "Reasonable Man"?

DIRECTOR OF PUBLIC PROSECUTIONS v. CAMPLIN

House of Lords, 1978.
2 All Eng.Rep. 168, 2 W.L.R. 679.

LORD DIPLOCK. * * * The respondent, Camplin, who was 15 years of age, killed a middle-aged Pakistani, Mohammed Lal Khan, by splitting his skull with a chapati pan, a heavy kitchen utensil like a rimless frying pan. At the time the two of them were alone together in Khan's flat. At Camplin's trial for murder * * * his only defence was that of provocation so as to reduce the offence to manslaughter. According to the story that he told in the witness box * * *, Khan had buggered him in spite of his resistance and had then laughed at him, whereupon Camplin had lost his self-control and attacked Kahn fatally with the chapati pan.

In his address to the jury on the defence of provocation, counsel for Camplin had suggested to them that when they addressed their minds to the question whether the provocation relied on was enough to make a reasonable man do as Camplin had done, what they ought to consider was not the reaction of a reasonable adult but the reaction of a reasonable boy of Camplin's age. The judge thought that this was wrong in law. So in this summing-up he took pains to instruct the jury that they must consider whether—

> the provocation was sufficient to make a reasonable man in like circumstances act as the defendant did. Not a reasonable boy, as

[counsel for Camplin] would have it, or a reasonable lad; it is an objective test—a reasonable man.

The jury found Camplin guilty of murder.   * * *

The point of law of general public importance involved in the case has been certified as being:

> Whether, on the prosecution for murder of a boy of 15, where the issue of provocation arises, the jury should be directed to consider the question * * * whether the provocation was enough to make a reasonable man do as he did by reference to a "reasonable adult" or by reference to a "reasonable boy of 15."   * * *

The "reasonable man" was a comparatively late arrival in the law of provocation.   As the law of negligence emerged in the first half of the 19th century he became the anthropomorphic embodiment of the standard of care required by the law.   It would appear that Keating in *R v Welsh* [(1869) 11 Co CC 36] was the first to make use of the reasonable man as the embodiment of the standard of self-control required by the criminal law of persons exposed to provocation * * *.

The reasonable man referred to by Keating was not then a term of legal art nor has it since become one in criminal law.   He (or she) has established his (or her) role in the law of provocation under a variety of different sobriquets in which the noun "man" is frequently replaced by "person" and the adjective "reasonable" by "ordinary," "average" or "normal."   * * *

My Lords, this was the state of law when *Bedder* [[1954] 2 All Eng.Rep. 801] fell to be considered by this House.   The accused had killed a prostitute.   He was sexually impotent.   According to his evidence he had tried to have sexual intercourse with her and failed.   She taunted him with his failure and tried to get away from his grasp.   In the course of her attempts to do so she slapped him in the face, punched him in the stomach and kicked him in the groin, whereupon he took a knife out of his pocket and stabbed her twice and caused her death.   The struggle that led to her death thus started because the deceased taunted the accused with his physical infirmity; but in the state of the law as it then was, taunts unaccompanied by any physical violence did not constitute provocation.   The taunts were followed by violence on the part of the deceased in the course of her attempt to get away from the accused, and it may be that this subsequent violence would have a greater effect on the self-control of an impotent man already enraged by the taunts than it would have had on a person conscious of possessing normal physical attributes.   So there might be some justification for the judge to instruct the jury to ignore the fact that the accused was impotent when they were considering whether the deceased's conduct amounted to such provocation as would cause a reasonable or ordinary person to lose his self-control.   * * *

* * * [But] Lord Simonds L.C. speaking on behalf of all the members of this House who sat on the appeal * * * went on to lay down the broader proposition that:

> It would be plainly illogical not to recognize an unusually excitable or pugnacious temperament in the accused as a matter to be taken into account but yet to recognise for that purpose some unusual physical characteristic, be it impotence or another.

Section 3 of the 1957 [Homicide] Act is in the following terms:

> Where on a charge of murder there is evidence on which the jury can find that the person charged was provoked (whether by things done or by things said or by both together) to lose his self-control, the question whether the provocation was enough to make a reasonable man do as he did shall be left to be determined by the jury; and in determining that question the jury shall take into account everything both done and said according to the effect which, in their opinion, it would have on a reasonable man.

My Lords, this section was intended to mitigate in some degree the harshness of the common law of provocation as it had been developed by recent decisions in this House. It recognises and retains the dual test: the provocation must not only have caused the accused to lose his self-control but also be such as might cause a reasonable man to react to it as the accused did. Nevertheless it brings about two important changes in the law. The first is it abolishes all previous rules of law as to what can or cannot amount to provocation and in particular the rule of law that * * * words unaccompanied by violence could not do so. Secondly it makes it clear that if there was any evidence that the accused himself at the time of the act which caused the death in fact lost his self-control in consequence of some provocation however slight it might appear to the judge, he was bound to leave to the jury the question, which is one of opinion not of law, whether a reasonable man might have reacted to that provocation as the accused did. * * *

The public policy that underlay the adoption of the "reasonable man" test in the common law doctrine of provocation was to reduce the incidence of fatal violence by preventing a person relying on his own exceptional pugnacity or excitability as an excuse for loss of self-control. The rationale of the test may not be easy to reconcile in logic with more universal propositions as to the mental element in crime. Nevertheless it has been preserved by the 1957 Act but falls to be applied now in the context of a law of provocation that is significantly different from what it was before the Act was passed.

Although it is now for the jury to apply the "reasonable man" test, it still remains for the judge to direct them what, in the new context of the section, is the meaning of this apparently inapt expression, since powers of ratiocination bear no obvious relationships to powers of self-control. * * *

As I have already pointed out, for the purposes of the law of provocation the "reasonable man" has never been confined to the adult male. It means an ordinary person of either sex, not exceptionally excitable or pugnacious, but possessed of such powers of self-control as everyone is entitled to expect that his fellow citizens will exercise in society as it is today. A crucial factor in the defence of provocation from earliest times has been the relationship between the gravity of provocation and the way in which the accused retaliated, both being judged by the social standards of the day. When Hale was writing in the 17th century pulling a man's nose was thought to justify retaliation with a sword; when *Mancini* [[1978] 1 All Eng.Rep. 1236] was decided by this House, a blow with a fist would not justify retaliation with a deadly weapon. But so long as words unaccompanied by violence could not in common law amount to provocation the relevant proportionality between provocation and retaliation was primarily one of degrees of violence. Words spoken to the accused before the violence started were not normally to be included in the proportion sum. But now that the law has been changed so as to permit of words being treated as provocation, even though unaccompanied by any other acts, the gravity of verbal provocation may well depend on the particular characteristics or circumstances of the person to whom a taunt or insult is addressed. To taunt a person because of his race, his physical infirmities or some shameful incident in his past may well be considered by the jury to be more offensive to the person addressed, however equable his temperament, if the facts on which the taunt is founded are true than it would be if they were not. It would stultify much of the mitigation of the previous harshness of the common law in ruling out verbal provocation as capable of reducing murder to manslaughter if the jury could not take into consideration all those factors which in their opinion would affect the gravity of taunts and insults when applied to the person to whom they are addressed. So to this extent at any rate the unqualified proposition accepted by this House in *Bedder* that for the purposes of the "reasonable man" test any unusual physical characteristics of the accused must be ignored requires revision as a result of the passing of the 1957 Act.

That he was only 15 years of age at the time of the killing is the relevant characteristic of the accused in the instant case. It is a characteristic which may have its effects on temperament as well as physique. If the jury think that the same power of self-control is not to be expected in an ordinary, average or normal boy of 15 as in an older person, are they to treat the lesser powers of self-control possessed by an ordinary, average or normal boy of 15 as the standard of self-control with which the conduct of the accused is to be compared?

It may be conceded that in strict logic there is a transition between treating age as a characteristic that may be taken into account in assessing the gravity of the provocation addressed to the accused and treating it as a characteristic to be taken into account in determining what is the degree of self-control to be expected of the ordinary person with whom the accused's conduct is to be compared. But to require old heads on young shoulders is inconsistent with the law's compassion of human infirmity to which Sir Michael Foster ascribed the doctrine of provocation more than two centuries ago. * * *

In my opinion a proper direction to a jury on the question left to their exclusive determination by Section 3 of the 1957 Act would be on the following lines. The judge should state what the question is, using the very terms of the section. He should then explain to them that the reasonable man referred to in the question is a person having the power of self-control to be expected of an ordinary person of the sex and age of the accused, but in other respects sharing such of the accused's characteristics as they think would affect the gravity of the provocation to him, and that the question is not merely whether such a person would in like circumstances be provoked to lose his self-control but also would react to the provocation as the accused did. * * *

LORD SIMON OF GLAISDALE. * * * [I]t is accepted that the phrase "reasonable man" really means "reasonable person," so as to extend to "reasonable woman." So, although this has never yet been a subject of decision, a jury could arguably * * * take the sex of the accused into account in assessing what might reasonably cause her to lose her self-control. * * * If so, this is already some qualification on the "reasonable person" as a pure abstraction devoid of any personal characteristics, even if such a concept were of any value to the law. This qualification might be crucial: take the insult "whore" addressed respectively to a reasonable man and a reasonable woman. Nevertheless, as counsel for the appellant sternly and cogently maintained, *Bedder* would preclude the jury from considering that the accused was, say, pregnant, or presumably undergoing menstruation or menopause. * * *

The original reasons in this branch of the law were largely reasons of the heart and of common sense, not the reasons of pure juristic logic. * * * But justice and common sense then demanded some limitation: it would be unjust that the drunk man or one exceptionally pugnacious or bad-tempered or over-sensitive should be able to claim that these matters rendered him peculiarly susceptible to the provocation offered, where the sober and even-tempered man would hang for his homicide. Hence, * * * the development of the concept of the reaction of a reasonable man to the provocation offered * * *. But it is one thing to invoke the reasonable man for the standard of self-control which the law requires; it is quite another to substitute some hypothetical being from whom all mental and physical attributes (except perhaps sex) have been abstracted. * * *

The provision that words alone can constitute provocation accentuates the anomalies, inconveniences and injustices liable to follow from the *Bedder* decision. The effect of an insult will often depend entirely on a characteristic of a person to whom the insult is directed. * * * [S]uch an expression as "Your character is as crooked as your back" would have a different connotation to a hunchback on the one hand and to a man with a back like a ramrod on the other. * * * In my judgment the reference to "a reasonable man" at the end of the section means "a man of ordinary self-control." If this is so the meaning satisfies what I have ventured to suggest as the reasons for importing into this branch of the law the concept of the reasonable man, namely to avoid the injustice of a man being entitled to rely on his exceptional excitability (whether idiosyncratic or by cultural environment or ethnic origin) or pugnacity or ill-temper or on his drunkenness (I do not purport to be exhaustive in this enumeration). * * *

I think that the standard of self-control which the law requires before provocation is held to reduce murder to manslaughter is still that of the reasonable person (hence his invocation in Section 3 of the 1957 Act), but that, in determining whether a person of reasonable self-control would lose it in the circumstances, the entire factual situation, which includes the characteristics of the accused, must be considered. * * *

Notes and Questions

1. *V* infuriates *N*, who is intoxicated, by making disparaging remarks about *N*'s mistress. *N* kills *V*. After *Camplin*, is *N* entitled to an instruction to the jury that it should measure his conduct against the standard of the "reasonable drunk man"? See Regina v. Newell, 71 Crim.App. 331 (1981).

2. *The "reasonable man" and self-control.* Why should the judge have instructed the jury to take into consideration Camplin's age? Isn't the point of the defendant's immaturity that he could not exercise ordinary self-control? If so, has the court accepted the principle that a jury should measure a short-tempered defendant's conduct against the standard of the "reasonable, short-tempered man"?

What about *adults* who lack the capacity to exercise ordinary self-control? One English scholar, surveying scientific literature on human aggression, has concluded that "[s]ome men are highly vulnerable to stress, others are strikingly resistant to it. * * * It seems likely * * * that a number of factors, some genetic, others environmental, combine to produce the differences of susceptibility and response." Peter Brett, *The Physiology of Provocation,* [1970] Crim.L.R. 634, 637. If he is correct, should short-tempered persons, perhaps born that way, still be held to the standard of the person of ordinary self-control?

Is it also possible that some persons, because of their cultural background, are more inclined than others to respond violently to provocations? If so, what standard of self-control should prevail in a multicultural society? In this context, do you approve of the following jury instruction given in *Regina v. Macdonald,* described by Colin Howard (*What Colour is the "Reasonable Man"?,* [1961] Crim.L.Rev. 41, 44) as an Australian case involving "a fight between two aborigines, one of [whom] went home and fetched two boomerangs with which he then returned and killed the other":

> The strict statement of the rule is that a reasonable man has to be deprived of his self-control. You may use these words, reasonable man, as meaning a reasonable native inhabitant of Australia. You may draw

a distinction between the amount of provocation which is needed before the ordinary reasonable human being, such as you are, would lose his self-control, and the lesser, if you think it applies, the lesser degree of provocation needed before an aboriginal of Australia loses his self-control.

3. *The sex of the "reasonable person."* According to Lord Diplock, "the reasonable man referred to * * * is a person having the power of self-control to be expected of an ordinary person of the sex * * * of the accused." Why is the sex of the defendant any more relevant than the hair color of the accused?

Is there any practical effect in taking into consideration the sex of the accused in determining the adequacy of the provocation? Note the following:

> [T]he legal standards that define adequate provocation and passionate "human" weakness reflect a male view of understandable homicidal violence. Homicide is overwhelmingly a male act. In 1984, eighty-seven percent of those arrested in the United States for homicide * * * were male. * * *
>
> > Women rarely kill. * * * Female homicide is so different from male homicide that women and men may be said to live in two different cultures, each with its own "subculture of violence."

Laurie J. Taylor, Comment, *Provoked Reason in Men and Women: Heat-of-Passion Manslaughter and Imperfect Self–Defense,* 33 UCLA L.Rev. 1679, 1679–81 (1986); see also Margo I. Wilson & Martin Daly, *Who Kills Whom In Spouse Killings? On the Exceptional Sex Ratio of Spousal Homicides in the United States,* 30 Criminology 189, 206 (1992) (reporting an asymmetry in "wives' and husbands' actions or motives" in spousal homicides; men frequently kill in response to revelations of infidelity, but that women rarely kill in such circumstances).

Is a woman who "acts like a man" by killing in response to infidelity likely to be benefitted or hurt by an instruction that the jury evaluate her actions by the standards of the "reasonable woman"?

4. According to Lord Simon, the Crown's attorney "sternly and cogently maintained" that the principles of *Bedder* would bar a jury from considering the fact that "the accused was, say, pregnant, or presumably undergoing menstruation or menopause." Is the implication of *Camplin* that a jury should now take into consideration such physical characteristics of the defendant? Should this be the case?

5. *Problem.* At a campsite, *C* killed *V* after he inadvertently discovered *V* participating in lesbian lovemaking. At his trial, *C* sought to introduce evidence regarding his psychosexual history, including the fact that his mother had been involved in a lesbian relationship, in order to show that his reaction was reasonable in light of his family history and consequent emotional state. Was *C* entitled to present such evidence? Commonwealth v. Carr, 398 Pa.Super. 306, 580 A.2d 1362 (1990).

c. Model Penal Code

PEOPLE v. CASASSA

Court of Appeals of New York, 1980.
49 N.Y.2d 668, 427 N.Y.S.2d 769, 404 N.E.2d 1310.

JASEN, JUDGE.

The significant issue on this appeal is whether the defendant, in a murder prosecution, established the affirmative defense of "extreme emotional disturbance" which would have reduced the crime to manslaughter in the first degree.

On February 28, 1977, Victoria Lo Consolo was brutally murdered. Defendant Victor Casassa and Miss Lo Consolo had been acquainted for some time prior to the latter's tragic death. They met in August, 1976 as a result of their residence in the same apartment complex. * * * The two apparently dated casually * * * until November, 1976 when Miss Lo Consolo informed defendant that she was not "falling in love" with him. Defendant claims that Miss Lo Consolo's candid statement of her feelings "devastated him."

Miss Lo Consolo's rejection of defendant's advances also precipitated a bizarre series of actions on the part of defendant which, he asserts, demonstrate the existence of extreme emotional disturbance upon which he predicates his affirmative defense. Defendant, aware that Miss Lo Consolo maintained social relationships with others, broke into the apartment below Miss Lo Consolo's on several occasions to eavesdrop. These eavesdropping sessions allegedly caused him to be under great emotional stress. Thereafter, on one occasion, he broke into Miss Lo Consolo's apartment while she was out. Defendant took nothing, but, instead, observed the apartment, disrobed and lay for a time in Miss Lo Consolo's bed. During this break-in, defendant was armed with a knife which, he later told police, he carried "because he knew that he was either going to hurt Victoria or Victoria was going to cause him to commit suicide."

Defendant's final visit to his victim's apartment occurred on February 28, 1977. Defendant brought several bottles of wine and liquor with him to offer as a gift. Upon Miss Lo Consolo's rejection of this offering, defendant produced a steak knife which he had brought with him, stabbed Miss Lo Consolo several times in the throat, dragged her body to the bathroom and submerged it in a bathtub full of water to "make sure she was dead." * * *

Defendant waived a jury and proceeded to trial before the County Court. * * * The defendant did not contest the underlying facts of the crime. Instead, the sole issue presented to the trial court was whether the defendant, at the time of the killing, had acted under the influence of "extreme emotional disturbance." (Penal Law, § 125.25, subd. 1, par. [a].) The defense presented only one witness, a psychiatrist, who testified, in essence, that the defendant had become obsessed with Miss Lo Consolo and that the course which their relationship had taken, combined with several personality attributes peculiar to defendant, caused him to be under the influence of extreme emotional disturbance at the time of the killing.

In rebuttal, the People produced several witnesses. Among these witnesses was a psychiatrist who testified that although the defendant was emotionally disturbed, he was not under the influence of "extreme emotional disturbance" * * * because his disturbed state was not the product of external factors but rather was "a stress he created from within himself, dealing mostly with a fantasy, a refusal to accept the reality of the situation."

The trial court in resolving this issue noted that the affirmative defense of extreme emotional disturbance may be based upon a series of events, rather than a single precipitating cause. In order to be entitled to the defense, the court held, a defendant must show that his reaction to such events was reasonable. In determining whether defendant's emotional reaction was reasonable, the court considered the appropriate test to be whether in the totality of the circumstances the finder of fact could understand how a person might have his reason overcome. Concluding that the test was not to be applied solely from the viewpoint of defendant, the court found that defendant's emotional reaction at the time of the commission of the crime was so peculiar to him that it could not be considered reasonable so as to reduce the conviction to manslaughter in the first degree. Accordingly, the trial court found defendant guilty of the crime of murder in the second degree. * * *

On this appeal defendant contends that the trial court erred in failing to afford him the benefit of the affirmative defense of "extreme emotional disturbance." It is argued that the defendant established that he suffered from a mental infirmity not arising to the level of insanity which disoriented his reason to the extent that his emotional reaction, from his own subjective point of view, was supported by a reasonable explanation or excuse. Defendant asserts that by refusing to apply a wholly subjective standard the trial court misconstrued section 125.25 of the Penal Law. We cannot agree.

Section 125.25 (subd. 1, par. [a]) of the Penal Law provides that it is an affirmative defense to the crime of murder in the second degree where "[t]he defendant acted under the influence of extreme emotional disturbance for which there was a reasonable explanation or excuse." This defense allows a defendant charged with the commission of acts which would otherwise constitute murder to demonstrate the existence of mitigating factors which indicate that, although he is not free from responsibility for his crime, he ought to be punished less severely by reducing the crime upon conviction to manslaughter in the first degree.

In enacting section 125.25, the Legislature adopted the language of the manslaughter provisions of the Model Penal Code. * * *

The "extreme emotional disturbance" defense is an outgrowth of the "heat of passion" doctrine which had for some time been recognized by New York as a distinguishing factor between the crimes of manslaughter and murder. However, the new formulation is significantly broader in scope than the "heat of passion" doctrine which it replaced.

For example, the "heat of passion" doctrine required that a defendant's action be undertaken as a response to some provocation which prevented him from reflecting upon his actions. Moreover, such reaction had to be immediate. The existence of a "cooling off" period completely negated any mitigating effect which the provocation might otherwise have had. In [*People v.*] *Patterson*[, 39 N.Y.2d 288, 383 N.Y.S.2d 573, 347 N.E.2d 898 (1976)], however, this court recognized that "[a]n action influenced by an extreme emotional disturbance is not one that is necessarily so spontaneously undertaken. Rather, it may be that a significant mental trauma has affected a defendant's mind for a substantial period of time, simmering in the unknowing subconscious and then inexplicably coming to the fore." * * *

The thrust of defendant's claim, however, concerns a question arising out of another perceived distinction between "heat of passion" and "extreme emotional disturbance" * * *, to wit: whether, assuming that the defense is applicable to a broader range of circumstances, the standard by which the reasonableness of defendant's emotional reaction is to be tested must be an entirely subjective one. * * *

Consideration of the Comments to the Model Penal Code, from which the New York statute was drawn, are instructive. The defense of "extreme emotional disturbance" has two principal components—(1) the particular defendant must have "acted under the influence of extreme emotional disturbance," and (2) there must have been "a reasonable explanation or excuse" for such extreme emotional disturbance, "the reasonableness of which is to be determined from the viewpoint of a person in the defendant's situation under the circumstances as the defendant believed them to be." The first requirement is wholly subjective—i.e., it involves a determination that the particular defendant did in fact act under extreme emotional disturbance, that the claimed explanation as to the cause of his action is not contrived or sham.

The second component is more difficult to describe—i.e., whether there was a reasonable explanation or excuse for the emotional disturbance. It was designed to sweep away "the rigid rules that have developed with respect to the sufficiency of particular types of provocation, such as the rule that words alone can never be enough," and "avoids a merely arbitrary limitation on the nature of the antecedent circumstances that may justify a mitigation." "The ultimate test, however, is objective; there must be 'reasonable' explanation or excuse for the actor's disturbance." In light of these comments and the necessity of articulating the defense in terms comprehensible to jurors, we conclude that the determination whether there was reasonable explanation or excuse for a particular emotional disturbance should be made by viewing the subjective, internal situation in which the defendant found himself and the external circumstances as he perceived them at the time, however inaccurate that perception may have been, and assessing from that standpoint whether the explanation or excuse for his emotional disturbance was reasonable, so as to entitle him to a reduction of the crime charged from murder in the second degree to manslaughter in the first degree.[2] We recognize that even such a description of the defense provides no precise guidelines and necessarily leaves room for the exercise of judgmental evaluation by the jury. This, however, appears to have been the intent of the draftsmen. "The purpose was explicitly to give full scope to what amounts to a plea in mitigation based upon a mental or emotional trauma of significant dimensions, with the jury asked to show whatever empathy it can." (Wechsler, Codification of Criminal Law in the United States: The Model Penal Code, 68 Col.L.Rev. 1425, 1446.) * * *

* * * In the end, we believe that what the Legislature intended in enacting the statute was to allow the finder of fact the discretionary power to mitigate the penalty when presented with a situation which, under the circumstances, appears to them to have caused an understandable weakness in one of their fellows. Perhaps the chief virtue of the statute is that it allows such discretion without engaging in a detailed explanation of individual circumstances in which the statute would apply, thus avoiding the "mystifying cloud of words" which Mr. Justice Cardozo abhorred.

We conclude that the trial court, in this case, properly applied the statute. The court apparently accepted, as a factual matter, that defendant killed Miss Lo Consolo while under the influence of "extreme emotional disturbance," a threshold question which must be answered in the affirmative before any test of reasonableness is required. The court, however, also recognized that in exercising its function as trier of fact, it must make a further inquiry into the reasonableness of that disturbance. In this regard, the court considered each of the mitigating factors put forward by defendant, including his claimed mental disability, but found that the excuse offered by defendant was so peculiar to him that it was unworthy of mitigation. The court obviously made a sincere effort to understand defendant's "situation" and "the circumstances as defendant believed them to be," but concluded that the murder in this case was the result of defendant's malevolence rather than an understandable human response deserving of mercy. We cannot say, as a matter of law, that the court erred in so concluding. Indeed, to do so would subvert the purpose of the statute.

In our opinion, this statute would not require that the jury or the court as trier of fact find mitigation on any particular set of facts, but, rather, allows the finder of fact the opportunity to do so, such opportunity being conditional only upon a finding of extreme emotional disturbance in the first instance. * * *

---

2. We emphasize that this test is to be applied to determine whether defendant's emotional disturbance, and not the act of killing, was supported by a reasonable explanation or excuse.

Notes and Questions

1. In the following cases, is the defendant entitled to a jury instruction on manslaughter under the Model Penal Code?

A. Defendant Raguseo lived in an apartment building in which each tenant had an assigned parking space. He took meticulous care of his spot, painting the lines on either side of the space, sweeping it regularly, and clipping the shrubbery nearby. One night Raguseo found someone else's car in his space. He called the police, who informed him that they did not have authority to tow a vehicle parked on private property. Two hours later, when the owner of the car returned, Raguseo stabbed him repeatedly, killing him. State v. Raguseo, 225 Conn. 114, 622 A.2d 519 (1993).

B. In a fit of rage, the defendant strangled to death his wife on their honeymoon cruise because she refused to stop eating sweets and because she did not know how to use the "complex" silverware settings aboard the cruise ship. United States v. Roston, 986 F.2d 1287 (9th Cir.1993).

C. The defendant killed Gerald because he reminded her of her ex-husband.

2. Reconsider *Carr* (Note 5, p. 233 supra): Under the Model Penal Code, is *C* entitled to a jury instruction on manslaughter? If so, should the jury consider the situation from the perspective of a person suffering from a sexual disturbance that makes him irrationally anti-homosexual, i.e., "from the viewpoint of a person in the actor's situation"? The Commentary explains the meaning of the latter language:

> The critical element in the Model Code formulation is the clause requiring that reasonableness be assessed "from the viewpoint of a person in the actor's situation." The word "situation" is designedly ambiguous. On the one hand, it is clear that personal handicaps and some external circumstances must be taken into account. Thus, blindness, shock from traumatic injury, and extreme grief are all easily read into the term "situation." This result is sound, for it would be morally obtuse to appraise a crime for mitigation of punishment without reference to these factors. On the other hand, it is equally plain that idiosyncratic moral values are not part of the actor's situation. An assassin who kills a political leader because he believes it is right to do so cannot ask that he be judged by the standard of a reasonable extremist. Any other result would undermine the normative message of the criminal law. In between these two extremes, however, there are matters neither as clearly distinct from individual blameworthiness as blindness or handicap nor as integral a part of moral depravity as a belief in the rightness of killing. Perhaps the classic illustration is the unusual sensitivity to the epithet "bastard" of a person born illegitimate. An exceptionally punctilious sense of personal honor or an abnormally fearful temperament may also serve to differentiate an individual actor from the hypothetical reasonable man, yet none of these factors is wholly irrelevant to the ultimate issue of culpability. The proper role of such factors cannot be resolved satisfactorily by abstract definition of what may constitute adequate provocation. The Model Code endorses a formulation that affords sufficient flexibility to differen-

tiate in particular cases between those special aspects of the actor's situation that should be deemed material for purpose of grading and those that should be ignored. There thus will be room for interpretation of the word "situation," and that is precisely the flexibility desired. * * * In the end, the question is whether the actor's loss of self-control can be understood in terms that arouse sympathy in the ordinary citizen. Section 210.3 faces this issue squarely and leaves the ultimate judgment to the ordinary citizen in the function of a juror assigned to resolve the specific case.

American Law Institute, Model Penal Code and Commentaries, Comment to § 210.3 at 62–63 (1980).

3. Model Penal Code § 210.3(1)(b) not only is a broader version of the heat-of-passion doctrine, but is intended to "allow an inquiry into areas which have been treated as part of the law of diminished responsibility or the insanity defense." Id. at 54. This aspect of the defense is considered at p. 641 infra.

4. *Problem.* Celerino Galicia, an adherent of *curanderismo,* "the Mexican belief in folk healing and spirits," believed that Roberta Martinez, his girlfriend, was a *bruja,* or female witch, who had cast a spell, an *embrujada,* over him. Galicia sought a healer to cleanse him of the embrujada. When he could not find one, he plunged a six-inch steak knife forty-four times into Martinez's chest, killing her. Adrienne Drell, *Witchcraft Murder Defense Fails,* A.B.A. J., May, 1993, at 40. Of what form of criminal homicide is Galicia guilty? Apply the Model Penal Code and the California Penal Code (see p. 197 supra).

C. UNINTENTIONAL KILLINGS: UNJUSTIFIED RISK–TAKING

BERRY v. SUPERIOR COURT

Court of Appeal, Sixth District, 1989.
208 Cal.App.3d 783, 256 Cal.Rptr. 344.[a]

AGLIANO, PRESIDING JUSTICE.

The People have charged Michael Patrick Berry, defendant, with the murder of two and one half year old James Soto who was killed by Berry's pit bull dog. Defendant also stands accused of * * * marijuana cultivation (Health & Saf.Code, § 11358); and misdemeanor keeping of a fighting dog. (Pen.Code, § 597.5, subd. (a)(1).) * * * [D]efendant seeks [pre-trial] dismissal of the charge[ ] of murder * * * He claims the evidence taken at the preliminary hearing falls legally short of establishing implied malice sufficient to [prosecute him] for murder * * *.

* * * Our task is to decide whether "a person of ordinary caution or prudence would be led to believe and conscientiously entertain a strong suspicion that defendant committed the crime charged." (*People v.*

a. Pursuant to Rule 976 of the California Rules of Court, the state supreme court ordered depublication of this case, i.e., the opinion is not published in the Official Reporter, nor may it be cited as authority in subsequent cases.

Watson (1981) 30 Cal.3d 290, 300, 179 Cal.Rptr. 43, 637 P.2d 279.)
* * *

The record shows that on June 13, 1987, James Soto, then aged two years and eight months, was killed by a pit bull dog named "Willy" owned by defendant. The animal was tethered near defendant's house but no obstacle prevented access to the dog's area. The victim and his family lived in a house which stood on the same lot, sharing a common driveway. The Soto family had four young children, then aged 10, 4½, 2½, and one year.

On the day of the child's death, his mother, Yvonne Nunez, left the child playing on the patio of their home for a minute or so while she went into the house, and when she came out the child was gone. She was looking for him when within some three to five minutes her brother-in-law, Richard Soto, called her and said defendant's dog had attacked James. Meanwhile the father, Arthur Soto, had come upon the dog Willy mauling his son. He screamed for defendant to come get the dog off the child; defendant did so. The child was bleeding profusely. Although an on-call volunteer fireman with paramedical training who lived nearby arrived within minutes and attempted to resuscitate the child, James died before an emergency crew arrived at the scene.

There was no evidence that Willy had ever before attacked a human being, but there was considerable evidence that he was bred and trained to be a fighting dog and that he posed a known threat to people. Defendant bought Willy from a breeder of fighting dogs, who informed defendant of the dog's fighting abilities, his gameness, wind, and exceptionally hard bite. The breeder told defendant that in a dog fight "a dog won't go an hour with Willy and live."

The police searched defendant's house after the death of James and found many underground publications about dog fighting; a pamphlet entitled "42 day keep" which set out the 6–week conditioning procedures used to prepare a dog for a match; a treadmill used to condition a dog and increase its endurance; correspondence with Willy's breeder, Gene Smith; photographs of dog fights; and a "break stick," used to pry fighting dogs apart since they will not release on command. One of Smith's letters dated December 7, 1984, described Willy as having an exceptionally hard bite.

Two women who knew defendant testified he told them he had raised dogs for fighting purposes and had fought pit bulls.

Richard Soto testified defendant told him he used the treadmill to increase the strength and endurance of his dogs. Defendant also told both Arthur and Richard Soto that he would not fight his dogs for less than $500 and he told Richard Willy had had matches as far away as South Carolina.

The victim's mother testified defendant had several dogs. He told her not to be concerned about the dogs, that they would not bother her children, except for "one that he had on the side of the house" which was behind a six foot fence. Defendant further said this dangerous dog was Willy but that she need not be concerned since he was behind a fence. There was a fence where the dog was tethered on the west side of defendant's house, but the fence was not an enclosure and did not prevent access to the area the dog could reach.

The police found some 243 marijuana plants growing behind defendant's house. Willy was tethered in such location that anyone wanting to approach the plants would have to cross the area the dog could reach. That area was readily accessible to anyone.

An animal control officer qualified as an expert on fighting dogs testified. He said pit bull dogs are selectively bred to be aggressive towards other animals. They give no warning of their attack, attack swiftly, silently and tenaciously. Although many recently bred pit bulls have good dispositions near human beings and are bred and raised to be pets, there are no uniform breeding standards for temperament and the animal control officers consider a pit bull dangerous unless proved otherwise. * * *

DISCUSSION

Whether Evidence Is Sufficient To Bind Over on Murder Charge

First, defendant claims that as a matter of law the record does not show implied malice sufficient to require him to stand trial for a charge of second degree murder. As stated above, the issue at this stage of the proceedings is not whether the evidence establishes guilt beyond a reasonable doubt, but rather whether the evidence is sufficient to lead a man of ordinary caution or prudence to believe and conscientiously entertain a strong suspicion of his guilt of this offense * * *.

The case of *People v. Watson, supra,* 30 Cal.3d 290, 179 Cal.Rptr. 43, 637 P.2d 279, * * * states that the test of implied malice in an unintentional killing is actual appreciation of a high degree of risk that is objectively present. There must be a high probability that the act done will result in death and it must be done with a base antisocial motive and with wanton disregard for life. The conduct in *Watson,* held sufficient to ground a finding of malice, was reckless speeding while intoxicated. Defendant had prior knowledge of the hazards of drunk driving.

The recent decision in *People v. Protopappas* (1988) 201 Cal.App.3d 152, 246 Cal.Rptr. 915 further elaborates the definition of implied malice. That case found sufficient evidence of implied malice to support the defendant dentist's convictions of the murders of three of his patients, who died because of his recklessness.[b] He clearly did not intend to kill them; as the decision pointed out, it was in his interests to keep them alive so that he could continue to collect fees from them. Further, his failure to provide proper treatment for them could be

b. In *Protopappas,* the defendant, on three occasions, administered anaesthesia to his patients prior to dental surgery, but ignored symptoms of medical distress and, in two cases, left them to tend to other patients.

characterized as an act of omission or neglect rather than an affirmative act of homicide. But the appellate court found sufficient evidence of malice because the jury could infer from his conduct that he actually appreciated the risk to his patients and exhibited extreme indifference to their welfare in failing to provide the proper treatment and care and in administering anaesthesia to them in grossly negligent fashion. The court found substantial evidence Protopappas's treatment of his patients was " ' "aggravated, culpable, gross, or reckless" neglect ... [which] involved such a high degree of probability that it would result in death that it constituted "a wanton disregard for human life" making it second degree murder.' " The *Protopappas* court further elaborated the requirements of implied malice thus: "wantonness, an extreme indifference to [the victim's] life, and subjective awareness of the very high probability of her death."

Interestingly, the court in *Protopappas* referred to the dentist's conduct as "the health care equivalent of shooting into a crowd or setting a lethal mantrap in a dark alley." Similarly here, the People seek to analogize defendant's manner of keeping Willy as the equivalent of setting a lethal mantrap, since anyone could have approached the dog and been at risk of attack.

Another decision which thoughtfully explores the nature of implied malice is *People v. Love* (1980) 111 Cal.App.3d 98, 168 Cal.Rtpr. 407. The facts of that case may be considered more aggravated than in this case or in *Protopappas, supra,* since in *Love* the defendant put a gun to the victim's temple and then claimed it went off accidentally. The analysis is nonetheless useful. The court discusses the "fine line between cases involving conduct consonant with the punishment to be imposed for second degree murder and those which are properly lesser crimes" and points out that the former cases all involve "an element of viciousness—an extreme indifference to the value of human life." Examples given of such conduct include the striking of a child, assault with a deadly weapon, or a father's neglect in caring for his son.

Love observes that the "continuum of death-causing behavior for which society imposes sanctions is practically limitless with the gradations of more culpable conduct imperceptibly shading into conduct for the less culpable. Our high court has drawn this line placing in the more culpable category not only those deliberate life-endangering acts which are done with a subjective awareness of the risk involved, but also life-endangering conduct which is 'only' done with the awareness the conduct is contrary to the laws of society. Although behavior in the latter category may not be as morally heinous as the former, the difference in culpability does not require the latter crime to be legally shifted into manslaughter slots. * * * One's felt sense of justice is not moved, much less outraged, when such life-endangering and death-causing conduct is labeled as second degree murder."

The decision in *Love* sets forth two prerequisites for affixing second degree murder liability upon an unintentional killing. One requirement is the defendant's extreme indifference to the value of human life, a condition which must be demonstrated by showing the probability that the conduct involved will cause death. Another requirement is awareness either (1) of the risks of the conduct, *or* (2) that the conduct is contrary to law. Here, evidence of the latter requirement is first, that the very possession of Willy may have constituted illegal keeping of a fighting dog. Second, there is evidence that defendant kept Willy to guard marijuana plants, also conduct with elements of illegality and antisocial purpose. Thus the second element which *Love* required could be satisfied here in a number of ways.

Defendant argues that the elements posited in *Love*—awareness of high risk or antisocial or illegal conduct—are insufficient. He says a further requirement is that the defendant have actively killed the victim, rather than being guilty of passive omissions which result in the death. * * *

However, despite defendant's argument that all second degree murders involve acts of commission rather than omission, * * * *Protopappas* * * * arguably rest[s] on reckless failure to provide proper care or treatment. The *Protopappas* court described the defendant's conduct there in precisely those terms. * * *

Almost any behavior can alternately be stated as a sin of omission or of commission. Therefore the distinction of active and passive behavior is not a reliable means of distinguishing intentional and unintentional homicide. * * * Rather, as the cases hold, attention is best focused on the difference in mental state, in the defendant's intent. Death by agency of an "abandoned and malignant heart," more precisely defined in *Watson, supra,* as a subjective appreciation of a high risk of death, is murder; by gross negligence alone is manslaughter.

Have we here evidence of the elements of second degree murder as described in these decisions, namely, the high probability the conduct will result in the death of a human being, a subjective appreciation of the risk, and a base antisocial purpose or motive? The People point to these facts: The homes of defendant and the victim's family shared a lot and were in close proximity, the Soto family had four very young children and defendant knew this; defendant knew the dog Willy was dangerous to the children, as evidenced by the mother's testimony that he told her that dog could be dangerous but was behind a fence; defendant in fact lulled Yvonne into a false sense of security by assuring her the dangerous dog was behind a fence when he was in fact accessible; defendant bred fighting dogs and had knowledge of the nature and characteristics of fighting pit bulls; defendant had referred to Willy as a "killer dog"; pit bulls in fact are sometimes dangerous and will attack unpredictably and without warning; and Willy was a proven savage fighting dog.

From this mass of evidence it is possible to isolate facts which standing alone would not suffice as the basis of a murder charge. For example, we do not believe that a showing that Willy was dangerous to other dogs, without more, would be sufficient to bind over his owner on a murder charge; there is no evidence in this record that dogs who are dangerous to their own kind are ipso facto dangerous to human beings and therefore there is no support for an inference that the owner of such a dog should be aware of any such danger. But the evidence amassed here goes beyond demonstrating that Willy was aggressive towards his own kind. We believe this record shows first, that Willy's owner may have been actually aware of the dog's potential danger to human beings. This mental state may be proved by showing he kept the dog chained, he warned the child's parents that the dog was dangerous to children, and he spoke of the dog as dangerous. Second, the testimony of the animal control officer could support an inference that fighting pit bull dogs are dangerous to human beings, and the record of defendant's extensive knowledge of the breed could support an inference that he knew such dogs are dangerous. * * *

We do not know the actual probability that a death could result from defendant's conduct in keeping the dog. Presumably that is a question of fact to be submitted to the court or jury upon appropriate instructions requiring that it find a high probability that death would result from the circumstances before it can convict of murder.

Defendant emphasizes the facts that Willy had never before attacked a human being and that he was kept chained on the premises. First, the fact that the dog was kept chained lessened little the risk which he posed, in view of the close proximity of very young children, the obvious risk of a child's wandering near, and indeed being attracted to a seemingly harmless pet, and the easy accessibility to his vicinity. * * * Also, the fact that defendant took the precaution of restraining the dog is a fact which might show he knew the dog was dangerous. * * *

We conclude that it is for the jury to resolve the factual issues of probability of death and subjective mental state. There is sufficient evidence to justify trial for murder on an implied malice theory. * * *

Notes and Questions

1. Is the court suggesting that Berry may be convicted of murder because he used the pit bull to guard his marijuana or may have been guilty of the misdemeanor of keeping a fighting dog? Does such conduct demonstrate "viciousness" or "an extreme indifference to the value of human life"? If a jury acquits Berry of these lesser offenses, should he still be convicted of second degree murder?

2. Does the evidence support the conclusion that Berry's conduct created a "very high probability of death"? What were the odds on that day that the tethered pit bull would maul someone to death? If there was only a one percent—or even 1/10th of one percent—chance of death, should that rule out a murder conviction?

On the other hand, is it sufficient to prove that the defendant was aware that his conduct created a very high probability of death? Suppose that a doctor, with appropriate consent, performs very dangerous experimental surgery in order to save the life of her extremely ill patient. If the patient dies from the surgery, has the surgeon acted with an "abandoned and malignant heart"? If not, what more must be proved to convict her of murder? Does the Model Penal Code provide an answer? See Section 2.02(2)(c).

3. The colorful phrase "abandoned and malignant heart," codified in California's murder statute, stems from the common law. Courts have struggled to define the phrase in a way that adequately explains to juries when hazardous conduct resulting in death constitutes murder.

The Utah Supreme Court has described this state of mind as "depraved indifference," i.e., "an utter callousness toward the value of human life and a complete and total indifference as to whether one's conduct will create the requisite risk of death * * * of another." State v. Standiford, 769 P.2d 254, 261 (Utah 1988). A person guilty of depraved indifference is one "bent on mischief" who "act[s] with a 'don't give a damn attitude,' in total disregard of the public safety." King v. State, 505 So.2d 403, 408 (Ala.Cr.App.1987).

The Model Penal Code abstains from such demonstrative language. In a Code jurisdiction, what would the prosecutor have to prove regarding Berry's state of mind in order to convict him of murder? Of manslaughter? If you were a juror in *Berry,* would you prefer to be instructed in Model Penal Code language or as the courts have done in *Standiford* and *King*?

4. *Problem.* Naomi wants to scare Bob by shooting a firearm in his direction, intending to miss him by just a hair. She hides behind a bush outside Bob's home, waiting for him to arrive. When he approaches, she fires the gun, accidentally killing him. In California, of what degree of murder is Naomi guilty? See People v. Laws, 12 Cal.App.4th 786, 15 Cal.Rptr.2d 668 (1993).

5. *Intent to cause grievous bodily injury.* At common law, a person acts with malice aforethought if, with the intent to cause grievous bodily injury, she accidentally kills another. Of what offense is such a person guilty under the Model Penal Code? The Commentary to the Code explains the drafters' views on this form of criminal homicide:

> Section 210.2 accords no special significance to an intent to cause grievous bodily harm, though such a purpose established malice aforethought at common law and thus sufficed for murder or, where murder was divided into degrees, for murder in the second degree under the usual formulation. The deletion of intent to injure as an independently sufficient culpability for murder rests on the judgment that it is preferable to handle such cases under the standards of extreme recklessness and recklessness contained in Sections 210.2(1)(b) and 210.3(1)(a). That the actor intended to cause injury of a particular nature or gravity is, of course, a relevant consideration in determining whether he acted with "extreme indifference to the value of human life" under Section 210.2(1)(b) or "recklessly" with respect to death of another under Section 210.3(1). Most traditional illustrations of murder based on intent to injure will fall within the recklessness category as defined in the Model Code. In the rare case of purposeful infliction of serious injury not involving recklessness with respect to death, the actor should be prosecuted for some version of aggravated assault or, perhaps, for negligent homicide.

American Law Institute, Model Penal Code and Commentaries, Comment to § 210.2 at 28–29 (1980).

STATE v. HERNANDEZ

Missouri Court of Appeals, 1991.
815 S.W.2d 67.

PER CURIAM.

A jury found Pedro M. Hernandez (defendant) guilty of involuntary manslaughter * * *.

* * * On September 12, 1988, Cecil Barrymore was killed as a result of a motor vehicle accident. Barrymore's employer, Robert Butcher, and the employer's son, Kevin Butcher, were also injured in the accident. Robert Butcher was driving a truck in which his son, Kevin, and Barrymore were passengers. The truck was traveling in a southerly direction on Highway 123 in Polk County when it was struck by a van that was traveling in the opposite direction on the same highway. The van was operated by defendant. When Robert Butcher first saw the van it was coming around a curve, sliding into the wrong lane of travel. Two of the van's wheels were off the ground. Butcher applied his brakes and pulled his truck as far to his right as possible. The van returned to its proper lane then came back into Butcher's lane of traffic and collided with Butcher's truck. The truck was knocked into the ditch that ran alongside the roadway and the van overturned in an adjacent field. Defendant was thrown from the van.

Other persons arrived at the scene of the accident shortly after it occurred. They included Sherry Howard, an employee of the Citizens Memorial Hospital Ambulance Service; * * * and Dr. Bill Matthews, a physician from a nearby town.

Sherry Howard attended to defendant. She asked defendant if he had been drinking. Defendant replied that he had drunk "a 12–pack and some whiskey." * * *

Dr. Matthews examined Cecil Barrymore at the scene and pronounced him dead. Dr. Matthews testified that Cecil Barrymore died as a result of injuries sustained from the accident.

The van operated by the defendant was registered to him and the insurance certificates for the vehicle were issued to him. The sun visor from the interior of the van was received in evidence over defendant's objection, as was a sign that had been attached to the back window of defendant's van. There were stickers and pins attached to the visor. The stickers, pins, and the sign had various slogans printed on them, including:

"The more I drink, the better you look";

"Reality is for those who can't stay drunk";

"Member beer drinkers hall of fame";

"I only drink to make other people more interesting";

"A woman drove me to drink. Now I can't thank her enough";

"I never drink before five ... it's too early in the morning!";

"Suds sucker";

"Hell on wheels";

"All American drinking team"; and

"I love older whiskey and younger women."

Defendant contends that the trial court erred in admitting into evidence the signs, stickers, and pins with the statements containing "drinking slogans." Defendant contends that those items were irrelevant to the criminal charges against him. He argues that the drinking slogans that were admitted in evidence were used to try to show him to be the "type" person who would commit the crime in question.

In order for evidence to be relevant, it must logically tend to support or establish a fact or issue between the parties. The elements of the offense of involuntary manslaughter that were required to be proven were: (1) * * * that defendant acted with criminal negligence; and [(2)] that, in so doing, defendant caused Cecil Barrymore's death. Thus, the issue on appeal is whether evidence of the drinking slogans logically tended to support or establish * * * one or [both] of those elements.

Criminal negligence refers to the degree of culpability of the defendant's mental state, § 562.016.5.[2] It is the least culpable of the defined mental states. * * *

The state argues that the drinking slogans are relevant because the remarks show that the defendant *"knew* that drinking large amounts of alcohol could distort his sense of reality and his driving skills." That argument fails because the defendant's knowledge of the effect of alcohol on him was not an issue. It was not something that the state had the burden to prove in order to show criminal negligence. The essence of * * * manslaughter—the factor that distinguishes it from other types of homicides—is the defendant's lack of awareness of the risk to others from his conduct. The state did not have to prove that the defendant knew of the effects of alcohol upon him. * * *

The state also argues that the drinking slogans were relevant because "they tended to prove that [defendant] did not accidentally or mistakenly drink alcohol, in that his display of such items indicated that [he] approved of excessive drinking." That is another way of saying that because defendant approves of excessive drinking, he is a bad person—he is a person of poor character. Reputation or character testimony is admissible only when a defendant has put his own reputation in issue.

---

2. § 562.016.5 provides:

5. A person **"acts with criminal negligence"** or is criminally negligent when he fails to be aware of a substantial and unjustifiable risk that circumstances exist or a result will follow, and such failure constitutes a gross deviation from the standard of care which a reasonable person would exercise in the situation.

In this case, defendant's reputation was not in issue. The trial court erred in admitting evidence of the drinking slogans. * * *

The conviction[ ] of involuntary manslaughter * * * [is] reversed. * * *

SHRUM, JUDGE, * * * dissenting in part.

* * * I dissent because I believe that three of the drinking slogans were relevant and admissible, and I believe the admission into evidence of the other drinking slogans was not prejudicial to the defendant.

In examining the criminal negligence element of involuntary manslaughter, the explanatory notes following § 2.02 of the Model Penal Code are instructive because the definition of criminal negligence found in § 562.016.5 is derived from that section of the code. * * *

The explanatory notes following Model Penal Code § 2.02 state, in pertinent part:

> A person acts negligently under this subsection when he inadvertently creates a substantial and unjustifiable risk of which he ought to be aware. He is liable if given the nature and degree of the risk, his failure to perceive it is, considering the nature and purpose of the actor's conduct and the circumstances known to him, a gross deviation from the care that would be exercised by a reasonable person in his situation.... The tribunal must evaluate the actor's failure of perception and determine whether, under all the circumstances, it was serious enough to be condemned. The jury must find fault, and must find that it was substantial and unjustified....

> [T]he jury is asked to perform two distinct functions. First, it is to examine the risk and the factors that are relevant to its substantiality and justifiability. In the case of negligence, these questions are asked not in terms of what the actor's perceptions actually were, but in terms of an objective view of the situation as it actually existed. Second, the jury is to make the culpability judgment, this time in terms of whether the failure of the defendant to perceive the risk justifies condemnation. Considering the nature and purpose of his conduct and the circumstances known to him, the question is whether the defendant's failure to perceive a risk involves a gross deviation from the standard of care that a reasonable person would observe in the actor's situation.

Model Penal Code and Commentaries, § 2.02 note 4 at 240–41 (American Law Institute 1985).

Under the approach described in the above quoted Model Penal Code commentary, the jury first had to determine that the defendant created a substantial and unjustifiable risk of which he ought to have been aware. Under the § 562.016.5 objective standard of care (that which a reasonable person would exercise in the situation), the jury reasonably could have concluded the defendant ought to have been aware that, in taking to the road in an intoxicated condition, he created the substantial and unjustifiable risk that he would cause the death of another person.

The second aspect of the criminal negligence inquiry requires the jury to decide whether the failure of the defendant to perceive the risk is a "gross deviation" from the reasonable person standard of care of § 562.016.5, and whether such failure of perception "justifies condemnation." The jury's inquiry now departs from the reasonable person standard and focuses on the defendant's actual perceptions. Under the Model Penal Code approach, the jury should consider "the circumstances known to [the defendant]" in deciding whether to condemn the failure of perception. In the case before us, in deciding whether to condemn the defendant's failure to perceive the risk that, if he drove in an intoxicated condition he would cause the death of another person, the jury should be allowed to consider "circumstances known to him" including his knowledge of how the consumption of alcohol would affect his ability to drive.

At least three of the drinking slogans displayed by the defendant in his van logically relate to his knowledge of how alcohol consumption would affect him, i.e., that it would (1) result in his loss of touch with reality ("Reality is for those who can't stay drunk"), (2) affect his ability to perceive ("The more I drink, the better you look"), and (3) alter his moods ("I only drink to make other people more interesting"). The jury could reasonably infer from his knowledge of the effects of alcohol consumption on his grasp of reality, his perceptions, and his moods that he also knew the effects of alcohol consumption on his ability to drive.

In deciding whether to condemn the defendant for his failure to perceive the risk that he would cause the death of another person if he drove in an intoxicated condition, the jury should have been permitted to consider the defendant's knowledge of how the consumption of alcohol might affect his perceptions thereby causing him to not perceive the risk. * * *

The remaining drinking slogans were not relevant to the offense and should not have been admitted into evidence. However, I believe no prejudice resulted to the defendant from their admission. * * *

Notes and Questions

1. What distinguishes criminal negligence, the state of mind necessary to prove involuntary manslaughter in *Hernandez,* from the mental state required to prove murder in *Berry* (p. 239 supra)? In light of the difference, was the prosecutor correct in not charging Hernandez with murder?

2. "Negligence" is considered an "objective" form of fault because liability is based on the actor's failure to live up to the external—objective—standard of care of the "reasonable person." The harmdoer is guilty although—indeed, because—she did not subjectively appreciate the dangerousness of her conduct, assuming that a reasonable person in her situation would have foreseen the risk. Nonetheless, as Holmes has explained, "negligence" does contain a subjective component:

The test of foresight is not what this very criminal foresaw, but what a man of reasonable prudence would have foreseen. [¶] On the other hand, there must be actual present knowledge of the present facts which make an act dangerous. The act is not enough by itself. * * *

* * * It is enough that such circumstances were actually known as would have led a man of common understanding to infer from them the rest of the group making up the present state of things. For instance, if a workman on a house-top at mid-day knows that the space below him is a street in a great city, he knows facts from which a man of common understanding would infer that there were people passing below. He is therefore bound to draw that inference, or, in other words, is chargeable with knowledge of that fact also, whether he draws the inference or not. If, then, he throws down a heavy beam into the street, he does an act which a person of ordinary prudence would foresee is likely to cause death, or grievous bodily harm, and he is dealt with as if he foresaw it, whether he does so in fact or not.

Oliver Wendell Holmes, The Common Law 53–55 (1881).

Based on Holmes's explanation, was Judge Shrum correct in stating that the three drinking slogans were relevant to the state's case of manslaughter?

STATE v. WILLIAMS

Court of Appeals of Washington, 1971.
4 Wash.App. 908, 484 P.2d 1167.

HOROWITZ, CHIEF JUDGE.

Defendants, husband and wife, were charged * * * with the crime of manslaughter for negligently failing to supply their 17–month child with necessary medical attention, as a result of which he died on September 12, 1968. Upon entry of findings, conclusions and judgment of guilty, sentences were imposed * * *. Defendants appeal.

The defendant husband, Walter Williams, is a 24–year old full-blooded Sheshont Indian with a sixth-grade education. His sole occupation is that of laborer. The defendant wife, Bernice Williams, is a 20–year–old part Indian with an 11th grade education. At the time of the marriage, the wife had two children, the younger of whom was a 14–month son. Both parents worked and the children were cared for by the 85–year–old mother of the defendant husband. The defendant husband assumed parental responsibility with the defendant wife to provide clothing, care and medical attention for the child. Both defendants possessed a great deal of love and affection for the defendant wife's young son.

The court expressly found:

That both defendants were aware that William Joseph Tabafunda was ill during the period September 1, 1968 to September 12, 1968. The defendants were ignorant. They did not realize how sick the baby was. They thought that the baby had a toothache and no layman regards a toothache as dangerous to life. They loved the baby and gave it aspirin in hopes of improving its condition. They did not take the baby to a doctor because of fear that the Welfare Department would take the baby away from them. They knew that medical help was available because of previous experience. They had no excuse that the law will recognize for not taking the baby to a doctor.

The defendants Walter L. Williams and Bernice J. Williams were negligent in not seeking medical attention for William Joseph Tabafunda.

That as a proximate result of this negligence, William Joseph Tabafunda died.

From these and other findings, the court concluded that the defendants were each guilty of the crime of manslaughter as charged.

Defendants * * * contend that the findings do not support the conclusions that the defendants are guilty of manslaughter as charged. * * *

Parental duty to provide medical care for a dependent minor child was recognized at common law and characterized as a natural duty. * * * The existence of the duty also is assumed * * * in statutes that provide special criminal and civil sanctions for the performance of that duty. * * * On the question of the quality or seriousness of breach of the duty, at common law, in the case of involuntary manslaughter, the breach had to amount to more than mere ordinary or simple negligence—gross negligence was essential. In Washington, however, RCW 9.48.060 [2] and RCW 9.48.150 [3] supersede both voluntary and involuntary manslaughter as those crimes were defined at common law. Under these statutes the crime is deemed committed even though the death of the victim is the proximate result of only simple or ordinary negligence.

The concept of simple or ordinary negligence describes a failure to exercise the "ordinary caution" necessary to make out the defense of excusable homicide. RCW 9.48.150. Ordinary caution is the kind of caution that a man of reasonable prudence would exercise under the same or similar conditions. If, therefore, the conduct of a defendant, regardless of his ignorance, good intentions and good faith, fails to measure up to the conduct required of a man of reasonable prudence, he is guilty of ordinary negligence because of his failure to use "ordinary caution." If such negligence proximately causes the death of the victim, the defendant, as pointed out above, is guilty of statutory manslaughter. * * *

The * * * issue of proximate cause requires consideration of the question of when the duty to furnish medical care became activated. If the duty to furnish such care was not activated until after it was too late

---

2. RCW 9.48.060 provided in part:

"In any case other than those specified in RCW 9.48.030, 9.48.040 and 9.48.050, homicide, not being excusable or justifiable, is manslaughter."

3. RCW 9.48.150 provides:

"Homicide is excusable when committed by accident or misfortune in doing any lawful act by lawful means, with ordinary caution and without any unlawful intent."

to save the life of the child, failure to furnish medical care could not be said to have proximately caused the child's death. Timeliness in the furnishing of medical care also must be considered in terms of "ordinary caution." The law does not mandatorily require that a doctor be called for a child at the first sign of any indisposition or illness. The indisposition or illness may appear to be of a minor or very temporary kind, such as a toothache or cold. If one in the exercise of ordinary caution fails to recognize that his child's symptoms require medical attention, it cannot be said that the failure to obtain such medical attention is a breach of the duty owed. * * *

It remains to apply the law discussed to the facts of the instant case. * * *

Dr. Gale Wilson, the autopsy surgeon and chief pathologist for the King County Coroner, testified that the child died because an abscessed tooth had been allowed to develop into an infection of the mouth and cheeks, eventually becoming gangrenous. This condition, accompanied by the child's inability to eat, brought about malnutrition, lowering the child's resistance and eventually producing pneumonia, causing the death. Dr. Wilson testified that in his opinion the infection had lasted for approximately 2 weeks, and that the odor generally associated with gangrene would have been present for approximately 10 days before death. He also expressed the opinion that had medical care been first obtained in the last week before the baby's death, such care would have been obtained too late to have saved the baby's life. Accordingly, the baby's apparent condition between September 1 and September 5, 1968 became the critical period for the purpose of determining whether in the exercise of ordinary caution defendants should have provided medical care for the minor child.

The testimony concerning the child's apparent condition during the critical period is not crystal clear, but is sufficient to warrant the following statement of the matter. The defendant husband testified that he noticed the baby was sick about 2 weeks before the baby died. The defendant wife testified that she noticed the baby was ill about a week and a half or 2 weeks before the baby died. The evidence showed that in the critical period the baby was fussy; that he could not keep his food down; and that a cheek started swelling up. The swelling went up and down, but did not disappear. In that same period, the cheek turned "a bluish color like." The defendants, not realizing that the baby was as ill as it was or that the baby was in danger of dying, attempted to provide some relief to the baby by giving the baby aspirin during the critical period and continued to do so until the night before the baby died. The defendants thought the swelling would go down and were waiting for it to do so; and defendant husband testified, that from what he had heard, neither doctors nor dentists pull out a tooth "when it's all swollen up like that." There was an additional explanation for not calling a doctor given by each defendant. Defendant husband testified that "the way the cheek looked, * * * and that stuff on his hair, they would think we were neglecting him and take him away from us and not give him back."

Defendant wife testified that the defendants were "waiting for the swelling to go down," and also that they were afraid to take the child to a doctor for fear that the doctor would report them to the welfare department, who, in turn, would take the child away. "It's just that I was so scared of losing him." They testified that they had heard that the defendant husband's cousin lost a child that way. The evidence showed that the defendants did not understand the significance or seriousness of the baby's symptoms. However, there is no evidence that the defendants were physically or financially unable to obtain a doctor, or that they did not know an available doctor, or that the symptoms did not continue to be a matter of concern during the critical period. Indeed, the evidence shows that in April 1968 defendant husband had taken the child to a doctor for medical attention.

In our opinion, there is sufficient evidence from which the court could find, as it necessarily did, that applying the standard of ordinary caution, * * * defendants were sufficiently put on notice concerning the symptoms of the baby's illness and lack of improvement in the baby's apparent condition in the period from September 1 to September 5, 1968 to have required them to have obtained medical care for the child. The failure so to do in this case is ordinary or simple negligence, and such negligence is sufficient to support a conviction of statutory manslaughter.

The judgment is affirmed.

Notes and Questions

1. Based on the finding that the Williamses were guilty of ordinary negligence in the death of the child, of what form of criminal homicide would they be guilty under the Model Penal Code?

2. *"Negligence": the debate.* Should persons be punished for negligently causing harm to others? The drafters of the Model Penal Code wrestled with this issue.

> It has been urged that inadvertent negligence is not a sufficient basis for criminal conviction, both on the utilitarian ground that threatened sanctions cannot influence the inadvertent actor and on the moral ground that criminal punishment should be reserved for cases involving conscious fault. The utilitarian argument is that the inadvertent actor by definition does not perceive the risks of his conduct, and thus cannot be deterred from risk creation. The moral argument is that the legitimacy of criminal condemnation is premised upon personal accountability of the sort that is usually and properly measured by an estimate of the actor's willingness consciously to violate clearly established societal norms. Those who hold this view argue that the actor who does not perceive the risks associated with his conduct presents a moral situation different in kind from that of the actor who knows exactly what he is doing and what risks he is running and who nevertheless makes a conscious choice condemned by the penal law.

American Law Institute, Model Penal Code and Commentaries, Comment to § 210.4 at 86 (1980).

Is the utilitarian argument against punishment for negligence persuasive? The drafters of the Code ultimately did not think so:

> When people have knowledge that conviction and sentence, not to speak of punishment, may follow conduct that inadvertently creates improper risk, they are supplied with an additional motive to take care before acting, to use their faculties and draw on their experience in gauging the potentialities of completed conduct. To some extent, at least, this motive may promote awareness and thus be effective as a measure of control.

Id., Comment to § 2.02 at 243 (1985).

Are you persuaded? Even if some people are more careful in their actions because of the threat or application of the criminal sanction for negligence, should an individual be punished if, because of a physical or mental disability, she lacked the capacity to act safely?

Capacity issues aside, should people be punished merely because they failed to satisfy an objective standard of due care? No, according to Jerome Hall:

> People differ regarding many ethical questions; therefore, all the more significant is the enduring agreement in the long history of ethics that *voluntary* harm-doing is the essence of fault. Accordingly, the proposal to exclude negligence from penal liability is far from being a radical innovation. That choice, and therefore (voluntary) action, are the *sine qua non* of fault was expounded by Plato, Aristotle, Kant, Hegel, and many succeeding philosophers. Most of the current polemics directly or covertly recognize that principle.
>
> The requirement of (voluntary) action becomes even more persuasive in penal law. For, certainly among moralists, *punishing* a human being is a very serious matter. No one should be punished unless he has clearly acted immorally, i.e., voluntarily harmed someone, and unless a criminal sanction is both suitable and effective. The implication is that if there is any doubt regarding any of the relevant criteria—voluntariness and the suitability and effectiveness of punishment—the issue should be resolved by narrowing penal liability.

Jerome Hall, *Negligent Behavior Should Be Excluded From Criminal Liability,* 63 Colum.L.Rev. 632, 635–36 (1963).

Do you agree with Professor Hall that one who negligently causes harm has not acted immorally? If Hernandez (p. 246 supra) explained his drunk driving by saying, "I just didn't think," how might his punishment on retributive "just desert" grounds be defended? Consider:

> If one focuses on the just desert of the offender, as do strict retributivists, one is likely to reason along the following lines. Justice requires that punishment be inflicted to the extent that the offender deserves punishment. To assess a man's just desert, we must fathom the kind of man he is; to do that within the criminal law, we must rely exclusively on the offender's illegal act as the index of his moral character. * * *
> [¶] * * * After all, insensitivity and egocentricity are moral flaws and both of these manifest themselves in incidents of negligent risk-taking.

George P. Fletcher, *The Theory of Criminal Negligence: A Comparative Analysis,* 119 U.Pa.L.Rev. 401, 417 (1971).

Professor Hall insists, however, that although blame is appropriate in cases of negligence, punishment for it is not:

> In sum, although many persons are frequently blamed, this does not warrant a leap from that commonplace fact to the conclusion that punishment for negligence is justified. "Blame" is a very wide notion and, like praise, it permeates all of daily life. Important differences exist between raising an eyebrow and putting a man in jail, between blame for not developing one's potentialities and blame for voluntarily harming a human being, between blame that can be rejected or that leaves the censured person free to do as he pleases and the blame signified in the inexorable imposition of a major legal privation, and, finally, between the blame expressed in a judgment for damages and the blame implied in punishing a criminal.

Jerome Hall, *Negligent Behavior Should Be Excluded From Criminal Liability,* supra, 63 Colum.L.Rev. at 641.

3. *"Criminal" versus "civil" negligence.* Even if punishment for criminal negligence is justified, should the law "blot[ ] the defendant's name with the ignominy of having been found a 'criminal killer'," Commonwealth v. Heck, 341 Pa.Super. 183, 491 A.2d 212, 223 (1985), on the basis of ordinary (civil) negligence, as in *Williams?* Appraise the following (id. at 223–26):

> To demonstrate the unreasonableness of such liability [liability based on ordinary negligence], let us clarify the nature of an act of simple negligence to show how far it differs from an act that would traditionally be thought of as a crime. Ordinary negligence is the "antithesis" of wilful or intentional conduct. * * *
>
> In a fundamental sense the harshness of criminal punishment is fitting only for * * * consciously inflicted wrongs, and so traditionally the criminal law has concerned itself exclusively with conscious wrongdoing. * * *
>
> [Nonetheless,] [i]t is not all that difficult to harmonize the idea of criminal negligence with the dominant theme of the criminal law to punish only acts done with a guilty mind. We must remember that criminal negligence [unlike ordinary negligence] involves a *gross* deviation from reasonable care such that it would be shocking to allow the actor's lack of awareness to excuse his actions in the circumstances. The criminally negligent act has been done so heedlessly, so indifferently, and so grossly contrary to common experience that it becomes intolerable to reasoning minds that the actor did not perceive the risk of harm created by his conduct. In such cases the law presumes wantonness even though the circumstances do not allow proof beyond a reasonable doubt of the actor's subjective awareness of wrongdoing. "Criminal negligence" is a breach of duty so flagrant * * * that we may safely indulge the legal fiction that it was committed with actual intent to injure; * * * it is far from mere ordinary negligence or inadvertence; it is "great" negligence incompatible with a proper regard for human

life * * *. The judicial conscience therefore does not revolt at labelling it criminal.

4. Sam and Tiffany are rich, well-educated social climbers. One weekend they become so preoccupied planning the "party of the decade" that they fail to notice the obvious fact that their young child is growing mortally ill. See Larry Alexander, *Reconsidering the Relationship Among Voluntary Acts, Strict Liability, and Negligence in Criminal Law,* 7 Soc.Phil. & Policy (Spring 1990) at 84, 100. Are these parents more deserving of punishment than the Williamses? If so, on what ground?

5. In Walker v. Superior Court, 47 Cal.3d 112, 253 Cal.Rptr. 1, 763 P.2d 852 (1988), *V, W* 's four-year-old daughter, experienced flu-like symptoms. Four days later, she complained of a stiff neck. Consistent with the tenets of *W* 's Christian Science faith, *W* treated *V* 's illness exclusively by prayer, even as *V* lost weight and became disoriented. After 17 days without medical treatment, *V* died of acute meningitis. Of what form of criminal homicide, if any, is *W* guilty?

In determining *W* 's culpability, should the jury evaluate her behavior from the perspective of a reasonable Christian Scientist? How would the Model Penal Code answer this question? See Section 2.02(2)(d), and weigh this explanation of it:

> The standard for ultimate judgment invites consideration of the "care that a reasonable person would observe in the actor's situation." There is an inevitable ambiguity in "situation." If the actor were blind or if he had just suffered a blow or experienced a heart attack, these would certainly be facts to be considered in a judgment involving criminal liability, as they would be under traditional law. But the heredity, intelligence or temperament of the actor would not be held material in judging negligence, and could not be without depriving the criterion of all its objectivity. The Code is not intended to displace discriminations of this kind, but rather to leave the issue to the courts.[27]

American Law Institute, Model Penal Code and Commentaries, Comment to § 2.02 at 242 (1985).

6. *Problem.* On an exceedingly cold day in Detroit, Leroy Lyons lit a torch made up of rolled newspapers in order to thaw frozen water pipes beneath his kitchen floor. Shortly thereafter, two friends showed up and asked Lyons to repay them for money they had furnished him so that he could buy illegal drugs for personal use. While an unseen fire smoldered under the kitchen floor, Lyons and his wife left the house for an hour in order to obtain the money to pay off his debt. Their seven young children remained alone in the house.

While the parents were away, the house was enveloped in flames. All of the children were killed when smoke trapped them in one room. Although there was a window in that room, it had bars on it to prevent burglaries.

---

27. There is a similar problem with recklessness. Though recklessness requires defendant's conscious disregard of risk, the determination whether he shall be held liable * * * turns on whether the disregard involves a gross deviation from the standard of conduct of a law-abiding person "in the actor's situation." Section 2.02(2)(c) thus requires the same discriminations demanded by the standard of negligence.

Jim Schaefer, Jeffrey S. Ghannam & Janet Wilson, *Father Started Tragic Blaze,* Detroit Free Press, Feb. 19, 1993, at A1.

If you were a prosecutor in Michigan, what homicide charges would you bring against the parents? Would it change your analysis if you learned that it never occurred to the Lyonses that they were exposing their children to danger by leaving them alone in the house that day?

D. UNINTENTIONAL KILLINGS: UNLAWFUL CONDUCT

1. THE FELONY–MURDER RULE

a. The Doctrine in Its Unlimited Form

SIR EDWARD COKE—THE THIRD PART OF THE INSTITUTES OF THE LAWS OF ENGLAND

(1797), 56

If the act be unlawful it is murder. As if A meaning to steale a Deere in the Park of B, shooteth at the Deere, and by the glance of the arrow killeth a boy, that is hidden in a bush: this is murder, for that the act was unlawful, although A had no intent to hurt the boy, nor knew not of him. But if B the owner of the Park had shot at his own Deere, and without any ill intent had killed the boy by the glance of his arrow, this had been homicide by misadventure, and no felony.

So if one shoot at any wild fowle upon a tree, and the arrow killeth any reasonable creature afar off, without any evill intent in him, this is *per infortunium:* for it was not unlawfull to shoot at the wilde fowle: but if he had shot at a Cock or Hen, or any tame fowle of another mans, and the arrow by mischance had killed a man, this had been murder, for the act was unlawfull.

AMERICAN LAW INSTITUTE, MODEL PENAL CODE AND COMMENTARIES, COMMENT TO § 210.2

(1980), 30–32

The classic formulation of the felony-murder doctrine declares that one is guilty of murder if a death results from conduct during the commission or attempted commission of any felony. Some courts have made no effort to qualify the application of this doctrine, and a number of earlier English writers also articulated an unqualified rule. At the time the Model Code was drafted, a number of American legislatures, moreover, perpetuated the original statement of the rule by statute. As thus conceived, the rule operated to impose liability for murder based on the culpability required for the underlying felony without separate proof of any culpability with regard to the death. The homicide, as distinct from the underlying felony, was thus an offense of strict liability. This rule may have made sense under the conception of *mens rea* as something approaching a general criminal disposition rather than as a specific attitude of the defendant towards each element of a specific offense. Furthermore, it was hard to claim that the doctrine worked injustice in an age that recognized only a few felonies and that punished each as a capital offense.[74]

In modern times, however, legislatures have created a wide range of statutory felonies. Many of these crimes concern relatively minor misconduct not inherently dangerous to life and carry maximum penalties far less severe than those authorized for murder. Application of the ancient rigor of the felony-murder rule to such crimes will yield startling results. For example, a seller of liquor in violation of a statutory felony becomes a murderer if his purchaser falls asleep on the way home and dies of exposure. And a person who communicates disease during felonious sexual intercourse is guilty of murder if his partner subsequently dies of the infection.

The prospect of such consequences has led to a demand for limitations on the felony-murder rule.

PEOPLE v. STAMP

Court of Appeal, Second District, 1969.
2 Cal.App.3d 203, 82 Cal.Rptr. 598.

COBEY, ASSOCIATE JUSTICE.   * * *

[Stamp, armed with a gun and blackjack, entered the victim's office and ordered him and his fellow employees to lie down on the floor and to remain there for five minutes while Stamp and an accomplice fled with the business's cash. Shortly thereafter, the victim, who suffered from an advanced case of heart disease, experienced heart palpitations and died. Three doctors testified at the defendant's trial that the victim's heart attack was precipitated by fright induced by the robbery.]

Appellant's contention that the felony-murder rule is inapplicable to the facts of this case is * * * without merit. Under the felony-murder rule of section 189 of the Penal Code, a killing committed in either the perpetration of or an attempt to perpetrate robbery is murder of the first degree. This is true whether the killing is wilfull, deliberate and premeditated, or merely accidental or unintentional, and whether or not the killing is planned as a part of the commission of the robbery. * * *

* * * This rule is a rule of substantive law in California and not merely an evidentiary shortcut to finding malice as it withdraws from the jury the requirement that they find either express malice or the implied malice which is manifested in an intent to kill. Under this rule

---

74. At common law all felonies were punishable by death. In a felony-murder situation, it made little difference whether the actor was convicted of murder or of the underlying felony because the sanction was the same. The primary use of the felony-murder rule at common law therefore was to deal with a homicide that occurred in furtherance of an attempted felony that failed. Since attempts were punished as misdemeanors, * * * the use of the felony-murder rule allowed the courts to punish the actor in the same manner as if his attempt had succeeded. Thus, a conviction for attempted robbery was a misdemeanor, but a homicide committed in the attempt was murder and punishable by death.

no intentional act is necessary other than the attempt to or the actual commission of the robbery itself. * * *

The doctrine is not limited to those deaths which are foreseeable. Rather a felon is held strictly liable for *all* killings committed by him or his accomplices in the course of the felony. As long as the homicide is the direct causal result of the robbery the felony-murder rule applies whether or not the death was a natural or probable consequence of the robbery. So long as a victim's predisposing physical condition, regardless of its cause, is not the only substantial factor bringing about his death, that condition, and the robber's ignorance of it, in no way destroys the robber's criminal responsibility for the death. * * *

PEOPLE v. FULLER

Court of Appeal, Fifth District, 1978.
86 Cal.App.3d 618, 150 Cal.Rptr. 515.

FRANSON, ACTING PRESIDING JUSTICE. * * *

This appeal challenges the California felony-murder rule as it applies to an unintentionally caused death during a high speed automobile chase following the commission of a nonviolent, daylight burglary of an unattended motor vehicle. Solely by force of precedent we hold that the felony-murder rule applies and respondents can be prosecuted for first degree murder. * * *

The pertinent facts are as follows: On Sunday, February 20, 1977, at about 8:30 a.m., uniformed Cadet Police Officer Guy Ballesteroz was on routine patrol in his vehicle * * *. As the officer approached the Fresno Dodge car lot, he saw an older model Plymouth parked in front of the lot. He also saw respondents rolling two tires apiece toward the Plymouth. His suspicions aroused, the officer radioed the dispatcher and requested that a police unit be sent.

* * * Ballesteroz made a U-turn and headed northbound on Blackstone. The respondents got into the Plymouth and drove away "really fast." Thereafter, a high speed chase ensued which eventually resulted in respondents' car running a red light * * * and striking another automobile which had entered the intersection. The driver of the other automobile was killed. Respondents were arrested at the scene. The chase from the car lot covered some seven miles and lasted approximately 10 to 12 minutes. * * *

Later investigation revealed that four locked Dodge vans at the car lot had been forcibly entered and the spare tires removed. Fingerprints from both of the respondents were found on the jack stands in some of the vans.

Penal Code section 189 provides, in pertinent part: "All murder ... which is committed *in the perpetration of,* or attempt to perpetrate, arson, rape, robbery, *burglary,* mayhem, or [lewd acts with a minor], is murder of the first degree; ...." (Emphasis added.) This statute imposes strict liability for deaths committed in the course of one of the enumerated felonies whether the killing was caused intentionally, negligently, or merely accidentally. * * *

Burglary falls expressly within the purview of California's first degree felony-murder rule. Any burglary within Penal Code section 459 [c] is sufficient to invoke the rule.

* * * Thus, the trial court erred in striking the murder count premised upon the felony-murder rule.

We deem it appropriate, however, to make a few observations concerning the irrationality of applying the felony-murder rule in the present case. * * *

If we were writing on a clean slate, we would hold that respondents should not be prosecuted for felony murder since * * * an automobile burglary is not dangerous to human life. The present case demonstrates why this is so. Respondents committed the burglary on vans parked in a dealer's lot on a Sunday morning. There were no people inside the vans or on the lot at the time. The respondents were not armed and presumably had no expectation of using violence during the burglary.

* * * [Under the felony-murder statute,] if a merchant in pursuit of a fleeing shoplifter is killed accidentally (by falling and striking his head on the curb or being hit by a passing automobile), the thief would be guilty of first degree felony murder assuming the requisite intent to steal at the time of the entry into the store. Such a harsh result destroys the symmetry of the law by equating an accidental killing resulting from a petty theft with a premeditated murder. In no sense can it be said that such a result furthers the ostensible purpose of the felony-murder rule which is to deter those engaged in felonies from killing negligently or accidentally. * * *

Notes and Questions

1. If the doors of the vans from which the tires were stolen had been shut but unlocked, would the defendants have been guilty of burglary? Would they have been guilty of first degree murder?

2. Could the court have avoided the outcome that it described as irrational? For example, could it have interpreted the statutory phrase "in the perpetration of" in a manner that would have taken this case outside the scope of the felony-murder rule? (See p. 279 infra.)

b. The Policy Debate

NELSON E. ROTH & SCOTT E. SUNDBY—THE FELONY–MURDER RULE: A DOCTRINE AT CONSTITUTIONAL CROSSROADS
70 Cornell Law Review 446, 446–55, 457–59

Few legal doctrines have been as maligned and yet have shown as great a resiliency as the felony-murder rule. Criticism of the rule

---

c. "Every person who enters any house, room, apartment, tenement, shop, warehouse, store, mill, barn, stable, outhouse, or other building, tent, vessel, railroad car, trailer coach, * * * [or] vehicle * * * when the doors of such vehicles are locked, * * * with the intent to commit larceny or any felony is guilty of burglary."

constitutes a lexicon of everything that scholars and jurists can find wrong with a legal doctrine: it has been described as "astonishing" and "monstrous," an unsupportable "legal fiction," "an unsightly wart on the skin of the criminal law," and as an "anachronistic remnant" that has " 'no logical or practical basis for existence in modern law.' " Perhaps the most that can be said for the rule is that it provides commentators with an extreme example that makes it easy to illustrate the injustice of various legal propositions.

Despite the widespread criticism, the felony-murder rule persists in the vast majority of states. Most states have attempted to limit the rule's potential harshness either by limiting the scope of its operation or by providing affirmative defenses. Such patchwork attempts to mitigate the rule's harshness, however, have been legitimately criticized because "they do not resolve [the rule's] essential illogic." * * * The United States thus remains virtually the only western country still recognizing a rule which makes it possible "that the most serious sanctions known to law might be imposed for accidental homicide." [12] * * *

I

The Conceptual Basis of the Felony-Murder Rule

A. *The Rule's Historical Development* * * *

The purpose of the felony-murder rule at common law is * * * vague. It is frequently argued that the rule's purpose was not fully articulated because all felonies at common law were punished by death and, therefore, the rule had little practical impact. * * *

Whatever the felony-murder rule's justification at common law, courts have attempted to provide the rule with a contemporary rationale. These post hoc rationalizations fall into four general categories: deterrence, transferred intent, retribution, and general culpability.

B. *Deterrence*

The deterrence rationale consists of two different strains. The first approach views the felony-murder rule as a doctrine intended to deter negligent and accidental killings during commission of felonies. Proponents argue that co-felons will dissuade each other from the use of violence if they may be liable for murder. Justice Holmes attempted to justify the rule on this basis by arguing that the rule would be justified if experience showed that death resulted disproportionately from the commission of felonies. Holmes added the caveat that "I do not ..., however, mean to argue that the rules under discussion arose on the

---

12. * * * England, where the doctrine originated, abolished the felony-murder rule in 1957. The Homicide Act, 1957, 5 & 6 Eliz. 2 ch. 11 § 1. The rule apparently never existed in France or Germany.

above reasoning, any more than that they are right, or would be generally applied in this country." [27]

The second view focuses not on the killing, but on the felony itself, and endorses the felony-murder rule as a deterrent to dangerous felonies. From this perspective, punishing both accidental and deliberate killings that result from the commission of a felony is "the strongest possible deterrent" to "undertaking inherently dangerous felonies."

Both of the deterrence justifications are logically flawed and neither has proven to have a basis in fact. The illogic of the felony-murder rule as a means of deterring killing is apparent when applied to accidental killings occurring during the commission of a felony. Quite simply, how does one deter an unintended act? * * * Moreover, any potential deterrence effect on unintentional killings is further reduced because few felons either will know that the felony-murder rule imposes strict liability for resulting deaths or will believe that harm will result from commission of the felony. Finally, statistical evidence has not borne out Holmes's proposed justification that a disproportionate number of killings occur during felonies. [34]

The purpose of deterring the commission of dangerous felonies through the felony-murder rule also lacks a legitimate basis. First, considerable doubt exists that serious crimes are deterred by varying the weight of the punishment. Second, the rule from this perspective uses the sanctions for murder to deter felonies, and "it is usually accepted as wiser to strike at the harm intended by the criminal rather than at the greater harm possibly flowing from his act which was neither intended nor desired by him." Where the killing is unintended, it would be far more sensible to enhance the sentence for conduct over which the felon had control, such as the carrying of a deadly weapon, rather than automatically to elevate the killing to murder. Finally, as with the other deterrence rationale, the felony-murder rule can have no deterrent effect if the felon either does not know how the rule works or does not believe a killing will actually result. * * *

C. Transferred Intent and Constructive Malice: The Felony–Murder Rule's Presumption of Culpability

The felony-murder rule may be conceptualized as a theory of "transferred or constructive intent." This theory posits that the intent to commit the felony is "transferred" to the act of killing in order to find culpability for the homicide. The rule thus serves "the purpose of . . . reliev[ing] the state of the burden of proving premeditation or malice."

Judges and commentators have criticized the transferred intent theory of felony murder as "an anachronistic remnant" that operates "fictitiously" to broaden unacceptably the scope of murder. The very

27. [O.W. Holmes, The Common Law 59 (1881).]

34. For instance, only one-half of one percent of all robberies result in homicide. The statistical data is summarized in Enmund v. Florida, 485 U.S. 782, 799–800 nn. 23–24 (1982).

concept of transferred intent has been criticized as having "no proper place in criminal law." * * *

The inapplicability of transferred intent to felony murder becomes evident when the crime's two different mens rea elements are examined: the intent to commit the felony and the culpability for the killing. The mental patterns are thus distinct and separate; for example, the intent to burglarize cannot be equated with the malice aforethought required for murder. The non-transferability of culpability is even more evident where the felony-murder rule allows elevation of the killing to first degree murder. In such a situation, the rule equates the intent to commit the felony with premeditation and deliberation, specific mental states that require proof of particular acts and thoughts. * * *

D. Retribution and General Culpability: A Strict Liability View of the Felony–Murder Rule

* * * An alternative approach is to view the rule as not requiring a separate mens rea element for the homicide, but as justifying conviction for murder simply on the basis that the defendant committed a felony and a killing occurred.

* * * The justifications advanced for this conceptualization are deterrence of the underlying felony, and the notion that the felon has exhibited an "evil mind" justifying severe punishment.

The "evil mind" theory of felony murder finds its roots in seventeenth and eighteenth century English notions of criminology. Mens rea was a less developed concept and judges focused on the harm resulting from a defendant's illegal act, rather than the maliciousness of his intent. The felony-murder rule thus partly operated on an unarticulated rationale that one who does bad acts cannot complain about being punished for their consequences, no matter how unexpected. Moreover, the felony-murder rule conceived from an "evil mind" perspective comported with the retribution theory of punishment prevailing at the time of the rule's development, which focused on the resulting harm, not on the actor's mental state, in deciding the appropriate punishment. A convict, therefore, bore responsibility for his felony and for any harmful result arising from the crime regardless of his specific intentions.

Continued reliance on a general culpability theory to justify the felony-murder rule has been described as a rather "primitive rationale" and as "a tribute to the tenacity of legal conceptions rooted in simple moral attitudes." The "evil mind" theory conflicts with the basic premise that "the criminal law is concerned not only with guilt or innocence in the abstract but also with the degree of criminal liability." Although the general culpability rationale was perhaps sufficient as long as a general intent of wrongdoing established malice aforethought, it conflicts with the progressive trend of categorizing homicide according to the degree of culpability. Indeed, the felony-murder rule viewed from a general culpability perspective effectively eliminates a mens rea element in convicting a felon for a killing occurring during the commission of a felony, and results in the rule operating as a strict liability crime: the occurrence of a killing is punished as murder regardless of the defendant's culpability.

DAVID CRUMP & SUSAN WAITE CRUMP— IN DEFENSE OF THE FELONY MURDER DOCTRINE

8 Harvard Journal of Law & Public Policy 359 (1985), 361–63, 367–72, 374–76

I. The Policies Supporting the Felony Murder Rule

A. *Rational Classification and Proportional Grading of Offenses: Actus Reus as an Element of Just Desert*

Classical theory divides the elements of crimes into two categories: mens rea and actus reus. Mens rea, or "guilty mind," is the mental state or states required to complete the offense. Actus reus may be translated literally as "the wrongful act," but it is better understood as referring to all of the physical elements of the crime, including the defendant's actions, the surrounding circumstances, and the consequences.

Differences in result must be taken into account as part of actus reus if classification and grading are to be rational. For example, murder and attempted murder may require similar mental states * * * but no common law jurisdiction treats the two offenses as one, and certainly none treats attempted murder more severely. The only difference justifying this classification is that death results in one offense but not in the other. Similarly, it is a misdemeanor for a person to operate a motor vehicle while impaired by drugs or alcohol, but if this conduct causes the death of a human being, the offense in some jurisdictions is elevated to the status of homicide. * * *

These classifications are the result of a concern for grading offenses so as to reflect societal notions of proportionality. * * *

The felony murder doctrine serves this goal, just as do the distinctions inherent in the separate offenses of attempted murder and murder, or impaired driving and vehicular homicide. Felony murder reflects a societal judgment that an intentionally committed robbery that causes the death of a human being is qualitatively more serious than an identical robbery that does not. Perhaps this judgment could have been embodied in a newly defined offense called "robbery-resulting-in-death"; but * * * such a proliferation of offense definitions is undesirable. Thus the felony murder doctrine reflects the conclusion that a robbery that causes death is more closely akin to murder than to robbery. If this conclusion accurately reflects societal attitudes, and if classification of crimes is to be influenced by such attitudes in order to avoid depreciation of the seriousness of the offense and to encourage respect for the law, then the felony murder doctrine is an appropriate classificatory device.

There is impressive empirical evidence that this classification does indeed reflect widely shared societal attitudes. * * *

B. Condemnation: Reaffirming the Sanctity of Human Life

A purpose of sentencing closely related to proportionality is that of condemnation. Some would regard proportional justice and condemnation as technically separate objectives, while others would view them as substantially equivalent. In any event, the purpose of condemnation or of expressing societal outrage deserves separate mention as a policy concern underlying the felony murder rule.

Condemnation itself is a multifaceted idea. It embodies the notion of reinforcement of societal norms and values as a guide to the conduct of upright persons, as opposed to less upright ones who presumably require the separate prod of "deterrence." The felony murder rule serves this purpose by distinguishing crimes that cause human deaths, thus reinforcing the reverence for human life. To put the argument differently, characterizing a robbery-homicide solely as robbery would have the undesirable effect of communicating to the citizenry that the law does not consider a crime that takes a human life to be different from one that does not—a message that would be indistinguishable, in the minds of many, from a devaluation of human life.

Another aspect of condemnation is the expression of solidarity with the victims of crime. If we as a society label a violent offense in a manner that depreciates its significance, we communicate to the victim by implication that we do not understand his suffering. * * * Felony murder is a useful doctrine because it reaffirms to the surviving family of a felony-homicide victim the kinship the society as a whole feels with him by denouncing in the strongest language of the law the intentional crime that produced the death.

Yet another facet of condemnation is expiation. A sound penal system attempts to provide the convicted defendant with a means by which he can "repay his debt to society" and thereby anticipate at least qualified readmittance—not only in the calculating eyes of the law as it measures his service of sentence, but in the hearts of fellow citizens, at least for crimes for which such repayment is possible. The felony murder rule may serve this purpose. * * *

C. Deterrence

Deterrence is often cited as one justification for the felony murder doctrine. * * * Deterrence is the policy most often recognized in the cases. Scholars, however, tend to dismiss this rationale, using such arguments as the improbability that felons will know the law, the unlikelihood that a criminal who has formed the intent to commit a felony will refrain from acts likely to cause death, or the assertedly small number of felony-homicides.

The trouble with these criticisms is that they underestimate the complexity of deterrence. There may be more than a grain of truth in the proposition that felons, if considered as a class, evaluate risks and benefits differently than members of other classes in society. The conclusion does not follow, however, that felons cannot be deterred, or that criminals are so different from other citizens that they are impervious to inducements or deterrents that would affect people in general. There is mounting evidence that serious crime is subject to deterrence if consequences are adequately communicated. The felony murder rule is just the sort of simple, commonsense, readily enforceable, and widely known principle that is likely to result in deterrence.

At the same time, the argument that felons may be ignorant of the law is unduly categorical. If it is meant to state that felons probably cannot quote the statutory language or cite the section number governing their actions contemporaneously with the event, the proposition is probably correct. Nevertheless, the general population, including felons, is probably more aware of the outlines of the felony murder doctrine than of many other, more common criminal concepts, if only because of the influence of television. * * *

The argument against deterrence often proceeds on the additional assumption that felony murder is addressed only to accidental killings and cannot result in their deterrence. By facilitating proof and simplifying the concept of liability, however, felony murder may deter intentional killings as well. The robber who kills intentionally, but who might claim under oath to have acted accidentally, is thus told that he will be deprived of the benefit of this claim. * * * The proposition that accidental killings cannot be deterred is inconsistent with the widespread belief that the penalizing of negligence, and even the imposition of strict liability, may have deterrent consequences.

D. Clear and Unambiguous Definition of Offenses and Sentence Consequences

Clear definition of crimes is advantageous. Imprecision in homicide definition is particularly prevalent and troublesome. Jury instructions on the presence or absence of premeditation, on conditions required for reduction to voluntary manslaughter, on the double misnomer embodied in "malice aforethought," and on the fine gradations between intent, knowledge, recklessness, and criminal negligence are typical sources of confusion. These concepts may be valuable because they relate to just desert and thus to proportionality, but the definitions of these terms, when given to lay jurors, may produce verdicts that differ more on account of jurors' understanding of words than on account of evidence of the crime. Hence unpredictable dispositions are a likely result.

If properly defined and applied, the felony murder doctrine sometimes provides the advantage of greater clarity. The mental state of intention to commit robbery, rape, or kidnapping is less ambiguous than the terms generally governing homicidal mental states. * * *

E. *Optimal Allocation of Criminal Justice Resources*

Another advantage of the felony murder rule * * * is that it may aid in the optimal allocation of criminal justice resources. * * * The efforts of judges, courtroom time, lawyering on both sides, and support services are all scarce resources. Although we resist thinking of criminal justice in these terms, and few would be willing to put a specific dollar price upon its proper function, the quality of our justice is limited by the scarcity of these resources and by the efficiency with which we allocate them. * * *

* * * The rule has beneficial allocative consequences because it clearly defines the offense, simplifies the task of the judge and jury with respect to questions of law and fact, and thereby promotes efficient administration of justice. Indeed, no less a tribunal than the California Supreme Court has stated this rationale:

> The Legislature has said in effect that this deterrent purpose [of the felony murder rule] outweighs the normal legislative policy of examining the individual state of mind of each person causing an unlawful killing to determine whether the killing was with or without malice, deliberate or accidental, and calibrating our treatment of the person accordingly. Once a person perpetrates or attempts to perpetrate one of the enumerated felonies, then in the judgment of the Legislature, he is no longer entitled to such fine judicial calibration, but will be deemed guilty of first degree murder for any homicide committed in the course thereof.[55] * * *

F. *Minimization of the Utility of Perjury*

Many crimes are defined more broadly than their harmful consequences alone might justify. For example, there are prohibitions upon the possession of heroin or the carrying of certain kinds of weapons, even though these actions, without use of the contraband, are not intrinsically harmful. A person might attempt to defend his possession of heroin by stating that he did not intend to use or distribute it (for example, he might explain that he collects controlled substances as others collect coins or stamps). This explanation, even if true, would be regarded as irrelevant under most statutes.

Such a result may be justified by the concern that any other approach would unduly reward perjury. The denial of harmful intent in such a situation is too facile. Sources of contrary evidence persuasive beyond reasonable doubt are likely to be absent even if the defensive theory is perjurious. If lack of intent to use an illegally possessed machine gun vitiated the possessory offense, the crime would be far more difficult to prosecute, and the ultimate harm that is the real concern would become that much more difficult to control. A similar rationale may underlie the felony murder rule; thus * * * the Pennsyl-

---

55. People v. Burton, 6 Cal.3d [375],   801–02 [(1971)].
388, 99 Cal.Rptr. [1], 9–10, 491 P.2d [793,]

vania Supreme Court justified its application of the felony murder rule to the circumstances before it with the observation, "It is rare ... that a criminal telephones or telegraphs his criminal intent...."

Scholars criticizing the felony murder rule sometimes argue or assume that juries will disbelieve false claims of accident. The criticism assumes too much: The accident claim need only rise to the level of reasonable doubt to be effective under conventional homicide law. Experienced trial lawyers would not deny the frequent occurrence of erroneous acquittals, given the standard of proof required. Moreover, the incentive to perjury is itself a liability. The law itself is brought into disrepute when it is defined so that perjury is frequent. Jurors might be induced to lose respect for the criminal justice system even as they acquit the defendant on his ambiguous claim of accident, which they disbelieve but cannot reject beyond a reasonable doubt.

Notes and Questions

1. The Michigan Supreme Court abolished that state's felony-murder rule in People v. Aaron, 409 Mich. 672, 299 N.W.2d 304 (1980). In doing so, it pointed out at 729–30, 299 N.W.2d at 327:

> From a practical standpoint, the abolition of the category of malice arising from the intent to commit the underlying felony should have little effect on the result of the majority of cases. In many cases where felony murder has been applied, the use of the doctrine was unnecessary because the other types of malice could have been inferred from the evidence.
>
> Abrogation of this rule does not make irrelevant the fact that a death occurred in the course of a felony. A jury can properly infer malice from evidence that a defendant intentionally set in motion a force likely to cause death or great bodily harm. Thus, whenever a killing occurs in the perpetration or attempted perpetration of an inherently dangerous felony, in order to establish malice the jury may consider the "nature of the underlying felony and the circumstances surrounding its commission." If the jury concludes that malice existed, they can find murder and, if they determine that the murder occurred in the perpetration or attempted perpetration of one of the enumerated felonies [in the first-degree murder statute], by statute the murder would become first-degree murder.

Look at Michigan Penal Code §§ 750.316–.317 (p. 198 supra). If a person recklessly kills another, of what degree of murder is she guilty? According to *Aaron,* if she recklessly kills another during the commission of an enumerated felony, of what degree is she guilty?

2. The Commentary to the Model Penal Code subjects the felony-murder doctrine to a thirteen page critique and concludes that the rule is "indefensible in principle." American Law Institute, Model Penal Code and Commentaries, Commentary to § 210.2, at 38–39 (1980).

What is left of the doctrine under the Code? What would be the result in *Stamp* and *Fuller?* Does the Code's solution "rest[ ] on no more secure a basis than the discarded rule"? Franklin E. Zimring & Gordon Hawkins,

Murder, the Model Code, and the Multiple Agendas of Reform, 19 Rutgers L.J. 773, 777 (1988).

c. *Limitations on the Rule*

i. *Overview*

AMERICAN LAW INSTITUTE, MODEL PENAL CODE AND COMMENTARIES, COMMENT TO § 210.2

(1980), 32–36

The prospect of [unjust] consequences has led to a demand for limitations on the felony-murder rule. American legislatures * * * responded to these demands at the time the Model Code was drafted primarily by dividing felony-homicides into two or more grades or by lowering the degree of murder for felony homicide.

In addition, the courts * * * imposed restrictions, both overt and covert, on the reach of the felony-murder doctrine. An example of covert limitation was the use of especially demanding interpretations of legal or proximate causation. The commentary to Section 2.03 discusses the problem of causation in general terms, but it is worth noting here that courts sometimes precluded liability for felony murder on the ground of insufficiently direct causal connection in circumstances where, had intent to kill been proved, the causation requirement would not have been construed to bar conviction. In other words, courts hostile to this strict liability species of murder sometimes introduced a culpability requirement through the back door of causation.

Other judicial limitations on the rule were accomplished by several different methods. First, courts required that the felony be "independent" of the homicide. * * * Other courts required that the felony be one recognized as such at common law. These offenses included arson, burglary, robbery, mayhem, larceny, rape, and sodomy. The rule was also applied by some courts only to felonies judged *mala in se* rather than *mala prohibitum.* * * * Still other courts narrowly construed the period during which the felony was in the process of commission as a method of limiting the operation of the rule. A few courts embarked on an effort to classify each felony according to whether that crime * * * was inherently dangerous to human life. * * * Finally, some courts have limited felony-murder liability to cases where the act of killing was committed by the defendant or his accomplice in the furtherance of the felony, and several modern statutes limit felony-murder liability to the killing of one other than a participant in the underlying felony.

ii. The "Inherently Dangerous Felony" Limitation

PEOPLE v. BURROUGHS

Supreme Court of California, 1984.
35 Cal.3d 824, 201 Cal.Rptr. 319, 678 P.2d 894.

GRODIN, JUSTICE.

Defendant Burroughs, a 77–year–old self-styled "healer," appeals from a judgment convicting him of * * * felony practicing medicine without a license (Bus. & Prof.Code, § 2053); and second degree felony murder (Pen.Code, § 187) in the treatment and death of Lee Swatsenbarg.

Burroughs challenges his second degree murder conviction by contending the felonious unlicensed practice of medicine is not an "inherently dangerous" felony, as that term has been used in our previous decisions to describe and limit the kinds of offenses which will support application of the felony-murder rule. * * *

Lee Swatsenbarg had been diagnosed by the family physician as suffering from terminal leukemia. Unable to accept impending death, the 24–year–old Swatsenbarg unsuccessfully sought treatment from a variety of traditional medical sources. He and his wife then began to participate in Bible study, hoping that through faith Lee might be cured. Finally, on the advice of a mutual acquaintance who had heard of defendant's ostensible successes in healing others, Lee turned to defendant for treatment.

During the first meeting between Lee and defendant, the latter described his method of curing cancer. This method included consumption of a unique "lemonade," exposure to colored lights, and a brand of vigorous massage administered by defendant. Defendant remarked that he had successfully treated "thousands" of people, including a number of physicians. He suggested the Swatsenbargs purchase a copy of his book, *Healing for the Age of Enlightenment.* If after reading the book Lee wished to begin defendant's unorthodox treatment, defendant would commence caring for Lee immediately. During the 30 days designated for the treatment, Lee would have to avoid contact with his physician.

Lee read the book, submitted to the conditions delineated by defendant, and placed himself under defendant's care. Defendant instructed Lee to drink the lemonade, salt water, and herb tea, but consume nothing more for the ensuing 30 days. At defendant's behest, the Swatsenbargs bought a lamp equipped with some colored plastic sheets, to bathe Lee in various tints of light. Defendant also agreed to massage Lee from time to time, for an additional fee per session.

Rather than improve, within two weeks Lee's condition began rapidly to deteriorate. He developed a fever, and was growing progressively weaker. Defendant counseled Lee that all was proceeding according to plan, and convinced the young man to postpone a bone marrow test urged by his doctor.

During the next week Lee became increasingly ill. He was experiencing severe pain in several areas, including his abdomen, and vomiting frequently. Defendant administered "deep" abdominal massages on two successive days, each time telling Lee he would soon recuperate.

* * * Three and a half weeks into the treatment, the couple spent the night at defendant's house, where Lee died of a massive hemorrhage of the mesentery in the abdomen. The evidence presented at trial strongly suggested the hemorrhage was the direct result of the massages performed by defendant.

* * * The trial court ruled that an underlying felony of unlicensed practice of medicine could support a felony-murder conviction because such practice was a felony "inherently dangerous to human life."[1] Consequently, the trial judge instructed the jury that if the homicide resulted directly from the commission of this felony, the homicide was felony murder of the second degree. This instruction was erroneous as a matter of law.

When an individual causes the death of another in furtherance of the perpetration of a felony, the resulting offense may be felony murder. This court has long held the felony-murder rule in disfavor. "We have repeatedly stated that felony murder is a 'highly artificial concept' which 'deserves no extension beyond its required application.' " For the reasons stated below, we hold that to apply the felony-murder rule to the facts of the instant case would be an unwarranted extension of this highly "anachronistic" notion.

At the outset we must determine whether the underlying felony is "inherently dangerous to human life." We formulated this standard because "[i]f the felony is not inherently dangerous, it is highly improbable that the potential felon will be deterred: he will not anticipate that injury or death might arise solely from the fact that he will commit the felony."

In assessing whether the felony is inherently dangerous to human life, "we look to the elements of the felony in the abstract, not the particular 'facts' of the case." This form of analysis is compelled because there is a killing in every case where the rule might potentially be applied. If in such circumstances a court were to examine the

1. Felony practicing medicine without a license violates section 2053 of the Business and Professions Code which states: "Any person who willfully, under circumstances or conditions which cause or create a risk of great bodily harm, serious physical or mental illness, or death, practices or attempts to practice, or advertises or holds himself or herself out as practicing, any system or mode of treating the sick or afflicted in this state, or diagnoses, treats, operates for, or prescribes for any ailment, blemish, deform- ity, disease, disfigurement, disorder, injury, or other physical or mental condition of any person, without having at the time of so doing a valid, unrevoked or suspended certificate as provided in this chapter, or without being authorized to perform such act pursuant to a certificate obtained in accordance with some other provision of law, is punishable by imprisonment in the county jail for not exceeding one year or in the state prison."

particular facts of the case prior to establishing whether the underlying felony is inherently dangerous, the court might well be led to conclude the rule applicable despite any unfairness which might redound to the defendant by so broad an application: the existence of the dead victim might appear to lead inexorably to the conclusion that the underlying felony is exceptionally hazardous. We continue to resist such unjustifiable bootstrapping.

In our application of the second degree felony-murder analysis we are guided by the bipartite standard articulated by this court in *People v. Henderson,* [(1977)], 19 Cal.3d 86, 137 Cal.Rptr. 1, 560 P.2d 1180. In *Henderson,* we stated a reviewing court should look first to the primary element of the offense at issue, then to the "factors elevating the offense to a felony," to determine whether the felony, taken in the abstract, is inherently dangerous to human life, or whether it possibly could be committed without creating such peril. In this examination we are required to view the statutory definition of the offense as a whole, taking into account even nonhazardous ways of violating the provisions of the law which do not necessarily pose a threat to human life.

The primary element of the offense in question here is the practice of medicine without a license. The statute defines such practice as "treating the sick or afflicted." One can certainly conceive of treatment of the sick or afflicted which has quite innocuous results—the affliction at stake could be a common cold, or a sprained finger, and the form of treatment an admonition to rest in bed and drink fluids or the application of ice to mild swelling. Thus, we do not find inherent dangerousness at this stage of our investigation.

The next level of analysis takes us to consideration of the factors which elevate the unlicensed practice of medicine to a felony: "circumstances or conditions which cause or create a risk of great bodily harm, serious mental or physical illness, *or death.*" That the Legislature referred to "death" as a separate risk, and in the disjunctive, strongly suggests the Legislature perceived that one may violate the proscription against the felonious practice of medicine without a license and yet not necessarily endanger human life. * * *

"Great bodily harm" is not defined in section 2053, but the closely analogous term "serious bodily injury" is defined in Penal Code section 243—which establishes appropriate punishments for the crime of battery when committed under various circumstances—as "[a] serious impairment of physical condition, including, but not limited to the following: loss of consciousness; concussion; bone fracture; protracted loss or impairment of function of any bodily member or organ; a wound requiring extensive suturing; and serious disfigurement." Pursuant to this definition, a broken arm or leg would constitute serious bodily injury—and by implication, great bodily harm as well. While painful and debilitating, such bone fractures clearly do not, by their nature, jeopardize the life of the victim. * * *

The statute at issue can also be violated by administering to an individual in a manner which threatens risk of serious mental or physical illness. Whether risk of serious physical illness is inherently dangerous to life is a question we do not reach; however, we believe the existence of the category of risk of serious mental illness also renders a breach of the statute's prohibitions potentially less than inherently dangerous to life. * * *

* * * It is not difficult, for example, to envision one who suffers from delusions of grandeur, believing himself to be the President of the United States. An individual who purports without the proper license to be able to treat such a person need not be placing the patient's life in jeopardy, though such treatment, if conducted, for example, without expertise, may lead to the need for more serious psychiatric attention.

Consequently, we are disinclined to rule today that the risks set forth in section 2053 are so critical as to render commission of this felony of necessity inherently dangerous to human life. * * *

Moreover, our analysis of precedent in this area reveals that the few times we have found an underlying felony inherently dangerous (so that it would support a conviction of felony murder), the offense has been tinged with malevolence totally absent from the facts of this case. In *People v. Mattison* (1971) 4 Cal.3d 177, 93 Cal.Rptr. 185, 481 P.2d 193, we held that poisoning food, drink, or medicine with intent to injure was inherently dangerous. * * *

To hold, as we do today, that a violation of section 2053 is not inherently so dangerous that by its very nature, it cannot be committed without creating a substantial risk that someone will be killed,[d] is consistent with our previous decisions in which the underlying felony has been held not inherently hazardous. We have so held where the underlying felony was felony false imprisonment (*People v. Henderson,* supra, 19 Cal.3d 86, 137 Cal.Rptr. 1, 560 P.2d 1180), * * * and in other, less potentially threatening circumstances.[4]

Finally, the underlying purpose of the felony-murder rule, to encourage felons to commit their offenses without perpetrating unnecessary violence which might result in a homicide, would not be served by applying the rule to the facts of this case. Defendant was or should have been aware he was committing a crime by treating Swatsenbarg in the first place. Yet, it is unlikely he would have been deterred from administering to Lee in the manner in which he did for fear of a prosecution for murder, given his published beliefs on the efficacy of massage in the curing of cancer. Indeed, nowhere is it claimed that

d. Subsequently, in People v. Patterson, 49 Cal.3d 615, 627, 262 Cal.Rptr. 195, 204, 778 P.2d 549, 558 (1989), the court defined as "inherently dangerous" any offense carrying "a high probability" of loss of life. Is this a stricter standard?

4. Including where the underlying felonies were grand theft by false pretenses (*People v. Phillips,* [(1966)], 64 Cal.2d 574, 51 Cal.Rptr. 225, 414 P.2d 353); and conspiracy to possess methedrine illegally (*People v. Williams,* [(1965)], 63 Cal.2d 452, 47 Cal.Rptr. 7, 406 P.2d 647).

defendant attempted to perform any action with respect to Swatsenbarg other than to heal him—and earn a fee for doing so.

This clearly is a case in which conviction of felony murder is contrary to our settled law, as well as inappropriate as a matter of sound judicial policy. * * *

Accordingly, defendant's second degree murder conviction is reversed. * * *

Notes and Questions

1. In People v. Patterson, 49 Cal.3d 615, 262 Cal.Rptr. 195, 778 P.2d 549 (1989), the state supreme court applied the inherently-dangerous-felony limitation to a Health and Safety Code provision that barred transportation, importation, sale, administration, or furnishing of "any controlled substance" to another, except by written prescription by a qualified medical professional. The proscribed controlled substances, about one hundred in number, were set out in other provisions of the Code and included medications as relatively benign as codeine and substances as dangerous as heroin. Patterson was charged with unlawfully furnishing cocaine to another.

The court distinguished this felony statute from the offense in *Burroughs,* practicing medicine without a license, which (*Patterson* explained) consisted of an "essentially single form of conduct." Therefore, in *Burroughs,* the court was required to examine the statute as a whole when determining dangerousness. In contrast, with the controlled substances law, "[i]t * * * appears that for the sake of convenience the Legislature has included * * * various offenses in one statute." Id. at 625, 262 Cal.Rptr. at 202, 778 P.2d at 556. As a consequence, the *Patterson* court severed the proscribed conduct in the instant case (furnishing of cocaine) from the other controlled substances included by reference in the law. It ruled that the "transportation, importation, sale, administration, or furnishing" of cocaine to another is inherently dangerous conduct, justifying the imposition of the felony-murder rule.

2. The inherently-dangerous-felony limitation stems from Regina v. Serné (1887) 16 Cox Crim.Cas. 311, 313, in which Judge James Stephen stated the felony-murder rule as follows:

> [I]nstead of saying that any act done with intent to commit a felony and which causes death amounts to murder, it would be reasonable to say that any act known to be dangerous to life, and likely in itself to cause death done for the purpose of committing a felony which caused death, should be murder.

If the felony-murder rule only applies to felonies of the sort described by Judge Stephen, is the rule needed to prove malice aforethought? In light of the rationale of the felony-murder doctrine, is the limitation sensible?

3. Many states that limit the felony-murder rule to dangerous felonies consider both the nature of the offense in the abstract *and* the circumstances surrounding its commission in the particular case. Unlike California, these states apply the felony-murder doctrine if the felony is inherently dangerous

under either standard. E.g., State v. Harrison, 90 N.M. 439, 564 P.2d 1321 (1977). Which method is preferable?

4. In *Henderson,* cited in *Burroughs, H* suspected *X* of stealing his television. *H* confronted *X* with a gun and demanded the return of his property. When *X* denied that he had taken it, *H* forced *X* into his car and drove him to a second destination, where he said that *V* would confirm the theft. When they arrived at *V*'s residence, *H* poked the gun in *X*'s back and used it to shove *X*. When *X* tried to move away, the gun accidentally discharged, killing *V*. False imprisonment, the felony underlying the murder charge, was defined as "imprisonment * * * effected by violence, menace, fraud, or deceit." Was the court correct in concluding that this offense is not inherently dangerous?

5. Are the following felonies inherently dangerous in the abstract?

A. "Every person who forcibly, or by any other means of instilling fear, steals or takes, or holds, detains, or arrests any person in this state, and carries the person into another country, state, or county, or into another part of the same county [is guilty of kidnapping] * * *." People v. Fleeton, 2 Cal.App.4th 421, 3 Cal.Rptr.2d 556 (1992); People v. Pearch, 229 Cal. App.3d 1282, 280 Cal.Rptr. 584 (1991).

B. "Any person who seizes, * * * kidnaps or carries away any individual by any means whatsoever with intent to hold or detain[ ] [the person] * * * for ransom [is guilty of kidnapping]." People v. Ordonez, 226 Cal. App.3d 1207, 277 Cal.Rptr. 382 (1991).

C. "Possession of a concealed firearm by a person previously convicted of a felony [is guilty of a felony]." People v. Satchell, 6 Cal.3d 28, 98 Cal.Rptr. 33, 489 P.2d 1361 (1971); State v. Underwood, 228 Kan. 294, 615 P.2d 153 (1980).

iii. The "Independent Felony" (or Merger) Doctrine

PEOPLE v. SMITH

Supreme Court of California, 1984.
35 Cal.3d 798, 201 Cal.Rptr. 311, 678 P.2d 886.

MOSK, JUSTICE.

Defendant appeals from a judgment convicting her of second degree murder (Pen.Code, § 187), [and] felony child abuse (§ 273a, subd. (1) * * *.

Defendant and her two daughters, three-and-a-half-year-old Bethany (Beth) and two-year-old Amy, lived with David Foster. On the day Amy died, she refused to sit on the couch instead of the floor to eat a snack. Defendant became angry, took Amy into the children's bedroom, spanked her and slapped her in the face. Amy then went towards the corner of the bedroom which was often used for discipline; defendant hit her repeatedly, knocking her to the floor. Foster then apparently joined defendant to "assist" in Amy's discipline. * * * Eventually, defendant knocked the child backwards and she fell, hitting her head on the closet door.

Amy stiffened and went into respiratory arrest. Defendant and Foster took her to the hospital * * *. Amy died that evening. * * *

* * * Defendant contends that on the facts of this case the crime of felony child abuse was an integral part of and included in fact within the homicide, and hence that it merged into the latter under the rule of *People v. Ireland* (1969) 70 Cal.2d 522, 538–540, 75 Cal.Rptr. 188, 450 P.2d 580. We agree.

Our opinions have repeatedly emphasized that felony murder, although the law of this state, is a disfavored doctrine * * *. * * * Accordingly, we have reiterated that this "highly artificial concept" "should not be extended beyond any rational function that it is designed to serve." "Applying this principle to various concrete factual circumstances, we have sought to insure that the [doctrine] ... be given the narrowest possible application consistent with its ostensible purpose—which is to deter those engaged in felonies from killing negligently or accidentally."

In accord with this policy, we restricted the scope of the felony-murder rule in *Ireland* by holding it inapplicable to felonies that are an integral part of and included in fact within the homicide. In that case the defendant and his wife were experiencing serious marital difficulties which eventually culminated in defendant's drawing a gun and killing his wife. The jury was instructed that it could find the defendant guilty of second degree felony murder if it determined that the homicide occurred during the commission of the underlying felony of assault with a deadly weapon. * * * We reasoned that "the utilization of the felony-murder rule in circumstances such as those before us extends the operation of that rule 'beyond any rational function that it is designed to serve.' [Citation.] To allow such use of the felony-murder rule would effectively preclude the jury from considering the issue of malice aforethought in all cases wherein homicide has been committed as a result of a felonious assault—a category which includes the great majority of all homicides. This kind of bootstrapping finds support neither in logic nor in law. We therefore hold that *a second degree felony-murder instruction may not properly be given when it is based upon a felony which is an integral part of the homicide and which the evidence produced by the prosecution shows to be an offense included in fact within the offense charged.*"

Very soon after *Ireland* we again had occasion to consider the question of merger in *People v. Wilson* (1969) 1 Cal.3d 431, 82 Cal.Rptr. 494, 462 P.2d 22. There the defendant forcibly entered his estranged wife's apartment carrying a shotgun. Once inside the apartment, he * * * proceeded to break into the bathroom where he killed his wife. * * *

* * * The jury was instructed on first degree felony murder on the theory that the homicide was committed in the course of a burglary because the defendant had entered the premises with intent to commit a felony, i.e., assault with a deadly weapon. We held that the felony-

murder rule cannot apply to burglary-murder cases in which "the entry would be nonfelonious but for the intent to commit the assault, and the assault is an integral part of the homicide and is included in fact in the offense charged. . . ." Because under *Ireland* the "elements of the assault were necessary elements of the homicide," the felony of burglary based on an intent to commit assault was included in fact in the homicide. We reasoned that "Where a person enters a building with an intent to assault his victim with a deadly weapon, he is not deterred by the felony-murder rule. That doctrine can serve its purpose only when applied to a felony independent of the homicide." * * *

In *People v. Sears* (1970) 2 Cal.3d 180, 84 Cal.Rptr. 711, 465 P.2d 847, we followed *Wilson* in a slightly different factual situation. There the defendant entered a cottage with the intent to assault his estranged wife. In the course of the assault, her daughter intervened and was killed by the defendant. The People argued that this situation was distinguishable on the ground that the felony of burglary with intent to assault the wife was "independent of the homicide" of the daughter and therefore the felony-murder rule could apply. We rejected the theory, holding that "It would be anomalous to place the person who intends to attack one person and in the course of the assault kills another inadvertently or in the heat of battle in a worse position than the person who from the outset intended to attack both persons and killed one or both." * * *

In *People v. Burton,* [(1971) 6 Cal.3d 375, 99 Cal.Rptr. 1, 491 P.2d 793], we refined the *Ireland* rule by adding the caveat that the felony-murder doctrine may nevertheless apply if the underlying offense was committed with an "independent felonious purpose." [In *Burton,* the underlying felony was armed robbery. The defendant asserted that the felony-murder rule did not apply because an armed robbery necessarily includes an assault with a deadly weapon. Therefore, the felony was an integral part of the homicide and included in fact within it.] Even if the felony was included within the facts of the homicide and was integral thereto, a further inquiry is required to determine if the homicide resulted "from conduct for an independent felonious purpose" as opposed to a "single course of conduct with a single purpose." In cases like *Ireland,* the "purpose of the conduct was the very assault which resulted in death"; on the other hand, "in the case of armed robbery, * * * there is an independent felonious purpose, namely * * * to acquire money or property belonging to another."

Our task is to apply the foregoing rules to the offense at issue here—felony child abuse defined by section 273a, subdivision (1).[4] We

---

4. Section 273a, subdivision (1), provided: "Any person who, under circumstances or conditions likely to produce great bodily harm or death, willfully causes or permits any child to suffer, or inflicts thereon unjustifiable physical pain or mental suffering, or having the care or custody of any child, willfully causes or permits the person or health of such child to be injured, or willfully causes or permits such child to be placed in such situation that its person or health is endangered, is punishable by imprisonment in the county jail not exceeding 1 year, or in

recognize that a violation of its terms can occur in a wide variety of situations: the definition broadly includes both active and passive conduct, i.e., child abuse by direct assault and child endangering by extreme neglect. Two threshold considerations, however, govern all types of conduct prohibited by this law: first, the conduct must be willful; second, it must be committed "under circumstances or conditions likely to produce great bodily harm or death." Absent either of these elements, there can be no violation of the statute.

The language of *Ireland, Wilson* and *Burton* bars the application of the felony-murder rule "where the purpose of the conduct was the very assault which resulted in death." In cases in which the violation of section 273a, subdivision (1), is a direct assault on a child that results in death (i.e., causing or permitting a child to suffer or inflicting thereon unjustifiable physical pain), it is plain that the purpose of the child abuse was the "very assault which resulted in death." It would be wholly illogical to allow this kind of assaultive child abuse to be bootstrapped into felony murder merely because the victim was a child rather than an adult, as in *Ireland.*

In the present case the homicide was the result of child abuse of the assaultive variety. Thus, the underlying felony was unquestionably an "integral part of" and "included in fact" in the homicide within the meaning of *Ireland.* Furthermore, we can conceive of no independent purpose for the conduct, and the People suggest none; just as in *Ireland,* the purpose here was the very assault that resulted in death. To apply the felony-murder rule in this situation would extend it "beyond any rational function that it is designed to serve." We reiterate that the ostensible purpose of the felony-murder rule is not to deter the underlying felony, but instead to deter negligent or accidental killings that may occur in the course of committing that felony. When a person *willfully* inflicts unjustifiable physical pain on a child under these circumstances, it is difficult to see how the assailant would be further deterred from killing negligently or accidentally in the course of that felony by application of the felony-murder rule. * * *

The People argue that the present case is controlled by *People v. Shockley,* [(1978)], 79 Cal.App.3d 669, 145 Cal.Rptr. 200, but that decision is distinguishable on its facts. In *Shockley,* the death followed from malnutrition and dehydration * * *. * * * Here the death of the child was directly caused by an assault that in turn was the basis of the charge of felony child abuse; on these facts, *Ireland* compels application of the merger rule.[7] * * *

Notes and Questions

1. Is the merger doctrine consistent with the underlying purpose of the felony-murder rule? In a state that applies both the merger doctrine and

the state prison for not less than 1 year nor more than 10 years."

7. Because of this factual distinction we need not address the question whether the merger doctrine applies when the defendant is guilty of felony child abuse of the non-assaultive variety, e.g., by extreme neglect—as in *Shockley*—or by failure to intervene when a child in his care or custody is placed in life-endangering situation.

the inherently-dangerous-felony limitation, what type of felony remains within the scope of the felony-murder rule?

2. The court stated in *Smith* that it "can conceive of no independent purpose for the [defendant's] conduct, and the People suggest none." What about the independent purpose of disciplining a child? See People v. Jackson, 172 Cal.App.3d 1005, 218 Cal.Rptr. 637 (1985) (in a felony-murder prosecution predicated on felony child abuse, the defendant's purpose was "to punish; to chastise; to bend the child's actions into conformity with [the parent's] idea of propriety").

3. How should the court resolve the issue left open in footnote 7? Is child abuse by omission any more "independent" than abuse by commission? Compare *Shockley,* cited in *Smith* (applying the felony-murder rule) with People v. Benway, 164 Cal.App.3d 505, 210 Cal.Rptr. 530 (1985) (applying the merger doctrine).

iv. Killings "in the Perpetration" or "in Furtherance" of a Felony

KING v. COMMONWEALTH

Court of Appeals of Virginia, 1988.
6 Va.App. 351, 368 S.E.2d 704.

COLEMAN, JUDGE.

[King and his co-pilot Bailey were flying a Beechcraft airplane containing more than 500 pounds of marijuana in the direction of a Virginia airport when they encountered heavy cloud cover and fog and became lost. In an effort to navigate through the bad weather, Bailey flew the plane to a lower altitude. The airplane crashed into a mountain, killing Bailey instantly. King survived the accident and was charged with felony murder of Bailey, based on their felony possession of marijuana.]

We consider whether the facts in this case constitute a violation of the felony-murder statute. * * * We hold that because the death was not caused by an act of the felons in furtherance of the felony, appellant is not criminally liable for the death. * * *

* * * The [felony-murder] doctrine was developed to elevate to murder a homicide committed during the course of a felony by imputing malice to the killing. The justification for imputing malice was the theory that the increased risk of death or serious harm occasioned by the commission of a felony demonstrated the felon's lack of concern for human life. * * *

* * * It does not follow * * * that any death of any person which occurs during the period in which a felony is being committed will subject the felon to criminal liability under the felony-murder rule. To construe our statute to encompass every accidental death occurring during the commission of a felony, regardless of whether it causally relates to or results from the commission of the felony, is to make felons absolutely liable for the accidental death of another even though such

death is fortuitous and the product of causes wholly unrelated to the commission of the felony. Recognizing the potentially harsh and far reaching effects of such a construction of the felony-murder doctrine, the Virginia courts, as well as others, have limited its application. * * *

One of the most significant factors in defining the scope of the felony-murder involves the causation required between the felony and the death. * * *

In Virginia, it is clear when the homicide is within the *res gestae* of the initial felony and emanates therefrom, it is committed in the perpetration of that felony. *Haskell v. Commonwealth*, 218 Va. 1033, 1041, 243 S.E.2d 477, 482 (1978). The Court explained that "the felony-murder statute applies where the killing is so closely related to the felony in time, place, and causal connection as to make it a part of the same criminal enterprise." Thus, the court in *Haskell* affirmed first degree murder convictions when the murder of a robbery victim was within five feet of the site of the robbery, within moments of the robbery, and was to facilitate the robbers' escape without being identified. Under these circumstances, the killing was obviously causally related to the robbery and was part of the same enterprise. * * *

In a leading case involving the felony-murder doctrine, * * * the Pennsylvania Supreme Court addressed the causation problem at length. Rejecting their previous standard of proximate cause, the court stated:

> In adjudging a felony-murder, it is to be remembered at all times that the thing which is imputed to a felon for a killing incidental to his felony is *malice* and *not the act of killing*. The mere coincidence of homicide and felony is not enough to satisfy the requirements of the felony-murder doctrine.... "Death must be a consequence of the felony ... and not merely coincidence."

Commonwealth v. Redline, 391 Pa. 486, 495, 137 A.2d 472, 476 (1958). * * *

In the present case, King and Bailey were in the airplane to further the felony of possession of marijuana with the intent to distribute. They were flying over the mountains while committing the felony. The time and the place of the death were closely connected with the felony. However, no causal connection exists between the felony of drug distribution and the killing by a plane crash. Thus, no basis exists to find that the accidental death was part or a result of the criminal enterprise. In the felony-murder cases cited above, death, to be considered an "accidental killing" within the statute, has resulted from a particular act which was an integral part of the felony or an act in direct furtherance of the felony—shooting a gun, striking a match, distributing cocaine. In this case, there is no such act which caused the death. * * * Bailey * * * was not killed * * * by any act of King which was in furtherance of the felony. * * * The felony-murder rule does not exist to enable courts to impute "the act of killing" where an accidental death results from fortuitous circumstances and the only connection with the felony is temporal.

The cause of Bailey's death was Bailey's piloting and adverse weather conditions. The accident stemmed not from the possession or distribution of drugs, but from fog, low cloud cover, pilot error, and inexperience. * * * The commission of the felony merely accounted for their presence at the location of the accident, and nothing directly related to the commission of the felony caused the accident. Thus, flying into the mountain was not a direct consequence of the felony. Had the plane been flying low or recklessly to avoid detection, for example, the crash would be a consequence or action which was directly intended to further the felony and a different result might obtain. * * *

Notes and Questions

1. George steals an automobile, drives it away, parks it, and then decides to return it. On the way back, he strikes and kills a pedestrian. Is this a killing "during the perpetration" or "in furtherance" of the felony theft? See State v. Diebold, 152 Wash. 68, 277 P. 394 (1929). Suppose that George kills the pedestrian one day after, and 280 miles from the scene of, the theft, before he decides to return the car? See Doane v. Commonwealth, 218 Va. 500, 237 S.E.2d 797 (1977).

2. *Problem.* Harding shot Jeffrey in the chest during a robbery, but Jeffrey survived. Harding was convicted of assault with intent to kill and armed robbery, and sentenced to prison. Jeffrey went on with his life. Four years later, however, while playing basketball, Jeffrey got into a minor scuffle, during which he suffered a fatal heart attack. The coroner's report disclosed that the death was a consequence of permanent damage to Jeffrey's heart suffered from the earlier gunshot wound. May Harding now be prosecuted for felony murder? See People v. Harding, 443 Mich. 693, 506 N.W.2d 482 (1993).

3. Other issues aside, how can King be guilty of murder for the death of co-felon Bailey? Didn't Bailey kill *himself* by his own poor piloting? The following materials consider this problem.

STATE v. BONNER

Supreme Court of North Carolina, 1992.
330 N.C. 536, 411 S.E.2d 598.

WHICHARD, JUSTICE.

[Defendants Bonner and Witherspoon, along with two others, attempted to rob a restaurant. During their effort, Dallas Pruitt, an off-duty police officer serving as a security guard, thwarted the felony by shooting and killing the other robbers. The defendants were charged with felony murder in the deaths of their confederates.]

* * * [T]he narrow issue is whether the common law theory of felony murder * * * will be extended to cover situations such as this, so that cofelons may be charged with first-degree murder as a result of the deaths of their accomplices at the hands of an adversary to the crimes. Based on long-standing precedent from this Court, and in accordance with the overwhelming majority of jurisdictions that have addressed this

issue, we hold that there is no felony murder liability on the facts of this case. * * *

The resolution of this issue is controlled by the principles enunciated in *State v. Oxendine,* 187 N.C. 658, 122 S.E. 568 (1924). In *Oxendine,* three men—Walter Oxendine, Clarence Oxendine, and Dock Wilkins—feloniously instigated a violent altercation with Proctor Locklear. The altercation escalated to gun play, and Robert Wilkins, an armed bystander, was killed as a result of a shot fired by Proctor Locklear. The trial court gave an instruction that permitted the jury to convict Walter Oxendine * * * regardless of whether the fatal shot was fired by Oxendine or his accomplices, or by Proctor Locklear. In reversing the conviction * * *, this Court said:

> It is unquestionably the law that where two or more persons conspire or confederate together or among themselves to commit a felony, each is criminally responsible for every crime committed by his coconspirators in furtherance of the original conspiracy, and which naturally or reasonably might have been anticipated as a result therefrom. And in the instant case, if the deceased had been killed by a shot from Walter Oxendine's pistol, each and every one of his confederates would have been equally responsible with him for the homicide. But Walter Oxendine and Proctor Locklear were not acting in concert; they were adversaries; and it is the general rule of law that a person may not be held criminally responsible for a killing unless the homicide were either actually or constructively committed by him; and in order to be his act, it must be committed by his own hand, or by some one acting in concert with him, or in furtherance of a common design or purpose.

Thus, the Court stated the general principle of accomplice liability and noted that had defendant Walter Oxendine, his accomplice, or his agent fired the fatal shot, there would be no question that all the participants would be responsible for the homicide. However, the general rule did not apply on the facts of *Oxendine* because Proctor Locklear, Oxendine's adversary, fired the deadly round. Therefore, the Court noted that a different general rule applied, *i.e.,* that criminal responsibility for a homicide is dependent on proof that the defendant or his agent did the killing. Because, as the Court said, "Walter Oxendine and Proctor Locklear were not acting in concert; they were adversaries," the instruction allowing defendant Walter Oxendine's conviction was fatally flawed and he was entitled to a new trial. * * *

In further illustrating its rationale for reversing Walter Oxendine's * * * conviction, the Court in *Oxendine* described the following hypothetical:

> Suppose, instead of killing an innocent bystander, Proctor Locklear had killed Dock Wilkins, one of his assailants, would the law, under these circumstances, hold the surviving assailants or confederates ... criminally responsible for the homicide? We think not. Each took his own chance of being injured or killed by Proctor

Locklear when the three made a common assault upon him. They would be responsible for what they did themselves, and such consequences as might naturally flow from their acts and conduct; but they never advised, encouraged or assented to the acts of Proctor Locklear, nor did they combine with him to do any unlawful act, nor did they, in any manner, assent to anything he did, and hence they could not be responsible for his conduct towards the deceased.

The Court's hypothetical is directly on point with the facts in the case at bar. As in the *Oxendine* hypothetical, the defendants here were aggressors who created a dangerous situation leading to a deadly response by Sergeant Pruitt. * * *

In light of its language, the reasoning behind its hypothetical, and the citation of authority in *Oxendine,* there can be no doubt that the rule of *Oxendine* requires reversal of the convictions here. * * * [T]hough defendants engaged in reckless and dangerous conduct, neither they nor their accomplices committed the fatal act. Instead, Sergeant Pruitt, an adversary to defendants and their accomplices, was responsible for the deaths of Stewart and Gainey. Pruitt was not the agent of defendants, nor did he act in concert with them in a manner that furthered a common design or purpose. On the contrary, his every action was in direct opposition to the criminal scheme in which defendants and their accomplices were engaged. * * *

The rule established in *Oxendine* is consistent with the prevailing rule in the overwhelming majority of states in this country * * *.

In * * * *State v. Canola*, 73 N.J. 206, 374 A.2d 20, defendant was convicted of felony murder when the robbery victim shot and killed one of defendant's cofelons. The court noted: * * *

> It is clearly the majority view throughout the country that, at least in theory, the doctrine of felony murder does not extend to a killing, although growing out of the commission of the felony, if directly attributable to the act of one other than the defendant or those associated with him in the unlawful enterprise.... This rule is sometimes rationalized on the "agency" theory of felony murder.

> A contrary view, which would attach liability under the felony murder rule for *any* death proximately resulting from the unlawful activity—even the death of a co-felon—notwithstanding the killing was by one resisting the crime, does not seem to have the present allegiance of any court.[1] * * *

Several appellate courts have noted the "justifiability" of a victim's lethal response as a factor foreclosing the presence of an "unlawful act" required under felony murder statutes. As stated by the Supreme Court of Pennsylvania in a case with similar facts:

1. The court in *Canola* perhaps overstated the dearth of authority supporting the "proximate cause" theory. Two states, Missouri and Florida, appear to follow the minority "proximate cause" theory. * * *

In the present instance, the victim of the homicide was one of the robbers who, while resisting apprehension in his effort to escape, was shot and killed by a policeman in the performance of his duty. Thus, the homicide was justifiable and, obviously, could not be availed of, on any rational legal theory, to support a charge of murder. How can anyone, no matter how much of an outlaw he may be, have a criminal charge lodged against him for the consequences of the lawful conduct of another person? The mere statement of the question carries with it its own answer.

Commonwealth v. Redline, 391 Pa. [486,] 509, 137 A.2d [472,] 483 [(1958)].

The State argues that for purposes of deterrence we should expand application of the felony murder rule to include cases such as these. Deterrence is a laudable objective of all aspects of the criminal law, but the proposition that criminal offenders not deterred by well-established and proper application of the felony murder rule will be deterred by the markedly broader version urged here is dubious at best. * * *

Notes and Questions

1. New Jersey imposes felony-murder liability when "the actor, acting either alone or with one or more other persons, is engaged in the commission of [an enumerated felony] * * * and in the course of such crime * * * any person causes the death of a person other than one of the participants." N.J.Stat.Ann. 2C–11–3 (1992).

In New Jersey, what would be the outcome in *Bonner?* In *Oxendine?* Suppose that one felon accidentally kills a co-felon? Is there any principled reason for limiting the felony-murder rule as New Jersey has done? See John S. Anooshian, Note, *Should Courts Use Principles of Justification and Excuse to Impose Felony–Murder Liability?,* 19 Rutgers L.J. 451 (1988).

2. In light of *Bonner,* is there an alternative way to hold a felon responsible for the killing of a co-felon at the hands of a third person? Yes, as seen in Taylor v. Superior Court, 3 Cal.3d 578, 91 Cal.Rptr. 275, 477 P.2d 131 (1970), overruled on other grounds in People v. Antick, 15 Cal.3d 79, 123 Cal.Rptr. 475, 539 P.2d 43 (1975).

In *Taylor, A* and *B,* robbers, entered a liquor store run by Mr. and Mrs. West. *C,* an accomplice in the robbery, remained outside in the getaway car. Inside, *A,* "chattering insanely," ordered Mr. West to put money in a bag, telling him repeatedly, "Don't move or I'll blow your head off. He's got a gun. He's got a gun." In response, Mrs. West picked up a gun and shot and killed *B. A* and *C* were prosecuted for *B* 's death.

As in *Bonner,* the court refused to apply the felony-murder doctrine. But, it concluded that *A* 's conduct in the store was malicious, i.e., reckless, and that his reckless behavior proximately caused the initiation of the gunfire by Mrs. West. Therefore, the court concluded that *A* could be convicted of murder for *B* 's death at Mrs. West's hands. *C,* sitting in the car, was also guilty, because *A* 's reckless conduct could be imputed to him under the agency (accomplice liability) doctrine.

As a practical matter, did it matter which theory—felony-murder or recklessness—was used to convict *A* and *C* ?

If Mrs. West had killed *A* rather than *B,* could *B* and *C* have been convicted of murder in *A* 's death? See *Antick,* supra, 15 Cal.3d at 93 n. 12, 123 Cal.Rptr. at 483 n. 12, 539 P.2d at 51 n. 12.

2. UNLAWFUL–ACT MANSLAUGHTER (THE "MISDEMEANOR MANSLAUGHTER" RULE)

An unintended homicide that occurs during the commission of an unlawful act not amounting to a felony constitutes common law involuntary manslaughter. As explained by the court in Comber v. United States, 584 A.2d 26, 49 (D.C.App.1990):

> The doctrine became known as the "misdemeanor-manslaughter rule," something of an analogue to the felony-murder rule. * * * Where the * * * doctrine applies, involuntary manslaughter liability attaches even where the defendant does not act with the degree of [culpability] ordinarily required for involuntary manslaughter predicated on criminally negligent behavior. In effect, the defendant's intentional commission of a misdemeanor supplies the culpability required to impose homicide liability.

Criticism of the unlawful-act doctrine parallels that of the felony-murder rule:

> Unlawful-act involuntary manslaughter has been severely criticized. The flaw in the concept is that a person may be convicted of unlawful-act manslaughter even though the person's conduct does not create a perceptible risk of death. Thus, a person is punished for the fortuitous result, the death, although the jury never has to determine whether the person was at fault with respect to the death. The concept violates the important principle that a person's criminal liability for an act should be proportioned to his or her moral culpability for that act. The wrongdoer should be punished for the unlawful act and for homicide if he or she is at fault with respect to the death, but should not be punished for a fortuitous result merely because the act was unlawful.

State v. Pray, 378 A.2d 1322, 1324 (Me.1977).

The extremity of the misdemeanor-manslaughter doctrine is evident from its application in real and hypothetical circumstances. For example, an automobile driver who non-negligently causes the death of a pedestrian due to the driver's failure to obey a stop sign, in violation of a traffic ordinance, is guilty of manslaughter. State v. Hupf, 48 Del. 254, 101 A.2d 355 (1953). Similarly, an actor is guilty of manslaughter if he unjustifiably pushes the victim in the chest with his forearm (a criminal battery) and the victim, intoxicated, falls down, strikes the back of his head on the pavement, and dies. See *Pray,* supra. In jurisdictions in which offensive contact constitutes misdemeanor battery, a person may be convicted of manslaughter "where a death freakishly results from spitting at another, putting one's hands on another in a sexually offensive manner, or lightly tapping another on the face." See *Comber, supra,* 584 A.2d at 50.

Manslaughter convictions have also been upheld for deaths arising from non-criminal, but morally wrongful, conduct. For example, in Commonwealth v. Mink, 123 Mass. 422 (1877), Lucy Mink attempted to kill herself with a gun in the presence of Charles Ricker. Ricker took hold of Mink in order to prevent her from shooting herself. A struggle ensued, during which Mink's pistol accidentally discharged, killing Ricker. Although attempted suicide was not an offense, the court held that Mink was guilty of criminal homicide because her conduct was morally wrongful. But see Commonwealth v. Catalina, 407 Mass. 779, 556 N.E.2d 973 (1990) (now limiting the unlawful-act doctrine to deaths resulting from batteries).

Because of the harshness of the rule, many courts limit the doctrine to deaths resulting from either *malum in se* misdemeanor conduct, Mills v. State, 13 Md.App. 196, 282 A.2d 147 (1971), or the commission of a "dangerous" misdemeanor, e.g., *Comber, supra,* 584 A.2d at 51 ("if the manner of its commission entails a reasonably foreseeable risk of appreciable physical injury"). Some states require proof that the death was a natural and probable consequence of the violation of the offense. The latter limitation "essentially converts the unlawful act type of manslaughter into culpable negligence manslaughter." Todd v. State, 594 So.2d 802, 804 (Fla.App.1992).

Led by the Model Penal Code, some states have abolished the misdemeanor-manslaughter rule.

E. CAPITAL MURDER

1. THE CONSTITUTIONAL AND POLICY DEBATE

INTRODUCTORY COMMENT

In Furman v. Georgia, 408 U.S. 238, 92 S.Ct. 2726, 33 L.Ed.2d 346 (1972), the Supreme Court, by a 5–4 margin, set aside death sentences in four Georgia cases. Although the judgment was announced in a brief statement of the Court, all nine justices filed opinions, taking up more than 200 pages, explaining their reasoning.

Justices Brennan and Marshall concluded that capital punishment is unconstitutional in all circumstances, regardless of the procedures used by the state to administer the penalty. Justices Douglas, Stewart, and White, also supporting the judgment, rejected this broad attack on capital punishment. They reasoned instead that because Georgia juries had unfettered discretion in determining who would be executed, there was too great a risk that the death penalty was being imposed arbitrarily, capriciously, or in a discriminatory manner. The four dissenters (Chief Justice Burger, and Justices Blackmun, Powell, and Rehnquist) rejected the *per se* and procedural attacks on the death penalty.

Although only two members of the Court took the abolitionist position, the effect of *Furman* was to end executions nationwide because all death penalty statutes were constitutionally infirm under the reasoning of the case. Thereafter, 35 states reformulated their sentencing provisions in an effort to overcome the Court's objections. In order to limit the discretion of the sentencing authority, as required by *Furman,* most of these states enacted death penalty legislation based on Model Penal Code § 210.6, which provides for a post-conviction sentencing hearing at which the parties may introduce evidence of statutory aggravating and mitigating factors relating to the murder and the defendant. The Supreme Court considered the constitutionality of such a statute in the next case.

GREGG v. GEORGIA

Supreme Court of the United States, 1976.
428 U.S. 153, 96 S.Ct. 2909, 49 L.Ed.2d 859.

Judgment of the Court, and opinion of MR. JUSTICE STEWART, MR. JUSTICE POWELL, and MR. JUSTICE STEVENS, announced by MR. JUSTICE STEWART.

The issue in this case is whether the imposition of the sentence of death for the crime of murder under the law of Georgia violates the Eighth and Fourteenth Amendments. * * *

I

[Gregg was convicted of intent-to-kill murder and armed robbery. At a post-conviction sentencing hearing, the jury imposed the death penalty after it found beyond a reasonable doubt that Gregg was guilty of two statutory aggravating circumstances.]

II

Before considering the issues presented it is necessary to understand the Georgia statutory scheme for the imposition of the death penalty. The Georgia statute * * * retains the death penalty for six categories of crime: murder, kidnaping for ransom or where the victim is harmed, armed robbery, rape, treason, and aircraft hijacking. The capital defendant's guilt or innocence is determined in the traditional manner, either by a trial judge or a jury, in the first stage of a bifurcated trial.

* * * After a verdict, finding, or plea of guilty to a capital crime, a presentence hearing is conducted before whoever made the determination of guilt. The sentencing procedures are essentially the same in both bench and jury trials. * * * The defendant is accorded substantial latitude as to the types of evidence that he may introduce. Evidence considered during the guilt stage may be considered during the sentencing stage without being resubmitted.

In the assessment of the appropriate sentence to be imposed the judge is also required to consider or to include in his instructions to the jury "any mitigating circumstances or aggravating circumstances otherwise authorized by law and any of [10] statutory aggravating circumstances which may be supported by the evidence...." * * * Before a convicted defendant may be sentenced to death * * * the jury, or the trial judge in cases tried without a jury, must find beyond a reasonable doubt one of the 10 aggravating circumstances specified in the statute.[9] The sentence of death may be imposed only if the jury (or judge) finds one of the statutory aggravating circumstances and then elects to impose that sentence. If the verdict is death, the jury or judge must specify the aggravating circumstance(s) found. In jury cases, the trial judge is bound by the jury's recommended sentence. * * *

III

We address initially the basic contention that the punishment of death for the crime of murder is, under all circumstances, "cruel and unusual" in violation of the Eighth and Fourteenth Amendments of the Constitution. * * *

It is clear * * * that the Eighth Amendment has not been regarded as a static concept. As Mr. Chief Justice Warren said, in an often-quoted phrase, "[t]he Amendment must draw its meaning from the evolving standards of decency that mark the progress of a maturing society." *Trop v. Dulles,* [356 U.S. 86, 101, 78 S.Ct. 590, 598, 2 L.Ed.2d 630 (1958)]. Thus, an assessment of contemporary values concerning

---

9. The statute provides in part: * * *

"(b) In all cases * * * for which the death penalty may be authorized, the judge shall consider, or he shall include in his instructions to the jury for it to consider, any mitigating circumstances or aggravating circumstances otherwise authorized by law and any of the following statutory aggravating circumstances which may be supported by the evidence:

"(1) The offense of murder, rape, armed robbery, or kidnapping was committed by a person with a prior record of conviction for a capital felony, or the offense of murder was committed by a person who has a substantial history of serious assaultive criminal convictions.

"(2) The offense of murder, rape, armed robbery, or kidnapping was committed while the offender was engaged in the commission of another capital felony, or aggravated battery, or the offense of murder was committed while the offender was engaged in the commission of burglary or arson in the first degree.

"(3) The offender by his act of murder, armed robbery, or kidnapping knowingly created a great risk of death to more than one person in a public place by means of a weapon or device which would normally be hazardous to the lives of more than one person.

"(4) The offender committed the offense of murder for himself or another, for the purpose of receiving money or any other thing of monetary value.

"(5) The murder of a judicial officer, former judicial officer, district attorney or solicitor or former district attorney or solicitor during or because of the exercise of his official duty.

"(6) The offender caused or directed another to commit murder or committed murder as an agent or employee of another person.

"(7) The offense of murder, rape, armed robbery, or kidnapping was outrageously or wantonly vile, horrible or inhuman in that it involved torture, depravity of mind, or an aggravated battery to the victim.

"(8) The offense of murder was committed against any peace officer, corrections employee or fireman while engaged in the performance of his official duties.

"(9) The offense of murder was committed by a person in, or who has escaped from, the lawful custody of a peace officer or place of lawful confinement.

"(10) The murder was committed for the purpose of avoiding, interfering with, or preventing a lawful arrest or custody in a place of lawful confinement, of himself or another. * * *"

the infliction of a challenged sanction is relevant to the application of the Eighth Amendment. * * * [T]his assessment does not call for a subjective judgment. It requires, rather, that we look to objective indicia that reflect the public attitude toward a given sanction.

But our cases also make clear that public perceptions of standards of decency with respect to criminal sanctions are not conclusive. A penalty also must accord with "the dignity of man," which is the "basic concept underlying the Eighth Amendment." This means, at least, that the punishment not be "excessive." When a form of punishment in the abstract (in this case, whether capital punishment may ever be imposed as a sanction for murder) rather than in the particular (the propriety of death as a penalty to be applied to a specific defendant for a specific crime) is under consideration, the inquiry into "excessiveness" has two aspects. First, the punishment must not involve the unnecessary and wanton infliction of pain. Second, the punishment must not be grossly out of proportion to the severity of the crime. * * *

* * * We now consider specifically whether the sentence of death for the crime of murder is a *per se* violation of the Eighth and Fourteenth Amendments to the Constitution. We note first that history and precedent strongly support a negative answer to this question.

The imposition of the death penalty for the crime of murder has a long history of acceptance both in the United States and in England. The common-law rule imposed a mandatory death sentence on all convicted murderers. * * *

It is apparent from the text of the Constitution itself that the existence of capital punishment was accepted by the Framers. At the time the Eighth Amendment was ratified, capital punishment was a common sanction in every State. * * *

For nearly two centuries, this Court, repeatedly and often expressly, has recognized that capital punishment is not invalid *per se*. * * *

The most marked indication of society's endorsement of the death penalty for murder is the legislative response to *Furman*. The legislatures of at least 35 States have enacted new statutes that provide for the death penalty for at least some crimes that result in the death of another person. And the Congress of the United States, in 1974, enacted a statute providing the death penalty for aircraft piracy that results in death. * * *

The jury also is a significant and reliable objective index of contemporary values because it is so directly involved. The Court has said that "one of the most important functions any jury can perform in making . . . a selection [between life imprisonment and death for a defendant convicted in a capital case] is to maintain a link between contemporary community values and the penal system." It may be true that evolving standards have influenced juries in recent decades to be more discriminating in imposing the sentence of death. But the relative infrequency of jury verdicts imposing the death sentence does not indicate rejection of capital punishment *per se*. Rather, the reluctance of juries in many cases to impose the sentence may well reflect the humane feeling that this most irrevocable of sanctions should be reserved for a small number of extreme cases. * * *

As we have seen, however, the Eighth Amendment demands more than that a challenged punishment be acceptable to contemporary society. The Court also must ask whether it comports with the basic concept of human dignity at the core of the Amendment. * * * [T]he sanction imposed cannot be so totally without penological justification that it results in the gratuitous infliction of suffering.

The death penalty is said to serve two principal social purposes: retribution and deterrence of capital crimes by prospective offenders.

In part, capital punishment is an expression of society's moral outrage at particularly offensive conduct. This function may be unappealing to many, but it is essential in an ordered society that asks its citizens to rely on legal processes rather than self-help to vindicate their wrongs. * * * "Retribution is no longer the dominant objective of the criminal law," *Williams v. New York*, 337 U.S. 241, 248, 69 S.Ct. 1079, 93 L.Ed. 1337 (1949), but neither is it a forbidden objective nor one inconsistent with our respect for the dignity of men. Indeed, the decision that capital punishment may be the appropriate sanction in extreme cases is an expression of the community's belief that certain crimes are themselves so grievous an affront to humanity that the only adequate response may be the penalty of death.

Statistical attempts to evaluate the worth of the death penalty as a deterrent to crimes by potential offenders have occasioned a great deal of debate. The results simply have been inconclusive. * * *

Although some of the studies suggest that the death penalty may not function as a significantly greater deterrent than lesser penalties, there is no convincing empirical evidence either supporting or refuting this view. We may nevertheless assume safely that there are murderers, such as those who act in passion, for whom the threat of death has little or no deterrent effect. But for many others, the death penalty undoubtedly is a significant deterrent. There are carefully contemplated murders, such as murder for hire, where the possible penalty of death may well enter into the cold calculus that precedes the decision to act. And there are some categories of murder, such as murder by a life prisoner, where other sanctions may not be adequate.

The value of capital punishment as a deterrent of crime is a complex factual issue the resolution of which properly rests with the legislatures, which can evaluate the results of statistical studies in terms of their own local conditions and with a flexibility of approach that is not available to the courts. * * *

Finally, we must consider whether the punishment of death is disproportionate in relation to the crime for which it is imposed. There is no question that death as a punishment is unique in its severity and irrevocability. * * * But we are concerned here only with the imposition of capital punishment for the crime of murder, and when a life has been taken deliberately by the offender, we cannot say that the punishment is invariably disproportionate to the crime. It is an extreme sanction, suitable to the most extreme of crimes.

We hold that the death penalty is not a form of punishment that may never be imposed, regardless of the circumstances of the offense, regardless of the character of the offender, and regardless of the procedure followed in reaching the decision to impose it. * * *

IV

We now consider whether Georgia may impose the death penalty on the petitioner in this case. * * *

While *Furman* did not hold that the infliction of the death penalty *per se* violates the Constitution's ban on cruel and unusual punishments, it did recognize that the penalty of death is different in kind from any other punishment imposed under our system of criminal justice. Because of the uniqueness of the death penalty, *Furman* held that it could not be imposed under sentencing procedures that created a substantial risk that it would be inflicted in an arbitrary and capricious manner. * * *

* * * [T]he concerns expressed in *Furman* * * * can be met by a carefully drafted statute that ensures that the sentencing authority is given adequate information and guidance. As a general proposition these concerns are best met by a system that provides for a bifurcated proceeding at which the sentencing authority is apprised of the information relevant to the imposition of sentence and provided with standards to guide its use of the information. * * *

We * * * turn to consideration of the constitutionality of Georgia's capital-sentencing procedures. * * *

These procedures require the jury to consider the circumstances of the crime and the criminal before it recommends sentence. No longer can a Georgia jury do as *Furman's* jury did: reach a finding of the defendant's guilt and then, without guidance or direction, decide whether he should live or die. Instead, the jury's attention is directed to the specific circumstances of the crime * * *. In addition, the jury's attention is focused on the characteristics of the person who committed the crime * * *. As a result, while some jury discretion still exists, "the discretion to be exercised is controlled by clear and objective standards so as to produce non-discriminatory application."

As an important additional safeguard against arbitrariness and caprice, the Georgia statutory scheme provides for automatic appeal of all death sentences to the State's Supreme Court. * * *

For the reasons expressed in this opinion, we hold that the statutory system under which Gregg was sentenced to death does not violate the Constitution. * * *

MR. JUSTICE WHITE, with whom THE CHIEF JUSTICE and MR. JUSTICE REHNQUIST join, concurring in the judgment.

* * * The issue in this case is whether the death penalty imposed for murder on petitioner Gregg under the new Georgia statutory scheme may constitutionally be carried out. I agree that it may. * * *

Petitioner's argument that there is an unconstitutional amount of discretion in the system which separates those suspects who receive the death penalty from those who receive life imprisonment, a lesser penalty, or are acquitted or never charged, seems to be in final analysis an indictment of our entire system of justice. Petitioner has argued, in effect, that no matter how effective the death penalty may be as a punishment, government, created and run as it must be by humans, is inevitably incompetent to administer it. This cannot be accepted as a proposition of constitutional law. Imposition of the death penalty is surely an awesome responsibility for any system of justice and those who participate in it. Mistakes will be made and discriminations will occur which will be difficult to explain. However, one of society's most basic tasks is that of protecting the lives of its citizens and one of the most basic ways in which it achieves the task is through criminal laws against murder. I decline to interfere with the manner in which Georgia has chosen to enforce such laws on what is simply an assertion of lack of faith in the ability of the system of justice to operate in a fundamentally fair manner. * * *

I therefore concur in the judgment of affirmance. * * *

MR. JUSTICE BLACKMUN, concurring in the judgment. * * *

MR. JUSTICE BRENNAN, dissenting.

The Cruel and Unusual Punishments Clause "must draw its meaning from the evolving standards of decency that mark the progress of a maturing society." * * *

* * * [T]he Clause forbidding cruel and unusual punishments under our constitutional system of government embodies in unique degree moral principles restraining the punishments that our civilized society may impose on those persons who transgress its laws. * * *

This Court inescapably has the duty, as the ultimate arbiter of the meaning of our Constitution, to say whether, when individuals condemned to death stand before our Bar, "moral concepts" require us to hold that the law has progressed to the point where we should declare that the punishment of death, like punishments on the rack, the screw, and the wheel, is no longer morally tolerable in our civilized society. My opinion in *Furman v. Georgia* concluded that our civilization and the law had progressed to this point and that therefore the punishment of death, for whatever crime and under all circumstances, is "cruel and unusual" in violation of the Eighth and Fourteenth Amendments of the Constitution. I shall not again canvass the reasons that led to that conclusion. I emphasize only that foremost among the "moral concepts" recognized in our cases and inherent in the Clause is the primary moral principle that the State, even as it punishes, must treat its citizens in a manner consistent with their intrinsic worth as human beings—a punishment must not be so severe as to be degrading to human dignity. * * *

The fatal constitutional infirmity in the punishment of death is that it treats "members of the human race as nonhumans, as objects to be toyed with and discarded. [It is] thus inconsistent with the fundamental premise of the Clause that even the vilest criminal remains a human being possessed of common human dignity." * * *

MR. JUSTICE MARSHALL, dissenting. * * *

Since the decision in *Furman,* the legislatures of 35 States have enacted new statutes authorizing the imposition of the death sentence for certain crimes, and Congress has enacted a law providing the death penalty for air piracy resulting in death. I would be less than candid if I did not acknowledge that these developments have a significant bearing on a realistic assessment of the moral acceptability of the death penalty to the American people. But if the constitutionality of the death penalty turns, as I have urged, on the opinion of an *informed* citizenry, then even the enactment of new death statutes cannot be viewed as conclusive. In *Furman,* I observed that the American people are largely unaware of the information critical to a judgment on the morality of the death penalty, and concluded that if they were better informed they would consider it shocking, unjust, and unacceptable. A recent study, conducted after the enactment of the post-*Furman* statutes, has confirmed that the American people know little about the death penalty, and that the opinions of an informed public would differ significantly from those of a public unaware of the consequences and effects of the death penalty.[1]

Even assuming, however, that the post-*Furman* enactment of statutes authorizing the death penalty renders the prediction of the views of an informed citizenry an uncertain basis for a constitutional decision, the enactment of those statutes has no bearing whatsoever on the conclusion that the death penalty is unconstitutional because it is excessive. An excessive penalty is invalid under the Cruel and Unusual Punishments Clause "even though popular sentiment may favor" it. The inquiry here, then, is simply whether the death penalty is necessary to accomplish the legitimate legislative purposes in punishment, or whether a less severe penalty—life imprisonment—would do as well.

The two purposes that sustain the death penalty as nonexcessive in the Court's view are general deterrence and retribution. In *Furman,* I canvassed the relevant data on the deterrent effect of capital punishment. The state of knowledge at that point, after literally centuries of debate, was summarized as follows by a United Nations Committee:

"It is generally agreed between the retentionists and abolitionists, whatever their opinions about the validity of comparative studies of

---

1. Sarat & Vidmar, Public Opinion, The Death Penalty, and the Eighth Amend-ment: Testing the Marshall Hypothesis, 1976 Wis.L.Rev. 171.

deterrence, that the data which now exist show no correlation
between the existence of capital punishment and lower rates of
capital crime."[3] * * *

The other principal purpose said to be served by the death penalty is
retribution. The notion that retribution can serve as a moral justification for the sanction of death * * * is * * * the most disturbing aspect
of today's unfortunate decisions.

The concept of retribution is a multifaceted one, and any discussion
of its role in the criminal law must be undertaken with caution. On one
level, it can be said that the notion of retribution or reprobation is the
basis of our insistence that only those who have broken the law be
punished, and in this sense the notion is quite obviously central to a just
system of criminal sanctions. But our recognition that retribution plays
a crucial role in determining who may be punished by no means requires
approval of retribution as a general justification for punishment. It is
the question whether retribution can provide a moral justification for
punishment—in particular, capital punishment—that we must consider.
* * *

The [plurality's] contentions—that society's expression of moral
outrage through the imposition of the death penalty preempts the
citizenry from taking the law into its own hands and reinforces moral
values—are not retributive in the purest sense. They are essentially
utilitarian in that they portray the death penalty as valuable because of
its beneficial results. These justifications for the death penalty are
inadequate because the penalty is, quite clearly I think, not necessary to
the accomplishment of those results.

There remains for consideration, however, what might be termed
the purely retributive justification for the death penalty—that the death
penalty is appropriate, not because of its beneficial effect on society, but
because the taking of the murderer's life is itself morally good. * * *

* * * [T]he taking of life "because the wrongdoer deserves it"
surely must fall, for such a punishment has as its very basis the total
denial of the wrongdoer's dignity and worth.

The death penalty, unnecessary to promote the goal of deterrence or
to further any legitimate notion of retribution, is an excessive penalty
forbidden by the Eighth and Fourteenth Amendments. * * *

Notes and Questions

1. *Mandatory death-penalty statutes.* Some states responded to *Furman* by eliminating jury discretion altogether. For example, North Carolina
redrafted its murder statute to impose the death penalty in all first degree
murder cases; a lesser penalty was set for second degree murder. On the
same day that *Gregg* was decided, the Supreme Court invalidated this

3. United Nations, Department of Eco-   ment, pt. II, ¶ 159, p. 123 (1968).
nomic and Social Affairs, Capital Punish-

statutory scheme. Woodson v. North Carolina, 428 U.S. 280, 96 S.Ct. 2978, 49 L.Ed.2d 944 (1976).

The Court stated that "there is general agreement that American juries have persistently refused to convict a significant portion of persons charged with first-degree murder * * * under mandatory death penalty statutes." Id. at 302, 96 S.Ct. at 2990, 49 L.Ed.2d at 959. The Court reasoned from this that, as a practical matter, North Carolina's system invited juries to determine which murderers would live (by convicting them of second degree murder) and which would die, without standards to guide them.

The Court recognized another constitutional shortcoming of the North Carolina statute:

[The shortcoming] is its failure to allow the particularized consideration of relevant aspects of the character and record of each convicted defendant before the imposition upon him of a sentence of death. * * * A process that accords no significance to [such factors] excludes * * * the possibility of compassionate or mitigating factors stemming from the diverse frailties of humankind. It treats all persons convicted of a designated offense not as uniquely human beings, but as members of a faceless, undifferentiated mass to be subjected to the blind infliction of the penalty of death.

Id. at 303–04, 96 S.Ct. at 2991, 49 L.Ed.2d at 960.

2. *Policy arguments: deterrence.* According to various studies, capital punishment does not have a general deterrent effect on the criminal homicide rate. Probably the most frequently cited study supporting the opposite view is Isaac Ehrlich, *The Deterrent Effect of Capital Punishment: A Question of Life and Death,* 65 Am.Econ.Rev. 397 (June 1975). Professor Ehrlich concluded that for the period from 1933 to 1967, each additional execution in the United States might have saved eight lives. The methods and conclusions of his study have been the subject of scholarly debate and, in some quarters, criticism. E.g., David C. Baldus & James W.L. Cole, *A Comparison of the Work of Thorsten Sellin & Isaac Ehrlich on the Deterrent Effect of Capital Punishment,* 85 Yale L.J. 170 (1975); William J. Bowers and Glenn L. Pierce, *The Illusion of Deterrence in Isaac Ehrlich's Research on Capital Punishment,* 85 Yale L.J. 187 (1975).

If the results from deterrence studies are inconclusive, as maintained by the *Gregg* plurality, should a utilitarian favor or oppose the death penalty? As a matter of institutional competence, who is better equipped to resolve the deterrence question, a legislature or a court?

3. *Policy arguments: retribution.* Is the death penalty justifiable on retributive grounds? Consider the remarks of Ernest van den Haag, *In Defense of the Death Penalty: A Legal–Practical–Moral Analysis,* 14 Crim. L.Bull. 51, 66–68 (1978):

"The life of each man should be sacred to each other man," the ancients tell us. They unflinchingly executed murderers. They realized it is not enough to proclaim the sacredness and inviolability of human life. * * * Does it not cheapen human life to punish the murderer by incarcerating him as one does a pickpocket? Murder differs in quality from other crimes and deserves, therefore, a punishment that differs in quality from other punishments.

If it were shown that no punishment is more deterrent than a trivial fine, capital punishment for murder would remain just, even if not useful. For murder is not a trifling offense. Punishment must be proportioned to the gravity of the crime, if only to denounce it and to vindicate the importance of the norm violated. Thus, all penal systems proportion punishments to crimes. The worse the crime the higher the penalty deserved. Why not the highest penalty—death—for the worst crime—wanton murder? Those rejecting the death penalty have the burden of showing that no crime deserves capital punishment—a burden which they have not so far been willing to bear.

Abolitionists are wrong when they insist that we all have an equally inalienable right to live to our natural term—that if the victim deserved to live, so does the murderer. That takes egalitarianism too far for my taste: The crime sets victim and murderer apart; if the victim died, the murderer does not deserve to live. The thought that there are some who think that murderers have as much right to live as their victims oppresses me. So does the thought that a Stalin or a Hitler should have the right to go on living. * * *

Never to execute a wrongdoer, regardless of how depraved his acts, is to proclaim that no act can be so irredeemably vicious as to deserve death—that no human being can be wicked enough to be deprived of life. Who actually believes that? I find it easier to believe that those who affect such a view do so because of a failure of nerve. They do not think themselves—and therefore anyone else—competent to decide questions of life and death. Aware of human frailty they shudder at the gravity of the decision and refuse to make it. * * * Such an attitude may be proper for inquiring philosophers and scientists. But not for courts. They can evade decisions on life and death only by giving up their paramount duties: to do justice, to secure the lives of the citizens, and to vindicate the norms society holds inviolable.

Is there an adequate response to the view that the death penalty is morally required for heinous murders? Reflect on John Kaplan, *The Problem of Capital Punishment,* 1983 U.Ill.L.Rev. 555, 565–67, 569–70:

The view that we should impose capital punishment because it is morally right is often phrased as an assertion that the person who would commit murder—or, more likely, some especially aggravated form of murder—should properly forfeit his own life. One problem with this argument is that it is usually supported simply by its assertion as a moral principle, rather than by any reasoning.

Often this kind of argument is phrased in terms of the victim and draws its emotional force from a feeling that somehow, by placing the defendant in the position that his victim now occupies, we will right some moral balance. Of course this is not a pragmatic argument; obviously nothing that we do to the defendant will do the victim any good. * * *

It is probable that the great majority of those who are sentenced to capital punishment have committed horrible crimes of the kind that the majority of us would agree deserved capital punishment, based simply on reading about them in the newspapers. * * *

In general, the people who commit those especially vicious, baffling, senseless crimes which do result in death sentences, fall into one of three categories. First of all there are those in whom the cultural connection between male sexuality and aggression and the need to dominate becomes unbalanced. This type of personality unfortunately exists throughout our society in more or less attenuated form. In extreme cases, sexuality becomes so unbalanced—indeed it can only be described as "perverted"—that the individual has a kind of sexual need to kill. Whether one defines this as a kind of mental illness, the perpetrators are far from normal. The next major kind of aggravated murderer is the person who is infused with a hatred which surfaces either almost continuously or else explosively on random occasions in a way that is virtually inexplicable. Finally, there is the person whose values can only be called feral. He looks upon the world as we envision a wild animal would look from the jungle. He feels no moral reason not to injure anyone, just as he feels that those around him have no moral reason not to injure him.

The interesting thing about all three of these kinds of people is that the more closely one examines their backgrounds and what has happened to them as they were growing up, the less one feels that it is morally necessary to kill them, any more than one would feel it was morally necessary to kill an escaped leopard from the zoo. They may be very, very dangerous people, but when one sees the kinds of backgrounds that the overwhelming majority of them have come from, the moral argument for executing them grows weaker. Though we certainly do not want anything to do with them, there appears to be no moral requirement that we injure further one whose humanity has been so diluted over the years by past injuries. * * *

One does not have to go so far as to say, with the French, "To understand all is to forgive all" in order to recognize that a great part of the moral imperative behind executing someone * * * disappears when we know about the conditions in which he was raised and the forces that shaped him. They may be as dangerous as an escaped leopard, but there is no moral imperative to executing such an animal if the danger can be handled in other ways.

* * * If we believe that everyone is responsible for his own acts, it is harder to regard those who perpetrate the most vicious killings as an exception to this. But the fact is we do not regard everyone as responsible for his acts. The huge edifice of mens rea in criminal law, which requires that for all serious crimes some blameworthy state of mind exist, is testament to that. * * *

More important, we recognize that many different conditions which do not prevent some responsibility for one's actions may nonetheless lessen that responsibility. Negligent homicide is virtually always treated as a lesser crime than intentional killing and even among those intentional homicides, those committed in hot blood or some kind of passion are less severely punished than more calculated killings. Under some circumstances, even though by no means an excuse, youth, drunkenness, mental retardation, previous blameless life, or extreme emotion all can lessen what would otherwise be seen as the proper punishment. If all these things are properly seen as mitigating factors, does not the history of [the usual "heinous" murderer] lessen the moral imperative of executing him?

4. *Executing the innocent.* Nobody knows precisely how many innocent people have been executed in the United States, nor is there hard data on the number of innocent persons who have been spared after a death sentence was imposed. One study purports to document 350 wrongful capital crime convictions, some of which resulted in death sentences that were carried out. Hugo Adam Bedau & Michael L. Radelet, *Miscarriages of Justice in Potentially Capital Cases,* 40 Stan.L.Rev. 21 (1987). The study is criticized by Stephen J. Markman & Paul G. Cassell, *Protecting the Innocent: A Response to the Bedau–Radelet Study,* 41 Stan.L.Rev. 121 (1988); see also the authors' reply, Hugo Adam Bedau & Michael L. Radelet, *The Myth of Infallibility: A Reply to Markman and Cassell,* 41 Stan.L.Rev. 161 (1988).

In view of human fallibility, the risk of executing an innocent person reaches near certainty over time. Does this fact alone justify the abolition of the death penalty? Our society constructs highways with full knowledge that innocent lives will be lost as a result. The benefits of public roads are thought to outweigh the drawbacks. Should we apply the same calculus to the death penalty issue?

Alternatively, should the issue be resolved on non-consequentialist grounds? For example, is it preferable to abolish the death penalty, in order to guarantee that innocent people will not be executed, even though the result is that many murderers do not get the punishment they (arguably) deserve according to retributivist standards? For example, suppose that one thousand persons are awaiting execution, and we are told that two of them— we do not know which ones—are definitely innocent. Is it morally preferable to execute all of them, since this means that 998 murderers receive their (arguably) just deserts, although two persons are unjustly treated; or should all one thousand persons be spared in order to protect the two innocent lives? This issue is considered by Richard O. Lempert, *Desert and Deterrence: An Assessment of the Moral Bases of the Case for Capital Punishment,* 79 Mich.L.Rev. 1177, 1225–31 (1981).

Policy issues aside, is the Constitution violated if the state executes a person who received a fair trial, but who was denied the post-conviction opportunity to present new evidence of his purported innocence? For example, in Herrera v. Collins, 506 U.S. ___, 113 S.Ct. 853, 122 L.Ed.2d 203 (1993), Leonel Herrera asserted an alibi defense at his Texas murder trial, but was convicted and sentenced to death in part on the basis of eyewitness testimony linking him to the crime. Years after his conviction, Herrera sought to introduce new evidence of his innocence, including an affidavit of a lawyer who swore that Leonel's now-deceased brother, Raul, had personally confessed to the crime. Also, Raul's son, nine years old at the time of the murder, was prepared to testify that he observed his father—not his uncle—

commit the offense. Because Texas law required that new evidence be presented to a court within 30 days after conviction, the state refused to consider Leonel's claim of innocence.

Herrera sought relief in the federal courts. On appeal to the United States Supreme Court, six justices ruled that the Constitution is violated by the execution of an innocent person. However, the Court held that a Death Row inmate does not have an automatic right to access to the federal courts to present his post-conviction claim of innocence. The prisoner must offer a "truly persuasive demonstration" of innocence before a federal court may consider his claim, which a majority of the justices concluded was not supplied in Herrera's case. Writing for the Court, Chief Justice Rehnquist declared that Herrera's remedy was to seek executive clemency.

Governor Ann Richards refused to grant a reprieve or to stay Herrera's execution. Telling onlookers, "I am innocent, innocent, innocent. Make no mistake about this * * *, something very wrong is taking place tonight," Herrera was executed on May 12, 1993. *Man in Case on Curbing New Evidence is Executed,* New York Times, May 13, 1993, at A14.

2. THE QUEST FOR RELIABLE PROCEDURES

INTRODUCTORY COMMENT

After *Gregg v. Georgia*, the Supreme Court was forced to give fuller meaning to its "first commandment" of capital sentencing jurisprudence, i.e., that the sentencer's discretion be narrowly guided as to the circumstances which justify the imposition of the death penalty.

Unfortunately, this commandment runs up against the Court's second commandment, evident from the mandatory death penalty cases (Note 1, p. 294 supra), namely, that death penalty sentencing should be individualized. Together, these two propositions constitute "the yin and the yang of the eighth amendment," Scott E. Sundby, *The Lockett Paradox: Reconciling Guided Discretion and Unguided Mitigation in Capital Sentencing*, 38 UCLA L.Rev. 1147, 1148 (1991). According to Justice Scalia, the two injunctions, "like * * * the twin objectives of good and evil * * * cannot be reconciled." Walton v. Arizona, 497 U.S. 639, 664, 110 S.Ct. 3047, 3068, 111 L.Ed.2d 511, 541–42 (1990) (concurring opinion).

Does the current system of guided discretion, but with individualized sentencing, work in a reliable manner? If not, which way should the Court turn—toward a system allowing more discretion or in the direction of previously rejected mandatory sentencing laws? Or, do these conflicting concerns suggest that there is no satisfactory way to make reliable death penalty determinations? The cases in this subsection raise two of the most important procedural issues in this regard.

a. The Lingering Question of Racial Discrimination

McCLESKEY v. KEMP

Supreme Court of the United States, 1987.
481 U.S. 279, 107 S.Ct. 1756, 95 L.Ed.2d 262.

Powell, J., delivered the opinion of the Court, in which Rehnquist, C.J., and White, O'Connor, and Scalia, JJ., joined. * * *

This case presents the question whether a complex statistical study that indicates a risk that racial considerations enter into capital sentencing determinations proves that petitioner McCleskey's capital sentence is unconstitutional under the Eighth or Fourteenth Amendment.

I

[Warren McCleskey, a black man, was convicted of the murder of a white police officer during the course of a robbery. In the post-conviction sentencing hearing, the jury recommended the death penalty after it found beyond a reasonable doubt the existence of two statutory aggravating circumstances (that the killing occurred during the commission of a robbery, and that the victim was a peace officer engaged in the performance of his duties) and no mitigating factors. The judge followed the recommendation and sentenced McCleskey to death. On appeal, the state supreme court affirmed the conviction and sentence.]

McCleskey next filed a petition for a writ of habeas corpus in the Federal District Court for the Northern District of Georgia. His petition raised 18 claims, one of which was that the Georgia capital sentencing process is administered in a racially discriminatory manner in violation of the Eighth and Fourteenth Amendments to the United States Constitution. In support of his claim, McCleskey proffered a statistical study performed by Professors David C. Baldus, Charles Pulaski, and George Woodworth, and (the Baldus study) that purports to show a disparity in the imposition of the death sentence in Georgia based on the race of the murder victim and, to a lesser extent, the race of the defendant. The Baldus study is actually two sophisticated statistical studies that examine over 2,000 murder cases that occurred in Georgia during the 1970's. The raw numbers collected by Professor Baldus indicate that defendants charged with killing white persons received the death penalty in 11% of the cases, but defendants charged with killing blacks received the death penalty in only 1% of the cases. The raw numbers also indicate a reverse racial disparity according to the race of the defendant: 4% of the black defendants received the death penalty, as opposed to 7% of the white defendants.

Baldus also divided the cases according to the combination of the race of the defendant and the race of the victim. He found that the death penalty was assessed in 22% of the cases involving black defendants and white victims; 8% of the cases involving white defendants and white victims; 1% of the cases involving black defendants and black victims; and 3% of the cases involving white defendants and black victims. Similarly, Baldus found that prosecutors sought the death penalty in 70% of the cases involving black defendants and white victims; 32% of the cases involving white defendants and white victims; 15% of the cases involving black defendants and black victims; and 19% of the cases involving white defendants and black victims.

Baldus subjected his data to an extensive analysis, taking account of 230 variables that could have explained the disparities on nonracial grounds. One of his models concludes that, even after taking account of 39 nonracial variables, defendants charged with killing white victims were 4.3 times as likely to receive a death sentence as defendants charged with killing blacks. According to this model, black defendants were 1.1 times as likely to receive a death sentence as other defendants. Thus, the Baldus study indicates that black defendants, such as McCleskey, who kill white victims have the greatest likelihood of receiving the death penalty. * * *

II

McCleskey's first claim is that the Georgia capital punishment statute violates the Equal Protection Clause of the Fourteenth Amendment. He argues that race has infected the administration of Georgia's statute in two ways: persons who murder whites are more likely to be sentenced to death than persons who murder blacks, and black murderers are more likely to be sentenced to death than white murderers. As a black defendant who killed a white victim, McCleskey claims that the Baldus study demonstrates that he was discriminated against because of his race and because of the race of his victim. In its broadest form, McCleskey's claim of discrimination extends to every actor in the Georgia capital sentencing process, from the prosecutor who sought the death penalty and the jury that imposed the sentence, to the State itself that enacted the capital punishment statute and allows it to remain in effect despite its allegedly discriminatory application. We agree with the Court of Appeals, and every other court that has considered such a challenge, that this claim must fail.

Our analysis begins with the basic principle that a defendant who alleges an equal protection violation has the burden of proving "the existence of purposeful discrimination." A corollary to this principle is that a criminal defendant must prove that the purposeful discrimination "had a discriminatory effect" on him. Thus, to prevail under the Equal Protection Clause, McCleskey must prove that the decisionmakers in *his* case acted with discriminatory purpose. He offers no evidence specific to his own case that would support an inference that racial considerations played a part in his sentence. Instead, he relies solely on the Baldus study. McCleskey argues that the Baldus study compels an inference that his sentence rests on purposeful discrimination. McCleskey's claim that these statistics are sufficient proof of discrimination, without regard to the facts of a particular case, would extend to all capital cases in Georgia, at least where the victim was white and the defendant is black.

The Court has accepted statistics as proof of intent to discriminate in certain limited contexts. First, this Court has accepted statistical disparities as proof of an equal protection violation in the selection of the jury venire in a particular district. * * * Second, this Court has accepted statistics in the form of multiple-regression analysis to prove statutory violations under Title VII of the Civil Rights Act of 1964 [relating to employment discrimination].

But the nature of the capital sentencing decision, and the relationship of the statistics to that decision, are fundamentally different from the corresponding elements in the venire-selection or Title VII cases. Most importantly, each particular decision to impose the death penalty is made by a petit jury selected from a properly constituted venire. Each jury is unique in its composition, and the Constitution requires that its decision rest on consideration of innumerable factors that vary according to the characteristics of the individual defendant and the facts of the particular capital offense. Thus, the application of an inference drawn from the general statistics to a specific decision in a trial and sentencing simply is not comparable to the application of an inference drawn from general statistics to a specific venire-selection or Title VII case. In those cases, the statistics relate to fewer entities, and fewer variables are relevant to the challenged decisions. * * *

Finally, McCleskey's statistical proffer must be viewed in the context of his challenge. McCleskey challenges decisions at the heart of the State's criminal justice system. "[O]ne of society's most basic tasks is that of protecting the lives of its citizens and one of the most basic ways in which it achieves the task is through criminal laws against murder." *Gregg v. Georgia,* 428 U.S. 153, 226, 96 S.Ct. 2909, 2949, 49 L.Ed.2d 859 (1976) (WHITE, J., concurring). Implementation of these laws necessarily requires discretionary judgments. Because discretion is essential to the criminal justice process, we would demand exceptionally clear proof before we would infer that the discretion has been abused. * * * Accordingly, we hold that the Baldus study is clearly insufficient to support an inference that any of the decisionmakers in McCleskey's case acted with discriminatory purpose. * * *

* * * Accordingly, we reject McCleskey's equal protection claims.

* * *

III

IV

[The court then turned to McCleskey's alternative argument that the Baldus study demonstrates that the Georgia capital sentencing system violates the Eighth Amendment.] * * *

To evaluate McCleskey's challenge, we must examine exactly what the Baldus study may show. Even Professor Baldus does not contend that his statistics *prove* that race enters into any capital sentencing decisions or that race was a factor in McCleskey's particular case.

Statistics at most may show only a likelihood that a particular factor entered into some decisions. There is, of course, some risk of racial prejudice influencing a jury's decision in a criminal case. There are similar risks that other kinds of prejudice will influence other criminal trials. The question "is at what point that risk becomes constitutionally unacceptable." McCleskey asks us to accept the likelihood allegedly shown by the Baldus study as the constitutional measure of an unacceptable risk of racial prejudice influencing capital sentencing decisions. This we decline to do. * * *

Individual jurors bring to their deliberations "qualities of human nature and varieties of human experience, the range of which is unknown and perhaps unknowable." The capital sentencing decision requires the individual jurors to focus their collective judgment on the unique characteristics of a particular criminal defendant. It is not surprising that such collective judgments often are difficult to explain. But the inherent lack of predictability of jury decisions does not justify their condemnation. On the contrary, it is the jury's function to make the difficult and uniquely human judgments that defy codification and that "buil[d] discretion, equity, and flexibility into a legal system."

McCleskey's argument that the Constitution condemns the discretion allowed decisionmakers in the Georgia capital sentencing system is antithetical to the fundamental role of discretion in our criminal justice system. Discretion in the criminal justice system offers substantial benefits to the criminal defendant. Not only can a jury decline to impose the death sentence, it can decline to convict or choose to convict of a lesser offense. Whereas decisions against a defendant's interest may be reversed by the trial judge or on appeal, these discretionary exercises of leniency are final and unreviewable. * * *

At most, the Baldus study indicates a discrepancy that appears to correlate with race. Apparent disparities in sentencing are an inevitable part of our criminal justice system. * * * As this Court has recognized, any mode for determining guilt or punishment "has its weaknesses and the potential for misuse." Specifically, "there can be 'no perfect procedure for deciding in which cases governmental authority should be used to impose death.'" Despite these imperfections, our consistent rule has been that constitutional guarantees are met when "the mode [for determining guilt or punishment] itself has been surrounded with safeguards to make it as fair as possible." Where the discretion that is fundamental to our criminal process is involved, we decline to assume that what is unexplained is invidious. In light of the safeguards designed to minimize racial bias in the process, the fundamental value of jury trial in our criminal justice system, and the benefits that discretion provides to criminal defendants, we hold that the Baldus study does not demonstrate a constitutionally significant risk of racial bias affecting the Georgia capital sentencing process.

V

Two additional concerns inform our decision in this case. First, McCleskey's claim, taken to its logical conclusion, throws into serious question the principles that underlie our entire criminal justice system. The Eighth Amendment is not limited in application to capital punishment, but applies to all penalties. Thus, if we accepted McCleskey's claim that racial bias has impermissibly tainted the capital sentencing decision, we could soon be faced with similar claims as to other types of penalty.[38] Moreover, the claim that his sentence rests on the irrelevant factor of race easily could be extended to apply to claims based on unexplained discrepancies that correlate to membership in other minority groups, and even to gender.[40] * * * As these examples illustrate, there is no limiting principle to the type of challenge brought by McCleskey. The Constitution does not require that a State eliminate any demonstrable disparity that correlates with a potentially irrelevant factor in order to operate a criminal justice system that includes capital punishment. * * *

Second, McCleskey's arguments are best presented to the legislative bodies. * * * Legislatures * * * are better qualified to weigh and "evaluate the results of statistical studies in terms of their own local conditions and with a flexibility of approach that is not available to the courts." * * *

JUSTICE BRENNAN, with whom JUSTICE MARSHALL, * * * JUSTICE BLACKMUN and JUSTICE STEVENS join * * *, * * * dissenting. * * *

At some point in this case, Warren McCleskey doubtless asked his lawyer whether a jury was likely to sentence him to die. A candid reply to this question would have been disturbing. First, counsel would have to tell McCleskey that few of the details of the crime or of McCleskey's past criminal conduct were more important than the fact that his victim was white. Furthermore, counsel would feel bound to tell McCleskey that defendants charged with killing white victims in Georgia are 4.3 times as likely to be sentenced to death as defendants charged with killing blacks. In addition, frankness would compel the disclosure that it was more likely than not that the race of McCleskey's victim would determine whether he received a death sentence * * *. Finally, the assessment would not be complete without the information that cases involving black defendants and white victims are more likely to result in a death sentence than cases featuring any other racial combination of defendant and victim. The story could be told in a variety of ways, but McCleskey could not fail to grasp its essential narrative line: there was a significant chance that race would play a prominent role in determining if he lived or died.

---

38. Studies already exist that allegedly demonstrate a racial disparity in the length of prison sentences. See, *e.g.*, Spohn, Gruhl, & Welch, The Effect of Race on Sentencing: A Reexamination of an Unsettled Question, 16 Law & Soc.Rev. 71 (1981–1982); Unnever, Frazier, & Henretta, Race Differences in Criminal Sentencing, 21 Sociological Q. 197 (1980).

40. See Chamblin, The Effect of Sex on the Imposition of the Death Penalty (speech given at a symposium of the American Psychological Association, entitled "Extra-legal Attributes Affecting Death Penalty Sentencing," New York City, Sept., 1979); Steffensmeier, Effects of Judge's and Defendant's Sex on the Sentencing of Offenders, 14 Psychology, Journal of Human Behavior, 3 (Aug. 1977).

The Court today holds that Warren McCleskey's sentence was constitutionally imposed. It finds no fault in a system in which lawyers must tell their clients that race casts a large shadow on the capital sentencing process. * * * The Court's evaluation of the significance of petitioner's evidence is fundamentally at odds with our consistent concern for rationality in capital sentencing * * *.

Considering the race of a defendant or victim in deciding if the death penalty should be imposed is completely at odds with [the] concern that an individual be evaluated as a unique human being. Decisions influenced by race rest in part on a categorical assessment of the worth of human beings according to color, insensitive to whatever qualities the individuals in question may possess. Enhanced willingness to impose the death sentence on black defendants, or diminished willingness to render such a sentence when blacks are victims, reflects a devaluation of the lives of black persons. When confronted with evidence that race more likely than not plays such a role in a capital sentencing system, it is plainly insufficient to say that the importance of discretion demands that the risk be higher before we will act—for in such a case the very end that discretion is designed to serve is being undermined. * * *

In fairness, the Court's fear that McCleskey's claim is an invitation to descend a slippery slope also rests on the realization that any humanly imposed system of penalties will exhibit some imperfection. Yet to reject McCleskey's powerful evidence on this basis is to ignore both the qualitatively different character of the death penalty and the particular repugnance of racial discrimination, considerations which may properly be taken into account in determining whether various punishments are "cruel and unusual." Furthermore, it fails to take account of the unprecedented refinement and strength of the Baldus study. * * *

Notes and Questions

1. Warren McCleskey was executed on September 26, 1991. Making eye contact with witnesses to his execution, McCleskey, who reportedly experienced a religious conversion in prison, stated that he was "deeply sorry for the lives that have been altered * * * because of my ignorance and stupidity." Mark Curriden, *McCleskey Put to Death After Hours of Delays, Final Apology,* Atlanta Journal and Constitution, Sept. 26, 1991, at D3.

2. Does the Baldus study suggest that persons undeserving of death are sentenced to die due to racial discrimination, or that persons deserving to die escape punishment due to racism, or both? Does this difference matter?

3. The issues raised by *McCleskey* are considered in Samuel R. Gross & Robert Mauro, *Patterns of Death: An Analysis of Racial Disparities in Capital Sentencing and Homicide Victimization,* 37 Stan.L.Rev. 27 (1984); Randall Kennedy, *McCleskey v. Kemp: Race, Capital Punishment, and the Supreme Court,* 101 Harv.L.Rev. 1388 (1988); Ronald J. Tabak, *Is Racism Irrelevant? Or Should The Fairness in Death Sentencing Act be Enacted to Substantially Diminish Racial Discrimination in Capital Sentencing?,* 18 N.Y.U.Rev.L. & Soc.Change 777 (1991).

b. Victim Impact Evidence

PAYNE v. TENNESSEE

Supreme Court of the United States, 1991.
501 U.S. ___, 111 S.Ct. 2597, 115 L.Ed.2d 720.

REHNQUIST, C.J. delivered the opinion of the court, in which WHITE, O'CONNOR, SCALIA, KENNEDY, and SOUTER, JJ. joined. * * *

In this case we reconsider our holdings in *Booth v. Maryland,* 482 U.S. 496, 107 S.Ct. 2529, 96 L.Ed.2d 440 (1987), and *South Carolina v. Gathers,* 490 U.S. 805, 109 S.Ct. 2207, 104 L.Ed.2d 876 (1989), that the Eighth Amendment bars the admission of victim impact evidence during the penalty phase of a capital trial.

The petitioner, Pervis Tyrone Payne, was convicted by a jury on two counts of first-degree murder and one count of assault with intent to commit murder in the first degree. He was sentenced to death for each of the murders, and to 30 years in prison for the assault.

The victims of Payne's offenses were 28–year–old Charisse Christopher, her 2–year–old daughter Lacie, and her 3–year–old son Nicholas. The three lived together in an apartment in Millington, Tennessee, across the hall from Payne's girlfriend, Bobbie Thomas. On Saturday, June 27, 1987, Payne * * * passed the morning and early afternoon injecting cocaine and drinking beer. * * * Sometime around 3 p.m., Payne * * * entered the Christophers' apartment, and began making sexual advances towards Charisse. Charisse resisted and Payne became violent. A neighbor who resided in the apartment directly beneath the Christophers * * * called the police after she heard a "blood curdling scream" from the Christopher apartment.

When the first police officer arrived at the scene, he immediately encountered Payne who was leaving the apartment building, so covered with blood that he appeared to be " 'sweating blood.' " * * *

Inside the apartment, the police encountered a horrifying scene. Blood covered the walls and floor throughout the unit. Charisse and her children were lying on the floor in the kitchen. Nicholas, despite several wounds inflicted by a butcher knife that completely penetrated through his body from front to back, was still breathing. Miraculously, he survived, but not until after undergoing seven hours of surgery and a transfusion of 1700 cc's of blood—400 to 500 cc's more than his estimated normal blood volume. Charisse and Lacie were dead.

Charisse's body was found on the kitchen floor on her back, her legs fully extended. She had sustained 42 direct knife wounds and 42 defensive wounds on her arms and hands. The wounds were caused by 41 separate thrusts of a butcher knife. None of the 84 wounds inflicted by Payne were individually fatal; rather, the cause of death was most likely bleeding from all of the wounds. * * *

During the sentencing phase of the trial, Payne presented the testimony of four witnesses: his mother and father, Bobbie Thomas, and * * * a clinical psychologist * * *. [Thomas and Payne's relatives testified that he attended church and was a person of good character. The psychologist testified that Payne scored low on an intelligence test and was "mentally handicapped."]

The State presented the testimony of Charisse's mother, Mary Zvolanek. When asked how Nicholas had been affected by the murders of his mother and sister, she responded:

> "He cries for his mom. He doesn't seem to understand why she doesn't come home. And he cries for his sister Lacie. He comes to me many times during the week and asks me, Grandmama, do you miss my Lacie. And I tell him yes. He says, I'm worried about my Lacie."

In arguing for the death penalty during closing argument, the prosecutor commented on the continuing effects of Nicholas' experience, stating:

> "But we do know that Nicholas was alive. And Nicholas was in the same room. Nicholas was still conscious. His eyes were open. He responded to the paramedics. He was able to follow their directions. He was able to hold his intestines in as he was carried to the ambulance. So he knew what happened to his mother and baby sister."

> "There is nothing you can do to ease the pain of any of the families involved in this case. There is nothing you can do to ease the pain of Bernice or Carl Payne, and that's a tragedy. * * * There is obviously nothing you can do for Charisse and Lacie Jo. But there is something that you can do for Nicholas.

> "Somewhere down the road Nicholas is going to grow up, hopefully. He's going to want to know what happened. And he is going to know what happened to his baby sister and his mother. He is going to want to know what type of justice was done. He is going to want to know what happened. With your verdict, you will provide the answer." * * *

The jury sentenced Payne to death on each of the murder counts. * * *

We granted certiorari, to reconsider our holdings in *Booth* and *Gathers* that the Eighth Amendment prohibits a capital sentencing jury from considering "victim impact" evidence relating to the personal characteristics of the victim and the emotional impact of the crimes on the victim's family.

In *Booth,* the defendant robbed and murdered an elderly couple. As required by a state statute, a victim impact statement was prepared based on interviews with the victims' son, daughter, son-in-law, and granddaughter. The statement, which described the personal characteristics of the victims, the emotional impact of the crimes on the family, and set forth the family members' opinions and characterizations of the crimes and the defendant, was submitted to the jury at sentencing. The jury imposed the death penalty. * * *

This Court held by a 5–to–4 vote that the Eighth Amendment prohibits a jury from considering a victim impact statement at the sentencing phase of a capital trial. The Court made clear that the admissibility of victim impact evidence was not to be determined on a case-by-case basis, but that such evidence was *per se* inadmissible in the sentencing phase of a capital case except to the extent that it "related directly to the circumstances of the crime." In *Gathers,* decided two years later, the Court extended the rule announced in *Booth* to statements made by a prosecutor to the sentencing jury regarding the personal qualities of the victim.

The *Booth* Court began its analysis with the observation that the capital defendant must be treated as a "uniquely individual human bein[g]," and therefore the Constitution requires the jury to make an individualized determination as to whether the defendant should be executed based on the "character of the individual and the circumstances of the crime." The Court concluded that while no prior decision of this Court had mandated that only the defendant's character and immediate characteristics of the crime may constitutionally be considered, other factors are irrelevant to the capital sentencing decision unless they have "some bearing on the defendant's 'personal responsibility and moral guilt.'" To the extent that victim impact evidence presents "factors about which the defendant was unaware, and that were irrelevant to the decision to kill," the Court concluded, it has nothing to do with the "blameworthiness of a particular defendant." Evidence of the victim's character, the Court observed, "could well distract the sentencing jury from its constitutionally required task [of] determining whether the death penalty is appropriate in light of the background and record of the accused and the particular circumstances of the crime." The Court concluded that, except to the extent that victim impact evidence relates "directly to the circumstances of the crime," the prosecution may not introduce such evidence at a capital sentencing hearing because "it creates an impermissible risk that the capital sentencing decision will be made in an arbitrary manner."

Booth and *Gathers* were based on two premises: that evidence relating to a particular victim or to the harm that a capital defendant causes a victim's family do not in general reflect on the defendant's "blameworthiness," and that only evidence relating to "blameworthiness" is relevant to the capital sentencing decision. However, the assessment of harm caused by the defendant as a result of the crime charged has understandably been an important concern of the criminal law, both in determining the elements of the offense and in determining the appropriate punishment. Thus, two equally blameworthy criminal defendants may be guilty of different offenses solely because their acts cause differing amounts of harm. "If a bank robber aims his gun at a guard, pulls the trigger, and kills his target, he may be put to death. If the gun unexpectedly misfires, he may not. His moral guilt in both cases is identical, but his responsibility in the former is greater." *Booth*, 482 U.S., at 519, 107 S.Ct., at 2541 (Scalia, J., dissenting).   * * *

Wherever judges in recent years have had discretion to impose sentence, the consideration of the harm caused by the crime has been an important factor in the exercise of that discretion * * *.   * * *

Payne echoes the concern voiced in *Booth*'s case that the admission of victim impact evidence permits a jury to find that defendants whose victims were assets to their community are more deserving of punishment that those whose victims are perceived to be less worthy. As a general matter, however, victim impact evidence is not offered to encourage comparative judgments of this kind—for instance, that the killer of a hardworking, devoted parent deserves the death penalty, but that the murderer of a reprobate does not. It is designed to show instead *each* victim's "uniqueness as an individual human being," whatever the jury might think the loss to the community resulting from his death might be. The facts of *Gathers* are an excellent illustration of this: the evidence showed that the victim was an out of work, mentally handicapped individual, perhaps not, in the eyes of most, a significant contributor to society, but nonetheless a murdered human being.   * * *

We are now of the view that a State may properly conclude that for the jury to assess meaningfully the defendant's moral culpability and blameworthiness, it should have before it at the sentencing phase evidence of the specific harm caused by the defendant. "[T]he State has a legitimate interest in counteracting the mitigating evidence which the defendant is entitled to put in, by reminding the sentencer that just as the murderer should be considered as an individual, so too the victim is an individual whose death represents a unique loss to society and in particular to his family." *Booth*, 482 U.S., at 517, 107 S.Ct., at 2540 (White, J., dissenting). By turning the victim into a "faceless stranger at the penalty phase of a capital trial," *Booth* deprives the State of the full moral force of its evidence and may prevent the jury from having before it all the information necessary to determine the proper punishment for a first-degree murder.   * * *

We thus hold that if the State chooses to permit the admission of victim impact evidence and prosecutorial argument on that subject, the Eighth Amendment erects no *per se* bar. A State may legitimately conclude that evidence about the victim and about the impact of the murder on the victim's family is relevant to the jury's decision as to whether or not the death penalty should be imposed. There is no reason to treat such evidence differently than other relevant evidence is treated. * * *

JUSTICE SOUTER, with whom JUSTICE KENNEDY joins, concurring. * * *

* * * Murder has foreseeable consequences. When it happens, it is always to distinct individuals, and after it happens other victims are left behind. Every defendant knows, if endowed with the mental competence for criminal responsibility, that the life he will take by his

homicidal behavior is that of a unique person, like himself, and that the person to be killed probably has close associates, "survivors," who will suffer harms and deprivations from the victim's death.   Just as defendants know that they are not faceless human ciphers, they know that their victims are not valueless fungibles, and just as defendants appreciate the web of relationships and dependencies in which they live, they know that their victims are not human islands, but individuals with parents or children, spouses or friends or dependents.   Thus, when a defendant chooses to kill, or to raise the risk of a victim's death, this choice necessarily relates to a whole human being and threatens an association of others, who may be distinctly hurt.   The fact that the defendant may not know the details of a victim's life and characteristics, or the exact identities and needs of those who may survive, should not in any way obscure the further facts that death is always to a "unique" individual, and harm to some group of survivors is a consequence of a successful homicidal act so foreseeable as to be virtually inevitable.

That foreseeability of the killing's consequences imbues them with direct moral relevance, and evidence of the specific harm caused when a homicidal risk is realized is nothing more than evidence of the risk that the defendant originally chose to run despite the kinds of consequences that were obviously foreseeable.   It is morally both defensible and appropriate to consider such evidence when penalizing a murderer, like other criminals, in light of common knowledge and the moral responsibility that such knowledge entails.   * * *

JUSTICE MARSHALL, with whom JUSTICE BLACKMUN joins, dissenting.

Power, not reason, is the new currency of this Court's decisionmaking.   Four Terms ago, a five-Justice majority of this Court held that "victim impact" evidence of the type at issue in this case could not constitutionally be introduced during the penalty phase of a capital trial. *Booth v. Maryland,* [supra].   By another 5–4 vote, a majority of this Court rebuffed an attack upon this ruling just two Terms ago.   *South Carolina v. Gathers,* [supra].   Nevertheless, today's majority overrules *Booth* and *Gathers* and credits the dissenting views expressed in those cases.   Neither the law nor the facts supporting *Booth* and *Gathers* underwent any change in the last four years.   Only the personnel of this Court did.   * * *

JUSTICE STEVENS, with whom JUSTICE BLACKMUN joins, dissenting.

* * * Justice Marshall is properly concerned about the majority's trivialization of the doctrine of *stare decisis*.   But even if *Booth* and *Gathers* had not been decided, today's decision would represent a sharp break with past decisions.   Our cases provide no support whatsoever for the majority's conclusion that the prosecutor may introduce evidence that sheds no light on the defendant's guilt or moral culpability, and thus serves no purpose other than to encourage jurors to decide in favor of death rather than life on the basis of their emotions rather than their reason.   * * *

* * * Evidence that serves no purpose other than to appeal to the sympathies or emotions of the jurors has never been considered admissible. Thus, if a defendant, who had murdered a convenience store clerk in cold blood in the course of an armed robbery, offered evidence unknown to him at the time of the crime about the immoral character of his victim, all would recognize immediately that the evidence was irrelevant and inadmissible. Evenhanded justice requires that the same constraint be imposed on the advocate of the death penalty. * * *

* * * [In] *Lockett v. Ohio,* 438 U.S. 586, 98 S.Ct. 2945, 57 L.Ed.2d 973 (1978), * * * Chief Justice Burger concluded that in a capital case, the sentencer must not be prevented "from considering, as a mitigating factor, any aspect of a defendant's character or record and any of the circumstances of the offense that the defendant proffers as a basis for a sentence less than death." * * *

Today's majority has obviously been moved by an argument that has strong political appeal but no proper place in a reasoned judicial opinion. Because our decision in *Lockett* recognizes the defendant's right to introduce all mitigating evidence that may inform the jury about his character, the Court suggests that fairness requires that the State be allowed to respond with similar evidence about the *victim.* This argument is a classic *non sequitur:* The victim is not on trial; her character, whether good or bad, cannot therefore constitute either an aggravating or mitigating circumstance. * * *

The premise that a criminal prosecution requires an even-handed balance between the State and the defendant is also incorrect. The Constitution grants certain rights to the criminal defendant and imposes special limitations on the State designed to protect the individual from overreaching by the disproportionately powerful State. * * *

The majority attempts to justify the admission of victim impact evidence by arguing that "consideration of the harm caused by the crime has been an important factor in the exercise of [sentencing] discretion." This statement is misleading and inaccurate. It is misleading because it is not limited to harm that is foreseeable. It is inaccurate because it fails to differentiate between legislative determinations and judicial sentencing. It is true that an evaluation of the harm caused by different kinds of wrongful conduct is a critical aspect in legislative definitions of offenses and determinations concerning sentencing guidelines. * * * But the majority cites no authority for the suggestion that unforeseeable and indirect harms to a victim's family are properly considered as aggravating evidence on a case-by-case basis. * * *

The notion that the inability to produce an ideal system of justice in which every punishment is precisely married to the defendant's blameworthiness somehow justifies a rule that completely divorces some capital sentencing determinations from moral culpability is incomprehensible to me. Also incomprehensible is the argument that such a rule is required for the jury to take into account that each murder victim is a "unique" human being. The fact that each of us is unique is a proposition so obvious that it surely requires no evidentiary support. What is not obvious, however, is the way in which the character or reputation in one case may differ from that of other possible victims. Evidence offered to prove such differences can only be intended to identify some victims as more worthy of protection than others. Such proof risks decisions based on the same invidious motives as a prosecutor's decision to seek the death penalty if a victim is white but to accept a plea bargain if the victim is black.

Given the current popularity of capital punishment in a crime-ridden society, the political appeal of arguments that assume that increasing the severity of sentences is the best cure for the cancer of crime, and the political strength of the "victims' rights" movement, I recognize that today's decision will be greeted with enthusiasm by a large number of concerned and thoughtful citizens. The great tragedy of the decision, however, is the danger that the "hydraulic pressure" of public opinion that Justice Holmes once described—and that properly influences the deliberations of democratic legislatures—has played a role * * * in the Court's * * * resolution of the constitutional issue involved. Today is a sad day for a great institution.

Notes and Questions

1. Suppose that a victim of a murder has fourteen school-aged children? Is that foreseeable? If not, is victim impact evidence admissible regarding the loss felt by each of the children?

2. Do emotions have a legitimate role to play in capital sentencing hearings? To the extent that conceptions of deserved punishment are at issue, should feelings such as compassion for the defendant and, under *Payne,* compassion for the victim, count for anything? What about moral outrage at the criminal? Samuel H. Pillsbury, *Emotional Justice: Moralizing the Passions of Criminal Punishment,* 74 Cornell L.Rev. 655, 710 (1989), believes that the deliberative process in death penalty cases should not be wholly rationalistic:

> The language of law is the language of rationality, of the cool and the deliberative. While this insistence upon rationalistic expression has general merit in the elucidation of critical issues, in some instances it obscures more than it reveals. Where, as in criminal punishment, the influence of emotions is too fundamental to ignore or entirely condemn, the law's vocabulary requires expansion to permit emotive discourse. * * * The heart has its reasons, which reason knows not.

According to Professor Pillsbury, judges should instruct jurors on the proper role of emotions, so as to minimize the risk of "moral error." Judges should tell jurors that there is "nothing wrong" with feelings of anger regarding murder, but that "anger can overwhelm proper judgment." He proposes that, in determining what sentence to recommend or impose, jurors be told to consider the defendant, and also the victim, "as you might a neighbor * * * or social acquaintance, someone that you know and care about." Id. at 704. Jurors should also be told "of their obligation to try to empathize with the offender as part of assessing deserved punishment." Id.

at 703. Do you believe that these instructions are helpful? Should jurors be told to empathize with the victims, or will they do that anyway?

3. SUBSTANTIVE LIMITATIONS ON THE DEATH PENALTY

TISON v. ARIZONA

Supreme Court of the United States, 1987.
481 U.S. 137, 107 S.Ct. 1676, 95 L.Ed.2d 127.

O'CONNOR, J., delivered the opinion of the Court, in which REHNQUIST, C.J., and WHITE, POWELL, and SCALIA, JJ., joined. * * *

The question presented is whether the petitioners' participation in the events leading up to and following the murder of four members of a family makes the sentences of death imposed by the Arizona courts constitutionally permissible although neither petitioner specifically intended to kill the victims and neither inflicted the fatal gunshot wounds.
* * *

I

Gary Tison was sentenced to life imprisonment as the result of a prison escape during the course of which he had killed a guard. After he had been in prison a number of years, Gary Tison's wife, their three sons Donald, Ricky, and Raymond, Gary's brother Joseph, and other relatives made plans to help Gary Tison escape again. The Tison family assembled a large arsenal of weapons for this purpose. Plans for escape were discussed with Gary Tison, who insisted that his cellmate, Randy Greenawalt, also a convicted murderer, be included in the prison break. * * *

On July 30, 1978, the three Tison brothers entered the Arizona State Prison at Florence carrying a large ice chest filled with guns. The Tisons armed Greenawalt and their father, and the group, brandishing their weapons, locked the prison guards and visitors present in a storage closet. The five men fled the prison grounds in the Tison's Ford Galaxy automobile. No shots were fired at the prison.

After leaving the prison, the men abandoned the Ford automobile and proceeded on to an isolated house in a white Lincoln automobile that the brothers had parked at a hospital near the prison. At the house, the Lincoln automobile had a flat tire * * *. The group decided to flag down a passing motorist and steal a car. Raymond stood out in front of the Lincoln; the other four armed themselves and lay in wait by the side of the road. One car passed by without stopping, but a second car, a Mazda occupied by John Lyons, his wife Donnelda, his 2–year–old son Christopher, and his 15–year–old niece, Theresa Tyson, pulled over to render aid.

[Shortly thereafter, Gary Tison and Greenawalt intentionally shot to death the Lyonses and Tyson. Ricky and Raymond Tison, the petitioners, were some distance away, filling a water jug, when the shootings occurred. They expressed surprise at the killings.]

The State then individually tried each of the petitioners for capital murder of the four victims as well as for the associated crimes of armed robbery, kidnaping, and car theft. The capital murder charges were based on Arizona felony-murder law providing that a killing occurring during the perpetration of robbery or kidnaping is capital murder, and that each participant in the kidnaping or robbery is legally responsible for the acts of his accomplices. Each of the petitioners was convicted of the four murders under these accomplice liability and felony-murder statutes. * * *

* * * [T]he judge sentenced both petitioners to death.

On direct appeal, the Arizona Supreme Court affirmed. The Court found:

> "The record establishes that both Ricky and Raymond Tison were present when the homicides took place and that they occurred as part of and in the course of the escape and continuous attempt to prevent recapture. The deaths would not have occurred but for their assistance. That they did not specifically intend that the Lyonses and Theresa Tyson die, that they did not plot in advance that these homicides would take place, or that they did not actually pull the triggers on the guns which inflicted the fatal wounds is of little significance." * * *

* * * We granted certiorari in order to consider the Arizona Supreme Court's application of *Enmund* [*v. Florida*, 458 U.S. 782, 102 S.Ct. 3368, 73 L.Ed.2d 1140 (1982)].

II

In *Enmund v. Florida*, this Court reversed the death sentence of a defendant convicted under Florida's felony-murder rule. Enmund was the driver of the "getaway" car in an armed robbery of a dwelling. The occupants of the house, an elderly couple, resisted and Enmund's accomplices killed them. * * *

This Court, citing the weight of legislative and community opinion, found a broad societal consensus, with which it agreed, that the death penalty was disproportional to the crime of robbery-felony murder "in these circumstances." The Court noted that although 32 American jurisdictions permitted the imposition of the death penalty for felony murders under a variety of circumstances, Florida was 1 of only 8 jurisdictions that authorized the death penalty "solely for participation in a robbery in which another robber takes life." Enmund was, therefore, sentenced under a distinct minority regime, a regime that permitted the imposition of the death penalty for felony murder *simpliciter*. * * *

After surveying the States' felony-murder statutes, the *Enmund* Court next examined the behavior of juries in cases like Enmund's in its attempt to assess American attitudes toward capital punishment in felony-murder cases. * * * The Court found the fact that only 3 of 739 death row inmates had been sentenced to death absent an intent to kill, physical presence, or direct participation in the fatal assault persuasive evidence that American juries considered the death sentence disproportional to felony murder *simpliciter.*

Against this background, the Court undertook its own proportionality analysis. Armed robbery is a serious offense, but one for which the penalty of death is plainly excessive * * *. Furthermore, the Court found that Enmund's degree of participation in *the murders* was so tangential that it could not be said to justify a sentence of death. It found that neither the deterrent nor the retributive purposes of the death penalty were advanced by imposing the death penalty upon Enmund. The *Enmund* Court was unconvinced "that the threat that the death penalty will be imposed for murder will measurably deter one who does not kill and has no intention or purpose that life will be taken." In reaching this conclusion, the Court relied upon the fact that killing only rarely occurred during the course of robberies, and such killing as did occur even more rarely resulted in death sentences if the evidence did not support an inference that the defendant intended to kill. The Court acknowledged, however, that "[i]t would be very different if the likelihood of a killing in the course of a robbery were so substantial that one should share the blame for the killing if he somehow participated in the felony."

That difference was also related to the second purpose of capital punishment, retribution. The heart of the retribution rationale is that a criminal sentence must be directly related to the personal culpability of the criminal offender. * * * Thus, in Enmund's case, "the focus [had to] be on *his* culpability, not on that of those who committed the robbery and shot the victims, for we insist on 'individualized consideration as a constitutional requirement in imposing the death sentence.'" Since Enmund's own participation in the felony murder was so attenuated and since there was no proof that Enmund had any culpable mental state, the death penalty was excessive retribution for his crimes. * * *

Petitioners [here] argue strenuously that they did not "intend to kill" as that concept has been generally understood in the common law. We accept this as true. Traditionally, "one intends certain consequences when he desires that his acts cause those consequences or knows that those consequences are substantially certain to result from his acts." As petitioners point out, there is no evidence that either Ricky or Raymond Tison took any act which he desired to, or was substantially certain would, cause death. * * *

* * * [Therefore,] [p]etitioners do not fall within the "intent to kill" category of felony murderers for which *Enmund* explicitly finds the death penalty permissible under the Eighth Amendment.

On the other hand, it is equally clear that petitioners also fall outside the category of felony murderers for whom *Enmund* explicitly held the death penalty disproportional: their degree of participation in the crimes was major rather than minor, and the record would support a finding of the culpable mental state of reckless indifference to human life. * * *

Raymond Tison brought an arsenal of lethal weapons into the Arizona State Prison which he then handed over to two convicted murderers, one of whom he knew had killed a prison guard in the course of a previous escape attempt. By his own admission he was prepared to kill in furtherance of the prison break. He performed the crucial role of flagging down a passing car occupied by an innocent family whose fate was then entrusted to the known killers he had previously armed. He robbed these people at their direction and then guarded the victims at gunpoint while they considered what next to do. He stood by and watched the killing, making no effort to assist the victims before, during, or after the shooting. Instead, he chose to assist the killers in their continuing criminal endeavors, ending in a gun battle with the police in the final showdown.

Ricky Tison's behavior differs in slight details only. * * *

These facts not only indicate that the Tison brothers' participation in the crime was anything but minor; they also would clearly support a finding that they both subjectively appreciated that their acts were likely to result in the taking of innocent life. The issue raised by this case is whether the Eighth Amendment prohibits the death penalty in the intermediate case of the defendant whose participation is major and whose mental state is one of reckless indifference to the value of human life. *Enmund* does not specifically address this point. * * *

A critical facet of the individualized determination of culpability required in capital cases is the mental state with which the defendant commits the crime. Deeply ingrained in our legal tradition is the idea that the more purposeful is the criminal conduct, the more serious is the offense, and, therefore, the more severely it ought to be punished. The ancient concept of malice aforethought was an early attempt to focus on mental state in order to distinguish those who deserved death from those who through "Benefit of ... Clergy" would be spared. * * * In *Enmund v. Florida,* the Court recognized again the importance of mental state, explicitly permitting the death penalty in at least those cases where the felony murderer intended to kill and forbidding it in the case of a minor actor not shown to have had any culpable mental state.

A narrow focus on the question of whether or not a given defendant "intended to kill," however, is a highly unsatisfactory means of definitively distinguishing the most culpable and dangerous of murderers. Many who intend to, and do, kill are not criminally liable at all—those who act in self-defense or with other justification or excuse. Other intentional homicides, though criminal, are often felt undeserving of the death penalty—those that are the result of provocation. On the other hand, some nonintentional murderers may be among the most dangerous and inhumane of all—the person who tortures another not caring whether the victim lives or dies, or the robber who shoots someone in the course of the robbery, utterly indifferent to the fact that the desire to rob may have the unintended consequence of killing the victim as well as taking the victim's property. This reckless indifference to the value of human life may be every bit as shocking to the moral sense as an "intent to kill." Indeed it is for this very reason that the common law and modern criminal codes alike have classified behavior such as occurred in this case along with intentional murders. * * * [W]e hold that the reckless disregard for human life implicit in knowingly engaging in criminal activities known to carry a grave risk of death represents a highly culpable mental state, a mental state that may be taken into account in making a capital sentencing judgment when that conduct causes its natural, though also not inevitable, lethal result.

The petitioners' own personal involvement in the crimes was not minor, but rather, as specifically found by the trial court, "substantial." Far from merely sitting in a car away from the actual scene of the murders acting as the getaway driver to a robbery, each petitioner was actively involved in every element of the kidnaping-robbery and was physically present during the entire sequence of criminal activity culminating in the murder of the Lyons family and the subsequent flight. The Tisons' high level of participation in these crimes further implicates them in the resulting deaths. * * *

* * * We will not attempt to precisely delineate the particular types of conduct and states of mind warranting imposition of the death penalty here. Rather, we simply hold that major participation in the felony committed, combined with reckless indifference to human life, is sufficient to satisfy the *Enmund* culpability requirement. * * *

JUSTICE BRENNAN, with whom JUSTICE MARSHALL * * *, JUSTICE BLACKMUN and JUSTICE STEVENS join * * * dissenting. * * *

Under the felony-murder doctrine, a person who commits a felony is liable for *any* murder that occurs during the commission of that felony, regardless of whether he or she commits, attempts to commit, or intended to commit that murder. The doctrine thus imposes liability on felons for killings committed by cofelons during a felony. This curious doctrine is a living fossil from a legal era in which all felonies were punishable by death; in those circumstances, the state of mind of the felon with respect to the murder was understandably superfluous, because he or she could be executed simply for intentionally committing the felony. Today, in most American jurisdictions and in virtually all European and Commonwealth countries, a felon cannot be executed for a murder that he or she did not commit or specifically intend or attempt to commit. In some American jurisdictions, however, the authority to impose death in such circumstances still persists. Arizona is such a jurisdiction. * * *

One reason the Court offers for its conclusion that death is proportionate punishment for persons falling within * * * [the recklessness] category is that limiting the death penalty to those who intend to kill "is a highly unsatisfactory means of definitively distinguishing the most culpable and dangerous of murderers." To illustrate that intention cannot be dispositive, the Court offers as examples "the person _who tortures_ another not caring whether the victim lives or dies, or the robber _who shoots_ someone in the course of the robbery, utterly indifferent to the fact that the desire to rob may have the unintended consequence of killing the victim as well as taking the victim's property." Influential commentators and some States have approved the use of the death penalty for persons, like those given in the Court's examples, _who kill_ others in circumstances manifesting an extreme indifference to the value of human life. * * * But the constitutionality of the death penalty for those individuals is no more relevant to this case than it was to _Enmund,_ because this case, like _Enmund,_ involves accomplices _who did not kill._ Thus, although some of the "most culpable and dangerous of murderers" may be those who killed without specifically intending to kill, it is considerably more difficult to apply that rubric convincingly to those who not only did not intend to kill, but who also have not killed.

It is precisely in this context—where the defendant has not killed—that a finding that he or she nevertheless intended to kill seems indispensable to establishing capital culpability. It is important first to note that such a defendant has not committed an _act_ for which he or she could be sentenced to death. The applicability of the death penalty therefore turns entirely on the defendant's mental state with regard to an act committed by another. Factors such as the defendant's major participation in the events surrounding the killing or the defendant's presence at the scene are relevant insofar as they illuminate the defendant's mental state with regard to the killings. They cannot serve, however, as independent grounds for imposing the death penalty.

Second, when evaluating such a defendant's mental state, a determination that the defendant acted with intent is qualitatively different from a determination that the defendant acted with reckless indifference to human life. The difference lies in the nature of the choice each has made. The reckless actor has not _chosen_ to bring about the killing in the way the intentional actor has. The person who chooses to act recklessly and is indifferent to the possibility of fatal consequences often deserves serious punishment. But because that person has not chosen to kill, his or her moral and criminal culpability is of a different degree than that of one who killed or intended to kill.

The importance of distinguishing between these different choices is rooted in our belief in the "freedom of the human will and a consequent ability and duty of the normal individual to choose between good and evil." _Morissette v. United States,_ 342 U.S. 246, 250, 72 S.Ct. 240, 243, 96 L.Ed. 288 (1952). To be faithful to this belief, which is "universal and persistent in mature systems of law," the criminal law must ensure that the punishment an individual receives conforms to the choices that individual has made. Differential punishment of reckless and intentional actions is therefore essential if we are to retain "the relation between criminal liability and moral culpability" on which criminal justice depends. The State's ultimate sanction—if it is ever to be used—must be reserved for those whose culpability is greatest. * * *

Notes and Questions

1. Accomplice law (Chapter 11 infra) provides that a person who intentionally assists in the commission of an offense is guilty of that crime, even if the perpetrator would have committed the offense without the accomplice's assistance. An accomplice whose assistance was unnecessary might be termed a "noncausal accessory." Various studies of actual jury behavior in death penalty cases and of mock juries suggest that "community sentiment discriminates between felony-murder triggermen and felony-murder non-causal accessories, with the latter being significantly less likely than the former to get the death penalty." Norman J. Finkel, *Capital Felony–Murder, Objective Indicia, and Community Sentiment,* 32 Ariz.L.Rev. 819, 888 (1990); see also Joshua Dressler, *The Jurisprudence of Death by Another: Accessories and Capital Punishment,* 51 U.Colo.L.Rev. 17 (1979); Norman J. Finkel & Kevin B. Duff, *Felony–Murder and Community Sentiment: Testing the Supreme Court's Assertion,* 15 Law & Hum.Behav. 405 (1991).

Is this community sentiment justifiable? For example, in terms of the death penalty, would you distinguish between the following three persons charged in the death of the victim during a bank robbery: (1) the triggerman in the bank robbery, who personally killed the victim; (2) the person who solicited the robbery, but who was not present during the commission of the robbery or homicide; and (3) the unarmed accomplice to the robbery, whose intentional assistance was limited to opening the door to the bank so that the triggerman could enter?

2. The Supreme Court has held that current standards of decency bar the execution of murderers who were under the age of 16 at the time of the homicide. Thompson v. Oklahoma, 487 U.S. 815, 108 S.Ct. 2687, 101 L.Ed.2d 702 (1988) (plurality opinion). However, the execution of a 16–year–old or 17–year–old killer does not constitute cruel and unusual punishment *per se,* although the defendant's age is a factor the sentencer is entitled to consider as a mitigating circumstance. Stanford v. Kentucky, 492 U.S. 361, 109 S.Ct. 2969, 106 L.Ed.2d 306 (1989).

Similarly, although a jury must be permitted to consider a murderer's mental retardation as a mitigating factor, the Eighth Amendment does not bar the execution of all persons with moderate mental deficiency. Penry v. Lynaugh, 492 U.S. 302, 109 S.Ct. 2934, 106 L.Ed.2d 256 (1989). However, the execution of a murderer who has lost his sanity while on Death Row is unconstitutional. (See p. 631 infra.)

Chapter 8

RAPE

A. SOCIAL CONTEXT

U.S. DEPT. OF JUSTICE, BUREAU OF JUSTICE
STATISTICS—FEMALE VICTIMS OF
VIOLENT CRIME

January 1991, NCJ–126826, 7–12

Rape for the NCS [National Crime Survey] is carnal knowledge through the use of force or the threat of force, including attempts. This definition excludes statutory rape. When a robber attempts to rape or rapes a victim, the offense is classified as a rape. When an offender assaults a woman and rapes or attempts to rape her, the offense is classified as a rape, even if the victim is injured or the offender carried a weapon.

- An estimated 155,000 women were raped each year between 1973 and 1987.

- From 1973 to 1987 there were annually 1.6 rapes per 1,000 women age 12 or older, meaning that 1 out of every 600 women was a rape victim each year.

- Rape and attempted rape are relatively rare crimes compared to robbery and assault, amounting to less than 3% of all violent crime measured by the NCS.

WHEN AND WHERE RAPES OCCURRED

- Almost two-thirds of rapes occurred at night. Completed rapes were more likely than attempted rapes to occur at night particularly between midnight and 6 a.m.

- Most rapes occurred at home. Four in ten completed rapes took place at the victim's home; 2 in 10 occurred at or near a friend's home, and 2 in 10, on the street.

- About 3 in 10 attempted rapes took place at home; 2 in 10 attempted rapes occurred on the street, and about 1 in 10 at a friend's house.

CHARACTERISTICS OF VICTIMS OF COMPLETED OR ATTEMPTED RAPE

• Black women were significantly more likely to be raped than white women, although a larger number of white women than the total of black, American Indian, Aleut, Eskimo, Asian, and Pacific Islander women were raped each year.

• Hispanic and non-Hispanic women were equally likely to be raped.

• Women age 16 to 24 were 3 times more likely to be raped than other women. This age pattern was similar for black and white women.

• Women who were separated or divorced or who had never married were 9 times more likely to be raped than those who were married or widowed.

• Among women of different residential localities, central city residents were the most likely to be raped; those who lived outside the metropolitan area were the least likely.

• Women who rented were more likely than those who owned their own homes to be raped.

• Women who lived in places like dormitories, halfway houses, and boarding houses and those in apartment houses with four or more units were more likely to be raped than were other women.

• Women who lived alone were more likely to be raped than those who lived with others.

• Unemployed women were 3 times more likely to be raped, and students 1½ times more likely, than women overall. Those who were retired or keeping house had the lowest rates of rape.

• About half of all rape victims and almost three-quarters of black rape victims were in the lowest third of the income distribution. Women in the low-income group were the most likely to be raped, and those in the top third, 15% of all victims, were the least likely.

• Black women with low incomes were more likely to be raped than black women with middle or high incomes; they were also more likely to be raped than white women in any income category. Middle-and upper-income women of all races had about the same likelihood of being raped.

REPORTING RAPE TO THE POLICE

• Of all attempted or completed rapes, 53% were reported to the police. Completed rapes and stranger rapes were reported more frequently than attempted rapes and those in which the offender and victim knew each other.

• The presence of a weapon increased the likelihood of the crime being reported to the police. Approximately 7 in 10 rapes were reported when the offender had had a weapon, and fewer than 5 in 10 when the rapist had been unarmed.

- When rape victims themselves reported the crime to the police, the reason they cited most frequently to NCS interviewers was to prevent the rape from happening again. Of the rape victims, 60% mentioned prevention, 47% said they wanted to punish the offender, and 31% said they wanted to stop the incident from happening.
  * * *

- When the police were not informed of a completed rape, victims gave three main reasons to the NCS: They considered the rape to be a private or personal matter or a matter that they wanted to resolve themselves (25%); they feared reprisal by the offender, his family, or friends (23%); and the police would be inefficient, ineffective, or insensitive (23%).

CHARACTERISTICS OF OFFENDERS * * *

- Rapists and their victims were likely to be of the same race. In rapes with one offender, about 7 of every 10 white victims were raped by a white offender, and about 8 of every 10 black victims were raped by a black offender. In rapes with two or more offenders, victims and offenders were of the same race 49% of the time for white victims and 72% of the time for black victims.
  * * *

- Rape is largely a crime of the older offender. In almost three-fourths of all rapes, the offenders were age 21 or older. * * *

- Most offenders were unarmed. A fourth of all rapists showed weapons. A tenth of the victims were unsure whether a weapon was present.

- Weapons were more likely to be present in completed rapes than in rape attempts. About the same percentage of offenders carried knives as carried guns.

- Most rape victims (about 8 in 10) tried to protect themselves. Those using self-protection were less likely to be victims of a completed rape than those not taking a self-protective measure.

- When victims were attacked and were thereby put at risk of injury, victims who tried to protect themselves were more likely to be injured (58%) than were those who took no measure (46%).

- Thirty percent of rape victims were threatened either with a weapon or verbally. About 45% of the victims of rape attempts were threatened; 55% were attacked. By definition, a completed rape is considered an attack.

- Victims of completed rapes were more likely to be injured than victims of rape attempts. Almost 60% of the victims of completed rape were injured: 14% seriously and 44% with minor injuries. These victims were more likely than victims of rape attempts to receive medical care.

- More than half of the victims of a completed rape received medical care for rape or injury; about a tenth of the victims of rape attempts received medical care. About 4 in 10 victims of a completed rape were treated in a hospital or emergency room, compared to fewer than 1 in 10 victims of attempted rape.

COMPARISON OF RAPE BY A NONSTRANGER AND BY A STRANGER

- Nonstranger rape usually occurred in the victim's home (48%) or in or near a friend's home (24%). About 3 in 10 rapes by strangers occurred on the street; about 2 in 10, at the victim's home.

- Offenders were less likely to have a weapon when their victims were known than when they were strangers. Strangers, who were more likely to have a weapon than nonstrangers, were especially more likely to have guns or knives.

- Victims of nonstrangers tried to protect themselves about as often as victims of strangers; that is, they were as likely to threaten, argue with, or try to reason with the offender and to use physical force, hit, chase, or throw objects when they knew their offender as when they did not.

- When rape victims knew their offenders, they were about as likely to be injured as victims of strangers. Just over a quarter of victims received medical care, whether or not the victim knew the offender.

SUSAN ESTRICH—RAPE

95 Yale Law Journal 1087 (1986), 1089–92

* * * The history of rape, as the law has been enforced in this country, is a history of both racism and sexism.[2] One could write an article of this length dealing only with the racism. * * * My focus is sexism.[3]

In recent years, rape has emerged as a topic of increasing research and attention among feminists, in both popular and scholarly journals.

2. The death penalty for rape in this country, now unconstitutional under Coker v. Georgia, 433 U.S. 584 (1977), was traditionally reserved for black men who raped white women. Between 1930 and 1967, 89% of the men executed for rape in this country were black. That figure includes 36% of the black men who were convicted of raping a white woman; only 2% of the defendants convicted of rape involving any other racial combination were executed. Professor Wolfgang, after a systematic analysis of 1,238 rape convictions between 1945 and 1965, concluded that race was the only factor that accounted for the disparities in the imposition of the death penalty. See Wolfgang, *Racial Discrimination in the Death Sentence for Rape,* in Executions in America 110–20 (W. Bowers ed. 1974). Although the death penalty for rape is now prohibited, at least one study has found that black men convicted of raping white women continue to receive the harshest penalties.

3. I am certain that some will say that I have not devoted enough attention to class either. I do not doubt that upper-class women fare better in the system when they are raped by lower-class men. I would suspect that class differences between victim and defendant may be more important than class itself in predicting disposition, although I have not seen any study of rape itself which confirms this. Beyond that, it seems to me that sex and sexism, not class, is far more useful as a focus in understanding the law of rape, certainly in theory but also in practice. Or, as some of my (upper-class male) friends put it to those who occasionally forget: "You may think you have it made, but you're still a woman."

But much of the feminist writing is not focused on an analysis of the *law* of rape, and some that is so focused is not very firmly grounded in the criminal law. At the same time, much of the writing about rape in the more traditional criminal law literature, with the exception of some recent articles (primarily student notes), does little more than mirror the condescension and misunderstanding, if not outright hostility to women, that have made rape a central part of the feminist agenda. * * *

To examine rape within the criminal law tradition is to expose fully the sexism of the law. Much that is striking about the crime of rape—and revealing of the sexism of the system—emerges only when rape is examined relative to other crimes * * *. * * *

The study of rape * * * also raises broader questions about the way conceptions of gender and the different backgrounds and perspectives of men and women should be encompassed within the criminal law. In one of his most celebrated essays, Oliver Wendell Holmes explained that the law does not exist to tell the good man what to do, but to tell the bad man what not to do.[8] Holmes was interested in the distinction between the good and bad man; I cannot help noticing that both are men. Most of the time, a criminal law that reflects male views and male standards imposes its judgment on men who have injured other men. It is "boys' rules" applied to a boys' fight.[9] In rape, the male standard defines a crime committed against women, and male standards are used not only to judge men, but also to judge the conduct of women victims. Moreover, because the crime involves sex itself, the law of rape inevitably treads on the explosive ground of sex roles, of male aggression and female passivity, of our understandings of sexuality—areas where differences between a male and a female perspective may be most pronounced. * * *

In considering [rape], my questions are * * *: How have the limits on the crime of rape been formulated? What do those limits signify? What makes it rape, as opposed to sex? In what ways is rape defined differently from other crimes? What do those differences tell us about the law's attitudes towards women, men, sex, and sexuality?

ROUNDTREE v. UNITED STATES

District of Columbia Court of Appeals, 1990.
581 A.2d 315.

STEADMAN, ASSOCIATE JUDGE: * * * [Opinion deleted.]

SCHWELB, ASSOCIATE JUDGE, concurring in part and dissenting in part:

* * * For many centuries, under a legal tradition established by men, female victims of rape and sexual abuse were treated harshly and

---

8. Holmes, *The Path of the Law,* 10 Harv.L.Rev. 457, 459 (1897).

9. In referring to "male" standards and "boys' rules," I do not mean to suggest that *every* man adheres to them. A "male view"

is nonetheless distinct from a "female view" not only by the gender of most of those who adhere to it, but also by the character of the life experiences and socialization which tend to produce it.

unfairly pursuant to a pervasive double standard of sexual morality. In a revealing passage in the Bible, rape was treated as an offense against an unmarried woman's father rather than against her; the rapist's punishment, besides having to pay fifty shekels to the "owner," was a forced marriage to the victim. *Deuteronomy* 22:28–29. The raped woman was obviously given no choice about becoming the perpetrator's wife. Some two millenia later, Sigmund Freud, the father of psychoanalysis, still viewed the "exclusive right of possession of a woman" as the "essence of monogamy," and the "demand that the girl shall bring with her into marriage with one man no memory of sexual relations with another" as a "logical consequence" of that right.[15] The notion that the world is divided into "bad girls", who do, and "good girls", who don't, was part of a climate of "romantic paternalism" which put women, in Justice Brennan's apt phrase, "not on a pedestal, but in a cage." *Frontiero v. Richardson,* 411 U.S. 677, 684, 93 S.Ct. 1764, 1769, 36 L.Ed.2d 583 (1973) (plurality opinion).[16] Nowhere was this cage more confining and oppressive to women than in relation to the law of sexual crimes.

Until quite recently, the complaining witness in a sexual assault case was presumed to be so lacking in credibility that special rules of corroboration, unheard of in relation to other crimes, were deemed to be necessary and appropriate. A defendant charged with a sexual offense could effectively put his victim on trial, for her entire sexual history and reputation were deemed "fair game" in relation to the issue of consent. The most private facts in a woman's life were thus exposed to the world for all, and especially those of prurient orientation, to see, denounce and deride. Despite their perceived "natural ... timidity and delicacy," women alleging rape were required to put up the "utmost resistance" to their assailants before a guilty verdict would be sustained. * * * Moreover, even if a woman did resist vigorously, this was often treated as evidence that she derived erotic pleasure from being overcome.[18]

That only a small percentage of cases of rape and sexual abuse were reported, and that fewer still resulted in conviction, is hardly surprising in light of the applicable "rules of the game" * * *. In reaction to these palpable injustices, the courts of this jurisdiction, like others elsewhere, took a number of measures to redress the balance. * * *

---

15. 4 S. Freud, Collected Papers 217 (Riviere trans. 1925), *quoted in* S. Estrich, *Rape,* 95 Yale L.J. 1087, 1141 n. 170 (1986).

16. *See, e.g.,* the concurring opinion of Justice Bradley in *Bradwell v. Illinois,* 83 U.S. (16 Wall) 130, 141, 21 L.Ed. 442 (1872), in which the Court sustained a prohibition against the practice of law by women:

> The natural and proper timidity and delicacy which belongs to the female sex evidently unfits it for many of the occupations of civil life ... The paramount destiny and mission of woman are to ful-

fill the noble and benign offices of wife and mother. This is the law of the Creator.

18. "Although a woman may desire sexual intercourse, it is customary for her to say "no, no, no" (although meaning "yes, yes, yes") and to expect the male to be the aggressor." Slovenko, *A Panoramic Overview: Sexual Behavior and the Law* in Sexual Behavior and the Law 5 (Slovenko ed. 1965), quoted in Note, *The Resistance Standard in Rape Legislation,* 18 Stan.L.Rev. 680, 682 (1966).

But the end does not justify the means. Our commitment to eradicating past and present wrongs may not be permitted to dilute our determination that all defendants, including those charged with sexual offenses, receive the fair trial which is their constitutional due. * * *

Notes and Questions

1. Professor Estrich describes rape law as sexist (and racist). Judge Schwelb in *Roundtree* warns against rape reform efforts that might deny an accused defendant his constitutional trial rights. In reading this chapter, consider whether Professor Estrich's accusations and/or Judge Schwelb's concerns are justified.

2. How serious an offense is rape? State laws vary, but forcible rape may carry a maximum sentence of life imprisonment, e.g., Mich.Comp.Laws Ann. § 750.520b (1991), or a substantial term of years, e.g., N.Y.—McKinney's Penal Law § 130.35 (1987) (rape in the first degree) and § 70.02(3)(a) (1982) (sentencing provisions) (imprisonment shall not exceed 25 years, nor be less than 6 years).

Are such penalties appropriate? Nearly all states treat rape as a more serious offense than battery, yet both crimes involve unwanted physical contact, and either crime may be aggravated by the use or display of a deadly weapon or a threat to cause grievous injury or death. Consequently, one scholar maintains that rape should be treated "as a variety of ordinary (simple or aggravated) battery because that is what rape is." Michael Davis, *Setting Penalties: What Does Rape Deserve?*, 3 Law & Phil. 61, 62–63 (1984).

Does this view of rape misstate the underlying harm of the offense? For example, is it true that "[w]hat is wrong with rape is that it is an act of the subordination of women to men"? Catherine MacKinnon, *Feminism, Marxism, Method, and the State: Toward Feminist Jurisprudence*, 8 Signs 635, 652 (1983). If so, should sexual intercourse even be an element of the offense?

3. Should "simple" (nonviolent) rapes be prosecuted at all? One commentator recommends mediation, rather than prosecution, in such circumstances:

> Rape is a frequent and serious occurrence in our society. Most rapes are simple rapes in which the victim and offender were acquainted prior to the rape and in which physical violence was absent. Simple rape causes serious emotional trauma for a victim, resulting in a need to regain self-esteem and control over her life. Shortcomings within the criminal justice system, however, discourage many victims of simple rape from reporting the crime. Even if a victim reports a simple rape, bias against victims of simple rape dramatically reduces the likelihood of a serious police investigation, trial, and conviction. When the criminal justice does deal with a simple rape case, the system fails to allow the parties control over their dispute. In addition, the criminal justice system deals ineffectively with underlying causes for the rape, and thus, fails to educate the parties or reform the offender. Mediation, a process in which the victim and the offender meet with the aid of a neutral third party, avoids the bias of the criminal justice system against the rape

victim. Mediation provides a victim with assistance in overcoming the feelings of powerlessness that resulted from the rape. Mediation also allows the victim and offender to confront each other and to deal with any miscommunication or misinterpretation of behavior that led to the rape. Ultimately, mediation allows an offender to face up to what he has done, while avoiding the stigma of a rape prosecution. Mediation, therefore represents a more effective and more healing solution than the court system to the problem of simple rape in our society. In addition, mediation holds the hope of changing societal causes of rape faster than the criminal justice system by changing individuals one by one.

Deborah Gartzke Goolsby, Comment, *Using Mediation in Cases of Simple Rape,* 47 Wash. & Lee L.Rev. 1183, 1213–14 (1990).

Another view is that a tort action may be a more effective remedy than a criminal prosecution in dealing with nonaggravated rapes. See Nora West, Note, *Rape in the Criminal Law and the Victim's Tort Alternative: A Feminist Analysis,* 50 U. Toronto Fac.L.Rev. 96 (1992). By suing, the rape victim is empowered vis-a-vis the attacker by personally "prosecuting" the offense. She retains greater control over the issues and proceedings than would be possible in a criminal action, because in the latter circumstance the prosecutor determines what charges to bring and may participate in plea bargaining with the defense, against the victim's wishes. With the lesser standard of proof in a civil action, as well, the plaintiff is better positioned than a public prosecutor to obtain redress, and the civil remedy of money damages may be a more satisfactory outcome for the victim of acquaintance rape than the imprisonment of the attacker.

B. ACTUS REUS

1. FORCIBLE RAPE

Rape is "the carnal knowledge of a woman forcibly and against her will." 4 Blackstone, Commentaries on the Law of England * 210 (1769).

a. *General Principles*

RUSK v. STATE

Court of Special Appeals of Maryland, 1979.
43 Md.App. 476, 406 A.2d 624.

THOMPSON, JUDGE.

We are called upon to review the sufficiency of the evidence to convict for rape. Whatever the law may have been before, it is now clear that our standard must be: Is the evidence sufficient for a finder of fact to conclude that the accused was guilty beyond a reasonable doubt? We hold that the evidence was not sufficient. In making this review we must look at the evidence in the light most favorable to the prosecution.

Edward Salvatore Rusk, the appellant, was convicted * * * of rape in the second degree and of assault. * * * The appellant does not challenge the conviction for assault * * *.

The prosecutrix was a twenty-one year old mother of a two-year-old son. She was separated from her husband but not yet divorced. Leaving her son with her mother, she attended a high school reunion after which she and a female friend, Terry, went bar hopping in the Fells Point area of Baltimore. They drove in separate cars. At the third bar the prosecutrix met appellant. * * * They had a five or ten minute conversation in the bar; at the end of which the prosecutrix said she was ready to leave. Appellant requested a ride home and she agreed. When they arrived at appellant's home, the prosecutrix parked at the curb on the side of the street opposite his rooming house but did not turn off the ignition. She put the car in park and appellant asked her to come up to his apartment. She refused. He continued to ask her to come up, and she testified she then became afraid. While trying to convince him that she didn't want to go to his apartment she mentioned that she was separated and if she did, it might cause her marital problems particularly if she were being followed by a detective. The appellant then took the keys out of the car and walked over to her side of the car, opened the door and said, "Now will you come up?" The prosecutrix then told him she would. She stated:

> "At that point, because I was scared, because he had my car keys. I didn't know what to do. I was someplace I didn't even know where I was. It was in the city. I didn't know whether to run. I really didn't think, at that point, what to do. Now, I know that I should have blown the horn. I should have run. There were a million things I could have done. I was scared, at that point, and I didn't do any of them."

The prosecutrix followed appellant into the rowhouse, up the stairs, and into the apartment. When they got into appellant's room, he said that he had to go to the bathroom and left the room for a few minutes.[a] The prosecutrix made no attempt to leave. When appellant came back, he sat on the bed while she sat on the chair next to the bed. He turned the light off and asked her to get on the bed with him. He started to pull her onto the bed and also began to remove her blouse. She stated she took off her slacks and removed his clothing because "he asked [her] to do it." After they both undressed, prosecutrix stated:

> "I was still begging him to please let, you know, let me leave. I said, 'you can get a lot of other girls down there, for what you want,' and he just kept saying, 'no,' and then I was really scared, because I can't describe, you know, what was said. It was more the look in his eyes; and I said, at that point—I didn't know what to say; and I said, 'If I do what you want, will you let me go without killing me?' Because I didn't know, at that point, what he was going to do; and I started to cry; and when I did, he put his hands on my throat, and started lightly to choke me; and I said, 'If I do what you want, will

---

a. Although there was evidence of a   fied that she did not notice one.
telephone in the room, the prosecutrix testi-

you let me go?' And he said, yes, and at that time, I proceeded to do what he wanted me to."

She stated that she performed oral sex and they then had sexual intercourse.[1] * * *

The Court of Appeals of Maryland last spoke on the amount of force required to support a rape conviction in *Hazel v. State,* 221 Md. 464, 469, 157 A.2d 922, 925 (1960), when the Court said:

> "Force is an essential element of the crime and to justify a conviction, the evidence must warrant a conclusion either that the victim resisted and her resistance was overcome by force or that she was prevented from resisting by threats to her safety."[2]

In all of the victim's testimony we have been unable to see any resistance on her part to the sex acts and certainly can we see no fear as would overcome her attempt to resist or escape as required by *Hazel.* Possession of the keys by the accused may have deterred her vehicular escape but hardly a departure seeking help in the rooming house or in the street. We must say that "the way he looked" fails utterly to support the fear required by *Hazel.* * * *

Appellee argues * * * that the issue as to whether or not intercourse was accompanied by force or threats of force is one of credibility to be resolved by the triers of the fact. We cannot follow the argument. As we understand the law, the trial judge in ruling on a motion to acquit must first determine that there is legally sufficient evidence for the jury to find the victim was reasonably in fear. That is the rule set forth in *Hazel* * * *.

Cases from other jurisdictions have followed the rule that the victim's fear which overcomes her will to resist must be a reasonable fear. * * *

* * * [W]e find the evidence legally insufficient to warrant a conclusion that appellant's words or actions created in the mind of the victim a reasonable fear that if she resisted, he would have harmed her, or that faced with such resistance, he would have used force to overcome it. The prosecutrix stated that she was afraid, and submitted because of

---

1. * * * After arriving home she said: "I sat in the car, thinking about it a while, and I thought I wondered what would happen if I hadn't of done what he wanted me to do. So I thought the right thing to do was to go report it, and I went from there to Hillendale to find a police car."

If, in quiet contemplation after the act, she had to wonder what would have happened, her submission on the side of prudence seems hardly justified. Indeed, if *she* had to wonder afterward, how can a fact finder reasonably conclude that she was justifiably in fear sufficient to overcome her will to resist, at the time.

2. Since *Hazel,* the Maryland Legislature has codified extensively the law pertaining to sexual offenses providing in Md. Code, Art. 27, § 463 as follows:

"(a) What constitutes.—A person is guilty of rape in the second degree if the person engages in vaginal intercourse with another person:

(1) By force or threat of force against the will and without the consent of the other person...."

The statute has made no change in the force as required by *Hazel.*

"the look in his eyes." After both were undressed and in the bed, and she pleaded to him that she wanted to leave, he started to lightly choke her. At oral argument it was brought out that the "lightly choking" could have been a heavy caress. We do not believe that "lightly choking" along with all the facts and circumstances in the case, were sufficient to cause a reasonable fear which overcame her ability to resist. In the absence of any other evidence showing force used by appellant, we find that the evidence was insufficient to convict appellant of rape.

WILNER, JUDGE, dissenting. * * *

The majority's error, in my judgment, is not in their exposition of the underlying principles of law that must govern this case, but rather in the manner that they have applied those principles. * * * Under the guise of judging the sufficiency of the evidence presented against appellant, they have tacitly—perhaps unwittingly, but nonetheless effectively—substituted their own view of the evidence (and the inferences that may fairly be drawn from it) for that of the judge and jury. In so doing, they have not only improperly invaded the province allotted to those tribunals, but, at the same time, have perpetuated and given new life to myths about the crime of rape that have no place in our law today. * * *

Md.Annot.Code art. 27, § 463(a) considers three types of conduct as constituting second degree rape. We are concerned only with the first: a person is guilty of rape in the second degree if he (1) engages in vaginal intercourse with another person, (2) by force or threat of force, (3) against the will, and (4) without the consent of the other person. There is no real question here as to the first, third, or fourth elements of the crime. The evidence was certainly sufficient to show that appellant had vaginal intercourse with the victim, and that such act was against her will and without her consent. The point at issue is whether it was accomplished by force or threat of force; and I think that in viewing the evidence, that point should remain ever clear. *Consent is not the issue here, only whether there was sufficient evidence of force or the threat of force.*

Unfortunately, courts, including in the present case a majority of this one, often tend to confuse these two elements—force and lack of consent—and to think of them as one. They are not. They mean, and require, different things. What seems to cause the confusion—what, indeed, has become a common denominator of both elements—is the notion that the victim must actively resist the attack upon her. If she fails to offer sufficient resistance (sufficient to the satisfaction of the judge), a court is entitled, or at least presumes the entitlement, to find that there was no force or threat of force, or that the act was not against her will, or that she actually consented to it, or some unarticulated combination or synthesis of these elements that leads to the ultimate conclusion that the victim was not raped. Thus it is that the focus is almost entirely on the extent of resistance—*the victim's acts, rather than those of her assailant.* Attention is directed not to the wrongful stimulus, but to the victim's reactions to it. Right or wrong, that seems to be the current state of the Maryland law; and, notwithstanding its uniqueness in the criminal law, and its illogic, until changed by statute or the Court of Appeals, I accept it as binding.

But what is required of a woman being attacked or in danger of attack? How much resistance must she offer? Where is that line to be drawn between requiring that she either risk serious physical harm, perhaps death, on the one hand, or be termed a willing partner on the other? * * *

From * * * pronouncements in *Hazel,* this Court has articulated what the majority refers to as a "rule of reason"—i.e., that "where the victim's story could not be corroborated by wounds, bruises or disordered clothing, the lack of consent could be shown by fear based upon reasonable apprehension." *Winegan v. State,* 10 Md.App. 196, 200, 268 A.2d 585, 588 (1970). As so phrased, I do not consider this to be a rule of reason at all; it is highly unreasonable, and again mixes the element of consent with that of force. But what I do accept is what the Court of Appeals said in *Hazel:* (1) if the acts and threats of the defendant were reasonably calculated to create in the mind of the victim—having regard to the circumstances in which she was placed—a real apprehension, due to fear, of imminent bodily harm, serious enough to impair or overcome her will to resist, then such acts and threats are the equivalent of force; (2) submission is not the equivalent of consent; and (3) the real test is whether the assault was committed without the consent and against the will of the prosecuting witness.

Upon this basis, the evidence against appellant must be considered. * * * The victim—I'll call her Pat—attended a high school reunion. * * *

* * * We know nothing about Pat and appellant. We don't know how big they are, what they look like, what their life experiences have been. We don't know if appellant is larger or smaller than she, stronger or weaker. We don't know what the inflection was in his voice as he dangled her car keys in front of her. We can't tell whether this was in a jocular vein or a truly threatening one. We have no idea what his mannerisms were. The trial judge and the jury could discern some of these things, of course, because they could observe the two people in court and could listen to what they said and how they said it. But all we know is that, between midnight and 1:00 a.m., in a neighborhood that was strange to Pat, appellant took her car keys, demanded that she accompany him, and most assuredly implied that unless she did so, at the very least, she might be stranded. * * *

How does the majority Opinion view these events? It starts by noting that Pat was a 21–year–old mother who was separated from her husband but not yet divorced, as though that had some significance. To me, it has none, except perhaps (when coupled with the further characterization that Pat and Terry had gone "bar hopping") to indicate an underlying suspicion, for which there is absolutely no support in the record, that Pat was somehow "on the make." Even more alarming, and unwarranted, however, is the majority's analysis [in footnote 1] of Pat's initial reflections on whether to report what had happened.

It is this type of reasoning—if indeed "reasoning" is the right word for it—that is particularly distressing. The concern expressed by Pat, made even more real by the majority Opinion of this Court, is one that is common among rape victims, and largely accounts for the fact that most incidents of forcible rape go unreported by the victim. If appellant had desired, and Pat had given, her wallet instead of her body, there would be no question about appellant's guilt of robbery. Taking the car keys under those circumstances would certainly have supplied the requisite threat of force or violence and negated the element of consent. No one would seriously contend that because she failed to raise a hue and cry she had consented to the theft of her money. Why then is such life-threatening action necessary when it is her personal dignity that is being stolen?

Rape has always been considered a most serious crime, one that traditionally carried the heaviest penalty. But until recently, it remained shrouded in the taboos and myths of a Victorian age, and little real attention was given to how rapes occur, how they may be prevented, and how a victim can best protect herself from injury when an attack appears inevitable. * * *

* * * As the result of the Battelle Study[8] we now know some things about this crime that we could only guess at before. * * *

Of particular significance is what was learned about resistance. The most common type of resistance offered by victims is verbal. Note: verbal resistance *is* resistance! In cases arising in the large cities, only 12.7% of the victims attempted flight, and only 12% offered physical resistance. The reason for this is apparent from the next thing learned: that "*[r]ape victims who resisted were more likely to be injured than ones who did not.*" * * *

Where does this leave us but where we started? A judge and a jury, observing the witnesses and hearing their testimony, concluded without dissent that there was sufficient evidence to find beyond a reasonable doubt that appellant had sexual intercourse with Pat by force or threat of force against her will and without her consent; in other words, that the extent of her resistance and the reasons for her failure to resist further were reasonable. No claim is made here that the jury was misinstructed on the law of rape. Yet a majority of this Court, without the ability to see and hear the witnesses, has simply concluded that, in their judgment, Pat's fear was not a reasonable one, or that there was no fear at all * * *. * * * Brushing all of this aside, they have counter-

8. This was a study conducted by the Battelle Memorial Institute Law and Justice Study Center under grant from the LEAA (National Institute of Law Enforce- ment and Criminal Justice). The Report of the study was published during 1977 and 1978. * * *

manded the judgment of the trial court and jury and declared Pat to have been, in effect, an adulteress.[17] * * *

STATE v. RUSK

Court of Appeals of Maryland, 1981.
289 Md. 230, 424 A.2d 720.

MURPHY, CHIEF JUDGE. * * *

We think the reversal of Rusk's conviction by the Court of Special Appeals was in error for the fundamental reason so well expressed in the dissenting opinion by Judge Wilner * * * that * * * the reasonableness of Pat's apprehension of fear was plainly a question of fact for the jury to determine. * * *

Judgment of the Court of Special Appeals reversed; case remanded to that court with directions that it affirm the judgment of the Criminal Court of Baltimore * * *.

COLE, JUDGE, dissenting:

I agree with the Court of Special Appeals that the evidence adduced at the trial of Edward Salvatore Rusk was insufficient to convict him of rape. * * *

While courts no longer require a female to resist to the utmost or to resist where resistance would be foolhardy, they do require her acquiescence in the act of intercourse to stem from fear generated by something of substance. She may not simply say, "I was really scared," and thereby transform consent or mere unwillingness into submission by force. These words do not transform a seducer into a rapist. She must follow the natural instinct of every proud female to resist, by more than mere words, the violation of her person by a stranger or an unwelcomed friend. She must make it plain that she regards such sexual acts as abhorrent and repugnant to her natural sense of pride. She must resist unless the defendant has objectively manifested his intent to use physical force to accomplish his purpose. The law regards rape as a crime of violence. The majority today attenuates this proposition. It declares the innocence of an at best distraught young woman. It does not demonstrate the defendant's guilt of the crime of rape.

My examination of the evidence in a light most favorable to the State reveals no conduct by the defendant reasonably calculated to cause the prosecutrix to be so fearful that she should fail to resist and thus, the element of force is lacking in the State's proof. * * *

I find it incredible for the majority to conclude that on these facts, without more, a woman was forced to commit oral sex upon the defen-

---

17. Interestingly, appellant was convicted of assault arising out of the same incident, but did not contest the sufficiency of the evidence supporting that conviction. It would seem that if there was not enough evidence of force, or lack of consent, to permit the rape conviction, there was an equal insufficiency to support the assault conviction. The majority is spared, in this case, the need to deal with that thorny dilemma.

dant and then to engage in vaginal intercourse. In the absence of any verbal threat to do her grievous bodily harm or the display of any weapon and threat to use it, I find it difficult to understand how a victim could participate in these sexual activities and not be willing. * * *

Notes and Questions

1. Regarding the majority opinion of the Court of Special Appeals, Professor Susan Estrich writes:

> In a very real sense, the "reasonable" woman under the view of the * * * judges who would reverse Mr. Rusk's conviction is not a woman at all. Their version of a reasonable person is one who does not scare easily, one who does not feel vulnerability, one who is not passive, one who fights back, not cries. The reasonable woman, it seems, is not a schoolboy "sissy." She is a real man.

Susan Estrich, *Rape,* 95 Yale L.J. 1087, 1114 (1986). Is this a fair critique of the judges' position?

2. Was Rusk guilty of rape because he used force to obtain intercourse or because he threatened to use force? If it is the former, would the outcome be same if he had not "lightly" touched the victim's neck? If he is guilty because he threatened Pat, was the threat expressed or implied? If it was the latter, how should the law deal with the possibility that a person might be convicted because his words or actions were misinterpreted?

3. *Resistance.* Why was Pat's lack of physical resistance an issue? Is it an element of the offense of rape? Is there any justification for the resistance requirement?

A few states now expressly provide that a victim need not resist her sexual assailant. E.g., Mich.Comp.Laws Ann. § 750.520i (1991). Another method of dealing with the issue is to provide that "[t]he prosecutor shall not be required to offer proof that the victim resisted * * *." N.J.Stat.Ann. 2C:14–5(a) (1982). Is there a practical difference between these approaches?

Model Penal Code § 213.1(1)(a) provides that a male who "compels" the victim "to submit by force or by threat of imminent death, serious bodily injury, extreme pain or kidnapping" is guilty of rape. This provision omits the element of "lack of consent" by the victim and is silent regarding the matter of resistance. Does this mean that these factors are irrelevant in a Model Code jurisdiction? See American Law Institute, Model Penal Code and Commentaries, Comment to § 213.1 at 304–07 (1980).

4. *Problem.* Consider the following facts:

> Weisberg, a 54–year–old manufacturer's representative for a clothing company, and the 39–year–old victim, P.C., were neighbors in a Vancouver, Washington, apartment complex. Weisberg and his wife lived three doors away from P.C. and he occasionally would see her in the common areas of the complex and stop to chat.

> On P.C.'s birthday, September 7, 1989, Weisberg offered P.C. a birthday gift—her choice of items from the racks and boxes of sample clothing in his apartment. She was interested and the next evening, Weisberg went to her apartment door and again invited her to come to

his apartment to make her clothing selection. P.C. accepted and, after calling to her roommate where she was going, willingly accompanied Weisberg to his apartment.

Once inside the Weisberg apartment, the two went upstairs to the defendant's bedroom where he kept the sample racks. As they were climbing the stairs Weisberg kissed P.C. on the cheek. In the bedroom, Weisberg helped P.C. choose two blouses and a skirt. P.C. said that she wanted to try on the items to make sure that they fit, and, in order to do so, she removed her shorts and her shirt. Weisberg assisted her and he suggested the clothing would fit better if P.C. removed her underclothing. When P.C. did not immediately take off her bra and panties, Weisberg removed them for her. There is no evidence that Weisberg used any force or threatened or suggested harm to P.C. if she did not remove the undergarments. Nor did P.C. ever attempt to leave Weisberg's apartment although the uncontested evidence was that his apartment doors were not locked from the inside and that her apartment door was not locked from the outside. P.C. testified that she did not try to stop Weisberg because she was afraid "that he might try to hurt me or something, and I didn't want to take the chance."

P.C. first tried on the blouses and then the skirt. After she removed the skirt and before she put her own clothes back on, Weisberg told her to lie down on his bed. When she said that she did not want to lie on the bed, Weisberg responded, "go ahead and lay on the bed anyway." * * *

Next Weisberg removed his clothes, rubbed P.C. with baby oil, and then had intercourse with her. When she told him to stop, that it was hurting her, he immediately stopped. He advised her to go take a shower to wash off the baby oil. P.C. showered, returned to the bedroom, dressed, and watched television in the bedroom while the defendant took his own shower. Weisberg returned to the bedroom, dressed and then went downstairs for a couple of soft drinks. The two had their drinks and watched a part of a movie on television. After approximately an hour in the apartment, Weisberg escorted P.C. downstairs and out the front door. P.C. testified that before she left, "he [Weisberg] turned around and said, 'Don't say anything to anybody what I did.' "

Sometime later the incident was reported to the police and Weisberg was arrested and charged with one count of rape in the second degree by forcible compulsion. * * *

The elements of rape in the second degree by forcible compulsion, as charged in this case, are set out in RCW 9A.44.050:

(1) A person is guilty of rape in the second degree when, under circumstances not constituting rape in the first degree, the person engages in sexual intercourse with another person:

(a) By forcible compulsion . . .

" 'Forcible compulsion' means physical force which overcomes resistance, or a threat, express or implied, that places a person in fear of

death or physical injury to herself or himself or another person, ... ''
RCW 9A.44.010(6).

State v. Weisberg, 65 Wash.App. 721, 723–25, 829 P.2d 252, 253–54 (1992).

Did the prosecutor prove forcible compulsion beyond a reasonable
doubt? In a footnote, the court disclosed that P.C. had a mental age of
approximately 9 to 11 years. The prosecutor did not claim that P.C. was
mentally incapable of consenting (an alternative basis for the rape prosecution), but does this put the claim of forcible compulsion in a different light?

STATE v. ALSTON

Supreme Court of North Carolina, 1984.
310 N.C. 399, 312 S.E.2d 470.

MITCHELL, JUSTICE.

The defendant raises on appeal the question whether the evidence of
his guilt of * * * second degree rape was sufficient to * * * support his
conviction * * *.

The State's evidence tended to show that at the time the incident
occurred the defendant and the prosecuting witness in this case, Cottie
Brown, had been involved for approximately six months in a consensual
sexual relationship. During the six months the two had conflicts at
times and Brown would leave the apartment she shared with the
defendant to stay with her mother. She testified that she would return
to the defendant and the apartment they shared when he called to tell
her to return. Brown testified that she and the defendant had sexual
relations throughout their relationship. Although she sometimes enjoyed their sexual relations, she often had sex with the defendant just to
accommodate him. On those occasions, she would stand still and remain
entirely passive while the defendant undressed her and had intercourse
with her.

Brown testified that at times their consensual sexual relations
involved some violence. The defendant had struck her several times
throughout the relationship when she refused to give him money or
refused to do what he wanted. Around May 15, 1981, the defendant
struck her after asking her for money that she refused to give him.
Brown left the apartment she shared with the defendant and moved in
with her mother. She did not have intercourse with the defendant after
May 15 until the alleged rape on June 15. After Brown left the
defendant, he called her several times and visited her at Durham
Technical Institute where she was enrolled in classes. When he visited
her they talked about their relationship. Brown testified that she did
not tell him she wanted to break off their relationship because she was
afraid he would be angry.

On June 15, 1981, Brown arrived at Durham Technical Institute by
taxicab to find the defendant standing close to the school door. The
defendant blocked her path as she walked toward the door and asked her
where she had moved. Brown refused to tell him, and the defendant

grabbed her arm, saying that she was going with him. Brown testified that it would have taken some effort to pull away. The two walked toward the parking lot and Brown told the defendant she would walk with him if he let her go. The defendant then released her. She testified that she did not run away from him because she was afraid of him. She stated that other students were nearby.

Brown stated that she and the defendant then began a casually paced walk in the neighborhood around the school. They walked, sometimes side by side, sometimes with Brown slightly behind the defendant. As they walked they talked about their relationship. Brown said the defendant did not hold her or help her along in any way as they walked. The defendant talked about Brown's "dogging" him and making him seem a fool and about Brown's mother's interference in the relationship. When the defendant and Brown left the parking lot, the defendant threatened to "fix" her face so that her mother could see he was not playing. While they were walking out of the parking lot, Brown told the defendant she wanted to go to class. He replied that she was going to miss class that day.

The two continued to walk away from the school. Brown testified that the defendant continually talked about their relationship as they walked, but that she paid little attention to what he said because she was preoccupied with her own thoughts. They passed several people. They walked along several streets and went down a path close to a wooded area where they stopped to talk. The defendant asked again where Brown had moved. She asked him whether he would let her go if she told him her address. The defendant then asked whether the relationship was over and Brown told him it was. He then said that since everyone could see her but him he had a right to make love to her again. Brown said nothing.

The two turned around at that point and began walking towards a street they had walked down previously. Changing directions, they walked in the same fashion they had walked before—side by side with Brown sometimes slightly behind. The defendant did not hold or touch Brown as they walked. Brown testified that the defendant did not say where they were going but that, when he said he wanted to make love, she knew he was going to the house of a friend. She said they had gone to the house on prior occasions to have sex. The defendant and Brown passed the same group of men they had passed previously. Brown did not ask for assistance because some of the men were friends of the defendant, and she assumed they would not help. The defendant and Brown continued to walk to the house of one of the defendant's friends, Lawrence Taylor.

When they entered the house, Taylor was inside. Brown sat in the living room while the defendant and Taylor went to the back of the house and talked. When asked why she did not try to leave when the defendant and Taylor were in the back of the house, Brown replied, "It was nowhere to go. I don't know. I just didn't." The defendant returned to the living room area and turned on the television. He attempted to fix a broken fan. Brown asked Taylor for a cigarette, and he gave her one.

The defendant began talking to Brown about another man she had been seeing. By that time Taylor had gone out of the room and perhaps the house. The defendant asked if Brown was "ready." The evidence tended to show that she told him "no, that I wasn't going to bed with him." She testified that she did not want to have sex with the defendant and did not consent to do so at any time on June 15.

After Brown finished her cigarette, the defendant began kissing her neck. He pulled her up from the chair in which she had been sitting and started undressing her. * * * He told her to lay down on a bed which was in the living room. She complied and the defendant pushed apart her legs and had sexual intercourse with her. Brown testified that she did not try to push him away. She cried during the intercourse. Afterwards they talked. * * *

* * * Brown made a complaint to the police the same day.

The defendant continued to call Brown after June 15, but she refused to see him. One evening he called from a telephone booth and told her he had to talk. When he got to her apartment he threatened to kick her door down and Brown let him inside. Once inside he said he had intended merely to talk to her but that he wanted to make love again after seeing her. Brown said she sat and looked at him, and that he began kissing her. She pulled away and he picked her up and carried her to the bedroom. He performed oral sex on her and she testified that she did not try to fight him off because she found she enjoyed it. The two stayed together until morning and had sexual intercourse several times that night. * * *

In his * * * assignment of error the defendant contends there was no substantial evidence that the sexual intercourse between Brown and him was by force and against her will. He argues that the evidence was insufficient to allow the trial court to submit the issue of his guilt of second degree rape to the jury. After a review of the evidence, we find this argument to have merit.

Second degree rape involves vaginal intercourse with the victim both by force and against the victim's will. G.S. 14-27.3. Consent by the victim is a complete defense, but consent which is induced by fear of violence is void and is no legal consent.

A defendant can be guilty of raping even his mistress or a "common strumpet." This is so because consent to sexual intercourse freely given can be withdrawn at any time prior to penetration. If the particular act of intercourse for which the defendant is charged was both by force and against the victim's will, the offense is rape without regard to the victim's consent given to the defendant for prior acts of intercourse.

Where as here the victim has engaged in a prior continuing consensual sexual relationship with the defendant, however, determining the victim's state of mind at the time of the alleged rape obviously is made more difficult. Although inquiry in such cases still must be made into the victim's state of mind at the time of the alleged rape, the State ordinarily will be able to show the victim's lack of consent to the specific act charged only by evidence of statements or actions by the victim which were clearly communicated to the defendant and which expressly and unequivocally indicated the victim's withdrawal of any prior consent and lack of consent to the particular act of intercourse.

In the present case the State introduced such evidence.   * * * Brown testified unequivocally that she did not consent to sexual intercourse with the defendant on June 15. She was equally unequivocal in testifying that she submitted to sexual intercourse with the defendant only because she was afraid of him. During their walk, she told the defendant that their relationship was at an end. When the defendant asked her if she was "ready" immediately prior to having sexual intercourse with her, she told him "no, that I wasn't going to bed with him." Even in the absence of physical resistance by Brown, such testimony by her provided substantial evidence that the act of sexual intercourse was against her will.

The State did not offer substantial evidence, however, of the element of force. As we have stated, actual physical force need not be shown in order to establish force sufficient to constitute an element of the crime of rape. Threats of serious bodily harm which reasonably induce fear thereof are sufficient. In the present case there was no substantial evidence of either actual or constructive force.

The evidence in the present case tended to show that, shortly after the defendant met Brown at the school, they walked out of the parking lot with the defendant in front. He stopped and told Brown he was going to "fix" her face so that her mother could see he was not "playing." This threat by the defendant and his act of grabbing Brown by the arm at the school, although they may have induced fear, appeared to have been unrelated to the act of sexual intercourse between Brown and the defendant. More important, the record is devoid of evidence that Brown was in any way intimidated into having sexual intercourse with the defendant by that threat or any other act of the defendant on June 15.   * * *

We note that the absence of an explicit threat is not determinative in considering whether there was sufficient force in whatever form to overcome the will of the victim. It is enough if the totality of the circumstances gives rise to a reasonable inference that the unspoken purpose of the threat was to force the victim to submit to unwanted sexual intercourse. The evidence introduced in the present case, however, gave rise to no such inference.   * * * Although Brown's general fear of the defendant may have been justified by his conduct on prior occasions, absent evidence that the defendant used force or threats to overcome the will of the victim *to resist the sexual intercourse alleged to* *have been rape,* such general fear was not sufficient to show that the defendant used the force required to support a conviction of rape. * * *

Notes and Questions

1. Why did the court conclude that Alston did not rape Brown? What element(s) of the offense did the prosecution supposedly fail to prove?

Suppose that Alston had called Brown on June 14 and told her, "The next time I see you, I intend to have sex with you, and if you don't cooperate, I'll kill you." If he did not repeat the threat on June 15—indeed, if he were outwardly pleasant—would this constitute forcible rape?

Even in the absence of force, was Alston's conduct on June 15 sufficiently threatening to constitute rape? Alternatively, would it be appropriate to convict him, even in the absence of threatening conduct, because of his "threatening capacity," i.e., his greater size, strength, and fighting ability? See Stephen J. Schulhofer, *Taking Sexual Autonomy Seriously: Rape Law and Beyond,* 11 Law & Phil. 35, 51 (1992).

2. Why were the post-June 15 actions of the parties introduced into evidence?

3. Was *Alston* properly decided? Consider the following remarks. Susan Estrich, *Rape,* 95 Yale L.J. 1087, 1111–12 (1986):

Decisions such as * * * *Alston* are vulnerable to attack on traditional doctrinal grounds. The courts' unwillingness to credit the victim's past experience of violence at the hands of the defendant stands in sharp contrast to the black letter law that a defendant's knowledge of his attacker's reputation for violence or ownership of a gun is relevant to the reasonableness of his use of deadly force in self-defense.

That these decisions depart so straightforwardly from established criminal law doctrine is noteworthy but not unusual in the law of rape. More interesting is the apparent paradox that they create. In [*Alston*], the court says—and this is explicit, not implicit—that sex was without the woman's consent. It also says that there was no force. In other words, the woman was not forced to engage in sex, but the sex she engaged in was against her will.

Such a paradox is almost inevitable if one adopts, and then enforces, the most traditional male notion of a fight as the working definition of "force." In a fight, you hit your assailant with your fists or your elbows or your knees. In a fight, the one attacked fights back. In these terms, there was no fight in *Alston.* Therefore, there was no force.

I am not at all sure how the judges who decided *Alston* would explain the victim's simultaneous refusal to consent and failure to resist. For myself, it is not at all difficult to understand that a woman who had been repeatedly beaten, who had been a passive victim of both violence and sex during the "consensual" relationship, who had sought to escape from the man, who is confronted and threatened by him, who summons the courage to tell him their relationship is over only to be answered by his assertion of a "right" to sex—a woman in such a position would not fight. She wouldn't fight; she might cry. Hers is the reaction of "sissies" in playground fights. Hers is the reaction of people who have already been beaten, or who never had the power to fight in the first instance. Hers is, from my reading, the most common reaction of women to rape. * * *

To say that there is no "force" in such a situation is to create a gulf between power and force, and to define the latter solely in schoolboy terms. Mr. Alston did not beat his victim—at least not with his fists. He didn't have to. She had been beaten—physically and emotionally—long before. But that beating was one that the court was willing to go to great lengths to avoid recognizing.

That the law prohibiting forced sex understands force in such narrow terms is frustrating enough for its women victims. Worse, however, is the fact that the conclusion that no force is present may emerge as a judgment not that the man did not act unreasonably, but as a judgment that the woman victim did.

Vivian Berger, *Not So Simple Rape,* 7 Crim.Just. Ethics (Winter/Spring 1988) at 69, 75–76:

I'm certain that Alston is a terrible person and that Cottie [Brown] should be pitied rather than blamed. But did he *rape* her? I share the doubts of the appellate court that reversed his conviction. Estrich does not. She argues eloquently, indeed angrily, that *Alston* represents yet another instance of schoolboy rules regarding force unjustly applied to defenseless women. * * *

* * * If the author means only to say that women more often cry than physically resist when confronted with male sexual aggression, I imagine that she may well be right and, as I have said, I don't quarrel with her overall view that a "no" without an actual fight can turn intercourse into rape. Yet if she means, as the sentence on "beaten" people suggests, that Cottie's global "reaction" to a difficult situation, not just her tears and lack of resistance, is "common" and makes what occurred "rape," I find myself somewhat troubled. * * *

I worry that a *too* "understanding" attitude toward the Cotties of the world by the legal system may backfire and ultimately damage the cause of women in general. * * * [W]e don't want the law to patronize women; when it did in a vast number of areas, we fought it and won significant victories. To treat as victims in a legal sense all of the female victims of life is at some point to cheapen, not celebrate, the rights to self-determination, sexual autonomy, and self- and societal respect of women. Naturally, no bright line exists to make the border separating justified use of rape law to safeguard female personhood and choice * * * from abuse of this law to "defend" women who abdicate self and will entirely. Because overprotection risks enfeebling instead of empowering women, the tension between reformist goals * * * seems to me to make cases like *Alston* a close call, not a springboard for moral outrage.

Thus, as to Cottie, I think it acceptable if not ineluctable to regard her as a pitiable woman, involved with an utterly contemptible man in a sick relationship, whose sexual dynamics included a course of conduct involving passivity, submission, and inconsistent response on her part, dominance and occasional violence on his. Had she taken Alston to court when he beat her, he ought to have been convicted of battery: vindicating her right to be free of physical injury would scarcely have amounted to undue solicitude for a weakling or depreciation of women as a group. But "rape" strikes me at least arguably as a misnomer for the event at issue here. Her stated "no," while not a "yes," bore greater resemblance to a mental reservation or a "do what you will" than to a firm and clear rejection, when viewed against the totality of the couple's ongoing interactions.

4. *Blaming the victim.* Approximately one-half of all sexual assaults go unreported to the police (p. 321 supra). One reason for this may be that society, and even rape victims, assign some blame for sexual assaults to the victim.

> A rape victim suffers an invasion of her bodily privacy in an intensely personal and unsettling manner, triggering a number of emotional and psychological reactions running the gamut from shock, fear, distrust and anger to guilt, shame, and disgust. * * *

> A common symptom * * * is self-doubt and agony over the role she—the victim—might have played in "bringing on" the rape. Susan Brownmiller addresses the cultural myths * * * that "she was asking for it" and "all women want to be raped" in her book *Against Our Will: Men, Women and Rape* [1975]. She states:

> > "She was asking for it" is the classic way a rapist shifts the burden of blame from himself to his victim. The popularity of the belief that a woman seduces ... a man into rape, or precipitates a rape by incautious behavior, is part of the smoke screen that men throw up to obscure their actions. The insecurity of women runs so deep that many, possibly most, rape victims agonize afterward in an effort to uncover what it was in their behavior, their manner, their dress that triggered this awful act against them. *Id.* at 312–13.
> > * * *

> Such soul-searching and working-through of the traumatic event is essential to full recovery, but is inhibited by the social stigma which, unfortunately, still attaches to the rape victim—family, friends and acquaintances frequently shun the victim, somehow blaming her (consciously or unconsciously) for her rape.

In re Pittsburgh Action Against Rape, 494 Pa. 15, 38, 40–41, 428 A.2d 126, 138–39 (1981) (Larsen J., dissenting).

Why do people assign blame to apparently innocent victims for their injuries? One explanation is that we want to believe that the world is just, i.e., that innocent persons—like ourselves—will not be victimized. Therefore, we rationalize that victims are partially responsible for their own fate. Melvin J. Lerner, *The Desire for Justice and Reactions to Victims* in Altruism and Helping Behavior 205 (J. Macaulay & L. Berkowitz eds. 1970).

In the context of rape, this blame-the-victim tendency is exacerbated by cultural attitudes about "proper" behavior by women. For example, in one attitudinal study, male and female college students received a fictional account of a forcible rape that occurred while the victim was walking home alone late at night through a college campus. The perceived respectability of the victim was manipulated: some students were told that she was a social worker living with her husband. Others learned that the victim was a divorced topless dancer, out on bail awaiting trial for possession of heroin with intent to distribute.

The experimenters found that female students, more than their male counterparts, focused on the role of chance (being in the wrong place at the wrong time) as an explanation for the rape. Nonetheless, both males and females attached some blame for the rape to the victim, but their reasons differed. On the whole, males focused on the victim's perceived character; females were more apt to emphasize the victim's behavior on the night of the crime (the fact that she chose to walk alone, late at night, through the campus). James Luginbuhl & Courtney Mullin, *Rape and Responsibility: How and How Much Is the Victim Blamed?*, 7 Sex Roles 547 (1981); see also L.G. Calhoun, J.W. Selby, A. Cann, & G.T. Keller, *The Effects of Victim Physical Attractiveness and Sex of Respondent on Social Reactions to Victims of Rape,* 17 Brit.J.Soc. & Clin.Psychol. 191 (1978) (reporting substantially similar results).

Sex differences also emerged when the students were asked to assign a penalty (from 1 to 99 years) for the rape. For females, the victim's degree of respectability was irrelevant to the penalty (43.8 years for the rape of the "respectable" victim, 45.8 years for the "unrespectable"). Males, however assigned significantly fewer years' penalty for the rape of the topless dancer (17.6 years, versus 53.7 years for the rape of the social worker).

Is there any point at which blame may *properly* be assigned to the victim in a forcible rape case? The reaction of jurors in rape trials sometimes suggests that the answer is yes. For example, a three-man and three-woman Florida jury acquitted a man of forcible rape, after he abducted the victim, who was dressed in a lace mini-skirt without underwear, at knife-point from outside a restaurant, and repeatedly had intercourse with her during a five-hour period. The male foreman of the jury stated that "[w]e felt she asked for it for the way she was dressed." A female juror explained, "[s]he was obviously dressed for a good time * * *." *Jury: Woman in Rape Case "Asked For It"*, Chicago Tribune, Oct. 6, 1989, at 11.

In response to the acquittal, the Florida legislature enacted legislation barring the introduction at trial of "evidence presented for the purpose of showing that [the] manner of dress of the victim at the time of the offense incited the sexual battery * * *." Fla.Stat.Ann. § 794.022 (1992). Would this rule have barred the introduction of evidence of the victim's clothing in the case that inspired it?

b. *"No" (or the Absence of "Yes") as "Force"?*

Always take "no" for an answer. Always stop when asked to stop. Never assume "no" means "yes." If her lips tell you "no" but there's "yes" in her eyes, keep in mind that her words, not her eyes, will appear in the court transcript.[b]

SUSAN ESTRICH—RAPE

95 Yale Law Journal 1087 (1986), 1092–93

* * * At one end of the spectrum is the "real" rape, what I will call the traditional rape: A stranger puts a gun to the head of his victim, threatens to kill her or beats her, and then engages in intercourse. In that case, the law—judges, statutes, prosecutors and all—generally acknowledge that a serious crime has been committed. But most cases deviate in one or many respects from this clear picture, making interpretation far more complex. Where less force is used or no other physical injury is inflicted, where threats are inarticulate, where the two know each other, where the setting is not an alley but a bedroom, where the initial contact was not a kidnapping but a date, where the woman says no but does not fight, the understanding is different. In such cases, the law, as reflected in the opinions of the courts, the interpretation, if not the words, of the statutes, and the decisions of those within the criminal justice system, often tell us that no crime has taken place and that fault, if any is to be recognized, belongs with the woman. In concluding that such acts—what I call, for lack of a better title, "non-traditional" rapes—are not criminal, and worse, that the woman must bear any guilt, the law has reflected, legitimized, and enforced a view of sex and women which celebrates male aggressiveness and punishes female passivity. And that vision, while under attack in recent years, continues to be a dominant force in our society and in the law of rape. * * *

Some of those who have written about rape from a feminist perspective intimate that nothing short of political revolution can redress the failings of the traditional approach to rape, that most of what passes for "sex" in our capitalist society is coerced, and that no lines can or should be drawn between rape and what happens in tens of millions of bedrooms across America.

So understood, this particular feminist vision of rape shares one thing with the most traditional sexist vision: the view that non-traditional rape is not fundamentally different from what happens in tens of millions of bedrooms across America. According to the radical feminist, all of it is rape; according to the traditionalist, it is all permissible sex and seduction. In policy terms, neither is willing to draw lines between rape and permissible sex. As a result, the two visions, contradictory in every other respect, point to the same practical policy implications.

My own view is different from both of these. I recognize that both men and women in our society have long accepted norms of male aggressiveness and female passivity which lead to a restricted understanding of rape. And I do not propose, nor do I think it feasible, to

b. Modern advice to men, according to Asa Barber, *The Stud Muffin Quiz*, Playboy, June 1992, at 36. As you read the following materials, consider whether this represents sensible and sufficient legal advice to men who wish to avoid prosecution and conviction for rape.

punish all of the acts of sexual intercourse that could be termed coerced. But lines can be drawn between these two alternatives. The law should be understood to prohibit claims and threats to secure sex that would be prohibited by extortion law and fraud or false pretenses law as a means to secure money. The law should evaluate the conduct of "reasonable" men, not according to a *Playboy*-macho philosophy that says "no means yes," but by according respect to a woman's words. If * * * silence does not negate consent, at least crying and saying "no" should.

SUSAN AGER—THE INCIDENT

Detroit Free Press Magazine, Mar. 22, 1992, p. 17

We were alone beneath the stars, high in the mountains, miles from the nearest light, our sleeping bags unrolled on the ground, weary from a long drive and anticipating sleep.

Or so I thought.

We were not lovers, merely acquaintances. We worked together. We respected each other. He owned a few acres in the mountains, and I admired that back-to-the-land streak in anyone. So we agreed to make this weekend camping trip together to his patch of earth.

A few days earlier, oh so briefly, I thought about saying something. Issuing a "don't-get-any-ideas" warning. But I didn't. I thought he'd feel insulted.

He did not worry so much about my feelings.

For hours on that starlit night he pestered me. Stroked me. Whispered to me first, then argued, then whined: "Oh, come on. You'll love it. Why'd you come up here with me then? Just once. It's such a beautiful night. You'll enjoy it, really. Come on. Please?"

I didn't scream, because there was no one to hear. I didn't fight, because there was nowhere to run. It was his car, and he had the keys. Instead, I curled up. I buried my head against my chest while he touched me. I slapped blindly at his touches, as if I were batting away mosquitos.

Because this happened more than a decade ago, I can't remember with precision how long he continued. * * * I wore no watch that night.

All I know is that he went on forever. Unrelenting.

Finally, weary and weepy, I gave up. I remember the sting of my tears rolling down my cheeks and into my ears as I lay on my back and he moaned.

Then, I fell instantly into sleep, as if from the top of a mountain.

Our weekend ended early, because I was sullen and that made him angry. There was nothing to say on the long ride home.

I never called what happened that night "rape." I still don't.

But it wasn't bliss, either.

I wonder why it has no name. Because it happens all the time: Men push. We submit.

No violence, no shouting, no cries of "rape" afterwards. Just sadness and defeat.

How many of us women have watched this sort of thing happen to us, as if we were outside our bodies, in the 30 years since a confluence of factors made sexual interaction easier, at least practically speaking?

That night in the mountains I surrendered for one reason: I was tired and wanted to escape.

But we surrender for reasons besides fatigue.

● Duty: Some women may feel an obligation to reward men who've been particularly kind, or patient, or ardent. Other women may feel an obligation to be a good-and-ready wife.

● Ambiguity: Part of us wants sex, the other part is wary. And as the train is moving toward the station, so to speak, we're still not sure. We may surrender at the same moment that we conclude, "No, this is stupid."

Some men claim not to understand this. But most women know there is a vast geography of shifting sentiment between Yes and No.

● Hope: Sometimes we surrender because our disinterest might turn into delight. A friend calls this the "No-but-I-could-be-convinced" approach. Sometimes it works. Often it doesn't, and we wonder why we gave in.

We make these excuses for our surrenders, but that's no consolation for the vanquished.

Years after that night in the mountains, I'm surprised to find how angry I am about it. Angrier than I was then. At both him and me, and the games people play.

Now, wiser and less polite, I would not whimper but shout! Not for help, but for my own integrity—to let him know how I felt about his boorish presumptions.

I would surrender only if he held me down and forced me to. And then I could call it rape.

STATE OF NEW JERSEY IN THE INTEREST OF M.T.S.

Supreme Court of New Jersey, 1992.
129 N.J. 422, 609 A.2d 1266.

HANDLER, J.

Under New Jersey law a person who commits an act of sexual penetration using physical force or coercion is guilty of second-degree sexual assault. The sexual assault statute does not define the words "physical force." The question posed by this appeal is whether the element of "physical force" is met simply by an act of non-consensual penetration involving no more force than necessary to accomplish that result.

That issue is presented in the context of what is often referred to as "acquaintance rape." The record in the case discloses that the juvenile, a seventeen-year-old boy, engaged in consensual kissing and heavy petting with a fifteen-year-old girl and thereafter engaged in actual sexual penetration of the girl to which she had not consented. There was no evidence or suggestion that the juvenile used any unusual or extra force or threats to accomplish the act of penetration.

The trial court determined that the juvenile was delinquent for committing a sexual assault. The Appellate Division reversed the disposition of delinquency, concluding that non-consensual penetration does not constitute sexual assault unless it is accompanied by some level of force more than that necessary to accomplish the penetration. We granted the State's petition for certification.

I

The issues in this case are perplexing and controversial. * * *

On Monday, May 21, 1990, fifteen-year-old C.G. was living with her mother, her three siblings, and several other people, including M.T.S. and his girlfriend. A total of ten people resided in the three-bedroom town-home at the time of the incident. M.T.S., then age seventeen, was temporarily residing at the home with the permission of the C.G.'s mother; he slept downstairs on a couch. C.G. had her own room on the second floor. At approximately 11:30 p.m. on May 21, C.G. went upstairs to sleep after having watched television with her mother, M.T.S., and his girlfriend. When C.G. went to bed, she was wearing underpants, a bra, shorts, and a shirt. At trial, C.G. and M.T.S. offered very different accounts concerning the nature of their relationship and the events that occurred after C.G. had gone upstairs. The trial court did not credit fully either teenager's testimony.

C.G. stated that earlier in the day, M.T.S. had told her three or four times that he "was going to make a surprise visit up in [her] bedroom." She said that she had not taken M.T.S. seriously and considered his comments a joke because he frequently teased her. She testified that M.T.S. had attempted to kiss her on numerous other occasions and at least once had attempted to put his hands inside of her pants, but that she had rejected all of his previous advances.

C.G. testified that on May 22, at approximately 1:30 a.m., she awoke to use the bathroom. As she was getting out of bed, she said, she saw M.T.S., fully clothed, standing in her doorway. According to C.G., M.T.S. then said that "he was going to tease [her] a little bit." C.G. testified that she "didn't think anything of it"; she walked past him, used the bathroom, and then returned to bed, falling into a "heavy" sleep within fifteen minutes. The next event C.G. claimed to recall of that morning was waking up with M.T.S. on top of her, her underpants and shorts removed. She said "his penis was into [her] vagina." As soon as C.G. realized what had happened, she said, she immediately slapped M.T.S. once in the face, then "told him to get off [her], and get out." She did not scream or cry out. She testified that M.T.S. complied in less than one minute after being struck; according to C.G., "he jumped right off of [her]." She said she did not know how long M.T.S. had been inside of her before she awoke.

C.G. said that after M.T.S. left the room, she "fell asleep crying" because "[she] couldn't believe that he did what he did to [her]." She explained that she did not immediately tell her mother or anyone else in the house of the events of that morning because she was "scared and in shock." According to C.G., M.T.S. engaged in intercourse with her "without [her] wanting it or telling him to come up [to her bedroom]." By her own account, C.G. was not otherwise harmed by M.T.S. * * *

According to M.T.S., he and C.G. had been good friends for a long time, and their relationship "kept leading on to more and more." He had been living at C.G.'s home for about five days before the incident occurred; he testified that during the three days preceding the incident they had been "kissing and necking" and had discussed having sexual intercourse. The first time M.T.S. kissed C.G., he said, she "didn't want him to, but she did after that." He said C.G. repeatedly had encouraged him to "make a surprise visit up in her room."

M.T.S. testified that at exactly 1:15 a.m. on May 22, he entered C.G.'s bedroom as she was walking to the bathroom. He said C.G. soon returned from the bathroom, and the two began "kissing and all," eventually moving to the bed. Once they were in bed, he said, they undressed each other and continued to kiss and touch for about five minutes. M.T.S. and C.G. proceeded to engage in sexual intercourse. According to M.T.S., who was on top of C.G., he "stuck it in" and "did it [thrust] three times, and then the fourth time [he] stuck it in, that's when [she] pulled [him] off of her." M.T.S. said that as C.G. pushed him off, she said "stop, get off," and he "hopped off right away."

According to M.T.S., after about one minute, he asked C.G. what was wrong; she replied with a back-hand to his face. He recalled asking C.G. what was wrong a second time, and her replying, "how can you take advantage of me or something like that." * * *

On May 23, 1990, M.T.S. was charged with conduct that if engaged in by an adult would constitute second-degree sexual assault of the victim, contrary to *N.J.S.A.* 2C:14–2c(1). * * *

Following a two-day trial on the sexual assault charge, M.T.S. was adjudicated delinquent. After reviewing the testimony, the court concluded that the victim had consented to a session of kissing and heavy petting with M.T.S. The trial court did not find that C.G. had been sleeping at the time of penetration, but nevertheless found that she had not consented to the actual sexual act. Accordingly, the court concluded that the State had proven second-degree sexual assault beyond a reasonable doubt. On appeal, * * * the Appellate Division determined that the absence of force beyond that involved in the act of sexual penetration precluded a finding of second-degree sexual assault. It therefore reversed the juvenile's adjudication of delinquency for that offense.

II

The New Jersey Code of Criminal Justice, *N.J.S.A.* 2C:14–2c(1), defines "sexual assault" as the commission "of sexual penetration" "with another person" with the use of "physical force or coercion."[1] An unconstrained reading of the statutory language indicates that both the act of "sexual penetration" and the use of "physical force or coercion" are separate and distinct elements of the offense. Neither the definitions section of *N.J.S.A.* 2C:14–1 to –8, nor the remainder of the Code of Criminal Justice provides assistance in interpreting the words "physical force." The initial inquiry is, therefore, whether the statutory words are unambiguous on their face and can be understood and applied in accordance with their plain meaning. * * *

The parties offer two alternative understandings of the concept of "physical force" as it is used in the statute. The State would read "physical force" to entail any amount of sexual touching brought about involuntarily. A showing of sexual penetration coupled with a lack of consent would satisfy the elements of the statute. The Public Defender urges an interpretation of "physical force" to mean force "used to overcome lack of consent." That definition equates force with violence and leads to the conclusion that sexual assault requires the application of some amount of force in addition to the act of penetration.

Current judicial practice suggests an understanding of "physical force" to mean "any degree of physical power or strength used against the victim, even though it entails no injury and leaves no mark." Resort to common experience or understanding does not yield a conclusive meaning. The dictionary provides several definitions of "force," among which are the following: (1) "power, violence, compulsion, or constraint exerted upon or against a person or thing," (2) "a general term for exercise of strength or power, esp. physical, to overcome resistance," or (3) "strength or power of any degree that is exercised without justifica-

---

1. The sexual assault statute, *N.J.S.A.*: 2C:14–2c(1), reads as follows:

c. An actor is guilty of sexual assault if he commits an act of sexual penetration with another person under any one of the following circumstances:

(1) The actor *uses physical force or coercion,* but the victim does not sustain severe personal injury;

(2) The victim is one whom the actor knew or should have known was physically helpless, mentally defective or mentally incapacitated;

(3) The victim is on probation or parole, or is detained in a hospital, prison or other institution and the actor has super-

visory or disciplinary power over the victim by virtue of the actor's legal, professional or occupational status;

(4) The victim is at least 16 but less than 18 years old and:

(a) The actor is related to the victim by blood or affinity to the third degree; or

(b) The actor has supervisory or disciplinary power over the victim; or

(c) The actor is a foster parent, a guardian, or stands in loco parentis within the household;

(5) The victim is at least 13 but less than 16 years old and the actor is at least 4 years older than the victim. * * *

tion or contrary to law upon a person or thing." *Webster's Third New International Dictionary* 887 (1961).

Thus, as evidenced by the disagreements among the lower courts and the parties, and the variety of possible usages, the statutory words "physical force" do not evoke a single meaning that is obvious and plain. * * * When a statute is open to conflicting interpretations, the court seeks the underlying intent of the legislature, relying on legislative history and the contemporary context of the statute. * * * We also remain mindful of the basic tenet of statutory construction that penal statutes are to be strictly construed in favor of the accused. Nevertheless, the construction must conform to the intent of the Legislature.

The provisions proscribing sexual offenses found in the Code of Criminal Justice, *N.J.S.A.* 2C:14–2c(1), became effective in 1979, and were written against almost two hundred years of rape law in New Jersey. The origin of the rape statute that the current statutory offense of sexual assault replaced can be traced to the English common law. Under the common law, rape was defined as "carnal knowledge of a woman against her will." American jurisdictions generally adopted the English view, but over time states added the requirement that the carnal knowledge have been forcible, apparently in order to prove that the act was against the victim's will. As of 1796, New Jersey statutory law defined rape as "carnal knowledge of a woman, forcibly and against her will." Those three elements of rape—carnal knowledge, forcibly, and against her will—remained the essential elements of the crime until 1979.

Under traditional rape law, in order to prove that a rape had occurred, the state had to show both that force had been used and that the penetration had been against the woman's will. Force was identified and determined not as an independent factor but in relation to the response of the victim, which in turn implicated the victim's own state of mind. "Thus, the perpetrator's use of force became criminal only if the victim's state of mind met the statutory requirement. The perpetrator could use all the force imaginable and no crime would be committed if the state could not prove additionally that the victim did not consent." National Institute of Law Enforcement and Criminal Justice, *Forcible Rape—An Analysis of Legal Issues* 5 (March 1978). Although the terms "non-consent" and "against her will" were often treated as equivalent, under the traditional definition of rape, both formulations squarely placed on the victim the burden of proof and of action. Effectively, a woman who was above the age of consent had actively and affirmatively to withdraw that consent for the intercourse to be against her will. As a Delaware court stated, "If sexual intercourse is obtained by milder means, or with the consent or silent submission of the female, it cannot constitute the crime of rape." *State v. Brown,* 83 A. 1083, 1084 (O.T.1912).

The presence or absence of consent often turned on credibility. To demonstrate that the victim had not consented to the intercourse, and also that sufficient force had been used to accomplish the rape, the state had to prove that the victim had resisted. According to the oft-quoted Lord Hale, to be deemed a credible witness, a woman had to be of good fame, disclose the injury immediately, suffer signs of injury, and cry out for help. 1 Matthew Hale, *History of the Pleas of the Crown* 633 (1st ed. 1847). Courts and commentators historically distrusted the testimony of victims, "assuming that women lie about their lack of consent for various reasons: to blackmail men, to explain the discovery of a consensual affair, or because of psychological illness." [Cynthia A. Wickstom, Note, *Focusing on the Offender's Forceful Conduct: A Proposal for the Redefinition of Rape Laws,* 56 Geo.Wash.L.Rev. 399 (1988)], at 403. Evidence of resistance was viewed as a solution to the credibility problem; it was the "outward manifestation of nonconsent, [a] device for determining whether a woman actually gave consent." Note, *The Resistance Standard in Rape Legislation,* 18 Stan.L.Rev. 680, 689 (1966). * * *

The judicial interpretation of the pre-reform rape law in New Jersey, with its insistence on resistance by the victim, greatly minimized the importance of the forcible and assaultive aspect of the defendant's conduct. Rape prosecutions turned then not so much on the forcible or assaultive character of the defendant's actions as on the nature of the victim's response. * * *

The importance of resistance as an evidentiary requirement set the law of rape apart from other common-law crimes, particularly in the eyes of those who advocated reform of rape law in the 1970s. * * *

To refute the misguided belief that rape was not real unless the victim fought back, reformers emphasized empirical research indicating that women who resisted forcible intercourse often suffered far more serious injury as a result. That research discredited the assumption that resistance to the utmost or to the best of a woman's ability was the most reasonable or rational response to a rape.

The research also helped demonstrate the underlying point of the reformers that the crime of rape rested not in the overcoming of a woman's will or the insult to her chastity but in the forcible attack itself—the assault on her person. Reformers criticized the conception of rape as a distinctly sexual crime rather than a crime of violence. They emphasized that rape had its legal origins in laws designed to protect the property rights of men to their wives and daughters. Although the crime had evolved into an offense against women, reformers argued that vestiges of the old law remained, particularly in the understanding of rape as a crime against the purity or chastity of a woman. The burden of protecting that chastity fell on the woman, with the state offering its protection only after the woman demonstrated that she had resisted sufficiently. * * *

Critics of rape law agreed that the focus of the crime should be shifted from the victim's behavior to the defendant's conduct, and particularly to its forceful and assaultive, rather than sexual, character.

Reformers also shared the goals of facilitating rape prosecutions and of sparing victims much of the degradation involved in bringing and trying a charge of rape. There were, however, differences over the best way to redefine the crime. Some reformers advocated a standard that defined rape as unconsented-to sexual intercourse, others urged the elimination of any reference to consent from the definition of rape. Nonetheless, all proponents of reform shared a central premise: that the burden of showing non-consent should not fall on the victim of the crime. In dealing with the problem of consent the reform goal was not so much to purge the entire concept of consent from the law as to eliminate the burden that had been placed on victims to prove they had not consented.

Similarly, with regard to force, rape law reform sought to give independent significance to the forceful or assaultive conduct of the defendant and to avoid a definition of force that depended on the reaction of the victim. In urging that the "resistance" requirement be abandoned, reformers sought to break the connection between force and resistance.

III

* * * The circumstances surrounding the actual passage of the current law reveal that it was conceived as a reform measure reconstituting the law to address a widely-sensed evil and to effectuate an important public policy. Those circumstances are highly relevant in understanding legislative intent and in determining the objectives of the current law.

In October 1971, the New Jersey Criminal Law Revision Commission promulgated a Final Report and Commentary on its proposed New Jersey Penal Code. The proposed Code substantially followed the American Law Institute's Model Penal Code (MPC) with respect to sexual offenses. See *M.P.C.* §§ 213.1 to 213.4. * * * The comments to the MPC, on which the proposed Code was based, state that "[c]ompulsion plainly implies non-consent," and that the words "compels to submit" require more than "a token initial resistance." A.L.I., *MPC,* § 213.1, comments at 306 (revised commentary 1980).

The Legislature did not endorse the Model Penal Code approach to rape. Rather, it passed a fundamentally different proposal in 1978 when it adopted the Code of Criminal Justice. The new statutory provisions covering rape were formulated by a coalition of feminist groups assisted by the National Organization of Women (NOW) National Task Force on Rape. * * * The NOW bill had been modeled after the 1976 Philadelphia Center for Rape Concern Model Sex Offense Statute. The Model Sex Offense Statute in turn had been based on selected provisions of the Michigan Criminal Sexual Conduct Statute * * *. The stated intent of the drafters of the * * * Model Statute had been to remove all features found to be contrary to the interests of rape victims. * * *

The reform statute defines sexual assault as penetration accomplished by the use of "physical force" or "coercion," but it does not define either "physical force" or "coercion" or enumerate examples of evidence that would establish those elements. * * * The task of defining "physical force" therefore was left to the courts.

That definitional task runs the risk of undermining the basic legislative intent to reformulate rape law. That risk was encountered by the Michigan Supreme Court in *People v. Patterson,* 428 *Mich.* 502, 410 *N.W.2d* 733 (1987). That court considered the sufficiency of the evidence of force or coercion in the prosecution of a sexual contact charge against a defendant who had placed his hands on the genital area of a seventeen-year-old girl while she was sleeping. A majority of the court concluded that the defendant had not used force as required by the statute because there was "no evidence of physical overpowering ... [and] there was no submission." Justice Boyle, in dissent, soundly criticized the majority's position as a distortion of the legislature's intent to protect the sexual privacy of persons from the use of force, coercion, or other undue advantage. Concluding that the statute did not require a showing of any extra force, Justice Boyle pointed out that in "defin[ing] force by measuring the degree of resistance by the victim," the majority had effectively "reintroduc[ed] the resistance requirement, when the proper focus ought to be on whether the contact was unpermitted."

Unlike the Michigan statute interpreted in *Patterson,* the New Jersey Code of Criminal Justice does not refer to force in relation to "overcoming the will" of the victim, or to the "physical overpowering" of the victim, or the "submission" of the victim. It does not require the demonstrated non-consent of the victim. * * *

The Legislature's concept of sexual assault and the role of force was significantly colored by its understanding of the law of assault and battery. As a general matter, criminal battery is defined as "the unlawful application of force to the person of another." The application of force is criminal when it results in either (a) a physical injury or (b) an offensive touching. * * * Thus, by eliminating all references to the victim's state of mind and conduct, and by broadening the definition of penetration to cover not only sexual intercourse between a man and a woman but a range of acts that invade another's body or compel intimate contact, the Legislature emphasized the affinity between sexual assault and other forms of assault and battery. * * *

* * * We are thus satisfied that an interpretation of the statutory crime of sexual assault to require physical force in addition to that entailed in an act of involuntary or unwanted sexual penetration would be fundamentally inconsistent with the legislative purpose to eliminate any consideration of whether the victim resisted or expressed non-consent. * * *

Because the statute eschews any reference to the victim's will or resistance, the standard defining the role of force in sexual penetration must prevent the possibility that the establishment of the crime will turn on the alleged victim's state of mind or responsive behavior. We conclude, therefore, that any act of sexual penetration engaged in by the defendant without the affirmative and freely-given permission of the victim to the specific act of penetration constitutes the offense of sexual assault. Therefore, physical force in excess of that inherent in the act of sexual penetration is not required for such penetration to be unlawful. The definition of "physical force" is satisfied under *N.J.S.A.* 2C:14–2c(1) if the defendant applies any amount of force against another person in the absence of what a reasonable person would believe to be affirmative and freely-given permission to the act of sexual penetration.

Under the reformed statute, permission to engage in sexual penetration must be affirmative and it must be given freely, but that permission may be inferred either from acts or statements reasonably viewed in light of the surrounding circumstances. Persons need not, of course, expressly announce their consent to engage in intercourse for there to be affirmative permission. Permission to engage in an act of sexual penetration can be and indeed often is indicated through physical actions rather than words. Permission is demonstrated when the evidence, in whatever form, is sufficient to demonstrate that a reasonable person would have believed that the alleged victim had affirmatively and freely given authorization to the act.   * * *

Today the law of sexual assault is indispensable to the system of legal rules that assures each of us the right to decide who may touch our bodies, when, and under what circumstances. The decision to engage in sexual relations with another person is one of the most private and intimate decisions a person can make. Each person has the right not only to decide whether to engage in sexual contact with another, but also to control the circumstances and character of that contact. No one, neither a spouse, nor a friend, nor an acquaintance, nor a stranger, has the right or the privilege to force sexual contact.   * * *

We emphasize as well that what is now referred to as "acquaintance rape" is not a new phenomenon. Nor was it a "futuristic" concept in 1978 when the sexual assault law was enacted. Current concern over the prevalence of forced sexual intercourse between persons who know one another reflects both greater awareness of the extent of such behavior and a growing appreciation of its gravity. Notwithstanding the stereotype of rape as a violent attack by a stranger, the vast majority of sexual assaults are perpetrated by someone known to the victim. One respected study indicates that more than half of all rapes are committed by male relatives, current or former husbands, boyfriends or lovers. Diana Russell, *The Prevalence and Incidence of Forcible Rape and Attempted Rape of Females,* 7 Victimology 81 (1982). Similarly, contrary to common myths, perpetrators generally do not use guns or knives and victims generally do not suffer external bruises or cuts. Although this more realistic and accurate view of rape only recently has achieved widespread public circulation, it was a central concern of the proponents of reform in the 1970s.   * * *

IV

In a case such as this one, in which the State does not allege violence or force extrinsic to the act of penetration, the factfinder must decide whether the defendant's act of penetration was undertaken in circumstances that led the defendant reasonably to believe that the alleged victim had freely given affirmative permission to the specific act of sexual penetration. Such permission can be indicated either through words or through actions that, when viewed in the light of all the surrounding circumstances, would demonstrate to a reasonable person affirmative and freely-given authorization for the specific act of sexual penetration.

In applying that standard to the facts in these cases, the focus of attention must be on the nature of the defendant's actions. * * * The role of the factfinder is to decide * * * whether the defendant's belief that the alleged victim had freely given affirmative permission was reasonable.

In these cases neither the alleged victim's subjective state of mind nor the reasonableness of the alleged victim's actions can be deemed relevant to the offense. The alleged victim may be questioned about what he or she did or said only to determine whether the defendant was reasonable in believing that affirmative permission had been freely given. * * *

In short, in order to convict under the sexual assault statute in cases such as these, the State must prove beyond a reasonable doubt that there was sexual penetration and that it was accomplished without the affirmative and freely-given permission of the alleged victim. * * * If there is evidence to suggest that the defendant reasonably believed that such permission had been given, the State must demonstrate either that defendant did not actually believe that affirmative permission had been freely-given or that such a belief was unreasonable under all of the circumstances. Thus, the State bears the burden of proof throughout the case. * * *

We acknowledge that cases such as this are inherently fact sensitive and depend on the reasoned judgment and common sense of judges and juries. The trial court concluded that the victim had not expressed consent to the act of intercourse, either through her words or actions. We conclude that the record provides reasonable support for the trial court's disposition.

Accordingly, we reverse the judgment of the Appellate Division and reinstate the disposition of juvenile delinquency for the commission of second-degree sexual assault.

For reversal and reinstatement—* * *—7.

Opposed—None.

Notes and Questions

1. Do you agree with Susan Ager that what she experienced was not rape? Should the boyfriend's conduct constitute a lesser criminal offense? On the other hand, does his breach of trust aggravate the harm?

2. Is *M.T.S.* rightly decided as a matter of statutory construction? As a matter of policy?

3. *Alternatives to the New Jersey approach.* Compare the New Jersey rape law, as interpreted in *M.T.S.*, to the statutory system in Washington. Under West's Rev.Code Wash.Ann. 9A.44.050(1)(a) (1993), rape in the second degree is committed when "the person engages in sexual intercourse with another person * * * by forcible compulsion." "Forcible compulsion" is defined as:

> [P]hysical force which overcomes resistance, or a threat, express or implied, that places a person in fear of death or physical injury to herself or himself or another person, or in fear that she or he or another person will be kidnapped. [Wash.Rev.Code 9A.44.010(6) (1993).]

Rape in the third degree occurs when "such person engages in sexual intercourse with another person, not married to the perpetrator * * * [w]here the victim did not consent * * * to sexual intercourse with the perpetrator and such lack of consent was clearly expressed by the victim's words or conduct * * *." West's Rev.Wash.Code 9A.44.060(1)(a) (1988).

Which statutory scheme do you prefer?

4. *"Criminal sexual contact."* New Jersey's sexual assault statute is patterned on the Michigan Penal Code. In Michigan and New Jersey, a person is guilty of a sexual assault (although of a lesser degree) if the defendant has "criminal sexual *contact* " with another person. In Michigan, the requisite "contact" includes:

> the intentional touching of the victim's or actor's intimate parts or the intentional touching of the clothing covering the immediate area of the victim's or actor's intimate parts, if that intentional touching can reasonably be construed as being for the purpose of sexual arousal or gratification. [Mich.Comp.Laws Ann. § 750.520a(k) (1991).]

Do you see any problems with prosecuting a person for criminal sexual contact under this definition?

5. In the past, male-dominant female-submissive "sexual courtship" was socially acceptable. One court observed, "[m]any men have been conditioned to believe that initial refusals [by women] are an essential part of the 'mating game' ritual which dictates that women must resist somewhat to make themselves more attractive to men * * *." Deborah S. v. Diorio, 153 Misc.2d 708, 714, 583 N.Y.S.2d 872, 877 (1992).

This "sexual script" might not be an historical relic. In one study of the behavior of 610 undergraduate women, 39% of the respondents admitted that they engaged in "token resistance," i.e., objecting and putting up mild resistance to the male's sexual overtures, even though they "had every intention to and [were] willing to engage in sexual intercourse." Charlene L. Muehlenhard & Lisa C. Hollabaugh, *Do Women Sometimes Say No When They Mean Yes? The Prevalence and Correlates of Women's Token Resistance to Sex,* 54 J. of Personality & Soc. Psychol. 872 (1988). Among the reasons given by the undergraduate women for their no-meant-yes behavior was fear of appearing promiscuous, self-consciousness or embarrassment, and game playing (e.g., "I wanted him to beg," "I wanted him to talk me into it," or "I wanted him to be more physically aggressive").

Even when "no means no," how far should the law take this formula? If a woman expresses her unwillingness to have intercourse with a man, is the "no" irrevocable on the present occasion? If not, how should the line be drawn between legitimate efforts to convince the woman to reconsider, on the one hand, and inappropriate pressures, cajolery, or manipulation of feelings, on the other hand? What about "a woman who says no to her lover before dinner and then changes her mind after several hours of relaxation and intimate conversation"? Stephen J. Schulhofer, *Taking Sexual Autonomy Seriously: Rape Law and Beyond,* 11 Law & Phil. 35, 43 (1992).

2. DECEPTIONS AND NON-PHYSICAL THREATS

BORO v. SUPERIOR COURT

Court of Appeal, First District, 1985.
163 Cal.App.3d 1224, 210 Cal.Rptr. 122.

NEWSOM, ASSOCIATE JUSTICE.

By timely petition filed with this court, petitioner Daniel Boro seeks a writ of prohibition to restrain further prosecution of Count II of the information on file against him * * * charging him with a violation of Penal Code section 261, subdivision (4), rape: "an act of sexual intercourse accomplished with a person not the spouse of the perpetrator, under any of the following circumstances: ... (4) Where a person is at the time unconscious of the nature of the act, and this is known to the accused."

Petitioner contends that his motion to dismiss should have been granted * * * because the evidence at the preliminary hearing proved that the prosecutrix, Ms. R., was aware of the "nature of the act" within the meaning of section 261, subdivision (4). The Attorney General contends the opposite, arguing that the victim's agreement to intercourse was predicated on a belief—fraudulently induced by petitioner—that the sex act was necessary to save her life, and that she was hence unconscious of the *nature* of the act within the meaning of the statute.

In relevant part the factual background may be summarized as follows. Ms. R., the rape victim, * * * received a telephone call from a person who identified himself as "Dr. Stevens" and said that he worked at Peninsula Hospital.

"Dr. Stevens" told Ms. R. that he had the results of her blood test and that she had contracted a dangerous, highly infectious and perhaps fatal disease; that she could be sued as a result; that the disease came from using public toilets; and that she would have to tell him the identity of all her friends who would then have to be contacted in the interest of controlling the spread of the disease.

"Dr. Stevens" further explained that there were only two ways to treat the disease. The first was a painful surgical procedure—graphically described—costing $9,000, and requiring her uninsured hospitalization for six weeks. A second alternative, "Dr. Stevens" explained, was to have sexual intercourse with an anonymous donor who had been injected with a serum which would cure the disease. The latter, non-surgical procedure would only cost $4,500. When the victim replied that she lacked sufficient funds the "doctor" suggested that $1,000 would suffice as a down payment. The victim thereupon agreed to the non-surgical alternative and consented to intercourse with the mysterious donor, believing "it was the only choice I had."

After discussing her intentions with her work supervisor, the victim proceeded to the Hyatt Hotel in Burlingame as instructed, and contacted "Dr. Stevens" by telephone. The latter became furious when he learned Ms. R. had informed her employer of the plan, and threatened to terminate his treatment, finally instructing her to inform her employer she had decided not to go through with the treatment. Ms. R. did so, then went to her bank, withdrew $1,000 and, as instructed, checked into another hotel and called "Dr. Stevens" to give him her room number.

About a half hour later the defendant "donor" arrived at her room. When Ms. R. had undressed, the "donor," petitioner, * * * had sexual intercourse with her.

At the time of penetration, it was Ms. R.'s belief that she would die unless she consented to sexual intercourse with the defendant: as she testified, "My life felt threatened, and for that reason and that reason alone did I do it." * * *

Upon the basis of the evidence just recounted, petitioner was charged * * *, as follows: Count I: section 261, subdivision (2)—rape: accomplished against a person's will by means of force or fear of immediate and unlawful bodily injury on the person or another. Count II: section 261, subdivision (4)—rape "[w]here a person is at the time unconscious of the nature of the act, and this is known to the accused. * * *

A * * * motion to set aside the information was granted as to Count[ ] I * * *. Petitioner's sole challenge is to denial of the motion to dismiss Count II.

The People's position is stated concisely: "We contend, quite simply, that at the time of the intercourse Ms. R., the victim, was 'unconscious of the nature of the act': because of [petitioner's] misrepresentation she believed it was in the nature of a medical treatment and not a simple, ordinary act of sexual intercourse." Petitioner, on the other hand, stresses that the victim was plainly aware of the *nature* of the act in which she voluntarily engaged, so that her motivation in doing so (since it did not fall within the proscription of section 261, subdivision (2)) is irrelevant.

Our research discloses sparse California authority on the subject. * * * In *People v. Minkowski* (1962) 204 Cal.App.2d 832, 23 Cal.Rptr. 92, the defendant was a physician who "treated" several victims for menstrual cramps. Each victim testified that she was treated in a position with her back to the doctor, bent over a table, with feet apart, in a dressing gown. And in each case the "treatment" consisted of the defendant first inserting a metal instrument, then substituting an instrument which "felt different"—the victims not realizing that the second instrument was in fact the doctor's penis. The precise issue before us was never tendered in *People v. Minkowski* because the petitioner there *conceded* the sufficiency of evidence to support the element of consciousness.

The decision is useful to this analysis, however, because it exactly illustrates certain traditional rules in the area of our inquiry. Thus, as a leading authority has written, "if deception causes a misunderstanding as to the fact itself (fraud in the *factum*) there is no legally-recognized consent because what happened is not that for which consent was given; whereas consent induced by fraud is as effective as any other consent, so far as direct and immediate legal consequences are concerned, if the deception relates not to the thing done but merely to some collateral matter (fraud in the inducement)." (Perkins & Boyce, Criminal Law (3d ed. 1982) ch. 9, § 3, p. 1079.)

The victims in *Minkowski* consented, not to sexual intercourse, but to an act of an altogether different nature, penetration by medical instrument. The consent was to a pathological, and not a carnal, act, and the mistake was, therefore, in the *factum* and not merely in the inducement.

Another relatively common situation in the literature on this subject—discussed in detail by Perkins (*supra,* at p. 1080) is the fraudulent obtaining of intercourse by impersonating a spouse. As Professor Perkins observes, the courts are not in accord as to whether the crime of rape is thereby committed. "[T]he disagreement is not in regard to the underlying principle but only as to its application. Some courts have taken the position that such a misdeed is fraud in the inducement on the theory that the woman consents to exactly what is done (sexual intercourse) and hence there is no rape; other courts, with better reason it would seem, hold such a misdeed to be rape on the theory that it involves fraud in the *factum* since the woman's consent is to an innocent act of marital intercourse while what is actually perpetrated upon her is an act of adultery. * * *"

In California, of course, we have by statute[3] adopted the majority view that such fraud is in the *factum,* not the inducement, and have thus held it to vitiate consent. It is otherwise, however, with respect to the conceptually much murkier statutory offense with which we here deal, and the language of which has remained essentially unchanged since its enactment.

The language itself could not be plainer. It defines rape to be "an act of sexual intercourse" with a non-spouse, accomplished where the victim is "at the time unconscious of the nature of the act ..." Nor, as

---

3. Section 261, subdivision (5) reads as follows: "Where a person submits under the belief that the person committing the act is the victim's spouse, and this belief is induced by any artifice, pretense, or concealment practiced by the accused, with intent to induce the belief."

we have just seen, can we entertain the slightest doubt that the Legislature well understood how to draft a statute to * * * specify * * * fraud in the inducement as vitiating consent. Moreover, courts of this state have previously confronted the general rule that fraud in the inducement does not vitiate consent. * * *

If the Legislature * * * had desired to correct the [gap in the law,] [5] it could certainly have done so. * * *

To so conclude is not to vitiate the heartless cruelty of petitioner's scheme, but to say that it comprised crimes of a different order than a violation of section 261, subdivision (4). * * *

SUSAN ESTRICH—RAPE

95 Yale Law Journal 1087 (1986), 1115–16, 1118–20

In *Goldberg v. State,* [77] a high-school senior working as a sales clerk was "sold a story" by the defendant that he was a free-lance agent and thought she was an excellent prospect to become a successful model. She accompanied him to his "temporary studio" where she testified that she engaged in intercourse because she was afraid. Her reasons for being afraid, according to the appellate court which reversed the conviction, were: "1) she was alone with the appellant in a house with no buildings close by and no one to help her if she resisted, and 2) the appellant was much larger than she was." According to the appellate court, "[i]n the complete absence of any threatening words or actions by the appellant, these two factors, as a matter of law, are simply not enough to have created a reasonable fear of harm so as to preclude resistance and be 'the equivalent of force.'"

The New York Supreme Court, sitting as the trier of fact in a rape case, reached a similar conclusion with respect to the threatening situation facing an "incredibly gullible, trusting, and naive" college sophomore. In *People v. Evans,* [80] the defendant posed as a psychologist conducting a sociological experiment, took the woman to a dating bar to "observe" her, and then induced her to come to an apartment he used as an "office." When she rejected his advances, he said to her: " 'Look where you are. You are in the apartment of a strange man. How do you know that I am really who I say I am? How do you know that I am really a psychologist? ... I could kill you. I could rape you. I could hurt you physically.'" The trial court found his conduct "reprehensible," describing it as "conquest by con job." But it was not criminal; the words were ambiguous, capable of communicating either a threat to use ultimate force or the chiding of a "foolish girl." While acknowl-

---

5. It is not difficult to conceive of reasons why the Legislature may have consciously wished to leave the matter where it lies. Thus, as a matter of degree, where consent to intercourse is obtained by promises of travel, fame, celebrity and the like—ought the liar and seducer to be chargeable as a rapist? Where is the line to be drawn?

77. 41 Md.App. 58, 395 A.2d 1213 (Ct. Spec.App.1979).

80. 85 Misc.2d 1088, 379 N.Y.S.2d 912 (Sup.Ct.1975), *aff'd,* 55 A.D.2d 858, 390 N.Y.S.2d 768 (1976).

edging that the victim might be terrified, the court was not persuaded beyond a reasonable doubt that the guilt of the defendant had been established. * * *

It is one thing to argue that * * * the men in these cases should not be considered in the same category (in terms of their blameworthiness, their dangerousness, or the harm caused by their actions), as the man who puts a gun to his victim's head and threatens to kill her if she refuses to have sex. It is quite another to argue that these men have committed no crime.

Most striking about these cases is the fact that had these men been seeking money instead of sex, their actions would plainly violate traditional state criminal prohibitions. Had Mr. Goldberg used his modeling agent story to secure money rather than sex, his would be a case of theft by deception or false pretenses. As for Mr. Evans, had he sought money rather than sex as part of his "sociological test," he too could have been found guilty of theft. Neither Goldberg nor Evans could have escaped liability on the ground that a "reasonable person" would not have been deceived, any more than a victim's leaving his front door unlocked or his keys in the automobile ignition serves as a defense to burglary or larceny. * * *

Lying to secure money is unlawful theft by deception or false pretenses, a lesser crime than robbery, but a crime nonetheless. Yet lying to secure sex is old-fashioned seduction—not first-degree rape, not even third-degree rape. A threat to expose sexual information has long been considered a classic case of extortion, if not robbery itself. But securing sex itself by means of a threat short of force has, in many jurisdictions, been considered no crime at all.

To the argument that it is either impossible or unwise for the law to regulate sexual "bargains" short of physical force, the law of extortion stands as a sharp rebuke: It has long listed prohibited threats in fairly inclusive terms.[95] While extortion may be a lesser offense than robbery, it is nonetheless prohibited.

It is almost certainly impossible to expect that the law could address all of the techniques of power and coercion which men use against women in sexual relations. I am not suggesting that we try.[96] Rather, I

---

95. Traditionally, robbery has been limited to threats of immediate bodily harms, threats to destroy the victim's home, or threats to accuse him of sodomy. Securing property through the use of other threats—threats to accuse an individual of a crime, to impair his credit or business repute, to take or withhold action as an official or cause an official to take or withhold action, to expose any secret tending to subject the person to contempt or ridicule—have been prohibited as the lesser offense of extortion or blackmail. Notably, extortion encompasses threats to do what is legal and even

desirable—to report a crime, for instance. It also encompasses threats to make public information which is true and accurate. Nonetheless, when those threats are used to secure money, in the absence of an honest claim of restitution or indemnification, they are prohibited as criminal.

96. Nor am I arguing that these cases must of necessity be considered in the same category as first degree, armed and brutal rape. I am more than willing to treat them as a lesser degree of "rape" and to impose lighter punishment in the same way that the unarmed robber, or the blackmailer, is

am suggesting that we do something that is actually quite easy—prohibit fraud to secure sex to the same extent we prohibit fraud to secure money, and prohibit extortion to secure sex to the same extent we prohibit extortion to secure money.

VIVIAN BERGER—NOT SO SIMPLE RAPE

7 Criminal Justice Ethics at 69 (Winter/Spring 1988), 76–77

The meager evidence of why [Estrich] advocates a crime of fraudulent rape and, relatedly, how she would understand it derive from her discussion of two decisions involving "con artist" defendants. By misrepresenting themselves, respectively, as a freelance modeling agent and a psychologist conducting an experiment, these men inveigled their way into the confidence of gullible young women with whom they later had sexual intercourse. The issue in the actual cases, *Goldberg v. State* and *People v. Evans,* was the same as that in *Rusk* and *Alston:* whether the record revealed sufficient force or threats to sustain a finding of guilt of rape. Both courts, one appellate, the other sitting as trier of fact, held for the accused. After criticizing these results in terms of the judges' insensitivity to the victim's sense of danger (as usual, the women ended by being stranded in a scary, unfamiliar environment), Estrich notes in passing that had the defendants been seeking money, not sex, they could have been convicted of theft by deception or false pretenses since, among other things, victim foolishness would have afforded them no defense.

That insight is true as far as it goes, but what bearing does it have on rape law? Does Estrich really mean to suggest that if, in a "*Goldberg* variation," the defendant has misrepresented himself as a talent scout and told the eighteen-year-old complainant, without any sort of intimidation, "Come to bed with me, and I'll make you a star," he should be convicted of *rape?* Fraud, perhaps; or mail fraud, if he wrote her a letter containing the lies—though I must confess to minimal sympathy for the idea that the law should protect, via criminal sanctions, the cheated expectations of women who sought to sleep their way to the top but discovered, too late, that they were dealing with swindlers. A *fortiori,* the notion that rape, one of the gravest possible infringements of human integrity, should be expanded to include situations where the woman attempts to sell her body and fails to receive the bargained-for price simply makes a mockery of women's long efforts to achieve autonomy, respect, and equality.

What, finally, would be the limits of liability for rape by fraud? Many females presumably yield to male advances because the man insists: "I love you." If false, is this representation "material"? To a "reasonable" woman? Does it matter whether the woman is reasonable? Whether her exploiter knows that she isn't? What if the man represents that he is rich and famous whereas, in truth, he is poor and unknown? Or to take a more earnest tack, suppose that a woman makes love with a man in reliance on his falsehood that he is AIDS-free?

---

treated as a less serious offender than the   one who uses a deadly weapon in a robbery.

In that case, the woman is surely a victim and the lying man, a despicable predator. But is he a rapist? The foregoing problems and many others would readily occur to thoughtful readers, not merely to nit-picking scholars. Estrich has failed to work them through. Thus, her approach to this tricky topic cannot, as it stands, be taken seriously. * * *

But what sorts of threats should qualify as the equivalent of "force" in rape? Surely, not all. Again, her treatment of a major issue is extremely sketchy. * * *

If Estrich really intends to propose that *any* threat sufficient to trigger a charge of extortion should serve to support a conviction of rape, then the latter crime could comprise obtaining sex by the following threatened actions: firing, or failing to hire, a woman; taking her canary; exposing her secret love affair; telling a prospective mortgagee that she frequently fails to honor her debts. Plainly, at some point (sooner, I would hope, where one's body, as opposed to one's money, is involved), the law should encourage the imposed-on woman to complain to the authorities or file civil suit (on grounds of sexual harassment, for instance) rather than yield. I believe that this seemingly harsher approach, at least to my more trivial examples, would demonstrate greater respect for women than "empower[ing] them with the weapon of a rape charge" and thereby implying that one should not expect weak females to defend their own sexual autonomy against any form of unpleasantness or pressure. I also believe that some threats of middling severity like loss of employment, especially to a person who depends on the income, might properly be criminalized as "coercion." But to call the resulting intercourse "rape" to my mind fails "to make clear that loss of bodily integrity" due to the gravest threats "is a different and greater injury" than its loss on account of lesser menaces, "and thus merits greater punishment," including the stigma of the label "rapist."

Notes and Questions

1. Since Boro told the victim that she had contracted a "perhaps fatal" disease, and the victim testified that "my life felt threatened," why was Count I (forcible rape) dismissed? Was Boro guilty of any non-rape offense? How would *Boro* be resolved under the Model Penal Code? See Sections 213.0–.5.

2. Is there any sound explanation for the common law *factum*/inducement distinction in rape prosecutions? In Bartell v. State, 106 Wis. 342, 82 N.W. 142 (1900), a man pretending to be a "magnetic healer" convinced an ailing female to undress and to be massaged by him for medical relief. Based on this fraud, he was convicted of battery. Similarly, a person is guilty of theft if she fraudulently induces another to part with his money. Why does fraud in the inducement negative the consent in these cases, but not in *Boro?*

3. Should a man be convicted of rape if he induces a woman to have intercourse with him as the result of any of the threats mentioned by Professor Berger in the last paragraph of her article?

Suppose that a college professor offers a student an "A" in his class if she sleeps with him. Rape? Is this different than if he tells her he will give her an "F" if she does not sleep with him? If so, why?

3. MARITAL IMMUNITY RULE

STATE v. SMITH

Supreme Court of New Jersey, 1981.
85 N.J. 193, 426 A.2d 38.

PASHMAN, J.

Since the enactment in New Jersey of the new Code of Criminal Justice, no person can claim that a sexual assault committed after the effective date of the Code * * * is exempt from prosecution because the accused and victim were husband and wife. The Criminal Code expressly excludes marriage to the victim as a defense against prosecution of sexual crimes. *N.J.S.A.* 2C:14–5(b). The criminal acts alleged in this case, however, occurred before the effective date of the Code. The issue before the Court is whether a defendant can be charged with and convicted of raping his wife under the former statute, *N.J.S.A.* 2A:138–1. We hold that, at least under the circumstances of this case, he can.

I

The State alleges that on October 1, 1975, defendant Albert Smith broke into the apartment of his estranged wife, Alfreda Smith, and repeatedly beat and raped her. On that date the accused and victim were legally married. They had been married for seven years but had lived separately for approximately one year. * * * It also appears from the record that the parties had not entered into a formal agreement setting down the terms of their separation, nor had either filed a complaint for divorce. * * *

After hearing testimony * * * the Essex County Grand Jury returned an indictment charging defendant with * * * rape. Defendant moved to dismiss the rape charge on the ground that he was legally married to the victim at the time of the incident. The trial judge reluctantly granted the motion. He believed that the common law included a marital exemption from the crime of rape, which was implicitly incorporated into this State's statutory definition of rape from early Revolutionary times to the present. Although the trial judge expressed unequivocal disapproval of such an anachronistic rule of law, he considered it the prerogative of the Legislature to change it. * * *

We granted the State's petition for certification to consider the reach of our former rape statute.

II

The rape statute under which defendant was charged provided in part:

> Any person who has carnal knowledge of a woman forcibly against her will ... is guilty of a high misdemeanor and shall be punished by a fine of not more than $5,000, or by imprisonment for not more than 30 years, or both.... [*N.J.S.A.* 2A:138–1 (repealed)]

The State argues that the statute covered the conduct of a husband against his wife because it applied to "any person."

This argument, although superficially appealing, does not resolve the issue before the Court. The marital exemption, if it existed, may have acted as a defense by negating some element of the crime. Thus the statute may well have applied to "any person," but a husband's forcible sexual intercourse with his wife was not rape because it did not include all three elements of the crime—carnal knowledge, force, and lack of consent. Similarly, the reference to "any person" could be construed not to include infants; insane persons, who lack the necessary state of mind to form an intent to rape; or women, at least as the principal actor. Thus, our inquiry must go beyond the "plain meaning" of the statute, the language of which alone does not reveal whether a husband was exempt from the charge of raping his wife.

Defendant * * * contends that the exemption was a rule of English common law which was incorporated into New Jersey's first rape statute in 1796 and remained unchanged throughout the time that *N.J.S.A.* 2A:138–1 was in effect.

The first State Constitution of New Jersey provided for * * * incorporation of English common and statutory law in existence at that time * * *. Thus, English common law as of 1776 became part of this State's law after the Revolution subject to change by the Legislature or except where in conflict with the State Constitution. * * *

[W]e must first consider whether there actually existed a marital exemption rule under pre-Revolutionary common law.

A

Sir Matthew Hale, a seventeenth century English jurist, wrote a treatise on English law which is invariably cited as authority for the rule. Hale discussed the crime of rape and possible defenses, stating:

> But the husband cannot be guilty of a rape committed by himself upon his lawful wife, for by their mutual matrimonial consent and contract the wife hath given up herself in this kind unto her husband, which she cannot retract. [1 Hale, *History of the Pleas of the Crown* *629]

Hale cited no authority for this proposition and we have found none in earlier writers. Thus the marital exemption rule expressly adopted by many of our sister states has its source in a bare, extra-judicial declaration made some 300 years ago. * * *

We need not decide, however, the broad question of whether a marital exemption existed under English common law. The narrower question here is whether such a marital exemption, even if it existed, would have applied inflexibly for as long as a marriage continued to exist in the legal sense. We think not.

We believe that Hale's statements concerning the common law of spousal rape derived from the nature of marriage at a particular time in history. Hale stated the rule in terms of an implied matrimonial consent to intercourse which the wife could not retract. This reasoning may have been persuasive during Hale's time, when marriages were effectively permanent, ending only by death or an act of Parliament. Since the matrimonial vow itself was not retractable, Hale may have believed that neither was the implied consent to conjugal rights. Consequently, he stated the rule in absolute terms, as if it were applicable without exception to all marriage relationships. In the years since Hale's formulation of the rule, attitudes towards the permanency of marriage have changed and divorce has become far easier to obtain. The rule, formulated under vastly different conditions, need not prevail when those conditions have changed.

Even in pre-Revolutionary England, matrimonial law permitted a wife to live apart from her husband. Judicial separation, sometimes called divorce *a mensa et thoro,* was available, and courts would also enforce mutual separation agreements. * * * If a wife had a right to live separately from her husband, it follows that she also had a right to refuse sexual intercourse with him at least while they were separated. Therefore, it would appear that Hale's rule was subject to an exception even in pre-Revolutionary England. * * *

B * * *

A common law rule of marital exemption was probably based on three major justifications, which might have constituted the common law principles adopted in this State.[4] The first of these, the notion that a woman was the property of her husband or father, *see* S. Brownmiller, *Against Our Will* 18–28 (1975), was never valid in this country. Rape laws may originally have protected a woman's chastity and therefore her value to her father or husband. In this State, however, rape statutes have always aimed to protect the safety and personal liberty of women. * * *

Second, the common law once included the concept that a husband and wife were one person, that after marriage a man and woman no longer retained separate legal existence. As a result of this concept, some have argued that a husband could not be convicted of, in effect, raping himself. This argument does not take into account how, in spite of marital unity, a husband could always be convicted of other crimes upon his wife, such as assault and battery. * * *

---

4. These are not the only justifications advanced by those favoring retention of marital exemption. Others, such as evidentiary problems, prospects of reconciliation, and availability of other criminal sanctions are discussed in Note. *The Marital Rape Exemption,* 52 *N.Y.U.L.Rev.* 306, 313–16 (1977).

The third and most prevalent justification for the exemption rule is the one utilized by Hale himself—that upon entering the marriage contract a wife consents to sexual intercourse with her husband. This irrevocable consent negates the third essential element of the crime of rape, lack of consent. We cannot say with certainty whether such a rationale was justified even in the seventeenth century.

More importantly, this implied consent rationale, besides being offensive to our valued ideals of personal liberty, is not sound where the marriage itself is not irrevocable. If a wife can exercise a legal right to separate from her husband and eventually terminate the marriage "contract," may she not also revoke a "term" of that contract, namely, consent to intercourse? Just as a husband has no right to imprison his wife because of her marriage vow to him, he has no right to force sexual relations upon her against her will. If her repeated refusals are a "breach" of the marriage "contract," his remedy is in a matrimonial court, not in violent or forceful self-help.

Changes in divorce laws have significantly affected judicial and legislative construction of marital exemption rules. Some jurisdictions have recognized that consent to intercourse does not automatically continue until a marriage is officially at an end. They have refused to exempt husbands from the charge of rape where a judicial decree of separation has been entered, where a spouse has filed for divorce or separate maintenance, or where the spouses are simply living apart.

Since the common law exemption supposedly operated by negating an essential element of the crime—lack of consent—it could not be applied where marital consent to sexual intercourse could be legally revoked. By 1975 our matrimonial laws recognized the right of a wife to withdraw consent prior to the dissolution of a marriage and even prior to a formal judicial order of separation. * * *

With none of the three major common law justifications viable under our laws at the time of defendant's conduct, it would be irrational to believe that a common law marital exemption for rape endured in this State while other laws had changed so dramatically. * * * Therefore, we hold that this State did not have a marital exemption rule for rape in 1975 that would have applied to this defendant and prevented his indictment and conviction on the charge of raping his wife. * * *

Notes and Questions

1. Approximately fourteen percent of the married women questioned in one survey stated that they had been the victim at least once of forced oral, anal, or vaginal penetration (or attempted penetration) by their husband. Diana E.H. Russell, Rape in Marriage 57 (1982).

2. The marital immunity rule is eroding. In 1991, the English House of Lords unanimously abolished it. R. v. R., [1991] 4 All Eng.Rep. 481. In the United States, a majority of states have repealed the exemption or have retained it in a modified form (e.g., permitting prosecution if the husband and wife were living apart at the time of the assault). See Rene I.

Augustine, *Marriage: The Safe Haven for Rapists,* 29 J.Fam.L. 559 (1991); Judith A. Lincoln, Note, *Abolishing the Marital Rape Exemption: The First Step in Protecting Married Women From Spousal Rape,* 35 Wayne L.Rev. 1219, 1227–30 (1989). The Model Penal Code, which was adopted by the American Law Institute before the rape reform movement, retains the rule.

Are there any legitimate reasons for retaining the marital immunity rule? Should the fact that the parties are married and living together serve as a mitigating factor in a rape prosecution? Suppose that a husband has intercourse with his sleeping wife. This would constitute rape in most states if the couple were not married. Should it be regarded as rape here? Or, reconsider *M.T.S.* (p. 346 supra): Should the holding in that case apply to married partners?

C. MENS REA

COMMONWEALTH v. SHERRY

Supreme Judicial Court of Massachusetts, 1982.
386 Mass. 682, 437 N.E.2d 224.

LIACOS, JUSTICE.

Each defendant was * * * convicted * * * of rape without aggravation. * * *

There was evidence of the following facts. The victim, a registered nurse, and the defendants, all doctors, were employed at the same hospital in Boston. The defendant Sherry, whom the victim knew professionally, with another doctor was a host at a party in Boston for some of the hospital staff on the evening of September 5, 1980. The victim was not acquainted with the defendants Hussain and Lefkowitz prior to this evening.

According to the victim's testimony, she had a conversation with Hussain at the party, during which he made sexual advances toward her. Later in the evening, Hussain and Sherry pushed her and Lefkowitz into a bathroom together, shut the door, and turned off the light. They did not open the door until Lefkowitz asked them to leave her in peace. At various times, the victim had danced with both Hussain and Sherry.

Some time later, as the victim was walking from one room to the next, Hussain and Sherry grabbed her by the arms and pulled her out of the apartment as Lefkowitz said, "We're going to go up to Rockport." The victim verbally protested but did not physically resist the men because she said she thought that they were just "horsing around" and that they would eventually leave her alone.[3] She further testified that once outside, Hussain carried her over his shoulder to Sherry's car and held her in the front seat as the four drove to Rockport. En route, she engaged in superficial conversation with the defendants. She testified that she was not in fear at this time. When they arrived at Lefkowitz's

---

3. The victim testified that she was not physically restrained as they rode down an elevator with an unknown fifth person, or as they walked through the lobby of the apartment building where other persons were present.

home in Rockport, she asked to be taken home. Instead, Hussain carried her into the house.

Once in the house, the victim and two of the men smoked some marihuana, and all of them toured the house. Lefkowitz invited them into a bedroom to view an antique bureau, and, once inside, the three men began to disrobe. The victim was frightened. She verbally protested, but the three men proceeded to undress her and maneuver her onto the bed. One of the defendants attempted to have the victim perform fellatio while another attempted intercourse. She told them to stop. At the suggestion of one of the defendants, two of the defendants left the room temporarily. Each defendant separately had intercourse with the victim in the bedroom. The victim testified, that she felt physically numbed and could not fight; she felt humiliated and disgusted. After this sequence of events, the victim claimed that she was further sexually harassed and forced to take a bath.

Some time later, Lefkowitz told the victim that they were returning to Boston because Hussain was on call at the hospital. On their way back, the group stopped to view a beach, to eat breakfast, and to get gasoline. The victim was taken back to where she had left her car the prior evening, and she then drove herself to an apartment that she was sharing with another woman. * * *

* * * The defendants * * * contend that because the judge failed to give two instructions exactly as requested, the judge's jury charge, considered as a whole, was inadequate and the cause of prejudicial error. The requested instructions in their entirety are set out in the margin.[8]

The defendants were not entitled to any particular instruction as long as the charge, as a whole, was adequate.

The instructions given by the trial judge placed before the jury the essential elements of the crime required to be proved. The judge instructed the jury that intercourse must be accomplished with force "such [as] to overcome the woman's will; that it be sufficient to accomplish the man's purpose of having sexual intercourse against her will" or by threats of bodily harm, inferred or expressed, which engendered fear "reasonable in the circumstances ... so that it was reasonable for her not to resist." * * *

These instructions correctly stated the elements of proof required for a rape conviction. * * *

To the extent the defendants * * * appear to have been seeking to raise a defense of good faith mistake on the issue of consent, the defendants' requested instruction would have required the jury to "find beyond a reasonable doubt that the accused had *actual knowledge* of [the victim's] lack of consent" (emphasis added). The defendants, on appeal,

8. "Unless you find beyond a reasonable doubt that [the victim] clearly expressed her lack of consent, or was so overcome by force or threats of bodily injury that she was incapable of consenting, and unless you find beyond a reasonable doubt that the accused had actual knowledge of [the victim's] lack of consent, then you must find them not guilty." * * *

argue that mistake of fact negating criminal intent is a defense to the crime of rape. The defense of mistake of fact, however, requires that the accused act in good faith and with reasonableness. Whether a reasonable good faith mistake of fact as to the fact of consent is a defense to the crime of rape has never, to our knowledge, been decided in this Commonwealth. We need not reach the issue whether a reasonable and honest mistake to the fact of consent would be a defense, for even if we assume it to be so, the defendants did not request a jury instruction based on a reasonable good faith mistake of fact. We are aware of no American court of last resort that recognizes mistake of fact, without consideration of its reasonableness as a defense; nor do the defendants cite such authority. There was no error. * * *

Notes and Questions

1. According to the trial judge, what did the prosecutor have to prove regarding Sherry's state of mind in order to convict him? According to the Supreme Judicial Court, what *mens rea* is required to convict a person of rape?

In the separate appeals of Lefkowitz and Hussain, a Massachusetts appeals court wrote:

> [T]he frequency with which the crime of rape has been described in the decisional law of this Commonwealth lead[s] to the inescapable conclusion that the prosecution has proved rape if the jury concludes that the intercourse was in fact non-consensual (that is effectuated by force or by threat of bodily injury), without any special emphasis on the defendant's state of mind. The scienter element of the offense thus equates with the scienter sufficient to convict of most crimes, a general intent. That element usually is not explained to the jury in the enumeration of the elements of the crime, being left to be inferred from all the evidence in the case.

Commonwealth v. Lefkowitz, 20 Mass.App.Ct. 513, 518, 481 N.E.2d 227, 231 (1985). Is this statement consistent with *Sherry?*

2. Should a defendant be acquitted of rape if he believes, as a reasonable person, that the victim consented? In Commonwealth v. Lefkowitz, id. at 521, 481 N.E.2d at 232, Justice Brown, concurring, expressed his view:

> The essence of the offense of rape is lack of consent on the part of the victim. I am prepared to say that when a woman says "no" to someone any implication other than a manifestation of non-consent that might arise in that person's psyche is legally irrelevant, and thus no defense. Any further action is unwarranted and the person proceeds at his peril. In effect, he assumes the risk. In 1985, I find no social utility in establishing a rule defining non-consensual intercourse on the basis of the subjective (and quite likely wishful) view of the more aggressive player in the sexual encounter.[1]

1. " 'No' must be understood to mean precisely that. Old cultural patterns—no matter how entrenched—must adapt to developing concepts of equality.... Surely [we] ... should understand that sexist stereotypes of 'no' meaning 'yes' can't justify aggression against women." Dershowitz,

In contrast, consider the following:

A requirement for an instruction based upon a reasonable and good faith but mistaken belief on the part of the defendant that the victim consented to sexual intercourse * * * would not be a surprising departure from established principles. Such a requirement would comport with general common law principles that some form of mens rea must be proved before there may be a criminal conviction. * * * Such a requirement would also comport with general notions of fairness; ordinarily one should not be held blameworthy for a felony for acting in accordance with his honest and reasonable beliefs created by the circumstances.

Commonwealth v. Simcock, 31 Mass.App.Ct. 184, 189, 575 N.E.2d 1137, 1141 (1991).[c]

3. A defendant is not entitled to a jury instruction regarding a defense unless evidence is introduced at the trial to support the claim. People v. Williams, 4 Cal.4th 354, 14 Cal.Rptr.2d 441, 841 P.2d 961 (1992) (holding: a mistake-of-fact instruction is not required in a rape prosecution if there is no substantial evidence of equivocal conduct by the woman warranting the instruction).

Was there any evidence in *Sherry* to support a mistake-of-fact claim? Can a mistake about consent ever be reasonable in a forcible rape prosecution?

4. According to Professor Susan Estrich, traditional rape law applies "boys' rules," by unfairly requiring women to act like reasonable men, e.g., physically to resist an unwanted sexual advance. On the issue of *mens rea,* however, are "boys' rules" more appropriate, i.e., should the defendant's culpability be determined on the basis of whether a reasonable *male* would have believed that the female consented?

D. PROVING RAPE

1. RAPE SHIELD LAWS

STATE v. HERNDON

Court of Appeals of Wisconsin, 1988.
145 Wis.2d 91, 426 N.W.2d 347.

MOSER, PRESIDING JUDGE. * * *

A DEFENDANT'S CONSTITUTIONAL RIGHT TO CONFRONT ADVERSE
WITNESSES AND PRESENT WITNESSES IN HIS BEHALF

The sixth amendment to the United States Constitution guarantees a defendant a fair trial by providing him with the right to cross-examine

New Rape Law Needed, Boston Herald American, June 24, 1985, at 19, col. 1.

c. Although the rule suggested by the court in *Simcock* is widely held in other jurisdictions, it is not the rule in Massachu- setts. Commonwealth v. Ascolillo, 405 Mass. 456, 541 N.E.2d 570 (1989) (declining to adopt the rule that a reasonable mistake of fact as to the victim's consent is a de- fense in a forcible rape prosecution).

all witnesses against him.[d] "The right of cross-examination is more than a desirable rule of trial procedure. It is implicit in the constitutional right of confrontation, and helps assure the 'accuracy of the truth-determining process'" by revealing any possible biases, prejudices or ulterior motives of the witness. * * *

The sixth amendment to the United States Constitution also guarantees a defendant the right to compulsory process of witnesses to testify in his behalf * * *. As the United States Supreme Court has stated, "[f]ew rights are more fundamental than that of an accused to present witnesses in his own defense." * * * A violation of this right may deprive the defendant of a fair trial.

The United States Supreme Court, when addressing a state statute that impinges on confrontation and compulsory process rights, has resorted to a balancing test [in which the state's interest in enacting a statute is weighed against the defendant's constitutional interests]. * * *

RAPE SHIELD LAWS AND DEFENDANTS' RIGHTS

Rape shield laws have been enacted by almost every state. Generally speaking, these laws deny a defendant in a sexual assault case the opportunity to examine the complainant concerning her prior sexual conduct or reputation. They also deny the defendant the opportunity to offer extrinsic evidence of the prior sexual conduct or reputation [22] of the complainant.

Rape shield laws were implemented to overcome the invidious and outrageous common law evidentiary rule allowing complainants to be asked in depth about their prior sexual experiences for the purpose of humiliation and harassment and to show unchastity. These statutes reflect the judgment that most evidence about chastity has far too little probative value on the issue of consent to justify extensive inquiry into the victim's sexual history.

Professor Harriett R. Galvin, in her survey of the nation's rape shield laws, has categorized the various types of legislation into four approaches: the Michigan, Texas, federal and California approaches.[25] * * *

The Michigan Approach

The rape shield laws which follow the Michigan approach are general prohibitions on prior sexual conduct or reputation evidence but have highly specific exceptions allowing for this evidence in those cir-

d. The Sixth Amendment reads, in part: "In all criminal prosecutions, the accused shall enjoy the right * * * to be confronted with the witnesses against him [and] to have compulsory process for obtaining witnesses in his favor * * *."

22. All references in this opinion to the complainant's reputation refer to her reputation for sexual conduct or practices.

25. Galvin, *Shielding Rape Victims in the State and Federal Courts: A Proposal for the Second Decade,* 70 Minn.L.Rev. 763, 773 (1985–86).

cumstances in which it is highly relevant and material to the presentation of a defense and therefore constitutionally required. * * *

[For example,] [u]nder the Massachusetts rape shield law, evidence of prior sexual conduct is generally prohibited. Exceptions are made for prior consensual acts with the defendant or recent conduct of the complainant which would explain her physical features, characteristics or conditions. The evidence must first be submitted to the trial court in an in camera hearing so that the court may weigh the relevancy of the evidence against its prejudicial effect on the victim. * * *

The policy underlying this [type of] rape shield law * * * is fourfold. First, the law prevents the defendant from harassing and humiliating the complainant with evidence of either her reputation for chastity or of specific prior sexual acts. Second, this type of evidence generally has no bearing on whether the complainant consented to sexual conduct with the defendant at the time in question. Third, exclusion of the evidence keeps the jury focused only on issues relevant to the case at hand. Finally, the law promotes effective law enforcement because a victim will more readily report and testify in sexual assault cases if she does not fear that her prior sexual conduct will be brought before the public.

The Texas, Federal and California Approaches

The rape shield laws written under the Texas, federal and California approaches each vary in their provisions from the laws written under the Michigan approach. Nevertheless, * * * the ultimate result concerning the admissibility of prior sexual conduct or reputation evidence is often very similar.

The laws written under the Texas approach are purely procedural in nature and often involve "untrammeled judicial discretion." For instance, Arkansas' rape shield law provides that, notwithstanding a general prohibition of opinion, reputation or specific sexual conduct evidence, evidence of the complainant's prior sexual conduct with the defendant or any other person may be used provided certain procedures are followed and the trial court determines that the probativeness of the evidence outweighs its prejudicial nature. * * *

Oregon's rape shield law is a good example of the federal approach. This approach has three key features: (1) a general prohibition of sexual conduct or reputation evidence; (2) exceptions allowing for this evidence in circumstances where the evidence is undeniably relevant to an effective defense; and (3) a general "catch-basin" provision allowing for the introduction of relevant evidence on a case-by-case basis. * * *

The key feature of the California approach is that the sexual conduct or reputation evidence is separated into two categories. Evidence offered to prove consent is generally inadmissible unless the evidence concerns prior sexual conduct between the complainant and the defendant. However, any sexual conduct or reputation evidence may be used to attack the complainant's credibility as long as the trial court determines that it is relevant to the issue. * * *

Since their creation, rape shield laws have generally passed constitutional muster despite challenges based upon the sixth amendment rights to confront adverse witnesses and present evidence in a defendant's behalf. Courts have almost always held that these rights are not absolute, and that evidence of the prior sexual conduct of the complainant is only marginally relevant. Because the probativeness of the evidence is so minuscule when weighed against the potential prejudice to the complaining witness that the receipt of such evidence may engender in the fact finders, the sixth amendment rights must bend to protect the innocent victims. On the other hand, the courts have also universally held that both cross-examination and witnesses brought on behalf of the defendant may show prior consensual sex if that evidence shows a complainant's unique pattern of conduct similar to the pattern of the case at hand or shows that the complainant may be biased or have a motive to fabricate the charges. In such cases, the issues of a witness' bias and credibility are not collateral, and the rape shield laws must give way to the defendant's sixth amendment rights. * * *

PEOPLE v. WILHELM

Michigan Court of Appeals, 1991.
190 Mich.App. 574, 476 N.W.2d 753.

PER CURIAM.

* * * Following a jury trial, defendant was convicted of third-degree criminal sexual conduct. Defendant was sentenced to from three years and nine months to ten years' imprisonment. Defendant appealed as of right. * * *

Defendant * * * claims that the trial court abused its discretion when it prohibited him from introducing certain testimony concerning alleged prior acts of the victim. Both the victim and defendant were in a bar. They were not together. Defendant claimed that he observed the victim lift her shirt and expose her breasts to two men who were sitting at her table. The victim also allegedly allowed one of the two men to "fondle" her breasts. Defendant claimed that another witness had also seen this activity.

During trial, the prosecutor learned that defendant intended to introduce this evidence. The prosecutor argued that the rape-shield statute [1] prohibited evidence of the victim's sexual conduct with another.

---

1. M.C.L. § 750.520j; M.S.A. § 28.-788(10) provides:

(1) Evidence of specific instances of the victim's sexual conduct, opinion evidence of the victim's sexual conduct, and reputation evidence of the victim's sexual conduct shall not be admitted * * * unless and only to the extent that the judge finds that the following proposed evi-

dence is material to a fact at issue in the case and that its inflammatory or prejudicial nature does not outweigh its probative value:

(a) Evidence of the victim's past sexual conduct with the actor.

(b) Evidence of specific instances of sexual activity showing the source or origin of semen, pregnancy, or disease.

Defendant moved to have this evidence admitted as relevant to the issue whether the victim had consented to intercourse with him later that same evening in his boat that was parked in his parents' driveway. * * *

Defendant argued that * * * another state's similar rape-shield statute had been held not to prohibit such evidence, citing *State v. Colbath*, 130 N.H. 316, 540 A.2d 1212 (1988). * * *

In *Colbath*, the defendant and the victim were in a tavern. The victim directed unspecified "sexually provocative attention" toward several men in the tavern, including the defendant. The defendant testified that he had felt the victim's breasts and bottom and that she had rubbed his crotch before they left the tavern and went to the defendant's trailer. There they had intercourse, which the defendant claimed was consensual and the victim claimed was not. While in the trailer, the defendant's live-in female companion came home, suspecting the defendant's infidelity. Upon discovering the pair, she violently assaulted the victim and dragged her outside by the hair. The trial court ruled that the evidence was inadmissible under New Hampshire's rape-shield law. Nonetheless, a state's witness testified that the victim had left the tavern in the company of various men several times during the afternoon and that the victim was "hanging all over everyone and making out with Richard Colbath and a few others." The trial court instructed the jury that the evidence was irrelevant. The New Hampshire Supreme Court declined the defendant's request to rule that its rape-shield law did not apply because the victim's right to privacy was not invaded by a discussion of acts that occurred in a bar open to the public. Instead, the court ruled that the defendant's right of confrontation required that the defendant be allowed to demonstrate that the probative value of statutorily inadmissible evidence in the context of his particular case outweighed its prejudicial effect on the victim. In doing so, the court noted:

> As soon as we address this process of assigning relative weight to prejudicial and probative force, it becomes apparent that the public character of the complainant's behavior is significant. On the one hand, describing a complainant's open, sexually suggestive conduct in the presence of patrons of a public bar obviously has far less potential for damaging the sensibilities than revealing what the same person may have done in the company of another behind a closed door. On the other hand, evidence of public displays of general interest in sexual activity can be taken to indicate a contemporaneous receptiveness to sexual advances that cannot be inferred from evidence of private behavior with chosen sex partners.

(2) If the defendant proposes to offer evidence described in subsection (1)(a) or (b), the defendant within 10 days after the arraignment on the information shall file a written motion and offer of proof.

The court may order an in camera hearing to determine whether the proposed evidence is admissible under subsection (1). * * *

In this case, for example, the jury could have taken evidence of the complainant's openly sexually provocative behavior toward a group of men as evidence of her probable attitude toward an individual within that group. Evidence that the publicly inviting acts occurred closely in time to the alleged sexual assault by one such man could have been viewed as indicating the complainant's likely attitude at the time of the sexual activity in question. It would, in fact, understate the importance of such evidence in this case to speak of it merely as relevant. We should recall that the fact of intercourse was not denied, and that the evidence of assault was subject to the explanation that the defendant's jealous living [sic? live-in] companion had inflicted the visible injuries. The companion's furious behavior had further bearing on the case, as well, for the jury could have regarded her attack as a reason for the complainant to regret a voluntary liaison with the defendant, and as a motive for the complainant to allege rape as a way to explain her injuries and excuse her undignified predicament. * * *

* * * [D]efendant claims that the public nature of the victim's activities should remove them from the protection of the rape-shield statute. We disagree. The statute itself does not make this distinction. Defendant treats the statute's purpose of protecting the victim's privacy as though it extends only to private acts. * * * [O]ne of the purposes of the law is to encourage victims to report and testify without fear that the trial court's proceedings would veer from an impartial examination of the accused's conduct on the date in question and instead take on the aspects of an inquisition during which the victim would be required to acknowledge and justify her sexual past. Moreover, we fail to see how a woman's consensual sexual conduct with another in public indicates to third parties that the woman would engage in similar behavior with them. * * * [E]vidence of a rape victim's unchastity is ordinarily insufficiently probative of her consent to intercourse with a defendant. * * *

Finally, defendant claims that the * * * preclusion of the evidence under the rape-shield law deprived him of his right of confrontation. We disagree. Evidence of a victim's sexual conduct with a third party is irrelevant to the issue whether she consented to sexual intercourse with the defendant. Defendant further argues that the victim's acts with the third persons were probative of the issue of consent because they occurred in a public place and shortly before the period of time during which he claims that the victim consented to sexual relations with him. Defendant apparently attempts to analogize his case with *Colbath*. We believe that *Colbath* is distinguishable. As noted therein, the victim's behavior constituted a public display of general interest in sexual activity in which the defendant was directly involved. Moreover, the victim in *Colbath* had left the bar with various men several times during the afternoon, and the beating she had received from the defendant's live-in companion in that case may have provided a motive for fabrication. * * * If believed, the victim's alleged conduct [in the present case] occurred with third parties and, although observed by defendant, was not relevant to the issue whether she consented to sexual intercourse with him later on the same evening. Because the evidence was irrelevant, defendant was not denied his right of confrontation. * * *

Notes and Questions

1. *Problem.* At *W*'s rape trial, *W* claimed that *V* consented to intercourse with him. In support of his claim, *W* sought to introduce evidence that *V* was a model for *Penthouse* magazine, that she acted in pornographic movies, and that prior to sexual intercourse with him, she had shown *W* the *Penthouse* photographs and discussed her sexual experiences with him. Wood v. Alaska, 957 F.2d 1544 (9th Cir.1992). As a matter of policy, should any or all of this evidence be excluded under a rape shield statute?

2. *Problem.* Lonnie was prosecuted for attempted rape of Melissa. Melissa testified that Lonnie entered her home uninvited and tried to rape her. In contrast, Lonnie testified that he and Melissa were participating in consensual sexual foreplay at her home when they decided to have intercourse. However, when he made a comment to her about her prior sexual practices, she became angry and told him to leave, which he did. The next day, she filed a police report accusing Lonnie of attempted rape.

Although the trial court allowed Lonnie to testify that he had said something to Melissa that made her angry, it did not permit him to specify what he said, which was that while they were engaged in intercourse "doggy fashion," Lonnie said to Melissa, "Don't you like it like this? Tim Hall said you did." Stephens v. Miller, 989 F.2d 264 (7th Cir.1993). Should the defendant have been permitted to tell the jury what he said to Melissa?

2. EXPERT TESTIMONY: RAPE TRAUMA SYNDROME

PEOPLE v. TAYLOR

Court of Appeals of New York, 1990.
75 N.Y.2d 277, 552 N.Y.S.2d 883, 552 N.E.2d 131.

WACHTLER, CHIEF JUDGE.

In these two cases, we consider whether expert testimony that a complaining witness has exhibited behavior consistent with "rape trauma syndrome" is admissible at the criminal trial of the person accused of the rape. Both trial courts admitted the testimony and the Appellate Division affirmed in both cases. We now affirm in *People v. Taylor,* and reverse in *People v. Banks.* While we recognize that the unchecked admission of expert testimony in this area has peculiar dangers, we believe that under certain circumstances and subject to certain limitations evidence of rape trauma syndrome is both relevant and admissible. We believe, however, that the trial court in *Banks* erred in allowing the expert to testify under the facts present in that case.

I. PEOPLE v. TAYLOR

On July 29, 1984, the complainant, a 19–year–old Long Island resident, reported to the town police that she had been raped and sodomized at gunpoint on a deserted beach near her home. * * *

The complainant arrived home around 11:00 P.M., woke her mother and told her about the attack. Her mother then called the police. Sometime between 11:30 P.M. and midnight, the police arrived at the complainant's house. At that time, the complainant told the police she did not know who her attacker was. She was taken to the police station where she described the events leading up to the attack and again repeated that she did not know who her attacker was. At the conclusion of the interview, the complainant was asked to step into a private room to remove the clothes that she had been wearing at the time of the attack so that they could be examined for forensic evidence. While she was alone with her mother, the complainant told her that the defendant John Taylor, had been her attacker. The time was approximately 1:15 A.M. The complainant had known the defendant for years, and she later testified that she happened to see him the night before the attack at a local convenience store.

Her mother summoned one of the detectives and the complainant repeated that the defendant had been the person who attacked her. The complainant said that she was sure that it had been the defendant because she had had ample opportunity to see his face during the incident. The complainant subsequently identified the defendant as her attacker in two separate lineups. * * *

The defendant's first trial ended without the jury being able to reach a verdict. At his second trial, the Judge permitted Eileen Treacy, an instructor at the City University of New York, Herbert Lehman College, with experience in counseling sexual assault victims, to testify about rape trauma syndrome. The prosecutor introduced this testimony for two separate purposes. First, Treacy's testimony on the specifics of rape trauma syndrome explained why the complainant might have been unwilling during the first few hours after the attack to name the defendant as her attacker where she had known the defendant prior to the incident. Second, Treacy's testimony that it was common for a rape victim to appear quiet and controlled following an attack, responded to evidence that the complainant had appeared calm after the attack and tended to rebut the inference that because she was not excited and upset after the attack, it had not been a rape. At the close of the second trial, the defendant was convicted * * *.

II. PEOPLE v. BANKS

On July 7, 1986, the defendant Ronnie Banks approached the 11–year–old complainant, who was playing with her friends in the City of Rochester. The complainant testified that the defendant told her to come to him and when she did not, he grabbed her by the arm and pulled her down the street. According to the complainant, the defendant took her into a neighborhood garage where he sexually assaulted her. The complainant returned to her grandmother's house, where she was living at the time. The next morning, she told her grandmother about the incident and the police were contacted. The defendant was arrested * * *.

At trial, the complainant testified that the defendant had raped and sodomized her. In addition, she and her grandmother both testified about the complainant's behavior following the attack. Their testimony revealed that the complainant had been suffering from nightmares, had been waking up in the middle of the night in a cold sweat, had been afraid to return to school in the fall, had become generally more fearful and had been running and staying away from home. Following the introduction of this evidence, the prosecution sought to introduce expert testimony about the symptoms associated with rape trauma syndrome.

Clearly, the prosecution, in an effort to establish that forcible sexual contact had in fact occurred, wanted to introduce this evidence to show that the complainant was demonstrating behavior that was consistent with patterns of response exhibited by rape victims. The prosecutor does not appear to have introduced this evidence to counter the inference that the complainant consented to the incident, since the 11–year-old complainant is legally incapable of consent. Unlike *Taylor,* the evidence was not offered to explain behavior exhibited by the victim that the jury might not understand; instead, it was offered to show that the behavior that the complainant had exhibited after the incident was consistent with a set of symptoms commonly associated with women who had been forcibly attacked. The clear implication of such testimony would be that because the complainant exhibited these symptoms, it was more likely than not that she had been forcibly raped.

The Judge permitted David Gandell, an obstetrician-gynecologist on the faculty of the University of Rochester, Strong Memorial Hospital, with special training in treating victims of sexual assault, to testify as to the symptoms commonly associated with rape trauma syndrome. After Gandell had described rape trauma syndrome he testified hypothetically that the kind of symptoms demonstrated by the complainant were consistent with a diagnosis of rape trauma syndrome. * * *

III. RAPE TRAUMA SYNDROME

In a 1974 study rape trauma syndrome was described as "the acute phase and long-term reorganization process that occurs as a result of forcible rape or attempted forcible rape. This syndrome of behavioral, somatic, and psychological reactions is an acute stress reaction to a life-threatening situation" (Burgess & Holmstrom, *Rape Trauma Syndrome,* 131 Am.J. Psychiatry 981, 982 [1974]). Although others had studied the reactions of rape victims prior to this publication, the Burgess and Holmstrom identification of two separate phases in a rape victim's recovery has proven enormously influential.

According to Burgess and Holmstrom, the rape victim will go through an acute phase immediately following the incident. The behavior exhibited by a rape victim after the attack can vary. While some women will express their fear, anger and anxiety openly, an equal number of women will appear controlled, calm, and subdued. Women in the acute phase will also experience a number of physical reactions. These reactions include the actual physical trauma that resulted from

the attack, muscle tension that could manifest itself in tension headaches, fatigue, or disturbed sleep patterns, gastrointestinal irritability
and genitourinary disturbance. Emotional reactions in the acute phase
generally take the form of fear, humiliation, embarrassment, fear of
violence and death, and self-blame.

As part of the long-term reorganizational phase, the victim will
often decide to make a change in her life, such as a change of residence.
At this point, the woman will often turn to her family for support.
Other symptoms that are seen in this phase are the occurrence of
nightmares and the development of phobias that relate to the circumstances of the rape. For instance, women attacked in their beds will
often develop a fear of being indoors, while women attacked on the street
will develop a fear of being outdoors.

While some researchers have criticized the methodology of the early
studies of rape trauma syndrome, Burgess and Holmstrom's model has
nonetheless generated considerable interest in the response and recovery
of rape victims and has contributed to the emergence of a substantial
body of scholarship in this area. The question before us today, then, is
whether the syndrome, which has been the subject of study and discussion for the past 16 years, can be introduced before a lay jury as relevant
evidence in these two rape trials.

We realize that rape trauma syndrome encompasses a broad range
of symptoms and varied patterns of recovery. Some women are better
able to cope with the aftermath of sexual assault than other women. It
is also apparent that there is no single typical profile of a rape victim and
that different victims express themselves and come to terms with the
experience of rape in different ways. We are satisfied, however, that the
relevant scientific community has generally accepted that rape is a
highly traumatic event that will in many women trigger the onset of
certain identifiable symptoms.

We note that the American Psychiatric Association has listed rape as
one of the stressors that can lead to posttraumatic stress disorder
(American Psychiatric Association, Diagnostic & Statistical Manual of
Mental Disorders 247, 248 [3d ed. rev. 1987] [DSM III–R]). According
to DSM III–R, there is an identifiable pattern of responses that can
follow an intensely stressful event. The victim who suffers from posttraumatic stress disorder will persistently reexperience the traumatic
event in a number of ways, as through dreams, flashbacks, hallucinations, or intense distress at exposure to events that resemble or symbol-
ize the traumatic event. The victim will also avoid stimuli that he or
she associates with the trauma. Finally, the victim will experience
"persistent symptoms of increased arousal," which could include difficulty in falling or staying asleep, sudden outbursts of anger, or difficulty
concentrating. While the diagnostic criteria for posttraumatic stress
disorder that are contained in DSM III–R have convinced us that the
scientific community has accepted that rape as a stressor can have
marked, identifiable effects on a victim's behavior, we would further

note that although rape trauma syndrome can be conceptualized as a posttraumatic stress disorder, victims of rape will often exhibit peculiar symptoms—like a fear of men—that are not commonly exhibited by victims of other sorts of trauma.

We are aware that rape trauma syndrome is a therapeutic and not a legal concept. Physicians and rape counselors who treat victims of sexual assault are not charged with the responsibility of ascertaining whether the victim is telling the truth when she says that a rape occurred. That is part of the truth-finding process implicated in a criminal trial. We do not believe, however, that the therapeutic origin of the syndrome renders it unreliable for trial purposes. Thus, although we acknowledge that evidence of rape trauma syndrome does not by itself prove that the complainant was raped, we believe that this should not preclude its admissibility into evidence at trial when relevance to a particular disputed issue has been demonstrated.

IV. The Law

Having concluded that evidence of rape trauma syndrome is generally accepted within the relevant scientific community, we must now decide whether expert testimony in this area would aid a lay jury in reaching a verdict. "[E]xpert opinion is proper when it would help to clarify an issue calling for professional or technical knowledge, possessed by the expert and beyond the ken of the typical juror."

Because cultural myths still affect common understanding of rape and rape victims and because experts have been studying the effects of rape upon its victims only since the 1970's, we believe that patterns of response among rape victims are not within the ordinary understanding of the lay juror. For that reason, we conclude that introduction of expert testimony describing rape trauma syndrome may under certain circumstances assist a lay jury in deciding issues in a rape trial.

In reaching our conclusions in this area, we note that an extensive body of case law has developed concerning the admissibility of this type of evidence. There is no uniform approach to the admission of evidence of rape trauma syndrome among the States that have considered the question. The Minnesota Supreme Court in one of the earliest rape trauma syndrome cases held such evidence inadmissible (*State v. Saldana,* 324 N.W.2d 227 [(1982)]). * * *

Among those States that have allowed such testimony to be admitted, the purpose for which the testimony was offered has proven crucial. A number of States have allowed testimony of rape trauma syndrome to be admitted where the defendant concedes that sexual intercourse occurred, but contends that it was consensual. * * *

Other States have permitted the admission of this testimony where it was offered to explain behavior exhibited by the complainant that might be viewed as inconsistent with a claim of rape. In *People v. Hampton,* 746 P.2d 947 [(1987)], the Colorado Supreme Court held that in a case where the complainant waited 89 days to report an attack, expert testimony that a rape victim who is assaulted by someone she knows is more reluctant to report an attack was admissible to explain the delay in reporting. The court noted that such evidence is not conclusive of rape, but that "[a]ny flaws present in the expert testimony go to the weight to be given the evidence rather than its admissibility and can be the subject of cross-examination of the expert witness." * * *

Having concluded that evidence of rape trauma syndrome can assist jurors in reaching a verdict by dispelling common misperceptions about rape, and having reviewed the different approaches taken by the other jurisdictions that have considered the question, we too agree that the reason why the testimony is offered will determine its helpfulness, its relevance and its potential for prejudice. In the two cases now before us, testimony regarding rape trauma syndrome was offered for entirely different purposes. We conclude that its admission at the trial of John Taylor was proper, but that its admission at the trial of Ronnie Banks was not.

As noted above, the complaining witness in *Taylor* had initially told the police that she could not identify her assailant. Approximately two hours after she first told her mother that she had been raped and sodomized, she told her mother that she knew the defendant had done it. The complainant had known the defendant for years and had seen him the night before the assault. We hold that under the circumstances present in this case, expert testimony explaining that a rape victim who knows her assailant is more fearful of disclosing his name to the police and is in fact less likely to report the rape at all was relevant to explain why the complainant may have been initially unwilling to report that the defendant had been the man who attacked her. Behavior of this type is not within the ordinary understanding of the jury and testimony explaining this behavior assists the jury in determining what effect to give to the complainant's initial failure to identify the defendant. This evidence provides a possible explanation for the complainant's behavior that is consistent with her claim that she was raped. As such, it is relevant.

Rape trauma syndrome evidence was also introduced in *Taylor* in response to evidence that revealed the complainant had not seemed upset following the attack. We note again in this context that the reaction of a rape victim in the hours following her attack is not something within the common understanding of the average lay juror. Indeed, the defense would clearly want the jury to infer that because the victim was not upset following the attack, she must not have been raped. This inference runs contrary to the studies cited earlier, which suggest that half of all women who have been forcibly raped are controlled and subdued following the attack. Thus, we conclude that evidence of this type is relevant to dispel misconceptions that jurors might possess regarding the ordinary responses of rape victims in the first hours after their attack. We do not believe that evidence of rape trauma syndrome, when admitted for that express purpose, is unduly prejudicial.

The admission of expert testimony describing rape trauma syndrome in *Banks,* however, was clearly error. As we noted earlier, this evidence was not offered to explain behavior that might appear unusual to a lay juror not ordinarily familiar with the patterns of response exhibited by rape victims. We conclude that evidence of rape trauma syndrome is inadmissible when it inescapably bears solely on proving that a rape occurred, as was the case here.

Although we have accepted that rape produces identifiable symptoms in rape victims, we do not believe that evidence of the presence, or indeed of the absence, of those symptoms necessarily indicates that the incident did or did not occur. Because introduction of rape trauma syndrome evidence by an expert might create such an inference in the minds of lay jurors, we find that the defendant would be unacceptably prejudiced by the introduction of rape trauma syndrome evidence for that purpose alone. We emphasize again that the therapeutic nature of the syndrome does not preclude its admission into evidence under all circumstances. We believe, however, that its usefulness as a fact-finding device is limited and that where it is introduced to prove the crime took place, its helpfulness is outweighed by the possibility of undue prejudice.
* * *

Notes and Questions

1. In most jurisdictions, expert testimony regarding a novel scientific concept is inadmissible unless it is "sufficiently established to have gained general acceptance in the particular field in which it belongs." Frye v. United States, 293 Fed. 1013, 1014 (D.C.Cir.1923) (See p. 448 infra.)

The unwillingness of some courts to admit evidence regarding rape trauma syndrome is the result of the controversial nature of the research in this field. See generally Patricia A. Frazier & Eugene Borgida, *Rape Trauma Syndrome: A Review of Case Law and Psychological Research,* 16 Law & Hum.Behav. 293 (1992). The Washington Supreme Court has summarized the key methodological objections:

> Among the shortcomings cited are the following: (1) differences in definitions and criteria for "rape"; (2) unrepresentative, biased, or inadequate sampling of victims; (3) inadequate means of eliciting information about victims; (4) lack of long-term assessments of victims; and (5) lack of a control group (i.e., a group of nonraped women) against which to compare the symptoms observed in rape victims.

State v. Black, 109 Wash.2d 336, 345, 745 P.2d 12, 17 (1987).

2. Victims of acquaintance rape often delay reporting the incident to the police. In light of this, consider the wisdom of the prompt complaint rule advanced by Model Penal Code § 213.6(4). Is there any justification for this special rule in the context of sexual offenses? Are you persuaded by the Institute's explanation for the requirement:

> The requirement of prompt complaint springs in part from a fear that unwanted pregnancy or bitterness at a relationship gone sour might convert a willing participant in sexual relations into a vindictive complainant. Barring prosecution if no report is made within a reason-

able time is one way of guarding against such fabrication. Perhaps more importantly, the provision limits the opportunity for blackmailing another by threatening to bring a criminal charge of sexual aggression. This objective is especially critical for those offenses involving consensual relations. The parents of an underage girl who has engaged in intercourse with an older male, for example, may forego public prosecution, which does nothing to enhance the reputation of their daughter, in favor of private gain. Requiring complaint within three months of learning of such an event reduces the ability of such persons to demand continuing payment for silence.

American Law Institute, Model Penal Code and Commentaries, Comment to § 213.6 at 421 (1980).

3. Should a defendant be permitted to introduce evidence that the complainant did *not* experience symptoms of rape trauma syndrome, in order to cast doubt on the claim that she was raped? See Henson v. State, 535 N.E.2d 1189 (Ind.1989); see generally Nicole R. Economou, Note, *Defense Expert Testimony on Rape Trauma Syndrome: Implications for the Stoic Victim*, 42 Hastings L.J. 1143 (1991).

3. CAUTIONARY JURY INSTRUCTION

STATE v. BASHAW

Supreme Court of Oregon, 1983.
296 Or. 50, 672 P.2d 48.

JONES, JUSTICE.

Defendant seeks reversal of his convictions for first degree rape and attempted rape in the first degree, contending that the trial court erred by refusing to give the following instruction:

> "A charge such as that made against the defendant in this case is one which is easily made and once made difficult to defend against even if the person accused is innocent. Therefore, the law requires that you examine the testimony of the female person named in the Information with caution."

* * * Considerable testimony flowed back and forth during the trial regarding the credibility of the victims. The defendant was able to present the testimony of several witnesses who impeached the [complainants] on certain points and several witnesses who offered damaging character testimony about the [complainants]. Further, the defendant also took the stand and categorically denied the rape and attempted rape allegations.

The instruction requested by the defendant should never be given in any rape case. Such an instruction may imply to a jury that the court is expressing reservations about the credibility of the alleged victim. It is the jury that is charged with the duty to weigh and evaluate the credibility of all witnesses. * * *

The requested instruction quoted above * * * was spawned in Oregon over 70 years ago in *State v. Friddles,* 62 Or. 209, 210, 123 P. 904 (1912). Justice Henry J. Bean, writing for the court, said, "The charge of rape is one which, as Lord Hale observes, is 'an accusation easily to be made, hard to be proved, and harder to be defended by the party accused though never so innocent."

We do not know what made Lord Chief Justice Matthew Hale an authority on defense against rape for his day, but his comment does not reflect contemporary thought or experience. His comment reflects a view of the rape victim and the crime of rape which simply is not borne out. The jury instruction which arose from this view assumes that the charge of rape is easily made. In fact, quite the opposite is true. * * * The crime is one of degradation as well as violence, and fear of reprisal and embarrassment contributes to the victim's hesitation to report it. Those who do report it must confront the trauma of the encounter with the police, the investigation of the crime and the ordeal of trial.

The instruction also states that the charge of rape is more difficult to defend against than other crimes. Once again, statistics throw doubt upon this assumption underlying the instruction:

> "* * * Of adults arrested, only sixty percent were charged. In almost half of these prosecutions, acquittals or dismissals ensued; in thirty-five percent, the defendant was convicted of rape; in sixteen percent, of some lesser offense. As compared with overall so-called 'Index Crime' statistics, these charging and conviction figures rank very low." Berger, *Man's Trial, Woman's Tribulation: Rape Cases in the Courtroom,* 77 Colum.L.Rev. 1, 6 (1977).[5]

In short, we find no reason to continue the institutional assumption that alleged rape victims are less trustworthy witnesses than other victims of crime. We note that we are among a growing number of jurisdictions that have jettisoned the cautionary instruction.

We do not say a trial court may never approve a cautionary instruction involving a witness. The interest of justice may require an appropriate instruction in a special situation. But, this is not such a case. A witness should not be cloaked with a judicially implied credibility taint simply because the witness claims to be the victim of a rape. We hold the trial court was correct in refusing to give the requested instruction. * * *

Notes and Questions

1. In more recent data from 12 states, rape convictions were obtained in sixty-four percent of the prosecutions; acquittals were secured in four

---

5. Prosecution and conviction rates for the other FBI index crimes (murder, non-negligent manslaughter, aggravated assault, burglary, larceny and motor vehicle theft) during the same time period were as follows: 81 percent of adults arrested were prosecuted; 70 percent were found guilty, 9 percent of a lesser charge. Recent reforms in the law of rape, changes in society's attitude toward the rape victim, and a recognition on the part of the law enforcement community of the severity of the crime, may contribute to a conviction rate more in keeping with that of other crimes of violence.

percent of the cases; and dismissals were granted in thirty-one percent of the prosecutions. These figures were virtually the same as for violent offenses overall. United States Department of Justice, Bureau of Justice Statistics, Sourcebook of Criminal Justice Statistics—1990 520 (1991).

2. Model Penal Code § 213.6(5) sets out two related requirements for conviction of a sexual offense: (1) corroboration of the complainant's testimony; and (2) a cautionary instruction to the jury similar to the one rejected in *Bashaw*. The Commentary explains:

> Special rules of this sort have excited considerable controversy in recent years and have become targets of bitter criticism by feminist reformers and their allies. This reaction springs from the fact that prior law imposed such requirements only for the crimes of rape and seduction. Thus, the alleged victim whose testimony had to be corroborated or received with caution was always a female, and the effect of special safeguards was consistently to discount female accusations against male defendants. It should be noted that the Model Code provision applies to all offenses defined in Article 213 without reference to the gender of the complaining witness. * * * As a practical matter, however, the vast majority of prosecutions under this article will continue to involve female complainants and male defendants. For that reason, enforcing special protections against fabricated accusations of sexual offenses is likely to remain an issue of special sensitivity in the penal law. * * *

> * * * One commentator identified three kinds of assertions advanced to justify a corroboration requirement for rape and related offenses.[57] First, many observers believe that false accusations are especially common in this context. The paradigm hypotheticals are the woman who, having yielded to entreaty, lashes out in bitterness when the man subsequently abandons the relationship and the underage girl who misidentifies the male responsible for pregnancy in order to protect her lover. No doubt such cases exist, just as analogous instances of false charges occur in other contexts. That they arise with exceptional frequency in sex offenses, however, is a matter of speculation. Additionally, some psychiatrists believe that many women fantasize rape and that it is easy for the neurotic "to translate their fantasies into actual beliefs and memory falsifications."[59] This analysis has been developed with force and detail by some scientists and attacked by others with equal verve and care. At best, it is a murky ground on which to base a corroboration requirement.

> A second kind of concern postulates likely prejudice to the defendant arising from the emotional hostility generated by the crime of rape. The idea is that rape is so heinous an event that judge and jury will be moved too quickly to express their outrage by conviction. Again, this argument has a paradigm case—trial of a black defendant for rape of a white woman. To the extent that the problem has a racial origin, one might expect that enforced non-discriminatory juror selection might

---

57. Note, *Rape Corroboration Requirement: Repeal Not Reform,* 81 Yale L.J. 1365, 1373 (1972).

59. 3A J. Wigmore, Evidence § 924a, at 744 (Chadbourn rev. ed. 1970) (quoting Dr. Karl Menninger). * * *

provide a partial answer. Beyond that context, it is difficult to believe that rape excites so much more emotional antipathy than murder that it requires a distinctive rule of law governing matters of proof. Moreover, experience fails to confirm the implication that rape convictions are especially easy to obtain.

The third and most persuasive consideration supporting a corroboration requirement is the difficulty of defending against false accusation of a sexual offense. * * * [T]here is undeniable point to the contention that proof of rape or other illicit intercourse involves special difficulty. In no other context is felony liability premised on conduct that under other circumstances may be welcomed by the "victim." The difference between criminal and non-criminal conduct depends ultimately on a question of attitude. Proof of this elusive issue often boils down to a confrontation of conflicting accounts. The corroboration requirement is an attempt to skew resolution of such disputes in favor of the defendant. It does not, or at least need not, rest on the assertion that one person's testimony is inherently more deserving of credence that another's. It certainly is not dependent on allegations that women generally fabricate such charges or that judges and juries regularly favor the complaining witness at the expense of justice. It is, rather, a determination to favor justice to the defendant, even at some cost to societal interest in effective law enforcement and to the personal demand of the victim for redress.

American Law Institute, Model Penal Code and Commentaries, Comment to § 213.6 at 422, 426–29 (1980).

In view of the embarrassment and trauma inherent in filing a police report for a sexual offense, false rape claims are not likely to be common. Occasionally, however, they occur. One of the most publicized cases in recent years involved Gary Dotson, who was accused by a teenage girl of forcible rape. She identified Dotson from a police photographic "mug shot" book and testified to the rape at the defendant's trial. Dotson asserted an alibi defense, but he was convicted and sentenced to imprisonment of from 25 to 50 years.

Six years later, Dotson's accuser recanted her prior testimony. She explained that, at the time, she was afraid that she was pregnant by a boyfriend (not Dotson), and she needed an explanation to justify her condition with her legal guardians. Therefore, she tore buttons off her shirt, ripped the zippers of her slacks, and put dirt on her clothing, to make it appear that she had been raped.

Based on the new evidence, Dotson moved for a new trial, but his motion was denied because the trial court did not believe the recantation. People v. Dotson, 163 Ill.App.3d 419, 114 Ill.Dec. 563, 516 N.E.2d 718 (1985). Thereafter, the governor commuted Dotson's sentence, although he said that he remained satisfied of the convicted man's guilt. In 1989, Dotson was exonerated on the basis of DNA genetic testing. Larry Green, *12–Year Legal Nightmare at an End; Recanted Testimony, High–Tech Help to Clear Gary Dotson,* Los Angeles Times, Aug. 15, 1989, pt. 1, at 5.

Chapter 9

GENERAL DEFENSES TO CRIMES

A. CATEGORIES OF DEFENSES

PAUL H. ROBINSON—CRIMINAL LAW DEFENSES: A SYSTEMATIC ANALYSIS

82 Columbia Law Review 199 (1982), 200, 202–05, 208–11, 213–14, 221, 229–32

Unlike many aspects of the criminal law, defenses have not yet been the subject of comprehensive conceptual analysis. The general nature and scope of most defenses have been perpetuated for centuries with little or no question. Current debates commonly focus on whether a particular defense should apply in a particular circumstance, but rarely consider the larger perspective. How do circumstances covered by one defense compare with those of other defenses? Do defenses overlap? If so, will the outcome in identical situations vary with the defense asserted? Should it? Are there gaps between defenses, that is, circumstances in which our common sense of justice suggests that the defendant should be exculpated, yet where no defense applies? Do defenses based on theoretically analogous grounds of exculpation generate analogous results? The general inquiry, which seems never to have been undertaken, is: how does the collection of recognized defenses operate as a system? * * *

There are, no doubt, many people who believe that defenses defy such systemization. Defenses, it might be argued, are the embodiment of such complex human notions of fairness and morality, tempered by the demands of utility and efficiency, that they are too complex and perhaps too illogical to be reduced to an integrated, comprehensive, and internally consistent system of exculpation. * * *

This Article attempts to provide some measure of conceptual organization for criminal law defenses * * *.

I. A SYSTEM OF DEFENSES

The term "defense" is commonly used, at least in a casual sense, to mean any set of identifiable conditions or circumstances which may prevent a conviction for an offense. * * * Upon examining the functions of and the rationales supporting these rules and doctrines, five general categories become apparent. They may be termed: failure of proof defenses, offense modification defenses, justifications, excuses, and nonexculpatory public policy defenses. * * *

A. *Failure of Proof Defenses*

Failure of proof defenses consist of instances in which, because of the conditions that are the basis for the "defense," all elements of the offense charged cannot be proven. They are in essence no more than the negation of an element required by the definition of the offense. * * *

Mistake provides a clear example * * *. Assume, for example, that incest is defined as having intercourse with a person the actor knows to be an ancestor, descendant, or sibling. If the actor honestly believes that the person with whom he is having intercourse in not a relative, one might term his mistake a "defense." In reality, the actor's mistaken belief prevents a state from proving the required mental element of knowledge of the familial relationship. When this sort of mistake of fact is recognized as a "defense," it is considered not a general mistake excuse, but only a failure of proof defense. * * *

B. *Offense Modifications*

Offense-modification defenses are real defenses in the sense that they do more than simply negate an element of an offense. They apply even where all elements of the offense are satisfied. They are distinguishable from general defenses (like self-defense or insanity), however, because they introduce criminalization decisions similar to those used in defining offenses, rather than giving effect to general principles of exculpation. They provide a more sophisticated account, when needed, of the harm or evil sought to be prohibited by the definition of the offense.

A parent, against the advice of police, pays a $10,000 ransom to the kidnapper of his child. A businessman pays monthly extortion payments to a racketeer. These persons may well satisfy the elements required for complicity in kidnapping and extortion, yet they will nonetheless have a defense to these charges. * * *

There is a single principle behind these modifications of the definition of an offense: while the actor has apparently satisfied all elements of the offense charged, he has not in fact caused the harm or evil sought to be prevented by the statute defining the offense. * * *

In many cases the defenses of this group are given no formal name, but exist only as accepted rules. For example, with regard to the kidnapping and extortion examples above, a common rule provides that the victim of a crime may not be held as an accomplice even though his conduct has in a significant sense aided the commission of the crime. * * *

Some offense modifications are considered defenses, rather than simply rules or doctrines, but they operate similarly to modify the definition of offenses. * * *

Offense modifications, like failure of proof defenses, commonly apply to only one specific offense. * * *

C. *Justifications*

Unlike failure of proof and offense modification defenses, justification defenses are not alterations of the statutory definition of the harm sought to be prevented or punished by an offense. The harm caused by the justified behavior remains a legally recognized harm which is to be avoided whenever possible. Under special justifying circumstances, however, that harm is outweighed by the need to avoid an even greater harm or to further a greater societal interest.

A forest fire rages toward a town of 10,000 unsuspecting inhabitants. The actor burns a field of corn located between the fire and the town; the burned field then serves as a firebreak, saving 10,000 lives. The actor has satisfied all elements of the offense of arson by setting fire to the field with the purpose of destroying it. The immediate harm he has caused—the destruction of the field—is precisely the harm which the statute serves to prevent and punish. Yet the actor is likely to have a complete defense, because his conduct and its harmful consequences were justified. The conduct in this instance is tolerated, even encouraged, by society. * * *

D. *Excuses*

Excuses, like justifications, are usually general defenses applicable to all offenses even though the elements of the offense are satisfied. Excuses admit that the deed may be wrong, but excuse the actor because conditions suggest that the actor is not responsible for his deed. For instance, suppose that the actor knocks the mailman over the head with a baseball bat because she believes he is coming to surgically implant a radio receiver which will take control of her body. The defendant has satisfied all elements of the offense of aggravated assault—she struck the mailman with a deadly weapon with the purpose of causing him bodily injury. This is precisely the harm sought to be prevented by the statute, and it is not outweighed by any greater societal harm avoided or greater societal interest furthered. It is conduct that society would in fact condemn and seek to prevent. The defendant is exculpated only because her condition at the time of the offense—her paranoid delusion—suggests that she has not acted through a meaningful exercise of free will and therefore is not an appropriate subject for criminal liability. * * *

E. Nonexculpatory Public Policy Defenses

In 1971 the actor forcibly takes a wallet from an old man at gun point. The crime goes unsolved until 1978 when he is identified and arrested. Although he has committed the offense, caused the harm sought to be prevented by the statute, and has no claim that his conduct is justified or excused, the actor may nonetheless have a defense. The statute of limitations may bar his conviction for robbery despite his clear culpability because by foregoing that conviction society furthers other, more important, public interests.

Time limitations on criminal prosecutions are often supported as fostering a more stable and forward-looking society. * * * These rationales may justify current statutes of limitations, but it must be noted that they are not based on a lack of culpability of the defendant. They are purely public policy arguments. * * *

Other public policy-based bars to prosecution include diplomatic immunity, judicial, legislative, and executive immunities, * * * and incompetency. Each of the * * * forms of immunity furthers important societal interests * * *.

This balancing of countervailing public policy interests, both societal and personal, should be distinguished from the balancing which occurs in justification defenses. In the latter, the harm done by defendant's act is outweighed by the societal benefit that it creates, and, as a result, he is not blameworthy. In nonexculpatory defenses, the defendant's conduct is harmful, and creates no societal benefit; the defendant is blameworthy. The societal benefit underlying the defense arises not from his conduct, but from foregoing his conviction. The defendant escapes conviction in spite of his culpability.

JOSHUA DRESSLER—JUSTIFICATIONS AND EXCUSES:
A BRIEF REVIEW OF THE CONCEPTS AND THE
LITERATURE

33 Wayne Law Review 1155 (1987), 1155, 1157–59, 1161–63, 1167–69, 1171–73

I. Introduction * * *

An important feature of the new literature regarding criminal law defenses is the rebirth of interest in the concepts of "justification" and "excuse." In early English common law the legal profession paid considerable attention to the differences between these doctrines. A practical reason may have inspired the interest: justifiable homicide (e.g., killing to prevent the commission of an atrocious felony) resulted in acquittal of the actor; excusable homicide (e.g., killing by a person suffering from an insane delusion) resulted in the forfeiture of the actor's property and a need for a pardon to avoid the death penalty.

Today, a successful claim of excuse has the same direct effect as a justification: acquittal of the defendant. Probably because of this, the interest of nineteenth and twentieth century lawyers and most legal scholars in the inherent differences between the two classes of exculpatory claims waned. Indeed, until recently, the absence of interest in the subject was nearly complete. American casebooks ignored the distinctions; the topic received scant attention in American law journals; and treatise authors ignored the differences or, perhaps worse, suggested that the differences were of no concern to lawyers. In light of this, it is not surprising that courts often use the words "justification" and "excuse" interchangeably.

In recent years, the academic landscape has changed. * * *

* * * The field is now fairly rich in literature that defines the contours of justification and excuse defenses or that uses the concepts to determine whether particular conduct should be justified, excused, or punished. * * *

II. JUSTIFICATION AND EXCUSE: THE BASICS

A person steeped in the justification-excuse debate or, indeed, any person who uses the English language with care is apt to wince upon hearing another say something like "the justification of self-defense *excuses* a person who injures an aggressor." The words "justification" and "excuse" are not interchangeable in the taxonomy of criminal law defenses or in proper English usage. A justification does not excuse conduct; an excuse does not justify conduct.

In its simplest form, and subject to substantial complexity and debate as to its precise contours, justified conduct is conduct that is "a good thing, or the right or sensible thing, or a permissible thing to do." A defendant who raises a justification defense in a criminal prosecution says, in essence, "I did nothing wrong for which I should be punished." To say that conduct is justified is to suggest that something which ordinarily would be considered wrong or undesirable—i.e., that would constitute "social harm,"—is, in light of the circumstances, socially acceptable or tolerable. A justification, in other words, negates the social harm of an offense.

An excuse is in the nature of a claim that although the actor has harmed society, she should not be blamed or punished for causing that harm. The criminal defendant who asserts an excusing defense says, in essence, "I admit, or you have proved beyond a reasonable doubt, that I did something I should not have done, but I should not be held criminally accountable for my actions." Whereas a justification negates the social harm of an offense, an excuse negates the moral blameworthiness of the actor for causing the harm. Just as we do not punish people for committing harmless acts, we ordinarily do not punish them for blamelessly causing harm. The existence of excuses in the law is evidence of this fact. * * *

III. WHY SHOULD WE CARE ABOUT ALL OF THIS?

A. *Generally*

Sir Henry Maine once observed that "nobody cares about criminal law except theorists and habitual criminals." Unfortunately, lawyers, judges, and lawmakers rarely are accused of being theorists, so it is difficult to convince the legal community that it should care about the justification-excuse distinction. The practical application of the distinction must be demonstrated.

Many of the scholars involved in the justification-excuse debate have sought, and I believe convincingly so, to demonstrate the importance of their work to the legal system. Some of their points suggest that, at least occasionally, a lawyer can take advantage of her knowledge of the justification-excuse dichotomy to win a criminal case. More significantly, the distinctions should prove valuable to those responsible for developing coherent and morally just rules of criminal responsibility. Some reasons why the subject should concern the legal community follow.

B.   Sending Clear Messages

Austin has observed that "words are our tools, and, as a minimum we should use clean tools: we should know what we mean and what we do not, and we must forearm ourselves against the traps that language sets us." [50]   These thoughts apply with special force to lawyers and judges. Words, after all, are their professional tools. As the words "justification" and "excuse" are not synonyms, the legal profession should not treat them as such. The importance of using clean tools is especially significant in the criminal law. Criminal statutes and rules of criminal responsibility express, or at least intend to express, the basic moral values of the community. Specifically, justification defenses reflect society's judgment that certain conduct is tolerable or desirable while excuse defenses recognize those circumstances in which society considers it morally unjust to punish and stigmatize wrongdoers. When the law fails to focus on the justification-excuse distinction it risks sending a false message.   * * *

C.   Providing Theoretical Consistency in the Criminal Law

Consideration of the justification-excuse distinction should be a valuable part of the process by which legislatures and courts coherently define criminal defenses. For example, * * * the heat-of-passion defense to murder suffers from a lack of sufficient consideration of the justification-excuse distinction by the courts that developed the doctrine.

Specifically, lawmakers failed to determine whether provoked killings are less serious offenses because the victim of the provocation is partially justified in killing the provoker—i.e., the victim's provocation results in partial moral forfeiture of her right to life—or whether she is partially excused for the homicide—i.e., the victim's life is fully valued but the actor's understandable passion reduces her moral blameworthiness. Unfortunately, some of the common law rules pertaining to the defense are based on a justification theory; other features fit the excuse

---

50.   J.L. Austin, [*A Plea for Excuses,* in   1961)], at 9.
Freedom and Responsibility (H. Morris ed.

mold. Only by alerting ourselves to the justification-excuse distinction can the elements of the defense be reconciled with the theory. * * *

D. Burden of Proof

A plausible argument can be made for the rule that legislatures ought to require the government to carry the burden of persuasion regarding justification defenses, but that the defendant should shoulder the burden with excuses.

The thesis is that the prosecutor is allocated the burden of proof regarding elements of a crime because no one should be punished if a reasonable doubt exists that she has committed an unlawful act. Justified conduct is lawful conduct. If the defendant is required to carry the burden of persuasion regarding a justification, she may be punished even though the factfinder is not satisfied beyond a reasonable doubt that she has acted wrongly. With excused conduct, however, all of the elements of the crime have been proved and the conduct was determined to be unjustifiable. In these circumstances, it is not unfair to require the defendant to persuade the jury that it should show compassion by excusing her for her unjustified, socially injurious conduct.

E. Accomplice Liability

In some cases, the liability of an accomplice to a crime could be affected by the justification-excuse distinction. If *A* provides *D* with a gun in order to kill *V,* and *D* is acquitted on the ground of self-defense, it follows that *A* should also be acquitted of the offense since she has aided the primary party to commit a socially acceptable act. If *D* is acquitted on the ground of an excuse—let us assume, insanity—no reason of logic or policy requires the acquittal of *A,* assuming that she is not also insane or otherwise excused. After all, *D* 's insanity acquittal does not negate the fact that *A* provided a gun to an insane person who committed a socially harmful act.

Notes and Questions

1. Most scholars reason that claims of justification are logically prior to pleas of excuse, i.e., if conduct is justified there is no reason to consider whether the actor is excused. E.g., Paul Robinson, *Criminal Law Defenses: A Systematic Analysis,* supra, at 332. Can you see why they say this? For the contrary view, see Douglas N. Husak, *The Serial View of Criminal Law Defenses,* 3 Crim.L.Forum 369 (1992).

B. BURDEN OF PROOF

INTRODUCTORY COMMENT

The Supreme Court declared in In re Winship, 397 U.S. 358, 90 S.Ct. 1068, 25 L.Ed.2d 368 (1970), that the due process clause of the United States Constitution requires the prosecutor to persuade the factfinder "beyond a reasonable doubt of every fact necessary to constitute the crime charged." (See p. 8 supra.)

What does *Winship* mean by the word "fact"? Must the government prove beyond a reasonable doubt the elements of the crime, as set out in the definition of the offense? Must it also prove the absence of any defenses to the defendant's conduct? The next case considers this question.

PATTERSON v. NEW YORK

Supreme Court of the United States, 1977.
432 U.S. 197, 97 S.Ct. 2319, 53 L.Ed.2d 281.

Mr. Justice White delivered the opinion of the Court.

The question here is the constitutionality under the Fourteenth Amendment's Due Process Clause of burdening the defendant in a New York State murder trial with proving the affirmative defense of extreme emotional disturbance as defined by New York law.

I

After a brief and unstable marriage, the appellant, Gordon Patterson, Jr., became estranged from his wife, Roberta. Roberta resumed an association with John Northrup, a neighbor to whom she had been engaged prior to her marriage to appellant. On December 27, 1970, Patterson borrowed a rifle from an acquaintance and went to the residence of his father-in-law. There, he observed his wife through a window in a state of semiundress in the presence of John Northrup. He entered the house and killed Northrup by shooting him twice in the head.

Patterson was charged with second-degree murder. In New York there are two elements of this crime: (1) "intent to cause the death of another person"; and (2) "caus[ing] the death of such person or of a third person." Malice aforethought is not an element of the crime. In addition, the State permits a person accused of murder to raise an affirmative defense that he "acted under the influence of extreme emotional disturbance for which there was a reasonable explanation or excuse."

New York also recognizes the crime of manslaughter. A person is guilty of manslaughter if he intentionally kills another person "under circumstances which do not constitute murder because he acts under the influence of extreme emotional disturbance." Appellant confessed before trial to killing Northrup, but at trial he raised the defense of extreme emotional disturbance.

The jury was instructed as to the elements of the crime of murder. Focusing on the element of intent, the trial court charged:

> "Before you, considering all of the evidence, can convict this defendant or anyone of murder, you must believe and decide that the People have established beyond a reasonable doubt that he intended, in firing the gun, to kill either the victim himself or some other human being.

* * *

"Always remember that you must not expect or require the defendant to prove to your satisfaction that his acts were done without the intent to kill. Whatever proof he may have attempted, however far he may have gone in an effort to convince you of his innocence or guiltlessness, he is not obliged, he is not obligated to prove anything. It is always the People's burden to prove his guilt, and to prove that he intended to kill in this instance beyond a reasonable doubt."

The jury was further instructed, consistently with New York law, that the defendant had the burden of proving his affirmative defense by a preponderance of the evidence. The jury was told that if it found beyond a reasonable doubt that appellant had intentionally killed Northrup but that appellant had demonstrated by a preponderance of the evidence that he had acted under the influence of extreme emotional disturbance, it had to find appellant guilty of manslaughter instead of murder.

The jury found appellant guilty of murder. * * * While appeal to the New York Court of Appeals was pending, this Court decided *Mullaney v. Wilbur,* 421 U.S. 684, 95 S.Ct. 1881, 44 L.Ed.2d 508 (1975), in which the Court declared Maine's murder statute unconstitutional. Under the Maine statute, a person accused of murder could rebut the statutory presumption that he committed the offense with "malice aforethought" by proving that he acted in the heat of passion on sudden provocation. The Court held that this scheme improperly shifted the burden of persuasion from the prosecutor to the defendant and was therefore a violation of due process. In the Court of Appeals appellant urged that New York's murder statute is functionally equivalent to the one struck down in *Mullaney* and that therefore his conviction should be reversed.

The Court of Appeals rejected appellant's argument, holding that the New York murder statute is consistent with due process. The Court distinguished *Mullaney* on the ground that the New York statute involved no shifting of the burden to the defendant to disprove any fact essential to the offense charged since the New York affirmative defense of extreme emotional disturbance bears no direct relationship to any element of murder. * * *

II

It goes without saying that preventing and dealing with crime is much more the business of the States than it is of the Federal Government, and that we should not lightly construe the Constitution so as to intrude upon the administration of justice by the individual States. * * *

In determining whether New York's allocation to the defendant of proving the mitigating circumstances of severe emotional disturbance is consistent with due process, it is * * * relevant to note that this defense is a considerably expanded version of the common-law defense of heat of passion on sudden provocation and that at common law the burden of proving the latter, as well as other affirmative defenses—indeed, "all . . . circumstances of justification, excuse or alleviation"—rested on the defendant. * * *

In 1895 the common-law view was abandoned with respect to the insanity defense in federal prosecutions. *Davis v. United States,* 160 U.S. 469, 16 S.Ct. 353, 40 L.Ed. 499 (1895). This ruling had wide impact on the practice in the federal courts with respect to the burden of proving various affirmative defenses, and the prosecution in a majority of jurisdictions in this country sooner or later came to shoulder the burden of proving the sanity of the accused and of disproving the facts constituting other affirmative defenses, including provocation. *Davis* was not a constitutional ruling, however, as *Leland v. Oregon,* [343 U.S. 790, 72 S.Ct. 1002, 96 L.Ed. 1302 (1952)], made clear.

At issue in *Leland v. Oregon* was the constitutionality under the Due Process Clause of the Oregon rule that the defense of insanity must be proved by the defendant beyond a reasonable doubt. Noting that *Davis* "obviously establish[ed] no constitutional doctrine," the Court refused to strike down the Oregon scheme, saying that the burden of proving all elements of the crime beyond reasonable doubt, including the elements of premeditation and deliberation, was placed on the State under Oregon procedures and remained there throughout the trial. To convict, the jury was required to find each element of the crime beyond a reasonable doubt, based on all the evidence, including the evidence going to the issue of insanity. Only then was the jury "to consider separately the issue of legal sanity *per se* . . . ." This practice did not offend the Due Process Clause even though among the 20 States then placing the burden of proving his insanity on the defendant, Oregon was alone in requiring him to convince the jury beyond a reasonable doubt.

In 1970, the Court declared that the Due Process Clause "protects the accused against conviction except upon proof beyond a reasonable doubt of every fact necessary to constitute the crime with which he is charged." *In re Winship,* 397 U.S. 358, 364, 90 S.Ct. 1068, 1073, 25 L.Ed.2d 368 (1970). Five years later, in *Mullaney v. Wilbur,* the Court further announced that under the Maine law of homicide, the burden could not constitutionally be placed on the defendant of proving by a preponderance of the evidence that the killing had occurred in the heat of passion on sudden provocation. The Chief Justice and Mr. Justice Rehnquist, concurring, expressed their understanding that the *Mullaney* decision did not call into question the ruling in *Leland v. Oregon, supra,* with respect to the proof of insanity.

Subsequently, the Court confirmed that it remained constitutional to burden the defendant with proving his insanity defense when it dismissed, as not raising a substantial federal question, a case in which the appellant specifically challenged the continuing validity of *Leland v. Oregon.* * * * *Rivera v. Delaware,* 429 U.S. 877, 97 S.Ct. 226, 50 L.Ed.2d 160 (1976) * * *.

III

We cannot conclude that Patterson's conviction under the New York law deprived him of due process of law. The crime of murder is defined by the statute, which represents a recent revision of the state criminal code, as causing the death of another person with intent to do so. The death, the intent to kill, and causation are the facts that the State is required to prove beyond a reasonable doubt if a person is to be convicted of murder. No further facts are either presumed or inferred in order to constitute the crime. The statute does provide an affirmative defense—that the defendant acted under the influence of extreme emotional disturbance for which there was a reasonable explanation—which, if proved by a preponderance of the evidence, would reduce the crime to manslaughter, an offense defined in a separate section of the statute. It is plain enough that if the intentional killing is shown, the State intends to deal with the defendant as a murderer unless he demonstrates the mitigating circumstances.

Here, the jury was instructed in accordance with the statute, and the guilty verdict confirms that the State successfully carried its burden of proving the facts of the crime beyond a reasonable doubt. * * * It seems to us that the State satisfied the mandate of *Winship* that it prove beyond a reasonable doubt "every fact necessary to constitute the crime with which [Patterson was] charged."

In convicting Patterson under its murder statute, New York did no more than *Leland* and *Rivera* permitted it to do without violating the Due Process Clause. Under those cases, once the facts constituting a crime are established beyond a reasonable doubt, based on all the evidence including the evidence of the defendant's mental state, the State may refuse to sustain the affirmative defense of insanity unless demonstrated by a preponderance of the evidence.

The New York law on extreme emotional disturbance follows this pattern. This affirmative defense * * * does not serve to negative any facts of the crime which the State is to prove in order to convict of murder. It constitutes a separate issue on which the defendant is required to carry the burden of persuasion; and unless we are to overturn *Leland* and *Rivera,* New York has not violated the Due Process Clause, and Patterson's conviction must be sustained.

We are unwilling to reconsider *Leland* and *Rivera.* But even if we were to hold that a State must prove sanity to convict once that fact is put in issue, it would not necessarily follow that a State must prove beyond a reasonable doubt every fact, the existence or nonexistence of which it is willing to recognize as an exculpatory or mitigating circumstance affecting the degree of culpability or the severity of the punishment. Here, in revising its criminal code, New York provided the affirmative defense of extreme emotional disturbance, a substantially expanded version of the older heat-of-passion concept; but it was willing to do so only if the facts making out the defense were established by the defendant with sufficient certainty. The State was itself unwilling to undertake to establish the absence of those facts beyond a reasonable doubt, perhaps fearing that proof would be too difficult and that too many persons deserving treatment as murderers would escape that punishment if the evidence need merely raise a reasonable doubt about the defendant's emotional state. It has been said that the new criminal code of New York contains some 25 affirmative defenses which exculpate or mitigate but which must be established by the defendant to be operative. The Due Process Clause, as we see it, does not put New York to the choice of abandoning those defenses or undertaking to disprove their existence in order to convict of a crime which otherwise is within its constitutional powers to sanction by substantial punishment.

The requirement of proof beyond a reasonable doubt in a criminal case is "bottomed on a fundamental value determination of our society that it is far worse to convict an innocent man than to let a guilty man go free." *Winship*, 397 U.S., at 372, 90 S.Ct., at 1077 (Harlan, J., concurring). The social cost of placing the burden on the prosecution to prove guilt beyond a reasonable doubt is thus an increased risk that the guilty will go free. While it is clear that our society has willingly chosen to bear a substantial burden in order to protect the innocent, it is equally clear that the risk it must bear is not without limits; and Mr. Justice Harlan's aphorism provides little guidance for determining what those limits are. Due process does not require that every conceivable step be taken, at whatever cost, to eliminate the possibility of convicting an innocent person. Punishment of those found guilty by a jury, for example, is not forbidden merely because there is a remote possibility in some instances that an innocent person might go to jail.

* * * If the State * * * chooses to recognize a factor that mitigates the degree of criminality or punishment, we think the State may assure itself that the fact has been established with reasonably certainty. To recognize at all a mitigating circumstance does not require the State to prove its non-existence in each case in which the fact is put in issue, if in its judgment this would be too cumbersome, too expensive, and too inaccurate.

We thus decline to adopt as a constitutional imperative, operative countrywide, that a State must disprove beyond a reasonable doubt every fact constituting any and all affirmative defenses related to the culpability of an accused. * * * We * * * will not disturb the balance struck in previous cases holding that the Due Process Clause requires the prosecution to prove beyond a reasonable doubt all of the elements included in the definition of the offense of which the defendant is charged. Proof of the nonexistence of all affirmative defenses has never been constitutionally required; and we perceive no reason to fashion such a rule in this case and apply it to the statutory defense at issue here.

This view may seem to permit state legislatures to reallocate burdens of proof by labeling as affirmative defenses at least some elements of the crimes now defined in their statutes. But there are obviously constitutional limits beyond which the States may not go in this regard. "[I]t is not within the province of a legislature to declare an individual guilty or presumptively guilty of a crime." *McFarland v. American Sugar Rfg. Co.,* 241 U.S. 79, 86, 36 S.Ct. 498, 500, 60 L.Ed. 899 (1916). The legislature cannot "validly command that the finding of an indictment, or mere proof of the identity of the accused, should create a presumption of the existence of all the facts essential to guilt." *Tot v. United States,* 319 U.S. 463, 469, 63 S.Ct. 1241, 1246, 87 L.Ed. 1519 (1943). * * * [T]he fact that a majority of the States have now assumed the burden of disproving affirmative defenses—for whatever reasons—[does not] mean that those States that strike a different balance are in violation of the Constitution.

IV

It is urged that *Mullaney v. Wilbur* necessarily invalidates Patterson's conviction. In *Mullaney* the charge was murder, which the Maine statute defined as the unlawful killing of a human being "with malice aforethought, either express or implied." * * * Malice as the statute indicated and as the court instructed, * * * was to be implied from "any deliberate, cruel act committed by one person against another suddenly ... or without a considerable provocation," in which event an intentional killing was murder unless by a preponderance of the evidence it was shown that the act was committed "in the heat of passion, on sudden provocation." The instructions emphasized that " 'malice aforethought and heat of passion on sudden provocation are two inconsistent things'; thus, by proving the latter the defendant would negate the former." * * *

* * * This Court, accepting the Maine court's interpretation of the Maine law, unanimously agreed with the Court of Appeals that Wilbur's due process rights had been invaded by the presumption casting upon him the burden of proving by a preponderance of the evidence that he had acted in the heat of passion upon sudden provocation.

Mullaney's holding, it is argued, is that the State may not permit the blameworthiness of an act or the severity of punishment authorized for its commission to depend on the presence or absence of an identified fact without assuming the burden of proving the presence or absence of that fact, as the case may be, beyond a reasonable doubt.[15] In our view, the *Mullaney* holding should not be so broadly read. * * *

Mullaney surely held that a State must prove every ingredient of an offense beyond a reasonable doubt, and that it may not shift the burden of proof to the defendant by presuming that ingredient upon proof of the

15. There is some language in *Mullaney* that has been understood as perhaps construing the Due Process Clause to require the prosecution to prove beyond a reasonable doubt any fact affecting "the degree of criminal culpability." It is said that such a rule would deprive legislatures of any discretion whatsoever in allocating the burden of proof, the practical effect of which might be to undermine legislative reform of our criminal justice system. * * * The Court did not intend *Mullaney* to have such far-reaching effect.

other elements of the offense. This is true even though the State's practice, as in Maine, had been traditionally to the contrary. Such shifting of the burden of persuasion with respect to a fact which the State deems so important that it must be either proved or presumed is impermissible under the Due Process Clause.

It was unnecessary to go further in *Mullaney*. The Maine Supreme Judicial Court made it clear that malice aforethought, * * * in the sense of the absence of provocation, was part of the definition of that crime. Yet malice, *i.e.,* lack of provocation, was presumed and could be rebutted by the defendant only by proving by a preponderance of the evidence that he acted with heat of passion upon sudden provocation. In *Mullaney* we held that however traditional this mode of proceeding might have been, it is contrary to the Due Process Clause as construed in *Winship*.

As we have explained, nothing was presumed or implied against Patterson; and his conviction is not invalid under any of our prior cases. The judgment of the New York Court of Appeals is

Affirmed.

MR. JUSTICE POWELL, with whom MR. JUSTICE BRENNAN and MR. JUSTICE MARSHALL join, dissenting.

In the name of preserving legislative flexibility, the Court today drains *In re Winship* of much of its vitality. Legislatures do require broad discretion in the drafting of criminal laws, but the Court surrenders to the legislative branch a significant part of its responsibility to protect the presumption of innocence.

I * * *

Mullaney held invalid Maine's requirement that the defendant prove heat of passion. The Court today, without disavowing the unanimous holding of *Mullaney,* approves New York's requirement that the defendant prove extreme emotional disturbance. The Court manages to run a constitutional boundary line through the barely visible space that separates Maine's law from New York's. It does so on the basis of distinctions in language that are formalistic rather than substantive.

This result is achieved by a narrowly literal parsing of the holding in *Winship:* "[T]he Due Process Clause protects the accused against conviction except upon proof beyond a reasonable doubt of every fact necessary to constitute the crime with which he is charged." The only "facts" necessary to constitute a crime are said to be those that appear on the face of the statute as a part of the definition of the crime. Maine's statute was invalid, the Court reasons, because it "defined [murder] as the unlawful killing of a human being 'with malice aforethought, either express or implied.'" "[M]alice," the Court reiterates, "in the sense of the absence of provocation, was part of the definition of that crime." *Winship* was violated only because this "fact"—malice— was "presumed" unless the defendant persuaded the jury otherwise by showing that he acted in the heat of passion. New York, in form presuming no affirmative "fact" against Patterson, and blessed with a statute drafted in the leaner language of the 20th century, escapes constitutional scrutiny unscathed even though the effect on the defendant of New York's placement of the burden of persuasion is exactly the same as Maine's.

This explanation of the *Mullaney* holding bears little resemblance to the basic rationale of that decision. But this is not the cause of greatest concern. The test the Court today establishes allows a legislature to shift, virtually at will, the burden of persuasion with respect to any factor in a criminal case, so long as it is careful not to mention the nonexistence of that factor in the statutory language that defines the crime. The sole requirement is that any references to the factor be confined to those sections that provide for an affirmative defense.

Perhaps the Court's interpretation of *Winship* is consistent with the letter of the holding in that case. But little of the spirit survives. Indeed, the Court scarcely could distinguish this case from *Mullaney* without closing its eyes to the constitutional values for which *Winship* stands. As Mr. Justice Harlan observed in *Winship*, "a standard of proof represents an attempt to instruct the factfinder concerning the degree of confidence our society thinks he should have in the correctness of factual conclusions for a particular type of adjudication." Explaining *Mullaney*, the Court says today, in effect, that society demands full confidence before a Maine factfinder determines that heat of passion is missing—a demand so insistent that this Court invoked the Constitution to enforce it over the contrary decision by the State. But we are told that society is willing to tolerate far less confidence in New York's factual determination of precisely the same functional issue. One must ask what possibly could explain this difference in societal demands. According to the Court, it is because Maine happened to attach a name—"malice aforethought"—to the absence of heat of passion, whereas New York refrained from giving a name to the absence of extreme emotional disturbance.

With all respect, this type of constitutional adjudication is indefensibly formalistic. A limited but significant check on possible abuses in the criminal law now becomes an exercise in arid formalities. * * * Nothing in the Court's opinion prevents a legislature from applying this new learning to many of the classical elements of the crimes it punishes.[8]
* * *

---

8. For example, a state statute could pass muster under the only solid standard that appears in the Court's opinion if it defined murder as mere physical contact between the defendant and the victim leading to the victim's death, but then set up an affirmative defense leaving it to the defendant to prove that he acted without culpable *mens rea*. The State, in other words, could be relieved altogether of responsibility for proving anything regarding the defendant's state of mind, provided only that the face of the statute meets the Court's drafting formulas.

To be sure, it is unlikely that legislatures will rewrite their criminal laws in this extreme form. * * * But it is completely foreign to this Court's responsibility for constitutional adjudication to limit the scope of judicial review because of the expectation—however reasonable—that legislative bodies will exercise appropriate restraint.

* * * This decision simply leaves us without a conceptual framework for distinguishing abuses from legitimate legislative adjustments of the burden of persuasion in criminal cases.

II

It is unnecessary for the Court to retreat to a formalistic test for applying *Winship*. Careful attention to the *Mullaney* decision reveals the principles that should control in this and like cases. * * * In *Mullaney* we concluded that heat of passion was one of the "facts" described in *Winship*—that is, a factor as to which the prosecution must bear the burden of persuasion beyond a reasonable doubt. We reached that result only after making two careful inquiries. First, we noted that the presence or absence of heat of passion made a substantial difference in punishment of the offender and in the stigma associated with the conviction. Second, we reviewed the history, in England and this country, of the factor at issue. Central to the holding in *Mullaney* was our conclusion that heat of passion "has been, almost from the inception of the common law of homicide, the single most important factor in determining the degree of culpability attaching to an unlawful homicide."

Implicit in these two inquiries are the principles that should govern this case. The Due Process Clause requires that the prosecutor bear the burden of persuasion beyond a reasonable doubt only if the factor at issue makes a substantial difference in punishment and stigma. * * * But a substantial difference in punishment alone is not enough. It also must be shown that in the Anglo–American legal tradition the factor in question historically has held that level of importance. If either branch of the test is not met, then the legislature retains its traditional authority over matters of proof. * * *

I hardly need add that New York's provisions allocating the burden of persuasion as to "extreme emotional disturbance" are unconstitutional when judged by these standards. "Extreme emotional disturbance" is * * * the direct descendant of the "heat of passion" factor considered at length in *Mullaney*. I recognize, of course, that the differences between Maine and New York law are not unimportant to the defendant; there is a somewhat broader opportunity for mitigation. But none of those distinctions is relevant here. The presence or absence of extreme emotional disturbance makes a critical difference in punishment and stigma, and throughout our history the resolution of this issue of fact, although expressed in somewhat different terms, has distinguished manslaughter from murder. * * *

Notes and Questions

1. *Burden of production.* Two burdens of proof arise in a criminal trial. The first is the burden of production (or the "burden of going forward"). The party on whom this burden is placed has the initial obligation to introduce evidence in support of the matter at issue. In general, the prosecutor is the party on whom the burden of production is

placed regarding the elements of a crime; the defendant has the burden relating to affirmative defenses. For example, in *Patterson,* the state was required to produce evidence that a human being died, that Patterson caused the death, and that he did so intentionally. Patterson had the burden of producing evidence regarding the affirmative defense of extreme emotional disturbance.

The quantum of evidence required to satisfy the burden of production varies by jurisdiction, but is rarely substantial. For example, some courts provide that the party on whom the burden of production is placed need present only "more than a mere scintilla" of evidence in support of the claim in question. United States v. Pratt, 913 F.2d 982, 988 (1st Cir.1990).

If the burden of production regarding an element or defense is met, the matter is properly before the factfinder, and the next burden to consider is the burden of *persuasion, i.e.,* the burden of convincing the factfinder of the truth of the claim being raised. This was the burden of proof at issue in *Winship, Mullaney,* and *Patterson.*

2. Consider the hypothetical murder statute set out in footnote 8 of Justice Powell's dissent. Does this statute satisfy the due process clause? If so, is there any other constitutional principle that this statute might offend? See John Calvin Jeffries, Jr. and Paul B. Stephan III, *Defenses, Presumptions, and Burden of Proof in the Criminal Law,* 88 Yale L.J. 1325, 1376–83 (1979).

3. *Problem.* Roberta is indicted for murder. State law provides that a person is guilty of murder if she "purposely, and with prior calculation and design, causes the death of another." Roberta introduces evidence at her trial that she killed Susan in self-defense. The judge intends to instruct the jury that in order to be acquitted on the ground of self-defense, Roberta must prove by a preponderance of the evidence that she "had an honest belief that she was in imminent danger of death or great bodily harm, and that her only means of escape from such danger was in the use of such force." You represent Roberta. What argument would you make that this proposed instruction violates the dictates of *Patterson?*

Suppose that murder were defined in the state as "purposely, and with prior calculation and design, causing the *unlawful* death of another." Does the addition of the italicized word change the burden-of-proof analysis? See Martin v. Ohio, 480 U.S. 228, 107 S.Ct. 1098, 94 L.Ed.2d 267 (1987).

4. Who has the burden of proof regarding defenses in Model Penal Code jurisdictions? Consider Sections 1.12 and 1.13(9).

C. PRINCIPLES OF JUSTIFICATION

1. STRUCTURE OF JUSTIFICATION DEFENSES

1 PAUL H. ROBINSON—CRIMINAL LAW DEFENSES
(1984) § 24(b), pp. 86–88[a]

All justification defenses have the same internal structure:

a. Reprinted from Criminal Law Defenses, Paul H. Robinson, copyright © 1984, with permission of the West Publishing Company.

triggering conditions permit a
necessary and *proportional response*

Triggering conditions are the circumstances that must exist before an actor will be eligible to act under a justification. For example, in defensive force justifications the justification is triggered if an aggressor presents a threat of unjustified harm to a protected interest, as by attempting to burn the defendant's chicken coop. * * *

The triggering conditions of a justification defense do not give an actor the privilege to act without restriction. To be justified, the responsive conduct must satisfy two requirements:

(1) it must be *necessary* to protect or further the interest at stake, and

(2) it must cause only a harm that is *proportional* or reasonable in relation to the harm threatened or the interest to be furthered.

The *necessity requirement* demands that the defendant act only when and to the extent necessary to protect or further the interest at stake. Thus, where an aggressor announces his intention to assault the actor at noon the next day, the threat provides the triggering condition for self-defense. But, if indeed the actor is in no danger at the time, he is not justified in immediately using physical force against the aggressor. * * *

The *proportionality requirement* places a limit on the maximum harm that may be used in protection or furtherance of an interest. It bars justification when the harm caused by the actor may be necessary to protect or further the interest at stake, but is too severe in relation to the value of the interest. Where an actor has no other option but deadly force to prevent the stealing of apples from her orchard, a jurisdiction that prohibits deadly force to protect property essentially requires the actor to sacrifice her apples out of regard for the thieves' lives.

2. SELF–DEFENSE

a. General Principles

UNITED STATES v. PETERSON

United States Court of Appeals, District of Columbia Circuit, 1973.
483 F.2d 1222.

SPOTTSWOOD W. ROBINSON, III, CIRCUIT JUDGE:

Indicted for second-degree murder, and convicted by a jury of manslaughter as a lesser included offense, Bennie L. Peterson [appeals] * * *. * * * He complains * * * that the judge twice erred in the instructions given the jury in relation to his claim that the homicide was committed in self-defense. One error alleged was an instruction that the jury might consider whether Peterson was the aggressor in the altercation that immediately foreran the homicide. The other was an instruction that a failure by Peterson to retreat, if he could have done so without jeopardizing his safety, might be considered as a circumstance bearing on the question whether he was justified in using the amount of force which he did. * * * [W]e affirm Peterson's conviction.

I

The events immediately preceding the homicide are not seriously in dispute. * * * Charles Keitt, the deceased, and two friends drove in Keitt's car to the alley in the rear of Peterson's house to remove the windshield wipers from the latter's wrecked car. While Keitt was doing so, Peterson came out of the house into the back yard to protest. After a verbal exchange, Peterson went back into the house, obtained a pistol, and returned to the yard. In the meantime, Keitt had reseated himself in his car, and he and his companions were about to leave.

Upon his reappearance in the yard, Peterson paused briefly to load the pistol. "If you move," he shouted to Keitt, "I will shoot." He walked to a point in the yard slightly inside a gate in the rear fence and, pistol in hand, said, "If you come in here I will kill you." Keitt alighted from his car, took a few steps toward Peterson and exclaimed, "What the hell do you think you are going to do with that?" Keitt then made an about-face, walked back to his car and got a lug wrench. With the wrench in a raised position, Keitt advanced toward Peterson, who stood with the pistol pointed toward him. Peterson warned Keitt not to "take another step" and, when Keitt continued onward shot him in the face from a distance of about ten feet. Death was apparently instantaneous. * * *

II * * *

III

More than two centuries ago, Blackstone, best known of the expositors of the English common law, taught that "all homicide is malicious, and of course, amounts to murder, unless ... *justified* by the command or permission of the law; *excused* on the account of accident or self-preservation; or *alleviated* into manslaughter, by being either the involuntary consequence of some act not strictly lawful, or (if voluntary) occasioned by some sudden and sufficiently violent provocation."

Tucked within this greatly capsulized schema of the common law of homicide is the branch of law we are called upon to administer today. No issue of justifiable homicide, within Blackstone's definition is involved.[35] But Peterson's consistent position is that as a matter of law

---

35. By the early common law, justification for homicide extended only to acts done in execution of the law, such as homicides in effecting arrests and preventing forcible felonies, and homicides committed in self-defense were only excusable. The distinction between justifiable and excusable homicide was important because in the latter case the slayer, considered to be not wholly free from blame, suffered a forfeiture of his goods. However, with the passage of 24 Henry VIII, ch. 5 (1532), the basis of justification was enlarged, and the distinction has largely disappeared. More

his conviction * * * was wrong, and that his act was one of self-preservation—excused homicide. * * *

Self-defense, as a doctrine legally exonerating the taking of human life, is as viable now as it was in Blackstone's time, and in the case before us the doctrine is invoked in its purest form. But "[t]he law of self-defense is a law of necessity;" the right of self-defense arises only when the necessity begins, and equally ends with the necessity; and never must the necessity be greater than when the force employed defensively is deadly.[40] The "necessity must bear all semblance of reality, and appear to admit of no other alternative, before taking life will be justifiable as excusable." Hinged on the exigencies of self-preservation, the doctrine of homicidal self-defense emerges from the body of the criminal law as a limited though important exception to legal outlawry of the arena of self-help in the settlement of potentially fatal personal conflicts.

So it is that necessity is the pervasive theme of the well defined conditions which the law imposes on the right to kill or maim in self-defense. There must have been a threat, actual or apparent, of the use of deadly force against the defender. The threat must have been unlawful and immediate. The defender must have believed that he was in imminent peril of death or serious bodily harm, and that his response was necessary to save himself therefrom. These beliefs must not only have been honestly entertained, but also objectively reasonable in light of the surrounding circumstances. It is clear that no less than a concurrence of these elements will suffice. * * *

IV * * *

* * The first of Peterson's complaints centers upon an instruction that the right to use deadly force in self-defense is not ordinarily available to one who provokes a conflict or is the aggressor in it. Mere words, the judge explained, do not constitute provocation or aggression; and if Peterson precipitated the altercation but thereafter withdrew from it in good faith and so informed Keitt by words or acts, he was justified in using deadly force to save himself from imminent danger or death or grave bodily harm. * * * Peterson contends that there was no evidence that he either caused or contributed to the conflict, and that the instructions on that topic could only [have] misled the jury.

It has long been accepted that one cannot support a claim of self-defense by a self-generated necessity to kill. The right of homicidal self-defense is granted only to those free from fault in the difficulty; it is denied to slayers who incite the fatal attack, encourage the fatal quarrel or otherwise promote the necessitous occasion for taking life. The fact that the deceased struck the first blow, fired the first shot or made the first menacing gesture does not legalize the self-defense claim if in fact

usually the terms are used interchangeably, each denoting a legally non-punishable act, entitling the accused to an acquittal.

40. When we speak of deadly force, we refer to force capable of inflicting death or serious bodily harm.

the claimant was the actual provoker. In sum, one who is the aggressor in a conflict culminating in death cannot invoke the necessities of self-preservation. Only in the event that he communicates to his adversary his intent to withdraw and in good faith attempts to do so is he restored to his right of self-defense.

This body of doctrine traces its origin to the fundamental principle that a killing in self-defense is excusable only as a matter of genuine necessity. Quite obviously, a defensive killing is unnecessary if the occasion for it could have been averted, and the roots of that consideration run deep with us. * * *

In the case at bar, the trial judge's charge fully comported with these governing principles. The remaining question, then, is whether there was evidence to make them applicable to the case. A recapitulation of the proofs shows beyond peradventure that there was.

It was not until Peterson fetched his pistol and returned to his back yard that his confrontation with Keitt took on a deadly cast. Prior to his trip into the house for the gun, there was, by the Government's evidence, no threat, no display of weapons, no combat. There was an exchange of verbal aspersions and a misdemeanor[57] against Peterson's property[58] was in progress but, at this juncture, nothing more. * * *

The evidence is uncontradicted that when Peterson reappeared in the yard with his pistol, Keitt was about to depart the scene. * * * The uncontroverted fact that Keitt was leaving shows plainly that so far as he was concerned the confrontation was ended. It demonstrates just as plainly that even if he had previously been the aggressor, he no longer was.

Not so with Peterson, however, as the undisputed evidence made clear. Emerging from the house with the pistol, he paused in the yard to load it, and to command Keitt not to move. He then walked through the yard to the rear gate and, displaying his pistol, dared Keitt to come in, and threatened to kill him if he did. While there appears to be no fixed rule on the subject, the cases hold, and we agree, that an affirmative unlawful act reasonably calculated to produce an affray foreboding injurious or fatal consequences is an aggression which, unless renounced, nullifies the right of homicidal self-defense. We cannot escape the abiding conviction that the jury could readily find Peterson's challenge to be a transgression of that character.

The situation at bar is not unlike that presented in *Laney* [294 F. 412 (1923)]. There the accused, chased along the street by a mob threatening his life, managed to escape through an areaway between two houses. In the back yard of one of the houses, he checked a gun he was carrying and then returned to the areaway. The mob beset him again, and during an exchange of shots one of its members was killed by a

---

57. It is well settled that deadly force cannot be employed to arrest or prevent the escape of a misdemeanant.

58. The law never tolerates the use of deadly force in the protection of one's property.

bullet from the accused's gun. In affirming a conviction of manslaughter, the court reasoned:

It is clearly apparent . . . that, when defendant escaped from the mob into the back yard . . . he was in a place of comparative safety, from which, if he desired to go home, he could have gone by the back way, as he subsequently did. The mob had turned its attention to a house on the opposite side of the street. According to Laney's testimony, there was shooting going on in the street. His appearance on the street at that juncture could mean nothing but trouble for him. Hence, when he adjusted his gun and stepped out into the areaway, he had every reason to believe that his presence there would provoke trouble. We think his conduct in adjusting his revolver and going into the areaway was such as to deprive him of any right to invoke the plea of self-defense.

Similarly, in Rowe v. United States [370 F.2d 240 (D.D.Cir.1966)], the accused was in the home of friends when an argument, to which the friends became participants, developed in the street in front. He left, went to his nearby apartment for a loaded pistol and returned. * * * [W]hen a group of five men began to move toward him, he began to shoot at them, killing two, and wounding a third. We observed that the accused "left an apparently safe haven to arm himself and return to the scene," and that "he inflamed the situation with his words to the men gathered there, even though he could have returned silently to the safety of the [friends'] porch." We held that

[t]hese facts could have led the jury to conclude that [the accused] returned to the scene to stir up further trouble, if not actually to kill anyone, and that his actions instigated the men into rushing him. Self-defense may not be claimed by one who deliberately places himself in a position where he has reason to believe "his presence . . . would provoke trouble."

We noted the argument "that a defendant may claim self-defense if he arms himself in order to proceed upon his normal activities, even if he realizes that danger may await him"; we responded by pointing out "that the jury could have found that the course of action defendant here followed was for an unlawful purpose." We accordingly affirmed his conviction of manslaughter over his objection that an acquittal should have been directed.

We are brought much the readier to the same conclusion here. We think the evidence plainly presented an issue of fact as to whether Peterson's conduct was an invitation to and provocation of the encounter which ended in the fatal shot. We sustain the trial judge's action in remitting that issue for the jury's determination.

V

The second aspect of the trial judge's charge as to which Peterson asserts error concerned the undisputed fact that at no time did Peterson endeavor to retreat from Keitt's approach with the lug wrench. The judge instructed the jury that if Peterson * * * could have safely retreated but did not do so, that failure was a circumstance which the jury might consider, together with all others, in determining whether he went further in repelling the danger, real or apparent, than he was justified in going.

Peterson contends that this imputation of an obligation to retreat was error, even if he could safely have done so. He points out that at the time of the shooting he was standing in his own yard, and argues he was under no duty to move. We are persuaded to the conclusion that in the circumstances presented here, the trial judge did not err in giving the instruction challenged.

Within the common law of self-defense there developed the rule of "retreat to the wall," which ordinarily forbade the use of deadly force by one to whom an avenue for safe retreat was open. This doctrine was but an application of the requirement of strict necessity to excuse the taking of human life, and was designed to insure the existence of that necessity. Even the innocent victim of a vicious assault had to elect a safe retreat, if available, rather than resort to defensive force which might kill or seriously injure.

In a majority of American jurisdictions, contrarily to the common law rule, one may stand his ground and use deadly force whenever it seems reasonably necessary to save himself. While the law of the District of Columbia on this point is not entirely clear, it seems allied with the strong minority adhering to the common law. * * *

That is not to say that the retreat rule is without exceptions. Even at common law it was recognized that it was not completely suited to all situations. Today it is the more so that its precept must be adjusted to modern conditions nonexistent during the early development of the common law of self-defense.[86] One restriction on its operation comes to the fore when the circumstances apparently foreclose a withdrawal with safety. The doctrine of retreat was never intended to enhance the risk to the innocent; its proper application has never required a faultless victim to increase his assailant's safety at the expense of his own. On the contrary, he could stand his ground and use deadly force otherwise appropriate if the alternative were perilous, or if to him it reasonably appeared to be. * * *

The trial judge's charge to the jury incorporated [this limit] on the retreat rule. Peterson, however, invokes another—the so-called "castle" doctrine. It is well settled that one who through no fault of his own is attacked in his home is under no duty to retreat therefrom. The oft-repeated expression that "a man's home is his castle" reflected the belief

---

86. " * * * Time, place, and conditions may create a situation which would clearly justify a modification of the rule. For example, the common-law rule, which required the assailed to retreat to the wall, had its origin before the general introduction of firearms. If a person is threatened with death or great bodily harm by an assailant, armed with a modern rifle, in open space, away from safety, it would be ridiculous to require him to retreat. Indeed, to retreat would be to invite almost certain death." Laney v. United States, *supra*.

in olden days that there were few if any safer sanctuaries than the home. The "castle" exception, moreover, has been extended by some courts to encompass the occupant's presence within the curtilage outside his dwelling. Peterson reminds us that when he shot to halt Keitt's advance, he was standing in his yard and so, he argues, he had no duty to endeavor to retreat.

Despite the practically universal acceptance of the "castle" doctrine in American jurisdictions wherein the point has been raised, its status in the District of Columbia has never been squarely decided. But whatever the fate of the doctrine in the District law of the future, it is clear that in absolute form it was inapplicable here. The right of self-defense, we have said, cannot be claimed by the aggressor in an affray so long as he retains that unmitigated role. It logically follows that any rule of no-retreat which may protect an innocent victim of the affray would, like other incidents of a forfeited right of self-defense, be unavailable to the party who provokes or stimulates the conflict. Accordingly, the law is well settled that the "castle" doctrine can be invoked only by one who is without fault in bringing the conflict on. That, we think, is the critical consideration here.

We need not repeat our previous discussion of Peterson's contribution to the altercation which culminated in Keitt's death. It suffices to point out that by no interpretation of the evidence could it be said that Peterson was blameless in the affair. * * *

Notes and Questions

1. *"Aggressor."* Under what circumstances is a person an "aggressor" for purposes of losing the right of self-defense? Apply *Peterson* to the following facts:

Dina ordinarily walked along a particular street in a residential area as part of her daily exercise regimen. One day Arthur, the resident bully, told her that if she came that way again he would kill her. Dina could just as conveniently have walked along another street, but reminiscent of Gary Cooper in High Noon,[b] she decided the next day to arm herself with a licensed gun and walk along the now forbidden route with her weapon visible to onlookers. Arthur appeared and came toward her menacingly. Dina shot and killed him. Who was the aggressor?

2. Based on *Peterson,* how does it appear that an aggressor regains the right of self-defense? In this regard, consider State v. Diggs, 219 Conn. 295, 592 A.2d 949 (1991): During an altercation on the street, Jim unlawfully pointed a rifle at Frank. Frank responded by throwing a punch at Jim and, while continuing to come at him, threatening additional injury. Frank's cousin, Rayford, arrived and attempted to defuse the argument. As he did,

---

b. High Noon (United Artists 1952). The movie tells the western yarn of an ex-marshall (Gary Cooper), whose wish to leave town and live a more peaceful life with his newlywed pacifist wife (Grace Kelly) was thwarted on the day of departure when he learned that a recently released killer was coming to town to shoot him. Cooper changed his plans, remained in town, and shot it out with the killer and his cohorts at "high noon."

*say he
wasn't going
to shoot*

Jim backed up the distance of a small front lawn, yelling to Rayford, "Tell your cousin to get out of my face. Come and get your cousin. Get back before I shoot." When Frank did not back down, Jim shot him. At the time of the shooting, who was the aggressor? If Jim was still the aggressor, what more did he have to do to regain his right of self-defense?

3. In *Diggs* (Note 2), Frank responded to Jim's unlawful deadly threat by using nondeadly force—by throwing a punch. Suppose that the situation were reversed: Jim unlawfully throws a punch at Frank, and Frank escalates the affair by pulling a gun on Jim. Should Jim, the initial aggressor, now have the right to kill Frank? The Commentary to the Model Penal Code explains the Model Code and non-Code approach to this situation:

> The typical case to be imagined is this: A attacks B with his fists; B defends himself, and manages to subdue A to the extent of pinning him to the floor. B then starts to batter A's head savagely against the floor. A manages to rise, and since B is still attacking him and A now fears that if he is thrown again to the floor he will be killed, A uses a knife. B is killed or seriously wounded.

> The solution to this situation under the provisions of this section is as follows: B is entitled to defend himself against A's attack, but only to the extent of using moderate, nondeadly force. He is given this privilege by Subsection (1). B exceeds the bounds of "necessary" force under that provision, however, when, after reducing A to helplessness, he batters A's head on the floor. Since this excessive force is, in its turn, unlawful, under Subsection (1) A is entitled to defend himself against it and, if he believes that he is then in danger of death or serious bodily harm without apparent opportunity for safe retreat, A is also entitled to use his knife in self-protection. A of course is criminally liable for his initial battery on B, but would have a justifying defense that he could raise against prosecution for the ultimate homicide or wounding. Subsection (2)(b)(i), depriving A of his justification on the ground of initial aggression, would not become operative unless A entered the encounter with the purpose of causing death or serious bodily harm.

> This conclusion—that an initial aggressor is accountable for his original unlawful use of force but not for his defense against a disproportionate return of force by his victim—is surely not unreasonable on its face. There is, however, much authority, both common law and statutory, demanding that a person claiming self-defense be free from fault in bringing on the difficulty. But the principle is not, on the whole, unqualified. The original aggressor is usually deemed to have a right of self-defense that is "imperfect"; before it may be exercised he must give notice of his wish to desist from the struggle and attempt in good faith to withdraw.

American Law Institute, Model Penal Code and Commentaries, Comment to § 3.04 at 49–51 (1985).

4. *Problem.* Calvin arrived at the house of his girlfriend, Donna, just as Edgar was leaving. Suspicious, Calvin asked Edgar whether he had been "fooling around" with Donna. Edgar responded by pointing a gun at Calvin. Calvin entered Donna's house and looked for his gun, which he had

previously left with Donna for her protection. Donna calmed Calvin down. Thirty minutes later, Calvin left with his gun in his possession. Outside, he unexpectedly discovered Edgar sitting in his (Edgar's) parked car. Calvin walked up, and again asked Edgar whether he had been "fooling around" with Donna. Edgar replied with a "mean smile." Calvin slapped Edgar with the back of his hand through the open car window. Edgar picked up his gun, which was sitting on the front seat, and started to get out of his car. As he did, Calvin shot Edgar. Self-defense? See State v. Corchado, 188 Conn. 653, 453 A.2d 427 (1982).

5. *The necessity requirement.* When is deadly force necessary? In State v. Dill, 461 So.2d 1130 (La.App.1984), the defendant (5′4″, 145 lbs) was in his car, preparing to leave a public parking lot, when the decedent (6′0″, 200 lbs.) walked over and requested help to start his own vehicle. The defendant said he would only help if the decedent paid him five dollars. After a verbal exchange, the decedent lunged at the defendant with a knife through the defendant's open car window. The defendant emerged with a gun and immediately shot the decedent in the head. If you were on the jury, would you acquit the defendant on the ground of self-defense? Was the shooting necessary? Did the defendant have any reasonable alternatives?

6. *Problem.* Garrison was visiting his sister's apartment when Jeremiah, the sister's former boyfriend, arrived in an intoxicated condition. The sister went into her bedroom and closed the door. Garrison tried to convince Jeremiah to leave, but the much larger man staggered menacingly toward Garrison with a gun in his waistband. Due to Jeremiah's intoxicated condition, Garrison was able to disarm him, but Jeremiah pulled a knife on Garrison. Garrison backed up a few feet and fired a shot with Jeremiah's gun, striking the man in the left ankle. When Jeremiah continued to come forward with the knife, Garrison stood his ground and fired a second, fatal shot. Self-defense? State v. Garrison, 203 Conn. 466, 525 A.2d 498 (1987).

7. *Retreat.* What are the arguments for and against the retreat rule set out in *Peterson?* Weigh these observations:

> The question whether one who is neither the aggressor nor a party to a mutual combat must retreat has divided the authorities. Self-defense is measured against necessity. From that premise one could readily say there was no necessity to kill in self-defense if the use of deadly force could have been avoided by retreat. The critics of the retreat rule do not quarrel with the theoretical validity of this conclusion, but rather condemn it as unrealistic. The law of course should not denounce conduct as criminal when it accords with the behavior of reasonable men. Upon this level, the advocates of no-retreat say the manly thing is to hold one's ground, and hence society should not demand what smacks of cowardice. Adherents of the retreat rule reply it is better that the assailed shall retreat than that the life of another be needlessly spent. They add that not only do right-thinking men agree, but further a rule so requiring may well induce others to adhere to that worthy standard of behavior. There is much dispute as to which view commands the support of ancient precedents, a question we think it would be profitless to explore.

Other jurisdictions are closely divided upon the retreat doctrine. * * * The Model Penal Code embraces the retreat rule while acknowledging that on numerical balance a majority of the precedents oppose it.

We are not persuaded to depart from the principle of retreat. We think it salutary if reasonably limited. Much of the criticism goes not to its inherent validity but rather to unwarranted applications of the rule. For example, it is correctly observed that one can hardly retreat from a rifle shot at close range. But if the weapon were a knife, a lead of a city block might well be enough. Again, the rule cannot be stated baldly, with indifference to the excitement of the occasion. As Mr. Justice Holmes cryptically put it, "Detached reflection cannot be demanded in the presence of an uplifted knife." Brown v. United States, 256 U.S. 335, 343, 41 S.Ct. 501, 502, 65 L.Ed. 961, 963 (1921). Such considerations, however, do not demand that a man should have the absolute right to stand his ground and kill in any and all situations. Rather they call for a fair and guarded statement of appropriate principles. * * *

We believe the following principles are sound:

1. The issue of retreat arises only if the defendant resorted to a deadly force. It is deadly force which is not justifiable when an opportunity to retreat is at hand. Model Penal Code [§ 3.04(2)(b)(ii)]. As defined in [§ 3.11(2),] a deadly force means "force which the actor uses with the purpose of causing or which he knows to create a substantial risk of causing death or serious bodily harm." * * *

2. What constitutes an opportunity to retreat which will defeat the right of self-defense? As [§ 3.04(2)(b)(ii)] of the Model Penal Code states, deadly force is not justifiable "if the actor _knows_ that he can avoid the necessity of using such force _with complete safety_ by retreating * * *." We emphasize "knows" and "with complete safety." One who is wrongfully attacked need not risk injury by retreating, even though he could escape with something less than serious bodily injury. It would be unreal to require nice calculations as to the amount of hurt, or to ask him to endure any at all. And the issue is not whether in retrospect it can be found the defendant could have retreated unharmed. Rather the question is whether he knew the opportunity was there, and of course in that inquiry the total circumstances including the attendant excitement must be considered.

State v. Abbott, 36 N.J. 63, 69–72, 174 A.2d 881, 884–86 (1961).

8. What is the rationale of the "castle" exception to the retreat doctrine? Is it that there is increased peril in retreating from one's home, or is the exception based on more "sentimental" (American Law Institute, Model Penal Code and Commentaries, Comment to § 3.04 at 56 (1985)) considerations?

Should there be an exception to this exception? Should an innocent person be required to retreat from her home if the aggressor also lives there? Notice Model Code § 3.04(2)(b)(ii)(A) in this regard: an innocent person "is not obliged to retreat from his dwelling or place of work, unless he * * * is assailed in his place of work by another person whose place of work the actor knows it to be." Why do you think the drafters distinguished between workplaces and dwellings? See American Law Institute, Model Penal Code and Commentaries, Comment to § 3.04 at 56 (1985).

9. *The proportionality requirement.* Deadly force may not be used to repel a nondeadly attack, even if this is the only way to avoid injury. For example, if Joshua unlawfully tries to strike Donald, and the only way Donald can avoid the blow is to push Joshua away, he may be justified in doing so, as the shove is a moderate response to a nondeadly assault. However, if the shove would likely cause death or serious bodily injury to Joshua, for example, if Donald pushes him into oncoming traffic on a busy street, then the common law requires Donald to suffer the assault, rather than to cause the death of the nondeadly aggressor. Should this be the rule?

10. *Self-defense and innocent aggressors.* Suppose that Rosa is on a hospital elevator between floors with Herman, a mental patient, when Herman, hallucinating that Rosa is a dangerous bear, threatens her with a knife. Is Rosa justified in killing Herman in self-defense? See Laurence A. Alexander, *Justification and Innocent Aggressors,* 33 Wayne L.Rev. 1177, 1177 (1987).

Should the fact that Herman is not morally to blame for his actions—almost certainly he is legally insane—affect Rosa's self-defense claim? If she is justified in using deadly force in these circumstances, is she justified in killing *two* innocent aggressors in self-defense? Ten innocent aggressors? Is there any limit? See George P. Fletcher, *Proportionality and the Psychotic Aggressor: A Vignette in Comparative Criminal Theory,* 8 Israel L.Rev. 367 (1973); Mordechai Kremnitzer, *Proportionality and the Psychotic Aggressor: Another View,* 18 Israel L.Rev. 178 (1983).

11. *Self-defense: rationale.* Why is killing in self-defense justifiable? Consider the following survey of justification theories of self-defense. Are you persuaded by any of them?

NANCY M. OMICHINSKI, COMMENT—APPLYING THE THEORIES OF JUSTIFIABLE HOMICIDE TO CONFLICTS IN THE DOCTRINE OF SELF–DEFENSE

33 Wayne Law Review 1447 (1987), 1447–53

Both utilitarian and retributive criminal law scholars acknowledge the right of an individual to kill another in self-defense. Self-defense, as a defense to a charge of murder or manslaughter, is treated almost universally as a justification rather than an excuse by those cognizant of the distinction. Although most commentators agree that self-defense is justified, they often disagree over which elements must be satisfied to assert a successful self-defense claim and whether the defense should be allowed under various circumstances. Such conflicts arise because commentators base their reasoning on different underlying theories of the justification of self-defense. * * *

Criminal law scholars have proposed various theories that might justify one person taking the life of another in certain circumstances. * * *

A. Public Duty

Originally, the common law condoned one person killing another only in situations that had "a strong public justice cast." William Blackstone recognized three types of justifiable homicide. First, a person commanded "in the execution of public justice" may kill another, for example, the public executioner is justified in putting "a malefactor to death." This justification arises because the executioner is acting under the *compulsion* of law.

Other types of justifiable homicide arise from conduct *permitted* by law. Thus, the law justifies "[h]omicides, committed for the advancement of public justice." Public officials, therefore, are justified in taking lives, if necessary, to stop riots, prevent prison escapes, or arrest thieves.

Finally, private citizens, as well as public officials, justifiably may kill another "for the prevention of any forcible and atrocious crime."
* * *

Blackstone specifically excluded self-defense as a justification. Even if he had not, however, it would be difficult to demonstrate that killing in self-defense is justified under Blackstone's theory. One might argue that, in killing an aggressor to save his own life, the person is preventing an "atrocious crime"—the murder of himself. This analysis, however, neglects to reflect the underlying value of Blackstone's theory: persons acting to promote the public good or benefit the community should be commended for their selfless conduct. Blackstone recognized that a person who kills in self-defense often is not completely blameless and, moreover, at best is acting to preserve himself. This theory, which justifies homicides committed by persons acting under a public duty, therefore, cannot explain properly why the use of deadly force in self-defense should be justified.

B. Moral Forfeiture of the Right to Life

A number of theories that justify homicide identify the moral rights at issue. The theory of moral forfeiture begins with the assertion that everyone has a right to life. Although the right to life traditionally has been regarded as inalienable, it may be forfeited; that is, a person may not voluntarily give or trade away her right to life, but she may lose it through her own fault or misconduct. * * *

In the context of self-defense, an aggressor, threatening to violate another's right to life, loses her own right to life, or loses the right to assert her right to life. Consequently, when a defender kills her in self-defense, the defender is not violating any right of the aggressor because the aggressor already has forfeited that right through her own wrongful conduct. To the extent that justified conduct implies that no social harm has occurred, this theory suggests that * * * "those who intentionally and cold-bloodedly try to kill others devalue themselves (or perhaps their interests) to the point that killing them is of little or no moral consequence." [25] * * *

C. *The Right to Preserve Personal Autonomy*

A different theory of justifiable homicide focuses on the rights of a defender, rather than on the rights of an aggressor. Again, the right to life provides the foundation * * *. The right to preserve personal autonomy, predominant in the German theory of self-defense, finds support in the political theory of John Locke. Locke analogized the standard self-defense situation—unlawful aggressor and innocent victim—to a "state of war." * * *

George Fletcher finds this theory of self-defense most convincing. He reasons that "the aggression breaches an implicit contract among autonomous agents, according to which each person ... is bound to respect the living space of all others. The intrusion upon someone's living space itself triggers a justified response." [33] Fletcher identifies the defender as "Right" and the aggressor as "Wrong"; the defender's autonomy is the "Law itself" and the aggressor is an "enemy of the Law." An innocent person is justified in using deadly force against an aggressor, not because the aggressor's life has no social value, but rather, because the defender is doing the "Right" thing in protecting himself.

D. *The Right to Resist Unlawful Aggression*

Another theory of justifiable homicide, proffered by Sanford Kadish, is the right to resist unlawful aggression.[35] This theory also stems from the right to life and, like the right to preserve personal autonomy, focuses on the rights of a defender, rather than on the rights of an aggressor. This theory, however, differs from the above theories in subtle yet significant ways.

The right to resist aggression is a right that an individual holds against the government, rather than against the aggressor. It begins with the assertion that when an individual moves from a state of nature into a state of society, he does not "surrender his fundamental freedom to preserve himself against aggression by the establishment of state authority." Instead, the state recognizes the individual's right to life and, in so doing, undertakes the duty to not violate that right and the responsibility to protect that right from violation by others. Because the state is not always able to meet this responsibility, it grants the individual the right to protect his life from aggression when the state fails to do so. * * *

---

25. Montague, [*Self–Defense and Choosing Between Lives,* 40 Phil.Stud. 207 (1981)], at 214.

33. Fletcher, *Proportionality and the Psychotic Aggressor: A Vignette in Compar-*

ative Criminal Theory, 8 Israel L.Rev. 367, 380 (1973).

35. Kadish, [*Respect for Life and Regard for Rights in the Criminal Law,* 64 Calif.L.Rev. 871 (1976)], at 884–86.

E. Lesser Evils Doctrine

The justification of "lesser evils," also referred to as "superior interest," * * * supplies another theory of justifiable homicide. Under this doctrine, conduct otherwise blameworthy is justified when a greater good or lesser evil results from the homicide, or when a superior interest is protected through the homicide. * * *

Can a theory of lesser evils justify killing in self-defense? * * *

One rationale is that the aggressor's wrongful conduct renders his life less valuable. Another explanation is that the defender is protecting the "general peace" as well as her own life and "this social interest must also be put on the defender's scale." Both explanations arguably tip the scale in favor of the defender, thus providing her with a justification for the use of deadly force in self-defense.

Notes and Questions

1. Why does it matter which theory is used to justify a killing in self-defense? One reason is that the applicability and scope of a criminal law defense should relate to its underlying rationale. For example, how would the difficult issues relating to innocent aggressors (Note 10, p. 415 supra) be resolved according to the various principles of justification explained in the preceding article?

Consider as well the proportionality requirement of self-defense. If one applies, for example, the moral forfeiture principle, is deadly force in response to a nondeadly attack justifiable? What if self-defense is based on the right of autonomy? What would be the utilitarian view?

2. *Self-defense: justification or excuse?* At the time of Blackstone, killing in self-protection constituted excusable homicide, based on "the great universal principle of self-preservation, which prompts every man to save his own life preferably to that of another, where one of them must inevitably perish." 4 Blackstone, Commentaries on the Law of England *186 (1769). Do you find the claim that a defensive killing is excusable more persuasive than that it is justifiable? On the other hand, on Blackstone's own terms, isn't it justifiable for a person to prefer her own life to that of a stranger?

Does it ultimately matter whether the defense is considered a justification or an excuse? The *Peterson* court did not think so (see footnote 35 at p. 406 supra). As you read the materials that follow, see if you agree.

b. "Reasonable Belief" Requirement

i. In General

PEOPLE v. GOETZ

Court of Appeals of New York, 1986.
68 N.Y.2d 96, 506 N.Y.S.2d 18, 497 N.E.2d 41.

CHIEF JUDGE WACHTLER.

A Grand Jury has indicted defendant on attempted murder, assault, and other charges for having shot and wounded four youths on a New

York City subway train after one or two of the youths approached him and asked for $5. The lower courts, concluding that the prosecutor's charge to the Grand Jury on the defense of justification was erroneous, have dismissed the attempted murder, assault and weapons possession charges. We now reverse and reinstate all counts of the indictment.

I.

The precise circumstances of the incident giving rise to the charges against defendant are disputed, and ultimately it will be for a trial jury to determine what occurred. We feel it necessary, however, to provide some factual background to properly frame the legal issues before us. Accordingly, we have summarized the facts as they appear from the evidence before the Grand Jury. * * *

On Saturday afternoon, December 22, 1984, Troy Canty, Darryl Cabey, James Ramseur, and Barry Allen boarded an IRT express subway train in The Bronx and headed south toward lower Manhattan. The four youths rode together in the rear portion of the seventh car of the train. Two of the four, Ramseur and Cabey, had screwdrivers inside their coats, which they said were to be used to break into the coin boxes of video machines.

Defendant Bernhard Goetz boarded this subway train * * * in Manhattan and sat down on a bench towards the rear section of the same car occupied by the four youths. Goetz was carrying an unlicensed .38 caliber pistol loaded with five rounds of ammunition in a waistband holster. * * *

* * * Canty approached Goetz, possibly with Allen beside him, and stated "give me five dollars." Neither Canty nor any of the other youths displayed a weapon. Goetz responded by standing up, pulling out his handgun and firing four shots in rapid succession. The first shot hit Canty in the chest; the second struck Allen in the back; the third went through Ramseur's arm and into his left side; the fourth was fired at Cabey, who apparently was then standing in the corner of the car, but missed, deflecting instead off of a wall of the conductor's cab. After Goetz briefly surveyed the scene around him, he fired another shot at Cabey, who then was sitting on the end bench of the car. The bullet entered the rear of Cabey's side and severed his spinal cord.

All but two of the other passengers fled the car when, or immediately after, the shots were fired. The conductor, who had been in the next car, heard the shots and instructed the motorman to radio for emergency assistance. The conductor then went into the car where the shooting occurred and saw Goetz sitting on a bench, the injured youths lying on the floor or slumped against a seat, and two women who had apparently taken cover, also lying on the floor. Goetz told the conductor that the four youths had tried to rob him.

While the conductor was aiding the youths, Goetz * * * jumped onto the tracks and fled. * * * Ramseur and Canty, initially listed in critical condition, have fully recovered. Cabey remains paralyzed, and has suffered some degree of brain damage.

On December 31, 1984, Goetz surrendered to police in Concord, New Hampshire * * *. Goetz admitted that he had been illegally carrying a handgun in New York City for three years. He stated that he had first purchased a gun in 1981 after he had been injured in a mugging. Goetz also revealed that twice between 1981 and 1984 he had successfully warded off assailants simply by displaying the pistol.

According to Goetz's statement, the first contact he had with the four youths came when Canty, sitting or lying on the bench across from him, asked "how are you," to which he replied "fine." Shortly thereafter, Canty, followed by one of the other youths, walked over to the defendant and stood to his left, while the other two youths remained to his right, in the corner of the subway car. Canty then said "give me five dollars." Goetz stated that he knew from the smile on Canty's face that they wanted to "play with me." Although he was certain that none of the youths had a gun, he had a fear, based on prior experiences, of being "maimed."

Goetz then established "a pattern of fire," deciding specifically to fire from left to right. His stated intention at that point was to "murder [the four youths], to hurt them, to make them suffer as much as possible." When Canty again requested money, Goetz stood up, drew his weapon, and began firing, aiming for the center of the body of each of the four. Goetz recalled that the first two he shot "tried to run through the crowd [but] they had nowhere to run." Goetz then turned to his right to "go after the other two." One of these two "tried to run through the wall of the train, but * * * he had nowhere to go." The other youth (Cabey) "tried pretending that he wasn't with [the others]" by standing still, holding on to one of the subway hand straps, and not looking at Goetz. Goetz nonetheless fired his fourth shot at him. He then ran back to the first two youths to make sure they had been "taken care of." Seeing that they had both been shot, he spun back to check on the latter two. Goetz noticed that the youth who had been standing still was now sitting on a bench and seemed unhurt. As Goetz told the police, "I said '[y]ou seem to be all right, here's another'," and he then fired the shot which severed Cabey's spinal cord. Goetz added that "if I was a little more under self-control * * * I would have put the barrel against his forehead and fired." He also admitted that "if I had had more [bullets], I would have shot them again, and again, and again."

II. * * *

* * * [T]he * * * Grand Jury filed a 10–count indictment, containing four charges of attempted murder, four charges of assault in the first degree, one charge of reckless endangerment in the first degree, and one charge of criminal possession of a weapon in the second degree. * * *

* * * Goetz moved to dismiss the charges * * * alleging, among other things, * * * that the prosecutor's instructions to that Grand Jury on the defense of justification were erroneous * * *.

[The trial court] * * * granted Goetz's motion * * *. The court, after inspection of the Grand Jury minutes, * * * held * * * that the prosecutor, in * * * elaborating upon the justification defense, had erroneously introduced an objective element into this defense by instructing the grand jurors to consider whether Goetz's conduct was that of a "reasonable man in [Goetz's] situation". The court * * * concluded that the statutory test for whether the use of deadly force is justified to protect a person should be wholly subjective, focusing entirely on the defendant's state of mind when he used such force. It concluded that dismissal was required for this error because the justification issue was at the heart of the case. * * *

On appeal by the People, a divided Appellate Division affirmed [the] dismissal of the charges. * * *

III.

Penal Law article 35 recognizes the defense of justification, which "permits the use of force under certain circumstances." One such set of circumstances pertains to the use of force in defense of a person, encompassing both self-defense and defense of a third person. Penal Law § 35.15(1) sets forth the general principles governing all such uses of force: "[a] person may * * * use physical force upon another person when and to the extent he *reasonably believes* such to be necessary to defend himself or a third person from what he *reasonably believes* to be the use or imminent use of unlawful physical force by such other person" (emphasis added).

Section 35.15(2) sets forth further limitations on these general principles with respect to the use of "deadly physical force": "A person may not use deadly physical force upon another person under circumstances specified in subdivision one unless (a) He *reasonably believes* that such other person is using or about to use deadly physical force * * * or (b) He *reasonably believes* that such other person is committing or attempting to commit a kidnapping, forcible rape, forcible sodomy or robbery" (emphasis added).

Thus, consistent with most justification provisions, Penal Law § 35.15 permits the use of deadly physical force only where requirements as to triggering conditions and the necessity of a particular response are met. As to the triggering conditions, the statute requires that the actor "reasonably believes" that another person either is using or about to use deadly physical force or is committing or attempting to commit one of certain enumerated felonies, including robbery. As to the need for the use of deadly physical force as a response, the statute requires that the actor "reasonably believes" that such force is necessary to avert the perceived threat.

Because the evidence before the * * * Grand Jury included statements by Goetz that he acted to protect himself from being maimed or to avert a robbery, the prosecutor correctly chose to charge the justification defense in section 35.15 to the Grand Jury. * * *

When the prosecutor had completed his charge, one of the grand jurors asked for clarification of the term "reasonably believes." The prosecutor responded by instructing the grand jurors that they were to consider the circumstances of the incident and determine "whether the defendant's conduct was that of a reasonable man in the defendant's situation." It is this response by the prosecutor—and specifically his use of "a reasonable man"—which is the basis for the dismissal of the charges by the lower courts. As expressed repeatedly in the Appellate Division's plurality opinion, because section 35.15 uses the term "*he* reasonably believes," the appropriate test, according to that court, is whether a defendant's beliefs and reactions were "reasonable *to him.*" Under that reading of the statute, a jury which believed a defendant's testimony that he felt that his own actions were warranted and were reasonable would have to acquit him, regardless of what anyone else in defendant's situation might have concluded. Such an interpretation defies the ordinary meaning and significance of the term "reasonably" in a statute, and misconstrues the clear intent of the Legislature, in enacting section 35.15, to retain an objective element as part of any provision authorizing the use of deadly physical force.

Penal statutes in New York have long codified the right recognized at common law to use deadly physical force, under appropriate circumstances, in self-defense. These provisions have never required that an actor's belief as to the intention of another person to inflict serious injury be correct in order for the use of deadly force to be justified, but they have uniformly required that the belief comport with an objective notion of reasonableness. * * *

In 1961 the Legislature established a Commission to undertake a complete revision of the Penal Law and the Criminal Code. * * * The drafting of the general provisions of the new Penal Law, including the article on justification, was particularly influenced by the Model Penal Code. While using the Model Penal Code provisions on justification as general guidelines, however, the drafters of the new Penal Law did not simply adopt them verbatim.

The provisions of the Model Penal Code with respect to the use of deadly force in self-defense reflect the position of its drafters that any culpability which arises from a mistaken belief in the need to use such force should be no greater than the culpability such a mistake would give rise to if it were made with respect to an element of a crime. Accordingly, under Model Penal Code § 3.04(2)(b), a defendant charged with murder (or attempted murder) need only show that he "*believe[d]* that [the use of deadly force] was necessary to protect himself against death, serious bodily injury, kidnapping or [forcible] sexual intercourse" to prevail on a self-defense claim (emphasis added). If the defendant's belief was wrong, and was recklessly, or negligently formed, however, he may be convicted of the type of homicide charge requiring only a reckless or negligent, as the case may be, criminal intent (*see,* Model Penal Code § 3.09[2]).

The drafters of the Model Penal Code recognized that the wholly subjective test set forth in section 3.04 differed from the existing law in most States by its omission of any requirement of reasonableness. * * *

New York did not follow the Model Penal Code's equation * * * choosing instead to use a single statutory section which would provide either a complete defense or no defense at all to a defendant charged with any crime involving the use of deadly force. The drafters of the new Penal Law adopted in large part the structure and content of Model Penal Code § 3.04, but, crucially, inserted the word "reasonably" before "believes."

The plurality below agreed with defendant's argument that the change in the statutory language from "reasonable ground," used prior to 1965, to "he reasonably believes" in Penal Law § 35.15 evinced a legislative intent to conform to the subjective standard contained in Model Penal Code § 3.04. This argument, however, ignores the plain significance of the insertion of "reasonably." Had the drafters of section 35.15 wanted to adopt a subjective standard, they could have simply used the language of section 3.04. * * *

We cannot lightly impute to the Legislature an intent to fundamentally alter the principles of justification to allow the perpetrator of a serious crime to go free simply because that person believed his actions were reasonable and necessary to prevent some perceived harm. To completely exonerate such an individual, no matter how aberrational or bizarre his thought patterns, would allow citizens to set their own standards for the permissible use of force. It would also allow a legally competent defendant suffering from delusions to kill or perform acts of violence with impunity, contrary to fundamental principles of justice and criminal law.

We can only conclude that the Legislature retained a reasonableness requirement to avoid giving a license for such actions. * * *

Goetz also argues that the introduction of an objective element will preclude a jury from considering factors such as the prior experiences of a given actor and thus, require it to make a determination of "reasonableness" without regard to the actual circumstances of a particular incident. This argument, however, falsely presupposes that an objective standard means that the background and other relevant characteristics of a particular actor must be ignored. To the contrary, we have frequently noted that a determination of reasonableness must be based on the "circumstances" facing a defendant or his "situation." Such terms encompass more than the physical movements of the potential assailant. As just discussed, these terms include any relevant knowledge the defendant had about that person. They also necessarily bring in the physical attributes of all persons involved, including the defendant.

[handwritten margin note: Change from reasonable ground to reasonable belief]

Furthermore, the defendant's circumstances encompass any prior experiences he had which could provide a reasonable basis for a belief that another person's intentions were to injure or rob him or that the use of deadly force was necessary under the circumstances. * * *

Accordingly, the order of the Appellate Division should be reversed, and the dismissed counts of the indictment reinstated.

Notes and Questions

1. Why did the prosecutor, rather than a judge, instruct the grand jurors on the law of self-defense? The answer lies in the fact that judges are not present during grand jury proceedings. A prosecutor presides: she subpoenas the witnesses she believes will provide relevant testimony in the investigation; she questions them in the jurors' presence; and, at the conclusion of the investigation, she instructs the grand jurors on the relevant law. The jurors then determine if there is probable cause to issue an indictment against one or more persons for a crime.

2. *The outcome.* Goetz was acquitted by the trial jury of all charges in the indictment except for possession of a concealed weapon, for which he received a one-year jail sentence. At his sentencing, Goetz told the judge, "I do feel that this case is really more about deterioration in society than it is about me." Anthony M. DeStefano, *Goetz Resentenced, Starts 1-Year Jail Term At Rikers,* Newsday, Jan. 14, 1989, at 3. Goetz was released from jail after eight months. For a fascinating analysis of the case, see George P. Fletcher, A Crime of Self Defense (1988).

3. *Making sense of the verdict.* Why did the jury acquit Goetz of attempted murder of the four youths? What message did the jury implicitly send by its verdict? Professor Stephen Carter believes that Goetz's attorney, and maybe the jurors, had one picture of Goetz, whereas the public that praised Goetz had another:

> As folk hero, * * * Bernhard Goetz is ultimately a disturbing figure. Even Mr. Goetz's defense painted him as something less than heroic. The defense was weakest on the issue of why he fired a second shot at a helpless Darrel Cabey * * *. [Goetz's] defense attorney offered a version of events in which, once the gun was drawn, Mr. Goetz's self-preserving instinct took command. Matters moved so quickly that his instinct would not let him stop * * *. In other words, his mind was not in control; he did not know what he was doing.
>
> The jury plainly accepted the rapid-fire theory as a reasonable explanation of Mr. Goetz's behavior. Mr. Goetz's public, however, the millions who apparently believe that they would have done precisely what he did and that the punks he shot got what they deserved, does not base its enthusiasm on the understanding he was out of control. On the contrary, the notion that he was *in* control is part of the appeal of the situation. To his public, Mr. Goetz was cool and calculating, showing the courage that millions of others would wish for themselves.

Stephen L. Carter, *When Victims Happen to be Black,* 97 Yale L.J. 420, 422–23 (1988).

4. *What does the "reasonable person" think about in a New York subway?* Are any of the following matters relevant in determining whether a reasonable person would have believed that the youths intended to seriously harm Goetz: (1) that two of the youths were armed with screwdrivers; (2) that the victims were young, African–American males; (3) that Goetz was a middle-aged white male; and (4) that Goetz had previously been mugged? Are there other matters that you, as a reasonable person, would have taken into consideration if you had been in Goetz's shoes?

The Goetz incident provoked a great deal of public discussion regarding the racial overtones of the case. Some examples follow.

Richard Cohen, Closing the Door on Crime, Washington Post Magazine, Sept. 7, 1986, at W13: In order to be admitted to certain Washington jewelry stores, customers have to ring a bell. The ring-back that opens the door is almost perfunctory. According to the owner of one store, only one type of person does not get admitted: Young black males. The owner says they are the ones who stick him up.

Nearby is a men's clothing shop—upscale, but not really expensive. When young black males enter this store, the sales help are instructed to leave their customers and, in the manner of defensive backs in football, "collapse" on the blacks. Politely, but firmly, they are sort of shooed out of the store. The owner's explanation for this? Young blacks are his shoplifters.

Are these examples of racism? The shopkeepers either think so or think they can be accused of it. * * *

Interestingly, though, a black colleague of mine thinks otherwise. He, too, would turn away young blacks if he owned a jewelry store, although he said he would make his judgments on more than race, sex and youth. He would also take into account such factors as dress and even walk. * * * For the record, though, another black colleague called the policies "racist"—a label she applied to black store owners who follow similar practices.

As for me, I'm with the store owners, although I was not at first. It took Bernhard Goetz, of all people, to expose my sloppy thinking. * * *

It was reasonable for Goetz to assume that he was about to be mugged. The youths asked for money, which, in New York and elsewhere, is just a boilerplate precede to a mugging. It was then that Goetz reportedly pulled his gun and shot them all—one allegedly in the back as the youth lay on the subway floor. You would have a hard time making the case that the last alleged squeeze of the trigger was "reasonable."

But how about the rest of his actions? There were some who yelled at the time that Goetz was motivated by racism—that he would not have pulled either the gun or its trigger if his putative assailants had been white. Maybe. But * * * [e]specially in cities like Washington and New York, the menace comes from young black males. Both blacks and whites believe those young black males are the ones most likely to bop them over the head. In the Goetz case, it matters not at all that the four men he shot had extensive arrest records. Goetz had no way of knowing that. As far as he was concerned, the four youths wore their records on their faces.

The Goetz case has its own complications * * *, but the factors present are the same the Washington storekeepers take into account when they decide how to treat a customer. Like Goetz, they are reacting out of fear to a combination of race, youth and sex. * * *

Of course, all policies based on generalities have their injustices. A storekeeper might not know that the youths he has refused to admit are theology students—rich ones at that. But then insurance companies had no way of knowing I was not a typical teen-age driver. I paid through the nose anyway.

A nation with our history is entitled to be sensitive to race and racism— and we are all wary of behavior that would bring a charge of racism. But the mere recognition of race as a factor—especially if those of the same race recognized the same factor—is not in itself racism. * * * Let he who would open the door throw the first stone.

Editorial, Fear of Blacks, Fear of Crime, New York Times, Dec. 28, 1986, pt. 4, at 10: It's very easy to spot a black person in this neighborhood, and whenever I see one, I know he's up to no good. They come in the neighborhood and rob everybody. It's a known fact. That's why everybody has a thing about them.

That's how a construction worker named Jimmy, from Howard Beach, Queens, tried to explain why a gang of teen-agers armed with bats and clubs last week chased and beat three blacks whose only apparent offense was to walk through his neighborhood.

The same crude presumption—that blackness indicates criminality— haunts the trial of Bernhard Goetz, who claims self-defense for shooting down four young blacks on a subway train. The presumption recently led a Louisiana sheriff to order deputies to stop and question all blacks on sight, and it produced furious debate in Washington, D.C. over whether local stores, fearing robbery, should refuse to admit black men. Signs on the doors of small shops on the upper East Side of Manhattan—"Men by appointment only"—also mask the ugly question: Shouldn't one assume that black men are up to no good?

Many whites would answer yes, observing that blacks, especially young black men, commit more than their share of crime. National surveys estimate that blacks commit robbery at a rate 10 times that of whites. Yet blacks cannot be faulted for denouncing the automatic assumption that the potential victim's viewpoint is the only one. What about the vast, innocent majority of blacks? * * *

The issue engages a classic dilemma of utilitarianism versus individual rights: At what point, if ever, should needs of the community as a whole be allowed to harm an innocent minority? John Rawls, the philosopher, suggests one widely respected answer: No one ought to endorse a social order that he could not accept if he were in the shoes of the most disadvantaged.

Who, then, is more disadvantaged, the innocent white subjected to crime and fear of crime, or the innocent black forced into humiliating inconvenience and heightened risk of violence from mistaken acts of self defense?

The innocent potential victim of crime has more options for protection against burglary and robbery—guards, locks, dogs, alarms and buzzers, legitimate community organizing. Innocent victims of discrimination based on popular fear can do little but submit. There is no reason to choose: discrimination, cumulatively, can be as poisonous as mugging or burglary. Both kinds of pain diminish the civility of modern life.

There is no remedy, only an approach, the one suggested by John Rawls. It's not hard for blacks to put themselves in the shoes of fearful shopkeepers and citizens; they are, too often, fearful citizens themselves. Fearful whites need to put themselves in the shoes of innocent blacks. Doing so will not dissipate the reasons for fear, but it can steadily inspire the understanding and reason that keep fear in its place.

Richard Cohen, Rational Fear, Irrational Act, Washington Post, June 18, 1987, at A23: There is a utility to stereotyping. The American ethic, not to mention the law, insists that we all be judged as individuals, but the city dweller especially knows better. Having been asked for $5 by four black youths shod for crime in high-top sneakers, Bernhard Goetz saw the stereotype and assumed he was about to be robbed. Many New Yorkers have applauded this rationality. * * *

But in Goetz's case, rational deductions were made by an irrational man. In the first place, he was illegally carrying a gun. Second, he machoed his way into the midst of the four youths while others in the subway car wisely kept their distance. His behavior was the urban equivalent of "smile when you say that, stranger"—the prologue to so many fights in so many movie westerns: almost a challenge in itself. * * *

The dilemma of the Goetz case lies in the difficulty of distinguishing between a rational fear based on a stereotype and the irrational behavior that can result. Life is too complicated, the city too menacing, to judge every person as an individual. A person of whatever race—black or white— is entitled to extrapolate on the basis of either experience or knowledge (crime statistics) to make certain judgments. Only a fool would treat Goetz's four boisterous black youths apparently looking for trouble as if they were four Iowa farm kids out to see the Big City.

Prudent, self-defensive behavior is not the same as aggressive, retributive action. What Goetz did was the moral equivalent of a white mob running through a black neighborhood, beating and, maybe, lynching the first person it encounters because a wholly different black had injured or killed a white. The fury of Goetz's attack was fueled not only by the demand for money, but by his previous mugging.

Race, but not necessarily conventional prejudice, undoubtedly played a role. The fear here is specific, not general—not an entire race, but just the young, male members of it who dress and act in a certain menacing way.

That always-moving, always-thin, line between rational fear and irrational action is one of civilization's essential threads. Pull it, and society begins to unravel. The fears of the urban American are real—as is the threat to him or, more likely, her. Crime and the threat of it have atomized our already weakened communities. People live in virtual vaults behind door locks and window bars. They will not walk their own streets at night, or, in some places, during the day. The old are tremulous, often victimized by the young. Cabs will not stop for certain people, and, for many, dogs are no longer pets, but weapons of self-defense.

But the law rightly insists that our actions be reasonable. It does not require you to be unafraid, not to dart or sneak out of harm's way or not to suspect the stranger. But it does uphold the worthy standard that you have no right to translate your fear into aggressive, dangerous action that is out of proportion to any threat. Bernhard Goetz did that.

He was right to suspect those four youths and even right to fear them. But when—one by one—he shot them, he committed a crime and so, in acquitting him, did his jury. It moved the line between rational fear and irrational action a little closer to the jungle.

Rosemary L. Bray, It's Ten O'clock and I Worry About Where My Husband Is, Glamour, April 1990, at 302: He phoned more than an hour ago, to say he was on his way home. But I have yet to hear the scrape of the iron gate, the rattling keys, so I worry.

Most married women fret about a tardy husband; young black women like myself worry more. For most people in New York—truth be told—the urban bogeyman is a young black man in sneakers. But we live in Central Harlem, where every young man is black and wears sneakers, so we learn to look into the eyes of young males and discern the difference between youthful bravado and the true dangers of the streets. No, I have other fears. I fear white men in police uniforms; white teenagers driving by in a car with Jersey plates; thin panicky, middle-aged white men on the subway. Most of all, I fear that their path and my husband's path will cross one night as he makes his way home.

Bob is tall—5'10" or so, dark, with thick hair and wire-rimmed glasses. He carries a knapsack stuffed with work from the office, old crossword puzzles, Philip Glass tapes, *Ebony Man* and *People* magazines. When it rains, he carries his good shoes in the bag and wears his Reebok sneakers. He cracks his knuckles a lot, and wears a peculiar grimace when his mind is elsewhere. He looks dear and gentle to me—but then, I have looked into those eyes for a long time.

I worry that some white person will see that grim, focused look of concentration and see the intent to victimize. I fear that some white person will look at him and see only his or her nightmare—another black man in sneakers. In fact, my husband *is* another black man in sneakers. He's also a writer, an amateur cyclist, a lousy basketball player, his parents' son, my life's companion. When I put aside the book I'm reading to peek out the window, the visions in my head are those of blind white panic at my husband's black presence, visions of a flashing gun, a gleaming knife: I see myself a sudden, horrified widow at thirty-four.

Once upon a time, I was vaguely ashamed of my paranoia about his safety in the world outside our home. After all, he is a grown man. But he is a grown black man on the streets alone, a menace to white New Yorkers—even the nice, sympathetic, liberal ones who smile at us when we're together. And I am reminded, over and over, how dangerous white people still can be, how their fears are a hazard to our health. When white people are ruled by their fears of everything black, every black woman is an addict, a whore; every black man is a rapist—even a murderer. * * *

So when it's ten o'clock and he's not home yet, my thoughts can't help but wander to other black men—husbands, fathers, sons, brothers—who never do make it home, and to other black women whose fingers no longer rest at a curtain's edge. Even after I hear the scrape of our iron gate, the key in the lock, even after I hear that old knapsack hit the floor of the downstairs hallway and Bob's voice calling to me, my thoughts return to them.

5. *"Reasonable belief": justification or excuse?* Contemplate the following standard jury instruction regarding the "reasonable belief" rule:

> If the defendant had reasonable grounds to believe and actually did believe that he was in imminent danger of death or serious bodily harm and that deadly force was necessary to repel such danger, he would be justified in using deadly force in self-defense, even though it may afterwards have turned out that the appearances were false. If these requirements are met he could use deadly force even though there was in fact neither purpose on the part of the person to kill him or do him serious bodily harm, nor imminent danger that it would be done, nor actual necessity that deadly force be used in self-defense.

Fresno Rifle and Pistol Club, Inc. v. Van de Kamp, 746 F.Supp. 1415, 1421 (E.D.Cal.1990) (quoting E. Devitt and C. Blackmar, Federal Jury Instructions § 41.20 (3d ed. 1977)).

How can it be justifiable to kill an innocent person, i.e., an apparent aggressor who actually means no harm? Some scholars contend that the common law "reasonable belief" standard is wrong. They reason that conduct is unjustifiable unless it is objectively right, e.g., unless the person against whom self-defensive action is taken *in fact* represents an imminent, unlawful threat. When a person acts on the basis of reasonable, but false, appearances, these commentators would excuse the actor, rather than justify the conduct. See George P. Fletcher, Rethinking Criminal Law 762–69 (1978); Paul H. Robinson, *A Theory of Justification: Societal Harm as a Prerequisite for Criminal Liability*, 23 UCLA L.Rev. 266, 271–73, 283–84 (1975).

Are these commentators correct? Or, is the common law "reasonable belief" principle defensible on the basis of one or more of the underlying theories of self-defense (see p. 415 supra)? See Joshua Dressler, *New Thoughts About the Concept of Justification in the Criminal Law: A Critique of Fletcher's Thinking and Rethinking*, 32 UCLA L.Rev. 61, 92–95 (1984); Kent Greenawalt, *Distinguishing Justifications From Excuses,* 49 Law & Contemp. Probs., Summer, 1986, at 89, 93–96, 101–03.

Does this dispute have practical implications? Suppose that Eunice reasonably, but incorrectly, believes that Violet is about to kill her. If Eunice pulls out a gun in order to kill Violet in "self-defense," may Violet kill *her* in self-defense? Why might Violet's right of self-defense depend on whether Eunice's claim is treated as a justification or an excuse?

6. *Unreasonable belief: "imperfect" defense?* The negative implication of the reasonable-belief rule is that a person who acts on the basis of a

genuine, but *unreasonable,* belief that deadly force is necessary for self-protection cannot successfully claim self-defense. Thus, an actor who mistakenly kills an innocent person or who uses more force than is necessary to combat real aggression will be acquitted if her mistake was reasonable, but will be convicted of murder if her mistake was unreasonable. Is this a sensible solution?

Many states now recognize "imperfect" or "incomplete" justification defenses. In these jurisdictions, for example, a defendant is guilty of manslaughter, rather than murder, if she kills the decedent while harboring a genuine, but unreasonable, belief that the decedent constitutes an imminent threat to her life. E.g., People v. Flannel, 25 Cal.3d 668, 160 Cal.Rptr. 84, 603 P.2d 1 (1979). How does the Model Penal Code handle this situation? See Sections 3.04 and 3.09.

Some states recognize an imperfect defense in other circumstances. For example, various jurisdictions allow a defendant to claim an imperfect defense if she uses deadly force in response to a nondeadly assault. E.g., State v. Clark, 69 Kan. 576, 77 P. 287 (1904). Other states allow the imperfect defense "where the homicide would fall within the perfect self defense doctrine but for the fault of the defendant in provoking or initiating the difficulty at the non-deadly force level." State v. Faulkner, 301 Md. 482, 489, 483 A.2d 759, 763 (1984); see also State v. McAvoy, 331 N.C. 583, 417 S.E.2d 489 (1992).

7. *Self-defense and innocent bystanders.* When Goetz shot the four youths, innocent subway passengers were sitting nearby. Suppose that an errant bullet from Goetz's gun had struck and killed one of the bystanders. Should Goetz's self-defense claim against the youths apply in a prosecution for the death of the bystander? See Smith v. State, 204 Ga.App. 173, 419 S.E.2d 74 (1992); People v. Mathews, 91 Cal.App.3d 1018, 154 Cal.Rptr. 628 (1979). How would the Model Penal Code answer this question? See Section 3.04 and 3.09.

Suppose that Alberto, holding Bob in front of him as a shield, aims his gun at Carl and prepares to shoot him. Under the Model Penal Code, may Carl (who has no place to retreat) shoot Alberto in self-defense, although he knows that Bob will die as a consequence?

ii. The Debate Continues: Objective, Subjective, or a Mixed Standard?

STATE v. WANROW

Supreme Court of Washington, 1977.
88 Wash.2d 221, 559 P.2d 548.

Utter, Associate Justice.

Yvonne Wanrow was convicted by a jury of second-degree murder * * *. She appealed her conviction * * *.

On the afternoon of August 11, 1972, defendant's (respondent's) two children were staying at the home of Ms. Hooper, a friend of defendant. Defendant's son was playing in the neighborhood and came back to Ms.

Hooper's house and told her that a man tried to pull him off his bicycle and drag him into a house. Some months earlier, Ms. Hooper's 7–year–old daughter had developed a rash on her body which was diagnosed as venereal disease. Ms. Hooper had been unable to persuade her daughter to tell her who had molested her. It was not until the night of the shooting that Ms. Hooper discovered it was William Wesler (decedent) who allegedly had violated her daughter. A few minutes after the defendant's son related his story to Ms. Hooper about the man who tried to detain him, Mr. Wesler appeared on the porch of the Hooper house and stated through the door, "I didn't touch the kid, I didn't touch the kid." At that moment, the Hooper girl, seeing Wesler at the door, indicated to her mother that Wesler was the man who had molested her. Joseph Fah, Ms. Hooper's landlord, saw Wesler as he was leaving and informed Shirley Hooper that Wesler had tried to molest a young boy who had earlier lived in the same house, and that Wesler had previously been committed to the Eastern State Hospital for the mentally ill. Immediately after this revelation from Mr. Fah, Ms. Hooper called the police who, upon their arrival at the Hooper residence, were informed of all the events which had transpired that day. Ms. Hooper requested that Wesler be arrested then and there, but the police stated, "We can't, until Monday morning." Ms. Hooper was urged by the police officer to go to the police station Monday morning and "swear out a warrant." Ms. Hooper's landlord, who was present during the conversation, suggested that Ms. Hooper get a baseball bat located at the corner of the house and "conk him over the head" should Wesler try to enter the house uninvited during the weekend. To this suggestion, the policeman replied, "Yes, but wait until he gets in the house." (A week before this incident Shirley Hooper had noticed someone prowling around her house at night. Two days before the shooting someone had attempted to get into Ms. Hooper's bedroom and had slashed the window screen. She suspected that such person was Wesler.)

That evening, Ms. Hooper called the defendant and asked her to spend the night with her in the Hooper house. At that time she related to Ms. Wanrow the facts we have previously set forth. The defendant arrived sometime after 6 p.m. with a pistol in her handbag. The two women ultimately determined that they were too afraid to stay alone and decided to ask some friends to come over for added protection. The two women then called the defendant's sister and brother-in-law, Angie and Chuck Michel. The four adults did not go to bed that evening, but remained awake talking and watching for any possible prowlers. There were eight young children in the house with them. At around 5 a.m., Chuck Michel, without the knowledge of the women in the house, went to Wesler's house, carrying a baseball bat. Upon arriving at the Wesler residence, Mr. Michel accused Wesler of molesting little children. Mr. Wesler then suggested that they go over to the Hooper residence and get the whole thing straightened out. Another man, one David Kelly, was also present, and together the three men went over to the Hooper house.

Mr. Michel and Mr. Kelly remained outside while Wesler entered the residence.

The testimony as to what next took place is considerably less precise. It appears that Wesler, a large man who was visibly intoxicated, entered the home and when told to leave declined to do so. A good deal of shouting and confusion then arose, and a young child, asleep on the couch, awoke crying. The testimony indicates that Wesler than approached this child, stating, "My what a cute little boy," or words to that effect, and that the child's mother, Ms. Michel, stepped between Wesler and the child. By this time Hooper was screaming for Wesler to get out. Ms. Wanrow, a 5'4" woman who at the time had a broken leg and was using a crutch, testified that she then went to the front door to enlist the aid of Chuck Michel. She stated that she shouted for him and, upon turning around to reenter the living room, found Wesler standing directly behind her. She testified to being gravely startled by this situation and to having then shot Wesler in what amounted to a reflex action. * * *

Reversal of respondent's conviction is * * * required by a * * * serious error committed by the trial court. * * *

In the opening paragraph of instruction No. 10, the jury, in evaluating the gravity of the danger to the respondent, was directed to consider only those acts and circumstances occurring "at or immediately before the killing ..." [7] This is not now, and never has been, the law of self-defense in Washington. On the contrary, the justification of self-defense is to be evaluated in light of *all* the facts and circumstances known to the defendant, including those known substantially before the killing.

In *State v. Ellis,* 30 Wash. 369, 70 P. 963 (1902), this court reversed a first-degree murder conviction obtained under self-defense instructions quite similar to that in the present case. The defendant sought to show that the deceased had a reputation and habit of carrying and using deadly weapons when engaged in quarrels. The trial court instructed that threats were insufficient justification unless " 'at the time of the alleged killing the deceased was making or immediately preceding the killing had committed some overt act ...' " This court found the instruction "defective and misleading", stating * * *[:]

[I]t is apparent that a man who habitually carries and uses such weapons in quarrels must cause greater apprehension of danger than one who does not bear such reputation ... The vital question is the reasonableness of the defendant's apprehension of danger ... The jury are [sic] entitled to stand as nearly as practicable in the

7. [The first paragraph of instruction] No. 10 reads:

"To justify killing in self-defense, there need be no actual or real danger to the life or person of the party killing, but there must be, or reasonably appear to be, at or immediately before the killing, some overt act, or some circumstances which would reasonably indicate to the party killing that the person slain, is, at the time, endeavoring to kill him or inflict upon him great bodily harm.["]

shoes of defendant, and from this point of view determine the character of the act.

Thus, circumstances predating the killing by weeks and months were deemed entirely proper, and in fact essential, to a proper disposition of the claim of self-defense. * * *

The second paragraph of instruction No. 10 contains an equally erroneous and prejudicial statement of the law. That portion of the instruction reads:

> However, when there is no reasonable ground for the person attacked to believe that *his* person is in imminent danger of death or great bodily harm, and it appears to *him* that only an ordinary battery is all that is intended, and all that *he* has reasonable grounds to fear from *his* assailant, *he* has a right to stand *his* ground and repel such threatened assault, yet *he* has no right to repel a threatened assault with naked hands, by the use of a deadly weapon in a deadly manner, unless *he* believes, *and has reasonable grounds* to believe, that *he* is in imminent danger of death or great bodily harm.

(Italics ours.) In our society women suffer from a conspicuous lack of access to training in and the means of developing those skills necessary to effectively repel a male assailant without resorting to the use of deadly weapons. Instruction No. 12 does indicate that the "relative size and strength of the persons involved" may be considered; however, it does not make clear that the defendant's actions are to be judged against her own subjective impressions and not those which a detached jury might determine to be objectively reasonable. * * *

The second paragraph of instruction No. 10 not only establishes an objective standard, but through the persistent use of the masculine gender leaves the jury with the impression the objective standard to be applied is that applicable to an altercation between two men. The impression created—that a 5'4" woman with a cast on her leg and using a crutch must, under the law, somehow repel an assault by a 6'2" intoxicated man without employing weapons in her defense, unless the jury finds her determination of the degree of danger to be objectively reasonable—constitutes a separate and distinct misstatement of the law and, in the context of this case, violates the respondent's right to equal protection of the law. The respondent was entitled to have the jury consider her actions in the light of her own perceptions of the situation, including those perceptions which were the product of our nation's "long and unfortunate history of sex discrimination." *Frontiero v. Richardson,* 411 U.S. 677, 684, 93 S.Ct. 1764, 1769, 36 L.Ed.2d 583 (1973). Until such time as the effects of that history are eradicated, care must be taken to assure that our self-defense instructions afford women the right to have their conduct judged in light of the individual physical handicaps which are the product of sex discrimination. To fail to do so is to deny the right of the individual woman involved to trial by the same rules which are applicable to male defendants. The portion of the instruction above quoted misstates our law in creating an objective standard of "reasonableness." It then compounds that error by utilizing language suggesting that the respondent's conduct must be measured against that of a reasonable male individual finding himself in the same circumstances. * * *

Notes and Questions

1. One scholar questions whether the events in *Wanrow* occurred as the defense claimed:

> The facts of *Wanrow* are quite * * * bizarre. The victim had been invited into a house in which the defendant, Wanrow, was staying precisely because she was afraid of [Wesler]. The ostensible purpose of the invitation [to Wesler] was to straighten the victim out, but the two men who were to do this "straightening" were outside the house at the time, leaving Wanrow and her small children alone in the house with one other woman. * * * It somewhat staggers the imagination to believe that a putative child molester, called into a house at 5 a.m. * * *, which he knew was surrounded by several men with weapons, would act in any way which would [cast] even suspicion upon him.

Richard Singer, *The Resurgence of Mens Rea: II—Honest but Unreasonable Mistake of Fact in Self Defense,* 28 B.C.L.Rev. 459, 498 n. 214 (1987).

2. Did the court correctly characterize the opening paragraph of Instruction 10: Does it actually direct jurors to consider only those acts and circumstances occurring at or immediately prior to the killing? If this is not its import, what do you think the trial judge had in mind?

3. Under *Wanrow,* is a woman's reaction to apparent aggression measured by the standard of a "reasonable woman" or according to her own subjective impression of what is reasonable under the circumstances?

4. *Feminist commentary on Wanrow.* *Wanrow* is treated by some commentators as "a case central to feminist commentary on self-defense." Shirley Sagawa, Note, *A Hard Case for Feminists: People v. Goetz,* 10 Harv.Wom.L.J. 253, 268 (1987). But, is the case really feminist in its perspective: Does the court's discussion of the effect of sex discrimination on women improperly "play on the stereotype of victimized and mistreated women that has historically limited women's claims for equal treatment and suggest that the court's responsiveness to Yvonne Wanrow's claim was shaped by patriarchal solicitude"? Elizabeth M. Schneider, *Describing and Changing: Women's Self–Defense Work and the Problem of Expert Testimony on Battering,* 9 Women's Rts.L.Rep. 195, 214 (1986). Is it fair to say that the implication of *Wanrow* is that "being a woman is an excuse" for acting in a manner that would be considered unreasonable if she were a man? See Shirley Sagawa, supra, at 273.

On the other hand, some feminist commentators believe that the holding in *Wanrow* is justified on the ground that traditional self-defense rules are male-oriented and, therefore, unfair to women who kill men, especially abusive men:

> Although, as compared to men, women rarely kill, it is significant that when women do kill, they frequently kill men whom they knew well,

often husbands or lovers. * * * It has been said that female homicide is
so different from male homicide that women and men may be said to
live in two difficult cultures, each with its own "subculture of violence."
If this is true then it should come as no surprise that laws created to
address male homicide * * * do not adequately address circumstances
under which women kill. * * *

    * * * The traditional elements of self-defense are based on the
paradigm of an encounter between two men of roughly equal physical
size and ability. The traditional model anticipates a one-time attack/de-
fense. The defendant is threatened with an attack that could potentially result in serious bodily harm or death and therefore is justified in
protecting himself. This model presumes that the authorities will step
in at the first possible opportunity; therefore, the defendant only need
defend himself as far as is necessary, at that moment, to keep the
aggressor at bay.

    This model * * * does not accommodate a scenario that includes
repeated attacks over time (battering), nor does it need to because men
are not, in significant numbers, subjected to repeated and vicious
physical abuse during the course of their *everyday lives*. This definition
of "necessity" does not contemplate having to live in an environment
dominated by regular, vicious, physical abuse without the possibility of
intervention or recourse to the law. Since necessity does not contemplate living with such physical abuse, the possibility of a fundamental
right to a life *free from abuse* never enters into the equation that
balances the rights of the attacker against the rights of a woman to
preserve her physical integrity.

Deborah Kochan, *Beyond the Battered Woman Syndrome: An Argument for
the Development of New Standards and the Incorporation of a Feminine
Approach to Ethics*, 1 Hastings Women's L.J. 89, 95–98 (1989).

    In light of the preceding observations, should women who kill men be
held to a different set of legal standards of self-defense than men who kill
other men? Specifically, should a woman (but not a man) be permitted to
use a deadly weapon to repel nondeadly force? Professor Susan Estrich
reflected on this question in her review of a book by Cynthia Gillespie
[Justifiable Homicide: Battered Women, Self–Defense and the Law (Ohio
State U. Press 1989)]:

    As every first-year law student learns, one is justified in using deadly
    force in self-defense only in response to a threat of death or serious
    bodily harm; only if the danger is "imminent" or immediately forth-
    coming; and in some states, and some locations (e.g., outside the home),
    only if there is no available path of safe retreat. None of these
    requirements is absolute in the sense that the defendant must, in
    hindsight, be proved *right* to prevail on a self-defense claim; rather,
    each test is based on the perspective of a reasonable man (the old cases)
    or person (the newer ones) in the defendant's position at the time.
    * * *

    In Gillespie's view, in a point she repeats often, these rules were
designed to define "manly behavior." But that is not so, really. In

many cases, the rules exist not so much to define manly behavior as to limit manly instincts—in order to preserve human life.

It might be "manly" to respond to a slight or an insult with deadly force, but the requirement that the threat be one of death or serious bodily harm does not permit it. Similarly, the imminence requirement is at least intended as a limit on vigilante revenge for attacks on one's family that occurred hours or days before. The retreat requirement is opposed by many precisely because it limits the manly instinct to stand one's ground and fight; it calls on men, and I think appropriately so, to sacrifice this aspect of manhood to the preservation of human life.

This is not to say that the automatic, unthinking application of these requirements to fights between men and women, or husbands and wives in particular, does not raise potential problems. The effect of the rule disallowing deadly response where nondeadly force is threatened may be particularly harsh for women, for their alternatives may be more limited. To expect or demand that women, who are likely to be smaller and less adept with their fists than most men, respond like schoolboys in the yard when attacked may be to leave them utterly without defenses.

A similar problem arises in rape law, where the requirement of force has been defined according to a woman's response, and where her failure to "fight back" in traditional, schoolboy terms—to use her hands or her fists to resist an unarmed man—leads some courts to conclude that there must have been no force in the first instance. But the answer, it seems to me, is a great deal easier in rape law: I have argued, as other have, that a woman should not be required to fight back with her hands and fists, that it should be enough if she *says* no, and that a man who proceeds in the face of such verbal resistance may fairly be held to have used force.

The hard question in self-defense cases, however, is not whether it will suffice for a woman to use *less* force than her male attacker; it is whether she is privileged to use more, to use deadly force when he may not. It is easy to characterize the current rule as one written by men and for men. But what should the rule for women be? Should a woman be privileged to respond to a fist with a gun? Cynthia Gillespie seems to say yes; indeed, she almost assumes it. But would she let a small, diminutive man do the same? Would she let a woman respond that way to the attack of her strong and aggressive sister? Should we? For me, at least, Gillespie's automatic response is not always so automatic; it requires careful consideration of the individual woman and the individual facts.

Susan Estrich, *Defending Women*, 88 Mich.L.Rev. 1430, 1431–32 (1990).

iii. Battered Woman Syndrome

INTRODUCTORY COMMENT

Statistically speaking, relatively little is known about the extent of violence within the family structure. Patsy A. Klaus & Michael R. Rand, Bureau of Justice Statistics, Special Report: Family Violence 1 (April

1984). However, we do know that in 1986 approximately thirty percent of all female homicide victims in the United States were killed by their husbands, ex-husbands, or boyfriends. *Report of the Gender Bias Study of the Supreme Judicial Court,* 23 Suffolk U.L.Rev. 575, 584 (1989) (citing U.S. Bureau of Justice Statistics). Moreover, in recent years, approximately one-fifth of all hospital emergency room admissions involved women battered by men. Susan A. MacManus & Nikki R. Van Hightower, *Limits of State Constitutional Guarantees: Lessons From Efforts to Implement Domestic Violence Policies,* 49 Pub.Admin.Rev. 269, 269 (1989).

On the other side of the homicidal coin, some experts estimate that 750 women a year kill their spouses or partners. In most of these cases, the woman was a victim of prior batterings by the decedent. Holly Maguigan, *Battered Women and Self–Defense: Myths and Misconceptions in Current Reform Proposals,* 140 U.Pa.L.Rev. 379, 397 & n. 67 (1991).

Until the 1980s, most police officers who answered "domestic disturbance" calls refused, often due to explicit departmental policy, to take men accused of battery into custody. Joan Zorza, *The Criminal Law of Misdemeanor Domestic Violence, 1970–1990,* 83 J.Crim.L. & Criminology 46, 48 (1992). In one department, for example, officers were taught at a training academy to "[a]void arrest if possible. Appeal to [the female complainant's] vanity." Del Martin, Battered Wives 93 (1981).

Police procedures have changed dramatically. In some communities, officers who respond to domestic violence calls are now required to arrest the batterer, with or without the approval (and even over the objection) of the victim. The results of such reforms are reported in Symposium on Domestic Violence, 83 J.Crim.L. & Criminology 1–253 (1992).

STATE v. NORMAN

Court of Appeals of North Carolina, 1988.
89 N.C.App. 384, 366 S.E.2d 586.

Parker, Judge.

* * * The primary issue presented on this appeal is whether the trial court erred in failing to instruct on self-defense. We answer in the affirmative and grant a new trial.

Facts

At trial the State presented the testimony of a deputy sheriff * * * who testified that * * * he was dispatched to the Norman residence. There, in one of the bedrooms, he found decedent, John Thomas "J.T." Norman (herein decedent or Norman) dead, lying on his left side on a bed. The State presented an autopsy report, stipulated to by both parties, concluding that Norman had died from two gunshot wounds to the head. The deputy sheriff also testified that * * * defendant told the officer that decedent, her husband, had been beating her all day, that she went to her mother's house nearby and got a .25 automatic pistol, that she returned to her house and loaded the gun, and that she shot her husband [while he slept.]   * * *

Defendant's evidence, presented through several different witnesses, disclosed a long history of verbal and physical abuse leveled by decedent against defendant.   Defendant and Norman had been married twenty-five years at the time of Norman's death.   Norman was an alcoholic.   He had begun to drink and to beat defendant five years after they were married.   The couple had five children * * *.   When defendant was pregnant with her youngest child, Norman beat her and kicked her down a flight of steps, causing the baby to be born prematurely the next day.

Norman, himself, had worked one day a few months prior to his death; but aside from that one day, witnesses could not remember his ever working.   Over the years and up to the time of his death, Norman forced defendant to prostitute herself every day in order to support him. If she begged him not to make her go, he slapped her.   Norman required defendant to make a minimum of one hundred dollars per day; if she failed to make this minimum, he would beat her.

Norman commonly called defendant "Dogs," "Bitches," and "Whores," and referred to her as a dog.   Norman beat defendant "most every day," especially when he was drunk and when other people were around, to "show off."   He would beat defendant with whatever was handy—his fist, a fly swatter, a baseball bat, his shoe, or a bottle; he put out cigarettes on defendant's skin; he threw food and drink in her face and refused to let her eat for days at a time; and he threw glasses, ashtrays, and beer bottles at her and once smashed a glass in her face. Defendant exhibited to the jury scars on her face from these incidents. Norman would often make defendant bark like a dog, and if she refused, he would beat her.   He often forced defendant to sleep on the concrete floor of their home and on several occasions forced her to eat dog or cat food out of the dog or cat bowl.

Norman often stated both to defendant and to others that he would kill defendant.   He also threatened to cut her heart out.

Witnesses for the defense also testified to the events in the thirty-six hours prior to Norman's death.   On or about the morning of 10 June 1985, Norman forced defendant to go to a truck stop or rest stop on Interstate 85 in order to prostitute to make some money.   * * * Some time later that day, Norman went to the truck stop, apparently drunk, and began hitting defendant in the face with his fist and slamming the car door into her.   He also threw hot coffee on defendant.   On the way home, Norman's car was stopped by police, and he was arrested for driving under the influence.

When Norman was released from jail the next morning, on 11 June 1985, he was extremely angry and beat defendant.   Defendant's mother said defendant acted nervous and scared.   Defendant testified that during the entire day, when she was near him, her husband slapped her, and when she was away from him, he threw glasses, ashtrays, and beer bottles at her.   Norman asked defendant to make him a sandwich; when defendant brought it to him, he threw it on the floor and told her to make him another. Defendant made him a second sandwich and brought it to him; Norman again threw it on the floor, telling her to put something on her hands because he did not want her to touch the bread. Defendant made a third sandwich using a paper towel to handle the bread. Norman took the third sandwich and smeared it in defendant's face.

On the evening of 11 June 1985, at about 8:00 or 8:30 p.m., a domestic quarrel was reported at the Norman residence. The officer responding to the call testified that defendant was bruised and crying and that she stated her husband had been beating her all day and she could not take it any longer. The officer advised defendant to take out a warrant on her husband, but defendant responded that if she did so, he would kill her. A short time later, the officer was again dispatched to the Norman residence. There he learned that defendant had taken an overdose of "nerve pills," and that Norman was interfering with emergency personnel who were trying to treat defendant. Norman was drunk and was making statements such as, " 'If you want to die, you deserve to die. I'll give you more pills,' " and " 'Let the bitch die.... She ain't nothing but a dog. She don't deserve to live.' " Norman also threatened to kill defendant, defendant's mother, and defendant's grandmother. * * * Defendant was taken to Rutherford Hospital.

The therapist on call at the hospital that night stated that defendant was angry and depressed and that she felt her situation was hopeless. On the advice of the therapist, defendant did not return home that night, but spent the night at her grandmother's house.

The next day, 12 June 1985, the day of Norman's death, Norman was angrier and more violent with defendant than usual. According to witnesses, Norman beat defendant all day long. Sometime during the day, Lemuel Splawn, Norman's best friend, called Norman and asked Norman to drive with him to Spartanburg, where Splawn worked, to pick up Splawn's paycheck. Norman arrived at Splawn's house some time later. Defendant was driving. During the ride to Spartanburg, Norman slapped defendant for following a truck too closely and poured a beer on her head. Norman kicked defendant in the side of the head while she was driving and told her he would " 'cut her breast off and shove it up her rear end.' "

Later that day, one of the Normans' daughters, Loretta, reported to defendant's mother that her father was beating her mother again. Defendant's mother called the sheriff's department, but no help arrived at that time. Witnesses stated that back at the Norman residence, Norman threatened to cut defendant's throat, threatened to kill her, and threatened to cut off her breast. Norman also smashed a doughnut on defendant's face and put out a cigarette on her chest.

In the late afternoon, Norman wanted to take a nap. He lay down on the larger of the two beds in the bedroom. Defendant started to lie down on the smaller bed, but Norman said, " 'No bitch ... Dogs don't sleep on beds, they sleep in [sic] the floor.'" Soon after, one of the Normans' daughters, Phyllis, came into the room and asked if defendant could look after her baby. Norman assented. When the baby began to cry, defendant took the child to her mother's house, fearful that the baby would disturb Norman. At her mother's house, defendant found a gun. She took it back to her home and shot Norman.

Defendant testified that things at home were so bad she could no longer stand it. She explained that she could not leave Norman because he would kill her. She stated that she had left him before on several occasions and that each time he found her, took her home, and beat her. She said that she was afraid to take out a warrant on her husband because he had said that if she ever had him locked up, he would kill her when he got out. She stated she did not have him committed because he told her he would see the authorities coming for him and before they got to him he would cut defendant's throat. Defendant also testified that when he threatened to kill her, she believed he would kill her if he had the chance.

The defense presented the testimony of two expert witnesses in the field of forensic psychology, Dr. William Tyson and Dr. Robert Rollins. Based on an examination of defendant and an investigation of the matter, Dr. Tyson concluded that defendant "fits and exceeds the profile, of an abused or battered spouse." Dr. Tyson explained that in defendant's case the situation had progressed beyond mere "'Wife battering or family violence'" and had become "torture, degradation and reduction to an animal level of existence, where all behavior was marked purely by survival...." Dr. Tyson stated that defendant could not leave her husband because she had gotten to the point where she had no belief whatsoever in herself and believed in the total invulnerability of her husband. He stated, "Mrs. Norman didn't leave because she believed, fully believed that escape was totally impossible.... She fully believed that [Norman] was invulnerable to the law and to all social agencies that were available; that nobody could withstand his power. As a result, there was no such thing as escape." Dr. Tyson stated that the incidences of Norman forcing defendant to perform prostitution and to eat pet food from pet dishes were parts of the dehumanization process. Dr. Tyson analogized the process to practices in prisoner-of-war camps in the Second World War and the Korean War.

When asked if it appeared to defendant reasonably necessary to kill her husband, Dr. Tyson responded, "I think Judy Norman felt that she had no choice, both in the protection of herself and her family, but to engage, exhibit deadly force against Mr. Norman, and that in so doing, she was sacrificing herself, both for herself and for her family."

Dr. Rollins was defendant's attending physician at Dorothea Dix Hospital where she was sent for a psychiatric evaluation after her arrest. Based on an examination of defendant, laboratory studies, psychological tests, interviews, and background investigation, Dr. Rollins testified that defendant suffered from "abused spouse syndrome." Dr. Rollins defined the syndrome in the following way:

> The "abused spouse syndrome" refers to situations where one spouse has achieved almost complete control and submission of the other by both psychological and physical domination. It's, to start with, it's usually seen in the females who do not have a strong sense of their own adequacy who do not have a lot of personal or occupational resources; it's usually associated with physical abuse over a long period of time, and the particular characteristics that interest us are that the abused spouse comes to believe that the other person is in complete control; that they themselves are worthless and they cannot get away; that there's no rescue from the other person.

When asked, in his opinion, whether it appeared reasonably necessary that defendant take the life of J.T. Norman, Dr. Rollins responded, "In my opinion, that course of action did appear necessary to Mrs. Norman." However, Dr. Rollins stated that he found no evidence of any psychotic disorder * * *.

LEGAL ANALYSIS * * *

The question * * * arising on the facts in this case is whether the victim's passiveness at the moment the [homicidal] act occurred precludes defendant from asserting * * * self-defense.

Applying the criteria of * * * self-defense to the facts of this case, we hold that the evidence was sufficient to submit an issue of * * * self-defense to the jury. An examination of the elements of * * * self-defense reveals that both subjective and objective standards are to be applied in making the crucial determinations. The first requirement that it appear to defendant and that defendant believe it necessary to kill the deceased in order to save herself from death or great bodily harm calls for a subjective evaluation. This evaluation inquires as to what the defendant herself perceived at the time of the shooting. The trial was replete with testimony of forced prostitution, beatings, and threats on defendant's life. The defendant testified that she believed the decedent would kill her, and the evidence showed that on the occasions when she had made an effort to get away from Norman, he had come after her and beat her. * * * Both experts testified that in their opinion, defendant believed killing the victim was necessary to avoid being killed. This evidence would permit a finding by a jury that defendant believed it necessary to kill the victim to save herself from death or serious bodily harm.

Unlike the first requirement, the second element of self-defense—that defendant's belief be reasonable * * *—is measured by the objective standard of the person of ordinary firmness under the same circumstances. Again, the record is replete with sufficient evidence to permit but not compel a juror, representing the person of ordinary firmness, to infer that defendant's belief was reasonable under the circumstances in which she found herself. Both expert witnesses testified that defendant exhibited severe symptoms of battered spouse syndrome, a condition that develops from repeated cycles of violence by the victim against the defendant. Through this repeated, sometimes constant, abuse, the battered spouse acquires what the psychologists denote as a state of "learned helplessness," defendant's state of mind as described by Drs. Tyson and Rollins. * * * The inability of a defendant to withdraw from the hostile situation and the vulnerability of a defendant to the victim are factors considered * * * in determining the reasonableness of a defendant's belief in the necessity to kill the victim. * * *

* * * Psychologists and sociologists report that battered spouse syndrome usually has three phases—the tension-building phase, the violent phase, and the quiet or loving phase. During the violent phase, the time when the traditional concept of self-defense would mandate that defendant protect herself, i.e., at the moment the abusing spouse attacks, the battered spouse is least able to counter because she is immobilized by fear, if not actually physically restrained.

Mindful that the law should never casually permit an otherwise unlawful killing of another human being to be justified or excused, this Court is of the opinion that with the battered spouse there can be, under certain circumstances, * * * killing of a passive victim that does not preclude the defense of * * * self-defense. Given the characteristics of battered spouse syndrome, we do not believe that a battered person must wait until a deadly attack occurs or that the victim must in all cases be actually attacking or threatening to attack at the very moment defendant commits the unlawful act for the battered person to act in self-defense. Such a standard, in our view, would ignore the realities of the condition. * * *

* * * Based on this evidence, a jury, in our view, could find that decedent's sleep was but a momentary hiatus in a continuous reign of terror by the decedent, that defendant merely took advantage of her first opportunity to protect herself, and that defendant's act was not without the provocation required for * * * self-defense.

Finally, the expert testimony considered with the other evidence would permit reasonable minds to infer that defendant did not use more force than reasonably appeared necessary to her under the circumstances to protect herself from death or great bodily harm. * * *

STATE v. NORMAN

Supreme Court of North Carolina, 1989.
324 N.C. 253, 378 S.E.2d 8.

MITCHELL, JUSTICE. * * *

The Court of Appeals granted a new trial, citing as error the trial court's refusal to submit a possible verdict of acquittal by reason of * * * self-defense. Notwithstanding the uncontroverted evidence that the defendant shot her husband three times in the back of the head as he lay sleeping in his bed, the Court of Appeals held that the defendant's evidence that she exhibited what has come to be called "the battered wife syndrome" entitled her to have the jury consider whether the homicide was an act of * * * self-defense and, thus, not a legal wrong.

We conclude that the evidence introduced in this case would not support a finding that the defendant killed her husband due to a reasonable fear of imminent death or great bodily harm, as is required before a defendant is entitled to jury instructions concerning * * * self-defense. Therefore, the trial court properly declined to instruct the jury on the law relating to self-defense. Accordingly, we reverse the Court of Appeals. * * *

The right to kill in self-defense is based on the necessity, real or reasonably apparent, of killing an unlawful aggressor to save oneself from *imminent* death or great bodily harm at his hands. Our law has recognized that self-preservation under such circumstances springs from a primal impulse and is an inherent right of natural law. * * *

The killing of another human being is the most extreme recourse to our inherent right of self-preservation and can be justified in law only by the utmost real or apparent necessity brought about by the decedent. For that reason, our law of self-defense has required that a defendant claiming that a homicide was justified * * * establish that she reasonably believed at the time of the killing she otherwise would have immediately suffered death or great bodily harm. Only if defendants are required to show that they killed due to a reasonable belief that death or great bodily harm was imminent can the justification for homicide remain clearly and firmly rooted in necessity. The imminence requirement ensures that deadly force will be used only where it is necessary as a last resort in the exercise of the inherent right of self-preservation. * * *

The term "imminent," as used to describe such perceived threats of death or great bodily harm as will justify a homicide by reason of * * * self-defense, has been defined as "immediate danger, such as must be instantly met, such as cannot be guarded against by calling for the assistance of others or the protection of the law." Black's Law Dictionary 676 (5th ed. 1979). * * *

The evidence in this case did not tend to show that the defendant reasonably believed that she was confronted by a threat of imminent death or great bodily harm. The evidence tended to show that no harm was "imminent" or about to happen to the defendant when she shot her husband. The uncontroverted evidence was that her husband had been asleep for some time when she walked to her mother's house, returned with the pistol, fixed the pistol after it jammed and then shot her husband three times in the back of the head. The defendant was not faced with an instantaneous choice between killing her husband or being killed or seriously injured. Instead, *all* of the evidence tended to show that the defendant had ample time and opportunity to resort to other means of preventing further abuse of her husband. * * *

Additionally, the lack of any belief by the defendant—reasonable or otherwise—that she faced a threat of imminent death or great bodily harm from the drunk and sleeping victim in the present case was illustrated by * * * her own expert witnesses when testifying about her subjective assessment of her situation at the time of the killing. * * *

Dr. Tyson * * * testified that the defendant "believed herself to be doomed . . . to a life of the worst kind of torture and abuse, degradation that she had experienced over the years in a progressive way; that it would only get worse, and that death was inevitable." Such evidence of the defendant's speculative beliefs concerning her remote and indefinite future, while indicating she had felt generally threatened, did not tend to show that she killed in the belief—reasonable or otherwise—that her husband presented a threat of *imminent* death or great bodily harm. * * *

We are not persuaded by the reasoning of our Court of Appeals in this case that when there is evidence of battered wife syndrome, neither an actual attack nor threat of attack by the husband at the moment the wife uses deadly force is required to justify the wife's killing of him in * * * self-defense. The Court of Appeals concluded that to impose such requirements would ignore the "learned helplessness," meekness and other realities of battered wife syndrome and would effectively preclude such women from exercising their right of self-defense. Other jurisdictions which have addressed this question under similar facts are divided in their views, and we can discern no clear majority position on facts closely similar to those of this case. * * *

* * * [S]tretching the law of self-defense to fit the facts of this case would require changing the "imminent death or great bodily harm" requirement to something substantially more indefinite than previously required and would weaken our assurances that justification for the taking of human life remains firmly rooted in real or apparent necessity. That result in principle could not be limited to a few cases decided on evidence as poignant as this. The relaxed requirements * * * proposed by our Court of Appeals would tend to categorically legalize the opportune killing of abusive husbands by their wives solely on the basis of the wives' testimony concerning their subjective speculation as to the probability of future felonious assaults by their husbands. Homicidal self-help would then become a lawful solution, and perhaps the easiest and most effective solution, to this problem. * * *

Reversed.

Martin, Justice, dissenting.

At the outset it is to be noted that the peril of fabricated evidence is not unique to the trials of battered wives who kill. The possibility of invented evidence arises in all cases in which a party is seeking the benefit of self-defense. Moreover, in this case there were a number of witnesses other than defendant who testified as to the actual presence of circumstances supporting a claim of self-defense. This record contains no reasonable basis to attack the credibility of evidence for the defendant. * * *

* * * Defendant does not seek to expand or relax the requirements of self-defense and thereby "legalize the opportune killing of allegedly abusive husbands by their wives," as the majority overstates. * * * The proper issue for this Court is to determine whether the evidence, viewed in the light most favorable to the defendant, was sufficient to require the trial court to instruct on the law of self-defense. I conclude that it was. * * *

Evidence presented by defendant described a twenty-year history of beatings and other dehumanizing and degrading treatment by her husband. In his expert testimony a clinical psychologist * * * described the defendant as a woman incarcerated by abuse, by fear, and by her conviction that her husband was invincible and inescapable * * *.

* * * This, in fact, is a state of mind common to the battered spouse, and one that dramatically distinguishes Judy Norman's belief in the imminence of serious harm from that asserted by [defendants in other cases]. * * * For the battered wife, if there is no escape, if there is no window of relief or momentary sense of safety, then the next attack, which could be the fatal one, is imminent. In the context of the doctrine of self-defense, "imminent" is a term the meaning of which must be grasped from the defendant's point of view. Properly stated, * * * the question is not whether the threat was *in fact* imminent, but whether defendant's belief in the impending nature of the threat, given the circumstances as she saw them, was reasonable in the mind of a person of ordinary firmness.

Defendant's intense fear * * * evident in the testimony of witnesses who recounted events of the last three days of the decedent's life * * * could have led a juror to conclude that defendant reasonably perceived a threat to her life as "imminent," even while her husband slept. * * *

In *State v. Wingler,* 184 N.C. 747, 115 S.E. 59 (1922), in which the defendant was found guilty for the murder of his wife, Justice * * * Stacy recognized the pain and oppression under which a woman suffers at the hands of an abusive husband: "The supreme tragedy of life is the immolation of woman. With a heavy hand, nature exacts from her a high tax of blood and tears." By his barbaric conduct over the course of twenty years, J.T. Norman reduced the quality of the defendant's life to such an abysmal state that, given the opportunity to do so, the jury might well have found that she was justified in acting in self-defense for the preservation of her tragic life. * * *

Notes and Questions

1. Judy Norman was convicted of voluntary manslaughter and sentenced to prison for six years. On July 9, 1989, two months after she entered the North Carolina Correctional Institute for Women, her sentence was commuted by the Governor of North Carolina. Judy Norman's plight and the issues raised by her case are considered in detail in Richard A.

Rosen, *On Self-Defense, Imminence, and Women Who Kill Their Batterers*, 71 N.C.L.Rev. 371 (1993).

2. Dr. Lenore Walker is the most prominent expert on the battered woman syndrome. Based on her book, The Battered Woman (1979), the New Jersey Supreme Court provided this synopsis of the syndrome:

> According to Dr. Walker, relationships characterized by physical abuse tend to develop battering cycles. Violent behavior directed at the woman occurs in three distinct and repetitive states that vary both in duration and intensity depending on the individuals involved.

> Phase one of the battering cycle is referred to as the "tension-building stage," during which the battering male engages in minor battering incidents and verbal abuse while the woman, beset by fear and tension, attempts to be as placating and passive as possible in order to stave off more serious violence.

> Phase two of the battering cycle is the "acute battering incident." At some point during phase one, the tension between the battered woman and the batterer becomes intolerable and more serious violence inevitable. The triggering event that initiates phase two is most often an internal or external event in the life of the battering male, but provocation for more severe violence is sometimes provided by the woman who can no longer tolerate or control her phase-one anger and anxiety.

> Phase three of the battering cycle is characterized by extreme contrition and loving behavior on the part of the battering male. During this period the man will often mix his pleas for forgiveness and protestations of devotion with promises to seek professional help, to stop drinking,[5] and to refrain from further violence. For some couples, this period of relative calm may last as long as several months, but in a battering relationship the affection and contrition of the man will eventually fade and phase one of the cycle will start anew.

> The cyclical nature of battering behavior helps explain why more women simply do not leave their abusers. The loving behavior demonstrated by the batterer during phase three reinforces hopes these women might have for their mate's reform and keeps them bound to the relationship.

> Some women may even perceive the battering cycle as normal, especially if they grew up in a violent household. Or they may simply not wish to acknowledge the reality of their situation.

> Other women, however, become so demoralized and degraded by the fact that they cannot predict or control the violence that they sink into a state of psychological paralysis and become unable to take any action at all to improve or alter the situation. There is a tendency in battered women to believe in the omnipotence or strength of their battering husbands and thus to feel that any attempt to resist them is hopeless.

State v. Kelly, 97 N.J. 178, 193–94, 478 A.2d 364, 371–72 (1984).

---

5. Alcohol is often an important component of violence toward women. * * *

3. In *Norman,* what was the Court of Appeals (or the dissent in the North Carolina Supreme Court) suggesting: (1) that an imminent deadly attack is not required in order to claim self-defense; (2) that the imminency requirement was satisfied in this case; (3) that a reasonable person in Judy Norman's situation would have believed that an attack was imminent, even though it was not; or (4), is the Kansas Supreme Court correct in stating that "[t]here is no doubt that the North Carolina [Court of Appeals] determined that the sleeping husband was an evil man who deserved the justice he received from his battered wife"?   State v. Stewart, 243 Kan. 639, 648, 763 P.2d 572, 578–79 (1988).

4. Rather than focus on the physical harm that Judy Norman was experiencing, should her acts be justified on the ground that she was defending herself against continued psychological degradation?   Professor Charles Ewing has proposed that the law permit the use of deadly force to prevent serious psychological injury, defined by him as "gross and enduring impairment of one's psychological functioning that significantly limits the meaning and value of one's physical existence."   Charles Patrick Ewing, *Psychological Self–Defense,* 14 Law & Hum.Behav. 579, 587 (1990); see Charles Patrick Ewing, Battered Women Who Kill: Psychological Self–Defense as Legal Justification (1987).

Ewing contends that such a rule would be consistent with the principle that, in order to avoid dishonor, a person may stand one's ground and kill an aggressor rather than retreat.   He reasons that his reform proposal "expresses a respect for human life even greater than that implicit in current self-defense doctrine," because it "would give equal priority to those vital aspects of human functioning that give meaning and value to such existence—in other words, those psychological attributes that make life worth living."   Ewing, *Psychological Self–Defense,* supra, at 590.   For a critique of the doctrine of psychological self-defense, see Stephen J. Morse, *The Misbegotten Marriage of Soft Psychology and Bad Law,* 14 Law & Hum.Behav. 595 (1990).

5. *The killing of a sleeping batterer: justified or excused?*   Was Judy Norman justified in killing her husband, or is her plea more in the nature of an excuse, i.e., that the killing was wrongful but society should hold her morally blameless for her actions?   If you believe that she was justified in killing her sleeping husband, what underlying rationale of self-defense supports your conclusion?   If you would not justify the killing, would you excuse Judy Norman?   Or, would you do as the jury ultimately did—convict her of manslaughter?   What might be the theoretical basis for such an outcome?

6. *Justification or excuse: does the label matter?*   If a battering victim may be acquitted of killing her abusive partner while he is asleep, does it matter whether her defense is labelled a "justification" or an "excuse"?   Is the message communicated by the acquittal the same?

Are there practical implications to treating the defense as a justification? Suppose that John Norman had awakened when his wife placed the gun at his temple.   At that moment, would *he* have been justified in killing *her*? Do his rights in this situation depend on how we describe her defense claim?

7. *Admissibility of expert testimony regarding the "battered woman syndrome."* Many courts apply a three-factor test for determining whether expert testimony is admissible in a criminal trial:

> (1) the subject matter "must be so distinctively related to some science, profession, business or occupation as to be beyond the ken of the average layman"; (2) "the witness must have sufficient skill, knowledge, or experience in that field or calling as to make it appear that his opinion or inference will aid the trier in his search for truth"; and (3) expert testimony is inadmissible if "the state of the pertinent art or scientific knowledge does not permit a reasonable opinion to be asserted even by an expert."

Dyas v. United States, 376 A.2d 827, 832 (D.C.App.1977) (quoting McCormick on Evidence § 13 (2d ed. E. Cleary 1972)).

The third prong is a major stumbling block when a party seeks to introduce novel scientific evidence. Under the traditional standard, scientific evidence is inadmissible unless the principle upon which it is based is "sufficiently established to have gained general acceptance in the particular field in which it belongs." Frye v. United States, 293 Fed. 1013, 1014 (D.C.Cir.1923).

In 1993, the Supreme Court held that the so-called *Frye* test no longer applies in federal courts. Scientific evidence is now admissible if the trial court determines that the expert's testimony rests on a reliable scientific foundation, even if the theory or technique in question lacks general acceptance. Daubert v. Merrell Dow Pharmaceuticals, Inc., 509 U.S. ___, 113 S.Ct. 2786, 125 L.Ed.2d 469 (1993).

Most states still apply the *Frye* standard. Whether they will continue to do so in light of *Daubert* remains to be seen. On the basis of *Frye,* however, some courts originally refused to allow testimony relating to the battered woman syndrome in self-defense cases. *Ibn–Tamas* is representative of the early concerns of trial and appellate judges.

IBN–TAMAS v. UNITED STATES

District of Columbia Court of Appeals, 1983.
455 A.2d 893.

[Ibn–Tamas was indicted for the murder of her abusive husband. The trial court refused to permit her to call Dr. Lenore Walker to testify regarding the battered woman syndrome. The defendant appealed. The Court of Appeals, 407 A.2d 626 (D.C.App.1979), ordered the trial court to conduct an evidentiary hearing to determine whether the proffered testimony satisfied the three-pronged test discussed in the preceding Note.

On remand, the trial court concluded "that defendant failed to establish a general acceptance by the expert's colleagues of the methodology used in the expert's study of battered women." The defendant appealed again. The Court of Appeals ruled that the trial judge did not abuse his discretion in excluding the evidence. What follows are remarks of a concurring judge.]

GALLAGHER, ASSOCIATE JUDGE, RETIRED, concurring:

I believe this proffered testimony on "battered women" is properly considered to be within the category of novel scientific evidence. Consequently, it falls within the underlying doctrine of *Frye v. United States,* 54 App.D.C. 46, 293 F. 1013 (1923). The essence of *Frye* is that there must be a reliable body of scientific opinion supporting a *novel scientific theory* before it is admissible in evidence.

Subsequent to the decision of this court in its first opinion, a book authored by Dr. Lenore E. Walker, whose expert testimony on "battered women" was proffered in *Ibn–Tamas, supra,* and which testimony is at the core of the issue on this appeal, was published, entitled, *The Battered Woman* (Harper & Rowe, 1979). In the introduction of that book, Dr. Walker made this statement:

> I think this research has raised more questions for me than it has answered. As a trained researcher, I felt uneasy about stating some of the conclusions in this book. They seemed too tentative to write down in the positive manner which I have used. Yet they are confirmed repeatedly by all the available data so far.

Dr. Walker went on to define the term: "A battered woman is a woman who is repeatedly subjected to any forceful physical *or psychological behavior* by a man in order to coerce her to do something he wants her to do without any concern for her rights." [emphasis added].

In discussing the viewpoint from which she wrote *The Battered Woman,* Dr. Walker said: "[I] view women as victims in order to understand what the toll of such domestic violence is like for them. Unfortunately, in doing so *I tend to place all men in an especially negative light,* instead of just those men who do commit such crimes." [emphasis added].

Initially, I must say that though there may be good reason for the light in which, for the sake of the study, Dr. Walker feels she must place "all men," it does give one a bit of a start. While it may be that "all men" are victims of the male role in society, it would seem one must establish the necessity for Dr. Walker's premise, which at first glance is a trifle disconcerting. It appears that the Doctor's approach would require tracing the man-woman relationship back to the roots of civilization—a subject which would require a little pondering, I should think.

In a case subsequent to *Ibn–Tamas I, supra,* the Supreme Court of Wyoming had misgivings about the "state of the art" on this subject. *Buhrle v. State of Wyoming,* 627 P.2d 1374 (1981). During the trial in that case, Dr. Walker was questioned on voir dire concerning the statement in her book that she felt uneasy about some of its conclusions and felt they were too tentative to write in the positive manner she had used. In explaining the statement, Dr. Walker testified she had received a research grant "to study the matter in a much more scientific way" and that her research was ongoing with completion to be in the future. For these and other reasons, the court went on to conclude that "research in 'the battered woman syndrome' is in its infancy." In so doing, the court did not rule out admissibility in the future if by then an adequate foundation is laid.

I agree. * * *

I do not mean to imply I believe that expert testimony on the "battered woman" will not lend itself to a recognition with sufficient scientific underpinning to warrant its admission into evidence in court. What I do say is that, as *Frye* soundly requires, more needs to be known by the court initially in the specific area of the science before its admissibility will be warranted. * * *

Notes and Questions

1. Dr. Walker has refined her definition of the term "battered woman." She now describes a battered woman as someone "in an intimate relationship with a man who repeatedly subjects * * * her to forceful physical and/or psychological abuse." "Repeatedly" is defined as "more than once"; "abuse" includes any of six categories of behavior, from life-threatening violence to "extreme verbal harassment and expressing comments of a derogatory nature with negative value judgments." Lenore Walker, The Battered Woman Syndrome 203 (2d ed. 1984).

One commentator has written that "[t]he breadth of Walker's definition has obvious value from the perspective of the clinical psychologist * * * [but that it] seems flagrantly overbroad from the perspective of traditional self-defense categories * * *." Stephen J. Schulhofer, *The Gender Question in Criminal Law*, 7 Soc. Phil. & Policy, Spring, 1990, at 105, 117. Do you agree?

2. Despite continued criticism from a few quarters regarding the validity of the research in this field, see, e.g., David L. Faigman, Note, *Battered Woman Syndrome and Self–Defense: A Legal and Empirical Dissent*, 72 Virg.L.Rev. 619 (1986), the overwhelming trend of the courts since *Ibn–Tamas* has been to admit battered woman syndrome testimony in appropriate self-defense cases.[c] Holly Maguigan, *Battered Women and Self–Defense: Myths and Misconceptions in Current Reform Proposals,* 140 U.Pa. L.Rev. 379, 429 (1991).

What are the "appropriate" cases? Homicide prosecutions of battered women generally fall into one of three categories. Seventy to ninety percent of all battered women who kill do so during a beating or when the batterer's actions prompt her to believe that an attack is immediately forthcoming. Id. at 384. The clear trend is to permit syndrome evidence is these so-called "confrontational" cases, assuming that the defendant has proven a history of abuse. See id. at 386, 427–29.

A second category of cases involves battered women who kill in "nonconfrontational" circumstances, i.e., while the abuser is asleep or during a significant lull in the violence. The courts are divided on whether the defendant is entitled to an instruction on self-defense in such circumstances, but if the defense may be claimed, expert testimony regarding the battered

---

c. Some states provide by statute for the admissibility of battered woman syn-   drome expert testimony. E.g., Ohio Rev. Code § 2901.06 (1993).

woman syndrome is usually admissible, either to show that the defendant subjectively perceived the danger facing her to be imminent or, more broadly, to demonstrate that her perception was reasonable under the circumstances. Id. at 415–16.

A few cases fall into a third grouping, in which the woman hires a third party to kill the batterer. An instruction on self-defense is not permitted in such circumstances. People v. Yaklich, 833 P.2d 758 (Colo.App.1991); State v. Leaphart, 673 S.W.2d 870 (Tenn.Cr.App.1983). Should this be the rule?

3. *Subjectivization of the "reasonable belief" standard: how far should the law go?* Is the purpose of permitting battered woman syndrome evidence to have the defendant's actions evaluated by the factfinder "in light of how the reasonably prudent *battered woman* would have perceived and reacted to [the decedent's] behavior"? Commonwealth v. Stonehouse, 521 Pa. 41, 65, 555 A.2d 772, 784 (1989). If so, what other characteristics of a defendant ought to be considered?

In State v. Simon, 231 Kan. 572, 646 P.2d 1119 (1982), the defendant, an elderly man, killed the decedent, a young man of Oriental ancestry, because he believed that the youth, by virtue of his ancestry, was an expert in the martial arts and dangerous. Under such circumstances, should jurors be instructed to measure the defendant's reactions by the standard of a "reasonably prudent elderly man who believes that all Oriental youths know the martial arts and are dangerous"?

In *Simon,* a clinical psychologist testified that the defendant was a "psychological invalid," "very tense and fearful," who was apt to "misjudge reality" and honestly see himself under attack. In view of this evidence, should the standard be what a "reasonably prudent, very tense and fearful psychological invalid" would believe in the defendant's situation?

Perhaps no court has gone as far in permitting a subjective standard of reasonableness than the North Dakota Supreme Court:

[A]n accused's actions are to be viewed from the standpoint of a person whose mental and physical characteristics are like the accused's and who sees what the accused sees and knows what the accused knows. For example, if the accused is a timid, diminutive male, the factfinder must consider these characteristics in assessing the reasonableness of his belief. If, on the other hand, the accused is a strong, courageous, and capable female, the factfinder must consider these characteristics in judging the reasonableness of her belief. * * *

Hence, a correct statement of the law of self-defense is one in which the court directs the jury to assume the physical and psychological properties peculiar to the accused, viz., to place itself as best it can in the shoes of the accused, and then decide whether or not the particular circumstances surrounding the accused at the time he used force were sufficient to create in his mind a sincere and reasonable belief that the use of force was necessary to protect himself from imminent and unlawful harm.

State v. Leidholm, 334 N.W.2d 811, 818 (N.D.1983); see also Nelson v. State, 42 Ohio App. 252, 181 N.E. 448, 449 (1932) (stating that because "[g]uilt is personal," a "nervous, timid, easily frightened individual is not measured by the same standard that a stronger, calmer, and braver man might be").

Does *Leidholm* go too far?

4. *Battered children and self-defense.* Lonnie Dutton, a 200–pound unemployed oilfield worker, lived in an 80–foot–long mobile home in Rush Springs, Oklahoma with his four children. The home had no electricity or running water and no telephone service.

Dutton regularly beat his children, sexually molested his daughter, and (until she secured a divorce) tortured his wife. He once ordered his two oldest boys to throw darts at their little sister and mother, and he poured jalepeño juice in his wife's eyes. Dutton obtained custody of the children after the divorce by telling the authorities that his wife had abused them.

One day, after Dutton's ten-year-old daughter told her brothers that "Daddy was messin' with me," two of them loaded their father's rifle, walked over to the couch where he was sleeping, and one of them (age 15) aimed the rifle at his father's right ear, while the other (age 12) pulled the trigger, killing him. Louis Sahagun, *Murder Case Opens Eyes to Horrific Tale of Child Abuse,* Los Angeles Times, Sept. 9, 1993, at A1; Sam Howe Verhovek, *Town Rallies Behind Boys Who Killed Father,* New York Times, July 25, 1993, Sec. 1, at 14.

The two youths were charged as juveniles with first degree murder and conspiracy to commit murder. Were their actions justified? Does the law of self-defense—the common law or the Model Penal Code—adequately protect the interests of abused children, such as the Duttons? If not, how should the law be re-framed? Should abused children be permitted to introduce evidence of the "battered child syndrome," a condition similar in many respects to the battered woman syndrome, to buttress their self-defense claim? See State v. Janes, 121 Wash.2d 220, 235, 850 P.2d 495, 502 (1993); Jahnke v. State, 682 P.2d 991 (Wyo.1984); Joelle Anne Moreno, *Killing Daddy: Developing a Self–Defense Strategy for the Abused Child,* 137 U.Pa. L.Rev. 1281 (1989); Diana J. Ensign, Note, *Links Between the Battered Woman Syndrome and the Battered Child Syndrome: An Argument for Consistent Standards in the Admissibility of Expert Testimony in Family Abuse Cases,* 36 Wayne L.Rev. 1619 (1990).

3. DEFENSE OF OTHERS

COMMONWEALTH v. MARTIN

Supreme Judicial Court of Massachusetts, 1976.
369 Mass. 640, 341 N.E.2d 885.

KAPLAN, JUSTICE.

The defendant * * * appeals * * * from his multiple convictions * * *,[1] arising from a clash between inmates and guards at Massachusetts Correctional Institution * * *. The issue on appeal is whether the

---

1. With regard to the alleged attack * * *, the defendant was convicted of assault and battery on a guard of a correc- tional institution, assault and battery with a dangerous weapon, and armed assault with intent to kill.

trial judge committed error in failing to instruct the jury with respect to the defendant's claimed justification or defense, namely, that the acts of which he was accused were part of an attempt on his part to come to the aid of a fellow inmate and friend, Gene Tremblay * * *, who was being unlawfully beaten by prison guards. * * *

1. We sketch very briefly the facts as they appeared at trial. * * *

According to the prosecution's case, a struggle erupted between two correction officers and two inmates as the inmates were being escorted from a second-floor segregation unit down to a first-floor area for showers and exercise. One of the inmates, Tremblay, fought with an officer near the stairwell and the officer fell or was shoved down the stairs, with Tremblay following him down. The fallen officer yelled to officers on the first floor for help, and one of them, John Quealey, restrained Tremblay, while others went to summon aid. Officer Quealey held Tremblay by the hair while pushing him toward and into an open cell on the first floor. * * *

Meantime the second inmate involved in the fight on the second floor had taken the cell keys from the other officer and released other inmates of the segregation unit. Several of the inmates, including the defendant, ran down the stairs and met officers who had arrived to give help. In the melee, Officer Quealey was stabbed a number of times in the chest and once on the arm. * * *

The defendant took the stand to give his version of the facts. He was corroborated in part by the codefendant Tremblay. Because the defendant's view was obstructed by a partition between the rows of cells on either side of the second floor, he had not been able to see the fight there and did not know who had started it. When his cell was opened, he walked to the end of the partition but, seeing blood on the floor and hearing sounds of a struggle on the stairs, he started back to his cell. He then heard Tremblay calling for help and surmised that Tremblay was in grave danger. The defendant raced down the stairs and saw Officer Quealey and two other officers striking Tremblay with clubs and a metal mop handle as he lay on the floor of an open cell. Tremblay had his arms over his head and was trying to fend off the blows. He was yelling for help. The defendant struck several officers, including * * * Quealey * * *, with his fists in his effort to pull the officers off Tremblay. The defendant denied that he had a knife at this time; he did not stab Officer Quealey * * * with a knife. * * *

The evidence on the part of the defendant, summarized above, was sufficient to lay a basis for a charge to the jury on the justification claimed by him * * *. It is of course immaterial that the triers might very well, in the end, lend no credence whatever to the defendant's version of the facts. * * *

2. The judge instructed the jury with respect to self-defense and even related these instructions to the question whether the defendant was privileged to use a dangerous weapon to protect himself from attack by Officer Quealey. But he gave the jury no instructions on the subject

of the privileged use of force to protect another. This failure seems to have been due to the judge's belief that the claimed justification was not recognized in the law of Massachusetts.

The defendant made due request in writing for jury instructions on the subject. * * * The main requested instruction * * * was * * *: "A person is justified in the use of force against another when and to the extent that he reasonably believes that such conduct is necessary to defend himself or another against such other's imminent use of unlawful force...." * * *

3. We hold that a justification corresponding roughly to that quoted [above] is recognized by the law of the Commonwealth. * * *

There is some but not much light in the decided cases in this jurisdiction about justified force used in aid of another. [The court briefly reviewed *Commonwealth v. Cooley,* 6 Gray 350 (1856) and *Commonwealth v. Malone,* 114 Mass. 295 (1973).] These cases are suggestive but laconic. The paucity of direct authority is perhaps explained by the likelihood that one coming to the defense of another may himself be, or come to be, under attack, and may thus simply claim self-defense, a less esoteric justification.[9]

Whatever the precise precedents, it is hardly conceivable that the law of the Commonwealth, or, indeed, of any jurisdiction, should mark as criminal those who intervene forcibly to protect others; for the law to do so would aggravate the fears which lead to the alienation of people from one another, an alienation symbolized for our time by the notorious Genovese incident [see p. 92 supra—ed.]. To the fear of "involvement" and of injury to oneself if one answered a call for help would be added the fear of possible criminal prosecution.

It becomes necessary to sketch the conditions justifying the use of intervening protective force. The essence is this: An actor is justified in using force against another to protect a third person when (a) a reasonable person in the actor's position would believe his intervention to be necessary for the protection of the third person, and (b) in the circumstances as that reasonable person would believe them to be, the third person would be justified in using such force to protect himself. The reasonableness of the belief may depend in part on the relationships among the persons involved (a matter to which we return below). The actor's justification is lost if he uses excessive force, e.g., aggressive or deadly force unwarranted for the protective purpose.

Of course, the subject cannot be exhausted in a paragraph. Without subscribing in advance to all the relevant provisions of the Model Penal Code * * *, we recommend it for study.[13] Accelerated by that Code, the trend, which is exemplified by legislation adopted in many States, has been to interweave closely the justification of defense of a third person

---

9. It has been suggested also that cases in which the justification of third-person defense might be available have been tried on a footing of preventing crime.

13. The principal sections of the Code to be consulted are §§ 3.05(1), 3.09(1)–(2), 3.04(1), (2)(a)(i), (b).

with self-defense; to eliminate some earlier authority restricting the justification of third-person defense to situations where the third person is seen retrospectively to have been entitled to use force in his own defense (regardless of the belief, which might be mistaken, of the "reasonable person" at the time),[15] and to remove earlier artificial or factitious restrictions of the justification, e.g., restrictions to protection of spouse, child, parent, master, or servant.

One such possible factitious restriction was rejected, we think correctly, in *United States v. Grimes,* 413 F.2d 1376 (7th Cir.1969), a case resembling the present. The defendant Grimes, an inmate of the Federal penitentiary in Marion, Illinois, seeing (as he claimed) a fellow inmate, Reid, being beaten by prison guards with metal flashlights, ran to Reid's aid and struck one of the guards. Grimes was indicted and convicted of assault upon an employee of a United States correctional institution. On appeal, it was held that the trial judge erred in refusing a jury instruction regarding justified use of force to protect a third person. The court spoke as follows to the point that, while the justification might be suitable generally, it should be rejected in the prison context because of its effect on institutional discipline: "We perceive no serious threat to prison discipline from a defense which merely protects inmates from unauthorized physical abuse by overzealous officials. Our decision in no way limits the power of prison officials to restrain or subdue unruly inmates, to carry out all reasonable orders necessary for the maintenance of prison discipline, or to cope with attempted assaults or escapes by prison inmates.["] * * *

We agree with the court in the *Grimes* case that the justification of a defense of a third person does not necessarily stop short at the prison gates. But the fact that an episode occurs in prison may have considerable significance. So the question of the reasonableness of a belief that an inmate would be justified in using force against a prison guard, thus justifying intervening protective force, is conditioned by the fact that the guard, by the nature of his job, is himself privileged to apply force to inmates when necessary to preserve order in the institution. Therefore the guard's mere taking an inmate into custody or holding him in custody would not be a proper occasion for intervening force. This may have an important bearing on the present case in the event of retrial.

Notes and Questions

1. In *People v. Young,* cited in footnote 15, Young intervened to assist someone he believed was being wrongfully attacked, but who actually was being placed under lawful arrest by a police officer dressed in civilian clothing. Young was charged with assault.

The New York Court of Appeals applied the common law and then-majority rule that "the right of a person to defend another ordinarily should not be greater than such person's right to defend himself." This is some-

---

15. In New York, for example, the restrictive decision of People v. Young, 11 N.Y.2d 274, 229 N.Y.S.2d 1, 183 N.E.2d 319 (1962), may be taken to be overruled by N.Y.Penal Law § 35.15 (McKinney 1975).

times called the "alter ego rule," in that it places the person who comes to the aid of another in the shoes of the individual for whom he was providing assistance. According to *Young,* the contrary position—that one may act on the basis of a reasonable belief—"would not be conducive to an orderly society." 11 N.Y.2d at 275, 229 N.Y.S.2d at 2, 183 N.E.2d at 319–320.

Which approach—*Martin* or *Young*—is preferable? Which rule is more likely to lead to a "more orderly society"? Do you agree with the observation that "citizens [are] reluctant—or afraid—to become 'involved' in deterring * * * violence," but that the reason for "[t]his reticence seem[s] to emanate less from fear of physical harm than from the potential consequences of a legal aftermath"? Alexander v. State, 52 Md.App. 171, 172, 447 A.2d 880, 881 (1982).

2. *Problem.* Paula, an undercover police officer, points a gun at Xavier, whom she is lawfully arresting for a murder. Sam, an innocent bystander, believing that Paula is an aggressor, comes to Xavier's assistance by pointing a licensed firearm at Paula, and yelling, "Drop your gun or I'll shoot!" Paula shoots and kills Sam. May she successfully claim self-defense? Apply the Model Penal Code.

3. Reconsider Note 10 (p. 415 supra), in which Rosa found herself on an elevator with an hallucinating mental patient, Herman, who was threatening her with a knife. If a third person had been on board, would he have been justified in killing Herman to defend Rosa?

4. DEFENSE OF PROPERTY/HABITATION AND LAW ENFORCEMENT DEFENSES

PEOPLE v. CEBALLOS

Supreme Court of California, 1974.
12 Cal.3d 470, 116 Cal.Rptr. 233, 526 P.2d 241.

BURKE, JUSTICE.

Don Ceballos was found guilty by a jury of assault with a deadly weapon. * * * He appeals from the judgment, contending primarily that his conduct was not unlawful because the alleged victim was attempting to commit burglary when hit by a trap gun mounted in the garage of defendant's dwelling and that the court erred in instructing the jury. We have concluded that the * * * judgment should be affirmed.

Defendant lived alone in a home in San Anselmo. The regular living quarters were above the garage, but defendant sometimes slept in the garage and had about $2,000 worth of property there.

In March 1970 some tools were stolen from defendant's home. On May 12, 1970, he noticed the lock on his garage doors was bent and pry marks were on one of the doors. The next day he mounted a loaded .22 caliber pistol in the garage. The pistol was aimed at the center of the garage doors and was connected by a wire to one of the doors so that the pistol would discharge if the door was opened several inches.

The damage to defendant's lock had been done by a 16–year–old boy named Stephen and a 15–year–old boy named Robert. On the afternoon of May 15, 1970, the boys returned to defendant's house while he was away. Neither boy was armed with a gun or knife. After looking in the windows and seeing no one, Stephen succeeded in removing the lock on the garage doors with a crowbar, and, as he pulled the door outward, he was hit in the face with a bullet from the pistol.

Stephen testified: He intended to go into the garage "[f]or musical equipment" because he had a debt to pay to a friend. His "way of paying that debt would be to take [defendant's] property and sell it" and use the proceeds to pay the debt. He "wasn't going to do it [i.e., steal] for sure, necessarily." He was there "to look around," and "getting in, I don't know if I would have actually stolen."

Defendant, testifying in his own behalf, admitted having set up the trap gun. * * *

When asked by the police shortly after the shooting why he assembled the trap gun, defendant stated that "he didn't have much and he wanted to protect what he did have."

As heretofore appears, the jury found defendant guilty of assault with a deadly weapon. An assault is "an unlawful attempt, coupled with a present ability, to commit a violent injury on the person of another." (Pen.Code, § 240.)

Defendant contends that had he been present he would have been justified in shooting Stephen since Stephen was attempting to commit burglary, that * * * defendant had a right to do indirectly what he could have done directly, and that therefore any attempt by him to commit a violent injury upon Stephen was not "unlawful" and hence not an assault. The People argue that * * * as a matter of law a trap gun constitutes excessive force, and that in any event the circumstances were not in fact such as to warrant the use of deadly force. * * *

At common law in England it was held that a trespasser, having knowledge that there are spring guns in a wood, cannot maintain an action for an injury received in consequence of his accidentally stepping on the wire of such gun. That [rule] aroused such a protest in England that it was abrogated seven years later by a statute, which made it a misdemeanor to set spring guns with intent to inflict grievous bodily injury but excluded from its operation a spring gun set between sunset and sunrise in a dwelling house for the protection thereof. (7 & 8 Geo. IV, ch. 18.)

In the United States, courts have concluded that a person may be held criminally liable under statutes proscribing homicides and shooting with intent to injure, or civilly liable, if he sets upon his premises a deadly mechanical device and that device kills or injures another. However, an exception to the rule that there may be criminal and civil liability for death or injuries caused by such a device has been recognized where the intrusion is, in fact, such that the person, were he present, would be justified in taking the life or inflicting the bodily harm with his own hands. The phrase "were he present" does not hypothesize the actual presence of the person, but is used in setting forth in an indirect manner the principle that a person may do indirectly that which he is privileged to do directly.

Allowing persons, at their own risk, to employ deadly mechanical devices imperils the lives of children, firemen and policemen acting within the scope of their employment, and others. Where the actor is present, there is always the possibility he will realize that deadly force is not necessary, but deadly mechanical devices are without mercy or discretion. Such devices "are silent instrumentalities of death. They deal death and destruction to the innocent as well as the criminal intruder without the slightest warning. The taking of human life [or infliction of great bodily injury] by such means is brutally savage and inhuman." (See State v. Plumlee, [177 La. 687,] 149 So. 425, 430.)

It seems clear that the use of such devices should not be encouraged. Moreover, whatever may be thought in torts, the foregoing rule setting forth an exception to liability for death or injuries inflicted by such devices "is inappropriate in penal law for it is obvious that it does not prescribe a workable standard of conduct; liability depends upon fortuitous results." (See Model Penal Code (Tent.Draft No. 8), § 3.06, com. 15.) We therefore decline to adopt that rule in criminal cases.

Furthermore, even if that rule were applied here, * * * defendant was not justified in shooting Stephen. Penal Code section 197 provides: "Homicide is ... justifiable ... 1. When resisting any attempt to murder any person, or to commit a felony, or to do some great bodily injury upon any person; or, 2. When committed in defense of habitation, property, or person, against one who manifestly intends or endeavors, by violence or surprise, to commit a felony...." Since a homicide is justifiable under the circumstances specified in section 197, *a fortiori* an attempt to commit a violent injury upon another under those circumstances is justifiable.

By its terms subdivision 1 of Penal Code section 197 appears to permit killing to prevent any "felony," but in view of the large number of felonies today and the inclusion of many that do not involve a danger of serious bodily harm, a literal reading of the section is undesirable. People v. Jones, 191 Cal.App.2d 478, 481, 12 Cal.Rptr. 777 * * * read into section 197, subdivision 1, the limitation that the felony be "some atrocious crime attempted to be committed by force." * * *

* * * [W]hatever may have been the very early common law, the rule developed at common law that killing or use of deadly force to prevent a felony was justified only if the offense was a forcible and atrocious crime. * * *

Examples of forcible and atrocious crimes are murder, mayhem, rape and robbery. In such crimes "from their atrocity and violence human life [or personal safety from great harm] either is, or is presumed to be, in peril."

Burglary has been included in the list of such crimes. However, in view of the wide scope of burglary under Penal Code section 459, as compared with the common law definition of that offense, in our opinion it cannot be said that under all circumstances burglary under section 459 constitutes a forcible and atrocious crime.[2]

Where the character and manner of the burglary do not reasonably create a fear of great bodily harm, there is no cause for exaction of human life, or for the use of deadly force. The character and manner of the burglary could not reasonably create such a fear unless the burglary threatened, or was reasonably believed to threaten, death or serious bodily harm.

In the instant case the asserted burglary did not threaten death or serious bodily harm, since no one but Stephen and Robert was then on the premises. A defendant is not protected from liability merely by the fact that the intruder's conduct is such as would justify the defendant, were he present, in believing that the intrusion threatened death or serious bodily injury. There is ordinarily the possibility that the defendant, were he present, would realize the true state of affairs and recognize the intruder as one whom he would not be justified in killing or wounding.

We thus conclude that defendant was not justified under Penal Code section 197, subdivisions 1 or 2, in shooting Stephen to prevent him from committing burglary. * * *

Defendant also argues that had he been present he would have been justified in shooting Stephen under subdivision 4 of Penal Code section 197, which provides, "Homicide is . . . justifiable . . . 4. When necessarily committed in *attempting,* by lawful ways and means, *to apprehend* any person for any felony committed. . . ." (Italics added.) The argument cannot be upheld. The words "attempting . . . to apprehend" contain the idea of acting for the purpose of apprehending. * * * Here no showing was made that defendant's intent in shooting was to apprehend a felon. Rather it appears from his testimony and extrajudicial statement heretofore recited that his intent was to prevent a burglary, to protect his property, and to avoid the possibility that a thief might get into defendant's house and injure him upon his return. * * *

Defendant also does not, and could not properly, contend that the intrusion was in fact such that, were he present, he would be justified under Civil Code section 50 in using deadly force. That section provides, "Any necessary force may be used to protect from wrongful injury the person or property of oneself. . . ." This section also should be read in the light of the common law, and at common law in general deadly force

---

2. At common law burglary was the breaking and entering of a mansion house in the night with the intent to commit a felony. Burglary under Penal Code section 459 differs from common law burglary in that the entry may be in the daytime and of numerous places other than a mansion house, and breaking is not required. For example, under section 459 a person who enters a store with the intent of committing theft is guilty of burglary. It would seem absurd to hold that a store detective could kill that person if necessary to prevent him from committing that offense.

could not be used solely for the protection of property. " 'The preservation of human life and limb from grievous harm is of more importance to society than the protection of property.' " * * *

At common law an exception to the foregoing principle that deadly force could not be used solely for the protection of property was recognized where the property was a dwelling house in some circumstances. "According to the older interpretation of the common law, even extreme force may be used to prevent dispossession [of the dwelling house]." (See Model Penal Code, *supra,* com. 8.) Also at common law if another attempted to burn a dwelling the owner was privileged to use deadly force if this seemed necessary to defend his "castle" against the threatened harm. Further, deadly force was privileged if it was, or reasonably seemed, necessary to protect the dwelling against a burglar.

Here we are not concerned with dispossession or burning of a dwelling, and, as heretofore concluded, the asserted burglary in this case was not of such a character as to warrant the use of deadly force. * * *

We conclude that as a matter of law the exception to the rule of liability for injuries inflicted by a deadly mechanical device does not apply under the circumstances here appearing. * * *

Notes and Questions

1. *Defense of property/habitation.* In view of the fact that deadly force in defense of property is unjustifiable, why does the common law permit its use to prevent an intrusion into the home? (In the latter circumstance, the defense is sometimes called the "defense of habitation," in order to distinguish it from the force used to defend personal property and real property other than the home.) Is the purpose of the defense to prevent death or serious injury to the occupants of the dwelling? If so, why not assert the defense of self-defense? Is it to prevent a crime from being committed inside? If so, why not invoke the defense of crime prevention? Is it to protect the occupant's right of privacy? If so, is deadly force a proportionate response to the harm threatened?

Various statutory and common law versions of the defense of habitation are recognized. In a few states the defense is expressed in very broad terms, such as the following:

> We think it may be safely laid down to be the law of this State that a man's habitation is one place where he may rest secure in the knowledge that he will not be disturbed by persons, coming within, without proper invitation or warrant, and that he may use all of the force apparently necessary to repel any invasion of his home.

People v. Eatman, 405 Ill. 491, 498, 91 N.E.2d 387, 390 (1950). See also State v. Reid, 3 Ohio App.2d 215, 221, 210 N.E.2d 142, 147 (1965) ("[I]t is the law that where * * * the home itself is attacked, [the dweller] may use such means as are necessary to * * * prevent his forcible entry, or material injury to his home, even to the taking of life.").

Is this too broad a defense? For example, assume that Leonard, after too long a night at the bar, becomes confused and tries to enter the unlocked front door of the house of his neighbor, Teresa, thinking it is his own. Teresa sees Leonard preparing to enter. She recognizes him and realizes that he is confused about his location. She calls out to him to stop, but he does not hear her. Under *Eatman,* may she shoot him? Under *Reid?*

A more common version of the defense authorizes the use of deadly force to prevent an uninvited entry into a home "if there exist reasonable and factual grounds to believe that unless so used, a felony would be committed." Falco v. State, 407 So.2d 203, 208 (Fla.1981). Under this rule, may Teresa shoot Leonard?

Some statutes only permit deadly force if the intruder represents an apparent threat to the safety of an occupant. How great must the threat be? Consider West's Colo.Rev.Stat.Ann. § 18–1–704.5 (1986), the so-called "Make My Day Law," which provides in part:

(1) The general assembly hereby recognizes that the citizens of Colorado have a right to expect absolute safety within their own homes.

(2) * * * [A]ny occupant of a dwelling is justified in using any degree of physical force, including deadly physical force, against another person when * * * the occupant has a reasonable belief that such other person has committed a crime in the dwelling in addition to the uninvited entry, or is committing or intends to commit a crime against a person or property in addition to the uninvited entry, and when the occupant reasonably believes that such other person might use any physical force, no matter how slight, against any occupant.

(3) Any occupant of a dwelling using physical force, including deadly force, in accordance with the provisions of subsection (2) of this section shall be immune from criminal prosecution for the use of such force.

In Colorado, suppose that Alex, drunken and boisterous, stands outside a house belonging to his neighbors, Nick and Nora, yelling obscenities and challenging Nick to come outside and fight. Nora opens the front door. Alex, standing just outside the doorway, puts his hand gently on Nora's shoulder and asks, "Where's your damn husband? I want him to come out." As Alex takes his hand off Nora's shoulder, Nick shoots him with .357 Magnum six-inch revolver. Is the killing justifiable? Procedurally, what is the implication of subsection (3)? See People v. Guenther, 740 P.2d 971 (Colo.1987).

Suppose that Alex had *not* put his hand on Nora's shoulder. Would this change the outcome? Suppose that he had put his hand on her shoulder, but Nora was standing just outside the house when it happened. What then?

In what ways is the defense of habitation in *Ceballos* narrower than any of the versions of the defense described in this Note? In what way is it *broader* than the defense of self-defense?

2. The defense of habitation is usually asserted when an occupant of a home uses deadly force to prevent an intrusion into her "castle." If the resident is justified in such circumstances, should she be permitted to kill the intruder after the entry is complete? See People v. Stombaugh, 52 Ill.2d 130, 284 N.E.2d 640 (1972) (permitting the defense); State v. McCombs, 297

N.C. 151, 253 S.E.2d 906 (1979) (disallowing the defense). What are the competing arguments?

3. *Problem.* People v. Godfrey, 80 N.Y.2d 860, 861–62, 587 N.Y.S.2d 594, 595, 600 N.E.2d 225, 226 (1992):

> [O]n the evening in question, [the defendant] and Marsh [the victim] became involved in a heated argument, and eventually agreed to physically settle their dispute at defendant's home. Upon arriving there, defendant—at Marsh's urging—immediately went to his bedroom to get his gun. Before he could return, however, Marsh entered the room and began approaching him. A violent struggle * * * ensued. When it finally subsided, defendant demanded that Marsh leave his house. Marsh * * * refused, and began walking toward defendant. As he did, he told defendant, "You got your gun, use it, if you don't, I will." Marsh then attempted to take defendant's gun from him, but defendant was able to "shove him off." Undeterred, Marsh again approached defendant. This time, however, defendant responded by shooting him.

The defendant requested jury instructions regarding self-defense and use of physical force to terminate a burglary. On the latter issue, what should be the result? Apply Model Penal Code § 3.06.

4. *Spring guns.* Do you agree with *Ceballos* that an occupant of a home should be punished for using a spring gun to prevent a forcible entry, even if she would be justified in personally killing the intruder? *Ceballos* explains why mechanical devices are undesirable, but what are the arguments for permitting their use?

5. *Short excursus on burglary.* As the materials demonstrate, deadly force is often justifiable as a means to thwart a common law burglary. Why is this? One way to think about this question is to consider why burglary is a felony. That is, what distinguishes a burglary from such misdemeanor offenses as trespass or unlawful entry? To answer this question you ought to consider the elements of the common law offense. Burglaries are limited to entries into dwelling-houses, as distinguished from commercial property. Why is this? The offense only applies to entries at night. Why? And why is the offense not complete unless the intruder enters with the specific intent to commit a felony inside?

Burglary laws are traditionally justified on three grounds. See Note, *A Rationale of the Law of Burglary,* 51 Colum.L.Rev. 1009 (1951). First, the fact of uninvited entry "gives rise to a probability of emotional distress on the part of the occupants." Id. at 1020. Second, entry into a home, particularly at night, creates a risk "that there will be violent resistance." Id.

Third, the offense functions as a remedy for perceived defects relating to the common law crime of attempt. To be guilty of an attempt (see Chapter 10 infra), a person must come fairly close to completing the intended crime. Therefore, one who breaks into a home in order to commit a crime inside, for example a theft, cannot usually be arrested for an attempt to commit the latter offense until she is already in the house, at which point it may be too late for the police to protect the dweller or her property. By making it an offense to break and enter a dwelling for a felonious purpose, the police may arrest an intruder before matters become too dangerous.

6. *Crime prevention.* There is limited support for the proposition that a police officer or private party may use deadly force, if necessary, to prevent the commission of *any* felony. E.g., State v. Sundberg, 611 P.2d 44 (Alaska 1980). However, most states, as in *Ceballos,* now limit the application of the crime prevention defense to forcible or atrocious felonies. Deadly force is never permitted to prevent a misdemeanor. Durham v. State, 199 Ind. 567, 574, 159 N.E. 145, 147 (1927).

Once a felony is committed, the defense of crime prevention no longer applies, i.e., there is no felony to prevent. However, a related law enforcement defense—one that justifies the use of force in order to effectuate an arrest or to prevent the escape of an arrestee—may apply. The next case concerns this defense.

TENNESSEE v. GARNER

Supreme Court of the United States, 1985.
471 U.S. 1, 105 S.Ct. 1694, 85 L.Ed.2d 1.

JUSTICE WHITE delivered the opinion of the Court.

This case requires us to determine the constitutionality of the use of deadly force to prevent the escape of an apparently unarmed suspected felon. We conclude that such force may not be used unless it is necessary to prevent the escape and the officer has probable cause to believe that the suspect poses a significant threat of death or serious physical injury to the officer or others.

I

At about 10:45 p.m. on October 3, 1974, Memphis Police Officers Elton Hymon and Leslie Wright were dispatched to answer a "prowler inside call." Upon arriving at the scene they saw a woman standing on her porch and gesturing toward the adjacent house. She told them she had heard glass breaking and that "they" or "someone" was breaking in next door. While Wright radioed the dispatcher to say that they were on the scene, Hymon went behind the house. He heard a door slam and saw someone run across the backyard. The fleeing suspect, * * * Edward Garner, stopped at a 6–feet–high chain link fence at the edge of the yard. With the aid of a flashlight, Hymon was able to see Garner's face and hands. He saw no sign of a weapon, and, though not certain, was "reasonably sure" and "figured" that Garner was unarmed. He thought Garner was 17 or 18 years old and about 5′5″ or 5′7″ tall.[2] While Garner was crouched at the base of the fence, Hymon called out "police, halt" and took a few steps toward him. Garner then began to climb over the fence. Convinced that if Garner made it over the fence

2. In fact, Garner, an eighth-grader, was 15. He was 5′4″ tall and weighed somewhere around 100 or 110 pounds.

he would elude capture,[3] Hymon shot him. The bullet hit Garner in the back of the head. Garner * * * died on the operating table. Ten dollars and a purse taken from the house were found on his body.

In using deadly force to prevent the escape, Hymon was acting under the authority of a Tennessee statute and pursuant to Police Department policy. The statute provides that "[i]f, after notice of the intention to arrest the defendant, he either flee or forcibly resist, the officer may use all the necessary means to effect the arrest." Tenn.Code Ann. § 40–7–108 (1982).[5] The Department policy was slightly more restrictive than the statute, but still allowed the use of deadly force in cases of burglary. The incident was reviewed by the Memphis Police Firearm's Review Board and presented to a grand jury. Neither took any action.

Garner's father then brought this action in the Federal District Court for the Western District of Tennessee, seeking damages under 42 U.S.C. § 1983 for asserted violations of Garner's constitutional rights.[d] The complaint alleged that the shooting violated the Fourth, Fifth, Sixth, Eighth, and Fourteenth Amendments of the United States Constitution. It named as defendants Officer Hymon, the Police Department, its Director, and the Mayor and city of Memphis. After a 3–day bench trial, the District Court entered judgment for all defendants. * * * It * * * concluded that Hymon's actions were authorized by the Tennessee statute, which in turn was constitutional. Hymon had employed the only reasonable and practicable means of preventing Garner's escape. Garner had "recklessly and heedlessly attempted to vault over the fence to escape, thereby assuming the risk of being fired upon." * * *

The Court of Appeals reversed and remanded. It reasoned that the killing of a fleeing suspect is a "seizure" under the Fourth Amendment,[6] and is therefore constitutional only if "reasonable." The Tennessee statute failed as applied to this case because it did not adequately limit the use of deadly force by distinguishing between felonies of different magnitudes—"the facts, as found, did not justify the use of deadly force under the Fourth Amendment." * * * *[7]

The State of Tennessee * * * appealed to this Court. * * *

---

3. When asked at trial why he fired, Hymon stated * * * that the area beyond the fence was dark, that he could not have gotten over the fence easily because he was carrying a lot of equipment and wearing heavy boots, and that Garner, being younger and more energetic, could have outrun him.

5. Although the statute does not say so explicitly, Tennessee law forbids the use of deadly force in the arrest of a misdemeanant.

d. Section 1983 provides: "Every person who, under color of [law] * * *, subjects, or causes to be subjected, any citizen of the United States * * * to the deprivation of any rights * * * secured by the Constitution * * *, shall be liable to the party injured in an action at law * * *."

6. "The right of the people to be secure in their persons ... against unreasonable searches and seizures, shall not be violated...." U.S. Const., Amdt. 4.

7. The Court of Appeals concluded that the rule set out in the Model Penal Code [§ 3.07(2)(b)] "accurately states Fourth Amendment limitations on the use of deadly force against fleeing felons." * * *

II

Whenever an officer restrains the freedom of a person to walk away, he has seized that person. While it is not always clear just when minimal police interference becomes a seizure, there can be no question that apprehension by the use of deadly force is a seizure subject to the reasonableness requirement of the Fourth Amendment.

A

A police officer may arrest a person if he has probable cause to believe that person committed a crime. Petitioners and appellant argue that if this requirement is satisfied the Fourth Amendment has nothing to say about *how* that seizure is made. This submission ignores the many cases in which this Court, by balancing the extent of the intrusion against the need for it, has examined the reasonableness of the manner in which a search or seizure is conducted. * * *

B

The same balancing process * * * demonstrates that, notwithstanding probable cause to seize a suspect, an officer may not always do so by killing him. The intrusiveness of a seizure by means of deadly force is unmatched. The suspect's fundamental interest in his own life need not be elaborated upon. The use of deadly force also frustrates the interest of the individual, and of society, in judicial determination of guilt and punishment. Against these interests are ranged governmental interests in effective law enforcement.[8] It is argued that overall violence will be reduced by encouraging the peaceful submission of suspects who know that they may be shot if they flee. Effectiveness in making arrests requires the resort to deadly force, or at least the meaningful threat thereof. * * *

Without in any way disparaging the importance of these goals, we are not convinced that the use of deadly force is a sufficiently productive means of accomplishing them to justify the killing of nonviolent suspects. The use of deadly force is a self-defeating way of apprehending a suspect and so setting the criminal justice mechanism in motion. If successful, it guarantees that that mechanism will not be set in motion. And while the meaningful threat of deadly force might be thought to lead to the arrest of more live suspects by discouraging escape attempts, the presently available evidence does not support this thesis. The fact is that a majority of police departments in this country have forbidden the use of deadly force against nonviolent suspects. If those charged with the enforcement of the criminal law have abjured the use of deadly force in arresting nondangerous felons, there is a substantial basis for doubting that the use of such force is an essential attribute of the arrest power in all felony cases. Petitioners and appellant have not persuaded us that

---

8. The dissent emphasizes that subsequent investigation cannot replace immediate apprehension. We recognize that this is so * * *. Nonetheless, it should be remembered that failure to apprehend at the scene does not necessarily mean that the suspect will never be caught. * * *

shooting nondangerous fleeing suspects is so vital as to outweigh the suspect's interest in his own life.

The use of deadly force to prevent the escape of all felony suspects, whatever the circumstances, is constitutionally unreasonable. It is not better that all felony suspects die than that they escape. Where the suspect poses no immediate threat to the officer and no threat to others, the harm resulting from failing to apprehend him does not justify the use of deadly force to do so. It is no doubt unfortunate when a suspect who is in sight escapes, but the fact that the police arrive a little late or are a little slower afoot does not always justify killing the suspect. A police officer may not seize an unarmed, nondangerous suspect by shooting him dead. The Tennessee statute is unconstitutional insofar as it authorizes the use of deadly force against such fleeing suspects.

It is not, however, unconstitutional on its face. Where the officer has probable cause to believe that the suspect poses a threat of serious physical harm, either to the officer or to others, it is not constitutionally unreasonable to prevent escape by using deadly force. Thus, if the suspect threatens the officer with a weapon or there is probable cause to believe that he has committed a crime involving the infliction or threatened infliction of serious physical harm, deadly force may be used if necessary to prevent escape, and if, where feasible, some warning has been given. As applied in such circumstances, the Tennessee statute would pass constitutional muster.

III

A

It is insisted that the Fourth Amendment must be construed in light of the common-law rule, which allowed the use of whatever force was necessary to effect the arrest of a fleeing felon, though not a misdemeanant. * * * Most American jurisdictions also imposed a flat prohibition against the use of deadly force to stop a fleeing misdemeanant, coupled with a general privilege to use such force to stop a fleeing felon. * * *

B

It has been pointed out many times that the common-law rule is best understood in light of the fact that it arose at a time when virtually all felonies were punishable by death.[11] "Though effected without the protections and formalities of an orderly trial and conviction, the killing of a resisting or fleeing felon resulted in no greater consequences than those authorized for punishment of the felony of which the individual was charged or suspected." American Law Institute, Model Penal Code

---

11. The roots of the concept of a "felony" lie not in capital punishment but in forfeiture. 2 F. Pollock & F. Maitland, The History of English Law 465 (2d ed. 1909). Not all felonies were always punishable by death. Nonetheless, the link was profound. Blackstone was able to write: "The idea of felony is indeed so generally connected with that of capital punishment, that we find it hard to separate them; and to this usage the interpretations of the law do now conform. And therefore if a statute makes any new offence felony, the law implies that is shall be punished with death, viz. by hanging, as well as with forfeiture...." 4 W. Blackstone, Commentaries *98.

§ 3.07, Comment 3, p. 56 (Tentative Draft No. 8, 1958). Courts have also justified the common-law rule by emphasizing the relative dangerousness of felons.

Neither of these justifications makes sense today. Almost all crimes formerly punishable by death no longer are or can be. And while in earlier times "the gulf between the felonies and the minor offences was broad and deep," 2 Pollock & Maitland 467, today the distinction is minor and often arbitrary. Many crimes classified as misdemeanors, or nonexistent, at common law are now felonies. These changes have undermined the concept, which was questionable to begin with, that use of deadly force against a fleeing felon is merely a speedier execution of someone who has already forfeited his life. They have also made the assumption that a "felon" is more dangerous than a misdemeanant untenable. Indeed, numerous misdemeanors involve conduct more dangerous than many felonies.[12]

There is an additional reason why the common-law rule cannot be directly translated to the present day. The common-law rule developed at a time when weapons were rudimentary. Deadly force could be inflicted almost solely in a hand-to-hand struggle during which, necessarily, the safety of the arresting officer was at risk. Handguns were not carried by police officers until the latter half of the last century. Only then did it become possible to use deadly force from a distance as a means of apprehension. As a practical matter, the use of deadly force under the standard articulation of the common-law rule has an altogether different meaning—and harsher consequences—now than in past centuries. * * *

In short, though the common-law pedigree of Tennessee's rule is pure on its face, changes in the legal and technological context mean the rule is distorted almost beyond recognition when literally applied.

C

In evaluating the reasonableness of police procedures under the Fourth Amendment, we have also looked to prevailing rules in individual jurisdictions. * * *

It cannot be said that there is a constant or overwhelming trend away from the common-law rule. In recent years, some States have reviewed their laws and expressly rejected abandonment of the common-law rule. Nonetheless, the long-term movement has been away from the rule that deadly force may be used against any fleeing felon, and that remains the rule in less than half the States.

This trend is more evident and impressive when viewed in light of the policies adopted by the police departments themselves. Overwhelmingly, these are more restrictive than the common-law rule. The Federal Bureau of Investigation and the New York City Police Department, for

12. White-collar crime, for example, poses a less significant physical threat than, say, drunken driving.

example, both forbid the use of firearms except when necessary to prevent death or grievous bodily harm. * * * A 1974 study reported that the police department regulations in a majority of the large cities of the United States allowed the firing of a weapon only when a felon presented a threat of death or serious bodily harm. * * * In light of the rules adopted by those who must actually administer them, the older and fading common-law view is a dubious indicium of the constitutionality of the Tennessee statute now before us.

D

Actual departmental policies are important for an additional reason. We would hesitate to declare a police practice of long standing "unreasonable" if doing so would severely hamper effective law enforcement. But the indications are to the contrary. There has been no suggestion that crime has worsened in any way in jurisdictions that have adopted, by legislation or departmental policy, rules similar to that announced today. * * *

Nor do we agree with petitioners and appellant that the rule we have adopted requires the police to make impossible, split-second evaluations of unknowable facts. We do not deny the practical difficulties of attempting to assess the suspect's dangerousness. However, similarly difficult judgments must be made by the police in equally uncertain circumstances. * * * Moreover, the highly technical felony/misdemeanor distinction is equally, if not more, difficult to apply in the field. An officer is in no position to know, for example, the precise value of property stolen * * *. * * *

IV

The District Court concluded that Hymon was justified in shooting Garner because state law allows, and the Federal Constitution does not forbid, the use of deadly force to prevent the escape of a fleeing felony suspect if no alternative means of apprehension is available. This conclusion made a determination of Garner's apparent dangerousness unnecessary. The court did find, however, that Garner appeared to be unarmed, though Hymon could not be certain that was the case. Restated in Fourth Amendment terms, this means Hymon had no articulable basis to think Garner was armed.

In reversing, the Court of Appeals accepted the District Court's factual conclusions and held that "the facts, as found, did not justify the use of deadly force." We agree. Officer Hymon could not reasonably have believed that Garner—young, slight, and unarmed—posed any threat. Indeed, Hymon never attempted to justify his actions on any basis other than the need to prevent an escape. The District Court stated in passing that "[t]he facts of this case did not indicate to Officer Hymon that Garner was 'non-dangerous.'" This conclusion is not explained, and seems to be based solely on the fact that Garner had broken into a house at night. However, the fact that Garner was a suspected burglar could not, without regard to the other circumstances, automatically justify the use of deadly force. Hymon did not have probable cause to believe that Garner, whom he correctly believed to be unarmed, posed any physical danger to himself or others.

The dissent argues that the shooting was justified by the fact that Officer Hymon had probable cause to believe that Garner had committed a nighttime burglary. While we agree that burglary is a serious crime, we cannot agree that it is so dangerous as automatically to justify the use of deadly force. The FBI classifies burglary as a "property" rather than a "violent" crime. See Federal Bureau of Investigation, Uniform Crime Reports, Crime in the United States 1 (1984). Although the armed burglar would present a different situation, the fact that an unarmed suspect has broken into a dwelling at night does not automatically mean he is physically dangerous. * * * In fact, the available statistics demonstrate that burglaries only rarely involve physical violence. During the 10–year period from 1973–1982, only 3.8% of all burglaries involved violent crime. Bureau of Justice Statistics, Household Burglary 4 (1985).

V

* * * We hold that the statute is invalid insofar as it purported to give Hymon the authority to act as he did. * * *

JUSTICE O'CONNOR, with whom THE CHIEF JUSTICE and JUSTICE REHNQUIST join, dissenting.

* * * Although the circumstances of this case are unquestionably tragic and unfortunate, our constitutional holdings must be sensitive both to the history of the Fourth Amendment and to the general implications of the Court's reasoning. By disregarding the serious and dangerous nature of residential burglaries and the longstanding practice of many States, the Court effectively creates a Fourth Amendment right allowing a burglary suspect to flee unimpeded from a police officer who has probable cause to arrest, who has ordered the suspect to halt, and who has no means short of firing his weapon to prevent escape. I do not believe that the Fourth Amendment supports such a right, and I accordingly dissent. * * *

The public interest involved in the use of deadly force as a last resort to apprehend a fleeing burglary suspect relates primarily to the serious nature of the crime. Household burglaries not only represent the illegal entry into a person's home, but also "pos[e] real risk of serious harm to others." According to recent Department of Justice statistics, "[t]hree-fifths of all rapes in the home, three-fifths of all home robberies, and about a third of home aggravated and simple assaults are committed by burglars." Bureau of Justice Statistics Bulletin, Household Burglary 1 (January 1985). * * * Victims of a forcible intrusion into their home by a nighttime prowler will find little consolation in the majority's confident assertion that "burglaries only rarely involve physical violence." Moreover, even if a particular burglary, when viewed in retrospect, does not involve physical harm to others, the "harsh potentialities for violence" inherent in the forced entry into a home preclude characterization of the crime as "innocuous, inconsequential, minor, or 'nonviolent.'"   * * *

Because burglary is a serious and dangerous felony, the public interest in the prevention and detection of the crime is of compelling importance.   Where a police officer has probable cause to arrest a suspected burglar, the use of deadly force as a last resort might well be the only means of apprehending the suspect.   * * *

Against the strong public interests justifying the conduct at issue here must be weighed the individual interests implicated in the use of deadly force by police officers.   The majority declares that "[t]he suspect's fundamental interest in his own life need not be elaborated upon." This blithe assertion hardly provides an adequate substitute for the majority's failure to acknowledge the distinctive manner in which the suspect's interest in his life is even exposed to risk.   For purposes of this case, we must recall that the police officer, in the course of investigating a nighttime burglary, had reasonable cause to arrest the suspect and ordered him to halt.   The officer's use of force resulted because the suspected burglar refused to heed this command and the officer reasonably believed that there was no means short of firing his weapon to apprehend the suspect.   Without questioning the importance of a person's interest in his life, I do not think this interest encompasses a right to flee unimpeded from the scene of a burglary.   * * *   The legitimate interests of the suspect in these circumstances are adequately accommodated by the Tennessee statute: to avoid the use of deadly force and the consequent risk to his life, the suspect need merely obey the valid order to halt.

A proper balancing of the interests involved suggests that use of deadly force as a last resort to apprehend a criminal suspect fleeing from the scene of a nighttime burglary is not unreasonable within the meaning of the Fourth Amendment.   Admittedly, the events giving rise to this case are in retrospect deeply regrettable.   No one can view the death of an unarmed and apparently nonviolent 15–year–old without sorrow, much less disapproval.   Nonetheless, the reasonableness of Officer Hymon's conduct for purposes of the Fourth Amendment cannot be evaluated by what later appears to have been a preferable course of police action.   The officer pursued a suspect in the darkened backyard of a house that from all indications had just been burglarized.   The police officer was not certain whether the suspect was alone or unarmed; nor did he know what had transpired inside the house.   He ordered the suspect to halt, and when the suspect refused to obey and attempted to flee into the night, the officer fired his weapon to prevent escape.   The reasonableness of this action for purposes of the Fourth Amendment is not determined by the unfortunate nature of this particular case; instead, the question is whether it is constitutionally impermissible for police officers, as a last resort, to shoot a burglary suspect fleeing the scene of the crime.   * * *

Notes and Questions

1. Although a police killing of a nonviolent felon is constitutionally unreasonable under the circumstances described in *Garner,* and therefore the homicide may justify a civil remedy (as in this case), a few courts have held that the Supreme Court did not intend, and lacks the authority, to compel states to change their criminal codes to punish such conduct. People v. Couch, 436 Mich. 414, 461 N.W.2d 683 (1990); see State v. Clothier, 243 Kan. 81, 753 P.2d 1267 (1988).

Even if *Garner* applies in the criminal law context, the Fourth Amendment only pertains to "state action," i.e., conduct by a public officer. Consequently, a statute that permits the use of deadly force by a private party against a nondangerous felon is not unconstitutional.

2. Constitutional questions aside, who has the better side of the policy arguments regarding the use of deadly force by police officers? One policy factor not mentioned in *Garner* is that racial minorities are victims of deadly force by police officers at a disproportionate rate. See James J. Fyfe, *Blind Justice: Police Shootings in Memphis,* 73 J.Crim.L. & Criminology 707, 707 (1982) (citing studies); Los Angeles v. Lyons, 461 U.S. 95, 116 n. 3, 103 S.Ct. 1660, 1672 n. 3, 75 L.Ed.2d 675, 693 n. 3 (1983) (Marshall, J., dissenting) ("Thus in a city where Negro males constitute 9% of the population, they have accounted for 75% of the deaths resulting from the [police] use of chokeholds.").

Even when police use of deadly force is justifiable, it can prove incendiary. According to one government report, "police use of firearms to apprehend suspects often strains community relations or even results in serious [racial] disturbances." President's Commission on Law Enforcement and Administration of Justice, *Task Force Report: The Police* 189 (1967); see Edward J. Littlejohn, *Deadly Force and its Effects on Community Relations,* 27 Howard L.J. 1131 (1984) (reporting on the use of deadly force, and its effect on community relations, by the Detroit Police Department).

3. *Use of force to make an arrest.* By arresting a suspect, a police officer is not guilty of false imprisonment is she has probable cause for the arrest, nor is she guilty of battery if she uses necessary nondeadly force while taking the suspect into custody, as long as she had probable cause to believe the arrestee committed a felony or a misdemeanor amounting to a breach of the peace.

A police officer has probable cause to arrest when the facts and circumstances within the officer's personal knowledge, and of which she has reasonably trustworthy information, would be sufficient to cause a prudent person to believe that an offense has been committed and that the suspect committed it. Joshua Dressler, Understanding Criminal Procedure 83 (1991). Under this standard, assuming probable cause, the arresting officer is justified in her actions, even if the person taken into custody turns out to be innocent of the crime.

4. *Problem.* In People v. Salemme, 2 Cal.App.4th 775, 3 Cal.Rptr.2d 398 (1992), the defendant entered a home with the consent of the occupant, for the felonious purpose of selling him fraudulent securities. He was prosecuted for violation of California Penal Code § 459, which provided in

pertinent part: "Every person who enters any house * * * or other building * * * with the intent to commit grand or petit larceny or any felony is guilty of burglary."

Suppose that the resident had discovered the sham, the defendant turned to flee, and the resident shot and killed him. Would the killing be justified under the defense of habitation, defense of property, crime prevention, or under the apprehension-of-a-felon rule? In view of *Ceballos,* how would you expect a California court to resolve the matter?

5. NECESSITY ("CHOICE OF EVILS")

a. *General Principles*

NELSON v. STATE

Supreme Court of Alaska, 1979.
597 P.2d 977.

MATTHEWS, JUSTICE.

Shortly after midnight on May 22, 1976, Dale Nelson drove his four-wheel drive truck onto a side road off the [highway] * * *. His truck became bogged down in a marshy area about 250 feet off the highway. Nelson testified that he was afraid the truck might tip over in the soft ground. He and his two companions, Lynnette Stinson and Carl Thompson, spent an hour unsuccessfully trying to free the vehicle. At about 1:00, Nelson began walking with Stinson down the highway. An acquaintance drove by and offered to help, but was unable to render much assistance. He then drove Nelson and Stinson to a Highway Department Yard where heavy equipment was parked. The yard was marked with "no-trespassing" signs. After waiting several hours for someone to come by, they decided to take a dump truck and use it to pull out Nelson's vehicle. The dump truck also became stuck.

At approximately 10:00 that morning a man identified only as "Curly" appeared. His vehicle was also stuck further down the highway. Curly offered to assist Nelson. They returned to the heavy equipment yard and took a front-end loader, which they used to free the dump truck. They then used the dump truck to free Curly's car. The dump truck was returned to the equipment yard, but when Nelson attempted to use the front-end loader to free his own truck the front-end loader also became bogged down.

Frustrated and tired after twelve hours of attempting to free his vehicle, Nelson and his companions quit and went to sleep. Two of them slept in a tent. One of them went to sleep in the truck. They were awakened by a Highway Department employee, who placed them under citizen's arrest.

Considerable damage was done to both the front-end loader and the dump truck as a result of Nelson's attempt to free his truck. * * * Nelson was convicted in district court of reckless destruction of personal property in violation of AS 11.20.515(b) [2] and joyriding in violation of AS 28.35.010.[3] This conviction was affirmed on appeal to the superior court.

The sole question presented is whether the jury was properly instructed on the defense of necessity. Nelson requested an instruction which read:

> You are instructed that the defendant is allowed to use a motor vehicle of another person without permission if the use is for an emergency in the case of immediate and dire need.

> You are further instructed that once the defendant has raised the issue of emergency or necessity, the state must prove the lack of emergency or necessity beyond a reasonable doubt.

Over Nelson's objection, the court gave an instruction on the necessity defense which read as follows:

> You are instructed that it is a defense to a crime such as joyriding or taking someone else's motor vehicle without his permission that the person acted out of necessity in a case of immediate and dire need. However, such a defense exists only when natural forces create a situation wherein it becomes necessary for a person to violate the law in order to avoid a greater evil to himself or his property. The harm which is to be avoided must be the greater harm and it must be immediate and dire. Where a reasonable alternative other than violating the law is available in order to avoid the harm the defense of necessity is not applicable.

Nelson argues that the jury instruction was erroneous because it allowed the jury to apply what he calls an "objective, after-the-fact" test of need and emergency, rather than a "subjective, reasonable man" test. By this we assume Nelson means that he was entitled to have explained to the jury that they must view the question of necessity from the standpoint of a reasonable person knowing all that the defendant did at the time he acted.

We affirm the conviction.   * * *

The defense of necessity may be raised if the defendant's actions, although violative of the law, were necessary to prevent an even greater harm from occurring.

2. AS 11.20.515(b) provides:

A person who wilfully interferes with or tampers with property not his own, with the purpose to harm the property of another person, or with reckless disregard for the risk of harm to or loss of the property, is guilty of malicious mischief and, upon conviction, is punishable by imprisonment for not more than one year, or by a fine of not less than $100 nor more than $5,000 or by both.

3. AS 28.35.010(a) provides in part:

Driving a vehicle without owner's consent. (a) A person who drives, tows away, or takes a vehicle not his own without the consent of the owner, with intent temporarily to deprive the owner of possession of the vehicle, or a person who is a party or accessory to or an accomplice in the driving or unauthorized taking is guilty of a misdemeanor, and upon conviction is punishable by imprisonment for not less than 30 days nor more than one year, and by a fine of not less than $100 nor more than $1,000.

The rationale of the necessity defense is not that a person, when faced with the pressure of circumstances of nature, lacks the mental element which the crime in question requires. Rather, it is this reason of public policy: the law ought to promote the achievement of higher values at the expense of lesser values, and sometimes the greater good for society will be accomplished by violating the literal language of the criminal law.

W. LaFave & A. Scott, *Criminal Law* § 50 at 382 (1972).

Commentators generally agree that there are three essential elements to the defense: 1) the act charged must have been done to prevent a significant evil; 2) there must have been no adequate alternative; 3) the harm caused must not have been disproportionate to the harm avoided.

The instruction given adequately describes these requirements for the jury. Nelson argues that he was entitled to wording which would explicitly allow the jury to find a necessity defense if a reasonable person at the time of acting would have believed that the necessary elements were present. Nelson is correct in stating that the necessity defense is available if a person acted in the reasonable belief that an emergency existed and there were no alternatives available even if that belief was mistaken. Moreover, the person's actions should be weighed against the harm reasonably foreseeable at the time, rather than the harm that actually occurs.[6]

Assuming that the instruction given was not worded adequately to convey these concepts to the jury, we would find the error harmless, for Nelson failed to make out a case for the necessity defense. The "emergency" situation claimed by Nelson to justify his appropriation of the construction equipment was the alleged danger that his truck, stuck in the mud, might tip over, perhaps damaging the truck top. However by the time Nelson decided to use the equipment the truck had already been stuck for several hours. The dire nature of the emergency may be judged by the fact that some twelve hours later, having unsuccessfully attempted to remove the vehicle from the mud, one of Nelson's companions fell asleep in the truck, which had still not tipped over.

Nor can it be said that Nelson had no lawful alternatives in his situation. The record shows that during the time Nelson was trying to free the vehicle people stopped on several different occasions and offered their services in the form of physical assistance, rides, or offers to telephone state troopers or a tow truck.

---

6. * * * [T]he defendant must also have acted in the belief that the reasonably foreseeable harm resulting from the violation would be less than the harm resulting from compliance with the law. However, here the defendant's belief is not by itself sufficient. An objective determination must be made as to whether the defendant's value judgment was correct, given the facts as he reasonably perceived them. The majority of jurisdictions appear to hold that this determination must be made, at least initially, by the court.

 Rule

Finally, it cannot be said that the harm sought to be avoided in this case—potential damage to Nelson's truck—was greater than the harm caused by Nelson's illegal actions. Even disregarding the actual damage to the equipment caused by Nelson's use, the seriousness of the offenses committed by Nelson were disproportionate to the situation he faced. The legislature has made this clear by making reckless destruction of personal property a crime punishable by imprisonment for up to one year and a $5,000 fine, and joyriding punishable by imprisonment for up to one year and a $1,000 fine. The equipment taken by Nelson was marked with no trespassing signs. Nelson's fears about damage to his truck roof were no justification for his appropriation of sophisticated and expensive equipment.

Affirmed.

AMERICAN LAW INSTITUTE, MODEL PENAL CODE AND COMMENTARIES, COMMENT TO § 3.02

(1985), 9–14

1. *Codification of a Principle of Necessity.* This section accepts the view that a principle of necessity, properly conceived, affords a general justification for conduct that would otherwise constitute an offense. It reflects the judgment that such a qualification on criminal liability, like the general requirements of culpability, is essential to the rationality and justice of the criminal law, and is appropriately addressed in a penal code. Under this section, property may be destroyed to prevent the spread of a fire. A speed limit may be violated in pursuing a suspected criminal. An ambulance may pass a traffic light. Mountain climbers lost in a storm may take refuge in a house or may appropriate provisions. Cargo may be jettisoned or an embargo violated to preserve the vessel. An alien may violate a curfew in order to reach an air raid shelter. A druggist may dispense a drug without the requisite prescription to alleviate grave distress in an emergency. A developed legal system must have better ways of dealing with such problems than to refer only to the letter of particular prohibitions, framed without reference to cases of this kind.

Although the point has not been entirely free from controversy, necessity seems clearly to have standing as a common law defense; such issue as there was related to its definition and extent. Because judicial decisions were rare, and the problems had received scant legislative attention, it was difficult to say even in a particular jurisdiction what the standing and scope of the defense might be. It was, therefore, believed essential to address the question in the formulation of an integrated code.

2. *Limitations on Scope of Defense.* The Code's principle of necessity is subject to a number of limitations. First, the actor must actually believe that his conduct is necessary to avoid an evil. If a druggist who sells a drug without a prescription is unaware that the recipient requires

it immediately to save his life, the actual necessity of the transaction will not exculpate the druggist. * * *

Second, the necessity must arise from an attempt by the actor to avoid an evil or harm that is greater than the evil or harm sought to be avoided by the law defining the offense charged. An equal or a lesser harm will not suffice. * * *

Third, the balancing of evils is not committed to the private judgment of the actor; it is an issue for determination at the trial. Thus, even if the defendant genuinely believes that the life of another is less valuable than his own financial security, his conduct would not be justified under Subsection (1)(a); for it requires that the harm or evil sought to be avoided be greater than that which would be caused by the commission of the offense, not that the defendant believe it to be so. * * * The Code does not resolve the question of how far the balancing of values should be determined by the court as a matter of law or submitted to the jury. There was disagreement in the Council of the Institute over the proper distribution of responsibility and it was decided that this question was best remitted to the law that generally governs the respective functions of the court and jury.

Fourth, under Subsections (1)(b) and (1)(c), the general choice of evils defense cannot succeed if the issue of competing values has been previously foreclosed by a deliberate legislative choice, as when some provision of the law deals explicitly with the specific situation that presents the choice of evils or a legislative purpose to exclude the claimed justification otherwise appears. * * * The legislature, so long as it acts within constitutional limits, is always free to make such a choice and have its choice prevail. * * *

The fifth limitation is dealt with in Subsection (2). * * *

When the actor has made a proper choice of values, his belief in the necessity of his conduct to serve the higher value will exculpate—unless the crime involved can be committed recklessly or negligently. When the latter is the case, recklessness or negligence in bringing about the situation requiring the choice of evils or in appraising the necessity for his conduct may be the basis for conviction. This treatment of the matter thus precludes conviction of a purposeful offense when the actor's culpability inheres in recklessness or negligence, while sanctioning conviction for a crime for which that level of culpability is otherwise sufficient to convict. What will constitute recklessness or negligence in the particular circumstances, of course, is an issue to be resolved under the definition of these terms in Section 2.02.

Notes and Questions

1. *Fault in creating the emergency.* In *Nelson,* assume that the defendant had an otherwise valid necessity claim. Would it affect the outcome if the prosecutor proved that the vehicle ran off the highway into the marsh because Nelson was driving recklessly? What would be the result under

Model Code § 3.02? What if Nelson had *purposely* driven off the road as a practical joke, hoping that he would get stuck?

2. Does Model Penal Code § 3.02(2) state a sensible limitation on the scope of the necessity defense? Suppose that Paul negligently starts a fire in a heavily wooded area that immediately threatens to burn down a row of occupied houses. Paul correctly concludes that the only way to save the homes is for him to burn down Jennifer's unoccupied house as a firebreak, which he does, thereby saving the other houses and, perhaps, lives. If Paul is prosecuted for arson, does he have a valid necessity claim? *Should* he be permitted the defense? See Paul H. Robinson, *Causing the Conditions of One's Own Defense: A Study in the Limits of Theory in Criminal Law Doctrine,* 71 Va.L.Rev. 1, 3–4, 8–13, 17–20 (1985).

3. *Problem.* At approximately 1:00 a.m., Paolello, an ex-felon, got into an argument with another man in a bar. Paolello left the bar, but the other man followed him. Outside, the two resumed their verbal exchange, after which the other man displayed a weapon. Paolello wrestled the gun away from him, and ran away with the firearm. He was arrested moments later, still in possession of the gun, and charged with violation of a statute that provided that "[i]t shall be [a felony] for any person who has been convicted * * * of a [felony] * * * to possess * * * any firearm * * *." Is Paolello entitled to an instruction under Model Penal Code § 3.02? If so, as a juror, would you acquit him of the offense? See United States v. Paolello, 951 F.2d 537 (3d Cir.1991).

Suppose that the original altercation in the bar began because Paolello called the other man "a coward, slimebag, and an infected vermin." How would this affect the analysis of Paolello's necessity claim? What if the insult had occurred two days earlier at the bar, but the other man was still seething from the insult and sought out Paolello?

4. *Problem.* People v. Brandyberry, 812 P.2d 674, 676 (Colo.App. 1991):

> Defendants * * * were charged * * * with conspiracy to kidnap and second degree kidnapping. Those charges arose from the forcible seizure and asportation of a * * * member of the Unification Church. * * *

> The evidence supporting the criminal charges was generally undisputed * * *. Defendants contracted with the victim's parents to plan and execute her removal from the influence of the church and its members. On May 26, 1987, in furtherance of that plan, defendant Whelan and other members of his "rescue team" forcibly seized the victim from a Denver street and transported her, against her will, to a * * * residence, where she was met by her parents, defendant Brandyberry, and other members of the "deprogramming team."

> The victim was then held in captivity by defendants * * * for several days while "deprogramming" was attempted. * * * [Thereafter, the victim escaped.]

> Defendants' * * * evidence was designed to show the existence of a pervasive pattern of fraudulent recruitment practices and "coercive persuasion" techniques allegedly used by the church to obtain, keep,

and control its members * * *. These practices and techniques * * * were calculated to so indoctrinate, enmesh, and involve recruited members * * * in church-sponsored ideology and activities as to undermine their abilities to think and act freely or independently in their own best interests. The destruction of the victim's ability to think and act freely and autonomously was claimed by the defendants as the injury they sought to avoid and eliminate by their * * * actions.

The defendants asserted the defense of necessity, defined by Colorado law as follows:

Conduct which would otherwise constitute an offense is justifiable and not criminal when it is necessary as an emergency measure to avoid an imminent public or private injury which is about to occur by reason of a situation occasioned or developed through no conduct of the actor, and which is of sufficient gravity that, according to the ordinary standards of intelligence and morality, the desirability and urgency of avoiding the injury clearly outweigh the desirability of avoiding the injury sought to be prevented by the statute defining the offense in issue. [West's Colo.Rev.Stat.A. § 18–1–702(1) (1986).]

Were the defendants entitled to a jury instruction on this defense? As a juror, is there additional information you need in order to determine whether the defendants acted justifiably?

b. Civil Disobedience

UNITED STATES v. SCHOON

United States Court of Appeals, Ninth Circuit, 1991.
971 F.2d 193.

BOOCHEVER, CIRCUIT JUDGE:

Gregory Schoon, Raymond Kennon, Jr., and Patricia Manning appeal their convictions for obstructing activities of the Internal Revenue Service Office in Tucson, Arizona, and failing to comply with an order of a federal police officer. Both charges stem from their activities in protest of United States involvement in El Salvador. They claim the district court improperly denied them a necessity defense. Because we hold the necessity defense inapplicable in cases like this, we affirm.

I.

On December 4, 1989, thirty people, including appellants, gained admittance to the IRS office in Tucson, where they chanted "keep America's tax dollars out of El Salvador," splashed simulated blood on the counters, walls, and carpeting, and generally obstructed the office's operation. After a federal police officer ordered the group, on several occasions, to disperse or face arrest, appellants were arrested.

At a bench trial, appellants proffered testimony about conditions in El Salvador as the motivation for their conduct. They attempted to assert a necessity defense, essentially contending that their acts in protest of American involvement in El Salvador were necessary to avoid further bloodshed in that country. While finding appellants motivated solely by humanitarian concerns, the court nonetheless precluded the defense as a matter of law, relying on Ninth Circuit precedent. The sole issue on appeal is the propriety of the court's exclusion of a necessity defense as a matter of law.

II.

A district court may preclude a necessity defense where "the evidence, as described in the defendant's offer of proof, is insufficient as a matter of law to support the proffered defense." *United States v. Dorrell*, 758 F.2d 427, 430 (9th Cir.1985). To invoke the necessity defense, therefore, the defendants colorably must have shown that: (1) they were faced with a choice of evils and chose the lesser evil; (2) they acted to prevent imminent harm; (3) they reasonably anticipated a direct causal relationship between their conduct and the harm to be averted; and (4) they had no legal alternatives to violating the law. * * *

The district court denied the necessity defense on the grounds that (1) the requisite immediacy was lacking; (2) the actions taken would not abate the evil; and (3) other legal alternatives existed. Because the threshold test for admissibility of a necessity defense is a conjunctive one, a court may preclude invocation of the defense if "proof is deficient with regard to any of the four elements."

While we could affirm substantially on those grounds relied upon by the district court, we find a deeper, systemic reason for the complete absence of federal case law recognizing a necessity defense in an indirect civil disobedience case. As used in this opinion, "civil disobedience" is the wilful violation of a law, undertaken for the purpose of social or political protest. * * * Indirect civil disobedience involves violating a law or interfering with a government policy that is not, itself, the object of protest. Direct civil disobedience, on the other hand, involves protesting the existence of a law by breaking that law or by preventing the execution of that law in a specific instance in which a particularized harm would otherwise follow. See Note, *Applying the Necessity Defense to Civil Disobedience Cases*, 64 N.Y.U.L.Rev. 79, 79–80 & n. 5 (1989). This case involves indirect civil disobedience because these protestors were not challenging the laws under which they were charged. In contrast, the civil rights lunch counter sit-ins, for example, constituted direct civil disobedience because the protestors were challenging the rule that prevented them from sitting at lunch counters. Similarly, if a city council passed an ordinance requiring immediate infusion of a suspected carcinogen into the drinking water, physically blocking the delivery of the substance would constitute direct civil disobedience: protestors would be preventing the execution of a law in a specific instance in which a particularized harm—contamination of the water supply—would otherwise follow.

* * * Today, we conclude, for the reasons stated below, that the necessity defense is inapplicable to cases involving indirect civil disobedience.

III.

Necessity is, essentially, a utilitarian defense. It therefore justifies criminal acts taken to avert a greater harm, maximizing social welfare by allowing a crime to be committed where the social benefits of the crime outweigh the social costs of failing to commit the crime. Pursuant to the defense, prisoners could escape a burning prison, a person lost in the woods could steal food from a cabin to survive, an embargo could be violated because adverse weather conditions necessitated sale of the cargo at a foreign port, a crew could mutiny where their ship was thought to be unseaworthy, and property could be destroyed to prevent the spread of fire.

What all the traditional necessity cases have in common is that the commission of the "crime" averted the occurrence of an even greater "harm." In some sense, the necessity defense allows us to act as individual legislatures, amending a particular criminal provision or crafting a one-time exception to it, subject to court review, when a real legislature would formally do the same under those circumstances. For example, by allowing prisoners who escape a burning jail to claim the justification of necessity, we assume the lawmaker, confronting this problem, would have allowed for an exception to the law proscribing prison escapes.

Because the necessity doctrine is utilitarian, however, strict requirements contain its exercise so as to prevent nonbeneficial criminal conduct. For example, " '[i]f the criminal act cannot abate the threatened harm, society receives no benefit from the criminal conduct.' " *Applying the Necessity Defense,* [supra], at 102 (quoting *United States v. Gant,* 691 F.2d 1159, 1164 (5th Cir.1982)). Similarly, to forgive a crime taken to avert a lesser harm would fail to maximize social utility. The cost of the crime would outweigh the harm averted by its commission. Likewise, criminal acts cannot be condoned to thwart threats, yet to be imminent, or those for which there are legal alternatives to abate the harm.

Analysis of three of the necessity defense's four elements leads us to the conclusion that necessity can never be proved in a case of indirect civil disobedience. We do not rely upon the imminent harm prong of the defense because we believe there can be indirect civil disobedience cases in which the protested harm is imminent.

A.

1. Balance of Harms

It is axiomatic that, if the thing to be averted is not a harm at all, the balance of harms necessarily would disfavor any criminal action. Indirect civil disobedience seeks first and foremost to bring about the repeal of a law or a change of governmental policy, attempting to mobilize public opinion through typically symbolic action. These protestors violate a law, not because it is unconstitutional or otherwise improper, but because doing so calls public attention to their objectives. Thus, the most immediate "harm" this form of protest targets is the *existence* of the law or policy. However, the mere existence of a constitutional law or governmental policy cannot constitute a legally cognizable harm. *See* Comment, *Political Protest and the Illinois Defense of Necessity,* 54 U.Chi.L.Rev. 1070, 1083 (1987) ("In a society based on democratic decision making, this is how values are ranked—a protester cannot simply assert that her view of what is best should trump the decision of the majority of elected representatives."); *cf. Dorrell,* 758 F.2d at 432 ("[T]he law should [not] excuse criminal activity intended to express the protestor's disagreement with positions reached by the lawmaking branches of the government.").

There may be, of course, general harms that result from the targeted law or policy. Such generalized "harm," however, is too insubstantial an injury to be legally cognizable. * * * The law could not function were people allowed to rely on their *subjective* beliefs and value judgments in determining which harms justified the taking of criminal action. *See United States v. Moylan,* 417 F.2d 1002, 1008–09 (4th Cir.1969) ("Exercise of a moral judgment based upon individual standards does not carry with it legal justification or immunity from punishment for breach of the law. . . . Toleration of such conduct would [be] inevitably anarchic.").

The protest in this case was in the form of indirect civil disobedience, aimed at reversal of the government's El Salvador policy. That policy does not violate the Constitution, and appellants have never suggested as much. There is no evidence that the procedure by which the policy was adopted was in any way improper; nor is there any evidence that appellants were prevented systematically from participating in the democratic processes through which the policy was chosen. The most immediate harm the appellants sought to avert was the existence of the government's El Salvador policy, which is not in itself a legally cognizable harm. Moreover, any harms resulting from the operation of this policy are insufficiently concrete to be legally cognizable as harms for purposes of the necessity defense.

Thus, as a matter of law, the mere existence of a policy or law validly enacted by Congress cannot constitute a cognizable harm. If there is no cognizable harm to prevent, the harm resulting from criminal action taken for the purpose of securing the repeal of the law or policy necessarily outweighs any benefit of the action.

2. *Causal Relationship Between Criminal Conduct and Harm to Be Averted*

This inquiry requires a court to judge the likelihood that an alleged harm will be abated by the taking of illegal action. In the sense that the likelihood of abatement is required in the traditional necessity cases, there will never be such likelihood in cases of indirect political protest. In the traditional cases, a prisoner flees a burning cell and averts death, or someone demolishes a home to create a firebreak and prevents the conflagration of an entire community. The nexus between the act undertaken and the result sought is a close one. Ordinarily it is the volitional illegal act alone which, once taken, abates the evil.

In political necessity cases involving indirect civil disobedience against congressional acts, however, the act alone is unlikely to abate the evil precisely because the action is indirect. Here, the IRS obstruction, or the refusal to comply with a federal officer's order, are unlikely to abate the killings in El Salvador, or immediately change Congress's policy; instead, it takes another *volitional* actor not controlled by the protestor to take a further step; Congress must change its mind.

3. Legal Alternatives

A final reason the necessity defense does not apply to these indirect civil disobedience cases is that legal alternatives will never be deemed exhausted when the harm can be mitigated by congressional action. As noted above, the harm indirect civil disobedience aims to prevent is the continued existence of a law or policy. Because congressional action can *always* mitigate this "harm," lawful political activity to spur such action will always be a legal alternative. * * *

The necessity defense requires the absence of any legal alternative to the contemplated illegal conduct which could reasonably be expected to abate an imminent evil. A prisoner fleeing a burning jail, for example, would not be asked to wait in his cell because someone might conceivably save him; such a legal alternative is ill-suited to avoiding death in a fire. In other words, the law implies a reasonableness requirement in judging whether legal alternatives exist.

Where the targeted harm is the existence of a law or policy, our precedents counsel that this reasonableness requirement is met simply by the possibility of congressional action. [Prior federal cases] * * * assumed * * * that the "possibility" that Congress will change its mind is sufficient in the context of the democratic process to make lawful political action a reasonable alternative to indirect civil disobedience. * * * Thus, indirect civil disobedience can never meet the necessity defense requirement that there be a lack of legal alternatives.

B. * * *

The real problem here is that litigants are trying to distort to their purposes an age-old common law doctrine meant for a very different set of circumstances. What these cases are really about is gaining notoriety for a cause—the defense allows protestors to get their political grievances discussed in a courtroom. It is precisely this political motive that has left some courts, like the district court in this case, uneasy. Because these attempts to invoke the necessity defense "force the courts to choose among causes they should make legitimate by extending the defense of necessity," and because the criminal acts, themselves, do not maximize social good, they should be subject to a *per se* rule of exclusion. * * *

FERNANDEZ, CIRCUIT JUDGE, concurring:

I agree with much of what the majority says regarding the application of the necessity defense to this type of case.

I do not mean to be captious in questioning whether the necessity defense is grounded on pure utilitarianism,[1] but fundamentally, I am not so sure that this defense of justification should be grounded on utilitarian theory alone rather than on a concept of what is right and proper conduct under the circumstances. * * *

STEVEN M. BAUER & PETER J. ECKERSTROM—THE STATE MADE ME DO IT: THE APPLICABILITY OF THE NECESSITY DEFENSE TO CIVIL DISOBEDIENCE

39 Stanford Law Review 1173 (1987), 1184–86, 1188–90, 1195–98

A. ARGUMENTS FOR THE POLITICAL NECESSITY DEFENSE * * *

To the theorist or reformer who bemoans the shrinking role of the individual in our society, the political necessity defense makes possible a much needed infusion of individual expression and grassroots political activity. The defense promotes a more vibrant and empowered political culture by amplifying individual viewpoints, by empowering a cross section of the community (the jury), and by increasing the quantity and quality of public discourse. Even considering the arguments against the political necessity defense, one might find these ends alluring enough to permit its use.

1. The Necessity Defense as Amplifier of Individual Viewpoints

The political necessity defense empowers the individual primarily by presenting a forum in which stifled minority or unheeded majority viewpoints receive a public hearing and a governmental response. * * *

The availability of an officially sanctioned hearing plays a significant role in remedying individual political discouragement. It conveys the symbolic message that our society highly values political input and gives special attention to apparent systemic failures in our form of democratic government. In particular, the hearing amplifies intensely held individual views: Since the civil disobedient risks criminal sanction to express his view, we can expect that view to be intensely held. Equally important, the political necessity defense presents a forum wherein an individual can demand a response from the government. While complaints directed at other governmental forums may be met with a form letter, shelved, or put off for study, the judicial process demands an immediate

---

1. For example, without questioning the defense itself, one might question the utility of permitting a condemned mass murderer to escape from a prison conflagration.

exploration and resolution of the issue involved. Here, the government must answer or dismiss its case. * * *

2. Empowering the Jury

The political necessity defense places the jury in a position to acquit the defendant, nullifying the effect of the law that has been broken. In its factual determination, the jury is called upon to weigh controversial political issues. * * *

The idea of empowering a jury to make significant case-by-case political decisions is neither novel nor foreign to the American legal tradition. During the colonial period, the jury became an important source of indigent political power set in opposition to the unpopular laws of the mother country. Well into the nineteenth century, American juries retained the power to decide questions of law as well as fact. Today, juries can still acquit criminal defendants against the evidence and the judge's instructions. Empowering the jury thus conforms with a longstanding American willingness to use citizens as a buffer between the defendant and the harsh and sometimes arbitrary enforcement of the law. * * *

3. Improving the Quality and Quantity of Public Discourse

The airing of political necessity arguments generally improves the quality and quantity of public discussion. Outside the courtroom, the trial draws attention both to the discrete issue raised by the civil disobedient and to the health of the democratic political process. Inside the courtroom, the quality of discourse improves through the patience of the court in hearing all arguments, the concreteness of the discussion, and the specificity required by evidentiary rules. This may also stimulate a higher quality of discussion outside the courtroom as the media reports on the trial's progress. * * *

B. ARGUMENTS AGAINST THE POLITICAL NECESSITY DEFENSE * * *

1. The philosophical inappropriateness of the political necessity defense.

Generally, civil disobedience is an unlawful act that is meant to urge reconsideration of a law or policy without threatening the structure of the community in which it is carried out. Three aspects of civil disobedience counsel that its practitioners should accept the legal consequences of their acts. First, civil disobedience pursues a civil society within the confines of the social contract. Second, it seeks social reform through persuasion. Third, it requires its practitioners, as moral political actors, to be ethically consistent. Accepting the punishment for the unlawful act is important to each of these premises. Attempting to avert punishment by raising necessity claims may undermine the justifications for civil disobedience; at the very least, the disobedient foregoes a strategically important symbolic event. * * *

* * * [T]he civil disobedient must accept enforcement of laws with which he disagrees if he is to expect enforcement of his prospective social agenda. For this reason, he must ritualize his respect for law in general, even as he uses the persuasive strategy of defying a particular law. The reformer can achieve this by accepting the punishment for his unlawful acts.

The civil disobedient must demonstrate his respect for law not only to demonstrate prospective philosophical consistency, but also to resolve the present philosophical dilemma of his own lawbreaking. In acting on conscience, the civil disobedient asserts a subjective moral vision. He cannot expect that vision to be binding on the rest of society unless it is endorsed through the democratic process. * * * By breaking the law while accepting its punishment, the civil disobedient can accommodate both his individual moral viewpoint and his ethical bond to accede to the mandate of the community.

2. Conflict With Democratic Values

Endorsing the necessity defense in civil disobedience cases runs counter to some important notions of American constitutional democracy. * * * [T]he political necessity defense rejects the legislative process altogether. * * * Just as arguments for jury nullification are excluded from the courtroom, so the necessity defense might be excluded in civil disobedience cases.

Jury decisions based on political necessity violate the principle of majority rule. As unelected minority tribunals, juries should not determine legal or political policy. Asking a jury to decide whether civil disobedience is justified because of an ill-conceived policy asks it to rule on the policy itself. Yet the Constitution vests policy-making powers in the legislative and executive branches which are, in theory, representative of and held accountable to the electorate. In contrast, juries do not represent either their local communities or the national electorate. And unlike legislators, jurors are accountable to no one and never have to justify the decisions they make during jury service. Unelected, unaccountable, unrepresentative jurors do not fulfill any standard conception of majority rule or representative government. * * *

The danger of the political necessity defense to democratic principles becomes clear when one considers possible cases in which civil disobedients might raise necessity. For instance, abortion clinic bombers could admit their crime yet avoid punishment by convincing a single juror that their strategy, however detestable, saved an unborn life. The national defense policies of elected officials could be greatly hampered if acts of vandalism and trespass were justified by political necessity, or even led to lengthy jury trials. Imagine the difficulty of enforcing civil rights legislation in certain cities if violators could plead political necessity before sympathetic racist juries. * * *

3. Inadequacies of the Forum

Closely related to the democratic objections to the political necessity defense are questions about whether, as a practical matter, juries have the ability to make fair and accurate policy decisions within the forum of the courtroom. * * *

The traditional realm of jury decisionmaking has not included overtly political questions. First, typical jurors are qualified as finders of fact but may not be qualified as policy formulators. Jurors have no special expertise in policymaking in general or in the challenged policy in particular. In fact, persons with expertise in the policy area will probably be struck from the jury, if not by the judge, then by one of the parties.

Second, the courtroom forum does not necessarily provide the jury with complete information regarding the challenged policy. Certainly, their information is more restricted than that of the primary lawmaking body, the legislature. * * *

Third, the manner in which the parties present evidence further twists an already contorted image and establishes a poor environment for the consideration of policy issues. Advocates and their paid experts present testimony in its most favorable light. Because the parties always present the evidence as advocates, the jurors must sort through subjective factual presentations rather than acquiring independent, objective factual interpretations.

Finally, factors that have nothing to do with the policy issue often enter into a jury's consideration. Subjective notions about the parties, actions by the judge, and the lawyers' ability to inflame the jury may influence its decision.

Notes and Questions

1. Should there be a *per se* rule of exclusion of the necessity defense in indirect civil disobedience cases?

Even without a *per se* rule of exclusion, state trial courts rarely instruct juries on the defense of necessity in indirect civil disobedience cases, a position approved by virtually all appellate courts. This does not mean, however, that the defense is never successfully used by protesters. Occasionally, a trial judge permits a defendant to raise the necessity claim, and the factfinder sends a "political message" by acquitting the defendant. See, e.g., City of Wichita v. Tilson, 253 Kan. 285, 855 P.2d 911 (1993) (in a bench trial, the judge absolved an anti-abortion protester of criminal trespass on the ground of necessity). Because a defendant may not constitutionally be retried after an acquittal, the prosecutor is barred from seeking a new trial on the ground that the judge erred in allowing the defense to be raised.

2. Should civil disobedients be convicted, but not punished? Do you agree that "[c]ivil resisters, for the most part, are people of passion and principle who are driven to lead by example. * * * It is unrealistic not to recognize that these individuals differ from the common egotistic criminal"? Matthew Lippman, *Reflections on Non–Violent Resistance and the Necessity*

Defense, 11 Hous.J.Int'l L. 277, 304 (1989). If so, is there a valid basis for punishing these people? Will punishment deter them or other similarly impassioned and principled opponents of government policies or laws? Is the justification for punishment that a disobedient's "[p]rofessed unselfish motivation, rather than a justification, actually identifies a form of arrogance which organized society cannot tolerate"? United States v. Cullen, 454 F.2d 386, 392 (7th Cir.1971).

3. *Problem.* In light of the preceding materials, consider the facts reported in Commonwealth v. Leno, 415 Mass. 835, 836–37, 616 N.E.2d 453, 454–55 (1993):

> In June, 1991, the defendants were arrested and charged with sixty-five counts of unauthorized possession of hypodermic needles and fifty-two counts of unauthorized possession of syringes. Each defendant also was charged with one count of distributing an instrument for the administration of a controlled substance. The defendants told the police they were exchanging clean syringes and needles for dirty, possibly contaminated ones to prevent the spread of AIDS.

> Defendant Leno is a fifty-five year old grandfather, who had been addicted to alcohol, cocaine, heroin, or various pills from age twelve to forty-five. At the time of trial, he was in his tenth year of recovery from addiction. Leno learned of needle exchange programs from a National AIDS Brigade lecturer. * * * Leno started a needle exchange program in Lynn in September, 1990, after realizing that "in my own back yard ... people were dying of AIDS ... and this particular service was not offered to them." Leno testified that he believed that by providing clean needles to addicts he was helping to stem the spread of AIDS, he was helping addicts, especially the homeless, to reach recovery, and that he was not helping addicts continue their habit.

> Defendant Robert Ingalls said that he is fifty-three years old and works as a landscaper. He joined Leno in operating a needle exchange program in Lynn as a matter of conscience: "I would have had a hard time with my conscience if I didn't do it without good reason. I [knew] people were dying of AIDS ... and when [Leno] told me what he was doing, I thought, well, maybe you could save a few lives.... [I]t's sort of an irresistible opportunity for me, if you can save a life."

> The two defendants legally purchased new sterile needles over-the-counter in Vermont. The defendants were at a specific location on Union Street in Lynn from 5 p.m. to 7 p.m. every Wednesday evening in 1991, until they were arrested * * *. They accepted dirty needles in exchange for clean needles; they exchanged between 150 and 200 needles each night, for fifty to sixty people. The defendants did not charge for the services or for the materials. * * *

> "[T]he application of the defense * * * is limited to the following circumstances: (1) the defendant is faced with a clear and imminent danger, not one which is debatable or speculative; (2) the defendant can reasonably expect that his [or her] action will be effective as the direct cause of abating the danger; (3) there is [no] legal alternative which will be effective in abating the danger; and (4) the Legislature has not acted

to preclude the defense by a clear and deliberate choice regarding the values at issue."

Does this case involve indirect civil disobedience? Under the definition of the defense set out above, are the defendants entitled to a jury instruction? If an instruction were given, would you acquit the defendants?

c. Defense to Murder?

THE QUEEN v. DUDLEY AND STEPHENS

Queen's Bench Division, 1884
14 Q.B.D. 273

LORD COLERIDGE, C.J.

[The facts are set out at p. 35 supra.]

* * * From these facts, stated with the cold precision of a special verdict, it appears sufficiently that the prisoners were subject to terrible temptation, to sufferings which might break down the bodily power of the strongest man, and try the conscience of the best. * * * But nevertheless this is clear, that the prisoners put to death a weak and unoffending boy upon the chance of preserving their own lives by feeding upon his flesh and blood after he was killed, and with the certainty of depriving *him* of any possible chance of survival. The verdict finds in terms that "if the men had not fed upon the body of the boy they would *probably* not have survived," and that "the boy being in a much weaker condition was *likely* to have died before them." They might possibly have been picked up next day by a passing ship; they might possibly not have been picked up at all; in either case it is obvious that the killing of the boy would have been an unnecessary and profitless act. It is found by the verdict that the boy was incapable of resistance, and, in fact, made none; and it is not even suggested that his death was due to any violence on his part attempted against, or even so much as feared by, those who killed him. Under these circumstances the jury say that they are ignorant whether those who killed him were guilty of murder, and have referred it to this Court to determine what is the legal consequence which follows from the facts which they have found. * * *

There remains to be considered the real question in the case—whether killing under the circumstances set forth in the verdict be or be not murder. The contention that it could be anything else was, to the minds of us all, both new and strange, and we stopped the Attorney General in his negative argument in order that we might hear what could be said in support of a proposition which appeared to us to be at once dangerous, immoral, and opposed to all legal principle and analogy. All, no doubt, that can be said has been urged before us, and we are now to consider and determine what it amounts to. First it is said that it follows from various definitions of murder in books of authority, which definitions imply, if they do not state, the doctrine, that in order to save your own life you may lawfully take away the life of another, when that other is neither attempting nor threatening yours, nor is guilty of any illegal act whatever towards you or any one else. But if these definitions be looked at they will not be found to sustain this contention. The earliest in point of date is the passage cited to us from Bracton, who lived in the reign of Henry III. * * * But in the very passage as to necessity, on which reliance has been placed, it is clear that Bracton is speaking of necessity in the ordinary sense—the repelling by violence, violence justified so far as it was necessary for the object, any illegal violence used towards oneself. * * *

It is, if possible, yet clearer that the doctrine contended for receives no support from the great authority of Lord Hale. * * * Lord Hale regarded the private necessity which justified, and alone justified, the taking the life of another for the safeguard of one's own to be what is commonly called "self-defence."

But if this could be even doubtful upon Lord Hale's words, Lord Hale himself has made it clear. For in the chapter in which he deals with the exemption created by compulsion or necessity he thus expresses himself:—"If a man be desperately assaulted and in peril of death, and cannot otherwise escape unless, to satisfy his assailant's fury, he will kill an innocent person then present, the fear and actual force will not acquit him of the crime and punishment of murder, if he commit the fact, for he ought rather to die himself than kill an innocent * * *." * * *

Is there, then, any authority for the proposition which has been presented to us? Decided cases there are none. * * *

The one real authority of former time is Lord Bacon, who, in his commentary * * * lays down the law as follows:—"Necessity carrieth a privilege in itself. * * * [I]f a man steal viands to satisfy his present hunger, this is no felony nor larceny. So if divers be in danger of drowning by the casting away of some boat or barge, and one of them get to some plank, or on the boat's side to keep himself above water, and another to save his life thrust him from it, whereby he is drowned, this is neither se defendendo or by misadventure, but justifiable." On this it is to be observed that Lord Bacon's proposition that stealing to satisfy hunger is no larceny is * * * expressly contradicted by Lord Hale * * *. And for the proposition as to the plank or boat, it is said to be derived from the canonists. At any rate he cites no authority for it, and it must stand upon his own. * * * There are many conceivable states of things in which it might possibly be true, but if Lord Bacon meant to lay down the broad proposition that a man may save his life by killing, if necessary, an innocent and unoffending neighbour, it certainly is not law at the present day. * * *

* * * Now it is admitted that the deliberate killing of this unoffending and unresisting boy was clearly murder, unless the killing can be justified by some well-recognised excuse admitted by the law. It is further admitted that there was in this case no such excuse, unless the killing was justified by what has been called "necessity." But the temptation to the act which existed here was not what the law has ever called necessity. Nor is this to be regretted. Though law and morality

are not the same, and many things may be immoral which are not necessarily illegal, yet the absolute divorce of law from morality would be of fatal consequence; and such divorce would follow if the temptation to murder in this case were to be held by law an absolute defence of it. It is not so. To preserve one's life is generally speaking a duty, but it may be the plainest and highest duty to sacrifice it. War is full of instances in which it is a man's duty not to live, but to die. The duty, in case of shipwreck, of a captain to his crew, of the crew to the passengers, of soldiers to women and children * * *; these duties impose on men the moral necessity, not of the preservation, but of the sacrifice of their lives for others, from which in no country, least of all, it is to be hoped, in England, will men ever shrink, as indeed, they have not shrunk. It is not correct, therefore, to say that there is any absolute or unqualified necessity to preserve one's life. * * * It is not needful to point out the awful danger of admitting the principle which has been contended for. Who is to be the judge of this sort of necessity? By what measure is the comparative value of lives to be measured? Is it to be strength, or intellect, or what? It is plain that the principle leaves to him who is to profit by it to determine the necessity which will justify him in deliberately taking another's life to save his own. In this case the weakest, the youngest, the most unresisting, was chosen. Was it more necessary to kill him than one of the grown men? The answer must be "No"—

"So spake the Fiend, and with necessity,

The tyrant's plea, excused his devilish deeds."

It is not suggested that in this particular case the deeds were "devilish," but it is quite plain that such a principle once admitted might be made the legal cloak for unbridled passion and atrocious crime. * * *

It must not be supposed that in refusing to admit temptation to be an excuse for crime it is forgotten how terrible the temptation was; how awful the suffering; how hard in such trials to keep the judgment straight and the conduct pure. We are often compelled to set up standards we cannot reach ourselves, and to lay down rules which we could not ourselves satisfy. But a man has no right to declare temptation to be an excuse, though he might himself have yielded to it, nor allow compassion for the criminal to change or weaken in any manner the legal definition of the crime. It is therefore our duty to declare that the prisoners' act in this case was wilful murder, that the facts as stated in the verdict are no legal justification of the homicide; and to say that in our unanimous opinion the prisoners are upon this special verdict guilty of murder.[1]

---

1. My brother Grove has furnished me with the following suggestion, too late to be embodied in the judgment but well worth preserving: "If the two accused men were justified in killing Parker, then if not rescued in time, two of the three survivors would be justified in killing the third, and of the two who remained the stronger would be justified in killing the weaker, so the three men might be justifiably killed to give the fourth a chance of surviving."—C.

The Court then proceeded to pass sentence of death upon the prisoners.[2]

Notes and Questions

1. Does *Dudley and Stephens* stand for the proposition that the killing of an innocent person, even to save the lives of a greater number of innocents, is never justifiable? If not, what is Lord Coleridge saying?

2. What *should* the law be in this regard? The Model Penal Code does not rule out the use of its choice-of-evils provision in homicide cases:

> The Model Code rejects any limitations on necessity cast in terms of particular evils to be avoided or particular evils to be justified * * *. * * * [T]his section reflects the view that the principle of necessity is one of general validity. It is widely accepted in the law of torts and there is even greater need for its acceptance in the law of crime. While there may be situations, such as rape, where it is hardly possible to claim that greater evil was avoided than that sought to be prevented by the law defining the offense, this is a matter that is safely left to the determination and elaboration of the courts.

> It would be particularly unfortunate to exclude homicidal conduct from the scope of the defense. For, recognizing that the sanctity of life has a supreme place in the hierarchy of values, it is nonetheless true that conduct that results in taking life may promote the very value sought to be protected by the law of homicide. Suppose, for example, that the actor makes a breach in a dike, knowing that it will inundate a farm, but taking the only course available to save a whole town. If he is charged with homicide of the inhabitants of the farm house, he can rightly point out that the object of the law of homicide is to save life, and that by his conduct he has effected a net saving of innocent lives. The life of every individual must be taken in such a case to be of equal value and the numerical preponderance in the lives saved compared to those sacrificed surely should establish legal justification for the act. * * * Although the view is not universally held that it is ethically preferable to take one innocent life than to have many lives lost,[15] most

---

2. This sentence was afterwards commuted by the Crown to six months' imprisonment.

15. Roman Catholic moralists have generally taken the position that one should not cause effects that are directly evil even if they are thought to be a necessary means to a greater good. Thus, it is considered wrong to terminate the life of a fetus even if that is the only way the mother can be saved and even if the fetus will die in any event. On the other hand, an ordinary operation designed directly to protect the mother's health is permissible, even if an inevitable effect is the death of the fetus, under the so-called principle of "double effect" that death is only permitted, not intended, and is not itself a means to saving the mother's life.

Many acts justifiable under this section would also be justifiable under the principle of "double effect." Diverting a flood to destroy a farmhouse instead of a town would be acceptable since the destruction of the farmhouse is not intended and is not a means of saving the town. Suppose, however, the citizens of a town receive a credible threat, say from a foreign invader, that everyone in the town will be killed unless the townspeople themselves kill their mayor, who is hiding. If the townspeople accede, they would have a substantial argument against criminal liability under this section but their act would be immoral under the double effect analysis, since they have intended to kill the mayor and it is his death that is the means to their safety.

persons probably think a net saving of lives is ethically warranted if the choice among lives to be saved is not unfair. Certainly the law should permit such a choice.

American Law Institute, Model Penal Code and Commentaries, Comment to § 3.02 at 14–15 (1985).

Is the implication of Section 3.02 that "[o]nce the justificatory theory of necessity is identified with utilitarianism, * * * it * * * imposes on the few a moral obligation to sacrifice themselves"? Alan Brudner, *A Theory of Necessity,* 7 Oxford J. Legal Studies 339, 342 (1987). That is, if Dudley and Stephens were justified in killing Parker, did the youth lose the right to kill them in self-defense? Should his right to life "yield[ ] to a utilitarian assessment in terms of net saving of lives"? Sanford H. Kadish, *Respect for Life and Regard for Rights in the Criminal Law,* 64 Cal.L.Rev. 871, 890 (1976).

Not all commentators agree with the Model Code's approach:

> On a utilitarian theory of justice, the matter is open to debate. The particular act did reduce aggregate harm: By killing one, three survived who probably otherwise would not have. However, * * * it is not clear whether a legal system which institutionalizes the permissibility of such killings would, on balance, prevent more harm than it causes. This is where the mariners and the Crown diverged—with the mariners concerned with increasing chances of survival in shipwrecks, and the Crown and the courts concerned with long-run risks of diluting the deterrent force of the homicide prohibition. It is difficult to imagine how one could obtain evidence supporting either contention.

> Once one begins to doubt a purely utilitarian theory of justice, however, the answer begins to change. It becomes questionable whether such killings could ever be justified. The German courts * * * have historically been influenced by Kantian ethics, and would probably interpret the choice-of-evils provision in the German code as not permitting homicide to save others' lives.

> While Kantian ethics once were largely ignored in American legal philosophy, that has ceased to be true in recent years. Many leading writers on ethics and jurisprudence are now explicitly Kantian in their insistence on the preeminent value of individuals. Each person's life is as important as the lives of other persons. Hence, it is not just to sacrifice A's existence in order to promote the interests—or even, to save the lives—of B, C, and D. * * * If correct, it means that Dudley and Stephens's act of homicide cannot be justifiable. * * * Were one to accept this conclusion, it would require amending the Model Penal Code's choice-of-evils provision. The principle of preferring the lesser evil * * * should have applicability only when the act invades interests of the victim that are of less importance for him than the interests the actor stands to lose from compliance: for example, when I break into your house and steal your food in order to prevent myself from starving. The principle should not apply when I exact the ultimate sacrifice from you.

Andrew von Hirsch, *Lifeboat Law,* 4 Crim.Just.Ethics (Summer/Fall 1985), at 88, 90.

In thinking about the issues raised by *Dudley and Stephens,* consider the following hypotheticals that involve the taking of an innocent life. Would you justify any or all of the homicides? Is there a useful way to distinguish these hypotheticals from each other and from *Dudley and Stephens?*

Hypothetical 1: A, B, and C, all strangers, are in a horse-drawn carriage in the countryside when they encounter a pack of hungry, ferocious animals. Because the horse is too slow to outrace the animals, A throws B out of the carriage. The animals stop and devour B, allowing A and C to escape. See Rollin M. Perkins, *Impelled Perpetration Restated,* 33 Hastings L.J. 403, 406 (1981).

Hypothetical 2: D and E are mountain climbers, roped together for safety. While they are moving along a narrow ledge, D falls off the ledge. E is not strong enough to pull D to safety. Because E is about to be dragged over the ledge by the dangling D, E cuts the rope. D falls to her death, E survives. Id.

Hypothetical 3: F engineers a trolley car. As the trolley rounds a bend, F sees five workers repairing the track. The only way to avoid striking and killing them is to stop the trolley, but the brakes unexpectedly fail. F sees a spur of track that would lead the trolley off to the right, but there is a single workman on the spur. F turns the trolley onto the spur, killing that workman, but saving the lives of the other five workers. Philippa Foot, *The Problem of Abortion and the Doctrine of Double Effect* in Virtues and Vices and Other Essays in Moral Philosophy 19 (1978).

Hypothetical 4: G is a surgeon with five desperately ill patients, two of whom need a lung transplant, two of whom require a kidney, and one of whom is waiting for a healthy heart. Each will die within 24 hours without the needed organ. H comes to the hospital for a routine physical. H is in excellent health, with the appropriate blood-type and tissue matches to allow his organs to be transplanted into all of the dying patients. Without H's consent, G harvests H's heart, lungs, and kidneys. H dies, but G's five patients survive and live long, healthy lives. Judith Jarvis Thomson, *The Trolley Problem,* 94 Yale L.J. 1395, 1396 (1985).

D. PRINCIPLES OF EXCUSE

1. WHY DO WE EXCUSE WRONGDOING?

SANFORD H. KADISH—EXCUSING CRIME

75 California Law Review 257 (1987), 263–65

Why we have excuses is less obvious than why we have other defenses. Let us start with Jeremy Bentham's explanation. He saw the point of excuses to be that they identified situations in which conduct is nondeterrable, so that punishment would be so much unnecessary evil. For since only the nondeterrable are excused, withholding punishment offers no comfort to those who are deterrable.[10] The trouble is, as is now widely appreciated, that this does not follow, for punishing all, whether or not they happen to be deterrable, closes off any hope a deterrable offender might otherwise harbor that he could convince a jury that he was among the nondeterrable. Moreover, without excuses, prosecutions would be faster and cheaper, convictions more reliable, and the deterrent threat more credible. Indeed, we have in our law a class of offenses, strict liability offenses, that dispenses with mens rea requirements on just these grounds. Have we not given up something of value for the increased effectiveness that strict liability arguably provides, something that is not captured in Bentham's rationale?

Professor Hart, in one of his early essays, offered a different account of excuses. He argued that by confining liability to cases in which persons have freely chosen, excuses serve to maximize the effect of a person's choices within the framework of coercive law, thereby furthering the satisfaction people derive in knowing that they can avoid the sanction of the law if they choose.[13]

This rationale is an improvement over Bentham, inasmuch as Hart gives us a reason why we might want to put up with the loss of deterrence caused by excuses. But does this account capture the full force of a system of excuses? Suppose we preferred the risk of accidentally being victims of law enforcement to the increased risk of being victims of crime. That would be a plausible choice, particularly for a public obsessed with rising crime rates. Would we then feel there was nothing more problematic in giving up excuses than that we would be trading one kind of satisfaction for another? I think not. Something is missing in this account.

Hart's account focuses on the interests and satisfactions of the great majority of us who never become targets of law enforcement—our security in knowing we will not be punished if we do not choose to break the law. What is missing is an account of the concern for the innocent person who is the object of a criminal prosecution. Hart's essay does refer to the satisfaction of the lawbreaker in knowing the price he must pay to get what he wants by breaking the law. But it is doubtful that this is a satisfaction the law has any interest in furthering, for the point of the criminal law is surely to keep people from engaging in prohibited conduct, not to give them a choice between complying with the law or suffering punishment. The law's concern is for the person accused who has not made a culpable choice to break the law, not with furthering the interests of persons who would like to.

To blame a person is to express a moral criticism, and if the person's action does not deserve criticism, blaming him is a kind of falsehood and

---

10. J. Bentham, An Introduction to the Principles of Morals and Legislation 160–62 (J. Burns & H.L.A. Hart ed. 1970); see discussion in H.L.A. Hart, *Legal Responsibility and Excuses,* in Punishment and Responsibility 41–43 (1968). For a modern version of the utilitarian argument, see Spriggs, *A Utilitarian Reply to McCloskey,* in Contemporary Utilitarianism 261, 291–92 (M. Bayles ed. 1968).

13. [*Legal Responsibility and Excuses,* in H.L.A. Hart, *supra* note 10,] at 28–53.

is, to the extent the person is injured by being blamed, unjust to him. It is this feature of our everyday moral practices that lies behind the law's excuses. Excuses, then, as Hart himself recognized in a later essay,[16] represent no sentimental compromise with the demands of a moral code; they are, on the contrary, of the essence of a moral code. * * *

Of course, one might escape excuses altogether by withdrawing the element of blame from a finding of criminality. Indeed, there are some—though not so many as there were a generation ago—who would prefer that the criminal law reject all backward-looking judgments of punishment, blame, and responsibility, and concern itself exclusively with identifying and treating those who constitute a social danger. Whether it would be desirable to loosen punishment from its mooring in blame is a large and much discussed question. I will confine myself here to two observations. First, such a dissociation would not likely succeed. People would continue to see state coercion as punishment, notwithstanding official declarations that the state's only interest is the individual's welfare and social protection. Second, it is very doubtful that we should want it to succeed, since blame and punishment give expression to the concept of personal responsibility which is a central feature of our moral culture.

Notes and Questions

1. Under what circumstances is a person morally blameless for committing a wrongful act? Three nonutilitarian answers, briefly described below, are often suggested. As you consider the excuse defenses described in this chapter, ask yourself which one of these explanations most accurately describes the law of excuses that has developed, and which one, if any, approximates your own judgments of moral culpability?

2. *Causal theory.* Professor Michael Moore describes the causal theory of excuses, which he ultimately rejects, this way:

> The causal theory is partly descriptive and partly normative. The descriptive part asserts that the established excuses of Anglo–American criminal law can best be understood in terms of causation. According to this part of the theory, when an agent is caused to act by a factor outside his control, he is excused; only those acts not caused by some factor external to his will are unexcused. The normative part of the theory asserts that the criminal law is morally right in excusing all those, and only those, whose actions are caused by factors outside their control. * * *
>
>   * * * The plausibility of such a moral principle should be readily apparent. What could be more unfair than punishing someone for something he could not help? Samuel Butler satirized the opposite view when, in *Erewhon,* he describes the "justice" of a trial for the crime of pulmonary consumption. The trial judge, anticipating a charge of

16. *Punishment and the Elimination of   10, at 174–77.
Responsibility,* in H.L.A. Hart, *supra* note

unfairness for meting out a severe sentence to the diseased defendant, responds:

> It is all very well for you to say that you came of unhealthy parents, and had a severe accident in your childhood which permanently undermined your constitution; excuses such as these are the ordinary refuge of the criminal; but they cannot for one moment be listened to by the ear of justice. I am not here to enter upon curious metaphysical questions as to the origin of this or that.... There is no question of how you came to be wicked, but only this—namely, are you wicked or not?

Our intuitions may well reject the moral premises of the Erewhonian legal system; it does matter to us how the crime originated. It seems plausible that if the crime was caused by events over which the accused had no control, he could not help committing the crime and therefore should be excused.

Michael S. Moore, *Causation and the Excuses,* 73 Cal.L.Rev. 1091, 1091, 1111–12 (1985).

Put in concrete terms, according to the causal principle of excuses, a person should be acquitted for criminal conduct arising from, for example, mental illness or drug addiction, assuming that the actor was not responsible for the illness or addiction. Do you see any problems with this approach?

3. *Character theory.* Joshua Dressler, *Reflections on Excusing Wrongdoers: Moral Theory, New Excuses and the Model Penal Code,* 19 Rutgers L.J. 671, 693–94 (1988):

> [S]ome scholars consider evaluation of an actor's character not just relevant, but central to the blaming-excusing process. George Fletcher [Rethinking Criminal Law 800 (1978)] has explained one version of the role of character this way:
>
> > (1) punishing wrongful conduct is just only if punishment is measured by the desert of the offender, (2) the desert of an offender is gauged by his character—i.e., the kind of person he is, (3) and therefore, a judgment about character is essential to the just attribution of punishment.
>
> Excuses in this construct are recognized in those circumstances in which bad character cannot be inferred from the offender's wrongful acts. Thus, we excuse an insane person because it is likely that the illness rather than his character was responsible for the criminal activity. Similarly, with duress * * *, the unlawful threat * * *, rather than the actor's character, may be responsible for the conduct. In such circumstances we believe that any person of good character in the same situation might or would have acted similarly.
>
> A wrongdoer's character may be relevant in determining blameworthiness in other ways:
>
> > [One] approach seeks to distinguish those aspects of character caused by unchosen influence and those that can fairly be attributed to the actor. Under this view, wrongful actions that stem from those aspects of character caused by other persons or natural forces should be

excused; wrongful actions that stem from character traits attributable to the individual should be punished. The approach builds on the common intuition that, while persons are generally responsible for their own character, extraordinary environmental or genetic influences may preclude such responsibility.[e] * * *

Finally, some character theories argue for a closer examination of the capacities necessary for moral decision making. For example, Peter Arenella contends that moral responsibility requires certain moral-emotional capacities beyond those mandated by chosen action. Although proponents differ on their definition of moral capacity, all give a central place to the ability to empathize. Without an ability to care for others, proponents argue that a person cannot deserve punishment, even if her harmful act was rational, intentional and uncoerced.

* * * The person with good character has empathy for others and can be self-critical. Since these qualities are needed to be good and since we blame offenders for failing to attain goodness, it seems to follow that these qualities are a prerequisite for responsible choice.

Samuel H. Pillsbury, *The Meaning of Deserved Punishment: An Essay on Choice, Character, and Responsibility,* 67 Ind.L.J. 719, 730–31, 733–34 (1992) (rejecting these versions of the character theory in favor of a choice-based concept of blameworthiness, as discussed in Note 4).

Professor Peter Arenella, mentioned in the preceding Pillsbury excerpt, has explained his character-based conception of moral agency, i.e., what it means to be a person who can fairly be held morally accountable for her actions, this way:

Our accounts of moral evil presuppose that the wrongdoer has the capacity for moral concern, judgment, and action. We view moral evil as a corruption of this moral potential. Our * * * attitudes of resentment and blame rest on such presuppositions. We find it difficult to sustain our initial reaction of blame towards an actor who has breached some moral norm when we come to believe that the actor, through no fault of her own, lacked these moral capacities. We blame people not just for morally bad acts, but for the morally objectionable attitudes that (we believe) the actor conveyed through such behavior. But the liberal model of moral responsibility insists that we should not blame someone for failing to show moral concern for the interests of others if the actor is incapable of feeling such concern or acting on its basis.

What enables us to be moral actors who can understand the moral norms implicated by the criminal law? What threshold capacities do we need before we are able to use these norms in our practical judgments? * * * I have argued that a moral agent must possess the following character-based abilities and attributes: the capacity to care for the interests of other human beings, the internalization of others' normative expectations (including self-identification as a participant in a culture's moral blaming practices), * * * the ability to subject one's non-moral

e. Is this *your* intuition? Do you believe that you are responsible for your character, i.e., for the type of person you have become? Are there aspects of your character for which you believe you should *not* be held responsible?

ends and values to moral evaluation, the capacity to respond to moral norms as a motivation for one's choices, and the power to manage those firmly entrenched aspects of character that impair one's ability to make an appropriate moral evaluation of the situation one is in and the choices open to one.

None of these attributes are properties, skills, or capacities whose development is totally a matter of our own responsible choices. Some of them can only develop through time and appropriate interpersonal relations and experiences with adults who nurture us. * * *

The character-based model of moral agency reminds us that "desert" does not "go all the way down." We neither choose nor control the process that determines whether we become moral agents. For the most part, our status as moral agents is a matter of constitutive and social luck.

Peter Arenella, *Convicting the Morally Blameless: Reassessing the Relationship Between Legal and Moral Accountability,* 39 UCLA L.Rev. 1511, 1609–10 (1992).

If Professor Arenella's observations in the last paragraph are correct, where does that leave the law of excuses?

4. *Free choice/practical reasoning/personhood theory.* Joshua Dressler, *Reflections on Excusing Wrongdoers: Moral Theory, New Excuses and the Model Penal Code,* supra, at 701:

We affix blame to people, but not to other living things, because we believe that humans are unique in their capacity to make moral decisions about how they will act. The concept of blame, in other words, is predicated on our view of persons as autonomous agents, whose "actions stand on an entirely different footing" from other events in the universe.

Desert is based on the principle that a specific blameworthy act can be imputed to the person—not just to the body of the person—who is in court if, but only if, he had the capacity and fair opportunity to function in a uniquely human way, i.e., freely to choose whether to violate the moral/legal norms of society.

"Free choice" exists if the actor has the substantial capacity and fair opportunity to (1) understand the pertinent facts relating to his conduct; (2) appreciate that his conduct violates society's moral or legal norms; and (3) conform his conduct to the law. Unless all three conditions for free choice are present, blame does not attach to the wrongdoer, as he lacks a critical attribute of personhood.

Professor Michael Moore describes the concept of personhood that he believes is at the core of excuse defenses this way:

[T]he excuses are all related to the exercise of the actor's practical reasoning capacities.

Reason is practical when it gives us reasons for actions rather than reasons for belief. At a bare minimum, the ability to reason practically involves: (1) the ability to form an object we desire to achieve through action, (2) the ability to form a belief about how certain actions will or will not achieve the objects of our desires, and (3) the ability to act on our desires and our beliefs so that our actions form the "conclusion" of a valid practical syllogism. * * *

The capacity to engage in practical-reasoning is one of the essential prerequisites of personhood. Some of the excuses deal with such profound defects in practical-reasoning capacities that the very actor's personhood is in question. * * *

Other excuses exist because persons whose practical reasoning capacities may be unimpaired nonetheless may not have the opportunity to use them. * * *

In one or another of * * * ways, our legal and moral excuses all reflect the moral judgment that responsibility can only be ascribed to an individual who has both the capacity and the opportunity to exercise the practical reasoning that is distinctive of his personhood.

Michael S. Moore, *Causation and the Excuses,* supra, at 1148–49.

How does this view of moral responsibility differ from the character theories described in the preceding Note? Which one of the excuse principles described above would exempt from punishment the broadest class of wrongdoers? Which approach to moral/legal responsibility is the narrowest?

2. DURESS

a. General Principles

UNITED STATES v. CONTENTO–PACHON

United States Court of Appeals, Ninth Circuit, 1984.
723 F.2d 691.

BOOCHEVER, CIRCUIT JUDGE.

This case presents an appeal from a conviction for unlawful possession with intent to distribute a narcotic controlled substance in violation of 21 U.S.C. § 841(a)(1) (1976). At trial, the defendant attempted to offer evidence of duress and necessity defenses. The district court excluded this evidence on the ground that it was insufficient to support the defenses. We reverse because there was sufficient evidence of duress to present a triable issue of fact.

I. FACTS

The defendant-appellant, Juan Manuel Contento–Pachon, is a native of Bogota, Colombia and was employed there as a taxicab driver. He asserts that one of his passengers, Jorge, offered him a job as the driver of a privately-owned car. Contento–Pachon expressed an interest in the job and agreed to meet Jorge and the owner of the car the next day.

Instead of a driving job, Jorge proposed that Contento–Pachon swallow cocaine-filled balloons and transport them to the United States. Contento–Pachon agreed to consider the proposition. He was told not to mention the proposition to anyone, otherwise he would "get into serious trouble." Contento–Pachon testified that he did not contact the police because he believes that the Bogota police are corrupt and that they are paid off by drug traffickers.

Approximately one week later, Contento–Pachon told Jorge that he would not carry the cocaine. In response, Jorge mentioned facts about Contento–Pachon's personal life, including private details which Contento–Pachon had never mentioned to Jorge. Jorge told Contento–Pachon that his failure to cooperate would result in the death of his wife and three year-old child.

The following day the pair met again. Contento–Pachon's life and the lives of his family were again threatened. At this point, Contento–Pachon agreed to take the cocaine into the United States.

The pair met two more times. At the last meeting, Contento–Pachon swallowed 129 balloons of cocaine. He was informed that he would be watched at all times during the trip, and that if he failed to follow Jorge's instruction he and his family would be killed.

After leaving Bogota, Contento–Pachon's plane landed in Panama. Contento–Pachon asserts that he did not notify the authorities there because he felt that the Panamanian police were as corrupt as those in Bogota. Also, he felt that any such action on his part would place his family in jeopardy.

When he arrived at the customs inspection point in Los Angeles, Contento–Pachon consented to have his stomach x-rayed. The x-rays revealed a foreign substance which was later determined to be cocaine.

At Contento–Pachon's trial, the government moved to exclude the defenses of duress and necessity. The motion was granted. We reverse.

A. Duress

There are three elements of the duress defense: (1) an immediate threat of death or serious bodily injury, (2) a well-grounded fear that the threat will be carried out, and (3) no reasonable opportunity to escape the threatened harm. * * *

* * * We examine the elements of duress.

Immediacy: The element of immediacy requires that there be some evidence that the threat of injury was present, immediate, or impending. "[A] veiled threat of future unspecified harm" will not satisfy this requirement. The district court found that the initial threats were not immediate because "they were conditioned on defendant's failure to cooperate in the future and did not place defendant and his family in immediate danger."

Evidence presented on this issue indicated that the defendant was dealing with a man who was deeply involved in the exportation of illegal substances. Large sums of money were at stake and, consequently, Contento–Pachon had reason to believe that Jorge would carry out his threats. Jorge had gone to the trouble to discover that Contento–Pachon was married, that he had a child, the names of his wife and child, and the location of his residence. These were not vague threats of possible future harm. According to the defendant, if he had refused to cooperate, the consequences would have been immediate and harsh.

Contento–Pachon contends that he was being watched by one of Jorge's accomplices at all times during the airplane trip. As a consequence, the force of the threats continued to restrain him. Contento–Pachon's contention that he was operating under the threat of immediate harm was supported by sufficient evidence to present a triable issue of fact.

Escapability: The defendant must show that he had no reasonable opportunity to escape. The district court found that because Contento–Pachon was not physically restrained prior to the time he swallowed the balloons, he could have sought help from the police or fled. Contento–Pachon explained that he did not report the threats because he feared that the police were corrupt. The trier of fact should decide whether one in Contento–Pachon's position might believe that some of the Bogota police were paid informants for drug traffickers and that reporting the matter to the police did not represent a reasonable opportunity of escape.

If he chose not to go to the police, Contento–Pachon's alternative was to flee. We reiterate that the opportunity to escape must be reasonable. To flee, Contento–Pachon, along with his wife and three year-old child, would have been forced to pack his possessions, leave his job, and travel to a place beyond the reaches of the drug traffickers. A juror might find that this was not a reasonable avenue of escape. Thus, Contento–Pachon presented a triable issue on the element of escapability. * * *

B. *Necessity*

The defense of necessity is available when a person is faced with a choice of two evils and must then decide whether to commit a crime or an alternative act that constitutes a greater evil. Contento–Pachon has attempted to justify his violation of 21 U.S.C. § 841(a)(1) by showing that the alternative, the death of his family, was a greater evil.

Traditionally, in order for the necessity defense to apply, the coercion must have had its source in the physical forces of nature. The duress defense was applicable when the defendant's acts were coerced by a human force. This distinction served to separate the two similar defenses. But modern courts have tended to blur the distinction between duress and necessity.

It has been suggested that, "the major difference between duress and necessity is that the former negates the existence of the requisite mens rea for the crime in question, whereas under the latter theory there is no actus reus." *United States v. Micklus,* 581 F.2d 612, 615 (7th Cir.1978). The theory of necessity is that the defendant's free will was properly exercised to achieve the greater good and not that his free will was overcome by an outside force as with duress.

The defense of necessity is usually invoked when the defendant acted in the interest of the general welfare. * * *

Contento–Pachon's acts were allegedly coerced by human, not physical forces. In addition, he did not act to promote the general welfare. Therefore, the necessity defense was not available to him. Contento–Pachon mischaracterized evidence of duress as evidence of necessity. The district court correctly disallowed his use of the necessity defense.

II. CONCLUSION

Contento–Pachon presented credible evidence that he acted under an immediate and well-grounded threat of serious bodily injury, with no opportunity to escape. Because the trier of fact should have been allowed to consider the credibility of the proffered evidence, we reverse. * * *

COYLE, DISTRICT JUDGE (dissenting in part and concurring in part): * * *

In * * * excluding the defense of duress, the trial court specifically found Contento–Pachon had failed to present sufficient evidence to establish the necessary elements of immediacy and inescapability. In its Order the district court stated:

> The first threat made to defendant and his family about three weeks before the flight was not immediate; the threat was conditioned upon defendant's failure to cooperate in the future and did not place the defendant and his family in immediate danger or harm. Moreover, after the initial threat and until he went to the house where he ingested the balloons containing cocaine, defendant and his family were not physically restrained and could have sought help from the police or fled. No such efforts were attempted by defendant. Thus, defendant's own offer of proof negates two necessary elements of the defense of duress.

* * * This finding is adequately supported by the record. * * *

I agree with the majority, however, that the district court properly excluded Contento–Pachon's necessity defense.

Notes and Questions

1. Joshua Dressler, *Exegesis of the Law of Duress: Justifying the Excuse and Searching For Its Proper Limits*, 62 S.Cal.L.Rev. 1331, 1335 (1989):

> Reduced to a[n] * * * easily digested analytic form, * * * [a defendant] will be acquitted of an offense other than murder on the basis of duress if he pleads and proves that (1) [another person] unlawfully threatened imminently to kill or grievously injure him or another person; and (2) he was not at fault in exposing himself to the threat.

2. *"Duress" as a justification defense.* In their influential treatise, Professors LaFave and Scott treat duress as a justification defense. See Wayne R. LaFave and Austin W. Scott, Jr., Criminal Law § 5.3 (2d ed.

1986). Are they correct in doing so? Look at the elements of the defense set out in Note 1, and consider the crimes for which the defense may be pleaded. Does duress appear to be a justification or an excuse? Which is it under the Model Penal Code?

If duress is a justification defense as LaFave and Scott suggest, how does it differ from the defense of necessity? According to *Contento–Pachon,* what distinguishes the two defenses?

Intuitively, is duress an excuse or a justification? For example, suppose that Agnes threatens to poke out an eye of Brian's infant daughter unless he rapes Cecilia, and Brian accedes to the threat. To the extent that we would be inclined to acquit him, is the reason that Brian did the right thing (justification) or is it that we do not believe it is just to hold him accountable for his actions under the circumstances (excuse)?

3. *"Duress" as an excuse defense.* If duress is an excuse, what is the rationale of the defense? According to the drafters of the Model Penal Code, condemnation of a coerced actor "is bound to be an ineffective threat; what is, however, more significant is that it is divorced from any moral base and is unjust." American Law Institute, Model Penal Code and Commentaries, Comment to § 2.09 at 375 (1985).

Jerome Hall disagrees with the deterrence argument. According to Hall, "it certainly has not been, and probably cannot be, established that the drive of self-preservation is irresistible, that conduct in such situations is inexorably fixed. * * * In many ordinary matters, it is a common experience to act against a very strong desire * * *." Jerome Hall, General Principles of Criminal Law 445–46 (2d ed. 1960). The wise course, he says, "is to proceed on the hypothesis that a substantial percentage of persons * * * will act against their instinctual desires * * *." Id., at 446–47. Do you agree? Even if a coerced actor cannot be deterred by the threat of punishment, is there still a utilitarian basis for abolishing the duress defense?

Regarding the "more significant" argument raised in the Model Code Commentary, namely, that it is morally unjust to punish a coerced actor, consider the following observations:

> A coerced wrongdoer is unlike the insane person. The coerced actor is a whole person, free of sickness. As such, he possess the capacity for free choice; he has practical reasoning skills. * * *
>
> Furthermore, the coerced actor not only possesses the capacity to understand the attendant factual and legal circumstances, but he does *in fact* realize what it is he is doing. When *D* steals a watch under duress, he knows that he is taking a watch; when he commits perjury, he realizes that he is uttering a falsehood under oath; and when he succumbs to a kill-or-be-killed command, he knows perfectly well that he is taking a human life. * * *
>
> Indeed, what most weakens the case for excuse is that the coerced actor *chooses* to violate the law. He chooses to commit the criminal offense rather than to accept the threatened consequences. He would not have chosen to commit the crime but for the threat, but it *is* still his

choice, albeit a hard and excruciatingly difficult choice. His act may be unwilling, but it is not unwilled.

In no other circumstances does the law excuse a person for his rational and intentionally chosen harmful acts. Only duress cases excuse one who "self-consciously subordinates [the law] to the primacy of the person who is the subject of the desire."

Joshua Dressler, *Exegesis of the Law of Duress: Justifying the Excuse and Searching For Its Proper Limits,* supra, at 1359–60.

If the preceding statement accurately describes duress, what is the moral foundation for excusing coerced wrongdoers? The Model Code Commentary provides the following explanation:

[L]aw is ineffective in the deepest sense, indeed * * * it is hypocritical, if it imposes on the actor who has the misfortune to confront a dilemmatic choice, a standard that his judges are not prepared to affirm that they should and could comply with if their turn to face the problem should arise.

American Law Institute, Model Penal Code and Commentaries, Comment to § 2.09 at 374–75 (1985).

Is this a satisfactory explanation? What about Lord Coleridge's observation in *Dudley and Stephens* (p. 490 supra) that "[w]e are often compelled to set up standards we cannot reach ourselves, and to lay down rules which we could not ourselves satisfy"?

4. *Problems.* Do the facts in the following cases state a valid claim of duress? Apply the common law and the Model Penal Code.

A. *R,* a police informant, obtained evidence against *X,* a narcotics dealer, upon a promise that the police would keep his identity confidential. After his identity was accidentally disclosed, *R* agreed to testify against *X,* but requested police protection. Before trial, armed assailants threatened to hurt *R* if he testified against *X,* and once *R* was nearly run over by a car, possibly driven by a confederate of *X.* *R* 's father, who feared for the safety of other family members, ordered *R* to move out of the family home. The police provided *R* with a bus ticket to another state and a small amount of money, but he was unable to find a job and returned. At *X*'s trial, *R* testified falsely, denying knowledge of *X*'s criminal activities. *R* was prosecuted for perjury. State v. Rosillo, 282 N.W.2d 872 (Minn.1979).

B. *T,* a chiropractor, originally refused, but ultimately aided others, to prepare a fraudulent insurance claim by making out a false medical report. *T* cooperated after receiving threatening telephone calls at home. In one call, he was told: "Remember, you just moved into a place that has a very dark entrance and you leave there with your wife. You and your wife are going to jump at shadows when you leave that dark entrance." State v. Toscano, 74 N.J. 421, 378 A.2d 755 (1977).

5. *"The person of reasonable firmness."* Model Penal Code § 2.09 measures the defendant's conduct against the standard of "a person of reasonable firmness." Since duress is an excuse, why is the test objective, rather than focusing on the subjective capacities of the coerced individual? For example, suppose that John wants to prove that he is a timid individual

and, therefore, had no choice but to commit a serious crime when a minor threat was issued? Is it fair to hold him to a standard that he cannot meet? The Commentary explains the drafters' reasoning:

> The case of concern here is that in which the actor makes a choice, but claims in his defense that he was so intimidated that he was unable to choose otherwise. Should such psychological incapacity be given the same exculpative force as the physical incapacity that may afford a defense under Section 2.01? * * *
>
> In favor of allowing the defense, it may be argued that the legal sanction cannot be effective in the case supposed and that the actor may not properly be blamed for doing what he had to choose to do. It seems clear, however, that the argument in its full force must be rejected. The crucial reason is the same as that which elsewhere leads to an unwillingness to vary legal norms with the individual's capacity to meet the standards they prescribe, absent a disability that is both gross and verifiable, such as the mental disease or defect that may establish irresponsibility [under § 4.01]. * * * To make liability depend upon the fortitude of any given actor would be no less impractical or otherwise impolitic than to permit it to depend upon such other variables as intelligence or clarity of judgment, suggestibility or moral insight.
>
> Moreover, the legal standard may gain in its effectiveness by being unconditional in this respect. * * * [L]egal norms and sanctions operate not only at the moment of the climactic choice, but also in the fashioning of values and of character.
>
> Though, for the foregoing reasons, the submission that the actor lacked the fortitude to make the moral choice should not be entertained as a defense, a different situation is presented if the claimed excuse is based upon the incapacity of men in general to resist the coercive pressures to which the individual succumbed.

American Law Institute, Model Penal Code and Commentaries, Comment to § 2.09 at 373–74 (1985).

Although Section 2.09 generally states an objective standard, some subjectivization is invited:

> The standard is not, however, wholly external in its reference; account is taken of the actor's "situation," a term that should here be given the same scope it is accorded in appraising recklessness and negligence. Stark, tangible factors that differentiate the actor from another, like his size, strength, age, or health, would be considered in making the exculpatory judgment. Matters of temperament would not.

Id. at 375.

6. *Duress and the battered woman.* Over a three week period, Lisa Dunn travelled with and assisted Daniel Remeta, with whom she was living, in a crime spree that included a kidnapping and murder. The cornerstone of Dunn's proposed trial defense was that she suffered from the battered woman syndrome and that, as a result, she felt compelled to participate in the crimes, even though Remeta never threatened her. Should syndrome evidence be admissible in support of a duress claim? If so, in what way is such evidence relevant? State v. Dunn, 243 Kan. 414, 758 P.2d 718 (1988),

habeas granted, Dunn v. Roberts, 768 F.Supp. 1442 (D.Kan.1991), affirmed 963 F.2d 308 (10th Cir.1992); see People v. Romero, 10 Cal.App.4th 1519, 13 Cal.Rptr.2d 332 (1992); United States v. Homick, 964 F.2d 899 (9th Cir. 1992).

b. Necessity Versus Duress

PEOPLE v. UNGER

Supreme Court of Illinois, 1977.
66 Ill.2d 333, 5 Ill.Dec. 848, 362 N.E.2d 319.

Ryan, Justice.

Defendant, Francis Unger, was charged with the crime of escape, and was convicted following a jury trial * * *. * * * The conviction was reversed upon appeal * * *. We * * * affirm the judgment of the appellate court.

At the time of the present offense, the defendant was confined at the Illinois State Penitentiary in Joliet, Illinois. Defendant was serving a one- to three-year term as a consequence of a conviction for auto theft in Ogle County. Defendant began serving this sentence in December of 1971. On February 23, 1972, the defendant was transferred to the prison's minimum security, honor farm. It is undisputed that on March 7, 1972, the defendant walked off the honor farm. Defendant was apprehended two days later in a motel room in St. Charles, Illinois.

At trial, defendant testified that prior to his transfer to the honor farm he had been threatened by a fellow inmate. This inmate allegedly brandished a six-inch knife in an attempt to force defendant to engage in homosexual activities. Defendant was 22 years old and weighed approximately 155 pounds. He testified that he did not report the incident to the proper authorities due to fear of retaliation. Defendant also testified that he is not a particularly good fighter.

Defendant stated that after his transfer to the honor farm he was assaulted and sexually molested by three inmates, and he named the assailants at trial. The attack allegedly occurred on March 2, 1972, and from that date until his escape defendant received additional threats from inmates he did not know. On March 7, 1972, the date of the escape, defendant testified that he received a call on an institution telephone. Defendant testified that the caller, whose voice he did not recognize, threatened him with death because the caller had heard that defendant had reported the assault to prison authorities. Defendant said that he left the honor farm to save his life and that he planned to return once he found someone who could help him. None of these incidents were reported to the prison officials. * * *

Defendant's first trial for escape resulted in a hung jury. The jury in the second trial returned its verdict after a five-hour deliberation. The following instruction (People's Instruction No. 9) was given by the trial court over defendant's objection.

"The reasons, if any, given for the alleged escape are immaterial and not to be considered by you as in any way justifying or excusing, if there were in fact such reasons."

The appellate court majority found that the giving of People's Instruction No. 9 was reversible error. Two instructions which were tendered by defendant but refused by the trial court are also germane to this appeal. Defendant's instructions Nos. 1 and 3 were predicated upon the affirmative defenses of compulsion and necessity. Defendant's instructions Nos. 1 and 3 read as follows:

"It is a defense to the charge made against the Defendant that he left the Honor Farm of the Illinois State Penitentiary by reason of necessity if the accused was without blame in occasioning or developing the situation and reasonably believed such conduct was necessary to avoid a public or private injury greater than the injury which might reasonably result from his own conduct."

"It is a defense to the charge made against the Defendant that he acted under the compulsion of threat or menace of the imminent infliction of death or great bodily harm, if he reasonably believed death or great bodily harm would be inflicted upon him if he did not perform the conduct with which he is charged."

The principal issue in the present appeal is whether it was error for the court to instruct the jury that it must disregard the reasons given for defendant's escape and to conversely refuse to instruct the jury on the statutory defenses of compulsion and necessity. * * * The State contends that, under the facts and circumstances of this case, the defenses of compulsion and necessity are, as a matter of law, unavailable to defendant. * * *

Proper resolution of this appeal requires some preliminary remarks concerning the law of compulsion and necessity as applied to prison escape situations. Traditionally, the courts have been reluctant to permit the defenses of compulsion and necessity to be relied upon by escapees. This reluctance appears to have been primarily grounded upon considerations of public policy. Several recent decisions, however, have recognized the applicability of the compulsion and necessity defenses to prison escapes. In *People v. Harmon* (1974), 53 Mich.App. 482, 220 N.W.2d 212, the defense of duress was held to apply in a case where the defendant alleged that he escaped in order to avoid repeated homosexual attacks from fellow inmates. In *People v. Lovercamp* (1974), 43 Cal. App.3d 823, 118 Cal.Rptr. 110, a limited defense of necessity was held to be available to two defendants whose escapes were allegedly motivated by fear of homosexual attacks.

As illustrated by *Harmon* and *Lovercamp,* different courts have reached similar results in escape cases involving sexual abuse, though the question was analyzed under different defense theories. A certain degree of confusion has resulted from the recurring practice on the part of the courts to use the terms "compulsion" (duress) and "necessity" interchangeably, though the defenses are theoretically distinct. It has been suggested that the major distinction between the two defenses is that the source of the coercive power in cases of compulsion is from human beings, whereas in situations of necessity the pressure on the defendant arises from the forces of nature. Also, * * * the defense of compulsion generally requires an impending, imminent threat of great bodily harm together with a demand that the person perform the specific criminal act for which he is eventually charged. Additionally, where the defense of compulsion is successfully asserted the coercing party is guilty of the crime.

It is readily discernible that prison escapes induced by fear of homosexual assaults and accompanying physical reprisals do not conveniently fit within the traditional ambits of either the compulsion or the necessity defense. However, it has been suggested that such cases could best be analyzed in terms of necessity. One commentator has stated that the relevant consideration should be whether the defendant chose the lesser of two evils, in which case the defense of necessity would apply, or whether he was unable to exercise a free choice at all, in which event compulsion would be the appropriate defense. Gardner, *The Defense of Necessity and the Right to Escape from Prison—A Step Towards Incarceration Free From Sexual Assault*, 49 S.Cal.L.Rev. 110, 133 (1975).

In our view, the defense of necessity is the appropriate defense in the present case. In a very real sense, the defendant here was not deprived of his free will by the threat of imminent physical harm which * * * appears to be the intended interpretation of the defense of compulsion as set out in * * * the Criminal Code. * * * Rather, if defendant's testimony is believed, he was forced to choose between two admitted evils by the situation which arose from actual and threatened homosexual assaults and fears of reprisal. Though the defense of compulsion would be applicable in the unlikely event that a prisoner was coerced by the threat of imminent physical harm to perform the specific act of escape, no such situation is involved in the present appeal. We, therefore, turn to a consideration of whether the evidence presented by the defendant justified the giving of an instruction on the defense of necessity.

The defendant's testimony was clearly sufficient to raise the affirmative defense of necessity. * * * Defendant testified that he was subjected to threats of forced homosexual activity and that, on one occasion, the threatened abuse was carried out. He also testified that he was physically incapable of defending himself and that he feared greater harm would result from a report to the authorities. Defendant further testified that just prior to his escape he was told that he was going to be killed, and that he therefore fled the honor farm in order to save his life. * * * It is clear that defendant introduced some evidence to support the defense of necessity. * * * [T]hat is sufficient to justify the giving of an appropriate instruction.

The State, however, would have us apply a more stringent test to prison escape situations. The State refers to the *Lovercamp* decision, where only a limited necessity defense was recognized. In *Lovercamp*, it was held that the defense of necessity need be submitted to the jury only where five conditions had been met. Those conditions are:

"(1) The prisoner is faced with a specific threat of death, forcible sexual attack or substantial bodily injury in the immediate future;

(2) There is no time for a complaint to the authorities or there exists a history of futile complaints which make any result from such complaints illusory;

(3) There is no time or opportunity to resort to the courts;

(4) There is no evidence of force or violence used towards prison personnel or other 'innocent' persons in the escape; and

(5) The prisoner immediately reports to the proper authorities when he has attained a position of safety from the immediate threat."

The State correctly points out that the defendant never informed the authorities of his situation and failed to report immediately after securing a position of safety. Therefore, it is contended that, under the authority of *Lovercamp,* defendant is not entitled to a necessity instruction. We agree with the State and with the court in *Lovercamp* that the above conditions are relevant factors to be used in assessing claims of necessity. We cannot say, however, that the existence of each condition is, as a matter of law, necessary to establish a meritorious necessity defense.

The preconditions set forth in *Lovercamp* are, in our view, matters which go to the weight and credibility of the defendant's testimony. * * * The absence of one or more of the elements listed in *Lovercamp* would not necessarily mandate a finding that the defendant could not assert the defense of necessity.

By way of example, in the present case defendant did not report to the authorities immediately after securing his safety. * * * However, defendant testified that he intended to return to the prison upon obtaining legal advice from an attorney and claimed that he was attempting to get money from friends to pay for such counsel. Regardless of our opinion as to the believability of defendant's tale, this testimony, if accepted by the jury, would have negated any negative inference which would arise from defendant's failure to report to proper authorities after the escape. The absence of one of the *Lovercamp* preconditions does not alone disprove the claim of necessity and should not, therefore, automatically preclude an instruction on the defense. * * *

Notes and Questions

1. Since prison escape cases do not neatly fit within the ambit of either the necessity or duress defense, does it matter which label is attached? If you represented a prison escapee, which defense would you prefer to use?

Balancing the interests. Does the choice-of-evils calculus involved in a necessity claim help or hurt an escapee's chances for acquittal? Does it matter whether the inmate was in prison for car theft or for rape? From the defendant's perspective, Professor George Fletcher sees problems with the necessity defense that can be avoided if the claim is couched in terms of duress:

> [T]here are several reasons why a contemporary Anglo–American court would be reluctant to label [an escapee's] conduct as right and proper. For one, it would be fashioning a rule that would seem to give other similarly maltreated inmates the right to walk out the front door. Further, judges today are likely to interweave two distinct questions of balancing: first, whether on balance the defendant did the right thing, and secondly, whether it would be right, on balance, to acquit the defendant. Looking at [a defendant's] conduct as a matter of interest-balancing readily blends with the court's balancing the benefits and burdens of deciding to acquit. Once the court starts focusing on the interests weighing against acquittal, [the defendant's] chances plummet. He would have been far better off if he could have anchored the debate to the limited inquiry whether his escape was excused by the [intolerable conditions]. He might then have kept the court's focus on the question of whether he could fairly be blamed for yielding to the pressure of the situation. By so directing the inquiry, he might have been able to divert judicial attention away from the prospective benefits and burdens of their decision and toward the requirements implicit in treating the individual defendant fairly. Yet at least for the last century, judges in England and the United States have been unreceptive to that mode of decision. The unequivocal preference is for a future-oriented assessment of the virtues of deciding for and against the defendant; there is little commitment to the imperative of treating the defendant justly—as a value independent of the resulting social benefits.
> * * *
> Like the draftsmen of the Model Penal Code, American judges are prone to insist that the only relevant dimension of necessity is the defense of lesser evils; thus the theoretical rationale for acquittal is whether, on balance, the defendant acted in the social interest. Yet that dimension rarely yields acquittals. And whenever a strong interest—like maintaining discipline in the prisons—emerges on the opposing scale, the judges are likely to frustrate the defendant's appeal to the greater good.

George P. Fletcher, *The Individualization of Excusing Conditions,* 47 S.Cal. L.Rev. 1269, 1285–87 (1974).

Professor David Dolinko disagrees with Professor Fletcher's appraisal:

> Despite its strength, Fletcher's argument is ultimately unconvincing for two reasons. First, if the argument is employed to suggest that the intolerable-conditions defense is better treated as duress than as necessity, it is open to the reply that there are equally strong grounds for believing that a duress defense would not work to the escapee's interest. Fletcher himself admits that English and American judges "have been unreceptive" to appeals to focus on the individual defendant's situation

rather than make "a future-oriented assessment of the virtues of deciding for and against the defendant." They may engage in such "future-oriented" speculation even when applying a duress defense. * * *

Secondly, although judges weighing the harm an escapee avoided against the harm to society from escapes can certainly give so great a weight to the societal interests as to preclude the defendant from a successful necessity defense, it is not inevitable that they will do so. Even in the nineteenth century, courts did not invariably apply the necessity defense with so little sensitivity to the individual defendant's situation. * * *

Certainly, contemporary courts are increasingly reluctant to assume that society's interests in preventing escapes must, in all but the most egregious cases, outweigh the interests of the individual defendant. * * * Indeed, the *Lovercamp* court explicitly rejected any automatic presumption that society's interests must prevail * * *. And the *Unger* court, which went even further in accommodating the escapee's individual interests by dropping the special prerequisites for admitting the intolerable-conditions plea, did so in applying a choice of evils defense.

David Dolinko, Comment, *Intolerable Conditions as a Defense to Prison Escapes*, 26 UCLA L.Rev. 1126, 1172–74 (1979).

Effect on third parties: the prison guard. Suppose that a prison guard had discovered Unger as he was escaping. Would she have been justified in preventing Unger's escape, by force if necessary? Would Unger have been justified in using defensive force against her? Do the answers to these questions depend on whether Unger's escape is justified or merely excused?

According to Professor Fletcher, a "determination that the conduct [of a prisoner] is justified presupposes a judgment about the superior social interest in the conflict. If the superior social interest is represented by the party seeking to [escape] * * *, it is also in the social interest to suppress resistance." George P. Fletcher, Rethinking Criminal Law 761 (1978). In short, if a prisoner is justified in escaping, a guard is not justified in preventing the escape. Again, Professor Dolinko disagrees:

The * * * serious consequence alleged to follow from conceding that a prisoner's escape was justified is that no one—including guards—should be entitled to resist the escape. * * * [T]his awkward result does not follow if the escape is merely excusable, since an excusable act is still wrongful and may be resisted. * * *

Whatever the validity of this argument as applied to justified actions in general, it neglects the special features present in an escape situation. * * *

* * * [E]ven if the lesser-evils principle is the basis for holding a prisoner's escape attempt justified, a prison guard can be justified by that same principle in foiling the escape. * * *

Suppose that a prisoner is attempting to escape in circumstances that justify his actions as the lesser evil. His escape would inflict a certain amount of harm, because to some degree it would weaken prison discipline, encourage other escape attempts, and possibly raise the level of tension and violence in the prison. This harm is by hypothesis outweighed by the harm the prisoner would avoid if he escapes: assume that this harm consists of a threatened sexual assault. Now consider a prison guard who discovers the inmate attempting to escape and acts to prevent the escape. The harm inflicted by the guard's action is precisely that which would have been avoided by the escape: subjecting the prisoner to sexual assault. But the harm that the guard's action averts is *not* necessarily the same as the harm which the escape would have inflicted—it may well be greater. The prisoner's escape, in itself, would have undermined prison discipline to some degree; but for a guard to witness a prisoner escaping and take no action to stop him would represent a much greater blow to discipline. Hence it is at least possible that the harm the guard's intervention averts might outweigh the harm of sexual assault on the inmate, even though that harm in turn outweighs the harm the escape would have wrought. If so, both the prisoner's escape attempt and the guard's intervention would be justified as choices of the lesser evil. Consequently, it is false to claim that interference with an action justified by the choice of evils principle (that is, by the defense of necessity) must be wrongful.

David Dolinko, *Intolerable Conditions as a Defense to Prison Escapes,* supra, at 1176, 1178, 1180–81.

Professor Fletcher replied:

Dolinko sees no difficulty in persons having incompatible rights. The pacifist may have a right not to kill; but the state may also have right to conscript him into active military service. The depressed man might arguably have a right to commit suicide, but his family has a right to intervene and prevent him from succumbing to his depression. The fetus may have a right to life, but the pregnant woman has a right to determine whether she will bear the fetus. These conflicts of plausible rights have always been with us; and so long as our legal system remains vital, they will be with us. But it does not follow that every right that appears plausible is a right in fact. The purpose of the legal system is precisely to resolve these conflicts based on plausible but inconsistent assertions of right. If the parties assert conflicting rights, then respect for their definition of the dispute requires that we search for the superior claim of right. * * *

If we leave aside the distortions produced by legally recognized rights departing from moral rights, then we have to recognize that every decision about rights entails a judgment about whether other parties have a right to prevent the rightful conduct. We cannot affirm a right in the prisoner to escape and at the same time grant the guard a right to keep him in prison. Conversely, if the guard has a right to keep convicted felons in prison, the inmates cannot have a right to escape.

Some people may have doubts about whether guards have a categorical right to keep all felons in prison, but I do not. Any rule we fashion about a "right to escape" must apply to convicted murderers as well as to prisoners doing time for possessing marijuana. It is not the office of prison guards to determine whether on balance it would be better for society to let a prisoner escape. Their duty as well as their right is to enforce the order of the courts committing convicted criminals to prison.

George P. Fletcher, *Should Intolerable Prison Conditions Generate a Justification or an Excuse for Escape?*, 26 UCLA L.Rev. 1355, 1364–65 (1979).

Effect on third parties: accomplices. Suppose that Unger had obtained help in escaping. Would his accomplice's liability depend on the nature of Unger's claim? (See p. 828 infra.)

2. *Model Penal Code.* How would *Unger* be decided under the Model Code? Could the defendant successfully raise either or both Sections 2.09 and 3.02?

Suppose that a guard had killed Unger because it was the only way to prevent the escape. In an ensuing murder prosecution, would the guard have had a valid defense? See Section 3.07(3). Would it matter whether the guard knew why Unger was fleeing?

c. Defense to Murder?

INTRODUCTORY COMMENT

Anglo–American courts frequently state in dictum that duress is not a defense to murder. In Director of Public Prosecutions for Northern Ireland v. Lynch [1975] App.Cas. 653, however, the House of Lords approved the assertion of the defense by a defendant who claimed that he was coerced by members of the Irish Republican Army to serve as an accomplice in the murder of a police officer, by driving the car used in the crime.

Lynch expressly reserved the question of whether to retain the no-defense rule in regard to a coerced *perpetrator* of a murder. Two years later, however, in Abbott v. The Queen [1977] App.Cas. 755, the Judicial Committee of the Privy Council held that the duress defense remained unavailable in such circumstances. In the following case, the House of Lords reconsidered the issue, this time (as in *Abbott*) in relation to a perpetrator of a murder.

REGINA v. HOWE

House of Lords, 1987.
1 App.Cas. 417.

[Howe was prosecuted along with three compatriots for various crimes, including the murder of a 19–year–old youth. Howe and the others took the victim to a secluded spot where they kicked and punched him. When ordered to do so by co-conspirator Murray, Howe strangled the victim. Howe claimed that if he had not complied, Murray would have beaten him to death.

The Court of Appeals certified three questions of law of general public importance to the House of Lords, the first one of which was: "Is duress available as a defence to a person charged with murder as a principal in the first degree (the actual killer)?" The House of Lords unanimously answered the question in the negative. Excerpts from the speech of one member of the House follows.]

LORD HAILSHAM OF ST. MARYLEBONE L.C. * * *

This leaves us free to discuss the first, and principal issue in the appeal which is the answer to be given to the first of the three certified questions. In my opinion, this must be decided on principle and authority, and the answer must in the end demand a reconsideration of *Lynch* and *Abbott.* * * *

I therefore consider the matter first from the point of view of authority. On this I can only say that at the time when *Lynch* was decided the balance of weight in an unbroken tradition of authority dating back to Hale and Blackstone seems to have been * * * that duress was not available to a defendant accused of murder. I quote only from Hale and Blackstone. Thus *Hale's Pleas of the Crown,* (1736), vol. 1, p. 51:

> "if a man be desperately assaulted, and in peril of death, and cannot otherwise escape, unless to satisfy his assailant's fury he will kill an innocent person then present, the fear and actual force will not acquit him of the crime and punishment of murder, if he commit the fact; for he ought rather to die himself, than kill an innocent: . . ."

Blackstone, Commentaries on the Laws of England, (1857 ed.), vol. 4, p. 28 was to the same effect. He wrote that a man under duress: "ought rather to die himself than escape by the murder of an innocent." * * *

I would only add that article 8 of the Charter of the International Military Tribunal, Treaty Series No. 27 of 1946 at Nuremberg, which was, at the time, universally accepted, save for its reference to mitigation, as an accurate statement of the common law both in England and the United States of America that:

> "The fact that the defendant acted pursuant to the order of his government or of a superior shall not free him from responsibility, but may be considered in mitigation of punishment if the tribunal determines that justice so requires."

"Superior orders" is not identical with "duress," but, in the circumstances of the Nazi regime, the difference must often have been negligible. * * *

What then is said on the other side? I accept, of course, that duress for almost all other crimes had been held to be a complete defence. I need not cite cases. They are carefully reviewed in *Lynch* and establish I believe that the defence is of venerable antiquity and wide extent. * * *

The other reported authority is the famous and important case of *Reg. v. Dudley and Stephens* (1884) 14 Q.B.D. 273. That is generally and, in my view correctly, regarded as an authority on the availability of the supposed defence of necessity rather than duress. But I must say frankly that, if we were to allow this appeal, we should, I think, also have to say that *Dudley and Stephens* was bad law. There is, of course, an obvious distinction between duress and necessity as potential defences; duress arises from the wrongful threats or violence of another human being and necessity arises from any other objective dangers threatening the accused. This, however, is, in my view a distinction without a relevant difference, since on this view duress is only that species of the genus of necessity which is caused by wrongful threats. I cannot see that there is any way in which a person of ordinary fortitude can be excused from the one type of pressure on his will rather than the other.

* * * But at this stage I feel that I should say that in *Abbott* I would have been prepared to accept a distinction between *Abbott* and *Lynch* * * *. I would not myself have immersed myself in the somewhat arcane terminology of accessory, principal in the second degree, and aiding and abetting. But it did seem to me then, and it seems to me now, that there is a valid distinction to be drawn in ordinary language between a man who actually participates in the irrevocable act of murder to save his own skin or that of his nearest and dearest and a man who simply participates before or after the event in the necessary preparation for it or the escape of the actual offender. It is as well to remember that, in *Abbott* the facts were that Abbott had dug a pit, thrown the victim into it, subjected her in co-operation with others to murderous blows and stab wounds and then buried her alive. It seems to me that those academics who see no difference between that case and the comparatively modest part alleged * * * in *Lynch* to have been played by the defendant under duress have parted company with a full sense of reality. Nevertheless and in spite of this, I do not think that the decision in *Lynch* can be justified on authority and that * * * I consider that the right course in the instant appeal is to restore the law to the condition in which it was almost universally thought to be prior to *Lynch*. * * *

This brings me back to the question of principle. I begin by affirming that, while there can never be a direct correspondence between law and morality, an attempt to divorce the two entirely is and has always proved to be, doomed to failure, and, in the present case, the overriding objects of the criminal law must be to protect innocent lives and to set a standard of conduct which ordinary men and women are expected to observe if they are to avoid criminal responsibility. * * *

In general, I must say that I do not at all accept in relation to the defence of murder it is either good morals, good policy or good law to suggest, as did the majority in *Lynch* and the minority in *Abbott* that the ordinary man of reasonable fortitude is not to be supposed to be capable of heroism if he is asked to take an innocent life rather than sacrifice his own. Doubtless in actual practice many will succumb to temptation, as they did in *Dudley and Stephens*. But many will not, and I do not believe that as a "concession to human frailty" the former should be exempt from liability to criminal sanctions if they do. I have known in my own lifetime of too many acts of heroism by ordinary human beings of no more than ordinary fortitude to regard a law as either "just or humane" which withdraws the protection of the criminal law from the innocent victim and casts the cloak of its protection upon the coward and the poltroon in the name of a "concession to human frailty."

I must not, however, underestimate the force of the arguments on the other side, advanced as they have been with such force and such persuasiveness by some of the most eminent legal minds, judicial and academic, in the country.

First, amongst these is, perhaps, the argument from logic and consistency. * * *

* * * Consistency and logic, though inherently desirable, are not always prime characteristics of a penal code based like the common law on custom and precedent. Law so based is not an exact science. All the same, I feel I am required to give some answer to the question posed. If duress is available as a defence to some crimes of the most grave why, it may legitimately be asked, stop at murder * * *? But surely I am entitled * * * to believe that some degree of proportionality between the threat and the offence must, at least to some extent, be a prerequisite of the defence under existing law. Few would resist threats to the life of a loved one if the alternative were driving across the red lights or in excess of 70 m.p.h. on the motorway. But, * * * it would take rather more than the threat of a slap on the wrist or even moderate pain or injury to discharge the evidential burden even in the case of a fairly serious assault. In such a case the "concession to human frailty" is no more than to say that in such circumstances a reasonable man of average courage is entitled to embrace as a matter of choice the alternative which a reasonable man could regard as the lesser of two evils. Other considerations necessarily arise where the choice is between the threat of death or a fortiori of serious injury and deliberately taking an innocent life. In such a case a reasonable man might reflect that one innocent human life is at least as valuable as his own or that of his loved one. In such a case a man cannot claim that he is choosing the lesser of two evils. Instead he is embracing the cognate but morally disreputable principle that the end justifies the means. * * *

Far less convincing than the argument based on consistency is the belief which appears in some of the judgments that the law must "move with the times" in order to keep pace with the immense political and social changes since what are alleged to have been the bad old days of Blackstone and Hale. * * * The argument is based on the false assumption that violence to innocent victims is now less prevalent than in the days of Hale or Blackstone. But I doubt whether this is so. We live in the age of the holocaust of the Jews, of international terrorism on the scale of massacre, of the explosion of aircraft in mid air, and murder sometimes at least as obscene as anything experienced in Blackstone's day. * * * Social change is not always for the better and it ill becomes those of us who have participated in the cruel events of the 20th century to condemn as out of date those who wrote in defence of innocent lives in the 18th century.

During the course of argument it was suggested that there was available * * * some sort of half way house between allowing these appeals and dismissing them. The argument ran that we might treat duress in murder as analogous to provocation, or perhaps diminished responsibility, and say that, in indictments for murder, duress might reduce the crime to one of manslaughter. I find myself quite unable to accept this. * * * Unlike the doctrine of provocation, which is based on emotional loss of control, the defence of duress * * * is put forward as a "concession to human frailty" whereby a conscious decision [is] coolly undertaken, to sacrifice an innocent human life * * *. * * *

Notes and Questions

1. Franklin is coerced to assist in a bank robbery, during the commission of which the bank teller accidentally is killed. Franklin is prosecuted for felony murder. Since duress is ordinarily a valid defense to robbery, does it also excuse the accidental killing? See State v. Lassen, 679 S.W.2d 363 (Mo.App.1984); State v. Ng, 110 Wash.2d 32, 750 P.2d 632 (1988).

2. The Model Penal Code does not bar the defense of duress in murder prosecutions. The drafters believed that "[i]t is obvious that even homicide may sometimes be the product of coercion that is truly irresistible * * *." American Law Institute, Model Penal Code and Commentaries, Comment to § 2.09 at 376 (1985). Under the Code, if a jury determines that a person of reasonable firmness would *not* have killed in the defendant's situation, of what crime is the defendant guilty?

3. *Necessity as an excuse.* Emergent conditions can justify the violation of a criminal law. Is there any reason why "necessity" may not also serve as an excuse? Consider the remarks of Canadian Supreme Court Justice Dickson in Perka v. Queen, [1984] 2 S.C.R. 232, 248–50:

> With regard to this conceptualization of a residual defense of necessity, I retain the skepticism I expressed [in an earlier case]. It is still my opinion that, "[n]o system of positive law can recognize any principle which would entitle a person to violate the law because of his view the law conflicted with some higher social value." * * *

> Conceptualized as an "excuse," however, the residual defense of necessity is, in my view, much less open to criticism. It rests on a realistic assessment of human weakness, recognizing that a liberal and humane criminal law cannot hold people to the strict obedience of laws in emergency situations where normal human instincts, whether of self-preservation or of altruism, overwhelmingly impel disobedience. The objectivity of the criminal law is preserved; such acts are still wrongful, but in the circumstances they are excusable. Praise is indeed not bestowed, but pardon is * * *.

George Fletcher, *Rethinking Criminal Law* (1978), describes this view of necessity as "compulsion of circumstance" which description points to the conceptual link between necessity as an excuse and the familiar criminal law requirement that in order to engage criminal liability, the actions constituting the *actus reus* of an offence must be voluntary. * * *

I agree with this formulation of the rationale for excuses in the criminal law. In my view this rationale extends beyond specific codified excuses and embraces the residual excuse known as the defence of necessity. At the heart of this defence is the perceived injustice of punishing violations of the law in circumstances in which the person had no other viable or reasonable choice available; the act was wrong but it is excused because it was realistically unavoidable.

If necessity may serve as an excuse, as Justice Dickson argues, does it follow that if the law excuses the killing of an innocent person as the result of a coercive human threat (duress), it should also excuse a killing that arises from natural conditions of an equally coercive nature ("compulsion of circumstances")? Was Lord Hailsham correct, in other words, when he observed that if the House of Lords had allowed Howe's appeal, it would have had to declare that the lifeboat case, *Dudley and Stephens* (p. 488 supra), was improperly decided?

The Model Code defense of duress is limited to coercion arising from the use or threatened use of "unlawful" force, which implies that coercive natural forces are not encompassed by the defense. The Commentary explains the drafters' reasoning:

> [S]ection [2.09], though plainly more liberal toward the victims of coercion than traditional law, does not reach one * * * situation that is arguably similar in principle to those it does reach. That is the case in which the danger to oneself or another arises from the effect of natural causes and an otherwise criminal act is performed to meet the danger. * * *
>
> At the time the Model Code was drafted, the Wisconsin Code contained a defense of necessity that, in effect, established a defense of duress from natural causes. The judgment of the Institute, however, was that such a defense should not be included. The general justification defense of Section 3.02 does apply to choices of evils required by natural causes. It will be an extraordinarily rare case in which a person will not be able to claim successfully that a response to natural causes was a choice of a lesser evil but could successfully claim that the choice was one a person of reasonable firmness would make. And there is a significant difference between the situations in which an actor makes the choice of an equal or greater evil under the threat of unlawful human force and when he does so because of a natural event. In the former situation, the basic interests of the law may be satisfied by the prosecution of the agent of unlawful force; in the latter circumstance, if the actor is excused, no one is subject to the law's application.

American Law Institute, Model Penal Code and Commentaries, Comment to § 2.09 at 377–79 (1985).

Others, including philosopher Robert Nozick, have drawn a similar distinction between human threats and natural forces:

> Robert Nozick * * * questions the difference between being confined in one's house by a lightning storm and being similarly imprisoned by a

person threatening to electrocute him if he leaves. His answer is that in the former case, one attributes the dweller's decision to his own will. In the latter case, however, "another's intentions are so closely linked with the action as to make it not fully one's own, less so than an act done in the face of equal costs due solely to inanimate nature." [233] Thus, in the sentence, "I, the coerced actor, am not to blame for the wrongdoing," the critical word becomes "I," and the assumption is that to excuse me there must be another person whose wrongful will is preempting mine.

* * *

But why should it be the case that before the criminal law excuses a person there must exist another actor with a wrongful will who potentially can be punished for the wrongdoing? Certainly, as a descriptive matter, this claim is inconsistent with other excuses. The pleas of insanity, infancy, involuntary intoxication, and mistake of law do not require the existence of a culpable party to whom legal responsibility may be shifted. In these contexts, the issue is whether the particular defendant deserves punishment, not whether someone else can be deservedly punished for the crime.

It should be kept in mind that the question at hand is whether the actor—the immediate law violator—had a fair chance to avoid acting unlawfully, i.e., whether a person of reasonable moral firmness would have resisted the human or natural threat. Assuming that natural and human threats are equal in coerciveness, the immediate actors' blameworthiness are also equal, as their opportunities to act lawfully were equally constrained.

Joshua Dressler, *Exegesis of the Law of Duress: Justifying the Excuse and Searching For Its Proper Limits,* 62 S.Cal.L.Rev. 1331, 1375–76 (1989).

4. *"Rotten social background" defense?* If "compulsion by circumstances" is recognized as an excuse, where should the line of personal responsibility be drawn? What if a person claims that because she grew up and continues to live in a terrible social environment, she could not resist turning to a life of crime? Should a jury be permitted to consider whether a person of reasonable firmness in the same situation would have acted in the same manner?

Yes, says Professor Richard Delgado:

An environment of extreme poverty and deprivation creates in individuals a propensity to commit crimes. In some cases, a defendant's impoverished background so greatly determines his or her criminal behavior that we feel it unfair to punish the individual. This sense of unfairness arises from the morality of the criminal law itself, in that "our collective conscience does not allow punishment where it cannot impose blame." And blame is inappropriate when a defendant's criminal behavior is caused by extrinsic factors beyond his or her control.

Richard Delgado, *"Rotten Social Background": Should the Criminal Law Recognize a Defense of Severe Environmental Deprivation?,* 3 Law & Inequality 9, 54–55 (1985) (citations deleted).

---

233. [R. Nozick, Philosophical Explanations (1981),] at 520.

No, according to Professor Sanford Kadish:

> Social deprivation may well establish a credible explanation of how the defendant has come to have the character he has. But it [does not] establish a moral excuse any more than a legal one, for there is a difference between explaining a person's wrongful behavior and explaining it away. Explanations are not excuses if they merely explain how the defendant came to have the character of someone who could do such a thing. Otherwise, there would be no basis for moral responsibility in any case where we knew enough about the person to understand him.

Sanford H. Kadish, *Excusing Crime,* 75 Cal.L.Rev. 257, 284 (1987).

An alternative argument for the defense is that a society that fosters or tolerates poor living conditions is not entitled "to sit in condemnation of [the criminal] with respect to the condemnable act [she committed]." David L. Bazelon, *The Morality of Criminal Law,* 49 S.Cal.L.Rev. 385, 388 (1976). Is this a suitable basis for recognizing an excuse defense?

3. INTOXICATION

a. *Voluntary (Self-Induced) Intoxication*

COMMONWEALTH v. GRAVES

Supreme Court of Pennsylvania, 1975.
461 Pa. 118, 334 A.2d 661.

Nix, Justice.

Daniel Lee Graves was convicted by a jury * * * for first degree murder, robbery and burglary. * * *

On September 28, 1971, Daniel Graves, appellant, and his cousins, Thomas and Edward Mathis, pursuant to a prior conceived plan, burglarized the residence of one Sebastiano Patiri, a 75 year old man and robbed him. During the course of the robbery and burglary, Mr. Patiri sustained injuries which resulted in his death.

Appellant Graves testified at trial that on the day of the incident he consumed a quart or more of wine and had taken a pill which was a form of Lysergic Acid Diephylanide (LSD). Appellant testified that he began hallucinating and saw "cars jumping over each other," as well as other strange phenomena. He then became unconscious and suffered limited amnesia, thus he contended that he had no recollection of the occurrence at the Patiri home.

The defense called a Dr. Sadoff, a professional psychiatrist who testified that * * * [a]s a result of [his] examination and evaluation, which included a polygraph and a sodium amytal test, he determined that Graves was telling the truth when he stated that he was under the influence of the wine and the LSD tablets during the afternoon of September 28, 1971. The doctor testified that in his opinion, appellant was under the influence of the two intoxicants and at the time of the Patiri attack "his mind was such that he wasn't able to form the proper conscious intent to take a life, to assault." Defense counsel then attempted to elicit from the doctor an opinion as to whether or not Graves at the time of the incident "could consciously form the specific intent to take or steal from a person or individual." An objection to this question was sustained and this ruling is assigned as error. Concomitantly, it is argued that the trial court erred in refusing a request to charge the jury that if they found Graves incapable of forming the intent to commit burglary or robbery because of the consumption of wine or the ingestion of the drug, or both, he could not be guilty of these offenses.

Relying on this Court's decision in Commonwealth v. Tarver, 446 Pa. 233, 284 A.2d 759 (1971), the trial court concluded that evidence of intoxication was irrelevant as to the robbery and burglary charges. Regrettably, although the trial court was adhering to a pronouncement of this Court, this ruling was erroneous and the judgments of sentence must now be reversed.

In Commonwealth v. Tarver, supra, this Court stated:

"If the charge is *felonious* homicide, intoxication, which is so great as to render the accused incapable of forming a wilful, deliberate and premeditated design to kill or incapable of judging his acts and their consequences, may properly influence a finding by the trial court that no specific intent to kill existed, and hence to conclude the killing was murder in the second degree. Although it is clear that this Court has employed the aforementioned rule to *lower the degree of guilt* within a crime, the crime still remains at murder. This Court has never extended the rule to lower murder in the second degree to voluntary manslaughter, nor has it applied this principle to any other crime outside of *felonious* homicide. Thus, exemplifying the fact that the rule has never been applied where its effect would change the nature of the crime, we have always limited its application to changing degrees within a crime. Since there are no analogous degrees of robbery, the principle has no application and defendant's acts are a felony, notwithstanding his alleged intoxication."

In reaching its conclusion that evidence of intoxication is limited to reducing the degree within a crime and may not be introduced to change the nature of the crime, the *Tarver* Court clearly misconceived the underlying basis for the relevance of evidence of intoxication in criminal matters. It is fundamental law in this jurisdiction that voluntary intoxication neither exonerates nor excuses criminal conduct. The only permissible probative value evidence of intoxication may have in criminal proceedings is where it is relevant to the question of the capacity of the actor to have possessed the requisite intent of the crime charged. Where the legislature, in its definition of a crime, has designated a particular state of mind as a material element of the crime, evidence of intoxication becomes relevant if the degree of inebriation has reached that point where the mind was incapable of attaining the state of mind required. It must be emphasized that although evidence of intoxication never provides a basis for exoneration or excuse, it may in some instances be relevant to establish that the crime charged in fact did not occur.[3]

Rejecting the view that an evidentiary rule relating to the introduction of evidence of intoxication must be strictly construed to avoid condoning voluntarily induced intoxication, most text writers have recognized the issue as being whether the crime in fact has been committed and considered the question accordingly:

> "Where a particular purpose, motive, or intent is a necessary element to constitute the particular kind or degree of crime, it is proper to consider the mental condition of accused, although produced by voluntary intoxication, and, where he lacked the mental capacity to entertain the requisite purpose, motive, or intent, such incapacity may constitute a valid defense to the particular crime charged, and the same rule applies to voluntary intoxication resulting in mental incapacity to indulge premeditation or deliberation, which precludes conviction of an offense wherein premeditation is essential. * * *
>
> The majority rule, holding intoxication to an extent precluding capacity to entertain a specific intent or to premeditate to be a defense, does so not because drunkenness excuses crime, but because, if the mental status required by law to constitute crime be one of specific intent or of deliberation and premeditation, and drunkenness excludes the existence of such mental state, then the particular crime charged has not in fact been committed. * * * "
> 22 C.J.S. Criminal Law § 68, pp. 217–219.[4]

Relying on a number of decisions that were *only concerned* with the application of intoxication evidence in felonious homicide cases, the *Tarver* Court concluded without precedent that intoxication evidence was only to be received to negate the specific intent to kill required by the crime of murder in the first degree. * * *

It has been argued that an extension in the allowance of the use of intoxication evidence would "only open wide the door to defenses built on frauds and perjuries, but would build a broad, easy turnpike for escape." The obvious fallacy of this argument is that we are not

---

3. "Suppose on the other hand *D* has been arrested for larceny, having been found walking off with *X*'s glass which he had no privilege or authority to carry away. Suppose again the only explanation he has to offer is that he was voluntarily drunk at the time and did not know what he was doing, the evidence indicating that he staggered away from the bar where he had been over-indulging and walked out into the street still clutching the glass from which he had been drinking, but too befuddled by liquor to know he was holding anything in his hand,—and when the glass was taken from him by the apprehending officer *D* stared at it blankly with no idea where it came from. The *actus reus* of larceny is the trespassory taking and carrying away of the personal property of another. *D* has done this and his voluntary intoxication is no excuse, but the facts stated fail to establish larceny." Perkins, Criminal Law, ch. 8, § 3 at 788 (1957).

4. Some text writers have even gone further and suggested that we should not limit the rule to those crimes which we have traditionally accepted as requiring a specific intent. * * * W. LaFave and A. Scott, Handbook on Criminal Law, Chapter 4, Section 45 (1972).

creating a new defense. Under our system of jurisprudence the legislature is charged with the responsibility of defining the elements of crimes. In discharging this responsibility they have required that the crimes of robbery and burglary must be accompanied by a specific intent. It is axiomatic that the presumption of innocence requires the Commonwealth to prove each element of the crime charged beyond a reasonable doubt.

It would clearly be an anomaly to suggest that although the Commonwealth must establish the existence of a mental state beyond a reasonable doubt, and that failure to sustain that burden requires an acquittal; yet preclude the defendant from producing relevant evidence to contest the issue.

There are instances in the law of evidence where testimony which may be relevant to a material fact in issue is nevertheless excluded. However, these instances are limited to that type of evidence that we have deemed to be inherently unreliable, e.g., results of polygraph tests. This admittedly is not the case with reference to evidence of intoxication and its effect on the mental capacity of the accused. For many years we have admitted this testimony in the most serious crime in this Commonwealth, i.e., murder in the first degree. To now contend that it would be less reliable in lesser offenses would be the height of absurdity.

We therefore conclude the *Tarver* decision, insofar as it suggested the evidence of intoxication offered for the purpose of negating the presence of specific intent may not be used in cases other than felonious homicide, is rejected. We also are constrained to find that the trial court committed reversible error in refusing to permit evidence and to charge the jury as to the possible effect of appellant's consumption of alcohol and ingestion of drugs upon his capacity to form the requisite intent required in the charges of robbery and burglary. Further, in view of the fact that the jury was given the option to consider the case under a theory of felony-murder, the finding of murder in the first degree must also be overturned. * * *

Notes and Questions

1. The court states that voluntary intoxication is not an excuse, but should this be so? "[I]f a man is punished for doing something when drunk that he would not have done when sober, is he not in plain truth punished for getting drunk?" Glanville Williams, Criminal Law: The General Part 564 (2d ed. 1961). If this observation is correct, is the effect of the law that a defendant may be punished for a crime of much greater seriousness than her moral culpability for becoming drunk? The Commentary to the Model Penal Code justifies the law this way:

> Yet it has been the consistent judgment of the common law that the simple infirmity of impaired control induced by intoxication offers no stronger a basis for formal adjustments in the grading of offenses or for complete exculpation than do infirmities produced by a variety of other causes. One could argue just as convincingly that the defendant's environment, his background or unusual mental stresses made contribu-

tions to his conduct that "in plain truth" make him less culpable than is reflected by the label attached to his crime. The traditional response to such contentions, and the one that appears correct in this context, has been to take such factors into account at sentencing, along with any other circumstances that suggest that the offense involved aberrant conduct of the actor rather than an expression of his settled personality and character.

American Law Institute, Model Penal Code and Commentaries, Comment to § 2.08 at 352 (1985).

2. At one time nearly all states applied the "specific intent"/"general intent" voluntary intoxication dichotomy declared in *Graves*. Today, however, this distinction is frequently rejected. Should it be? If so, what should the new rule be? The next case considers these questions.

STATE v. STASIO

Supreme Court of New Jersey, 1979.
78 N.J. 467, 396 A.2d 1129.

SCHREIBER, J.

[Defendant Stasio was found guilty by a jury of assault with intent to rob. He appealed his conviction on various grounds, including that the trial judge erroneously instructed the jury that "voluntary intoxication was not a defense to any act by the defendant in this matter."]

The major issue on this appeal is whether voluntary intoxication constitutes a defense to a crime, one element of which is the defendant's intent. * * *

This Court last considered the culpability of an individual who had committed an illegal act while voluntarily under the influence of a drug or alcohol in *State v. Maik*, 60 N.J. 203, 287 A.2d 715 (1972). There the defendant *Maik* had been charged with the first degree murder of his friend, a fellow college student. The defense was insanity at the time of the killing. Evidence at the trial had suggested that the defendant was schizophrenic and that a psychotic episode may have been triggered by the defendant's voluntary use of LSD or hashish. The trial court had charged the jury that if it found that the underlying psychosis had been activated by the voluntary use of either narcotic, the defense of insanity would not stand.

On appeal Chief Justice Weintraub, writing for a unanimous Court, began by discussing generally the concept of criminal responsibility. After pointing out that although there was a difference in the treatment of sick and bad offenders, he noted that notwithstanding that difference "the aim of the law is to protect the innocent from injury by the sick as well as the bad." It was in that context that a decision would have to be made whether the voluntary use of alcoholic beverages or drugs should support a viable defense. He then stated the generally accepted proposition that criminal responsibility was not extinguished when the offender was under the influence of a drug or liquor and the reasons for that rule:

It is generally agreed that a defendant will not be relieved of criminal responsibility because he was under the influence of intoxicants or drugs voluntarily taken. This principle rests upon public policy, demanding that he who seeks the influence of liquor or narcotics should not be insulated from criminal liability because that influence impaired his judgment or his control. The required element of badness can be found in the intentional use of the stimulant or depressant. Moreover, to say that one who offended while under such influence was sick would suggest that his sickness disappeared when he sobered up and hence he should be released. Such a concept would hardly protect others from the prospect of repeated injury.

The Chief Justice set forth four exceptions to the general rule. First, when drugs being taken for medication produce unexpected or bizarre results, no public interest is served by punishing the defendant since there is no likelihood of repetition. Second, if intoxication so impairs a defendant's mental faculties that he does not possess the wilfulness, deliberation and premeditation necessary to prove first degree murder, a homicide cannot be raised to first degree murder. Under this exception the influence of liquor "no matter how pervasive that influence may be, will not lead to an acquittal. It cannot reduce the crime below murder in the second degree, and this because of the demands of public security." Third, a felony homicide will be reduced to second degree murder when intoxication precludes formation of the underlying felonious intent. * * * [C]onsiderations of fairness indicate that such a defendant should be treated the same as one charged with ordinary first degree homicide requiring premeditation. Fourth, the defense of insanity is available when the voluntary use of the intoxicant or drug results in a fixed state of insanity after the influence of the intoxicant or drug has spent itself. * * *

A difference of opinion has been expressed in the Appellate Division as to the meaning of Chief Justice Weintraub's discussion of intoxication in *Maik*. In *State v. Del Vecchio,* 142 N.J.Super. 359, 361 A.2d 579 (1976), a conviction for breaking and entering with intent to steal was reversed on the ground that the jury had improperly been charged that voluntary intoxication was not a defense to a crime requiring a specific intent. The Appellate Division reasoned that, when a specific intent was an element of an offense, voluntary intoxication may negate existence of that intent. * * * The Appellate Division also held that the only principle to be derived from *Maik* was the proposition that voluntary intoxication may be relevant in determining whether a murder may be raised to first degree. * * *

In our opinion the Chief Justice in *Maik* enunciated a principle applicable generally to all crimes and, unless one of the exceptions to the general rule is applicable, voluntary intoxication will not excuse criminal conduct. The need to protect the public from the prospect of repeated injury and the public policy demanding that one who voluntarily subjects himself to intoxication should not be insulated from criminal responsibility are strongly supportive of this result. We reject the approach adopted by *Del Vecchio* because, although it has surface appeal, it is based on an unworkable dichotomy, gives rise to inconsistencies, and ignores the policy expressed in *Maik*.

Del Vecchio would permit the intoxication defense only when a "specific" as distinguished from a "general" intent was an element of the crime. However, that difference is not readily ascertainable. * * * Professor Hall has deplored the attempted distinction in the following analysis:

> The current confusion resulting from diverse uses of "general intent" is aggravated by dubious efforts to differentiate that from "specific intent." Each crime * * * has its distinctive *mens rea, e.g.* intending to have forced intercourse, intending to break and enter a dwellinghouse and to commit a crime there, intending to inflict a battery, and so on. It is evident that there must be as many *mentes reae* as there are crimes. And whatever else may be said about an intention, an essential characteristic of it is that it is directed towards a definite end. To assert therefore that an intention is "specific" is to employ a superfluous term just as if one were to speak of a "voluntary act." [J. Hall, *General Principles of Criminal Law* 142 (2d ed. 1960)] * * *

Moreover, distinguishing between specific and general intent gives rise to incongruous results by irrationally allowing intoxication to excuse some crimes but not others. In some instances if the defendant is found incapable of formulating the specific intent necessary for the crime charged, such as assault with intent to rob, he may be convicted of a lesser included general intent crime, such as assault with a deadly weapon. In other cases there may be no related general intent offense so that intoxication would lead to acquittal. * * *

Finally, where the more serious offense requires only a general intent, such as rape, intoxication provides no defense, whereas it would be a defense to an attempt to rape, specific intent being an element of that offense. Yet the same logic and reasoning which impels exculpation due to the failure of specific intent to commit an offense would equally compel the same result when a general intent is an element of the offense. * * *

The *Del Vecchio* approach may free defendants of specific intent offenses even though the harm caused may be greater than in an offense held to require only general intent. This course thus undermines the criminal law's primary function of protecting society from the results of behavior that endangers the public safety. This should be our guide rather than concern with logical consistency in terms of any single theory of culpability, particularly in view of the fact that alcohol is significantly involved in a substantial number of offenses. The demands of public safety and the harm done are identical irrespective of the offender's reduced ability to restrain himself due to his drinking. "[I]f a person casts off the restraints of reason and consciousness by a voluntary act, no wrong is done to him if he is held accountable for any crime which he may commit in that condition. Society is entitled to this protection." *McDaniel v. State,* 356 So.2d 1151, 1160–1161 (Miss.1978).

Until a stuporous condition is reached or the entire motor area of the brain is profoundly affected, the probability of the existence of intent remains. The initial effect of alcohol is the reduction or removal of inhibitions or restraints. But that does not vitiate intent. The loosening of the tongue has been said to disclose a person's true sentiments— "*in vino veritas.*" One commentator has noted:

> The great majority of moderately to grossly drunk or drugged persons who commit putatively criminal acts are probably aware of what they are doing and the likely consequences. In the case of those who are drunk, alcohol may have diminished their perceptions, released their inhibitions and clouded their reasoning and judgment, but they still have sufficient capacity for the conscious mental processes required by the ordinary definitions of all or most specific *mens rea* crimes. For example, a person can be quite far gone in drink and still capable of the conscious intent to steal, which is an element of common law larceny. [Murphy, "Has Pennsylvania Found a Satisfactory Intoxication Defense?", 81 *Dick.L.Rev.* 199, 208 (1977)]

When a defendant shows that he was comatose and therefore could not have broken and entered into the home or committed some other unlawful activity, such stage of intoxication may be relevant in establishing a general denial. But short of that, voluntary intoxication, other than its employment to disprove premeditation and deliberation in murder, should generally serve as no excuse. In this fashion the opportunities of false claims by defendants may be minimized and misapplication by jurors of the effect of drinking on the defendant's responsibility eliminated. * * *

[The court reversed the conviction on other grounds.]

HANDLER, J., concurring.

If a defendant's state of mind is a material factor in determining whether a particular crime has been committed—and if a degree of intoxication so affects the defendant's mental faculties as to eliminate effectively a condition of the mind otherwise essential for the commission of a crime—intoxication should be recognized as a defense in fact.

* * * I subscribe to the reasoning expressed in *State v. Maik,* and endorsed by this Court, which denigrated the attempted differentiation between so-called specific intent and general intent crimes. It is an unhelpful, misleading and often confusing distinction. * * *

Adherence to the distinction between specific and general intent crimes, and the availability of voluntary intoxication as a defense in terms of that distinction, has led to anomalous results. * * * Inconsistent applications of the intoxication defense and disparate results can be avoided or reduced by rejecting the dichotomy between specific intent and general intent crimes.

The Model Penal Code of the American Law Institute has eschewed this distinction. It deals with *mens rea* primarily in terms of purpose and knowledge and calls for an analysis of the elements of the criminal offense in relation to these components. See Model Penal Code § 2.08. * * * This approach, in my view, enables a trier of fact to assimilate proof of a defendant's intoxication in a more realistic perspective and to reach a more rational determination of the effect of intoxication upon criminal responsibility, particularly in terms of consciousness and purpose. * * *

The majority of this Court repudiates the intoxication defense on grounds of general deterrence and a ubiquitous need to protect society from drunken criminals. This approach mirrors a commendable impulse, which I share. But, it fails to consider that enforcement of the criminal law must be fair and just, as well as strict and protective.

The criminal laws need not be impotent or ineffective when dealing with an intoxicated criminal. The question should always be whether under particular circumstances a defendant ought to be considered responsible for his conduct. This involves a factual determination of whether he has acted with volition. Intoxication, in this context, would constitute a defense if it reached such a level, operating upon the defendant's mind, so as to deprive him of his will to act. I would accordingly require, in order to generate a reasonable doubt as to a defendant's responsibility for his acts, that it be shown he was so intoxicated that he could not think, or that his mind did not function with consciousness or volition. * * *

* * * I do not share the pessimism of the Court that voluntary intoxication as a recognized defense will wreak havoc in criminal law enforcement * * *. The fear of condoning criminals, who are also drunks, can be addressed, I respectfully suggest, by imposing a heavy burden of proof upon defendants to show a degree of intoxication capable of prostrating the senses. Drunkenness which does not have this effect does not diminish responsibility and should not serve to excuse criminality. * * *

Today's holding by the majority * * * stands logic on its head. This Court and the Legislature have long adhered to the view that criminal sanctions will not be imposed upon a defendant unless there exists a " 'concurrence of an evil-meaning mind with an evil-doing hand.' " The policies underlying this proposition are clear. A person who intentionally commits a bad act is more culpable than one who engages in the same conduct without any evil design. The intentional wrongdoer is also more likely to repeat his offense, and hence constitutes a greater threat to societal repose. A sufficiently intoxicated defendant is thus subject to less severe sanctions not because the law "excuses" his conduct but because the circumstances surrounding his acts have been deemed by the Legislature to be less deserving of punishment. * * *

Just as the lack of premeditation, willfulness, or deliberation precludes a conviction for first-degree murder, so should the lack of intent to rob or steal be a defense to assault and battery with intent to rob, or breaking and entering with intent to steal. The principle is the same in both situations. If voluntary intoxication negates an element of the offense, the defendant has not engaged in the conduct proscribed by the criminal statute, and hence should not be subject to the sanctions imposed by that statute. * * *

Notes and Questions

1. Two of the four exceptions to the no-acquittal-for-intoxication rule set out in *Maik,* as explained in *Stasio,* do not involve claims of voluntary intoxication. The first listed exception, frequently described as "pathological intoxication," constitutes *involuntary* intoxication, the subject of the next chapter subsection.

The fourth listed exception is the "settled insanity" doctrine of intoxication, which arises when the defendant's long-term, excessive use of alcohol or drugs brings on a mental infirmity that remains even after the short-term effects of the substance have worn off. Almost all jurisdictions recognize a defense in such circumstances, even if the defendant possesses the requisite *mens rea* for the offense, but the defense is that of *insanity,* not intoxication, even if the actor was intoxicated at the time of the crime. E.g., People v. Chapman, 165 Mich.App. 215, 418 N.W.2d 658 (1987); Jones v. State, 648 P.2d 1251 (Okla.Crim.App.1982).

Should a person be excused if her insanity was induced by regular, voluntary ingestion of alcohol or narcotics? Over a dissent, the Colorado Supreme Court answered this question in the negative in Bieber v. People, 856 P.2d 811, 817 (1993):

As a matter of public policy * * * we cannot excuse a defendant's actions which endanger others in his or her community, based upon a mental disturbance or illness that he or she actively and voluntarily contracted. There is no principled basis to distinguish between the short-term and long-term effects of voluntary intoxication by punishing the first and excusing the second. If anything, the moral blameworthiness would seem to be even greater with respect to the long-term effects of many, repeated instances of voluntary intoxication occurring over an extended period of time.

The dissent criticized the majority for "contraven[ing] long established principles of criminal responsibility and chart[ing] a course contrary to all other jurisdictions that have addressed this issue." Id. at 823. What principles of criminal responsibility do you believe that it had in mind? See generally Lawrence P. Tiffany, *The Drunk, The Insane, and the Criminal Courts: Deciding What to Make of Self–Induced Insanity,* 69 Wash.U.L.Q. 221 (1991).

2. *Voluntary intoxication in murder prosecutions.* Several jurisdictions only allow voluntary intoxication to serve as a "defense" to first degree murder, to reduce the offense to second degree. 1 Paul H. Robinson, Criminal Law Defenses § 65(a) at 292 (1984). But, if a person is so

intoxicated "that he does not possess the wilfulness, deliberation and premeditation necessary to prove first degree murder" (*Stasio*), how is he guilty of second degree murder? One court has explained:

> There seems to be a paradox here, but careful recent analysis has resolved the apparent dilemma. Intoxication sufficient to erode the capacity to form a premeditated specific intent to kill (first-degree murder) would, *ipso facto,* erode the capacity to form a non-premeditated specific intent to kill (second-degree murder * * *). One incapable of arriving at a decision (to kill) slowly is hardly capable of arriving at the same decision instantaneously, yet that is just what a hasty glance at the case law would seem to suggest. * * *

> The logical explanation as to why voluntary intoxication may negate first-degree murder but not second-degree murder has been provided by W. LaFave & A. Scott, *Criminal Law* (1972). Recognizing that there are four forms of murderous *mens rea*—1) intent to kill, 2) intent to inflict grievous bodily harm, 3) felony-murder, and 4) depraved-heart— the authors have explained that the absence of a specific intent to kill would, of necessity, obviate a conviction for that variety of murder in either of its degrees but could nonetheless support a second-degree murder conviction upon the "depraved-heart" theory, which requires only wanton recklessness and does not require any specific intent. * * *

> Thus, the erosion, through voluntary intoxication, of the specific intent to kill does not * * * move the crime *down* from a higher level of blameworthiness (first degree) to a lower level of blameworthiness (second degree) within the context of the same murderous *mens rea* (intent to kill), but rather moves the crime *down and over* from a murderous *mens rea* requiring a specific intent to a different murderous *mens rea* not requiring such specific intent.

Cirincione v. State, 75 Md.App. 166, 170 n. 1, 540 A.2d 1151, 1153 n. 1 (1988).

3. Model Penal Code § 2.08(1) provides that intoxication is a defense if it "negatives an element of the offense." The Code does not distinguish between "general intent" and "specific intent" crimes. As a practical matter, however, is the exculpatory effect of voluntary intoxication under Section 2.08 any different than the effect according to the traditional common law rule? For example, suppose that Christopher consumes ten to twelve bottles of beer and several "shots" of hard liquor in a short period of time at a bar, after which he gets into his car, drives in an exceedingly dangerous manner, and unintentionally kills Lori, a pedestrian in the crosswalk. Under the common law, of what form of criminal homicide would Christopher likely be guilty? Of what is he guilty under the Model Penal Code? See Section 2.08(2).

The Commentary explains the rationale of subsection (2):

> The * * * difficult question relates to recklessness, where awareness of the risk created by the actor's conduct ordinarily is requisite for liability under Section 2.02. The problem is whether intoxication ought

to be accorded a significance coextensive with its relevance to disprove such awareness, as in the case of purpose or knowledge * * *.

It is clear that this is the result that should ensue unless a special rule of liability is formulated on the subject * * *.

Those who oppose a special rule for drunkenness in relation to awareness of the risk in recklessness draw strength * * * from the proposition that it is precisely the awareness of the risk in recklessness that is the essence of its moral culpability—a culpability dependent upon the magnitude of the specific risk knowingly created. When that risk is greater in degree than that which the actor perceives at the time of getting drunk, as is frequently the case, the result of a special rule is bound to be a liability disproportionate to culpability. Hence the solution urged is to dispense with any special rule, relying rather on the possibility of proving foresight at the time of drinking and, when this cannot be proved, upon a generalized prohibition of being drunk and dangerous, with sanctions appropriate for such behavior. This approach would also permit prosecution for negligence if negligent commission of the act in question was sufficient to establish criminal liability. With respect to negligence, the essence of the culpability is the failure to perceive a risk that the actor should have perceived. The actor's culpability in failing to perceive a risk would be judged against the standard of a man in normal possession of his faculties. Thus, the fact that the defendant was drunk will not exculpate him from a charge of negligence. Indeed, often drunkenness would be substantial evidence that he had acted negligently.

The case thus made is worthy of respect, but there are strong considerations on the other side. There is first the weight of the antecedent law which here, more clearly than in England, has tended toward a special rule for drunkenness in this context. Beyond this, there is the fundamental point that awareness of the potential consequences of excessive drinking on the capacity of human beings to gauge the risks incident to their conduct is by now so dispersed in our culture that it is not unfair to postulate a general equivalence between the risks created by the conduct of the drunken actor and the risks created by his conduct in becoming drunk. Becoming so drunk as to destroy temporarily the actor's powers of perception and judgment is conduct that plainly has no affirmative social value to counterbalance the potential danger. The actor's moral culpability lies in engaging in such conduct. Added to this are the impressive difficulties posed in litigating the foresight of any particular actor at the time when he imbibes and the relative rarity of cases where intoxication really does engender unawareness as distinguished from imprudence. These considerations led to the conclusion, on balance, that the Model Code should declare that unawareness of risks, of which the actor would have been aware had he been sober, is immaterial. Most states with revised codes have taken a similar position.

American Law Institute, Model Penal Code and Commentaries, Comment to § 2.08 at 358–59 (1985).

4. *Problem.* Velez puffed twice on a marijuana cigarette, unaware that it contained an hallucinogenic drug. The drug rendered him unconscious, during which state he brutally attacked the victim with a screwdriver. Velez was prosecuted for assault with a deadly weapon. State law provided in pertinent part:

(a) No act committed by a person while in a state of voluntary intoxication is less criminal by reason of his having been in such condition. Evidence of voluntary intoxication shall not be admitted to negate the capacity to form any mental states for the crimes charged * * *.

(b) Evidence of voluntary intoxication is admissible solely on the issue of whether or not the defendant actually formed a required specific intent, premeditated, deliberated, or harbored malice aforethought, when a specific intent crime is charged.

Does Velez have a basis for acquittal of the offense charged? See People v. Velez, 175 Cal.App.3d 785, 221 Cal.Rptr. 631 (1985). What would be the outcome under the Model Penal Code? See American Law Institute, Model Penal Code and Commentaries, Comment to § 2.08 at 353 (1985).

b. *Involuntary Intoxication*

CITY OF MINNEAPOLIS v. ALTIMUS

Supreme Court of Minnesota, 1976.
306 Minn. 462, 238 N.W.2d 851.

KELLY, JUSTICE.

Defendant * * * was found guilty by a * * * jury of careless driving, and hit and run as to an attended vehicle * * *. On this appeal from judgment of conviction, defendant contends that he should receive a new trial because * * * the trial court erred in refusing to instruct the jury on the defense of involuntary intoxication * * *.

* * * [D]efendant, driving south on Hiawatha Avenue, made an illegal left turn from the right-hand lane and crashed into a garbage truck proceeding northward on Hiawatha. Immediately after impact, defendant backed up and drove easterly on Lake Street at a slow speed. This slow speed resulted from the fact that the automobile defendant was driving had been badly damaged in the collision. Policemen who observed the accident followed defendant and stopped him about a block from the point of impact. Defendant * * * appeared to one of the officers to be somewhat confused * * *. In response to questions by the officers, defendant, who gave "William Jones" as his name, stated that he did not have his driver's license with him but showed the officers a paper purporting to be a transfer of title from Robert Altimus to William Jones. * * *

At trial, the defense did not dispute the evidence adduced by the state, but introduced evidence designed to show that defendant did not have the requisite state of mind to be guilty of * * * the * * * traffic charges. Defendant testified that on September 25, 1973, three days before the incident, he had seen a doctor at the Veterans Administration

Hospital for treatment of a back problem and the flu and that the doctor had prescribed Valium, which he had taken as prescribed. He testified that on September 28 the Valium began to have a strange effect on him, making it impossible for him to control himself. He testified that he did not know who owned the automobile which he had driven, and that he remembered nothing about the accident or the events that followed.

The only other defense witness was Dr. Humberto Ortiz, the doctor who treated defendant at the Veterans Administration Hospital. He testified that he prescribed the Valium because it was a skeletal muscle relaxant and was the type of drug which would relieve the acute back pain defendant had been experiencing. * * * Dr. Ortiz listed drowsiness, fatigue, ataxia, and confusion as the normal side effects of Valium. He testified, however, that hyperexcitability, although more rare, was also a possible side effect. On cross-examination, he stated that he did not know if the drug might cause one to be confused as to his identity; but in response to a hypothetical question stating the facts of the case, he expressed the opinion that defendant might have been suffering from the effects of the drug.

* * * [T]he defense requested the trial court to instruct on the defense of involuntary intoxication * * *, but the trial court refused * * *. * * *

The general rule * * * is that voluntary intoxication is a defense to a criminal charge * * * only if * * * the trier of fact concluded that the defendant's intoxication deprived him of the specific intent or purpose requisite to the alleged offense. Because of traffic offenses with which defendant was charged do not require a specific intent to do a prohibited act, the defense of voluntary intoxication cannot and does not apply to those offenses.

While general traffic offenses do not require that the wrongdoer specifically intend to commit the crime for which he is charged, we have held that before criminal liability can attach it is essential that the defendant intentionally or negligently do the act which constitutes the crime. * * * The unusual issue presented on this appeal is whether the defendant is entitled to assert the defense of involuntary intoxication if due to such intoxication he unintentionally and nonnegligently did the acts for which he is charged. * * *

* * * The common-law rule was that voluntary intoxication was never a defense to a criminal charge. * * * The common law distinguished involuntary from voluntary intoxication, however, and found the former to be a defense to criminal liability if it caused the defendant to become temporarily insane. * * * The defense of involuntary intoxication has long been recognized by the courts in England and the United States.

Four different kinds of involuntary intoxication have been recognized: Coerced intoxication, pathological intoxication, intoxication by innocent mistake, and unexpected intoxication resulting from the ingestion of a medically prescribed drug. Coerced intoxication is intoxication involuntarily induced by reason of duress or coercion. Some courts have declared in general terms that coerced intoxication may be a complete defense to all criminal liability. See, e.g., *Burrows v. State,* 38 Ariz. 99, 297 P. 1029 (1931). In *Burrows,* the Arizona Supreme Court approved the trial court's instruction which stated that involuntary intoxication would be a complete defense if the defendant was compelled to drink against his will and "his reason was destroyed" so "that he did not understand and appreciate the consequences of his act." Courts have strictly construed the requirement of coercion, however, so that acquittal by reason of coerced intoxication is an exceedingly rare result.

Pathological intoxication has been defined as "intoxication grossly excessive in degree, given the amount of the intoxicant, to which the actor does not know he is susceptible." Model Penal Code, § 2.08(5)(c). Pathologically intoxicated offenders have been held not criminally responsible for their acts when they ingested the intoxicant not knowing of their special susceptibility to its effects. The defense of pathological intoxication has been limited in some jurisdictions, however, by the requirement that the intoxicated defendant must be deprived of mental capacity to the degree necessary for an insanity defense.

Involuntary intoxication may also occur when intoxication results from an innocent mistake by the defendant about the character of the substance taken, as when another person has tricked him into taking the liquor or drugs. See, *People v. Penman,* 271 Ill. 82, 110 N.E. 894 (1915). In *Penman,* the defendant killed his victim after apparently taking cocaine tablets which, due to the deception of another, he believed to be breath purifiers. The Illinois Supreme Court held that this would constitute involuntary intoxication and a full defense to criminal liability if it caused the defendant to become temporarily insane.

The last kind of involuntary intoxication recognized in the case law arises when the defendant is unexpectedly intoxicated due to the ingestion of a medically prescribed drug. * * *

Appellant asserts that due to the ingestion of a prescribed drug, Valium, he was unexpectedly intoxicated to the point of unconsciousness, incapable of controlling his actions, and thus not criminally responsible for his actions. To assess fully the merits of this claim, it is necessary to review carefully the circumstances in which a defense of involuntary intoxication due to ingestion of a prescribed drug is properly available.

The first requirement is that the defendant must not know, or have reason to know, that the prescribed drug is likely to have an intoxicating effect. If the defendant knows, or has reason to know, that the prescribed drug will have an intoxicating effect, then he is voluntarily intoxicated. * * *

The second requirement is that the prescribed drug, and not some other intoxicant, is in fact the cause of defendant's intoxication at the time of his alleged criminal conduct.

The third requirement is that the defendant, due to involuntary intoxication, is temporarily insane. * * *

Involuntary intoxication, we note in summary, is a most unusual condition. The circumstances in which an instruction on the defense of involuntary intoxication will be appropriate will accordingly be very rare. We hold, nevertheless, that in the instant case such an instruction was necessary because defendant introduced evidence sufficient to raise the defense of temporary insanity due to involuntary intoxication. * * *

ROGOSHESKE, JUSTICE (concurring specially).

I agree that this case must be reversed and remanded for a new trial due to a failure below to instruct on the defense of involuntary intoxication. I cannot join the majority opinion, however, because I neither believe that involuntary intoxication is a type of insanity nor that an instruction couched in terms of an insanity defense fits defendant's asserted defense in this unique case.

The premise underlying the defense of involuntary intoxication is that a person should not be held criminally liable in the absence of volitional fault, that is, conscious fault. * * * Stated in other words, "persons should not be punished if they could not have done otherwise, *i.e.*, had neither the capacity nor a fair opportunity to act otherwise." Hart, Punishment and Responsibility, p. 153. See, Rawls, A Theory of Justice, p. 241. * * *

I would apply the above principle to the case at bar by instructing the jury that defendant should be excused from criminal liability if defendant establishes by the preponderance of the evidence that due to the ingestion of Valium he was intoxicated to such an extent that he was incapable of exercising reasonable care in operating his automobile, and that he did not know or have reasonable grounds to foresee that in taking the Valium pursuant to his doctor's prescription his mental condition would become such as to render him incapable of exercising reasonable care in driving an automobile.

The majority opinion declares that involuntary intoxication is a defense only when it causes temporary insanity as insanity is defined [by state law]. * * *

In my opinion, the defense of involuntary intoxication does not rest upon so tenuous a statutory basis. Involuntary intoxication is a defense anchored firmly in the theory of mens rea, which has long been a part of Anglo–American common law. * * *

Notes and Questions

1. Involuntary intoxication is a true excuse, that is, a defendant who raises the defense will be acquitted, even if she possessed the specific mental state required in the definition of the offense, as long as she satisfies the jurisdiction's insanity standard. Essentially, the defendant's claim is one of temporary, intoxication-induced mental disorder, except that the defendant

asserts the defense of intoxication rather than insanity, and thus is not subject to post-trial civil commitment proceedings, as are insanity acquittees.

Should the involuntary intoxication defense be limited to circumstances in which the actor is legally insane, or is concurring Justice Rogosheske's approach preferable?

2. Would the defendant in *Altimus* have been entitled to assert the defense of involuntary intoxication if he had been charged with driving under the influence of an intoxicant, a strict liability offense in most jurisdictions? See State v. Miller, 309 Or. 362, 788 P.2d 974 (1990); Model Penal Code § 2.05.

3. Is D entitled to raise the defense of involuntary intoxication in the following circumstances?

A. D took prescribed medication for migraine headaches. The prescription provided that he should take two pills four times a day, but D took five dosages of five pills each during a 26–hour period. On prior occasions, D had taken more than the prescribed medication because the additional pills provided headache relief. In the past, the extra medication made him drowsy, but this time it caused intoxication, and he committed a crime. People v. Turner, 680 P.2d 1290 (Colo.App.1983).

B. D, an alcoholic, took Anabuse, a prescription drug for his alcoholism, and Serax, a pain medication prescribed for physical injuries D sustained. D's physician warned him that Serax, when taken with Anabuse and even small amounts of alcohol, could cause bizarre behavior. While taking the medications, D purchased and consumed two pints of vodka in one morning, suffered a severe reaction from the medicine, and committed an armed robbery. People v. Gerrior, 155 Ill.App.3d 949, 108 Ill.Dec. 542, 508 N.E.2d 1119 (1987).

c. *Alcoholism and Drug Addiction as an Excuse*

PEOPLE v. TOCCO

Supreme Court, Bronx County, 1988.
138 Misc.2d 510, 525 N.Y.S.2d 137.

DOMINIC R. MASSARO, JUSTICE.

The novel question presented here is whether imbibing by a chronic alcoholic can rise to the level of misconduct making for recklessness per se. The court, absent any scientific standard of proof to the contrary, is disinclined to equate alcoholism with involuntariness; notwithstanding, it seeks some limiting principle whereby application of the cruel and unusual punishment prohibition [of the United States Constitution] does not result in exoneration of the chronic alcoholic for criminal conduct.

The defendant here is charged with arson in the second degree, and reckless endangerment in the first degree. More specifically, he is alleged to have set fire to the apartment in which he resided with his ex-wife and children.

Tried before the court, without jury, it is clear from the evidence adduced that the People have proved beyond a reasonable doubt that the

defendant did, in fact, set two separate fires in the apartment. * * *
The evidence further establishes that the defendant is an alcoholic of
classic dimension, caught in the vortex of a severe drinking problem that
has determined his behavior, despite the constancy and regularity of
violent consequences over which he has no control, for upwards of 15
years. Albeit sincere efforts to which he testified, the defendant has
failed "to reclimb the slope."[1] The evidence likewise is conclusive that
he was severely intoxicated on April 24, 1986, at the time that the
premises were set ablaze.

Indeed, the defense admits the act. It contends that the defendant
* * * was incapable of formulating the requisite intent necessary to
subject him to liability for the crime of arson in the second degree.
While not conceding this point, the People urge the court to consider in
its deliberations the lesser included offense of reckless arson, that is,
arson in the fourth degree. * * *

It is estimated that 10 million Americans suffer from some form of
alcoholism (U.S. Dept. of Health, Education and Welfare, *The Alcohol,
Drug Abuse, and Mental Health National Data Book* 15 [1980]).

In New York, there are 1.4 million alcoholics, 9.3% of the State's
population. The scourge of highway deaths caused by intoxicated drivers distracts from other reflections of the serious depths the problem
presents, including the fact that one-third of all general hospital admissions are related to the misuse of alcohol and one quarter of all
suicides—approximately 30 times that of the general population—involve
alcoholic abusers. These statistics only begin to illustrate the scope of
the problem of alcoholism facing our citizenry.

Alcoholism is generally defined as the chronic, pathological use of
alcohol. There is a thirty year consensus in the medical profession that
such pathological use of alcohol is a disease. The American Medical
Association first described the disease as appropriate for medical treatment in 1956, stating that:

> Alcoholism is an illness characterized by preoccupation with alcohol
> and loss of control over its consumption such as to lead usually to
> intoxication if drinking is begun; by chronicity; by progression; and
> by tendency toward relapse. It is typically associated with physical
> disability and impaired emotional, occupational and/or social adjust-
> ments as a direct consequence of persistent and excessive use
> (American Medical Association, *Manual on Alcoholism,* 6 [1957]).

Even were our courts inclined to accept the disease thesis advanced
by the medical profession, ignorance largely prevails as to its etiology.

Whatever the factors of alcoholism, the characteristic lack of control
over drinking and the resulting dysfunction beyond the control of the

---

1. The reference is to Virgil, and apt:

The descent to hell is easy

   The gates stand open day and night
But to reclimb the slope

And escape to the upper air

This is labor ...

The Aeneid.

alcoholic individual gives rise to issues both philosophical and legal, clearly of major social and judicial concern. * * *

As we have seen, there is a recognition among physicians that alcoholism is a disease characterized by loss of control over the consumption of alcoholic beverages. Can then an alcoholic's inebriated state(s) ever be considered truly voluntary? * * *

Some commentators have speculated that courts will be required, some time in the future, to meet the argument that the intoxication of a chronic alcoholic is, on its face, involuntary. If such were the case, the chronic alcoholic could never be held liable for crimes that he committed while in a severely intoxicated state. As of yet, no court has extended the defense to preclude prosecution of an alcoholic for non-alcohol-related crimes committed while in an intoxicated state. * * *

* * * [I]t would appear that any change in the law would find basis only in conclusive medical evidence spurred by growing social concern, rather than constitutional pivots. Yet, if alcoholism is a disease characterized by an inability to control the consumption of alcoholic beverages, then the imposition of criminal liability for acts performed while drunk would at first blush defy logic.

Separating the physical act of drinking from the causative condition, alcoholism, is the distinguishing factor to which we must pay heed. Alcoholics should be held responsible for their conduct; they should not be penalized for their condition. An enlightened society cannot otherwise justify itself.

If an alcoholic knows that he is prone to commit criminal acts while drunk and that the consumption of even one drink will destroy his ability to resist further drinking, to the point of intoxication, as in the instant case, it must follow that his voluntarily imbibing of the first drink is the very initiation of a reckless act—and the concomitant disregard of the substantial and unjustifiable risk attendant thereto. If so, under our law the consumption of said drink by such alcoholic raises the act to the level of recklessness per se, subjecting him to strict accountability for crimes such as reckless arson and/or reckless endangerment now before the court. * * *

Arguendo, if we accept alcoholism as a disease, the hypothesis suggests that some (though probably not all) alcoholics lack the ability to control the taking of even the first drink. In paralleling the instant case, exculpatory legal argument on the proposition that the defendant's addictive conduct was involuntary—whether psychological, biochemical, genetic, cultural and/or environmental—has not been shown. Nothing in the record was offered to explain or illuminate the defendant's condition. * * *

Accepting the law as it now stands, then, it is clear that intoxication will negative the specific intent required in some crimes, but will not act as even a partial defense in general intent crimes. Moreover, though the law may evolve as new medical research on the nature of alcoholism becomes available, alcoholism is not, according to the prevailing view, accepted as a defense to any crime.

Accordingly, upon the evidence adduced at the trial of this action, this court finds the defendant not guilty of arson in the second degree, which is defined as "intentionally [damaging] a building * * * by starting a fire," as he lacked the specific intent to damage a building. However, the court finds the defendant guilty of the lesser included offense of arson in the fourth degree, which is defined as "recklessly [damaging] a building * * * by intentionally starting a fire."

Further, and likewise, this court finds the defendant guilty of reckless endangerment in the first degree. Here, the defendant voluntarily commenced a reckless course of action (i.e., the act of his taking an alcoholic beverage), a risk in itself, the natural consequences of which, the unjustifiable endangerment of the lives of others, thus being intended. The court opines that the chronic alcoholism of this defendant combines with the totality of circumstances extant to make his conduct of disregard that of recklessness per se. Even were this not the court's finding, the defendant's having committed the arsonous act (i.e., lighting the fire[s]) would, nonetheless, make out the elements of the offense.

ROBINSON v. CALIFORNIA

Supreme Court of the United States, 1962.
370 U.S. 660, 82 S.Ct. 1417, 8 L.Ed.2d 758.

MR. JUSTICE STEWART delivered the opinion of the Court.

A California statute makes it a criminal offense for a person to "be addicted to the use of narcotics." [1] This appeal draws into question the constitutionality of that provision of the state law, as construed by the California courts in the present case.

The appellant was convicted after a jury trial in the Municipal Court of Los Angeles. * * * Officer Brown testified that he had had occasion to examine the appellant's arms one evening on a street in Los Angeles some four months before the trial. The officer testified that at that time he had observed "scar tissue and discoloration on the inside" of the appellant's right arm, and "what appeared to be numerous needle marks and a scab which was approximately three inches below the crook of the elbow" on the appellant's left arm. The officer also testified that the appellant under questioning had admitted to the occasional use of narcotics. * * *

The judge * * * instructed the jury that the appellant could be convicted under a general verdict if the jury agreed *either* that he was of

---

1. The statute is § 11721 of the California Health and Safety Code. It provides: "No person shall use, or be under the influence of, or be addicted to the use of narcotics, excepting when administered by or under the direction of a person licensed by the State to prescribe and administer narcotics. * * * Any person convicted of violating any provision of this section is guilty of a misdemeanor and shall be sentenced to serve a term of not less than 90 days nor more than one year in the county jail. * * * In no event does the court have the power to absolve a person who violates this section from the obligation of spending at least 90 days in confinement in the county jail."

the "status" *or* had committed the "act" denounced by the statute. "All that the People must show is either that the defendant did use a narcotic in Los Angeles County, or that while in the City of Los Angeles he was addicted to the use of narcotics * * *."

Under these instructions the jury returned a verdict finding the appellant "guilty of the offense charged." * * * We noted probable jurisdiction of this appeal because it squarely presents the issue whether the statute as construed by the California courts in this case is repugnant to the Fourteenth Amendment of the Constitution.

The broad power of a State to regulate the narcotic drugs traffic within its borders is not here in issue. * * *

Such regulation, it can be assumed, could take a variety of valid forms. A State might impose criminal sanctions, for example, against the unauthorized manufacture, prescription, sale, purchase, or possession of narcotics within its borders. In the interest of discouraging the violation of such laws, or in the interest of the general health or welfare of its inhabitants, a State might establish a program of compulsory treatment for those addicted to narcotics. Such a program of treatment might require periods of involuntary confinement. And penal sanctions might be imposed for failure to comply with established compulsory treatment procedures. Or a State might choose to attack the evils of narcotics traffic on broader fronts also—through public health education, for example, or by efforts to ameliorate the economic and social conditions under which those evils might be thought to flourish. In short, the range of valid choice which a State might make in this area is undoubtedly a wide one, and the wisdom of any particular choice within the allowable spectrum is not for us to decide. Upon that premise we turn to the California law in issue here.

It would be possible to construe the statute under which the appellant was convicted as one which is operative only upon proof of the actual use of narcotics within the State's jurisdiction. But the California courts have not so construed this law. Although there was evidence in the present case that the appellant had used narcotics in Los Angeles, the jury were instructed that they could convict him even if they disbelieved that evidence. The appellant could be convicted, they were told, if they found simply that the appellant's "status" or "chronic condition" was that of being "addicted to the use of narcotics." And it is impossible to know from the jury's verdict that the defendant was not convicted upon precisely such a finding. * * *

This statute, therefore, is not one which punishes a person for the use of narcotics, for their purchase, sale or possession, or for antisocial or disorderly behavior resulting from their administration. It is not a law which even purports to provide or require medical treatment. Rather, we deal with a statute which makes the "status" of narcotic addiction a criminal offense, for which the offender may be prosecuted "at any time before he reforms." California has said that a person can be continuously guilty of this offense, whether or not he has ever used or possessed any narcotics within the State, and whether or not he has been guilty of any antisocial behavior there.

It is unlikely that any State at this moment in history would attempt to make it a criminal offense for a person to be mentally ill, or a leper, or to be afflicted with a venereal disease. A State might determine that the general health and welfare require that the victims of these and other human afflictions be dealt with by compulsory treatment, involving quarantine, confinement, or sequestration. But, in the light of contemporary human knowledge, a law which made a criminal offense of such a disease would doubtless be universally thought to be an infliction of cruel and unusual punishment in violation of the Eighth and Fourteenth Amendments.

We cannot but consider the statute before us as of the same category. In this Court counsel for the State recognized that narcotic addiction is an illness.[8] Indeed, it is apparently an illness which may be contracted innocently or involuntarily.[9] We hold that a state law which imprisons a person thus afflicted as a criminal, even though he has never touched any narcotic drug within the State or been guilty of any irregular behavior there, inflicts a cruel and unusual punishment in violation of the Fourteenth Amendment. * * * Even one day in prison would be a cruel and unusual punishment for the "crime" of having a common cold. * * *

Reversed.

MR. JUSTICE DOUGLAS, concurring.

While I join the Court's opinion, I wish to make more explicit the reasons why I think it is "cruel and unusual" punishment in the sense of the Eighth Amendment to treat as a criminal a person who is a drug addict. * * *

As stated by Dr. Isaac Ray many years ago:

"Nothing can more strongly illustrate the popular ignorance respecting insanity than the proposition, equally objectionable in its humanity and its logic, that the insane should be punished for criminal acts, in order to deter other insane persons from doing the same thing." Treatise on the Medical Jurisprudence of Insanity (5th ed. 1871), p. 56.

Today we have our differences over the legal definition of insanity. But however insanity is defined, it is in end effect treated as a disease. While afflicted people may be confined either for treatment or for the protection of society, they are not branded as criminals.

Yet terror and punishment linger on as means of dealing with some diseases. As recently stated:

8. In its brief the appellee stated: "Of course it is generally conceded that a narcotic addict, particularly one addicted to the use of heroin, is in a state of mental and physical illness. So is an alcoholic." * * *

9. Not only may addiction innocently result from the use of medically prescribed narcotics, but a person may even be a narcotics addict from the moment of his birth.

" * * * the idea of basing treatment for disease on purgatorial acts and ordeals is an ancient one in medicine. It may trace back to the Old Testament belief that disease of any kind, whether mental or physical, represented punishment for sin; and thus relief could take the form of a final heroic act of atonement. This superstition appears to have given support to fallacious medical rationales for such procedures as purging, bleeding, induced vomiting, and blistering, as well as an entire chamber of horrors constituting the early treatment of mental illness. The latter included a wide assortment of shock techniques, such as the 'water cures' (dousing, ducking, and near-drowning), spinning in a chair, centrifugal swinging, and an early form of electric shock. All, it would appear, were planned as means of driving from the body some evil spirit or toxic vapor." Action for Mental Health (1961), pp. 27–28.

That approach continues as respects drug addicts. Drug addiction is more prevalent in this country than in any other nation of the western world. It is sometimes referred to as "a contagious disease." But those living in a world of black and white put the addict in the category of those who could, if they would, forsake their evil ways.

The first step toward addiction may be as innocent as a boy's puff on a cigarette in an alleyway. It may come from medical prescriptions. Addiction may even be present at birth. * * *

The impact that an addict has on a community causes alarm and often leads to punitive measures. Those measures are justified when they relate to acts of transgression. But I do not see how under our system *being an addict* can be punished as a crime. If addicts can be punished for their addiction, then the insane can also be punished for their insanity. Each has a disease and each must be treated as a sick person. * * *

The Eighth Amendment expresses the revulsion of civilized man against barbarous acts—the "cry of horror" against man's inhumanity to his fellow man.

By the time of Coke, enlightenment was coming as respects the insane. Coke said that the execution of a madman "should be a miserable spectacle, both against law, and of extreame inhumanity and cruelty, and can be no example to others." 6 Coke's Third Inst. (4th ed. 1797), p. 6. Blackstone endorsed this view of Coke.

We should show the same discernment respecting drug addiction. The addict is a sick person. He may, of course, be confined for treatment or for the protection of society. Cruel and unusual punishment results not from confinement, but from convicting the addict of a crime. * * * A prosecution for addiction, with its resulting stigma and irreparable damage to the good name of the accused, cannot be justified as a means of protecting society, where a civil commitment would do as well. * * * We would forget the teachings of the Eighth Amendment if we allowed sickness to be made a crime and permitted sick people to be punished for being sick. This age of enlightenment cannot tolerate such barbarous action.

Mr. Justice Harlan, concurring.

I am not prepared to hold that on the present state of medical knowledge it is completely irrational and hence unconstitutional for a State to conclude that narcotics addiction is something other than an illness nor that it amounts to cruel and unusual punishment for the State to subject narcotics addicts to its criminal law. Insofar as addiction may be identified with the use or possession of narcotics within the State (or, I would suppose, without the State), in violation of local statutes prohibiting such acts, it may surely be reached by the State's criminal law. But in this case the trial court's instructions permitted the jury to find the appellant guilty on no more proof than that he was present in California while he was addicted to narcotics. Since addiction alone cannot reasonably be thought to amount to more than a compelling propensity to use narcotics, the effect of this instruction was to authorize criminal punishment for a bare desire to commit a criminal act.

* * * Accordingly, I agree that the application of the California statute was unconstitutional in this case and join the judgment of reversal.

[The dissenting opinion of Mr. Justice Clark is deleted.]

Mr. Justice White, dissenting.

If appellant's conviction rested upon sheer status, condition or illness or if he was convicted for being an addict who had lost his power of self-control, I would have other thoughts about this case. But this record presents neither situation. * * *

I am not at all ready to place the use of narcotics beyond the reach of the States' criminal laws. I do not consider appellant's conviction to be a punishment for having an illness or for simply being in some status or condition, but rather a conviction for the regular, repeated or habitual use of narcotics immediately prior to his arrest and in violation of the California law.[3] * * *

* * * The Fourteenth Amendment is today held to bar any prosecution for addiction regardless of the degree or frequency of use, and the Court's opinion bristles with indications of further consequences. If it is "cruel and unusual punishment" to convict appellant for addiction, it is difficult to understand why it would be any less offensive to the Fourteenth Amendment to convict him for use on the same evidence of use which proved he was an addict. It is significant that in purporting to

---

3. This is not a case where a defendant is convicted "even though he has never touched any narcotic drug within the State or been guilty of any irregular behavior there." The evidence was that appellant lived and worked in Los Angeles. He admitted before trial that he had used narcotics for three or four months, three or four times a week, usually at his place with his friends. He stated to the police that he had last used narcotics * * * in the City of Los Angeles on January 27, 8 days before his arrest. * * *

reaffirm the power of the States to deal with the narcotics traffic, the Court does not include among the obvious powers of the State the power to punish for the use of narcotics. I cannot think that the omission was inadvertent. * * *

Notes and Questions

1. The constitutional significance of *Robinson* cannot be fully understood without considering the next case, *Powell v. Texas.* However, standing alone, what is the apparent holding of *Robinson?* Why is it constitutionally impermissible for the State of California to punish Robinson?

2. In view of *Robinson,* what common law elements of criminal responsibility might constitutionally be mandated?

POWELL v. TEXAS

Supreme Court of the United States, 1968.
392 U.S. 514, 88 S.Ct. 2145, 20 L.Ed.2d 1254.

MR. JUSTICE MARSHALL announced the judgment of the Court and delivered an opinion in which THE CHIEF JUSTICE, MR. JUSTICE BLACK, and MR. JUSTICE HARLAN join.

In late December 1966, appellant was arrested and charged with being found in a state of intoxication in a public place, in violation of Vernon's Ann.Texas Penal Code, Art. 477 (1952), which reads as follows:

"Whoever shall get drunk or be found in a state of intoxication in any public place, or at any private house except his own, shall be fined not exceeding one hundred dollars."

* * * His counsel urged that appellant was "afflicted with the disease of chronic alcoholism," that "his appearance in public [while drunk was] * * * not of his own volition," and therefore that to punish him criminally for that conduct would be cruel and unusual, in violation of the Eighth and Fourteenth Amendments to the United States Constitution.

The trial judge * * * sitting without a jury * * * ruled as a matter of law that chronic alcoholism was not a defense to the charge. He found appellant guilty, and fined him $50. * * *

I.

The principal testimony was that of Dr. David Wade, a Fellow of the American Medical Association, duly certificated in psychiatry. * * * Dr. Wade sketched the outlines of the "disease" concept of alcoholism; noted that there is no generally accepted definition of "alcoholism"; alluded to the ongoing debate within the medical profession over whether alcohol is actually physically "addicting" or merely psychologically "habituating"; and concluded that in either case a "chronic alcoholic" is an "involuntary drinker," who is "powerless not to drink," and who "loses his self-control over his drinking." He testified that he had examined appellant, and that appellant is a "chronic alcoholic," who "by the time he has reached [the state of intoxication] * * * is not able to control his behavior, and [who] * * * has reached this point because he has an uncontrollable compulsion to drink." Dr. Wade also responded in the negative to the question whether appellant has "the willpower to resist the constant excessive consumption of alcohol." He added that in his opinion jailing appellant without medical attention would operate neither to rehabilitate him nor to lessen his desire for alcohol.

On cross-examination, Dr. Wade admitted that when appellant was sober he knew the difference between right and wrong, and he responded affirmatively to the question whether appellant's act in taking the first drink in any given instance when he was sober was a "voluntary exercise of his will." Qualifying his answer, Dr. Wade stated that "these individuals have a compulsion, and this compulsion, while not completely overpowering, is a very strong influence, an exceedingly strong influence, and this compulsion coupled with the firm belief in their mind that they are going to be able to handle it from now on causes their judgment to be somewhat clouded."

Appellant testified concerning the history of his drinking problem. He reviewed his many arrests for drunkenness; testified that he was unable to stop drinking; stated that when he was intoxicated he had no control over his actions and could not remember them later, but that he did not become violent; and admitted that he did not remember his arrest on the occasion for which he was being tried. On cross-examination, appellant admitted that he had had one drink on the morning of the trial and had been able to discontinue drinking. * * *

* * * The State made no effort to obtain expert psychiatric testimony of its own, or even to explore with appellant's witness the question of appellant's power to control the frequency, timing, and location of his drinking bouts, or the substantial disagreement within the medical profession concerning the nature of the disease, the efficacy of treatment and the prerequisites for effective treatment. It did nothing to examine or illuminate what Dr. Wade might have meant by his reference to a "compulsion" which was "not completely overpowering," but which was "an exceedingly strong influence," or to inquire into the question of the proper role of such a "compulsion" in constitutional adjudication. * * *

Following this abbreviated exposition of the problem before it, the trial court indicated its intention to disallow appellant's claimed defense of "chronic alcoholism." Thereupon defense counsel submitted, and the trial court entered, the following "findings of fact":

> "(1) That chronic alcoholism is a disease which destroys the afflicted person's will power to resist the constant, excessive consumption of alcohol.

> "(2) That a chronic alcoholic does not appear in public by his own volition but under a compulsion symptomatic of the disease of chronic alcoholism.

"(3) That Leroy Powell, defendant herein, is a chronic alcoholic who is afflicted with the disease of chronic alcoholism."

Whatever else may be said of them, those are not "findings of fact" in any recognizable, traditional sense in which that term has been used in a court of law; they are the premises of a syllogism transparently designed to bring this case within the scope of this Court's opinion in Robinson v. State of California. Nonetheless, the dissent would have us adopt these "findings" without critical examination; it would use them as the basis for a constitutional holding that "a person may not be punished if the condition essential to constitute the defined crime is part of the pattern of his disease and is occasioned by a compulsion symptomatic of the disease."

The difficulty with that position, as we shall show, is that it goes much too far on the basis of too little knowledge. In the first place, the record in this case is utterly inadequate to permit the sort of informed and responsible adjudication which alone can support the announcement of an important and wide-ranging new constitutional principle. We know very little about the circumstances surrounding the drinking bout which resulted in this conviction, or about Leroy Powell's drinking problem, or indeed about alcoholism itself. * * *

Furthermore, the inescapable fact is that there is no agreement among members of the medical profession about what it means to say that "alcoholism" is a "disease." One of the principal works in this field states that * * * "*a disease is what the medical profession recognizes as such.*" In other words, there is widespread agreement today that "alcoholism" is a "disease," for the simple reason that the medical profession has concluded that it should attempt to treat those who have drinking problems. There the agreement stops. * * *

Nor is there any substantial consensus as to the "manifestations of alcoholism." E.M. Jellinek, one of the outstanding authorities on the subject, identifies five different types of alcoholics which predominate in the United States, and these types display a broad range of different and occasionally inconsistent symptoms. Moreover, wholly distinct types, relatively rare in this country, predominate in nations with different cultural attitudes regarding the consumption of alcohol. Even if we limit our consideration to the range of alcoholic symptoms more typically found in this country, there is substantial disagreement as to the manifestations of the "disease" called "alcoholism." * * *

The trial court's "finding" that Powell "is afflicted with the disease of chronic alcoholism," which "destroys the afflicted person's will power to resist the constant, excessive consumption of alcohol" covers a multitude of sins. Dr. Wade's testimony that appellant suffered from a compulsion which was an "exceedingly strong influence," but which was "not completely overpowering" is at least more carefully stated, if no less mystifying. * * * [C]onceptual clarity can only be achieved by distinguishing carefully between "loss of control" once an individual has commenced to drink and "inability to abstain" from drinking in the first place. Presumably a person would have to display both characteristics in order to make out a constitutional defense, should one be recognized. Yet the "findings" of the trial court utterly fail to make this crucial distinction, and there is serious question whether the record can be read to support a finding of either loss of control or inability to abstain. * * *

It is one thing to say that if a man is deprived of alcohol his hands will begin to shake, he will suffer agonizing pains and ultimately he will have hallucinations; it is quite another to say that a man has a "compulsion" to take a drink, but that he also retains a certain amount of "free will" with which to resist. It is simply impossible, in the present state of our knowledge, to ascribe a useful meaning to the latter statement. This definitional confusion reflects, of course, not merely the undeveloped state of the psychiatric art but also the conceptual difficulties inevitably attendant upon the importation of scientific and medical models into a legal system generally predicated upon a different set of assumptions.

II.

Despite the comparatively primitive state of our knowledge on the subject, it cannot be denied that the destructive use of alcoholic beverages is one of our principal social and public health problems. * * *

There is as yet no known generally effective method for treating the vast number of alcoholics in our society. * * * Thus it is entirely possible that, even were the manpower and facilities available for a full-scale attack upon chronic alcoholism, we would find ourselves unable to help the vast bulk of our "visible"—let alone our "invisible"—alcoholic population.

However, facilities for the attempted treatment of indigent alcoholics are woefully lacking throughout the country. It would be tragic to return large numbers of helpless, sometimes dangerous and frequently unsanitary inebriates to the streets of our cities without even the opportunity to sober up adequately which a brief jail term provides. * * *

One virtue of the criminal process is, at least, that the duration of penal incarceration typically has some outside statutory limit; this is universally true in the case of petty offenses, such as public drunkenness, where jail terms are quite short on the whole. "Therapeutic civil commitment" lacks this feature; one is typically committed until one is "cured." Thus, to do otherwise than affirm might subject indigent alcoholics to the risk that they may be locked up for an indefinite period of time under the same conditions as before, with no more hope than before of receiving effective treatment and no prospect of periodic "freedom."

Faced with this unpleasant reality, we are unable to assert that the use of the criminal process as a means of dealing with the public aspects of problem drinking can never be defended as rational. The picture of the penniless drunk propelled aimlessly and endlessly through the law's "revolving door" of arrest, incarceration, release and re-arrest is not a pretty one. But before we condemn the present practice across-the-board, perhaps we ought to be able to point to some clear promise of a better world for these unfortunate people. Unfortunately, no such promise has yet been forthcoming. If, in addition to the absence of a coherent approach to the problem of treatment, we consider the almost complete absence of facilities and manpower for the implementation of a rehabilitation program, it is difficult to say in the present context that the criminal process is utterly lacking in social value. * * *

III. * * *

Appellant * * * seeks to come within the application of the Cruel and Unusual Punishment Clause announced in Robinson v. State of California * * *.

On its face the present case does not fall within that holding, since appellant was convicted, not for being a chronic alcoholic, but for being in public while drunk on a particular occasion. The State of Texas thus has not sought to punish a mere status, as California did in *Robinson;* nor has it attempted to regulate appellant's behavior in the privacy of his own home. Rather, it has imposed upon appellant a criminal sanction for public behavior which may create substantial health and safety hazards, both for appellant and for members of the general public, and which offends the moral and esthetic sensibilities of a large segment of the community. This seems a far cry from convicting one for being an addict, being a chronic alcoholic, being "mentally ill, or a leper * * *."

Robinson so viewed brings this Court but a very small way into the substantive criminal law. And unless *Robinson* is so viewed it is difficult to see any limiting principle that would serve to prevent this Court from becoming, under the aegis of the Cruel and Unusual Punishment Clause, the ultimate arbiter of the standards of criminal responsibility, in diverse areas of the criminal law, throughout the country.

It is suggested in dissent that *Robinson* stands for the "simple" but "subtle" principle that "[c]riminal penalties may not be inflicted upon a person for being in a condition he is powerless to change." In that view, appellant's "condition" of public intoxication was "occasioned by a compulsion symptomatic of the disease" of chronic alcoholism, and thus, apparently, his behavior lacked the critical element of *mens rea*. Whatever may be the merits of such a doctrine of criminal responsibility, it surely cannot be said to follow from *Robinson*. The entire thrust of *Robinson's* interpretation of the Cruel and Unusual Punishment Clause is that criminal penalties may be inflicted only if the accused has committed some act, has engaged in some behavior, which society has an interest in preventing, or perhaps in historical common law terms, has committed some *actus reus*. It thus does not deal with the question of whether certain conduct cannot constitutionally be punished because it is, in some sense, "involuntary" or "occasioned by a compulsion." * * *

Ultimately, then, the most troubling aspects of this case, were *Robinson* to be extended to meet it, would be the scope and content of what could only be a constitutional doctrine of criminal responsibility. In dissent it is urged that the decision could be limited to conduct which is "a characteristic and involuntary part of the pattern of the disease as it afflicts" the particular individual, and that "[i]t is not foreseeable" that it would be applied "in the case of offenses such as driving a car while intoxicated, assault, theft, or robbery." That is limitation by fiat. In the first place, nothing in the logic of the dissent would limit its application to chronic alcoholics. If Leroy Powell cannot be convicted of public intoxication, it is difficult to see how a State can convict an individual for murder, if that individual, while exhibiting normal behavior in all other respects, suffers from a "compulsion" to kill, which is an "exceedingly strong influence," but "not completely overpowering." * * *

Traditional common-law concepts of personal accountability and essential considerations of federalism lead us to disagree with appellant. We are unable to conclude, on the state of this record or on the current state of medical knowledge, that chronic alcoholics in general, and Leroy Powell in particular, suffer from such an irresistible compulsion to drink and to get drunk in public that they are utterly unable to control their performance of either or both of these acts and thus cannot be deterred at all from public intoxication. And in any event this Court has never articulated a general constitutional doctrine of *mens rea.*

We cannot cast aside the centuries-long evolution of the collection of interlocking and overlapping concepts which the common law has utilized to assess the moral accountability of an individual for his antisocial deeds. The doctrines of *actus reus, mens rea,* insanity, mistake, justification, and duress have historically provided the tools for a constantly shifting adjustment of the tension between the evolving aims of the criminal law and changing religious, moral, philosophical, and medical views of the nature of man. This process of adjustment has always been thought to be the province of the States.

Nothing could be less fruitful than for this Court to be impelled into defining some sort of insanity test in constitutional terms. Yet, that task would seem to follow inexorably from an extension of *Robinson* to this case. If a person in the "condition" of being a chronic alcoholic cannot be criminally punished as a constitutional matter for being drunk in public, it would seem to follow that a person who contends that, in terms of one test, "his unlawful act was the product of mental disease or mental defect," Durham v. United States, 94 U.S.App.D.C. 228, 241, 214 F.2d 862, 875, 45 A.L.R.2d 1430 (1954), would state an issue of constitutional dimension with regard to his criminal responsibility had he been tried under some different and perhaps lesser standard, e.g., the right-wrong test of *M'Naghten's Case.* * * * But formulating a constitutional rule would reduce, if not eliminate, that fruitful experimentation, and freeze the developing productive dialogue between law and psychiatry into a rigid constitutional mold. It is simply not yet the time to write the Constitutional formulas cast in terms whose meaning, let alone relevance, is not yet clear either to doctors or to lawyers.

Affirmed.

MR. JUSTICE BLACK, whom MR. JUSTICE HARLAN joins, concurring.
* * *

Those who favor the change now urged upon us rely on their own notions of the wisdom of this Texas law to erect a constitutional barrier, the desirability of which is far from clear. To adopt this position would significantly limit the States in their efforts to deal with a widespread and important social problem and would do so by announcing a revolutionary doctrine of constitutional law that would also tightly restrict state power to deal with a wide variety of other harmful conduct.

I.   * * *

Jailing of chronic alcoholics is definitely defended as therapeutic, and the claims of therapeutic value are not insubstantial. As appellee notes, the alcoholics are removed from the streets, where in their intoxicated state they may be in physical danger, and are given food, clothing, and shelter until they "sober up" and thus at least regain their ability to keep from being run over by automobiles in the street. * * *

Apart from the value of jail as a form of treatment, jail serves other traditional functions of the criminal law. For one thing, it gets the alcoholics off the street, where they may cause harm in a number of ways to a number of people, and isolation of the dangerous has always been considered an important function of the criminal law. In addition, punishment of chronic alcoholics can serve several deterrent functions— it can give potential alcoholics an additional incentive to control their drinking, and it may, even in the case of the chronic alcoholic, strengthen his incentive to control the frequency and location of his drinking experiences.

These values served by criminal punishment assume even greater significance in light of the available alternatives for dealing with the problem of alcoholism. Civil commitment facilities may not be any better than the jails they would replace. * * *

* * * From what I have been able to learn about the subject, it seems to me that the present use of criminal sanctions might possibly be unwise, but I am by no means convinced that *any* use of criminal sanctions would inevitably be unwise or, above all, that I am qualified in this area to know what is legislatively wise and what is legislatively unwise.

II.

I agree with Mr. Justice Marshall that the findings of fact in this case are inadequate to justify the sweeping constitutional rule urged upon us. I could not, however, consider any findings that could be made with respect to "voluntariness" or "compulsion" controlling on the question whether a specific instance of human behavior should be immune from punishment as a constitutional matter. When we say that appellant's appearance in public is caused not by "his own" volition but rather by some other force, we are clearly thinking of a force that is nevertheless "his" except in some special sense.[1] The accused undoubtedly commits the proscribed act and the only question is whether the act can be attributed to a part of "his" personality that should not be regarded as criminally responsible. Almost all of the traditional purposes of the criminal law can be significantly served by punishing the person who in fact committed the proscribed act, without regard to whether his action was "compelled" by some elusive "irresponsible" aspect of his personality. As I have already indicated, punishment of such a defendant can clearly be justified in terms of deterrence, isolation, and treatment. * * * For these reasons, much as I think that criminal sanctions should in many situations be applied only to those whose conduct is morally blameworthy, I cannot think the States should be held constitutionally required to make the inquiry as to what part of a defendant's personality is responsible for his actions and to excuse anyone whose action was, in some complex, psychological sense, the result of a "compulsion."

III.

The rule of constitutional law urged by appellant is not required by Robinson v. State of California. In that case we held that a person could not be punished for the mere status of being a narcotics addict. * * *

Punishment for a status is particularly obnoxious, and in many instances can reasonably be called cruel and unusual, because it involves punishment for a mere propensity, a desire to commit an offense; the mental element is not simply one part of the crime but may constitute all of it. This is a situation universally sought to be avoided in our criminal law; the fundamental requirement that some action be proved is solidly established even for offenses most heavily based on propensity, such as attempt, conspiracy, and recidivist crimes. * * *

The reasons for this refusal to permit conviction without proof of an act are difficult to spell out, but they are nonetheless perceived and universally expressed in our criminal law. Evidence of propensity can be considered relatively unreliable and more difficult for a defendant to rebut; the requirement of a specific act thus provides some protection against false charges. Perhaps more fundamental is the difficulty of distinguishing, in the absence of any conduct, between desires of the day-dream variety and fixed intentions that may pose a real threat to society; extending the criminal law to cover both types of desire would be unthinkable, since "[t]here can hardly be anyone who has never thought evil. When a desire is inhibited it may find, expression in fantasy; but it would be absurd to condemn this natural psychological mechanism as illegal."

---

1. If an intoxicated person is actually carried into the street by someone else, "he" does not do the act at all, and of course he is entitled to acquittal. E.g., Martin v. State, 31 Ala.App. 334, 17 So.2d 427 (1944).

In contrast, crimes that require the State to prove that the defendant actually committed some proscribed act involve none of these special problems. In addition, the question whether an act is "involuntary" is, as I have already indicated, an inherently elusive question, and one which the State may, for good reasons, wish to regard as irrelevant. In light of all these considerations, our limitation of our *Robinson* holding to pure status crimes seems to me entirely proper.

IV.

The rule of constitutional law urged upon us by appellant would have a revolutionary impact on the criminal law, and any possible limits proposed for the rule would be wholly illusory. If the original boundaries of *Robinson* are to be discarded, any new limits too would soon fall by the wayside and the Court would be forced to hold the States powerless to punish any conduct that could be shown to result from a "compulsion," in the complex, psychological meaning of that term. * * *

The real reach of any such decision, however, would be broader still, for the basic premise underlying the argument is that it is cruel and unusual to punish a person who is not morally blameworthy. I state the proposition in this sympathetic way because I feel there is much to be said for avoiding the use of criminal sanctions in many such situations. But the question here is one of constitutional law. The legislatures have always been allowed wide freedom to determine the extent to which moral culpability should be a prerequisite to conviction of a crime. The criminal law is a social tool that is employed in seeking a wide variety of goals, and I cannot say the Eighth Amendment's limits on the use of criminal sanctions extend as far as this viewpoint would inevitably carry them. * * *

MR. JUSTICE WHITE, concurring in the result.

If it cannot be a crime to have an irresistible compulsion to use narcotics, Robinson v. State of California, I do not see how it can constitutionally be a crime to yield to such a compulsion. Punishing an addict for using drugs convicts for addiction under a different name. Distinguishing between the two crimes is like forbidding criminal conviction for being sick with flu or epilepsy but permitting punishment for running a fever or having a convulsion. Unless *Robinson* is to be abandoned, the use of narcotics by an addict must be beyond the reach of the criminal law. Similarly, the chronic alcoholic with an irresistible urge to consume alcohol should not be punishable for drinking or for being drunk.

Powell's conviction was for the different crime of being drunk in a public place. * * *

The trial court said that Powell was a chronic alcoholic with a compulsion not only to drink to excess but also to frequent public places when intoxicated. Nothing in the record before the trial court supports the latter conclusion, which is contrary to common sense and to common knowledge. The sober chronic alcoholic has no compulsion to be on the public streets; many chronic alcoholics drink at home and are never seen drunk in public. Before and after taking the first drink, and until he becomes so drunk that he loses the power to know where he is or to direct his movements, the chronic alcoholic with a home or financial resources is as capable as the nonchronic drinker of doing his drinking in private, of removing himself from public places and, since he knows or ought to know that he will become intoxicated, of making plans to avoid his being found drunk in public. For these reasons, I cannot say that the chronic alcoholic who proves his disease and a compulsion to drink is shielded from conviction when he has knowingly failed to take feasible precautions against committing a criminal act, here the act of going to or remaining in a public place. On such facts the alcoholic is like a person with smallpox, who could be convicted for being on the street but not for being ill, or, like the epileptic, who would be punished for driving a car but not for his disease.

The fact remains that some chronic alcoholics must drink and hence must drink *somewhere*. Although many chronics have homes, many others do not. * * * For some of these alcoholics I would think a showing could be made that resisting drunkenness is impossible and that avoiding public places when intoxicated is also impossible. As applied to them this statute is in effect a law which bans a single act for which they may not be convicted under the Eighth Amendment—the act of getting drunk.

It is also possible that the chronic alcoholic who begins drinking in private at some point becomes so drunk that he loses the power to control his movements and for that reason appears in public. The Eighth Amendment might also forbid conviction in such circumstances, but only on a record satisfactorily showing that it was not feasible for him to have made arrangements to prevent his being in public when drunk and that his extreme drunkenness sufficiently deprived him of his faculties on the occasion in issue. * * *

Mr. Justice Fortas, with whom Mr. Justice Douglas, Mr. Justice Brennan, and Mr. Justice Stewart join, dissenting. * * *

The issue posed in this case is a narrow one. There is no challenge here to the validity of public intoxication statutes in general or to the Texas public intoxication statute in particular. * * *

The sole question presented is whether a criminal penalty may be imposed upon a person suffering the disease of "chronic alcoholism" for a condition—being "in a state of intoxication" in public—which is a characteristic part of the pattern of his disease and which, the trial court found, was not the consequence of appellant's volition but of "a compulsion symptomatic of the disease of chronic alcoholism." * * *

Robinson stands upon a principle which, despite its subtlety, must be simply stated and respectfully applied because it is the foundation of individual liberty and the cornerstone of the relations between a civilized state and its citizens: Criminal penalties may not be inflicted upon a person for being in a condition he is powerless to change. In all probability, Robinson at some time before his conviction elected to take narcotics. But the crime as defined did not punish this conduct.[29] The statute imposed a penalty for the offense of "addiction"—a condition which Robinson could not control. Once Robinson had become an addict, he was utterly powerless to avoid criminal guilt. He was powerless to choose not to violate the law.

In the present case, appellant is charged with a crime composed of two elements—being intoxicated and being found in a public place while in that condition. The crime, so defined, differs from that in *Robinson*. The statute covers more than a mere status. But the essential constitutional defect here is the same as in *Robinson*, for in both cases the particular defendant was accused of being in a condition which he had no capacity to change or avoid. * * *

* * * [H]ere the findings of the trial judge call into play the principle that a person may not be punished if the condition essential to constitute the defined crime is part of the pattern of his disease and is occasioned by a compulsion symptomatic of the disease. This principle, narrow in scope and applicability, is implemented by the Eighth Amendment's prohibition of "cruel and unusual punishment," as we construed that command in *Robinson*. * * *

Notes and Questions

1. If Powell had been homeless, would the outcome in the case have been the same?

2. Is *Powell* consistent with the holding of *Robinson*? Is the underlying rationale of *Powell* consistent with the reasoning of *Robinson*? If not, why do you think the Supreme Court changed directions?

3. In light of *Powell*, reconsider Note 2 (p. 544 supra). Specifically, would it be constitutional for a state to make it a crime "to be HIV Positive," i.e., to be infected with Human Immunodeficiency Virus, the causative agent of Acquired Immunodeficiency Syndrome (AIDS)? Would it be constitutional to punish a person for "being a prostitute"? What if a state makes it a crime to have an epileptic seizure?

4. In United States v. Moore, 486 F.2d 1139 (D.C.Cir.1973), a heroin addict "with an overpowering need to use heroin," appealed his conviction under two federal statutes for possession of heroin. In considering the defendant's claim, Circuit Judge J. Skelly Wright observed:

> Although *Powell* left unsettled the precise relationship between criminal responsibility and the Constitution, no member of the Court expressed even the slightest disagreement with the basic proposition that the Eighth Amendment provides only the floor and not the ceiling for development of common law notions of criminal responsibility.

29. The Court noted in *Robinson* that narcotic addiction "is apparently an illness which may be contracted innocently or involuntarily." In the case of alcoholism it is even more likely that the disease may be innocently contracted, since the drinking of alcoholic beverages is a common activity, generally accepted in our society, while the purchasing and taking of drugs are crimes. * * *

* * * Thus, no matter what interpretation of *Powell* * * * is adopted, the decision must "be read not as a bar, but as an exhortation toward further experiment with common-law doctrines of criminal responsibility."

Id. at 1240 (dissenting opinion).

Is the law's failure to recognize an addiction defense consistent with current criminal law doctrine? For example, if it is proper to excuse a person for criminal conduct because she was subjected to compelling forces that a person of reasonable firmness would have been unable to resist, is it fair to punish a drug addict for possession of drugs? Aren't the physiological forces of addiction as compelling as a gun pointed at the defendant's head or a threat of serious harm to a third party?

On the other hand, if you would permit an addiction defense in a prosecution for simple possession or acquisition of an illegal drug, are you similarly required to acquit the addict of more serious crimes, such as robbery or murder, if they are also motivated by the compulsive need to obtain the drugs to feed the addiction? Can you provide a principled distinction?

Notes 5 and 6 concern the question of whether the law ought to recognize a defense to criminal conduct that stems from the actor's alcoholism or drug addiction.

5. *Retributivism.* In assessing an individual's responsibility for a crime from a retributivist perspective, is the pertinent issue whether the actor is to blame for becoming an alcoholic or addict? If we conclude that she is not to blame for her condition, does it inevitably follow that she does not deserve to be punished for the criminal "symptoms" or ordinary consequences of the disease? Reflect on Circuit Judge Wilkey's characterization of the issue, as set out in United States v. Moore, 486 F.2d 1139, 1145 (D.C.Cir.1973)?

> In the case of any addict there are two factors that go to make up the "self control" (or absence thereof) which governs his activities, and which determines whether or not he will perform certain acts, such as crimes, to obtain drugs. One factor is the physical craving to have the drug. The other is what might be called the addict's "character," or his moral standards. * * *

> * * * Putting [the issue] in mathematical terms, if the addict's craving is 4 on a scale of 10, and his strength of character is only 3, he will have a resulting loss of self-control and commit some illegal act to acquire drugs * * *. For a different example, let us assume a medically induced addict, whose craving is 6, but whose strength of character is 8; with him there will be no resulting loss of self-control, and presumably no illegal acts of any kind.

> In * * * these examples the legally important factor is the resulting loss of self-control. Drug addiction of varying degrees may or may not result in loss of self-control, depending on the strength of character opposed to the drug craving.

What is the implication of this analysis from a "just deserts" perspective?

Suppose that a person *is* to blame for becoming an addict. Does it follow from this that she deserves to be punished for her later, arguably involuntary, addiction-related conduct? Yes, according to the following anti-drug message to adolescents:

> Here * * * is the truth about crack, and many other drugs. If you do it once, you are significantly more likely to mess up your life than you otherwise would have been. If you do it a second time, the chances rise again. And so on. At some point * * * continued use entails some degree of ongoing damage to your life and the chances of something truly catastrophic happening becomes high. * * * At a certain point it may in some sense be beyond your power to step back from the brink. *Still, when catastrophe strikes, it's all your fault, for * * * you knew, or should have known, the odds when you went into the game * * *.*

"The Barry Bust," *The New Republic,* Vol. 202, No. 7, Feb. 12, 1990, at 8, 9 (emphasis added).

Do you agree with the italicized conclusion? Or, do you find Circuit Judge Wright's observation in *Moore,* supra, at 1243, more persuasive:

> It is of course true that there may have been a time in the past before the addict lost control when he made a conscious decision to use drugs. But imposition of punishment on this basis would violate the long-standing rule that "[t]he law looks to the immediate, and not to the remote cause; to the actual state of the party, and not to the causes, which remotely produced it." * * * "A sick person is a sick person though he exposed himself to contagion." I would adhere to that view today, for no matter how the addict came to be addicted, once he has reached that stage he clearly is sick, and a bare desire for vengeance cannot justify his treatment as a criminal.

6. *Utilitarianism.* Steven S. Nemerson, *Alcoholism, Intoxication, and the Criminal Law,* 10 Cardozo L.Rev. 393, 439–42 (1988):

> Punishing individuals who are actually blameless as a result of alcoholism-induced intoxication may * * * serve to maximize utility by its effects on pre-crime drinking by some alcoholics.

> * * * [P]sychological denial of their inability to control the amount and results of their drinking "immunizes" [alcoholics] from the deterrent force of the threat or imposition of punishment. But punishment for crime by intoxicated alcoholics is not necessarily inefficacious as to all those in this class. Some do entertain limited doubts about their control over their own drinking and subsequent conduct. Some at least realize that in the past their drinking has led to unpredicted, undesired, and perhaps even criminal, consequences. To the extent that such doubts exist—to the extent that they acknowledge their own "problem drinking"—such individuals may be amenable to the deterrent force of punishment. * * *

> While an alcoholic not undergoing treatment has little or no control over whether he will drink, he does retain some control over when he will begin to drink. To the extent that drinking under certain conditions or in certain settings is more likely to result in criminal behavior,

punishment of alcoholics for their crimes may serve to channel alcoholics's drinking into less potentially dangerous environments. * * *

In addition, a system of laws that punishes alcoholics * * * also serves to reduce the likelihood that *nonalcoholic* culpable offenders will escape incarceration because they happen to be intoxicated when they committed a crime. While such individuals do not necessarily engage in crime with the intention of fabricating an alcoholism defense if apprehended, upon being charged with an offense they may well seek to establish that excuse. * * *

* * * [P]unishment of alcoholics for their crimes can, and often does, play a causal role in rehabilitation. * * * [A]lcoholism is very much a disease of denial. Subjective unwillingness to acknowledge an inability to control the degree or effects of drinking is a hallmark of alcoholism. * * *

The fact that the alcoholic may not be morally blameworthy for his criminal acts does not negate the practical effect of imposing punishment for those acts. Treating the offender *as if he were morally responsible* serves to promote rehabilitation.

4. INSANITY

a. *Procedural Context*

i. *Competency to Stand Trial*

A criminal trial may not proceed if the defendant is incompetent to stand trial. A person can be incompetent for a variety of reasons, including that she is severely mentally ill or disabled, suffers from amnesia, or is unable to communicate with her attorney due to physical handicaps, such as the inability to speak. Although statutory language varies, generally speaking, a defendant is incompetent to stand trial unless she has sufficient present ability to consult with her lawyer "with a reasonable degree of rational understanding" and has "a rational as well as factual understanding of the proceedings" against her. Dusky v. United States, 362 U.S. 402, 402, 80 S.Ct. 788, 789, 4 L.Ed.2d 824, 825 (1960) (internal quotation marks omitted).

The issue of competency, should it arise, ordinarily is considered at the defendant's initial appearance before a magistrate, but it may be raised at any time during the proceedings, including at trial. Unless the parties agree that the defendant is incompetent, the judge ordinarily will appoint at least one psychiatrist to examine the defendant, during which time the accused may be committed to a hospital or other suitable facility for the testing. E.g., Model Penal Code § 4.05.

There is no settled view as to where the burden of proof lies at a competency hearing. Some states place the burden on the party raising the competency issue, others allocate the burden to the defense to prove the defendant's inability to stand trial, and still others provide that the burden rests with the prosecutor to demonstrate competency. See Medina v. California, 505 U.S. ___, 112 S.Ct. 2572, 120 L.Ed.2d 353

(1992) (upholding the constitutionality of a statute placing the burden of proof on the defendant, and summarizing current law).

If a judge determines that the defendant is incompetent to stand trial, criminal proceedings are suspended, and the defendant is committed to a mental health facility, where she may be held until she regains competency, a period of time that sometimes exceeds the maximum sentence that may be imposed for the offense charged.

Constitutional issues arise when the defendant cannot be restored to competency. For example, in Jackson v. Indiana, 406 U.S. 715, 92 S.Ct. 1845, 32 L.Ed.2d 435 (1972), the defendant was described as a "mentally defective deaf mute with a mental level of a pre-school child," who could neither read, write, nor communicate to others except through very limited sign language. The examining doctors described the defendant's prognosis for competency as "rather dim." As defense counsel pointed out, the defendant's commitment under such circumstances amounted to a life sentence without a criminal trial.

The Supreme Court ruled that "[a]t the least, due process requires that the nature and duration of commitment bear some reasonable relation to the purpose for which the individual is committed." Id. at 738, 92 S.Ct. at 1858, 32 L.Ed.2d at 451. Therefore, the Court held:

> [A] person charged by the State with a criminal offense who is committed solely on account of his incapacity to proceed to trial cannot be held more than the reasonable period of time necessary to determine whether there is a substantial probability that he will attain the capacity in the foreseeable future. If it is determined that this is not the case, then the State must either institute the customary civil commitment proceeding that would be required to commit indefinitely any other citizen, or release the defendant.

Release of an incompetent defendant can endanger society. In one well publicized case, Donald Lang, an illiterate deaf-mute, was arrested for the murder of a prostitute. He was released after it was determined that he probably would never be competent to stand trial. See People ex rel. Myers v. Briggs, 46 Ill.2d 281, 263 N.E.2d 109 (1970). Within five months he was arrested again for murder. Although he was convicted of this crime, the judgment was reversed after an appellate court determined that Lang's disabilities deprived him of a fair trial. People v. Lang, 26 Ill.App.3d 648, 325 N.E.2d 305 (1975). Criminal proceedings were never reinstituted, but Lang was committed to a mental institution through civil proceedings. People v. Lang, 225 Ill.App.3d 229, 167 Ill.Dec. 221, 587 N.E.2d 490 (1992).

Severely psychotic defendants sometimes can be restored to competency by the administration of antipsychotic drugs. May the state, therefore, require such a person to undergo administration of such medication in order to render her competent to stand trial? As a constitutional matter, "[t]he forcible injection of medication into a nonconsenting person's body represents a substantial interference with that person's liberty" interest, under the due process clause. Washington v. Harper, 494 U.S. 210, 229, 110 S.Ct. 1028, 1041, 108 L.Ed.2d 178, 203 (1990).

Nonetheless, due process is satisfied if the state proves that the coerced administration of drugs before or during trial is "medically appropriate and, considering less intrusive alternatives, essential for the sake of [the defendant's] own safety or the safety of others." Riggins v. Nevada, 504 U.S. ___, ___, 112 S.Ct. 1810, 1815, 118 L.Ed.2d 479, 489 (1992). And, the Supreme Court has suggested that "the State *might* * * * [also be] able to justify medically appropriate, involuntary treatment with [an antipsychotic] drug by establishing that it could not obtain an adjudication of [the defendant's] guilt or innocence by using less intrusive means." Id. at ___, 112 S.Ct. at 1815, 118 L.Ed.2d at 489–90 (emphasis added).

Issues of competency aside, the use of antipsychotic drugs, whether they are administered voluntarily or not, may affect the trial by changing the defendant's demeanor before the jury. According to one criminal defense lawyer, "[i]t's difficult to convince a jury that a person who is an ordinary-looking human being, who is not frothing at the mouth and throwing himself on the floor, suffers from a mental illness so severe that it overpowers his ability to discern right from wrong." Peter J. Howe, *Insanity Plea Difficult in Massachusetts,* Boston Globe, Sept. 28, 1990, at 18 (quoting John P. White, Jr.).

ii. Pre-trial Assertion of the Insanity Plea

Many states have instituted special procedures that must be followed if a defendant wishes to assert the insanity defense at trial. For example, a defendant who intends to claim insanity must often assert a special plea of "not guilty by reason of insanity," rather than (or in conjunction with) the general plea of "not guilty." Courts are divided on the question of whether a trial judge may interpose an insanity plea over the objections of a competent defendant. See David S. Cohn, *Offensive Use of the Insanity Defense: Imposing the Insanity Defense Over the Defendant's Objection,* 15 Hastings Const.L.Q. 295 (1988).

In some states and in the federal courts, a defendant who intends to introduce expert testimony relating to her mental condition at the time of the crime must notify the prosecutor of her plan within a specified period of time before trial, and submit to a psychiatric evaluation by a court appointed expert. If the defendant fails to comply with such rules, the judge may bar the party's expert testimony at trial. E.g., Fed. R.Crim.P. 12.2.

iii. Burden of Proof at Trial

Because insanity is an affirmative defense, the legislature may constitutionally require the defendant to persuade the factfinder that she was insane at the time of the crime. Leland v. Oregon, 343 U.S. 790, 72 S.Ct. 1002, 96 L.Ed. 1302 (1952). Nonetheless, until the 1980s, most states and the federal courts required the prosecutor to carry the burden of proof regarding the defendant's sanity. 2 Paul H. Robinson, Criminal Law Defenses § 173(a) at 284–85 (1984).

As a result of public anger stemming from the insanity acquittal of John W. Hinckley, the attempted assassin of President Ronald Reagan, see United States v. Hinckley, 525 F.Supp. 1342 (D.D.C.1981), clarified 529 F.Supp. 520 (D.D.C.), affirmed 672 F.2d 115 (D.C.Cir.1982), a majority of states and Congress now place the burden of persuasion regarding sanity on the defendant.

The prosecutor retains the constitutional obligation to prove beyond a reasonable doubt all of the elements of the offense charged. Consequently, the same testimony introduced by the defendant in support of her insanity claim may also raise a reasonable doubt as to her capacity to form the requisite mental state of the offense, or it may cast doubt on whether her conduct included a voluntary act. In light of this, is it proper for a judge to instruct the jury to consider the defendant's insanity defense *before* it considers her "guilt or innocence of the crimes charged"? See State v. McMullin, 421 N.W.2d 517 (Iowa 1988).

iv. *Post–Trial Disposition of Insanity Acquittees*

Many members of the public believe that defendants who are found not guilty by reason of insanity go free immediately or within a short period of time following trial. National Mental Health Association, Myths and Realities: A Report of the National Commission on the Insanity Defense 24 (1983). In reality, as early as in Blackstone's time, the view was that, "in the case of absolute madmen, as they are not answerable for their actions, they should not be permitted the liberty of acting unless under proper control; and, in particular, they ought not to be suffered to go loose, to the terror of the king's subjects." 4 William Blackstone, Commentaries on the Law of England *25 (1769).

In some jurisdictions a person found not guilty by reason of insanity is automatically committed by the criminal court to a psychiatric facility for custody, care, and treatment of her mental illness. E.g., D.C.Code 1981, § 24–301(d)(1); Model Penal Code § 4.08. In other states, commitment does not occur automatically, but it is common for local law to permit or require the criminal court to order the acquittee temporarily detained in a mental health facility for observation and determination of whether she remains mentally ill and subject to civil commitment. E.g., Mich.Comp.Laws Ann. § 330.2050 (1990).

In Addington v. Texas, 441 U.S. 418, 99 S.Ct. 1804, 60 L.Ed.2d 323 (1979), the Supreme Court ruled that a person may not be civilly committed to a mental institution unless the state proves by clear and convincing evidence that the individual is presently mentally ill and dangerous to herself or others. However, in Jones v. United States, 463 U.S. 354, 103 S.Ct. 3043, 77 L.Ed.2d 694 (1983), the Supreme Court held that when a person charged with a crime (in this case, shoplifting) is found not guilty by reason of insanity, the state may properly commit the person on the lesser standard of proof of preponderance of the evidence.

Why does the clear-and-convincing-evidence standard for proving mental illness and dangerousness not apply to an insanity acquittee? The Court explained:

> A verdict of not guilty by reason of insanity establishes two facts: (i) the defendant committed an act that constitutes a criminal offense, and (ii) he committed the act because of mental illness. * * *
>
> The fact that a person has been found, beyond a reasonable doubt, to have committed a criminal act certainly indicates dangerousness. * * * Indeed, this concrete evidence generally may be at least as persuasive as any predictions about dangerousness that might be made in a civil-commitment proceeding. We do not agree with petitioner's suggestion that the requisite dangerousness is not established by proof that a person committed a non-violent crime against property. This Court never has held that "violence" * * * is a prerequisite for a constitutional commitment.
>
> Nor can we say that it was unreasonable for Congress to determine that the insanity acquittal supports an inference of continuing mental illness. It comports with common sense to conclude that someone whose mental illness was sufficient to lead him to commit a criminal act is likely to remain ill and in need of treatment.

Id. at 363–65, 103 S.Ct. at 3049–50, 77 L.Ed.2d at 705–06.

The *Jones* Court also held that a person found not guilty by reason of insanity may be held in custody as long as she remains both mentally ill and dangerous, although this may result in hospitalization for a period of time longer than the detainee could have been incarcerated if convicted. On other hand, the state violates due process if it holds a person against her will in a mental institution once it is determined that she is no longer mentally ill, even if she remains dangerous to the community or herself. Foucha v. Louisiana, 504 U.S. ___, 112 S.Ct. 1780, 118 L.Ed.2d 437 (1992). Thus, Model Penal Code § 4.08(3), which authorizes release only when the committed person proves that she may safely be discharged, is unconstitutional.

b. Struggling for a Definition: The Tests of Insanity

i. Why Do We Excuse the Insane?: Initial Thoughts

UNITED STATES v. FREEMAN

United States Court of Appeals, Second Circuit, 1966.
357 F.2d 606.

KAUFMAN, CIRCUIT JUDGE: * * *

We are here seeking a proper test of criminal responsibility. That we are not instead deciding the initial question—whether lack of such responsibility, however defined, should be a defense in criminal prosecutions—itself seems significant and worthy of at least some brief comment.

The criminal law * * * is an expression of the moral sense of the community. The fact that the law has, for centuries, regarded [insane] wrong-doers as improper subjects for punishment is a testament to the extent to which that moral sense has developed. Thus, society has recognized over the years that none of the three asserted purposes of the criminal law—rehabilitation, deterrence and retribution—is satisfied when the truly irresponsible * * * are punished.

What rehabilitative function is served when one who is mentally incompetent and found guilty is ordered to serve a sentence in prison? Is not any curative or restorative function better achieved in such a case in an institution designed and equipped to treat just such individuals? And how is deterrence achieved by punishing the incompetent? Those who are substantially unable to restrain their conduct are, by definition, undeterrable and their "punishment" is no example for others; those who are [insane] * * * can hardly be expected rationally to weigh the consequences of their conduct. Finally, what segment of society can feel its desire for retribution satisfied when it wreaks vengeance upon the incompetent? Although an understandable emotion, a need for retribution can never be permitted in a civilized society to degenerate into a sadistic form of revenge.

Notes and Questions

1. Holloway v. United States, 148 F.2d 665, 666–67 (D.C.Cir.1945):

To punish a man who lacks the power to reason is as undignified and unworthy as punishing an inanimate object or an animal. A man who cannot reason cannot be subject to blame. Our collective conscience does not allow punishment where it cannot impose blame.

2. Is Judge Kaufman correct in asserting that punishment of the insane is incompatible with principles of rehabilitation, deterrence, and retribution?

3. Controversies have always swirled around the insanity defense. Should the defense be abolished? Should it be very narrowly framed? Or, does the defense not go far enough in exculpating mentally disordered persons? In light of competing social currents and developments in our understanding of human psychology, courts have struggled over the past two centuries to devise a suitable definition of insanity. As you read the following materials, consider the weaknesses and strengths of each formulation of the insanity defense. Ask yourself which standard best serves the utilitarian and retributive principles of the criminal law.

ii. The M'Naghten Rule

[handwritten: only: Knowing right from wrong]

DANIEL M'NAGHTEN'S CASE

House of Lords, 1843.
10 Cl. & F. 200, 8 Eng.Rep. 718.

[M'Naghten was indicted for the murder of Edward Drummond, secretary to Prime Minister Robert Peel. As the defendant explained upon his arrest, he intended to kill the Prime Minister because "[t]he tories in my city follow and persecute me wherever I go, and have entirely destroyed my peace of mind. * * * [T]hey do everything to harass and persecute me; in fact they wish to murder me." The defendant shot Drummond by mistake, believing he was Peel.

At trial, the defense called expert and lay witnesses who testified that M'Naghten was obsessed with "morbid delusions" and suffered from insanity. The presiding judge, Lord Chief Justice Tindal, instructed the jury regarding insanity as follows:

The question to be determined is, whether at the time the act in question was committed, the prisoner had or had not the use of his understanding, so as to know that he was doing a wrong or wicked act. If the jurors should be of opinion that the prisoner was not sensible, at the time he committed it, that he was violating the laws both of God and man, then he would be entitled to a verdict in his favour: but if, on the contrary, they were of opinion that when he committed the act he was in a sound state of mind, their verdict must be against him.

The jury returned a verdict of "not guilty, on the ground of insanity." The acquittal resulted in public outrage, deep concern by Queen Victoria (who had been subjected to assassination attempts herself), and debate in the House of Lords, where the judges were asked to respond to five questions of law. The *"M'Naghten* rule" is found in Lord Chief Justice Tindal's answers to the second and third questions propounded to him.]

Your Lordships are pleased to inquire of us, secondly, "What are the proper questions to be submitted to the jury, where a person alleged to be afflicted with insane delusion respecting one or more subjects or persons, is charged with the commission of a crime (murder, for example), and insanity is set up as a defence?" And, thirdly, "In what terms ought the question to be left to the jury as to the prisoner's state of mind at the time when the act was committed?" And as these two questions appear to us to be more conveniently answered together, we have to submit our opinion to be, that the jurors ought to be told in all cases that every man is to be presumed to be sane, and to possess a sufficient degree of reason to be responsible for his crimes, until the contrary be proved to their satisfaction; and that to establish a defence on the ground of insanity, it must be clearly proved that, at the time of the committing of the act, the party accused was labouring under such a defect of reason, from disease of the mind, as not to know the nature and quality of the act he was doing; or, if he did know it, that he did not know he was doing what was wrong. The mode of putting the latter part of the question to the jury on these occasions has generally been, whether the accused at the time of doing the act knew the difference between right and wrong * * *.

UNITED STATES v. FREEMAN

United States Court of Appeals, Second Circuit, 1966.
357 F.2d 606.

KAUFMAN, CIRCUIT JUDGE: * * *

M'Naghten and its antecedents can, in many respects, be seen as examples of the law's conscientious efforts to place in a separate category, people who cannot be justly held "responsible" for their acts. As far back as 1582, William Lambard of Lincolns' Inn set forth what can be viewed as the forerunner of the M'Naghten test as we know it: "If a man or a natural fool, or a lunatic in the time of his lunacy, or a child who apparently has no knowledge of good or evil do kill a man, this is no felonious act * * * for they cannot be said to have any understanding will." By 1724, the language had shifted from "good or evil" to the more familiar emphasis on the word "know." Thus, in Rex v. Arnold, 16 How.St.Tr. 695, 764 the "Wild Beast" test was enunciated. It provided for exculpation if the defendant "doth not *know* what he is doing, no more than * * * a wild beast."

By modern scientific standards the language of these early tests is primitive. In the 18th Century, psychiatry had hardly become a profession, let alone a science. Thus, these tests and their progeny were evolved at a time when psychiatry was literally in the Dark Ages.

In the pre–M'Naghten period, the concepts of phrenology and monomania were being developed and had significant influence on the right and wrong test. Phrenologists believed that the human brain was divided into thirty-five separate areas, each with its own peculiar mental function. The sixth area, for example, was designated "destructiveness." It was located, we are told, above the ear because this was the widest part of the skull of carnivorous animals. Monomania, on the other hand, was a state of mind in which one insane idea predominated while the rest of the thinking processes remained normal.

Of course, both phrenology and monomania are rejected today as meaningless medical concepts since the human personality is viewed as a fully integrated system. But, by an accident of history, the rule of M'Naghten's case froze these concepts into the common law just at a time when they were becoming obsolete. * * *

After a lengthy trial in 1843, M'Naghten was found "not guilty by reason of insanity." M'Naghten's exculpation from criminal responsibility was most significant for several reasons. His defense counsel had relied in part upon Dr. Isaac Ray's historic work, Medical Jurisprudence of Insanity which had been published in 1838. This book, which was used and referred to extensively at the trial, contained many enlightened views on the subject of criminal responsibility in general and on the weaknesses of the right and wrong test in particular. Thus, for example, the jury was told that the human mind is not compartmentalized and that a defect in one aspect of the personality could spill over and affect other areas. * * * [T]he court was so impressed with this and other medical evidence of M'Naghten's incompetency that Lord Chief Justice Tindal practically directed a verdict for the accused.

For these reasons, M'Naghten's case could have been the turning point for a new approach to more modern methods of determining criminal responsibility. But the Queen's ire was raised by the acquittal and she was prompted to intervene. * * * Consequently, the fifteen judges of the common law courts were called in a somewhat extraordinary session under a not too subtle atmosphere of pressure to answer five prolix and obtuse questions on the status of criminal responsibility in England. Significantly, it was Lord Chief Justice Tindal who responded for fourteen of the fifteen judges, and thus articulated what has come to be known as the M'Naghten Rules or M'Naghten test. Rather than relying on Dr. Ray's monumental work which had apparently impressed him at M'Naghten's trial, Tindal, with the Queen's breath upon him, reaffirmed the old restricted right-wrong test despite its 16th Century roots and the fact that it, in effect, echoed such uninformed concepts as phrenology and monomania. In this manner, Dr. Ray's insights were to be lost to the common law for over one hundred years except in the small state of New Hampshire.[31] * * *

But the principal objection to M'Naghten is not that it was arrived at by this extraordinary process. Rather, the rule is faulted because it has several serious deficiencies which stem in the main from its narrow scope. Because M'Naghten focuses only on the cognitive aspect of the personality, i.e., the ability to know right from wrong, we are told by eminent medical scholars that it does not permit the jury to identify those who can distinguish between good and evil but who cannot control their behavior. The result is that instead of being treated at appropriate mental institutions for a sufficiently long period to bring about a cure or sufficient improvement so that the accused may return with relative safety to himself and the community, he is ordinarily sentenced to a prison term as if criminally responsible and then released as a potential recidivist with society at his mercy. To the extent that these individuals continue to be released from prison because of the narrow scope of M'Naghten, that test poses a serious danger to society's welfare.

Similarly, M'Naghten's single track emphasis on the cognitive aspect of the personality recognizes no degrees of incapacity. Either the defendant knows right from wrong or he does not and that is the only choice the jury is given. But such a test is grossly unrealistic; our

---

31. Because of the influence of Dr. Ray, New Hampshire adopted a test which was a precursor of the modern *Durham* rule. [See subsection iv, infra.]

mental institutions, as any qualified psychiatrist will attest, are filled with people who to some extent can differentiate between right and wrong, but lack the capacity to control their acts to a substantial degree. * * *

A further fatal defect of the M'Naghten Rules stems from the unrealistically tight shackles which they place upon expert psychiatric testimony. When the law limits a testifying psychiatrist to stating his opinion whether the accused is capable of knowing right from wrong, the expert is thereby compelled to test guilt or innocence by a concept which bears little relationship to reality. He is required thus to consider one aspect of the mind as a "logic-tight compartment in which the delusion holds sway leaving the balance of the mind intact. * * *"

Prominent psychiatrists have expressed their frustration when confronted with such requirements. Echoing such complaints, Edward de Grazia has asked, "How [does one] translate 'psychosis' or 'psychopathy' or 'dementia praecox' or even 'sociopathy' or 'mental disorder' or 'neurotic character disorder' or 'mental illness' into a psychiatric judgment of whether the accused knew 'right' from 'wrong.'" In stronger and more vivid terms, Dr. Lawrence Kolb, Director of the New York Psychiatric Institute, * * * expressed a similar viewpoint when he declared that "answers supplied by a psychiatrist in regard to questions of rightness or wrongness of an act or 'knowing' its nature constitute a professional perjury." * * *

The tremendous growth of psychiatric knowledge since the Victorian origins of M'Naghten and even the near-universal disdain in which it is held by present-day psychiatrists are not by themselves sufficient reasons for abandoning the test. At bottom, the determination whether a man is or is not held responsible for his conduct is not a medical but a legal, social or moral judgment. Ideally, psychiatrists—much like experts in other fields—should provide grist for the legal mill, should furnish the raw data upon which the legal judgment is based. It is the psychiatrist who informs as to the mental state of the accused—his characteristics, his potentialities, his capabilities. But once this information is disclosed, it is society as a whole, represented by judge or jury, which decides whether a man with the characteristics described should or should not be held accountable for his acts. In so deciding, it cannot be presumed that juries will check their common sense at the courtroom door. * * *

The true vice of M'Naghten is not, therefore, that psychiatrists will feel constricted in artificially structuring their testimony but rather that the ultimate deciders—the judge or the jury—will be deprived of information vital to their final judgment. For whatever the social climate of Victorian England, today's complex and sophisticated society will not be satisfied with simplistic decisions, based solely upon a man's ability to "know" right from wrong. * * *

Notes and Questions

1. Although psychiatrists and legal scholars have subjected the *M'Naghten* rule to withering criticism, nearly all American jurisdictions originally adopted the test and, except for a brief time in the 1980s, the *M'Naghten* standard or a variation of it has retained majority rule status in this country.

iii. *Expanding M'Naghten: The "Irresistible Impulse" Test*

PARSONS v. STATE

Supreme Court of Alabama, 1887.
81 Ala. 577, 2 So. 854.

SOMERVILLE, J.   In this case the defendants have been convicted of the murder of Bennett Parsons, by shooting him with a gun; one of the defendants being the wife and the other the daughter of the deceased. The defense set up in the trial was the plea of insanity, the evidence tending to show that the daughter was an idiot, and the mother and wife a lunatic, subject to insane delusions, and that the killing on her part was the offspring and product of those delusions.

The rulings of the court raise some questions of no less difficulty than of interest; for, as observed by a distinguished American judge, "of all medico-legal questions, those connected with insanity are the most difficult and perplexing." It has become of late a matter of comment among intelligent men, including the most advanced thinkers in the medical and legal professions, that the deliverances of the law courts on this branch of our jurisprudence have not heretofore been at all satisfactory, either in the soundness of their theories, or in their practical application.   * * *

The question, then, presented seems to be whether an old rule of legal responsibility shall be adhered to, based on theories of physicians promulgated a hundred years ago, which refuse to recognize any evidence of insanity, except the single test of mental capacity to distinguish right and wrong, or whether the courts will recognize as a possible fact, if capable of proof by clear and satisfactory testimony, the doctrine, now alleged by those of the medical profession who have made insanity a special subject of investigation, that the old test is wrong, and that there is no single test by which the existence of the disease, to that degree which exempts from punishment, can in every case be infallibly detected. * * *

It is everywhere admitted, and as to this there can be no doubt, that an idiot, lunatic, or other person of diseased mind, who is afflicted to such extent as not to know whether he is doing right or wrong, is not punishable for any act which he may do while in that state. Can the courts justly say, however, that the only test or rule of responsibility in criminal cases is the power to distinguish right from wrong, whether in the abstract, or as applied to the particular case? Or may there not be insane persons, of a diseased brain, who, while capable of perceiving the difference between right and wrong, are, as matter of fact, so far under *the duress of such disease* as to destroy *the power to choose* between right and wrong? * * *

* * * No one can deny that there must be two constituent elements of legal responsibility in the commission of every crime, and no rule can be just and reasonable which fails to recognize either of them: (1) Capacity of intellectual discrimination; and (2) freedom of will. * * * If therefore, it be true, as matter of fact, that the disease of insanity can, in its action on the human brain through a shattered nervous organization, or in any other mode, so affect the mind as to subvert the freedom of the will, and thereby destroy the power of the victim *to choose* between the right and wrong, although he perceive it,—by which we mean the power of volition to adhere in action to the right and abstain from the wrong,— is such a one criminally responsible for an act done under the influence of such controlling disease? We clearly think not, and such as we believe to be the just, reasonable, and humane rule, towards which all the modern authorities in this country, legislation in England, and the laws of other civilized countries of the world, are gradually but surely tending * * *.

We next consider the question as to the *probable existence of such a disease,* and the *test of its presence,* in a given case. * * *

In *State v. Felter,* 25 Iowa, 68, the capacity to distinguish between right and wrong was held not to be a safe test of criminal responsibility in all cases; and it was accordingly decided that, if a person commit a homicide knowing it to be wrong, but do so under the influence of an uncontrollable and irresistible impulse, arising not from natural passion, but from an insane condition of the mind, he is not criminally responsible. "If," said Chief Justice Dillon, "by the observation and concurrent testimony of medical men who make the study of insanity a specialty, it shall be definitely established to be true that there is an unsound condition of the mind, that is, a diseased condition of the mind, in which, though a person abstractly knows that a given act is wrong, he is yet, by an *insane impulse,* that is, an impulse proceeding from a diseased intellect, irresistibly driven to commit it, the law must modify its ancient doctrines, and recognize the truth, and give to this condition, when it is satisfactorily shown to exist, its exculpatory effect." * * *

* * * This inquiry, as we have said, and here repeat, is a question of fact for the determination of the jury in each particular case. It is not a matter of law to be decided by the courts. We think it sufficient if the insane delusion—by which we mean the delusion proceeding from a *diseased mind* —sincerely exists at the time of committing the alleged crime, and the defendant, believing it to be real, is so influenced by it as either to render him incapable of perceiving the true nature and quality of the act done, by reason of the depravation of the reasoning faculty, or so subverts his will as to destroy his free agency by rendering him powerless to resist by reason of *the duress of the disease.* In such a case, in other words, there must exist either one of two conditions: (1) Such

mental defect as to render the defendant unable to distinguish between right and wrong in relation to the particular act; or (2) the overmastering of defendant's will in consequence of the insane delusion under the influence of which he acts, produced by disease of the mind or brain.
* * *

Notes and Questions

1. The irresistible impulse test has not lacked for critics. The original criticism was that it was too narrow:

> As it has commonly been employed, * * * we find the "irresistible impulse" test to be inherently inadequate and unsatisfactory. Psychiatrists have long questioned whether "irresistible impulses" actually exist; the more basic legal objection is that it is too narrow, and carries the misleading implication that a crime impulsively committed must have been perpetrated in a sudden and explosive fit. Thus, the * * * test is unduly restrictive because it excludes far more numerous instances of crimes committed after excessive brooding and melancholy by one who is unable to resist sustained psychic compulsion or to make any real attempt to control his conduct. In seeking one isolated and indefinite cause for every act, moreover, the test is unhappily evocative of the notions which underlay M'Naghten—unfortunate assumptions that the problem can be viewed in black and white absolutes and in crystal-clear causative terms.
>
> In so many instances the criminal act may be the reverse of impulsive; it may be coolly and carefully prepared yet nevertheless the result of a diseased mind. The "irresistible impulse" test is therefore little more than a gloss on M'Naghten, rather than a fundamentally new approach to the problem of criminal responsibility.

United States v. Freeman, 357 F.2d 606, 620–21 (2d Cir.1966).

A more recent criticism of the test is that there is no reliable way to distinguish an irresistible impulse from an impulse that simply was not resisted. See p. 580 infra.

iv. Abandonment of M'Naghten: The Durham ("Product") Test

DURHAM v. UNITED STATES

United States Court of Appeals,
District of Columbia Circuit, 1954.
214 F.2d 862.

BAZELON, CIRCUIT JUDGE.

Monte Durham was convicted of housebreaking, by the District Court sitting without a jury. The only defense asserted at the trial was that Durham was of unsound mind at the time of the offense. We are now urged to reverse the conviction (1) because the trial court did not correctly apply existing rules governing the burden of proof on the defense of insanity, and (2) because existing tests of criminal responsibility are obsolete and should be superseded.

[The court overturned Durham's conviction, and remanded the case for a new trial because the trial court improperly placed the burden of proof of the defendant's sanity on the accused. Discussion of the second issue follows.]

It has been ably argued by counsel for Durham that the existing tests in the District of Columbia for determining criminal responsibility, *i.e.*, the so-called right-wrong test supplemented by the irresistible impulse test, are not satisfactory criteria for determining criminal responsibility. We are urged to adopt a different test to be applied on the retrial of this case. This contention has behind it nearly a century of agitation for reform. * * *

Medico-legal writers in large number * * * present convincing evidence that the right-and-wrong test is "based on an entirely obsolete and misleading conception of the nature of insanity." The science of psychiatry now recognizes that a man is an integrated personality and that reason, which is only one element in that personality, is not the sole determinant of his conduct. The right-wrong test, which considers knowledge or reason alone, is therefore an inadequate guide to mental responsibility for criminal behavior. * * *

* * * By its misleading emphasis on the cognitive, the right-wrong test requires court and jury to rely upon what is, scientifically speaking, inadequate, and most often, invalid and irrelevant testimony in determining criminal responsibility.

The fundamental objection to the right-wrong test, however, is not that criminal irresponsibility is made to rest upon an inadequate, invalid or indeterminable symptom or manifestation, but that it is made to rest upon *any* particular symptom. In attempting to define insanity in terms of a symptom, the courts have assumed an impossible role, not merely one for which they have no special competence. * * * In this field of law as in others, the fact finder should be free to consider all information advanced by relevant scientific disciplines. * * *

* * * We find that the "irresistible impulse" test is also inadequate in that it gives no recognition to mental illness characterized by brooding and reflection and so relegates acts caused by such illness to the application of the inadequate right-wrong test. We conclude that a broader test should be adopted. * * *

The rule we now hold must be applied on the retrial of this case and in future cases is not unlike that followed by the New Hampshire court since 1870.[47] It is simply that an accused is not criminally responsible if his unlawful act was the product of mental disease or mental defect.

We use "disease" in the sense of a condition which is considered capable of either improving or deteriorating. We use "defect" in the sense of a condition which is not considered capable of either improving or deteriorating and which may be either congenital, or the result of injury, or the residual effect of a physical or mental disease. * * *

47. State v. Pike, 1870, 49 N.H. 399.

The questions of fact under the test we now lay down are as capable of determination by the jury as, for example, the questions juries must determine upon a claim of total disability under a policy of insurance where the state of medical knowledge concerning the disease involved, and its effects, is obscure or in conflict. * * * Testimony as to such "symptoms, phases or manifestations," along with other relevant evidence, will go to the jury upon the ultimate questions of fact which it alone can finally determine. Whatever the state of psychiatry, the psychiatrist will be permitted to carry out his principal court function which * * * "is to inform the jury of the character of [the accused's] mental disease [or defect]." The jury's range of inquiry will not be limited to, but may include, for example, whether an accused, who suffered from a mental disease or defect did not know the difference between right and wrong, acted under the compulsion of an irresistible impulse, or had "been deprived of or lost the power of his will * * *."

Finally, in leaving the determination of the ultimate question of fact to the jury, we permit it to perform its traditional function which * * * is to apply "our inherited ideas of moral responsibility to individuals prosecuted for crime * * *." Juries will continue to make moral judgments, still operating under the fundamental precept that "Our collective conscience does not allow punishment where it cannot impose blame." But in making such judgments, they will be guided by wider horizons of knowledge concerning mental life. * * *

The legal and moral traditions of the western world require that those who, of their own free will and with evil intent (sometimes called *mens rea*), commit acts which violate the law, shall be criminally responsible for those acts. Our traditions also require that where such acts stem from and are the product of a mental disease or defect as those terms are used herein, moral blame shall not attach, and hence there will not be criminal responsibility. The rule we state in this opinion is designed to meet these requirements. * * *

Notes and Questions

1. Generally speaking, mental health professionals applauded *Durham*. Psychiatrists believed that they had won a significant battle in their "cold war" with lawyers regarding the proper role of psychiatry in the criminal justice system. One of the most influential combatants was Dr. Karl Menninger, Chairman of the Board of Trustees of the Menninger Foundation in Topeka, Kansas. He explained the fundamental disagreement between psychiatrists and lawyers this way:

> Medicine and law are both represented by intelligent, learned men and women. Both professions have ancient traditions and high ideals. Both are concerned with and feel a sense of responsibility for public safety. Both deal constantly with the tendency of people to get out of line, to deviate or threaten to deviate from the acceptable code of behavior. This common theoretical interest should be a keystone bringing together their skills and knowledge in a cooperative effort.

> But it does not work that way. * * *

* * * The law assumes that when a person, regardless of his earlier experiences, reaches the age of discretion, he sees the wisdom—as it were—of being discreet, and so exercises appropriate control of his behavior except when overcome by passion or temptation. He and all other men are "equal" in the eyes of the law. But Freud showed that men are extremely unequal in respect to endowment, discretion, equilibrium, self-control, aspiration, and intelligence—differences depending not only on inherited genes and brain-cell configurations but also on childhood conditioning. * * *

Lawyers are concerned with placing or rebutting *blame* for specific acts of deviant, prohibited behavior; psychiatrists are interested in correcting total patterns of behavior. Instead of seeking for the *blame* or the exculpation of an accused, doctors seek the etiology, the explanation, the underlying motives, and contributing facts in the commission of certain undesirable acts. Lawyers and psychiatrists speak two different languages in regard to professional matters, and hence their common English tongue is of little help in meaningful communication with one another. * * *

For example, the word *justice,* which is so dear to lawyers, is one which the doctor *qua* scientist simply does not use or readily understand. No one thinks of justice as applying to the phenomena of physics. There is no "justice" in chemical reactions, in illness, or in behavior disorder.

Free will—to a lawyer—is not a philosophical theory or a religious concept or a scientific hypothesis. It is a "given," a *basic* assumption in legal theory and practice. To the psychiatrist, this position is preposterous; he seeks clear operational definitions of *free* and of *will.* On the other hand, the psychiatrist's assumption that motivation and mentation can go on *unconsciously* is preposterous to lawyers, constituting a veritable self-contradiction in terms. * * *

Trying to get around the absurdity of the M'Naghten criteria has invited the ingenuity of many lawyers, judges, and psychiatrists for a century. No substantial progress was made until 1954 when the famous Durham decision rule was enunciated by Judge David Bazelon * * *

The Durham decision was a definite advance over the medievalism represented by the M'Naghten rule, and psychiatrists welcomed it for that reason.

Karl Menninger, The Crime of Punishment 90–92, 96–97, 115 (1968).

According to Dr. Menninger, "[t]he very word *justice* irritates scientists. No surgeon expects to be asked if an operation for cancer is just or not." Id. at 17. Do you think that a psychiatrist expects to be asked if criminal conduct was the "product" of a mental disease or defect? Is the psychiatrist's conception of "product" likely to be the same as the lawyer's?

v. The American Law Institute Rule and Beyond

UNITED STATES v. BRAWNER

United States Court of Appeals,
District of Columbia Circuit, 1972.
471 F.2d 969.

LEVENTHAL, CIRCUIT JUDGE:

The principal issues raised on this appeal * * * relate to appellant's defense of insanity. * * *

In the course of our reconsideration of the rule governing the insanity defense, we have studied the opinions of other courts, particularly but not exclusively the opinions of the other Federal circuits, and the views of the many scholars who have thoughtfully pondered the underlying issues. * * *

We have stretched our canvas wide; and the focal point of the landscape before us is the formulation of the American Law Institute. The ALI's primary provision is stated thus in its Model Penal Code, see § 4.01(1).

Section 4.01 Mental Disease or Defect Excluding Responsibility.

(1) A person is not responsible for criminal conduct if at the time of such conduct as a result of mental disease or defect he lacks substantial capacity either to appreciate the criminality [wrongfulness] of his conduct or to conform his conduct to the requirements of the law.

We have decided to adopt the ALI rule as the doctrine excluding responsibility for mental disease or defect * * *.

History looms large in obtaining a sound perspective for a subject like this one. But the cases are numerous. And since our current mission is to illuminate the present, rather than to linger over the past, it suffices for our purposes to review a handful of our opinions on the insanity defense.

The landmark opinion was written by Judge Bazelon in Durham v. United States. * * *

Few cases have evoked as much comment as *Durham*. * * * It has been hailed as a guide to the difficult and problem-laden intersection of law and psychiatry, ethics and science. It has been scored as an unwarranted loophole through which the cunning criminal might escape from the penalty of the law. We view it more modestly, as the court's effort, designed in the immemorial manner of the case method that has built the common law, to alleviate two serious problems with the previous rule.

The first of these was a problem of language which raised an important symbolic issue in the law. We felt that the language of the old right-wrong/irresistible impulse rule for insanity was antiquated, no longer reflecting the community's judgment as to who ought to be held criminally liable for socially destructive acts. * * *

The second vexing problem that *Durham* was designed to reach related to the concern of the psychiatrists called as expert witnesses for their special knowledge of the problem of insanity, who often and typically felt that they were obliged to reach outside of their professional expertise when they were asked, under the traditional insanity rule established in 1843 by *M'Naghten's* Case, whether the defendant knew right from wrong. They further felt that the narrowness of the traditional test, which framed the issue of responsibility solely in terms of cognitive impairment, made it impossible to convey to the judge and jury the full range of information material to an assessment of defendant's responsibility.

Discerning scholarship now available asserts that the experts' fears and concerns reflected a misapprehension as to the impact of the traditional standard in terms of excluding relevant evidence.

> Wigmore states the rule to be that when insanity is in issue, "any and all conduct of the person is admissible in evidence." And the cases support Wigmore's view. The almost unvarying policy of the courts has been to admit *any* evidence of abberational behavior so long as it is probative of the defendant's mental condition, without regard to the supposed restrictions of the test used to define insanity for the jury.[5]

Moreover if the term "know" in the traditional test of "know right from wrong" is taken as denoting affective knowledge, rather than merely cognitive knowledge, it yields a rule of greater flexibility than was widely supposed to exist.

We need not occupy ourselves here and now with the question whether, and to what extent, the *M'Naghten* rule, ameliorated by the irresistible impulse doctrine, is susceptible of application to include medical insights and information as justice requires. In any event, the experts felt hemmed in by the traditional test * * *.

The rule as reformulated in *Durham* permitted medical experts to testify on medical matters properly put before the jury for its consideration, and to do so without the confusion that many, perhaps most, experts experienced from testimony structured under the *M'Naghten* rule. That was a positive contribution to jurisprudence—and one that was retained when the American Law Institute undertook to analyze the problem and proposed a different formulation.

A difficulty arose under the *Durham* rule in application. The rule was devised to facilitate the giving of testimony by medical experts in the context of a legal rule, with the jury called upon to reach a composite conclusion that had medical, legal and moral components. However the

---

5. A. Goldstein, The Insanity Defense 54 (1967), *citing* 1 Wigmore Evidence § 228   (1940) and numerous cases.

pristine statement of the *Durham* rule opened the door to "trial by label." *Durham* did distinguish between "disease," * * * and "defect." But the court failed to explicate what abnormality of mind was an essential ingredient of these concepts. In the absence of a definition of "mental disease or defect," medical experts attached to them the meanings which would naturally occur to them—medical meanings—and gave testimony accordingly. The problem was dramatically highlighted by the weekend flip flop case, In re Rosenfield, 157 F.Supp. 18 (D.D.C. 1957). The petitioner was described as a sociopath. A St. Elizabeths psychiatrist testified that a person with a sociopathic personality was not suffering from a mental disease. That was Friday afternoon. On Monday morning, through a policy change at St. Elizabeths Hospital, it was determined as an administrative matter that the state of a psychopathic or sociopathic personality did constitute a mental disease.

The concern that medical terminology not control legal outcomes culminated in McDonald v. United States, 114 U.S.App.D.C. 120, 312 F.2d 847, 851 (en banc, 1962), where this court recognized that the term, mental disease or defect, has various meanings, depending upon how and why it is used, and by whom. Mental disease means one thing to a physician bent on treatment, but something different, if somewhat overlapping, to a court of law. We provided a legal definition of mental disease or defect, and held that it included "any abnormal condition of the mind which substantially affects mental or emotional processes and substantially impairs behavior controls." * * *

The *Durham* rule also required explication along other lines, notably the resolution of the ambiguity inherent in the formulation concerning actions that were the "product" of mental illness. It was supplemented in Carter v. United States, 102 U.S.App.D.C. 227 at 234, 235, 252 F.2d 608 at 615–616 (1957):

> The simple fact that a person has a mental disease or defect is not enough to relieve him of responsibility for a crime. There must be a relationship between the disease and the criminal act; and the relationship must be such as to justify a reasonable inference that the act would not have been committed if the person had not been suffering from the disease.

Thus *Carter* clarified that the mental illness must not merely have entered into the production of the act, but must have played a necessary role. *Carter* identified the "product" element of the rule with the "but for" variety of causation.

The pivotal "product" term continued to present problems, principally that it put expert testimony on a faulty footing. Assuming that a mental disease, in the legal sense, had been established, the fate of the defendant came to be determined by what came to be referred to by the legal jargon of "productivity." On the other hand, it was obviously sensible if not imperative that the experts having pertinent knowledge should speak to the crucial question whether the mental abnormality involved is one associated with aberrant behavior. But since "productivity" was so decisive a factor in the decisional equation, a ruling permitting experts to testify expressly in language of "product" raised in a different context the concern lest the ultimate issue be in fact turned over to the experts rather than retained for the jurors representing the community. * * *

It was in this context that the court came to the decision in Washington v. United States, 129 U.S.App.D.C. 29, 390 F.2d 444 (1967), which forbade experts from testifying as to productivity altogether. * * *

The American Law Institute's Model Penal Code expressed a rule which has become the dominant force in the law pertaining to the defense of insanity. The ALI rule is eclectic in spirit, partaking of the moral focus of *M'Naghten,* the practical accommodation of the "control rules" (a term more exact and less susceptible of misunderstanding than "irresistible impulse" terminology), and responsive, at the same time, to a relatively modern, forward-looking view of what is encompassed in "knowledge." * * *

The core rule of the ALI has been adopted, with variations, by all save one of the Federal circuit courts of appeals, and by all that have come to reconsider the doctrine providing exculpation for mental illness. Their opinions have been exceptionally thoughtful and thorough in their expositions of the interests and values protected. * * *

The position of the Fourth Circuit was announced by Chief Judge Haynsworth in [United States v. Chandler, 393 F.2d 920 (4th Cir.1968)]:

> The American Law Institute's formulation has achieved wide acceptance. * * * [I]t is, in our opinion, the preferred formulation. With appropriate balance between cognition and volition, it demands an unrestricted inquiry into the whole personality of a defendant who surmounts the threshold question of doubt of his responsibility. Its verbiage is understandable by psychiatrists; it imposes no limitation upon their testimony, and yet, to a substantial extent, it avoids a diagnostic approach and leaves the jury free to make its findings in terms of a standard which society prescribes and juries may apply. * * *

* * * Having paused to study the rulings in the other circuits, we turn to our comments, and to our reflections following the extensive, and intensive, exposure of this court to insanity defense issues. * * *

A principal reason for our decision to depart from the *Durham* rule is the undesirable characteristic, surviving even the *McDonald* modification, of undue dominance by the experts giving testimony. * * * The difficulty is rooted in the circumstance that there is no generally accepted understanding, either in the jury or the community it represents, of the concept requiring that the crime be the "product" of the mental disease.

When the court used the term "product" in *Durham* it likely assumed that this was a serviceable, and indeed a natural, term for a rule defining criminal responsibility—a legal reciprocal, as it were, for the familiar term "proximate cause," used to define civil responsibility. But if concepts like "product" are, upon refinement, reasonably understood, or at least appreciated, by judges and lawyers, and perhaps philosophers, difficulties developed when it emerged that the "product" concept did not signify a reasonably identifiable common ground that was also shared by the nonlegal experts,[10] and the laymen serving on the jury as the representatives of the community. * * *

The expert witnesses—psychiatrists and psychologists—are called to adduce relevant information concerning what may for convenience be referred to as the "medical" component of the responsibility issue. But the difficulty * * * is that the medical expert comes, by testimony given in terms of a non-medical construct ("product"), to express conclusions that in essence embody ethical and legal conclusions. There is, indeed, irony in a situation under which the *Durham* rule, which was adopted in large part to permit experts to testify in their own terms concerning matters within their domain which the jury should know, resulted in testimony by the experts in terms not their own to reflect unexpressed judgments in a domain that is properly not theirs but the jury's. The irony is heightened when the jurymen, instructed under the esoteric "product" standard, are influenced significantly by "product" testimony of expert witnesses really reflecting ethical and legal judgments rather than a conclusion within the witnesses' particular expertise.

It is easier to identify and spotlight the irony than to eradicate the mischief. The objective of *Durham* is still sound—to put before the jury the information that is within the expert's domain, to aid the jury in making a broad and comprehensive judgment. But when the instructions and appellate decisions define the "product" inquiry as the ultimate issue, it is like stopping the tides to try to halt the emergence of this term in the language of those with a central role in the trial—the lawyers who naturally seek to present testimony that will influence the jury who will be charged under the ultimate "product" standard, and the expert witnesses who have an awareness, gained from forensic psychia-

---

10. A difference in language perception probably contributed to the development that psychiatric testimony concerning "product" causal relationship did not develop along the lines presaged by legal students of the problem. Early critiques in journals asserted that a but-for test of "product" would rarely, if ever, permit a psychiatrist to testify as to the existence of mental illness coexisting with a lack of "product" causal relationship to the crime. * * * As events have developed, however, it has become almost commonplace that psychiatrists testifying as to the presence of mental disease have nevertheless found an absence of "product" causal relation with the crime, or at least expressed substantial doubt as to such relationship. Perhaps more to the point, it has become commonplace for psychiatrists called by Government and defense to be in agreement on the mental disease aspects of their testimony and to differ on the issue of "product" relationship. This is not intended, in any way, as a criticism of any particular testimony. There is often a genuine and difficult question as to the relationship between a particular mental disease and particular offense. What is our concern, however, is that the inherent difficulty of this core problem has been intensified, and the sources of confusion compounded, by a kind of mystique that came to surround the "product" test, and testimony cast in that language.

try and related disciplines, of the ultimate "product" standard that dominates the proceeding.

The experts have meaningful information to impart, not only on the existence of mental illness or not, but also on its relationship to the incident charged as an offense. In the interest of justice this valued information should be available, and should not be lost or blocked by requirements that unnaturally restrict communication between the experts and the jury. The more we have pondered the problem the more convinced we have become that the sound solution lies not in further shaping of the *Durham* "product" approach in more refined molds, but in adopting the ALI's formulation as the linchpin of our jurisprudence.

The ALI's formulation retains the core requirement of a meaningful relationship between the mental illness and the incident charged. The language in the ALI rule is sufficiently in the common ken that its use in the courtroom, or in preparation for trial, permits a reasonable three-way communication—between (a) the law-trained, judges and lawyers; (b) the experts and (c) the jurymen—without insisting on a vocabulary that is either stilted or stultified, or conducive to a testimonial mystique permitting expert dominance and encroachment on the jury's function. There is no indication in the available literature that any such untoward development has attended the reasonably widespread adoption of the ALI rule in the Federal Courts and a substantial number of state courts. * * *

AMERICAN LAW INSTITUTE, MODEL PENAL CODE AND COMMENTARIES COMMENT TO § 4.01

(1985), 168–72

The Model Code formulation is based on the view that a sense of understanding broader than mere cognition, and a reference to volitional incapacity should be achieved directly in the formulation of the defense, rather than left to mitigation in the application of M'Naghten. The resulting standard relieves the defendant of responsibility under two circumstances: (1) when, as a result of mental disease or defect, the defendant lacked substantial capacity to appreciate the criminality [wrongfulness] of his conduct; (2) when, as a result of mental disease or defect, the defendant lacked substantial capacity to conform his conduct to the requirements of law.

The use of "appreciate" rather than "know" conveys a broader sense of understanding than simple cognition. The proposal as originally approved in 1955 was cast in terms of a person's lack of capacity to appreciate the "criminality" of his conduct, but the Institute accepted "wrongfulness" as an appropriate substitute for "criminality" in the Proposed Final Draft. * * *

The part of the Model Code test relating to volition is cast in terms of capacity to conform one's conduct to the requirements of the law. Application of the principle calls for a distinction, inevitable for a standard addressed to impairment of volition, between incapacity and mere indisposition.[17] In drawing this distinction, the Model Code formulation effects a substantial improvement over pre-existing standards.

In contrast to the M'Naghten and "irresistible impulse" criteria, the Model Code formulation reflects the judgment that no test is workable that calls for complete impairment of ability to know or to control. The extremity of these conceptions had posed the largest difficulty for the administration of the old standards. Disorientation, psychiatrists indicated, might be extreme and still might not be total; what clinical experience revealed was closer to a graded scale with marks along the way. Hence, an examiner confronting a person who had performed a seemingly purposive act might helpfully address himself to the extent of awareness, understanding and control. If, on the other hand, he had to speak to utter incapacity vel non under the M'Naghten test, his relevant testimony would be narrowly limited to the question of whether the defendant suffered from delusional psychosis, where the act would not be criminal if the facts were as the defendant deludedly supposed them to be. A test requiring an utter incapacity for self-control imposes a comparably unrealistic restriction on the scope of the relevant inquiry. To meet these difficulties, it was thought that the criterion should ask if the defendant, as a result of mental disease or defect, was deprived of "substantial capacity" to appreciate the criminality (or wrongfulness) of his conduct or to conform his conduct to the requirements of law, meaning by "substantial" a capacity of some appreciable magnitude when measured by the standard of humanity in general, as opposed to the reduction of capacity to the vagrant and trivial dimensions characteristic of the most severe afflictions of the mind.

The adoption of the standard of substantial capacity may well be the Code's most significant alteration of the prevailing tests. It was recognized, of course, that "substantial" is an open-ended concept, but its quantitative connotation was believed to be sufficiently precise for purposes of practical administration.

---

17. The Institute considered but did not approve an alternative formulation supported by a minority of its Council. Under that formulation:

> A person is not responsible for criminal conduct if at the time of such conduct as a result of mental disease or defect he lacks substantial capacity to appreciate the criminality of his conduct or is in such state that the prospect of conviction and punishment cannot constitute a significant restraining influence upon him.

MPC T.D. 4, at 27 (alternative (b)).

Instead of asking whether the defendant had capacity to conform his conduct to the requirements of law, this alternative formulation asks whether, in consequence of mental disease or defect, the threat of punishment could not exercise a significant restraining influence upon him. To some extent, of course, these are the same inquiries. To the extent that they diverge, the latter asks a narrower and harder question, involving the assessment of capacity to respond to a single influence, the threat of punishment. Both Dr. Guttmacher and Dr. Overholser considered the assessment of responsiveness to this one influence too difficult for psychiatric judgment. Hence, though the issue framed by the alternative may well be thought to state the question that is most precisely relevant for legal purposes, the inquiry was deemed impolitic on this ground. Insofar as nondeterrability is the determination that is sought, it must be reached by probing general capacity to conform to the requirements of law.

The alternative formulation has not been adopted in any jurisdiction.

Notes and Questions

1. By the early 1980s, the American Law Institute (ALI) standard had been adopted by more than half of the states and by all but one of the federal circuits. The trend away from *M'Naghten* and toward the ALI test seemed unstoppable.

Then, along came the 1981 attempt on the life of President Ronald Reagan and the 1982 insanity acquittal of his would-be assassin, John W. Hinckley. Three states responded to public outrage by abolishing the insanity defense. See Idaho Code § 18–207(a) (1987); Mont.Code Ann. 46–14–102, 46–14–214, 46–14–301 (1992); and Utah Code Ann. 76–2–305 (1990). More often, however, legislatures and courts that had adopted the ALI rule returned to the "unvarnished *M'Naghten* standard." Sanders v. State, 585 A.2d 117, 124 (Del.1990). The following case illustrates the reasoning underlying the latter movement.

UNITED STATES v. LYONS

United States Court of Appeals, Fifth Circuit, 1984.
731 F.2d 243.

GEE, CIRCUIT JUDGE: * * *

For the greater part of two decades our Circuit has followed the rule that a defendant is not to be held criminally responsible for conduct if, at the time of that conduct and as a result of mental disease or defect, he lacked substantial capacity either to appreciate the wrongfulness of his conduct *or to conform his conduct to the requirements of the law.* *Blake v. United States,* 407 F.2d 908, 916 (5th Cir.1969) (en banc). * * *

* * * Following the example of sister circuits, we embraced this standard in lieu of our former one, * * * because we concluded that then current knowledge in the field of behavioral science supported such a result. Unfortunately, it now appears our conclusion was premature—that the brave new world that we foresaw has not arrived.

Reexamining the *Blake* standard today, we conclude that the volitional prong of the insanity defense * * * does not comport with current medical and scientific knowledge, which has retreated from its earlier, sanguine expectations. Consequently, we now hold that a person is not responsible for criminal conduct on the grounds of insanity only if at the time of that conduct, as a result of a mental disease or defect, he is unable to appreciate the wrongfulness of that conduct.[9]

9. We employ the phrase "is unable" in preference to our earlier formulation "lacks substantial capacity" for reasons well stated in the Commentary of the American Bar Association Standing Committee:

Finally, it should be pointed out that the standard employs the term "unable" in lieu of the "substantial capacity" language of the ALI test. This approach has been taken both to simplify the formulation and to reduce the risk that juries will

interpret the test too loosely. By using the "substantial capacity" language, the drafters of the ALI standard were trying to avoid the rigidity implicit in the M'Naughten formulation. They correctly recognize that it is rarely possible to say that a mentally disordered person was totally unable to "know" what he was doing or to "know" that it was wrong; even a psychotic person typically retains some grasp of reality. However, the

We do so for several reasons. First, as we have mentioned, a majority of psychiatrists now believe that they do not possess sufficient accurate scientific bases for measuring a person's capacity for self-control or for calibrating the impairment of that capacity. Bonnie, *The Moral Basis of the Insanity Defense*, 69 ABA J. 194, 196 (1983). "The line between an irresistible impulse and an impulse not resisted is probably no sharper than between twilight and dusk." *American Psychiatric Association Statement on the Insanity Defense*, 11 (1982) [APA Statement]. Indeed, Professor Bonnie states:

> There is, in short, no objective basis for distinguishing between offenders who were undeterrable and those who were merely undeterred, between the impulse that was irresistible and the impulse not resisted, or between substantial impairment of capacity and some lesser impairment.

In addition, the risks of fabrication and "moral mistakes" in administering the insanity defense are greatest "when the experts and the jury are asked to speculate whether the defendant had the capacity to 'control' himself or whether he could have 'resisted' the criminal impulse." Bonnie, *supra*, at 196. Moreover, psychiatric testimony about volition is more likely to produce confusion for jurors than is psychiatric testimony concerning a defendant's appreciation of the wrongfulness of his act. It appears, moreover, that there is considerable overlap between a psychotic person's inability to understand and his ability to control his behavior. Most psychotic persons who fail a volitional test would also fail a cognitive test, thus rendering the volitional test superfluous for them. * * *

One need not disbelieve in the existence of Angels in order to conclude that the present state of our knowledge regarding them is not such as to support confident conclusions about how many can dance on the head of a pin. In like vein, it may be that some day tools will be discovered with which reliable conclusions about human volition can be fashioned. It appears to be all but a certainty, however, that despite earlier hopes they do not lie in our hands today. When and if they do, it will be time to consider again to what degree the law should adopt the sort of conclusions that they produce. But until then, we see no prudent course for the law to follow but to treat all criminal impulses—including those not resisted—as resistible. To do otherwise in the present state of medical knowledge would be to cast the insanity defense adrift upon a sea of unfounded scientific speculation, with the palm awarded case by case to the most convincing advocate of that which is presently unknown—and may remain so, because unknowable. * * *

ALVIN B. RUBIN, CIRCUIT JUDGE, with whom TATE, CIRCUIT JUDGE, joins dissenting. * * *

phrase "substantial capacity" is not essential to take into account these clinical realities. Sufficient flexibility is provided by the term "appreciate."

Commentary (revised November, 1983) to Standards 7–6.1(a) and 7–6.9(b), ABA Standing Committee on Association Standards for Criminal Justice (to be published).

The majority's fear that the present test invites "moral mistakes" is difficult to understand. The majority opinion concedes that some individuals cannot conform their conduct to the law's requirements. Other writers have concluded that a strictly cognitive insanity test will overlook some individuals who would be covered by a control test. Without citing any data that verdicts in insanity cases decided under a control test are frequently inaccurate, the majority embraces a rule certain to result in the conviction of at least some who are not morally responsible and the punishment of those for whom retributive, deterrent, and rehabilitative penal goals are inappropriate. A decision that virtually ensures undeserved, and therefore unjust, punishment in the name of avoiding moral mistakes rests on a peculiar notion of morality. * * *

Judges are not, and should not be, immune to popular outrage over this nation's crime rate. Like everyone else, judges watch television, read newspapers and magazines, listen to gossip, and are sometimes themselves victims. They receive the message trenchantly described in a recent book criticizing the insanity defense: "Perhaps the bottom line of all these complaints is that *guilty people go free*—guilty people who do not have to accept judgment or responsibility for what they have done and are not held accountable for their actions.... These are not cases in which the defendant is alleged to have committed a crime. *Everyone knows he did it.*"[25] Although understandable as an expression of uninformed popular opinion, such a viewpoint ought not to serve as the basis for judicial decisionmaking; for it misapprehends the very meaning of guilt.

Guilt is the legal embodiment of moral and philosophical concepts. * * * [T]hose concepts presuppose a morally responsible agent to whom guilt can be attributed. By definition, guilt cannot be attributed to an individual unable to refrain from violating the law. When a defendant is properly acquitted by reason of insanity under the control test, the guilty does not go free. * * *

In sum, I cannot join in a decision that, without supporting data, overturns a widely used rule that has not been shown to be working badly in order to adopt a change that will likely produce little or no practical benefit to society as a whole, conflicts with the fundamental moral predicates of our criminal justice system, and may inflict undeserved punishment on a few hapless individuals.

Notes and Questions

1. The Hinckley acquittal also served as the political impetus for the passage of the Insanity Defense Reform Act of 1984, in which Congress codified a federal insanity defense, governed now by 18 U.S.C. § 17 (1992):

> (a) Affirmative defense. It is an affirmative defense to a prosecution under any Federal statute that, at the time of the commission of the acts constituting the offense, the defendant, as a result of a severe mental disease or defect, was unable to appreciate the nature and

25. W. Winslade & J. Ross, The Insanity Plea 2–3 (1983).

quality or the wrongfulness of his acts. Mental disease or defect does not otherwise constitute a defense.

(b) Burden of proof. The defendant has the burden of proving the defense of insanity by clear and convincing evidence.

In what ways does this test differ from the *M'Naghten* and ALI tests? See Jodie English, *The Light Between Twilight and Dusk: Federal Criminal Law and the Volitional Insanity Defense*, 40 Hastings L.J. 1 (1988).

2. In view of the various criticisms directed at each of the insanity tests, which version of the defense do you find most appealing? Or, should the defense be formulated in still another way? In *United States v. Brawner*, supra, Judge Bazelon, author of *Durham*, suggested an alternative standard:

> It is clear that *Durham* focused the jury's attention on the wrong question—on the relationship between the act and the impairment rather than on the blameworthiness of the defendant's action measured by prevailing community standards. If the ALI test is indeed an improvement, it is not because it focuses attention on the *right* question, but only because it makes the *wrong* question so obscure that jurors may abandon the effort to answer it literally.

> Instead of asking the jury whether the act was caused by the impairment, our new test asks the jury to wrestle with such unfamiliar, if not incomprehensible, concepts as the capacity to appreciate the wrongfulness of one's action, and the capacity to conform one's conduct to the requirements of law. The best hope for our new test is that jurors will regularly conclude that no one—including the experts—can provide a meaningful answer to the questions posed by the ALI test. And in their search for some semblance of an intelligible standard, they may be forced to consider whether it would be just to hold the defendant responsible for his action. By that indirect approach our new test may lead juries to disregard (or at least depreciate) the conclusory testimony of the experts, and to make the "intertwining moral, legal, and medical judgments" on which the resolution of the responsibility question properly depends. * * *

> The Court's approach may very well succeed and encourage jurors to look behind the testimony and recommendations of the experts. But, * * * there is also a significant possibility that our new test will leave the power of the experts intact—or even make possible an enlargement of their influence. In my opinion, an instruction that tells the jurors candidly what their function is, is the instruction most likely to encourage the jurors to resist encroachments on that function. * * *

> Our instruction to the jury should provide that a defendant is not responsible *if at the time of his unlawful conduct his mental or emotional processes or behavior controls were impaired to such an extent that he cannot justly be held responsible for his act*. This test would ask the psychiatrist a single question: what is the nature of the impairment of the defendant's mental and emotional processes and behavior controls? It would leave for the jury the question whether that impairment is

sufficient to relieve the defendant of responsibility for the particular act charged.

The purpose of this proposed instruction is to focus the jury's attention on the legal and moral aspects of criminal responsibility, and to make clear why the determination of responsibility is entrusted to the jury and not the expert witnesses.

Brawner, 471 F.2d 969, 1031–32 (D.C.Cir.1972) (concurring in part, dissenting in part).

Judge Leventhal expressed the majority's reasons for rejecting this proposal:

[T]here is a substantial concern that an instruction overtly cast in terms of "justice" cannot feasibly be restricted to the ambit of what may properly be taken into account but will splash with unconfinable and malign consequences. The Government cautions that "explicit appeals to 'justice' will result in litigation of extraneous issues and will encourage improper arguments to the jury phrased solely in term of 'sympathy' and 'prejudice.' "

Nor is this solely a prosecutor's concern.

Mr. Flynn, counsel appointed to represent defendant, puts it that even though the jury is applying community concepts of blameworthiness "the jury should not be left at large, or asked to find out for itself what those concepts are." * * *

We are impressed by the observation of Professor Abraham S. Goldstein, one of the most careful students of the problem:

[The] overly general standard may place too great a burden upon the jury. If the law provides no standard, members of the jury are placed in the difficult position of having to find a man responsible for no other reason than their personal feelings about him. Whether the psyches of individual jurors are strong enough to make that decision, or whether the "law" should put that obligation on them, is open to serious question. It is far easier for them to perform the role assigned to them by legislatures and courts if they know—or are able to rationalize—that their verdicts are "required" by law.[28]

Id. at 987–88.

3. *Do* jurors perform the role assigned to them, i.e., do they evaluate the defendant's state of mind in conformity with the instructions given to them? One study of jury behavior in mock trials found that jurors poorly comprehended legal instructions regarding the insanity defense. Furthermore, regardless of the legal standard used, jurors generally focused on the same factors, including the defendant's history of mental illness, ability to recall events from the offense, degree of remorse, and cognitive and volitional capacities. James R.P. Ogloff, *A Comparison of Insanity Defense Standards on Juror Decision Making,* 15 Law & Hum.Behav. 509 (1991).

In view of these findings, researcher Ogloff observed that "the 'justly responsible' test is one formulation * * * that is surprisingly consistent with

---

28. A. Goldstein, The Insanity Defense 81–82 (1967).

the conclusion that jurors apply their own sense of justice when determining whether to find a defendant [not guilty by reason of insanity]." Id. at 527. See also Norman J. Finkel & Sharon F. Handel, *How Jurors Construe "Insanity"*, 13 Law & Hum.Behav. 41 (1989) (finding that jurors' constructs of insanity were more sophisticated than the legal definitions).

c. The Move to Abolish the Defense

AMERICAN LAW INSTITUTE, MODEL PENAL CODE AND COMMENTARIES COMMENT TO § 4.01

(1985), 182–83

A variety of reasons for abolition have been advanced from quite different ideological perspectives. Though it oversimplifies matters somewhat, it clarifies understanding to distinguish two basic positions in favor of abolition. The first position is perhaps epitomized by President Nixon's support of abolition, which he said was * * * to curb "unconscionable abuse" of the insanity defense which had taken place under prior standards. This position does not challenge the traditional assumption that an important function of the system of criminal justice is to label serious wrongdoers as blameworthy; it asserts that the insanity defense is a device by which too many wrongdoers are escaping punishment. * * *

The other attack on the insanity defense is more complex and it goes to the roots of the criminal law. It shares with the first position a skepticism that distinctions can sensibly be made between those who are responsible and those who are not. Critics taking this view cite the rarity of the employment of the defense as evidence that most mentally ill defendants are being convicted despite the availability of the defense. They doubt that the stigma of those convicted and subsequently treated as mentally disturbed is any worse than the stigma of those who commit criminal acts and are committed to high security institutions for the mentally ill without undergoing trial or after being acquitted on grounds of insanity. They argue that there is little basis for withholding condemnation of those whose mental illness causes them to act criminally when those whose deprived economic and social background causes them to act criminally are condemned. They regard the adversarial debate over the responsibility of particular defendants as wasteful, confusing for the jury, and possibly harmful for those defendants who are mentally disturbed. They think psychiatric diagnosis should be employed primarily after conviction to determine what sort of correctional treatment is appropriate instead of prior to conviction to determine criminal responsibility. Ideally, in the view of some of these critics, criminal convictions generally should not be regarded as stigmatizing, but as determinants of dangerousness to which the community must respond.

Notes and Questions

1. Public attitudinal studies reveal that abolitionism is founded on both retributive and utilitarian values. One study conducted a year after

John Hinckley's acquittal found that among opponents of the insanity defense, "[m]any * * * do not agree that punishing the insane is morally wrong. Most [also] believe that procedures now in place are largely ineffective in protecting them from insane criminals." Valerie P. Hans, *An Analysis of Public Attitudes Toward the Insanity Defense,* 24 Criminology 393, 407 (1986). The following materials speak to these dual concerns.

UNITED STATES v. LYONS

United States Court of Appeals, Fifth Circuit, 1984.
739 F.2d 994.

ALVIN B. RUBIN, CIRCUIT JUDGE, with whom TATE, CIRCUIT JUDGE, joins dissenting: * * *

* * * Public opposition to any insanity-grounded defense is often based, either explicitly or implicitly, on the view that the plea is frequently invoked by violent criminals who fraudulently use it to evade just punishment. Some critics perceive the insanity defense as an opportunity for criminals to use psychiatric testimony to mislead juries. This perception depicts an insanity trial as a "circus" of conflicting expert testimony that confuses a naive and sympathetic jury. And it fears insanity acquittees as offenders who, after manipulating the criminal justice system, are soon set free to prey once again on the community.

Despite the prodigious volume of writing devoted to the plea, the empirical data that are available provide little or no support for these fearsome perceptions and in many respects directly refute them. Both the frequency and the success rate of insanity pleas are grossly overestimated by professionals and lay persons alike; the plea is rarely made, and even more rarely successful.[8] * * *

The perception that the defendant who successfully pleads insanity is quickly released from custody is also based only on assumption. Although an acquittal by reason of insanity ends the criminal jurisdic-

---

8. For example, one extensive study examined the opinions held by college students, the general public, state legislators, law enforcement officers, and mental health personnel in Wyoming. Estimates of the frequency with which criminal defendants entered the plea ranged from 13% to 57%. During the time period considered, however, the actual frequency was only 0.47%: one case in 200. Similarly, although estimates of its success rate varied from 19% to 44%, during the relevant period only one of the 102 defendants who entered the plea was acquitted by reason of insanity. One compendious British study, encompassing selected periods from 1740 to 1930, found the frequency of the plea to range between .29% to 1.30% with a success rate varying between 28.5% and 69.6%. 1 N. Walker, *Crime and Insanity in England* 67 (1968);

2 N. Walker and S. McCabe, Crime and Insanity in England (1973).

A somewhat dated survey of major metropolitan areas in the United States reported similar conclusions, finding that insanity pleas were rarely entered. The highest figures were obtained in California and the District of Columbia, where the data showed the plea was invoked in 1.3% and 5.1% of all felony dispositions respectively. A. Matthews, *Mental Disability and the Law* 26–30 (1970).

One source estimates fewer than 100 successful insanity pleas out of 50,000 federal criminal cases brought annually. Dershowitz, *Abolishing the Insanity Defense: The Most Significant Feature of the Administration's Proposed Criminal Code—An Essay,* 9 Crim.L.Bull. 434, 436 (1973).

tion of * * * the courts of a few states, the acquittee is not simply set free. "The truth is that in almost every case, the acquittee is immediately hospitalized and evaluated for dangerousness. Usually, the acquittee remains hospitalized for an extended time." [9]

In sum, the available evidence belies many of the assumptions upon which much popular criticism of the insanity defense are based. The plea is rarely invoked, usually fails, and, when it is successful, the acquittees rarely go free.

Another set of objections to the plea is based on the thesis that factfinders—especially juries—are confused and manipulated by the vagueness of the legal standards of insanity and the notorious "battle of the experts" who present conclusory, superficial, and misleading testimony. These conditions, the argument runs, conspire to produce inconsistent and "inaccurate" verdicts.

Let us first put these objections in perspective. Most cases involving an insanity plea do not go to trial; instead, like most other criminal cases, they are settled by a plea bargain. In many of the cases that do go to trial, psychiatric testimony is presented by deposition, without disagreement among experts, and without opposition by the prosecution. And in the few cases in which a contest does develop, the defendant is usually convicted. Hence the stereotypic "circus tent" may be raised in only a handful of cases.

The manipulated-jury argument is supported largely by declamation, not data. Although there is some evidence to support the assertion that the wording of the insanity defense has little impact on trial outcomes, one major study of jury reactions to criminal cases involving the insanity defense reached conclusions contrary to the assumption that the jury function is usurped by expert testimony. That study found that jurors responsibly and carefully consider the evidence presented, do recognize that the final responsibility for the defendant's fate rests with them, do appreciate the limits and proper use of expert testimony, and do grasp the instructions given them.[13] Although the evidence does not warrant the conclusion that juries function better in insanity trials than in other criminal cases, it certainly does not appear that they function *less* effectively. * * *

Notes and Questions

1. As Judge Rubin conceded in footnote 13, not all studies support his claim that jurors grasp the meaning of insanity instructions given to them. See Note 3, p. 584 supra. Also contrary to Judge Rubin's remarks, some social science literature suggests that jurors are heavily influenced by expert

---

9. Rappeport, The Insanity Plea Scapegoating the Mentally Ill—Much Ado About Nothing?, 24 So.Tex.L.J. 687, 698 (1983). * * *

13. R. Simon, *The Jury and the Defense of Insanity* 89, 175–77 (1967). Rita Simon's study re-enacted actual criminal cases be-

fore subject juries drawn from local jury pools. Another study, however, found poor comprehension rates among most juries exposed to various instructions on the insanity defense. Arens, Granfield, & Susman, *Jurors, Jury Charges and Insanity,* 14 Catholic L.Rev. 1 (1965). * * *

psychiatric testimony.   See James R.P. Ogloff, *A Comparison of Insanity Defense Standards on Juror Decision Making,* 15 Law & Hum. Behav. 509 (1991) (reporting on his own research, and citing similar findings by others).

Regarding the frequency-of-use and success-rate figures for the insanity defense, "[w]hat is as startling as any other fact unearthed by empiricists is the realization that * * * officials in twenty states could provide no information whatsoever about the use of the plea." Michael L. Perlin, *Unpacking the Myths: The Symbolism Mythology of Insanity Defense Jurisprudence,* 40 Case W.Res.L.Rev. 599, 649 (1990). Such figures that do exist, however, suggest that the insanity-plea incidence is fairly uniformly low, but that the success rate of the defense is "quite variable." Richard A. Pasewark & Hugh McGinley, *Insanity Plea: National Survey of Frequency and Success,* 13 J. Psychiatry & Law 101, 101 (1985).

UNITED STATES v. TORNIERO

United States District Court, D. Connecticut, 1983.
570 F.Supp. 721.

JOSE A. CABRANES, DISTRICT JUDGE:

[Torniero was charged with interstate transportation of stolen goods. After the defendant noticed his intention to raise the insanity defense, the government filed a Motion to Reconsider the Law of Insanity, in which it called on the trial court to abolish the defense.

Judge Cabranes conducted a hearing on the matter, but ultimately concluded that he lacked authority to grant the relief requested. In the following excerpt, he summarizes the government's argument in favor of the abolition of the insanity plea, and provides his conceptualization of the purpose and significance of the defense.]

Legal and philosophical writers have generally agreed that the criminal justice system has five major objectives * * *. The first objective is that of *isolation,* the separation of the criminal from the rest of society as a physical check on the criminal's ability to do further injury. The second objective is that of *general deterrence,* the prevention of crimes by other individuals through the exemplary punishment of the convicted offender. The third objective, that of *specific deterrence,* looks to the prevention of future crimes by the offender himself, with the impact of his punishment continuing to impress him after his release. The fourth objective is that of *rehabilitation.* * * * Finally, there is the objective of *retribution.* * * *

The Government has argued that none of those objectives is served by the insanity defense.

With respect to isolation, the Government points out that in state criminal justice systems, the consequence of a successful assertion of the insanity defense—*i.e.,* an acquittal by reason of insanity—is, usually, the initiation of civil commitment proceedings. In a federal court, such as the present one, however, acquittal by reason of insanity leads to freedom for the defendant, despite the unresolved possibility that the defendant might pose a significant danger to other members of society.

Hence, in federal courts, the objective of isolation is not advanced at all by maintenance of the insanity defense. Even in state criminal justice systems, the Government argues, the objective of isolation is not well-served, for * * * a civil commitment proceeding, if it leads to institution-alization, usually results in hospitalization; most hospitals, however, are not organized to isolate patients. In the end, civil commitment may do very little to promote isolation of those persons who have been adjudicated insane.

General deterrence is undermined, the Government argues, by the insanity defense, because successful assertion of the defense encourages other members of the public to believe that it is possible to commit a criminal act yet evade criminal responsibility.

The objective of specific deterrence, claims the Government, would be better served by abandonment of the insanity defense. The Government argues that the significance of the insanity defense lies in the fact that it may be asserted by defendants who understood the nature of their actions and, with respect to the particular acts with which they are charged, could have behaved otherwise. The individual who suffers from delusions or hallucinations and who, consequently, cannot apprehend the reality of his acts need not rely on the insanity defense; in his case, the Government will not be able to prove that he had the particularized intention to do something he knew to be wrong, the *mens rea,* necessary for a criminal conviction. In this context, the Government argues that even individuals suffering from mental disease or defect are capable of understanding that certain specific acts are associated with unpleasant consequences and thus of learning not to engage in such acts. Thus, the Government claims, the objective of specific deterrence would be advanced by retention of the usual sanctions for criminal offenses, even when committed by persons who, though having the requisite *mens rea,* are mentally disordered.

Maintenance of the insanity defense, it can be argued, has little bearing on the question of rehabilitation, as a convicted defendant can always be sentenced under conditions providing for appropriate professional treatment. Abolition or restriction of the insanity defense would merely shift the place of psychiatric testimony from trial itself to the post-trial sentencing proceedings.

Finally, the Government contends that the achievement of retribution, satisfaction of the community's sense of justice, is gravely undermined by the insanity defense. The Government points to the public reactions to such widely-publicized trials as those of John W. Hinckley Jr. (1982), and Robert H. Torsney, a white New York City policeman who killed a black youth (1977) (both acquitted by reason of insanity), * * * and argues that the criminal justice system risks loss of public confidence and a populist turn toward extreme responses.

Though the Government's argument in favor of outright "abolition" of the insanity defense is tightly-woven and backed with scholarly authorities and statistics, as well as anecdotal evidence, it is not ultimately persuasive. To see why that is so, it is necessary to understand the proper justification for the insanity defense. * * *

* * * [T]he * * * question of sanctions is not the appropriate one to raise in seeking to distinguish sane from insane. That is why the Government's analysis of the five objectives of the criminal justice system, objectives realized in terms of sanctions, is, ultimately, beside the point.

In sentencing a criminal defendant after conviction, the court properly considers what pressures can be brought to bear in the name of society that will benefit the community, whether by assuaging its feelings of outrage or by influencing the behavior of other members of society or by modifying the defendant's own behavior. In convicting a defendant, however, a jury undertakes a very different task; it makes a finding of guilt.

The finding of guilt has often been misunderstood. To some extent, the jury that finds a defendant guilty finds that he did those acts with which he has been charged. But that description does not exhaust what we mean when we speak of a finding of guilt.

The idea of guilt is not, of course, originally a legal concept. Apart from its meaning at the bar, guilt has an important place in society. The ability of members of society to rely on their fellow citizens to engage in everyday activities in predictable, normal ways—that is, in civilized fashion—depends upon the capacity of individuals to recognize their own moral transgressions and respond by feeling guilt. * * *

In the modern day, the sentencing judge * * * asks himself what external pressures can be brought to bear upon the convicted defendant in order to achieve one or another purpose of the criminal justice system. The jury does not ask itself that question. Rather, the jury asks itself whether the defendant ought to feel guilt—whether, in short, the defendant ought to be instructed, in the name of society, to face the *internal* pressure of a recognition of his own immorality. All that the jury can impose upon the defendant, apart from committing him to the judge's disposition, is the judgment of society that one who has acted as the defendant has acted ought to understand himself as guilty.

Because of the moral character of the jury's findings, because it represents such a significant social intrusion into the life of the person who stands accused, our legal system has sought to ensure that the jury will determine guilt only where it can comprehend the defendant's understanding of his acts. As the jury may ultimately have to determine that the defendant ought to feel guilt, the jury must be confident that it can understand how the defendant thinks and feels. The jury's comprehension does not amount to *condonation* of the defendant. On the contrary, the jury's understanding of the defendant may lead to the harshest condemnation of the accused. The jury's verdict constitutes a determination that the defendant ought to feel guilt; thus, our law limits the jury's consideration to those cases in which an understanding of the defendant sufficient to make that determination can be achieved.

The legal condition of insanity, then, occurs when the state of the defendant's mind is such that it is alienated from ordinary human experience. We cannot understand the outlook of the insane person; the barrier of mental disease or defect interrupts the possibility of the jury's comprehension. Faced with such a defendant, modern society has determined that a judgment of conviction would be a travesty of the ideal of justice that inspires our criminal law.

Accordingly, society has established the insanity defense. In putting forward that defense, the accused claims that the state of his mind at the time of the offense * * * was such that the jury, composed of persons with the normal array of human experiences, could not comprehend his view of the world at that moment. * * *

Notes and Questions

1. Are you persuaded by Judge Cabranes's conceptualization of the defense? Suppose that a defendant tells the jury that he beat the victim to death because "I feel good when I hear the sound of human bones cracking." See Peter Arenella, *Convicting the Morally Blameless: Reassessing the Relationship Between Legal and Moral Accountability,* 39 UCLA L.Rev. 1511, 1547 n. 66 (1992) (so describing a former client's explanation for his criminal conduct). Could the jury comprehend *this* "view of the world"? If not, does this mean that the killer should be excused? Is Adolph Hitler insane under Judge Cabranes's "definition"? *Should* he be considered "too crazy" to be held accountable for his actions?

2. One influential critic of the insanity defense is Professor Norval Morris, "a man of the liberal center, a former law school dean, a world-renowned scholar, and an influential pragmatic reformer." Phillip E. Johnson, *Book Review,* 50 U.Chi.L.Rev. 1534, 1536 (1983). Morris states that "the defense of insanity is a tribute * * * to our hypocrisy rather than to our morality." Norval Morris, Madness and the Criminal Law 64 (1982). According to Morris, at id., the defense produces

> a morally unsatisfactory classification on the continuum between guilt and innocence. It applies in practice to only a few mentally ill criminals, thus omitting many others with guilt-reducing relationships between their mental illness and their crime; it excludes other powerful pressures on human behavior, thus giving excessive weight to the psychological over the social.

According to Professor Morris, social disadvantage is more criminogenic than mental illness, yet the former condition—properly, he believes—is not an excuse for criminal conduct. He reasons that the defendant's mental condition, as well as social adversities, should be taken into account, but only at the sentencing stage.

How might a proponent of the insanity plea defend the current law against Professor Morris's attack? Is there a suitable justification for recognizing a mental illness, but not a social deprivation, defense? See Stephen J. Morse, *Excusing the Crazy: The Insanity Defense Reconsidered,* 58 S.Cal.L.Rev. 777, 788–90 (1985).

3. Does it violate the Constitution to convict and punish an insane person for her wrongdoing? Reconsider *Powell v. Texas* (p. 544 supra). Are there other constitutional arguments that might be advanced? See State v. Searcy, 118 Idaho 632, 798 P.2d 914 (1990); State v. Korell, 213 Mont. 316, 690 P.2d 992 (1984).

d. Issues in Applying the Insanity Test

i. The Right–Wrong Prong of M'Naghten

PEOPLE v. SERRAVO

Supreme Court of Colorado, 1992.
823 P.2d 128.

JUSTICE QUINN delivered the Opinion of the Court.

We granted certiorari to review the decision of the court of appeals, in order to determine the meaning of the phrase "incapable of distinguishing right from wrong" in Colorado's statutory definition of insanity codified at section 16–8–101(1), 8A C.R.S. (1986). The trial court, in the insanity phase of a criminal prosecution, instructed the jury that the phrase "incapable of distinguishing right from wrong" refers to a person who appreciates that his conduct is criminal but, due to a mental disease or defect, believes that the conduct is morally right. The prosecution, pursuant to section 16–12–102(1), 8A C.R.S. (1986), appealed the trial court's ruling on the question of law, and the court of appeals approved the ruling.[1] * * *

I.

Serravo was charged in a multi-count information with crimes of attempt to commit first degree murder after deliberation, assault in the first degree, and the commission of crimes of violence. The charges arose out of the stabbing his wife, Joyce Serravo, on May 10, 1987. After the charges were filed, Serravo entered a plea of not guilty by reason of insanity and was thereafter examined by several psychiatrists. The issue of legal insanity was tried to a jury, which returned a verdict of not guilty by reason of insanity.

The evidence at the insanity trial established that the stabbing occurred under the following circumstances. On the evening of May 9, 1987, Serravo, who was a King Soopers union employee, visited striking employees at the King Soopers store near his home. Serravo returned home at approximately 12:30 a.m. on May 10. After sitting in the kitchen and reading the Bible, he went upstairs to the bedroom where his wife was sleeping, stood over her for a few minutes, and then stabbed her in the back just below the shoulder blade. When his wife awoke, Serravo told her that she had been stabbed by an intruder and that she should stay in bed while he went downstairs to call for medical help.

---

1. Section 16–12–102(1), 8A C.R.S. (1986), authorizes the prosecution to appeal   any decision in a criminal case upon any question of law.

Police officers were later dispatched to the home. Serravo told the officers that he had gone to the King Soopers store and had left the garage door open, that the door leading to the house from the garage was unlocked, that when he returned from King Soopers and was reading the Bible he heard his front door slam, and that he went upstairs to check on his wife and children and saw that his wife was bleeding from a wound in her back. Serravo signed a consent to search his home and gave the police clothes that he was wearing at the time of his discovery of his wife's injury.

Several weeks after the stabbing Serravo's wife found letters written by Serravo. In these letters Serravo admitted the stabbing, stating that "[o]ur marriage was severed on Mother's Day when I put the knife in your back," that "I have gone to be with Jehovah in heaven for three and one-half days," and that "I must return for there is still a great deal of work to be done." After reading the letters, Serravo's wife telephoned him in order to confront him about the letters. Serravo told his wife that God had told him to stab her in order to sever the marriage bond. Mrs. Serravo informed the police of these facts and Serravo was thereafter arrested and charged.

The prosecution presented expert psychiatric testimony on Serravo's sanity at the time of the stabbing. Doctor Ann Seig * * * examined Serravo pursuant to a court ordered evaluation of his mental state. Serravo gave the doctor a history of having worked on a plan, inspired by his relationship to God, to establish a multi-million dollar sports complex called Purely Professionals. This facility, according to Serravo, would enable him to achieve his goal of teaching people the path to perfection. On the night of the stabbing, Serravo, according to the history given to Doctor Seig, was excited because he finally believed that he had received some positive encouragement in his endeavor from some King Soopers union members, but he was discouraged by some inner "evil spirits" who kept raising troublesome questions about how he would deal with his wife's lack of encouragement and support. Doctor Seig diagnosed Serravo as suffering either from an organic delusional disorder related to left temporal lobe damage as a result of an automobile accident some years ago or paranoid schizophrenia.[6] Either diagnosis, in Doctor Seig's opinion, would adequately account for Serravo's delusional belief that he had a privileged relationship with God as the result of which he was in direct communication with God. Doctor Seig testified that Serravo was operating under this delusional system when he stabbed his wife and these delusions caused him to believe that his act was morally justified.

6. A standard mental health diagnostic manual published by the American Psychiatric Association, *Diagnostic and Statistical Manual of Mental Disorders,* Third Edition Revised (1987) (DSM IIIR), defines paranoid schizophrenia as a "major disturbance in the content of thought involv[ing] delusions that are often multiple, fragmented or bizarre...." *Id.* at 188. A preoccupation with grandiose or religious delusions is a symptom of paranoid schizophrenia. *Id.* The DSM IIIR defines a delusional disorder as the presence of a persistent thematic delusion. A person laboring under a grandiose delusion is convinced that he or she has a great talent or insight, or has a special relationship with a prominent person or deity.

Doctor Seig, however, was of the view that Serravo, because he was aware that the act of stabbing was contrary to law, was sane at the time of the stabbing.

Serravo presented four psychiatrists and a clinical psychologist on the issue of his legal insanity. The first psychiatrist, Doctor Frederick Miller, was of the opinion that on the night of the stabbing Serravo was under the psychotic delusion that it was his divine mission to kill his wife and that he was morally justified in stabbing her because God had told him to do so. Doctor Miller was not quite certain whether Serravo's psychotic disorder was paranoid schizophrenia, a paranoid delusional disorder, or an organic delusional disorder. Although uncertain of the exact diagnostic label applicable to Serravo, Doctor Miller was of the opinion that Serravo's mental illness made it impossible for him to distinguish right from wrong even though Serravo was probably aware that such conduct was legally wrong.

Another psychiatrist, Doctor Eric Kaplan, * * * supervised Doctor Ann Seig during her examination of Serravo and also made an independent evaluation of Serravo's mental condition. It was Doctor Kaplan's opinion that Serravo was suffering from paranoid schizophrenia at the time of the stabbing and was laboring under the paranoid delusion that his wife stood in the way of his divine mission of completing the large sports complex, that Serravo believed that the stabbing was the right thing to do, and that Serravo, as a result of his mental illness, was unable to distinguish right from wrong with respect to the stabbing. Two other psychiatrists, Doctor Geoffrey Heron and Doctor Seymour Sundell, offered the opinion that Serravo, at the time of the stabbing, was suffering from paranoid schizophrenia and a paranoid delusion about God which so affected his cognitive ability as to render him incapable of distinguishing right from wrong as normal people would be able to do in accordance with societal standards of morality.

Doctor Leslie Cohen, a clinical psychologist, also testified about Serravo's mental condition at the time of the stabbing. Having conducted extensive psychological testing of Serravo, Doctor Cohen was able to offer an opinion on Serravo's reality testing, his emotional reactivity, and his volition, all of which were relevant to the functioning of his conscience. The doctor was of the opinion that Serravo's conscience was based on a false belief or delusion about his magical powers as a result of his direct communication with God. Serravo, in the doctor's view, was suffering from a psychotic disorder that rendered him incapable of distinguishing right from wrong at the time of the stabbing. Although Doctor Cohen acknowledged that Serravo appeared to cover up his conduct when the police arrived at his home, the doctor explained that conduct as the product of a small part of his still intact reality testing. According to Doctor Cohen, Serravo is "not an incoherent man who can't figure out what's going on," but rather "senses that people don't understand his reasoning very well" and thus apparently believed that the police "wouldn't understand the complex reasoning that went behind the stabbing and that it would be better if he kept it to himself."

At the conclusion of the evidence, the trial court instructed the jury, in accordance with the statutory definition of insanity, that a person "is not accountable who is so diseased or defective in mind at the time of the commission of the act as to be incapable of distinguishing right from wrong, with respect to the act." The court also gave the following jury instruction, to which the prosecution objected, on the meaning of the phrase "incapable of distinguishing right from wrong":

Instruction No. 5

As used in the context of the statutory definition of insanity as a criminal defense, the phrase "incapable of distinguishing right from wrong" includes within its meaning the case where a person appreciates that his conduct is criminal, but, because of a mental disease or defect, believes it to be morally right.

In objecting to the jury instruction, the prosecution stated that it would permit the jury to return an insanity verdict based solely on a purely subjective moral standard rather than a legal standard of right and wrong. * * *

The jury returned a verdict of not guilty by reason of insanity at the time of the commission of the alleged crimes, and the court committed Serravo to the custody of the Department of Institutions until such time as he is found to be eligible for release. * * *

II.

We initially consider whether the phrase "incapable of distinguishing right from wrong" should be measured by legal right and wrong, as argued by the People, or instead, should be measured by a societal standard of morality, as determined by the court of appeals. The phrase in question appears in section 16–8–101, 8A C.R.S. (1986), which defines legal insanity as follows:

The applicable test of insanity shall be, and the jury shall be so instructed: "A person who is so diseased or defective in mind at the time of the commission of the act as to be incapable of distinguishing right from wrong with respect to that act is not accountable. But care should be taken not to confuse such mental disease or defect with moral obliquity, mental depravity, or passion growing out of anger, revenge, hatred, or other motives, and kindred evil conditions, for when the act is induced by any of these causes the person is accountable to the law.["]

Because Colorado's statutory definition of insanity is based on the right-wrong test of legal insanity articulated in *M'Naghten's Case,* 8 Eng.Rpt. 718 (1843), our resolution of the issue before us must begin with a review of that case.

A.

In 1843 Daniel M'Naghten shot and killed Edward Drummond, the private secretary to Sir Robert Peel. * * * M'Naghten claimed at trial that he was insane and could not be held responsible because his delusion caused him to commit the act. The jury was instructed that it was to decide whether M'Naghten "had or had not the use of his understanding, so as to know that he was doing a wrong or wicked act," and that if the jury found that he "was not sensible, at the time he committed it, that he was violating the laws both of God and man," then the jury should return a verdict of not guilty by reason of insanity. The jury found M'Naghten not guilty by reason of insanity, and the House of Lords thereafter debated the proper standard of legal insanity and posed five questions to the judges of the Queen's Bench in an attempt to better formulate the insanity defense. The judges' answers to these questions, which were appended to the report of the original case, have come to be considered as if they were the law of the case.

The initial question asked of the judges was the following:

1st. What is the law respecting alleged crimes committed by persons afflicted with insane delusion, in respect of one or more particular subjects or persons: as, for instance, where at the time of the commission of the alleged crime, the accused knew he was acting contrary to law, but did the act complained of with a view, under the influence of insane delusion, of redressing or revenging some supposed grievance or injury, or of producing some supposed public benefit?

The judges answered that a person under the influence of an insane delusion who believes that the act will redress or revenge a supposed grievance will "nevertheless [be] punishable according to the nature of the crime committed, if he knew at the time of committing such crime that he was acting contrary to law; by which expression we understand Your Lordships to mean the law of the land."

The next two questions asked of the judges were answered as one question, and the answer qualifies the reference to "the law of the land" in the first answer. The second and third questions asked in *M'Naghten* were as follows:

2d. What are the proper questions to be submitted to the jury, when a person alleged to be afflicted with insane delusion respecting one or more particular subjects or persons, is charged with the commission of a crime (murder, for example), and insanity is set up as a defence?

3d. In what terms ought the question be left to the jury, as to the prisoner's state of mind at the time when the act was committed?

Id. at 720. The answer to these questions was as follows:

[T]he jurors ought to be told in all cases that every man is to be presumed to be sane, and to possess a sufficient degree of reason to be responsible for his crimes, until the contrary be proved to their satisfaction; and that to establish a defence on the ground of insanity, it must be clearly proved that, at the time of the committing of the act, the party accused was labouring under such a defect of reason, from disease of the mind, as not to know the nature and quality of the act he was doing; or, if he did know it, that he did not know he was doing what was wrong. The mode of putting the latter part of the question to the jury on these occasions has generally been, whether the accused at the time of doing the act knew the difference between right and wrong: which mode, though rarely, if ever, leading to any mistake with the jury, is not, as we conceive, so accurate when put generally and in the abstract, as when put with reference to the party's knowledge of right and wrong, in respect to the very act with which he is charged. *If the question were to be put as to the knowledge of the accused solely and exclusively with reference to the law of the land, it might tend to confound the jury, by inducing them to believe that an actual knowledge of the law of the land was essential in order to lead to a conviction; whereas the law is administered upon the principle that everyone must be taken conclusively to know it, without proof that he does know it. If the accused was conscious that the act was one which he ought not to do, and if that act was at the same time contrary to the law of the land, he is punishable; and the usual course therefore has been to leave the question to the jury, whether the party accused had a sufficient degree of reason to know that he was doing an act that was wrong: and this course we think is correct, accompanied with such observations and explanations as the circumstances of each particular case may require.*

Id. at 722–23 (emphasis added).

B.

The judges' answer to the second and third questions in *M'Naghten* suggests that a person may be considered legally sane as long as the person commits an act contrary to law and knows that the act is morally wrong without regard to the person's actual knowledge of its legality under positive law. Such an interpretation, in our view, is eminently sound.

We acknowledge that some cases subsequent to *M'Naghten* have interpreted the right-wrong test as limiting the insanity defense to a cognitive inability to distinguish legal right from legal wrong, with the result that a person's simple awareness that an act is illegal is a sufficient basis for finding criminal responsibility. We believe, however, that such an analysis injects a formalistic legalism into the insanity equation to the disregard of the psychological underpinnings of legal insanity. A person in an extremely psychotic state, for example, might be aware that an act is prohibited by law, but due to the overbearing effect of the psychosis may be utterly without the capacity to comprehend that the act is inherently immoral. A standard of legal wrong would render such person legally responsible and subject to imprisonment for the conduct in question notwithstanding the patent injustice of such a disposition. Conversely, a person who, although mentally ill, has the cognitive capacity to distinguish right from wrong and is aware that an act is morally wrong, but does not realize that it is illegal, should nonetheless be held responsible for the act, as ignorance of the law is no excuse.

Construing the term "wrong" as moral wrong finds support in several cases which have basically followed the well-reasoned opinion of the New York Court of Appeals in *People v. Schmidt,* 216 N.Y. 324, 110 N.E. 945 (1915).[9] The *Schmidt* opinion, written by then Judge Benjamin Cardozo, rejected the view that the term "wrong" means "contrary to the law of the state." After a careful analysis of *M'Naghten* and the history of the insanity defense, Judge Cardozo remarked:

> The [M'Naghten] judges expressly held that a defendant who knew nothing of the law would none the less be responsible if he knew that the act was wrong, by which, therefore, they must have meant, if he knew that it was morally wrong. Whether he would also be responsible if he knew that it was against the law, but did not know it to be morally wrong, is a question that was not considered. In most cases, of course, knowledge that an act is illegal will justify the inference of knowledge that it is wrong. But none the less it is the knowledge of wrong, conceived of as moral wrong, that seems to have been established by that decision as the controlling test. That must certainly have been the test under the older law when the capacity to distinguish between right and wrong imported a capacity to distinguish between good and evil as abstract qualities.[10] There is nothing to justify the belief that the words right and wrong, when they became limited by [M']Naughten's Case to the right and wrong

---

9. One line of cases interpreting the *M'Naghten* test seems to require that the defendant know that the act is wrong under societal standards of morality *and* is also illegal. *E.g., State v. Crenshaw,* 98 Wash.2d 789, 659 P.2d 488, 494 (1983). This conjunctive formulation of the *M'Naghten* test would appear to be unnecessarily rigid and would apparently exonerate a person by reason of insanity when the person knew the act was morally wrong but, as a result of a mental disease or defect, was not aware that the act was contrary to law. At least one court has held that the *M'Naghten* test requires a person to be able to distinguish moral *or* legal right from moral *or* legal wrong. *E.g., State v. Thorne,* 239 S.C. 164, 121 S.E.2d 623 (1961); *State v. Torrence,* 406 S.E.2d 315, 328 n. 5 (S.C.1991). Such a disjunctive formulation of the test is inherently ambiguous and can only foster uncertainty in application.

10. In the early nineteenth century, prior to *M'Naghten,* English law treated the phrase "good and evil," which connotes the moral quality of an act, as synonymous and

interchangeable with the phrase "right and wrong."

> The first known substitution of "right and wrong" for "good and evil" was in *Parker's Case* (1812), in which the Attorney–General argued that "before it could have any weight in rebutting a charge [treason] so clearly made out, the jury must be perfectly satisfied, that at the time when the crime was committed, the person did not really know right from wrong." In *Bellingham's Case* (1812), both phrases were used, and Lord Chief Justice Mansfield instructed the jury that "the single question was, whether, at the time this fact [murder] was committed, [the defendant] ... possessed a sufficient degree of understanding to distinguish good from evil, right from wrong." In the United States, these two phrases were also used synonymously in both infancy and insanity cases.

Platt & Diamond, *The Origins of the "Right and Wrong" Test of Criminal Responsibility and Its Subsequent Development in the United States: An Historical Survey,* 54 Calif.L.Rev. 1227, 1237 (1966).

of the particular act, cast off their meaning as terms of morals, and became terms of pure legality.

In resolving the ostensible tension between the legal standard of wrong in the answer to the first *M'Naghten* question (i.e., a person is legally responsible if the person acted with knowledge that an act is contrary to the "law of the land") and the moral standard suggested in the answer to the second and third *M'Naghten* questions (i.e., actual knowledge of codified law is not required for a conviction, but rather a person may be punished for conduct if the person knows that the act is one that "he ought not do"), the *Schmidt* opinion stated that the first answer "presupposes the offender's capacity to understand that violation of the law is wrong" and that the offender is sane except for a delusion that his act will redress a supposed grievance or attain some public benefit. The first *M'Naghten* answer, in other words, "applies only to persons who 'are not in other respects insane.'" The delusion that an act will redress a supposed grievance or result in a public benefit, in Cardozo's words, "has no such effect in obscuring moral distinctions as a delusion that God himself has issued a command," inasmuch as "[t]he one delusion is consistent with knowledge that the act is a moral wrong, [but] the other is not." * * *

In urging that the phrase "incapable of distinguishing right from wrong" in section 16–8–101, 8A C.R.S. (1986), should be limited to legal right and wrong, the People focus on that part of the insanity definition which states that "care should be taken not to confuse such mental disease or defect with moral obliquity" and argue that this statutory language manifests a legislative intent to define legal insanity in terms of an incapacity to distinguish legal right from legal wrong. We acknowledge, as asserted by the People, that the term "moral obliquity" refers to a deviation from moral rectitude. *Webster's Third New International Dictionary* 1557 (1986). Accepting that definition, however, does not lead us to the construction urged by the People.

The purpose served by the statutory reference to "moral obliquity" is not to provide a definitional component for legal insanity, which has been defined in the preceding sentence of section 16–8–101 * * *. Rather, the purpose served by the reference to "moral obliquity" is to distinguish, on the one hand, an act committed by a person capable of distinguishing right from wrong but nonetheless acting out of a perverse and culpable rejection of prevailing moral standards and, on the other hand, an act committed by a person in a state of mental illness that renders the person incapable of distinguishing right from wrong with respect to the act. In the case of a person acting out of moral obliquity, rather than a mental disease or defect rendering the actor incapable of distinguishing right from wrong, the person is accountable to the law. * * * If the General Assembly intended otherwise, we reasonably may assume that it would have cast the statutory definition of insanity in terms of an incapacity to distinguish "legality from illegality" or "lawfulness from unlawfulness" rather than in terms of an incapacity to distinguish "right from wrong" with respect to the act charged as a crime. * * *

C.

Moral wrong can be measured either by a purely personal and subjective standard of morality or by a societal and presumably more objective standard. We believe that the better reasoned interpretation of "wrong" in the term "incapable of distinguishing right from wrong" refers to a wrongful act measured by societal standards of morality.

The concepts of "right" and "wrong" are essentially ethical in character and have their primary source in the existing societal standards of morality, as distinguished from the written law. A person's awareness and appreciation of right and wrong derive primarily from a variety of experiences and relationships including, but not necessarily limited to, behavioral rules endorsed by the social culture as well as ethical principles transmitted through the family, the community, the formal educational process, and religious associations. Simply put, legal insanity combines concepts of law, morality and medicine with the moral concepts derived primarily from the total underlying conceptions of ethics shared by the community at large. Defining "wrong" in terms of a purely personal and subjective standard of morality ignores a substantial part of the moral culture on which our societal norms of behavior are based. * * *

D.

We turn then to Jury Instruction No. 5, which stated that the phrase "incapable of distinguishing right from wrong" includes the case of a person who "appreciates that his conduct is criminal but, because of a mental disease or defect, believes it to be morally right." Although the court of appeals concluded that this instruction did not incorporate a "subjective moral standard to the determination of whether defendant understood right from wrong," we are of a contrary view. Jury Instruction No. 5 was cast in terms so general that it well could have been interpreted by the jury to incorporate a personal and subjective standard of moral wrong rather than a societal standard of right and wrong. * * *

III.

We next consider the relationship between the so-called "deific-decree" delusion and Colorado's test of legal insanity. The court of appeals, after holding that the term "wrong" in the statutory definition of insanity refers not to legal wrong but moral wrong under societal standards of morality, held that the "deific-decree" delusion was an exception to the societal standards of moral wrong. Drawing on the opinion of the Washington Supreme Court in *State v. Crenshaw,* 98 Wash.2d 789, 659 P.2d 488 (1983),[12] the court of appeals limited the so-

---

12. In *Crenshaw,* the Supreme Court of Washington carved out the deific exception   from Justice Cardozo's reference in *Schmidt* to a mother insanely obeying

called deific-decree exception to those situations "in which a person commits a criminal act, knowing it is illegal and morally wrong according to society's standards but, because of a mental defect, believes that God has decreed the act." This exception, the court of appeals went on to conclude, must be distinguished from the case "in which a person acts in accordance with a duty imposed by a particular faith." In our view, the "deific-decree" delusion is not so much an exception to the right-wrong test measured by the existing societal standards of morality as it is an integral factor in assessing a person's cognitive ability to distinguish right from wrong with respect to the act charged as a crime.

* * * If a person insanely believes that "he has a command from the Almighty to kill, it is difficult to understand how such a man can know that it is wrong for him to do it." *Schmidt*, 110 N.E. at 948 (quoting *Guiteau's Case*, 10 Fed. 161, 182 (1882)). A person acting under such a delusion is no less insane even though the person might know that murder is prohibited by positive law. It thus seems clear to us that a person is legally insane if that person's cognitive ability to distinguish right from wrong with respect to the act has been destroyed as a result of a psychotic delusion that God has commanded the act. * * *

JUSTICE VOLLACK dissenting: * * *

The majority concludes, relying on what is essentially *dicta* from * * * *People v. Schmidt*, that "wrong" means whether the defendant knows that an act is wrong by society's morals. The express language of the *M'Naghten* decision, however, supports neither the majority's nor the *Schmidt* opinion, but instead indicates that "right from wrong" was meant to be legal right from wrong.

First, nowhere in any of the *M'Naghten* judges' answers does the word "moral" appear. Secondly, the *M'Naghten* judges' answer to the first question clearly expresses the view that a person is punishable if that person "knew at the time of committing their crime that he was acting contrary to law." Both the *Schmidt* court and the majority, however, relied on the answer to the second and third questions in *M'Naghten* to support their conclusion. * * *

Relying on the tenuous reasoning in *Schmidt*, the majority states that the *M'Naghten* judges' answer to the second and third questions "qualifies the reference to 'law of the land' in the first answer." * * *

The answer to the second and third questions does not "qualify" the first answer, as the majority states, but instead explains the first answer

God's command to kill her child. The *Crenshaw* court, citing *Schmidt,* stated that although the woman who kills her infant child under an insane delusion that God has ordered the act might know "that the law and society condemn the act, it would be unrealistic to hold her responsible for the crime, since her free will has been subsumed by her belief in the deific decree." *Crenshaw* appears to have judicially embroidered the *Schmidt* opinion, since *Schmidt* contains no reference to the volitional or free will aspect of the insanity defense. On the contrary, Judge Cardozo in *Schmidt* specifically states that New York's test of insanity does not contain an irresistible impulse component. It thus appears that the *Crenshaw* court added a volitional component to the "deific-decree" exception which is not supported by *Schmidt.*

by stating how the jury should be instructed. The best way to demonstrate this is with the aid of a hypothetical. A defendant is charged with murder and pleads insanity. In such a case, the *M'Naghten* judges state that the question of the defendant's sanity should not be put to the jury "generally and in the abstract." By this they meant that the jury should not be asked whether the defendant knew that *murder* was against the law. If the court submits the instruction "generally and in the abstract," the court would be asking the jury, on the one hand, whether the defendant actually knew murder was against the law, while on the other hand, the defendant is presumed to know the law. Such a request would confuse the jury.

To avoid such confusion, the judges stated that the question should be put to the jury "with reference to the party's knowledge of right and wrong, in respect to the very act with which he is charged." By this they meant whether the defendant was "conscious" that the particular act he or she committed (whatever it is labeled by the state) was against the law.[14] Such an interpretation flows logically from a reading of the answer to the second and third questions and complements, instead of conflicts with, the answer to the first question. * * *

Notes and Questions

1.   Do you believe that Serravo feigned mental illness? If not, is there any justification for punishing him?

2.   Regarding the moral/legal right-and-wrong distinction, whose interpretation of the Colorado insanity statute and *M'Naghten* do you find more persuasive? What about as a matter of sound policy?

3.   In State v. Crenshaw, 98 Wash.2d 789, 659 P.2d 488 (1983), Crenshaw (who had a long history of psychiatric care) took his newlywed wife to a motel room, beat her unconscious, and then stabbed her 24 times, killing her. Thereafter, he cut off her head, chatted with the motel manager over a beer, and then placed his wife's remains in his car and drove away. Later, Crenshaw picked up two hitchhikers and enlisted their aid in disposing of the body. Afterward, they reported the incident to the police.

Upon arrest, Crenshaw confessed. He explained that he followed the "Moscovite" religious faith, which provided that it was morally proper to kill an adulterous wife. Crenshaw told the police that on the day of the murder he sensed that his wife had been unfaithful and, therefore, he killed her.

Under the deific decree standard announced in *Serravo,* was Crenshaw insane?

---

ii.   Convincing the Jury

STATE v. GREEN
Court of Criminal Appeals of Tennessee, 1982.
643 S.W.2d 902.

---

14. Thus, if a defendant knows that stabbing his wife is against the law, he is conscious that the act was one he ought not to do.

DAUGHTREY, JUDGE.

The sole issue raised by this appeal is the sufficiency of the evidence to support the defendant's first degree murder conviction for the slaying of a Chattanooga police officer. At trial the defense offered both lay and expert testimony to establish that 18 year old Steven Green was insane at the time he committed the offense. After a review of the record, we find that the State's rebuttal evidence was not sufficient to refute the overwhelming proof of defendant Green's insanity.

We do not reach this conclusion lightly. As the United States Supreme Court noted in *Burks v. United States,* "[w]hen the basic issue before the appellate court concerns the sufficiency of the Government's proof of a defendant's sanity (as it did here), a reviewing court should be most wary of disturbing the jury verdict." 437 U.S. 1, 17 n. 11, 98 S.Ct. 2141, 2150 n. 11; 57 L.Ed.2d 1 (1978). However, as the *Burks* court also pointed out, "[t]here may be cases where the facts adduced as to the existence and impact of an accused's mental condition may be so over-whelming as to require a judge to conclude that no reasonable juror could entertain a reasonable doubt." We think the matter before us is one of those rare cases.

Tennessee law utilizes the American Law Institute's Model Penal Code § 4.01 to determine the question of an accused's sanity. * * * At trial the State disputed the fact that the defendant in this case suffered from a mental disease or disorder. On appeal the State argues that Green had the capacity to know right from wrong and to control his behavior at will. As to both contentions, the evidence in the record shows otherwise.

On the evening of January 18, 1979, Chattanooga police found the body of Officer Harry Wilcox in a restroom at Warner Park. The corpse, clothed in a blue park police uniform, was lying face down in a pool of blood. The victim had been shot twice in the head, and his police revolver was missing. On the victim's back officers found a plastic bag containing a note. The note, addressed to Agent Ray Hanrahan of the FBI, contained a meaningless string of words and phrases, including reference to an "ousiograph." * * *

Police were led to Green by contacting FBI agent Hanrahan, who had talked to Green a few weeks before the murder and whose notes of their conversation included Green's name. At trial Hanrahan testified that Green had come to the FBI office in the Commerce Union Bank Building and told the agent that some people in New York were talking to him, sending messages to his brain, and "directing" him. Green told Hanrahan that a doctor in New York had invented a machine called an "oustograph" or "ousiograph" that could detect these matters. He asked Hanrahan to find out about the oustograph for him. Hanrahan looked up the word in a dictionary and contacted a radio technician, but could not learn anything about such a machine. Hanrahan said he thought the defendant "had [mental] problems," and he suggested to Green at the time that he go to Erlanger Hospital to seek help.

Hanrahan's perception of the precariousness of Green's mental health was indeed accurate. Green had first received psychiatric treatment at the age of seven when as a child in New York City he was suspended from school for picking fights with other children "for no reason at all . . ., beat[ing] them up really viciously." At that time he began seeing a psychiatrist who diagnosed his problem as paranoia. After treating the defendant for over two years, the psychiatrist pronounced Green "all right" but warned that the condition could recur during his teenage years. At age twelve, Green attacked his mother with a knife and again received psychiatric treatment.

By the time Green was sixteen, he had become a loner. He refused to go to school, remained in bed all day, and stayed out all night. He refused to bathe. He would not talk to anyone, and when spoken to, he would not respond or would laugh hysterically. Green carried a bag around with him, explaining to his parents that the bag "kept him company." He complained that the television talked back at him. At first Green insisted there was nothing wrong with him, but he eventually agreed to accept psychiatric treatment. After he was hospitalized for more than a month in 1978, his family reached the limits of their insurance coverage, and Green was transferred to an out-patient clinic. During this period he was heavily medicated and "was just like a zombie." Because the medication made Green so drowsy he could not study, he stopped taking the medicine and refused to visit the out-patient clinic.

Green enrolled in a Navy reserve program, returned to school, and managed to graduate from high school in June 1978. Immediately after graduation, he reported for Navy training, but a few weeks later the Navy discharged him for failure to adapt to regulations. When he returned home from the Navy, Green resumed his old behavior patterns. He stayed in bed during the day and walked the streets at night. He had a fight with his brother and cut him on the leg with a knife. He said that other people in the apartment building had a machine that tampered with his brain. He felt that the television talked back at him; he thought people talked about him; and he was suspicious whenever the telephone rang. The defendant would not bathe or change his clothes. Toward the end of August 1978, he stole the family's household money and left home.

In September 1978, the defendant turned up in Chicago. From there he called an uncle, Noah Green, who arranged for the defendant to come to Memphis. Green stayed with his uncle in Memphis for six to seven weeks. At trial Noah Green described his nephew's bizarre behavior during that time. When the defendant first arrived in Memphis he had not bathed, and during the course of his stay, Noah Green had to insist that he wash. The defendant told his uncle about an "oustograph," a kind of machinery that dealt with the mind, and asked his uncle why people were following him. The defendant would stay in his room all day and only went outside when his uncle insisted. He would pace the house at night. Sometimes he locked himself in the bathroom, but ran the shower without bathing. Green laughed at inappropriate times, and he would stare into space and move his mouth without saying anything. Twice the defendant visited a mental health clinic, but each time he refused to cooperate with the doctors. The medical staff told his family that because Green had not yet exhibited violent tendencies, he could not be hospitalized involuntarily. By November 1978, Green's behavior had become so bizarre that Noah Green feared for the safety of his young children and asked his nephew to leave. Green then went to stay with an aunt, Julia McNair, who also lived in Memphis.

Green lived in McNair's home for two weeks. She testified that during that time he never went out, he kept her apartment in darkness, and he refused to bathe. He would not talk to other people but laughed and talked to himself constantly.

When a psychologist at the local mental health center told McNair that the defendant needed to be hospitalized and that he might "go off at any time" and "do anything," she became frightened. She told her nephew that he would have to leave her home if he did not seek medical help immediately. When he refused, she called her brother, the defendant's father, and told him to come get Green and take him back to New York City. When Green's father arrived in Memphis, the defendant insisted that he did not need treatment and refused to return to New York. * * *

Some two months later, in January 1979, the defendant was arrested and charged with the Wilcox murder. * * *

In March 1979, John Littleton was hired as local counsel for Green and went to the jail to interview his client. Despite the lawyer's efforts to establish rapport with Green, he found none of the interest usually displayed by an accused in the handling of his case. Instead, Littleton said, Green was "extremely apprehensive and afraid, also very unresponsive, very disturbed, ..., very withdrawn, [and] would hardly talk at all other than to acknowledge who he was." Littleton said Green stared at the walls as though he might have been hearing voices. Littleton immediately asked for a psychiatric examination of Green, which was ordered by the trial court * * *.

As a result of the court order, Green was first seen by Dr. Stanley Speal, a forensic psychologist * * *. Speal saw Green on several occasions * * * and diagnosed the defendant as paranoid schizophrenic, a condition which is characterized by irrational thinking, feelings inappropriate to the situation, an overly suspicious nature, hostility, and delusions of grandeur and of persecution.

Although Green was initially thought competent to stand trial, no immediate evaluation was made concerning his mental condition at the time of the offense. However, Green "steadily refused medication ...

and his condition deteriorated as a result," so that by May 1979 it was necessary to hospitalize him for a reevaluation of his competency.

Green was * * * found to be incompetent to stand trial. The staff of the Forensic Services Division also concluded that he was insane at the time of the offense, as well as committable and in need of maximum security. * * * [Six months later], however, he was found to be "greatly improved," his paranoid schizophrenia was noted as being in remission, and the hospital staff recommended that he be returned to Chattanooga for trial.

At Green's trial in November 1980, various members of his family from New York City and Memphis outlined the defendant's social and psychiatric history, beginning with his initial treatment at age seven, up to the time he left Memphis in November 1978. FBI Agent Hanrahan then described his interview with Green in November or December 1978, an event which led him to the conclusion that Green needed hospitalization for his mental problems. * * *

The observations and conclusions of these lay witnesses were confirmed by several expert witnesses who testified at trial, including Dr. Samuel Pieper and clinical nurse Robin Shanks, both of whom were on the staff at Middle Tennessee Mental Health Institute. The expert testimony establishing Green's insanity in January 1979 is clear, consistent, and convincing, and the State offered no corresponding expert testimony to refute it. The medical experts in this case had the benefit of reports by other professionals who had examined and treated the defendant in New York City and Memphis, as well as Bellevue Hospital records from his 1978 hospitalization. They testified, and there is no evidence to the contrary, that they and all the other professional staff members who came in contact with Green after his arrest agreed unanimously that he was insane at the time of the offense.

Dr. Speal saw Green on six separate occasions between March 16, 1979, and September 17, 1980. He administered tests in March 1979 that showed that Green was psychotic at that time, "without a clear perception of reality, prone to delusional thinking." These delusions were of both the persecution and grandeur varieties, indicating a condition of paranoid schizophrenia. Describing a person in this condition, Speal said that:

> ... his thinking is irrational, he will say words that don't mean anything at times, he can't think logically ..., his feelings [are] not appropriate to the situation. He may be extremely angry if someone just bats an eyelash or doesn't look at him right. . . .

Dr. Speal further indicated that Green was suffering from auditory hallucinations when he examined him and that he appeared to have a history of such hallucinations; Speal reached the conclusion that "[i]t was a result of these voices that the killing took place." He described Green's delusion concerning the "oustograph" and Green's fear that this "mind control device" was monitoring his brain from New York. In Speal's opinion Green "was in great pain at that time because of this delusion [that he was being controlled by unknown people in New York]." Dr. Speal concluded on the basis of his 18 month contact with Green that the defendant had been insane at the time the offense was committed.

Dr. Pieper, a neurologist and psychiatrist at Middle Tennessee Mental Health Institute, was a member of the medical team that evaluated Green. In addition to the defendant's grandiose and persecutory delusions, the doctor said Green suffered from "bizarre delusions," i.e., those "in which things are so odd that we simply use the word bizarre to describe them.., [as w]hen you think that a TV set controls your mind and sends messages into your mind." Pieper said that Green's delusion concerning the oustograph fell into this category.
* * *

Dr. Pieper noted Green's "quite pervasive" and "consistent pattern" of psychosis with paranoid delusional thinking, originating in his early teenage years. He concluded that at the time Green killed Wilcox he was acting under the control of delusions or hallucinations or both, that he therefore did not understand that his act was wrong and could not conform his conduct to the requirements of law. * * *

The State's rebuttal evidence, offered to establish the defendant's sanity at the time of the offense, consisted of testimony by five Chattanooga police officers and a former county employee. The first of these witnesses was Terry Slaughter, the detective who arrested Green on January 20, 1978, for the Wilcox killing. He described Green as "cooperative," "coherent," and "intelligent," but said that Green did not want to discuss the shooting. In the two hours he spent with Green, Slaughter noticed no bizarre behavior nor any sign that Green was "under delusion." * * *

Officer Janus Marlin, a Warner Park patrolman and a colleague of the victim's, found Green huddled in a phone booth in the park on December 27, 1979. Green had taken refuge there to get out of the cold and told Marlin he had "no place to go." The officer took him to a nearby rescue mission. Asked if there was "anything out of the ordinary" about Green at the time, Marlin said no, but also testified that "he was dirty and he smelled."

Officer John Bishop arrested Green for vagrancy on the night of December 19, 1978, when he found him sleeping in a city courtroom. He arrested Green a second time on December 29 for loitering in a service station restroom and begging from customers. * * * Asked by the prosecution if he noticed anything out of the ordinary about Green, Officer Bishop said only that the defendant was "fairly quiet," "very polite," and "just answered the questions."

Officer Richard Alexander arrested Green for vagrancy on January 20, two days after the Wilcox killing, as Green "was walking the streets at [a] late hour of the night ... trying to find someplace to stay warm." The officer described Green as coherent, but said that he apparently "[j]ust ... had a lack of concern about anything."[3]   In response to a question by the prosecution concerning evidence that Green "was under any delusions or hallucinations at the time," the officer responded negatively, saying that he was with Green for about 40 minutes. He did note, however, that Green was unkempt and dirty.

Another Warner Park patrolman, Sam Foster, saw Green in the early part of December. * * * Officer Foster said Green acted "normally."

Finally, the State offered testimony by a former county employee, William Cox, who gave Green a ride in his county-owned transportation van near the Hamilton County garage on January 18, 1979, the day Officer Wilcox was killed. * * * During the 45 minutes they were in the van together, Cox said, they engaged in "small talk." In response to a question by the prosecution, the witness agreed that he noticed nothing out of the ordinary about Green.

From this testimony, the State took the position that Green was "not insane and crazy and bizarre at the time [the Wilcox killing] happened," but was just "a little bit different." However, the testimony of the various State witnesses, all of whom had had only brief contact with Green over a period of several weeks and described him as "normal," is not inconsistent with a determination that Green was insane at the time of the offense. The medical experts testified, and their testimony is unrefuted, that a paranoid schizophrenic can operate in a *seemingly* normal way. As Dr. Speal put it, "as long as you have a distant relationship with them, they can almost appear normal." Dr. Pieper concurred in this conclusion, saying that a paranoid schizophrenic can "function in a manner which appears to be normal and it's accepted as normal by the general public." Going further, he noted:

> Paranoid schizophrenic people have a characteristic of what we call encapsulated delusions. That is they may have some abnormal thoughts that are about a very particular area and as long as you stay out of that area everything looks pretty good. When you get inside this area, then you realize that this doesn't make sense, it's illogical, it's bizarre, you know, it just doesn't make sense. When the person is functioning in areas which don't require any thinking about that particular problem, they can look pretty normal. They can get on a bus and ride the bus and no problem. But if somebody asks them a question or says something or makes a movement that they regard as threatening, suddenly all of this bizarre thinking takes charge and at that point they may react in any sort of way

3. This description of apathetic behavior is consistent with the symptoms of schizophrenia outlined in *Sampson v. State,* 553 S.W.2d 345, 347 (Tenn.1977): "The outstanding features of these disorders are the bizarre thought content and the odd behavior of the patient, his apparent alienation from the world of reality, *an apathetic flat-* *tening of mood which may at intervals be punctuated by apparently inappropriate periods of great intensity,* the presence of delusions (false beliefs), illusions (false interpretations of stimuli), and hallucinations (perception of external stimuli not present)."

that's totally unexpected and totally irrational. The only time that I was ever hit by a patient in working with them for fifteen years was by a paranoid schizophrenic who suddenly and for no reason at all, the best I could tell, swung and hit me. Now, in retrospect I knew that that might occur, but I couldn't predict when it was going to occur.   * * *

Given the nature of the evidence offered by the defendant, the burden of proof in this case fell squarely on the State to establish the defendant's sanity beyond a reasonable doubt.   * * *

* * * [T]he State argues that the nature of the defendant's condition was not sufficient to meet the * * * two-prong [insanity] test * * *. First, the State says, evidence that the defendant fled from the scene of the crime and hid the weapon involved in the shooting proves that he knew the wrongfulness of his act. The most obvious response to this argument is that the record shows only that the defendant left the scene at some point after the shooting and that Officer Wilcox's revolver was never recovered; neither of these facts establishes beyond a reasonable doubt that the defendant was attempting to conceal his identity or complicity from police, or that he otherwise was able to appreciate the wrongfulness of what he had done.   * * *

But even if it were conceded that by his post-event behavior Green evidenced some appreciation of the wrongfulness of his conduct, the record is wholly devoid of any evidence that at the time he shot Wilcox, Green was able to conform his conduct to the dictates of law. The State's only argument in response to overwhelming evidence of Green's incapacity in this respect is that his failure to react violently toward other police officers with whom he came into contact proves that he was able to conform his conduct to the law with respect to Officer Wilcox. * * * This argument, of course, not only begs the question (that is, whether under this analysis any initial violent behavior could ever be the product of insanity), but it also ignores the nature of paranoid schizophrenia, as described by experts in this and other cases.   * * *

The State correctly points out that a jury is not bound by expert testimony, even when it is non-conflicting. However, the Tennessee Supreme Court has clearly delineated what proof the State must produce to meet and overcome evidence of insanity:

> Th[e] burden can be met by the state through the introduction of expert testimony on the issue [of insanity], or through lay testimony where a proper foundation for the expressing of an opinion is laid, or through the showing of acts or statements of the petitioner, at or very near the time of the commission of the crime, which are consistent with sanity *and inconsistent with insanity.*

In this case, although the acts of the defendant at or near the time of the killing were arguably "consistent with sanity," quite obviously they were not also "inconsistent with insanity."   * * * [W]e have no choice but to set aside Green's conviction.   * * *

Notes and Questions

1. Since the prosecutor had the burden of proof regarding Green's sanity, Tennessee applied the relatively broad ALI standard of insanity, and all of the experts testified that Green was insane, how do you explain the jury's verdict? Even if the jury verdict was wrong, did the Court of Criminal Appeals overstep the bounds of proper appellate review?

2. Green refused the medication prescribed to him at an outpatient psychiatric clinic, and he later refused outpatient care entirely. Do you agree with the suggestion of one commentator that defendants in such circumstances should be barred from relying on the insanity defense if they are prosecuted for a crime of negligence or recklessness, including reckless homicide? Michael D. Slodov, Comment, *Criminal Responsibility and the Noncompliant Psychiatric Offender: Risking Madness,* 40 Case West.Res. L.Rev. 271 (1989).

3. In *Green,* the state relied exclusively on lay testimony to rebut the defendant's experts. Should a finding of sanity ever be permitted in such circumstances? See People v. Banks, 17 Ill.App.3d 746, 308 N.E.2d 261 (1974); Groseclose v. State, 440 So.2d 297 (Miss.1983); Olivier v. State, 850 S.W.2d 742 (Tex.App.1993).

What about the converse? For example, suppose that Green's attorney had merely introduced evidence of the defendant's bizarre behavior from age seven until the time of the offense, but called no experts to the stand to testify regarding Green's mental state at the time of the crime. Should this be enough to justify a jury instruction on insanity? See Pacheco v. State, 757 S.W.2d 729 (Tex.Cr.App.1988), remanded, 770 S.W.2d 834 (Ct.App. 1989).

4. The proper role of mental health experts in criminal trials is a major source of controversy. One court articulated their role this way:

[I]n *State v. Johnson* [121 R.I. 254, 266–67, 399 A.2d 469, 476 (1979)] * * * [w]e explained the role of expert opinion as follows:

"Ideally, psychiatrists—much like experts in other fields—should provide grist for the legal mill, should furnish the raw data upon which the legal judgment is based. It is the psychiatrist who informs as to the mental state of the accused—his characteristics, his potentialities, his capabilities. But once this information is disclosed, it is society as a whole, represented by judge or jury, which decides whether a [person] with the characteristics described should or should not be held accountable for his acts." (quoting *United States v. Freeman,* 357 F.2d [606,] 619–20 [(2d Cir.1966)]).

In addition the *Johnson* opinion gave specific directions aimed at preserving the proper role for the jury. We stated that "the charge to the jury must include unambiguous instructions stressing that regardless of the nature and extent of the experts' testimony, the issue of exculpation remains at all times a legal and not a medical question." Under the *Johnson* formulation, the jury should hear all relevant expert testimony regarding a defendant's mental condition. The trial justice, however, must instruct the jury to weigh the credibility of the experts, make its own independent decision concerning whether the defendant suffered from a mental defect at the time of the perpetration of the crime, and determine whether * * * [the defendant was insane at the time of the offense].

State v. Gardner, 616 A.2d 1124, 1126–27 (R.I.1992).

Based on *Johnson,* the *Gardner* court held that the defendant's expert could not only testify that the defendant suffered from schizotypal personality disorder, but that he suffered from this mental defect at the time of the crime. The court explained:

> In this case expert testimony concerning defendant's mental state at the time of the offenses is exactly the type of "grist for the legal mill" that *Johnson* contemplated would come before the jury. As noted above, the jury must determine whether defendant suffered from a mental defect at the time of the perpetration of the crimes. The jury should not perform this function in a vacuum; it should hear testimony on this issue from both prosecution and defense expert witnesses, assess the credibility of their testimony, and determine if the defendant in fact suffered from this mental defect.
>
> The state argues that to admit this evidence would result in expert testimony that encroaches on an area left to the jury. * * * Nothing in our *Johnson* opinion, however, suggested that because the jury must determine the defendant's mental state at the time of the crime, experts could not testify on this issue. To the contrary, *Johnson's* direction to allow experts to provide the jury with a full and accurate picture of a defendant's mental state strongly indicates that this evidence is admissible.

Id. at 1127.

Do psychiatrists play too great a role in criminal trials? Consider the following remarks of Stephen Morse, then Professor of Law and Professor of Psychiatry at the University of Southern California.

STEPHEN J. MORSE—CRAZY BEHAVIOR, MORALS, AND SCIENCE: AN ANALYSIS OF MENTAL HEALTH LAW

51 Southern California Law Review 527 (1978), 554–60

* * * "Is the person normal in the mental health sense?" It should * * * be recognized that for mental health law this question really should mean, in operational terms, "Does this person behave sufficiently crazily to warrant special legal treatment on moral and social grounds?" Once the nature of the question is clear, one can analyze how it should properly be answered. The major thesis * * * is that the question, "Who is sufficiently crazy?" is a social question, and that *for legal purposes* it can and should be answered by laypersons. * * *

Let us consider some examples to analyze * * * the question of "who is crazy?" and how it should be answered. Suppose an adult walks down the street, accosting passersby and loudly uttering strange epithets. Asked why he is engaging in this behavior, he sincerely replies that electrochemical rays shot at him by supernatural beings are forcing him to behave in this way. This person clearly has a mental disorder according to the American Psychiatric Association,[48] but do we need an expert to tell us that he is crazy? Clearly not. * * *

Let us now consider a much harder example: a man who is extremely neat, punctual, and precise. Indeed, he spends so much time ensuring that he is neat, punctual, and precise that he often accomplishes considerably less in his love life and work life than he might like, a fact that makes him unhappy. Despite his discontent, he finds that for some reason he feels that he just has to be that way, and in any case, he gets along all right with his family and his job. This person suffers from a mental disorder according to the currently dominant diagnostic scheme.[49] Indeed, excessive concern with neatness, punctuality, or anything else is a little crazy in the loosest colloquial sense. On the other hand, many persons would probably be inclined to say about this person, "Oh, so and so has some quirks like all of us, but that's just the way he is." * * * Is this person normal? Again, does the ability to answer this question require medical expertise or merely common sense based on social rules and expectations?

Mental health experts are a bit more inclined than the average person to declare that particular behaviors are abnormal and evidence mental disorder. Even so, most experts and laypersons would agree in their assessment of our second example. He is a person with some personality quirks (or in "psychiatrese," characterological symptoms) that interfere to some extent with his successful functioning. Thus, the final question of normality in this borderline case is simply, "How quirky must a person be before he or she will be labeled *abnormal*?" There is no scientific answer to this question. There exists no objectively identifiable underlying abnormal condition that distinguishes this person from those with fewer, different, or no quirks. Even if there were an identifiable underlying condition, for legal purposes the answer depends on social tolerance for quirkiness or on social value preferences concerning how much a person can "normally" hinder his own functioning by quirkiness before we consider him crazy.

A final example is a person whose sexual orientation is exclusively homosexual but who maintains adequate interpersonal relations, whose work life is generally unimpaired, and who has no significantly maladaptive personality quirks. This case illustrates the difficulty in answering the question "who is crazy?" and exemplifies the process by which professionals sometimes decide such questions.

Our example is a person who would be regarded as quite normal by both experts and laypersons except for his homosexuality. But is this person normal in the mental health sense? * * * Until 1973, the

---

48. The diagnosis would probably be "Schizophrenia, Paranoid Type," according to * * * DSM–III [American Psychiatric Association, Diagnostic and Statistical Manual of Mental Disorders (3d ed.)].

49. The diagnosis would probably be * * * "Compulsive personality disorder" according to DSM–III.

American Psychiatric Association, the organization responsible for the promulgation of the currently dominant diagnostic scheme of mental disorders, considered homosexuality per se a mental disorder. In that year, by a vote of its membership, the Association decided that homosexuality was not a mental disorder. The nature of homosexuality did not change, nor were there any startling breakthroughs in the scientific understanding of homosexual behavior. * * *

What changed were the *values* of a professional group empowered to affix labels of deviancy. Historically, many societies considered homosexuality sinful. The ascendancy of the medical model of deviant behavior led to a redefinition of this deviant behavior as sick. The majority of mental health experts, although by no means all, now view homosexuality per se as neither sick nor bad; rather, it is viewed as one possible form of human sexual orientation. A homosexual may still be considered mentally disordered, but not on the basis of homosexuality per se. * * *

* * * Homosexuals are no longer officially considered sick not because of a scientific finding, but because a majority of professionals with the power to affix the "sick" label changed their minds. If the decision of whether homosexual behavior is abnormal really reduces to a statement of value preferences, however, the assistance professionals can give to laypersons to discern such abnormalities is negligible.

Mental health experts are neither moral experts nor social value experts, nor even experts on any mental health issue about which there is little scientific data or agreement * * *.

The best measuring instrument for determining if a person is crazy is to find out as much as possible about the actor from those persons who have had an opportunity to observe him directly in a wide variety of circumstances. When much is learned about how the actor has behaved at many different times and in many different circumstances, or at a particular time and in particular circumstances, then all members of society will be competent to judge if the person is crazy in general or if he was crazy at the particular time in question. The current deference the law accords mental health experts is misplaced. For legal purposes, the question of who is crazy must be recognized as a social and moral judgment that must be decided as such.

Notes and Questions

1. More recently, Professor Morse has opined that "[e]xperts should be limited to offering both full, rich, clinical descriptions of [the defendant's] thoughts, feelings and actions and relevant data based on sound scientific studies." But, he suggests, "[t]o remedy the 'circus atmosphere' of insanity trials, experts should be prohibited from offering diagnoses, unvalidated explanations, and ultimate legal conclusions." Stephen J. Morse, *Excusing the Crazy: The Insanity Defense Reconsidered,* 58 S.Cal.L.Rev. 777, 823 (1985).

iii. Sociopaths

Consider Robert Alton Harris. In front of his younger brother, Harris shot to death two youths, one at point-blank range. After murdering them, he took their lunch bag, calmly ate the remainder of their meal, amused himself imagining what it would be like to be the police officer who reports the victims' deaths to their families, and laughed at his brother for not having the stomach to join him in the meal. Harris was convicted of murder and sentenced to death. See People v. Harris, 28 Cal.3d 935, 171 Cal.Rptr. 679, 623 P.2d 240 (1981).

Harris committed countless other acts of violence before these murders and while on Death Row. He was so unpopular in prison that other Death Row inmates promised to celebrate when he was executed.[f] They said of Harris, "The guy's a misery, a scumbag; we're going to party when he [gets executed]. He doesn't care about life, he doesn't care about others, he doesn't care about himself." Miles Corwin, *Icy Killer's Life Steeped in Violence,* Los Angeles Times, May 16, 1982, at 1. In short, Harris's "ears [were] not deaf, but his heart [was] frozen." Gary Watson, *Responsibility and the Limits of Evil* in Responsibility, Character, and the Emotions 271 (F. Schoeman ed. 1987).

The inmates' description of Harris is consistent with the conclusion that he suffered from so-called "sociopathy" or "psychopathy," or what the American Psychiatric Association now describes as "antisocial personality disorder." The essential feature of the condition is "a pattern of irresponsible and antisocial behavior beginning in childhood or early adolescence and continuing into adulthood." American Psychiatric Association, *Diagnostic and Statistical Manual of Mental Disorders* 342 (3d ed. Revised 1987).

Sociopaths tend to be aggressive, impulsive, reckless, habitual liars, and without feelings of remorse for their wrongdoing. The disorder is far more common in males than in females. Predisposing factors include Attention–Deficit Hyperactivity Disorder, abuse as a child, and growing up without parental figures of both sexes. A genetic connection may also be involved, as the disorder is five times more common among immediate relatives of males with the disorder than among the general population. Id. at 343. Although a sociopath understands what he is doing and suffers from no irresistible impulses—i.e., he is sane under the usual insanity standard—he typically feels no emotional connection to others, and may lack the capacity to care for anyone else but himself.

Assuming that Harris had these sociopathic characteristics, does this make him sick or evil? Does he deserve blame, condemnation and punishment, or should he be held criminally nonresponsible for his actions? One scholar has argued that at least some sociopaths are not

---

f. They got their wish on April 12, 1992, when Harris was executed in California's gas chamber. Jane Meredith Adams, *Killer*   *Executed After High Court Intervenes,* Chicago Tribune, April 22, 1992, at 3.

moral agents: because they lack fundamental attributes of human nature, such as the capacity to care for others and to make moral evaluations, they are not properly subject to moral condemnation. See Peter Arenella, *Convicting the Morally Blameless: Reassessing the Relationship Between Legal and Moral Accountability,* 39 UCLA L.Rev. 1511 (1992).

Do you agree that a person who lacks the capacity for moral concern is not a proper subject of blame? If so, what should society do with a sociopath? He cannot be committed to a mental institution unless he is both dangerous *and* mentally ill. Foucha v. Louisiana, 504 U.S. ___, 112 S.Ct. 1780, 118 L.Ed.2d 437 (1992). The general view of the psychiatric community, however, is that antisocial personality disorder is not a mental disease and is untreatable. If you would punish a sociopath, what about the basic premise of the insanity defense, that "[o]ur collective conscience does not allow punishment where it cannot impose blame"? Holloway v. United States, 148 F.2d 665, 666–67 (D.C.Cir. 1945).

Is Professor Jeffrie Murphy correct when he states that "from the moral point of view, it is * * * implausible to regard [sociopaths] as *persons* at all." Therefore, they "are in no position to claim any rights on grounds of moral merit or desert." Jeffrie G. Murphy, *Moral Death: A Kantian Essay on Psychopathy,* 82 Ethics 284, 294 (1972). Thus, according to Murphy, we may deal with a sociopath as we would any dangerous, uncontrollable animal, such as by humanely killing him if necessary. Should *that* trouble our collective conscience?

iv. Multiple Personality Disorder

KIRKLAND v. STATE

Court of Appeals of Georgia, 1983.
166 Ga.App. 478, 304 S.E.2d 561.

BIRDSONG, JUDGE. * * *

The conditions of multiple personality [disorder] and its less refined cousin, psychogenic fugue, are extremely rare and certainly not fully understood * * * by psychiatry. In general, the affected individual unconsciously "develops" alternate personalities to deal with trauma (e.g., child or sexual abuse) that the individual otherwise cannot endure. The alternate personalities are separate identities with highly individualized traits, behavior patterns, and complex social activities, even to the point of possessing different family histories, different ages, or even different nationalities. When faced with stressful situations, the individual may be dominated by one or more separate personalities; the "core" individual most often has no knowledge of the existence of any other personalities, but may sometimes hear "voices" and will "lose time." She may wake up in a strange city thousands of miles from home, and find herself in possession of unfamiliar and uncharacteristic clothing and objects. The "core" personality has no control over the personality which is in domination, or consciousness; the transition to the alternate is involuntary and unknowing; she has no memory of what the other personality does. The alternate personality may stay in control for hours, months or years. A particular alternate personality may be, and often is, as its raison d'etre, a well-developed and complete personality in itself, rational and quite functional. Naturally the core personality stays often confused, and may even ultimately abdicate altogether in favor of another (or a platoon of others) who will separately function in society to the limit of their respective abilities.

PEOPLE v. WADE

Supreme Court of California, 1987.
43 Cal.3d 366, 233 Cal.Rptr. 48, 729 P.2d 239.

THE COURT:

Defendant Melvin Meffery Wade (hereafter appellant) appeals from a judgment imposing the death penalty following his conviction of first degree murder * * *. * * *

A. PROCEDURAL HISTORY

Trial commenced on February 1, 1982. Following the presentation of the prosecution's case in chief, the trial court permitted appellant to enter a plea of not guilty by reason of insanity. The jury convicted appellant of first degree murder * * *.

* * * The jury found appellant to be sane at the time of the offense. [At the time, California applied the ALI test of insanity.]

Following the penalty phase, the jury returned a verdict of death.

B. GUILT PHASE EVIDENCE

Appellant was 24 years old at the time of the offense. In April 1981, appellant and his wife, Irabell "Cookie" Strong, were living in a one-bedroom apartment at the Mission Motel in San Bernardino. Four of Cookie's five children—Penny (age twelve), Joyce (age ten), Alexis (age nine), and Syeeta (age eight)—were also living with them.

According to Cookie, appellant was kind to the children at first, but as time went by he began to abuse them more and more. Appellant was easily upset and was "quick to hit" the children and punish them. He beat them with his fists, hit them with a paddle, made them stand on one foot for extended periods of time, and ordered them to kneel on top of a dresser and take cold showers. He also forced Joyce and Alexis to drink their own urine and mixtures of milk and salt to induce vomiting.

[The court recounted the awful events leading up to Joyce's death. Over a 22–hour period, Wade beat the girl with his fists and a wooden board, choked her with dog chain, threw her against a wall, put her in the attic in a duffle bag, and, finally, killed her with a kick to the stomach while she was lying unconscious.] During this time, appellant consumed a bottle of wine and shouted that he was "Michael the

Archangel" and that he would kill Joyce because she was a "devil."
* * *

The motel manager, hearing a disturbance in the apartment occupied by appellant and his family, eventually called the police. [Appellant fled the scene.] * * *

Moments after the police arrived, appellant returned. He walked through the parking lot with his hands up in the air and said: "Here I am. I'm the one you want. I guess I hit her too hard. I guess I hit her too hard." Appellant was then placed under arrest.

Following his arrest, appellant gave a statement to the police. He asked if Joyce were dead and said that he had killed an innocent person but that he did not mean to hit her so hard. He admitted hitting Joyce with his fists, striking her with a paddle, and hitting her head against the wall. He also admitted putting her in the crawl space to punish her. He denied using a dog leash on her or making her stand against the wall. Appellant said that he loved Joyce, but that she had been a constant discipline problem. He also related that he was under pressure, was seeing a psychiatrist, had been a prisoner of war in Vietnam, and was on welfare.

Four doctors—psychiatrists Ralph Allison, Ethel Chapman and Robert Summerour and clinical psychologist Craig Rath—were called by the defense to testify about appellant's psychiatric background and his mental state at the time of the offense. They testified in great detail about appellant's background. They reported that from the age of three, appellant was physically and sexually abused by his mother's boyfriend, Jack. Jack would also lock appellant in a closet for hours. While in the closet, appellant would talk to an imaginary friend. Gradually, this friend, called "Othello," began to talk back to him.

At the age of 12, appellant began to experience blackouts. He described events in his past which he could not explain, such as finding himself in bed with a 46-year-old woman, who kept calling him "Othello." Throughout the 1970's, appellant received psychological counseling. He also attempted suicide three times.

The defense doctors attempted to determine if appellant was a multiple personality. Each of them supposedly encountered a personality called "Othello." Drs. Rath and Allison also reportedly spoke with personalities named "Joe" and "Michael." When the doctors asked to speak with "Othello," appellant would close his eyes, lower his head and, shortly thereafter, the personality of "Othello" would emerge.[4]

The doctors described Melvin Wade as mild-mannered, polite, soft-spoken and cooperative. "Othello," on the other hand, was hostile, boisterous, arrogant, vulgar and violent. He supposedly disliked Melvin intensely.

4. One of Dr. Allison's sessions with appellant, during which more than one personality was interviewed, was videotaped and played for the jury.

"Othello," also referred to as the "Son of Fire" and "Son of Satan," was born in Greece and fed on "germs of loneliness and despair." "Othello" was the devil's assassin employed by the council of 12 archdemons to kill Cookie. On the day of Joyce's killing, "Othello" had tried to force Cookie to sacrifice herself by threatening Joyce's life. "Othello" explained that he really wanted to kill Cookie but Joyce got in the way. "Othello" was also assigned to kill Melvin.

Melvin's body also contained a personality named "Joe." "Joe" is "Othello's" son and secretary, and a "devil in training" "waiting around for a body to occupy." The doctors described "Joe" as young, weak, friendly, soft-spoken, mischievous and devilish. "Joe" was the personality who surrendered and confessed to the police after the killing. He had apparently "fouled up his part of the assignment."

A fourth personality is "Michael the Archangel." The doctors described "Michael" as angelic, weak and mild. "Michael" holds a rank in the "archangel group" equivalent to "Othello's" rank as a demon and is "Othello's" arch enemy. He tries to help Melvin fight against "Othello." He is strongest on Sundays and was unable to prevent Joyce's death because it occurred on a Saturday, "Othello's" "strongest" day.[5]

All four defense doctors concluded that appellant suffered from a dissociative disorder. Drs. Rath and Chapman firmly diagnosed him as a multiple personality, unable to harbor malice or to form the intent to kill at the time of the offense. Dr. Summerour diagnosed him as having a probable multiple personality dissociative disorder. Dr. Allison, on the other hand, opined that appellant did not have a multiple personality, but rather suffered from "possession syndrome," an atypical dissociative disorder which occurs when the person believes he is possessed by demons from an outside source. Drs. Rath and Allison concluded that appellant was legally insane at the time of the offense.

The findings of the defense doctors were disputed by the prosecution who called three psychiatrists. These doctors, Robert Flanagan, Frederick Hacker and Anthony Oliver, had also examined appellant. Dr. Hacker believed that appellant did not have the intent to kill at the time of the offense. He described appellant as an "emotionally immature and disturbed person." Dr. Oliver opined that appellant was a pathological liar and that his multiple personality was malingered. He also diagnosed appellant as being schizotypal and having a mixed personality disorder with antisocial components. Dr. Flanagan stated that appellant was legally sane. * * *

---

5. Several lay witnesses also testified about appellant's background. His wife Cookie stated that appellant sometimes called himself "Othello Mulet Metheen" and said he was from Greece. On a number of occasions, he also referred to himself as "Michael the Archangel." At those times, Cookie described appellant as being "dead serious." She also related that appellant had blacked out on several occasions.

Cookie's daughter Penny testified that appellant said his name was "Othello" sometimes and boasted that he knew many languages. She also stated that appellant had blacked out on a number of occasions.

Two employees of the Hordis Glass Company, who had previously worked with appellant, also testified on rebuttal. They described appellant as a quick-learner who regularly read books, magazines and newspapers. They never heard appellant call himself "Othello," "Joe" or "Michael."

The defense presented two lay witnesses on surrebuttal to corroborate the existence of multiple personalities. From ages 15 to 20, appellant lived with the family of Ella Mae Edwards. Mrs. Edwards testified that she believed appellant was a split personality. He once told her his full name was "Othello Mulet Metheen," that he had been in the Green Berets, and that he was employed as a hit man.

Ted Sanders, a county jail inmate who observed appellant's behavior during the period of the trial, described two incidents when appellant's behavior changed abruptly. On the first occasion, while a number of inmates were watching television, appellant suddenly attacked Sanders and threatened to kill him without provocation. Sanders described how appellant's eyes seemed to grow larger and his voice rougher. When Sanders subsequently mentioned the incident to appellant, he insisted that he had taken no part in it. The second incident occurred three weeks later, when appellant assaulted another inmate in a similar sudden, unprovoked fashion. Again, appellant assertedly could not recall the incident when it was brought to his attention.

C. Penalty Phase Evidence

Appellant was the only witness to testify at the penalty phase. He corroborated the earlier psychiatric testimony about "Othello." He maintained that he was unaware of killing Joyce, of inflicting any of the previously described "methods of discipline" upon the children, of ever talking to the police about the killing, or of attacking other inmates in the jail. Appellant stated that he loved Joyce and her mother, Cookie. He expressed sadness over Joyce's death.

Appellant recalled being sexually and physically abused and locked in a closet as a child. He recalled occasions in his life when he had memory lapses. Whenever he questioned "Othello" about these lapses, "Othello" would tell him it was none of his business. Appellant further testified that he did not believe in demons, but that he did believe in God. He asked for God's forgiveness for what his body had done and expressed his desire not to continue living if he had to coexist with "Othello."

At defense counsel's request, "Othello" emerged on the witness stand and testified before the jury. Unlike Melvin, "Othello" used profane language throughout his testimony. He stated that Melvin was his enemy, that he did not believe in God, and that he felt no sorrow for Joyce's death. He maintained that he was the devil's disciple and that he wanted the jury to kill Melvin. * * *

RALPH B. ALLISON, M.D.—THE POSSESSION
SYNDROME ON TRIAL

6 American Journal of Forensic Psychiatry 46 (1985), 48–52 [g]

[Dr. Allison's trial testimony is summarized in *Wade,* supra. In this article the author describes his pre-trial evaluation of Wade, identified here as "Leroy Jackson." In the article, Cookie, Wade's wife, is "Candy"; Joyce is "Darnell."]

The [defense] attorney called me when he felt he had heard enough to interject an insanity plea in the middle of the ongoing trial. Prior to my arrival, he contracted with a local forensic psychologist to examine Leroy, which he did the day before I came to town. I met with the psychologist and the attorney. The psychologist [reported] that Leroy could well have MPD [multiple personality disorder], as he had met "Othello Mulett Metheen," a possible alter-personality during the interview. While Leroy consistently claimed amnesia for the day of the crime plus the six days following, Othello readily admitted to having done the killing. I conducted my first interview with Leroy that evening, gathering all the history of dissociative episodes he could recall.

The following day, Saturday, March 13, 1982, the attorney and I conducted a videotaped interview with Leroy in the [attorney's] office for the purpose of being able to safely present evidence of Leroy's mental state to the court. The taping before noon was a recap of what Leroy had told me the night before, focusing on the several episodes prior to his arrest for which he claimed amnesia. These included three suicide attempts and a tonsillectomy. I then asked him to prepare to let out Othello after lunch, and he agreed, having been aware of Othello for years by virtue of his long conversations with him in the fields. Leroy insisted on being handcuffed behind his back, for our safety. Two deputies were also stationed at the door and window to prevent his escape from the office.

The afternoon taping was of Othello, who managed to twist his handcuffs under his buttocks and got his hands in front of him, where he banged the metal cuffs on the attorney's expensive table, trying to get them off. In a blustering, bragging fashion, he told of killing Darnell, though he would have preferred to have done in her mother, Candy, instead. He showed no remorse and indicated that Leroy had nothing to do with the crime, but he would kill him at a later date.

After Othello's confession, I asked to talk to Michael, the Archangel, but this was unsuccessful. When I tried the procedure used to persuade multiples to switch to a non-dangerous personality, I only succeeded in getting Leroy back. We then showed the videotape to Leroy, as he claimed complete amnesia for that part of the session.

The following Monday I testified that I could make only a provisional diagnosis of the MPD in this case, but I did consider him to be legally insane under current California law. I was unwilling to be definite in my diagnosis until I knew the origin of Othello. I felt that I needed to come back later for another series of interviews when I could pursue the questions that had been raised so far.

During the following month, both sides called in their best forensic psychiatrists and psychologists, nine in all. When I returned five weeks later I was able to read all the reports and discovered that there was a split verdict. Four experts said that the defendant was a multiple; four said he was mentally ill but not a multiple; one said he was faking the whole thing. I was to be the last psychiatrist to testify for the defense prior to submission of the case to the jury.

This trip I spent most of Saturday and Sunday (April 17–18, 1982) interviewing Leroy in the county jail. After meeting Leroy briefly I asked to talk to Othello, whom he promptly produced, as he had been produced for any examiner who had asked to talk to him. For the first time, Othello mentioned his son, Joe, so I asked to talk to him. When I met Joe I found an entity who claimed to be the same age as Leroy. He reported being the "snitch" who had told many of the previous examiners what had happened, while they thought they were talking to Leroy. He was willing to tell all about the events relating to the crimes, as well as Leroy's prior experiences, as he had been the former assistant to Othello in doing his evil deeds.

Joe claimed to be a spirit who had last had his own body as a boy in Aukland, New Zealand. He stated that he had fallen off a cliff at the age of 14 and died. He identified Othello as being Lucifer's agent and the one who had accepted the contract from the Council of 12 Archdemons to kill Leroy's wife, Candy. According to the Council, Candy had been backsliding in her participation in satanic worship services. After breakfast on the day of the crime, Othello took over the body from Leroy and began to threaten Candy by attacking her daughter. His message was, "Agree to be executed, or I'll kill Darnell. I'm knuckling under for nobody." His last threatening act toward Darnell was putting her in a duffle bag and then carrying her to the attic. When that failed to bring Candy around, Othello felt he had to kill somebody to fulfill the contract, so [h]e bashed Darnell's head into the wall, finally killing her.

When Darnell was pulled out of the attic, Joe lost awareness of what was happening. The next thing he remembered was hearing Othello's urgent instructions to run from the police. * * * As he sprinted away, he looked over his shoulder and saw the glint of gunmetal in the officers' hands. Deciding he wanted to stay alive, he turned and surrendered and was then told that Darnell had died. Prior to that time, he thought she was still alive. * * *

Joe explained the first appearance of Othello to Leroy, at age four. Leroy's divorced mother worked all day and left her children in the care of Jack, her brutal boyfriend. Jack locked Leroy in a closet while he sexually molested Leroy's sisters. Finally, neighbors called police who removed the children from the home, but they missed Leroy in the closet. His mother came home to find her children gone, a note from the police on the kitchen table and Leroy still hiding in the closet under the clothes hems. As Joe said, "A person feels like he has been mistreated and thrown around, sexually assaulted. This builds up and makes a four-year-old turn away. They said there is a God. How come you don't do something? He doesn't understand. Here's a male doll in a dark closet. Used it for a type of voodoo. He took it, talked to it as a friend and wished. He talked to the doll. Why was Jack doing what he was doing? How could he get back? He felt lonely, not many playmates. Othello came in from the outside and gave orders. Son of fire, water and ice."

Joe explained that archdemons are strongest on Wednesdays and Saturdays. (The killing took place on a Saturday.) That is why I came to see him on a Sunday, which was the strongest day of the week for Michael, the Archangel. This time when I asked to talk to Michael, I was successful, in spite of [interference] from Othello.

Here are his words: "I am Michael. I am a warrior. I've been with him five years now."

I asked why.

"For a young man who was born possessed with the evilness of Lucifer, for the life that was cast away, like the fire that burns away. Now the child is grown and the days are shorter. For then Othello exists. The battle continues till lives are taken. No more blood shall be stricken from the earth."

I asked, "Why didn't you prevent the murder?"

"You have twelve demons who exist. I don't win every battle that exists."

I asked, "Did Leroy make you?"

"He didn't make me."

I asked, "Where are you?"

"Like an angel, as in the Bible, I am in that rank."

The next day in court, Leroy was in legal chains and handcuffs since Othello was determined to come out and give a statement, invited or not. He did take over the body, as manifested with intense shuffling and muttering, in contrast to Leroy's usual quiet and passive behavior. In my testimony I concluded that Leroy Jackson [suffered from] * * * the Possession Syndrome, an Atypical Dissociative Disorder. My theory was that what we had observed was a creation of Leroy's unconscious mind and was simply a dramatic picture of what he wished to be and do but could not see as himself.

Following my testimony, the jury found him guilty of first degree murder with special circumstances. During the penalty phase, Othello was allowed to testify. He told the all white "honky jury" that he didn't care what they said since Leroy was going to die by his, Othello's, hand that December on his twin son's birthday. Then he, Othello, would move on to another living body.

Notes and Questions

1. If you had been appointed to represent Wade, who was indigent, would you have relied exclusively on the defense of insanity?

2. Based on what you know, if you had been a juror, would you have found Wade insane under the ALI insanity standard? Under *M'Naghten? Durham?* The federal definition of insanity (p. 582 supra)? Under Judge Bazelon's proposed "justly responsible" test (p. 583 supra)? Which of these standards, if any, comes closest to permitting the result you believe is most sensible in this case?

3. *Who must be insane in a multiple-personality case?* In answering Note 2, is the issue whether Wade, when he was "himself," knew right from wrong and/or could conform his conduct to the requirements of the law? Or, should the issue be whether Wade could have prevented Othello from taking control of his mind and body? Or, is the question whether *Othello* knew right from wrong and could control his conduct? Or, is it meaningless to treat Wade as if a person's identity could be segmented in this way?

In this regard, appraise United States v. Denny–Shaffer, 2 F.3d 999 (10th Cir.1993). The defendant was charged with kidnapping an infant from a hospital nursery in New Mexico and taking him to Texas and, later, to Minnesota. The court summarized the psychiatric testimony:

> Dr. Conroy [the expert for the government] and Dr. McCarty [the defense's expert] * * * agreed that, at the time of the kidnapping, defendant was suffering from MPD and that her dominant or host personality, "Gidget," did not consciously participate in the abduction. Neither expert, however, could establish that the alter personality in control of defendant at the time of the offense ["Rina" and, perhaps, "Bridget"] was legally insane * * *. * * *
>
> From these underlying conclusions, Dr. Conroy's report stated that there were two possible views on legal responsibility: (1) that in light of the presence of a host personality and several alter personalities, if the [insanity] statute means that all alters, or at least the host personality, must be fully aware of the nature, quality, and wrongfulness of an act, then Denny–Shaffer was not responsible at the time of the abduction; and (2) on the other hand, if an MPD victim is viewed as a single individual with varying personality components, and not divided as separate people, the issue changes; in such a case the question would be whether the personality in control at the time of the offense was unable to understand the nature, quality, and wrongfulness of her acts. If this is the proper interpretation of the statute, then the defendant did suffer from a significant mental illness, but it was not such as to render her unable to understand the nature, quality, and wrongfulness of her acts.
>
> Dr. McCarty, on the other hand, was unable to render an opinion one way or another about the controlling alter or alters' being able to appreciate the nature and quality or wrongfulness of their conduct.

Id. at 1008.

The trial court ruled that the second view of legal responsibility outlined by Dr. Conroy applied, i.e., that the question is whether the alter personality in control at the time of the offense satisfies the federal definition of insanity. As a consequence the trial court held that there was insufficient evidence to raise the insanity defense. On appeal, the Tenth Circuit reviewed MPD law:

> Decisions regarding proper construction of insanity defense statutes where MPD was involved are not numerous. We have been unable to find any federal case where such a defense involving MPD was asserted * * *. Moreover, the state cases involving this mental disorder are few in number and of limited assistance because of the variance in the nature of the insanity defenses in the states.
>
> The government relies on *State of Ohio v. Grimsley,* 3 Ohio App.3d 265, 444 N.E.2d 1071 (1982), and its progeny. There the argument was made that the defendant's MPD state was such that she was not acting consciously or voluntarily at the time of the offense of driving under the influence of alcohol and could not be guilty. The court held that the defense failed. The claim that the defendant was dissociated from her primary to a secondary personality and thus was not acting consciously or voluntarily was rejected as not supported by the evidence. Without analysis, the court said there was only one person driving and one person accused of drunken driving and that the "evidence failed to demonstrate that Jennifer [the alter] was unconscious or otherwise acting involuntarily." * * *
>
> The government also relies on *State of Hawaii v. Rodrigues,* 67 Haw. 70, 679 P.2d 615 (1984). * * *
>
> * * * The statement of the [*Rodrigues*] court relied on by the government was that "recent cases dealing with the multiple personality defense have held it is immaterial whether the defendant was in one state of consciousness or another, so long as in the personality then controlling the behavior, the defendant was conscious and his or her actions were a product of his or her own volition." [h]

Denny–Shaffer, 2 F.3d at 1017–18.

The appellate court rejected *Grimsley* and *Rodrigues* as "unpersuasive," reasoning instead as follows:

> Our criminal justice system punishes those it convicts for many reasons, chief among them being retribution against the criminal, deterrence of future crimes, and rehabilitation of the criminal. However, we hold accountable only those who are morally culpable for their conduct * * *. * * *
>
> * * * Whatever the specific formulation of the defense has been throughout history, it has always been the case that the law has been loath to assign criminal responsibility to an actor who was unable, at the

---

h. See also Kirkland v. State, 166 Ga. App. 478, 480, 304 S.E.2d 561, 564 (1983): "[W]e will not begin to parcel criminal ac- countability out among the various inhabit- ants of the mind."

time he or she committed the crime, to know either what was being done or that it was wrong. This basic tenet has apparently been entirely unaffected by advances in medicine or psychology. * * *

The defendant argues that the judge erred in his ruling construing [the federal insanity statute]. She maintains that the proof was sufficient to raise a submissible insanity defense with a reasonable and proper interpretation of the Act. We agree. We are convinced that the proof was sufficient * * * for the trier of fact to find that the defendant had shown by clear and convincing evidence that * * * she was not guilty by reason of insanity since her dominant or host personality was neither aware of nor in control of the commission of the offense and thus was unable to appreciate the nature and quality or wrongfulness of the conduct which the alter or alters carried out. * * *

Here there was substantial evidence presented by the defendant that the defendant's host or dominant personality was unaware there was to be an abduction by an alter personality and was not capable of preventing it. Thus not only was the host personality unable to appreciate the nature of the abduction, she did not even grasp that it was being committed. Yet the government would have us hold that, because one or more of the alter personalities knew what was happening and the experts are unable to say that those personalities could not appreciate the nature and quality or wrongfulness of the acts, the defense is wholly unavailable to Denny–Shaffer.

We find no support for such a restrictive interpretation in the wording of [the insanity statute] or in the legislative history. * * *

Our conclusion is further supported by the principle that penal statutes are to be strictly construed against the government. * * *

Id. at 1012–14. Are you persuaded?

The *Denny–Shaffer* court confronted an additional problem. Kidnapping is a continuing offense, i.e. even if an alter personality seized the infant, the defendant could be convicted of the crime if the host personality later became aware of the crime and unlawfully retained the child. The court observed:

There is evidence in the record * * * which could support inferences that the defendant violated [the kidnapping statute] while the host or dominant personality was active * * *. * * * [W]e should consider the evidence as to actions in Texas and Minnesota as a basis for inferences that the host personality became aware of the wrongfulness of confining and holding the baby after the host learned that it was in possession of the child. * * *

On the other hand, there is * * * expert testimony by Dr. McCarty that MPD victims tend to cover up acts committed by their alters.[24]

---

24. Dr. McCarty testified that one of the effects of MPD is to cause the host personality to try to "cover for" or ignore the actions of the alters.

The host personality generally does not know about the existence of the alters.

This leads * * * to the host actively denying evidence of the existence of alters, and may even cause the host to flee from treatment when confronted with evidence of alters. What the MPD victim does know is that, like Denny–Shaffer, they blank out or

This proof, * * * and the proof discussed earlier of the severity of this MPD case, all raised a question of fact on the insanity defense for the jury. We are convinced that the substantial showing of the disorder in defendant's mental perceptions presented a genuine issue whether the defendant's host or dominant personality * * * was unable to appreciate the nature and quality or wrongfulness of her acts during the subsequent confinement and holding of the child. * * *

We note that several of the actions in question before and after the abduction of the infant here were arguably steps that aided or abetted the accomplishment of the kidnapping. This might suggest that the host personality could be found liable for aiding or abetting the alter or alters who abducted the child. Since the case is to be remanded for a new trial, we will note that no aiding and abetting theory in these circumstances should be submitted to the jury. "One must ... aid or abet someone else to commit a substantive offense. One cannot aid or abet himself." *United States v. Martin,* 747 F.2d 1404, 1407 (11th Cir.1984). We are not persuaded that in determining liability for aiding and abetting, alter personalities should be recognized as distinct legal persons, with independent status under the criminal laws, who may be aided and abetted.

Id. at 1019–20.

Regarding the issues raised in this Note, see Elyn R. Saks, *Multiple Personality Disorder and Criminal Responsibility,* 25 U.C. Davis L.Rev. 383 (1992); Michael S. Moore, Law and Psychiatry: Rethinking the Relationship 387–415 (1984).

4. *Did Wade's lawyer adequately represent his client?* A defendant has a constitutional right to competent representation. Strickland v. Washington, 466 U.S. 668, 104 S.Ct. 2052, 80 L.Ed.2d 674 (1984). Moreover, as a matter of professional ethics, as well as constitutional law, a criminal defense lawyer must act in the best interests of her client. The American Bar Association's Model Code of Professional Responsibility (1969), EC [Ethical Consideration] 7–1 provides: "The duty of a lawyer, both to his client and to the legal system, is to represent his client zealously within the bounds of the law * * *."

California Supreme Court Chief Justice Rose Bird, herself once a public defender, was sharply critical of Melvin Wade's trial counsel:

Counsel began his guilt phase closing argument by informing the jury, for no apparent good reason, that he had been appointed by the court to represent appellant. He explained that the "court is not in the same hierarchy as, say the service, for instance, where if a general tells you and a captain to do something, or if you're [*sic*] admiral tells you as a commander to do something, or as an enlisted person you say, 'Yes, sir,' or 'Aye-aye.' Courts don't carry that much weight. But it behooves an attorney as one of his duties to, if a court requests him to [do]

lose time and are later accused of doing things they deny having done. When they are confronted with such situations as "'waking up' in the middle of conversa-

tions [with] people whom they do not know," they simply do not know what to think and attempt to cover up to avoid others discovering their "problems."

something, in my opinion it's his ethical duty to accept the appointment." * * *

* * * Throughout the rest of the argument counsel placed his concern with preserving his own image as a responsible lawyer and good citizen above his duty to advocate on behalf of his client. This is not only evident from counsel's repeated allusions to his appointed status, but from the remarks that "[t]here's nothing that *I* have done that *I* feel ashamed of with respect to the defense of this case," and "there's nothing that *I* have done to in any way serve to make a mockery of that child's death." (Emphasis added.)

Other statements confirm the view that counsel was more concerned with distancing himself from his client than with representing him. "And even though it may have been wiser for me professionally to turn down this kind of a case and to better serve my interests as an attorney or as a human being to turn down this case, *it was my duty to take on the defense of a defenseless person.*" (Emphasis added.) "It is your duty as a juror individually to look at the facts in the case. Just as it is my duty as an attorney not to be swayed by public feeling or opinion *against me* for representing Melvin Meffery Wade." (Emphasis added.)

Several times, counsel indicated that he had presented defense evidence out of duty rather than conviction. "But it is my duty as an attorney, if doctors present evidence to me that indicates that the defendant that *I'm charged with representing* has a mental disease or mental defect, I have no alternative but to present that issue to you ladies and gentlemen of the jury. I can't turn my back on that issue, whether *I'm accused of contriving the defense,* whether *I'm accused of staging the defense,* or *I'm the director and producer of the defense. As my ethical duty* I must present that issue for your consideration." (Emphasis added.) * * *

Counsel then attempted to deny the prosecutor's charge that the defense was "sensational." Instead of simply stating this point, he went further and told the jury that *"[i]t's a pitiful defense when you say that your client is insane.* And that's all we're saying in this case. * * * "* (Emphasis added.) * * *

Counsel further told how his wife shared his revulsion. She opposed his involvement in the case, he related, and "had some derogatory remark to make about it, said I was defending him. *I corrected her saying that I was representing him.* And she asked me not to confuse her with any of my legalisms. [¶] As the conversation continued she started to cry, and she informed me that [she] had read an account in the newspaper about how the family [of] Irabell [Cookie] Strong needed money for food and lodging and whatever. *But she didn't send any money and she informed me that she sent my money, and a sizable sum of it, to buy flowers to decorate the grave of that little thing, as she put it, because she could not see Joyce Toliver going to her grave without some flowers* . . . ." (Emphasis added.) * * *

As though counsel's performance at [the guilt phase was] not enough, counsel compounded his errors and omissions in his penalty phase closing. There, he virtually asked the jury to return a death sentence, closing with these words: "... considering the disorder, the emotional disturbance that the evidence has suggested to you by way of the physicians in this case and the psychologists, I don't think that Melvin Wade, Melvin Meffery Wade, can actually, can be said to lose this case. [¶] As has been expressed to me by Melvin on many occasions, he can't live with that beast from within any longer and *if in your wisdom you think the appropriate punishment is death, you may be also giving an escape once again by analogy the gift of life to Melvin Meffery Wade to be free from his horror that he and only he knows so well.*" (Emphasis added.) It is unlikely that a defense attorney who argues death as "an escape" and "the gift of life" for his client had any overall tactical purpose in mind.

People v. Wade, 43 Cal.3d 366, 233 Cal.Rptr. 48, 61–62, 66, 729 P.2d 239, 252–53, 257 (1987) (dissenting opinion).

Do you believe that Wade's attorney violated his ethical responsibilities to his client? Or, do you agree with the majority opinion in *Wade*:

> [T]rial counsel, faced with defending an appalling crime and responding to the prosecutor's pointed suggestions of a fabricated defense, made a tactical choice to candidly admit his client's guilt, acknowledge the heinous nature of the offense, and concentrate upon the theory that appellant indeed was plagued with multiple personalities or dissociative disorders, and was insane or incapable of forming the requisite criminal intent when the offense was committed. The fact that this argument ultimately failed is no negative reflection upon counsel's competence.

Id. at 53, 729 P.2d at 244.

5. *Postscript to Wade.* Dr. Allison met with "Leroy Jackson" on Death Row after his conviction:

> Two years after his conviction, * * * I conducted a four-hour interview with Leroy in a locked contact booth in the prison's visiting area. Leroy arrived, appearing cheerful, sporting a mustache and reading glasses. The interview lasted four hours. During this time I also reviewed matters with Othello and Joe, both of whom appeared with the cooperation of Leroy. No one knew what had happened to Archangel Michael, and he did not make an appearance at that time. Overall, there seemed to be no change in the balance of forces I had observed during the trial, since three of the entities were still in attendance and had been active during the previous years of incarceration.

> Leroy was very proud to report that he had learned to read, write and type in prison. * * *

> The patient is getting along well with all staff and the civilized inmates, but some of the inmates do know him as Othello. He stays in his cell most of the time since he cannot risk letting Othello out among other inmates. He is still communicating with Othello regularly, but, as he says, "on my own terms." Leroy is still experiencing amnesic episodes. Othello did not execute him on his son's birthday in December, 1982, as threatened in court, however Leroy did awaken in his cell

with multiple bleeding slash wounds of his right forearm on January 13, 1984 and required hospitalization. Leroy believes that Othello is trying to tear away at his body, bit by bit. He exhibited to me the 20 gash wound scars on his right inner forearm.

Leroy made no requests for me to intervene in any way in his situation. He reiterated orally what he had earlier written to me: "I still have this problem and all I want is to die; then I won't have to live like this."

When I asked Leroy to let me talk to Othello, he reluctantly agreed but stalled as long as he could. Finally, his face became expressionless with his eyes wide open for a minute. Then, the voice I knew to be Othello's came forth, with its usual gutter language, in contrast to Leroy's polite English. * * *

It was apparent to me, now that Othello was out, that he would prefer to stay out, but that was not to my liking. I did not dare let him out into the visiting area where he could easily ruin Leroy's good reputation with the correctional officers. Also, I was locked into this steel and plexiglass booth and had no way to leave if Othello should get angry with me. I asked him to let Joe come out for his turn, but he was not eager to give way to that traitor, and I had to devise a strategy to get him to leave on his own accord when I was done with him. * * *

* * * I held a long conversation with Joe about current events. His job is to protect the body from harm and to do all he can to get a better deal for Leroy. Although he has no hope that Leroy can be cured of his "cancer" of 28 years, he is the entity who meets with the defense attorneys to develop legal strategies for further hearings on Leroy's case. * * *

When Leroy awoke he wondered why he had not been wearing his glasses. (Neither Othello nor Joe needs glasses.) [i] * * * A friendly correctional officer came by and, like friendly associates, they gleefully waved to each other. After locating an officer who would unlock the door, I said farewell and returned to the outside world.

Ralph B. Allison, *The Possession Syndrome on Trial,* 6 Am.J.Forens. Psychiatry 46, 53–58 (1985).[j]

     6. *Postscript to the postscript.* In *Wade,* the state supreme court voted, 4–3, to affirm the defendant's conviction for first-degree murder. However, by a similar vote, 4–3, it overturned Wade's death sentence because of an incorrect instruction to the jury during the penalty phase.

---

i. In MPD cases "personalities can be so different that the differences may show up through physical symptoms. * * * [D]ifferent alters often require different eyeglass prescriptions. Different personalities may speak different languages, be different-handed, respond differently to physical tests such as electroencephalograms (EEGs) and Galvanic Skin Response tests, respond differently to medications, and score differ-ently on psychological tests such as Rorschach tests and MMPIs (Minnesota Multiphasic Personality Inventories). See Elyn R. Saks, *Multiple Personality Disorder and Criminal Responsibility,* 25 U.C. Davis L.Rev. 383, 396–97 & nn. 44–45 (1992)." U.S. v. Denny–Shaffer, 2 F.3d 999, 1009 n. 8 (10th Cir.1993).

     j. See footnote g (p. 620 supra).

After the death sentence was reversed, the prosecutor petitioned the state supreme court to rehear the case. Petitions of this sort are normally denied, but in the interim, Chief Justice Bird and two other members of the court were defeated in their re-election bids. After the governor appointed their replacements, the "new" court voted to rehear the matter. This time it voted 6–1 to affirm the judgment of guilt and the death sentence. People v. Wade, 44 Cal.3d 975, 244 Cal.Rptr. 905, 750 P.2d 794 (1988).

Wade's new lawyers filed a petition for a writ of *habeas corpus* in the federal district court, in which they alleged 17 constitutional grounds for overturning the conviction or death sentence. One stated basis was that Wade was denied effective assistance of counsel at trial.

On June 22, 1989, nineteen hours before Wade was scheduled to go to the gas chamber, District Judge Manuel Real granted a stay of execution in order to consider Wade's federal petition. Kim Murphy, *Killer Gets Stay With 19½ Hours Left to Live,* Los Angeles Times, June 23, 1989, pt. 2, at 3. On October 18, 1990, however, Judge Real denied the petition. He ruled that none of the grounds for reversal was supported by credible evidence. Wade v. Vasquez, 752 F.Supp. 931 (C.D.Cal.1990).

Wade's lawyers appealed the denial of the petition to the Ninth Circuit of the United States Court of Appeals. At oral arguments, the judges appeared interested in the ineffective assistance of counsel claim. One member of the three-judge panel expressed concern that Wade's trial lawyer had called Dr. Allison as a witness, although the psychiatrist did not believe that Wade suffered from MPD.[k] Another judge remarked that defense counsel's penalty phase closing argument sounded like a call for the death penalty. Richard Barbieri, *After Mason, Few Prisoners Near Execution in California,* The Recorder, Aug. 24, 1993, at 1.

As this casebook goes to press, the Ninth Circuit panel has not announced its ruling on Wade's petition. If Wade's death sentence is affirmed, he is near the top of the execution list on California's heavily populated Death Row. Katherine Bishop, *No Rush to More California Executions,* New York Times, April 27, 1992, at B10.

e. *"Guilty but Mentally Ill" Verdict*

A growing number of states now permit the factfinder to return a verdict of "guilty but mentally ill" (GBMI) in any case in which it could return a verdict of "not guilty by reason of insanity" (NGRI). E.g., Mich.Comp.Law Ann. § 768.36(3) (1991); N.M.Stat.Ann. § 31–9–4 (1992); Utah Code Ann. 77–13–1 (1990). A GBMI verdict is allowed if the prosecutor proves beyond a reasonable doubt all of the elements of the crime, no defenses (including insanity) are proven, and the defendant suffers from a mental illness.

Under the prototypical Michigan system, a GBMI-verdict defendant receives a sentence suitable for one who is found guilty of the offense for

---

k. Since Dr. Allison testified that he believed that Wade was insane, albeit as a result of "possession syndrome," should Wade's counsel be faulted for calling him to the stand?

which she has been convicted. Upon sentencing, however, the defendant is evaluated to determine if psychiatric treatment is indicated. If it is, care may be provided in the prison or a mental health facility. If treatment is finished before the defendant's sentence of imprisonment is completed, the inmate is returned to the prison's jurisdiction to serve the balance of the sentence.

According to one observer, "[t]he verdict has been the target of virtually-unanimous academic criticism," both on constitutional and policy grounds. Michael L. Perlin, *Unpacking the Myths: The Symbolism Mythology of Insanity Defense Jurisprudence,* 40 Case West.Res. L.Rev. 599, 637 n. 166 (1989); see Roger George Frey, Note, *The Guilty But Mentally Ill Verdict and Due Process,* 92 Yale L.J. 475 (1983); but see Ira Mickenberg, *A Pleasant Surprise: The Guilty But Mentally Ill Verdict Has Both Succeeded In Its Own Right and Successfully Preserved the Traditional Role of the Insanity Defense,* 55 U.Cin.L.Rev. 943 (1987) (supporting the defense). However, despite criticisms, GBMI laws have withstood constitutional attack. See Debra T. Landis, *"Guilty But Mentally Ill" Statutes: Validity and Construction,* 71 A.L.R.4th 702 (1992).

Studies of jury verdicts in Michigan indicate that implementation of the GBMI law did not result in a reduction of NGRI verdicts in that state. E.g., Gare A. Smith & James A. Hall, *Evaluating Michigan's Guilty But Mentally Ill Verdict: An Empirical Study,* 16 U.Mich.J.L.Ref. 77 (1982); Lynn W. Blunt & Harley Stock, *"Guilty But Mentally Ill": An Alternative Verdict,* 3 Behav. Sci. & Law 49 (1985). However, in Pennsylvania the number of successful insanity pleas dropped significantly after the GBMI verdict was instituted. R.D. Mackay & Jerry Kopelman, *The Operation of the "Guilty But Mentally Ill" Verdict in Pennsylvania,* 16 J. Psychiatry & Law 247 (Summer, 1988). Also, studies of mock juries suggest that the GBMI option may reduce markedly the number of psychotic defendants found NGRI. Caton F. Roberts, Stephen L. Golding, & Frank D. Fincham, *Implicit Theories of Criminal Responsibility,* 11 Law & Hum. Behav. 207 (1987).

f. Execution of the Insane

The Supreme Court held in Ford v. Wainwright, 477 U.S. 399, 106 S.Ct. 2595, 91 L.Ed.2d 335 (1986), that the Eighth Amendment proscription on cruel and unusual punishment prohibits a state from imposing the death penalty upon a person who is insane at the time of execution. Although the Court did not define the term "insane" in this context, Justice Marshall wrote:

> The bar against executing a prisoner who has lost his sanity bears impressive historical credentials; the practice consistently has been branded "savage and inhuman." 4 W. Blackstone, Commentaries * 24–* 25. * * *

As is often true of common-law principles, the reasons for the rule are less sure and less uniform that the rule itself. One explanation is that the execution of an insane person simply offends humanity; another, that it provides no example to others and thus contributes nothing to whatever deterrence value is intended to be served by capital punishment. Other commentators postulate religious underpinnings: that it is uncharitable to dispatch an offender "into another world, when he is not of a capacity fit himself for it." It is also said that execution serves no purpose in these cases because madness is its own punishment * * *. More recent commentators opine that the community's quest for "retribution" * * * is not served by execution of an insane person, which has a "lesser value" than that of the crime for which he is to be punished. Unanimity of rationale, therefore, we do not find. "But whatever the reason of the law is, it is plain the law is so."

Id. at 406–08, 106 S.Ct. at 2600–01, 91 L.Ed.2d at 344–45.

Do any of these justifications persuade you? For purposes of this rule, how should a court define "insane"? Is it constitutional to execute a person found to be "guilty but mentally ill"? See Sanders v. State, 585 A.2d 117 (Del.1990); State v. Wilson, 306 S.C. 498, 413 S.E.2d 19 (1992); see Anne S. Emanuel, *Guilty But Mentally Ill Verdicts and the Death Penalty: An Eighth Amendment Analysis,* 68 N.C.L.Rev. 37 (1989).

5. DIMINISHED CAPACITY

STEPHEN J. MORSE—UNDIMINISHED CONFUSION IN DIMINISHED CAPACITY

75 Journal of Criminal Law & Criminology 1 (1984), 1, 5–7, 20–21

The diminished capacity doctrine allows a criminal defendant to introduce evidence of mental abnormality at trial either to negate a mental element of the crime charged, thereby exonerating the defendant of that charge, or to reduce the degree of crime for which the defendant may be convicted, even if the defendant's conduct satisfied all the formal elements of a higher offense. The first variant of diminished capacity, which I shall refer to as the "mens rea" variant, is the dominant approach in the United States. The second, which I shall refer to as the "partial responsibility" variant, is the rule in Great Britain and in indirect form has been adopted in a substantial number of American jurisdictions. * * *

A. THE MENS REA VARIANT

The prosecution always bears the burden of proving beyond a reasonable doubt its prima facie case, the definitional elements necessary to find the defendant guilty of the crime charged or lesser included offenses.[13] Cases of strict liability aside, all crimes include a mental element, a mens rea, that the prosecution must prove. If the prosecu-

---

13. *In re* Winship, 397 U.S. 358, 364 (1970).

tion fails to carry its persuasion burden on a requisite mental element, the defendant must be acquitted of any crime that includes such an element in its definition. As a matter of constitutional law, the defendant is entitled to introduce competent and relevant evidence to disprove any element of any crime charged subject to few and limited exceptions.

In light of these elementary principles of criminal law, it is clear that the mens rea variant of diminished capacity is not a separate defense that deserves to be called "diminished capacity" or any other name connoting that it is some sort of special, affirmative defense. The defendant is simply introducing evidence, in this case evidence of mental abnormality, to make the following claim: "I did not commit the crime charged because I did not possess the requisite mens rea." * * * Further, a defendant claiming no mens rea because of mental disorder is not asserting some lesser form of legal insanity, that is, he is not claiming that he is partially or less responsible for the crime charged. Rather, the defendant is straightforwardly denying the prosecution's prima facie case by attempting to cast doubt on the prosecution's claim that a requisite mental element was present at the time of the offense. He is claiming that he is not guilty of that crime at all, although he may be guilty of a lesser crime if all the elements of the latter are proven. It is as if, for example, a defendant charged with murder on an intent-to-kill theory pleads not guilty on the ground that he thought he was shooting at a tree and therefore lacked the requisite intent to kill.

The moral logic of the mens rea variant is as compelling and straightforward as the technical logic. In our system of criminal justice, culpability is dependent upon a finding of both an act *and* a requisite mental state. Moreover, culpability for the same act varies according to the accompanying mental state. * * * A defendant who lacks a required element is not blameworthy for an offense that includes that element, and it would be unjust as well as unconstitutional to punish him for it.

Many courts and legislatures have been convinced of the fundamental fairness and consequent necessity of allowing defendants to attempt to cast doubt on the prosecution's case using evidence of mental abnormality,[17] but they have usually placed illogical limitations on the defendant's ability to do so. A smaller number of courts and legislatures have refused to permit the admission of any evidence of mental abnormality, except on the issue of legal insanity.[19] * * *

B. THE PARTIAL RESPONSIBILITY VARIANT

Partial responsibility is a form of lesser legal insanity: The defendant is claiming that, as a result of mental abnormality, he is not fully responsible for the crime proven against him. Even if the technical

---

17. The Model Penal Code was an early proponent of this view. Model Penal Code § 4.02.

19. * * * Unfortunately, courts constantly confuse partial responsibility with the mens rea variant and then reject the mens rea variant on the ground that the insanity defense is the only doctrine that considers nonresponsibility caused by mental abnormality.

elements of an offense are satisfied, the defendant is less culpable and should be convicted of a lesser crime, or, at least, should be punished less severely. * * *

The rationales for holding a defendant partially responsible and for excusing him by reason of insanity differ only in degree. The preconditions for moral and legal responsibility are, *inter alia,* that the actor is reasonably rational and in control of his actions. Actors, such as small children, who lack reasonable cognitive or volitional capacity through no fault of their own may be dangerous, but are not considered fully responsible as moral agents. This basic intuition about the way cognitive and volitional capacity relate to responsibility is tracked by the insanity defense tests * * *.

Although the law draws a bright line for legal responsibility, human cognitive and volitional capacities and behaviors are clearly distributed along a very lengthy continuum of competence. All legally sane defendants will not be equally rational or equally in possession of self-control at the time of the prohibited act. When a legally sane defendant has impaired rationality or self-control because of mental abnormality—a cause he is allegedly unable to control—an argument for some form of lessened responsibility arises. * * *

In * * * American law, partial responsibility has been adopted in [three] basic forms: (1) * * * the "extreme emotional disturbance" doctrine promulgated in the Model Penal Code and now adopted in a substantial number of American jurisdictions; [(2)] de facto partial responsibility adopted in the guise of interpreting mens rea elements; and [(3)] the use of mental disorder to reduce sentences.

CHESTNUT v. STATE

Supreme Court of Florida, 1989.
538 So.2d 820.

GRIMES, JUSTICE.

* * * The district court certified the following question as one of great public importance:

Is evidence of an abnormal mental condition not constituting legal insanity admissible for the purpose of proving either that the accused could not or did not entertain the specific intent or state of mind essential to proof of the offense, in order to determine whether the crime charged, or a lesser degree thereof, was in fact committed?

* * * We answer the question in the negative.

Chestnut and two codefendants * * * robbed and killed the victim * * * as the result of a robbery/murder scheme. * * *

The state filed a pretrial motion seeking to prohibit anticipated testimony by defense witnesses who would present evidence concerning appellant's mental condition below that standard recognized by the *M'Naghten* rule. The trial court granted the state's motion finding that

" 'absent an insanity plea, expert testimony as to mental status, especially when offered to bolster an affirmative defense would be improper in and of itself since it would only tend to confuse the jury.' "

At trial, counsel proffered expert testimony seeking to establish that Chestnut did not have the mental state required for premeditated first-degree murder. The proffered testimony revealed that Chestnut's intelligence was in the lowest five percent of the general population. Further, it showed that, several years earlier, appellant was kicked in the head by a bull, sustaining a fractured skull and brain damage which caused a posttraumatic seizure disorder that required medication. Chestnut also proffered evidence that he has diminished mental capacity with moderate impairment of verbal memory and has a passive personality which causes him to avoid physical confrontation; as a result, he is easily led and manipulated. * * *

The issue presented by this case is not a new one. In his article entitled "Psychiatric Evidence in Criminal Cases for Purposes Other Than the Defense of Insanity," Professor Lewin explains:

> Partial responsibility has been recognized for at least 100 years but it was not until the late 1950's that the Supreme Court of California in a series of decisions promulgated the modern concept and excited the imaginations of forensic psychiatrists, behavioral scientists and related scholars. Simply stated, the theory is that if because of mental disease or defect a defendant cannot form the specific state of mind required as an essential element of a crime, he may be convicted only of a lower grade of the offense not requiring that particular mental element. For example, if D is charged with the premeditated slaying of V, partial responsibility would enable a psychiatrist to testify that a mental disease interfered with D's capacity to formulate a plan. Thus a jury could find that D acted impulsively and without premeditation and therefore find D guilty of a lesser grade of homicide. The defense is thus available to reduce first degree murder requiring the specific intent elements of deliberation, premeditation and intent to kill to second degree murder, or even to manslaughter. Although generally applied to first degree murder cases, it is in theory applicable to any crime requiring proof of a specific intent, such as larceny or robbery.

26 Syracuse L.Rev. 1051, 1054–55 (1975). * * *

Following the lead of California, approximately one-half the states and federal jurisdictions now approve the defense. Yet, it was recently noted in *State v. Wilcox,* 70 Ohio St.2d 182, 186, 436 N.E.2d 523, 525 (1982):

> At this juncture, however, it appears that enthusiasm for the diminished capacity defense is on the wane and that there is, if anything, a developing movement away from diminished capacity although the authorities at this point are still quite mixed in their views. See . . . generally, Annotation, 22 A.L.R.3d 1223.

It is also clear that a state is not constitutionally compelled to recognize the doctrine of diminished capacity.

The adoption of the principle of diminished capacity has usually been justified on the premise that mentally deficient persons should be treated in the same manner as intoxicated persons. *See United States v. Brawner,* 471 F.2d 969 (D.C.Cir.1972). However, several recent cases have sharply rejected this analogy. Thus, in *Bethea v. United States,* 365 A.2d 64, 88 (D.C.App.1976), the court said:

> We recognize that there are exceptions to the basic principle that all individuals are presumed to have a similar capacity for mens rea. The rule that evidence of intoxication may be employed to demonstrate the absence of specific intent figured prominently in the *Brawner* court's advocacy of consistency in the treatment of expert evidence of mental impairment. The asserted analogy is flawed, however, by the fact that there are significant evidentiary distinctions between psychiatric abnormality and the recognized incapacitating circumstances. Unlike the notion of partial or relative insanity, conditions such as intoxication, medication, epilepsy, infancy, or senility are, in varying degrees, susceptible to quantification or objective demonstration, and to lay understanding. * * *

In the same vein, the court in *State v. Wilcox* said:

> It takes no great expertise for jurors to determine whether an accused was " 'so intoxicated as to be mentally unable to intend anything (unconscious),' " ... whereas the ability to assimilate and apply the finely differentiated psychiatric concepts associated with diminished capacity demands a sophistication (or as critics would maintain a sophistic bent) that jurors (and officers of the court) ordinarily have not developed. We are convinced as was the *Bethea* court, that these "significant evidentiary distinctions" preclude treating diminished capacity and voluntary intoxication as functional equivalents for purposes of partial exculpation from criminal responsibility.

The adverse consequences of adopting the defense of diminished capacity were recognized by the court in *Bethea v. United States:*

> Under the present statutory scheme, a successful plea of insanity avoids a conviction, but confronts the accused with the very real possibility of prolonged therapeutic confinement. If, however, psychiatric testimony were generally admissible to cast a reasonable doubt upon whatever degree of mens rea was necessary for the charged offense, thus resulting in outright acquittal, there would be scant reason indeed for a defendant to risk such confinement by arguing the greater form of mental deficiency. Thus, quite apart from the argument that the diminished capacity doctrine would result in a considerably greater likelihood of acquittal for those who by traditional standards would be held responsible, the future safety of the offender as well as the community would be jeopardized by the possibility that one who is genuinely dangerous might obtain his

complete freedom merely by applying his psychiatric evidence to the threshold issue of intent.

To permit the defense of diminished capacity would invite arbitrary applications of the law because of the nebulous distinction between specific and general intent crimes. Moreover, a recognition of the defense would open the door to consequences which could seriously affect our society. In a case of first-degree premeditated murder,* a finding of diminished mental capacity would serve to reduce the conviction to a lesser homicide. However, in the case of robbery, which was held to be a specific intent crime * * *, the application of diminished capacity could result in an absolute acquittal of any crime whatsoever. This is so because the only necessarily lesser included offense of robbery is petit theft and that, too, is a specific intent crime. * * * Since burglary is also a specific intent crime, one acquitted of that offense could only be convicted, if at all, of trespass. Unlike the case where one is found not guilty by reason of insanity, there would be no authority to commit these persons for treatment except through the use of civil remedies and its concomitant burdens. * * *

We acknowledge the cogent reasons expressed in *Bethea* for declining to adopt the defense of diminished capacity:

> The concept of insanity is simply a device the law employs to define the outer limits of that segment of the general population to whom these presumptions concerning the capacity for criminal intent shall not be applied. The line between the sane and the insane for the purposes of criminal adjudication is not drawn because for one group the actual existence of the necessary mental state (or lack thereof) can be determined with any greater certainty, but rather because those whom the law declares insane are demonstrably so aberrational in their psychiatric characteristics that we choose to make the assumption that they are incapable of possessing the specified state of mind. Within the range of individuals who are not "insane," the law does not recognize the readily demonstrable fact that as between individual criminal defendants the nature and development of their mental capabilities may vary greatly.... By contradicting the presumptions inherent in the doctrine of mens rea, the theory of diminished capacity inevitably opens the door to variable or sliding scales of criminal responsibility. We should not lightly undertake such a revolutionary change in our criminal justice system. * * *

It could be said that many, if not most, crimes are committed by persons with mental aberrations. If such mental deficiencies are sufficient to meet the definition of insanity, these persons should be acquitted on that ground and treated for their disease. Persons with less serious mental deficiencies should be held accountable for their crimes just as everyone else. If mitigation is appropriate, it may be accomplished through sentencing, but to adopt a rule which creates an oppor-

---

* Ironically, the defense might not be available to one charged with first-degree felony murder providing the underlying felony was not a specific intent crime.

tunity for such persons to obtain immediate freedom to prey on the public once again is unwise. * * *

OVERTON, JUSTICE, dissenting.

In my view, it is totally unreasonable and illogical to allow a defendant to present evidence of *voluntary* intoxication and drug use as a defense to the element of specific intent to commit first-degree premeditated murder, but then to prohibit another defendant from presenting objective evidence of *involuntary* organic brain damage on the same issue. This results in a clear injustice. * * *

The issue here should be rephrased and limited to the evidentiary question of whether a defendant may introduce objective evidence of organic brain damage to establish that he lacked the requisite mental state of first-degree premeditated murder. I totally disagree with the characterization of the issue as one of whether we should adopt the diminished capacity doctrine. * * *

In the case primarily relied on by the majority, *Bethea v. United States,* that court, while emphatically rejecting subjective psychiatric evidence, expressly recognized that objective evidence of epilepsy and senility was a proper matter to be presented to the jury concerning mens rea * * *.

Clearly, epilepsy and senility are no different from other objective evidence of brain damage. While I could agree that it is justifiable to reject subjective evidence of an abnormal mental condition, I find no justification for rejecting objective evidence of organic brain damage. * * *

Notes and Questions

1. Based on the question certified to the state supreme court, which version of diminished capacity—*mens rea* or partial responsibility—did the district court have in mind when it questioned the admissibility of evidence relating to an "abnormal mental condition not constituting legal insanity"? Which version did the state supreme court have in mind? Which version is the dissent talking about? Would the defendant's proffered testimony, if believed, have supported either a *mens rea* or partial responsibility variant of diminished capacity?

2. In Bunney v. State, 603 So.2d 1270 (Fla.1992), the state supreme court held that evidence of the defendant's epilepsy was admissible to demonstrate his lack of specific intent to commit first degree felony murder and kidnapping. Is *Bunney* consistent with *Chestnut?*

3. One concern of some courts and scholars is that the effect of recognizing the doctrine of diminished capacity is to "transform criminal trials into psychiatric shouting matches." State v. Wilcox, 70 Ohio St.2d 182, 198, 436 N.E.2d 523, 533 (1982). Is this a greater concern with diminished capacity than in insanity trials?

Are there other reasons for disallowing psychiatric testimony in diminished capacity cases? At least as to the *mens rea* variant, Professor Peter Arenella sees little place for expert testimony:

The only difficulty with the *mens rea* model is its assumption that psychiatric analysis is directly relevant to the criminal law's state of mind elements. This premise is usually erroneous because most expert testimony does not speak to the criminal law's conception of intent.

Consider the following hypothetical. Assume Mr. Fanatic believes that God has ordered him to kill his neighbor because the neighbor is an agent of the devil. Mr. Fanatic buys a gun and ammunition, invites his neighbor over for tea, and calmly blows his brains out, killing him instantly. Psychiatrists testify that Mr. Fanatic was suffering from paranoid schizophrenia as evidenced by his delusion that God had ordered the killing. * * * Mr. Fanatic would be exculpated under the insanity rule of the Model Penal Code. Yet the same evidence of mental abnormality would not refute the existence of either the specific intent to kill or premeditation and deliberation. Mr. Fanatic certainly intended to kill and his objective acts clearly evidenced a preconceived design to effectuate that intent in a calm, deliberate manner.

Is this an illogical result? How can the defendant be insane, and therefore entitled to a complete defense, and yet not qualify for what is considered a "partial" defense? The simple answer is that there is no necessary connection between a judgment about the defendant's criminal responsibility and his mental capacity to entertain the state of mind required by the crime. As long as the *mens rea* element is defined in terms of the conscious mind's cognitive and affective functions, it is perfectly plausible that the defendant entertained the specific mental state but was still insane. In fact, most mentally abnormal offenders are fully capable of thinking about their criminal act before they do it, turning it over in their minds, planning the act, and then performing it in accordance with their preconceived plan. Evidence of how Fanatic's mental abnormality impaired his behavior controls or made it difficult for him to appreciate the act's gravity does not negate the existence of the required mental states; it merely explains them. Therefore, a psychiatric explanation of how a defendant's personality development led to his deviant behavior which does not dispute the presence of this conscious intent should not be admissible evidence under the strict *mens rea* model.

Admittedly, there will be occasional cases in which the expert testimony establishes that the defendant was incapable of entertaining the requisite intent. But given the criminal law's minimal definition of *mens rea*, the only type of mental abnormality that could establish such incapacity would be a severe mental disability that substantially interfered with the defendants reality-testing functions. However, evidence that the defendant's reality-testing functions were so impaired by mental illness that he did not realize what he was doing would also establish his insanity under either the *M'Naughton* or Model Penal Code tests. Thus, our analysis suggests that if courts administer the *mens rea* model honestly and only admit evidence that establishes that the defendant did not entertain the requisite mental state, the strict *mens rea* variant will rarely serve any purpose not satisfied by the insanity defense.

Peter Arenella, *The Diminished Capacity and Diminished Responsibility Defenses: Two Children of a Doomed Marriage,* 77 Colum.L.Rev. 827, 833–35 (1977).

4. In *Chestnut,* the question certified by the district court was whether evidence was admissible "for the purpose of proving either that the accused *could not or did not* entertain" the requisite intent. Should the law distinguish between psychiatric testimony relating to an actor's *capacity* to form the requisite intent and evidence relating to whether the actor *in fact* formed the intent? If so, which type of evidence should be allowed? Professor Stephen Morse explains the distinction this way:

Another cause of trouble with expert testimony on the mens rea variant is the conceptualization of the issue in terms of the defendant's *capacity* to form a mens rea, rather than whether he formed it *in fact.* In California, this distinction is colloquially referred to as the difference between "capacity" and "actuality" evidence.[140] On the face of it, the capacity conceptualization appears to make sense. Although the law requires proof of whether a defendant formed a mens rea in fact, if he lacked the capacity to form it, he could not have formed it in fact. There are * * * problems, however. * * *

Much as mental disorder virtually never negates mens rea in fact, it also seldom negates the capacity to form it. A mens rea is a relatively simple mental state; it requires little cognitive capacity to intend to do something or to know legally relevant facts * * *. A mentally abnormal person may not form a requisite intent or have the required knowledge, but it will rarely be because he lacked the capacity to form the mens rea. For example, suppose a mentally disordered person abroad in the streets becomes disorganized and lost in a deserted part of town on a cold evening. Lacking the resources to find his way to proper shelter, he breaks into a building to get out of the cold. Caught by the police while doing so, he is charged with burglary on the theory that he intended to steal. Our poor defendant is innocent of burglary because he lacks the mens rea for theft—he only wanted to stay warm, not to steal—but he does not lack mens rea because he did not have the capacity to form it. He was perfectly capable of intending to steal; it is simply the case, however, that he did not intend to do so on this occasion. The defendant's mental disorder is relevant to proving that he lacked mens rea, for it is the reason he became disorganized, got lost, and needed to get warm, but his mental disorder did not affect his capacity to form the mens rea. * * *

* * * Except in the extremely rare case in which it is possible that the defendant truly lacked the capacity to form mens rea, the capacity issue is largely irrelevant, and courts would do better to focus entirely on the actuality question. Even in those rare cases, it will still be better

---

140. This usage is derived from the language of § 28(a) of the California Penal Code, which reads as follows:

Evidence of mental disease, mental defect or mental disorder shall not be admitted to negate the *capacity* to form any mental state.... Evidence of mental dis-

ease, mental defect, or mental disorder is admissible solely on the issue whether or not the accused *actually* formed a required specific intent, premeditated, deliberated, or harbored malice aforethought, when a specific intent crime is charged. * * *

to avoid the capacity issue, because innocence can be more directly and certainly proven by showing that no mens rea was formed in fact, and also because testimony about capacity is generally too speculative to be admissible.

Stephen J. Morse, Undiminished Confusion in Diminished Capacity, 75 J.Crim.L. & Criminology 1, 42–43 (1984).

5. Should the law recognize the partial responsibility variant of the diminished capacity doctrine? Assume that there are two sane killers, Alice and Bob, each of whom intentionally and unjustifiably takes the life of another person. Alice possesses normal mental capacities, whereas Bob suffers from some mental abnormality, e.g., moderate mental illness or retardation. In light of Bob's mental condition, should the criminal law treat his crime as a lesser offense than that committed by Alice?

Professor Morse would treat the two killers the same:

> Analysis of responsibility usually begins by asking about all the difficulties, burdens, problems, and misfortunes suffered by the perpetrator, all the criminogenic reasons why obeying the law seemed so hard, why offending seemed so inevitable. But suppose we start with a different question: How hard is it not to offend the law? How hard is it not to kill, burgle, rob, rape, and steal? The ability to resist the temptation to violate the law is not akin to the ability required to be a fine athlete, artist, plumber, or doctor. The person is not being asked to exercise a difficult skill; rather, he or she is being asked simply to refrain from engaging in antisocial conduct. Think, too, of all the factors mitigating against such behavior: parental, religious, and school training; peer pressures and cultural expectations; internalized standards ("superego"); fear of capture and punishment; fear of shame; and a host of others. Not all such factors operate on all actors or with great strength: there will be wide individual differences based on life experiences and, perhaps, biological factors. Nonetheless, for all persons there are enormous forces arrayed against lawbreaking. It is one thing to yield to a desire to engage in undesirable conduct such as to gossip, brag, or treat one's fellows unfairly; it is another to give in to a desire to engage in qualitatively more harmful conduct such as to kill, rape, burgle, rob, or burn.

> The substantive criminal law sets minimal ethical and legal standards that ask very little of us and are easy to meet. Even if an actor has rationality or self-control problems, it is not hard for a legally responsible person to avoid offending. This is a morally relevant empirical claim that cannot be rigorously confirmed or disconfirmed, but I believe the assumption is every bit as plausible as the opposite and I wish to rely on it. If the empirical claim is correct, the differences that exist between offenders convicted of the same crime are morally insignificant compared to the similarities. The great value of this position, placing the burden of persuasion on those who believe it is hard to obey the law, is that it treats people with greater respect and dignity than the opposing view, which treats them as helpless puppets buffeted by forces that rob them of responsibility for their deeds. Moreover, I do not believe it is a harshly unrealistic view. Rather, it goes to the heart of

what it means to be a responsible person in a world that cannot exist without vast amounts of restraint and forbearance towards our fellows.

As long as the function of conviction and sentencing is to punish the actor for what he has done, rather than for who he is, there is no injustice in treating alike actors whose behavior satisfies the elements of the same crime and meets the low threshold standard for legal responsibility.

Id. at 30–32.

What are the broader implications of Professor Morse's views? Are there other currently recognized defenses that are unjustifiable according to his reasoning?

The Journal published a reply to Professor Morse:

We should not punish persons for possessing bad character, nor should we mitigate or exculpate because of good character. But we ought to consider explanations for behavior that indicate that the actors' personal blameworthiness for the events—their moral accountability for the harm—is less than we ordinarily would expect.[47]

The difference between insanity and diminished capacity is one of degree. Just as we differentially punish people because of gradations in mens rea, no principled basis exists for ignoring gradations here. The [proffered] evidence is no less reliable in the case of diminished capacity than with insanity. As long as the jury, not the "expert," resolves the moral issues of accountability, there is no good reason for closing our eyes to partial responsibility claims.

* * * [Consider] this * * * case [50][:] the defendant, Fisher, intentionally strangled a librarian. Fisher was not insane. Under Professor Morse's all-or-nothing approach, he was properly convicted of murder. * * * Yet, Fisher was mentally subnormal. * * * [H]e suffered from an aggressive psychopathic condition that affected his behavior. He killed suddenly, but intentionally; yet, he acted only after the victim called him a "black nigger." Are these factors individually or collectively irrelevant to his moral guilt and deserved punishment? Is it wrong for the jury to be permitted to evaluate their moral relevance? The Court said yes. Morse would say yes. I would say no. I agree with the observations of Justice Frankfurter:

A shocking crime puts law to its severest test.... Fisher is not the name of a theoretical problem. We are not hear [sic] dealing with an abstract man.... Murder cases are apt to be peculiarly individualized.... The bite of law is in its enforcement. This is

47. This does not confuse the issue of causation with that of moral responsibility. * * * I do not suggest that we treat defendants more leniently merely because they suffer from some mental abnormality, or even because the abnormality is causally related to their behavior. When the abnormality impairs free will in a substantial and verifiable way, however, we ought to consider the abnormality. Choice-making capabilities are impaired if the defendant's mental or emotional condition substantially affects volitional or cognitive functions. * * *

50. Fisher v. United States, 328 U.S. 463 (1946).

especially true when careful or indifferent judicial administration has consequences so profound as ... life and death.[53]

Fisher's impairment, and the victim's racial epithet, may not have been the legal causes of his conduct. His free will acts were the cause. Because he had free will, and chose to kill, he should be punished. But my intuition tells me that the information [proffered] by the defense would have been highly relevant to morally sensitive jurors in their decision regarding Fisher's degree of moral guilt. Jurors might conclude that it was harder for Fisher than for the juror *not* to kill.

It is easy for any of us to give in to our fear of crime and to our natural anger at those who perpetrate it. It is much easier to defend the interests of the victim than those of the perpetrator. But, as Ramsey Clark has warned: "Reason fades as fear deprives us of any concern or compassion for others. When fear turns our concern entirely to self-protection ... this can destroy our desire for justice itself." [55]

Joshua Dressler, *Reaffirming the Moral Legitimacy of the Doctrine of Diminished Capacity: A Brief Reply to Professor Morse,* 75 J.Crim.L. & Criminology 953, 960–61 (1984).

6. INFANCY

IN RE DEVON T.

Court of Special Appeals of Maryland, 1991.
85 Md.App. 674, 584 A.2d 1287.

MOYLAN, JUDGE.

In a world dizzy with change, it is reassuring to find Daniel M'Naghten alive and well in juvenile court. It was, of course, M'Naghten's bungled attempt to assassinate Prime Minister Sir Robert Peel, killing by mistake Sir Robert's private secretary Edward Drummond, that led to his prosecution for murder and the assertion of his now eponymic insanity defense. When the House of Lords placed its imprimatur upon the jury's acquittal by reason of insanity, "the M'Naghten test" was impressed indelibly upon the Common Law of Anglo–America.

The M'Naghten test, by name, crossed to New England within the year. It was adopted by the Court of Appeals in 1888 as the controlling standard in Maryland, * * * and remained the exclusive criterion of criminal insanity in this state until supplanted by the Acts of 1967, ch. 709.[1] * * *

What has not been adequately noted in the case law is that this cognitive capacity to distinguish right from wrong in the language of M'Naghten was not a characteristic of the insanity defense exclusively. It has traditionally been the common denominator criterion for a whole

---

53. *Id.* at 477, 478, 484 (Frankfurter, J., dissenting).

55. R. Clark, Crime in America 19 (1970).

1. The 1967 legislation, then codified as Md.Ann.Code art. 59, § 9(a), adopted the test for criminal insanity recommended by the American Law Institute and contained in § 4.01 of the Model Penal Code. * * *

family of defenses based upon mental incapacity—insanity, infancy, mental retardation, intoxication (at least of the involuntary variety). The cause of the mental incapacity might vary from one such defense to the next but the ultimate nature of the resulting incapacity was a constant. In any of its manifestations, criminal responsibility traditionally turned and largely still turns upon the difference between a mind doli capax (capable of malice or criminal intent) and a mind doli incapax (incapable of malice or criminal intent). Capability or capacity might be eroded in various ways but the ultimate quality of the required mental capacity itself was unchanging. * * *

Hence, we tentatively advance the traditional M'Naghten test as pertinent to our present review of an adjudication of juvenile delinquency in the Circuit Court for Baltimore City. For the moment, however, let Daniel M'Naghten retire to the wings as we bring onto the stage the contemporary players.

THE PRESENT CASE

The juvenile appellant, Devon T., was charged with committing an act which, if committed by an adult, would have constituted the crime of possession of heroin with intent to distribute. In the Circuit Court for Baltimore City, Judge Roger W. Brown found that Devon was delinquent. The heart of the case against Devon was that when on May 25, 1989, Devon was directed to empty his pockets by the security guard at the Booker T. Washington Middle School, under the watchful eye of the Assistant Principal, the search produced a brown bag containing twenty zip-lock pink plastic bags which, in turn, contained heroin. * * *

THE INFANCY DEFENSE GENERALLY

At the time of the offense, Devon was 13 years, 10 months, and 2 weeks of age. He timely raised the infancy defense. * * *

The case law and the academic literature alike conceptualize the infancy defense as but an instance of the broader phenomenon of a defense based upon lack of moral responsibility or capacity. The criminal law generally will only impose its retributive or deterrent sanctions upon those who are morally blameworthy—those who know they are doing wrong but nonetheless persist in their wrongdoing.

After several centuries of pondering the criminal capacity of children and experimenting with various cut-off ages, the Common Law settled upon its current resolution of the problem by late Tudor and early Stuart times. As explained by LaFave & Scott, *Criminal Law,* (2d ed. 1986), at 398, the resolution was fairly simple:

> "At common law, children under the age of seven are conclusively presumed to be without criminal capacity, those who have reached the age of fourteen are treated as fully responsible, while as to those between the ages of seven and fourteen there is a rebuttable presumption of criminal incapacity."

The authors make clear that infancy was an instance of criminal capacity generally:

> "The early common law infancy defense was based upon an unwillingness to punish those thought to be incapable of forming criminal intent and not of an age where the threat of punishment could serve as a deterrent."

* * *

Clark & Marshall, *A Treatise on the Law of Crimes,* (6th Wing. ed. 1958), emphasizes that the mental quality that is the *sine qua non* of criminal responsibility is the capacity to distinguish right from wrong.
* * *

The reasoning behind the rule is made very clear, at 391:

> "A child is not criminally responsible unless he is old enough, and intelligent enough, to be capable of entertaining a criminal intent; and to be capable of entertaining a criminal intent he must be capable of distinguishing between right and wrong as to the particular act."

Walkover, *The Infancy Defense in the New Juvenile Court,* 31 UCLA L.Rev. 503, 507 (1984), distills the rationale to a single sentence:

> "The infancy defense was an essential component of the common law limitation of punishment to the blameworthy."

* * *

THE INFANCY DEFENSE IN JUVENILE COURT

With the creation shortly after the turn of the present century of juvenile courts in America, diverting many youthful offenders from criminal courts into equity and other civil courts, the question arose as to whether the infancy defense had any pertinence to a juvenile delinquency adjudication. Under the initially prevailing philosophy that the State was acting in delinquency cases as *parens patriae* (sovereign parent of the country), the State was perceived to be not the retributive punisher of the child for its misdeeds but the paternalistic guardian of the child for its own best interests. Under such a regime, the moral responsibility or blameworthiness of the child was of no consequence. Morally responsible or not, the child was in apparent need of the State's rehabilitative intervention and the delinquency adjudication was but the avenue for such intervention.

This was the philosophy that persuaded this Court * * * to forbear from extending the defense of infancy to juvenile court proceedings as an inapposite criterion. * * *

Over the course of the century, however, buffeted by unanticipated urban deterioration and staggering case loads, the reforming vision of * * * the * * * founders of the movement faded. Although continuing to stress rehabilitation over retribution more heavily than did the adult criminal courts, delinquency adjudications nonetheless took on, in practice if not in theory, many of the attributes of junior varsity criminal trials. The Supreme Court, in *In re Gault,* 387 U.S. 1, 87 S.Ct. 1428, 18 L.Ed.2d 527 (1967), and *In re Winship,* 397 U.S. 358, 90 S.Ct. 1068, 25 L.Ed.2d 368 (1970), acknowledged this slow but inexorable transformation of the juvenile court apparatus into one with increasingly penal overtones. It ultimately guaranteed, therefore, a juvenile charged with delinquency most of the due process protections afforded an adult charged with crime. * * *

In terms of the applicability of the infancy defense to delinquency proceedings, the implications of the new dispensation are clear. A finding of delinquency, unlike other proceedings in a juvenile court, unmistakably connotes some degree of blameworthiness and unmistakably exposes the delinquent to, whatever the gloss, the possibility of unpleasant sanctions. Clearly, the juvenile would have as an available defense to the delinquency charge 1) the fact that he was too criminally insane to have known that what he did was wrong, 2) that he was too mentally retarded to have known that what he did was wrong, or 3) that he was too involuntarily intoxicated through no fault of his own to have known that what he did was wrong. It would be inconceivable that he could be found blameworthy and suffer sanctions, notwithstanding precisely the same lack of understanding and absence of moral accountability, simply because the cognitive defect was caused by infancy rather than by one of the other incapacitating mechanisms. * * *

In a juvenile delinquency adjudication, * * * the defense of infancy is now indisputably available in precisely the same manner as it is available in a criminal trial. * * *

What Is Criminal Capacity in an Infant?

Before the juvenile master, the appellant timely raised the infancy defense. One party or the other (it matters not which) introduced the undisputed fact * * * that at the time of the allegedly delinquent act, Devon was 13 years, 10 months, and 2 weeks of age. Thus, the issue of mental incapacity due to infancy was properly generated and before the court.

On that issue, Devon initially had the benefit of presumptive incapacity. The presumption having been generated, the State had the burdens (of both production and persuasion) of rebutting that presumption. * * *

To overcome the presumption of incapacity, then, what precisely was that quality of Devon's mind as to which the State was required to produce legally sufficient evidence? It was required to produce evidence permitting the reasonable inference that Devon—the Ghost of M'Naghten speaks:—"at the time of doing the act knew the difference between right and wrong." * * *

The analogy between incapacity due to infancy and incapacity due to insanity, mental retardation, or involuntary intoxication has lost some of its original symmetry to the extent that those latter incapacities have been broadened (directly or indirectly) to include a volitional as well as a cognitive component. The infancy defense retains its exclusive concern with the cognitive element. * * *

In short, when Devon walked around the Booker T. Washington Middle School with twenty zip-lock bags of heroin, apparently for sale or other distribution, could Devon pass the M'Naghten test? Was there legally sufficient data before him to permit Judge Brown to infer that Devon knew the difference between right and wrong and knew, moreover, that what he was doing was wrong?

The Legal Sufficiency of the Evidence to Prove Devon's Knowledge of Right and Wrong

As we turn to the legal sufficiency of the evidence, it is important to know that the only mental quality we are probing is the cognitive capacity to distinguish right from wrong. Other aspects of Devon's mental and psychological make-up, such as his scholastic attainments, his I.Q., his social maturity, his societal adjustment, his basic personality, etc., might well require evidentiary input from psychologists, from parents, from teachers or other school authorities, etc. On knowledge of the difference between right and wrong, however, the general case law, as well as the inherent logic of the situation, has established that that particular psychic phenomenon may sometimes permissibly be inferred from the very circumstances of the criminal or delinquent act itself. * * *

On the issue of Devon's knowledge of the difference between right and wrong, if all we knew in this case were that Devon's age was at some indeterminate point between his seventh birthday and his fourteenth birthday, the State's case would be substantially weaker than it is now. The evidence before Judge Brown that Devon, at the time of the allegedly delinquent act, was 13 years, 10 months, and 2 weeks of age was substantial, although not quite sufficient, proof of his cognitive capacity.

The applicable common law on doli incapax with relation to the infancy defense establishes that on the day before their seventh birthday, no persons possess cognitive capacity. (0 per cent). It also establishes that on the day of their fourteenth birthday, all persons (at least as far as age is concerned) possess cognitive capacity. (100 per cent). On the time scale between the day of the seventh birthday and the day before the fourteenth birthday, the percentage of persons possessing such capacity steadily increases. The statistical probability is that on the day of the seventh birthday, at most a tiny fraction of one per cent will possess cognitive capacity. Conversely, on the day before the fourteenth birthday, only a tiny fraction of one per cent will lack such cognitive capacity. Assuming a steady rate of climb,[6] the midpoint

---

6. The climb in cognitive capacity from the seventh birthday through the fourteenth birthday, of course, has not been charted with actuarial precision by the so- cial sciences. The rise in maturity of the group as a whole may be a linear progression at a regular rate of climb. There may, however, be plateaus interrupting the up-where fifty per cent of persons will lack cognitive capacity and fifty per cent will possess it would be at 10 years and 6 months of age. That is the scale on which we must place Devon.

We stress that the burden in that regard, notwithstanding the probabilities, was nonetheless on the State. * * * The fact that the quantum of proof necessary to overcome presumptive incapacity diminishes in substantially the same ratio as the infant's age increases only serves to lessen the State's burden, not to eliminate it. * * *

We hold that the State successfully carried that burden. A minor factor, albeit of some weight, was that Devon was essentially at or near grade level in school. The report of the master, received and reviewed by Judge Brown, established that at the time of the offense, Devon was in middle school, embracing grades 6, 7, and 8. The report of the master, indeed, revealed that Devon had flunked the sixth grade twice, with truancy and lack of motivation as apparent causes. That fact nonetheless revealed that Devon had initially reached the sixth grade while still eleven years of age. That would tend to support his probable inclusion in the large majority of his age group rather than in a small and subnormal minority of it.

We note that the transcript of the hearing before the juvenile master shows that the master was in a position to observe first-hand Devon's receiving of legal advice from his lawyer, his acknowledgement of his understanding of it, and his acting upon it. His lawyer explained that he had a right to remain silent and that the master would not infer guilt from his exercise of that right. He acknowledged understanding that right. His lawyer also advised him of his right to testify but informed him that both the assistant state's attorney and the judge might question him about the delinquent act. Devon indicated that he wished to remain silent and say nothing. Although reduced to relatively simple language, the exchange with respect to the risk of self-incrimination and the privilege against self-incrimination forms a predicate from which an observer might infer some knowledge on Devon's part of the significance of incrimination. * * *

The transcript that was received and reviewed by Judge Brown revealed yet a further exchange between the juvenile master and Devon, also not without some significance. After Devon and his companion

ward progression. There might even be a parabolic curve, concentrating much of the statistical advance of the group as a whole into the last year or two rather than having it spread evenly across the course of the seven years.

Whatever the configuration of the maturity chart, however, Devon had moved 98.2 per cent of the way, on the timeline of his life, from his seventh birthday to his fourteenth birthday. Assuming a regular linear progression, simply for illustrative purposes, that would mean that of all persons in Devon's particular age group, 98.2 per cent would be expected to possess cognitive capacity and 1.8 per cent would be expected to lack it. The State's burden, therefore, would not be to prove that Devon was precociously above average but only to satisfy the court that Devon fell within the upper 98.2 per cent of his age group and not within the subnormal 1.8 per cent of it.

In any event, whatever the statistical rate of progress or the maturity curve might be, Devon had moved 98.2 per cent of the way from its beginning point to its terminus.

Edward had already been adjudicated delinquent and when no further risk of incrimination inhered, the master, prior to disposition, asked each of the two what, if anything, he would like to say and was met by "stonewalling" * * *. This inferable allegiance to the Underworld's "Code of Silence" suggests that Devon and Edward were no mere babies caught up in a web they did not comprehend. The permitted inference, rather, was that they were fully conscious of the ongoing war between lawful authority and those who flout it and had deliberately chosen to adhere to the latter camp.

We turn, most significantly, to the circumstances of the criminal act itself. * * *

* * * The case broke when a grandmother, concerned enough to have had her own live-in grandson institutionalized, complained to the authorities at Booker T. Washington Middle School that several of her grandson's classmates were being truant on a regular basis and were using her home, while she was out working, as the "hide out" from which to sell drugs. * * * Children who are unaware that what they are doing is wrong have no need to hide out or to conceal their activities.

The most significant circumstance was the very nature of the criminal activity in which Devon engaged. It was not mere possession of heroin. It was possession of twenty packets of heroin with the intent to distribute. This was the finding of the court and it was supported by the evidence. There were no needle marks or other indications of personal use on Devon's body. * * *

We hold that the surrounding circumstances here were legally sufficient to overcome the slight residual weight of the presumption of incapacity due to infancy. * * *

Notes and Questions

1. In light of the fact that Maryland shifted to the American Law Institute test of insanity, why did the court apply *M'Naghten?* Isn't one reason for treating youths differently than adults the fact that children find it more difficult than adults to resist "childish urges."

2. Under English common law, a special rule of incapacity applied in rape cases: a boy under the age of fourteen years was *conclusively* presumed to be incapable of committing rape. The most often stated reason for this rule was that young males in pre-industrial England did not reach puberty until the age of fourteen; perhaps a stronger motive for the rule was a desire to protect boys from the death penalty mandated at common law. Commonwealth v. Walter R., 414 Mass. 714, 715–16, 610 N.E.2d 323, 324 (1993). Most jurisdictions in this country refused from the outset to recognize the conclusive presumption. See Commonwealth v. A Juvenile, 399 Mass. 451, 504 N.E.2d 1049 (1987).

Chapter 10

INCHOATE OFFENSES

A. OVERVIEW

AMERICAN LAW INSTITUTE—MODEL PENAL
CODE AND COMMENTARIES COMMENT
TO ARTICLE 5

(1985), 293–294

Article 5 [of the Model Penal Code] undertakes to deal systematically with [the crimes of] attempt, solicitation and conspiracy. These
offenses have in common the fact that they deal with conduct that is
designed to culminate in the commission of a substantive offense, but
has failed in the discrete case to do so or has not yet achieved its
culmination because there is something that the actor or another still
must do. The offenses are inchoate in this sense.

These, to be sure, are not the only crimes so defined that their
commission does not rest on proof of the occurrence of the evil that it is
the object of the law to prevent; many specific, substantive offenses also
have a large inchoate aspect. This is true not only with respect to
crimes of risk creation, such as reckless driving, or specific crimes of
preparation, such as possession with unlawful purpose. It is also true,
at least in part, of crimes like larceny, forgery, kidnapping and even
arson, not to speak of burglary, where a purpose to cause greater harm
than that which is implicit in the actor's conduct is an element of the
offense. This reservation notwithstanding, attempt, solicitation and
conspiracy have such generality of definition and of application as
inchoate crimes that it is useful * * * to confront the common problems
they present.

* * * General deterrence is at most a minor function to be served in
fashioning provisions of the penal law addressed to these inchoate
crimes; that burden is discharged upon the whole by the law dealing
with the substantive offenses.

Other and major functions of the penal law remain, however, to be
served. They may be summarized as follows:

First: When a person is seriously dedicated to commission of a crime, a firm legal basis is needed for the intervention of the agencies of law enforcement to prevent its consummation. In determining that basis, there must be attention to the danger of abuse; equivocal behavior may be misconstrued by an unfriendly eye as preparation to commit a crime. It is no less important, on the other side, that lines should not be drawn so rigidly that the police confront insoluble dilemmas in deciding when to intervene, facing the risk that if they wait the crime may be committed while if they act they may not yet have any valid charge.

Second: Conduct designed to cause or culminate in the commission of a crime obviously yields an indication that the actor is disposed towards such activity, not alone on this occasion but on others. There is a need, therefore, subject again to proper safeguards, for a legal basis upon which the special danger that such individuals present may be assessed and dealt with. They must be made amenable to the corrective process that the law provides.

Third: Finally, and quite apart from these considerations of prevention, when the actor's failure to commit the substantive offense is due to a fortuity, as when the bullet misses in attempted murder or when the expected response to solicitation is withheld, his exculpation on that ground would involve inequality of treatment that would shock the common sense of justice. Such a situation is unthinkable in any mature system designed to serve the proper goals of penal law.

Notes and Questions

1. Ira P. Robbins, *Double Inchoate Crimes*, 26 Harv.J. on Legis. 1, 3–4 (1989):

> The inchoate crimes of attempt, conspiracy, and solicitation are well established in the American legal system. "Inchoate" offenses allow punishment of an actor even though he has not consummated the crime that is the object of his efforts. * * *

> Most American jurisdictions treat inchoate offenses as substantive crimes, distinct and divorced from the completed crimes toward which they tend. Accordingly, attempt, conspiracy, and solicitation are defined broadly to encompass acts leading to the commission of any completed crime. Rather than try to enumerate every act to which inchoate liability attaches, however, legislatures have enacted relatively short statutes containing abstract conceptual terms with universal application. The Model Penal Code's provision for attempt liability, for example, represents a middle-ground approach to this problem. It prohibits an act that constitutes a "substantial step" toward the completed offense. The Code then fleshes out the abstract term "substantial step" by listing several nonexclusive examples that have application to numerous completed crimes. It has fallen to the courts to elaborate on the scope of inchoate offenses and decide when to administer them.

> Thus, the concept of substantive inchoate crimes, by requiring a high degree of judicial interpretation, has vested great discretion in the judiciary. This discretion is similar to that of earlier courts in creating

common-law offenses. In both circumstances, the court analyzes the policies underlying the criminal law and decides whether those policies require courts to punish certain acts.

2. Professor Robbins points out (Note 1) that because inchoate offenses are defined broadly and abstractly, the judiciary is vested with tremendous interpretative discretion. For the same reason, police officers who come upon activities they regard as suspicious have considerable enforcement discretion. For example, consider the incident described in McQuirter v. State, 36 Ala.App. 707, 63 So.2d 388 (1953):

One summer evening, a woman walked with her two children and a neighbor's child past a parked truck in which a man, McQuirter, "said something unintelligible, opened the truck door, and placed his foot on the running board." McQuirter followed the woman and children, approaching within two or three feet of them. Fearful, the woman stopped at a friend's house. After ten minutes, she proceeded on her way, but McQuirter was still there and "came toward her from behind a telephone pole." The woman instructed the children to run to an acquaintance's house, which they did. When the resident of the house came out and investigated, McQuirter turned and walked away.

Suppose that a police officer had observed the preceding events. Should she have arrested McQuirter? If so, for what crime? Alternatively, should the officer have detained McQuirter to inquire as to his intentions? The difficulty with this option is that an officer may not constitutionally detain someone against his will unless she has reason to suspect that crime is afoot. Terry v. Ohio, 392 U.S. 1, 88 S.Ct. 1868, 20 L.Ed.2d 889 (1968). Do the facts here support a reasonable inference that McQuirter intended to commit a crime? What crime?

In actuality, no police officer was present, the woman arrived home safely, and McQuirter went to his home. Nonetheless, he was arrested, prosecuted and convicted of the inchoate offense of "attempt to commit an assault with intent to rape." Is this a good outcome,[a] or do you believe that McQuirter was punished for innocent conduct "misconstrued by an unfriendly eye"? Does your outlook on the case change when you learn that McQuirter was an African–American and the woman, described by the Alabama court as "Mrs. Ted Allen," was white?[b]

What does this case suggest about inchoate offenses in general? For example, do such laws come unacceptably close to punishing persons for criminal thoughts? Is there too great a risk that innocent people will be punished for suspicious-appearing behavior? On the other hand, can a society adequately protect itself without punishing inchoate conduct?

a. Does your outlook on the case change when you learn that the Chief of Police testified at McQuirter's trial that the defendant confessed that he intended to rape the woman? McQuirter, however, denied making these statements.

b. The appellate court believed that these facts were relevant: "In determining the question of intention the jury may consider social conditions and customs founded upon racial differences, such as that the prosecutrix was a white woman and defendant was a Negro man." Id. at 709, 63 So.2d at 390.

Keep these questions in the forefront of your mind as you consider the materials in this chapter. Also, ask yourself whether the courts have adequately resolved the conflicting policy concerns encountered in the enforcement of inchoate crimes.

B. ATTEMPT

1. GENERAL PRINCIPLES

IRA P. ROBBINS, DOUBLE INCHOATE CRIMES
26 Harvard Journal on Legislation 1 (1989), 9–12

Although the law of attempt has roots in the early English law, its formulation as a general substantive offense is a relatively recent development.[22] * * * Many American jurisdictions now make specific provisions for the punishment of attempts to commit certain offenses, and almost all cover the rest of the field with a general attempt statute. With a few exceptions, these general statutes cover attempts to commit any felony or misdemeanor.

Among modern American jurisdictions, * * * the rule of merger operates * * * to the extent that a defendant cannot be convicted of both a completed offense and an attempt to commit it. All jurisdictions treat attempt as a lesser included offense of the completed crime. Moreover, many jurisdictions have held that a defendant may be convicted of the attempt if the state proves the completed crime, and several states so provide by statute.

* * * The principal purpose behind punishing an attempt * * * is not deterrence. The threat posed by the sanction for an attempt is unlikely to deter a person willing to risk the penalty for the object crime. Instead, the primary function of the crime of attempt is to provide a basis for law-enforcement officers to intervene before an individual can commit a completed offense.

Notes and Questions

1. Criminal attempts are of two varieties—incomplete and complete. In the former case, the actor does some of the acts that she set out to do, but

---

22. The modern doctrine of attempt has its origin in the case of Rex v. Scofield, Cald.Mag.Rep. 397 (1784). In *Scofield,* the court indicted the defendant on a charge of placing a lighted candle and combustible material on another's house with intent to set fire to it, even though the house did not burn. Such conduct clearly would constitute an attempt to commit arson in modern law. Prior to *Scofield,* however, the courts imposed attempt liability only for two categories of offenses: attempted treason and attempts to subvert justice, such as subornation of perjury and attempted bribery of the King's officials.

The court in *Scofield* established the premises that a criminal intent may make criminal an act that was otherwise innocent in itself, and, conversely, that the completion of an act, criminal in itself, was not necessary to constitute a crime.

Rex v. Higgins, 102 Eng.Rep. 269 (1801), extended the decision in *Scofield.* In *Higgins,* * * * [t]he court ruled that it could indict a person for any act or attempt that tended "to the prejudice of the community."

then desists or is prevented from continuing by an extraneous factor, e.g., the intervention of a police officer. In contrast, with a completed attempt, the actor does every act planned, but is unsuccessful in producing the intended result, e.g., she shoots and misses the intended victim.

Professor Robbins states that the primary purpose of attempt laws is to provide a basis for police intervention before an offense is completed. This rationale might explain incomplete attempts, but what is the basis for punishing a completed attempt?

2. *The role of "harm" in criminal attempts.* Is there any social harm in a criminal attempt? For example, if Oscar lies in wait to kill Paul, but is arrested before he can pull the trigger—perhaps before Paul even arrives on the scene—what harm has Oscar caused? Or, if Quentin, with the intent to kill, stabs and slightly wounds Roxanne, her physical injuries are encompassed in the ordinary battery statute, so the question remains: Is there harm, beyond the battery, that justifies Quentin's prosecution for attempted murder? Or, suppose that Tammy fires a gun at Ursula who is asleep, but the gun misfires. Tammy, disgusted, abandons her efforts to kill Ursula. Ursula goes about the rest of her life untouched by the events. Where is the harm in Tammy's actions? If there is no harm, are we punishing harmless conduct because of the actor's illicit thoughts?

Regarding the fundamental significance of social harm to the criminal law, Professor Paul H. Robinson writes:

> If the criminal law is extended to punish bad intent alone or the mere possibility of harmful conduct, it goes beyond its accepted role, appears unfair and overreaching, and ultimately loses its credibility and integrity.
>
> If one views deterrence as the proper function of the criminal law, a harm requirement is appropriate. To the extent that the criminal law punishes nonharmful conduct, it weakens the stigma and deterrent effect of criminal conviction for harmful conduct. If a defendant who has caused no harm feels that he is punished unjustifiably, rehabilitative efforts will be hampered. Indeed, one may ask: If no harm has been caused, what harm will be deterred by punishment, and what harm-causing characteristic will be rehabilitated? If one believes that the role of the criminal law is to provide retribution, a harm requirement is also proper; in the absence of harm there is nothing for which to seek retribution. * * * The consistency of a requirement of harm with these fundamental purposes of the criminal law is reflected in the fact that harm has, from the earliest of civilized times, been treated as a de facto requirement.

Paul H. Robinson, *A Theory of Justification: Societal Harm as a Prerequisite for Criminal Liability*, 23 UCLA L.Rev. 266, 266–67 (1975).

If social harm is a de facto requirement of the criminal law, are laws punishing attempts unjustifiable? The following article considers this question.

ANDREW ASHWORTH, CRIMINAL ATTEMPTS AND THE ROLE OF RESULTING HARM UNDER THE CODE, AND IN THE COMMON LAW

19 Rutgers Law Journal 725 (1988), 734–38

What is the justification for criminalising incomplete attempts? Prevention is surely the main reason for penalising preliminary steps on the way to inflicting a prohibited harm. The law should authorise agents of law enforcement to intervene before the major harm is done. This is one of the few ways in which criminal law can realistically provide protection of rights. But to justify intervention (by arrest and perhaps overnight detention) is not to justify punishment. What has the incomplete attempter done that is wrong?

The answer depends on the chosen rationale for criminal punishment. Modern retributivist theories purport to justify punishment if and insofar as it tends to "restore an order of fairness which was disrupted by the criminal's criminal act." A crime disturbs the order of things ordained by law. The offender deserves punishment because he has chosen to disturb this order in a prohibited way. The punishment is necessary so as to restore, at least symbolically, that order.

This general theory of "just deserts," however, is not sufficiently specific to be applied to the incomplete attempter. It can be developed in either of two ways. A "harm-based" form of retributivism would link the justification for punishment to the culpable causing of harm: both the justification for and the measure of punishment derive from the culpable causing of a prohibited harm. This would seem to indicate impunity for incomplete attempters on the ground that, whatever their culpability, they have not yet caused the prohibited harm. The only way to circumvent this would be to argue for an extended definition of harm, * * * whereby a preliminary act manifesting an intent to commit a substantive crime is presumed to cause apprehension or fear in others. Some systems of criminal law do contain offences of this kind, but the actual or possible causation of apprehension in other persons does not generally form part of the definition of attempts. Thus, the harm-based version of retributivism * * * does not readily yield a justification for punishing incomplete attempts.

An intent-based form of retributivism would start with the proposition that the technique of the criminal law is to impose on individuals in society various duties of self-restraint, in order to provide a basic security of person, property, amenity, and so on. A person who voluntarily casts off this burden of self-restraint deserves punishment, in that he or she has used unfair means to gain an advantage over law-abiding citizens. The purpose of criminal punishment then is to counterbalance, at least symbolically, a voluntary breaking of the rules. Since fairness is an integral element in this "just deserts" approach, it would be wrong to allow random or chance factors to determine the threshold of criminal liability or the quantum of punishment. In criminal endeavours, as in other spheres of life, things do not always turn out as one expects. The emphasis in criminal liability should be upon what D was trying to do, intended to do and believed he was doing, rather than upon the actual consequences of his conduct. The point may be restated in terms of the "intent principle" and the "belief principle": the intent principle is that individuals should be held criminally liable for what they intended to do, and not according to what actually did or did not occur; the belief principle is that individuals should be judged on the basis of what they believed they were doing, not on the basis of actual facts and circumstances which were not known to them at the time.

Applying the intent principle, one must ask whether a person who takes substantial steps towards the commission of the substantive offence, with intent to commit that offence, has already manifested sufficient non-self-restraint so as to deserve punishment (subject to debate about the stage required as the actus reus of an attempt). Whether the endeavour is successful, in terms of committing the substantive offence, may well depend on matters which to D are pure chance—whether the police learn about the plan and intervene before D does all that was planned; whether something fails to work in the way D envisaged; whether the victim behaves unexpectedly, and so on. The fact that D appears in court for the substantive offence and E (who set out to commit the same crime) is charged only with an attempt may have been determined simply by twists of fate, unrelated to the efforts they made or to their relative culpability. The actual outcomes of their efforts should not make the difference between criminal liability and no liability at all * * *. For the intent-based retributivist, * * * once D has reached a sufficient stage in acting with the settled purpose of committing a substantive offence, criminal liability is individually deserved and socially fair.

How do the two versions of retributive theory apply to complete attempts, in which D has done all the acts intended without producing the prohibited outcome? Harm-based retributivism might be thought to tell more strongly here than for incomplete attempts, since a complete attempt may sometimes create more apprehension and alarm. Yet the absence of apprehension from the definition of attempts, together with the fact that many impossible attempts may be completed without causing alarm to anyone, weakens this argument. Intent-based retributivism, on the other hand, has its clearest application here. In a complete attempt D has done everything planned, and the non-occurrence of the consequence is unexpected and often outside his control. It can therefore be maintained that there is no relevant moral difference, for the purposes of punishment as distinct from compensation, between D's culpability and that of the substantive offender whose attempt succeeded. They equally deserve to be convicted of a crime, even if their offences are labelled differently.

Turning to consequentialist justifications, there is little difficulty in supporting the conviction of the incomplete attempter. Assuming that D has done a sufficient preliminary act and that it can be established that he intended to commit the substantive offence, this may be accepted as sufficient evidence of a dangerous disposition, and it supplies a good reason for intervening so as to prevent the consummation of the attempt. For the consequentialist, it is not a sufficient justification for punishment that it is said to be deserved. Since punishment involves the infliction of unpleasant consequences, it must be clear that any penalty will have a preventive (or other beneficial) effect which is not outweighed by any negative consequences it may have. As one measure of social defence, punishment must be aimed at those who have shown a disposition to cause prohibited harms. The complete attempter has unambiguously shown his willingness to try to bring about a proscribed consequence. The fact that chance interposed itself on this occasion and the result failed to follow does not reduce the dangerousness of this individual to any significant extent.

* * * Thus, both incomplete and complete attempts may support, although to a different extent, similar predictions about the defendant's propensities to do harm as may the substantive offence.

Notes and Questions

1. *"Objectivism" and "subjectivism."* In his influential book, Rethinking Criminal Law (1978), Professor George Fletcher describes two "patterns of criminality" that are important to understanding the development of criminal law doctrine.

The critical feature of one pattern—he calls it "the pattern of manifest criminality"—is that the offense "be objectively discernible at the time that it occurs. The assumption is that a neutral third-party observer could recognize the activity as criminal even if he had no special knowledge about the offender's intention." Id. at 115–16. Following this pattern, the actor's mental state does not arise as a legal issue unless and until the wrongfulness of her conduct is demonstrated by her actions. In the context of criminal attempts, Fletcher call this the "objectivist" theory of attempts, because it focuses on the actor's conduct, and "does not presuppose a prior determination of the actor's intent." Id. at 138.

The competing pattern, "subjective criminality," focuses on the actor's intentions, rather than on externalities. In the realm of attempts, the subjectivist theory suggests that "the act of execution is important so far as it verifies the firmness of the intent," but has no independent significance. Id. Any act that verifies the person's commitment to carry out her criminal plan is sufficient to justify the criminal sanction.

In considering criminal attempts, reflect on whether objectivist or subjectivist patterns of criminality have predominated.

2. GRADING CRIMINAL ATTEMPTS

AMERICAN LAW INSTITUTE, MODEL PENAL CODE AND COMMENTARIES, COMMENT TO § 5.05

(1985), 485–86, 489–90

1. *Background.* Earlier law reflected no general or coherent theory for determining the sanctions that should be authorized upon conviction of attempt, solicitation or conspiracy. The maxima for these crimes were frequently fixed lower than for the substantive offense that was the actor's object * * *. * * *

The former statutes fitted into a number of identifiable patterns, some of which have been carried over in recent revisions. One common provision set specific maximum penalties, ranging from 10 to 50 years, for attempts to commit crimes punishable by death or life imprisonment, and fixed the penalty for all other attempts at one half of the maximum for the completed crime. * * *

2. *Grading.* Subsection (1) of 5.05 departs from the law that preceded promulgation of the Model Code by treating attempt, solicitation and conspiracy on a parity for purposes of sentence and by determining the grade or degree of the inchoate crime by the gravity of the most serious offense that is its object. Only when the object is a capital crime or a felony of the first degree does the Code deviate from this solution, grading the inchoate offense in that case as a felony of the second degree.

The theory of this grading system may be stated simply. To the extent that sentencing depends upon the antisocial disposition of the actor and the demonstrated need for a corrective sanction, there is likely to be little difference in the gravity of the required measures depending on the consummation or the failure of the plan. It is only when and insofar as the severity of sentence is designed for general deterrent purposes that a distinction on this ground is likely to have reasonable force. It is doubtful, however, that the threat of punishment for the inchoate crime can add significantly to the net deterrent efficacy of the sanction threatened for the substantive offense that is the actor's object, which he, by hypothesis, ignores. Hence, there is a basis for economizing in use of the heaviest and most afflictive sanctions by removing them from the inchoate crimes. The sentencing provisions for second degree felonies, including the provision for extended terms, should certainly suffice to meet whatever danger is presented by the actor.

Notes and Questions

1. Should an attempt be treated as a less serious offense than the target crime, or as one of equal seriousness? How would a utilitarian answer this question? A retributivist?

2. *Problems.* Answer according to Model Penal Code §§ 5.05, 6.01, and 6.06:

A. Kynette starts a fire at Lydia's home, with the intent of destroying it. If convicted of arson (M.P.C. § 220.1), what punishment may she receive?

B. The same as A., except that Kynette is arrested as she attempts to start the fire. Kynette is convicted of attempted arson.

C. Lance purposely shoots and kills Mason. If convicted of murder (M.P.C. § 210.2), what punishment may be imposed?

D. Same as C., except that Mason survives the attack. Lance is convicted of attempted murder.

3. MENS REA

The word "attempt" means to try; it implies an effort to bring about a desired result. Hence an attempt to commit any crime requires a specific intent to commit that particular offense.[c]

PEOPLE v. GENTRY

Appellate Court of Illinois, First District, 1987.
157 Ill.App.3d 899, 109 Ill.Dec. 895, 510 N.E.2d 963.

JUSTICE LINN delivered the opinion of the court:

Following a jury trial, defendant, Stanley Gentry, was convicted of attempt murder (Ill.Rev.Stat.1983, ch. 38, par. 8–4(a)).[d] * * *

On appeal, Gentry asserts that his conviction should be reversed because * * * the trial court's instruction regarding the intent necessary for attempt murder was prejudicially erroneous * * *.

The record indicates that on December 13, 1983, Gentry and Ruby Hill, Gentry's girlfriend, were in the apartment they shared * * *. At approximately 9:00 p.m. the couple began to argue. During the argument, Gentry spilled gasoline on Hill, and the gasoline on Hill's body ignited. Gentry was able to smother the flames with a coat, but only after Hill had been severely burned. Gentry and Hill were the only eyewitnesses to the incident. * * *

The victim, Ruby Hill, * * * testified at trial. Hill stated that she and Gentry had been drinking all afternoon and that both of them were "pretty high." She further testified that Gentry had poured gasoline on her and that the gasoline ignited only after she had gone near the stove in the kitchen. Hill also related how Gentry tried to snuff the fire out by placing a coat over the flames. * * *

At the close of the presentation of evidence in this case, the following instructions were given. First, the trial court defined "attempt" as it relates to the underlying felony of murder:

c. Rollin M. Perkins, *Criminal Attempt and Related Problems,* 2 UCLA L.Rev. 319, 340 (1955).

d. Paragraph 8–4(a) read: "A person commits an attempt when, with the intent to commit a specific offense, he does any act which constitutes a substantial step toward the commission of that offense."

"A person commits the offense of murder when he, *with intent to commit the offense of murder* does any act which constitutes a substantial step toward the commission of the offense of murder. The offense attempted need not have been completed."

Second, * * * the trial court defined the crime of murder, including all four culpable mental states:

"A person commits the crime of murder where he kills an individual if, in performing the acts which cause the death, he intends to kill *or* do great bodily harm to that individual; *or* he knows that such acts will cause death to that individual; *or* he knows that such acts create a strong probability of death or great bodily harm to that individual."

Gentry contends that the inclusion of all the alternative states of mind in the definitional murder instruction was erroneous because the crime of attempt murder requires a showing of specific intent to kill. Gentry posits that inclusion of all four alternative states of mind permitted the jury to convict him of attempt * * * upon a finding that he intended to harm Hill, or acted with the knowledge that his conduct created a strong probability of death or great bodily harm to Hill, even if the jury believed that Gentry did not act with specific intent to kill. We agree with Gentry's position that the jury was misinstructed in this case.

Our supreme court has repeatedly held that a finding of specific intent to kill is a necessary element of the crime of attempt murder. Indeed, a trial court instructing a jury on the crime * * * must make it clear that specific intent to kill is the pivotal element of that offense, and that intent to do bodily harm, or knowledge that the consequences of defendant's act may result in death or great bodily harm, is not enough. * * *

* * * The State labels as illogical those cases which distinguish between the specific intent to kill and the three other alternative states of mind also found in the definitional murder instruction.

The State would read the attempt * * * instruction as requiring a showing of any of the alternative mental states sufficient for a conviction of murder. In other words, the State makes no distinction between the mental state required to prove murder and the mental state required to prove attempt murder. We find the State's analysis and conclusion to be erroneous and lacking in legal substance since it fails to contain the judicial reasoning which recognizes the distinction between the intent elements of murder and attempt murder.

Specifically, we cite the *Kraft* case, where defendant's attempt murder conviction was reversed where the jury instructions would have permitted a conviction without a finding of specific intent to kill. (133 Ill.App.3d 294, 88 Ill.Dec. 546, 478 N.E.2d 1154.) In reversing the defendant's attempt murder conviction in that case, the *Kraft* court analyzed the distinction between the culpable mental states required for murder and attempt * * * noting as follows:

"Our criminal code contains separate statutory definitions for the four culpable mental states of intent, knowledge, recklessness, and negligence, with knowledge encompassing a distinct and less purposeful state of mind than intent * * *. [O]ur state legislature manifested a desire to treat intent and knowledge as distinct mental states when imposing criminal liability for conduct * * *. Knowledge is not intent as defined by our statutes and the jury instructions should reflect this distinction. Accordingly, in a prosecution for attempted murder, where alternative culpable mental states will satisfy the target crime of murder, but only one is compatible with the mental state imposed by our attempt statute, the incompatible elements must be omitted from the jury instructions."

Consequently, it is sufficient only for us to say that we recognize the distinction between the alternative states of mind delineated in the definitional murder instruction, as well as the fact that only the specific intent to kill satisfies the intent element of the crime of attempt murder. * * *

* * * [W]e reverse defendant's conviction and sentence, and remand this cause for a new trial in front of a properly instructed jury.

Notes and Questions

1. The court's application of the Illinois attempt statute tracks the common law. Since an attempt is usually punished less severely, and never more severely, than the target offense, why does the common law require a *more* culpable state of mind for an attempted murder than for the completed crime?

Is the intent requirement appropriate in view of the purposes of attempt laws? Do you agree with the following observation by Holmes?

Acts should be judged by their tendency under the known circumstances, not by the actual intent which accompanies them. ¶ It may be true that in the region of attempts, as elsewhere, the law began with cases of actual intent, as those cases are the most obvious ones. But it cannot stop with them, unless it attaches more importance to the etymological meaning of the word *attempt* than to the general principles of punishment.

Oliver Wendell Holmes, The Common Law 66 (1881).

2. Assume that the prosecutor introduced evidence at Gentry's trial that the gasoline was ignited from a match the defendant lit and tossed at Hill after he doused her with the fuel. Based on this version of the facts, if the prosecution had arisen in a Model Penal Code jurisdiction, would Gentry have been guilty of attempted murder if he had set Hill on fire: (a) in order to kill her; (b) in order to "teach her a lesson," which he knew might result in her death; or (c) without realizing how dangerous his actions were? Would Gentry be guilty of any other Model Code offense relating to Hill's injuries? Look at Article 211 for possibilities.

3. Bob wants to demolish a building. He realizes that people are in the structure and believes that they will be killed in the demolition, although

he does not want them to die. He detonates a bomb, but it proves defective. At common law, is Bob guilty of attempted murder? What would be the outcome under the Model Penal Code? See American Law Institute, Model Penal Code and Commentaries, Comment to § 5.01 at 304–05 (1985).

BRUCE v. STATE

Court of Appeals of Maryland, 1989.
317 Md. 642, 566 A.2d 103.

MURPHY, CHIEF JUDGE.

The question presented is whether "attempted felony murder" is a crime in this State.

On December 2, 1986, three men entered Barry Tensor's shoe store. One man, later identified as Leon Bruce, was masked and armed with a handgun. He ordered Tensor to open the cash register. * * * Upon finding it empty, Bruce demanded to know where the money could be found. Tensor testified:

"I said it's empty, that is all there is and then he took the gun and aimed it right at my face, at my head. And he said I'm going to kill you in a very serious voice, and the gun was continuously held right at my face.

"At that point, I was incredibly afraid and I just tucked my head down and kind of tried to get out of the way and ducked down and moved forward. And at that point, I guess I banged into him or something and he shot me."

Tensor was hospitalized for five weeks from a gunshot wound to his stomach.

* * * A jury * * * found [Bruce] * * * guilty of attempted first degree felony murder, guilty of robbery with a deadly weapon, and guilty of * * * two handgun charges. * * *

On appeal * * *, Bruce argued that attempted felony murder was not a crime in Maryland. We granted certiorari * * * to consider the significant issue raised in the case.

Maryland Code Article 27, § 407 provides that murder "perpetrated by means of poison, or lying in wait, or by any kind of wilful, deliberate and premeditated killing shall be murder in the first degree." Section 410—the so-called felony murder statute—provides that all murder committed in the perpetration of, or attempt to perpetrate, certain designated felonies, of which robbery is one, is also murder in the first degree. These statutes do not create new statutory crimes but rather divide the common law crime of murder into degrees for purposes of punishment.

* * * To secure a conviction for first degree murder under the felony murder doctrine, the State is required to prove a specific intent to commit the underlying felony and that death occurred in the perpetration or attempt to perpetrate the felony; it is not necessary to prove a

specific intent to kill or to demonstrate the existence of wilfulness, deliberation, or premeditation. * * *

In determining whether attempted felony murder is a crime in Maryland, we note that criminal attempts are * * * applicable to any existing crime, whether statutory or common law. *Cox v. State,* 311 Md. 326, 329–30, 534 A.2d 1333 (1988). Under Maryland law, a criminal attempt consists of a specific intent to commit the offense coupled with some overt act in furtherance of the intent which goes beyond mere preparation.

In *Cox,* the question presented was whether an individual could be convicted of attempted voluntary manslaughter. Recognizing that criminal attempt is a specific intent crime, we held that an individual may be convicted of the crime of attempted voluntary manslaughter since the substantive offense is "an *intentional* homicide, done in a sudden heat of passion, caused by adequate provocation." On the other hand, we noted that involuntary manslaughter is an *"unintentional* killing done without malice, by doing some unlawful act endangering life, or in negligently doing some act lawful in itself"; accordingly, we held that it may not form the basis of a criminal conviction for attempt.

* * * Because a conviction for felony murder requires no specific intent to kill, it follows that because a criminal attempt is a specific intent crime, attempted felony murder is not a crime in Maryland. * * *

Notes and Questions

1. Nearly all states that have considered the question agree with *Bruce,* but a contrary result was reached in Amlotte v. State, 456 So.2d 448, 449–50 (Fla.1984). In *Amlotte, A* fired a gun at *V* during the commission of a burglary. *A* was not hit. The court, upholding a conviction of attempted felony murder, announced the following rule:

> [W]henever an individual perpetrates or attempts to perpetrate an enumerated felony, and during the commission of the felony the individual commits * * * a specific overt act which could, but does not, cause the death of another, that individual will have committed the crime of attempted felony murder.

Under this rule, would *A* have been guilty of attempted felony murder if he had *not* fired his gun at *V,* but *V* had suffered a fear-induced heart attack during the burglary, from which he recovered?

2. In Simmons v. State, 151 Fla. 778, 10 So.2d 436 (1942), the accused attempted to have sexual intercourse with a female under the age of eighteen years, but desisted when he learned that she was under the age of legal consent. Is the accused guilty of attempted statutory rape? In what manner does the *mens rea* issue here differ from that in *Bruce* ?

3. *Model Penal Code.* How would *Simmons* (Note 2) be resolved under Model Penal Code § 5.01(1)? The Commentary explains:

> The requirement of purpose extends to the conduct of the actor and to the results that his conduct causes, but his purpose need not encompass

all of the circumstances included in the formal definition of the substantive offense.[9] As to them, it is sufficient that he acts with the culpability that is required for commission of the completed crime.

* * * Assume, for example, a statute that provides that sexual intercourse with a female under a prescribed age is an offense, and that a mistake as to age will not afford a defense no matter how reasonable its foundation. The policy of the substantive offense as to age, therefore, is one of strict liability, and if the actor has sexual intercourse with a female, he is guilty or not, depending upon her age and irrespective of his views as to her age. Suppose, however, that he is arrested before he engages in the proscribed conduct, and that the charge is an attempt to commit the offense. Should he then be entitled to rely on a mistake as to age as a defense? Or should the policy of the substantive crime on this issue carry over to the attempt as well? * * *

Under the formulation in Subsection (1)(c),[11] the proffered defense would not succeed * * *. In the statutory rape example, the actor must engage in sexual intercourse with a female [12] in order to be charged with the attempt, and must engage in a substantial step in a course of conduct planned to culminate in his commission of that act. With respect to the age of the victim, however, it is sufficient if he acts "with the kind of culpability otherwise required for the commission of the crime," which in the case supposed is none at all. Since, therefore, mistake as to age is irrelevant with respect to the substantive offense, it is likewise irrelevant with respect to the attempt. * * *[13]

The judgment is thus that if the defendant manifests a purpose to engage in the type of conduct or to cause the type of result that is forbidden by the criminal law, he has sufficiently exhibited his danger-

9. The "circumstances" of the offense refer to the objective situation that the law requires to exist, in addition to the defendant's act or any results that the act may cause. The elements of "nighttime" in burglary, "property of another" in theft, "female not his wife" in rape, and "dwelling" in arson are illustrations. "Conduct" refers to "breaking and entering" in burglary, "taking" in theft, "sexual intercourse" in rape and "burning" in arson. Results, of course, include "death" in homicide. While these terms are not airtight categories, they have served as a helpful analytical device in the development of the Code.

11. Subsection (1)(a) would not apply * * * because * * * the defendant would have committed the substantive offense if he had successfully completed his conduct. [Since] he did not complete his planned course of conduct, Subsection (1)(c) would apply. * * *

12. It is assumed that the culpability standard for the "female" element of the offense is knowledge, and thus it would be the same for the attempt.

It should also be noted that the language "under the circumstances as he believes them to be," as well as its counterpart language in Subsections (1)(a) and (1)(b), does not affect the analysis of cases like the one[ ] posed. This language is designed to deal with the so-called "impossibility" cases [see p. 685 infra], where the actor believes an element of the offense to exist but where in fact it does not. In that situation, the actor is measured by "the circumstances as he believes them to be." In cases like [the statutory rape illustration], the actor's mistaken belief as to the particular circumstances is made irrelevant by law.

13. It should be noted that while offenses involving strict liability were chosen for clarity of illustration, the analysis would be the same for circumstance elements where the culpability level is set at recklessness or negligence. For example, if negligence as to age * * * were required and sufficient for the substantive offense, the same would hold true for the attempt.

ousness to justify the imposition of criminal sanctions, so long as he otherwise acts with the kind of culpability that is sufficient for the completed offense. The objective is to select out those elements of the completed crime that, if the defendant desires to bring them about, indicate with clarity that he poses the type of danger to society that the substantive offense is designed to prevent. This objective is well served by the Code's approach, followed in a number of recently enacted and proposed revisions, of allowing the policy of the substantive offense to control with respect to circumstance elements.

American Law Institute, Model Penal Code and Commentaries, Comment to § 5.01 at 301–03 (1985).

4. *Problem.* N.Y.—McKinney's Penal Law § 125.27(1)(a)(i) provides that a person is guilty of murder in the first degree when "with intent to cause the death of another person, he causes the death of such person; and * * * the victim was a police officer * * * killed in the course of performing his official duties * * *."

Assume that Alice unjustifiably attempts to kill Barbara, unaware that Barbara is an undercover police officer performing her official duties. Barbara survives the attack. Is Alice guilty of attempted murder under the New York statute? Assume that New York applies Model Code attempt law.

5. *Proving intent.* Even if a party unambiguously intends to commit an offense, it is sometimes difficult to identify the target offense. Evaluate People v. Terrell, 99 Ill.2d 427, 429–32, 77 Ill.Dec. 88, 89–91, 459 N.E.2d 1337, 1338–40 (1984):

> The evidence revealed that on August 7, 1980, at approximately 6:15 a.m., an anonymous telephone call was received by the Kankakee City police. The caller stated that two men, armed with guns, were hiding behind a service station. This report was dispatched and was responded to by Officer Whitehead in one patrol car, and Officers Pepin and Rokus, who were patrolling the area, in another car.
>
> A diagram, entered into evidence, shows that the service station is located on the southwest corner of Erzinger and Maple streets. The first building south of the station, facing Maple Street, is a construction company. Further south is a tool company. To the rear of the buildings is a large grassy lot which extends to an alley running parallel to the buildings.
>
> Officer Whitehead arrived at the scene within minutes of the radio dispatch and only seconds before Officers Rokus and Pepin. Whitehead pulled into the alley and onto the empty lot behind the station, where he immediately observed a man, crouched in the weeds, 20 to 30 feet from the station. As the officer got out of his car, the defendant, who he saw carrying a gun, jumped up from the weeds, ran towards the fence, climbed to the other side and proceeded south down Maple Street. * * * [T]he defendant disposed of the gun sometime before he scaled the fence, although he could not remember seeing it being dropped.
>
> Twelve to fifteen minutes after he was initially observed, Officer Pepin discovered the defendant hiding in the weeds behind the tool company, approximately 280 feet from the service station. The defen-

dant had removed his shirt and was lying on it. A black nylon stocking with a knot in the end of it was found in his pocket. Although the defendant claimed that he was going to the gas station to buy cigarettes, the officer found no money on defendant's person. * * *

* * * It is unclear from the record if the station was open at the time the officers arrived on the scene. Officer Whitehead did notice, however, that the station was open at some time during his search of the area. * * *

While the defendant, in the instant case, does not deny the presence of "some" criminal intent, he maintains that the evidence fails to "imply a design to commit an armed robbery at the station." He suggests a list of alternative targets and offenses which includes the crime of burglary as opposed to armed robbery. In addition, he finds it significant that the State failed to establish that the gas station was open when he was initially discovered.

We find this argument unpersuasive. It is unreasonable to expect a trier of fact to infer intent to commit burglary, rather than armed robbery when confronted with a suspect who was seen carrying a loaded revolver and in possession of a ladies' stocking but no burglary tools. In addition, the trial court could reasonably infer that the service station was the object of defendant's plan. The defendant was observed in close proximity to the station, by Officer Whitehead, as he arrived on the scene. This observation was in conformity with the initial tip from the telephone caller who specifically indicated that the suspects were hiding behind the service station. As for the victim necessary for an armed robbery, the trier of fact may reasonably have inferred that the defendant was awaiting the attendant's arrival before taking the final step in his plan.

Following the court's reasoning, if the gas station had been open and attended by a female, could a jury reasonably conclude that the defendant intended to rape the attendant and not rob the station?

Justice Simon dissented in *Terrell*:

The crime of attempt has two unambiguous requirements—"*intent* to commit a specific offense," and an "act which constitutes a *substantial step* toward the commission of that offense." I do not believe that either * * * requirement * * * [has] been met in this case.

The few facts proved here suggest, at most, a general intent to engage in some form of mischief in the general area in which defendant was arrested. The majority uses the same facts to establish both intent to commit a specific armed robbery, and a substantial step in the commission of that robbery. These facts are defendant's presence in the vicinity of the station, and his possession of a gun and of a woman's stocking capable of being used as a face mask. * * *

The defendant's actions here were preliminary activities, consistent with a number of different outcomes. * * * There was no evidence in the record that there was anyone in the service station during the time defendant was hiding in the weeds. There is also no evidence as to the customary opening time either of the station, or of the other nearby businesses. There is no indication whether anyone was present in any of the other business establishments, or whether anyone was walking on the street, in the alleyway, or in the empty lot. Potential armed-robbery victims could have been located in any of those places. Further, I do not find it "unreasonable to expect a trier of fact to infer intent to commit burglary, rather than armed robbery when confronted with [this] suspect." Many burglaries are committed without special tools; defendants enter through open windows or throw rocks found in empty lots to break windows, to give but two of many examples. Too, burglars often wear masks to hide their identities in the event that they are inadvertently discovered. Guns are also carried by burglars in case they unexpectedly encounter other people.

The problem in defining attempt is to allow police to intervene in an unfolding course of criminal conduct before the intended harm is actually done, while at the same time avoiding punishment for equivocal acts which may or may not eventually lead to criminal harm. It is always difficult to draw this line so as to properly balance the conflicting needs of the police and the public at large against the rights of the individual citizen. Our legislature has drawn the line at the point where the defendant has taken a substantial step toward commission of the crime. This court cannot interfere with the legislature's decision and with that balance by moving the line further in the direction of mere preparation and undefined intent.

Id. at 436–37, 439–41, 77 Ill.Dec. at 93, 95, 459 N.E.2d at 1342, 1344.

Following Justice Simon's reasoning, what should the officers have done when they spotted Terrell lurking in the weeds? Assuming *arguendo* that the facts do not support a finding beyond a reasonable doubt that Terrell intended to rob the gas station, is there any reasonable doubt that he intended to commit *some* offense? If that much is clear, is the defendant prejudiced by being convicted of attempted armed robbery of the gas station if, in fact, he intended to commit some other offense there or intended to commit an armed robbery of a different victim down the road?

4. ACTUS REUS

a. *General Principles*

UNITED STATES v. MANDUJANO

United States Court of Appeals, Fifth Circuit, 1974.
499 F.2d 370.

RIVES, CIRCUIT JUDGE. * * *

Section 846 of Title 21, entitled "Attempt and conspiracy," provides that,

"Any person who attempts or conspires to commit any offense defined in this subchapter is punishable by imprisonment or fine or both which may not exceed the maximum punishment prescribed for the offense, the commission of which was the object of the attempt or conspiracy." * * *

Apparently there is no legislative history indicating exactly what Congress meant when it used the word "attempt" in section 846. * * * In United States v. Noreikis, 7 Cir.1973, 481 F.2d 1177, * * * the court commented that,

> "While it seems to be well settled that mere preparation is not sufficient to constitute an attempt to commit a crime, it seems equally clear that the semantical distinction between preparation and attempt is one incapable of being formulated in a hard and fast rule. The procuring of the instrument of the crime might be preparation in one factual situation and not in another. * * *"
> * * *

The courts in many jurisdictions have tried to elaborate on the distinction between mere preparation and attempt. See the Comment at 39–48 of Tent. Draft No. 10, 1960 of the Model Penal Code.[5] In cases involving statutes other than section 846, the federal courts have confronted this issue on a number of occasions. * * *

In United States v. Coplon, 2 Cir.1950, 185 F.2d 629, * * * Judge Learned Hand surveyed the law and addressed the issue of what would constitute an attempt:

> "Because the arrest in this way interrupted the consummation of the crime one point upon the appeal is that her conduct still remained in the zone of 'preparation,' and that the evidence did not prove an 'attempt.' This argument it will be most convenient to answer at the outset. A neat doctrine by which to test when a person, intending to commit a crime which he fails to carry out, has 'attempted' to commit it, would be that he has done all that it is within his power to do, but has been prevented by intervention from outside; in short, that he has passed beyond any *locus pœnitentiae.* Apparently that was the original notion, and may still be law in England; but it is certainly not now generally the law in the United States, for there are many decisions which hold that the accused has

---

5. This comment to the Model Penal Code catalogues a number of formulations which have been adopted or suggested, including the following:

(a) The physical proximity doctrine—the overt act required for an attempt must be proximate to the completed crime, or directly tending toward the completion of the crime, or must amount to the commencement of the consummation.

(b) The dangerous proximity doctrine—a test given impetus by Mr. Justice Holmes whereby the greater the gravity and probability of the offense, and the nearer the act to the crime, the stronger is the case for calling the act an attempt.

(c) The indispensable element test—a variation of the proximity tests which em-

phasizes any indispensable aspect of the criminal endeavor over which the actor has not yet acquired control.

(d) The probable desistance test—the conduct constitutes an attempt if, in the ordinary and natural course of events, without interruption from an outside source, it will result in the crime intended.

(e) The abnormal step approach—an attempt is a step toward crime which goes beyond the point where the normal citizen would think better of his conduct and desist.

(f) The res ipsa loquitur or unequivocality test—an attempt is committed when the actor's conduct manifests an intent to commit a crime.

passed beyond 'preparation,' although he has been interrupted before he has taken the last of his intended steps. * * * "

In Mims v. United States, 5 Cir.1967, 375 F.2d 135, 148, we noted that, "Much ink has been spilt in an attempt to arrive at a satisfactory standard for telling where preparations ends [sic] and attempt begins," and that the question had not been decided by this Court. The Court in *Mims,* did note that the following test from People v. Buffum, 40 Cal.2d 709, 256 P.2d 317, 321, has been "frequently approved":

" 'Preparation alone is not enough, there must be some *appreciable fragment* of the crime committed, it must be in such progress that it will be consummated unless interrupted by circumstances independent of the will of the attempter, and the act must not be equivocal in nature. * * *' "

Notes and Questions

1. Here are some other not entirely consistent observations about the line between preparation and perpetration:

A. United States v. Oviedo, 525 F.2d 881, 884–85 (5th Cir.1976):

When the question before the court is whether certain conduct constitutes mere preparation * * * or an attempt * * *, the possibility of error is mitigated by the requirement that the objective acts of the defendant evidence commitment to the criminal venture and corroborate the *mens rea.* To the extent that this requirement is preserved it prevents the conviction of persons engaged in innocent acts on the basis of a *mens rea* proved through speculative inferences, unreliable forms of testimony, and past criminal conduct.

Courts could have approached the preparation-attempt determination in another fashion, eliminating any notion of particular objective facts, and simply could have asked whether the evidence at hand was sufficient to prove the necessary intent. But this approach has been rejected for precisely the reasons set out above, for conviction upon proof of mere intent provides too great a possibility of speculation and abuse. * * *

Thus, we demand that in order for a defendant to be guilty of a criminal attempt, the objective acts performed, without any reliance on the accompanying *mens rea,* mark the defendant's conduct as criminal in nature. The acts should be unique rather than so commonplace that they are engaged in by persons not in violation of the law.

B. Stokes v. State, 92 Miss. 415, 46 So. 627, 629 (1908):

At last, it is the safety of the public and their protection which is to be guarded. * * * ¶ When the intent to commit crime, or, to put it more accurately, when the only proof is that it is the declared intention of a person to commit a crime merely, with no act done in furtherance of the intent, however clearly may be proved this intention, it does not amount to an attempt, and it cannot be punished as such. But, whenever the design of a person to commit crime is clearly shown, slight acts done in furtherance of this design will constitute an attempt, and this court will not destroy the practical and commonsense administration of the law with subtleties as to what constitutes preparation and what an act done toward the commission of a crime. * * * Too many loopholes have been made whereby parties are enabled to escape punishment for that which is known to be criminal in its worse sense.

C.   State v. Otto, 102 Idaho 250, 257, 629 P.2d 646, 653 (1981) (Bakes, C.J., dissenting):

The [court] * * * attempts to distinguish between acts of preparation and acts of perpetration. Although this type of analysis has been accepted by * * * courts, the distinction is in fact highly artificial, since all acts leading up to the ultimate consummation of a crime are by their very nature preparatory. The real question is whether acts of preparation when coupled with intent have reached a point at which they pose a danger to the public so as to be worthy of law's notice.

D.   Arnold N. Enker, *Impossibility in Criminal Attempts—Legality and the Legal Process,* 53 Minn.L.Rev. 665, 674 (1969):

Because attempt is a relational crime—it is defined in relation to the statutorily defined substantive crime allegedly attempted—there is available a judicial technique for deciding individual cases, namely the technique of analogy. Cases arising along the preparation-attempt spectrum are handled in terms of their similarities to and differences from the substantive crime attempted, and in terms of analogy to previously decided or hypothetical attempt cases. In deciding, the court weighs several factors, principally: whether the act at issue is sufficiently close to the substantive crime or close enough to potential irreparable harm so as to preclude any further postponement of official intervention; whether the defendant's conduct has progressed to the point that one may be reasonably certain that he is firmly committed to a specific illegal venture rather than merely contemplating the possible future commission of a crime; and whether the act is sufficiently unambiguous to demonstrate the actor's illegal intent.

AN INITIAL EFFORT AT DRAWING THE PREPARATION– PERPETRATION LINE

1.   On January 15, at 3:00 p.m., Anne decides to kill Bob, who lives twenty miles away.

2.   At 3:15 p.m., Anne places ammunition in her gun.

3.   At 3:30 p.m., Anne begins her 25–minute drive to Bob's house.

4.   At 3:55 p.m. Anne reaches Bob's house. She parks on the street, gets out of her car, and surveys the area. She knows that Bob ordinarily arrives home from work by car at 5:20 p.m., so she decides that just before he arrives she will hide behind a tall bush near his driveway and shoot Bob as soon as he reaches his front door.

5.   In the interim, Anne returns to her parked car and reads a newspaper.

6.   At 5:15 p.m., Anne stations herself behind the bush.

7.   Bob does not arrive home at 5:20 p.m. At 5:35 p.m., Anne leaves.

8. Bob arrives home at 5:40 p.m. [*Alternative 8A: Bob is out of town, and does not return home for 24 hours.*] [*Alternative 8B: Bob did not go to work that day due to illness, and was in bed asleep throughout the preceding events.*]

9. On January 18, at 5:15 p.m., Anne returns to Bob's house and stations herself behind the bush.

10. At 5:20 p.m., Bob drives his car into the driveway.

11. Bob gets out of his car.

12. Bob's young daughter runs out of the house and hugs him in the driveway.

13. Anne decides not to kill Bob at this time, because she does not want to traumatize the girl by having her see the shooting.

14. While driving home, Anne decides that killing Bob, and thus leaving his daughter without a father, is morally wrong, and she abandons her plan.

Notes and Questions

1. Is Anne guilty of attempted murder on January 15? On January 18? On both dates? If she is guilty, at precisely what point did the attempt(s) occur. What is your justification for drawing the line where you did? Do alternatives 8A and 8B affect your analysis?

2. Suppose Step 1 and the final sentence of Step 4 are deleted, i.e., you know nothing of Anne's intentions except by way of her actions. Does your answer change?

b. Common Law Tests

COMMONWEALTH v. PEASLEE

Supreme Judicial Court of Massachusetts, 1901.
177 Mass. 267, 59 N.E. 55.

HOLMES, C.J. This is an indictment for an attempt to burn a building and certain goods therein, with intent to injure the insurers of the same. * * * The defense is that the overt acts alleged and proved do not amount to an offense. It was raised by a motion to quash, and also by a request to the judge to direct a verdict for the defendant. We will consider the case in the first place upon the evidence, apart from any question of pleading, and afterwards will take it up in connection with the indictment as actually drawn.

The evidence was that the defendant had constructed and arranged combustibles in the building in such a way that they were ready to be lighted, and if lighted would have set fire to the building and its contents. To be exact, the plan would have required a candle which was standing on a shelf six feet away to be placed on a piece of wood in a pan of turpentine and lighted. The defendant offered to pay a younger man in his employment if he would go to the building, seemingly some miles from the place of the dialogue, and carry out the plan. This was refused. Later the defendant and the young man drove towards the building, but when within a quarter of a mile the defendant said that he had changed his mind, and drove away. This is as near as he ever came to accomplishing what he had in contemplation.

The question on the evidence, more precisely stated, is whether the defendant's acts come near enough to the accomplishment of the substantive offense to be punishable. * * * The most common types of an attempt are either an act which is intended to bring about the substantive crime, and which sets in motion natural forces that would bring it about in the expected course of events, but for the unforeseen interruption, as, in this case, if the candle had been set in its place and lighted, but had been put out by the police, or an act which is intended to bring about the substantive crime, and would bring it about but for a mistake of judgment in a matter of nice estimate or experiment, as when a pistol is fired at a man, but misses him, or when one tries to pick a pocket which turns out to be empty. In either case the would-be criminal has done his last act.

Obviously new considerations come in when further acts on the part of the person who has taken the first steps are necessary before the substantive crime can come to pass. In this class of cases there is still a chance that the would-be criminal may change his mind. In strictness, such first steps cannot be described as an attempt, because that word suggests an act seemingly sufficient to accomplish the end, and has been supposed to have no other meaning. That an overt act, although coupled with an intent to commit the crime, commonly is not punishable if further acts are contemplated as needful, is expressed in the familiar rule that preparation is not an attempt. But some preparations may amount to an attempt. It is a question of degree. If the preparation comes very near to the accomplishment of the act, the intent to complete it renders the crime so probable that the act will be a misdemeanor, although there is still a locus poenitentiae, in the need of a further exertion of the will to complete the crime. As was observed in a recent case, the degree of proximity held sufficient may vary with circumstances, including, among other things, the apprehension which the particular crime is calculated to excite. Com. v. Kennedy, 170 Mass. 18, 22, 48 N.E. 770. See also, Com. v. Willard, 22 Pick. 476. * * *

Under the cases last cited, we assume that there was evidence of a crime, and perhaps of an attempt. The latter question we do not decide. Nevertheless on the pleadings [which failed to allege the solicitation of the employee to set the fire] a majority of the court is of opinion that the exceptions must be sustained. A mere collection and preparation of materials in a room for the purpose of setting fire to them, unaccompanied by any present intent to set the fire, would be too remote. If the accused intended to rely upon his own hands to the end, he must be shown to have had a present intent to accomplish the crime without much delay, and to have had this intent at a time and place where he was able to carry it out. We are not aware of any carefully considered case that has gone further than this. We assume, without deciding, that that is the meaning of the indictment; and it would have been proved if, for instance, the evidence had been that the defendant had been frightened by the police as he was about to light the candle. On the other hand, if the offense is to be made out by showing a preparation of the room, and a solicitation of some one else to set the fire, which solicitation, if successful, would have been the defendant's last act, the solicitation must be alleged as one of the overt acts. * * * If the indictment had been properly drawn, we have no question that the defendant might have been convicted.

Exceptions sustained.

Notes and Questions

1. Suppose that the employee had agreed to set the fire by himself, and that it was he, not Peaslee, who turned back a quarter of a mile from the building. Should that affect *Peaslee's* guilt for attempt?

2. Based on the evidence introduced at his trial, was Peaslee guilty of attempt under either the "probable desistance" or "abnormal step" tests of attempt, as these standards are summarized in footnote 5 of *Mandujano*, p. 668 supra?

The drafters of the Model Penal Code were critical of these two tests:

Probable Desistance Test. Oriented largely toward the dangerousness of the actor's conduct * * * [t]his test seemed to require a judgment in each case that the actor had reached a point where it was unlikely that he would have voluntarily desisted from his efforts to commit the crime. But in cases applying this test no inquiry was made into the personality of the particular offender before the court. Rather, the question was whether *anyone* who went so far would stop short of the final step. * * *

Accepting for the time being the underlying assumption that probability of desistance, or actual abandonment of the criminal endeavor, negatives dangerousness sufficiently to warrant immunity from attempt liability, this test still does not appear to provide a workable standard. Is there an adequate empirical basis for predicting whether desistance is probable at various points in various type of cases? The opinion has been voiced that one who has undertaken a criminal endeavor and performed an act pursuant to that purpose would not be likely to stop short of the final step. And in actual operation the probable desistance test is linked entirely to the nearness of the actor's conduct to completion, this being the sole basis of unsubstantiated judicial appraisals of the probabilities of desistance. The test as applied appears to be little more than the physical proximity approach.

Abnormal Step Approach. * * * Despite its proper orientation, this approach has several serious deficiencies. First, with respect to some and probably with respect to most crimes, any step toward the crime is a departure from the conduct of the normal citizen. Thus this approach would effect a major revolution in attempt liability, since under this definition of attempt almost any act undertaken for the purpose of committing a crime would constitute an attempt. * * * Finally, who is to judge where the normal citizen would stop and what kind of proof would be appropriate for such a determination? The test is oriented toward singling out dangerous personalities but is virtually impossible of application.

American Law Institute, Model Penal Code and Commentaries, Comment to § 5.01 at 324–26 (1985).

3. *Peaslee* is sometimes cited as an application of the "dangerous proximity" test (see footnote 5 of *Mandujano*). Oliver Wendell Holmes originally explained the doctrine in The Common Law 67–69 (1881):

> [L]ighting a match with intent to set fire to a haystack has been held to amount to a criminal attempt to burn it, although the defendant blew out the match on seeing that he was watched. * * *

> * * * If a man starts from Boston to Cambridge for the purpose of committing a murder when he gets there, but is stopped by the draw [bridge] and goes home, he is no more punishable than if he had sat in his chair and resolved to shoot somebody, but on second thoughts had given up the notion. * * *

> Eminent judges have been puzzled where to draw the line, or even to state the principle on which it should be drawn, between the two sets of cases. But the principle is believed to be similar to that on which all other lines are drawn by the law. Public policy, that is to say, legislative considerations, are at the bottom of the matter; the considerations being, in this case, the nearness of the danger, the greatness of the harm, and the degree of apprehension felt.

PEOPLE v. RIZZO

Court of Appeals of New York, 1927.
246 N.Y. 334, 158 N.E. 888.

CRANE, J. The police of the city of New York did excellent work in this case by preventing the commission of a serious crime. It is a great satisfaction to realize that we have such wide-awake guardians of our peace. Whether or not the steps which the defendant had taken up to the time of his arrest amounted to the commission of a crime, as defined by our law, is, however, another matter. He has been convicted of an attempt to commit the crime of robbery in the first degree and sentenced to State's prison. There is no doubt that he had the intention to commit robbery if he got the chance. An examination, however, of the facts is necessary to determine whether his acts were in preparation to commit the crime if the opportunity offered, or constituted a crime in itself, known to our law as an attempt to commit robbery in the first degree. Charles Rizzo, the defendant, appellant, with three others, * * * planned to rob one Charles Rao of a payroll valued at about $1,200 which he was to carry from the bank for the United Lathing Company. These defendants, two of whom had firearms, started out in an automobile, looking for Rao or the man who had the payroll on that day. Rizzo claimed to be able to identify the man and was to point him out to the others who were to do the actual holding up. The four rode about in their car looking for Rao. They went to the bank from which he was supposed to get the money and to various buildings being constructed by the United Lathing Company. At last they came to One Hundred and Eightieth street and Morris Park avenue. By this time they were watched and followed by two police officers. As Rizzo jumped out of the car and ran into the building all four were arrested. The defendant was taken out from the building in which he was hiding. Neither Rao nor a man named Previti, who was also supposed to carry a payroll, were at the place at the time of the arrest. The defendants had not found or seen the man they intended to rob; no person with a payroll was at any of the places where they had stopped and no one had been pointed out or identified by Rizzo. * * *

Does this constitute the crime of an attempt to commit robbery in the first degree? * * *

In Hyde v. U.S., 225 U.S. 347, 32 S.Ct. 793, 56 L.Ed. 1114, it was stated that the act amounts to an attempt when it is so near to the result that the danger of success is very great. "There must be dangerous proximity to success." * * *

Commonwealth v. Peaslee, 177 Mass. 267, 59 N.E. 55, refers to the acts constituting an attempt as coming *very near* to the accomplishment of the crime.

How shall we apply this rule of immediate nearness to this case? * * * To constitute the crime of robbery the money must have been taken from Rao by means of force or violence, or through fear. The crime of attempt to commit robbery was committed if these defendants did an act tending to the commission of this robbery. Did the acts above described come dangerously near to the taking of Rao's property? Did the acts come so near the commission of robbery that there was reasonable likelihood of its accomplishment but for the interference? Rao was not found; the defendants were still looking for him; no attempt to rob him could be made, at least until he came in sight * * *. In a word, these defendants had planned to commit a crime and were looking around the city for an opportunity to commit it, but the opportunity fortunately never came. * * *

For these reasons, the judgment of conviction of this defendant, appellant, must be reversed and a new trial granted. * * *

Notes and Questions

1. Based on the dangerous proximity test, should *D* be convicted of attempt in the following cases?

A. *D* paid *X*, an undercover agent, a fee to procure a young female for him, with whom he planned to have sexual intercourse. *D* selected a girl from a collection of photographs displayed to him, after which he rented a room where the sexual acts would occur. *X* arrested *D* as they approached the building where the non-existent girl was supposed to be waiting. Attempted sexual assault? Van Bell v. State, 105 Nev. 352, 775 P.2d 1273 (1989).

B. *X,* an undercover investigator, observed *D,* who did not possess the requisite barbering license, unlock the rear door of his shop and enter. Shortly thereafter, *X* went to the front door and asked *D* if the shop was open. *D* unlocked the door, admitted *X,* walked over to the barber's chair, put on his smock, and offered the chair to *X.* Attempt to practice barbering without a license? People v. Paluch, 78 Ill.App.2d 356, 222 N.E.2d 508 (1966).

C. *D* agreed to perform an illegal abortion on *X. X* paid *D* his $250 fee. *D* administered a sedative to *X. X* removed her shoes and began to unbutton her blouse. At this time, the kitchen table was covered with a sheet, medical instruments were in a pan on the oven being sterilized, and other surgical equipment were set out on a small table. Before *X* got on the table, a police officer arrested *D.* Attempted abortion? People v. Woods, 24 Ill.2d 154, 180 N.E.2d 475 (1962).

D. *D* met with *X,* a police informant, to arrange the purchase of an illegal drug from *X.* At their second meeting, *D* and *X* reached agreement on the terms of the sale. However, *D* had insufficient cash on his person, and the cocaine was not properly packaged. Therefore, they scheduled to meet again later that day "in a distant parking lot," in order to conclude their business. However, *D* was arrested at the conclusion of the second meeting. Attempted possession of a controlled substance? People v. Warren, 66 N.Y.2d 831, 498 N.Y.S.2d 353, 489 N.E.2d 240 (1985).

E. *D* ordered cocaine from a supplier, admitted a drug courier into her home, examined the product, but ultimately rejected it because of perceived defects in its quality. Attempted possession of a controlled substance? People v. Acosta, 80 N.Y.2d 665, 593 N.Y.S.2d 978, 609 N.E.2d 518 (1993).

F. After extensive negotiations, *D* hired burglars to stage a fake theft of various antiquities he owned, in order that he could fraudulently recover $18 million in insurance proceeds from Lloyd's of London. *D* provided the burglars with a diagram of the warehouse where the valuables were stored. Two days later, the burglars broke into the warehouse, but they were arrested before the antiquities could be removed. *D* was charged, along with others, with attempting to commit grand larceny by obtaining insurance proceeds under false pretenses. People v. Mahboubian, 74 N.Y.2d 174, 544 N.Y.S.2d 769, 543 N.E.2d 34 (1989).

2. How should *Mahboubian* (Note 1F.) be resolved under the indispensable element test (footnote 5 of *Mandujano*)? That standard is explained by the American Law Institute:

> Some decisions seem to stand for the proposition that if the successful completion of a crime requires the assent or action of some third person, that assent or action must be forthcoming before the actor can be guilty of an attempt. Thus, if A and B plan to defraud a life insurance company by pretending that A, the insured, is dead, and if C, the beneficiary, must file a formal claim before any proceeds can be paid, it has been held that the acts of A and B cannot amount to an attempt to

defraud the insurance company until C files a claim or agrees to file a claim. * * *

An analogous group of cases supports the view that a person cannot be guilty of an attempt if he lacks a means essential to completion of the offense. Thus, it has been held that one cannot be guilty of an attempt * * * to vote illegally until he obtains a ballot.

American Law Institute, Model Penal Code and Commentaries, Comment to § 5.01 at 323–24 (1985).

PEOPLE v. MILLER

Supreme Court of California, 1935.
2 Cal.2d 527, 42 P.2d 308.

SHENK, JUSTICE.

The defendant was charged by * * * amended information * * * with "attempt to commit murder, in that on or about the 17th day of March, 1934, * * * he did, then and there, wilfully, unlawfully and feloniously, attempt to murder one Albert Jeans." The jury found the defendant guilty as charged in the amended information. * * *

The evidence is practically without conflict. On the day in question, the defendant, somewhat under the influence of liquor and in the presence of others at the post office in the town of Booneville, threatened to kill Albert Jeans * * *. On that day Jeans was employed on the hop ranch of Ginochio, who was the constable of Booneville. About 4 o'clock that afternoon, while Constable Ginochio, Jeans, and others were planting hops, the defendant entered the hop field of Ginochio carrying a .22–caliber rifle. Ginochio was about 250 or 300 yards away and Jeans about 30 yards beyond him. The defendant walked in a direct line toward Ginochio. When the defendant had gone about 100 yards, he stopped and appeared to be loading his rifle. At no time did he lift his rifle as though to take aim. Jeans, as soon as he perceived the defendant, fled on a line at about right angles to Miller's line of approach, but whether before or after the stopping motion made by the defendant is not clear. The defendant continued toward Ginochio, who took the gun into his own possession; the defendant offering no resistance. The gun was found to be loaded with a .22–caliber long, or high-speed, cartridge. The foregoing are the salient facts stated without the color afforded by the epithets and language used by the defendant in making his threats. * * *

We are mindful of the fact that language appearing in Stokes v. State, 92 Miss. 415, 46 So. 627, 629, that, "whenever the design of a person to commit crime is clearly shown, slight acts done in furtherance of this design will constitute an attempt," has received approval. The statement, however, * * * is not in conflict with the usual statements of the tests applied to aid in drawing the line at the point where preparation leaves off and execution has commenced. It still presupposes some direct act or movement in execution of the design, as distinguished from mere preparation, which leaves the intended assailant only in the condition to commence the first direct act toward consummation of his design. The reason for requiring evidence of a direct act, however slight, toward consummation of the intended crime, is * * * that in the majority of cases up to that time the conduct of the defendant, consisting merely of acts of preparation, has never ceased to be equivocal; and this is necessarily so, irrespective of his declared intent. It is that quality of being equivocal that must be lacking before the act becomes one which may be said to be a commencement of the commission of the crime, or an overt act, or before any fragment of the crime itself has been committed, and this is so for the reason that, so long as the equivocal quality remains, no one can say with certainty what the intent of the defendant is. * * *

* * * In the present case, up to the moment the gun was taken from the defendant, no one could say with certainty whether the defendant had come into the field to carry out his threat to kill Jeans or merely to demand his arrest by the constable. Under the authorities, therefore, the acts of the defendant do not constitute an attempt to commit murder. * * *

Notes and Questions

1. Was the defendant's conduct equivocal? If not, what act(s) convince you that he intended to kill Jeans? If you agree with the court, what additional facts or change in circumstances would have made the defendant's conduct unequivocal?

Miller is controversial, even in its home state. According to one California court, "[o]ther jurisdictions have not stood in line for a chance to follow *Miller*'s logic. * * * It could be argued that in this jurisdiction, *Miller*'s command is treated as a request to create grounds to ignore it." People v. Jimimez, 235 Cal.App.3d 88, 92–93, 279 Cal.Rptr. 157, 160 (1991).

2. Under the strict version of the unequivocality standard, an act does not constitute an attempt unless the actor's specific criminal purpose is evident from her conduct, without considering any statement she may have made before, during, or after the incident regarding her state of mind.

Is this a sensible test? Although ultimately critical of this version of the doctrine, the American Law Institute offers these justifications for the standard:

> [T]he res ipsa loquitur rule * * * may be viewed entirely as a matter of procedure, as a device to prevent liability based solely on confessions and other representations of purpose [119] because of the risks they raise when considered with the other probative weaknesses [120] incident to

119. Statements made by the actor before or during the act are not reliable because the actor may have been bluffing or he may have entertained an idea or inclination without really acting on it, the act in question being motivated by a noncriminal purpose.

120. There are a number of differences between the conduct questioned in an at-

tempt case and the conduct questioned in a case involving the completed crime. In an attempt case the conduct involved is noncausal, so at the outset there is the opportunity to charge a crime where nothing is amiss. There is no corpus delicti to verify the fact that somebody has caused some sort of trouble. Moreover, in a case of a completed crime the last proximate act

attempt liability. Whether the requirement of unequivocality is considered part of the substantive definition of attempt or as a separate rule of evidence, it can be realistically administered only by means of a procedural mechanism—by excluding from the jury, in whole or in part, the actor's incriminating representations of purpose. If problems of proof are the basis of the preparation-attempt distinction, then the res ipsa loquitur approach has some merit. * * *

A second point of departure in considering the * * * test is its relation to the manifested dangerousness of the actor. * * * The assumption underlying [the test] * * * is that there is some relationship between the actor's state of mind and the external appearance of his acts. While the actor's behavior is externally equivocal the criminal purpose in his mind is likely to be unfixed—a subjective equivocality. But once the actor must desist or perform acts that he realizes would incriminate him if all external facts were known, in all probability a firmer state of mind exists.

American Law Institute, Model Penal Code and Commentaries, Comment to § 5.01 at 326–29 (1985).

Does the unequivocality doctrine work as it should? What if a person enters a neighbor's barn, walks up to a haystack, and pulls out a match. Does this unequivocally demonstrate the actor's intention to set a fire, or must she light the match first? If she lights the match, is it now unequivocal? Suppose that she then pulls out a cigar, lights it, and sits down on the floor of the barn and reads a newspaper. See Glanville Williams, Criminal Law: The General Part 630 (2d ed. 1961).

3. In United States v. Buffington, 815 F.2d 1292 (9th Cir.1987), the police learned from an informant that *D1*, *D2*, and *D3* intended to rob a specific bank, and that *D3*, a male, would be dressed as a female. The police put the area under surveillance, during which time they observed three persons, including a male dressed as a female, drive slowly past the bank, look in, drive to an adjacent street, turn around, and again peer into the bank.

As the police continued to watch, the driver parked the car 150 feet from a drug store, and about 50 feet from the bank. *D1* entered the drug store and walked to a window overlooking the bank. He did not inspect or purchase goods there, but after three minutes stood in a cashier's line at the store.

Simultaneously, *D2* got out of the parked car, wearing a large coat, hat, and long scarf. (The weather that day was inclement.) *D3*, the male in female clothing, then exited and stood by the car door. Both faced the drug store. By coincidence, a major power outage occurred in the area at that moment, causing bank employees to lock their doors. The three men reentered the car and left. The police stopped the vehicle and arrested the occupants. Inside the car, the police discovered two weapons, and found

must be proved. * * * Thus, as to any substantive crime, the chances are that more steps will have to be proved if the completed crime is involved than if the attempt is charged.

that *D2* was wearing five layers of coats or jackets.   Attempted bank robbery?

c. The Model Penal Code and Beyond

UNITED STATES v. JACKSON

United States Court of Appeals, Second Circuit, 1977.
560 F.2d 112.

FREDERICK VAN PELT BRYAN, SENIOR DISTRICT JUDGE:

Robert Jackson, William Scott, and Martin Allen appeal from judgments of conviction entered * * * in the United States District Court for the Eastern District of New York after a trial before Chief Judge Jacob Mishler without a jury.

Count one of the indictment alleged that between June 11 and June 21, 1976 the appellants conspired to commit an armed robbery of the Manufacturers Hanover Trust * * *.   Counts two and three each charged appellants with an attempted robbery of the branch on June 14 and on June 21, 1976, respectively * * *.   * * *

Appellants' principal contention is that the court below erred in finding them guilty on counts two and three.   While they concede that the evidence supported the conspiracy convictions on count one, they assert that, as a matter of law, their conduct never crossed the elusive line which separates "mere preparation" from "attempt."   * * *

[The government's evidence at trial consisted largely of the testimony of Vanessa Hodges, an unindicted co-conspirator, and of federal agents who put the Manufacturers Hanover Bank under surveillance on June 21, 1976.

On June 11, 1976, Hodges told defendant Allen of her interest in robbing the Manufacturers Hanover Bank on June 14.   She proposed that they rob it when it opened, by grabbing the weekend deposits when the bank manager arrived.   Allen agreed to assist.

On June 14, Hodges, Allen, and defendant Jackson, who drove Allen's car, arrived at the bank.   In the back seat of the car were weapons, ammunition, materials intended as masks, and handcuffs to bind the bank manager.   However, they arrived after the weekend deposits had been placed in a vault, so they went to a nearby restaurant and discussed their next move.   They determined that it was too risky to rob the bank without another person, so they left and secured the assistance of defendant Scott.

When the four returned on the same day, Allen entered the bank to check the surveillance cameras.   Jackson placed a fake license plate on the get-away car.   However, because the bank was now too busy, they rescheduled the robbery for June 21.

On June 18, Hodges was arrested on an unrelated robbery charge and began cooperating with the government.   She related the events of

June 14, and warned them of the plan to rob the bank on June 21. Although the defendants learned of Hodges' arrest, they decided to go ahead without her.

On June 21, as the police watched the area, the three defendants, driving in a car with a fake license plate, circled the block where the bank was situated, and parked nearby. One defendant walked in front of the bank, holding a container of coffee, and then returned to the car. Over the next hour or so, they repeatedly drove around the area. On their final drive-around, they spotted the police and fled. The police pursued and arrested the occupants of the car. Inside the vehicle they discovered weapons, ammunition, a toy revolver, handcuffs, a mask, and the genuine automobile license plate for the car.]

In his memorandum of decision, Chief Judge Mishler * * * characterized the question of whether the defendants had attempted a bank robbery as charged in counts two and three or were merely engaged in preparations as "a close one." * * * He concluded that on June 14 and again on June 21, the defendants took substantial steps, strongly corroborative of the firmness of their criminal intent, toward commission of the crime of bank robbery and found the defendants guilty on each of the two attempt counts. These appeals followed. * * *

Chief Judge Kaufman, writing for [this] court, [previously] selected the two-tiered inquiry of *United States v. Mandujano*,[6] [499 F.2d 370 (5th Cir.1974)] * * * as stating the proper test for determining whether the foregoing conduct constituted an attempt. He observed that this analysis "conforms closely to the sensible definition of an attempt proffered by the American Law Institute's Model Penal Code." [The court quoted § 5.01 in full.] * * *

The draftsmen of the Model Penal Code recognized the difficulty of arriving at a general standard for distinguishing acts of preparation from acts constituting an attempt. * * * The problem then was to devise a standard more inclusive than one requiring the last proximate act before attempt liability would attach, but less inclusive than one which would make every act done with the intent to commit a crime criminal. * * *

The formulation upon which the draftsmen ultimately agreed required, in addition to criminal purpose, that an act be a substantial step in a course of conduct designed to accomplish a criminal result, and that it be strongly corroborative of criminal purpose in order for it to constitute such a substantial step. The following differences between this test and previous approaches to the preparation-attempt problem were noted:

6. The *Mandujano* test was paraphrased as follows:

Initially, the defendant must have been acting with the kind of culpability otherwise required for the commission of the crime he is charged with attempting.

Then, the defendant must have engaged in conduct which constitutes a substantial step toward commission of the crime, conduct strongly corroborative of the firmness of the defendant's criminal intent.

First, this formulation shifts the emphasis from what remains to be done—the chief concern of the proximity tests—to what the actor *has already done*. The fact that further major steps must be taken before the crime can be completed does not preclude a finding that the steps already undertaken are substantial. It is expected, in the normal case, that this approach will broaden the scope of attempt liability.

Second, although it is intended that the requirement of a substantial step will result in the imposition of attempt liability only in those instances in which some firmness of criminal purpose is shown, no finding is required as to whether the actor would probably have desisted prior to completing the crime. * * *

Finally, the requirement of proving a substantial step generally will prove less of a hurdle for the prosecution than the *res ipsa loquitur* approach, which requires that the actor's conduct must itself manifest the criminal purpose. The difference will be illustrated in connection with the present section's requirement of corroboration. Here it should be noted that, in the present formulation, the two purposes to be served by the *res ipsa loquitur* test are, to a large extent, treated separately. Firmness of criminal purpose is intended to be shown by requiring a substantial step, while problems of proof are dealt with by the requirement of corroboration (although, under the reasoning previously expressed, the latter will also tend to establish firmness of purpose).

Model Penal Code § 5.01, Comment at 47 (Tent. Draft No. 10, 1960).

The draftsmen concluded that, in addition to assuring firmness of criminal design, the requirement of a substantial step would preclude attempt liability, with its accompanying harsh penalties, for relatively remote preparatory acts. At the same time, however, by not requiring a "last proximate act" or one of its various analogues it would permit the apprehension of dangerous persons at an earlier stage than the other approaches without immunizing them from attempt liability. * * *

We cannot say that [the] conclusions which Chief Judge Mishler reached as the trier of fact as to what the evidence before him established were erroneous. * * * [T]he criminal intent of the appellants was beyond dispute. The question remaining then is the substantiality of the steps taken on the dates in question, and how strongly this corroborates the firmness of their obvious criminal intent. This is a matter of degree.

On * * * separate occasions, appellants reconnoitered the place contemplated for the commission of the crime and possessed the paraphernalia to be employed in the commission of the crime—loaded sawed-off shotguns, extra shells, a toy revolver, handcuffs, and masks—which was specially designed for such unlawful use and which could serve no lawful purpose under the circumstances. Under the Model Penal Code formulation, * * * either type of conduct, standing alone, was sufficient as a matter of law to constitute a "substantial step" if it strongly corroborated their criminal purpose. Here both types of conduct coincided on both June 14 and June 21, along with numerous other elements strongly corroborative of the firmness of appellants' criminal intent. The steps taken toward a successful bank robbery thus were not "insubstantial" as a matter of law, and Chief Judge Mishler found them "substantial" as a matter of fact. We are unwilling to substitute our assessment of the evidence for his, and thus affirm the convictions for attempted bank robbery on counts two and three.[9] * * *

Notes and Questions

1. Model Penal Code § 5.01(2) is intended to "give some definite content to the 'substantial step' requirement" of subsection (1)(c), which applies in cases of incomplete attempts. American Law Institute, Model Penal Code and Commentaries, Comment to § 5.01 at 332 (1985). If the prosecutor establishes that any one of the situations enumerated in subsection (2) has occurred, the trial judge is required to instruct the jury pursuant to subsection (1)(c), and must accept a verdict of guilty unless she determines that, as a matter of law, the conduct is not "strongly corroborative of the actor's criminal purpose."

A small number of states and some federal courts have adopted the substantial step formula of subsection (1)(c), but subsection (2) has not been widely followed. Id. at 331, 332.

2. Since the *Jackson* defendants only intended to rob the bank once, is it fair to convict them of two counts of attempt? As noted by the court (footnote 9), the double jeopardy clause was not violated by the dual convictions, because the attempts involved separate criminal episodes. In contrast, if they had entered the bank on June 14, and had taken money from two bank tellers, only one count of bank robbery would have been proper, because the victim of the offense would have been the bank, not the two tellers.

3. *Problem.* J traveled from Oklahoma to St. Louis with $22,000, in order to purchase cocaine from X, an undercover government agent. After they agreed on a price for the sale, J demanded that X open the plastic bag containing the purported cocaine before he displayed his money. When X refused, J broke off the deal and flew home. Is there sufficient evidence under the Model Penal Code to convict J of attempted possession of cocaine? See United States v. Joyce, 693 F.2d 838 (8th Cir.1982).

Suppose that the reason X refused to open the plastic bag was that the substance inside was fake cocaine. Suppose, also, that upon arrest J was found to be in possession of relatively little cash. Should this affect the outcome? See United States v. McDowell, 705 F.2d 426, petition for rehearing denied with opinion, 714 F.2d 106 (11th Cir.1983).

---

9. Since Chief Judge Mishler was justified on the facts of this case in construing the June 14 and June 21 attempts as distinct criminal transactions or episodes, rather than simultaneous violations, the concurrent sentences on counts two and three were not improper. We feel impelled here, however, to remind the Government that it may face valid double jeopardy claims if it tries to fragment what is in fact a single crime into its components and punish each separately.

4. *Problem.* While being observed at all times by police officers in an unmarked car and by helicopter, *M,* who was dressed in dark clothing, left his home one evening and drove twenty miles to another residential area where he drove slowly down several residential streets. He parked his car at an apartment complex, got out, walked a short distance, and disappeared from police view into the yards of a row of houses. He reappeared six minutes later, and then disappeared again for one minute behind some other houses. When a marked police car coincidentally drove through the area, *M* fled by foot. No evidence was presented at trial of any attempted break-ins of any homes in the area. Should *M* be convicted of attempted burglary? Apply the common law and the Model Penal Code. See Commonwealth v. Melnyczenko, 422 Pa.Super. 363, 619 A.2d 719 (1992).

5. *Punishing pre-attempt conduct.* Even under the Model Penal Code, which broadens the scope of attempt liability, the police do not have authority to arrest for insubstantial acts, even if the actor's dangerousness is manifest. As a result, legislatures have enacted laws that make criminal certain kinds of pre-attempt conduct. For example, West's Ann.Cal.Penal Code § 422 (1993) provides in part:

Any person who wilfully threatens to commit a crime which will result in death or great bodily injury to another person, with the specific intent that the statement is to be taken as a threat, even if there is no intent of actually carrying it out, which, on its face and under the circumstances in which it is made, is so unequivocal, unconditional, immediate, and specific as to convey to the person threatened a gravity of purpose and an immediate prospect of execution of the threat, and thereby caused that person reasonably to be in sustained fear for his or her safety, or for his or her immediate family's safety, shall be punished by imprisonment * * * not to exceed one year.

Does this statute apply to the following facts: In 1985, *H* began writing letters, sending flowers and other gifts, and telephoning *L,* a Los Angeles television news anchorwoman. *L* ignored the communications, but she reported *H*'s behavior to her supervisor, who unsuccessfully attempted to have it stopped. The letters and gifts continued to arrive for nearly five years. On August 9, 1989, *H* told *X* that he was going to the television studio at which *L* worked to kill her. Because *X* observed that *H* was in possession of ammunition for a gun, he believed that the threat was real. *X* informed the police, who in turn told the television station, which contacted *L* at her home. *L,* frightened, arranged for 24–hour armed guards at her home. The following afternoon, *H* was arrested.

If you represented *H,* could you plausibly argue that your client's conduct falls outside the scope of the statute? People v. Hudson, 5 Cal.App. 4th 131, 6 Cal.Rptr.2d 690 (1992).

The preceding statute gave birth to "anti-stalking" laws passed throughout the country. West's Ann.Cal.Penal Code § 646.9 (1993) is typical of this genre:

(a) Any person who wilfully, maliciously, and repeatedly follows or harasses another person and who makes a credible threat with the intent to place that person in reasonable fear of death or great bodily injury or to place that person in reasonable fear of the death or great bodily injury of his or her immediate family is guilty of the crime of stalking, punishable by imprisonment in a county jail for not more than one year or by a fine of not more than one thousand dollars * * *, or by both * * *. * * *

(e) For purposes of this section, "harasses" means a knowing and willful course of conduct directed at a specific person which seriously alarms, annoys, or harasses the person, and which serves no legitimate purpose. The course of conduct must be such as would cause a reasonable person to suffer substantial emotional distress, and must actually cause substantial emotional distress to the person. "Course of conduct" means a pattern of conduct composed of a series of acts over a period of time, however short, evidencing a continuity of purpose. * * *

(f) For purposes of this section, "a credible threat" means a threat made with the intent and the apparent ability to carry out the threat so as to cause the person who is the target of the threat to reasonably fear for his or her safety or the safety of his or her immediate family. * * *

Was *H* guilty of stalking *L* in *Hudson?*

5. SPECIAL DEFENSES

a. *Impossibility*

UNITED STATES v. THOMAS

Court of Military Appeals, 1962.
13 U.S.C.M.A. 278, 32 C.M.R. 278.

KILDAY, JUDGE:

[The defendants, Thomas and McClellan, were tried by general court-martial. Each was charged with the offenses of conspiracy to commit rape, rape, and lewd and lascivious conduct, in violation of the Uniform Code of Military Justice. Each was acquitted of rape, but the court-martial found them guilty of attempted rape, contrary to Article 80 of the Uniform Code, and likewise convicted them of the other two charges upon which they were brought to trial. However, the board of review set aside the convictions of attempted rape and conspiracy as to both accused.]

* * * The case is before this Court on the following [question] certified to us by the Acting The Judge Advocate General of the Navy * * *:

"I. Was the Board of Review correct in setting aside, with respect to both accused, the findings of guilty of Charge I, attempted rape? * * * *"

The evidence adduced at the trial presents a sordid and revolting picture which need not be discussed in detail other than as necessary to decide the certified [issue]. In brief, both these * * * accused * * * started their fateful evening on a "bar hopping" spree. They were accompanied by an eighteen-year-old companion, Abruzzese * * *. The latter was a co-actor in these offenses, but was granted immunity from prosecution for his criminality in the incidents, and testified as a witness for the Government.

After several stops the trio entered a tavern known as "Taylor's Place" where McClellan began dancing with a girl. Almost at once she collapsed in McClellan's arms. Thereafter, he, with his two companions, volunteered to take her home. They placed the apparently unconscious female in McClellan's car and left. * * * Before they had proceeded very far McClellan, in frank, expressive language, suggested that this was a good chance for sexual intercourse as apparently this woman was just drunk and would never know the difference. Each of the three subsequently did or attempted to consummate this act and then started their return to town. The three became concerned as the woman had not regained consciousness.

In the meantime they dropped Abruzzese off at the USO. The accused, unable to find the female's home and becoming more concerned about her condition, stopped at a service station seeking help. The attendant called the police who, upon arriving at the service station, examined the girl and determined she was dead. An ambulance was called and she was taken to a hospital for further examination. An autopsy, later performed, revealed that she apparently died of "acute interstitial myocarditis." In general terms this is a weakening of the heart muscles with edema and inflammation which occurs more in young people without its presence being suspected. It was the general undisputed opinion that her death probably occurred at the time she collapsed on the dance floor at Taylor's Place or very shortly thereafter. * * * [T]he accused were unaware of the fact she was dead. * * *

Before the board of review, appellate defense counsel contended that the law officer erred in his instructions to the court * * *. In support of that position, the defense argued that where circumstances beyond the accused's control make it legally impossible to commit a crime, as distinguished from factual impossibility to do so, there can be no attempt * * * to commit the substantive offense.

In substance, then, the question thus presented to the board of review was, whether the law officer was correct in his instructions to the court-martial that a finding the victim was alive was not essential to a conviction for attempt as a lesser included offense of rape. * * *

* * * [A]s a backdrop against which to consider the problem, we deem it appropriate to explore the intricacies of the civilian holdings in the area.

As might be anticipated, a subject so intriguing has frequently received the attention of legal scholars as reflected by numerous articles and papers appearing in law school publications. * * *

In practically all of the * * * articles and texts, the specific question involved in this case—impossibility of completion of the substantive crime—is discussed at very considerable length. The two reasons for "impossibility" are treated in this connection: (1) If the intended act is not criminal, there can be no criminal liability for an attempt to commit the act. This is sometimes described as a "legal impossibility." (2) If the intended substantive crime is impossible of accomplishment because of some physical impossibility unknown to the accused, the elements of a criminal attempt are present. This is sometimes described as "impossibility in fact."

The authorities seem to be in fair accord that (1), above, is not punishable as an attempt. There is some considerable conflict of authority as to whether (2), above, is punishable as an attempt, but the preponderance seems to be that such instances do constitute attempts. What is abundantly clear, however, is that it is most difficult to classify any particular state of facts as positively coming within one of these categories to the exclusion of the other.

Practically all writers on this subject, whether in law journal articles, texts, or judicial opinions, cite and discuss the same relatively limited number of decisions. These decisions are generally placed in the two following categories:

1. "Legal impossibility" in which attempt convictions have been set aside on the ground that it was legally impossible for the accused to have committed the crime contemplated. These are as follows:

(a) A person accepting goods which he believed to have been stolen, but which were not then "stolen" goods, was not guilty of an attempt to receive stolen goods. People v. Jaffe, 185 N.Y. 497, 78 N.E. 169 (1906).

(b) An accused who offered a bribe to a person believed to be a juror, but who was not a juror, could not be said to have attempted to bribe a juror. State v. Taylor, 345 Mo. 325, 133 S.W.2d 336 (1939).

(c) An official who contracted a debt which was unauthorized and a nullity, but which he believed to be valid, could not be convicted of an attempt to illegally contract a valid debt. Marley v. State, 58 N.J.L. 207, 33 A. 208 (1895).

(d) A hunter who shot a stuffed deer believing it to be alive had not attempted to take a deer out of season. State v. Guffey, 262 S.W.2d 152 (Mo.) (1953).

(e) It is not an attempt to commit subornation of perjury where the false testimony solicited, if given, would have been immaterial to the case at hand and hence not perjurious. People v. Teal, 196 N.Y. 372, 89 N.E. 1086 (1909).

2. Instances in which a claim of impossibility has been rejected and convictions sustained, are included below. Apparently these can all be classified as "impossibility in fact." These decisions are:

(a) It is now uniformly held that one is guilty if he attempts to steal from an empty pocket. The same is true as to an empty receptacle, and an empty house. * * *

(b) One can attempt to possess narcotics, even though accused obtained possession of talcum believing it to be narcotics. People v. Siu, 126 Cal.App.2d 41, 271 P.2d 575 (1954). * * *

(c) An accused may be guilty of attempted murder who, suspecting that a policeman on the roof was spying upon him through a hole, but ignorant that the policeman was then upon another part of the roof, fired at the hole with intent to kill. People v. Lee Kong, 95 Cal. 666, 30 Pac. 800 (1892). It is attempted murder to shoot into the intended victim's bed believing he is there asleep when in fact he is some place else. State v. Mitchell, 173 Mo. 633, 71 S.W. 175 (1902). An accused is not absolved from the charge of attempted murder when he points an unloaded gun at his wife's head and pulls the trigger, if he actually thought at the time that it was loaded. State v. Damms, 9 Wis.2d 183, 100 N.W.2d 592 (1960).

(d) In attempted abortion cases an accused may be guilty in the absence of proof that the woman was pregnant. Commonwealth v. Tibbetts, 157 Mass. 519, 32 N.E. 910 (1893). * * *

The lack of logic between some of the holdings, supra; the inherent difficulty in assigning a given set of facts to a proper classification; the criticism of existing positions in this area; and, most importantly, the denial of true and substantial justice by these artificial holdings have led, quite naturally, to proposals for reform in the civilian legal concepts of criminal attempts.

In addition to a progressive and modern view now evident in some judicial decisions and writings, The American Law Institute in its * * * "Model Penal Code" defines Criminal Attempts, in Article 5.01 * * *. The import of that * * * statute is made clear in Tentative Draft No. 10 of the Model Penal Code of The American Law Institute, supra, at page 25, where it is stated [that one major purpose of the Article is "to extend the criminality of attempts by sweeping aside the defense of impossibility (including the distinction between so-called factual and legal impossibility)."]

After having given this entire question a great deal more than casual attention and study, we are forced to the conclusion that the law of attempts in military jurisprudence has tended toward the advanced and modern position, which position will be achieved for civilian jurisprudence if The American Law Institute is completely successful in its advocacy of this portion of the Model Penal Code. * * *

We hold, therefore, * * * that in this instance the fact that the female, upon whom these detestable acts were performed, was already dead at the time of their commission, is no bar to conviction for attempted rape.

However, for purposes of clarity, we should make mention of that portion of paragraph 159, Manual for Courts–Martial, which reads:

"It is not an attempt when every act intended by the accused could be completed without committing an offense, even though the accused may at the time believe he is committing an offense."

That provision has no reference to questions we have here discussed. Such language says no more than that if what an accused believed to be a substantive crime was actually no crime at all, he cannot be guilty of an attempt to commit such crime. That is, when the intended action, even if completed, is not an offense despite the fact accused believed otherwise, he cannot be held for a criminal attempt. Under those circumstances a substantive offense is nonexistent, and an accused's acts, whether carried to fruition or not, constitute wholly lawful conduct. It is interesting to observe that the same situation will exist under the Model Penal Code. See Tentative Draft No. 10, page 31, which states, in the commentary:

"Of course, it is still necessary that the result desired or intended by the actor constitute a crime. If, according to his beliefs as to facts and legal relationships, the result desired or intended is not a crime, the actor will not be guilty of an attempt even though he firmly believes that his goal is criminal." * * *

The certified [issue is] answered in the negative, and the decision of the board of review is reversed. * * *

FERGUSON, JUDGE (* * * dissenting in part):

Professor Jerome Hall traces the difficulty in analyzing the defense of impossibility in criminal attempts to Baron Bramwell's original use of illustrative fact situations "from Never–Never Land" in Regina v. Collins, 9 Cox C.C. 497, 169 Eng.Rep. 1477 (1864). Hall, General Principles of Criminal Law, 2d ed., page 593. I am inclined to attribute it to a growing tendency on the part of legal theoreticians to attach more importance to the evilness of a man's intent than to his acts—a belief, if you will, that the law should punish sinful thoughts if accompanied by any sort of antisocial conduct which evidences the design to execute forbidden acts. When certain courts adopt such broad penal theories and others reject them, the result is the legal morass to which my brothers refer.

The path which they have found out of this bog of theory, speculation, and learned dissertations is indeed tempting, for it eliminates any need to concern ourselves with the close and intricate question whether accused's actions fall within the area of legal impossibility. But I cannot in good conscience agree with a position which adopts a[n] * * * approach to the law of criminal attempts without the slightest indication that such was the intent of Congress in passing Uniform Code of Military Justice. * * *

* * * I find nothing in the Manual's discussion of criminal attempts which indicates that it was believed that the defense of legal—as opposed to factual—impossibility was abolished upon enactment of the Uniform Code. * * *

* * * I suggest, therefore, that it is necessary to meet the problem before us head on and to descend into the whirlpool of commentaries, articles, and opinions which surround the [issue]. * * *

It should be noted at the outset that we are all in agreement that the offense of rape itself cannot be committed upon the body of a dead person. * * * The statute requires an act of sexual intercourse by the accused "with a female not his wife." A female is a living human being. * * *

As it is, therefore, an utter impossibility for the consummated offense of rape to be committed upon the body of a dead person, may the accused who commits all the acts necessary to such offense upon a dead body, with the requisite *mens rea,* be convicted of an attempt to rape? The authorities in point have been cited at length in the principal opinion. * * *

Impossibility cases have generally involved homicide, larceny and related crimes, rape, and what might be classified as a hodgepodge of statutory offenses, ranging from abortion to corruption of jurors.

The homicide cases have usually involved the absence of the victim. In State v. Mitchell, it was established that the defendant fired two shots into his intended victim's bedroom for the purpose of slaying him. The victim, however, was elsewhere in the house, and the attack went for nought. Rejecting the contention that accused should not have been convicted of attempted murder, the court stated:

"... So in this case the intent evidenced by the firing into the bedroom with a deadly weapon, accompanied by a present capacity in defendant to murder Warren if he were in the room, and the failure to do so only because Warren happily retired upstairs instead of in the bed into which defendant fired, made out a perfect case of an attempt within the meaning of the statute...." * * *

In People v. Jaffe, it was concluded that the defendant could not be guilty of an attempt to receive stolen property when the cloth which he received was in fact not stolen. In the *Jaffe* case, the court noted:

"... In passing upon the question here presented for our determination, it is important to bear in mind precisely what it was that the defendant attempted to do. He simply made an effort to purchase certain specific pieces of cloth. He believed the cloth to be stolen property, but it was not such in fact. The purchase, therefore, if it had been completely effected, could not constitute the crime of receiving stolen property, knowing it to be stolen, since there could be no such thing as knowledge on the part of the defendant of a nonexistent fact, although there might be a belief on his part that the fact existed. As Mr. Bishop well says, it is a mere truism that there can be no receiving of stolen goods which have not been stolen. 2 Bishop's New Crim. Law, § 1140. It is equally difficult to perceive how there can be an attempt to receive stolen goods, knowing them to have been stolen, when they have not been stolen in fact.

*"The crucial distinction between the case before us and the pickpocket cases, and others involving the same principle, lies not in the possibility or impossibility * * * of the commission of the crime, but in the fact that, in the present case, the act, which it was doubtless the intent of the defendant to commit, would not have been a crime if it had been consummated."* [Emphasis supplied.] * * *

Charges of attempted rape seem uniformly to have allowed legal impossibility as a defense when a juridical impediment was found to prevent the consummation of the crime. Thus, in Frazier v. State, 48 Tex.Crim. 142, 86 S.W. 754 (1905), it was concluded to be legally impossible for a husband to be convicted of the attempted criminal violation of his wife's person. And in Foster v. Commonwealth, 96 Va. 306, 31 S.E. 503 (1898), a jurisdiction applying the common-law's conclusive presumption of legal incapacity of a boy under the age of fourteen to commit rape determined that, because of such presumption, he could not be convicted of attempted rape. * * *

It seems to me that, from the foregoing authorities—representative as they are of the welter of decisions in this field—definite principles may be derived which, when applied to the facts depicted in the record before us, lead inevitably to the conclusion that accused's conviction of attempted rape must be vitiated on the basis of legal impossibility. In the homicide cases, we find in every instance a victim in being upon whom the crime could have been committed and, except in [one case], in proximity to the scene of the actual attempt. * * * In short, the intended victim's absence is simply a factual matter. * * *

The same is true of one who possesses or uses milk sugar, believing it to be a narcotic preparation. People v. Siu, supra. There is no legal impediment to conviction, for the accused has merely made a factual mistake concerning the identity of the supposed contraband, just as does the defendant who seizes a woman, intending to ravish her, but finds himself, for physical reasons, unable to effect penetration.

In contrast to these cases * * * are those in which there is, so to speak, no "victim in being." Thus, we find that one cannot attempt to influence a juror who is not a juror. One cannot attempt to pursue a deer which is nothing more than a stuffed hide. State v. Guffey, supra. One cannot attempt to kill by firing into a corpse or commit rape upon a mannequin. 1 Bishop, A Treatise on Criminal Law, 9th ed., § 742; State v. Guffey, supra. Nor can one attempt to receive stolen goods which are not in fact stolen, People v. Jaffe, supra, or attempt rape where he legally has no capacity so to act, Foster v. Commonwealth, supra.

In each of these instances, there is simply no "victim" or thing which the particular law intended to be broken is designed to protect. * * *

In like manner, the barrier to consummation of the crime charged here is not factual but legal. Indeed, accused did everything they set out to do, but they admittedly could not commit the actual crime of rape because their victim was dead and thus outside the protection of the law appertaining to that offense. Because the objective of their loathsome attentions was no longer subject to being raped, it seems to me that there cannot be any liability for an attempt, for, just as in the case of the lad under the age of fourteen, the stuffed "deer," and the nonjuror, a legal rather than a factual impediment existed to the offense's consummation. In brief, this is not the case of an empty pocket but one in which there was no pocket to pick. * * *

Notes and Questions

1. United States v. Oviedo, 525 F.2d 881, 883 (5th Cir.1976):

Legal impossibility occurs when the actions which the defendant performs or sets in motion, even if fully carried out as he desires, would not constitute a crime. Factual impossibility occurs when the objective of the defendant is proscribed by the criminal law but a circumstance unknown to the actor prevents him from bringing about that objective.

Based on these definitions, is *Thomas* a case of factual or legal impossibility?

2. Assuming *arguendo* that the cases summarized in the majority opinion were correctly decided, can you provide a coherent explanation for the difference between factual impossibility and legal impossibility? Is the dissent's explanation of the distinction satisfactory? For example, why is it a case of "factual impossibility" to shoot at an empty bed (*Mitchell*), but it is "legal impossibility" to shoot a stuffed dummy (*Guffey*)? Does this mean that, in *Mitchell*, if the would-be victim, aware of the impending bedroom assault, had put a mannequin in his bed, the defendant would not have been guilty of attempted murder when he shot it? Suppose that the defendant, acting in the dark, had not seen the mannequin when he fired his gun?

3. *Jaffe and non-stolen goods.* The dissent in *Thomas* makes much of *People v. Jaffe,* a leading legal impossibility case, in which the defendant received non-stolen property, believing it was stolen. Look again at the *Jaffe* court's explanation (pp. 690–691 supra), in particular the italicized language, for reversing the attempt conviction: Is the New York court's reasoning persuasive? Not according to one scholar:

The critics of *Jaffe* have not found much difficulty in demolishing the analysis contained in this passage. It has been pointed out that the *Jaffe* court's statement that "the act, which it was doubtless the intent of the defendant to commit would not have been a crime if it had been consummated" is very questionable and turns upon a choice of what is relevant in establishing what his intention was. It certainly seems no defiance of ordinary language to say that Jaffe intended to receive stolen goods, for, in speaking of a person's intention, we frequently incorporate his mistaken view of a situation, since belief and intent cannot be neatly separated. So, if I am sitting in a plane flying from New York to Los Angeles, which I mistakenly think is flying to London—my desired destination—it would be a perfectly reasonable statement to say that, at least until the mistake is pointed out to me, it was my intention to reach London on that plane. The rejection of *Jaffe* * * * is not only supported by such a view of intent but also by the policy underlying the law of attempts. Jaffe, in this way of looking at the facts, intended to commit an offense known to the law, so this is not a case of legal impossibility. Where the prosecution can discharge its burden of proof by showing beyond a reasonable doubt that an accused had such an intent, expressed in a sufficient overt act, then in terms of the prohibitions of the criminal law such a person is socially dangerous and deserves punishment.[e]

4. *The saga of Lady Eldon.* Consider the following story:

Lady Eldon, when traveling with her husband on the Continent, bought what she supposed to be a quantity of French lace, which she hid, concealing it from Lord Eldon in one of the pockets of the coach. The package was brought to light by a custom officer at Dover. The lace turned out to be an English manufactured article of little value and, of course, not subject to duty. Lady Eldon had bought it at a price vastly above its value, believing it to be genuine, intending to smuggle it into England.

1 Wharton, Criminal Law § 225, at 304 n. 9 (12th ed. 1932).

Assume that despite her elevated social position in England, Lady Eldon was charged with the offense of attempting to smuggle a dutiable item into the country. Factual or legal impossibility?

5. *Abolition of the impossibility defense.* The Model Penal Code sweeps aside the defense of impossibility. Is abolition a good idea? The reporters of the Code have explained the drafters' rationale:

Insofar as it has not rested on conceptual tangles that have been largely independent of policy considerations, the defense of impossibility seems to have been employed to serve a number of functions. First, it has been used to verify criminal purpose; if the means selected were absurd, there is good ground for doubting that the actor really planned to commit a crime. Similarly, if the defendant's conduct, objectively viewed, is ambiguous, there may be ground for doubting the firmness of his purpose to commit a criminal offense. A general defense of impossibility is, however, an inappropriate way of assuring that the actor has a true criminal purpose. * * *

[Another] consideration that has been advanced in support of an impossibility defense is the view that the criminal law need not take notice of conduct that is innocuous, the element of impossibility preventing any dangerous proximity to the completed crime. The law of attempts, however, should be concerned with manifestations of danger-

e. Graham Hughes, *One Further Footnote on Attempting the Impossible,* 42 N.Y.U.L.Rev. 1005, 1009 (1967). Copyright © 1967, New York University. Reprinted by permission.

ous character as well as with preventive arrests; the fact that particular conduct may not create an actual risk of harmful consequences, though it would if the circumstances were as the defendant believed them to be, should not therefore be conclusive. The innocuous character of the particular conduct becomes relevant only if the futile endeavor itself indicates a harmless personality, so that immunizing the conduct from liability would not result in exposing society to a dangerous person.

American Law Institute, Model Penal Code and Commentaries, Comment to § 5.01 at 315–16 (1985).

Is it true, as the drafters claim (id. at 309) that "[i]n all of these cases [that recognize the defense] the actor's criminal purpose has been clearly demonstrated; he went as far as he could in implementing that purpose; and, as a result, his 'dangerousness' is plainly manifested"? Reconsider Lady Eldon's lace (Note 4 supra) and *Jaffe* (Note 3) in light of the following observations:

> The argument that Lady Eldon should be convicted of attempted smuggling is that having gone beyond preparatory acts to the point where she has committed the very act defined by the crime—importing the lace—it is clear that she is fully committed to her illegal escapade. Only the accidental absence of an external circumstance required by the statute—that the imported goods be dutiable—precludes liability for the substantive crime. Since she thought the goods were dutiable, intended to avoid paying the duty, and did all the acts that would have supported substantive liability had the facts been as she thought, she should be guilty of an attempt.

> But, we are entitled to ask, if Lady Eldon's handkerchief really is cheap linen, how do we know that she thought it was expensive dutiable lace? The facts state that she "hid" the lace, "concealing" it in a pocket, but those are loaded words that assume the very thing at issue, namely that she sought to avoid a duty she mistakenly believed due. Where there are present two objective factors—lace subject to import duty and an act of concealment—the coincidence of an objective motive to smuggle and conduct consistent with that motive and supportive of that goal is fair ground for the conclusion that Lady Eldon in fact intended to avoid paying the duty. If we remove the objective existence of the motive, the evidentiary basis for the conclusion that she intended to evade a duty believed due is correspondingly weakened.　* * *

> Let us apply a similar analysis to another famous legal impossibility case, *People v. Jaffe* * * *

> Those who would eliminate the defense of legal impossibility from the legal lexicon and would convict Jaffe of attempted possession of stolen goods because he thought they were stolen presumably would convict any other defendant of the same crime with respect to goods that had never been stolen if it could be proved that the defendant thought they were stolen. Having dispensed with the need for establishing the circumstance that the goods are stolen, they must permit this result if there is evidence of guilty belief. Assume two cases in which the sole direct evidence of the defendant's alleged belief that the goods are stolen is a confession or a testimony of an informer or an

accomplice. In one case the goods possessed are in fact stolen; in the other they are not. It is reasonably clear that most of us would rest easier with a conviction in the first case than in the second although we might have a difficult time articulating reasons for this distinction. * * * [I]t may * * * be that possession of stolen goods furnishes some evidence of belief that they are stolen while, clearly, possession of goods not in fact stolen furnishes no reason to believe that the defendant thought they were stolen.

The draftsmen of the Model Penal Code have argued that while eliminating legal impossibility as a defense, the Code adequately takes care of these problems by its separate provision requiring that the defendant's act corroborate his mens rea. But the Model Penal Code's requirement that the act corroborate the mens rea [Section 5.01(1)(c)-ed.] applies only to cases in the preparation-attempt continuum. Cases such as *Jaffe* and Lady Eldon are covered by separate provision [Section 5.01(1)(a)-ed.] which provides that where the defendant does any act which would constitute a crime under the circumstances as he thought them to be, he is guilty of an attempt. The corroboration requirement of section 5.01(2) does not apply to this section. Perhaps the draftsmen assumed that doing the act defined in the substantive crime will always supply at least as much corroboration of mens rea as is present in the substantive crime itself. If so, what they have failed to see is that the act in its narrow sense of the defendant's physical movements can be perfectly innocent in itself—possession of goods, bringing goods into the country—and that what gives the act character as corroborative of mens rea is often the objective element or the attendant circumstances that the goods possessed are in fact stolen, or that the goods brought into the country are in fact dutiable, or that the goods possessed are in fact narcotics.

Arnold N. Enker, *Impossibility in Criminal Attempts—Legality and the Legal Process,* 53 Minn.L.Rev. 665, 677, 679–80, 682–83 (1969).

The reporters of the Code responded in part to Professor Enker's criticism this way:

[I]t should * * * be noted how unlikely it is that persons will be prosecuted on the basis of admissions alone; the person who has behaved in a wholly innocuous way is not a probable subject of criminal proceedings. So the issue posed over Subsections (1)(a) and (1)(b) is more theoretical than practical.

American Law Institute, Model Penal Code and Commentaries, Comment to § 5.01 at 319–20 (1985).

At least occasionally, however, prosecutions based solely on guilty admissions do occur. For example, in Anderton v. Ryan, [1985] 1 App.Cas. 560, 2 All Eng.Rep. 355, overruled by Regina v. Shivpuri, [1986] 1 App.Cas. 1, 2 All Eng.Rep. 334, *R* reported a theft of her video cassette recorder to the police. Later, she told the investigating officer, "I may as well be honest, it was a stolen one I bought, I should not have phoned you."

R was prosecuted for "dishonestly handling stolen property knowing or believing it is stolen." Because the video recorder was never recovered, the prosecutor could not prove that it had been stolen before *R* bought it. The issue facing the House of Lords, therefore, was whether *R* could be convicted of an attempted violation of the statute. Under the Model Code, could she be? As a policy matter, *should* she be?

6. *Impossibility and "illusory crimes."* In Wilson v. State, 85 Miss. 687, 38 So. 46 (1905), *W* tampered with a check by altering the numbers on it, so that a draft made out to him for "$2.50" read "$12.50." He attempted to cash it, but the bank teller, noticing the discrepancy (the words on the check continued to read "two dollars and fifty cents"), refused to pay him.

W was prosecuted for forgery. The trial judge instructed the jury that it could not properly convict the defendant of forgery, an offense that required proof of a "material" alteration of the instrument, because "the marginal numbers and figures [that *W* altered] are not part of the instrument." The jury, therefore, returned a verdict of *attempted* forgery. Should the conviction be sustained? Does it matter whether impossibility is a defense? In this regard, consider the following:

> Legal impossibility describes a situation in which the objective of the accused * * * does not constitute an offense known to the law, even though the accused may mistakenly believe the law to be other than it is. Mistake of law may not generally excuse, but neither can it in itself be a sufficient ground for indictment. So an American on a visit to England might quite reasonably have the mistaken belief that fornication is a crime in England since it is one in the American jurisdiction in which he resides. Such a mistaken belief clearly cannot subject him to prosecution for a nonexistent crime of committing the sexual act, and it would be a strange notion to talk of a prosecution for attempting to commit a crime which is not on the statute book. How after all could the indictment be drafted, unless we recognized the existence of a general offense of doing what one mistakenly believed to be a crime? It will be noticed that the argument here does not essentially depend on the concept of attempt in the usual sense of that word, for it is not necessarily a case of trying and failing. The inappropriateness of convicting such a person remains whether he has committed sexual intercourse or only attempted it. The reason for not convicting him has nothing to do with the failure of the enterprise, but rather with the absence of any prohibition of the conduct whether completed or not.[f]

7. *"Inherent" impossibility.* Leroy Ivy, a prison inmate, obtained a photograph of the judge who sentenced him to prison. Ivy intended to obtain a lock of the judge's hair from a person working in the judge's home, and then send it and the picture to a voodoo priest who would cast a death curse on the judge. Ivy was arrested before he could secure the lock of hair. Mark Curriden, *Voodoo Attempt?*, 75 A.B.A. J., Sept. 1989, at 48.

Suppose that Ivy had obtained the lock of hair and mailed it to the priest, who cast the curse, but the judge did not die. Would the priest (and Ivy, under concepts of complicity considered in Chapter 11) be guilty of attempted murder?

---

f. Graham Hughes, *One Further Footnote on Attempting the Impossible,* 42 N.Y.U.L.Rev. 1005, 1006 (1967). Copyright © 1967, New York University. Reprinted by permission.

Most commentators believe that an attempt prosecution should not lie in such circumstances:

> As Justice Holmes aptly said in Com. v. Kennedy, 170 Mass. 18, 48 N.E. 770: "As the aim of the law is not to punish sins, but is to prevent certain external results, the act done must come pretty near to accomplishing that result before the law will notice it." * * *
>
> * * * [A case like this] belongs to the category of "trifles," with which "the law is not concerned." Even though a "voodoo doctor" * * * actually believed that his malediction would surely bring death to the person on whom he was invoking it, [in light of the lack of proximity to the result] I cannot conceive of an American court upholding a conviction of such a maledicting "doctor" for attempted murder or even attempted assault and battery.

Commonwealth v. Johnson, 312 Pa. 140, 152, 167 A. 344, 348 (1933) (Maxes, J. dissenting).

Is this reasoning faulty? How is the use of a voodoo curse any less proximate to the result than firing an unloaded gun?

Would Ivy be guilty of attempted murder under the Model Penal Code? See Sections 5.05 and 6.12.

b. *Abandonment*

COMMONWEALTH v. McCLOSKEY

Superior Court of Pennsylvania, 1975.
234 Pa.Super. 577, 341 A.2d 500.

HOFFMAN, JUDGE:

Appellant contends that the Commonwealth's evidence at trial was insufficient to sustain his conviction for an attempted prison breach.

At the time of the alleged offense, appellant was serving a one- to three-year sentence for larceny in the Luzerne County Prison. At about 12:15 a.m., on December 26, 1972, James Larson, a Guard Supervisor at the prison, heard an alarm go off that indicated that someone was attempting an escape in the recreation area of the prison. The alarm was designed so that it could be heard in the prison office, but not in the courtyard. Larson immediately contacted Guards Szmulo and Banik. Initially, the guards checked the prison population, but found no one missing. The three men then conducted a search of the area where the alarm had been "tripped." Near the recreation yard between two wings of the prison, they found one piece of barbed wire that had been cut. In addition, Guard Szmulo found a laundry bag filled with civilian clothing. The bags are issued by the prison and are marked with a different number for each prisoner. A check revealed that the bag belonged to appellant.

At approximately 5:15 a.m., on December 26, the appellant voluntarily approached Larson. Appellant had spent that night on the nine p.m. to five a.m. shift at work in the boiler room, situated near the point where the alarm had been triggered. Appellant explained to Larson "I was gonna make a break last night, but I changed my mind because I thought of my family, and I got scared of the consequences." Appellant testified at trial that he had become depressed prior to his decision to escape because he had been denied a Christmas furlough on December 24, 1972. His testimony at trial was consistent with Larson's version of the episode: "... in the yard, I realized that I had shamed my family enough, and I did not want to shame them any more.... So I went back to the boiler room and continued working."

On April 18, 1973, the grand jury returned an indictment charging the appellant with prison breach. Appellant went to trial * * * before a judge sitting without a jury and was found guilty of attempted prison breach. * * * This appeal followed. * * *

In the instant case, the evidence on the record indicates that appellant scaled a fence within the prison walls that led to the recreation yard and then to the prison wall. * * * The Commonwealth's evidence supports the appellant's claim that he went only as far as the yard before giving up his plan to escape. * * * Thus appellant was still within the prison, still only contemplating a prison breach, and not yet attempting the act. He was thus in a position to abandon the criminal offense of attempted prison breach voluntarily, thereby exonerating himself from criminal responsibility.

Judgment of sentence is vacated and appellant ordered discharged on the conviction of attempted prison breach. * * *

CERCONE, JUDGE (concurring):

I agree with the majority that appellant's conviction for attempted prison breach should not be permitted to stand. However, I disagree with the basis for the majority's conclusion, that the acts done by appellant prior to his decision to abandon his escape were insufficient to constitute an attempt. I would have found little difficulty, for instance, in affirming appellant's conviction had he been apprehended by the guards immediately after he had snipped the barbed wire and crossed the inner fence. To hold otherwise is to require that prisoners must literally be plucked from the prison wall before their conduct may be characterized as attempted prison breach.

I respectfully suggest that the majority has fallen into a trap peculiarly common to the law of attempts. As Professor Perkins has stated in discussing when conduct ceases to be merely preparatory and becomes perpetration:

"The preparatory-perpetrating dichotomy is useful in discussing situations of a rather general nature, but the actual dividing line between the two is shadowy in the extreme. There is reason to believe that *in close cases the decision is based upon other considerations* and that the label attached is that appropriate to the conclusion reached—after it is reached." R. Perkins, Criminal Law 561 (2d ed. 1969). [Emphasis added.]

The "other consideration" which has influenced the majority herein is appellant's voluntary abandonment of his escape plan. In my opinion, appellant's abandonment of his plan is a sufficient defense to the crime of attempted prison breach and should be recognized as such.

As a practical matter, it has long been recognized that plans voluntarily abandoned are less likely to be found to be attempts than are plans carried to the same point, but interrupted by the apprehension of the perpetrators. Unfortunately, in jurisdictions where voluntary abandonment or renunciation of a criminal purpose has not been recognized as an affirmative defense, the courts have sought to give effect to the defendant's abandonment, *sub silentio,* by characterizing his conduct as "preparatory." That is precisely the error which the majority has made in the instant case. The difficulty with this position is that, with regard to the preparation-perpetration dichotomy, it breeds results superficially inconsistent. If voluntary abandonment is to be given effect in attempt cases, it should not be done covertly.

For some time the trend in the law has been to recognize voluntary abandonment as an affirmative and complete defense to a charge of attempt, despite the exhortations to the contrary by some commentators. And, in following this trend our legislature substantially adopted section 5.01 of the Model Penal Code in drafting the attempt provisions in our recently enacted Crimes Code. Our Code now recognizes that abandonment under circumstances indicating voluntariness, is a complete defense to a charge of attempt. Appellant, however, was charged under our old Penal Code which did not speak to whether voluntary abandonment was a defense to a charge of attempt. * * *

It is clear that this court long ago perceived voluntary abandonment to be an affirmative defense to the crime of attempt * * *.

Sound policy reasons also underlie the recognition of voluntary abandonment as an affirmative defense. As the drafters of the Model Penal Code have pointed out, the defense of complete and permanent abandonment should be allowed because voluntary abandonment negates the conclusion that the accused continues to be dangerous; and, the knowledge that voluntary abandonment exonerates one from criminal liability provides a motive to desist prior to completion of the crime.

Thus, I have concluded that the law in Pennsylvania recognized voluntary abandonment as an affirmative defense even prior to the adoption of the Crimes Code. In any event, the trend in the United States is so profoundly in favor of such a defense that we should have recognized its existence in the instant case even had the Crimes Code not been enacted. * * *

Notes and Questions

1. How do you respond to the following argument against the abandonment defense?

[T]he traditional view [is] that voluntary abandonment is not a defense where the elements of an attempt are already established, although it may be relevant to the issue of whether defendant possessed the requisite intent in the first place. Under this view, once a defendant has gone so far as to have committed a punishable attempt, the crime is "complete" and he or she cannot then abandon the crime and avoid liability anymore than a thief can abandon a larceny by returning the stolen goods.

People v. Kimball, 109 Mich.App. 273, 281, 311 N.W.2d 343, 347 (1981).

In a jurisdiction in which abandonment is a defense to an attempt, should the defense apply to a *completed* offense? For example, should a thief who voluntarily returns the goods she stole be permitted a defense? What about a burglar who, after breaking into a dwelling, voluntarily leaves without committing a felony therein? Are such cases distinguishable from attempts? See Paul R. Hoeber, *The Abandonment Defense to Criminal Attempt and Other Problems of Temporal Individuation,* 74 Cal.L.Rev. 377, 418–26 (1986); Daniel G. Moriarty, *Extending the Defense of Renunciation,* 62 Temple L.Rev. 1, 38–58 (1989).

2. *Problem.* People v. McNeal, 152 Mich.App. 404, 408–09, 393 N.W.2d 907, 909–10 (1986):

> The victim in this case was a sixteen-year-old girl who was walking to a bus stop where she would pick up a bus to her high school. She provided the only testimony regarding the incident leading to defendant's convictions. She testified that on the morning of the incident it was foggy and she was alone. A man, later identified as defendant, grabbed her by the neck and stuck a butcher knife to her side. He forced her to walk a couple of blocks and told her that he had a gun in his pocket. Shortly before the two arrived at defendant's intended destination, he wrapped a towel around her eyes and put his jacket hood on her. Minutes later, they arrived at a house which defendant unlocked with a key. Once inside, the victim asked defendant why he had grabbed her. His reply was that she was a black woman. At some point after they entered the house, the victim began to cry and defendant told her to shut up because "he hadn't had [her] pants down yet." Defendant then threw her on a couch. For the next hour and a half, the victim and defendant talked. Defendant spoke of black women he had dated who had treated him badly. The victim tried to keep defendant talking.

> After the talk, defendant laid himself down on the couch next to the victim and began kissing her on the lips and neck. He then rubbed her on the top part of her thighs and on the side of her stomach, but nowhere else. During the episode, the victim asked defendant several times to let her go. Once, he told her that she should finish her education. She replied that she had two tests to take at school that day and that he should let her go. He said that he did not know if he should, but she promised that, if he did, she would not tell anyone. Finally, he took the towel and hood off her and took her to the bathroom so that she could fix her hair. Then he walked her to the bus stop, waited with her, and told her that he was sorry and that he would never do it again.

The defendant was prosecuted for kidnapping and attempted rape. Should he be convicted of the attempt? Do these facts establish the defense of renunciation of criminal purpose under Model Penal Code § 5.01(4)?

Should the abandonment defense apply if a would-be rapist desists from having intercourse because: (1) the victim tearfully told him that her young daughter would be home from school "any time," and that "I am all she has because her daddy is dead," see Ross v. State, 601 So.2d 872 (Miss.1992); (2) the victim convinced him that "you could be my boyfriend, and you do not have to have it this way"? People v. Taylor, 80 N.Y.2d 1, 586 N.Y.S.2d 545, 598 N.E.2d 693 (1992); or (3) the victim was pregnant, see Le Barron v. State, 32 Wis.2d 294, 145 N.W.2d 79 (1966).

3. Suppose that a felon, while voluntarily abandoning an attempted robbery, accidentally kills the robbery victim. In a state that recognizes the abandonment defense, may she use the defense to avoid conviction of attempted robbery and, therefore, of felony murder? See Sheckles v. State, 501 N.E.2d 1053 (Ind.1986).

4. When is it too late to abandon an attempt? For example, suppose that the defendant, with the intent to kill, stabs another person during an altercation, feels immediate remorse, and rushes the victim to a hospital where timely life-saving medical care is provided. In an attempted murder prosecution, should she be able to claim the defense of abandonment? See State v. Smith, 409 N.E.2d 1199 (Ind.App.1980); American Law Institute, Model Penal Code and Commentaries, Comment to § 5.01 at 360 (1985).

C. ASSAULT

STATE v. BOUTIN

Supreme Court of Vermont, 1975.
133 Vt. 531, 346 A.2d 531.

BILLINGS, JUSTICE.

After trial by jury, Raymond Boutin was tried and convicted * * * of simple assault in violation of 13 V.S.A. § 1023(a)(1) in that he did then and there attempt to cause bodily injury to another. * * * He now appeals on the ground that even taking the evidence in the light most favorable to the State, the jury could not have found the defendant guilty beyond a reasonable doubt of attempting to cause bodily injury to another.

The facts disclose that on the evening of August 29, 1973, the defendant and Gary Moore were involved in a scuffle in front of Al's Pizza in Island Pond, Vermont. Following the scuffle, the defendant picked up a bottle from a trash can nearby, while Moore grabbed a rock from the street. Two town constables heard the disturbance and, on investigating, found the defendant and Moore ten feet apart, with the defendant walking towards Moore with the bottle raised over his head and Moore backing away across the street. The constables requested the defendant to put down the bottle, and then the defendant turned on the officers. At no time did the defendant attempt to strike Moore or to throw the bottle or lunge towards Moore, nor did he ever get in closer proximity than ten feet.

The simple assault statute * * * reads as follows:

§ 1023. Simple Assault

(a) A person is guilty of simple assault if he:

(1) attempts to cause or purposely, knowingly or recklessly causes bodily injury to another; ...

To constitute an attempt to commit a crime, the act must be of such a character as to advance the conduct of the actor beyond the sphere of mere intent. It must reach far enough towards the accomplishment of the desired result to amount to the commencement of the consummation. Here the holding of a bottle in one hand ten feet from the intended victim does not make it likely to end in the consummation of the crime intended. Although equivocal testimony is for the jury's evaluations, there first must be some testimony in a case evidencing criminal conduct as charged and sufficient to justify a finding of guilty beyond a reasonable doubt. Since the evidence failed to establish all of the elements essential to constitute the alleged offense, the trial court should have granted the motion for directed verdict.

Reversed.

AMERICAN LAW INSTITUTE, MODEL PENAL CODE AND COMMENTARIES, COMMENT TO § 211.1
(1980), 175–78, 183–84

Mayhem and Battery. The common law punished actual injury to another as mayhem or battery, depending upon the kind of harm caused. Mayhem, a common-law felony, originally consisted of injury permanently impairing the victim's ability to defend himself or to annoy his adversary. * * *

Battery was a common-law misdemeanor of far broader scope. It covered any unlawful application of force to the person of another wilfully or in anger. The requirement of force could be satisfied directly, as by a blow of the fist or indirectly, as by the use of a mechanical agent. Moreover, the notion of force was not limited to actual violence but included any kind of offensive and unlawful contact. Offensive contact was rendered unlawful chiefly by lack of consent. Thus, common-law battery covered unwanted sexual advance as well as physical attack. * * * [I]t was not uncommon * * * for American statutes to consolidate battery with the offense of assault.

Assault. Originally, common-law assault was simply an attempt to commit a battery. * * * Typical legislation described the offense as "an unlawful attempt, coupled with a present ability, to commit a violent injury on the person of another." Under such an approach, no assault would be committed if the alleged assailant had no intent to injure or if his gun were unloaded. The requirement of "present ability," moreover, imported into the offense an even stricter notion of proximity to the completed act than characterized the law of criminal attempt. Thus, some actions that went far enough to have constituted an attempt would nevertheless fail to satisfy the more stringent proximity required of an assault.

It was recognized early in the development of the private law of damages that an action could be maintained against one who intentionally placed another in fear of bodily injury, even if he acted without any purpose to carry out the threat. The majority of jurisdictions at the time the Model Code was drafted had assimilated this civil notion of assault into the criminal law. In these jurisdictions, assault thus consisted either of an actual attempt to commit a battery or of an intentional subjection of another to reasonable apprehension of receiving a battery. The assault offense was thus expanded to include menacing as well as actual attempts to do physical harm to another. It also generally included so-called conditional assaults, *i.e.,* situations where the actor threatened violence without justification or excuse if the victim did not engage in conduct demanded by the actor. * * *

The Model Code Approach. Section 211.1 of the Model Code undertakes a substantial restructuring of prior law. It eliminates the common-law categories and many of the antecedent statutory variations in favor of a single integrated provision. * * *

Subsections (1)(a), (1)(c), and (2) include attempts as well as completed offenses, thus achieving a consolidation of what former law treated as the separate crimes of assault and battery, as well as their more serious counterparts. The special feature of the former law of assault requiring greater proximity to success than for a normal attempt is discarded, however, in favor of the normal application of attempt principles. References in Section 211.1 to "attempts" are meant to incorporate the terms of Section 5.01, which defines attempt generally.

Notes and Questions

1. Did Boutin commit an assault according to Model Penal Code § 211.1?

2. Suppose that Boutin had been armed with a gun, rather than a bottle. Would he have been guilty of common law assault, as he walked toward Moore, with the gun pointed at him? Was he any closer to completion of the offense than with a bottle?

Suppose that Boutin had said, "S.O.B., I am going to kill you," as he walked toward Moore with the gun pointed. Assault? See State v. Brooks, 44 Ohio St.3d 185, 542 N.E.2d 636 (1989). If Boutin's gun proved to be unloaded, although he believed it was loaded when he uttered the threat, would he be guilty of assault? Of attempted murder?

3. Practical joker Roberto blindfolds himself, stands outside a crowded room, aims his gun inside the room, and fires three times, at five second intervals, hitting nobody. Under the Model Penal Code, is Roberto guilty of assault or of reckless endangerment (Section 211.2)?

4. Is there a crime of "attempted assault"? No, according to State v. Wilson, 53 Ga. 205, 206 (1874):

Is there any such crime? The Code, section 4357, defines an assault to be "an attempt to commit a violent injury on the person of another." Under section 4712, to make out an attempt to commit a crime it must appear that the accused has done some act towards the commission of it, and either fail in the perpetration thereof, or be prevented or intercepted in executing the same. As an assault is itself an attempt to commit a crime, an attempt to make an assault can only be an attempt to attempt to do it, or to state the matter still more definitely, it is to do any act towards doing an act towards the commission of the offense. This is simply absurd. As soon as any act is done towards committing a violent injury on the person of another, the party doing the act is guilty of an assault, and he is not guilty until he has done the act. Yet it is claimed that he may be guilty of an attempt to make an assault, when, under the law, he must do an act before the attempt is complete. The refinement and metaphysical acumen that can see a tangible idea in the words an attempt to act is too great for practical use. It is like conceiving of the beginning of eternity or the starting place of infinity.

Professor Perkins disagrees:

[I]t is apparent that reference may be made to an "attempt to assault" without logical absurdity. There is nothing absurd in referring to an attempt to frighten, which would constitute, if successful, a criminal assault in most jurisdictions. Where an attempt to commit a battery with present ability is the only basis on which a criminal assault may be established, an "attempt to assault" would mean in substance an attempt to commit a battery without present ability. Even where a criminal assault still has its original meaning as an attempt to commit a battery, reference to an attempt to assault is not necessarily absurd. Because of the recognized difference between the requirement of proximity for an assault and for a general criminal attempt, an attempt to assault would indicate an effort to accomplish a battery that had proceeded beyond the stage of preparation, but had not come close enough to completion to constitute an assault. It is not surprising, therefore, that there is a tendency to break away from the ancient view that there is no such offense known to the law as an attempt to commit an assault.

Rollin M. Perkins, *An Analysis of Assault and Attempts to Assault,* 47 Minn.L.Rev. 71, 81–82 (1962).

People v. O'Connell, 14 N.Y.S. 485 (1891) is an example of an attempted assault of the "attempted battery" variety. In *O'Connell, O* threatened *V* with an ax. The court reasoned that to be guilty of an assault, *O* had to be within reaching distance of *V,* but that such proximity was not needed for an attempted assault.

Even if an "attempted attempted battery" is not logically impossible and not too speculative to determine, are there policy reasons to worry about recognition of double inchoate offenses of this sort? Reconsider McQuirter v. State, 36 Ala.App. 707, 63 So.2d 388 (1953) (p. 652 supra).

D. SOLICITATION

1. GENERAL PRINCIPLES

STATE v. MANN

Supreme Court of North Carolina, 1986.
317 N.C. 164, 345 S.E.2d 365.

MARTIN, JUSTICE. * * *

Solicitation involves the asking, enticing, inducing, or counselling of another to commit a crime. The solicitor conceives the criminal idea and furthers its commission via another person by suggesting to, inducing, or manipulating that person. As noted by Weschler, Jones, and Korn in *The Treatment of Inchoate Crimes in the Model Penal Code of the American Law Institute: Attempt, Solicitation and Conspiracy,* 61 Colum.L.Rev. 571, 621–22 (1961), "the solicitor, working his will through one or more agents, manifests an approach to crime more intelligent and masterful than the efforts of his hireling," and a solicitation, "an attempt to conspire," may well be more dangerous than an attempt. Indeed, a solicitor may be more dangerous than a conspirator; a conspirator may merely passively agree to a criminal scheme, while the solicitor plans, schemes, suggests, encourages, and incites the solicitation. Further, the solicitor is morally more culpable than a conspirator; he keeps himself from being at risk, hiding behind the actor. * * *

Notes and Questions

1. At common law, a solicitation to commit any felony or a misdemeanor involving a breach of the peace or obstruction of justice, was indictable as a misdemeanor. Until the Model Penal Code was drafted, however, few state penal codes included a general criminal solicitation statute, although many states prohibited specific forms of solicitation, e.g., solicitation to commit murder. Consequently, in states that abolished common law offenses, most solicitations went unpunished. Today, however, most states include a general prohibition on criminal solicitations. American Law Institute, Model Penal Code and Commentaries, Comment to § 5.02 at 366–70 (1985).

Solicitation is a controversial crime because the offense is complete as soon as the solicitor asks, entices, or encourages another to commit the target offense. As observed in *Mann,* a solicitation may consist of nothing more than an attempt to conspire with another to commit an offense, which essentially makes solicitation a double inchoate crime. Nonetheless, the American Law Institute adopted a broad solicitation statute for the reasons stated in *Mann.*

2. The offense of solicitation merges into the crime solicited if the latter offense is committed or attempted by the solicited party. For example, if Agnes solicits Ben to murder Camille, and Ben refuses, Agnes is guilty of solicitation; if Ben agrees and kills or attempts to murder Camille, Agnes is guilty of murder or attempted murder, respectively, under complicity

principles (see Chapter 11 infra), rather than of the offense of solicitation. If Ben agrees, but is arrested before the attempt, Agnes and Ben may be prosecuted for conspiracy to commit murder (see subsection E. infra). Agnes's solicitation would merge into the conspiracy.

STATE v. COTTON

Court of Appeals of New Mexico, 1990.
109 N.M. 769, 790 P.2d 1050.

DONNELLY, JUDGE.

Defendant appeals his convictions of two counts of criminal solicitation. * * *

In 1986, defendant, together with his wife Gail, five children, and a stepdaughter, moved to New Mexico. A few months later, defendant's wife and children returned to Indiana. Shortly thereafter, defendant's fourteen-year-old stepdaughter moved back to New Mexico to reside with him. In 1987, the Department of Human Services investigated allegations of misconduct involving defendant and his stepdaughter. * * *

In May 1987, defendant was arrested and charged with multiple counts of criminal sexual penetration of a minor and criminal sexual contact of a minor. While in the Eddy County Jail awaiting trial on those charges defendant discussed with his cell-mate James Dobbs * * * his desire to persuade his stepdaughter not to testify against him. During his incarceration defendant wrote numerous letters to his wife; in several of his letters he discussed his strategy for defending against the pending criminal charges.

On September 23, 1987, defendant addressed a letter * * * to his wife. In that letter he requested that she assist him in defending against the pending criminal charges by persuading his stepdaughter not to testify at his trial. The letter also urged his wife to contact the stepdaughter and influence her to return to Indiana or that she give her money to leave the state so that she would be unavailable to testify. After writing this letter defendant gave it to Dobbs and asked him to obtain a stamp for it so that it could be mailed later. Unknown to defendant, Dobbs removed the letter from the envelope, replaced it with a blank sheet of paper, and returned the sealed stamped envelope to him. Dobbs gave the original letter written by defendant to law enforcement authorities, and it is undisputed that defendant's original letter * * * was never in fact mailed nor received by defendant's wife.

On September 24 and 26, 1987, defendant composed another letter * * * to his wife. * * * The letter stated that * * * his wife should try to arrange for his stepdaughter to visit her in Indiana for Christmas; and that his wife should try to talk the stepdaughter out of testifying or to talk her into testifying favorably for defendant. Defendant also said in the letter that his wife should "warn" his stepdaughter that if she did testify for the state "it won't be nice * * * and she'll make [New Mexico] news," and that, if the stepdaughter was not available to testify, the prosecutor would have to drop the charges against defendant.

* * * It is * * * undisputed that the second letter * * * was never mailed to defendant's wife.   * * *

The offense of criminal solicitation as provided in NMSA Section 30–28–3 (Repl.Pamp.1984), is defined in applicable part as follows:

> A. Except as to bona fide acts of persons authorized by law to investigate and detect the commission of offenses by others, a person is guilty of criminal solicitation if, with the intent that another person engage in conduct constituting a felony, he solicits, commands, requests, induces, employs or otherwise attempts to promote or facilitate another person to engage in conduct constituting a felony within or without the state.

Defendant contends that the record fails to contain the requisite evidence to support the charges of criminal solicitation against him because defendant's wife, the intended solicitee, never received the two letters, * * *

* * * The state reasons that even in the absence of evidence indicating that the solicitations were actually communicated to or received by the solicitee, under our statute, proof of defendant's acts of writing the letters, attempts to mail or forward them, together with proof of his specific intent to solicit the commission of a felony constitutes sufficient proof to sustain a charge of criminal solicitation. We disagree.

The offense of criminal solicitation, as defined in Section 30–28–3 by our legislature, adopts in part, language defining the crime of solicitation as set out in the Model Penal Code promulgated by the American Law Institute. * * * As enacted by our legislature, however, Section 30–28–3 significantly omits one section of the Model Penal Code, Section 5.02(2), which pertains to the effect of an uncommunicated criminal solicitation.

The commentary to the American Law Institute Model Penal Code explains that "[g]eneral statutory provisions punishing solicitations were not common before the Model Penal Code." [1] Model Penal Code § 5.02, commentary 2, § 5.02, at 367 (1985). The Commentary further notes in Section 5.02 of its proposed draft of criminal solicitation that:

> Under Subsection (2) [of proposed Section 5.02 of the Model Penal Code], conduct "designed to effect" communication of the culpable message is sufficient to constitute criminal solicitation and there is therefore no need for a crime of attempted solicitation.

> One reason for treating the crimes of solicitation and attempt in separate provisions was the judgment, reflected in Subsection (2), that the last proximate act to effect communication with the party

---

1. As observed by the drafters of the Model Penal Code in their commentary to Section 5.02, prior to the promulgation of the American Law Institute proposed Criminal Solicitation statute, uncommunicated messages by a defendant could under some circumstances constitute attempted solicitation, but "it [is] considered doubtful whether an uncommunicated message could constitute a solicitation."

whom the actor intends to solicit should be required before liability attaches on this ground. * * *

However, as enacted by our legislature, Section 30–28–3 sets out the offense of criminal solicitation in a manner which differs in several material respects from the proposed draft of the Model Penal Code. Among other things, * * * Section 30–28–3 specifically omits that portion of the Model Penal Code subsection declaring that an uncommunicated solicitation to commit a crime may constitute the offense of criminal solicitation.[2] The latter omission, we conclude, indicates an implicit legislative intent that the offense of solicitation requires some form of actual communication from the defendant to either an intermediary or the person intended to be solicited, indicating the subject matter of the solicitation. * * *

The question posed in the instant case is also discussed by the authors, W. LaFave and A. Scott. "What if the solicitor's message never reaches the person intended to be solicited, as where the intermediary fails to pass on the communication or the solicitee's letter is intercepted before it reaches the addressee? The act is nonetheless criminal, *although it may be that the solicitor must be prosecuted for an attempt to solicit on such facts.*" [Footnotes omitted; emphasis added.] 2 W. LaFave & A. Scott, *Substantive Criminal Law* § 6.1 (1986). We apply a similar result in the present case. * * *

* * * Defendant's convictions for solicitation are reversed and the cause is remanded with instructions to set aside the convictions * * *.

Notes and Questions

1. Did the court correctly apply Section 30–28–3? If you had been the prosecutor, to what language in the statute would you have pointed in support of the claim that uncommunicated solicitations are punishable as solicitations?

2. Alice and Beverly are cellmates. Alice, thinking aloud, says, "I ought to kill Corina" (another prisoner). Beverly thinks about Alice's comments, and realizes that she, too, would like Corina dead. Beverly tells Alice, "I agree. I will kill Corina." Is Alice guilty of solicitation to commit murder under Section 30–28–3? See Monoker v. State, 321 Md. 214, 582 A.2d 525 (1990).

3. Alice and Beverly are cellmates. Alice wants Corina, another prisoner, killed. Alice knows that Beverly, a convicted murderer, is angry with Corina for a prior offense and is considering violent action against her. Therefore, Alice "lets drop" the information that "Corina snitched on Beverly last week to the guards." Based on this new information, Beverly decides to kill Corina. Is Alice guilty of solicitation to commit murder under Model Code § 5.02(1)? See American Law Institute, Model Penal Code and Commentaries, Comment to § 5.02 at 372 (1985).

---

2. The American Law Institute, Model Criminal Code, Section 5.02(2) provides: "It is immaterial under Subsection (1) of this Section that the actor fails to communicate with the person he solicits to commit a crime if his conduct was designed to effect such communication." * * *

4. Francisco asks Georgia to furnish him with tools so that he may burglarize Harold's house. Georgia refuses. Is Francisco guilty of solicitation under Section 30–28–3? Is he guilty of solicitation under the Model Penal Code? See Sections 5.02(1) and 2.06(3).

5. People v. Vandelinder, 192 Mich.App. 447, 449–50, 481 N.W.2d 787, 788 (1992):

> The charges [of solicitation to kidnap, solicitation to rape, and solicitation to commit murder] arose out of defendant's offer to an undercover police officer to pay $1,000 for the kidnapping, rape, and possible murder of his estranged wife. Defendant's alternative aims were either to reconcile with his wife or to get rid of her. He told the supposed kidnapper to videotape several people raping the victim in order to have some leverage against her if she agreed to his demands to reconcile on his terms. In the event she did not agree, the kidnapper was to kill the victim.

Is the defendant guilty of the solicitation charges under the Model Penal Code? See Sections 5.02(1) and 2.02(6). See American Law Institute, Model Penal Code and Commentaries, Comment to § 2.02 at 247 (1985).

2. WHEN IS SOLICITATION AN ATTEMPT?

STATE v. OTTO

Supreme Court of Idaho, 1981.
102 Idaho 250, 629 P.2d 646.

McFADDEN, JUSTICE.

The appellant appeals his conviction of attempted first degree murder based on his hiring of an undercover police officer to kill Captain Ailor of the Lewiston Police Department. Appellant had been under investigation by Captain Ailor concerning the disappearance of the appellant's wife in August, 1976.

On October 24, 1976, appellant was in the Long Branch Saloon owned by Stan Kuykendall. Mr. Kuykendall testified that during a conversation appellant expressed a desire to find a "hit-man" to kill Captain Ailor because Ailor had been harassing him over Mrs. Otto's disappearance. Mr. Kuykendall reported this to the Lewiston Police Department. Following this report an officer telephoned appellant and said he was a "hit-man." This officer later testified that appellant stated he was willing to spend $500 to have the killing done, but after dickering a price of $1,000 was agreed upon.

The Lewiston police called in members of the Idaho State Police to assist them in investigating the matter. It was decided that Officer Watts of the Idaho State Police would wear a "bug" and attempt to record his conversations with appellant. On the afternoon of October 26, 1976, Officer Watts, wearing the transmitter, met with appellant at the Long Branch as prearranged earlier in the day. During this conversation, Watts agreed to kill Captain Ailor for $250 "up front" if he were to receive an additional $750 after the killing. It was agreed that appellant would place the $250 in a cup in Watts pickup, which appellant was seen to do later in the day. Appellant was arrested on October 27 and charged with attempted murder in the first degree.

The essential question before this court is whether the appellant's conduct amounted to more than solicitation of another to murder and reached the extent or degree of an attempt under accepted principles of criminal law. We hold it did not and thus the conviction must be reversed. * * *

It is recognized, of course, that a close relationship exists between solicitation and attempt. In the early stages of criminal activity, the two offenses may run parallel courses. However, there exists an accepted and distinct difference between them in law, the strength of which cannot be muted by a few courts erroneously treating the terms and concepts as interchangeable.

It is supported beyond contradiction that, regardless how heinous, no man can be convicted for having criminal intent alone. An *actus reus* is essential. And in the sphere of inchoate criminal offenses, it is clear that not every act will, when combined with criminal intent, suffice to establish the basis for an attempt. In the voluminous jurisprudence on attempts in the criminal law, some well supported tenets have been established in regard to the act required. * * *

While the distinction between acts of preparation and those of commission (or as is more commonly phrased "perpetration") may be difficult to make in many situations, courts have widely adopted the differentiation.[2]

The general rule in regard to solicitations within the context of the preparatory-perpetratory acts sufficient for an attempt [4] is well stated by the Tennessee Supreme Court in *Gervin v. State,* 212 Tenn. 653, 371 S.W.2d 449 (1963):

"The weight of American authority holds, as a general proposition, that mere criminal solicitation of another to commit a crime does not constitute an attempt. * * *

The "weight of authority," *supra,* is not composed solely of treatise authors, though clearly they have done the most exhaustive work on the subject. The majority of jurisdictions considering the issue have also held that solicitation is not an attempt. A few courts, however, have held that solicitation can be sufficient predicate for an attempt to commit the crime solicited. *Braham v. State,* 571 P.2d 631 (Alaska 1977); *State v. Gay,* 4 Wash.App. 834, 486 P.2d 341 (1971); *State v. Mandel,* 78 Ariz. 226, 278 P.2d 413 (1954). Since the state relies primarily on the minority view expressed in these last cited cases to

2. The essential focus in regard to this distinction is upon the proximity of the act, both spatially and temporally, to the completion of the criminal design. * * *

4. The prerequisite to an understanding of the general rule is the recognition that

solicitation is in the nature of the incitement or encouragement of another to commit a crime in the future. Thus it is essentially preparatory to the commission of the targeted offense.

support appellant's conviction, a brief discussion of this line of authority is called for.

These decisions rely heavily upon the proposition that when the intent that a crime be committed is clearly shown, "slight acts" on the part of the solicitor will make him liable for an attempt to commit that target crime. This theory in turn rests primarily upon the case of *Stokes v. State,* 92 Miss. 415, 46 So. 627 (1908). * * *

It appears, however, that the language in *Stokes* as to the sufficiency of slight acts in attempt prosecutions is gratuitous. In *Stokes,* both solicitor and solicitee planned the murder, proceeded to the designated spot from which the attack was to be made, and were apprehended as the solicitor was handing the murder weapon he had earlier procured to the solicitee. An attempt, under the generally accepted rules of perpetration and proximity, had been committed * * *. * * *

We disagree with the reasoning in the case of *State v. Gay.* While that court noted that a "mere" solicitation is not an attempt, the court there held that the transfer of "consideration," i.e., the partial payment for the contracted killing, was a "slight" yet sufficient act upon which an attempt could be found. (This is the same "slight act" relied on in part by the *Mandel* court, *supra.*

Facially there would appear to be no persuasive reason why a request to kill, however phrased or whatever enticement offered, should be treated differently under the law merely because part of the agreed upon fee has passed hands. There is no greater proximity, no significantly greater likelihood of consummation, and no act of a nature other than the incitement or preparation inherent in the solicitation itself. * * *

In *State v. Braham, supra,* the most recent adoption of the minority position, the Alaska court also recognized that there must be an overt act beyond mere preparation. Yet, after noting the disparate lines of authority, that court elected to join with the Arizona and Washington courts. In the factual context of the *Braham* case, the court found the requisite overt act in the solicitee's visit to the intended victim at the urging of the solicitor for the purpose of gaining the victim's confidence. At that time, the solicitee was still committed to the planned murder; it was only upon later realizing that the police were well informed of the circumstances of the planned murder that the solicitee became an informer. There thus appears to be a valid basis for the Alaska decision holding the solicitor guilty of an attempt. * * * It is well accepted that when the parties are acting in furtherance of a plan, the solicitor shares any attempt liability that accrues due to the actions of his agent.

While the concept of "slight acts" is doubtlessly appealing in some respects, especially to those seeking to punish reprehensible acts when criminal intent is clear, use of this phrase in the manner of the *Gay* and *Mandel* decisions is improper. The solicitor of another, assuming neither solicitor nor solicitee proximately acts toward the crime's commission, cannot be held for an attempt. He does not by his incitement of another to criminal activity commit a dangerously proximate act of perpetration. The extension of attempt liability back to the solicitor destroys the distinction between preparation and perpetration. * * * It is foreseeable that jurisdictions faced with a general attempt statute and no means of severely punishing a solicitation to commit a felony might resort to the device of transforming the solicitor's urgings into a proximate attempted commission of the crime urged but doing so violates the very essence of the requirement that a sufficient *actus reus* be proven before criminal liability will attach.

In light of the foregoing discussion, the facts in appellant's situation take on additional clarity. Here appellant desired to have Captain Ailor murdered. In structuring his plan, he solicited an agent to commit the actual act, and in this regard he paid $250 and promised him a larger sum after the crime had been committed. Neither appellant nor the agent ever took any steps of perpetration in dangerous proximity to the commission of the offense planned. The conversation in the Long Branch at which appellant solicited the undercover policeman, and the payment of part of the agreed upon fee, are not acts of perpetration at all but are clearly the preparatory acts of incitement of another to commit a crime, i.e., of mere solicitation. These acts are not sufficient under the law above discussed to support a conviction on the charge of attempted murder. * * *

Appellant's conviction on the charge of attempted first degree murder is reversed.

BISTLINE, JUSTICE, dissenting.

I do not find it necessary to engage in a debate which is largely centered around attempting to determine when solicitation leaves off and attempt takes over, or to distinguish between overt acts and slightly overt acts, or to find the line of demarcation between perpetration and preparation. * * *

Murder may be accomplished in many ways, and it may be attempted in many ways. Of a twenty volume work on the history of mankind, at least two volumes could be devoted to discussing the multitude of ingenious ways man has devised to kill his fellow man, and seventeen volumes could be written dealing in general with man's inhumanity to man in doing so. The point I lead to is that a man may take it upon himself to effect the death of another person in several ways. He may undertake to commit the murder. * * * Others, desiring the commission of a murder, however, may lack the fortitude to make a direct attack, or may deceive themselves into believing that there is less risk involved if someone else does the dastardly deed. Such persons accordingly may connive to bring about the murder through an agent. If the agent fails to accomplish the act, is it any less an attempt on the part of the principal? Such is the simple question before us.

Whether a person takes on for himself the task of trying to kill another person, or tries to bring about that killing through hiring another to perform the deed, is in actuality nothing but a matter of personal choice. While the principal is guilty of murder when the contract is performed, an attempt has been made when the bargain is struck. Such to me appears to be the essence of the Washington court's holding in *State v. Gay*. Nor does there appear to be any sound reason for demanding that there be an exchange of consideration. * * * If criminals are going to contract out their services, and if there are persons who will retain those services, there is no reason why the criminal courts should decline to respect those contracts. Here, of course, Otto did pay a consideration, and there is no reason to dwell in depth on what might be the case if he had not. Such is better saved for a case where no consideration changes hands. * * *

I am unable to see that the principal is to be relieved of his criminal liability simply because his agent fails in the purpose of his agency either by fouling up, by dishonesty, or by turning out to be a police officer.

Where it has come to pass in this country that we have people who will accept a contract for a killing, it is only fair and just that, where others agree to purchase such services, those contracts should be accorded the intent contemplated by the contracting parties.

The judgment of conviction should be affirmed.

Notes and Questions

1. American Law Institute, Model Penal Code and Commentaries, Comment to § 5.02 at 368–69 (1985):

> Whether the solicitation to commit a crime constitutes an attempt by the solicitor is a question that has been answered in several ways. One approach to the problem treats every solicitation as a specific type of attempt to be governed by ordinary attempt principles, the solicitation being an overt act that alone or together with other overt acts may surpass preparation and result in liability. A second position is that a naked solicitation is not an attempt, but a solicitation accompanied by other overt acts, for example, the offer of a reward or the furnishing of materials, does constitute an attempt. The third view is similar to the second except that in order to find the solicitor guilty of an attempt the other overt acts must proceed beyond what would be called preparation if the solicitor planned to commit the crime himself. Finally, there is the view that no matter what acts the solicitor commits, he cannot be guilty of an attempt because it is not his purpose to commit the offense personally. Although there has been considerable conflict, even among the decisions of the same jurisdiction, the trend has seemed to be toward the last two solutions * * *.

2. Would Otto be guilty of attempted murder under the Model Penal Code? In particular, consider Section 5.01, subsection (2)(g) ("soliciting an innocent agent to engage in conduct constituting an element of the offense"). The Commentary provides the following example of an "innocent agent": *D* unlawfully tells *E* to set fire to *F*'s haystack, and gives him a match to do it. *D* knows that *E* mistakenly believes that it is *D*'s haystack. Under these facts, *E* is an innocent agent, and *D* is guilty of attempted arson

rather than solicitation. American Law Institute, Model Penal Code and Commentaries, Comment to § 5.01 at 346–47 (1985).

Was Officer Watts an innocent agent of Otto? Why does it matter whether he is or is not? That is, in what sense is solicitation of an innocent agent a "substantial step in a course of conduct planned to culminate in * * * commission of the crime," but solicitation of another not necessarily a substantial step?

3. *Problem.* United States v. Church, 32 M.J. 70, 73 (CMA 1991):

Essentially, appellant, who was stationed in North Dakota, had been in the market for several months for someone to kill his estranged wife. She lived in Michigan with the couple's 20-month-old son, and her parents, brothers, sisters, and grandfather. Eventually some of appellant's associates in whom he had confided began to take him seriously, and they reported the matter to the Office of Special Investigations (OSI). Shortly thereafter, an undercover OSI agent was presented as a "hit man," and appellant fell for it.

In a motel room meeting in North Dakota, appellant provided the agent with a partial payment; expense money for the round trip flight; annotated street maps of the vicinity of Mrs. Church's residence; diagrams of the house; photographs of Mrs. Church and their son; descriptions of all the people in the house, including where they slept, what kind of cars they drove, and what their work schedules were; as well as the locations of the guns and dogs. Appellant also approved use of the weapon the agent presented, a .22-caliber semi-automatic pistol with silencer, and he expressed a preference where on the victim he wanted the shots placed. The job was to be done while appellant was conspicuously on duty in North Dakota. Unbeknownst to appellant, the entire conversation was video and audio taped.

Two days later, the agent called appellant from Michigan with the news that appellant's wife had moved and that it would cost more to locate her and accomplish the job. Appellant was apologetic and promptly agreed to the higher amount. He also caused a friend in North Dakota to call telephone Information and obtain his wife's new phone number. The next day the agent called back to tell appellant that he had located the intended victim and that the job would be done shortly. Appellant expressed satisfaction and promised to continue efforts to raise the additional money.

Two days after that, appellant was notified through command channels that his wife had been murdered. Appellant put on "a Class A act" of grief in the unit. That same day, he was notified by the undercover agent to meet him at the North Dakota motel. Appellant arrived, expressed satisfaction with the job done, paid the agent as much of the balance as he had raised, and identified his wife's "body" from a staged photograph. Appellant was then apprehended.

Should these facts support a conviction for attempted murder or only of solicitation? What result under the Model Penal Code? What result at common law?

E. CONSPIRACY

1. GENERAL PRINCIPLES

Whether a definition of conspiracy should be attempted has been doubted because of the question of whether it is possible to frame one in such a manner that it will include every wrong of this nature without including matters which do not belong therein.[g]

The modern crime of conspiracy is so vague that it almost defies definition. Despite certain elementary and essential elements, it also, chameleon-like, takes on a special coloration from each of the many independent offenses on which it may be overlaid.[h]

The law of conspiracy is so irrational, its implications so far removed from ordinary human experience or modes of thought, that like the Theory of Relativity it escapes just beyond the boundaries of the mind. One can dimly understand it while an expert is explaining it, but minutes later it is not easy to tell it back.[i]

PEOPLE v. CARTER

Supreme Court of Michigan, 1982.
415 Mich. 558, 330 N.W.2d 314.

* * * JUSTICE BLAIR MOODY, JR. * * *

Criminal conspiracy occupies a unique place in our criminal justice system. It is defined as "a partnership in criminal purposes," a mutual agreement or understanding, express or implied, between two or more persons to commit a criminal act or to accomplish a legal act by unlawful means. While the offense has its origins in the common law, it is now specifically proscribed by statute, which sets forth the penalties for its commission.

"The gist of the offense of conspiracy lies in the unlawful agreement." The crime is complete upon formation of the agreement; * * * it is not necessary to establish any overt act in furtherance of the conspiracy as a component of the crime.[3] However, a twofold specific intent is required for conviction: intent to combine with others, and intent to accomplish the illegal objective. * * *

It is a settled principle of black-letter law that conspiracy is a crime that is separate and distinct from the substantive crime that is its object. The guilt or innocence of a conspirator does not depend upon the accomplishment of the goals of the conspiracy. More importantly * * *,

---

g. Rollin M. Perkins & Ronald M. Boyce, Criminal Law 681 (3d ed. 1982).

h. Krulewitch v. United States, 336 U.S. 440, 446–47, 69 S.Ct. 716, 720, 93 L.Ed. 790, 796 (1949) (Jackson, J., concurring).

i. Jessica Mitford, The Trial of Dr. Spock 61 (1969).

3. Many * * * states do require, as an element of proof of the crime, that an overt act in pursuance of the conspiratorial end be taken. The overt-act requirement tends to be relatively easy to meet; virtually any act, no matter how insignificant, may suffice.

a conviction of conspiracy does not merge with a conviction of the completed offense. Thus, a defendant may be convicted and punished for both the conspiracy and the substantive crime. * * *

Notes and Questions

1. *Rationale of the crime.* Peter Buscenni, Note, *Conspiracy: Statutory Reform Since the Model Penal Code,* 75 Colum.L.Rev. 1122, 1122 n. 5 (1975):

> Typically, conspiracy is said to perform a dual function. [First,] [i]n its aspect as an inchoate * * * crime, conspiracy has been employed to fill the gap created by a law of attempt too narrowly conceived. Where, in order to constitute attempt, preparation has had to proceed so far toward actual commission of a crime as to itself create an intolerable danger to society, conspiracy has entered the breach and provided an opportunity for earlier official intervention. [Second,] [i]n its role as weapon against group criminal activity, conspiracy has been used to combat the extraordinary dangers allegedly presented by multi-member criminal undertakings. In this guise, the offense has been characterized by vague definition and loose procedural standards. The usual response to criticism has been that such features are necessary to cope with the special threats posed by organized criminal conduct.

Of these two stated justifications, "the heart of the rationale lies in the fact—or at least the assumption—that collective action toward an antisocial end involves a greater risk to society than individual action toward the same end." *Developments in the Law—Criminal Conspiracy,* 72 Harv.L.Rev. 920, 923–24 (1959). The Supreme Court has presented the classic defense of this rationale:

> The distinctiveness between a substantive offense and a conspiracy to commit [it] is a postulate of our law. "It has long been recognized by the Court that the commission of the substantive offense and a conspiracy to commit it are separate and distinct offenses." * * *
>
> This settled principle derives from the reason of things in dealing with socially reprehensible conduct: collective criminal agreement— partnership in crime—presents a greater potential threat to the public than individual delicts. Concerted action both increases the likelihood that the criminal object will be successfully attained and decreases the probability that the individuals involved will depart from their path of criminality. Group association for criminal purposes often, if not normally, makes possible the attainment of ends more complex than those which one criminal could accomplish. Nor is the danger of a conspiratorial group limited to the particular end toward which it has embarked. Combination in crime makes more likely the commission of crimes unrelated to the original purpose for which the group was formed. In sum, the danger which a conspiracy generates is not confined to the substantive offense which is the immediate aim of the enterprise.

Callanan v. United States, 364 U.S. 587, 593–94, 81 S.Ct. 321, 325, 5 L.Ed.2d 312, 317 (1961).

Is this argument convincing? One critic states:

> Though these assumed dangers from conspiracy have a romantically individualistic ring, they have never been verified empirically. It is hardly likely that a search for such verification would end in support of [the] suggestion that combination alone is *inherently* dangerous. This view is immediately refuted by reference to our own society, which is grounded in organization and agreement. More likely, empirical investigation would disclose that there is as much reason to believe that a large number of participants will increase the prospect that the plan will be leaked as that it will be kept secret; or that the persons involved will share their uncertainties and dissuade each other as that each will stiffen the others' determination. Most probably, however, the factors ordinarily mentioned as warranting the crime of conspiracy would be found to add to the danger to be expected from a group in certain situations and not in others; the goals of the group and the personalities of its members would make any generalization unsafe and hence require some other explanation for treating conspiracy as a separate crime in all cases.

Abraham S. Goldstein, *Conspiracy to Defraud the United States,* 68 Yale L.J. 405, 414 (1959).

2. As Justice Moody noted in *Carter,* a criminal conspiracy at common law involves an agreement to commit a crime or *to commit a lawful act in an unlawful manner.* The italicized language means that "it will be enough if the acts contemplated are corrupt, dishonest, fraudulent, or immoral * * *." State v. Kemp, 126 Conn. 60, 78, 9 A.2d 63, 71–72 (1939). Thus, two persons who merely agree to perform an immoral (but not criminal) act, may be punished for conspiracy, although one person, acting by herself, would be guilty of no criminal offense if she did the immoral act.

3. Suppose that April and Bill conspire to rob First State Bank, and subsequently rob it. According to *Carter,* are April and Bob guilty of both conspiracy to rob the bank and of robbery, or only of robbery? What would be the result under the Model Penal Code? See Section 1.07(1).

In a Model Code jurisdiction, does the conspiracy merge into the completed offense if Alice and Bob conspire to rob banks—not simply to rob a specific bank—and they are arrested after robbing First State Bank, but before they commit any further robberies? See American Law Institute, Model Penal Code and Commentaries, Comment to § 1.07 at 109 (1985).

4. *"Conspiracy" and "attempt."* Is there an offense of conspiracy to attempt to commit an offense? What is the argument for the view that such a crime is logically inconsistent? See Townes v. State, 314 Md. 71, 548 A.2d 832 (1988).

Is "attempted conspiracy" a cognizable offense, or is that simply another way of describing the crime of solicitation? Can you suggest a scenario in which a person who attempts to conspire (as "conspiracy" is defined in *Carter*) is *not* guilty of the offense of solicitation?

KRULEWITCH v. UNITED STATES

Supreme Court of the United States, 1949.
336 U.S. 440, 69 S.Ct. 716, 93 L.Ed. 790.

MR. JUSTICE BLACK delivered the opinion of the Court.

A federal district court indictment charged in three counts that petitioner and a woman defendant had (1) induced and persuaded another woman to go on October 20, 1941, from New York City to Miami, Florida, for the purpose of prostitution, in violation of 18 U.S.C. § 399; (2) transported or caused her to be transported from New York to Miami for that purpose, in violation of 18 U.S.C. § 398 [the Mann Act]; and (3) conspired to commit those offenses in violation of 18 U.S.C. § 88. Tried alone, the petitioner was convicted on all three counts of the indictment. The Court of Appeals affirmed. We granted certiorari limiting our review to consideration of alleged error in admission of certain hearsay testimony against petitioner over his timely and repeated objections.

The challenged testimony was elicited by the Government from its complaining witness, the person whom petitioner and the woman defendant allegedly induced to go from New York to Florida for the purpose of prostitution. The testimony narrated the following purported conversation between the complaining witness and petitioner's alleged co-conspirator, the woman defendant. "She asked me, she says, 'You didn't talk yet?' And I says, 'No.' And she says, 'Well, don't,' she says, 'until we get you a lawyer.' And then she says, 'Be very careful what you say.' And I can't put it in exact words. But she said, 'It would be better for us two girls to take the blame than Kay (the defendant) because he couldn't stand it, he couldn't stand to take it.' "

The time of the alleged conversation was more than a month and a half after October 20, 1941, the date the complaining witness had gone to Miami. Whatever original conspiracy may have existed between petitioner and his alleged co-conspirator to cause the complaining witness to go to Florida in October, 1941, no longer existed when the reported conversation took place in December, 1941. For on this latter date the trip to Florida had not only been made—the complaining witness had left Florida, had returned to New York, and had resumed her residence there. Furthermore, at the time the conversation took place, the complaining witness, the alleged co-conspirator, and the petitioner had been arrested. * * *

It is beyond doubt that the central aim of the alleged conspiracy— transportation of the complaining witness to Florida for prostitution— had either never existed or had long since ended in success or failure when and if the alleged co-conspirator made the statement attributed to her. The statement plainly implied that petitioner was guilty of the crime for which he was on trial. It was made in petitioner's absence and the Government made no effort whatever to show that it was made with his authority. The testimony thus stands as an unsworn, out-of-court declaration of petitioner's guilt. This hearsay declaration, attributed to a co-conspirator, was not made pursuant to and in furtherance of objectives of the conspiracy charged in the indictment, because if made, it was after those objectives either had failed or had been achieved. Under these circumstances, the hearsay declaration attributed to the alleged co-conspirator was not admissible on the theory that it was made in furtherance of the alleged criminal transportation undertaking.

Although the Government recognizes that the chief objective of the conspiracy—transportation for prostitution purposes—had ended in success or failure before the reported conversation took place, it nevertheless argues for admissibility of the hearsay declaration as one in furtherance of a continuing subsidiary objective of the conspiracy. Its argument runs this way. Conspirators about to commit crimes always expressly or implicitly agree to collaborate with each other to conceal facts in order to prevent detection, conviction and punishment. Thus the argument is that even after the central criminal objectives of a conspiracy have succeeded or failed, an implicit subsidiary phase of the conspiracy always survives, the phase which has concealment as its sole objective. The Court of Appeals adopted this view. * * *

We cannot accept the Government's contention. There are many logical and practical reasons that could be advanced against a special evidentiary rule that permits out-of-court statements of one conspirator to be used against another. But however cogent these reasons, it is firmly established that where made in furtherance of the objectives of a going conspiracy, such statements are admissible as exceptions to the hearsay rule. * * * We are not persuaded to adopt the Government's implicit conspiracy theory which in all criminal conspiracy cases would create automatically a further breach of the general rule against the admission of hearsay evidence. * * *

Mr. Justice Jackson, concurring in the judgment and opinion of the Court.

This case illustrates a present drift in the federal law of conspiracy which warrants some further comment because it is characteristic of the long evolution of that elastic, sprawling and pervasive offense. Its history exemplifies the "tendency of a principle to expand itself to the limit of its logic." The unavailing protest of courts against the growing habit to indict for conspiracy in lieu of prosecuting for the substantive offense itself, or in addition thereto, suggests that loose practice as to this offense constitutes a serious threat to fairness in our administration of justice.

The modern crime of conspiracy is so vague that it almost defies definition. Despite certain elementary and essential elements, it also, chameleon-like, takes on a special coloration from each of the many independent offenses on which it may be overlaid. It is always "predominantly mental in composition" because it consists primarily of a meeting of minds and an intent.

The crime comes down to us wrapped in vague but unpleasant connotations. It sounds historical undertones of treachery, secret plotting and violence on a scale that menaces social stability and the security of the state itself. "Privy conspiracy" ranks with sedition and rebellion in the Litany's prayer for deliverance. Conspiratorial movements do indeed lie back of the political assassination, the *coup d'etat,* the *putsch,* the revolution, and seizures of power in modern times, as they have in all history.

But the conspiracy concept also is superimposed upon many concerted crimes having no political motivation. It is not intended to question that the basic conspiracy principle has some place in modern criminal law, because to unite, back of a criminal purpose, the strength, opportunities and resources of many is obviously more dangerous and more difficult to police than the efforts of a lone wrongdoer. It also may be trivialized, as here, where the conspiracy consists of the concert of a loathsome panderer and a prostitute to go from New York to Florida to ply their trade, and it would appear that a simple Mann Act prosecution would vindicate the majesty of federal law. However, even when appropriately invoked, the looseness and pliability of the doctrine present inherent dangers which should be in the background of judicial thought wherever it is sought to extend the doctrine to meet the exigencies of a particular case.

Conspiracy in federal law aggravates the degree of crime over that of unconcerted offending. The act of confederating to commit a misdemeanor, followed by even an innocent overt act in its execution, is a felony and is such even if the misdemeanor is never consummated. The more radical proposition also is well-established that at common law and under some statutes a combination may be a criminal conspiracy even if it contemplates only acts which are not crimes at all when perpetrated by an individual or by many acting severally.

Thus the conspiracy doctrine will incriminate persons on the fringe of offending who would not be guilty of aiding and abetting or of becoming an accessory, for those charges only lie when an act which is a crime has actually been committed. * * *

A recent tendency has appeared in this Court to expand this elastic offense and to facilitate its proof. In Pinkerton v. United States, 328 U.S. 640, 66 S.Ct. 1180, 90 L.Ed. 1489, it sustained a conviction of a substantive crime where there was no proof of participation in or knowledge of it, upon the novel and dubious theory that conspiracy is equivalent in law to aiding and abetting.

Doctrines of conspiracy are not only invoked for criminal prosecution, but also in civil proceedings for damages or for injunction, and in administrative proceedings to apply regulatory statutes. They have been resorted to by military commissions and on at least one notable occasion when civil courts were open at the time and place to punish the offense. This conspiracy concept was employed to prosecute laborers for combining to raise their wages and formed the basis for abuse of the labor injunction. * * *

The interchangeable use of conspiracy doctrine in civil as well as penal proceedings opens it to the danger, absent in the case of many crimes, that a court having in mind only the civil sanctions will approve tax practices which later are imported into criminal proceedings. * * * Further, the Court has dispensed with even the necessity to infer any definite agreement, although that is the gist of the offense. * * *

Of course, it is for prosecutors rather than courts to determine when to use a scatter gun to bring down the defendant, but there are procedural advantages from using it which add to the danger of unguarded extension of the concept.

An accused, under the Sixth Amendment, has the right to trial "by an impartial jury of the State and district wherein the crime shall have been committed." The leverage of a conspiracy charge lifts this limitation from the prosecution and reduces its protection to a phantom, for the crime is considered so vagrant as to have been committed in any district where any one of the conspirators did any one of the acts, however innocent, intended to accomplish its object. The Government may, and often does, compel one to defend at a great distance from any place he ever did any act because some accused confederate did some trivial and by itself innocent act in the chosen district. * * *

When the trial starts, the accused feels the full impact of the conspiracy strategy. Strictly, the prosecution should first establish *prima facie* the conspiracy and identify the conspirators, after which evidence of acts and declarations of each in the course of its execution are admissible against all. But the order of proof of so sprawling a charge is difficult for a judge to control. As a practical matter, the accused often is confronted with a hodgepodge of acts and statements by others which he may never have authorized or intended or even known about, but which help to persuade the jury of existence of the conspiracy itself. In other words, a conspiracy often is proved by evidence that is admissible only upon assumption that conspiracy existed. * * *

The trial of a conspiracy charge doubtless imposes a heavy burden on the prosecution, but it is an especially difficult situation for the defendant. The hazard from loose application of rules of evidence is aggravated where the Government institutes mass trials.[20] * * *

A co-defendant in a conspiracy trial occupies an uneasy seat. There generally will be evidence of wrongdoing by somebody. It is difficult for the individual to make his own case stand on its own merits in the minds

---

20. An example is afforded by Allen v. United States, 7 Cir., 4 F.2d 688. At the height of the prohibition frenzy, seventy-five defendants were tried on charges of conspiracy. A newspaper reporter testified to going to a drinking place where he talked with a woman, behind the bar, whose name he could not give. There was not the slightest identification of her nor showing that she knew or was known by any defendant. But it was held that being back of the bar showed her to be a co-conspirator and, hence, her statements were admissible against all. He was allowed to relate incriminating statements made by her.

of jurors who are ready to believe that birds of a feather are flocked together. If he is silent, he is taken to admit it and if, as often happens, co-defendants can be prodded into accusing or contradicting each other, they convict each other. There are many practical difficulties in defending against a charge of conspiracy which I will not enumerate. * * *

There is, of course, strong temptation to relax rigid standards when it seems the only way to sustain convictions of evildoers. But statutes authorize prosecution for substantive crimes for most evil-doing without the dangers to the liberty of the individual and the integrity of the judicial process that are inherent in conspiracy charges. * * * And I think there should be no straining to uphold any conspiracy conviction where prosecution for the substantive offense is adequate and the purpose served by adding the conspiracy charge seems chiefly to get procedural advantages to ease the way to conviction. * * *

PHILLIP E. JOHNSON—THE UNNECESSARY CRIME OF CONSPIRACY

61 California Law Review 1137 (1973), 1137–41

The literature on the subject of criminal conspiracy reflects a sort of rough consensus. Conspiracy, it is generally said, is a necessary doctrine in some respects, but also one that is overbroad and invites abuse.

The overbreadth of conspiracy and its potential for abuse have been extensively discussed in the literature. One principal theme of criticism, best illustrated by Mr. Justice Jackson's opinion in *Krulewitch v. United States,* emphasizes the difficulties which the ordinary criminal defendant may face when charged with conspiracy. The advantages which conspiracy provides the prosecution are seen as disadvantages for the defendant so serious that they may lead to unfair punishment unfairly determined. Critics taking this approach typically propose to trim conspiracy doctrine just enough to provide protection for defense interests without disturbing those rules deemed genuinely important for effective law enforcement. The leading reform proposal of this type is the conspiracy section of the American Law Institute's Model Penal Code * * *.

The other major line of criticism stresses the dangers that conspiracy law raises for first amendment freedoms. Prosecutions of political dissidents, including labor organizers, Communist Party leaders, and contemporary radicals, typically have been conspiracy prosecutions. The law of conspiracy is intended, after all, to make it easier to impose criminal punishment on members of groups that plot forbidden activity. Insofar as it accomplishes this end, it unavoidably increases the likelihood that persons will be punished for what they say rather than for what they do, or for associating with others who are found culpable. Critics who are alarmed at the resulting threat to freedom of speech and freedom of association typically have proposed new constitutional doctrines derived from the first amendment to curtail the use of conspiracy charges in cases having some "political" element.

Unfortunately, the proposals for legislative or constitutional reforms of conspiracy law are inadequate. It will not do simply to reform conspiracy legislatively by removing its most widely deplored overextensions, or to reform it judicially by engrafting new doctrines derived from the first amendment. Such measures are appropriate for improving a doctrine that is basically sound, but in need of some adjustment at the edges. The law of criminal conspiracy is not basically sound. It should be abolished, not reformed.

The central fault of conspiracy law and the reason why any limited reform is bound to be inadequate can be briefly stated. What conspiracy adds to the law is simply confusion, and the confusion is inherent in the nature of the doctrine. The confusion stems from the fact that conspiracy is not only a substantive inchoate crime in itself, but the touchstone for invoking several independent procedural and substantive doctrines. We ask whether a defendant agreed with another person to commit a crime initially for the purpose of determining whether he may be convicted of the offense of conspiracy even when the crime itself has not yet been committed. If the answer to that question is in the affirmative, however, we find that we have also answered a number of other questions that would otherwise have to be considered independently. Where there is evidence of conspiracy, the defendant may be tried jointly with his criminal partners and possibly with many other persons whom he has never met or seen, the joint trial may be held in a place he may never have visited, and hearsay statements of other alleged members of the conspiracy may be used to prove his guilt. Furthermore, a defendant who is found guilty of conspiracy is subject to enhanced punishment and may also be found guilty of any crime committed in furtherance of the conspiracy, whether or not he knew about the crime or aided in its commission.

Each of these issues involves a separate substantive or procedural area of the criminal law of considerable importance and complexity. The essential vice of conspiracy is that it inevitably distracts the courts from the policy questions or balancing of interests that ought to govern the decision of specific legal issues and leads them instead to decide those issues by reference to the conceptual framework of conspiracy. Instead of asking whether public policy or the interests of the parties requires a particular holding, the courts are led instead to consider whether the theory of conspiracy is broad enough to permit it. What is wrong with conspiracy, in other words, is much more basic than the overbreadth of a few rules. The problem is not with particular results, but with the use of a single abstract concept to decide numerous questions that deserve separate consideration in light of the various interests and policies they involve. * * *

* * * Conspiracy became the monster it now is by a process of judicial improvisation. Whatever may have been the justification for this patchwork process, the problems it meant to remedy can now be resolved by more specific doctrines with a firmer basis in policy. Hence it is particularly disappointing that the * * * Model Penal Code retains a

general conspiracy doctrine. * * * The reforms touch mainly upon matters that are of little importance, while the major sources of abuse are left untouched. Moreover, the history of conspiracy to date, which is one of almost constant expansion, gives little reason to hope that any partial retrenchment will be lasting.

Notes and Questions

1. Professor Johnson has lamented that "[t]he outstanding fact is * * * that the law has moved in precisely the opposite direction from that which I recommended in my long-ago article." Paul Marcus, *Criminal Conspiracy Law: Time to Turn Back From An Ever Expanding, Ever More Troubling Area.* 1 Wm. & Mary Bill of Rts. J. 1, 5 (1992) (quoting a letter, dated January 25, 1991, from Johnson to Marcus).

2. One of the more confusing features of conspiracy law is that "conspiracy" is not simply an inchoate offense, but is also a basis for holding a person accountable for the criminal actions of others. Some jurisdictions state that a conspirator may be convicted of every crime committed by a co-conspirator in furtherance of the conspiracy, even if the conspirator did not aid in the commission of the substantive offense(s) for which she is charged. The relationship of conspiracy to accomplice liability is considered in Chapter 11.

2. MENS REA

a. General Principles

PEOPLE v. HORN

Supreme Court of California, 1974.
12 Cal.3d 290, 115 Cal.Rptr. 516, 524 P.2d 1300.

TOBRINER, JUSTICE.

Defendants Wilmout Horn and Virgil Lee Feltner appeal from convictions, following jury verdict, of conspiracy to commit first degree murder (Pen.Code § 182), of arson, and of unlawful manufacture of a fire bomb. Evidence submitted at the trial showed that at the time of the conspiracy defendants were so intoxicated that they may have lacked the capacity to entertain malice aforethought, and consequently that the conspiracy should be classed as one to commit voluntary manslaughter. The trial court, however, erroneously refused to instruct the jury that diminished capacity arising from intoxication can reduce a homicide to manslaughter and erroneously compelled the jury to choose between finding defendants guilty of conspiracy to commit first degree murder or innocent of any conspiracy at all. The court's error in instructions and the form of verdict seriously prejudiced the defense to the conspiracy count and requires a reversal of that conviction. * * *

On the evening of May 10, 1970, defendants and Billy Horn, the brother of defendant Wilmout Horn, decided "to get rid of Elmer [Damron]." Upon meeting four juveniles, defendant Horn offered to pay them $20 each to bomb or burn "a house"; the juveniles agreed.

Defendant Horn drove the juveniles to Elmer Damron's home, and there defendants Horn and Feltner described how they wanted the house blown up.

Defendants, Billy Horn, and the juveniles then went to Billy's house where they made five or six fire bombs. Defendants and the juveniles returned to the vicinity of Damron's house. The juveniles lit the bombs, throwing them at the house; they then ran down an alley where Billy Horn picked them up in his car.

Awakened by the explosions, Damron called the fire department. Outside the house the firemen and policemen found three fire bombs which had failed to explode, and fragments of other bombs.   * * *

Defendants Horn and Feltner testified that they consumed large quantities of liquor and beer during the afternoon and evening of May 10, and at the time of the conspiracy were highly intoxicated. This testimony was corroborated by * * * other persons who had observed defendants during the evening.

The trial court instructed the jury that conspiracy to commit murder "is an agreement between two or more persons to commit the public offense of murder and with the specific intent to commit such offense...." It defined murder as "the unlawful killing of a human being with malice aforethought"; further instructions defined "malice" and "aforethought." Noting that conspiracy requires specific intent, the court instructed that "if the evidence shows that the defendant was intoxicated at the time of the alleged offense, the jury should consider his state of intoxication in determining if defendant had such specific intent."   * * *

The trial court did not instruct the jury * * * that diminished capacity caused by intoxication may reduce a homicide below first degree murder. * * * The jury found defendants guilty of conspiracy to commit first degree murder * * *. Defendants were sentenced to life imprisonment.

* * * [P]roof of a conspiracy to commit a specific offense requires proof that the conspirators intended to bring about the elements of the conspired offense. Since evidence of diminished mental capacity can show that a homicide was committed without premeditation or malice aforethought, reducing that homicide to second degree murder or manslaughter, such evidence may also serve to classify a conspiracy to commit a homicide as one to commit second degree murder or manslaughter.   * * *

Penal Code section 182, after listing certain felonies, not including murder or manslaughter, provides that when two or more persons "conspire to commit any other felony, they shall be punishable in the same manner and to the same extent as is provided for the punishment of the said felony. If the felony is one for which different punishments are prescribed for different degrees, the jury or court which finds the defendant guilty thereof shall determine the degree of the felony defendant conspired to commit. If the degree is not so determined, the punishment for conspiracy to commit such felony shall be that prescribed for the lesser degree, except in the case of conspiracy to commit murder, in which case the punishment shall be that prescribed for murder in the first degree." To comply with this section, the trier of fact must determine the identity of the conspired felony, and if that felony is divided into degrees, the degree of the felony.

Homicide itself is not a crime, but a class of crimes, graduated according to the mental state and personal turpitude of the offender. Consequently, when the case involves a conspiracy to commit a homicide, the duty will devolve upon the jury to determine whether the homicide that the defendants conspired to commit was a first degree murder—a killing characterized by malice aforethought. Plainly a jury could not properly discharge its duty if it were ignorant of the relationship between diminished capacity arising from intoxication and the classes and degrees of homicide.

The Attorney General, however, argues that conspiracy is a crime without degrees or lesser included offenses, and hence that the defense of diminished capacity goes not to the conspired homicide but only to the conspirators' capacity to agree among themselves. This argument mistakes the element of intent in the crime of conspiracy, and overlooks the duty of the jury under Penal Code section 182 to determine the crime, and the degree of the crime, which defendants conspired to commit.

Conspiracy is a "specific intent" crime. The specific intent required divides logically into two elements: (a) the intent to agree, or conspire, and (b) the intent to commit the offense which is the object of the conspiracy. To sustain a conviction for conspiracy to commit a particular offense, the prosecution must show not only that the conspirators intended to agree but also that they intended to commit the elements of that offense. * * *

It is contended that since defendants are charged with conspiracy, not with murder, that only two issues arise: did defendants conspire, and did they have the capacity to conspire? But resolution of only those two issues does not dispose of the case. *Under Penal Code section 182 the jury must also determine which felony defendants conspired to commit,* and if that felony is divided into degrees, which degree of the felony they conspired to commit. The jury cannot perform that task unless it is instructed on the elements of both the offense defendants are charged with conspiring to commit, and any lesser offense defendants assert to be the true object of the conspiracy.[4] * * *

4. Assume, for example, that defendants, accused of conspiracy to commit grand theft, admit the conspiracy but alleged the object was a petty theft. Obviously the jury would have to be instructed on the difference between the two crimes. Or that defendants, accused of conspiracy to commit burglary, ask the jury to fix that crime as a burglary of the second degree; obviously the court would have to instruct on the difference between first and second degree burglary. Likewise here, in which defendants assert that the object of their conspiracy was manslaughter, the jury should be instructed on the mental state

The Attorney General contends, however, that any conspiracy to commit a homicide is, of logical necessity, a conspiracy to commit first degree murder. He relies on People v. Kynette (1940) 15 Cal.2d 731, 104 P.2d 794, which stated that "a conspiracy to commit murder can only be a conspiracy to commit murder of the first degree for the obvious reason that the agreement to murder necessarily involves the 'wilful, deliberate, and premeditated' intention to kill a human being." * * *[5]

Perhaps as of 1940, when *Kynette* was decided, one could argue that proof that a defendant entered into an agreement to commit a homicide demonstrated beyond reasonable doubt his capacity to premeditate and to entertain malice aforethought. But today premeditation no longer means merely advance planning of the crime; it requires proof that the defendant "could maturely and meaningfully reflect upon the gravity of his contemplated act." (People v. Wolff (1964) 61 Cal.2d 795, 821, 40 Cal.Rptr. 271, 287, 394 P.2d 959, 975.) Furthermore, a conviction of murder in any degree requires proof of malice aforethought; since People v. Gorshen (1959) 51 Cal.2d 716, 727, 336 P.2d 492, malice can be rebutted "by a showing that the defendant's mental capacity was reduced by mental illness, mental defect or intoxication."

In view of these decisions, it can no longer be successfully argued that objective proof that defendants planned a homicide in advance conclusively proves that homicide was a first degree murder. The planning itself may have been affected by a defendant's * * * intoxication. Consequently the fact that a killing was planned in advance, whether individually or in concert, does not prove that the planner acted with malice or after meaningful reflection upon the gravity of his contemplated act. If, gripped by mental illness, intoxication, or heat of passion, a man kills without malice, he commits manslaughter; it necessarily follows that if this same man, under those same circumstances, conspires to kill, he conspires to commit manslaughter. Even though his befuddled brain still possesses the bare capacity to agree to the conspiracy, his inability to appreciate the gravity of his act, or to harbor malice aforethought compels us to classify the object of his conspiracy as a manslaughter.

There is another fundamental reason why we cannot treat all conspiracies to commit homicide as conspiracies to commit first degree

which distinguishes manslaughter and murder.

5. *Kynette's* assertion that a conspiracy to commit murder is always a conspiracy to commit first degree murder is inconsistent with the present language of Penal Code section 182. When *Kynette* was decided, section 182 provided simply that conspirators to commit a felony "shall be punishable in the same manner and to the same extent as is provided for the punishment [of the commission] of the said felony." The current section 182, enacted in 1955, is much more specific * * *.

As * * * written and punctuated, it plainly authorizes the trier of fact to return a verdict finding conspiracy to commit murder in the second degree. *Only* if the trier of fact fails to determine the degree is a conspiracy to commit murder punished as one to commit first degree murder. Since the Legislature has authorized a verdict of conspiracy to commit second degree murder, it clearly does not believe that crime to be a logical impossibility.

murder. In People v. Holt (1944) 25 Cal.2d 59, 89, 153 P.2d 21, 37, we stated that "Dividing intentional homicides into murder and voluntary manslaughter was a recognition of the infirmity of human nature. Again dividing the offense of murder into two degrees is a further recognition of that infirmity and of difference in the quantum of personal turpitude of the offenders. The difference is basically in the offenders. . . ." Since the punishment for conspiracy to commit a homicide is the same as the punishment for the conspired felony, we must undertake this same delicate weighing of personal turpitude of conspirators to commit homicide. If because of intoxication or mental incapacity the personal turpitude of a conspirator indicates a classification of manslaughter, it would be wholly unjust to punish him as a first degree murderer solely because he acted in concert with another person of equal diminished capacity. * * *

Mosk, Justice.

I dissent.

Under California law there are no degrees of conspiracy. Defendants tried for the crime of conspiracy are either guilty as charged or not guilty; the trier of fact has no comfortable option of reducing conspiracy to a lesser offense.

But, argue the majority, Penal Code section 182 provides that if the felony the defendants conspire to commit consists of degrees, then the trier of fact must ascertain the degree. True enough. But where the majority [then] go awry is in leaping from the code section to the untenable conclusion that the defendants' *mental capacity to conspire* is to be determined by consideration of the planned subordinate felony, rather than solely by reference to the crime itself: conspiracy. * * *

Of course, diminished capacity is an issue in this case. But where the majority fall into error is in relating diminished capacity to murder, instead of to the charge of conspiracy. * * *

A conspiracy is a combination of two or more persons to commit a crime or to do any of the other acts forbidden by Penal Code section 182. The law speaks of a conspiracy as an agreement plus an overt act in furtherance of the agreement. Conspiracy is a totally independent accusation based upon the criminality attached to an unlawful agreement followed by some act in pursuance of the joint design. The key to the offense is the agreement, not the crime which the conspirators purportedly agree to commit. * * *

Thus we must look to the capacity of the defendants to conspire, i.e., to agree between themselves. It seems obvious that the criminal act they agreed to commit is unrelated to their mental ability to agree. The issue is: *was their capacity to conspire diminished?* The jury was properly instructed on that query, and by its verdict of guilt found the defendants to have adequate capacity to negotiate a criminal agreement.

But, say the majority, two persons may have the ability to conspire but lack the ability to complete the offense they conspire to commit;

therefore they can be convicted of conspiring to commit some lesser offense. In this instance the majority hold that lacking the capacity to conspire to commit first degree murder, the defendants nevertheless may have the capacity to conspire to commit manslaughter. I confess the rationale of this esoteric concept escapes me. If the defendants are unable to conspire to commit one crime because of mental incapacity, it would seem to follow that they would be equally unable to conspire to commit another crime. By the simple device of changing the crime alleged to have been conspiratorially contemplated the law cannot elevate, *mirabile dictu*, the mental capacity of the defendants. * * *

This case is not as distressingly complicated as the unique theory of the majority attempts to make it. There are two simple questions and equally easy answers. First, did the defendants enter into an agreement, i.e., conspiracy to commit an unlawful act? The jury answered affirmatively * * *. Second, did the defendants have the capacity to enter into an agreement, i.e., conspiracy? The jury, properly instructed * * *, answered affirmatively * * *.

Notes and Questions

1. Suppose that at the time of the conspiracy Horn had been severely intoxicated, but Feltner had been sober. How would Justice Tobriner have handled this situation? What about Justice Mosk?

2. In People v. Barajas, 198 Mich.App. 551, 499 N.W.2d 396 (1993), *B* agreed to purchase one kilogram of cocaine from *X*. The parties, arrested before the delivery occurred, were prosecuted for conspiracy to possess over 650 grams of cocaine, in violation of state law. (Possession of 650 or fewer grams of cocaine constituted a lesser offense.) As it turned out, *X* intended to defraud *B*: the box that he intended to deliver contained only 26 grams of cocaine, mixed with baking soda. Are the parties guilty as charged? Does the answer depend on when *X* decided to defraud *B*?

3. Jacob and Ken agree to detonate a bomb in a building they both know is occupied, in order to destroy it. Although they do not want anybody to die, they believe that people will be killed as a result of their actions. If the bomb explodes and occupants die, of what form of criminal homicide are they guilty? If the bomb does not go off, are they guilty of attempted murder? In either case, are they guilty of conspiracy to commit murder? Answer under the Model Penal Code. See American Law Institute, Model Penal Code and Commentaries, Comment to § 5.03 at 407–08 (1985).

b. *Intent: "Purpose" or "Knowledge"?*

PEOPLE v. LAURIA

California Court of Appeal, Second District, 1967.
251 Cal.App.2d 471, 59 Cal.Rptr. 628.

FLEMING, ASSOCIATE JUSTICE.

In an investigation of call-girl activity the police focused their attention on three prostitutes actively plying their trade on call, each of whom was using Lauria's telephone answering service, presumably for business purposes.

On January 8, 1965, Stella Weeks, a policewoman, signed up for telephone service with Lauria's answering service. Mrs. Weeks, in the course of her conversation with Lauria's office manager, hinted broadly that she was a prostitute concerned with the secrecy of her activities and their concealment from the police. She was assured that the operation of the service was discreet and "about as safe as you can get." It was arranged that Mrs. Weeks need not leave her address with the answering service, but could pick up her calls and pay her bills in person.

On February 11, Mrs. Weeks talked to Lauria on the telephone and told him her business was modelling and she had been referred to the answering service by Terry, one of the three prostitutes under investigation. She complained that because of the operation of the service she had lost two valuable customers, referred to as tricks. Lauria defended his service and said that her friends had probably lied to her about having left calls for her. * * * In the course of his talk he said "his business was taking messages." * * *

On April 1 Lauria and the three prostitutes were arrested. Lauria complained to the police that this attention was undeserved, stating that * * * he kept separate records for known or suspected prostitutes for the convenience of himself and the police. * * * However, his service didn't "arbitrarily tell the police about prostitutes on our board. As long as they pay their bills we tolerate them." In a subsequent voluntary appearance before the Grand Jury Lauria * * * admitted he knew some of his customers were prostitutes, and he knew Terry was a prostitute because he had personally used her services, and he knew she was paying for 500 calls a month.

Lauria and the three prostitutes were [indicted] for conspiracy to commit prostitution, and nine overt acts were specified. Subsequently the trial court set aside the indictment as having been brought without reasonable or probable cause. The People have appealed, claiming that a sufficient showing of an unlawful agreement to further prostitution was made.

To establish agreement, the People need show no more than a tacit, mutual understanding between coconspirators to accomplish an unlawful act. Here the People attempted to establish a conspiracy by showing that Lauria, well aware that his codefendants were prostitutes who received business calls from customers through his telephone answering service, continued to furnish them with such service. This approach attempts to equate knowledge of another's criminal activity with conspiracy to further such criminal activity, and poses the question of the criminal responsibility of a furnisher of goods or services who knows his product is being used to assist the operation of an illegal business. Under what circumstances does a supplier become a part of a conspiracy to further an illegal enterprise by furnishing goods or services which he knows are to be used by the buyer for criminal purposes?

The two leading cases on this point face in opposite directions. In United States v. Falcone, 311 U.S. 205, 61 S.Ct. 204, 85 L.Ed. 128, the sellers of large quantities of sugar, yeast, and cans were absolved from participation in a moonshining conspiracy among distillers who bought from them, while in Direct Sales Co. v. United States, 319 U.S. 703, 63 S.Ct. 1265, 87 L.Ed. 1674, a wholesaler of drugs was convicted of conspiracy to violate the federal narcotic laws by selling drugs in quantity to a codefendant physician who was supplying them to addicts. The distinction between these two cases appears primarily based on the proposition that distributors of such dangerous products as drugs are required to exercise greater discrimination in the conduct of their business than are distributors of innocuous substances like sugar and yeast.

In the earlier case, *Falcone,* the sellers' knowledge of the illegal use of the goods was insufficient by itself to make the sellers participants in a conspiracy with the distillers who bought from them. Such knowledge fell short of proof of a conspiracy, and evidence on the volume of sales was too vague to support a jury finding that respondents knew of the conspiracy from the size of the sales alone.

In the later case of *Direct Sales,* the conviction of a drug wholesaler for conspiracy to violate federal narcotic laws was affirmed on a showing that it had actively promoted the sale of morphine sulphate in quantity and had sold codefendant physician, who practiced in a small town in South Carolina, more than 300 times his normal requirements of the drug, even though it had been repeatedly warned of the dangers of unrestricted sales of the drug. The court contrasted the restricted goods involved in *Direct Sales* with the articles of free commerce involved in *Falcone:* "All articles of commerce may be put to illegal ends," said the court. "But all do not have inherently the same susceptibility to harmful and illegal use. * * * This difference is important for two purposes. One is for making certain that the seller knows the buyer's intended illegal use. The other is to show that by the sale he intends to further, promote and cooperate in it. This intent, when given effect by overt act, is the gist of conspiracy. While it is not identical with mere knowledge that another purposes unlawful action, it is not unrelated to such knowledge. * * * The step from knowledge to intent and agreement may be taken. There is more than suspicion, more than knowledge, acquiescence, carelessness, indifference, lack of concern. There is informed and interested cooperation, stimulation, instigation. And there is also a 'stake in the venture' which, even if it may not be essential, is not irrelevant to the question of conspiracy."

While *Falcone* and *Direct Sales* may not be entirely consistent with each other in their full implications, they do provide us with a framework for the criminal liability of a supplier of lawful goods or services put to unlawful use. Both the element of *knowledge* of the illegal use of the goods or services and the element of *intent* to further that use must be present in order to make the supplier a participant in a criminal conspiracy.

Proof of *knowledge* is ordinarily a question of fact and requires no extended discussion in the present case. The knowledge of the supplier was sufficiently established when Lauria admitted he knew some of his customers were prostitutes and admitted he knew that Terry, an active subscriber to his service, was a prostitute. * * * Because Lauria knew in fact that some of his customers were prostitutes, it is a legitimate inference he knew they were subscribing to his answering service for illegal business purposes and were using his service to make assignations for prostitution. On this record we think the prosecution is entitled to claim positive knowledge by Lauria of the use of his service to facilitate the business of prostitution.

The more perplexing issue in the case is the sufficiency of proof of *intent* to further the criminal enterprise. The element of intent may be proved either by direct evidence, or by evidence of circumstances from which an intent to further a criminal enterprise by supplying lawful goods or services may be inferred. Direct evidence of participation, such as advice from the supplier of legal goods or services to the user of those goods or services on their use for illegal purposes, * * * provides the simplest case. * * * But in cases where direct proof of complicity is lacking, intent to further the conspiracy must be derived from the sale itself and its surrounding circumstances in order to establish the supplier's express or tacit agreement to join the conspiracy. * * *

In examining precedents in this field we find that sometimes, but not always, the criminal intent of the supplier may be inferred from his knowledge of the unlawful use made of the product he supplies. Some consideration of characteristic patterns may be helpful.

1. Intent may be inferred from knowledge, when the purveyor of legal goods for illegal use has acquired a stake in the venture. For example, in Regina v. Thomas, (1957), 2 All.E.R. 181, 342, * * * when the accused rented a room at a grossly inflated rent to a prostitute for the purpose of carrying on her trade, a jury could find he was living on the earnings of prostitution. * * *

2. Intent may be inferred from knowledge, when no legitimate use for the goods or services exists. The leading California case is People v. McLaughlin, 111 Cal.App.2d 781, 245 P.2d 1076, in which the court upheld a conviction of the suppliers of horse-racing information by wire for conspiracy to promote bookmaking, when it had been established that wire-service information had no other use than to supply information needed by bookmakers to conduct illegal gambling operations. * * *

In such cases the supplier must necessarily have an intent to further the illegal enterprise since there is no known honest use for his goods. * * *

3. Intent may be inferred from knowledge, when the volume of business with the buyer is grossly disproportionate to any legitimate demand, or when sales for illegal use amount to a high proportion of the seller's total business. In such cases an intent to participate in the

illegal enterprise may be inferred from the quantity of the business done. For example, in *Direct Sales,* supra, the sale of narcotics to a rural physician in quantities 300 times greater than he would have normal use for provided potent evidence of an intent to further the illegal activity. * * *

Yet there are cases in which it cannot reasonably be said that the supplier has a stake in the venture or has acquired a special interest in the enterprise, but in which he has been held liable as a participant on the basis of knowledge alone. * * * It seems apparent from these cases that a supplier who furnishes equipment which he *knows* will be used to commit a serious crime may be deemed from that knowledge alone to have intended to produce the result. Such proof may justify an inference that the furnisher intended to aid the execution of the crime and that he thereby became a participant. For instance, we think the operator of a telephone answering service with positive knowledge that his service was being used to facilitate the extortion of ransom, the distribution of heroin, or the passing of counterfeit money who continued to furnish the service with knowledge of its use, might be chargeable on knowledge alone with participation in a scheme to extort money, to distribute narcotics, or to pass counterfeit money. * * *

Logically, the same reasoning could be extended to crimes of every description. Yet we do not believe an inference of intent drawn from knowledge of criminal use properly applies to the less serious crimes classified as misdemeanors. The duty to take positive action to dissociate oneself from activities helpful to violations of the criminal law as far stronger and more compelling for felonies than it is for misdemeanors or petty offenses. In this respect, as in others, the distinction between felonies and misdemeanors, between more serious and less serious crime, retains continuing vitality. * * *

From this analysis of precedent we deduce the following rule: the intent of a supplier who knows of the criminal use to which his supplies are put to participate in the criminal activity connected with the use of his supplies may be established by (1) direct evidence that he intends to participate, or (2) through an inference that he intends to participate based on, (a) his special interest in the activity, or (b) the aggravated nature of the crime itself.

When we review Lauria's activities in the light of this analysis, we find no proof that Lauria took any direct action to further, encourage, or direct the call-girl activities of his codefendants and we find an absence of circumstances from which his special interest in their activities could be inferred. Neither excessive charges for standardized services, nor the furnishing of services without a legitimate use, nor an unusual quantity of business with call girls, are present. The offense which he is charged with furthering is a misdemeanor, a category of crime which has never been made a required subject of positive disclosure to public authority. Under these circumstances, although proof of Lauria's knowledge of the criminal activities of his patrons was sufficient to charge him with that fact, there was insufficient evidence that he intended to further their criminal activities, and hence insufficient proof of his participation in a criminal conspiracy with his codefendants to further prostitution. * * *

Notes and Questions

1. A merchant sells "fuzz busters" (a mechanism installed in a motor vehicle that emits a signal in proximity of a police speed-radar device) in his store. The box in which the device is sold states in bold and large lettering, "KEEPS YOU ONE STEP AHEAD OF THE POLICE." Under *Lauria,* is the merchant guilty of conspiracy to violate traffic speed laws? If so, who are the other parties to the conspiracy?

2. Should a gun dealer be subject to prosecution for conspiracy to commit murder if she lawfully sells a firearm to a customer who states, "I need a gun to kill my neighbor, who is getting on my nerves"? Is she guilty under Model Penal Code § 5.03?

c. Attendant Circumstances

UNITED STATES v. FEOLA

Supreme Court of the United States, 1975.
420 U.S. 671, 95 S.Ct. 1255, 43 L.Ed.2d 541.

MR. JUSTICE BLACKMUN delivered the opinion of the Court.

This case presents the issue whether knowledge that the intended victim is a federal officer is a requisite for the crime of conspiracy, under 18 U.S.C. § 371, to commit an offense violative of 18 U.S.C. § 111,[1] that is, an assault upon a federal officer while engaged in the performance of his official duties.

Respondent Feola and three others * * * were indicted for violations of §§ 371 and 111. A jury found all four defendants guilty of both charges. * * * [T]he United States Court of Appeals affirmed the judgment of conviction on the substantive charges, but reversed the conspiracy convictions. * * *

I

The facts reveal a classic narcotics "rip-off." The details are not particularly important for our present purposes. We need note only that the evidence shows that Feola and his confederates arranged for a sale of heroin to buyers who turned out to be undercover agents for the Bureau

---

1. "§ 111. Assaulting, resisting, or impeding certain officers or employees.

"Whoever forcibly assaults, resists, opposes, impedes, intimidates, or interferes with any person designated in section 1114 of this title while engaged in or on account of the performance of his official duties, shall be fined not more than $5,000 or imprisoned not more than three years, or both.

"Whoever, in the commission of any such acts uses a deadly or dangerous weapon, shall be fined not more than $10,000 or imprisoned not more than ten years, or both."

Among the persons "designated in section 1114" of 18 U.S.C. is "any officer or employee ... of the Bureau of Narcotics and Dangerous Drugs."

of Narcotics and Dangerous Drugs. The group planned to palm off on the purchasers, for a substantial sum, a form of sugar in place of heroin and, should that ruse fail, simply to surprise their unwitting buyers and relieve them of the cash they had brought along for payment. The plan failed when one agent, his suspicions being aroused, drew his revolver in time to counter an assault upon another agent from the rear. Instead of enjoying the rich benefits of a successful swindle, Feola and his associates found themselves charged, to their undoubted surprise, with conspiring to assault, and with assaulting, federal officers.

At the trial, the District Court, without objection from the defense, charged the jurors that, in order to find any of the defendants guilty on either the conspiracy count or the substantive one, they were not required to conclude that the defendants were aware that their quarry were federal officers.

The Court of Appeals reversed the conspiracy convictions on a ground not advanced by any of the defendants. Although it approved the trial court's instructions to the jury on the substantive charge of assaulting a federal officer, it nonetheless concluded that the failure to charge that knowledge of the victim's official identity must be proved in order to convict on the conspiracy charge amounted to plain error. The court perceived itself bound by a line of cases, commencing with Judge Learned Hand's opinion in United States v. Crimmins, 123 F.2d 271 (CA2 1941), all holding that scienter of a factual element that confers federal jurisdiction, while unnecessary for conviction of the substantive offense, is required in order to sustain a conviction for conspiracy to commit the substantive offense. Although the court noted that the *Crimmins* rationale "has been criticized," and, indeed, offered no argument in support of it, it accepted "the controlling precedents somewhat reluctantly."

II

The Government's plea is for symmetry. It urges that since criminal liability for the offense described in 18 U.S.C. § 111 does not depend on whether the assailant harbored the specific intent to assault a federal officer, no greater scienter requirement can be engrafted upon the conspiracy offense, which is merely an agreement to commit the act proscribed by § 111. Consideration of the Government's contention requires us preliminarily to pass upon its premise, the proposition that responsibility for assault upon a federal officer does not depend upon whether the assailant was aware of the official identity of his victim at the time he acted.

That the "federal officer" requirement is anything other than jurisdictional [9] is not seriously urged upon us; indeed, both Feola and

9. We are content to state the issue this way despite its potential to mislead. Labeling a requirement "jurisdictional" does not necessarily mean, of course, that the requirement is not an element of the offense Congress intended to describe and to punish. Indeed, a requirement is sufficient to confer jurisdiction on the federal courts for

the Court of Appeals concede that scienter is not a necessary element of the substantive offense under § 111. Although some early cases were to the contrary, the concession recognizes what is now the practical unanimity of the Courts of Appeals. * * *

* * * All [Section 111] requires is an intent to assault, not an intent to assault a federal officer. A contrary conclusion would give insufficient protection to the agent enforcing an unpopular law, and none to the agent acting under cover.

This interpretation poses no risk of unfairness to defendants. It is no snare for the unsuspecting. Although the perpetrator of a narcotics "rip-off," such as the one involved here, may be surprised to find that his intended victim is a federal officer in civilian apparel, he nonetheless knows from the very outset that his planned course of conduct is wrongful. The situation is not one where legitimate conduct becomes unlawful solely because of the identity of the individual or agency affected. In a case of this kind the offender takes his victim as he finds him. The concept of criminal intent does not extend so far as to require that the actor understand not only the nature of his act but also its consequence for the choice of a judicial forum. * * *

We hold, therefore, that in order to incur criminal liability under § 111 an actor must entertain merely the criminal intent to do the acts therein specified. We now consider whether the rule should be different where persons conspire to commit those acts.

III

Our decisions establish that in order to sustain a judgment of conviction on a charge of conspiracy to violate a federal statute, the Government must prove at least the degree of criminal intent necessary for the substantive offense itself. Respondent Feola urges upon us the proposition that the Government must show a degree of criminal intent in the conspiracy count greater than is necessary to convict for the substantive offense; he urges that even though it is not necessary to show that he was aware of the official identity of his assaulted victims in order to find him guilty of assaulting federal officers, in violation of 18 U.S.C. § 111, the Government nonetheless must show that he was aware that his intended victims were undercover agents, if it is successfully to prosecute him for conspiring to assault federal agents. * * *

what otherwise are state crimes precisely because it implicates factors that are an appropriate subject for federal concern. With respect to the present case, for example, a mere general policy of deterring assaults would probably prove to be an undesirable or insufficient basis for federal jurisdiction; but where Congress seeks to protect the integrity of federal functions and the safety of federal officers, the interest is sufficient to warrant federal involvement.

The significance of labeling a statutory requirement as "jurisdictional" is not that the requirement is viewed as outside the scope of the evil Congress intended to forestall, but merely that the existence of the fact that confers federal jurisdiction need not be one in the mind of the actor at the time he perpetrates the act made criminal by the federal statute. The question, then, is not whether the requirement is jurisdictional, but whether it is jurisdictional only.

The general conspiracy statute, 18 U.S.C. § 371, offers no textual support for the proposition that to be guilty of conspiracy a defendant in effect must have known that his conduct violated federal law. The statute makes it unlawful simply to "conspire ... to commit any offense against the United States." A natural reading of these words would be that since one can violate a criminal statute simply by engaging in the forbidden conduct, a conspiracy to commit that offense is nothing more than an agreement to engage in the prohibited conduct. Then where, as here, the substantive statute does not require that an assailant know the official status of his victim, there is nothing on the face of the conspiracy statute that would seem to require that those agreeing to the assault have a greater degree of knowledge. * * *

With no support on the face of the general conspiracy statute * * *, respondent relies solely on the line of cases commencing with United States v. Crimmins, 123 F.2d 271 (CA2 1941), for the principle that the Government must prove "antifederal" intent in order to establish liability under § 371. In *Crimmins,* the defendant had been found guilty of conspiring to receive stolen bonds that had been transported in interstate commerce. Upon review, the Court of Appeals pointed out that the evidence failed to establish that Crimmins actually knew the stolen bonds had moved into the State. Accepting for the sake of argument the assumption that such knowledge was not necessary to sustain a conviction on the substantive offense, Judge Learned Hand nevertheless concluded that to permit conspiratorial liability where the conspirators were ignorant of the federal implications of their acts would be to enlarge their agreement beyond its terms as they understood them. He capsulized the distinction in what has become well known as his "traffic light" analogy:

> "While one may, for instance, be guilty of running past a traffic light of whose existence one is ignorant, one cannot be guilty of conspiring to run past such a light, for one cannot agree to run past a light unless one supposes that there is a light to run past."

Judge Hand's attractive, but perhaps seductive, analogy has received a mixed reception in the Courts of Appeals. The Second Circuit, of course, has followed it; others have rejected it. * * * We conclude that the analogy, though effective prose, is, as applied to the facts before us, bad law.[24]

The question posed by the traffic light analogy is not before us, just as it was not before the Second Circuit in *Crimmins.* Criminal liability, of course, may be imposed on one who runs a traffic light regardless of whether he harbored the "evil intent" of disobeying the light's command; whether he drove so recklessly as to be unable to perceive the light; whether, thinking he was observing all traffic rules, he simply

24. The Government rather effectively exposes the fallacy of the *Crimmins* traffic light analogy by recasting it in terms of a jurisdictional element. The suggested example is a traffic light on an Indian reservation. Surely, one may conspire with others to disobey the light but be ignorant of the fact that it is on the reservation. As applied to a jurisdictional element of this kind the formulation makes little sense.

failed to notice the light; or whether, having been reared elsewhere, he thought that the light was only an ornament. Traffic violations generally fall into that category of offenses that dispense with a *mens rea* requirement. * * * The traffic light analogy poses the question whether it is fair to punish parties to an agreement to engage intentionally in apparently innocent conduct where the unintended result of engaging in that conduct is the violation of a criminal statute.

But this case does not call upon us to answer this question, and we decline to do so * * *. We note in passing, however, that the analogy comes close to stating what has been known as the *"Powell* doctrine," originating in People v. Powell, 63 N.Y. 88 (1875), to the effect that a conspiracy, to be criminal, must be animated by a corrupt motive or a motive to do wrong. Under this principle, such a motive could be easily demonstrated if the underlying offense involved an act clearly wrongful in itself; but it had to be independently demonstrated if the acts agreed to were wrongful solely because of statutory proscription. Interestingly, Judge Hand himself was one of the more severe critics of the *Powell* doctrine.

That Judge Hand should reject the *Powell* doctrine and then create the *Crimmins* doctrine seems curious enough. Fatal to the latter, however, is the fact that it was announced in a case to which it could not have been meant to apply. In *Crimmins,* the substantive offense, namely, the receipt of stolen securities that had been in interstate commerce, proscribed clearly wrongful conduct. Such conduct could not be engaged in without an intent to accomplish the forbidden result. So, too, it is with assault, the conduct forbidden by the substantive statute, § 111, presently before us. One may run a traffic light "of whose existence one is ignorant," but assaulting another "of whose existence one is ignorant," probably would require unearthly intervention. Thus, the traffic light analogy, even if it were a correct statement of the law, is inapt, for the conduct proscribed by the substantive offense, here assault, is not of the type outlawed without regard to the intent of the actor to accomplish the result that is made criminal. If the analogy has any vitality at all, it is to conduct of the latter variety; that, however, is a question we save for another day. We hold here only that where a substantive offense embodies only a requirement of *mens rea* as to each of its elements, the general federal conspiracy statute requires no more.

The *Crimmins* rule rests upon another foundation: that it is improper to find conspiratorial liability where the parties to the illicit agreement were not aware of the fact giving rise to federal jurisdiction, because the essence of conspiracy is agreement and persons cannot be punished for acts beyond the scope of their agreement. This "reason" states little more than a conclusion, for it is clear that one may be guilty as a conspirator for acts the precise details of which one does not know at the time of the agreement. The question is not merely whether the official status of an assaulted victim was known to the parties at the time of their agreement, but whether the acts contemplated by the conspirators are to be deemed legally different from those actually performed solely because of the official identity of the victim. Put another way, does the identity of the proposed victim alter the legal character of the acts agreed to, or is it no more germane to the nature of those acts than the color of the victim's hair?

Our analysis of the substantive offense in Part II, supra, is sufficient to convince us that for the purpose of individual guilt or innocence, awareness of the official identity of the assault victim is irrelevant. We would expect the same to obtain with respect to the conspiracy offense unless one of the policies behind the imposition of conspiratorial liability is not served where the parties to the agreement are unaware that the intended target is a federal law enforcement official.

* * * Our decisions have identified two independent values served by the law of conspiracy. The first is protection of society from the dangers of concerted criminal activity. * * * Given the level of criminal intent necessary to sustain conviction for the substantive offense, the act of agreement to commit the crime is no less opprobrious and no less dangerous because of the absence of knowledge of a fact unnecessary to the formation of criminal intent. Indeed, unless imposition of an "anti-federal" knowledge requirement serves social purposes external to the law of conspiracy of which we are unaware, its imposition here would serve only to make it more difficult to obtain convictions on charges of conspiracy, a policy with no apparent purpose.

The second aspect is that conspiracy is an inchoate crime. * * *

Again, we do not see how imposition of a strict "anti-federal" scienter requirement would relate to this purpose of conspiracy law. Given the level of intent needed to carry out the substantive offense, we fail to see how the agreement is any less blameworthy or constitutes less of a danger to society solely because the participants are unaware which body of law they intend to violate. Therefore, we again conclude that imposition of a requirement of knowledge of those facts that serve only to establish federal jurisdiction would render it more difficult to serve the policy behind the law of conspiracy without serving any other apparent social policy.

We hold, then, that assault of a federal officer pursuant to an agreement to assault is not, even in the words of Judge Hand, "beyond the reasonable intendment of the common understanding," United States v. Crimmins, 123 F.2d at 273. The agreement is not thereby enlarged, for knowledge of the official identity of the victim is irrelevant to the essential nature of the agreement, entrance into which is made criminal by the law of conspiracy. * * *

Notes and Questions

1. If 18 U.S.C. § 111 were interpreted according to Model Penal Code standards, what level of culpability, if any, would be required as to the victim's federal identity? Consider Model Penal Code §§ 1.13(10) and 2.02.

Assuming *arguendo* that knowledge of the identity of the officers is not an element of the federal assault statute, would the Model Penal Code nonetheless require proof of such knowledge to convict the defendants of conspiracy? The Commentary provides an overview to the issues raised in *Feola* :

> The fact that conspiracy is defined in terms of an agreement produces difficulties * * * with respect to the requisite awareness by the conspirator of those circumstance elements regarding which something less than knowledge suffices for the substantive crime. The problem has arisen most often in federal cases in which some circumstance that affords a basis for federal jurisdiction, such as use of the mails or crossing state lines, is made an element of the crime. Prior to * * * *United States v. Feola* * * *, most decisions involving such offenses held that although knowledge of the jurisdictional element is unnecessary for guilt of the substantive crime, it is necessary for guilt of conspiracy to commit that crime. In a prosecution for use of the mails to defraud, for example, it is sufficient if the mails were in fact used for the purpose of furthering the scheme, while for conspiracy to commit that crime it was said that the defendants must have contemplated that the mails would be so used. * * * Federal crimes based on the transportation of stolen goods through interstate commerce were treated similarly; although strict liability as to the interstate element sufficed for the substantive crime, a conspirator had to be aware of the past or contemplate the future passage of the goods through interstate commerce.

> The problem in these cases could have been greatly simplified if the Congress had viewed these circumstances not as an element of the respective crimes, but frankly as a basis for establishing federal jurisdiction. * * *

> Traditionally, however, Congress and the courts combined to treat the jurisdictional circumstance as an element of the crime, with the result that even though the mails were in fact used or a state line was in fact crossed, conspiracy could not be adjudged unless this factor was in contemplation at the time of combination * * *.

> The conspiracy provision in the Code does not attempt to solve the problem by explicit formulation, nor have the recent legislative revisions. * * * [I]t was believed that the matter is best left to judicial resolution as cases that present the question may arise, and that the formulations proposed afford sufficient flexibility for satisfactory decision. Under Subsection (1) of Section 5.03 it is enough that the object of the agreement is "conduct that constitutes the crime," which can be held to import no more than the mental state required for the substantive offense into the agreement to commit it. Although the agreement must be made "with the purpose of promoting or facilitating the commission of the crime," it is arguable, though by no means certain, that such a purpose may be proved although the actor did not know of the existence of a circumstance, which did exist in fact, when knowledge of the circumstance is not required for the substantive offense. Rather than press the matter further in this section, the Institute deliberately left the matter to interpretation in the context in which the issue is presented.

American Law Institute, Model Penal Code and Commentaries, Comment to § 5.03 at 409–11, 413–14 (1985).

2. Suppose that Jack and Jill agree to attack the next person who walks through the door of their office. That person turns out to be a federal officer, whom they assault. Under *Feola,* are they guilty of conspiracy to assault a federal officer? What if nobody enters?

3. *Feola* mentions the *"Powell"* (or "corrupt motive") doctrine. In *Powell,* the defendants, municipal officials, were charged with conspiracy to violate a statute that required them to advertise for bids before purchasing supplies. The defendants asserted that they should be acquitted of conspiracy because they were unaware of the underlying statute and, therefore, were acting in good faith when they agreed to purchase supplies for which bids had not been obtained.

The court agreed. It reasoned that a corrupt motive "is implied in the meaning of the word conspiracy." Therefore, an agreement to do an act "innocent in itself" is not criminal unless the parties entering into the agreement possess a corrupt motive, as distinguished from an intent merely "to do the act prohibited in ignorance of the prohibition." People v. Powell, 63 N.Y. 88, 92 (1875).

Justice Blackmun described as "curious" the fact that Judge Learned Hand rejected the *Powell* doctrine, yet was the author of *Crimmins* (the "traffic light" analogy). Were he alive today, how might Judge Hand distinguish the two cases?

3. ACTUS REUS

ABRAHAM S. GOLDSTEIN—CONSPIRACY TO DEFRAUD THE UNITED STATES

68 Yale Law Journal 405 (1959), 409–12

The agreement represents the actualization of the intent contemplated by the act-intent maxim. It is the "act" which expresses in concrete form the threat to society of an intent shared by two or more persons. Vicarious liability is imputed and hearsay admitted, statute of limitations tolled and venue attained—all by virtue of the terms of that agreement.

Yet "agreement" is almost as much a theoretical construct as the "intent" it is supposed to carry over the threshold from fancy to fact. Indeed, in most cases, it is proved by the very same evidence from which intent will be inferred. Thus, instead of anchoring intangible intent to a tangible act, the law of conspiracy makes intent an appendage of the equally intangible agreement. By pouring the same proof into the mold of "agreement" and by calling that "agreement" an "act"—passive though it may be—courts foster the already elaborate illusion that conspiracy reaches actual, not potential, harm.

The illusory quality of agreement is increased by the fact that it, like intent, must inevitably be based upon assumptions about what people acting in certain ways must have had in mind. It is ordinarily fashioned by a jury out of bits and pieces of circumstantial evidence, usually styled "overt acts," offered to prove that two or more persons are (or were) pursuing a given unlawful purpose. The sensation that the proof consists of little more than "bits and pieces" is, of course, intensified by the fact that acts and statements of each of several defendants are being offered into evidence as imputable to each of the other defendants. And overshadowing the entire proceeding is the uneasy feeling that the evidence may be taking the form cast for it in the indictment quite as much because the parties are seated together in the courtroom as defendants in a common trial as because they did, in fact, agree. This is not to say that words of caution are not uttered by judge to jury. Indeed, conspiracy cases are among the rare instances in which trial judges ask juries to be mindful of the vagaries of the process in which they are participating.

More important, however, jurors are also told that the existence of a conspiracy may be inferred from the unfolding of events over an extended period of time and that, though evidence like unexplained meetings of defendants is insufficient in and of itself, such evidence must be used if the crime is ever to be discovered. Judicial folklore is also shared. Conspirators, juries are advised, do not shout their plans from the rooftops. Nor do they cast them in written form or announce them in the presence of witnesses. The net effect of such commentary is to free juries from the automatic compliance with "law" which instructions ordinarily demand and to invite a "guilty" verdict on less evidence than might otherwise be required.

Notes and Questions

1. *Developments in the Law—Criminal Conspiracy*, 72 Harv.L.Rev. 920, 933 (1959):

> The basic principle that a conspiracy is not established without proof of an agreement has been weakened, or at least obscured, by * * * the courts' unfortunate tendency to overemphasize a rule of evidence at the expense of a rule of law. Conspiracy is by nature a clandestine offense. It is improbable that the parties will enter into their illegal agreement openly; it is not necessary, in fact, that all the parties ever have direct contact with one another, or know one another's identity, or even communicate verbally their intention to agree. It is therefore unlikely that the prosecution will be able to prove the formation of the agreement by direct evidence, and the jury must usually infer its existence from the clear co-operation among the parties. But in their zeal to emphasize that the agreement need not be proved directly, the courts sometimes neglect to say that it need be proved at all.

COMMONWEALTH v. AZIM

Superior Court of Pennsylvania, 1983.
313 Pa.Super. 310, 459 A.2d 1244.

PER CURIAM:

Appellant Charles Azim * * * seeks dismissal of all the charges brought against him. * * *

Appellant was arrested, along with Mylice James and Thomas Robinson * * * for simple assault, robbery, and conspiracy. The victim of the robbery was Jerry Tennenbaum, a Temple University student. Appellant drove a car in which the other two men were passengers. Appellant stopped the car, Robinson called Tennenbaum over to the curb, the two passengers got out of the car, inflicted bodily injury on Tennenbaum, took his wallet which had fallen to the ground, and immediately left the scene in the same car driven by appellant. Robinson and appellant were tried to a jury and convicted as co-defendants * * *. * * *

In this appeal, appellant * * * argues that because his conspiracy conviction was not supported by sufficient evidence against him, the charges of assault and robbery must also fail.

* * * In *Commonwealth v. Volk,* 298 Pa.Super. 294, 444 A.2d 1182 (1982) * * * our Court maintained that * * *:

* * * "The essence of criminal conspiracy is a common understanding, no matter how it came into being, that a particular criminal objective be accomplished." *Commonwealth v. Carter,* 272 Pa.Superior Ct. 411, 416 A.2d 523 (1979). By its very nature, the crime of conspiracy is frequently not susceptible of proof except by circumstantial evidence. And although a conspiracy cannot be based upon mere suspicion or conjecture, a conspiracy "may be inferentially established by showing the relationship, conduct or circumstances of the parties, and the overt acts on the part of the co-conspirators have uniformly been held competent to prove that a corrupt confederation has in fact been formed." Commonwealth v. Carter, supra.

At trial, the prosecution presented evidence that established that appellant was the driver of the car in which James and Robinson (the men who demanded money from Tennenbaum and beat and choked him) rode. Robinson was seated on the front seat, next to appellant. Robinson rolled down the car window, twice beckoned to the victim to come close to the car, and when Tennenbaum refused, the two passengers got out, assaulted Tennenbaum, and took his wallet. Appellant sat at the wheel, with the engine running and lights on, and the car doors open, while the acts were committed in the vicinity of the car. He then drove James and Robinson from the scene.

Among those circumstances relevant to proving conspiracy are association with alleged conspirators, knowledge of the commission of the crime, presence at the scene of the crime, and, at times, participation in the object of the conspiracy. Conspiracy to commit burglary has been found where the defendant drove codefendants to the scene of a crime and then later picked them up. * * * We find no merit in appellant's claim that he was merely a hired driver, with no knowledge of his passengers' criminal activity.

We hold that a rational factfinder could find, beyond a reasonable doubt, that appellant conspired with James and Robinson to commit assault and robbery. * * *

Once conspiracy is established and upheld, a member of the conspiracy is also guilty of the criminal acts of his co-conspirators * * *. * * *

Notes and Questions

1. *Problem.* Assume that the following facts are proven at trial: X talked for a minute to D, a "known criminal," outside a liquor store. X entered the store, bought nothing, and, a few moments later, came out. X stood by himself, approximately 50 feet away from D. Five minutes later, X re-entered the store. About thirty seconds later, D entered. While X robbed the store, D nervously stood near the front door. After X took money from the clerk, he and D fled by foot, running in opposite directions. Conspiracy?

COMMONWEALTH v. COOK

Appeals Court of Massachusetts, 1980.
10 Mass.App.Ct. 668, 411 N.E.2d 1326.

GREANEY, JUSTICE.

The defendant [Dennis Cook] was tried before a jury * * * on an indictment charging conspiracy to commit rape. His motion for a required finding of not guilty was filed and denied at the conclusion of the Commonwealth's case, and he was subsequently convicted and sentenced on the indictment. On appeal he claims error in the denial of the motion. We hold that the evidence introduced up to the time the Commonwealth rested was insufficient to warrant his conviction of conspiracy and that, as a result, the judgment must be reversed. A summary of the Commonwealth's evidence follows.

At approximately 8:00 P.M. on the evening of July 16, 1977, the victim, age seventeen, went to Chicopee to visit some friends and to see her boyfriend. Upon discovering that her friends were not at home, she proceeded to the housing project where her boyfriend resided. As she passed the area of the project office, the defendant and his brother Maurice Cook attempted to engage her in conversation. Not knowing the Cooks, she spurned an invitation to join them and instead walked to her boyfriend's residence. After ascertaining that he was not at home, she reversed her route, intending to stay at her friends' home to await their return. As she passed the office area for the second time, she accepted the Cooks' renewed invitation to socialize, and she sat with the two brothers on a platform talking for approximately forty-five minutes. The area apparently was used as a common meeting point for informal socializing, and while the victim was there several other people were in the vicinity, one of whom recognized the victim and called her by name. There was evidence that the Cooks smoked marihuana and drank beer but that the victim declined to smoke marihuana because her boyfriend disliked her "flying high." She did take a drink of beer. The defendant told her that he and his brother were caring for a nearby home whose occupants were away on vacation. Because the victim was having difficulty remembering their names, the defendant told her that he worked at Smith and Wesson. He also showed her his plant identification card with his picture on it, and his brother informed her of his employer and his address and displayed his driver's license.

About 9:00 P.M. Maurice Cook indicated that he was out of cigarettes and suggested that the three walk to a convenience store located about a minute and a half away. The victim agreed. To reach the store, the trio proceeded along the street to a narrow path or trail located behind the project office. This path led down a hill through a wooded area to the rear of a well-lit service station adjacent to the convenience store. As they "walk[ed] towards the path" single file (with Maurice in front, the victim in the middle and the defendant in the rear), the victim "slipped . . . fell or something." She sat on the ground for a few seconds laughing when "Maurice turned around and jumped on me . . . and told me I was going to love it." After she screamed, Maurice covered her mouth with his hand, took off his belt and gave it to the defendant seated nearby. Maurice then scratched her with a stick or blunt object and said, "No blood, no blood." The defendant was overheard laughing and saying, "The bitch doesn't want to bleed, we'll make her bleed." Maurice then forcibly raped her. During the assault the victim lost consciousness. She awoke about 11:00 P.M. and went directly to her friends' home. The incident was subsequently reported to the police, and the Cooks were arrested. Maurice was indicted for rape and the defendant, in addition to the conspiracy indictment, was charged as an accessory to the rape.

1. A combination of two or more persons who seek by some concerted action to accomplish a criminal act may be punished as a conspiracy. It is essential to a conviction that the Commonwealth prove the existence of an agreement, because "[t]he gravamen of . . . conspiracy . . . is the unlawful agreement." * * * "It must [also] be shown that the defendant was aware of the objective of the conspiracy which was alleged." Proof of a conspiracy may rest entirely or mainly on circumstantial evidence, but "some record evidence" is not enough, and an acquittal must be ordered if any essential element of the crime is left to surmise, conjecture or guesswork.

We are of the opinion that the evidence, tested against the foregoing principles, was insufficient to establish a conspiracy. The circumstances under which the victim and the Cooks met and socialized were not indicative of a preconceived plan between the defendant and his brother to commit a sexual assault. Rather, the meeting and subsequent engagement were consistent with a chance social encounter common between young persons. The area where the group stayed prior to setting out for the store was used frequently as a gathering spot, and there was no evidence either that the Cooks attempted to conceal from others the fact that they were with the victim or that they consciously attempted to mislead her as to their identities. The evidence cuts directly against any such inference because of the special efforts made by the defendant and his brother to identify themselves by disclosing their names and places of employment, and by showing the victim their photographs. We do not think it plausible to infer that this conduct was an attempt by the Cooks to lull the victim into a false sense of security. Moreover, since all the conversation at the platform occurred in the victim's presence, the jury could not have properly inferred that a clandestine plan to commit an assault had been formulated during that period. While openness will not automatically sanitize a conspiracy, highly visible conduct has to be considered inconsistent with the shadowy environment which usually shrouds the crime. The purpose for leaving the area was on its face innocuous and was suggested by Maurice, not the defendant. While the route chosen was arguably suspicious, the evidence established that it also was selected by Maurice, not the defendant. There was evidence that the path provided a short, reasonably direct route to a gasoline station which was nearby, well-lighted, and visible from the crest of the hill. We do not think that the events up to the time the victim fell were sufficient to establish a criminal agreement or to warrant the jury in inferring the state of facts that the Commonwealth claims to have existed.

Nor was the prosecution's case strengthened by the circumstances surrounding the assault itself. There was no evidence that the defendant (or his brother for that matter) had anything to do with the victim's falling to the ground. The fact that Maurice's attack began immediately after the victim found herself in a compromising situation suggests spontaneity of action on his part rather than the purposeful execution of a predetermined plan. From that point on, the defendant's conduct fits the classic paradigm of an accomplice adding encouragement to a crime in progress. The fact that the defendant may have aided and abetted the crime does not * * * establish a conspiracy, particularly where the evidence shows that prior planning is not an inherent facet of the crime. "[N]either association with [a criminal] nor knowledge of illegal activity constitute proof of participation in a conspiracy."

In reaching our conclusion, we are mindful of the principle that proof of a tacit agreement to commit a crime may be enough to establish a conspiracy. But in this case it is just as reasonable to conclude that the defendant became implicated in the crime as an accomplice after it had commenced without any advance knowledge that it was to occur, as it is to infer that the minds of the parties had met in advance "understandingly, so as to bring about an intelligent and deliberate agreement to ... commit the offense charged." "[W]hen the evidence tends to sustain either of two inconsistent propositions, neither ... can be said to have been established by legitimate proof."

2. The remaining question raised by the Commonwealth's argument is whether the defendant can be convicted of conspiracy *solely* on the evidence tending to show his complicity as an accomplice in the commission of the substantive crime. We think on the evidence in this case such a conclusion would be unjustified.

Accomplice and conspiratorial liability are not synonymous, and one can be an accomplice aiding in the commission of a substantive offense without necessarily conspiring to commit it. The holdings which conceptually and practically separate the two types of criminal activity do so because of fundamental distinctions between them. As has already been discussed, the gist of conspiracy rests in the "agree[ment] [between the conspirators] to work in concert for the criminal or corrupt or unlawful purpose," and it is that agreement which constitutes the criminal act and which generally serves to manifest the requisite criminal intent. * * * Absent from the formulation of accomplice liability is the necessity of establishing an agreement or consensus in the same sense as those terms are used in describing the agreement or combination which hallmarks a conspiracy.[3] When a defendant is convicted of conspiring with others to commit a crime, the conviction stems from, and is designed to punish, the unlawful agreement which preexists commission of the substantive offense. This is why proof of the conspiracy typically involves circumstantial evidence aimed at establishing a consensus prior to the commission of the target offense. Execution of the crime thus represents performance of the agreement. But because the conspiracy for practical purposes is at least one step removed from the substantive offense, the offense does not substitute for the agreement and the factfinder's analysis of the conspiracy evidence is logically directed at ascertaining whether an underlying agreement exists. As the Second Circuit stated, in a different factual context: "To warrant a conviction for conspiracy ... the evidence must disclose something further than participating in the offense which is the object of the conspiracy; there must be proof of the unlawful agreement, either express or implied, and participation with knowledge of the agreement." *Dickerson v. United States,* 18 F.2d 887, 893 (8th Cir.1927). * * * Implicit support for our conclusion is also contained in the following statement from *Commonwealth v. Stasiun,* 349 Mass. 38, 48, 206 N.E.2d 672 (1965): "[P]unishment [for conspiracy] is imposed for entering into the combination. This is not the same thing as participating in the substantive offense which was the object of the conspiracy." A contrary holding on the facts we are considering would confuse certain settled aspects of the law of conspiracy and would tend unnecessarily to expand its already elastic and pervasive definition by "blur[ring] the demarcation line between a conspiracy to commit an offense and the substantive offense which is the object of the conspiracy." * * * "[A]cts of aiding and abetting clearly make each actor a principal in the substantive offense ... but cannot, without [more],[8] also make each other actor a principal in the crime of

3. The Commonwealth's argument meshing the two concepts perhaps derives from misplaced reliance on Mr. Justice Holmes' famous epigram that a conspiracy is "a partnership in criminal purposes." *United States v. Kissel,* 218 U.S. 601, 608, 31 S.Ct. 124, 126, 54 L.Ed. 1168 (1910). Styling every joint venture crime as a type of partnership would automatically make each actor at the scene a member of a conspiracy. But a partnership contemplates the partners' arriving at an agreement before the partnership engages in its business. To avoid reasoning along such lines, the Model Penal Code rejected inclusion of "the analogy of partnership ... in the formal definition [of conspiracy]" and instead rested "the core of the conspiracy idea ... on the primordial conception of agreement." Model Penal Code, comments to § 5.03, at 116–117 (Proposed Official Draft 1962). * * *

8. Of course, a factfinder can consider and permissibly infer the existence of a conspiracy from the circumstances sur-

conspiracy to commit such offense. . . ." We conclude that in this case the evidence of the confederation at the scene was insufficient to warrant the defendant's conviction of conspiracy. * * *

Notes and Questions

1. Is *Cook* consistent with *Azim* ?

2. *Developments in the Law—Criminal Conspiracy,* 72 Harv.L.Rev. 920, 934–35 (1959):

> [A] verbal ambiguity * * * leads courts to deal with the crime of conspiracy as though it were a group rather than an act. If a "conspiracy" consists of the people who are working toward a proscribed object, and if one who aids and abets a substantive offense becomes liable as a principal thereto, then it follows that one who aids and abets these men in the attainment of their object becomes liable as a conspirator. * * * [T]his reasoning from a faulty premise * * * [is] difficult to discover since it is assumed rather than articulated * * *. But to aid and abet a crime it is necessary not merely to help the criminal, but to help him in the commission of the particular criminal offense. A person does not aid and abet a conspiracy by helping the "conspiracy" to commit a substantive offense, for the crime of conspiracy is separate from the offense which is its object. It is necessary to help the "conspiracy" in the commission of the crime of conspiracy, that is, in the commission of the act of agreement. Only then is it justifiable to dispense with the necessity of proving commission of the act of agreement by the defendant himself.

3. *Problem.* X and Y discuss with Z, an undercover police officer, their plan to import marijuana into the country. Later, D drives X and Y to the airport in a pickup truck loaded with household appliances, where they meet Z. Z asks Y who D is, and is told that "he will be at the off-loading site in the U.S." Z asks D if this is true. D smiles, nods his head in agreement, and unloads the appliances. Is D guilty of conspiracy with X and Y to import marijuana? United States v. Alvarez, 610 F.2d 1250, reversed 625 F.2d 1196 (5th Cir.1980) (en banc).

4. *Problem.* Federal agents observe a small plane enter United States airspace from Columbia and, after being intercepted in the air by the agents, drop bales of marijuana into the Gulf of Mexico. On the ground, customs officers discover that the interior of the plane was smeared with chunks of fresh pineapple to mask the odor of the prior cargo. The five occupants—the pilot and four illegal aliens from Columbia—are prosecuted for conspiracy to import marijuana. Should they be convicted? United States v. Reyes, 595 F.2d 275 (5th Cir.1979).

rounding the commission of the crime. For example, the sophistication surrounding the execution of the Brinks' robbery (*Commonwealth v. Geagan,* 339 Mass. 487, 159 N.E.2d 870 [1959]), would warrant a conclusion that its perpetrators had conspired and prepared in advance to commit it. But there the facts establishing the "more" necessary to convict the accomplices of conspiracy consisted of the numerous incidental circumstances manifested at the scene of the crime and elsewhere which demonstrated planning and pursuit of a prearranged systematic course of action. * * *

4. CONSPIRACY: BILATERAL OR UNILATERAL?

PEOPLE v. FOSTER

Supreme Court of Illinois, 1983.
99 Ill.2d 48, 75 Ill.Dec. 411, 457 N.E.2d 405.

UNDERWOOD, JUSTICE:

Following a jury trial * * * the defendant, James Foster, was convicted of conspiracy to commit robbery, and sentenced to an extended term of six years' imprisonment. * * *

On September 28, 1981, defendant initiated his plan to commit a robbery when he approached John Ragsdale in a Rantoul bar and asked Ragsdale if he was "interested in making some money." Defendant told Ragsdale of an elderly man, A.O. Hedrick, who kept many valuables in his possession. Although Ragsdale stated that he was interested in making money he did not believe defendant was serious until defendant returned to the bar the next day and discussed in detail his plan to rob Hedrick. In an effort to gather additional information, Ragsdale decided to feign agreement to defendant's plan but did not contact the police.

On October 1, defendant went to Ragsdale's residence to find out if Ragsdale was "ready to go." Since Ragsdale had not yet contacted the police he told defendant that he would not be ready until he found someone else to help them. Ragsdale informed the police of the planned robbery on October 3. Defendant and Ragsdale were met at Hedrick's residence the following day and arrested.

The appellate court determined that the conspiracy statute (Ill.Rev. Stat.1981, ch. 38, par. 8–2) required actual agreement between at least two persons to support a conspiracy conviction. Reasoning that Ragsdale never intended to agree to defendant's plan but merely feigned agreement, the court reversed defendant's conviction.

On appeal to this court the State argues that under the conspiracy statute it suffices if only one of the participants to the alleged conspiracy actually intends to agree to commit an offense. * * *

The question is whether the Illinois legislature, in amending the conspiracy statute in 1961, intended to adopt the unilateral theory of conspiracy. To support a conspiracy conviction under the unilateral theory only one of the alleged conspirators need intend to agree to the commission of an offense. Prior to the 1961 amendment the statute clearly encompassed the traditional, bilateral theory, requiring the actual agreement of at least two participants. The relevant portion of the former statute is as follows:

"If any *two or more persons* conspire or *agree together* * * * to do any illegal act * * * they shall be deemed guilty of a conspiracy." (Emphasis added.)

The amended version of the statute provides:

"*A person* commits conspiracy when, with intent that an offense be committed, *he agrees* with another to the commission of that offense." (Emphasis added.)

Since the statute is presently worded in terms of "a person" rather than "two or more persons" it is urged by the State that only one person need intend to agree to the commission of an offense. In support of its position the State compares the Illinois statute with the Model Penal Code conspiracy provision and the commentary thereto. The Model Penal Code provision is similar to section 8–2(a) in that it is also worded in terms of "a person":

"*A person* is guilty of conspiracy with another person or persons to commit a crime if with the purpose of promoting or facilitating its commission *he* :

(a) *agrees* with such other person or persons that they or one or more of them will engage in conduct which constitutes such crime or an attempt or solicitation to commit such crime * * *." (Emphasis added.) Model Penal Code sec. 5.03.

The commentary following section 5.03 expressly indicates the drafters' intent to adopt the unilateral theory of conspiracy. * * *

There is no question that the drafters of section 8–2(a) were aware of this provision since several references were made to the Model Penal Code in the committee comments to section 8–2. Consequently, the State reasons that the drafters would not have deleted the words "two or more persons" if they had intended to retain the bilateral theory. Similar reasoning was employed in *State v. Marian* (1980), 62 Ohio St.2d 250, 405 N.E.2d 267, and *State v. St. Christopher* (1975), 305 Minn. 226, 232 N.W.2d 798, where the courts were asked to interpret statutory provisions analogous to section 8–2(a). In each of those decisions it was determined that deletion of the words "two or more persons" from the State's conspiracy statute reflected a legislative intent to abandon the bilateral theory. The Ohio court, however, also relied to a considerable degree upon the absence from Ohio criminal law of a statute making solicitation to commit a crime an offense. Illinois does have such a statute.

While impressed with the logic of the State's interpretation of section 8–2(a), we are troubled by the committee's failure to explain the reason for deleting the words "two or more persons" from the statute. The committee comments to section 8–2 detail the several changes in the law of conspiracy that were intended by the 1961 amendment. The comments simply do not address the unilateral/bilateral issue. The State suggests that the new language was so clear on its face that it did not warrant additional discussion. We doubt, however, that the drafters could have intended what represents a rather profound change in the law of conspiracy without mentioning it in the comments to section 8–2. * * *

As earlier noted, Illinois does have a solicitation statute which embraces virtually every situation in which one could be convicted of conspiracy under the unilateral theory. Moreover, the penalties for solicitation and conspiracy are substantially similar. There would appear to have been little need for the legislature to adopt the unilateral theory of conspiracy in light of the existence of the solicitation statute. Even though the Model Penal Code also contains a separate solicitation offense and still provides for the unilateral theory, its commentary makes explicit its intent to do so. The absence of similar comments upon our statute seems difficult to explain if the intent was the same.

We cannot agree with the State's argument that section 8–2(b) of the statute supports a unilateral interpretation of section 8–2(a). Section 8–2(b) provides:

"It shall not be a defense to conspiracy that the person or persons with whom the accused is alleged to have conspired:

* * *

(4) Has been acquitted, or

(5) Lacked the capacity to commit an offense."

The State argues that subsections (4) and (5) focus on the culpability of only one of the conspirators and are therefore consistent with a legislative intent to adopt the unilateral theory. However, the committee comments clearly indicate that the limited purpose of those subsections is to avoid the recurrent problems inherent in conducting separate trials:

"Previously, acquittal of all other conspirators absolved the remaining one, since, theoretically, there must be at least two guilty parties to a conspiracy. [Citation.] However, this rationale was rejected as being too technical and overlooking the realities of trials which involve differences in juries, contingent availability of witnesses, the varying ability of different prosecutors and defense attorneys, etc."

Additionally, if the drafters had intended to adopt the unilateral theory in section 8–2(a), it would have been unnecessary to include section 8–2(b) in the statute, since the provisions of section 8–2(b) are encompassed by the unilateral theory.

* * * We are also mindful of the rule of construction * * * which requires us to resolve statutory ambiguities in favor of criminal defendants.

For the above reasons we conclude that section 8–2(a) encompasses the bilateral theory of conspiracy. * * *

Notes and Questions

1. Some courts disapprove of the unilateral theory:

The rationale behind making conspiracy a crime also supports [the bilateral] rule. Criminal conspiracy is an offense separate from the actual criminal act because of the perception "that collective action toward an antisocial end involves a greater risk to society than individual action toward the same end." In part, this view is based on the perception that group activity increases the likelihood of success of the criminal act and of future criminal activity by members of the group, and is difficult for law enforcement officers to detect. * * * Such dangers, however, are nonexistent when a person "conspires" only with a government agent.

United States v. Escobar de Bright, 742 F.2d 1196, 1199 (9th Cir.1984).

How would advocates of the unilateral conspiracy rule respond? See American Law Institute, Model Penal Code and Commentaries, Comment to § 5.03 at 400 (1985).

2. *Foster* alludes to the "recurrent problems" that arise in bilateral conspiracy jurisdictions when separate trials of alleged conspirators are held. For example, in Commonwealth v. Byrd, 490 Pa. 544, 550–53, 417 A.2d 173, 176–77 (1980), Byrd and Smith, charged with conspiracy, were tried separately. Byrd was convicted. Smith was later acquitted. Byrd then sought to overturn his conviction as a result of Smith's acquittal. The Pennsylvania Supreme Court rejected the claim:

> There is no doubt that the crime of conspiracy requires proof of more than a single participant. As Justice Cardozo once noted: "It is impossible in the nature of things for a man to conspire with himself." *Morrison v. California,* 291 U.S. 82, 92, 54 S.Ct. 281, 285, 78 L.Ed. 664 (1934). Nevertheless, such generalizations do not require that a valid conviction for conspiracy against one defendant must be held in limbo pending the outcome of the separate trial or trials of all alleged co-conspirators. Nor do they require that a valid conspiracy conviction must subsequently be nullified by the acquittal of the other or others charged.

> At the outset it is important to emphasize certain already well-established principles in this area. There is no doubt, for example, that one convicted of conspiracy is not entitled to relief simply because others charged have not yet been tried. That the prosecution has *nolle prossed* charges against one or all of the others indicted is equally insufficient to afford a single convicted conspirator any relief. So too, that the only other co-conspirators have been granted immunity and so cannot be tried does not bar conviction of the remaining defendant. And, indeed, it is established that where the other alleged co-conspirators are unapprehended, unindicted, dead, or even, in some instances, unknown, there is no basis to disturb a valid conviction for conspiracy. The only question still apparently open to any debate is whether an acquittal of all alleged co-conspirators should produce a different result. At least in the case, such as this, of a subsequent acquittal, we do not believe that it should.

> Admittedly, some authority * * * does assert that the acquittal of all but one conspirator requires the discharge of the remaining defendant. This rule, however, had its origins at a time when co-conspirators were jointly tried. In that circumstance a single jury would hear the evidence of conspiracy and, rightly, would not be permitted to find the evidence sufficient to prove a conspiracy involving only one of those charged. The acquittal rule that developed was thus clearly a rule of

verdict consistency. * * * In the case of separate trials, however, this consistency rule loses much if not all of its force.

An acquittal at any trial is never a guarantee that no crime has been committed. Rather it signifies only that the Commonwealth has not proved its case to the satisfaction of the jury. Thus in the present case, different verdicts may well have been due solely to the different composition of the two juries. Alternatively, the difference may have been due to a variety of other circumstances, including a difference in the proof offered at trial. * * * It is error to assume that the failure of a jury to convict one conspirator necessarily invalidates the Commonwealth's verdict, won from a different jury, at a separate trial.

In bilateral jurisdictions, the general rule is that a conviction of a single conspirator may not stand if the remaining defendants are acquitted *at the same trial*. Should this be the outcome in a state that defines conspiracy in unilateral terms? What is the position of the Model Penal Code? See American Law Institute, Model Penal Code and Commentaries, Comment to § 5.03 at 402 (1985).

5. SCOPE OF AN AGREEMENT: PARTY AND OBJECT DIMENSIONS

AMERICAN LAW INSTITUTE, MODEL PENAL CODE AND COMMENTARIES, COMMENT TO § 5.03

(1985), 422–24

* * * Much of the most perplexing litigation in conspiracy has been concerned less with the essential elements of the offense than with the scope to be accorded to a combination, i.e., the singleness or multiplicity of the conspiratorial relationships in a large, complex, and sprawling network of crime. The question here differs from that discussed above in that in most of these cases it is clear that each defendant has committed or conspired to commit one or more crimes; the question now is, to what extent is he a conspirator with each of the persons involved in the larger criminal network to commit the crimes that are their objects.

A narcotics operation may involve smugglers, distributors, and many retail sellers and may result in numerous instances of the commission of different types of crimes, as, for example, importing, possessing, and selling the narcotics. A vice ring may involve an overlord, lesser officers, and numerous runners and prostitutes; it may comprehend countless instances of the commission of such crimes as prostitution, placing a female in a house of prostitution, and receiving money from her earnings. Has a retailer conspired with the smugglers to import the narcotics? Has a prostitute conspired with the leaders of the vice ring to commit the acts of prostitution of each other prostitute who is controlled by the ring?

The inquiry may be crucial for a number of purposes. These include not only defining each defendant's liability, but also the propriety of joint prosecution, admissibility against a defendant of the hearsay acts and declarations of others, questions of multiple prosecution or conviction and double jeopardy, satisfaction of the overt act requirement or statutes of limitation, or rules of jurisdiction and venue, and possibly liability for substantive crimes executed pursuant to the conspiracy. The scope problem is thus central to the concern of courts and commentators about the use of conspiracy, a concern based on the conflict between the need for effective means of prosecuting large criminal organizations, and the dangers of prejudice to individual defendants.

KILGORE v. STATE

Supreme Court of Georgia, 1983.
251 Ga. 291, 305 S.E.2d 82.

BELL, JUSTICE.

Kilgore was convicted * * * for the murder of Roger Norman and was given a life sentence. He appeals.

In the early morning hours of July 8, 1981, the victim, Roger Norman, was traveling south on Interstate 59 (I–59) * * * to his home in Alabama. While driving, he was shot in the head and killed. * * *

At trial, the state introduced evidence of a conspiracy to kill Roger Norman. In particular, it introduced evidence of three previous attempts on Norman's life. As to the first attempt, David Oldaker testified that on February 6, 1981 Greg Benton, his cousin, asked him to go with him to Menton, Alabama, Norman's home. He testified that the purpose of the trip was to kill Norman and that Benton told him a crippled man named Tom who sold pharmaceuticals and lived in Soddy–Daisy, Tennessee, was the man who wanted Norman killed. This testimony was admitted over the hearsay objection of defense counsel. Tom Carden, who died on July 16, 1981, was Norman's brother in law and lived in Soddy–Daisy. He was a paraplegic. Oldaker and Benton went to Norman's home, where they unsuccessfully attempted to kill him. Kilgore was in no way implicated in this attempt.

Evidence did specifically connect Kilgore with the second attempt. Ed Williams, an employee of a truck stop located just off the interstate near Trenton, Georgia, testified that on the evening of June 8, 1981 he saw two cars traveling close to each other while crossing a bridge over I–59; that he heard sounds like a car backfiring; and that Norman's car pulled into the truck stop while the other car turned north on I–59. Norman, who had been on his way home from work, had been shot in the upper back. Sheriff Steele of Dade County testified that based on what Norman told him, he posted a lookout for a 1962 or 1963 Rambler with a dark bottom, white top, and Tennessee tags.

Constance Chambers, Kilgore's ex-girlfriend who lived with him from April through September of 1981, testified that on June 8, 1981, Kilgore and his cousin, Lee Berry, borrowed her 1964 Rambler. It had a dark green body, white top, and Tennessee tags. She testified that Kilgore returned to her apartment around 4:00 a.m. the next morning and told her they had killed a man near Trenton, Georgia. Later that day, Chambers testified that Kilgore received a phone call from Tom Carden, during which she heard Kilgore say "apparently we didn't get him" * * *. * * *

Concerning the circumstances leading up to Norman's death on July 8, 1981, Chambers' testimony shows the continuation of a conspiracy to kill Norman. She testified that on June 15, 1981 Kilgore received a phone call from Carden, during which she heard Kilgore tell Carden he needed more money to obtain a faster car and another man to help him. Shortly thereafter, Kilgore went to Carden's and picked up fifteen hundred dollars. Chambers also testified that on July 5, 1981 Kilgore received another call from Carden, after which she and Kilgore drove to Carden's trailer where Kilgore took fifteen thousand dollars from the mailbox. According to her testimony, they left Carden's and drove to a V.F.W. post where they met a friend of Kilgore's, Bob Price. She testified that Kilgore took a rifle out of his car, put it in Price's van, and left with him, while she drove home alone. * * *

Chambers testified that on July 7, 1981, the day preceding the murder, Kilgore and Price left her apartment about 6:00 p.m., each in a separate vehicle but driving in the same direction. She did not see Kilgore until noon the next day, July 8, when, she testified, he returned driving a blue Lincoln. * * *

Kilgore and Chambers spent several days in Florida, and Chambers testified that on the way home Kilgore told her that "all mighty hell is going to break loose.... we killed a man"; that they [he and Price] had killed him on I–59 * * *. * * *

Kilgore appeals and enumerates fifty-one errors. * * *

Kilgore apparently contends that the state did not prove he actually committed the murder, and that consequently, it must have been proceeding on the theory that his guilt was based upon a conspiracy; yet, he argues, the state did not prove a conspiracy because it did not prove an overt act occurred in Georgia. * * * However, * * * the conspiracy was merely an evidentiary tool used by the state to help prove Kilgore guilty of the murder of Norman. In fact, Kilgore could not have been tried for conspiracy since the object of the conspiracy was completed.[j] * * *

He next argues that the trial court erred in admitting over objection the hearsay testimony of David Oldaker that Benton told him that the man who wanted Norman killed was a crippled man named Tom who sold pharmaceuticals and lived in a trailer in Soddy–Daisy, Tennessee. This testimony was the only evidence connecting Tom Carden to the February 1981 attempt. For the reasons which follow, we find that this hearsay testimony was inadmissible.

The testimony could only be admissible under the exception to the hearsay rule which provides that the out-of-court statements of one conspirator are admissible against all conspirators. Therefore, this

j. Under Georgia law, the crime of conspiracy merged into the completed offense.

testimony was only admissible if Oldaker, Benton, and Kilgore were co-conspirators.

To have a conspiracy, there must be an agreement between two or more persons to commit a crime. Here, there is no question that the evidence shows that Oldaker and Benton and Carden were co-conspirators in their attempt to kill Norman, and that Kilgore and Price and Carden were co-conspirators in the murder of Norman, but the question is whether Kilgore, who did not know of or communicate with Oldaker and Benton, and Oldaker and Benton, who likewise did not know of or communicate with Kilgore, can be considered to have agreed to and become co-conspirators in the murder of Norman. We find that they cannot.

The type of agreement necessary to form a conspiracy is not the "meeting of the minds" necessary to form a contract and may be a "mere tacit understanding between two or more people that they will pursue a particular criminal objective." Kurtz, Criminal Offenses in Georgia, Conspiracy, pp. 53, 55 (1980). LaFave & Scott, Handbook on Criminal Law, § 61, p. 461 (1972). See *Cunningham v. State,* supra, 248 Ga. p. 835, 286 S.E.2d 427. Also, "there need not be any written statement or even a speaking of words which expressly communicates agreement. It is possible for various persons to be parties to a single agreement (and thus one conspiracy) even though they do not know the identity of one another, and even though they are not all aware of the details of the plan of operation." LaFave & Scott, supra, p. 461.

However, limitations have been imposed upon the concept that persons who do not know each other can "agree" to commit a crime. An agreement, and thus one conspiracy, is more likely to be inferred in what have been termed "chain" conspiracies, "usually involving the distribution of narcotics or other contraband, in which there is successive communication or cooperation . . . ." LaFave & Scott, supra, p. 480. Because the parties should know by the large, ongoing nature of the conspiracy that the other members exist, and because the various "links" have a community of interest in that the success of one member's part is dependent upon the success of the whole enterprise, courts have treated links as co-conspirators despite a lack of communication or contact with one another. *United States v. Bruno,* 105 F.2d 921, 922 (2d Cir.1939), rev'd on other grounds, 308 U.S. 287, 60 S.Ct. 198, 84 L.Ed. 257 (1939). In *Bruno,* because of these considerations the court found but one conspiracy among many smugglers, middlemen, and retailers in a drug smuggling operation.

The "chain" conspiracy contrasts with the "wheel" conspiracy in which there is usually a "hub," or common source of the conspiracy, who deals individually with different persons, "spokes," who do not know each other. It is more difficult to infer an agreement among these spokes than among the links of a "chain" conspiracy because they are less likely to have a community of interest or reason to know of each other's existence since one spoke's success is usually not dependent on the other spokes' success, but instead on his dealings with the hub. This is the type of conspiracy, if any, with which we deal in this case. *Kotteakos v. United States,* [328 U.S. 750, 66 S.Ct. 1239, 90 L.Ed. 1557 (1946),] is the classic case of a "wheel" conspiracy. There, Brown, the hub, agreed with various persons, the spokes, on an individual basis to fraudulently procure loans for them for a 5% commission. Because most of the spokes had no connection with and had not aided each other, the court found that there was no common purpose or interest among the spokes and, thus, that they were not co-conspirators. * * *

In the instant case, we conclude that Kilgore was not a co-conspirator of Benton and Oldaker. Here, there was no community of interests between Benton and Oldaker on the one hand and Kilgore on the other. The success of Benton's and Oldaker's attempt to kill Norman was not dependent in any way on Kilgore. Likewise, the success of Kilgore's attempt to kill Norman was not aided by Oldaker and Benton, especially considering that they did not assist in further efforts to kill Norman.

In addition, Benton and Oldaker, as one spoke, and Kilgore, as another or replacement spoke, had no knowledge of and no reason to know of each other such that an agreement can be inferred between them. There was no reason for Kilgore to know of the previous attempt on Norman's life, as his success was not dependent on it. Likewise, Oldaker and Benton had no reason to know of another spoke. It could be argued that Oldaker and Benton should have known that if they failed Carden would find another spoke, and that, therefore, they can be deemed to have "agreed" with this spoke. However, we find this reasoning to be too speculative a ground on which to infer such an agreement.

For the above reasons, we find that Kilgore and Oldaker and Benton were not co-conspirators. Consequently, it was error to admit the hearsay testimony of Oldaker. * * *

Notes and Questions

1. People v. Macklowitz, 135 Misc.2d 232, 236, 514 N.Y.S.2d 883, 886 (1987):

> Numerous labels have been used in an effort to categorize different types of conspiracies. Chains, links, wheels, hubs and spokes are just a few of the terms utilized where there are several layers of actors involved with various, albeit related, roles and objectives. The most common distinction made is between wheel conspiracies and chain conspiracies. A wheel conspiracy involves an individual (or small group)—the hub, who transacts illegal dealings with the various other individuals—the spokes. The most common evidentiary issue in a wheel conspiracy is whether the separate transactions between the hub and individual spokes can be merged to form a single conspiracy.

> In contrast, the chain conspiracy usually involves several layers of personnel dealing with a single subject matter, as opposed to a specific person. Drug trafficking is often cited as a classic example of a chain

conspiracy inasmuch as it is characterized by manufacturing links, wholesaling links and retailing links. A single conspiracy can be proven if each link knew or must have known of the other links in the chain, and if each defendant intended to join and aid the larger enterprise. * * *

This structural analysis is not without confusion, as some conspiracies may be classified as chain/spoke combinations. For example, in narcotics trafficking, the links at either end might be comprised of a number of persons "... who may have no reason to know that others are performing a role similar to theirs—in other words the extreme links of a chain conspiracy may have elements of the spoke conspiracy."

Perhaps a more accurate way to visualize a complex conspiracy case would be to view it as a three-dimensional organic chemistry molecule with each part interacting continuously with another thereby forming and adhering to the whole, for a common purpose.

2. In *Kilgore,* according to the prosecutor's theory of the case, who were the parties to the conspiracy to kill Norman? Structurally, what would the conspiracy look like? What does the conspiracy look like under the court's interpretation of the facts?

3. In United States v. Bruno, 105 F.2d 921 (2d Cir.1939) (cited in *Kilgore*), Bruno was indicted with 87 others for conspiracy to import, sell and possess narcotics. The government proved that various members of the conspiracy smuggled narcotics into the port of New York, that these smugglers received compensation for the narcotics from middlemen, who in turn sold the drugs to retailers in New York and to a retail group working the Texas–Louisiana region. In turn, the retailers dispensed the drugs on the street or distributed them to smaller-level peddlers. The evidence did not disclose any cooperation or communication between the smugglers and the retailers; however, the smugglers were aware that the middlemen with whom they dealt sold to retailers, and the retailers knew that the middlemen were buying the drugs from importers. Is this a single wheel conspiracy, a single chain conspiracy, or something else?

4. In Kotteakos v. United States, 328 U.S. 750, 66 S.Ct. 1239, 90 L.Ed. 1557 (1946), also cited in *Kilgore,* the indictment charged a single 32–person conspiracy, in which it was alleged that Brown, the key figure in the scheme, obtained federal loans for at least eight sets of persons by assisting them in making false representations in their loan applications. Apparently, none of Brown's customers were aware of his arrangements with the others. The Supreme Court determined that this was a wheel conspiracy: in essence Brown was at the hub, with eight spokes emanating outward, but with no rim connecting the spokes. Under this interpretation, Brown should have been charged with at least eight counts of conspiracy, based on each fraudulent loan application.

Why do you think the prosecutor sought to treat the events as a single conspiracy, rather than as eight separate agreements? What additional facts, if proven, would have established a single conspiracy?

5. *Problem.* Stern was engaged in the business of performing illegal abortions. He solicited 26 abortion referrals from 17 physicians, druggists,

and nurses, to whom he paid a fee for their referrals. If you were the prosecutor, of what offense(s) and against whom would you seek an indictment? Stern v. Superior Court, 78 Cal.App.2d 9, 177 P.2d 308 (1947); Anderson v. Superior Court, 78 Cal.App.2d 22, 177 P.2d 315 (1947).

BRAVERMAN v. UNITED STATES

Supreme Court of the United States, 1942.
317 U.S. 49, 63 S.Ct. 99, 87 L.Ed. 23.

MR. CHIEF JUSTICE STONE delivered the opinion of the Court. * * *

Petitioners were indicted, with others, on seven counts, each charging a conspiracy to violate a separate and distinct internal revenue law of the United States.[1] On the trial there was evidence from which the jury could have found that for a considerable period of time petitioners, with others, collaborated in the illicit manufacture, transportation, and distribution of distilled spirits involving the violations of statutes mentioned in the several counts of the indictment. At the close of the trial petitioners renewed a motion which they had made at the beginning to require the Government to elect one of the seven counts of the indictment upon which to proceed, contending that the proof could not and did not establish more than one agreement. In response the Government's attorney took the position that the seven counts of the indictment charged as distinct offenses the several illegal objects of one continuing conspiracy, that if the jury found such a conspiracy it might find the defendants guilty of as many offenses as it had illegal objects, and that each such offense the two-year statutory penalty could be imposed.

The trial judge submitted the case to the jury on that theory. The jury returned a general verdict finding petitioners "guilty as charged," and the court sentenced each to eight years' imprisonment. On appeal the Court of Appeals for the Sixth Circuit affirmed * * *. It found that "From the evidence may be readily deduced a common design of appellant and others, followed by concerted action" to commit the several unlawful acts specified in the several counts of the indictment. It concluded that the fact that the conspiracy was "a general one to violate all laws repressive of its consummation does not gainsay the separate identity of each of the seven conspiracies." * * *

1. The seven counts respectively charged them with conspiracy, in violation of § 37 of the Criminal Code, unlawfully (1) to carry on the business of wholesale and retail liquor dealers without having the special occupational tax stamps required by statute, 26 U.S.C.A. Int.Rev.Code § 3253; (2) to possess distilled spirits, the immediate containers of which did not have stamps affixed denoting the quantity of the distilled spirits which they contained and evidencing payment of all Internal Revenue taxes imposed on such spirits, 26 U.S.C.A. Int.Rev. Code § 2803; (3) to transport quantities of distilled spirits, the immediate containers of which did not have affixed the required stamps, 26 U.S.C.A. Int.Rev.Code § 2803; (4) to carry on the business of distillers without having given bonds as required by law, 26 U.S.C.A. Int.Rev.Code § 2833; (5) to remove, deposit and conceal distilled spirits in respect whereof a tax is imposed by law, with intent to defraud the United States of such tax, 26 U.S.C.A. Int.Rev.Code § 3321; (6) to possess unregistered stills and distilling apparatus, 26 U.S.C.A. Int. Rev.Code § 2810; and (7) to make and ferment mash, fit for distillation, on unauthorized premises, 26 U.S.C.A. Int.Rev.Code § 2834.

Both courts below recognized that a single agreement to commit an offense does not become several conspiracies because it continues over a period of time, and that there may be such a single continuing agreement to commit several offenses. But they thought that in the latter case each contemplated offense renders the agreement punishable as a separate conspiracy.

The question whether a single agreement to commit acts in violation of several penal statutes is to be punished as one or several conspiracies is raised on the present record, not by the construction of the indictment, but by the Government's concession at the trial and here, reflected in the charge to the jury, that only a single agreement to commit the offenses alleged was proven. Where each of the counts of an indictment alleges a conspiracy to violate a different penal statute it may be proper to conclude, in the absence of a bill of exceptions bringing up the evidence, that several conspiracies are charged rather than one, and that the conviction is for each. But it is a different matter to hold, as the court below appears to have done in this case, that even though a single agreement is entered into, the conspirators are guilty of as many offenses as the agreement has criminal objects.

The gist of the crime of conspiracy as defined by the statute is the agreement or confederation of the conspirators to commit one or more unlawful acts * * *.

For when a single agreement to commit one or more substantive crimes is evidenced by an overt act, as the statute requires, the precise nature and extent of the conspiracy must be determined by reference to the agreement which embraces and defines its objects. Whether the object of a single agreement is to commit one or many crimes, it is in either case that agreement which constitutes the conspiracy which the statute punishes. The one agreement cannot be taken to be several agreements and hence several conspiracies because it envisages the violation of several statutes rather than one. * * *

Notes and Questions

1. *Problem.* Terry and Luis murder Carol on January 1, murder Daniel on January 2, and rob and murder Elaine on January 3. Assuming that they acted conspiratorially, of how many counts of conspiracy are they guilty under *Braverman?*

2. In Albernaz v. United States, 450 U.S. 333, 101 S.Ct. 1137, 67 L.Ed.2d 275 (1981), the defendants were convicted of violations of two drug conspiracy statutes, 21 U.S.C. § 963 (1988) (punishing conspiracies to import illegal narcotics), and 21 U.S.C. § 846 (1988) (punishing conspiracies to distribute illegal narcotics). The judge imposed consecutive sentences on each count.

The Supreme Court held that the defendants could be convicted and punished under both statutes, although the government did not prove the existence of separate conspiratorial agreements to import and distribute the drugs. The Court reasoned that, in light of the separate conspiracy statutes,

Congress intended to permit imposition of separate penalties for violations of the two offenses. The Court distinguished *Braverman* on the ground that the defendants in that case were charged under a general conspiracy statute.

3. *Model Penal Code.* The Model Code method of determining the parties to, and objects of, a conspiracy does not track the common law, in part because of its unilateral view of conspiracy. As the Commentary explains:

> The combined operation of Subsections (1), (2), and (3) is relied upon to delineate the identity and scope of a conspiracy. All three provisions focus on the culpability of the individual actor. Subsections (1) and (2) limit the scope of his conspiracy both in terms of its criminal objectives, to those crimes that he had the purpose of promoting or facilitating, and in terms of parties, to those with whom he agreed, except when the same crime that he conspired to commit is, to his knowledge, also the object of a conspiracy between one of his co-conspirators and another person or persons. Subsection (3) provides that his conspiracy is a single one despite a multiplicity of criminal objectives, as long as such crimes are the object of the same agreement or continuous conspiratorial relationship.

American Law Institute, Model Penal Code and Commentaries, Comment to § 5.03 at 425 (1985).

Under the Model Penal Code, of how many counts of conspiracy are Terry and Luis (Note 1) guilty? How would the Code's methodology work with the facts of United States v. Bruno, 105 F.2d 921 (2d Cir.1939) (Note 3, p. 758 supra)? See American Law Institute, Model Penal Code and Commentaries, Comment to § 5.03 at 425–30 (1985).

6. DEFENSES

IANNELLI v. UNITED STATES

Supreme Court of the United States, 1975.
420 U.S. 770, 95 S.Ct. 1284, 43 L.Ed.2d 616.

MR. JUSTICE POWELL delivered the opinion of the Court.

This case requires the Court to consider Wharton's Rule, a doctrine of criminal law enunciating an exception to the general principle that a conspiracy and the substantive offense that is its immediate end are discrete crimes for which separate sanctions may be imposed.

I

Petitioners were tried under a six-count indictment alleging a variety of federal gambling offenses. Each of the eight petitioners, along with seven unindicted coconspirators and six codefendants, was charged, *inter alia,* with conspiring to violate and violating 18 U.S.C. § 1955, a federal gambling statute making it a crime for five or more persons to conduct, finance, manage, supervise, direct, or own a gambling business prohibited by state law. Each petitioner was convicted of both offenses, and each was sentenced under both the substantive and conspiracy counts. The Court of Appeals for the Third Circuit affirmed, finding that a recognized exception to Wharton's Rule permitted prosecution and punishment for both offenses. * * * For the reasons now to be stated, we affirm.

II

Wharton's Rule owes its name to Francis Wharton, whose treatise on criminal law identified the doctrine and its fundamental rationale:

> "When to the idea of an offense plurality of agents is logically necessary, conspiracy, which assumes the voluntary accession of a person to a crime of such a character that it is aggravated by a plurality of agents, cannot be maintained. ... In other words, when the law says, 'a combination between two persons to effect a particular end shall be called, if the end be effected, by a certain name,' it is not lawful for the prosecution to call it by some other name; and when the law says, such an offense—*e.g.*, adultery—shall have a certain punishment, it is not lawful for the prosecution to evade this limitation by indicting the offense as conspiracy." 2 F. Wharton, Criminal Law § 1604, p. 1862 (12th ed. 1932).[5]

The Rule has been applied by numerous courts, state and federal alike. It also has been recognized by this Court, although we have had no previous occasion carefully to analyze its justification and proper role in federal law.

The classic formulation of Wharton's Rule requires that the conspiracy indictment be dismissed before trial. * * * Federal courts earlier adhered to this literal interpretation and thus sustained demurrers to conspiracy indictments. More recently, however, some federal courts have differed over whether Wharton's Rule requires initial dismissal of the conspiracy indictment. * * * In this case, and in United States v. Kohne, 347 F.Supp. 1178, 1186 (WD Pa.1972), * * * the courts held that the Rule's purposes can be served equally effectively by permitting the prosecution to charge both offenses and instructing the jury that a conviction for the substantive offense necessarily precludes conviction for the conspiracy.

Federal courts likewise have disagreed as to the proper application of the recognized "third-party exception," which renders Wharton's Rule inapplicable when the conspiracy involves the cooperation of a greater number of persons than is required for commission of the substantive offense. In the present case, the Third Circuit concluded that the third-party exception permitted prosecution because the conspiracy involved more than the five persons required to commit the substantive offense * * *. The Seventh Circuit reached the opposite result, however, rea-

---

5. The current edition of Wharton's treatise states the Rule more simply:

"An agreement by two persons to commit a particular crime cannot be prosecuted as a conspiracy when the crime is of such a nature as to necessarily require the participation of two persons for its commission." 1 R. Anderson, Wharton's Criminal Law and Procedure § 89, p. 191 (1957).

soning that since § 1955 also covers gambling activities involving more than five persons, the third-party exception is inapplicable.

The Courts of Appeals are at odds even over the fundamental question whether Wharton's Rule ever applies to a charge for conspiracy to violate § 1955. * * *

As this brief description indicates, the history of the application of Wharton's Rule to charges for conspiracy to violate § 1955 fully supports the Fourth Circuit's observation that "rather than being a rule, [it] is a concept, the confines of which have been delineated in widely diverse fashion by the courts." With this diversity of views in mind, we turn to an examination of the history and purposes of the Rule.

III
A

Traditionally the law has considered conspiracy and the completed substantive offense to be separate crimes. Conspiracy is an inchoate offense, the essence of which is an agreement to commit an unlawful act. Unlike some crimes * * * the conspiracy to commit an offense and the subsequent commission of that crime normally do not merge into a single punishable act. Thus, it is well recognized that in most cases separate sentences can be imposed for the conspiracy to do an act and for the subsequent accomplishment of that end. Indeed, the Court has even held that the conspiracy can be punished more harshly than the accomplishment of its purpose.

The consistent rationale of this long line of decisions rests on the very nature of the crime of conspiracy. This Court repeatedly has recognized that a conspiracy poses distinct dangers quite apart from those of the substantive offense.

> "This settled principle derives from the reason of things in dealing with socially reprehensible conduct: collective criminal agreement—partnership in crime—presents a greater potential threat to the public than individual delicts. * * *"

As Mr. Justice Jackson, no friend of the law of conspiracy, see Krulewitch v. United States, 336 U.S. 440, 445, 69 S.Ct. 716, 719, 93 L.Ed. 790 (1949), observed: "The basic rationale of the law of conspiracy is that a conspiracy may be an evil in itself, independently of any other evil it seeks to accomplish."

B

The historical difference between the conspiracy and its end has led this Court consistently to attribute to Congress "a tacit purpose—in the absence of any inconsistent expression—to maintain a long-established distinction between offenses essentially different,—a distinction whose practical importance in the criminal law is not easily overestimated." Wharton's Rule announces an exception to this general principle. * * *

Wharton's Rule first emerged at a time when the contours of the law of conspiracy were in the process of active formulation. The general question whether the conspiracy merged into the completed felony offense remained for some time a matter of uncertain resolution. That issue is now settled, however, and the Rule currently stands as an exception to the general principle that a conspiracy and the substantive offense that is its immediate end do not merge upon proof of the latter. If the Rule is to serve a rational purpose in the context of the modern law of conspiracy, its role must be more precisely identified.

C

This Court's prior decisions indicate that the broadly formulated Wharton's Rule * * * has current vitality only as a judicial presumption, to be applied in the absence of legislative intent to the contrary. The classic Wharton's Rule offenses—adultery, incest, bigamy, duelling—are crimes that are characterized by the general congruence of the agreement and the completed substantive offense. The parties to the agreement are the only persons who participate in commission of the substantive offense,[15] and the immediate consequences of the crime rest on the parties themselves rather than on society at large. Finally, the agreement that attends the substantive offense does not appear likely to pose the distinct kinds of threats to society that the law of conspiracy seeks to avert. It cannot, for example, readily be assumed that an agreement to commit an offense of this nature will produce agreements to engage in a more general pattern of criminal conduct.

The conduct proscribed by § 1955 is significantly different from the offenses to which the Rule traditionally has been applied. Unlike the consequences of the classic Wharton's Rule offenses, the harm attendant upon the commission of the substantive offense is not restricted to the parties to the agreement. Large-scale gambling activities seek to elicit the participation of additional persons—the bettors—who are parties neither to the conspiracy nor to the substantive offense that results from it. Moreover, the parties prosecuted for the conspiracy need not be the same persons who are prosecuted for commission of the substantive offense. An endeavor as complex as a large-scale gambling enterprise might involve persons who have played appreciably different roles, and whose level of culpability varies significantly. It might, therefore, be appropriate to prosecute the owners and organizers of large-scale gambling operations both for the conspiracy and for the substantive offense

---

15. An exception to the Rule generally is thought to apply in the case in which the conspiracy involves more persons than are required for commission of the substantive offense. For example, while the two persons who commit adultery cannot normally be prosecuted both for that offense and for conspiracy to commit it, the third-party exception would permit the conspiracy charge where a "matchmaker"—the third party— had conspired with the principals to encourage commission of the substantive offense. The rationale supporting this exception appears to be that the addition of a third party enhances the dangers presented by the crime. Thus, it is thought that the legislature would not have intended to preclude punishment for a combination of greater dimension than that required to commit the substantive offense.

Our determination that Congress authorized prosecution and conviction for both offenses in all cases, see Part IV, *infra*, makes it unnecessary to decide whether the exception to Wharton's Rule could properly be applied to conspiracies to violate § 1955 involving more than five persons. * * *

but to prosecute the lesser participants only for the substantive offense. Nor can it fairly be maintained that agreements to enter into large-scale gambling activities are not likely to generate additional agreements to engage in other criminal endeavors. * * * [T]he legislative history of § 1955 provides documented testimony to the contrary.

Wharton's Rule applies only to offenses that *require* concerted criminal activity, a plurality of criminal agents. In such cases, a closer relationship exists between the conspiracy and the substantive offense because *both* require collective criminal activity. The substantive offense therefore presents some of the same threats that the law of conspiracy normally is thought to guard against, and it cannot automatically be assumed that the Legislature intended the conspiracy and the substantive offense to remain as discrete crimes upon consummation of the latter. Thus, absent legislative intent to the contrary, the Rule supports a presumption that the two merge when the substantive offense is proved.

But a legal principle commands less respect when extended beyond the logic that supports it. In this case, the significant differences in characteristics and consequences of the kinds of offenses that gave rise to Wharton's Rule and the activities proscribed by § 1955 counsel against attributing significant weight to the presumption the Rule erects. More important, * * * the Rule * * * must defer to a discernible legislative judgment. We turn now to that inquiry.

IV

The basic purpose of the Organized Crime Control Act of 1970 was "to seek the eradication of organized crime in the United States by strengthening the legal tools in the evidence-gathering process, by establishing new penal prohibitions, and by providing enhanced sanctions and new remedies to deal with the unlawful activities of those engaged in organized crime." The content of the Act reflects the dedication with which the Legislature pursued this purpose. * * *

Major gambling activities were a principal focus of congressional concern. Large-scale gambling activities were seen to be both a substantive evil and a source of funds for other criminal conduct. * * *

* * * We conclude, therefore, that the history and structure of the Organized Crime Control Act of 1970 manifest a clear and mistakable legislative judgment that more than outweighs any presumption of merger between the conspiracy to violate § 1955 and the consummation of that substantive offense. * * *

Notes and Questions

1. Does Wharton's Rule apply in the following cases?

A. Conspiracy by *D1* to "barter, exchange, or offer" an illegal narcotic to *D2*. State v. Cavanaugh, 23 Conn.App. 667, 583 A.2d 1311 (1990). What about conspiracy by *D3* to sell an illegal drug to *D4?* Or, conspiracy to "possess a controlled substance with intent to deliver"? Johnson v. State, 587 A.2d 444 (Del.1991).

B. Conspiracy by *D5* (tax preparer) and *D6* (taxpayer) to violate the following statute, which provides that any person who:

> [w]ilfully aids or assists in, or procures, counsels, or advises the preparation or presentation under * * * the internal revenue laws, of a return * * * which is fraudulent or is false as to any material matter, whether or not such falsity or fraud is with the knowledge or consent of the person authorized to present such return [shall be guilty of a felony].

United States v. Gruberg, 493 F.Supp. 234 (S.D.N.Y.1979).

C. Conspiracy by *D7* and *D8* that *D7* shall "receive, retain, or dispose" of *D8*'s property, knowing or believing that the property is stolen. See Guyer v. State, 453 A.2d 462 (Del.1982).

D. Conspiracy by *D9,* a public official, and *D10,* a private party, to commit bribery, which is defined as the "giving and receiving of money or property to a public official in order to influence the official's vote or judgment on a public matter." See People v. Wettengel, 98 Colo. 193, 58 P.2d 279 (1936). What if the statute prohibits an "offer to give or receive" a bribe? See People v. Incerto, 180 Colo. 366, 505 P.2d 1309 (1973).

GEBARDI v. UNITED STATES

Supreme Court of the United States, 1932.
287 U.S. 112, 53 S.Ct. 35, 77 L.Ed. 206.

MR. JUSTICE STONE delivered the opinion of the Court.

This case is here on certiorari, to review a judgment of conviction for conspiracy to violate the Mann Act ([18 USCA § 397 et seq.]). Petitioners, a man and a woman, not then husband and wife, were indicted for conspiring together, and with others not named, to transport the woman from one state to another for the purpose of engaging in sexual intercourse with the man. At the trial * * * there was evidence from which the court could have found that the petitioners had engaged in illicit sexual relations in the course of each of the journeys alleged; that the man purchased the railway tickets for both petitioners for at least one journey; and that in each instance the woman, in advance of the purchase of the tickets, consented to go on the journey and did go on it voluntarily for the specified immoral purpose. There was no evidence supporting the allegation that any other person had conspired. The trial court * * * gave judgment of conviction * * *.

The only question which we need consider here is whether * * * the evidence was sufficient to support the conviction. * * *

Section 2 of the Mann Act, violation of which is charged by the indictment here as the object of the conspiracy, imposes the penalty upon "any person who shall knowingly transport or cause to be transported, or aid or assist in obtaining transportation for, or in transporting, in interstate or foreign commerce * * * any woman or girl for the purpose of prostitution or debauchery, or for any other immoral purpose.

* * *'' Transportation of a woman or girl whether with or without her consent, or causing or aiding it, or furthering it in any of the specified ways, are the acts punished, when done with a purpose which is immoral within the meaning of the law.

The act does not punish the woman for transporting herself; it contemplates two persons—one to transport and the woman or girl to be transported. For the woman to fall within the ban of the statute she must, at the least, "aid or assist" some one else in transporting or in procuring transportation for herself. But such aid and assistance must * * * be more active than mere agreement on her part to the transportation and its immoral purpose. For the statute is drawn to include those cases in which the woman consents to her own transportation. Yet it does not specifically impose any penalty upon her, although it deals in detail with the person by whom she is transported. In applying this criminal statute we cannot infer that the mere acquiescence of the woman transported was intended to be condemned by the general language punishing those who aid and assist the transporter, any more than it has been inferred that the purchaser of liquor was to be regarded as an abettor of the illegal sale. The penalties of the statute are too clearly directed against the acts of the transporter as distinguished from the consent of the subject of the transportation. * * *

* * * We come thus to the main question in the case, whether, admitting that the woman by consenting, has not violated the Mann Act, she may be convicted of a conspiracy with the man to violate it. * * *

* * * [W]e perceive in the failure of the Mann Act to condemn the woman's participation in those transportations which are effected with her mere consent, evidence of an affirmative legislative policy to leave her acquiescence unpunished. We think it a necessary implication of that policy that when the Mann Act and the conspiracy statute came to be construed together, as they necessarily would be, the same participation which the former contemplates as an inseparable incident of all cases in which the woman is a voluntary agent at all, but does not punish, was not automatically to be made punishable under the latter. It would contravene that policy to hold that the very passage of the Mann Act effected a withdrawal by the conspiracy statute of that immunity which the Mann Act itself confers.

It is not to be supposed that the consent of an unmarried person to adultery with a married person, where the latter alone is guilty of the substantive offense, would render the former an abettor or a conspirator, or that the acquiescence of a woman under the age of consent would make her a co-conspirator with the man to commit statutory rape upon herself. The principle, determinative of this case, is the same.

On the evidence before us the woman petitioner has not violated the Mann Act and, we hold, is not guilty of a conspiracy to do so. As there is no proof that the man conspired with anyone else to bring about the transportation, the convictions of both petitioners must be

Reversed.

Notes and Questions

1. What would be the result under the Model Penal Code?

PEOPLE v. SCONCE

California Court of Appeal, Second District, 1991.
228 Cal.App.3d 693, 279 Cal.Rptr. 59.

KLEIN, PRESIDING JUSTICE.

The People filed an information charging * * * David Wayne Sconce (Sconce) with conspiracy to commit murder. The trial court set the information aside [prior to trial] because it found Sconce effectively had withdrawn from the conspiracy. The People appeal. * * *

FACTUAL * * * BACKGROUND

This case involves Sconce's alleged formation of a conspiracy [with Bob Garcia] to kill Elie Estephan (Estephan). * * *

[Sconce offered Bob Garcia $10,000 to kill Estephan, the estranged husband of Cindy Strunk Estephan. Sconce told Garcia that he, Cindy, and a man named Sallard were plotting the murder. Garcia agreed to find someone to kill Estephan or to do it himself. Pursuant to the agreement, Garcia contacted ex-convict Herbert Dutton and offered him $5,000 to carry out the killing. Subsequently, Garcia and Dutton went to Estephan's house to inspect the area. They decided that Dutton would plant a bomb under Estephan's car.]

* * * Approximately three weeks after Sconce's initial conversation with Garcia, Sconce "just called it off. He said just forget about it, disregard doing it." Garcia did not see Dutton after the night they drove to Estephan's house. Although Garcia did not know it at the time Sconce told him not to kill Estephan, Dutton had been arrested on a parole violation. * * *

CONTENTIONS

The People contend the trial court erroneously set aside the information because Sconce's withdrawal from the conspiracy, although it might insulate him from liability for future conspiratorial acts, does not constitute a defense to liability for the conspiracy itself. * * *

DISCUSSION * * *

" 'Once the defendant's participation in the conspiracy is shown, it will be presumed to continue unless he is able to prove, as a matter of defense, that he effectively withdrew from the conspiracy. * * *' " (*People v. Lowery* (1988) 200 Cal.App.3d 1207, 1220, 246 Cal.Rptr. 443.)

Withdrawal from a conspiracy requires "an affirmative and bona fide rejection or repudiation of the conspiracy, communicated to the coconspirators." (*People v. Crosby,* [(1962) 58 Cal.2d 713], 730–731, 25 Cal.Rptr. 847, 375 P.2d 839.) * * *

Under California law withdrawal is a complete defense to conspiracy only if accomplished before the commission of an overt act, or, where it is asserted in conjunction with the running of the statute of limitations.[3]
* * *

"The requirement of an overt act before conspirators can be prosecuted and punished exists, ... to provide a *locus p[o]enitentiae* —an opportunity for the conspirators to reconsider, terminate the agreement, and thereby avoid punishment for the conspiracy."

Obviously, the inverse of this rule is that once an overt act has been committed in furtherance of the conspiracy the crime of conspiracy has been completed and no subsequent action by the conspirator can change that.

Thus, even if it be assumed Sconce effectively withdrew from the conspiracy * * *, withdrawal merely precludes liability for subsequent acts committed by the members of the conspiracy. The withdrawal does not relate back to the criminal formation of the unlawful combination. In sum, conspiracy is complete upon the commission of an overt act.
* * *

The rationale in favor of terminating liability is the one relied upon by the trial court, i.e., the reasons for allowing withdrawal as a defense to conspiracy—encouraging abandonment and thereby weakening the group—continue to apply after the commission of an overt act.

However, the rule remains that withdrawal avoids liability only for the target offense, or for any subsequent act committed by a coconspirator in pursuance of the common plan. "[I]n respect of the conspiracy itself, the individual's change of mind is ineffective; he cannot undo that which he has already done." (4 Wharton's Criminal Law, (14th ed. 1981) *Conspiracy,* § 734, pp. 555–557.) [4]

Even if this court were inclined to agree with the trial court, we are bound to follow the foregoing settled rule. Any change in the law is a matter for the Legislature.[5]

---

3. Because there is no statute of limitations applicable to the crime of conspiracy to commit murder in California, Sconce cannot assert the statute of limitations in this instance.

4. The Model Penal Code recognizes a defense which it refers to as renunciation. The Model Penal Code states: "It is an affirmative defense that the actor, after conspiring to commit a crime, thwarted the success of the conspiracy, under circumstances manifesting a complete and voluntary renunciation of his [or her] criminal purpose." (Model Pen.Code, § 5.03, subd. (6).)

The defense of renunciation is not the same as withdrawal. "One difference is immediately apparent: In renunciation, the defendant must 'thwart the success' of the conspiracy. Another important difference is that renunciation is a complete defense, relieving liability for all prior involvement in the conspiracy." (Note, *Withdrawal from Conspiracy: A Constitutional Allocation of Evidentiary Burdens* (1982) 51 Fordham L.Rev. 438, 440, fn. 12.)

Renunciation is not available as a defense in California.

5. Although it is therefore unnecessary to wrestle with the policy concerns underlying the current rule, we note that avoidance of criminal liability for the target offense and for all future acts of the conspiracy continues to provide incentive for a conspirator to withdraw, assuming the legal fiction the conspirator is knowledgeable in the law of conspiracy.

Because we conclude Sconce's withdrawal from the conspiracy is not a valid defense to the completed crime of conspiracy, we need not determine whether the evidence showed that Sconce, in fact, withdrew from the conspiracy and communicated that withdrawal to each coconspirator. * * *

Notes and Questions

1. *Impossibility: a defense to conspiracy?* Reconsider *United States v. Thomas* (p. 685 supra), in which the defendants had intercourse with an "unconscious" (but actually dead) female. They were convicted of attempted rape. Were they also guilty of conspiracy to commit rape? In a state that retains the common law defense of legal impossibility in attempt cases, is there a plausible argument for rejecting the defense in conspiracy prosecutions? Or might the case for the impossibility defense be *stronger* with conspiracies? See People v. Tinskey, 394 Mich. 108, 228 N.W.2d 782 (1975); State v. Houchin, 235 Mont. 179, 765 P.2d 178 (1988); and State v. Moretti, 52 N.J. 182, 244 A.2d 499 (1968).

7. RICO: THE SPRAWLING SON–OF–CONSPIRACY STATUTE

TITLE 18, UNITED STATES CODE, CHAPTER 96— RACKETEER INFLUENCED AND CORRUPT ORGANIZATIONS (RICO)

(1993)

§ 1961 Definitions

As used in this chapter—

(1) "racketeering activity" means (A) any act or threat involving murder, kidnaping, gambling, arson, robbery, bribery, extortion, dealing in obscene matter, or dealing in narcotic or other dangerous drugs, which is chargeable under State law and punishable by imprisonment for more than one year; (B) any act which is indictable under any of the following provisions of title 18, United States Code: [various enumerated criminal statutes]; * * *; * * *

(3) "person" includes any individual or entity capable of holding a legal or beneficiary interest in property;

(4) "enterprise" includes any individual, partnership, corporation, association, or other legal entity, and any union or group of individuals associated in fact although not a legal entity;

(5) "pattern of racketeering activity" requires at least two acts of racketeering activity, one of which occurred after the effective date of this chapter and the last of which occurred within ten years (excluding any period of imprisonment) after the commission of a prior act of racketeering activity; * * *.

§ 1962 Prohibited Activities

(a) It shall be unlawful for any person who has received any income derived, directly or indirectly, from a pattern of racketeering activity or though collection of an unlawful debt in which such person has participated * * *, to use or invest, directly or indirectly, any part of such income, or the proceeds of such income, in acquisition of any interest in, or the establishment or operation of, any enterprise which is engaged in, or the activities of which affect, interstate or foreign commerce. * * *

(b) It shall be unlawful for any person through a pattern of racketeering activity or through collection of an unlawful debt to acquire or maintain, directly or indirectly, any interest in or control of any enterprise which is engaged in, or the activities of which affect, interstate or foreign commerce.

(c) It shall be unlawful for any person employed by or associated with any enterprise engaged in, or the activities of which affect, interstate or foreign commerce, to conduct or participate, directly or indirectly, in the conduct of such enterprise's affairs through a pattern of racketeering activity or collection of unlawful debt.

(d) It shall be unlawful for any person to conspire to violate any of the provisions of subsection (a), (b), or (c) of this section.

§ 1963   Criminal Penalties

(a) Whoever violates any provision of section 1962 of this chapter shall be fined * * * or imprisoned not more than 20 years (or for life if the violation is based on racketeering activity for which the maximum penalty includes life imprisonment), or both, and shall forfeit to the United States, irrespective of any provision of State law—

(1) any interest the person has acquired or maintained in violation of section 1962;

(2) any (A) interest in; (B) security of; (C) claim against; or (D) property or contractual right of any kind affording a source of influence over;

any enterprise which the person has established, operated, controlled, conducted, or participated in the conduct of in violation of section 1962; and

(3) any property constituting, or derived from, any proceeds which the person obtained, directly or indirectly, from racketeering activity or unlawful debt collection in violation of section 1962.

The court, in imposing sentence on such person shall order, in addition to any other sentence imposed * * *, that the person forfeit to the United States all property described in this subsection. In lieu of a fine otherwise authorized by this section, a defendant who derives profit or other proceeds from an offense may be fined not more than twice the gross profits or other proceeds. * * *

(c) All right, title, and interest in property described in subsection (a) vests in the United States upon the commission of the act giving rise to forfeiture under this section. * * *

GERALD E. LYNCH—RICO: THE CRIME OF BEING A CRIMINAL, PARTS I & II

87 Columbia Law Review 661 (1987), 661–63

One of the most controversial statutes in the federal criminal code is that entitled "Racketeer–Influenced and Corrupt Organizations," known familiarly by its acronym, RICO. Passed in 1970 as title IX of the Organized Crime Control Act of 1970, RICO has attracted much attention because of its draconian penalties, including innovative forfeiture provisions; its broad draftsmanship, which has left it open to a wide range of applications, not all of which were foreseen or intended by the Congress that enacted it; and the sometimes dramatic prosecutions that have been brought in its name.[3]

RICO's complexity has attracted several efforts to unscramble the many issues of interpretation it poses. The potency of its sanctions and the procedural advantages it bestows on prosecutors have drawn polemics of praise and criticism from practitioners and scholars with ties to law enforcement or defense practice. Yet there has been little discussion of the fundamental questions RICO poses concerning some of our basic assumptions about criminal law and procedure.

One reason for this lack of discussion may be that the uses of RICO that most starkly raise the issues I have in mind were not contemplated in the congressional debates about the statute and have become more clearly dominant with the passage of time. Congress viewed RICO principally as a tool for attacking the specific problem of infiltration of legitimate business by organized criminal syndicates. As such, RICO has hardly been a dramatic success. Few notable RICO prosecutions have dealt directly with this sort of criminal activity.

Instead, prosecutors have seized on the virtually unlimited sweep of the language of RICO to bring a wide variety of different prosecutions in the form of RICO indictments. All but ignoring those subsections of RICO that directly prohibit the act of infiltrating legitimate business by investment of illicit profits or by illegitimate tactics, prosecutors have relied principally on the expansive prohibition of the operation of an enterprise through a pattern of racketeering activity to strike at those— whether or not they fit any ordinary definition of "racketeer" or "organized criminal"—who commit crimes in conducting the affairs of businesses, labor unions, and government offices.

More importantly, a large proportion of RICO prosecutions, and the greatest number of the most visible ones, have been directed at the

---

3. In the Southern District of New York alone, RICO has been used to prosecute members of the Black Liberation Army for a series of armed bank robberies, a band of Croatian terrorists for bombings and extortion, the heads of New York's "Five Families" of organized crime for constituting the ruling "Commission" of the Mafia, several of New York City's most powerful politicians for corrupting the award of contracts by its Parking Violations Bureau, and international commodities trader Marc Rich and associated entities and individuals for evasion of federal energy regulations and "the largest known criminal scheme to avoid paying taxes in history."

operations of illegitimate criminal enterprises themselves. Through an expansive (though quite literal) interpretation of section 1962(c), prosecutors have moved directly against "organized crime" itself, in both the narrow and broad senses of the term. In cases of this sort, defendants have been tried for engaging with others in series of crimes having looser connections than have traditionally been permitted even in conspiracy prosecutions. Although particular "predicate acts" must be proven, such prosecutions tend to focus not on the defendant's particular antisocial acts, but on whether an examination of broad stretches of the defendant's criminal career and those of his associates reveals that he has associated himself with a criminal combine. Necessarily, RICO prosecutions put before the jury charges that a particular defendant engaged in not just one but several, often very loosely related, crimes, and frequently also present an equally ill-assorted set of charges against codefendants.

Notes and Questions

1. Look carefully at the provisions of RICO. Section 1962 states the prohibited activities: subsections (a) through (c) are the substantive provisions; subsection (d) creates a RICO conspiracy offense.

Most RICO litigation has centered on the meaning of the terms "pattern of racketeering activity" and "enterprise," as they are defined in Section 1961. The next two Notes concern these terms. For a helpful introduction to the statute, see Stephen D. Brown and Alan M. Lieberman, *RICO Basics: A Primer,* 35 Vill.L.Rev. 865 (1990).

2. *"Enterprise."* Although the original purpose of RICO was to attack the infiltration of lawful enterprises by organized crime, the Supreme Court ruled in United States v. Turkette, 452 U.S. 576, 101 S.Ct. 2524, 69 L.Ed.2d 246 (1981), that the term "enterprise" includes illegal enterprises.

Does this mean that if the government proves that an enterprise is criminal in nature, a "pattern of racketeering activity" thereby exists? Not necessarily, as *Turkette* explained, id. at 583, 101 S.Ct. at 2528–29, 69 L.Ed.2d at 254:

> That a wholly criminal enterprise comes within the ambit of the statute does not mean that a "pattern of racketeering activity" is an "enterprise." In order to secure a conviction under RICO, the Government must prove both the existence of an "enterprise" and the connected "pattern of racketeering activity." The enterprise is an entity, for present purposes a group of persons associated together for a common purpose of engaging in a course of conduct. The pattern of racketeering activities is, on the other hand, a series of criminal acts as defined by the statute. 18 U.S.C. § 1961(1). The former is proved by evidence of an ongoing organization, formal or informal, and by evidence that the various associates function as a continuing unit. The latter is proved by evidence of the requisite number of acts of racketeering committed by the participants in the enterprise. While the proof used to establish these separate elements may in particular cases coalesce, proof of one does not necessarily establish the other. * * * The existence of an

enterprise at all times remains a separate element which must be proved by the Government.

3. *"Pattern of racketeering activity."* If an enterprise [k] murders two people on separate occasions, is this a "pattern of racketeering activity"? See Section 1961(5). The Supreme Court provides the following interpretive warning:

> As many commentators have pointed out, the definition of a "pattern of racketeering activity" differs from the other provisions in § 1961 in that it states that a pattern *"requires* at least two acts of racketeering activity," not that it "means" two such acts. The implication is that while two acts are necessary, they may not be sufficient. Indeed, in common parlance two of anything do not generally form a "pattern." The legislative history supports the view that two isolated acts of racketeering activity do not constitute a pattern. As the Senate Report explained: "The target of [RICO] is thus not sporadic activity. The infiltration of legitimate business normally requires more than one 'racketeering activity' and the threat of continuing activity to be effective. It is this factor of *continuity plus relationship* which combines to produce a pattern." Similarly, the sponsor of the Senate bill * * * pointed out * * * that "[t]he term 'pattern' itself requires the showing of a relationship.... So, therefore, proof of two acts of racketeering activity, without more, does not establish a pattern...." Significantly, in defining "pattern" in a later provision of the same bill, Congress was more enlightening: "[C]riminal conduct forms a pattern if it embraces criminal acts that have the same or similar purposes, results, participants, victims, or methods of commission, or otherwise are interrelated by distinguishing characteristics and are not isolated events." 18 U.S.C. § 3537(e). This language may be useful in interpreting other sections of the Act.

Sedima, S.P.R.L. v. Imrex Co., Inc., 473 U.S. 479, 496 n. 14, 105 S.Ct. 3275, 3285 n. 14, 87 L.Ed.2d 346, 358 n. 14 (1985).

In this regard, consider United States v. Indelicato, 865 F.2d 1370 (2d Cir.1989). Indelicato was named in two counts of a 25–count indictment that charged him and seven others with various crimes arising out of the operations of an organization known as the "Commission" of La Costa Nostra, purportedly the ruling body of organized crime families throughout the United States. The indictment alleged that the Commission was an "enterprise" within the meaning of the RICO statute. Indelicato was charged in one count of the indictment with violation of Section 1962, subsection (c), based on the claim that he participated in the nearly simultaneous murders of three persons belonging to a competing organized crime family. No other predicate acts were alleged. Is Indelicato guilty?

4. *Problem.* Licavoli and others were charged with violation of Section 1962, subsection (c). In order to establish that they engaged in a pattern of racketeering activity, the government proved two predicate acts: (1) conspiracy to murder one Danny Greene; and (2) murder of Danny Greene. Does the conspiracy charge count? Should it matter that, under state procedural

---

k. An "enterprise" may be one person. See Section 1961(4).

rules, a person may not be convicted and punished for both conspiracy and murder? See United States v. Licavoli, 725 F.2d 1040 (6th Cir.1984).

5. Section 1962, subsection (c) is the most controversial of the three substantive provisions of the RICO statute. Compare it to subsections (a) and (b). Can you see why it tests the outer limits of traditional criminal law doctrine? Professor Lynch discusses this subsection in the following article excerpt.

GERALD E. LYNCH—RICO: THE CRIME OF BEING A CRIMINAL, PARTS III & IV

87 Columbia Law Review 920 (1987), 932–34, 936–41

In order to understand RICO's value in prosecuting diversified illicit enterprises, and the potential abuses of such prosecutions, we must first understand the limits imposed on criminal prosecutions by our conventional understanding of what a crime is, and the potential of RICO to explode those limitations.

Fundamental to our traditional law of crimes * * * is a conception of crime that is transaction-bound. Synthesizers of the common-law tradition tell us that the core of any definition of crime is a particular act or omission. That act or omission is conceived as taking place in an instant of time so precise that it can be associated with a particular mental state of intention, awareness of risk, or neglect of due care. The verbs that form the heart of the definitions of particular offenses ("takes and carries away," "engages in sexual intercourse," "damages by starting a fire," "sells a controlled substance") typically refer to single rather than repeated actions, completed in a brief span of time. Where the verbs in penal statutes instead refer to causing a particular result ("causes the death of another human being," "causes serious physical injury")—a process that can extend over a period of time—the focus of inquiry into a defendant's culpability must nevertheless be a specific, momentary act or omission. Even the crime of conspiracy, which in practice may permit an examination of an extended course of conduct by one or more individuals, does so in the guise of using that course of conduct as evidence from which to infer that a particular act of "agreement" occurred, presumably at a specific, if not precisely ascertainable, moment in time. * * *

The focus on particular events in defining crimes is not merely a linguistic convention. The requirement that criminal punishment be based on a specific act has deep roots. The very nature of criminal punishment, as distinct from other uses of the compulsive power of the state (such as mandatory treatment for physical or mental illness), requires that a person not be punished for bad character, tendency to commit crime, or even a specifically formulated intention to commit some particular prohibited act. Before the state can deprive a citizen of liberty in a *punitive* way, the individual must manifest that character or tendency by the commission of some concrete prohibited act.

In significant part, the purpose of this limitation is the protection of an individual from punishment for thoughts or traits not yet exemplified by actual harmful conduct. But the moral basis of the focus on particular acts extends beyond this problem. Even for those accused of committing what is unquestionably a concrete, particular offense, we are careful to guard against the possibility that a defendant may be convicted and punished for bad character rather than for the particular act charged. * * *

Indeed, the power of this model * * * is so strong that some proponents of the "just deserts" model of punishment have argued that the focus on the individual incident rather than on the character of the offender should be extended even into the sentencing process. On this view, a defendant's past conduct or overall character would have no relevance at all in determining an appropriate sentence, giving especially concrete content to the idea of punishing the crime and not the criminal. At this point, however, our tradition until recently has balked, and the sentencing decision has been seen, within limits set by a vague principle of proportionality and by concrete maximum sentences devised by legislatures in correlation to the seriousness of particular offenses, as including appropriate attention to treatment and incapacitation goals based in part on the general character of the offender. The prevalence of legislative proposals for less discretionary, more conduct-based sentencing systems may suggest that the retributive view of crime may be weakening even the citadel of sentencing discretion. * * *

RICO prosecutions of criminal enterprises present a serious challenge to the substantive and procedural implications of this transaction-based model of crime.

This challenge is partially apparent on the face of the statute. Ordinary criminal statutes, as we have seen, define the conduct they prohibit in terms of rather concrete actions that can be committed in an identifiable moment of time. Indeed, two of the three substantive prohibitions imposed by the RICO statute in essence follow this very model. Those sections make it a crime to "use or invest" money from particular sources in a particular way, and to "acquire ... any interest" in an enterprise by means of certain conduct. While the necessity of proving a "pattern of racketeering activity" may well permit proof of a variety of (possibly only distantly related) criminal acts, the act that constitutes the offense is a single, specific action—acquisition of a business interest. The particular moment at which an individual commits the prohibited act can, in theory and usually in practice, be identified. Past acts of racketeering are relevant to the offense charged only if they bear directly on the particular acquisition of an interest charged in the indictment.

Section 1962(c), in contrast, makes it a crime to "conduct or participate, directly or indirectly, in the conduct" of the affairs of any "enterprise[ ] ... through a pattern of racketeering activity." The very words of the statute reveal an intent to prohibit not any particular, time-bound action, but a course of conduct extending over a potentially lengthy period of time. Although the predicate acts of racketeering are conventional crimes, defined in terms of specific conduct, the actual RICO violation is not identifiable by the physical contours of a particular action or effect. Rather, the defining characteristic of the "pattern of racketeering" is the relationship of certain conduct to other conduct and to the "enterprise," which itself is an abstract construct of certain interpersonal relationships. Whether or not this definition is vague in the technical legal sense of the word, the level of abstraction in the definition permits the offense to cover a wide variety of conduct for which ordinary language does not supply a single common term. * * *

Moreover, it is the fact that RICO does define a crime that entails some of its most dramatic procedural and evidentiary consequences. Since section 1962(c) defines participating in the affairs of an enterprise through a pattern of racketeering as a crime separate and apart from the predicate acts, it does not merely enhance the statutory penalty for the predicate acts, but rather permits the imposition of consecutive sentences for the RICO offense and the predicates. Because the RICO offense is a separate crime, the statute of limitations runs only from its completion; thus, every additional racketeering offense committed in furtherance of the enterprise's affairs within ten years of a previous one extends the statute of limitations for another five years for prosecution of the entire pattern. A RICO indictment thus may hold a defendant accountable for acts that took place twenty or more years before the date of the indictment—not for the penalty attached to the predicate crime, but for the separately defined RICO offense.

Even within the ordinary limits of the double jeopardy principle and the statute of limitations, a prosecutor can use section 1962(c) to place before a single jury in a single trial offenses that could not otherwise be included in the same indictment or admitted into evidence at the same trial. Suppose, for example, the authorities develop evidence that the same defendant from whom they have recently made an undercover purchase of narcotics is a member of an organized crime family who committed a contract killing three years earlier. Under our ordinary, transaction-bound rules of procedure and evidence, the defendant would have to be tried separately for each offense. Since the earlier crime is plainly not part of the same course of events as the later, joinder of the two crimes would not be possible; if the homicide had taken place in another state, jurisdictional or venue problems would also prevent joinder.

In a trial on the narcotics charge alone, moreover, the evidence of a prior homicide committed by the defendant would likely be excluded as irrelevant and highly prejudicial. Evidence that the defendant in a narcotics trial was part of the "Mafia" would surely be excluded as merely prejudicial evidence of the defendant's character and associations. And the prosecutor presumably would not even think about trying to elicit evidence of crimes that some *other* member of the same crime family had committed, in which this particular defendant was not personally involved. Evidence of the defendant's involvement in organized crime or of the murder he may have committed might finally surface after the defendant's conviction, as part of an argument for a severe sentence.

If the case could be indicted and tried under RICO, however, all of the evidence regarding this defendant's activities could easily be presented in the same trial. Since the government would have to allege and prove a pattern of racketeering activity, the murder and the narcotics offense could be alleged as elements of the same crime, the violation of section 1962(c). The rules precluding admission of evidence of other crimes, consequently, would simply have no application—evidence of the homicide would not be evidence of a *prior* crime, but evidence of the very offense charged in the indictment.

Jurisdictional and venue problems disappear, as well. It is irrelevant that the federal government lacks jurisdiction to prosecute ordinary homicides; the crime charged here is racketeering that affects interstate commerce, not murder. The single crime of racketeering, like any other crime, can be prosecuted in any district where a portion of the crime was committed, so any venue problem with combining crimes committed in different districts disappears.

Notes and Questions

1. *Private RICO actions.* Title 18 U.S.C. § 1964 authorizes private RICO causes of actions, as well as suits initiated by the Attorney General, to obtain civil remedies. Under Section 1964, a district court may enjoin racketeering activities, order anyone to divest her interest in a RICO enterprise, and/or impose treble damages for any harm sustained as a result of racketeering activities.

Section 1964 has stimulated a rush of private RICO civil suits. In one such action, a health center that performed abortions alleged that Operation Rescue, an anti-abortion organization, sought to shut down the plaintiff's clinic by blocking entry to it, by entering and causing property damage, and by assaulting employees. Northeast Women's Center, Inc. v. McMonagle, 939 F.2d 57 (3d Cir.1991). Is this a proper use of RICO, or should the law be limited to enterprises with an overriding economic motive for their predicate acts? See National Organization for Women, Inc. v. Scheidler, 968 F.2d 612 (7th Cir.1992), reversed, ___ U.S. ___, 114 S.Ct. 798, 127 L.Ed.2d 99 (1994).

UNITED STATES v. ELLIOTT

United States Court of Appeals, Fifth Circuit, 1978.
571 F.2d 880.

SIMPSON, CIRCUIT JUDGE:

In this case we deal with the question of whether and, if so, how a free society can protect itself when groups of people, through division of labor, specialization, diversification, complexity of organization, and the accumulation of capital, turn crime into an ongoing business. Congress fired a telling shot at organized crime when it passed the Racketeer Influenced and Corrupt Organizations Act of 1970, popularly known as RICO. Since the enactment of RICO, the federal courts, guided by constitutional and legislative dictates, have been responsible for perfecting the weapons in society's arsenal against criminal confederacies.

Today we review the convictions of six persons accused of conspiring to violate the RICO statute, two of whom were also accused and convicted of substantive RICO violations. The government admits that in this prosecution it has attempted to achieve a broader application of RICO than has heretofore been sanctioned. Predictably, the government and the defendants differ as to what this case is about. According to the defendants, what we are dealing with is a leg, a tail, a trunk, an ear—separate entities unaffected by RICO proscriptions. The government, on the other hand, asserts that we have come eyeball to eyeball with a single creature of behemoth proportions, securely within RICO's grasp. After a careful, if laborious study of the facts and the law, we accept, with minor exceptions, the government's view. * * *

I. THE FACTS

Simply stated, this is a case involving a group of persons informally associated with the purpose of profiting from criminal activity. The facts giving rise to this generalization, however, are considerably more complex. Evidence presented during the 12 day trial implicated the six defendants and 37 unindicted co-conspirators in more than 20 different criminal endeavors. * * *

[The criminal endeavors, which occurred over a seven-year period, included arson of a nursing home; supplying counterfeit titles to stolen cars; numerous thefts, including one of a truckload of Hormel meat; efforts to influence the outcome of a jury trial relating to the Hormel meat theft; illegal drug transactions; intimidation; and murder.

The indictment charged the six defendants—James Elliott, Robert Delph, Jr., William Foster, Recea Hawkins, John Clayburn Hawkins (known as "J.C."), and John Taylor—with conspiring with each other, 37 unindicted co-conspirators, and with "others to the grand jury known and unknown," to violate Section 1962, subsection (c), of RICO. The essence of the conspiracy charge was that the defendants agreed to participate, directly and indirectly, in the conduct of the affairs of an enterprise whose purposes were to commit thefts, fence stolen goods, illegally traffic in narcotics, obstruct justice, and engage in "other criminal activities."

The trial evidence supported the government's claim that all of the defendants were involved in one or more of the criminal endeavors. However, at no time did more than three of the defendants participate in any specific criminal endeavor, although J.C. Hawkins was linked to all of the crimes.]

Here, the government proved beyond a reasonable doubt the existence of an enterprise comprised of at least five of the defendants.[18] This enterprise can best be analogized to a large business conglomerate. Metaphorically speaking, J.C. Hawkins was the chairman of the board, functioning as the chief executive officer and overseeing the operations of many separate branches of the corporation. An executive committee in charge of the "Counterfeit Title, Stolen Car, and Amphetamine Sales Department" was comprised of J.C., Delph, and Taylor, who supervised the operations of lower level employees * * *. Another executive committee, comprised of J.C., Recea and Foster, controlled the "Thefts From Interstate Commerce Department," arranging the purchase, concealment, and distribution of such commodities as meat, dairy products, "Career Club" shirts, and heavy construction equipment. An offshoot of this department handled subsidiary activities, such as murder and obstruction of justice, intended to facilitate the smooth operation of its primary activities. Each member of the conglomerate, with the exception of Foster, was responsible for procuring and wholesaling whatever narcotics could be obtained. The thread tying all of these departments, activities, and individuals together was the desire to make money. * * *

IV. THE RICO CONSPIRACY COUNT

* * * In this appeal, all defendants, with the exception of Foster, argue that while the indictment alleged but one conspiracy, the government's evidence at trial proved the existence of several conspiracies, resulting in a variance which substantially prejudiced their rights and requires reversal, citing *Kotteakos v. United States,* 328 U.S. 750, 66 S.Ct. 1239, 90 L.Ed. 1557 (1946). Prior to the enactment of the RICO statute, this argument would have been more persuasive. However, as we explain below, RICO has displaced many of the legal precepts traditionally applied to concerted criminal activity. Its effect in this case is to free the government from the strictures of the multiple conspiracy doctrine and to allow the joint trial of many persons accused of diversified crimes.

A. *Prior Law: Wheels and Chains*

1. Kotteakos *and the Wheel Conspiracy Rationale:* The Court in *Kotteakos* held that proof of multiple conspiracies under an indictment alleging a single conspiracy constituted a material variance requiring reversal where a defendant's substantial rights had been affected. At issue was "the right not to be tried *en masse* for the conglomeration of distinct and separate offenses committed by others". *Kotteakos* thus protects against the "spill-over effect," the transference of guilt from members of one conspiracy to members of another.

---

18. As we explain below, we hold that the evidence was insufficient to tie James Elliott to the enterprise or to a conspiracy to violate the Act. The number of persons making up an enterprise is irrelevant, however, in that even a single individual may be considered an "enterprise" under the statutory definition. 18 U.S.C. § 1961(4). * * *

The facts of *Kotteakos* [l] * * * led the Court to speak in terms of a "wheel conspiracy," in which one person, the "hub" of the wheel, was accused of conspiring with several others, the "spokes" of the wheel. * * *

2. Blumenthal *and the Chain Conspiracy Rationale:* The impact of *Kotteakos* was soon limited by the Court in *Blumenthal v. United States,* 332 U.S. 539, 68 S.Ct. 248, 92 L.Ed. 154 (1947), where the indictment charged a single conspiracy to sell whiskey at prices above the ceiling set by the Office of Price Administration. The owner of the whiskey, through a series of middlemen, had devised an intricate scheme to conceal the true amount he was charging for the whiskey. Although some of the middlemen had no contact with each other and did not know the identity of the owner, they had to have realized that they were indispensible cogs in the machinery through which this illegal scheme was effectuated. The Court concluded that "in every practical sense the unique facts of this case reveal a single conspiracy of which the several agreements were essential and integral steps". Thus the "chain conspiracy" rationale evolved.

The essential element of a chain conspiracy—allowing persons unknown to each other and never before in contact to be jointly prosecuted as co-conspirators—is interdependence. The scheme which is the object of the conspiracy must depend on the successful operation of each link in the chain. "An individual associating himself with a 'chain' conspiracy knows that it has a 'scope' and that for its success it requires an organization wider than may be disclosed by his personal participation". * * *

3. *Limits of the Chain Conspiracy Rationale:* The rationale of *Blumenthal* applies only insofar as the alleged agreement has "a common end or single unified purpose." Generally, where the government has shown that a number of otherwise diverse activities were performed to achieve a single goal, courts have been willing to find a single conspiracy. This "common objective" test has most often been used to connect the many facets of drug importation and distribution schemes. The rationale falls apart, however, where the remote members of the alleged conspiracy are not truly interdependent or where the various activities sought to be tied together cannot reasonably be said to constitute a unified scheme. * * *

Applying pre-RICO conspiracy concepts to the facts of this case, we doubt that a single conspiracy could be demonstrated. Foster had no contact with Delph and Taylor during the life of the alleged conspiracy. Delph and Taylor, so far as the evidence revealed, had no contact with Recea Hawkins. The activities allegedly embraced by the illegal agreement in this case are simply too diverse to be tied together on the theory that participation in one activity necessarily implied awareness of others. Even viewing the "common objective" of the conspiracy as the raising of revenue through criminal activity, we could not say, for example, that

---

l. See Note 4, p. 758 supra.

Foster, when he helped to conceal stolen meat, had to know that J.C. was selling drugs to persons unknown to Foster, or that Delph and Taylor, when they furnished counterfeit titles to a car theft ring, had to know that the man supplying the titles was also stealing goods out of interstate commerce. The enterprise involved in this case probably could not have been successfully prosecuted as a single conspiracy under the general federal conspiracy statute, 18 U.S.C. § 371.

B. *RICO to the Rescue: The Enterprise Conspiracy*

In enacting RICO, Congress found that "organized crime continues to grow" in part "because the sanctions and remedies available to the Government are unnecessarily limited in scope and impact." Thus, one of the express purposes of the Act was "to seek the eradication of organized crime ... by establishing new penal prohibitions, and by providing enhanced sanctions and new remedies to deal with the unlawful activities of those engaged in organized crime." Pub.L. 91–452, § 1, 84 Stat. 922 (1970). Against this background, we are convinced that, through RICO, Congress intended to authorize the single prosecution of a multi-faceted, diversified conspiracy by replacing the inadequate "wheel" and "chain" rationales with a new statutory concept: the enterprise.

To achieve this result, Congress acted against the backdrop of hornbook conspiracy law. Under the general federal conspiracy statute,

> the precise nature and extent of the conspiracy must be determined by reference to the agreement which embraces and defines its objects. Whether the object of a single agreement is to commit one or many crimes, it is in either case that agreement which constitutes the conspiracy which the statute punishes. *Braverman v. United States,* 317 U.S. 49, 53, 63 S.Ct. 99, 102, 87 L.Ed. 23 (1942).

In the context of organized crime, this principle inhibited mass prosecutions because a single agreement or "common objective" cannot be inferred from the commission of highly diverse crimes by apparently unrelated individuals. RICO helps to eliminate this problem by creating a substantive offense which ties together these diverse parties and crimes. Thus, the object of a RICO conspiracy is to violate a substantive RICO provision—here, to conduct or participate in the affairs of an enterprise through a pattern of racketeering activity—and not merely to commit each of the predicate crimes necessary to demonstrate a pattern of racketeering activity. The gravamen of the conspiracy charge in this case is not that each defendant agreed to commit arson, to steal goods from interstate commerce, to obstruct justice, and to sell narcotics; rather, it is that each agreed to participate, directly and indirectly, in the affairs of the enterprise by committing two or more predicate crimes. Under the statute, it is irrelevant that each defendant participated in the enterprise's affairs through different, even unrelated crimes, so long as we may reasonably infer that each crime was intended to further the enterprise's affairs. To find a single conspiracy, we still must look for agreement on an overall objective. What Congress did was to define that objective through the substantive provisions of the Act.

C. Constitutional Considerations

The "enterprise conspiracy" is a legislative innovation in the realm of individual liability for group crime. We need to consider whether this innovation comports with the fundamental demand of due process that guilt remain "individual and personal." *Kotteakos, supra,* 328 U.S. at 772, 66 S.Ct. at 1252.

The substantive proscriptions of the RICO statute apply to insiders *and outsiders*—those merely "associated with" an enterprise—who participate directly *and indirectly* in the enterprise's affairs through a pattern of racketeering activity. 18 U.S.C. § 1962(c). Thus, the RICO net is woven tightly to trap even the smallest fish, those peripherally involved with the enterprise. This effect is enhanced by principles of conspiracy law also developed to facilitate prosecution of conspirators at all levels. Direct evidence of agreement is unnecessary * * *. Additionally, once the conspiracy has been established, the government need show only "slight evidence" that a particular person was a member of the conspiracy. * * *

Undeniably, then, under the RICO conspiracy provision, remote associates of an enterprise may be convicted as conspirators on the basis of purely circumstantial evidence. We cannot say, however, that this section of the statute demands inferences that cannot reasonably be drawn from circumstantial evidence or that it otherwise offends the rule that guilt be individual and personal. The Act does not authorize that individuals "be tried *en masse* for the conglomeration of distinct and separate offenses committed by others". Nor does it punish mere association with conspirators or knowledge of illegal activity; its proscriptions are directed against conduct, not status. To be convicted as a member of an enterprise conspiracy, an individual, by his words or actions, must have objectively manifested an agreement to participate, directly or indirectly, in the affairs of an enterprise *through the commission of two or more predicate crimes.* One whose agreement with the members of an enterprise did not include this vital element cannot be convicted under the Act. Where, as here, the evidence establishes that each defendant, over a period of years, committed several acts of racketeering activity in furtherance of the enterprise's affairs, the inference of an agreement to do so is unmistakable.

It is well established that "[t]he government is not required to prove that a conspirator had full knowledge of all the details of the conspiracy; knowledge of the essential nature of the plan is sufficient." * * *

In the instant case, it is clear that "the essential nature of the plan" was to associate for the purpose of making money from repeated criminal activity. Defendant Foster, for example, hired J.C. Hawkins to commit arson, helped him to conceal large quantities of meat and shirts stolen from interstate commerce, and bought a stolen forklift from him.

It would be "a perversion of natural thought and of natural language" to deny that these facts give rise to the inference that Foster knew he was directly involved in an enterprise whose purpose was to profit from crime. As we noted in *United States v. Gonzalez,* 491 F.2d 1202, 1206 (5th Cir.1974), "persons so associating and forming organizations for furthering such illicit purposes do not normally conceive of the association as engaging in one unlawful transaction and then disbanding. Rather the nature of such organizations seems to be an ongoing operation ..." Foster also had to know that the enterprise was bigger than his role in it, and that others unknown to him were participating in its affairs. He may have been unaware that others who had agreed to participate in the enterprise's affairs did so by selling drugs and murdering a key witness. That, however, is irrelevant to his own liability, for he is charged with agreeing *to participate* in the enterprise through his own crimes, not with agreeing *to commit* each of the crimes through which the overall affairs of the enterprise were conducted. We perceive in this no significant extension of a co-conspirator's liability. When a person "embarks upon a criminal venture of indefinite outline, he takes his chances as to its content and membership, so be it that they fall within the common purposes as he understands them."

Our society disdains mass prosecutions because we abhor the totalitarian doctrine of mass guilt. We nevertheless punish conspiracy as a distinct offense because we recognize that collective action toward an illegal end involves a greater risk to society than individual action toward the same end. That risk is greatly compounded when the conspirators contemplate not a single crime but a career of crime. "There are times when of necessity, because of the nature and scope of the particular federation, large numbers of persons taking part must be tried together or perhaps not at all.... When many conspire, they invite mass trial by their conduct." *Kotteakos, supra,* 328 U.S. at 773, 66 S.Ct. at 1252.

We do not lightly dismiss the fact that under this statute four defendants who did not commit murder have been forced to stand trial jointly with, and as confederates of, two others who did. Prejudice inheres in such a trial; great Neptune's ocean could not purge its taint. But the Constitution does not guarantee a trial free from the prejudice that inevitably accompanies any charge of heinous group crime; it demands only that the potential for transference of guilt be minimized to the extent possible under the circumstances in order "to individualize each defendant in his relation to the mass." The RICO statute does not offend this principle. Congress, in a proper exercise of its legislative power, has decided that murder, like thefts from interstate commerce and the counterfeiting of securities, qualifies as racketeering activity. This, of course, ups the ante for RICO violators who personally would not contemplate taking a human life. Whether there is a moral imbalance in the equation of thieves and counterfeiters with murderers is a question whose answer lies in the halls of Congress, not in the judicial conscience. * * *

[The court proceeded to uphold the RICO conspiracy convictions of Delph, Foster, Recea Hawkins, J.C. Hawkins, and Taylor.]

As to James Elliott: The evidence relevant to James Elliott as we view the record, was not sufficient to permit the jury to conclude that he conspired with the other five defendants to violate the RICO statute. Accordingly, his conviction * * * must be reversed. * * *

Viewed in a light most favorable to the government, the evidence against Elliott proved the following:

(1) Early in the spring of 1971, Joe Fuchs gave Elliott a bottle of 500 amphetamine capsules without a prescription.

(2) Shortly thereafter, Elliott negotiated a deal with Fuchs for Joe Breland to build an enclosed porch and for Fuchs to repay Elliott and Breland with amphetamine pills. During the next year, Fuchs delivered the pills in installments of 400.

(3) In April, 1972, Elliott, apparently as a favor for J.C., either sold or gave to Fuchs a 50 pound piece of stolen Hormel meat.

(4) In May, 1973, Elliott, serving as a juror in the trial of Rudolph Flanders for possession of meat from the same stolen shipment, held out for acquittal, causing a mistrial. No evidence was presented that Elliott had been contacted in advance about how he would vote in the Flanders case, although J.C. had told others that he felt Elliott would cooperate.

(5) In January, 1976, Elliott encouraged Fuchs to lie to a federal grand jury about how he acquired the stolen meat given to him by Elliott in 1972.

This evidence could not be taken to support, to the exclusion of all other reasonable hypotheses, a conclusion by the jury that Elliott agreed to participate, directly or indirectly, in the affairs of an enterprise through a pattern of racketeering activity. At best, this evidence discloses that Elliott used a close friend, Joe Fuchs, as a personal source of amphetamines and that he became peripherally involved in a stolen meat deal, an involvement he later attempted to conceal. The government failed to prove that Elliott's amphetamine transactions with Fuchs were in any way connected with the affairs of the enterprise. The Hormel meat, on the other hand, undeniably was acquired as a result of enterprise activity, but Elliott's cooperation with J.C. Hawkins in disposing of a small portion of the meat is insufficient to prove beyond a reasonable doubt that Elliott knowingly and intentionally joined the broad conspiracy to violate RICO. Elliott's acts are equally consistent with the hypothesis that he conspired with J.C. and Fuchs for the limited purpose of aiding in the distribution of stolen meat, an offense with which he was not charged in this case. Under this hypothesis, Elliott agreed to participate in the affairs of the enterprise, but not through a *pattern* of racketeering activity, hence, not in violation of the Act. Similarly, Elliott's two subsequent attempts to cover up the facts in the Hormel meat case are subject to two interpretations: (1) as possible overt acts in furtherance of an agreement to participate in the enterprise's affairs through a pattern of racketeering activity, or (2) as efforts at concealment undertaken after the object of his more limited conspiracy with J.C. and Fuchs had been accomplished, on the theory that "every conspiracy will inevitably be followed by actions taken to cover the conspirators' traces." To allow these predictable acts of concealment to be construed as independent evidence that Elliott agreed to conduct a pattern of racketeering activity would unjustifiably broaden the already pervasive scope of the RICO statute. We hold, then, that the more reasonable conclusion dictated by these facts is that, while Elliott may have conspired to distribute stolen meat, the jury could not reasonably conclude that he conspired to violate RICO. * * *

Notes and Questions

1. Did Congress intend, as *Elliott* suggests, to permit RICO conspiracy convictions that are barred under general conspiracy doctrine? The Fifth Circuit reconsidered the question in United States v. Sutherland, 656 F.2d 1181 (5th Cir.1981), in which three defendants—Sutherland, Walker and Maynard—were indicted under RICO Section 1962, subsection (d), for conspiracy to violate subsection (c).

The indictment charged that the defendants agreed that Walker and Maynard would collect traffic tickets from their friends and associates, along with the statutory fine plus a small premium ($10); they would deliver the tickets to Sutherland, a judge of the Municipal Court of El Paso, who would have the cases transferred to his docket and then favorably dispose of them; and that the money collected would be split between Sutherland and whichever other defendant delivered the ticket. As alleged, the conspiracy consisted of an agreement to associate with and to participate in the conduct of an enterprise (the Municipal Court of the City of El Paso) through a pattern of racketeering activity (bribery of a state official, in violation of state law).

The government conceded on appeal that it failed to prove that a single agreement existed. Rather, it established two bribery conspiracies, one between Sutherland and Walker and a second between Sutherland and Maynard. The government did not show that either bribery scheme was dependent on, or benefitted from, the other, nor did it prove that Walker or Maynard knew, or should have known, of the other.

The *Sutherland* court explained the government's theory of the RICO prosecution and discussed the meaning of *Elliott:*

> The government does not defend its joint trial in this case on the basis of traditional conspiracy law, i.e., by arguing either that the evidence connected the spokes of a wheel conspiracy by common knowledge or agreement, or that the evidence demonstrates a chain conspiracy. Instead, the government argues that despite the apparent relevance to this case of the traditional multiple conspiracy doctrine, the defendants were properly tried together for a single "enterprise conspiracy" under RICO. The government contends, in brief, that a single conspiracy to violate a substantive RICO provision may be comprised of a pattern of agreements that absent RICO would constitute multiple conspiracies. The government contends that this is so even where, as

here, there is no agreement of any kind between the members of the two separate conspiracies. According to the government, these otherwise multiple conspiracies are tied together by the RICO "enterprise:" so long as the object of each conspiracy is participation in the same enterprise in violation of RICO, it matters not that the different conspiracies are otherwise unrelated. Thus, the government argues that it need not demonstrate any connection between Walker and Maynard because the two conspiracies at issue each involved the same RICO enterprise—the Municipal Court of the City of El Paso.

For this proposition the government relies on *United States v. Elliott.* * * *

Read out of context, without attention to the facts of the case or to the court's rationale, *Elliott* does seem to support the government's position, i.e., that the defendants' participation in the same RICO enterprise is enough to tie otherwise multiple conspiracies together even where, as here, there is no agreement of any kind between the members of the two separate conspiracies. Indeed, *Elliott* has been thus read by some courts and commentators (and, as so read, has been uniformly criticized). * * *

Elliott does indeed hold that on the facts of that case a series of agreements that under pre-RICO law would constitute multiple conspiracies could under RICO be tried as a single "enterprise" conspiracy. But the language of *Elliott* explains that what ties these conspiracies together is not the mere fact that they involve the same enterprise, but is instead—as in any other conspiracy—an "agreement on an overall objective." What RICO does is to provide a new criminal objective by defining a new substantive crime. In *Elliott,* as here, that crime consists of participation in an enterprise through a pattern of racketeering activity. The defendants in *Elliott* could not have been tried on a single conspiracy count under pre-RICO law because the defendants had not agreed to commit any particular crime. They were properly tried together under RICO only because the evidence established an agreement to commit a substantive RICO offense, i.e., an agreement to participate in an enterprise through a pattern of racketeering activity.

To be sure, the government did not prove in *Elliott* that each of the conspirators had explicitly agreed with all of the others to violate the substantive RICO provision at issue. However, the government did prove that, as in a traditional "chain" conspiracy, the nature of the scheme was such that each defendant must necessarily have known that others were also conspiring to participate in the same enterprise through a pattern of racketeering activity. We found the facts sufficient to demonstrate that the defendants knew they were "directly involved in an enterprise whose purpose was to profit from crime," and that each knew "that the enterprise was bigger than his role in it, and that others unknown to him were participating in its affairs." The agreement among all of the defendants in *Elliott* was an implicit one, but it was an agreement nonetheless.

* * * *Elliott* does not stand for the proposition that multiple conspiracies may be tried on a single "enterprise conspiracy" count under

RICO merely because the various conspiracies involve the same enterprise. What *Elliott* does state is two-fold: (1) a pattern of agreements that absent RICO would constitute multiple conspiracies may be joined under a single RICO conspiracy count if the defendants have agreed to commit a substantive RICO offense; and (2) such an agreement to violate RICO may, as in the case of a traditional "chain" or "wheel" conspiracy, be established on circumstantial evidence, i.e., evidence that the nature of the conspiracy is such that each defendant must necessarily have known that others were also conspiring to violate RICO.

Id. at 1191–94.

Chapter 11

LIABILITY FOR THE CONDUCT OF ANOTHER

A. ACCOMPLICE LIABILITY

1. GENERAL PRINCIPLES

a. *Common Law Terminology and Its Significance*

STATE v. WARD

Court of Appeals of Maryland, 1978.
284 Md. 189, 396 A.2d 1041.

ORTH, JUDGE.

With the common law of England * * * came the doctrine of accessoryship applicable to felonies. Although the common law may be changed by legislative act or judicial decision, the doctrine has not been altered in this jurisdiction. Maryland is one of the few, if not the only state, which has retained this doctrine in virtually the same form as it existed at the time of William Blackstone in the 18th century, and it represents the law of Maryland at the present time.

Accompanying the common law doctrine across the Atlantic were certain highly technical procedural rules, not altogether logical, which had developed from the distinction between principals and accessories before the fact. These rules operate to the advantage of the accused and the detriment of the prosecution, for they "tended to shield accessories from punishment notwithstanding overwhelming evidence of their criminal assistance." W. LaFave & A. Scott, Handbook on Criminal Law § 63, pp. 498–499. * * *

"In the field of felony the common law divided guilty parties into principals and accessories." Principals came to be classified as in the first degree (perpetrators) or in the second degree (abettors) and accessories as before the fact (inciters) or after the fact (criminal protectors).[13]

---

13. "According to the ancient analysis only the actual perpetrator of the felonious deed was a principal. Other guilty parties were called 'accessories', and to distinguish

A *principal in the first degree* is one who actually commits a crime, either by his own hand, or by an inanimate agency, or by an innocent human agent. A *principal in the second degree* is one who is guilty of felony by reason of having aided, counseled, commanded or encouraged the commission thereof in his presence, either actual or constructive. An *accessory before the fact* is one who is guilty of felony by reason of having aided, counseled, commanded or encouraged the commission thereof, without having been present either actually or constructively at the moment of perpetration. An *accessory after the fact* is one who, with knowledge of the other's guilt, renders assistance to a felon in the effort to hinder his detection, arrest, trial or punishment. * * *

At the common law the principal in the second degree may be tried and convicted prior to the trial of the principal in the first degree, or even after the latter has been tried and acquitted. Furthermore, a principal in the second degree may be convicted of a higher crime or a lower crime than the principal in the first degree. With respect to accessories, however, the common law took a different path. An accessory cannot be tried, without his consent, before the principal.[16] And an accessory could not be convicted of a higher crime than his principal. * * *

Notes and Questions

1. Two additional felony principal-accessory distinctions, besides those mentioned in *Ward,* developed in the common law era. First, an accessory could only be prosecuted in the jurisdiction in which the accessorial acts took place, rather than where the crime occurred. No similar rule applied to principals in the second degree. Second, strict rules of pleading and proof

among these with reference to time and place they were divided into three classes: (1) accessories before the fact, (2) accessories at the fact, and (3) accessories after the fact. At a relatively early time the party who was originally considered an accessory at the fact ceased to be classed in the accessorial group and was labeled a principal. To distinguish him from the actual perpetrator of the crime he was called a principal in the second degree. Thereafter, in felony cases there were two kinds of principals, first degree and second degree, and two kinds of accessories, before the fact and after the fact." Perkins, Criminal Law 643 (2d ed. 1969).

"There is some authority for using the word 'accomplice' to include all principals and all accessories, but the preferred usage is to include all principals and accessories before the fact, but to exclude accessories after the fact." *Id.* at 648. * * *

16. Even when the accessory waives the right, and may be tried before the principal, if he is convicted it is necessary to respite judgment until the trial of the principal

because a subsequent acquittal of the latter would annul this conviction.

The principal and the accessory may be tried jointly, unless the accessory is entitled to a severance, but if they are tried together the trier of fact must first inquire into the guilt of the principal, and, if it finds him not guilty, the accessory must be acquitted. Only upon finding the principal guilty may the trier of fact consider whether the accessory is guilty. An acquittal of the principal, of course, bars a subsequent trial of the accessory. Professor Perkins finds this aspect of the principal-accessory concept to be "quite absurd." He points out: "Anything which prevents conviction of the principal makes impossible the conviction of the accessory. Hence, if the principal is never apprehended, or if before the moment of conviction he should die or be pardoned, the accessory must go free although his guilt may be well known and easy to prove. Furthermore, if both are convicted in due course, but the conviction of the principal is thereafter reversed, the conviction of the accessory cannot stand." [Perkins] at 673.

applied: a defendant charged as an accessory could not be convicted as a principal, and vice versa. These technicalities were avoided in misdemeanor and treason prosecutions, because all parties to such crimes were denominated as principals.

Why did common law judges formulate and apply the technical rules described in *Ward* and this Note? According to Professor Perkins, the courts were satisfied with the relatively minor penalties imposed for misdemeanors, and they considered death an appropriate punishment for all parties to treason, but they did not believe that all participants in other felonies should be executed, as was then required. As a consequence, they devised intricate rules to shield some parties, primarily accessories, from conviction. Rollin M. Perkins, *Parties to Crime,* 89 U.Pa.L.Rev. 581, 607 (1941).

Most states, by legislation, have expressly abrogated the common law distinction between principals and accessories before the fact. Other states have reached substantially the same outcome by permitting accessories before the fact to be tried and punished without regard to the status of the principal's prosecution. E.g., Model Penal Code § 2.06(7).

In general, an accessory *after* the fact is no longer treated as a party to the crime committed by the principal in the first degree, but rather is subject to prosecution for a separate, lesser offense, such as "hindering apprehension or prosecution." Model Penal Code § 242.3. See Wayne R. LaFave & Austin W. Scott, Jr., Criminal Law § 6.9 (2d ed. 1986).

b. *Theoretical Foundation: Derivative Liability*

Although some early statutes treated accessories "as guilty of a separate substantive offense, * * * this is an undesirable fiction." Rollin M. Perkins, *Parties to Crime,* 89 U.Pa.L.Rev. 581, 587 (1941). An accomplice (i.e., at common law, a principal in the second degree or accessory before the fact) is not guilty of the crime of "aiding and abetting," but is guilty of the substantive offense committed by the perpetrator (the principal in the first degree). Professor Kadish explains:

> [T]he doctrine of complicity (sometimes referred to as the law of aiding and abetting, or accessorial liability) emerges to define the circumstances in which one person (to whom I will refer as the secondary party or actor, accomplice, or accessory) becomes liable for the crime of another (the primary party or actor, or the principal). * * *
>
> The nature of complicity liability follows from the considerations that called it forth. The secondary party's liability is derivative, which is to say, it is incurred by virtue of a violation of law by the primary party to which the secondary party contributed. It is not direct [liability] * * *. One who "aids and abets" [the primary party] to do those acts * * * can be liable for doing so, but not because he has thereby caused the actions of the principal or because the actions of the principal are his acts. His liability must

rest on the violation of law by the principal, the legal consequences of which he incurs because of his own actions.

It is important not to misconstrue derivative liability as imparting vicarious liability. Accomplice liability does not involve imposing liability on one party for the wrongs of another solely because of the relationship between the parties. Liability requires action by the secondary actor * * * that makes it appropriate to blame him for what the primary actor does. The term "derivative" as used here merely means that his liability is dependent on the principal violating the law.

Sanford H. Kadish, *Complicity, Cause and Blame: A Study in the Interpretation of Doctrine,* 73 Cal.L.Rev. 323, 336–37 (1985).

Professor Kadish's explanation of accomplice liability raises three related questions: (1) What makes a person an accomplice, i.e., what does an accomplice do, and with what state of mind, to justify holding her accountable for the actions of the primary party?; (2) In view of the fact accomplices derive their liability from the primary party, are there cases in which it is justifiable to convict a secondary party, although there is no liability to derive from the primary actor, or to convict the accomplice of a more serious offense than may be derived from the principal?; and (3) Under what circumstances, if any, may an accomplice avoid liability despite her participation in criminal activity? The materials in this chapter consider these questions.

2. "ELEMENTS" OF ACCOMPLICE LIABILITY: IN GENERAL

STATE v. HOSELTON

Supreme Court of Appeals of West Virginia, 1988.
179 W.Va. 645, 371 S.E.2d 366.

PER CURIAM:

This case is before the Court upon the appeal of Kevin Wayne Hoselton from his conviction of entering without breaking a vessel, with intent to commit larceny, pursuant to *W.Va.Code,* 61–3–12 [1923].[1] * * *

The accused was charged * * * as a principal in the first degree for either breaking and entering or entering without breaking a storage unit on a docked barge with intent to commit larceny. He was eighteen years old at the time, and was with several friends, each of whom was separately indicted as a principal in the first degree. The accused was convicted of entering without breaking, as charged in the indictment.

---

1. *W.Va.Code,* 61–3–12 [1923] reads, in pertinent part:

If any person shall, at any time, break and enter, or shall enter without breaking, any ... steamboat or other boat or vessel, within the jurisdiction of any county in this State, with intent to commit a felony or any larceny, he shall be deemed guilty of a felony, and, upon conviction, shall be confined in the penitentiary not less than one nor more than ten years....

The only evidence used to link the accused to the crime was his voluntary statement. The pertinent answers given by the accused in his voluntary statement were, as follows:

Q. Were you with some individuals that broke into the barge?

A. Yes, sir.

Q. Once you got to the barges, what happened?

A. We all walked up on that, and I was standing outside there. Mike, he tried to get the big door open, and he couldn't do it.

Q. M[...] A[...]?

A. Yes, sir. And I heard a couple of other people back there—I don't know who it was—trying to get in.

Q. Why couldn't you see them?

A. Because I was standing at the end of the barge there.

Q. Were you keeping a look-out?

A. You could say that. I just didn't want to go down in there.

Q. Do you know who actually gained entry to the barge[?]

A. No, sir, I'm not sure.

Q. Kevin, did you know at the time that you were down there that you all were committing a crime?

A. Yes, I did know that, but—

The items stolen from the storage unit were tools, grease guns, grease and a battery charger. None of these items, or profits on their resale, were given to the accused. In both his statement and his trial testimony, the accused stated that he, standing at one end of the barge, with an obstructed view of the storage unit, was unaware of his friends' intent to steal the items until he heard the opening of the storage unit door. He then walked to the unit and saw his friends handling the goods. He then returned to the other end of the barge and went to an automobile, owned and operated by one of his friends, who remained in the storage facility. His friends returned to the automobile with the goods. The accused did not assist the others in placing the goods in the automobile. He was then immediately driven home.

The accused testified that he and his friends frequently trespassed upon the barge for fishing. * * *

On appeal, the accused contends that the evidence is insufficient to support a conviction for entering with intent to commit larceny. Therefore, the trial judge erred when he denied the accused's motions for acquittal and new trial. * * *

The State contends there was sufficient evidence to establish that the accused was a lookout, therefore, the conviction for breaking and entering as a principal in the first degree should stand.

A lookout is one who is "by prearrangement, keeping watch to avoid interception or detection or to provide warning during the perpetration of the crimes and thereby participating in the offenses charged ..."

This Court has consistently held that lookouts are aiders and abettors, principals in the second degree.

Principals in the second degree are punishable as principals in the first degree. *W.Va.Code,* 61–11–6 [1923].

An aider and abettor, or principal in the second degree must "in some sort associate himself with the venture, that he participate in it as something that he wishes to bring about, that he seek[s] by his action to make it succeed."

> It is well established that in order for a defendant to be convicted as an aider and abettor, and thus a principal in the second degree, the prosecution must demonstrate that he or she shared the criminal intent of the principal in the first degree. * * *

State v. Harper, 365 S.E.2d 69, 74 (1987).[4]

Therefore, if the State establishes evidence that an accused acted as a lookout, it has necessarily established the requisite act and mental state to support a conviction of aiding and abetting. * * *

In this case, the only evidence that suggested the accused was a lookout was his response to the investigating officer's questioning: "Q. Were you a lookout? A. You could say that. I just didn't want to go down there."

In both his voluntary statement and during his testimony at trial, the accused stated that he had no prior knowledge of his friends' intentions to steal anything from the barge. When he heard the door open to the storage unit and saw his friends removing the goods, the accused left the barge and returned to the car. The accused never received any of the stolen property, which was later retrieved by the police from the other defendants. * * *

* * * [T]he accused's response that "[y]ou could say" he was a lookout, standing completely alone, does not establish that the accused was an aider and abettor by participating in, and wishing to bring about the entering with intent to commit larceny.

Viewed in the light most favorable to the prosecution, the State did not prove that the accused was a lookout. * * *

We therefore reverse and set aside the accused's conviction for entering without breaking.

4. *See also* LaFave & Scott, *Substantive Criminal Law,* § 6 (1986) * * * Professor Scott writes:

[i]t is useful to give separate consideration to whether a person has engaged in the requisite acts (or omissions) and to whether he had the requisite mental state. . . . It may generally be said that one is liable as an accomplice to the crime of another if he (a) gave assistance or encouragement or failed to perform a legal duty to prevent it (b) with the intent thereby to promote or facilitate commission of the crime. * * *

Notes and Questions

1. Although "aiding and abetting" is not itself a crime, courts and commentators frequently discuss accomplice liability in terms ordinarily reserved for offenses. For example, the secondary party's assistance is the *"actus reus"* of accomplice liability; the intent to promote or facilitate the commission of the crime is the *"mens rea."*

Subject to exceptions and clarifications considered in the next chapter subsection, the *mens rea* of the accomplice is sometimes described as a "dual intent," i.e., the intent to assist the primary party *and* the intent that the offense charged be committed. State v. Harrison, 178 Conn. 689, 694, 425 A.2d 111, 113 (1979). The *actus reus* of accomplice liability (see subsection 4, infra) can take the form of solicitation of the offense, active assistance in the commission of the crime, encouragement of the offense, or failure to prevent the commission of the crime if the secondary party has the legal duty to make such an effort.

In this regard, look carefully at the structure of Model Penal Code § 2.06, the complicity provision. Subsection (1) provides that a person may be guilty of an offense by his own conduct (direct accountability) and/or "by the conduct of another person for which he is legally accountable" (indirect accountability). Subsection (2) sets out three ways in which indirect accountability may arise. One way—subsection (2)(c)—is to be an "accomplice of such other person in the commission of the offense."

Subsection (3) defines the term "accomplice" for purposes of accountability under subsection (2)(c). Under subsection (3)(a), the required state of mind ("the purpose of promoting or facilitating the commission of the offense") is set out first; the *actus reus* is set out in three alternative subsection ((3)(a)(i)–(iii)).

2. In *Hoselton,* would Kevin have been an accomplice in the commission of the charged offense in the following circumstances? Apply common law doctrine and Model Penal Code § 2.06 (as both are discussed in Note 1).

A. Kevin's friends told him to wait in the car while they entered the barge. They falsely told Kevin (who believed their claims) that they were entering in order to pick up a television set the barge owner borrowed from them.

B. Kevin's friends falsely told him that they had come to the barge "just to fool around." They asked him, and he agreed, to stay in the car and honk if he spotted the police. He spotted a police officer and honked. His friends hurried out of the barge, but were caught before they could escape.

C. Same as (B), except that Kevin knew that his friends intended to steal property from the barge. His friends did not ask him to do anything, but he helped them by honking the horn when the police arrived.

D. Same as (C), except that when he honked the horn, his friends did not hear him and were arrested by the police in the barge.

E. Same as (B), except that his friends told him the truth, i.e., that they had come to steal items from the barge. No police officer arrived, so Kevin did not need to honk the horn.

F. Same as (A), except that Kevin knew what his friends intended to do. While waiting in the car, he observed a telephone nearby, considered calling the police, but declined to do so.

G. Kevin did not know what was going on when his friends entered the barge. Thereafter, they brought some of the stolen goods to the car. Kevin now agreed to serve as a lookout as they returned to the barge to pick up more items they had pulled out of the storage unit. See People v. Escobar, 7 Cal.App.4th 1430, 9 Cal.Rptr.2d 770 (1992).

3. MENS REA

a. "Intent": "Purposely" or Knowingly"?

PEOPLE v. LAURIA

California Court of Appeal, Second District, 1967.
251 Cal.App.2d 471, 59 Cal.Rptr. 628.

[For the opinion in this case, see p. 729 supra.]

Notes and Questions

1. Assume that Lauria had been prosecuted as an accomplice in the acts of prostitution committed by the women who used his answering service. Should guilt be assigned on the basis of knowing assistance, or should accountability as an accomplice require proof that the actor assisted with the purpose of facilitating the commission of the offense(s)? Is there any reason why the law might require *purposive* conduct in conspiracy prosecutions, but convict of the substantive offenses on the basis of *knowledge* under accomplice doctrine, or vice versa?

As with conspiracy law, the purpose-versus-knowledge debate is apparent in the case of accomplice liability. For example, in United States v. Peoni, 100 F.2d 401, 402 (2d Cir.1938), Circuit Judge Learned Hand wrote:

> It will be observed that all [the] definitions [of the terms in the federal accomplice liability statute] have nothing whatever to do with the probability that the forbidden result would follow upon the accessory's conduct; and that they all demand that he in some sort associate himself with the venture, that he participate in it as in something that he wishes to bring about, that he seek by his action to make it succeed. All the words used—even the most colorless, "abet"—carry an implication of purposive attitude towards it.

Another federal court saw the matter differently:

> Guilt as an accessory depends, not on "having a stake" in the outcome of the crime * * * but on aiding and assisting the perpetrators; and those who make a profit by furnishing to criminals, whether by sale or otherwise, the means to carry on their nefarious undertakings aid them just as truly as if they were actual partners with them, having a stake in the fruits of their enterprise. * * * One who sells a gun to another knowing that he is buying it to commit murder, would hardly escape conviction as an accessory to the murder by showing that he received full price for the gun; and no difference in principle can be

drawn between such a case and any other case of a seller who knows that the purchaser intends to use the goods which he is purchasing in the commission of felony.

Backun v. United States, 112 F.2d 635, 637 (4th Cir.1940).

Who is correct? May the answer lie in looking more deeply at the underlying rationale of accomplice liability?

> The theory of the intentionality requirement is not obvious. One possible explanation is social policy; namely, that it would be undesirable to draw the circle of criminal liability any wider. A pall would be cast on ordinary activity if we had to fear criminal liability for what others might do simply because our actions made their acts more probable. This has been the dominant consideration in recent debates over proposals to extend liability to those who know their actions will assist another to commit a crime but who act for reasons other than to further those criminal actions—the supplier of materials, for example, who knows that a buyer plans to use them to commit a crime. The argument that people otherwise lawfully conducting their affairs should not be constrained by fear of liability for what their customers will do has tended to prevail over the argument that it is proper for the criminal law to prohibit conduct that knowingly facilitates the commission of crime. * * *

> These policy considerations, however, may not be the whole story. * * *

> The explanation for the intention requirement must be found elsewhere. It may reside in the notion of agreement as the paradigm mode by which a principal in agency law (the secondary party in the terminology of the criminal law) becomes liable for the acts of another person. The liability of the principal in civil law rests essentially on his consent to be bound by the actions of his agent, whom he vests with authority for this purpose. * * *

> Insofar as manifesting consent to be bound by the acts of another is a general requirement for holding one person liable for the actions of another, the requirement of intention for complicity liability becomes more readily explicable. Obviously, in the context of the criminal law, literal consent to be criminally liable is irrelevant. But by intentionally acting to further the criminal actions of another, the secondary party voluntarily identifies himself with the principal party. The intention to further the acts of another, which creates liability under the criminal law, may be understood as equivalent to manifesting consent to liability under the civil law.

Sanford H. Kadish, *Complicity, Cause and Blame: A Study in the Interpretation of Doctrine,* 73 Cal.L.Rev. 323, 353–55 (1985).

On the rationale of accomplice liability, weigh this observation regarding Professor Kadish's remarks:

> [T]he concept of agency explains a great deal about why we feel justified in punishing an accomplice as if she were the perpetrator. Perhaps, however, our feelings may be described better in terms of "forfeited personal identity." Ordinarily a person is held criminally responsible

for his own actions. However, when an accomplice chooses to become a part of the criminal activity of another, she says in essence, "your acts are my acts," and forfeits her personal identity. We euphemistically * * * impute the actions of the perpetrator to the accomplice by "agency" doctrine; in reality, we demand that she who chooses to aid in a crime [forfeit] her right to be treated as an individual. Thus, * * * distinctions between parties are rendered irrelevant. We pretend the accomplice is no more than an incorporeal shadow.

Joshua Dressler, *Reassessing the Theoretical Underpinnings of Accomplice Liability: New Solutions to an Old Problem,* 37 Hastings L.J. 91, 111 (1985); see People v. Luparello, 187 Cal.App.3d 410, 440, 231 Cal.Rptr. 832, 849 (1986) (invoking the "forfeited personal identity" concept).

2. Suppose that a gun dealer sells a weapon to a person she knows does contract killings for "organized crime." Assuming that knowledge is sufficient to impose liability, is the dealer guilty of *all* the murders committed with the weapon she sold?

3. The *Lauria* court suggested that knowing aid should be sufficient for liability if the offense is serious in nature, but not otherwise. Are there more desirable distinctions? For example, should the law distinguish between assistance motivated by ordinary profit motives (e.g., the gun dealer who sells a gun to someone she knows intends to use the weapon to commit a murder) and similar assistance for non-commercial reasons (e.g., a person who furnishes the gun out of friendship)? If so, who should be held to the higher *mens rea* standard?

Should the law instead devise a sliding scale of accountability, in which the greater the actor's assistance, the less culpable she must be in order to be held responsible for the primary party's actions? For example, if a landlord rents a room to a gambler, he would be guilty of the tenant's illegal gambling activities as long as he acted with knowledge of the tenant's criminal use of the room, whereas the stationer who sells the gambler paper used for recordkeeping would only be accountable if she acted with the purpose of promoting or facilitating the commission of the offense. See United States v. Giovannetti, 919 F.2d 1223, 1227 (7th Cir.1990).

4. *Lawyers as criminal accomplices of their clients.* Lawyers have an ethical duty to represent their clients zealously, but only within the bounds of the law. When does zealous advocacy cross the line to criminal assistance? Consider Nix v. Whiteside, 475 U.S. 157, 160–61, 106 S.Ct. 988, 991, 89 L.Ed.2d 123, 130–31 (1986):

Whiteside was charged with murder * * *. * * * Gary L. Robinson was * * * appointed [to represent him] and immediately began an investigation. Whiteside gave him a statement that he had stabbed [the decedent] Love as the latter "was pulling a pistol from underneath the pillow on the bed." Upon questioning by Robinson, however, Whiteside indicated that he had not actually seen a gun, but that he was convinced that Love had a gun. No pistol was found on the premises; shortly after the police search following the stabbing, which had revealed no weapon, the victim's family had removed all of the victim's possessions from the apartment. Robinson interviewed Whiteside's companions who were present during the stabbing, and none had seen a gun during the incident. Robinson advised Whiteside that the existence of a gun was not necessary to establish the claim of self-defense, and that only a reasonable belief that the victim had a gun nearby was necessary even though no gun was actually present.

Until shortly before trial, Whiteside consistently stated to Robinson that he had not actually seen a gun, but that he was convinced that Love had a gun in his hand. About a week before trial, during preparation for direct examination, Whiteside for the first time told Robinson and his associate Donna Paulsen that he had seen something "metallic" in Love's hand. When asked about this, Whiteside responded:

> "[I]n Howard Cook's case there was a gun. If I don't say I saw a gun, I'm dead."

Robinson told Whiteside that such testimony would be perjury and repeated that it was not necessary to prove that a gun was available but only that Whiteside reasonably believed that he was in danger. On Whiteside's insisting that he would testify that he saw "something metallic" Robinson told him, according to Robinson's testimony:

> "[W]e could not allow him to [testify falsely] because that would be perjury, and as officers of the court we would be suborning perjury if we allowed him to do it; . . . I advised him that if he did do that it would be my duty to advise the Court of what he was doing and that I felt he was committing perjury; also, that I probably would be allowed to attempt to impeach that particular testimony."

Robinson also indicated he would seek to withdraw from the representation if Whiteside insisted on committing perjury.

As a result of Robinson's warnings, Whiteside backed down and testified only that he had "known" that Love had a gun and that he had believed that Love was reaching for a gun when he stabbed him. The jury apparently did not believe Whiteside, as they convicted him of murder.

The Supreme Court approved of Robinson's conduct:

[W]e [have] recognized counsel's duty of loyalty and his "overarching duty to advocate the defendant's cause." Plainly, that duty is limited to legitimate, lawful conduct compatible with the very nature of a trial as a search for truth. Although counsel must take all reasonable lawful means to attain the objectives of the client, counsel is precluded from taking steps or in any way assisting the client in presenting false evidence or otherwise violating the law. This principle has consistently been recognized in most unequivocal terms by expositors of the norms of professional conduct since the first Canons of Professional Ethics were adopted by the American Bar Association in 1908. * * *

* * * The more recent Model Rules of Professional Conduct (1983) * * * admonish attorneys to obey all laws in the course of representing a client:

> "RULE 1.2   Scope of Representation
>
> . . . .

"(d) A lawyer shall not counsel a client to engage, or assist a client, in conduct that the lawyer knows [a] is criminal or fraudulent...." [b]

Id. at 166–68, 106 S.Ct. at 994–95, 89 L.Ed.2d at 134–35.

Suppose that attorney Robinson, as he did, had warned Whiteside not to commit perjury, but further suppose that he had not threatened to report his suspicions to the judge or to withdraw from the case. On these facts, if Robinson had called Whiteside as a witness, and the defendant testified to seeing "something metallic" in Love's hand, would Robinson be guilty of unethical behavior?

Suppose on these hypothetical facts, Whiteside had been acquitted of murder. If he were later charged with perjury, should Robinson be held as an accomplice? In a jurisdiction that permits accomplice liability on the basis of knowledge, is Robinson guilty? Suppose that Robinson, in his defense, explained, "I suspected my client was perjuring himself, but I couldn't know for sure without asking him directly whether he was lying. If I had done that, he would have clammed up and I would have jeopardized the attorney-client relationship." Do you agree with the remark of Judge Friendly, who observed that lawmakers "could not have intended that men holding themselves out as members of [this] ancient profession[ ] should be able to escape criminal liability on a plea of ignorance when they have shut their eyes to what was plainly to be seen * * *"? United States v. Benjamin, 328 F.2d 854, 863 (2d Cir.1964).

Because of their professional responsibilities to their clients, should criminal defense lawyers be "cut some slack" and held to a more lenient standard of accomplice liability? Or, should they be held to a higher standard because they are also officers of the court? In United States v. Cintolo, 818 F.2d 980, 996 (1st Cir.1987), the court observed:

[W]e emphatically reject the notion that a law degree, like some sorcerer's amulet, can ward off the rigors of the criminal law. No spells of this sort are cast by the acceptance of a defendant's retainer. We decline to chip some sort of special exception for lawyers into the brickwork of [the law]. * * * As sworn officers of the court, lawyers should not seek to avail themselves of relaxed rules of conduct. To the exact contrary, they should be held to the very highest standards in promoting the cause of justice. See ABA Model Code of Professional Responsibility EC 1–5 ("A lawyer should maintain high standards of professional conduct and should encourage fellow lawyers to do likewise."); EC 9–6 ("Every lawyer owes a solemn duty to uphold the integrity and honor of his profession; to encourage respect for the law and for the courts and judges thereof; . . . to conduct himself so as to reflect credit on the legal profession and to inspire the confidence, respect, and trust of his clients and of the public").

a. The Scope and Terminology section of the Model Rules provides: " 'Knows' denotes actual knowledge of the fact in question. A person's knowledge may be inferred from circumstances."

b. The rule continues: "[B]ut a lawyer may discuss the legal consequences of any proposed course of conduct with a client and may counsel or assist a client to make a good faith effort to determine the validity, scope, meaning or application of the law."

We have carefully examined the avowed fears of the [bar] * * * that a decision upholding [an attorney's] conviction * * * may * * * somehow chill the criminal defense bar in zealous advocacy on behalf of clients. We find such concerns to be grossly overstated.

b. When Is "Intent" Not Required?

i. *Offenses Not Requiring Intent*

STATE v. FOSTER

Supreme Court of Connecticut, 1987.
202 Conn. 520, 522 A.2d 277.

SANTANIELLO, ASSOCIATE JUDGE.

The defendant, Michael Foster, was convicted in a jury trial of kidnapping in the second degree in violation of General Statutes § 53a–94, assault in the third degree in violation of General Statutes § 53a–61, and being an accessory to criminally negligent homicide in violation of General Statutes §§ 53a–8 and 53a–58. * * * He claims on appeal that the trial court erred in: (1) instructing the jury on the crime of being an accessory to criminally negligent homicide and in denying his post-trial motions for judgment of acquittal and in arrest of judgment; [and] (2) denying his motion for judgment of acquittal on the third count because there was insufficient evidence to support a conviction * * *.

The jury could reasonably have found the following facts. In June, 1982, the defendant was living with his girlfriend and their child in an apartment near the Martin Luther King School in Hartford. At approximately 7:30 p.m. in the evening of June 16, 1982, while walking near the school, the defendant's girlfriend was robbed and raped by a young black male who held a straight-edged razor to her throat. During the one half hour encounter, she observed her attacker's features and later that night described him and the clothes he was wearing to the police. She also described the assailant, with specific identifiable features, to the defendant.

The defendant, who was "bitter" about the attack, purposely went looking for his girlfriend's attacker. On June 22, 1982, the defendant and a friend, Otha Cannon, after visiting with the defendant's girlfriend for a short period of time, went walking in the vicinity where the rape and robbery had occurred. Near the Martin Luther King School, the defendant saw a man he thought matched the description of the assailant. After telling Cannon "[t]his is the guy who raped my lady," the defendant and Cannon confronted the suspected rapist, later identified as William Jack Middleton, in an alleyway next to the school. Upon being approached, Middleton became frightened and denied any involvement in the robbery or rape. He attempted to flee and a fight ensued; the defendant beat Middleton about the face, eye, chest and head with his fist and a blunt instrument, knocking him to the ground. The defendant, desiring to bring his girlfriend to the scene to make an identification, told Middleton to "wait here" while he left to get her.

Although Middleton agreed to wait, the defendant, suspecting that he might flee, gave a knife to Cannon and told him to stay with Middleton to prevent his escape. Thereafter, while waiting for the defendant to return, Middleton, as he was reaching for something in his pocket, apparently charged at Cannon. As Middleton ran toward him, Cannon held out the knife that the defendant had given him and fatally stabbed Middleton. The victim had a straight-edged razor in his pocket which was later identified by the defendant's girlfriend as the one wielded by her assailant during the rape incident. * * *

The defendant first claims that the trial court erred in (1) instructing the jury as to the crime of being an accessory to criminally negligent homicide, and (2) denying his posttrial motions for judgment of acquittal and in arrest of judgment. We disagree.

General Statutes § 53a–8 provides in relevant part that "[a] person, acting with the mental state required for the commission of an offense, who ... intentionally aids another person to engage in conduct which constitutes an offense shall be criminally liable for such conduct ... as if he were the principal offender." We have previously stated that a conviction under § 53a–8 requires proof of a dual intent, i.e., "that the accessory have the intent to *aid* the principal *and* that in so aiding he intend to *commit* the offense with which he is charged."

Citing this "dual intent" requirement, and relying on *State v. Almeda,* 189 Conn. 303, 455 A.2d 1326 (1983), and *State v. Beccia,* 199 Conn. 1, 505 A.2d 683 (1986), cases which held that persons cannot attempt or conspire to commit an offense that requires an unintended result, the defendant argues that a person cannot be convicted as an accessory to criminally negligent homicide. He reasons that because accessorial liability requires an accused, in aiding a principal, to "intend to commit the offense with which he is charged" and because criminally negligent homicide requires that an unintended death occur, the crime of being an accessory to criminally negligent homicide is a logical impossibility in that it would require a defendant, in aiding another, to intend to commit a crime in which an unintended result occurs.

We find the defendant's argument unpersuasive. The defendant's reliance upon *Almeda* and *Beccia,* and the concept of "dual intent," is misplaced. Attempt and conspiratorial liability differ substantially from the liability imposed on an accessory. First, both attempt and conspiracy are offenses in and of themselves, while accessorial liability is not. Attempt is a distinct, inchoate offense and a defendant may be punished for attempting to commit a substantive offense without actually committing the crime. Likewise, conspiracy has been recognized as being a crime distinct from the commission of the substantive offense. * * *

There is, however, no such crime as "being an accessory." The defendant is charged with committing one substantive offense; "[t]he accessory statute merely provides alternate means by which a substantive crime may be committed."

Second, the intent required for attempt or conspiratorial liability is distinguishable from the requisite intent for accessorial liability. * * *

Intentional conduct is defined as conduct "with respect to a result or to conduct described by a statute defining an offense when [a person's] *conscious objective is to cause such a result* or to engage in such conduct." (Emphasis added.) General Statutes § 53a–3(11). Thus, to be guilty of attempt, a defendant's conscious objective must be to cause the result which would constitute the substantive crime. A person cannot attempt to commit a crime which requires that an unintended result occur, such as involuntary manslaughter, because it is logically impossible for one to intend to bring about an unintended result. *State v. Almeda,* supra. Similarly, to be guilty of conspiracy, the defendant, upon entering an agreement, must intend that his conduct achieve the requisite criminal result. When the substantive crime requires an unintended result, a person cannot conspire to commit that crime because it is logically impossible to agree to achieve a specific result unintentionally. *State v. Beccia,* supra.

Contrary to the defendant's assertions, and unlike attempt or conspiratorial liability, accessorial liability does not require that a defendant act with the conscious objective to cause the result described by a statute. Although we have stated that the defendant, in intentionally aiding another, must have the intent to commit the substantive offense[,] this language must be read in context. All the cases which speak of this "dual intent" involve crimes that require a defendant to act with a specific intent to commit the crime. * * * Because the substantive crime with which the person was charged in those cases required that the accessory specifically intend to act or bring about a result, it is logical to state that the accessory, in aiding another, must have "intend[ed] to commit the offense with which he is charged."

Section 53a–8, however, is not limited to cases where the substantive crime requires the specific intent to bring about a result. General Statutes § 53a–8 merely requires that a defendant have the *mental state required for the commission of a crime* while intentionally aiding another. * * * Accordingly, an accessory may be liable in aiding another if he acts intentionally, knowingly, recklessly or with criminal negligence toward the result, depending on the mental state required by the substantive crime. When a crime requires that a person act with criminal negligence, an accessory is liable if he acts "with respect to a result or to a circumstance described by a statute defining an offense when he fails to perceive a substantial and unjustifiable risk that such result will occur or that such circumstance exists." General Statutes § 53a–3(14).

This interpretation is consistent with the underlying principles of accessorial liability. Such liability is designed to punish one who intentionally aids another in the commission of a crime and not one whose innocent acts in fact aid one who commits an offense. * * * Thus, accessorial liability is predicated upon the actor's state of mind at the time of his actions, and whether that state of mind is commensurate to the state of mind required for the commission of the offense. If a person, in intentionally aiding another, acts with the mental culpability required for the commission of a crime—be it "intentional" or "criminally negligent"—he is liable for the commission of that crime.

Moreover, because accessorial liability is not a distinct crime, but only an alternative means by which a substantive crime may be committed, it would be illogical to impose liability on the perpetrator of the crime, while precluding liability for an accessory, even though both possess the mental state required for the commission of the crime. Connecticut "long ago adopted the rule that there is no practical significance in being labeled an 'accessory' or a 'principal' for the purpose of determining criminal responsibility. * * * [14]"

Therefore, a person may be held liable as an accessory to a criminally negligent act if he has the requisite culpable mental state for the commission of the substantive offense, and he intentionally aids another in the crime. For the above reasons, we find that being an accessory to criminally negligent homicide is a cognizable crime under Connecticut law. Accordingly, the trial court did not err either in instructing the jury with respect to the crime or in denying the defendant's post-trial motions.

---

14. Accessorial liability has been addressed by § 2.06 of the Model Penal Code, which states in relevant part:

"Section 2.06. LIABILITY FOR CONDUCT OF ANOTHER; COMPLICITY. * * *

"(3) A person is an accomplice of another person in the commission of an offense if:

"(a) with the purpose of promoting or facilitating the commission of the offense, he

"(i) solicits such other person to commit it, or

"(ii) aids or agrees or attempts to aid such other person in planning or committing it, or

"(iii) having a legal duty to prevent the commission of the offense, fails to make proper effort so to do; or

"(b) his conduct is expressly declared by law to establish his complicity.

"(4) When causing a particular result is an element of an offense, an accomplice in the conduct causing such result is an accomplice in the commission of that offense if he acts with the kind of culpability, if any, with respect to that result that is sufficient for the commission of the offense...."

In discussing the liability of an accessory, when a particular result is an essential element to the commission of a crime, comment 7 of § 2.06 states:

"[S]ubsection (4) makes it clear that complicity in conduct causing a particular criminal result entails accountability for that result so long as the accomplice is personally culpable with respect to the result to the extent demanded by the definition of the crimes. * * *

"The most common situation in which Subsection (4) will become relevant is where unanticipated results occur from conduct for which the actor is responsible under Subsection (3). His liability for unanticipated occurrences rests upon two factors: his complicity in the conduct that caused the result, and his culpability towards the result to the degree required by the law, that makes the result criminal. Accomplice liability in this event is thus assimilated to the liability for the principal actor; the principal actor's liability for unanticipated results, of course, would turn on the extent to which he was reckless or negligent, as required by the law defining the offense, toward the result in question...."

"This formulation combines the policy that accomplices are equally accountable within the range of their complicity with the policies underlying those crimes defined according to results."

The defendant next contends that even if the crime of being an accessory to criminally negligent homicide does exist, there was insufficient evidence to support a verdict of guilty and therefore the trial court erred in denying his motion for judgment of acquittal. We disagree. * * *

From the evidence presented, the jury could reasonably have found that the defendant intentionally had aided Cannon by giving him the knife. Additionally, the jury could reasonably have inferred that the defendant had failed to perceive a substantial and unjustifiable risk that death would occur by handing Cannon the knife to prevent Middleton from escaping. * * * Because the jury could have found the defendant guilty beyond a reasonable doubt if it found the state's evidence credible, the trial court did not err in denying the defendant's motion for judgment of acquittal. * * *

Notes and Questions

1. Not all courts agree with *Foster*. E.g., State v. Etzweiler, 125 N.H. 57, 65, 480 A.2d 870, 874–75 (1984) (applying a complicity statute similar to Model Penal Code § 2.06):

> To satisfy the requirements of [the complicity statute], the State must establish that Etzweiler's acts were designed to aid Bailey in committing negligent homicide. Yet under the negligent homicide statute, Bailey must be unaware of the risk of death that his conduct created. We cannot see how Etzweiler could intentionally aid Bailey in a crime that Bailey was unaware that he was committing. Thus, we hold, as a matter of law, that, in the present context of the Criminal Code, an individual may not be an accomplice to negligent homicide.

Is this reasoning persuasive?

2. *Problem.* Alice informs Bob, a taxicab driver, that she is late for her airplane flight and that "you should drive as fast as necessary to get me to the airport on time. If I make it on time, you will get a very large tip." Is Alice an accomplice in the commission of negligent homicide by Bob, in the following two cases?

A. Bob exceeds the speed limit. As a consequence, he unintentionally strikes Carl's car from behind, causing it to strike a tree, killing Carl.

B. Bob exceeds the speed limit. At one intersection, while speeding, Bob runs through a red light, striking Carl's car, killing Carl.

ii. Natural-and-Probable-Consequences Doctrine

STATE v. LINSCOTT

Supreme Judicial Court of Maine, 1987.
520 A.2d 1067.

SCOLNIK, JUSTICE.

William Linscott appeals from a judgment following a jury-waived trial * * *, convicting him of one count of murder, and one count of robbery. He contends that his conviction of intentional or knowing murder as an accomplice under the accomplice liability statute, 17–A M.R.S.A. § 57(3)(A) (1983), violated his constitutional right to due process of law in that he lacked the requisite intent to commit murder. * * *

The facts are not in dispute. On December 12, 1984, the defendant, then unemployed, and two other men—the defendant's step-brother, Phillip Willey, and Jeffrey Colby—drove * * * to the house of a friend, Joel Fuller. Fuller, with a sawed-off shotgun in his possession, joined the others. The defendant drove to the residence of Larry Ackley, where Fuller obtained 12–gauge shotgun shells.

Later that evening, Fuller suggested that the four men drive to the house of a reputed cocaine dealer, Norman Grenier * * *, take Grenier by surprise, and rob him. The defendant agreed to the plan, reasoning that Grenier, being a reputed drug dealer, would be extremely reluctant to call the police and request they conduct a robbery investigation that might result in the discovery of narcotics in his possession. Fuller stated that Grenier had purchased two kilograms of cocaine that day, and that Grenier had been seen with $50,000 in cash. Fuller guaranteed the defendant $10,000 as his share of the proceeds of the robbery.

The four drove up to Grenier's house, which was situated in a heavily wooded rural area on a dead-end road in Swanville. The defendant and Fuller left the car and approached the house. The defendant carried a hunting knife and switchblade, and Fuller was armed with the shotgun. * * *

The defendant and Fuller walked around to the back of Grenier's house. At that time, Grenier and his girlfriend were watching television in their living room. The defendant and Fuller intended to break in the back door in order to place themselves between Grenier and the bedroom, where they believed Grenier kept a loaded shotgun. Because the back door was blocked by snow, the two men walked around to the front of the house. Under their revised plan the defendant was to break the living room picture window whereupon Fuller would show his shotgun to Grenier, who presumably would be dissuaded from offering any resistance.

The defendant subsequently broke the living room window with his body without otherwise physically entering the house. Fuller immediately fired a shot through the broken window, hitting Grenier in the chest. Fuller left through the broken window after having removed about $1,300 from Grenier's pants pocket, later returning to the house to retrieve an empty shotgun casing. * * *

* * * At a jury-waived trial, * * * the defendant testified that he knew Fuller to be a hunter and that it was not unusual for Fuller to carry a firearm with him, even at night. He nevertheless stated that he had no knowledge of any reputation for violence that Fuller may have had. The defendant further testified that he had no intention of causing anyone's death in the course of the robbery.

At the completion of the trial * * * the trial justice found the defendant guilty of robbery and, on a theory of accomplice liability, found him guilty of murder. The court specifically found that the defendant possessed the intent to commit the crime of robbery, that Fuller intentionally or at least knowingly caused the death of Grenier, and that this murder was a reasonably foreseeable consequence of the defendant's participation in the robbery. However, the court also found that the defendant did not intend to kill Grenier, and that the defendant probably would not have participated in the robbery had he believed that Grenier would be killed in the course of the enterprise.

The sole issue raised on appeal is whether the defendant's conviction pursuant to the second sentence of subsection 3–A of the accomplice liability statute, 17–A M.R.S.A. § 57 (1983),[1] unconstitutionally violates his right to due process under Article I, section 6–A of the Maine Constitution and the Fourteenth Amendment of the United States Constitution. "[T]he Due Process Clause protects the accused against conviction except upon proof beyond a reasonable doubt of every fact necessary to constitute the crime with which he is charged." *In re Winship*, 397 U.S. 358, 364, 90 S.Ct. 1068, 1072, 25 L.Ed.2d 368 (1970). The defendant contends that the accomplice liability statute impermissibly allows the State to find him guilty of murder, which requires proof beyond a reasonable doubt that the murder was committed either intentionally or knowingly, without having to prove either of these two culpable mental states. Instead, the defendant argues, the accomplice liability statute permits the State to employ only a mere negligence standard in convicting him of murder in violation of his right to due process. We find the defendant's argument to be without merit.

The second sentence of section 57(3)(A) endorses the "foreseeable consequence" rule of accomplice liability. *See State v. Goodall*, 407 A.2d 268, 278 (Me.1979).[2] In that case we stated that

> [t]he history of the statute demonstrates that the legislature indeed intended to impose liability upon accomplices for those crimes that were the reasonably foreseeable consequence of their criminal enterprise, *notwithstanding an absence on their part of the same culpability required for conviction as a principal to the crime.*

1. 17–A M.R.S.A. § 57(3)(A) (1983) provides:

3. A person is an accomplice of another person in the commission of a crime if:

A. With the intent of promoting or facilitating the commission of the crime, he solicits such other person to commit the crime, or aids or agrees to aid or attempts to aid such other person in planning or committing the crime. *A person is an accomplice under this subsection to any crime the commission of which was a reasonably foreseeable consequence of his conduct* ...

(Emphasis added).

2. The "foreseeable consequence" or "natural and probable consequence" rule in complicity law has been stated as follows: "an accessory is liable for any criminal act which in the ordinary course of things was the natural or probable consequence of the crime that he advised or commanded, although such consequence may not have been intended by him." 22 C.J.S. *Criminal Law* § 92 (1961) (footnote omitted). * * *

Id. (emphasis added). Accordingly, we have stated that section 57(3)(A) is to be interpreted as follows: Under the first sentence of that section, which is to be read independently of the second sentence,

> liability for a "primary crime" ... [here, robbery] is established by proof that the actor intended to promote or facilitate that crime. Under the second sentence, liability for any "secondary crime" ... [here, murder] that may have been committed by the principal is established upon a two-fold showing: (a) that the actor intended to promote the *primary crime,* and (b) that the commission of the secondary crime was a "foreseeable consequence" of the actor's participation in the primary crime.

Id. at 277–278. We have consistently upheld this interpretation of section 57(3)(A). We discern no compelling reason to depart from this construction of the statute.

Furthermore, the foreseeable consequence rule as stated in Section 57(3)(A) merely carries over the objective standards of accomplice liability as used in the common law. Thus, a rule allowing for a murder conviction under a theory of accomplice liability based upon an *objective* standard, despite the absence of evidence that the defendant possessed the culpable *subjective* mental state that constitutes an element of the crime of murder, does not represent a departure from prior Maine law. * * *

We also do not find fundamentally unfair or disproportionate the grading scheme for sentencing purposes * * * [of] murder premised on a theory of accomplice liability * * *. The potential penalty of life imprisonment for murder under a theory of accomplice liability based on an objective standard "does not denote such punitive severity as to shock the conscience of the public, nor our own respective or collective sense of fairness." * * *

For the foregoing reasons, we find no constitutional defect in this statutory provision, nor any fundamental unfairness in its operation. * * *

Notes and Questions

1. People v. Woods, 8 Cal.App.4th 1570, 1586, 11 Cal.Rptr.2d 231, 239 (1992):

> To determine a defendant's guilt or innocence based on aider and abettor liability, a jury must employ a four-part analysis (assuming the aider and abettor is charged with the crime originally contemplated by the perpetrator as well as other crimes which allegedly were reasonably foreseeable consequences of the original crime). Although the perpetrator and the aider and abettor need not be tried jointly, the jury first must determine the crimes and degrees of crimes originally contemplated and committed, if any, by the perpetrator. Next, the jury must decide whether the aider and abettor knew of the perpetrator's intent to commit the originally contemplated criminal acts and whether the aider and abettor intended to encourage or facilitate the commission of those

acts. In other words, the jury must determine if the aider and abettor is liable vicariously for, i.e., guilty of, the crime or crimes originally contemplated. Then the jury must determine whether other crimes and degrees of crimes charged against the aider and abettor were committed by the perpetrator. If so, the jury must determine whether those crimes, although not necessarily contemplated at the outset, were reasonably foreseeable consequences of the original criminal acts encouraged or facilitated by the aider and abettor. In other words, the jury must determine if the aider and abettor is liable vicariously for, i.e., guilty of, other crimes beyond those contemplated originally.

2. Suppose that Joshua intentionally assists Marge, a life-long pacifist, to commit petty larceny in a department store, by driving her to the scene. To Joshua's utter surprise, Marge walks up to a clerk, pulls a knife, and orders him to hand over a bottle of cologne in the clerk's hand, which he does. Of what offense is Marge guilty? Of what offense, if any, is Joshua guilty? In this regard, consider *Woods*, id. at 1587–88, 11 Cal.Rptr.2d at 240:

> The analysis of aider and abettor liability would be relatively simple if the prosecution were required to charge not only the greatest crime committed by the perpetrator but also every necessarily included crime * * *. However, the prosecution need not file charges for every necessarily included offense. * * *

> Therefore, in determining aider and abettor liability for crimes of the perpetrator beyond the act originally contemplated, the jury must be permitted to consider uncharged, necessarily included offenses where the facts would support a determination that the greater crime was not a reasonably foreseeable consequence but the lesser offense was such a consequence.

3. In State v. Fitch, 600 A.2d 826 (Me.1991), the defendant was an accomplice in a robbery, during which a death ensued. The trial court instructed the jury with respect to the defendant's liability for murder in accordance with Maine's complicity statute (see footnote 1 in *Linscott*). During deliberations, the jury requested re-instruction on the subject. The trial judge, over the defendant's objection, explained to the jury that it could convict the defendant of murder if, "[d]uring the course of defendant's conduct in the participation of the offense of robbery, [it] was * * * a reasonably foreseeable consequence of that conduct that the murder of [the victim] could occur." Is the latter instruction correct?

iii. Attendant Circumstances

BOWELL v. STATE

Court of Appeals of Alaska, 1986.
728 P.2d 1220.

SINGLETON, JUDGE * * *

[Bowell was convicted as an accomplice of James Thomas in the commission of first degree sexual assault of the victim, B.S., in violation of Alaska Statute 11.41.410(a)(1), which provided that a person is guilty of sexual assault if he "engages in sexual penetration with [sic] another person without consent of that person." On appeal, Bowell attacked his conviction on the ground that the state's accomplice statute, AS 11.16.-110, was constitutionally defective for failing to require a culpable mental state.]

Bowell reasons that AS 11.16.110(2)(B) creates a legal accountability for a person who aids or abets another person in the commission of a criminal offense, but is deficient in failing to provide a "mental element" for "aiding or abetting."

Alaska Statute 11.16.110 provides as follows:

> *Legal accountability based upon the conduct of another: Complicity.*
>
> A person is legally accountable for the conduct of another constituting an offense if
>
> ... (2) with intent to promote or facilitate the commission of the offense, the person
>
> ... (B) aids or abets the other in planning or committing the offense.

The state counters that Bowell has misread the statute, and that the introductory language to AS 11.16.110(2)(B), "with intent to promote or facilitate the commission of the offense" supplies the *mens rea* for accomplice liability, while "aids or abets" describes the *actus reus* of the offense. The state's position finds support * * * in the Commentary to the Model Penal Code provision from which our statute is derived, A.L.I., *Model Penal Code and Commentaries* Part I § 2.06 (1985). The Commentary states in relevant part:

> Subsection (3)(a) requires that the actor have the purpose of promoting or facilitating the commission of the offense, i.e., that he have as his conscious objective the bringing about of conduct that the Code has declared to be criminal. This is not to say that he must know of the criminality of the conduct; there is no more reason here to require knowledge of the criminal law than there is with the principal actor. But he must have the purpose to promote or facilitate the particular conduct that forms the basis for the charge, and thus he will not be liable for conduct that does not fall within this purpose.

In summary, in order to be liable as an accomplice for Thomas' sexual assault on B.S., it was necessary that the state prove beyond a reasonable doubt that Bowell was aware that Thomas intended to have sexual intercourse with B.S. and, intending to facilitate Thomas in achieving his goal, performed some act of aid or encouragement. While the statute interpreted in this way will adequately provide both the *mens rea* and an *actus reus* for most offenses, it does present certain difficulties in connection with crimes such as first-degree sexual assault, which include the circumstances surrounding an offender's conduct as an element of the offense. The Commentary to the Model Penal Code discusses this problem as follows:

> There is a deliberate ambiguity as to whether the purpose requirement [the requirement that in order to be guilty as an accomplice, the actor have the purpose of promoting or facilitating the commission of the offense] extends to circumstance elements of the contemplated offense or whether, as in the case of attempts, the policy of the substantive offense on this point should control. The reasoning is the same as in the case of conspiracy, which is set forth in some detail in Section 5.03 Comment 2(c)(ii).[c] The result, therefore, is that the actor must have a purpose with respect to the proscribed conduct or the proscribed result, with his attitude towards the circumstances to be left to resolution by the courts.
> * * *

A.L.I., *Model Penal Code and Commentaries* Part I § 2.06 n. 37, at 311 (1985).

     * * * In *Reynolds v. State,* 664 P.2d 621 (Alaska App.1983), we held that the state must prove a culpable mental state regarding the "circumstance"—lack of consent—in order to convict a principal of the offense of first-degree sexual assault. "In order to prove a violation of AS 11.41.-410(a)(1), the state must prove that the defendant knowingly engaged in sexual intercourse and recklessly disregarded the victim's lack of consent." 664 P.2d at 625. Similar reasoning leads us to conclude that the state must prove the same element in order to convict a person of first-degree sexual assault as an accomplice. In other words, in order to convict Bowell as an accomplice of Thomas' first-degree sexual assault of B.S., the state was required to prove that Bowell knew that Thomas' intended to engage in sexual intercourse with B.S., that he intentionally engaged in conduct facilitating Thomas' efforts, and that at the time he aided Thomas, he recklessly disregarded B.S.'s lack of consent to Thomas' overtures.

Notes and Questions

     1. Suppose that Bowell intentionally assisted Thomas to have intercourse with a female whom he did not realize, nor had reason to know, was under the age of consent. Under the reasoning of this case, would Bowell be an accomplice in the commission of the offense of statutory rape? Does the answer depend on whether the principal, Thomas, knew that the female with whom he had intercourse was underage? Does the answer depend on any other facts not stated in this hypothetical?

4. ACTUS REUS

INTRODUCTORY COMMENT

     What must a person *do* to be convicted as an accomplice in the commission of an offense? The "blackletter" law may be explained this way:

---

c. See p. 740 supra.

A person is a party to an offense * * * if he either [1] actually commits the offense or [2] does some act which forms a part thereof, or [3] if he assists in the actual commission of the offense or of any act which forms part thereof, or [4] directly or indirectly counsels or procures any person to commit the offense or to do any act forming a part thereof.[d]

The legal definition of the word "aider" is not different from its meaning in common parlance. It means one who assists, supports, or supplements the efforts of another. The word "abettor" means in law one who instigates, advises or encourages the commission of a crime. Thus the word "abet" may import that one is present at the commission of a crime without giving active assistance. * * * To be an aider or abettor it is not essential that there be a prearranged concert of action, although, in the absence of such action, it is essential that one should in some way advocate or encourage[e] the commission of the crime.[f]

In many, perhaps most, multi-party prosecutions, the *actus reus* component of accomplice liability is clear cut, e.g., the secondary party solicited the offense, furnished an instrumentality used in the commission of the crime, or provided other significant aid in the perpetration of the offense. However, as the following cases demonstrate, difficult issues of fact and policy arise when the secondary party's participation is comparatively slight.

STATE v. VAILLANCOURT

Supreme Court of New Hampshire, 1982.
122 N.H. 1153, 453 A.2d 1327.

PER CURIAM.

The only issue presented in this case is whether the Trial Court * * * erred in ruling that the indictment against the defendant was sufficient on its face. We hold that the court's ruling was erroneous, and we reverse.

The factual backdrop of the case involves an attempted burglary on the morning of December 8, 1980, at the O'Connor residence in Manchester. On that day, a neighbor observed two young men, allegedly the defendant, David W. Vaillancourt, and one Richard Burhoe, standing together on the O'Connors' front porch. The men were ringing the doorbell and conversing with one another. Because they remained on the porch for approximately ten minutes, the neighbor became suspicious and began to watch them more closely. She saw them walk around to the side of the house where Burhoe allegedly attempted to break into a basement window. The defendant allegedly stood by and

d. State v. Keller, 268 N.C. 522, 526, 151 S.E.2d 56, 58 (1966).

e. "[T]he word 'encourage' [has] no technical meaning. [Prior cases] adopted Webster's definition of 'encourage' to mean

'giving courage to; inspiring with courage, spirit, or hope.'" Seward v. State, 208 Md. 341, 347, 118 A.2d 505, 507 (1955).

f. Anello v. State, 201 Md. 164, 168, 93 A.2d 71, 72–73 (1952).

watched his companion, talking to him intermittently while the companion tried to pry open the window. The neighbor notified the police, who apprehended the defendant and Burhoe as they were fleeing the scene.

Shortly thereafter, a grand jury indicted the defendant for accomplice liability * * *. The indictment alleged, in pertinent part, as follows:

"[T]hat David W. Vaillancourt ... with the purpose of promoting and facilitating the commission of the offense of attempted burglary, did purposely aid Richard Burhoe ... *by accompanying him to the location of said crime and watching* as the said Richard Burhoe [attempted to commit the crime of burglary]...."

(Emphasis added.) Prior to trial, the defendant filed a motion to dismiss, claiming that the indictment failed to allege criminal conduct on his part. The trial court denied the motion, and a jury subsequently found the defendant guilty as charged. The defendant now contests the sufficiency of his indictment.

The defendant bases his argument on the axiomatic principle that an indictment must allege some criminal activity. He specifically contends that his indictment was insufficient because, even if the facts alleged in it were true, they would not have satisfied the elements necessary for accomplice liability or for any other crime. We agree.

The crime of accomplice liability * * * requires the actor to have solicited, aided, agreed to aid, or attempted to aid the principal in planning or committing the offense. The crime thus necessitates some active participation by the accomplice. We have held that knowledge and mere presence at the scene of a crime could not support a conviction for accomplice liability because they did not constitute sufficient affirmative acts to satisfy the actus reus requirement of the accomplice liability statute.

In the instant case, other than the requisite *mens rea,* the State alleged only that the defendant aided Burhoe "by accompanying him to the location of the crime and watching ..." Consistent with our rulings with respect to "mere presence," we hold that accompaniment and observation are not sufficient acts to constitute "aid" * * *.

BOIS, JUSTICE, with whom BROCK, JUSTICE, joins, dissenting:

I cannot accept the majority's conclusion that accompaniment and observation are insufficient acts to constitute "aid" under the accomplice liability statute * * *. Although I agree that "mere presence" would be an insufficient factual allegation, the indictment in this case alleged more than "mere presence." As the majority concedes, the indictment alleged the requisite *mens rea.* It also alleged accompaniment, which connotes presence *and* some *further connection* between the accomplice and the principal. While not a customary form of assistance, "accompaniment with the purpose of aiding" implies the furnishing of moral support and encouragement in the performance of a crime, thereby "aiding" a principal in the commission of an offense. * * * I would therefore hold that the indictment in this case sufficiently alleged criminal conduct on the part of the defendant.

Notes and Questions

1. Why is presence at the site of an offense, with the intent to assist, insufficient to create accomplice liability? What more is needed? The United States Supreme Court has suggested one possible answer to the latter question:

> We understand [the jury instruction] to mean that where an accomplice is present for the purpose of aiding and abetting in a murder, but refrains from so aiding and abetting * * *, he is equally guilty as if he had actively participated by words or acts of encouragement. Thus understood, the statement might, in some instances, be a correct instruction. Thus, if there had been evidence sufficient to show that there had been a previous conspiracy between Rowe [the perpetrator] and Hicks [the alleged accomplice] to waylay and kill [the victim], Hicks, if present at the time of the killing, would be guilty, even if it was found unnecessary for him to act. But the error of such an instruction, in the present case, is in the fact there was no evidence on which to base it.

Hicks v. United States, 150 U.S. 442, 450, 14 S.Ct. 144, 147, 37 L.Ed. 1137, 1141 (1893).

Why is presence coupled with a prior arrangement (conspiracy) sufficient? Based on *Hicks*, was the majority or the dissent correct in *Vaillancourt?* As a practical matter, does *Hicks* render the "presence alone" rule a nullity?

2. *Problem.* Francis is driving his car. His wife, their two infant children, and George, a friend, are passengers. With his wife's permission, Francis picks up a hitchhiker, who enters the backseat with George and one of the children. Subsequently, George pulls out a knife and takes the hitchhiker's wallet and watch. Francis says and does nothing during the episode and continues to drive. Is he an accomplice to the robbery? What about his wife? Compare Pace v. State, 248 Ind. 146, 224 N.E.2d 312 (1967) with State v. Parker, 282 Minn. 343, 164 N.W.2d 633 (1969). What would be the result under the Model Penal Code?

WILCOX v. JEFFERY

King's Bench Division, 1951.
1 All England Law Reports 464.

LORD GODDARD, C.J.: * * * Herbert William Wilcox, the proprietor of a periodical called "Jazz Illustrated," was charged on an information that "on Dec. 11, 1949, he did unlawfully aid and abet one Coleman Hawkins in contravening art. 1(4) of the Aliens Order, 1920, by failing to comply with a condition attached to a grant of leave to land, to wit, that the said Coleman Hawkins should take no employment paid or unpaid while in the United Kingdom, contrary to art. 18(2) of the Aliens Order, 1920." Under the Aliens Order, art. 1(1), it is provided that

> "... an alien coming ... by sea to a place in the United Kingdom—*(a)* shall not land in the United Kingdom without the leave of an immigration officer ..."

It is provided by art. 1(4) that:

> "An immigration officer, in accordance with general or special directions of the Secretary of State, may, by general order or notice or otherwise, attach such conditions as he may think fit to the grant of leave to land, and the Secretary of State may at any time vary such conditions in such manner as he thinks fit, and the alien shall comply with the conditions so attached or varied ..."

If the alien fails to comply, he is to be in the same position as if he has landed without permission, *i.e.,* he commits an offence.

The case is concerned with the visit of a celebrated professor of the saxophone, a gentleman by the name of Hawkins who was a citizen of the United States. He came here at the invitation of two gentlemen of the name of Curtis and Hughes, connected with a jazz club which enlivens the neighbourhood of Willesden. They, apparently, had applied for permission for Mr. Hawkins to land and it was refused, but, nevertheless, this professor of the saxophone arrived with four French musicians. When they came to the airport, among the people who were there to greet them was the appellant. He had not arranged their visit, but he knew they were coming and he was there to report the arrival of these important musicians for his magazine. So, evidently, he was regarding the visit of Mr. Hawkins as a matter which would be of interest to himself and the magazine which he was editing and selling for profit. Messrs. Curtis and Hughes arranged a concert at the Princes Theatre, London. The appellant attended that concert as a spectator. He paid for his ticket. Mr. Hawkins went on stage and delighted the audience by playing the saxophone. The appellant did not get up and protest in the name of the musicians of England that Mr. Hawkins ought not to be here competing with them and taking the bread out of their mouths or the wind out of their instruments. It is not found that he actually applauded, but he was there having paid to go in, and, no doubt, enjoying the performance, and then, lo and behold, out comes his magazine with a most laudatory description, fully illustrated, of this concert. On those facts the magistrate has found that he aided and abetted. * * *

There was not accidental presence in this case. The appellant paid to go to the concert and he went there because he wanted to report it. He must, therefore, be held to have been present, taking part, concurring, or encouraging, whichever word you like to use for expressing this conception. It was an illegal act on the part of Hawkins to play the saxophone or any other instrument at this concert. The appellant clearly knew that it was an unlawful act for him to play. He had gone there to hear him, and his presence and his payment to go there was an encouragement. He went there to make use of the performance, because he went there, as the magistrate finds and was justified in finding, to get "copy" for his newspaper. It might have been entirely different, as I say, if he had gone there and protested, saying: "The musicians' union do not like you foreigners coming here and playing and you ought to get off the stage." If he had booed, it might have been some evidence that he was not aiding and abetting. If he had gone as a member of a *claque* to try to drown the noise of the saxophone, he might very likely be found not guilty of aiding and abetting. In this case it seems clear that he was there, not only to approve and encourage what was done, but to take advantage of it by getting "copy" for his paper. In those circumstances there was evidence on which the magistrate could find that the appellant aided and abetted, and for these reasons I am of opinion that the appeal fails. * * *

Notes and Questions

1. In *Wilcox,* are all of the spectators who did not boo, create a disruption, or walk out in protest, accomplices? If so, why was Wilcox singled out for prosecution? If not, what distinguishes him from the other members of the audience?

2. *Problem.* On March 6, 1983, a young woman entered a tavern in New Bedford, Massachusetts to purchase cigarettes. Sixteen customers, fifteen of whom were male, and the male bartender were present. The victim spoke for a few moments to the other woman present. After the other female left, the victim started to leave. Two men approached her, knocked her to the ground, tore off her clothing, and over a 75–minute period forced her to commit various sexual acts on both of them, which she resisted. During this period, while the victim frequently cried out for help, some of the customers cheered the rapists on. None of the customers, nor the bartender, came to her aid or called the police during the assaults. See Commonwealth v. Vieira, 401 Mass. 828, 519 N.E.2d 1320 (1988); Commonwealth v. Cordeiro, 401 Mass. 843, 519 N.E.2d 1328 (1988).

Regarding the rapes, what is the liability, if any, of: (1) the cheering customers; (2) the bartender; (3) the non-cheering customers? Regarding the cheering customers, does their liability depend on whether the rapists heard the cheers? Would they be liable if the perpetrators heard the cheering, but would not have desisted even if the customers had remained silent or yelled at them to stop?

STATE v. HELMENSTEIN

Supreme Court of North Dakota, 1968.
163 N.W.2d 85.

STRUTZ, JUDGE.

* * * The defendant was [prosecuted] * * * on a charge of burglary of a grocery store in Hannover. * * * Trial by jury was waived * * *. After trial, the court found the defendant guilty of the offense as charged. This appeal is from the judgment of conviction and from an order denying the defendant's motion for new trial. * * *

The record discloses that, on the night of the alleged burglary, two groups of young people had been driving around in the vicinity of Center, North Dakota. During the evening, these two groups met at the park in Center. Someone in one of the groups had obtained some beer, and this was passed around and all of them drank some of it. After a while, they all decided to get into one of the automobiles and ride around. They got into the defendant's car. A short time later, someone suggested that they drive to Hannover, about six miles west of Center, and break into the store at that place. When this suggestion was made, one person in the party said she wanted some bananas. Someone else expressed a desire for other articles which could be secured at the store. They drove over to Hannover and parked the car some distance from the store, and three of the party, including the defendant, went to the store, broke in, and returned with beer, cigarettes, candy, and bananas. They then drove back toward Center. On the way, the parties all agreed on what story they would tell the officers of the law if any of them should be questioned. At Center, they divided the loot and separated.

At the trial, five of the young people who had been in this party testified for the State against the defendant. The only witness other than those who were in the party on the night of the burglary was Harold Henke, the owner of the store that had been burglarized. His testimony established that he owned the store, that on the morning following the burglary he found that the store had been entered during the night, and that approximately $130 worth of merchandise had been taken. His testimony in no way connected the defendant with the offense, but merely established the fact that a crime had been committed.

The trial court found the defendant guilty. * * *

The first question for us to consider is whether there was competent evidence against the defendant sufficient to sustain the judgment of conviction. Our statute provides that a conviction may not be had upon the testimony of an accomplice unless his testimony is corroborated by such other evidence as tends to connect the defendant with the commission of the offense, and the corroboration is not sufficient if it merely shows the commission of the offense or the circumstances thereof. * * *

Now, in the light of these rules, let us examine the record before us to determine the status of the witnesses who testified for the State and who were members of the party of young people on the night of the burglary. Carol Weiss contends that she was against the burglary, but she kept her feelings to herself and did not express them. The record discloses that when the burglary was planned she expressed a desire for some bananas. * * * This clearly would make her an accomplice * * *.

Janice Zahn also was called as a witness by the State. She testified that when someone suggested that they break into the store at Hannover, everybody agreed. Thus she admitted that she herself agreed to the burglary when it was suggested, and we believe this makes her, as well as every other person in the party, an accomplice.

Another witness called by the State, who was in the party on the night of the burglary, was Kenneth Cahoon. He admitted that he took part in the actual burglary of the store with the defendant and with one Clem Rohrich. So his status clearly is that of an accomplice. * * *

* * * The only testimony, therefore, which could possibly have corroborated the testimony of the above-named persons—all of whom have clearly been shown to be accomplices—would be the testimony of the witness Glen Zahn. The decision in this case therefore depends entirely upon whether Glen Zahn was an accomplice. * * *

Let us therefore examine the testimony of Glen Zahn to see what he * * * said. He contends that he had secret objections to the burglary which he did not express to anyone. He further testified that he was asleep when the burglary was committed and that he did not take part in the actual burglary of the store. The trial court found that Glen had had too much to drink and that he was asleep during the time of the burglary and in no way aided or abetted or encouraged the crime. Zahn's own testimony, however, discloses that he does not claim to have fallen asleep until the three members of the party left the parked car for the store, for he remembers their leaving. After the burglary had been accomplished, all of them together made up a story to tell to investigating officers in case any of them should be questioned. Zahn admits that he helped make up the story to mislead the officers of the law, and he says, "Well, we all made a story together." Why would Zahn feel it necessary to make up a story to mislead the officers if he had no part in the offense? We believe that the record clearly shows that the burglary in this case was the result of a plan in which each of the parties had a part, and that each of these young people encouraged and countenanced the offense and that each of them thus was concerned in its commission. * * *

Since we hold Zahn to be an accomplice, there is no evidence in this case, other than that of persons who also are accomplices, connecting the defendant with the commission of the offense with which he is charged. Therefore, the evidence against him is insufficient to sustain the judgment of conviction. * * *

Notes and Questions

1. Virtually every state has a corroboration rule similar to that applied in *Helmenstein.* What policy justifies a rule that can result in the acquittal of a person against whom there is substantial evidence of guilt? See Christine J. Saverda, Note, *Accomplices in Federal Court: A Case for Increased Evidentiary Standards,* 100 Yale L.J. 785 (1990).

2. *Causation and complicity.* How significant to the commission of the burglary was the assistance of each of the accomplices? Can we sensibly say, for example, that but for Weiss's "assistance" of asking for the bananas the crime would not have occurred? If not, are we punishing accomplices in the absence of a causal link between the secondary party's assistance and the offense? If causation is not required, what justifies such an outcome?

A. *Is causation required?* No, say the courts:

We are therefore clear to the conclusion that, before Judge Tally can be found guilty of aiding and abetting the Skeltons to kill Ross, it must appear that his [participation] * * * aided them to kill Ross, contributed to Ross's death, in point of physical fact * * *.

The assistance given, however, need not contribute to the criminal result in the sense that but for it the result would not have ensued. It is quite sufficient if it facilitated a result that would have transpired without it. It is quite enough if the aid merely rendered it easier for the principal actor to accomplish the end intended by him and the aider and abettor, though in all human probability the end would have been attained without it.[g]

[I]f one commits a crime and another is * * * aiding, abetting, assisting, or encouraging its commission, the latter thereby becomes a participant * * * and his culpability is determined by his motives, and not by the degree of his influence over the former.[h]

[H]ere the record provides ample evidence to establish that appellant was * * * an active participant in the criminal [homicide]. * * * Once it has been determined that appellant was an accomplice, proof that the *principal* caused the death satisfies the requirement of establishing the causal relationship of the accomplice. Here the fact that [the principal] fired the fatal shots is not challenged. Thus the challenge to sufficiency, relating to the asserted failure to establish the element of causation [as to the accomplice], is without merit.[i]

Does the Model Penal Code require a causal connection between the accomplice's assistance and the commission of the crime?

B. *Is the no-causation-requirement principle justifiable?* Reflect on the following observation:

The common law is wedded to the concept of personal, rather than vicarious, responsibility for crimes. Professor Sayre has described the notion that criminal liability is "intensely personal" as "deep rooted." Our demand that responsibility be personal is the result of the "inarticulate, subconscious sense of justice of the man on the street." Personal responsibility is the "only sure foundation of law." Causation * * * is the instrument we employ to ensure that responsibility is personal. It links the actor to the harm. It helps us to understand who should be punished by answering how the harm occurred. * * *

Sine qua non causation serves a second, more sophisticated, role: assuring that those who are legally blameworthy are given their retributively deserved punishment. * * *

This second role of causation must be explained carefully. The theologian or ethicist frequently makes moral judgments based on a person's intentions and motives. The externality of those intentions has only secondary value to him. On the other hand, any nonutilitarian juridical conception of blame focuses initially and primarily on the external harm caused by the criminal actor. The harm or actus reus of the crime is the indispensable justification for punitive intervention.

---

g. State ex rel. Martin v. Tally, 102 Ala. 25, 69, 15 So. 722, 738–39 (1894).

h. Fuson v. Commonwealth, 199 Ky. 804, 809, 251 S.W. 995, 997 (1923).

i. Commonwealth v. Smith, 480 Pa. 524, 528–29, 391 A.2d 1009, 1011 (1978) (emphasis added).

Harm is the measure of the actor's degree of legal guilt and of his deserved punishment. To the adherent of a retributory philosophy, guilt and punishment must be initially proportional to the value of the harm the actor caused. It is to that degree to which the moral equilibrium of society has been disturbed. This is presumably the maximum amount of redress to which society is entitled. * * *

Sine qua non causation, therefore, serves as the link between the indispensable factor of harm and the actor responsible for it. It ensures both that guilt and punishment are based on personal involvement and that the stigma of criminal conviction and the pain of criminal punishment that follows are apportioned in relation to the degree each person has disturbed society's equilibrium. * * *

Accomplice law, then, might be unjustified in ignoring causation. * * * It holds persons accountable for the actions of others. As a result, although the accomplice is punished because of her own conduct, she is punished to the extent of another's. She can be punished for harm she did not cause. If accomplice law is to be defended, one must * * * find a sound basis for distinguishing legal accountability of accomplices from other criminal law doctrines, or reform accomplice law.

Joshua Dressler, *Reassessing the Theoretical Underpinnings of Accomplice Liability: New Solutions to an Old Problem,* 37 Hastings L.J. 91, 103–04, 106, 108 (1985).

Can you suggest a "sound basis" for the no-causation principle?

3. The criminal law generally treats accomplices alike, i.e., each accomplice is guilty of the offense committed by the primary party and is subject to the same punishment as the primary actor. However, are there certain categories of accomplices who are *inherently* less dangerous or less deserving of punishment than the primary party and other accomplices?

For example, should principals in the second degree be punished more severely than accessories before the fact, on the ground that their presence at the scene demonstrates that they are more dangerous or more culpable? Or, should a categorical distinction be made between those who provide significant assistance and those whose help is minimal? In the latter case, how might the line be drawn? See Dressler, id. at 124–40 (distinguishing between "causal" and "noncausal" accomplices, and recommending that the latter be punished less severely than the former).

4. *Accomplice liability by attempting to aid.* Suppose that Sadie unlocks the front door of Roger's house in order to facilitate Paul's later burglary. However, Paul enters through a window, unaware of Sadie's earlier action. Is Sadie an accomplice in the commission of Paul's burglary?

At common law, Sadie is not an accomplice. Sanford H. Kadish, *Complicity, Cause and Blame: A Study in the Interpretation of Doctrine,* 73 Cal.L.Rev. 323, 359 (1985). An actor is an accomplice in the commission of an offense if she intentionally aids—no matter how minimally—the primary party. Nonetheless, she must *in fact* assist. In Sadie's case, she attempted to aid Paul by unlocking the door. Since he did not use this avenue of ingress, however, her efforts to assist failed.

Would Sadie be guilty as an accomplice under the Model Penal Code?

Can attempting to aid constitute a crime in itself? Consider the next case.

PEOPLE v. GENOA

Court of Appeals of Michigan, 1991.
188 Mich.App. 461, 470 N.W.2d 447.

SHEPHERD, PRESIDING JUDGE.

The prosecution appeals * * * a lower court order dismissing a charge against defendant of attempted possession with intent to deliver 650 grams or more of cocaine. We affirm.

The charge against defendant stemmed from a June 6, 1988, transaction in which an undercover agent of the Michigan State Police met with defendant at a hotel and proposed that if defendant gave him $10,000 toward the purchase of a kilogram of cocaine, which the police agent claimed he would then sell, the agent would repay defendant the $10,000, plus $3,500 in profits and a client list. Defendant accepted the proposal and later returned with the $10,000. After defendant left, the police agent turned the money over to the Michigan State Police, and defendant was subsequently arrested.

The district court judge * * * dismissed the charge against defendant on the ground that because the police agent never intended to commit the contemplated crime and, indeed, never did commit it, defendant, though he believed he was giving money for an illegal enterprise, financed nothing. * * *

While the prosecution did not necessarily concede it below, it is readily apparent that the only theory by which it could prosecute defendant was that defendant attempted to aid and abet the crime of possession with intent to deliver cocaine. Defendant certainly could not be shown to have even attempted to constructively possess the cocaine himself, in that the evidence simply indicated that defendant was to help finance the proposed venture. And, while Michigan does not distinguish between principals and accessories for purposes of culpability, certain elements must be established to show someone aided and abetted the commission of a crime. Those elements are that: (1) the underlying crime was committed by either the defendant or some other person, (2) the defendant performed acts or gave encouragement which aided and assisted the commission of the crime, and (3) the defendant intended the commission of the crime or had knowledge that the principal intended its commission at the time of giving aid or encouragement.

Thus, while the conviction of the principal is not necessary to a conviction of an accessory, the prosecution must prove that the underlying crime was committed by someone, and that the defendant either committed or aided and abetted the commission of that crime. However, in the case at bar, it is clear that the underlying crime was never committed by anyone. The absence of this element made it legally impossible for defendant to have committed any offense.

It is apparent to us that the inability to charge or prosecute defendant results from a gap in legislation. * * *

Notes and Questions

1. How would *Genoa* be resolved under the Model Penal Code? See Sections 2.06 and 5.01(3).

2. *Entrapment.* Issues of accomplice liability aside, should Genoa be prosecuted for the commission of an offense that an undercover agent set up? Every jurisdiction in the United States recognizes the criminal law defense of entrapment by a law enforcement officer. (The defense does not apply if the entrapper is a private, i.e., nongovernmental, party.) Most states and the federal courts apply the "subjective" test of entrapment. According to this standard, entrapment is proved if a government agent induces an innocent person, i.e., one not predisposed to commit the type of offense charged, to violate the law, so that she can be prosecuted. A person is predisposed to commit the offense if she is "ready and willing" to commit the type of crime charged, if presented with a favorable opportunity to do so. Sherman v. United States, 356 U.S. 369, 78 S.Ct. 819, 2 L.Ed.2d 848 (1958).

The alternative, "objective" test of entrapment focuses on the police conduct used to ensnare the defendant. By this standard, entrapment occurs when "the police conduct * * * falls below standards, to which common feelings respond, for the proper use of governmental power." Id. at 382, 78 S.Ct. at 825, 2 L.Ed.2d at 856 (Frankfurter, J., concurring). Police conduct falls below acceptable standards when it "is likely to induce to the commission of crime [those] * * * who would normally avoid crime and through self-struggle resist ordinary temptations." Id. at 384, 78 S.Ct. at 826, 2 L.Ed.2d at 857. See generally Joshua Dressler, Understanding Criminal Procedure §§ 170–174 (1991).

Should entrapment be a defense? Is it a justification defense, an excuse, or something else?

5. DISTINGUISHING DIRECT FROM ACCOMPLICE LIABILITY

There cannot be a secondary party to a crime in the absence of a principal in the first degree; but an apparent secondary party may himself, on closer inspection, be the principal in the first degree.[j]

BAILEY v. COMMONWEALTH

Supreme Court of Virginia, 1985.
229 Va. 258, 329 S.E.2d 37.

Carrico, Chief Justice.

* * * The question on appeal is whether it was proper to convict Bailey of involuntary manslaughter when, in his absence, the victim was killed by police officers responding to reports from Bailey concerning the victim's conduct.

j. Glanville Williams, Criminal Law:
The General Part 350 (2d ed. 1961).

The death of the victim, Gordon E. Murdock, occurred during the late evening of May 21, 1983, in the aftermath of an extended and vituperative conversation between Bailey and Murdock over their citizens' band radios. During the conversation, which was to be the last in a series of such violent incidents, Bailey and Murdock cursed and threatened each other repeatedly.

Bailey and Murdock lived about two miles apart * * *. On the evening in question, each was intoxicated. Bailey had consumed a "twelve-pack" of beer and a "fifth of liquor" since mid-afternoon; a test of Murdock's blood made during an autopsy showed alcoholic content of ".271% ... by weight." Murdock was also "legally blind," with vision of only 3/200 in the right eye and 2/200 in the left. Bailey knew that Murdock had "a problem with vision" and that he was intoxicated on the night in question.

Bailey also knew that Murdock owned a handgun and had boasted "about how he would use it and shoot it and scare people off with it." Bailey knew further that Murdock was easily agitated and that he became especially angry if anyone disparaged his war hero, General George S. Patton. During the conversation in question, Bailey implied that General Patton and Murdock himself were homosexuals.

Also during the conversation, Bailey persistently demanded that Murdock arm himself with his handgun and wait on his front porch for Bailey to come and injure or kill him. Murdock responded by saying he would be waiting on his front porch, and he told Bailey to "kiss [his] mother or [his] wife and children good-bye because [he would] never go back home."

Bailey then made two anonymous telephone calls to the Roanoke City Police Department. In the first, Bailey reported "a man ... out on the porch [at Murdock's address] waving a gun around." A police car was dispatched to the address, but the officers reported they did not "see anything."

Bailey called Murdock back on the radio and chided him for not "going out on the porch." More epithets and threats were exchanged. Bailey told Murdock he was "going to come up there in a blue and white car"[1] and demanded that Murdock "step out there on the ... porch" with his gun "in [his] hands" because he, Bailey, would "be there in just a minute."

Bailey telephoned the police again. This time, Bailey identified Murdock by name and told the dispatcher that Murdock had "a gun on the porch," had "threatened to shoot up the neighborhood," and was "talking about shooting anything that moves." Bailey insisted that the police "come out here and straighten this man out." Bailey refused to

1. Bailey owned a blue and white vehicle; the police vehicles were also blue and white.

identify himself, explaining that he was "right next to [Murdock] out here" and feared revealing his identity.

Three uniformed police officers, Chambers, Beavers, and Turner, were dispatched to Murdock's home. None of the officers knew that Murdock was intoxicated or that he was in an agitated state of mind. Only Officer Beavers knew that Murdock's eyesight was bad, and he did not know "exactly how bad it was." Beavers also knew that Murdock would get "a little 10–96 (mental subject) occasionally" and would "curse and carry on" when he was drinking.

When the officers arrived on the scene, they found that Murdock's "porch light was on" but observed no one on the porch. After several minutes had elapsed, the officers observed Murdock come out of his house with "something shiny in his hand." Murdock sat down on the top step of the porch and placed the shiny object beside him.

Officer Chambers approached Murdock from the side of the porch and told him to "[l]eave the gun alone and walk down the stairs away from it." Murdock "just sat there." When Chambers repeated his command, Murdock cursed him. Murdock then reached for the gun, stood up, advanced in Chambers' direction, and opened fire. Chambers retreated and was not struck.

All three officers returned fire, and Murdock was struck. Lying wounded on the porch, he said several times, "I didn't know you was the police." He died from "a gunshot wound of the left side of the chest."
* * *

In an instruction granted below and not questioned on appeal, the trial court told the jury it should convict Bailey if it found that his negligence or reckless conduct was so gross and culpable as to indicate a callous disregard for human life and that his actions were the proximate cause or a concurring cause of Murdock's death. Bailey concedes that the evidence at trial, viewed in the light most favorable to the Commonwealth, would support a finding that his actions constituted negligence so gross and culpable as to indicate a callous disregard for human life. He contends, however, that he "did not kill Murdock."

Bailey argues that his conviction can be sustained only if he was a principal in the first degree, a principal in the second degree, or an accessory before the fact to the killing of Murdock. The Attorney General concedes that Bailey was not a principal in the second degree or an accessory before the fact, but maintains that he was a principal in the first degree.

Countering, Bailey argues he was not a principal in the first degree because only the immediate perpetrators of crime occupy that status. Here, Bailey says, the immediate perpetrators of Murdock's killing were the police officers who returned Murdock's fire.[2] He was in his own home two miles away, Bailey asserts, and did not control the actors in the confrontation at Murdock's home or otherwise participate in the

---

2. Bailey admits the officers acted in self-defense.

events that occurred there. Hence, Bailey concludes, he could not have been a principal in the first degree.

We have adopted the rule in this Commonwealth, however, that one who effects a criminal act through an innocent or unwitting agent is a principal in the first degree. *Collins v. Commonwealth,* 226 Va. 223, 233, 307 S.E.2d 884, 890 (1983) * * *.

Bailey argues that the present case is distinguishable from *Collins.* There, Bailey says, the accused and the undercover policewoman were working in concert, pursuing a common goal of soliciting and collecting fees for sexual favors; although the policewoman was innocent of the crime of pandering because she had no intent to perform sexual acts, the accused was guilty nevertheless because the fees were collected on his behalf. Here, Bailey asserts, he and the police shared no common scheme or goal. Neither, Bailey says, did he share a common goal with Murdock; indeed, "Murdock's intent was to kill Bailey."

The question is not, however, whether Murdock was Bailey's innocent or unwitting agent but whether the police officers who responded to Bailey's calls occupied that status. And, in resolving this question, we believe it is irrelevant whether Bailey and the police shared a common scheme or goal. What is relevant is whether Bailey undertook to cause Murdock harm and used the police to accomplish that purpose, a question which we believe must be answered affirmatively.

Knowing that Murdock was intoxicated, nearly blind, and in an agitated state of mind, Bailey orchestrated a scenario on the evening of May 21, 1983, whose finale was bound to include harmful consequences to Murdock, either in the form of his arrest or his injury or death. * * *

From a factual standpoint, it is clear from the sum total of Bailey's actions that his purpose in calling the police was to induce them to go to Murdock's home and unwittingly create the appearance that Bailey himself had arrived to carry out the threats he had made over the radio. And, from a legal standpoint, it is clear that, for Bailey's mischievous purpose, the police officers who went to Murdock's home and confronted him were acting as Bailey's innocent or unwitting agents.

But, Bailey argues, he cannot be held criminally liable in this case unless Murdock's death was the natural and probable result of Bailey's conduct. Bailey maintains that either Murdock's own reckless and criminal conduct in opening fire upon the police or the officers' return fire constituted an independent, intervening cause absolving Bailey of guilt.

We have held, however, that "[a]n intervening act which is reasonably foreseeable cannot be relied upon as breaking the chain of causal connection between an original act of negligence and subsequent injury." Here, under instructions not questioned on appeal, the jury determined that the fatal consequences of Bailey's reckless conduct could reasonably have been foreseen and, accordingly, that Murdock's death was not the result of an independent, intervening cause but of Bailey's misconduct.

At the least, the evidence presented a jury question on these issues. * * *

Notes and Questions

1. Why is Bailey not an accessory before the fact? Would he be an accomplice under Model Penal Code § 2.06?

2. *Innocent agency doctrine.* Some applications of the "innocent agency" or "innocent instrumentality" doctrine applied in *Bailey* are straightforward. For example, if *D*, intending to kill *V*, his infant son, hands *X*, his seven-year-old daughter, poisoned candy and instructs her to feed it to *V* (which she does, killing *V*), *D* is the principal in the first degree. *X*, who lacked the intent to kill and who, in any case, would be excused on the ground of infancy, is *D* 's innocent agent. *X* is no more the principal in the first degree than is a gun or a pit bull used by one person to kill another. *D* 's liability is predicated on *X* 's actions (as *D* 's putative agent), coupled with *D* 's own mental state.

The doctrine has been invoked in cases not nearly as straightforward. For example, in Regina v. Tyler, 173 Eng.Rep. 643 (1838), *X*, an insane man, assembled a group (including *T*) and, as its leader, killed *V*. *X* was found not guilty of murder due to his insanity. *T* was convicted as a principal in the first degree. Is this a correct use of the innocent agency doctrine?

Was the court in *Bailey* correct in applying the innocent agency doctrine? Are there any problems in imputing the police officers' conduct to the defendant?

3. In *Bailey*, suppose that Murdock had killed one of the officers before being shot to death by the police. Would *Bailey* be guilty of criminal homicide of the officer? If so, would he be guilty as an accomplice or as the primary party?

4. *Problem. Bailey* cited *Collins v. Commonwealth* in support of the innocent agency doctrine. In that case, *C* operated an escort service, in which he arranged for female escorts to date male customers for a fee. *C* received the fee and a portion of any "tips" provided by the customers for sexual services performed by the escorts. *X*, an undercover agent, met *C* and agreed to be employed by him as an escort. Thereafter, she proceeded to a male customer's apartment, collected the fee, agreed to perform sexual intercourse, and then arrested the customer.

Based on the preceding evidence, *C* was prosecuted for pandering, which was defined by state law as: "receiv[ing] any money * * * on account of procuring for or placing in a house of prostitution or elsewhere any person for the purpose of causing such person to engage in unlawful sexual intercourse." Is *C* a principal in the first degree or an accessory before the fact? Should his guilt be justified on the grounds of the innocent agency doctrine?

5. *Problem.* Suppose that Harold, a visitor at a state prison, abducts Ira, an inmate, and coerces him to leave the prison. If Harold and Ira are prosecuted for escape, is Ira guilty? Is Harold? Apply Model Penal Code § 242.6(1) (escape).

If Harold is guilty, is he guilty as an accomplice or as the primary party? In this regard, look carefully at Section 242.6(1): Why might it seem odd to say that Harold is the principal in the first degree of this offense? See Sanford H. Kadish, *Complicity, Cause and Blame: A Study in the Interpretation of Doctrine,* 73 Cal.L.Rev. 323, 373 (1985).

6. *Problem.* In Jacobs v. State, 184 So.2d 711 (Fla.App.1966), *A, B* and *C* agreed to "drag race" on a public road at excessive and unlawful rates of speed. During the race, *A* negligently struck *V*'s vehicle, causing his own death and that of *V*. Are *B* and *C* guilty of manslaughter in *A*'s death? In *V*'s death? Are they guilty as accomplices or as principals in the first degree?

6. RELATIONSHIP OF THE LIABILITY OF THE ACCOMPLICE TO THE PRINCIPAL

a. *If the Principal Is Acquitted or Not Prosecuted*

STATE v. HAYES

Supreme Court of Missouri, 1891.
105 Mo. 76, 16 S.W. 514.

THOMAS, J. * * *

[Defendant Hayes proposed to Hill that Hill assist him in the burglary of a store. Unknown to Hayes, Hill was a stepson of the store owner. Hill feigned agreement and informed the owner of Hayes's intentions. On the night of the planned burglary, Hayes opened a window and helped Hill inside. Hill picked up a side of bacon and handed it out to Hayes. Hayes assisted Hill out of the window, whereupon the two men took 15 to 20 steps (with Hayes holding the bacon) before the police arrived. Hayes was convicted of burglary and larceny. Hill was not arrested.]

* * * It will be seen the trial court told the jury * * * that defendant was guilty of burglary if he, with a felonious intent, assisted and aided Hill to enter the building, notwithstanding Hill himself may have had no such intent. In this [instruction] we think the court erred. One cannot read this record without being convinced beyond a reasonable doubt that Hill did not enter the warehouse with intent to steal. * * *

* * * We may assume, then, for the sake of the argument, that Hill committed no crime in entering the warehouse. The act of Hill, however, was by the instruction of the court imputed to defendant. This act, according to the theory of the instructions, so far as Hill was concerned, was not a criminal act, but when it was imputed to defendant it became criminal because of the latter's felonious intent. This would probably be true if Hill had acted under the control and compulsion of defendant, and as his passive and submissive agent in this transaction. But he was not a passive agent in this transaction. He was an active one. He acted of his own volition. * * * To make defendant responsible for the acts of

Hill, they must have had a common motive and common design. The design and the motives of the two men were not only distinct, but dissimilar, even antagonistic. * * *

* * * The court should instruct the jury that if Hill broke into and entered the wareroom with a felonious intent, and defendant was present, aiding him with the same intent, then he is guilty; but if Hill entered the room with no design to steal, but simply to entrap defendant, and capture him in the commission of crime, and defendant did not enter the room himself, then he is not guilty of burglary and larceny as charged. * * * The judgment is reversed * * *.

Notes and Questions

1.   Why was Hayes not prosecuted as the principal in the first degree through the innocent agency doctrine?

2.   In light of the result in this appeal, what advice would you give to a person in Hill's shoes, who wishes to ensnare a criminal "red-handed" in a burglary?

3.   Is Hayes guilty of *any* common law offense, inchoate or complete? Of what, if anything, is Hayes guilty under the Model Penal Code?

UNITED STATES v. LOPEZ

United States District Court, N.D. California, 1987.
662 F.Supp. 1083.

LYNCH, DISTRICT JUDGE.

[Ronald McIntosh landed a helicopter on the grounds of the Federal Correctional Institution in order to effect the escape of his girlfriend, Samantha Lopez, whose life allegedly was unlawfully threatened by prison authorities. The two were apprehended ten days later and prosecuted for various offenses, including prison escape. Prior to their trial, which is reported in a subsequent appeal, 885 F.2d 1428 (9th Cir.1989), McIntosh and Lopez indicated their intent to raise a "necessity/duress" defense based on the claimed threats to Lopez's life. The following is an excerpt from the trial court's ruling on the government's motion *in limine* for an order barring the presentation of evidence on the defense of necessity or duress.]

* * * In response to the government's motion, each defendant has filed a written offer of proof *in camera*. By these offers of proof, defendants seek to establish the prima facie case required to be shown before defendants are entitled to an instruction on the defense of necessity/duress. The parties agree that if Lopez makes a prima facie showing of each element of the necessity/duress defense, she will be entitled to an instruction on that defense. * * *

McIntosh requests the following jury instruction: "If you find defendant Samantha Lopez not guilty of escape because she acted under necessity/duress, then you must also find defendant McIntosh not guilty of aiding and abetting her alleged escape." The government contends that McIntosh can be convicted of aiding and abetting Lopez' escape even if Lopez succeeds on her necessity/duress defense.

* * * The general rule is that a defendant can be convicted of aiding and abetting even if the principal is not identified or convicted; however, an aider and abettor may not be held liable absent proof that a criminal offense was committed by a principal. "The fact that the principal need not be identified or convicted has never been thought to obviate the need for proof showing that an underlying crime was committed by someone." *United States v. Powell,* 806 F.2d 1421, 1424 (9th Cir.1986).

This Court must therefore determine whether Lopez committed a criminal offense if her necessity/duress defense succeeds. This determination requires an examination of the theoretical distinctions between two categories of defenses: justification and excuse. Lopez' alleged defense of necessity/duress must then be classified as either a justification or an excuse.

Justification defenses are those providing that, although the act was committed, it is not wrongful. For example, a forest fire is burning toward a town of 10,000 residents. An actor burns a field of corn located between the fire and the town in order to set up a firebreak. By setting fire to the field with the intent to destroy it, the actor satisfies all the elements of the crime of arson; however, he most likely will have a complete defense because his conduct is justified. Burning the field avoided a greater societal harm; therefore, the act is not a crime.

When a defense is categorized as an excuse, however, the result is that, although the act is wrongful, the actor will not be held accountable. * * * Thus, an insane person who robs a bank will be excused from liability. * * *

The classification of a defense as a justification or an excuse has an important effect on the liability of one who aids and abets the act. A third party has the right to assist an actor in a justified act. Therefore, a third party could not be held liable for aiding and abetting the arson described in the hypothetical above. In contrast, a sane getaway driver could be convicted of aiding and abetting an insane person's bank robbery. Excuses are always personal to the actor.

The defense of duress or coercion traditionally arises when a person unlawfully commands another to do an unlawful act using the threat of death or serious bodily injury. * * *

The defense of necessity may be raised in a situation in which the pressure of natural physical forces compels an actor to choose between two evils. The actor may choose to violate the literal terms of the law in order to avoid a greater harm. The defense of necessity is categorized as a justification.

In the context of prison escapes, the distinction between duress/coercion and necessity has been hopelessly blurred. In fact, courts seem to use the two terms interchangeably. * * *

This Court believes, however, that the defense asserted by Lopez, under the facts of this case, most nearly resembles necessity, which is a justification to the alleged crime. In the present case, Lopez' claim is not that the alleged threats overwhelmed her will so that her inability to make the "correct" choice should be excused. Instead, Lopez claims that she, in fact, did make the correct choice. * * *

Accordingly, if the jury finds Lopez not guilty of escape by reason of her necessity defense, her criminal act will be justified. * * * No criminal offense will have been committed by a principal. McIntosh is therefore entitled to his requested jury instruction. * * *

Notes and Questions

1. Is the court's analysis too simplistic? Should the classification of the primary party's defense as a justification or an excuse be dispositive on the issue of accomplice's liability? See Douglas N. Husak, *Justifications and the Criminal Liability of Accessories*, 80 J.Crim.L. & Criminology 491 (1989). For example, suppose that Yolanda, a young child armed with a loaded gun that she thinks is a toy, threatens to kill Nancy. Assuming that Nancy would be justified in killing Yolanda to save her own life, does it necessarily follow that a stranger to both parties is justified in assisting Nancy in killing the child?

On the other hand, are there circumstances in which the accomplice should be justified, although the principal is culpable? For example, suppose that in a retreat jurisdiction an aggressor threatens to stab Nancy, who is unarmed. Nancy could retreat to a known place of safety, but she does not. Should the fact that she is not entitled to claim self-defense preclude a third person from assisting Nancy by tossing her a knife?

b. If the Principal Is Convicted

REGINA v. RICHARDS

Court of Appeal, Criminal Division, 1974.
[1974] Q.B. 776.

JAMES L.J.

[Isabelle Christina Richards was indicted along with two men, Alan Bryant and Paul Squires, for the offense of wounding her husband with intent to do grievous bodily harm, under section 18 of the Offenses against the Person Act (Count 1), and of the alternative and lesser charge, under section 20, of wounding, not involving the specific intent to do grievous bodily harm (Count 2). The men were found not guilty of Count 1 and convicted of Count 2. Richards was convicted of Count 1. This appeal followed.]

The facts of the matter can be stated quite shortly. On the evening of February 25, 1973, the defendant's husband, Mr. Richards, left his home in Weymouth in order to go to work. Shortly afterwards in a lane not far away he was attacked by two men, who were wearing black balaclavas over their heads. He was struck on the back of his head. He tried to escape but was grabbed by the coat sleeves. Eventually he struggled free from his assailants. The medical evidence was that he sustained a laceration on the top of his scalp which required two stitches. There was no need for him to be detained in hospital; it was not a serious injury in fact.

On February 26 the defendant was arrested and at the police station she explained that, according to her, her marriage had been deteriorating, she had become very depressed and started drinking. She was asked if it was at her suggestion that her co-accused Bryant (known as Alan) and Squires (known as Paul) attacked her husband, and to that she replied that she had made the suggestion but in fact she did not want them to hurt him. * * * But in her statement she admitted in these words: "I told them that I wanted them to beat him up bad enough to put him in hospital for a month." She agreed that she had told them that she would give them £5 if they would beat up her husband. She also admitted that she had suggested the appropriate time that her husband might be attacked, namely, when he went out to work, and that she would give a signal by putting on the kitchen light in the house where they lived so that those lying in wait would know when he was setting off for work. As it turned out, there was a power cut at the time so she could not put the light on; she had to hold a candle up to the window, but she played her part as she had promised.

None of the accused gave evidence at the trial and they were content to rest upon the basis that the jury might find them guilty of the second less serious offence. Thus in the upshot the two persons who committed the acts which were the foundation of the offence alleged in count 2 were guilty of an offence under section 20; the defendant, who committed no physical act upon the victim herself at all, was convicted of the more serious offence.

Mr. Aplin's submissions [for the defendant] are brief. He says that looking at the facts of this case the defendant is in the position of one who aided and abetted, or counselled and procured, to use the old language, the other two to commit the offence, and that she cannot be guilty of a graver crime than the crime of which the two co-accused were guilty. There was only one offence that was committed, committed by the co-accused, an offence under section 20, and therefore there is no offence under section 18 of the Act of which his client can properly be found guilty on the facts of this case.

Mr. Purvis [for the Crown] has referred us to a number of authorities in support of his submissions and argument that it is possible, and it should be on the facts of this case, that a person who did no physical act herself by way of assault should nevertheless be guilty of the graver crime of wounding with intent if it is established that she had that specific intent, although persons who were acting at her counselling and command did not have the specific intent that she had and therefore are not themselves guilty of the graver offence.

In support of this argument Mr. Purvis invites our attention * * * to *Smith and Hogan, Criminal Law,* 2nd ed. (1969), in particular * * * on p. 92 * * *:

"... if there were malice in the abettor, and none in the person who struck the party, it will be murder as to the abettor, and manslaughter only as to the other."

There the person who is an abettor, * * * not actually doing the physical act himself, is said to be guilty possibly of the more serious crime than the crime of which the person acting is guilty. But it is right to observe that * * * the authority for that proposition * * * confines that to a case in which the person who is said to be capable of being guilty of the more serious offence is an abettor, a different situation from one who is in the position of an accessory [before the fact] * * *.

Mr. Purvis says that here one can properly look at the actus reus, that is the physical blows struck upon Mr. Richards, and separately the intention with which the blows were struck. The defendant, he says, is responsible for the blows being struck, the actus reus, because they were struck at her request by the co-accused. If, as Mr. Purvis says is the case, the specific intention of the defendant was different from the specific intention if any proved to be entertained on the part of the co-accused, then it is proper that the defendant should be convicted of the section 18 offence if that specific intention goes so far as to amount to intent to cause grievous bodily harm, although that intention was never in the minds of the persons who committed the acts at her request.

We do not take that view. Looking at the facts of this case the acts were perpetrated at some distance from where the defendant was. She was not truly in a position which would earlier have been described as an abettor of those who did the acts. There is proved on the evidence in this case one offence and one offence only, namely, the offence of unlawful wounding without the element of specific intent. We do not think it right that one could say that that which was done can be said to be done with the intention of the defendant who was not present at the time and whose intention did not go to the offence which was in fact committed. That is the short point in the case as we see it. If there is only one offence committed, and that is the offence of unlawful wounding, then the person who has requested that offence to be committed, or advised that that offence be committed, cannot be guilty of a graver offence than that in fact which was committed.

For those reasons we think that this conviction cannot stand. * * * [W]hat this court will do is to quash the conviction that was sustained and substitute a conviction for unlawful wounding. * * *

Notes and Questions

1. Is *Richards* properly decided? English scholars Smith and Hogan state that "[i]t is submitted that *Richards* is wrongly decided. * * * The true principle, it is suggested, is that where the principal has caused an *actus reus,* the liability of each of the secondary parties should be assessed

according to his own *mens rea.*" J.C. Smith and Brian Hogan, Criminal Law 140 (5th ed. 1983).

Professor Kadish defends *Richards:*

The case has been criticized, and insofar as the decision rested on the distinction between whether the secondary party was present or not, the criticism is well taken. But the decision is supportable, it would seem, on the ground that Mrs. Richards did not *cause* the actions of the men.

Critics of the *Richards* decision have taken a different view. Smith and Hogan, for example, argue by analogy to a person, *D,* who gives poison to another, *E,* to administer to the deceased, telling *E* it is an emetic that will cause only discomfort. They argue that if *D* had told *E* that the poison was medicine the deceased needed, *D* would unquestionably be guilty of murder. It should make no difference that *D* told *E* the poison was an emetic, which, since *E*'s action would then have been an intentional assault, would have made *E* guilty of manslaughter. * * *

Their conclusion that *D* is liable for murder is sound, but the generalization they adduce to support it is questionable. It is not a "true principle" that the secondary party's liability is assessed according to his own mens rea when the primary party "has caused an *actus reus.*" This is true only when the secondary party can be said to have caused the actions of the primary party, thereby bringing into play the doctrine of causation which, unlike the doctrine of complicity, does not rest on a derivative theory of liability. In Smith and Hogan's hypothetical this is the case, since *D* used *E* as his unwitting instrument. But it is not the case with Mrs. Richards. She made no misrepresentation to the men she hired. They were not her unwitting instruments, but freely chose to act as they did. Hence their actions, as such, could not be attributed to Mrs. Richards. The innocent-agency doctrine is inapplicable because she did not cause their action.

It is a further question whether Mrs. Richards *should* be liable for assault with intent to do grievous injury, even if I am right that existing doctrine precludes that result. Surely the strongest argument for liability is that the culpability of her hirelings is irrelevant to *her* culpability. But that argument proves too much. If her hirelings committed no assault, but instead went to the police, it is incontrovertible that Mrs. Richards could not be found liable for any assault, let alone an aggravated assault. Yet whether her hirelings chose to do as she bade them or to go to the police is also irrelevant to her culpability. The point would be that however culpable her intentions she could not be blamed for an assault that did not take place. The same retort is applicable on the facts of the case: an actual assault took place (and Mrs. Richards is liable for it) but an aggravated assault did not take place. * * * She could properly be held liable for solicitation to commit an aggravated assault, not for aggravated assault.

Sanford H. Kadish, *Complicity, Cause and Blame: A Study in the Interpretation of Doctrine,* 73 Cal.L.Rev. 323, 388–89 (1985).

Professor Glanville Williams agrees with Smith and Hogan. He contends that the men were "semi-innocent" agents of Mrs. Richards. Therefore, their lesser culpability should not bar punishment of the fully culpable accessory. Glanville Williams, Textbook on Criminal Law 322–23 (1978). In what sense were they "semi-innocent"?

2. *Richards* was overruled in Regina v. Howe, [1987] 1 App.Cas. 417, [1987] 1 All Eng.Rep. 771. In *Howe, H,* acting under duress imposed by *X,* killed *V. H* was convicted of manslaughter. The court, under the impression that *X* could not then be convicted of murder under *Richards,* overruled the latter case. Is there a way, however, to distinguish *Richards*? See Peter Alldridge, *The Doctrine of Innocent Agency,* 2 Crim.L.Forum 45, 65 (1990).

7. LIMITS TO ACCOMPLICE LIABILITY

ROBINSON v. STATE

Court of Appeals of Texas, 1991.
815 S.W.2d 361.

JONES, JUSTICE.

These appeals present a question of first impression in Texas: does a purchaser of a controlled substance become, by virtue of the law of parties, criminally responsible for the seller's delivery? A jury convicted [purchaser Robinson] of delivery of marihuana in an amount greater than five pounds but less than fifty pounds. The trial court assessed punishment * * * at thirty years' imprisonment. * * *

[Danny Hinkle, an undercover police officer, persuaded Ricardo Castro to find a buyer for a large quantity of marihuana Hinkle claimed he wanted to sell. Castro talked with Robinson, who agreed to purchase fifteen pounds of Hinkle's marihuana. The transfer of the marihuana was made from Hinkle to Robinson, whereupon Robinson was arrested for delivery of marihuana. Under state law, "[e]xcept as authorized * * *, a person commits an offense if the person knowingly or intentionally delivers marihuana." Tex.Health & Safety Code Ann. § 481.120(a) (West 1991).]

* * * The indictment of Robinson charged that he

did then and there, acting with intent to promote and assist the intentional and knowing delivery, by actual transfer, from Danny Hinkle to the said Michael Anthony Robinson of marihuana in an amount of more than five pounds but less than 50 pounds, intentionally and knowingly solicit, encourage, direct, aid, and attempt to aid the said Danny Hinkle to commit said offense, and the said Danny Hinkle did then and there intentionally and knowingly deliver, by actual transfer, to the said Michael Anthony Robinson, marihuana in an amount of more than five pounds but less than 50 pounds.

At trial, the court charged the jury * * * that

A person is criminally responsible as a party to an offense if the offense is committed by his own conduct, by the conduct of another for which he is criminally responsible, or by both.

A person is criminally responsible for an offense committed by the conduct of another if, acting with intent to promote or assist the commission of the offense, he solicits, encourages, directs, aids, or attempts to aid the other person to commit the offense.

Mere presence alone will not constitute one a party to an offense. * * *

The trial court gave the jury a technically accurate charge as to the law of complicity, usually referred to as the "law of parties." * * *

We recognize that, as a general proposition, the law of parties applies to a prosecution for the delivery of a controlled substance. Such application is not without exception, however. We believe Professor LaFave correctly states the general rule regarding exceptions to the law of complicity:

> There are ... some exceptions to the general principle that a person who assists or encourages a crime is also guilty as an accomplice. For one, the victim of the crime may not be held as an accomplice even though his conduct in a significant sense has assisted in the commission of the crime....
>
> *Another exception is where the crime is so defined that participation by another is inevitably incident to its commission.* It is justified on the ground that the legislature, by specifying the kind of individual who was guilty when involved in a transaction necessarily involving two or more parties, must have intended to leave the participation by the others unpunished.... Thus, under this exception one having intercourse with a prostitute is not liable as a party to the crime of prostitution, *a purchaser is not a party to the crime of illegal sale,....*

2 W. LaFave & A. Scott, *Substantive Criminal Law* § 6.8(e) at 165–66 (1986) (citations omitted) (emphasis added). * * *

Numerous jurisdictions have addressed the question presented here, and all have reached the same result. [Citations.] The opinion of the Supreme Court of Wyoming in *Wheeler* [691 P.2d 599, 602 (Wyo.1984)] provides a good example of the reasoning employed in these decisions:

> There is a definite distinction between a seller and a buyer. Their separate acts may result in a single transaction, but the buyer is not aiding the "selling act" of the seller and the seller is not aiding the "buying act" of the buyer. The buyer and seller act from different poles. They are not in association or confederacy. An accomplice is one who participates in the same criminal conduct as the defendant, not one whose conduct is the antithesis of the defendant, albeit the conduct of both is involved in a single transaction. * * *

The few Texas courts that have addressed analogous questions also have reached the same result. For example, when it was unlawful to perform an abortion in Texas, it was nonetheless well established that a woman on whom an abortion was performed, even if she consented to the procedure, was not an accomplice to the offense. Likewise, * * *

Texas courts held that one who was merely a customer of a prostitute was not guilty of the offense of prostitution.

When the legislature adopted the current Penal Code in 1974, it abolished the distinction between "principals" and "accomplices," replacing those terms with the more modern concepts of "complicity" and "criminal responsibility for the conduct of another." We have found nothing, however, in the language or legislative history of the Code to indicate that the legislature intended to repudiate the long-standing precedent set by Texas courts in their treatment of accomplices to the offenses of prostitution and abortion. We conclude that, except where otherwise provided by express legislative enactment, this "exception" to the law of parties was carried into the current Penal Code.   * * *

Notes and Questions

1.   Under the reasoning of *Robinson,* is a mother who pays a ransom an accomplice in the kidnapping of her child ("the unlawful removal or confinement of another person for a substantial period of time for the purpose of obtaining a ransom")? Is there another basis for acquitting her?

PEOPLE v. BROWN

Appellate Court of Illinois, Third District, 1980.
90 Ill.App.3d 742, 46 Ill.Dec. 591, 414 N.E.2d 475.

ALLOY, PRESIDING JUSTICE:

After a jury trial, in which Brown was found guilty of attempt burglary, the trial court sentenced Brown to a term of four years imprisonment. On appeal, the defense argues that the conviction should be reversed because * * * the evidence established that the defendant voluntarily abandoned his criminal activity and purpose.   * * *

* * * Assistant State's Attorney for Tazewell County, William Brown, was the key witness for the State. According to State's Attorney Brown, the defendant Barry Brown (no relation) had asked to speak to an attorney in the State's Attorney's office in the early morning hours of September 5, 1979, after he and two other persons had been arrested by police, while they were in a pick-up truck, on property next to Hillside Motors in Creve Coeur. The back door of Hillside Motors had been kicked in during the early morning hours of September 5. According to William Brown, defendant Brown told him that on the night of September 4, 1979, he and another man, Randall Schultz, had been driving around Peoria in Schultz' truck. They had picked up Maxwell Babcock, another young man, who defendant Brown had not previously known. While in Peoria, Babcock suggested that they steal a car and go out and wreck it. He said he knew a place where they could steal a car.

Defendant Brown informed attorney Brown that he and Schultz didn't really want to commit the burglary but that they went along to Hillside Motors in Creve Coeur, the place where the theft was to occur. When they arrived there, Babcock told the two to go around to the back of the building and kick the door in, while he stood lookout in front.

Babcock, according to his plan, was then to enter the building, take keys and money, while the other two stood lookout in front. Following the plan, Brown and Schultz went around to the back of the building and Brown kicked at the door twice, but it did not open. Schultz kicked once and it came open. At this point, Brown told the Assistant State's Attorney, he got "scared" and decided to end his participation in the crime. He and Schultz, without entering the building at all, went to the front of the building to Babcock. They told him that they were leaving, that the burglary was "bullshit" and that they were taking their truck with them. Babcock did not want to leave, but the other two told him they were going and the truck was, too. Babcock then got in the truck with Brown and Schultz.

As they were leaving the parking lot of the service station, next to Hillside Motors, the police arrived and stopped them. * * *

The defense' first argument is that the defendant's acts in kicking the door were mere preparation and did not constitute a substantial step toward the commission of the burglary. By this argument, the defense seeks to counter the State's contention that the attempt burglary was completed once the door was kicked in by defendants Brown and Schultz. We find, without difficulty, that the kicking in of the door was not merely preparation to the burglary but that it was a substantial step towards its completion. Once the door has been opened, the only step remaining is the entry into the building. * * *

The defense counter argument is that even if the evidence was sufficient to show attempt burglary, the conviction should not have been entered because of the fact that defendant Brown was not acting as a principal and because he effectively withdrew from the criminal enterprise, while at the same time preventing its completion. Reliance is thus put upon the accountability statute (Ill.Rev.Stat.1979, ch. 38, par. 5–2), which states in pertinent part:

"A person is legally accountable for the conduct of another when:

* * *

(c) Either before or during the commission of an offense, and with intent to promote or facilitate such commission, he solicits, aids, abets, agrees or attempts to aid, such other person in the planning or commission of the offense. However a person is not so accountable, unless the statute defining the offense provides otherwise, if:

* * *

(3) Before the commission of the offense, he terminates his effort to promote or facilitate such commission, and does one of the following: wholly deprives his prior efforts of effectiveness in such commission, or gives timely warning to the proper law enforcement authorities, or otherwise makes proper effort to prevent the commission of the offense."

The defense argues the applicability of the withdrawal provision of subsection (c)(3) to the defendant's conduct in this case. It is argued that the uncontradicted evidence indicates that prior to completion of the burglary, defendant Brown, along with Schultz, terminated participation in the crime and made a proper effort to prevent the commission of the offense, the latter by informing Babcock that they were leaving and taking the truck with them. Based upon the withdrawal, the defense contends that the defendant ought not have been convicted of attempt burglary. * * * The State contends that the defendant's withdrawal has no effect upon his responsibility for the offense of attempt burglary because that offense, as opposed to the burglary offense, was completed prior to his withdrawal. It is argued that the requirements of subsection (c)(3) of the statute were not satisfied in that the withdrawal did not come "before the commission of the offense."

* * * We turn initially to the accountability section and its withdrawal provisions. * * * Under this provision, as noted, Brown may be held accountable for Babcock's actions and intent because of his aid prior to and during the commission of the offense. However, subsection (c)(3), as already noted, removes accountability if before the commission of "the offense" (emphasis added), the person terminates his efforts to promote such commission and makes a proper effort to prevent the commission of the offense. * * * Clearly, from the context of its use, the referent for "the offense" is set forth in subsection (c), being that offense in which the defendant aids or abets another. So, the question of withdrawal must focus upon the offense or offenses which the defendant aided or abetted "in the planning or commission of." In the factual context of the instant case, both burglary and attempt burglary are possible referents under the statute. * * * As to the burglary offense, Brown's withdrawal would have been effective, in that it occurred prior to the commission of any burglary. However, as to the offense of attempt burglary, his withdrawal was ineffective to prevent application of accountability to his actions, for the reason that such withdrawal did not occur before the commission of the attempt burglary. We conclude that the withdrawal provisions of the accountability statute were not applicable to the attempt burglary charge in that the evidence supported a finding that the offense had occurred prior to the time of the defendant's withdrawal. * * *

Notes and Questions

1. Was Brown an accomplice in the attempted burglary, as the prosecutor charged, or was he actually the perpetrator of the attempt?

2. Suppose that Babcock had stayed at the scene after Brown and Schultz left, and he had entered the door of the building that Schultz had broken open. Would Brown and Schultz have been guilty of Babcock's burglary?

8. A SPECIAL PROBLEM: AIDING AND ABETTING A SUICIDE

a. Drawing Lines: When Does Suicide Assistance Constitute Murder?

PEOPLE v. CAMPBELL

Court of Appeals of Michigan, 1983.
124 Mich.App. 333, 335 N.W.2d 27.

HOEHN, JUDGE.

Defendant, Steven Paul Campbell, was charged with * * * murder, in connection with the suicide death of Kevin Patrick Basnaw. Following a preliminary examination in district court on March 10, 1981, defendant was bound over to circuit court for trial. Defendant moved to quash the information and dismiss the defendant on the ground that providing a weapon to a person, who subsequently uses it to commit suicide, does not constitute the crime of murder. The motion to quash was denied by the circuit court, and this Court granted leave to appeal.

The concise statement of facts is as follows.

On October 4, 1980, Kevin Patrick Basnaw committed suicide. On the night in question, Steven Paul Campbell went to the home of the deceased. They were drinking quite heavily.

The testimony indicates that late in the evening the deceased began talking about committing suicide. He had never talked about suicide before.

About two weeks before, the defendant, Steven Paul Campbell, caught the deceased in bed with defendant's wife, Jill Campbell. Some time during the talk of suicide, Kevin said he did not have a gun. At first the defendant, Steven Paul Campbell, indicated Kevin couldn't borrow or buy one of his guns. Then he changed his mind and told him he would sell him a gun, for whatever amount of money he had in his possession. Then the deceased, Kevin Basnaw, indicated he did not want to buy a gun, but Steve Campbell continued to encourage Kevin to purchase a gun, and alternately ridiculed him.

The defendant and the deceased then drove to the defendant's parent's home to get the weapon, leaving Kimberly Cleland, the deceased's girlfriend, alone. Even though she knew of the plan, she did not call anyone during this period of time. She indicated she thought the defendant was saying this to get a ride home.

The defendant and the deceased returned in about fifteen minutes with the gun and five shells. The deceased told his girlfriend to leave with the defendant because he was going to kill himself. He put the shells and the gun on the kitchen table and started to write a suicide note.

The defendant and the deceased's girlfriend left about 3 to 3:30 a.m. When they left, the shells were still on the table.

Steven, out of Kevin's presence and hearing, told Kimberly not to worry, that the bullets were merely blanks and that he wouldn't give Kevin real bullets. Kimberly and Steven prepared to leave.

On the way home, Kimberly asked Steven if the bullets he had given Kevin were really blanks. Steven said that they were and said "besides, the firing pin doesn't work." The girlfriend indicated that both defendant and deceased were about equally intoxicated at this point. The deceased's blood alcohol was found to be .26 percent. * * *

Next morning, one Billy Sherman arrived at about 11:30 a.m. and he and the deceased's roommate found the deceased slumped at the kitchen table with the gun in his hand. Dr. Kopp, the county Pathologist, listed the cause of death as suicide; self-inflicted wound to the temple. * * *

The prosecutor and the trial court relied on *People v. Roberts,* 211 Mich. 187, 178 N.W. 690 (1920), to justify trying defendant for open murder.

In that case, Mr. Roberts' wife had terminal multiple sclerosis. She was in great pain. In the past, she had unsuccessfully attempted suicide by ingesting carbolic acid. At his wife's request, Mr. Roberts made a potion of water and poison and placed it within her reach.

Defendant Roberts was convicted of murder in the first degree.

We are not persuaded by defendant's attempts to distinguish this case from *Roberts, supra.* * * *

The *Roberts* case, without discussion, assumed that a murder had occurred and considered only the degree of that crime. It then determined that the act of placing poison within the reach of the deceased constituted the administration of poison within the meaning of * * * M.C.L. § 750.316; M.S.A. § 28.548, which provided:

> "All murder which shall be perpetrated by means of poison, or lying in wait, or any other kind of wilful, deliberate and premeditated killing, or which shall be committed in the perpetration, or attempt to perpetrate any arson, rape, robbery or burglary, shall be deemed murder of the first degree, and shall be punished by solitary confinement at hard labor in the state prison for life."

The prosecutor argues that inciting to suicide, coupled with the overt act of furnishing a gun to an intoxicated person, in a state of depression, falls within the prohibition, "or other wilful, deliberate and premeditated killing." * * *

The term suicide excludes by definition a homicide. Simply put, the defendant here did not kill another person.

A second ground militates against requiring the defendant to stand trial for murder.

"Courts might well emphasize that juries can convict of murder only when they are convinced beyond a reasonable doubt that (1) the defendant intended * * * to kill * * *." *People v. Morrin,* 31 Mich.App. 301, 323, 187 N.W.2d 434 (1971).

Defendant had no present intention to kill. He provided the weapon and departed. Defendant hoped Basnaw would kill himself but hope alone is not the degree of intention requisite to a charge of murder.

The common law is an emerging process. When a judge finds and applies the common law, hopefully he is applying the customs, usage and moral values of the present day. It is noted that in none of the cases decided [outside Michigan] since 1920 has a defendant, guilty of incitement to suicide, been found guilty of murder. Instead, they have been found guilty of crimes ranging from the equivalent of negligent homicide to voluntary manslaughter. * * *

A number of legislatures have considered the problem and have enacted legislation which may be accepted as evidence of present day social values in this area. A number of states have made, or proposed making, incitement to suicide a crime. * * *

Incitement to suicide has not been held to be a crime in two-thirds of the states of the United States. In the states where incitement to suicide has been held to be a crime, there has been no unanimity as to the nature of severity of the crime. * * *

No Legislature has classified such conduct as murder. * * *

Whether incitement to suicide is a crime under the common law is extremely doubtful.

The Court finds no unanimity of custom or usage strong enough to be given the title of "common law." * * *

While we find the conduct of the defendant morally reprehensible, we do not find it to be criminal under the present state of the law.

The remedy for this situation is in the Legislature. We invite them to adopt legislation on the subject * * *.

The trial court is reversed and the case is remanded with instructions to quash the information and warrant and discharge the defendant.

Notes and Questions

1. Of what offense, if any, is Campbell guilty under the Model Penal Code? See Section 210.5. If Basnaw had failed in his effort to kill himself, would *he* have been guilty of attempted suicide under the Model Code? If attempted suicide is not an offense, is there any justification for punishing a person who assists in a non-offense?

2. The Michigan legislature did not initially accept the invitation of the *Campbell* court to fill in the perceived gap in that state's criminal code. As a consequence, Michigan prosecutors and trial courts were compelled to deal with thorny problems arising from the *Roberts* and *Campbell* cases. Is there a principled way to distinguish between the following two Michigan cases?

Case 1. Bertram Harper, believing that suicide assistance was lawful in Michigan in light of *Campbell,* came to the state with his cancer-stricken wife, Virginia, in order to assist her in her suicide attempt. They went to a hotel near the airport, where Virginia took an overdose of sleeping pills and then pulled a plastic bag over her head. Due to discomfort, she asked her husband to pull the bag off, which he did. When she fell asleep from the pills, Bertram put the bag back over her head, secured it with rubber bands, and waited for her to die. He then notified the police. *Death Pact Fulfilled Her Trust, Husband Testifies,* Detroit Free Press, May 9, 1991, at 1A.

Case 2. Janet Adkins, an Oregon woman suffering from the early stages of Alzheimer's disease, came to Michigan with her husband so that Dr. Jack Kevorkian, a pathologist and advocate of euthanasia, could assist her in committing suicide. In the husband's presence, Kevorkian connected her to a homemade suicide device. After explaining the process to Ms. Adkins, she pushed a button on the machine, which caused lethal drugs to enter a vein in her arm through an intravenous tube. She died within minutes. Isabel Wilkerson, *Inventor of Suicide Machine Arrested on Murder Charge,* New York Times, December 4, 1990, at A1.

In Case 1, Harper was indicted for murder, but acquitted by a jury. Cecil Angel, *"I Knew In My Heart I Was Right",*[k] Detroit Free Press, May 11, 1991, at 1A; Juliana Reno, Comment, *A Little Help From My Friends: The Legal Status of Assisted Suicide,* 25 Creighton L.Rev. 1151 (1992). In Case 2, Kevorkian was indicted for murder, but the trial court quashed the indictment, citing *Campbell,* supra. People v. Kevorkian, No. 90–20157 (52nd Dist.Ct.Mich.1991); Susan K. Jezewski, Comment, *Can a Suicide Machine Trigger the Murder Statute?,* 37 Wayne L.Rev. 1921 (1991).[l]

The Michigan saga, in particular Dr. Kevorkian's participation in suicide attempts, did not end with the Adkins case. See Note 4, p. 852 infra.

b. May (and Should) Suicide Assistance be Punished?

DONALDSON v. LUNDGREN

Court of Appeal of California, Second District, 1992.
2 Cal.App.4th 1614, 4 Cal.Rptr.2d 59.

GILBERT, ASSOCIATE JUSTICE.

Plaintiff Thomas Donaldson wishes to die in order to live. He suffers from an incurable brain disease. He wishes to commit suicide with the assistance of plaintiff Carlos Mondragon so that his body may be cryogenically preserved. It is Donaldson's hope that sometime in the future, when a cure for his disease is found, his body may be brought back to life.

k. Is that what the acquittal implies?

l. In a pre-trial hearing, Dr. Kevorkian testified that although Janet Adkins threw the switch that turned on the machine, the lethal drugs began to slow down in the intravenous tube after she lost consciousness. The prosecutor asked Kevorkian, "Did you do anything to help [the drugs] continue?" Kevorkian testified, "I shook the bottles [to] make sure its flow [was] correct." Arthur Caplan, *Murder Charge is Appropriate in Kevorkian Case,* Detroit Free Press, Jan. 1, 1991, at 2D. Based on this testimony, was the murder charge appropriate?

He and Mondragon appeal a judgment dismissing their action for declaratory and injunctive relief. Despite our sympathy for Donaldson, we must affirm and hold he has no constitutional right to either premortem cryogenic suspension or an assisted suicide. * * *

F<small>ACTS</small> * * *

Plaintiff Thomas Donaldson, a mathematician and computer software scientist, suffers from a malignant brain tumor, diagnosed by physicians as a grade 2 astrocytoma. The astrocytoma, a "space occupying lesion," is inoperable and continues to grow and invade brain tissue. The tumor has caused Donaldson weakness, speech impediments and seizures. Ultimately, continued growth of the tumor will result in Donaldson's persistent vegetative state and death. Physicians have predicted his probable death by August 1993, five years from initial diagnosis.

Donaldson desires to be cryogenically suspended, premortem, with the assistance of Mondragon and others. This procedure would freeze Donaldson's body to be later reanimated when curative treatment exists for his brain cancer. Following cryogenic suspension, Donaldson will suffer irreversible cessation of circulatory and respiratory function and irreversible cessation of all brain function.

He will be dead according to the definition of death set forth in Health and Safety Code section 7180. That section provides: "(a) An individual who has sustained either (1) irreversible cessation of circulatory and respiratory functions, or (2) irreversible cessation of all functions of the entire brain, including the brain stem, is dead...."

Donaldson seeks a judicial declaration that he has a constitutional right to cryogenic suspension premortem with the assistance of others. Alternatively, he asserts he will end his life by a lethal dose of drugs. Mondragon will "advise and encourage" Donaldson through suicide "to minimize the time between his legal death and the onset of the cryonic suspension process."

Recognizing that Mondragon will be committing a homicide, or alternatively, aiding and advising a suicide, Donaldson and Mondragon seek an injunction protecting Mondragon from criminal prosecution. In order not to destroy his chance of reanimation, they also seek a court order to prevent the county coroner from examining Donaldson's remains. * * *

D<small>ISCUSSION</small> * * *

Whatever Donaldson's motivations are for dying, * * * he argues his right to privacy and self-determination are paramount to any state interest in maintaining life. He reasons the state has no logical, secular motive to demand his continued existence, given his medical condition and prognosis. Therefore, there should be no balancing of interests where the state has only an abstract interest in preserving life in general as opposed to Donaldson's specific and compelling interest in ending his particular life. * * *

A person has a constitutionally protected interest in refusing unwanted medical treatment or procedures. (*Cruzan v. Director, Mo. Health Dept.,* 497 U.S. 261, 110 S.Ct. 2841, 2851, 111 L.Ed.2d 224, 241 (1990).) This constitutionally secured right derives from a liberty interest found in the Fourteenth Amendment to the United States Constitution and, in California, from the right of privacy in article 1, section 1 of the California Constitution. The right of patient autonomy has been described as "the ultimate exercise of one's right to privacy."

This right to medical self-determination also derives from the legal doctrine of informed consent to medical treatment. A logical corollary of the doctrine is that a patient possesses the right not to consent and to refuse treatment.

Whether asserting rights resting upon the United States or California Constitution or the decisional law of informed consent, a patient may refuse treatment even though withholding of treatment creates a life-threatening situation. (*Bouvia v. Superior Court,* 179 Cal.App.3d 1127, 1137, 225 Cal.Rptr. 297 [(1986)].) Moreover, the right to refuse treatment or life-sustaining measures is not limited to those who are terminally ill. * * *

To determine whether Donaldson has suffered a violation of his constitutional rights, we must balance his interests against any relevant state interests. Pertinent state interests include preserving human life, preventing suicide, protecting innocent third parties such as children, and maintaining the ethical integrity of the medical profession. * * * (Alexander, *Death by Directive* (1988) 28 Santa Clara L.Rev. 67, 78 (hereafter *Death by Directive*).) The state may also decline to assess the quality of a particular human life and assert an unqualified general interest in the preservation of human life to be balanced against the individual's constitutional rights.

Decisions regarding the right to refuse life-sustaining treatment, including hydration and nourishment, distinguish between artificial life support in the face of inevitable death and self-infliction of deadly harm (suicide). Likewise, decisions hold a physician incurs no criminal liability by terminating life support measures when a patient chooses to abandon such treatment. The rationale of these decisions is that natural death from underlying illness is merely forestalled by life support measures.

Donaldson acknowledges these decisions concern patients in persistent vegetative states or patients otherwise dependent upon life-sustaining measures, but argues a refusal of further medical treatment is a legal fiction for suicide: "As is often true in times of social transition, case law has created fictions to avoid affronting previously accepted norms. [Fn. omitted.] In life support termination, there is a fiction of medical determinism. Patients are seen as passive victims of their illness. They do not choose to die; death overtakes them. Their physicians do nothing to help them die. Death overwhelms them, too." (*Death by Directive, supra,* at p. 82.)

Donaldson argues that the doctor who disconnects the support system is taking affirmative action that in fact causes the death of the patient. He points out that even if the doctor assists the patient to die by doing nothing, he or she is actively participating in ending the patient's life. " 'Not doing anything is doing something. It is a decision to act every bit as much as deciding for any other deed. If I decide not to eat or drink anymore, knowing what the consequence will be, I have committed suicide as surely as if I had used a gas oven.' J. FLETCHER, HUMANHOOD: ESSAYS IN BIOMEDICAL ETHICS 157 (1979)." (Note, *Suicidal Competence and the Patient's Right to Refuse Lifesaving Treatment* (1987) 75 Cal.L.Rev. 707, 740, fn. 213.)

There may be an apparent similarity between the patient and doctor, and Donaldson and Mondragon, but in fact there is a significant difference. The patient, for example, who is being kept alive by a life-support system has taken a detour that usually postpones an immediate encounter with death. In short, the medical treatment has prolonged life and prevented death from overtaking the patient. Stopping the treatment allows the delayed meeting with death to take place.

Donaldson is asking that we sanction something quite different. Here there are no life-prolonging measures to be discontinued. Instead, a third person will simply kill Donaldson and hasten the encounter with death. No statute or judicial opinion countenances Donaldson's decision to consent to be murdered or to commit suicide with the assistance of others.

Donaldson, however, may take his own life. He makes a persuasive argument that his specific interest in ending his life is more compelling than the state's abstract interest in preserving life in general. No state interest is compromised by allowing Donaldson to experience a dignified death rather than an excruciatingly painful life.

Nevertheless, even if we were to characterize Donaldson's taking his own life as the exercise of a fundamental right, it does not follow that he may implement the right in the manner he wishes here. It is one thing to take one's own life, but quite another to allow a third person assisting in that suicide to be immune from investigation by the coroner or law enforcement agencies.

In such a case, the state has a legitimate competing interest in protecting society against abuses. This interest is more significant than merely the abstract interest in preserving life no matter what the quality of that life is. Instead, it is the interest of the state to maintain social order through enforcement of the criminal law and to protect the lives of those who wish to live no matter what their circumstances. This interest overrides any interest Donaldson possesses in ending his life through the assistance of a third person in violation of the state's penal laws. We cannot expand the nature of Donaldson's right of privacy to provide a protective shield for third persons who end his life.

Donaldson argues that his right to die is like a citizen's right to vote. An invalid, for example, may need the assistance of a third person to get to the polling booth. Donaldson argues that in similar fashion his claimed right to take his life carries with it the right to assistance in exercising that right.

In the example of the invalid voter, the state has no competing interest to prevent assistance. Quite the contrary, the state's interest is to encourage its citizens to vote. In the case of assisted suicides, however, the state has an important interest to ensure that people are not influenced to kill themselves. The state's interest must prevail over the individual because of the difficulty, if not the impossibility, of evaluating the motives of the assister or determining the presence of undue influence. * * *

It is unfortunate for Donaldson that the courts cannot always accommodate the special needs of an individual. We realize that time is critical to Donaldson, but the legal and philosophical problems posed by his predicament are a legislative matter rather than a judicial one. * * *

Notes and Questions

1. In Bouvia v. Superior Court, 179 Cal.App.3d 1127, 225 Cal.Rptr. 297 (1986), cited in *Donaldson,* Elizabeth Bouvia sought the removal of a nasogastric tube inserted and maintained against her will for the purpose of keeping her alive.

Bouvia, 28 years old at the time of the law suit, was a quadriplegic suffering from severe cerebral palsy. She was bedridden, nearly immobile, and dependent on others for all of her basic needs. She also suffered from painful degenerative arthritis. The arthritic pain was reduced by the insertion of a tube in her chest, which periodically injected doses of morphine into her body. Bouvia wanted the doctors to remove the nasogastric tube so that she could die, but she wanted the hospital to maintain the morphine doses so that her death would not be painful.

The hospital refused to comply, and a trial court denied her petition for relief. On appeal, the state appellate court held that a mentally competent patient who understands the risks involved has a constitutional right to refuse treatment. The court ruled that the state's legitimate interest in preserving life was outweighed by Bouvia's right to refuse treatment.

2. Cruzan v. Director, Missouri Dept. of Health, 497 U.S. 261, 110 S.Ct. 2841, 111 L.Ed.2d 224 (1990), also cited in *Donaldson,* involved Nancy Cruzan, a young woman brain damaged from a car accident, who was kept alive for eight years in a state hospital in a "chronic vegetative state."

Once it became apparent that there was no meaningful chance that Cruzan would regain consciousness, her parents requested that hospital personnel disconnect their daughter's artificial feeding and hydration equipment so that she could die. When the hospital refused, the parents sought relief from a trial court, which granted their petition. The trial court ruled that a person in Cruzan's condition has a constitutional right to demand the withdrawal of "death prolonging procedures." It also found that, while healthy, Cruzan had told a friend that she would not wish to continue her life in a vegetative state.

The state supreme court reversed the judgment of the trial court. It ruled that the parents' petition should not be granted in the absence of clear and convincing evidence of the patient's wishes. Cruzan's statements to a friend were deemed "unreliable for the purpose of determining her intent." Cruzan v. Harmon, 760 S.W.2d 408, 424 (Mo.1988).

On further appeal, the United States Supreme Court ruled that a competent person has a liberty interest under the due process clause in refusing unwanted medical treatment, an interest which must be balanced against the state's interest in preserving life. The high court assumed, although it did not hold, that the interest of a competent person in refusing lifesaving hydration and nutrition outweighs the state's interests.

The Court held, however, that in the case of an incompetent person, such as Cruzan, a state may properly require clear and convincing evidence of the patient's wishes regarding the withdrawal of life-sustaining treatment. Moreover, the due process clause does not require a state to accept the "substituted judgment" of close family members in the absence of clear and convincing evidence of the incompetent patient's wishes.

3. *Euthanasia.* Recent initiative measures in California and Washington intended to permit "physician aid-in-dying" were defeated by voters in those states.[m] The Washington initiative provided, in part:

Sec. 1.   * * * In recognition of the dignity and privacy which patients have a right to expect, the people hereby declare that the laws of the state of Washington shall recognize the right of an adult person to make a written directive instructing such person's physician to withhold or withdraw life-sustaining procedures in the event of a terminal condition, and/or to request and receive aid-in-dying under the provisions of this chapter.

Sec. 2.   * * * Unless the context clearly requires otherwise, the definitions contained in this section shall apply throughout this chapter. * * *

(6) "Qualified patient" means a patient diagnosed and certified in writing to be afflicted with a terminal condition by two physicians[,] one of whom shall be the attending physician, who have personally examined the patient.

(7) "Terminal condition" means an incurable or irreversible condition which, in the written opinion of two physicians having examined the patient and exercising reasonable medical judgment, will result in

---

m. In Michigan, however, where Dr. Kevorkian was active in assisting in a large number of suicides (see Note 4 infra), a survey found that state residents, by a 58–31% margin, favored "legislation that would permit doctors to help a patient commit suicide if the patient is terminally ill." Detroit Free Press, Feb. 10, 1992, at 1A.

This attitude may not be limited to Michigan or to suicide assistance. In mock-jury murder prosecutions of defendants charged with euthanasia, investigators reported sizable nullifications of the law (25% not guilty verdicts) and partial nullifications (39% found guilty of lesser offenses). Norman J. Finkel, Marie L. Hurabiell, and Kevin C. Hughes, *Right to Die, Euthanasia, and Community Sentiment: Crossing the Public/Private Boundary,* 17 Law & Hum. Behav. 487 (1993).

death within six months, or a condition in which the patient has been determined in writing by two physicians as having no reasonable probability of recovery from an irreversible coma or persistent vegetative state. * * *

(9) "Aid-in-dying" means aid in the form of a medical service provided in person by a physician that will end the life of a conscious and mentally competent qualified patient in a dignified, painless and humane matter, when requested voluntarily by the patient through a written directive in accordance with this chapter * * *.

Sec. 3. [Provides for an adult person to execute a revocable directive, to be witnessed by two persons who are neither related to the declarant nor entitled to any portion of the estate of the declarant, which directs the physician to provide aid-in-dying if the patient lacks the ability to give directions regarding the use of life-sustaining procedures, while in an irreversible coma or persistent vegetative state.] * * *

Sec. 5. * * * No physician [or other licensed health personnel, acting under the direction of a physician] or health facility which, acting in good faith in accordance with the requirements of this chapter, causes the withholding or withdrawing of life-sustaining procedures from a qualified patient, shall be subject to civil [or criminal] liability therefrom [or] * * * be guilty of any * * * unprofessional conduct. * * *

Sec. 8. * * * The act of withholding or withdrawing life-sustaining procedures or providing aid-in-dying, when done pursuant to a directive described [herein] * * * shall not be construed to be an intervening force or to affect the chain of proximate cause between the conduct of any person that placed the declarer in a terminal condition and the death of a declarer. * * *

From a criminal law perspective, would this initiative have done more than simply immunize medical personnel from prosecutions for suicide assistance? Does this initiative permit euthanasia, i.e., the "merciful" killing of another? If so, is such a law desirable? Much of the debate in this regard relates to "sanctity of life" and "quality of life" considerations.

Professor Philip Peters has articulated (although he does not endorse) the basic claim of those who assert that a state has an overriding interest in protecting the sanctity of life:

> For some people, especially those with a deep faith in God, life itself may have an intrinsic value that makes intentionally ending it morally wrong, at least in the absence of an equally compelling moral excuse. This view may reflect a belief that all humans, like Job, have a responsibility to live out their lives and that they lack the authority or the capacity to judge either the value of their own lives or the value of the lives of their wards. * * *

> Most importantly, this moral mandate partly explains the past criminality of suicide. At common law, suicide was *malum in se,* like murder, an offense against God and nature. Self-destruction was unnatural because it was contrary to the instinct for self-preservation. Suicide offended God because it breached God's proscription "Thou

shalt not kill." It usurped God's right to end life. Suicide also cheapened life by treating it as alienable.

Disentangling the state's interest in the sanctity or intrinsic value of life from other policies served by the state's interest in the preservation of life is difficult, and, perhaps, a little unfair. The phrase "sanctity of life" itself has many possible meanings. At its core lies the idea that all life is equally valuable and worthy of respect regardless of age, handicap, race, or other attribute. In this respect, it constitutes a widely shared liberal ideal, demanding protection of the vulnerable against error and abuse. * * * But sanctity of life objections often run deeper than fears of error or extension. * * * Under this view, a preference for death is itself morally wrong and the state may legitimately refuse to condone it. Even though this viewpoint may be interwoven with concerns about abuse and extension, it seems appropriate to consider the moral objection in isolation from its related concerns.

Philip G. Peters, Jr., *The State's Interest in the Preservation of Life: From Quinlan to Cruzan,* 50 Ohio St.L.J. 891, 951–52 (1989).

The quality-of-life argument runs as follows:

For the severely, irreversibly ill, a rational choice for euthanasia promotes control over the end of life. At stake, observes Sheldon Kurtz, is a "matter of vital, exclusive importance: the timing, manner and circumstance of one's death." [87] The choice has practical, philosophical and spiritual ingredients.

Opponents of euthanasia often emphasize the spiritual nature of their views, rooting their opposition in the idea that life is a gift of God. The cliche about "playing God" when making life and death decisions is meant to restrain decisions favoring death. But it is wrong to leave the spiritual ground to euthanasia opponents. Decisions about death are inherently philosophical and, for believers in God, religious. Believers who contemplate euthanasia must necessarily resolve for themselves spiritual questions as to life's meaning and the proper realms of God and man. * * *

One's appreciation of life may lead to an acceptance of its end in circumstances that promote ideals of love, kindness and human connection. Dr. Timothy Quill, in his account of his [terminally ill] patient Diane,[n] noted that once [he provided her with] a supply of drugs * * * to end her life, she was relieved of the fear of painful and dependent death. She was then able to make "deep, personal connections with her family and close friends." * * *

Disease and its treatment rob the individual of a great deal. Some conditions cause a host of extreme physical effects: bones so brittle they easily break, severely impaired breathing, constant exhaustion, emaciation, paralysis, blindness, recurrent nausea and vomiting, persistent fever and inability to eat or sleep. Physical problems often come in

---

87. *Should Physicians Perform Euthanasia?* [Am. Med. News 12 (Jan. 7, 1991)], at 13 (response of Sheldon F. Kurtz).

n. Timothy E. Quill, *Death and Dignity: A Case of Individualized Decision Making,* 324 N. Eng. J. Med. 691 (1991).

multiples, with increasing bodily degradation and pain. Mental deterioration adds a different cluster of problems, from loss of memory and ability to perform everyday tasks to the inability to communicate with or even recognize others. Treatments for serious diseases often have their own toxic side effects, intensifying physical and mental suffering.

The magnitude of psychological suffering that accompanies dire medical conditions is easily underestimated. The varied sources of psychic pain that grip the victim of catastrophic illness include losses of privacy, lifestyle and established routines; the destruction of one's sense of security and sense of normalcy; the painful awareness of one's former physical powers and present incapacities; the dreaded anticipation of future mental and physical deterioration; the loss of control over one's life and life plans; the unwanted dependence on machines and doctors; the loss of home and of social roles in the outside world brought about by hospitalization; and the loss of hope, of optimism about the future, and of pleasure in life. For some there is the pain of knowing that one is destined, in Samuel Gorovitz's words, "to witness and endure a final stage not as an effective agent, but merely a deteriorating object." [96]
* * *

Finally, people have an interest in how they will be remembered. The manner of one's death may overshadow other facets of one's life, to the point of haunting loved ones who witness an intolerable death.

Stephen A. Newman, *Euthanasia: Orchestrating "The Last Syllable of . . . Time,"* 53 U.Pitt.L.Rev. 153, 179–82 (1991).

Another feature of the euthanasia debate concerns the "slippery slope" or "wedge principle." The concern is that even if passive euthanasia (e.g., omitting lifesaving medical treatment so that a person may die) is morally permissible, its toleration would lead to acceptance of active voluntary euthanasia (e.g., killing a person who requests it) and, ultimately, of active *involuntary* euthanasia.

One of the richest debates in this regard took place in the 1950s with the publication of Professor Glanville Williams's book, The Sanctity of Life and the Criminal Law (1957), in which he advocated legalization of voluntary euthanasia. Professor Yale Kamisar responded:

> Look, when the messenger cometh, shut the door, and hold him fast at the door; is not the sound of his master's feet behind him? [210]

> This is the "wedge principle," the "parade of horrors" objection, if you will, to voluntary euthanasia. * * * I agree with Williams that if a first step is "moral" it is moral wherever a second step may take us. The real point, however, the point that Williams sloughs, is that whether or not the first step is precarious, is perilous, is worth taking, rests in part on what the second step is likely to be.

---

96. Samuel Gorovitz, Doctors' Dilemma: Moral Conflict and Medical Care 153 (1982) *quoted in* M. Pabst Battin, *The Least Worth Death,* Hastings Center Rep. 15 (April, 1983).

210. II *Kings,* VI, 32, quoted and applied in Sperry, *The Case Against Mercy Killing,* 70 Am.Mercury 271, 276 (1950).

It is true that the "wedge" objection can always be advanced, the horrors can always be paraded. But it is no less true that on some occasions the objection is much more valid than it is on others. One reason why the "parade of horrors" cannot be too lightly dismissed in this particular instance is that Miss Voluntary Euthanasia is not likely to be going it alone for very long. Many of her admirers * * * would be neither surprised nor distressed to see her joined by Miss Euthanatize the Congenital Idiots and Miss Euthanatize the Permanently Insane and Miss Euthanatize the Senile Dementia. * * *

Another reason why the "parade of horrors" argument cannot be too easily dismissed in this particular instance, it seems to me, is that the parade *has* taken place in our time and the order of procession has been headed by the killing of "incurables" and the "useless":

> Even before the Nazis took open charge in Germany, a propaganda barrage was directed against the traditional compassionate nine-teenth-century attitudes toward the chronically ill, and for the adoption of a utilitarian, Hegelian point of view. * * * The begin-nings at first were merely a subtle shift in emphasis in the basic attitude of the physicians. *It started with the acceptance of the attitude, basic in the euthanasia movement, that there is such a thing as life not worthy to be lived.* This attitude in its early stages concerned itself merely with the severely and chronically sick. Gradually the sphere of those to be included in this category was enlarged to encompass the socially unproductive, the ideologically unwanted, the racially unwanted and finally all non-Germans.
> * * * [213]

It can't happen here. Well, maybe it cannot, but no small part of our Constitution and no small number of our Supreme Court opinions stem from the fear that *it can happen here unless we darn well make sure that it does not* by adamantly holding the line, by swiftly snuffing out what are or might be small beginnings of what we do not want to happen here.

Yale Kamisar, *Some Non–Religious Views Against Proposed "Mercy–Killing" Legislation*, 42 Minn.L.Rev. 969, 1030–32, 1038 (1958).

Professor Williams replied:

> Kamisar's particular bogey, the racial laws of Nazi Germany, is an effective one in the democratic countries. Any reference to the Nazis is a powerful weapon to prevent change in the traditional taboo on * * * euthanasia. * * *
>
> But it is insufficient to answer the "wedge" objection in general terms; we must consider the particular fears to which it gives rise. Kamisar professes to fear certain other measures that the Euthanasia societies may bring up if their present measure is conceded to them. Surely, these other measures, if any, will be debated on their merits? Does he seriously fear that anyone in the United States is going to

---

213. Alexander, *Medical Science Under Dictatorship*, 241 New England Journal of   Medicine 39, 44, 50 (1949) (emphasis add-ed). * * *

propose the extermination of people of a minority race or religion? Let us put aside such ridiculous fancies and discuss practical politics.

The author is quite right in thinking that a body of opinion would favour the legalization of the involuntary euthanasia of hopelessly defective infants, and some day a proposal of this kind may be put forward. The proposal would have distinct limits, just as the proposal for voluntary euthanasia of incurable sufferers has limits. I do not think that any responsible body of opinion would now propose the euthanasia of insane adults, for the perfectly clear reason that any such practice would greatly increase the sense of insecurity felt by the borderline insane and by the large number of insane persons who have sufficient understanding on this particular matter.

Kamisar expresses distress at a concluding remark in my book in which I advert to the possibility of old people becoming an overwhelming burden on mankind. I share his feeling that there are profoundly disturbing possibilities here; and if I had been merely a propagandist, intent upon securing agreement for a specific measure of law reform, I should have done wisely to have omitted all reference to this subject. Since, however, I am merely an academic writer, trying to bring such intelligence as I have to bear on moral and social issues, I deemed the topic too important and threatening to leave without a word. I think I have made it clear * * * that I am not for one moment proposing any euthanasia of the aged in the present society; such an idea would shock me as much as it shocks Kamisar and would shock everybody else. Still, the fact that we may one day have to face is that medical science is more successful in preserving the body than in preserving the mind. It is not impossible that, in the foreseeable future, medical men will be able to preserve the mindless body until the age, say, of 1000, while the mind itself will have lasted only a tenth of that time. What will mankind do then? It is hardly possible to imagine that we shall establish huge hospital-mausolea where the aged are kept in a kind of living death. Even if it is desired to do this, the cost of the undertaking may make it impossible.

This is not an immediately practical problem, and we need not yet face it. The problem of maintaining persons afflicted with senile dementia is well within our economic resources as the matter stands at present. Perhaps some barrier will be found to medical advance which will prevent the problem from becoming more acute.

Glanville Williams, *"Mercy–Killing" Legislation—A Rejoinder,* 43 Minn. L.Rev. 1, 10–12 (1958).

4. *A legislative effort to prohibit suicide assistance.* As voters in California and Washington were considering measures to permit some forms of suicide assistance and/or euthanasia (Note 3), legislators in Michigan were moving in the opposite direction. In 1993, after Dr. Jack Kevorkian assisted a fifteenth person to commit suicide in that state (his first effort is chronicled in Note 2, p. 842 supra), the state legislature passed a law reading in pertinent part:

(1) A person who has knowledge that another person intends to commit or attempt to commit suicide and who intentionally does either

of the following is guilty of criminal assistance to suicide, a felony punishable by imprisonment for not more than 4 years or by a fine of not more than $2,000.00, or both:

(a) Provides the physical means by which the other person attempts or commits suicide;

(b) Participates in a physical act by which the other person attempts or commits suicide.

(2) Subsection (1) shall neither be applicable to nor deemed to affect any other laws that may be applicable to withholding or withdrawing medical treatment by a licensed health care professional.

(3) A licensed health care professional who administers, prescribes, or dispenses medications or procedures to relieve a person's pain or discomfort, even if the medication or procedure may hasten or increase the risk of death, is not guilty of assistance to suicide under this section unless the medications or procedures are knowingly and intentionally administered, prescribed, or dispensed to cause death. [Mich.Comp. Law.Ann. § 752.1027 (1993).] *o*

How broad is the scope of this law? Assume that Paul commits suicide. Under which of the following circumstances would Quincy be guilty of suicide assistance under Section 752.1027?

A. When Paul said that he intended to shoot himself, Quincy attempted to dissuade him. When Quincy failed in that effort, he convinced Paul to kill himself "less painfully" by taking an overdose of sleeping pills, which he furnished.

B. Quincy helped Paul to compose a suicide letter to his wife, immediately before Paul took his life.

C. Quincy sat with Paul, holding his hand and comforting him, while Paul took his own life.

D. Quincy stood by and watched Paul, his suicidal teenage son, take an overdose of pills.

E. Same as D., but Quincy said to his son as he was ingesting the pills, "Good, I'm glad you're killing yourself."

F. After Paul's house was burglarized, Quincy, Paul's neighbor, loaned him a gun for self-protection. At the time, Paul was suffering from inoperable cancer, and Quincy knew that Paul intended to kill himself when the condition became more severe. Nine months later, Paul committed suicide with Quincy's gun.

As you now understand the scope of the statute, does it go too far? Not far enough? How would *Campbell* (p. 839 supra) be decided under this statute? What about *Roberts,* discussed in *Campbell?*

---

o. In the same legislation, Michigan created a commission to develop recommendations for further laws relating to issues of death and dying, and to submit the recommendations within 15 months from the effective date of the Act. The law provides for automatic repeal of the criminal provisions set out above, six months following the submission of the recommendations.

B. LIABILITY OF CONSPIRATORS
INTRODUCTORY COMMENT

In many jurisdictions, "conspiracy," an inchoate offense, also constitutes a basis independent of accomplice liability for holding a person accountable for the actions of others. As the following materials suggest, not only is it conceptually possible (although uncommon) for a person to be a co-conspirator without being an accomplice, but conspiracy liability can be broader than accomplice liability.

PINKERTON v. UNITED STATES
Supreme Court of the United States, 1946.
328 U.S. 640, 66 S.Ct. 1180, 90 L.Ed. 1489.

MR. JUSTICE DOUGLAS delivered the opinion of the Court.

Walter and Daniel Pinkerton are brothers who live a short distance from each other on Daniel's farm. They were indicted for violations of the Internal Revenue Code. The indictment contained ten substantive counts and one conspiracy count. The jury found Walter guilty on nine of the substantive counts and on the conspiracy count. It found Daniel guilty on six of the substantive counts and on the conspiracy count. * * *

A single conspiracy was charged and proved. * * * Each of the substantive offenses found was committed pursuant to the conspiracy. * * *

It is contended that there was insufficient evidence to implicate Daniel in the conspiracy. But we think there was enough evidence for submission of the issue to the jury.

There is, however, no evidence to show that Daniel participated directly in the commission of the substantive offenses on which his conviction has been sustained, although there was evidence to show that these substantive offenses were in fact committed by Walter in furtherance of the unlawful agreement or conspiracy existing between the brothers. The question was submitted to the jury on the theory that each petitioner could be found guilty of the substantive offenses, if it was found at the time those offenses were committed petitioners were parties to an unlawful conspiracy and the substantive offenses charged were in fact committed in furtherance of it.[6]

Daniel relies on United States v. Sall [116 F.2d 745 (3rd Cir.1940)]. That case held that participation in the conspiracy was not itself enough to sustain a conviction for the substantive offense even though it was committed in furtherance of the conspiracy. The court held that, in addition to evidence that the offense was in fact committed in furtherance of the conspiracy, evidence of direct participation in the commission of the substantive offense or other evidence from which participation might fairly be inferred was necessary.

---

6. * * * Daniel was not indicted as an aider or abettor, nor was his case submitted to the jury on that theory.

We take a different view. We have here a continuous conspiracy. There is here no evidence of the affirmative action on the part of Daniel which is necessary to establish his withdrawal from it. * * * And so long as the partnership in crime continues, the partners act for each other in carrying it forward. It is settled that "an overt act of one partner may be the act of all without any new agreement specifically directed to that act." United States v. Kissel, 218 U.S. 601, 608, 31 S.Ct. 124, 126, 54 L.Ed. 1168. * * *

A different case would arise if the substantive offense committed by one of the conspirators was not in fact done in furtherance of the conspiracy, did not fall within the scope of the unlawful project, or was merely a part of the ramifications of the plan which could not be reasonably foreseen as a necessary or natural consequence of the unlawful agreement. But as we read this record, that is not this case.

Affirmed.

Mr. Justice Rutledge, dissenting in part.

The judgment concerning Daniel Pinkerton should be reversed. In my opinion it is without precedent here and is a dangerous precedent to establish.

* * * The proof showed that Walter alone committed the substantive crimes. There was none to establish that Daniel participated in them, aided and abetted Walter in committing them, or knew that he had done so. Daniel in fact was in the penitentiary, under sentence for other crimes, when some of Walter's crimes were done. * * *

The court's theory seems to be that Daniel and Walter became general partners in crime by virtue of their agreement and because of that agreement without more on his part Daniel became criminally responsible as a principal for everything Walter did thereafter in the nature of a criminal offense of the general sort the agreement contemplated, so long as there was not clear evidence that Daniel had withdrawn from or revoked the agreement. Whether or not his commitment to the penitentiary had that effect, the result is a vicarious criminal responsibility as broad as, or broader than, the vicarious civil liability of a partner for acts done by a co-partner in the course of the firm's business.

Such analogies from private commercial law and the law of torts are dangerous, in my judgment, for transfer to the criminal field. Guilt there * * * remains personal, not vicarious, for the more serious offenses. It should be kept so. * * *

Notes and Questions

1. In *Pinkerton,* Daniel conspired with Walter, but did not aid and abet in the commission of the substantive offenses. Can you suggest a scenario in which a person is an accomplice, but not a conspirator?

2. *Pinkerton v. accomplice liability.* Is the dissent in *Pinkerton* correct in objecting to the rule announced by the majority? In light of the natural-

and-probable-consequences rule applicable to accomplices (see p. 805 supra), is there any practical difference between the *Pinkerton* rule and accomplice liability?

In this regard, consider People v. Luciano, 277 N.Y. 348, 14 N.E.2d 433 (1938). *L* was the head of a prostitution ring. He and four managers of the criminal enterprise were convicted of 62 counts of prostitution, each count involving a specific instance of placing a woman in a house of prostitution, receiving money for so doing, or receiving money from her earnings. The court justified the convictions for the substantive offenses as follows:

> If five men meet in a room, and the leader directs that one shall commit a burglary on a bank one night; that another commit a burglary on a jewelry store the next; and that the others commit a burglary in a fur shop on another night, can it be possible that the leader who directs and superintends all these burglaries can only be tried for a conspiracy * * *? Of course not. He is guilty, although he never left that room, of all these three burglaries, and by proving this conspiracy, which need not be alleged in the indictment, he could be convicted of the crimes of burglary committed on these three different nights.

Id. at 359, 14 N.E.2d at 435–36.

The court's burglary hypothetical obscures the controversial nature of the *Pinkerton* doctrine. In the hypothetical, the leader of the burglary ring could be convicted of the substantive offenses on traditional accomplice grounds. The more intriguing question is whether the prostitutes in *Luciano* could be held responsible under *Pinkerton* as co-conspirators for every criminal act committed by every other prostitute. Could they be? Realistically, could they be convicted of these offenses on the basis of accomplice liability?

The *Pinkerton* rule was applied to lesser functionaries in Anderson v. Superior Court, 78 Cal.App.2d 22, 177 P.2d 315 (1947), in which an abortionist (Stern) performed illegal abortions on pregnant women sent to him by Anderson and sixteen co-conspirators, who received fees for their referrals. Stern, Anderson, and the sixteen other contacts were prosecuted for conspiracy to perform abortions and for twenty-six separate counts of abortion. That is, Anderson was prosecuted not only for the abortions performed on the women she directed to Stern, but also for those performed on those sent to Stern by others. Could she have been convicted of these offenses as an accomplice?

3. At the time of the adoption of the Model Penal Code, minor parties to conspiracies were infrequently held responsible for substantive offenses over which they exerted no influence. According to the American Law Institute:

> The cases that declare the [*Pinkerton*] doctrine normally involve defendants who have had a hand in planning, directing, or executing the crimes charged. When that is so, the other principles of accessorial liability establish guilt * * *. Indeed, when that is not so, courts may be expected to seek ways to avoid the conclusion of complicity, though traditional [*Pinkerton*] doctrine hardly points the way.

American Law Institute, Model Penal Code and Commentaries, Comment to § 2.06 at 308–09 (1985).

According to one scholar, however, "the most striking change in the conspiracy area during the past two decades has been the enormous number of cases involving many defendants * * * and dozens and dozens of complicated [substantive] charges." Paul Marcus, *Criminal Conspiracy Law: Time to Turn Back From an Ever Expanding, Ever More Troubling Area,* 1 Wm. & Mary Bill of Rts. J. 1, 10 (1992).

The drafters of the Code believed that the "law would lose all sense of just proportion if simply because of the conspiracy itself each [conspirator] were held accountable for thousands of additional offenses of which he was completely unaware and which he did not influence at all." American Law Institute, Model Penal Code and Commentaries, Comment to § 2.06 at 307 (1985).

Do you agree? Or do you concur in the statement that "[a]lthough it may appear to some that this rule is unduly harsh, such harshness may be considered as an occupational hazard confronting those who might be tempted to engage in a criminal conspiracy * * *"? State v. Barton, 424 A.2d 1033, 1038 (R.I.1981).

4. How would Daniel's liability for Walter's actions in *Pinkerton* be resolved under Model Penal Code § 2.06? See American Law Institute, Model Penal Code and Commentaries, Comment to § 2.06 at 307 (1985).

C. VICARIOUS LIABILITY

COMMONWEALTH v. KOCZWARA

Supreme Court of Pennsylvania, 1959.
397 Pa. 575, 155 A.2d 825.

COHEN, JUSTICE.

This is an appeal from the judgment of the Court of Quarter Sessions of Lackawanna County sentencing the defendant to three months in the Lackawanna County Jail, a fine of five hundred dollars and the costs of prosecution, in a case involving violations of the Pennsylvania Liquor Code.

John Koczwara, the defendant, is the licensee and operator of an establishment on Jackson Street in the City of Scranton known as J.K.'s Tavern. At that place he had a restaurant liquor license issued by the Pennsylvania Liquor Control Board. The Lackawanna County Grand Jury indicted the defendant on [four] counts for violations of the Liquor Code. The first and second counts averred that the defendant permitted minors, unaccompanied by parents, guardians or other supervisors, to frequent the tavern on February 1st and 8th, 1958; the third count charged the defendant with selling beer to minors on February 8th, 1958; [and] the fourth charged the defendant with permitting beer to be sold to minors on February 8th, 1958 * * *. * * *

At the conclusion of the Commonwealth's evidence, count three of the indictment, charging the sale by the defendant personally to the minors, was removed from the jury's consideration by the trial judge on the ground that there was no evidence that the defendant had personally participated in the sale or was present in the tavern when sales to the minors took place. Defense counsel then demurred to the evidence as to the other three counts. The demurrer was overruled. Defendant thereupon rested without introducing any evidence and moved for a directed verdict of acquittal. The motion was denied, the case went to the jury and the jury returned a verdict of guilty as to each of the remaining three counts: two counts of permitting minors to frequent the licensed premises without parental or other supervision, and the count of permitting sales to minors. * * *

Defendant raises two contentions, both of which, in effect, question whether the undisputed facts of this case support the judgment and sentence imposed by the Quarter Sessions Court. Judge Hoban found as fact that "in every instance the purchase [by minors] was made from a bartender, not identified by name, and service to the boys was made by the bartender. There was no evidence that the defendant was present on any one of the occasions testified to by these witnesses, nor that he had any personal knowledge of the sales to them or to other persons on the premises." We, therefore, must determine the criminal responsibility of a licensee of the Liquor Control Board for acts committed by his employees upon his premises, without his personal knowledge, participation, or presence, which acts violate a valid regulatory statute passed under the Commonwealth's police power.

While an employer in almost all cases is not criminally responsible for the unlawful acts of his employees, unless he consents to, approves, or participates in such acts, courts all over the nation have struggled for years in applying this rule within the framework of "controlling the sale of intoxicating liquor." At common law, any attempt to invoke the doctrine of *respondeat superior* in a criminal case would have run afoul of our deeply ingrained notions of criminal jurisprudence that guilt must be personal and individual.[1] In recent decades, however, many states have enacted detailed regulatory provisions in fields which are essentially non-criminal, e.g., pure food and drug acts, speeding ordinances, building regulations, and child labor, minimum wage and maximum hour legislation. Such statutes are generally enforceable by light penalties, and although violations are labelled crimes, the considerations applicable to them are totally different from those applicable to true crimes, which involve moral delinquency and which are punishable by imprisonment or another serious penalty. Such so-called statutory crimes are in reality an attempt to utilize the machinery of criminal

---

1. The distinction between *respondeat superior* in tort law and its application to the criminal law is obvious. In tort law, the doctrine is employed for the purpose of settling the incidence of loss upon the party who can best bear such loss. But the criminal law is supported by totally different concepts. We impose penal treatment upon those who injure or menace social interests, partly in order to reform, partly to prevent the continuation of the anti-social activity and partly to deter others. If a defendant has personally lived up to the social standards of the criminal law and has not menaced or injured anyone, why impose penal treatment?

administration as an enforcing arm for social regulations of a purely civil nature, with the punishment totally unrelated to questions of moral wrongdoing or guilt. It is here that the social interest in the general well-being and security of the populace has been held to outweigh the individual interest of the particular defendant. The penalty is imposed despite the defendant's lack of a criminal intent or mens rea.

Not the least of the legitimate police power areas of the legislature is the control of intoxicating liquor. * * * It is abundantly clear that the conduct of the liquor business is lawful only to the extent and manner permitted by statute. Individuals who embark on such an enterprise do so with knowledge of considerable peril, since their actions are rigidly circumscribed by the Liquor Code.

Because of the peculiar nature of this business, one who applies for and receives permission from the Commonwealth to carry on the liquor trade assumes the highest degree of responsibility to his fellow citizens. As the licensee of the Board, he is under a duty not only to regulate his own personal conduct in a manner consistent with the permit he has received, but also to control the acts and conduct of any employee to whom he entrusts the sale of liquor. Such fealty is the *quid pro quo* which the Commonwealth demands in return for the privilege of entering the highly restricted and, what is more important, the highly dangerous business of selling intoxicating liquor.

In the instant case, the defendant has sought to surround himself with all the safeguards provided to those within the pale of criminal sanctions. He has argued that a statute imposing criminal responsibility should be construed strictly, with all doubts resolved in his favor. While the defendant's position is entirely correct, we must remember that we are dealing with a statutory crime within the state's plenary police power. In the field of liquor regulation, the legislature has enacted a comprehensive Code aimed at regulating and controlling the use and sale of alcoholic beverages. The question here raised is whether the legislature intended to impose vicarious criminal liability on the licensee-principal for acts committed on his premises without his presence, participation or knowledge.

This Court has stated, as long ago as Commonwealth v. Weiss, 139 Pa. 247, 251, 21 A. 10 (1891), that "whether a criminal intent, or a guilty knowledge, is a necessary ingredient of a statutory offense ... is a matter of construction. It is for the legislature to determine whether the public injury, threatened in any particular matter, is such and so great as to justify an absolute and indiscriminate prohibition."

In the Liquor Code, Section 493, the legislature has set forth twenty-five specific acts which are condemned as unlawful, and for which penalties are provided in Section 494. Subsections (1) and (14) of Section 493 contain the two offenses charged here. In neither of these subsections is there any language which would require the prohibited acts to have been done either knowingly, wilfully or intentionally, there being a significant absence of such words as "knowingly, wilfully, etc."

* * * The omission of any such word in the subsections of Section 494 is highly significant. It indicates a legislative intent to eliminate both knowledge and criminal intent as necessary ingredients of such offenses. * * *

As the defendant has pointed out, there is a distinction between the requirement of a mens rea and the imposition of vicarious absolute liability for the acts of another. It may be that the courts below, in relying on prior authority, have failed to make such a distinction.[5] In any case, we fully recognize it. Moreover, we find that the intent of the legislature in enacting this Code was not only to eliminate the common law requirement of a mens rea, but also to place a very high degree of responsibility upon the holder of a liquor license to make certain that neither he nor anyone in his employ commit any of the prohibited acts upon the licensed premises. Such a burden of care is imposed upon the licensee in order to protect the public from the potentially noxious effects of an inherently dangerous business. We, of course, express no opinion as to the *wisdom* of the legislature's imposing vicarious responsibility under certain sections of the Liquor Code. There may or may not be an economic-sociological justification for such liability on a theory of deterrence. Such determination is for the legislature to make, so long as the constitutional requirements are met.

Can the legislature, consistent with the requirements of due process, thus establish absolute criminal liability? Were this the defendant's first violation of the Code, and the penalty solely a minor fine of from $100–$300, we would have no hesitation in upholding such a judgment. Defendant, by accepting a liquor license, must bear this financial risk. Because of a prior conviction for violations of the Code, however, the trial judge felt compelled under the mandatory language of the statute to impose not only an increased fine of five hundred dollars, but also a three month sentence of imprisonment. Such sentence of imprisonment in a case where liability is imposed vicariously cannot be sanctioned by this Court consistently with * * * Section 9, Article I of the Constitution of the Commonwealth of Pennsylvania.

The Courts of the Commonwealth have already strained to permit the legislature to carry over the civil doctrine of *respondeat superior* and to apply it as a means of enforcing the regulatory scheme that covers the liquor trade. We have done so on the theory that the Code established petty misdemeanors involving only light monetary fines. It would be unthinkable to impose vicarious criminal responsibility in cases involving true crimes. Although to hold a principal criminally liable might possibly be an effective means of enforcing law and order, it would do violence to our more sophisticated modern-day concepts of justice. Liability for all true crimes, wherein an offense carries with it a jail sentence, must be based exclusively upon personal causation. It can be readily imagined that even a licensee who is meticulously careful in the choice of his

---

5. We must also be extremely careful to distinguish the present situation from the question of *corporate* criminal liability. * * *

employees cannot supervise every single act of the subordinates.   A man's liberty cannot rest on so frail a reed as whether his employee will commit a mistake in judgment.   * * *

* * * [W]e are * * * holding that so much of the judgment as calls for imprisonment is invalid, and we are leaving intact the five hundred dollar fine imposed by Judge Hoban under the subsequent offense section.   * * *

MUSMANNO, JUSTICE (dissenting).

The Court in this case is doing what it has absolutely no right to do. * * *

The Majority of this Court is doing something which can find no justification in all the law books which ornament the libraries and enlighten the judges and lawyers in this Commonwealth. It sustains the conviction of a person for acts admittedly not committed by him, not performed in his presence, not accomplished at his direction, and not even done within his knowledge. It is stigmatizing him with a conviction for an act which, in point of personal responsibility, is as far removed from him as if it took place across the seas. The Majority's decision is so novel, so unique, and so bizarre that one must put on his spectacles, remove them to wipe the lenses, and then put them on again in order to assure himself that what he reads is a judicial decision proclaimed in Philadelphia, the home of the Liberty Bell, * * * and the place where the fathers of our country met to draft the Constitution of the United States, the Magna Charta of the liberties of Americans and the beacon of hope of mankind seeking justice everywhere.   * * *

The Majority builds its superstructure of rationalization on a spongy foundation of fallacy and misconception. The Majority Opinion says:

> "It is abundantly clear that the conduct of the liquor business is lawful only to the extent and manner permitted by statute."

This is only affirming what was said more fully by the Trial Court, namely:

> "The liquor business is an unlawful business and its conduct is only lawful to the extent and manner permitted by statute and the licensing of persons to sell liquor and other alcoholic beverages is an exercise of the police power."

The liquor business is *not* an unlawful business. If it is unlawful, then the Commonwealth of Pennsylvania is engaged in an illegal business. Obviously this cannot be so. The liquor business is as lawful as any other business conducted openly in the Commonwealth. The Majority does not save its broad statement that the liquor business is unlawful by adding that it "is lawful only to the extent and manner permitted by statute." In fact, this supposed modification only accentuates the absurdity of the major premise. What the Majority says about the liquor business can equally be said of the milk business because the milk business obviously is lawful only to the extent that those who engage in milking cows, filling milk bottles and distributing them for profit, abide by the laws and regulations of the Commonwealth controlling and regulating the milk business.

* * * That people abuse the consumption of liquor is evident by a glance into any tavern, cocktail lounge or convention, and this includes conventions of people dedicated to upholding the law. However, the imprudently over-abundant individual consumption of liquor has nothing to do with the legality of the business itself. * * *

The Majority introduces into its discussion a proposition which is shocking to contemplate. It speaks of "vicarious criminal liability." Such a concept is as alien to American soil as the upas tree. There was a time in China when a convicted felon sentenced to death could offer his brother or other close relative in his stead for decapitation. The Chinese law allowed such "vicarious criminal liability." I never thought that Pennsylvania would look with favor on anything approaching so revolting a barbarity.

The Majority Opinion attempts to give authority to its legislative usurpation by referring to twenty-five specific acts which are designated as unlawful in Section 494 of the Liquor Code. It is true that the General Assembly has enumerated certain proscribed situations, but nowhere has the Legislature said that a person may be tried and convicted for a personal act committed in the darkness of his absence and in the night of his utter lack of knowledge thereof. * * *

* * * The Majority Opinion finds the imprisonment part of the sentence contrary to law. Thus, in addition to the other things I have had to say about the Majority Opinion, I find myself compelled to pin on it the bouquet of inconsistency. * * * [I]f the Majority cannot sanction the incarceration of a person for acts of which he had no knowledge, how can it sanction the imposition of a fine? How can it sanction a conviction at all? * * *

* * * If it is wrong to send a person to jail for acts committed by another, is it not wrong to convict him at all? There are those who value their good names to the extent that they see as much harm in a degrading criminal conviction as in a jail sentence. The laceration of a man's reputation, the blemishing of his good name, the wrecking of his prestige by a criminal court conviction may blast a person's chances for honorable success in life to such an extent that a jail sentence can hardly add much to the ruin already wrought to him by the conviction alone. * * *

Notes and Questions

1. The court states that it recognizes the difference between strict liability and vicarious liability. What is the difference? Also, how does vicarious liability differ from accomplice liability?

2. *Model Penal Code.* Section 2.06(2)(b) of the Model Penal Code provides that a person is legally accountable for the conduct of another when "he is made accountable for the conduct of such other person by the Code or by the law defining the offense." This provision permits a legislative

decision to impose vicarious liability. The Commentary to Section 2.06 warns that "[t]he latitude afforded by Subsection (2)(b) does not reflect a judgment that vicarious liability should be encouraged." American Law Institute, Model Penal Code and Commentaries, Comment to § 2.06 at 305–06 (1985). Any statute that imposes vicarious liability, however, is subject to the restrictive conditions of Section 2.05.

D. CORPORATE LIABILITY
AMERICAN LAW INSTITUTE—MODEL PENAL CODE AND COMMENTARIES, COMMENT TO § 2.07
(1985), 332

The law of corporate criminal responsibility is of comparatively recent origin, the modern development having occurred almost entirely within the last century and a quarter. In the early years the recognition of corporate responsibility was inhibited by certain * * * conceptual notions. The most persistent * * * was the idea that a corporation might not be held for a crime involving criminal intent. In recent years most of these limitations have been swept aside. The modern development, however, has proceeded largely without reference to any intelligible body of principle and the field is characterized by the absence of articulate analysis of the objectives thought to be attainable by imposing criminal fines on corporate bodies.

STATE v. CHRISTY PONTIAC–GMC, INC.
Supreme Court of Minnesota, 1984.
354 N.W.2d 17.

Simonett, Justice.   * * *

In a bench trial, defendant-appellant Christy Pontiac–GMC, Inc., was found guilty of two counts of theft by swindle and two counts of aggravated forgery, and was sentenced to a $1,000 fine on each of the two forgery convictions. Defendant argues that as a corporation it cannot, under our state statutes, be prosecuted or convicted for theft or forgery and that, in any event, the evidence fails to establish that the acts complained of were the acts of the defendant corporation.

Christy Pontiac is a Minnesota corporation, doing business as a car dealership. It is owned by James Christy, a sole stockholder, who serves also as president and as director. In the spring of 1981, General Motors offered a cash rebate program for its dealers. A customer who purchased a new car delivered during the rebate period was entitled to a cash rebate, part paid by GM and part paid by the dealership. GM would pay the entire rebate initially and later charge back, against the dealer, the dealer's portion of the rebate. Apparently it was not uncommon for the dealer to give the customer the dealer's portion of the rebate in the form of a discount on the purchase price.

At this time Phil Hesli was employed by Christy Pontiac as a salesman and fleet manager. On March 27, 1981, James Linden took delivery of a new Grand Prix for his employer, Snyder Brothers. Although the rebate period on this car had expired on March 19, the salesman told Linden that he would still try to get the $700 rebate for Linden. Later, Linden was told by a Christy Pontiac employee that GM had denied the rebate. Subsequently, it was discovered that Hesli had forged Linden's signature twice on the rebate application form submitted by Christy Pontiac to GM, and that the transaction date had been altered and backdated to March 19 on the buyer's order form. Hesli signed the order form as "Sales Manager or Officer of the Company."

On April 6, 1981, Ronald Gores purchased a new Le Mans, taking delivery the next day. The rebate period for this model car had expired on April 4, and apparently Gores was told he would not be eligible for a rebate. Subsequently, it was discovered that Christy Pontiac had submitted a $500 cash rebate application to GM and that Gores' signature had been forged twice by Hesli on the application. It was also discovered that the purchase order form had been backdated to April 3. This order form was signed by Gary Swandy, an officer of Christy Pontiac.

Both purchasers learned of the forged rebate applications when they received a copy of the application in the mail from Christy Pontiac. Both purchasers complained to James Christy, and in both instances the conversations ended in angry mutual recriminations. Christy did tell Gores that the rebate on his car was "a mistake" and offered half the rebate to "call it even." After the Attorney General's office made an inquiry, Christy Pontiac contacted GM and arranged for cancellation of the Gores rebate that had been allowed to Christy Pontiac. Subsequent investigation disclosed that of 50 rebate transactions, only the Linden and Gores sales involved irregularities.

In a separate trial, Phil Hesli was acquitted of three felony charges but found guilty on the count of theft for the Gores transaction and was given a misdemeanor disposition. An indictment against James Christy for theft by swindle was dismissed, * * * for lack of probable cause. Christy Pontiac, the corporation, was also indicted, and the appeal here is from the four convictions on those indictments. * * *

I.

Christy Pontiac argues on several grounds that a corporation cannot be held criminally liable for a specific intent crime. Minn.Stat. § 609.52, subd. 2 (1982), says "whoever" swindles by artifice, trick or other means commits theft. Minn.Stat. § 609.625, subd. 1 (1982), says "whoever" falsely makes or alters a writing with intent to defraud, commits aggravated forgery. Christy Pontiac agrees that the term "whoever" refers to persons, and it agrees that the term "persons" *may* include corporations, *see* Minn.Stat. § 645.44, subd. 7 (1982), but it argues that when the word "persons" is used here, it should be construed to mean only natural persons. This should be so, argues defendant, because the legislature has defined a crime as "conduct which is prohibited by statute and for which the actor may be sentenced to imprisonment, with or without a fine," Minn.Stat. § 609.02, subd. 1 (1982), and a corporation cannot be imprisoned. Neither, argues defendant, can an artificial person entertain a mental state, let alone have the specific intent required for theft or forgery.

We are not persuaded by these arguments. The Criminal Code is to "be construed according to the fair import of its terms, to promote justice, and to effect its purposes." Minn.Stat. § 609.01, subd. 1 (1982). The legislature has not expressly excluded corporations from criminal liability and, therefore, we take its intent to be that corporations are to be considered persons within the meaning of the Code in the absence of any clear indication to the contrary. We do not think the statutory definition of a crime was meant to exclude corporate criminal liability; rather, we construe that definition to mean conduct which is prohibited and, if committed, *may* result in imprisonment. Interestingly, the specific statutes under which the defendant corporation was convicted, sections 609.52 (theft) and 609.625 (aggravated forgery), expressly state that the sentence may be either imprisonment *or* a fine.

Nor are we troubled by any anthropomorphic implications in assigning specific intent to a corporation for theft or forgery. There was a time when the law, in its logic, declared that a legal fiction could not be a person for purposes of criminal liability, at least with respect to offenses involving specific intent, but that time is gone. If a corporation can be liable in civil tort for both actual and punitive damages for libel, assault and battery, or fraud, it would seem it may also be criminally liable for conduct requiring specific intent. Most courts today recognize that corporations may be guilty of specific intent crimes. Particularly apt candidates for corporate criminality are types of crime, like theft by swindle and forgery, which often occur in a business setting.

We hold, therefore, that a corporation may be prosecuted and convicted for the crimes of theft and forgery.

II.

There remains, however, the evidentiary basis on which criminal responsibility of a corporation is to be determined. Criminal liability, especially for more serious crimes, is thought of as a matter of personal, not vicarious, guilt. One should not be convicted for something one does not do. In what sense, then, does a corporation "do" something for which it can be convicted of a crime? The case law, as illustrated by the authorities above cited, takes differing approaches. If a corporation is to be criminally liable, it is clear that the crime must not be a personal aberration of an employee acting on his own; the criminal activity must, in some sense, reflect corporate policy so that it is fair to say that the activity was the activity of the corporation. * * *

We believe, first of all, the jury should be told that it must be satisfied beyond a reasonable doubt that the acts of the individual agent constitute the acts of the corporation. Secondly, as to the kind of proof required, we hold that a corporation may be guilty of a specific intent crime committed by its agent if: (1) the agent was acting within the course and scope of his or her employment, having the authority to act for the corporation with respect to the particular corporate business which was conducted criminally; (2) the agent was acting, at least in part, in furtherance of the corporation's business interests; and (3) the criminal acts were authorized, tolerated, or ratified by corporate management.

This test is not quite the same as the test for corporate vicarious liability for a civil tort of an agent. The burden of proof is different, and, unlike civil liability, criminal guilt requires that the agent be acting at least in part in furtherance of the corporation's business interests. Moreover, it must be shown that corporate management authorized, tolerated, or ratified the criminal activity. Ordinarily, this will be shown by circumstantial evidence, for it is not to be expected that management authorization of illegality would be expressly or openly stated. Indeed, there may be instances where the corporation is criminally liable even though the criminal activity has been expressly forbidden. What must be shown is that from all the facts and circumstances, those in positions of managerial authority or responsibility acted or failed to act in such a manner that the criminal activity reflects corporate policy, and it can be said, therefore, that the criminal act was authorized or tolerated or ratified by the corporation. * * *

III.

This brings us, then, to the third issue, namely, whether under the proof requirements mentioned above, the evidence is sufficient to sustain the convictions. We hold that it is.

The evidence shows that Hesli, the forger, had authority and responsibility to handle new car sales and to process and sign cash rebate applications. Christy Pontiac, not Hesli, got the GM rebate money, so that Hesli was acting in furtherance of the corporation's business interests. Moreover, there was sufficient evidence of management authorization, toleration, and ratification. Hesli himself, though not an officer, had middle management responsibilities for cash rebate applications. When the customer Gores asked Mr. Benedict, a salesman, about the then discontinued rebate, Benedict referred Gores to Phil Hesli. Gary Swandy, a corporate officer, signed the backdated retail buyer's order form for the Linden sale. James Christy, the president, attempted to negotiate a settlement with Gores after Gores complained. Not until after the Attorney General's inquiry did Christy contact divisional GM headquarters. As the trial judge noted, the rebate money "was so obtained and accepted by Christy Pontiac and kept by Christy Pontiac until somebody blew the whistle * * *." We conclude the evidence establishes that the theft by swindle and the forgeries constituted the acts of the corporation.

We wish to comment further on two aspects of the proof. First, it seems that the state attempted to prosecute both Christy Pontiac and James Christy, but its prosecution of Mr. Christy failed for lack of evidence. We can imagine a different situation where the corporation is the alter ego of its owner and it is the owner who alone commits the crime, where a double prosecution might be deemed fundamentally unfair. Secondly, it may seem incongruous that Hesli, the forger, was acquitted of three of the four criminal counts for which the corporation was convicted. Still, this is not the first time different trials have had different results. * * *

PAMELA H. BUCY—CORPORATE ETHOS: A STANDARD FOR IMPOSING CORPORATE CRIMINAL LIABILITY

75 Minnesota Law Review 1095 (1991), 1102–1105

American jurisprudence has employed two major standards to determine when a corporation should be criminally liable. Both impose vicarious liability by imputing the criminal acts and intent of corporate agents to the corporation. The traditional or respondeat superior approach is a common law rule developed primarily in the federal courts and adopted by some state courts. Derived from agency principles in tort law, it provides that a corporation "may be held criminally liable for the acts of any of its agents [who] (1) commit a crime (2) within the scope of employment (3) with the intent to benefit the corporation." As construed by most courts, the latter two requirements are almost meaningless. Courts deem criminal conduct to be "within the scope of employment" even if the conduct was specifically forbidden by a corporate policy and the corporation made good faith efforts to prevent the crime. Similarly, courts deem criminal conduct by an agent to be "with the intent to benefit the corporation" even when the corporation received no actual benefit from the offense and no one within the corporation knew of the criminal conduct at the time it occurred. With these latter two requirements thus weakened, a corporation may be criminally liable whenever one of its agents (even an independent contractor in some circumstances) commits a crime related in almost any way to the agent's employment.

The American Law Institute's Model Penal Code (MPC) provides the major alternative standard for corporate criminal liability currently found in American jurisprudence. * * * The type of criminal offense charged determines which standard applies. The option that applies to the majority of criminal offenses [25] provides that a court may hold a corporation criminally liable if the criminal conduct was "authorized, requested, commanded, performed or recklessly tolerated by the board of directors or by a high managerial agent acting in behalf of the corporation within the scope of his office or employment." This standard still

---

25. The MPC includes two additional standards of corporate liability. Section 2.07(1)(a) applies to minor infractions and non-Code penal offenses "in which a legislative purpose to impose liability on corporations plainly appears." The standard in § 2.07(1)(a) is broad respondeat superior, for the corporation is held liable whenever "the conduct is performed by an agent of the corporation acting in behalf of the corporation within the scope of his office or employment." Section 2.07(1)(b) applies to omissions and provides strict liability for the corporation that fails to "discharge a specific duty" imposed by law. * * *

uses a respondeat superior model, but in a limited fashion: the corporation will be liable for conduct of only some agents (its directors, officers, or other higher echelon employees).

The critical weakness in both the traditional respondeat superior and MPC standards of liability is that they fail to sufficiently analyze corporate intent. Cases where a corporate employee acted contrary to express corporate policy and yet the court still held the corporation liable best exemplify this weakness. *United States v. Hilton Hotels Corp.*[27] provides an apt example. The purchasing agent at a Hilton Hotel in Portland, Oregon, threatened a supplier of goods with the loss of the hotel's business if the supplier did not contribute to an association that was formed to attract conventions to Portland. The corporate president testified that such action was contrary to corporate policy. Both the manager and assistant manager of the Portland Hilton Hotel also testified that they specifically told the purchasing agent not to threaten suppliers. Nevertheless, the court convicted the Hilton Hotel Corporation of antitrust violations under the respondeat superior standard of liability.

Because the respondeat superior standard focuses solely on an individual corporate agent's intent and automatically imputes that intent to the corporation, a corporation's efforts to prevent such conduct are irrelevant. Under this approach all corporations, honest or dishonest, good or bad, are convicted if the government can prove that even one maverick employee committed criminal conduct.

The MPC's requirement that a higher echelon employee commit, or recklessly supervise, the criminal conduct is an improvement over the traditional respondeat superior approach. Recognizing the unfairness of holding a corporation liable for the acts of all its agents, the MPC views the corporation as the embodiment of the acts and intent of only its "high managerial agent[s]." High managerial agents are those individuals "having duties of such responsibility that [their] conduct may fairly be assumed to represent the policy of the corporation or association."[33]

The MPC's refinement of traditional respondeat superior suffers from three serious problems, however. The first problem, the maverick employee, still arises because the MPC uses the same conceptual paradigm as does respondeat superior—that is, the MPC automatically imputes the intent of individual corporate agents (albeit only the higher echelon agents) to the corporation. * * *

The second problem with the MPC standard is that even if a clear corporate policy caused a lower echelon employee to commit an offense, the corporation is liable only if there is evidence that a specific higher echelon official recklessly tolerated this conduct. Injustice also results from this problem but here the liability is too narrow: a corporation is not held criminally liable when it should be.

27. 467 F.2d 1000 (9th Cir.1972), *cert. denied,* 409 U.S. 1125 (1973).

33. * * * § 2.07(4)(c).

The third problem with the MPC standard is [that it] * * * encourages higher echelon officials to insulate themselves from knowledge of corporate employee activity. Under this standard, if higher echelon officials can maintain unawareness of illegal conduct by corporate employees, it is difficult to prove that they tolerated such conduct, and therefore nearly impossible to hold the corporation criminally liable. By encouraging such unawareness, the MPC discourages corporations from policing themselves.

Notes and Questions

1. Professor Bucy is critical of the Model Penal Code and common law for failure to sufficiently analyze corporate intent. What does she mean by "corporate intent"? Can a corporation "intend" anything? What does it mean to say, as Professor Bucy does, that the current law punishes all corporations, "good or bad," for the acts of a maverick employee. Is it meaningful to speak of a corporation, as distinguished from the human beings who represent it, as "good or bad"?

More generally, when the issue is whether a corporation, as distinguished from one of its officers or employees, should be convicted of a criminal offense, do criminal law principles developed with natural persons in mind have any place in the analysis?

Professor Bucy proposes in her article that corporate criminal liability depend on proof beyond a reasonable doubt of a "corporate ethos" or "corporate culture" within the organization that encouraged the criminal conduct by the agents of the corporation. A "corporate culture" may be defined as "an attitude, policy, rule, course of conduct or practice existing within the body corporate generally or within the area of the body corporate in which the relevant activities take place." Australian Criminal Law Officers, Committee of the Standing Committee of Attorney–General, Final Draft Model Criminal Code § 501.2.2 (Dec. 1992).

What do you think of her suggestion? Do you think Christy Pontiac was guilty under this standard? What type of information would you need to determine Christy's corporate culture?

2. *Problem.* A corporation inadvertently sells a dangerously defective product. The defect comes to the attention of the board of directors after learning of four deaths caused by the defect. After a careful investigation, the board determines that the cost of conducting a product recall with its attendant bad publicity, and of manufacturing the product in a non-defective manner, would be greater than the cost of paying money judgments in civil suits as they arise. Consequently, the corporation continues to manufacture and sell the product in its defective condition. Under the common law, is the corporation guilty of criminal homicide for the ensuing deaths? What would be the result under the Model Penal Code?

3. The "hornbook" law is that a corporation cannot be imprisoned or killed and, therefore, may not be indicted for any crime for which imprisonment and/or death are the only punishments set out by the legislature. But does that follow?

At least one court believes that it is possible to incarcerate a corporation. In United States v. Allegheny Bottling Company, 695 F.Supp. 856 (E.D.Va.1988), the corporate defendant was convicted along with three individuals of price fixing. In announcing his sentence, id. at 858–61, District Judge Doumar wrote:

The Lord Chancellor of England said some two hundred years ago, "Did you ever expect a corporation to have a conscience, when it has no soul to be damned, and no body to be kicked?" * * * Certainly, this Court does not expect a corporation to have a conscience, but it does expect it to be ethical and abide by the law. This Court will deal with this company no less severely than it will deal with any individual who similarly disregards the law.

For the reasons stated, Allegheny Bottling Company is sentenced to three (3) years imprisonment and a fine of One Million Dollars ($1,-000.00). Execution of the sentence of imprisonment is suspended and all but $950,000.00 of said fine is suspended, and the defendant is placed on probation for a period of three (3) years. * * *

* * * A crucial issue in this case is whether the imprisonment term in this statute applies to corporations. Before the Court addresses that issue, however, another issue will be disposed of—the lingering idea that a corporation cannot be imprisoned. This Court today specifically holds that a corporation can be "imprisoned" * * *, contrary to the traditional view. * * *

The term "imprisonment" is defined by Webster to include "constraint of a person either by force or by such other coercion as restrains him within limits against his will." *Webster's Third New International Dictionary* at 1137. * * * The key to corporate imprisonment is this: imprisonment simply means *restraint.* * * *

Corporate imprisonment requires only that the Court restrain or immobilize the corporation. * * * [C]orporate imprisonment can be accomplished by simply placing the corporation in the custody of the United States Marshal. The United States Marshal would restrain the corporation by seizing the corporation's physical assets or part of the assets or restricting its actions or liberty in a particular manner. When this sentence was contemplated, the United States Marshal for the Eastern District of Virginia, Roger Ray, was contacted. When asked if he could imprison Allegheny * * *, he stated that he could. He stated that he restrained corporations regularly for bankruptcy court. He stated that he could close the physical plant itself and guard it. He further stated that he could allow employees to come and go and limit certain actions or sales if that is what the Court imposes. * * *

Cases in the past have *assumed* that corporations cannot be imprisoned, without any cited authority for that proposition. This Court, however, has been unable to find any case which actually held that corporate imprisonment is illegal, unconstitutional or impossible. * * *

Allegheny Bottling Company appealed its conviction and sentence. The Fourth Circuit affirmed the conviction but remanded the cause to the District Judge "to correct the sentence." 870 F.2d 655 (4th Cir.1989).

If the implicit message of the Fourth Circuit is that "incarceration" of a corporation is impermissible, does this mean that the only penal remedy available is a monetary fine? [p] If so, can fines satisfy retributive conceptions of justice, or is retribution a meaningless concept in this context? If the goal of corporate punishment is to promote socially acceptable conduct by businesses, is a fine an adequate remedy? Consider the next article.

JOHN C. COFFEE, JR.—"NO SOUL TO DAMN: NO BODY TO KICK": AN UNSCANDALIZED INQUIRY INTO THE PROBLEM OF CORPORATE PUNISHMENT

79 Michigan Law Review 386 (1981), 386–397, 399–402

Did you ever expect a corporation to have a conscience, when it has no soul to be damned, and no body to be kicked? [1]

Edward, First Baron Thurlow 1731–1806

The Lord Chancellor of England quoted above was neither the first nor the last judge to experience frustration when faced with a convicted corporation. American sentencing judges are likely to face a similar dilemma with increasing frequency in the near future, for a number of signs indicate that corporate prosecutions will become increasingly commonplace. * * * [T]he problem of corporate punishment seems perversely insoluble: moderate fines do not deter, while severe penalties flow through the corporate shell and fall on the relatively blameless. * * *

The literature on corporate sanctions sometimes seems to consist of little more than the repeated observation that the fines imposed on convicted corporations have historically been insignificant. True as this point undoubtedly is, it is also a short-sighted critique. It ignores both the judiciary's reasons for declining to impose more severe penalties and the possibility that a monetary penalty sufficiently high to deter the corporation may be infeasible or undesirable. Once these possibilities are considered, the problem of corporate criminal behavior becomes radically more complex. Three independent, but overlapping perspectives each suggest that monetary penalties directed at the corporation will often prove inadequate to deter illegal behavior. * * *

A. THE DETERRENCE TRAP

* * * Economists generally agree that an actor who contemplates committing a crime will be deterred only if the "expected punishment cost" of a proscribed action exceeds the expected gain. This concept of the expected punishment cost involves more than simply the amount of the penalty. Rather, the expected penalty must be discounted by the likelihood of apprehension and conviction in order to yield the expected punishment cost. For example, if the expected gain were $1 million and the risk of apprehension were 25%, the penalty would have to be raised to $4 million in order to make the expected punishment cost equal the

---

p. Is it impossible to impose a death sentence on a corporation?

1. *Quoted in* M. King, Public Policy and the Corporation 1 (1977). * * *

expected gain. One may well question the adequacy of this simple formula when applied to individual defendants, because the stigmatization of a criminal conviction constitutes an additional and severe penalty for the white-collar defendant. But this loss of social status is a less significant consideration for the corporate entity, and we are thus forced to rely largely on monetary sanctions.

The crux of the dilemma arises from the fact that the maximum meaningful fine that can be levied against any corporate offender is necessarily bounded by its wealth. Logically, a small corporation is no more threatened by a $5 million fine than by a $500,000 fine if both are beyond its ability to pay. In the case of an individual offender, this wealth ceiling on the deterrent threat of fines causes no serious problem because we can still deter by threat of incarceration. But for the corporation, which has no body to incarcerate, this wealth boundary seems an absolute limit on the reach of deterrent threats directed at it. If the "expected punishment cost" necessary to deter a crime crosses this threshold, adequate deterrence cannot be achieved. For example, if a corporation having $10 million of wealth were faced with an opportunity to gain $1 million through some criminal act or omission, such conduct could not logically be deterred by monetary penalties directed at the corporation *if the risk of apprehension were below 10%*. That is, if the likelihood of apprehension were 8%, the necessary penalty would have to be $12.5 million (*i.e.,* $1 million times 12.5, the reciprocal of 8%). Yet such a fine exceeds the corporation's ability to pay. In short, our ability to deter the corporation may be confounded by our inability to set an adequate punishment cost which does not exceed the corporation's resources.

The importance of this barrier (* * * the "deterrence trap") depends on whether rates of apprehension for corporate crimes are typically low. Although there are exceptions, most corporate crimes seem highly concealable. This is so because, unlike victims of classically under-reported crimes (such as rape or child abuse), victims of many corporate crimes do not necessarily know of their injury. The victim of price-fixing may never learn that he has overpaid; the consumer of an unsafe, toxic, or carcinogenic product typically remains unaware of the hazards to which he has been exposed. Even the government or a fellow competitor may rarely discover the tax fraud or illegal bribe which has cost it a substantial loss in revenues. * * *

Beyond ease of concealment, legal and behavioral characteristics distinguish price-fixing from other corporate crimes: safety and environmental violations involve questions of judgment which the participants can rationalize without consciously (or at least explicitly) engaging in behavior they know to be illegal. In addition, many, if not most, forms of corporate crime require some element of intent (*i.e.,* "knowingly" or "willfully") which can be exceedingly difficult to prove in the context of prosecuting a white-collar worker for a "regulatory" offense. * * *

The final element in the deterrence equation requires little emphasis: corporate misbehavior involves high stakes. A $50,000 bribe may secure a $50 million defense contract, a failure to report a safety or design defect in a product may avert a multi-million dollar recall, and the suppression of evidence showing a newly discovered adverse side effect of a popular drug may save its manufacturer an entire product market. Thus, when all the elements of the equation are combined, it is not unrealistic to predict that cases will arise in which the expected gain may be $10 million or higher, while the likelihood of apprehension is under 10%. If so, a mechanical application of the economist's deterrence formula suggests that only penalties of $100 million or above could raise the "expected punishment cost" to a level in excess of the expected gain. Few corporations, if any, could pay such a fine * * *.

B. THE BEHAVIORAL PERSPECTIVE

An abstract quality surrounds the foregoing economic analysis. Lucid as its logic seems, it ignores the organizational dynamics within the firm and treats the corporation as a "black box" which responds in a wholly amoral fashion to any net difference between expected costs and benefits. Students of organizational decision-making have always rejected this "black box" model of the firm and have been quick to point out that a fundamental incongruence may exist between the aims of the manager and those of the firm. Indeed, this assertion is but a corollary of the famous Berle–Means thesis that control and ownership have been divorced in the modern public corporation.[23] Given this separation, it follows that the "real world" corporation manager may view corporate participation in criminal activities from the standpoint of how to maximize his own ends, rather than those of the firm.

Does the behavioral perspective indicate that corporate misbehavior may be easier to deter than the foregoing economic analysis suggests? Regrettably, the reverse may be the case: for several reasons, the behavioral perspective suggests that it may be extraordinarily difficult to prevent corporate misconduct by punishing only the firm. First, from such a perspective, it seems clear that the individual manager may perceive illegal conduct to be in his interest, even if the potential costs to which it exposes the firm far exceed the potential corporate benefits. For example, the executive vice president who is a candidate for promotion to president may be willing to run risks which are counterproductive to the firm as a whole because he is eager to make a record profit for his division or to hide a prior error of judgment. Correspondingly, the lower echelon executive with a lackluster record may deem it desirable to resort to illegal means to increase profits (or forestall losses) in order to prevent his dismissal or demotion. * * *

* * * [I]t is important to move from theoretical to empirical arguments. The theoreticians of deterrence tend to assume that the actor

23. A. Berle & G. Means, The Modern 1967). * * *
Corporation and Private Property (rev. ed.

has perfect knowledge, or at least can calculate with reasonable accuracy the odds of apprehension. In reality, we lack even an approximate estimate of how much white-collar crime occurs or how often it results in conviction. Because an accurate calculation of the cost/benefit calculus which the microeconomic approach utilizes is thus improbable, the critical variable becomes the actor's attitude toward risk. Is he a risk averter or a risk preferrer? Other things being equal, the risk-averse manager tends to be deterred by high penalties even when they are associated with low rates of apprehension, while a risk-preferring manager would look at the same combination of penalties and probabilities and not be deterred. Knowing only that apprehension is a longshot, the risk preferrer will be likely to chance profitable illegal behavior, even though an apprehension would devastate his career.

Although some theorists have argued that the typical corporate manager is risk averse, some empirical evidence points in the opposite direction. Repeated studies have detected a phenomenon known as the "risky shift"; businessmen participating in role-playing experiments have shown a pronounced tendency to make "riskier" decisions when acting in a small group than when acting alone. That is, the degree of risk they are willing to accept increases dramatically when the decision is reached collectively within a small group—exactly the context in which most business decisions are made. * * *

Finally, the behavioral perspective highlights one of the most basic causes of misbehavior within organizations: individuals frequently act out of loyalty to a small group within the firm with which they identify. Thus, engineers working on the development of a particular project may develop an intense dedication to it which leads them to suppress negative safety findings. Similarly, a plant manager may falsify environmental data out of a fear that the prohibitive costs of bringing the plant into compliance might result in its closing. This pattern is consistent with a considerable body of social science data which suggests that the individual's primary loyalty within any organization is to his immediate work group. Within this group, he will engage in candid disclosure and debate, but he will predictably edit and screen data before submitting them to superiors in order to cast his sub-unit in a favorable light.

From this perspective, the following generalization becomes understandable: the locus of corporate crime is predominantly at the lower to middle management level. Although public interest groups are vocal in their denunciations of "crime in the suites," in truth the most shocking safety and environmental violations are almost exclusively the product of decisions at lower managerial levels. Senior executives may still bear some causal responsibility, but the chain of causation is remote, and their influence on decisions is only indirect. * * *

To sum up, in the modern public corporation it is not only ownership and control that are divorced (as Berle and Means recognized long ago), but also strategic decision-making and operational control. In an era of finance capitalism, the manager responsible for operational and production decisions is increasingly separated by organization, language, goals, and experience from the financial manager who today plans and directs the corporation's future. This tends both to insulate the upper echelon executive (who may well desire that the sordid details of "meeting the competition" or "coping with the regulators" not filter up to his attention) and to intensify the pressures on those below by denying them any forum in which to explain the crises they face. This generalization helps to explain both the infrequency with which corporate misconduct can be traced to senior levels and the limited effort made to date within many firms to develop a system of legal auditing which approaches the sophistication of financial auditing. * * *

C. THE EXTERNALITY PROBLEM

The idea of externalities as applied to the actions of public bodies is probably best illustrated by the common practice of most highway departments in liberally dumping salt on frozen roads. This technique cures their problem of ice-coated roads at a relatively low cost, but it also imposes an "external cost" on landowners and drivers: plants die along the borders of such roadways, and cars rust and deteriorate more quickly because of the effect of the salt on their exteriors. This cost, however, is not borne by the highway department, and thus is externalized in the same sense that a manufacturer traditionally never bore the cost of his pollution that fell on the adjoining landowners downwind. * * *

The problem of external costs is present in the case of corporate punishment, and comes into focus when we consider the incidence of financial penalties imposed on the corporation. As a moment's reflection reveals, the costs of deterrence tend to spill over onto parties who cannot be characterized as culpable. Axiomatically, corporations do not bear the ultimate cost of the fine; put simply, when the corporation catches a cold, someone else sneezes. This overspill of the penalty initially imposed on the corporation has at least four distinct levels, each progressively more serious. First, stockholders bear the penalty in the reduced value of their securities. Second, bondholders and other creditors suffer a diminution in the value of their securities which reflects the increased riskiness of the enterprise. * * * The analysis, however, needs to be carried several steps further: the third level of incidence of a severe financial penalty involves parties even less culpable than the stockholders. As a class, the stockholders can at least sometimes be said to have received unjust enrichment from the benefits of the crime; this arguably justifies their indirectly bearing a compensating fine. However, if the fine is severe enough to threaten the solvency of the corporation, the predictable response will be a cost-cutting campaign, involving reductions in the work force through layoffs of lower echelon employees who received no benefit from the earlier crime. Severe financial penalties thus interfere with public goals of full employment and minority recruitment by restricting corporate expansion. * * * Finally, there is the fourth level of incidence of a financial penalty: it may be passed onto the consumer. * * * If this happens, the "wicked" corporation not only goes unpunished, but the intended beneficiary of the criminal statute (*i.e.,* the consumer) winds up bearing its penalty.

Notes and Questions

1. Are there socially cheaper methods of punishing corporations? Among the strategies outlined in Professor Coffee's article are: implementation of "equity fines," whereby a corporation is ordered to authorize and issue shares of the corporation to a state crime victim compensation fund in sufficient number that their expected market value is equivalent to the cash fine necessary to deter illegal activity; authorization of private law suits with treble damage penalties following government prosecution; and increased plea bargaining by prosecutors, whereby corporations would be required to provide restitution to injured victims in exchange for dismissal of criminal charges.

Chapter 12

THEFT

INTRODUCTORY COMMENT

In the very early years of English legal history, theft of property was not a criminal offense. Only forcible appropriations of property, i.e., robberies, were punishable. During the middle ages, however, as economic conditions mandated a change in the law, the common law of crimes was expanded to include nonforcible, nonconsensual takings, i.e. larceny. As with all other common law felonies, grand larceny was a capital crime.

Larceny law did not develop in a simple or smooth manner. On the one hand, common law jurists did not consider death an appropriate penalty for many thefts, so they often construed the offense narrowly and developed technical rules that allowed some thieves to escape conviction. On the other hand, the courts were sensitive to pressures from commercial interests to broaden the scope of the law, which they did over time.

The courts did not act fast enough to suit English lawmakers. Beginning in the eighteenth century, Parliament intervened and filled in various gaps in the law of theft. However, rather than redefine larceny, the legislators enacted new offenses, primarily the crimes of embezzlement and obtaining property by false pretenses.

For more than a century, English and American courts struggled to make sense of the larceny/embezzlement/false-pretenses trichotomy. Only partially successful in this effort, many states sought to simplify the law by combining these and other property crimes (e.g., receiving stolen property) into a single, consolidated theft statute. See, e.g., Model Penal Code § 223.1. Unfortunately, even in states that have reformed their law, the simplification process has been incomplete, as courts frequently draw on the common law and its intricate distinctions to interpret the modern offense of theft.

A. LARCENY

1. ACTUS REUS

a. "Trespassory Taking (Caption) and Carrying Away (Asportation) * * *"

LEE v. STATE

Court of Special Appeals of Maryland, 1984.
59 Md.App. 28, 474 A.2d 537.

Bell, J. * * *

Distinctions among larceny, embezzlement, obtaining by false pretenses, * * * and the other closely related theft offenses * * * can be explained by a brief exposition of the historical role criminal law played in protecting property. The history of these theft related offenses commenced with the common law courts' concern for crimes of violence (e.g. robbery) and for protecting society against breaches of peace; then expanded by means of the ancient quasi-criminal writ of trespass to cover all taking of another's property from his possession without his consent, even though no force was used. This latter misconduct was punished as larceny. Larceny at common law was defined as the trespassory taking and carrying away of personal property of another with intent to steal the same. The requirement of a trespassory taking made larceny an offense against possession;[1] and thus, a person such as a bailee who had rightfully obtained possession of property from its owner could not be guilty of larceny even if he used the property in a manner inconsistent with the owner's expectations.

Because of this narrow interpretation of larceny, the courts gradually broadened the offense by manipulating the concept of possession to embrace misappropriation by a person who with the consent of the owner already had physical control over the property. * * *

REX v. CHISSER

Court of King's Bench, 1678.
T. Raym. 275, 83 Eng.Rep. 142.

Upon a special verdict the jury find that on the day, and at the place in the indictment mentioned, Abraham Chisser came to the shop of Anne Charteris * * *, and asked for to see two crevats * * *, which she shewed to him, and delivered them into his hands, and thereupon he asked the price of them, to which she answered 7s, whereupon the said Abraham Chisser offered her 3s and immediately run out of the said

---

1. "Trespassory taking" under common law principles focused on the physical aspect of taking and obtaining possession. Under this traditional approach to larceny, the rule of "possessorial immunity" was fundamental in defining the contours of larceny. This rule provided that transferring possession of an object conferred immunity from the criminal law on the party receiving possession, for subsequent misuse or misappropriation of the entrusted object. This immunity terminated when the possessor (usually the bailee) returned possession to the owner or delivered the goods to another party.

shop, and took away the said goods openly in her sight, but whether this be felony, or not, is the question. * * *

And I am of opinion, that this act of Chisser is felony * * *.

* * * Although these goods were delivered to Chisser by the owner, yet they were not out of her possession by such delivery, till the property should be altered by the perfection of the contract, which was but inchoated and never perfected between the parties; and when Chisser run away with the goods, it was as if he had taken them up, lying in the shop, and run away with them. * * *

Notes and Questions

1. *"Physical" versus "constructive" possession.* With *Chisser's Case,* we see the common law at work, effectively broadening the law of larceny, by developing the distinction between physical possession of personal property—which Chisser certainly had—and constructive possession, which remained with shop owner Charteris. In the later language of the courts, Chisser had *custody* of the goods; Charteris had *possession*. He trespassorily took possession of the goods from Charteris, however, when he fled with the shop owner's property: he now had custody *and* wrongful possession of the property.

In theory, this legal fiction could have been applied in the context of bailments, mentioned in *Lee.* That is, the English courts could have stated that a bailor retained constructive possession of her property even after she delivered it to a bailee, but the rule was clearly in place by the time of *Chisser* that full possession—physical and constructive—passed to the bailee by means of the bailment.

How were the courts going to deal with dishonest bailees? And, what about a dishonest employee (servant), who received property belonging to his employer (master) in the course of employment, and then converted it to his personal use? The common law courts came to the rescue of property owners and employers, as the next case demonstrates.

UNITED STATES v. MAFNAS

United States Court of Appeals, Ninth Circuit, 1983.
701 F.2d 83.

PER CURIAM:

Appellant (Mafnas) was convicted in the U.S. District Court of Guam of stealing money from two federally insured banks in violation of 18 U.S.C. § 2113(b) which makes it a crime to "... take ... with intent to steal ... any money belonging to ... any bank...."

Mafnas was employed by the Guam Armored Car Service (Service), which was hired by the Bank of Hawaii and the Bank of America to deliver bags of money.

On three occasions Mafnas opened the bags and removed money. As a result he was convicted of three counts of stealing money from the banks.

This Circuit has held that § 2113(b) applies only to common law larceny which requires a trespassory taking. Mafnas argues * * * he had lawful possession of the bags, with the consent of the banks, when he took the money.

This problem arose centuries ago, and common law has evolved to handle it. The law distinguishes between possession and custody. 3 Wharton's Criminal Law 346–57 (C. Torcia, 14th ed. 1980).

> Ordinarily, ... if a person receives property for a limited or temporary purpose, he is only acquiring custody. Thus, if a person receives property from the owner with instructions to deliver it to the owner's house, he is only acquiring custody; therefore, his subsequent decision to keep the property for himself would constitute larceny.

3 Wharton's Criminal Law, at 353.

The District Court concluded that Mafnas was given temporary custody only, to deliver the money bags to their various destinations. The later decision to take the money was larceny, because it was beyond the consent of the owner, who retained constructive possession until the custodian's task was completed. This rationale was used in *United States v. Pruitt,* 446 F.2d 513, 515 (6th Cir.1971). There, Pruitt was employed by a bank as a messenger. He devised a plan with another person to stage a fake robbery and split the money which Pruitt was delivering for the bank. The Sixth Circuit found that Pruitt had mere custody for the purpose of delivering the money, and that his wrongful conversion constituted larceny.

Mafnas distinguishes *Pruitt* because the common law sometimes differentiates between employees, who generally obtain custody only, and others (agents), who acquire possession. Although not spelled out, Mafnas essentially claims that he was a bailee, and that the contract between the banks and Service resulted in Service having lawful possession, and not mere custody over the bags. *See Lionberger v. United States,* 371 F.2d 831, 840, 178 Ct.Cl. 151 (Ct.Cl.) *cert. denied,* 389 U.S. 844, 88 S.Ct. 91, 19 L.Ed.2d 110 (1967) ("A bailment situation is said to arise where an owner, while retaining title, delivers personalty to another for some particular purpose upon an express or implied contract.")

The common law also found an answer to this situation. A bailee who "breaks bulk" commits larceny.

> Under this doctrine, the bailee-carrier was given possession of a bale, but not its contents. Therefore, when the bailee pilfered the entire bale, he was not guilty of larceny; but when he broke open the bale and took a portion or all of the contents, he was guilty of larceny because his taking was trespassory and it was from the constructive possession of another.

3 Wharton's Criminal Law 353–54.

Either way, Mafnas has committed the common law crime of larceny, replete with trespassory taking.

Mafnas also cannot profit from an argument that any theft on his part was from Service and not from the banks. Case law is clear that since what was taken was property belonging to the banks, it was property or money "in the care, custody, control, management, or possession of any bank" within the meaning of 18 U.S.C. § 2113(b), notwithstanding the fact that it may have been in the possession of an armored car service serving as a bailee for hire.

Therefore, his conviction is Affirmed.

Notes and Questions

1. *Employers and employees.* Assume that *R*, an employer, asks *E*, her employee, to take the business's pickup truck to *X*, a mechanic, for brake repair. In which of the following cases is *E* guilty of larceny of *R*'s pickup truck, when he takes it out of town, with the intent to steal it?

A. Upon receiving the pickup truck from *R*, *E* drives it out of town.

B. As instructed by *R*, *E* drives the vehicle to *X* for repair. The next day, *E* returns, receives the vehicle from *X*, pays for the repairs, drives it toward *R*'s business, and then decides to steal it.

C. Suppose in B., *X* instructs *E* to remain at the repair shop while the brakes are fixed. An hour later, *E* receives the repaired vehicle, pays for it, drives it toward *R*'s business, and then decides to steal it.

2. *Bailees.* A purchases a television set from *X Company*. *X* hires *B*, a bailee, to deliver the set in its original box to *A*. In which of the following circumstances is *B* guilty of larceny?

A. *B* picks up the television set from *X*, takes it to her own home, removes the set from the box, and keeps it.

B. *B* receives the television set from *X*. On the way to *A*'s house, she decides to give the television set to *C*, a friend of hers. She tells *C*, "Enjoy the television, it is my gift to you." *B* leaves. Later, *C* opens the box and removes the television.

C. *B* receives the television set from *X* and delivers it to *A*, as instructed. At *A*'s request, *B* removes the set from its box, decides to keep the television, and flees with it.

3. *Asportation.* In *Mafnas*, the defendant opened the money bags and "removed" the money. Suppose Mafnas had been arrested immediately after the removal, but before he fled with the cash. Would he have been guilty of larceny or only of attempted larceny?

Notice that the offense of larceny is incomplete unless the property taken is "carried away." The slightest "carrying away" movement suffices: a shoplifter who takes property but is caught before he leaves the store is guilty of larceny, People v. Olivo, 52 N.Y.2d 309, 438 N.Y.S.2d 242, 420 N.E.2d 40 (1981); the requisite asportation is satisfied if a person yanks off an earring from the victim's pierced ear, and moves it only a few inches before it gets caught in the victim's hair, Rex v. Lapier, 1 Leach 320, 168 Eng.Rep. 263 (1784); [a] and larceny is proved if the thief, intending to steal a

a. Of what offense other than larceny might the culprit be guilty?

heavy leather bag containing various parcels, lifts the top of the bag from the floor, but drops it before he can get a full grasp of it, Rex v. Walsh, 1 Mood. 14, 168 Eng.Rep. 1166 (1824).

In view of the slight-movement rule, how do you explain the unanimous view of twelve judges in Rex v. Coslet, 1 Leach 236, 168 Eng.Rep. 220 (1782) that the following did not constitute asportation by the accused of linen cloth contained in a bag:

> [The bag] contained linen, packed up in the form of a long square; and was put into a waggon travelling the Acton Road; it laid lengthways in the waggon; the prisoner set it up on one end, for the greater convenience of taking the linen out; and cut the cloth or wrapper all the way down with intent to take out the contents, but he was discovered and apprehended before he had taken anything out of it.

4. *Trespass.* Until now we have assumed that the caption and asportation elements of larceny occurred as the result of a trespass. But, what is a "trespass"? The next two cases provide an answer.

TOPOLEWSKI v. STATE

Supreme Court of Wisconsin, 1906.
130 Wis. 244, 109 N.W. 1037.

The accused was charged with having stolen three barrels of meat, the property of the Plankinton Packing Company, of the value of $55.20, and was found guilty. * * *

The evidence was to this effect: The Plankinton Packing Company suspected the accused of having by criminal means possessed himself of some of its property and of having a purpose to make further efforts to that end. A short time before the 14th day of October, 1905, one Mat Dolan, who was indebted to the accused in the sum of upwards of $100.00, was discharged from the company's employ. Shortly theretofore the accused pressed Dolan for payment of the aforesaid indebtedness and the latter, being unable to respond, the former conceived the idea of solving the difficulty by obtaining some of the company's meat products through Dolan's aid and by criminal means, Dolan to participate in the benefits of the transaction by having the value of the property credited upon his indebtedness. A plan was accordingly laid by the two to that end, which Dolan disclosed to the company. Such plan was abandoned. Thereafter various methods were discussed of carrying out the idea of the accused, Dolan participating with the knowledge and sanction of the company. Finally a meeting was arranged between Dolan and the accused to consider the subject, the packing company requesting the former to bring it about, and with knowledge of Dolan causing one of its employés to be in hiding where he could overhear whatever might be said, the arrangement being made on the part of the company by Mr. Layer[,] the person in charge of its wholesale department. At such interview the accused proposed that Dolan should procure some packages of the company's meat to be placed on their loading platform, as was customary in delivering meat to customers, and that he should drive to such platform, ostensibly as a customer, and remove such packages. Dolan agreed to the proposition and it was decided that the same should be consummated early the next morning, all of which was reported to Mr. Layer. He thereupon caused four barrels of meat to be packed and put in the accustomed condition for delivery to customers and placed on the platform in readiness for the accused to take them. He set a watch over the property and notified the person in charge of the platform, who was ignorant of the reason for so placing the barrels, upon his inquiring what they were placed there for, to let them go; that they were for a man who would call for them. About the time appointed for the accused to appear he drove to the platform and commenced putting the barrels in his wagon. The platform boss supposing, as the fact was, that the accused was the man Mr. Layer said was to come for the property, assumed the attitude of consenting to the taking. He did not actually help load the barrels on to the wagon, but he was by, consented by his manner and when the accused was ready to go, helped him arrange his wagon and inquired what was to be done with the fourth barrel. The accused replied that he wanted it marked and sent up to him with a bill. He told the platform boss that he ordered the stuff the night before through Dolan. He took full possession of the three barrels of meat with intent to deprive the owner permanently thereof and without compensating it therefor, wholly in ignorance, however, of the fact that Dolan had acted in the matter on behalf of such owner and that it had knowingly aided in carrying out the plan for obtaining the meat.

MARSHALL, J. (after stating the facts). * * *

* * * So in the circumstances characterizing the taking of the barrels of meat from the loading platform the case comes down to this: If a person procures another to arrange with a third person for the latter to consummate, as he supposes, larceny of the goods of such person and such third person in the course of negotiations so sanctioned by such person suggests the plan to be followed, which is agreed upon between the two, each to be an actor in the matter, and subsequently that is sanctioned secretly by such person, the purpose on the part of the latter being to entrap and bring to justice one thought to be disposed to commit the offense of larceny, and such person carries out a part of such plan necessary to its consummation assigned to such other in the agreement aforesaid, such third person not knowing that such person is advised of the impending offense, and at the finality causes one of its employés, to, tacitly at least, consent to the taking of the goods, not knowing of the real nature of the transaction, is such third person guilty of the crime of larceny, or does the conduct of such person take from the transaction the element of trespass or nonconsent essential to such crime?

It will be noted that the plan for depriving the packing company of its property originated with the accused, but that it was wholly impracticable of accomplishment without the property being placed on the loading platform and the accused not being interfered with when he attempted to take it. When Dolan agreed to procure such placing the packing company in legal effect agreed thereto. Dolan did not expressly consent nor did the agreement he had with the packing company authorize him to do so, to the misappropriation of the property. Did the agreement in legal effect with the accused to place the property of the packing company on the loading platform, where it could be appropriated by the accused * * * constitute consent to such appropriation?

The case is very near the border line, if not across it, between consent and nonconsent to the taking of the property. Reg. v. Lawrence, 4 Cox C.C. 438, it was held that if the property was delivered by a servant to the defendant by the master's direction the offense cannot be larceny, regardless of the purpose of the defendant. In this case the property was not only placed on the loading platform, as was usual in delivering such goods to customers, with knowledge that the accused would soon arrive, having a formed design to take it, but the packing company's employé in charge of the platform, Ernst Klotz, was instructed that the property was placed there for a man who would call for it. Klotz from such statement had every reason to infer, when the accused arrived and claimed the right to take the property, that he was the one referred to and that it was proper to make delivery to him and he acted accordingly. While he did not physically place the property, or assist in doing so, in the wagon, his standing by, witnessing such placing by the accused, and then assisting him in arranging the wagon, as the evidence shows he did, and taking the order, in the usual way, from the accused as to the disposition of the fourth barrel, and his conduct in respect thereto amounted, practically, to a delivery of the three barrels to the accused.

In Rex v. Egginton, 2 P. & P. 508, we have a very instructive case on the subject under discussion here. A servant informed his master that he had been solicited to aid in robbing the latter's house. By the master's discretion the servant opened the house, gave the would-be thieves access thereto and took them to the place where the intended subject of the larceny had been laid in order that they might take it. All this was done with a view to the apprehension of the guilty parties after the accomplishment of their purpose. The servant by direction of the master not only gave access to the house but afforded the would-be thieves every facility for taking the property, and yet the court held that the crime of larceny was complete, because there was no direction to the servant to deliver the property to the intruders or consent to their taking it. They were left free to commit the larceny, as they had purposed doing, and the way was made easy for them to do so, but they were neither induced to commit the crime, nor was any act essential to the offense done by any one but themselves. * * *

We cannot well escape the conclusion that this case falls under the condemnation of the rule that where the owner of property by himself or his agent, actually or constructively, aids in the commission of the offense, as intended by the wrongdoer, by performing or rendering unnecessary some act in the transaction essential to the offense, the would-be criminal is not guilty of all the elements of the offense. * * *

The logical basis for the doctrine above discussed is that there can be no larceny without a trespass. So if one procures his property to be taken by another intending to commit larceny, or delivers his property to such other, the latter purposing to commit such crime, the element of trespass is wanting and the crime not fully consummated however plain may be the guilty purpose of the one possessing himself of such property. That does not militate against a person's being free to set a trap to catch one whom he suspects of an intention to commit the crime of larceny, but the setting of such trap must not go further than to afford the would-be thief the amplest opportunity to carry out his purpose, formed without such inducement on the part of the owner of the property, as to put him in the position of having consented to the taking. * * *

If the accused had merely disclosed to Dolan, his ostensible accomplice, a purpose to improve the opportunity when one should present itself to steal barrels of meat from the packing company's loading platform, and that had been communicated by Dolan to the company and it had then merely furnished the accused the opportunity he was looking for to carry out such purpose, and he had improved it, the situation would be quite different. * * *

REX v. PEAR

Central Criminal Court, 1780.
1 Leach 212, 168 Eng.Rep. 208.

The prisoner was indicted for stealing a black horse, the property of Samuel Finch. It appeared in evidence that Samuel Finch was a Livery–Stable–keeper in the Borough; and that the prisoner, on the 2d of July 1779, hired the horse of him to go to Sutton, in the county of Surry, and back again, saying on being asked where he lived, that he lodged at No. 25 in King-street, and should return about eight o'clock the same evening. He did not return; and it was proved that he had sold the horse on the very day he had hired it, to one William Hollist, in Smithfield Market; and that he had no lodging at the place to which he had given the prosecutor directions.

The learned Judge said: There had been different opinions on the law of this class of cases; that the general doctrine then was that if a horse be let for a particular portion of time, and after that time is expired, the party hiring, instead of returning the horse to its owner, sell it and convert the money to his own use, it is felony, because there is then no privity of contract subsisting between the parties; that in the present case the horse was hired to take a journey into Surry, and the prisoner sold him the same day, without taking any such journey; that there were also other circumstances which imported that at the time of the hiring the prisoner had it in intention to sell the horse, as his saying that he lodged at a place where in fact he was not known. He therefore left it with the Jury to consider, Whether the prisoner meant at the time of the hiring to take such journey, but was afterwards tempted to sell the horse? for if so he must be acquitted; but that if they were of opinion that at the time of the hiring the journey was a mere pretence to get the horse into his possession, and he had no intention to take such journey but intended to sell the horse, they would find that fact specially for the opinion of the Judges.

The Jury found that the facts above stated were true; and also that the prisoner had hired the horse with a fraudulent view and intention of selling it immediately.

The question was referred to the Judges, Whether the delivery of the horse by the prosecutor to the prisoner, had so far changed the possession of the property, as to render the subsequent conversion of it a mere breach of trust, or whether the conversion was felonious?

The Judges differed greatly in opinion on this case; and delivered their opinions *seriatim* upon it at Lord Chief Justice De Gray's house on 4th February 1780 and on the 22nd of the same month Mr. Baron Perryn delivered their opinion on it. The majority of them thought, That the question, as to the original intention of the prisoner in hiring the horse, had been properly left to the jury; and as they had found, that his view in so doing was fraudulent, the parting with the property had not changed the nature of the possession, but that it remained unaltered at the time of the conversion; and that the prisoner was therefore guilty of felony.

Notes and Questions

1. Pear's offense has come to be known as "larceny by trick." When did the offense occur in *Pear?* Another way of asking the question is: when did the defendant trespassorily take possession of the horse? Assuming that Pear intended to steal the horse from the outset, did the larceny occur the moment he rode away on the animal, or only when he acted in violation of the real owner's interests, i.e., when he sold it? What are the practical implications of the former interpretation?

BROOKS v. STATE

Supreme Court of Ohio, 1878.
35 Ohio.St. 46.

The plaintiff in error, George Brooks, * * * was convicted of larceny in stealing $200 in bank bills, the property of Charles B. Newton. It appears from the evidence, that Newton * * *, on the 24th of October, 1878, * * * came to the city of Warren in a buggy to attend to some business. He fastened his horse to a hitching post on Market street. On his way home, in the forenoon of the same day, he discovered that he had lost the package of bank bills in question. He made search for it in various places where he had been, but failed to find it. He looked where he hitched his horse on Market street, but he states that he did not look there very carefully, as there was a team of horses hitched there at the time. Notice of the loss was published in the two newspapers printed in Warren, and in one printed in Leavittsburgh, which also had a circulation in Warren.

On Wednesday, the 20th of November following, the defendant, who resided in Warren, while working on Market street, near the post at which Newton hitched his horse, found the roll or package of bank bills. The package was found "five or six feet from the hitching post." He was, at the time, working in company with several other laborers. At the time he found the money one of these laborers was within ten feet and another within twenty feet of him, but he did not let any of them know that he had found the money. He states, in his testimony, that he put it in his pocket as soon as he found it. Just after finding the package, he picked up a one dollar bill, which he did show to them. This bill was wet and muddy, and he sold it to one of them for twenty-five cents, saying if none of them bought it he would keep it himself. He testifies the reason he sold it was that he did not want them to know at the time that he had found the other money. This bill was shown to several persons at the time, and was put on the hitching post to dry. Within a half hour after finding the money, at the time of stopping for dinner, he quit work, and, at his request, was paid off. He spent part of the money, the same day, for a pair of boots, and for other purposes, and let a Mrs. Lease have fifty dollars of it the same day, with which to purchase furniture for his wife, and for other purposes. * * *

Evidence was also given that the defendant, with his wife, shortly afterward left Warren, and that he attempted to secrete himself before he left. The evidence did not show that the defendant saw any of the notices of the loss of the money published in the newspapers, or that he had any notice of the loss by Newton at the time it was found. Much other evidence was given, but the foregoing is sufficient to show the character of the legal questions raised. * * *

WHITE, J. * * *

Larceny may be committed of property that is casually lost as well as of that which is not. The title to the property, and its constructive possession, still remains in the owner; and the finder, if he takes possession of it for his own use, and not for the benefit of the owner, would be guilty of trespass, unless the circumstances were such as to show that it had been abandoned by the owner.

The question is, under what circumstances does such property become the subject of larceny by the finder?

In Baker v. The State, 29 Ohio St. 184, the rule * * * was there laid down, that "when a person finds goods that have actually been lost, and takes possession with intent to appropriate them to his own use, really believing, at the time, or having good ground to believe, that the owner can be found, it is larceny."

It must not be understood from the rule, as thus stated, that the finder is bound to use diligence or to take pains in making search for the owner. His belief, or grounds of belief, in regard to finding the owner, is not to be determined by the degree of diligence that he might be able to use to accomplish that purpose, but by the circumstances apparent to him at the time of finding the property. If the property has not been abandoned by the owner, it is the subject of larceny by the finder, when, at the time he finds it, he has reasonable ground to believe, from the nature of the property, or the circumstances under which it is found, that if he does not conceal but deals honestly with it, the owner will appear or be ascertained. But before the finder can be guilty of larceny, the intent to steal the property must have existed at the time he took it into his possession. * * *

The case was fairly submitted to the jury; and from an examination of the evidence, we find no ground for interfering with the action of the court below in refusing a new trial.

OKEY, J., dissenting.

I do not think the plaintiff was properly convicted. * * * [The bills] had lain there several weeks, and the owner had ceased to make search for it. The evidence fails to show that the plaintiff had any information of a loss previous to the finding, and in his testimony he denied such notice. There was no mark on the money to indicate the owner, nor was there any thing in the attending circumstances pointing to one owner more than another. * * *

No doubt the plaintiff was morally bound to take steps to find the owner. An honest man would not thus appropriate money, before he had made the finding public, and endeavored to find the owner. But in violating the moral obligation, I do not think the plaintiff incurred criminal liability. * * *

The obligation * * * that the finder must deal "honestly" with the money, is too indefinite; and the opinion contains no satisfactory explanation of it. This leaves both law and fact to the jury, without any rule to guide them. What one jury might think was honest dealing, another jury might think was the reverse. * * *

Notes and Questions

1. Suppose that Brooks had turned in the package of bank bills to legal authorities, but (as he did here) sold the wet and muddy one-dollar-bill to a fellow worker. On these facts, is Brooks guilty of petty larceny? Suppose that it could be proved that the bill belonged to Newton, but that it had become separated from the original package.

2. Cliff, a wealthy man, discovers an extremely valuable watch on the road. He picks it up intending to keep it for a few days so that he can impress his even-richer friends, and then turn it over to the police. After impressing his friends, he decides to keep the watch. Is Cliff guilty of larceny?

b. "* * * Of the Personal Property of Another * * *"

LUND v. COMMONWEALTH

Supreme Court of Virginia, 1977.
217 Va. 688, 232 S.E.2d 745.

I'ANSON, CHIEF JUSTICE.

Defendant, Charles Walter Lund, was charged in an indictment with the theft of keys, computer cards, computer printouts and using "without authority computer operation time and services of Computer Center Personnel at Virginia Polytechnic Institute and State University [V.P.I. or University] ... with intent to defraud, such property and services having a value of one hundred dollars or more." Code §§ 18.1–100 and 18.1–118 were referred to in the indictment as the applicable statutes. Defendant * * * was found guilty of grand larceny and sentenced to two years in the State penitentiary. * * *

Defendant was a graduate student in statistics and a candidate for a Ph.D. degree at V.P.I. The preparation of his dissertation on the subject assigned to him by his faculty advisor required the use of computer operation time and services of the computer center personnel at the University. His faculty advisor neglected to arrange for defendant's use of the computer, but defendant used it without obtaining the proper authorization.

The computer used by the defendant was leased on an annual basis by V.P.I. from the IBM Corporation. The rental was paid by V.P.I. which allocates the cost of the computer center to various departments within the University by charging it to the budget of that department. This is a bookkeeping entry, and no money actually changes hands. The departments are allocated "computer credits [in dollars] back for their use [on] a proportional basis of their [budgetary] allotments." Each department manager receives a monthly statement showing the allotments used and the running balance in each account of his department.

An account is established when a duly authorized administrator or "department head" fills out a form allocating funds to a department of the University and an individual. When such form is received, the computer center assigns an account number to this allocation and provides a key to a locked post office box which is also numbered to the authorized individual and department. The account number and the post office box number are the access code which must be provided with each request before the computer will process a "deck of cards" prepared by the user and delivered to computer center personnel. The computer print-outs are usually returned to the locked post office box. When the product is too large for the box, a "check" is placed in the box, and it is used to receive the print-outs at the "computer center main window."

Defendant came under surveillance on October 12, 1974, because of complaints from various departments that unauthorized charges were being made to one or more of their accounts. When confronted by the University's investigator, defendant initially denied that he had used the computer service, but later admitted that he had. He gave to the investigator seven keys for boxes assigned to other persons. One of these keys was secreted in his sock. He told the investigating officer he had been given the keys by another student. A large number of computer cards and print-outs were taken from defendant's apartment.

The director of the computer center testified that the unauthorized sum spent out of the accounts associated with the seven post office box keys, amounted to $5,065. He estimated that on the basis of the computer cards and print-outs obtained from the defendant, as much as $26,384.16 in unauthorized computer time had been used by the defendant. He said, however, that the value of the cards and print-outs obtained from the defendant was "whatever scrap paper is worth."

Defendant testified that he used the computer without specific authority. He stated that he knew he was a large computer user, but, because he was doing work on his doctoral dissertation, he did not consider this use excessive or that "he was doing anything wrong."

Four faculty members testified in defendant's behalf. They all agreed that computer time "probably would have been" or "would have been" assigned to defendant if properly requested. * * *

The defendant contends that his conviction of grand larceny of the keys, computer cards, and computer print-outs cannot be upheld under the provisions of Code § 18.1–100 because (1) there was no evidence that the articles were stolen, or that they had a value of $100 or more, and (2) computer time and services are not the subject of larceny under the provisions of Code §§ 18.1–100 or 18.1–118.

Code § 18.1–100 provides as follows:

"Any person who: (1) Commits larceny from the person of another of money or other thing of value of five dollars or more, or

(2) Commits simple larceny not from the person of another of goods and chattels of the value of one hundred dollars or more, shall be deemed guilty of grand larceny ...."

Section 18.1–118 provides as follows:

"If any person obtain, by any false pretense or token, from any person, with intent to defraud, money or other property which may be the subject of larceny, he shall be deemed guilty of larceny thereof; ...."

The Commonwealth concedes that the defendant could not be convicted of grand larceny of the keys and computer cards because there was no evidence that those articles were stolen and that they had a market value of $100 or more. The Commonwealth argues, however, that the evidence shows the defendant violated the provisions of § 18.1–118 when he obtained by false pretense or token, with intent to defraud, the computer print-outs which had a value of over $5,000.

Under the provisions of Code § 18.1–118, for one to be guilty of the crime of larceny by false pretense, he must make a false representation of an existing fact with knowledge of its falsity and, on that basis, obtain from another person money or other property which may be the subject of larceny, with the intent to defraud.

At common law, larceny is the taking and carrying away of the goods and chattels of another with intent to deprive the owner of the possession thereof permanently. Code § 18.1–100 defines grand larceny as a taking from the person of another money or other thing of value of five dollars or more, or the taking not from the person of another goods and chattels of the value of $100 or more. The phrase "goods and chattels" cannot be interpreted to include computer time and services in light of the often repeated mandate that criminal statutes must be strictly construed.

At common law, labor or services could not be the subject of the crime of false pretense because neither time nor services may be taken and carried away. * * * Some jurisdictions have amended their criminal codes specifically to make it a crime to obtain labor or services by means of false pretense. We have no such provision in our statutes.

Furthermore, the unauthorized use of the computer is not the subject of larceny. Nowhere in Code § 18.1–100 or § 18.1–118 do we find the word "use." The language of the statutes connotes more than just the unauthorized use of the property of another. It refers to a taking and carrying away of a certain concrete article of personal property. * * *

We hold that labor and services and the unauthorized use of the University's computer cannot be construed to be subjects of larceny under the provisions of Code §§ 18.1–100 and 18.1–118.

The Commonwealth argues that even though the computer print-outs had no market value, their value can be determined by the cost of the labor and services that produced them. We do not agree.

The cost of producing the print-outs is not the proper criterion of value for the purpose here. Where there is no market value of an article that has been stolen, the better rule is that its actual value should be proved. * * *

Here the evidence shows that the print-outs had no ascertainable monetary value to the University or the computer center. Indeed, the director of the computer center stated that the print-outs had no more value than scrap paper. * * * Hence, the evidence was insufficient to convict the defendant of grand larceny under either Code § 18.1–100 or § 18.1–118.

For the reasons stated, the judgment of the trial court is reversed, and the indictment is quashed.

Notes and Questions

1. In People v. Tansey, 156 Misc.2d 233, 593 N.Y.S.2d 426 (1992), two high ranking officers in the State Police, without authority to do so, obtained

telephone authorization codes issued to other members of the police force, which they used to place calls from pay phones and their homes. They were prosecuted for various offenses, including knowing possession of stolen property (the authorization codes). You represent the defendants. What argument would you make to support the claim that your clients are not guilty of this offense?

2. Roberta comes onto Samantha's land without permission, chops down a tree, and immediately carts off the timber for firewood. Is this common law larceny? Suppose, instead, that after Roberta chops down the tree, she realizes that there is too much to take away at that time. She leaves and returns the next day with a pickup truck, at which time she carts off the timber. Larceny? See Rollin M. Perkins & Ronald N. Boyce, Criminal Law 293 (3d ed. 1982).

3. Tom takes his car to a mechanic for repair. Later, he refuses to pay the repair bill and, late at night, comes to the garage and drives the automobile home. Assuming that he acted with the requisite *mens rea,* is Tom guilty of larceny?

But, *did* Tom have the requisite *mens rea*? Read on.

2. *MENS REA*: " * * * WITH THE INTENT TO STEAL THE PROPERTY"

PEOPLE v. BROWN

Supreme Court of California, 1894.
105 Cal. 66, 38 P. 518.

GAROUTTE, J. The appellant was convicted of the crime of burglary, alleged by the information to have been committed in entering a certain house with intent to commit grand larceny. The entry is conceded, and also it is conceded that appellant took therefrom a certain bicycle, the property of the party named in the information, and of such a value as to constitute grand larceny. The appellant is a boy of 17 years of age, and, for a few days immediately prior to the taking of the bicycle, was staying at the place from which the machine was taken, working for his board. He took the stand as a witness, and testified: "I took the wheel to get even with the boy, and, of course, I didn't intend to keep it. I just wanted to get even with him. The boy was throwing oranges at me in the evening, and he would not stop when I told him to, and it made me mad, and I left Yount's house Saturday morning. I thought I would go back and take the boy's wheel. He had a wheel, the one I had the fuss with. Instead of getting hold of his, I got Frank's, but I intended to take it back Sunday night; but, before I got back, they caught me. I took it down by the grove, and put it on the ground, and covered it with brush, and crawled in, and Frank came and hauled off the brush, and said: 'What are you doing here?' Then I told him * * * I covered myself up in the brush so that they could not find me until evening, until I could take it back. I did not want them to find me. I expected to remain there during the day, and not go back until evening." Upon the foregoing state of facts, the court gave the jury the following instruction: "I think it is not necessary to say very much to you in this case. I may say, generally, that I think counsel for the defense here stated to you in his argument very fairly the principles of law governing this case, except in one particular. In defining to you the crime of grand larceny, he says it is essential that the taking of it must be felonious. That is true; the taking with the intent to deprive the owner of it; but he adds the conclusion that you must find that the taker intended to deprive him of it permanently. I do not think that is the law. I think in this case, for example, if the defendant took this bicycle, we will say for the purpose of riding twenty-five miles, for the purpose of enabling him to get away, and then left it for another to get it, and intended to do nothing else except to help himself away for a certain distance, it would be larceny, just as much as though he intended to take it all the while. A man may take a horse, for instance, not with the intent to convert it wholly and permanently to his own use, but to ride it to a certain distance, for a certain purpose he may have, and then leave it. He converts it to that extent to his own use and purpose feloniously.'' This instruction is erroneous, and demands a reversal of the judgment. If the boy's story be true, he is not guilty of larceny in taking the machine; yet, under the instruction of the court, the words from his own mouth convicted him. The court told the jury that larceny may be committed, even though it was only the intent of the party taking the property to deprive the owner of it temporarily. We think the authorities form an unbroken line to the effect that the felonious intent must be to deprive the owner of the property permanently. The illustration contained in the instruction as to the man taking the horse is too broad in its terms as stating a correct principle of law. Under the circumstances depicted by the illustration, the man might, and again he might not, be guilty of larceny. It would be a pure question of fact for the jury, and dependent for its true solution upon all the circumstances surrounding the transaction. But the test of law to be applied to these circumstances for the purpose of determining the ultimate fact as to the man's guilt or innocence is, did he intend to permanently deprive the owner of his property? If he did not intend so to do, there is no felonious intent, and his acts constitute but a trespass. While the felonious intent of the party taking need not necessarily be an intention to convert the property to his own use, still it must in all cases be an intent to wholly and permanently deprive the owner thereof. * * *

Notes and Questions

1. In *Brown,* the trial judge instructed the jury that it is larceny for a man to take another's horse, "ride it a certain distance * * * and then leave it." The appellate court agreed that this hypothetical conduct might constitute larceny. Why? If the "felonious intent" of larceny is the intent *permanently* to deprive the owner of his property, in what sense can it be said that the man in the illustration acted with felonious intent? See State v. Davis, 38 N.J.L. 176 (1875).

2. Suppose that the youth in *Brown* had decided to keep the bicycle after he took it. Under ordinary principles of criminal law doctrine (see p. 191 supra), he could not be convicted of larceny because the intent to steal (the *mens rea* of the offense) did not concur in time with earlier trespassory taking and carrying away of the bicycle (the *actus reus* of the offense).

Common law jurists avoided this outcome by developing the legal fiction of "continuing trespass." Under this doctrine, the initial trespass continues as long as the wrongdoer remains in possession of the property that is the subject of the prosecution. State v. Somerville, 21 Me. 14, 19 (1842). It is as if a new trespassory taking occurs at every moment in time. Thus, in *Brown,* if the youth, after wrongfully "borrowing" the bicycle (a trespassory taking), decided to deprive the owner of it permanently, the law would treat this new, felonious state of mind as concurring with the trespassory taking occurring at that instant.

In light of the continuing trespass doctrine, reconsider the liability of Cliff, the finder of the lost watch (Note 2, p. 888 supra).

JUPITER v. STATE

Court of Appeals of Maryland, 1992.
328 Md. 635, 616 A.2d 412.

Rodowsky, Judge.

At issue here is whether forcibly taking from a licensed seller of alcoholic beverages beer that the seller intended to sell to legally eligible members of the public constitutes robbery where full payment is made.

After a day's duck hunting, and after helping three friends drink two and one-half cases of beer, the Petitioner, John Mitchell Jupiter (Jupiter), went to Captain John's Crab House and Marina and asked to purchase a six-pack of beer. Warren Yates (Yates), the owner of Captain John's, refused to do so. Yates told Jupiter that he was refused service because he was intoxicated. Jupiter then asked if Yates would sell him a single beer, and Yates again refused. Jupiter went to his vehicle parked outside and then reentered Captain John's carrying a shotgun. It was later determined that there was one shell in the chamber. Jupiter placed the shotgun on the counter, pointed it at Yates, and asked, "Are you going to sell it to me now?" Yates said, "Yes, sir," and produced a six-pack of Budweiser from a cooler behind the counter. Jupiter put a twenty dollar bill on the counter. Yates took the bill and gave Jupiter sixteen dollars change. An employee of Captain John's telephoned the police. * * *

In submitting that his conduct was not robbery, Jupiter relies entirely on *The Fisherman's Case,* decided in sixteenth-century England, and on some widely scattered commentary about that case. The earliest reference to *The Fisherman's Case* that Jupiter presents is from M. Dalton, *The Country Justice* 364 (1690). The accused met a fisherman who was going to market with some fish to sell. The fisherman refused to sell fish to the defendant, "whereupon the other took away some of the Fishermans Fishes against his will, and gave him more Mony for them than they were worth; but the Fisherman was thereby put in fear: Whereupon the other was indicted.... But Judgment was respited, for that the Court doubted whether it were Felony or no."

There has been a longstanding difference of opinion as to the holding in this case.

Blackstone and a few other early English commentators refer to *The Fisherman's Case* for the proposition that one who forces a sale of goods intended for sale is not guilty of robbery. * * *

Other commentators, however, have criticized the case, and several conclude that *The Fisherman's Case* stands for the proposition that its facts present a question of fact as to the defendant's intent.

Jupiter contends that *The Fisherman's Case* established a common law principle that has never been altered, and that the case is controlling authority here. He argues that the facts of *The Fisherman's Case* portray the lack, as a matter of law, of the mens rea necessary to support common law larceny or robbery. In *West v. State,* 312 Md. 197, 202, 539 A.2d 231, 233 (1988), we described robbery as "the felonious taking and carrying away of the personal property of another, from his person or in his presence, by violence or putting in fear...." "The word 'felonious' when used in connection with the taking of property means a taking with the intent to steal." *Williams v. State,* 302 Md. 787, 792–93, 490 A.2d 1277, 1280 (1985). Thus, Jupiter argues that as a matter of law the evidence was insufficient to prove that he had an intent to steal.

Even if we assume that *The Fisherman's Case* was decided as a matter of law, the facts here do not present *The Fisherman's Case.* Whatever the vitality of that 400 year old decision, the facts of this case are different. It was not because of the "[p]erverseness of his [h]umor" that Yates refused to sell beer to Jupiter. W. Hawkins, *Pleas of the Crown* 97 (4th ed. 1762). Yates was prohibited by law from selling to intoxicated persons. * * * Yates told Jupiter that he could not sell him beer, and he told him why. Hence the evidence clearly was sufficient to support jury findings that Jupiter knew that he did not have a right to purchase beer, that he intended to take it in any event, and that he took it away with the intent permanently to deprive the owner of it. Ordinarily those findings sufficiently support an ultimate finding of an intent to steal.

For Jupiter to derive a complete defense from *The Fisherman's Case* requires a more particularized analysis than merely asserting that one who forces a seller of goods to sell them at their price cannot have the mens rea for robbery. * * *

Jupiter also apparently argues that he had a "claim of right" to the beer. He does not particularize that argument, but claim of right is another possible explanation of *The Fisherman's Case.* The drafters of the Model Penal Code, for instance, apparently viewed *The Fisherman's*

Case as a claim of right case. *See* Model Penal Code § 223.1(3) & commentary at 158 (1980). * * *

Jupiter, arguing within the reported facts of *The Fisherman's Case,* contends that those who force merchants of goods to sell their goods do not commit robbery because the merchants have been forced only to do what the merchants held themselves out as willing to do. The argument appears to be that Jupiter did not have the mens rea for robbery because he had a good faith claim of right to acquire the goods by paying for them; *i.e.,* he relied upon the "supposed consent" of the seller to yield the goods upon tender of the full price. * * *

We shall assume that the holding of *The Fisherman's Case* is that the evidence of mens rea was insufficient as a matter of law to convict the fish "purchaser" because of a claim of right. But the facts in the case before us are not those of *The Fisherman's Case.* Here there is ample evidence that Jupiter knew that the seller was legally prohibited from selling the beer, and that Jupiter nevertheless forced the sale. Those facts in this case at least raise a jury question as to the good faith of any claim of right.

Moreover, claim of right as a defense to robbery has been limited in the 400 years since *The Fisherman's Case* was decided. There are strong public policy reasons why self-help, involving the use of force against a person, should not be condoned. For that reason most courts have tended to apply claim of right strictly under those circumstances. Courts have held that the defense does not apply unless the defendant was attempting to retrieve a specific chattel that was the subject of a prior claim of right; the defendant may not attempt to take money or property of equivalent value. Courts have held that the defense does not apply where the defendant attempted to retake the proceeds of illegal activity. A few courts have suggested that the claim of right defense should be abrogated altogether as a defense to robbery, although there is no consensus on this point.

These limitations on the defense are sometimes logically problematic. Courts rarely explain how removing the defense in robbery cases is consistent with the mens rea for the included crime of larceny, or why other criminal proscriptions, such as the ones against assault or extortion, are insufficient deterrents. Nonetheless, the public policy underlying these decisions is sound. In a complex and crowded world, legal process is necessarily the preferred alternative.

We need not undertake to describe specific instances in which the claim of right defense should not apply to robbery, and we decline the State's invitation to abrogate the defense altogether. It is sufficient for the purposes of this case to hold that the defense is not applicable to robbery when the transaction that the robbery effects would be illegal even if it were consensual. * * *

ELDRIDGE, JUDGE, dissenting.

I cannot agree with the majority's holding that a larcenous intent, which is a requisite for conviction of common law robbery, is not negated by the fact of full payment for goods held out for sale.

It is firmly established that larceny is an essential element of the common law crime of robbery. Moreover, this Court has not eliminated the intent requirement of common law larceny. * * *

Although the majority attempts to cloud the matter somewhat, it is clear as a common law principle that one who forces a sale of goods, which are held out for sale, is not guilty of robbery because there is no underlying larceny. As the authorities make clear, when the goods involved are generally held out for sale, when the defendant is willing to pay the full price for the goods, and when the defendant has the present ability to pay the full price, the "intent to steal" element of larceny is missing and the transaction is not a robbery. * * *

The majority concludes, however, that a statutory regulation *aimed at the seller,* prohibiting him from selling alcohol to an intoxicated purchaser, alters this settled principle. Thus, the majority holds that where goods are held out for sale, and where a purchaser pays for the goods, but where a regulatory statute would preclude the *vendor* from selling the goods under the particular circumstances, then the *purchaser* who takes and pays for the goods without the vendor's acquiescence commits a larceny. If force is used, the purchaser also commits robbery.

The majority does not even attempt to explain how, under this scenario, the *purchaser's* intent becomes different, or how the presence of the regulatory statute aimed at the vendor supplies an intent to steal on the part of the purchaser. * * *

Furthermore, if the majority intends to change the mens rea element of larceny only under certain circumstances where a regulatory statute is involved and where the defendant purchaser takes and pays for goods without the seller's acquiescence, the majority fails to set forth any guiding and logical principles for identifying those circumstances where the "intent to steal" element is abrogated. On the other hand, if the majority contemplates the abrogation of the element of larcenous intent whenever a regulatory statute would proscribe the particular sale, the ramifications of its holding may be quite substantial. For example, suppose an underage youth enters [a] convenience store which sells alcohol, and the clerk on duty is away from the counter. The youth picks up a six pack of beer, which costs $5.15. He brings it to the counter, waits a few minutes, and then, leaving $6.00 on the counter, leaves the store. Apparently under the majority's view, because the clerk would have been statutorily prohibited from making the sale, the youth is guilty of larceny. * * *

Although I would reverse the robbery conviction, I note that the defendant in this case was properly found guilty of a serious crime, namely assault. There is no need to distort the common law of larcenous intent beyond recognition in order to respond severely to the dangerousness of the defendant's act. Under Maryland law, the maxi-

mum term of imprisonment for assault is greater than the ten year
sentence which was imposed in the instant case for robbery.   * * *

Notes and Questions

1. How would this case be resolved under the Model Penal Code?

B. EMBEZZLEMENT

REX v. BAZELEY

Central Criminal Court, 1799.
2 Leach 835, 168 Eng.Rep. 517.

[Bazeley, the prisoner, was the principal teller at a bank run by
Esdaile and Hammett, the prosecutors of this action.[b] Bazeley's duty
was to receive and pay money, notes and bills, at the counter.   In
January, 1799, he received bank-notes and cash for deposit from William
Gilbert, through his servant, George Cock. Bazeley credited Gilbert's
account, but placed a bank-note in his pocket, which he later appropriated to his own use.]

Const and Jackson, the prisoner's Counsel, * * * proceeded to argue
the case upon the following points.

First, That the prosecutors cannot, in contemplation of law, be said
to have had a constructive possession of this Bank-note, at the time the
prisoner is charged with having tortiously converted it to his own use.

Secondly, That supposing the prosecutors to have had the possession
of this note, the prisoner, under the circumstances of this case, cannot be
said to have tortiously taken it from that possession with a felonious
intention to steal it.

Thirdly, That the relative situation of the prosecutors and the
prisoner makes this transaction merely a breach of trust; and,

Fourthly, That this is not one of those breaches of trust which the
Legislature has declared to be felony.

The first point, viz. That the prosecutor cannot, in contemplation
of law, be said to have had a constructive possession of this Bank-note at
the time the prisoner is charged with having tortiously converted it to
his own use.—To constitute the crime of larceny, the property must be
taken from the possession of the owner; this possession must be either
actual or constructive; it is clear that the prosecutors had not, upon the
present occasion, the actual possession of the Bank-note, and therefore
the inquiry must be, whether they had the constructive possession of it?
or, in other words, whether the possession of the servant was, under the
circumstances of this case, the possession of the master? Property in
possession is said by Sir William Blackstone to subsist only where a man
hath both the right to, and also the occupation of, the property. The
prosecutors in the present case had only a right or title to possess the
note, and not the absolute or even qualified possession of it. It was

b. In England, private parties are permitted to prosecute some criminal actions.

never in their custody or under their controul. * * * Suppose the prisoner had not parted with the note, but had merely kept it in his own custody, and refused, on any pretence whatever, to deliver it over to his employers, they could only have recovered it by means of an action of trover or detinue, the first of which presupposes the person against whom it is brought, to have obtained possession of the property by lawful means, as by delivery, or finding; and the second, that the right of property only, and not the possession of it, either really or constructively, is in the person bringing it. The prisoner received this note by the permission and consent of the prosecutors, while it was passing from the possession of Mr. Gilbert to the possession of Messrs. Esdaile's and Hammett's; and not having reached its destined goal, but having been thus intercepted in its transitory state, it is clear that it never came to the possession of the prosecutors. It was delivered into the possession of the prisoner, upon an implied confidence on the part of the prosecutors, that he would deliver it over into their possession, but which, from the pressure of temporary circumstances, he neglected to do: at the time therefore of the supposed conversion of this note, it was in the legal possession of the prisoner. To divest the prisoner of this possession, it certainly was not necessary that he should have delivered this note into the hands of the prosecutors, or of any other of their servants personally; for if he had deposited it in the drawer kept for the reception of this species of property, it would have been a delivery of it into the possession of his masters; but he made no such deposit: and instead of determining in any way his own possession of it, he conveyed it immediately from the hand of Mr. Gilbert's clerk into his own pocket. Authorities are not wanting to support this position. * * *

Secondly, Supposing the prosecutor to have had the possession of this note, yet the prisoner, under the circumstances of this case, cannot be said to have tortiously taken it from that possession with a felonious intent to steal it. * * * In the present case there was no evidence whatever to shew that any such intention existed in his mind at the time the note came to his hands * * *. Besides, the prisoner had given a bond to account faithfully for the monies that should come to his hands: he was the agent of a trading company, and had the means of converting bills into cash, which would have enabled him, at the time, to repay to the prosecutor the £100, which he detained for his own use; but if, at the very time he received the note, he had no intent to steal it, it is no felony; for Sir Edward Coke and all the writers on Crown Law agree, that the intent to steal must be when the property comes to his hands or possession; and that if he have the possession of it once lawfully, though he hath the *animus furandi* afterwards, when he carrieth it away, it is no larceny.

But, thirdly, the situation which the prisoner held, and the capacity in which he acted in the banking-house of the prosecutors, make this transaction only a breach of trust. * * *

Fourthly, But a breach of trust is not, either by the Common Law or by Act of Parliament, in this case, felony. * * * [I]f there be such a

Dressler C&M On Criminal Law -21

consent of the owner of the property as argues a trust in the prisoner, and gives him a possession against all strangers, then his breaking that trust, or abusing that possession, though to the owner's utter deceit of all his interest in those goods, it will not be felony * * *. * * * Taking it, therefore, as a settled point, that a breach of trust cannot, by the rules of the common law, be converted into a felonious taking, the next and last inquiry will be, in what cases the Legislature has made this particular breach of trust felony? There are only four statutes upon this subject, viz. the 21 Hen. VIII. c. 7; the 15 Geo. II. c. 13, s. 12; the 5 Geo. III. c. 35, s. 17; and 7 Geo. III. c. 50. The two last Acts relate entirely and exclusively to breaches of trust committed by servants employed in the business of the Post–Offices; and the second to breaches of trust committed by servants employed in the business of the Bank of England, and of course, cannot affect, in any manner whatever, the present case. Nor can the case of the prisoner be construed within the statute 21 Hen. VIII. c. 7, * * * for it has been determined upon this statute, that it is strictly confined to such goods as are delivered by the master to the servant to keep. But this Bank-note, as has been already shewn, was not in the possession of the master, and therefore it cannot have been delivered by him; it being impossible for a man to deliver, either by himself or his agent, a thing of which he is neither actually nor constructively possessed; but, even admitting that it had been in the master's possession, and delivered by him to the prisoner, it would not have been delivered to him to keep, but for the purpose of entering it faithfully in the book, and handing it over to the Bank-note cashier. * * *

Fielding, for the Crown, argued the case entirely on the question, Whether the prosecutors, Esdaile and Hammett, had such a constructive possession of the Bank-note as to render the taking of it by the prisoner felony? He insisted, that in the case of personal chattels, the possession in law follows the right of property; and, that as Gilbert's clerk did not deposit the notes with Bazeley as a matter of trust to him; for they were paid at the counter, and in the banking-house of the prosecutors, of which Bazeley was merely one of the organs; and, therefore, the payment to him was in effect a payment to them, and his receipt of them vested the property *eo instanter* in their hands, and gave them the legal possession of it. * * *

The Judges, it is said, were of opinion * * * that this Bank-note never was in the legal custody or possession of the prosecutors, Messrs. Esdailes and Hammett; but no opinion was ever publicly delivered; and the prisoner was included in the Secretary of State's letter as a proper object for a pardon.

But in consequence of this case the statute 39 Geo. III. c. 85 was passed, entitled, "An Act to protect Masters and others against Embezzlement, by their Clerks or Servants"; and after reciting, that ["]whereas Bankers, Merchants, and others, are, in the course of their dealings and transactions, frequently obliged to entrust their servants, clerks, and persons employed by them in the like capacity, with receiving, paying, negotiating, exchanging, or transferring money, goods, bonds, bills, notes, bankers' drafts, and other valuable effects and securities; that doubts had been entertained, whether the embezzling the same by such servants, clerks, and others, so employed by their masters, amounts to felony by the laws of England; and that it is expedient that such offences should be punished in the same manner in both parts of the United Kingdom"; it enacts and declares, "That if any servant or clerk, or any person employed for the purpose in the capacity of a servant or clerk to any person or persons whomsoever, or to any body corporate or politic, shall, by virtue of such employment, receive or take into his possession any money, goods, bond, bill, note, banker's draft, or other valuable security or effects, for or in the name, or on the account of his master or masters, or employer or employers, and shall fraudulently embezzle, secrete, or make away with the same, or any part thereof; every such offender shall be deemed to have feloniously stolen the same from his master or masters, employer or employers, for whose use, or in whose name or names, or on whose account, the same was or were delivered to, or taken into the possession of, such servant, clerk, or other person so employed, although such money, & c. was or were no otherwise received into the possession of such master or masters, employer or employers, than by the actual possession of his or their servant, clerk, or other person so employed; and every such offender his adviser, procurer, aider or abettor, shall be liable to be transported for any term not exceeding fourteen years, in the discretion of the Court."

Notes and Questions

1. In states that have not reformed their theft laws, embezzlement is a statutory offense, separate from larceny, that fills the gap left by *Bazeley*. Although embezzlement statutes vary by jurisdiction, in general they make criminal the conversion of property received by the wrongdoer in a nontrespassory manner. Usually, however, there must also be an element of entrustment, i.e., the actor must have received the property in trust for another, such that the embezzler's conversion of the property implicates a breach of that trust.

2. In Commonwealth v. Ryan, 155 Mass. 523, 523, 30 N.E. 364, 364 (1892), Justice Holmes described as follows the events resulting in an embezzlement prosecution:

> The defendant was employed by one Sullivan to sell liquor for him in his store. Sullivan sent two detectives to the store, with marked money of Sullivan's, to make a feigned purchase from the defendant. One detective did so. The defendant dropped the money into the money-drawer of a cash-register, which happened to be open in connection with another sale made and registered by the defendant, but he did not register the sale, as was customary, and afterwards—it would seem within a minute or two—he took the money from the drawer. The question presented is whether it appears as matter of law that the defendant was not guilty of embezzlement, but was guilty of larceny, if of anything.

How should the court answer the question?

3. Reconsider *Brooks* (p. 886 supra): Suppose that Brooks had picked up the lost money with the intention of turning it in, but then decided to keep it. Would he be guilty of embezzlement?

C. FALSE PRETENSES

PEOPLE v. LONG

Supreme Court of Michigan, 1980.
409 Mich. 346, 294 N.W.2d 197.

PER CURIAM.

Defendant was charged with two counts of larceny in a building. [H]e was convicted, as charged, by a jury. He was sentenced to serve from 14 months to 4 years imprisonment * * *. We conclude that the charged conduct, as outlined by the evidence introduced at trial, will not sustain the convictions of larceny.

I

Evidence introduced by the prosecution at trial indicated that the defendant was involved in a scheme whereby he short-changed two cashiers $10 each. He did so by creating confusion and impliedly representing that he was giving them an amount of money equal to that which he was receiving. By distracting them and asking for various amounts of change, he induced them to give him $10 more than they received from him.

Prior to trial, defendant moved to quash the information on the basis that larceny, as charged, required a taking against the will and without the consent of the owner. Contending that there was a voluntary exchange of money, counsel argued that the proper charge was either obtaining money under false pretenses or larceny by trick [3] rather than larceny in a building. The trial court denied the motion to quash, agreeing with the prosecutor's view that the evidence at the preliminary examination would support the charge of larceny by trick and that the prosecutor had the discretion and power to bring the charge of larceny in a building.

* * * The Court of Appeals affirmed the defendant's conviction in an unpublished memorandum opinion. * * * [W]e remanded to the Court of Appeals for amplification of the facts and the reasons underlying its decision. In its amplified opinion the Court of Appeals, observing that the distinction between the crime of larceny by trick and that of obtaining property under false pretenses turns upon the intent of the owner to part with the property, *People v. Martin,* 116 Mich. 446, 74 N.W. 653 (1898), concluded:

3. The common-law offense of larceny by trick is included in the general larceny statute.

"In the instant case the cashiers did not knowingly transfer an extra $10 to the defendant relying on some false representations of the defendant. Rather, the cashiers, believing they had transferred only an amount equal to that received in making change for the defendant, were induced by trick or artifice of the defendant to part with possession of the extra $10.

"Taking into consideration the intention of the parties, it is obvious that the cashiers intended only to exchange various denominations of money with the defendant *quid pro quo*. The cashiers had no intention to transfer possession or title to any money in excess of that received. The defendant, on the other hand, intended to obtain through use of artifice possession of the extra $10 and intended thereby to relieve the owner of her possession.

"The absence of intent on the part of the cashiers to knowingly and voluntarily transfer possession or title to any money in excess of that received, places the defendant's conduct within the ambit of larceny rather than obtaining property under false pretenses."

II

In our view, the Court of Appeals has incorrectly construed and applied the rule of *People v. Martin* in distinguishing between larceny and false pretenses. We find this case to be one of false pretenses.

In *People v. Martin,* this Court identified the distinction between larceny and false pretenses as follows:

"It is sometimes difficult to determine in a given case whether the offense is larceny or whether it is a case of false pretenses. We think the rule to be gathered from the authorities may be stated to be: In larceny, the owner of the thing stolen has no intention to part with his property therein; in false pretenses, the owner does intend to part with his property in the thing, but this intention is the result of fraudulent contrivances. If the owner did not part with his property in the thing, but simply delivered the possession, the ownership remaining unchanged, for the purpose of having the person to whom the property was delivered use it for a certain special and particular purpose, for the owner, the title would not pass, and its felonious conversion would be larceny. A distinction is made between a bare charge for special use of the thing, and a general bailment; and it is not larceny if the owner intends to part with the property and deliver the possession absolutely, although he has been induced to part with the goods by fraudulent means. If, by trick or artifice, the owner of property is induced to part with the possession to one who receives the property with felonious intent, the owner still meaning to retain the right of property, the taking will be larceny; but if the owner part with not only the possession, but right of property also, the offense of the party obtaining the thing will not be larceny, but that of obtaining the goods by false pretenses. * * * "

The rule noted in *Martin* governs characterization of defendant's offense in the present case. By distracting the cashiers and asking them for various amounts of change, defendant induced them to give him $10 more than they received from him. The partings were induced by defendant's fraudulent representations that he had received an inadequate amount of change. While undoubtedly the cashiers would not have parted with the "additional" sum had they recognized it as such, it is apparent that the partings were voluntary and advertent. At the time of their occurrence, the partings represented a surrendering of possession accompanied by an intention, however hastily or ill-advisedly formed, to transfer title. Because both possession and title were intended to be transferred, defendant's offense was that of obtaining money under false pretenses.

The creation of the offense of false pretenses by statute had its historical origins in the lawmaker's need to fill a void in the common law which existed by virtue of the fact that common-law larceny did not extend to punish the party who, without taking and carrying away, had obtained both possession and title to another's property. Against this historical background, our Legislature early chose to recognize the offense. The conduct charged against defendant falls within the legislatively recognized category; thus marked, it is distinct from larceny.

Reversed and defendant is ordered discharged.

RYAN, JUSTICE, dissenting.

I dissent. * * *

In the case before us the scheme employed by the defendant is known as "ringing the changes" and is analyzed as follows:

> " 'Ringing the changes', a trick frequently practiced on shopkeepers and salesmen, is effected by tendering a large bill or coin in payment of a small purchase, and, after the correct change has been given, asking for other change and repeating the request until, in the confusion of mind created by so many operations, the thief obtains more money than he should. This is held to be larceny, notwithstanding in each operation the shopkeeper or salesman voluntarily delivered the money asked for, *since it is obvious that he intended to part with the title to only such money as constituted the correct change.*" (Emphasis supplied.) 52A CJS, Larceny, § 36, p. 465.

Stated another way, the literal meaning of "false pretense" connotes the receiving of the victim's property by virtue of a misrepresentation of fact which induces the victim to voluntarily relinquish both possession and title. In the "ringing the changes" scheme, the accused never makes any representation to the victim at all, and the victim never realizes that he is losing the money delivered in excess of the correct change. Thus, while the victim voluntarily relinquishes possession, he does not relinquish title to that portion of the money that exceeds the correct change. This absence of intent of the victim to pass title renders the taking trespassory, thereby supplying the primary necessary element in larceny which is absent in false pretenses. All authorities concur in substantiating the foregoing analysis. * * *

Notes and Questions

1. Rollin M. Perkins & Ronald N. Boyce, Criminal Law 364 (3d ed. 1982):

> The statutes of the various states, while by no means uniform, * * * suggest the following definition: The crime of false pretenses is knowingly and designedly obtaining the property of another by means of untrue representations of fact with intent to defraud.

Assuming that title to the extra money passed to Long, as the majority stated, is he guilty of false pretenses under this definition?

2. Suppose that Brooks (p. 886 supra), attempting to return the lost money, had handed over the bills to Xavier, who fraudulently claimed to have lost the money. Of what offense, if any, would *Xavier* be guilty?

3. Suppose that Long had gone to the bank where his money was deposited and had closed out his account, which contained ten dollars. Of what offense—larceny by trick, embezzlement, or false pretenses—if any, would he have been guilty in the following circumstances?

A. The teller, mistakenly believing that Long had twenty dollars in his account, handed him two $10 bills. Long was unaware of the teller's mistake until he left the bank, at which time he decided to keep the extra money.

B. Same as A., except that Long was aware of the teller's mistake as the money was handed to him. He failed to disclose the error and left with the extra cash.

C. The teller, aware that Long was entitled to only ten dollars, inadvertently delivered to him two $10 bills, the second bill of which was stuck to the first bill. Long was unaware of the situation until he left the bank, at which time he decided to keep the extra bill.

D. Same as C., except that Long was aware of the teller's mistake as the cash was handed to him. He failed to disclose the error and left with the extra money.

4. Does all of this leave you with a queasy feeling in your stomach?

Appendix

AMERICAN LAW INSTITUTE
MODEL PENAL CODE

(Official Draft, 1962)

PART I. GENERAL PROVISIONS
Article 1. Preliminary

SECTION 1.01. [*Omitted*]

SECTION 1.02. PURPOSES; PRINCIPLES OF CONSTRUCTION

(1) The general purposes of the provisions governing the definition of offenses are:

(a) to forbid and prevent conduct that unjustifiably and inexcusably inflicts or threatens substantial harm to individual or public interests;

(b) to subject to public control persons whose conduct indicates that they are disposed to commit crimes;

(c) to safeguard conduct that is without fault from condemnation as criminal;

(d) to give fair warning of the nature of the conduct declared to constitute an offense;

(e) to differentiate on reasonable grounds between serious and minor offenses.

(2) The general purposes of the provisions governing the sentencing and treatment of offenders are:

(a) to prevent the commission of offenses;

(b) to promote the correction and rehabilitation of offenders;

(c) to safeguard offenders against excessive, disproportionate or arbitrary punishment;

(d) to give fair warning of the nature of the sentences that may be imposed on conviction of an offense;

(e) to differentiate among offenders with a view to a just individualization in their treatment;

(f) to define, coordinate and harmonize the powers, duties and functions of the courts and of administrative officers and agencies responsible for dealing with offenders;

(g) to advance the use of generally accepted scientific methods and knowledge in the sentencing and treatment of offenders;

(h) to integrate responsibility for the administration of the correctional system in a State Department of Correction [or other single department or agency].

(3) The provisions of the Code shall be construed according to the fair import of their terms but when the language is susceptible of differing constructions it shall be interpreted to further the general purposes stated in this Section and the special purposes of the particular provision involved. The discretionary powers conferred by the Code shall be exercised in accordance with the criteria stated in the Code and, insofar as such criteria are not decisive, to further the general purposes stated in this Section.

SECTION 1.03.   [*Omitted*]

SECTION 1.04.   CLASSES OF CRIMES; VIOLATIONS

(1) An offense defined by this Code or by any other statute of this State, for which a sentence of [death or of] imprisonment is authorized, constitutes a crime.   Crimes are classified as felonies, misdemeanors or petty misdemeanors.

(2) A crime is a felony if it is so designated in this Code or if persons convicted thereof may be sentenced [to death or] to imprisonment for a term that, apart from an extended term, is in excess of one year.

(3) A crime is a misdemeanor if it is so designated in the Code or in a statute other than this Code enacted subsequent thereto.

(4) A crime is a petty misdemeanor if it is so designated in this Code or in a statute other than this Code enacted subsequent thereto or if it is defined by a statute other than this Code that now provides that persons convicted thereof may be sentenced to imprisonment for a term of which the maximum is less than one year.

(5) An offense defined by this Code or by any other statute of this State constitutes a violation if it is so designated in this Code or in the law defining the offense or if no other sentence than a fine, or fine and forfeiture or other civil penalty is authorized upon conviction or if it is defined by a statute other than this Code that now provides that the offense shall not constitute a crime.   A violation does not constitute a crime and conviction of a violation shall not give rise to any disability or legal disadvantage based on conviction of a criminal offense.

(6) Any offense declared by law to constitute a crime, without specification of the grade thereof or of the sentence authorized upon conviction, is a misdemeanor.

(7) An offense defined by any statute of this State other than this Code shall be classified as provided in this Section and the sentence that may be imposed upon conviction thereof shall hereafter be governed by the Code.

SECTION 1.05. ALL OFFENSES DEFINED BY STATUTE; APPLICATION OF GENERAL PROVISIONS OF THE CODE

(1) No conduct constitutes an offense unless it is a crime or violation under this Code or another statute of the State.

(2) The provisions of Part I of the Code are applicable to offenses defined by other statutes, unless the Code otherwise provides.

(3) This Section does not affect the power of a court to punish for contempt or to employ any sanction authorized by law for the enforcement of an order or a civil judgment or decree.

SECTION 1.06. [*Omitted*]

SECTION 1.07. METHOD OF PROSECUTION WHEN CONDUCT CONSTITUTES MORE THAN ONE OFFENSE

(1) *Prosecution for Multiple Offenses; Limitation on Convictions.* When the same conduct of a defendant may establish the commission of more than one offense, the defendant may be prosecuted for each such offense. He may not, however, be convicted of more than one offense if:

(a) one offense is included in the other, as defined in Subsection (4) of this Section; or

(b) one offense consists only of a conspiracy or other form of preparation to commit the other; or

(c) inconsistent findings of fact are required to establish the commission of the offenses; or

(d) the offenses differ only in that one is defined to prohibit a designated kind of conduct generally and the other to prohibit a specific instance of such conduct; or

(e) the offense is defined as a continuing course of conduct and the defendant's course of conduct was uninterrupted, unless the law provides that specific periods of such conduct constitute separate offenses.

(2) *Limitation on Separate Trials for Multiple Offenses.* Except as provided in Subsection (3) of this Section, a defendant shall not be subject to separate trials for multiple offenses based on the same conduct or arising from the same criminal episode, if such offenses are known to the appropriate prosecuting officer at the time of the commencement of the first trial and are within the jurisdiction of a single court.

(3) *Authority of Court to Order Separate Trials.* When a defendant is charged with two or more offenses based on the same conduct or arising from the same criminal episode, the Court, on application of the prosecuting attorney or of the defendant, may order any such charge to be tried separately, if it is satisfied that justice so requires.

(4) *Conviction of Included Offense Permitted.* A defendant may be convicted of an offense included in an offense charged in the indictment [or the information]. An offense is so included when:

(a) it is established by proof of the same or less than all the facts required to establish the commission of the offense charged; or

(b) it consists of an attempt or solicitation to commit the offense charged or to commit an offense otherwise included therein; or

(c) it differs from the offense charged only in the respect that a less serious injury or risk of injury to the same person, property or public interest or a lesser kind of culpability suffices to establish its commission.

(5) *Submission of Included Offense to Jury.* The Court shall not be obligated to charge the jury with respect to an included offense unless there is a rational basis for a verdict acquitting the defendant of the offense charged and convicting him of the included offense.

SECTIONS 1.08.–1.11. [*Omitted*]

SECTION 1.12. PROOF BEYOND A REASONABLE DOUBT; AFFIRMATIVE DEFENSES; BURDEN OF PROVING FACT WHEN NOT AN ELEMENT OF AN OFFENSE; PRESUMPTIONS

(1) No person may be convicted of an offense unless each element of such offense is proved beyond a reasonable doubt. In the absence of such proof, the innocence of the defendant is assumed.

(2) Subsection (1) of the Section does not:

(a) require the disproof of an affirmative defense unless and until there is evidence supporting such defense; or

(b) apply to any defense which the Code or another statute plainly requires the defendant to prove by a preponderance of evidence.

(3) A ground of defense is affirmative, within the meaning of Subsection (2)(a) of the Section, when:

(a) it arises under a section of the Code that so provides; or

(b) it relates to an offense defined by a statute other than the Code and such statute so provides; or

(c) it involves a matter of excuse or justification peculiarly within the knowledge of the defendant on which he can fairly be required to adduce supporting evidence.

(4) When the application of the Code depends upon the finding of a fact which is not an element of an offense, unless the Code otherwise provides:

(a) the burden of proving the fact is on the prosecution or defendant, depending on whose interest or contention will be furthered if the finding should be made; and

(b) the fact must be proved to the satisfaction of the Court or jury, as the case may be.

(5) When the Code establishes a presumption with respect to any fact that is an element of an offense, it has the following consequences:

(a) when there is evidence of the facts that give rise to the presumption, the issue of the existence of the presumed fact must be submitted to the jury, unless the Court is satisfied that the evidence as a whole clearly negatives the presumed fact; and

(b) when the issue of the existence of the presumed fact is submitted to the jury, the Court shall charge that while the presumed fact must, on all the evidence, be proved beyond a reasonable doubt, the law declares that the jury may regard the facts giving rise to the presumption as sufficient evidence of the presumed fact.

(6) A presumption not established by the Code or inconsistent with it has the consequences otherwise accorded it by law.

SECTION 1.13. GENERAL DEFINITIONS

In this Code, unless a different meaning plainly is required:

(1) "statute" includes the Constitution and a local law or ordinance of a political subdivision of the State;

(2) "act" or "action" means a bodily movement whether voluntary or involuntary;

(3) "voluntary" has the meaning specified in Section 2.01;

(4) "omission" means a failure to act;

(5) "conduct" means an action or omission and its accompanying state of mind, or, where relevant, a series of acts and omissions;

(6) "actor" includes, where relevant, a person guilty of an omission;

(7) "acted" includes, where relevant, "omitted to act";

(8) "person," "he" and "actor" include any natural person and, where relevant, a corporation or an unincorporated association;

(9) "element of an offense" means (i) such conduct or (ii) such attendant circumstance or (iii) such a result of conduct as

(a) is included in the description of the forbidden conduct in the definition of the offense; or

(b) establishes the required kind of culpability; or

(c) negatives an excuse or justification for such conduct; or

(d) negatives a defense under the statute of limitations; or

(e) establishes jurisdiction or venue;

(10) "material element of an offense" means an element that does not relate exclusively to the statute of limitations, jurisdiction, venue or to any other matter similarly unconnected with (i) the harm or evil, incident to conduct, sought to be prevented by the law defining the offense, or (ii) the existence of a justification or excuse for such conduct;

(11) "purposely" has the meaning specified in Section 2.02 and equivalent terms such as "with purpose," "designed" or "with design" have the same meaning;

(12) "intentionally" or "with intent" means purposely;

(13) "knowingly" has the meaning specified in Section 2.02 and equivalent terms such as "knowing" or "with knowledge" have the same meaning;

(14) "recklessly" has the meaning specified in Section 2.02 and equivalent terms such as "recklessness" or "with recklessness" have the same meaning;

(15) "negligently" has the meaning specified in Section 2.02 and equivalent terms such as "negligence" or "with negligence" have the same meaning;

(16) "reasonably believes" or "reasonable belief" designates a belief which the actor is not reckless or negligent in holding.

Article 2. General Principles of Liability

SECTION 2.01. REQUIREMENT OF VOLUNTARY ACT; OMISSION AS BASIS OF LIABILITY; POSSESSION AS AN ACT

(1) A person is not guilty of an offense unless his liability is based on conduct which includes a voluntary act or the omission to perform an act of which he is physically capable.

(2) The following are not voluntary acts within the meaning of this Section:

(a) a reflex or convulsion;

(b) a bodily movement during unconsciousness or sleep;

(c) conduct during hypnosis or resulting from hypnotic suggestion;

(d) a bodily movement that otherwise is not a product of the effort or determination of the actor, either conscious or habitual.

(3) Liability for the commission of an offense may not be based on an omission unaccompanied by action unless:

(a) the omission is expressly made sufficient by the law defining the offense; or

(b) a duty to perform the omitted act is otherwise imposed by law.

(4) Possession is an act, within the meaning of this Section, if the possessor knowingly procured or received the thing possessed or was aware of his control thereof for a sufficient period to have been able to terminate his possession.

SECTION 2.02. GENERAL REQUIREMENTS OF CULPABILITY

(1) *Minimum Requirements of Culpability.* Except as provided in Section 2.05, a person is not guilty of an offense unless he acted purposely, knowingly, recklessly or negligently, as the law may require, with respect to each material element of the offense.

(2) *Kinds of Culpability Defined.*

(a) *Purposely.* A person acts purposely with respect to a material element of an offense when:

(i) if the element involves the nature of his conduct or a result thereof, it is his conscious object to engage in conduct of that nature or to cause such a result; and

(ii) if the element involves the attendant circumstances, he is aware of the existence of such circumstances or he believes or hopes that they exist.

(b) *Knowingly.* A person acts knowingly with respect to a material element of an offense when:

(i) if the element involves the nature of his conduct or the attendant circumstances, he is aware that his conduct is of that nature or that such circumstances exist; and

(ii) if the element involves a result of his conduct, he is aware that it is practically certain that his conduct will cause such a result.

(c) *Recklessly.* A person acts recklessly with respect to a material element of an offense when he consciously disregards a substantial and unjustifiable risk that the material element exists or will result from his conduct. The risk must be of such a nature and degree that, considering the nature and purpose of the actor's conduct and the circumstances known to him, its disregard involves a gross deviation from the standard of conduct that a law-abiding person would observe in the actor's situation.

(d) *Negligently.* A person acts negligently with respect to a material element of an offense when he should be aware of a substantial and unjustifiable risk that the material element exists or will result from his conduct. The risk must be of such a nature and degree that the actor's failure to perceive it, considering the nature and purpose of his conduct and the circumstances known to him, involves a gross deviation from the standard of care that a reasonable person would observe in the actor's situation.

(3) *Culpability Required Unless Otherwise Provided.* When the culpability sufficient to establish a material element of an offense is not prescribed by law, such element is established if a person acts purposely, knowingly or recklessly with respect thereto.

(4) *Prescribed Culpability Requirement Applies to All Material Elements.* When the law defining an offense prescribes the kind of culpability that is sufficient for the commission of an offense, without distinguishing among the material elements thereof, such provision shall apply to all the material elements of the offense, unless a contrary purpose plainly appears.

(5) *Substitutes for Negligence, Recklessness and Knowledge.* When the law provides that negligence suffices to establish an element of an offense, such element also is established if a person acts purposely, knowingly or recklessly. When recklessness suffices to establish an element, such element also is established if a person acts purposely or knowingly. When acting knowingly suffices to establish an element, such element also is established if a person acts purposely.

(6) *Requirement of Purpose Satisfied if Purpose Is Conditional.* When a particular purpose is an element of an offense, the element is established although such purpose is conditional, unless the condition negatives the harm or evil sought to be prevented by the law defining the offense.

(7) *Requirement of Knowledge Satisfied by Knowledge of High Probability.* When knowledge of the existence of a particular fact is an element of an offense, such knowledge is established if a person is aware of a high probability of its existence, unless he actually believes that it does not exist.

(8) *Requirement of Wilfulness Satisfied by Acting Knowingly.* A requirement that an offense be committed wilfully is satisfied if a person acts knowingly with respect to the material elements of the offense, unless a purpose to impose further requirements appears.

(9) *Culpability as to Illegality of Conduct.* Neither knowledge nor recklessness or negligence as to whether conduct constitutes an offense or as to the existence, meaning or application of the law determining the elements of an offense is an element of such offense, unless the definition of the offense or the Code so provides.

(10) *Culpability as Determinant of Grade of Offense.* When the grade or degree of an offense depends on whether the offense is committed purposely, knowingly, recklessly or negligently, its grade or degree shall be the lowest for which the determinative kind of culpability is established with respect to any material element of the offense.

SECTION 2.03. CAUSAL RELATIONSHIP BETWEEN CONDUCT AND RESULT; DIVERGENCE BETWEEN RESULT DESIGNED OR CONTEMPLATED AND ACTUAL RESULT OR BETWEEN PROBABLE AND ACTUAL RESULT

(1) Conduct is the cause of a result when:

(a) it is an antecedent but for which the result in question would not have occurred; and

(b) the relationship between the conduct and result satisfies any additional causal requirements imposed by the Code or by the law defining the offense.

(2) When purposely or knowingly causing a particular result is an element of an offense, the element is not established if the actual result is not within the purpose or the contemplation of the actor unless:

(a) the actual result differs from that designed or contemplated, as the case may be, only in the respect that a different person or different property is injured or affected or that the injury or harm designed or contemplated would have been more serious or more extensive than that caused; or

(b) the actual result involves the same kind of injury or harm as that designed or contemplated and is not too remote or accidental in its occurrence to have a [just] bearing on the actor's liability or on the gravity of his offense.

(3) When recklessly or negligently causing a particular result is an element of an offense, the element is not established if the actual result is not within the risk of which the actor is aware or, in the case of negligence, of which he should be aware unless:

(a) the actual result differs from the probable result only in the respect that a different person or different property is injured or affected or that the probable injury or harm would have been more serious or more extensive than that caused; or

(b) the actual result involves the same kind of injury or harm as the probable result and is not too remote or accidental in its occurrence to have a [just] bearing on the actor's liability or on the gravity of his offense.

(4) When causing a particular result is a material element of an offense for which absolute liability is imposed by law, the element is not established unless the actual result is a probable consequence of the actor's conduct.

SECTION 2.04. IGNORANCE OR MISTAKE

(1) Ignorance or mistake as to a matter of fact or law is a defense if:

(a) the ignorance or mistake negatives the purpose, knowledge, belief, recklessness or negligence required to establish a material element of the offense; or

(b) the law provides that the state of mind established by such ignorance or mistake constitutes a defense.

(2) Although ignorance or mistake would otherwise afford a defense to the offense charged, the defense is not available if the defendant would be guilty of another offense had the situation been as he supposed. In such case, however, the ignorance or mistake of the defendant shall reduce the grade and degree of the offense of which he may be convicted to those of the offense of which he would be guilty had the situation been as he supposed.

(3) A belief that conduct does not legally constitute an offense is a defense to a prosecution for that offense based upon such conduct when:

(a) the statute or other enactment defining the offense is not known to the actor and has not been published or otherwise reasonably made available prior to the conduct alleged; or

(b) he acts in reasonable reliance upon an official statement of the law, afterward determined to be invalid or erroneous, contained in (i) a statute or other enactment; (ii) a judicial decision, opinion or judgment; (iii) an administrative order or grant of permission; or (iv) an official interpretation of the public officer or body charged by law with responsibility for the interpretation, administration or enforcement of the law defining the offense.

(4) The defendant must prove a defense arising under Subsection (3) of this Section by a preponderance of evidence.

SECTION 2.05. WHEN CULPABILITY REQUIREMENTS ARE INAPPLICABLE TO VIOLA-
TIONS AND TO OFFENSES DEFINED BY OTHER STATUTES; EFFECT OF
ABSOLUTE LIABILITY IN REDUCING GRADE OF OFFENSE TO VIOLATION

(1) The requirements of culpability prescribed by Sections 2.01 and 2.02 do not apply to:

(a) offenses which constitute violations, unless the requirement involved is included in the definition of the offense or the Court determines that its application is consistent with effective enforcement of the law defining the offense; or

(b) offenses defined by statutes other than the Code, insofar as a legislative purpose to impose absolute liability for such offenses or with respect to any material element thereof plainly appears.

(2) Notwithstanding any other provision of existing law and unless a subsequent statute otherwise provides:

(a) when absolute liability is imposed with respect to any material element of an offense defined by a statute other than the Code and a conviction is based upon such liability, the offense constitutes a violation; and

(b) although absolute liability is imposed by law with respect to one or more of the material elements of an offense defined by a statute other than the Code, the culpable commission of the offense may be charged and proved, in which event negligence with respect to such elements constitutes sufficient culpability and the classification of the offense and the sentence that may be imposed therefor upon conviction are determined by Section 1.04 and Article 6 of the Code.

SECTION 2.06. LIABILITY FOR CONDUCT OF ANOTHER; COMPLICITY

(1) A person is guilty of an offense if it is committed by his own conduct or by the conduct of another person for which he is legally accountable, or both.

(2) A person is legally accountable for the conduct of another person when:

(a) acting with the kind of culpability that is sufficient for the commission of the offense, he causes an innocent or irresponsible person to engage in such conduct; or

(b) he is made accountable for the conduct of such other person by the Code or by the law defining the offense; or

(c) he is an accomplice of such other person in the commission of the offense.

(3) A person is an accomplice of another person in the commission of an offense if:

(a) with the purpose of promoting or facilitating the commission of the offense, he

(i) solicits such other person to commit it; or

(ii) aids or agrees or attempts to aid such other person in planning or committing it; or

(iii) having a legal duty to prevent the commission of the offense, fails to make proper effort so to do; or

(b) his conduct is expressly declared by law to establish his complicity.

(4) When causing a particular result is an element of an offense, an accomplice in the conduct causing such result is an accomplice in the commission of that offense, if he acts with the kind of culpability, if any, with respect to that result that is sufficient for the commission of the offense.

(5) A person who is legally incapable of committing a particular offense himself may be guilty thereof if it is committed by the conduct of another person for which he is legally accountable, unless such liability is inconsistent with the purpose of the provision establishing his incapacity.

(6) Unless otherwise provided by the Code or by the law defining the offense, a person is not an accomplice in an offense committed by another person if:

(a) he is a victim of that offense; or

(b) the offense is so defined that his conduct is inevitably incident to its commission; or

(c) he terminates his complicity prior to the commission of the offense and

(i) wholly deprives it of effectiveness in the commission of the offense; or

(ii) gives timely warning to the law enforcement authorities or otherwise makes proper effort to prevent the commission of the offense.

(7) An accomplice may be convicted on proof of the commission of the offense and of his complicity therein, though the person claimed to have committed the offense has not been prosecuted or convicted or has been convicted of a different offense or degree of offense or has an immunity to prosecution or conviction or has been acquitted.

SECTION 2.07. LIABILITY OF CORPORATIONS, UNINCORPORATED ASSOCIATIONS AND PERSONS ACTING, OR UNDER A DUTY TO ACT, IN THEIR BEHALF

(1) A corporation may be convicted of the commission of an offense if:

(a) the offense is a violation or the offense is defined by a statute other than the Code in which a legislative purpose to impose liability on corporations plainly appears and the conduct is performed by an agent of the corporation acting in behalf of the corporation within the scope of his office or employment, except that if the law defining the offense designates the agents for whose conduct the corporation is accountable or the circumstance under which it is accountable, such provisions shall apply; or

(b) the offense consists of an omission to discharge a specific duty of affirmative performance imposed on corporations by law; or

(c) the commission of the offense was authorized, requested, commanded, performed or recklessly tolerated by the board of directors or by a high managerial agent acting in behalf of the corporation within the scope of his office or employment.

(2) When absolute liability is imposed for the commission of an offense, a legislative purpose to impose liability on a corporation shall be assumed, unless the contrary plainly appears.

(3) An unincorporated association may be convicted of the commission of an offense if:

(a) the offense is defined by a statute other than the Code which expressly provides for the liability of such an association and the conduct is performed by an agent of the association acting in behalf of the association within the scope of his office or employment, except that if the law defining the offense designates the agents for whose conduct the association is accountable or the circumstances under which it is accountable, such provisions shall apply; or

(b) the offense consists of an omission to discharge a specific duty of affirmative performance imposed on associations by law.

(4) As used in the Section:

(a) "corporation" does not include an entity organized as or by a governmental agency for the execution of a governmental program;

(b) "agent" means any director, officer, servant, employee or other person authorized to act in behalf of the corporation or association and, in the case of an unincorporated association, a member of such association;

(c) "high managerial agent" means an officer of a corporation or an unincorporated association, or, in the case of a partnership, a partner, or any other agent of a corporation or association having duties of such responsibilities that his conduct may fairly be assumed to represent the policy of the corporation or association.

(5) In any prosecution of a corporation or an unincorporated association for the commission of an offense included within the terms of Subsection (1)(a) or Subsection (3)(a) of this Section, other than an offense for which absolute liability has been imposed, it shall be a defense if the defendant proves by a preponderance of evidence that the high managerial agent having supervisory responsibility over the subject matter of the offense employed due diligence to prevent its commission. This paragraph shall not apply if it is plainly inconsistent with the legislative purpose in defining the particular offense.

(6)(a) A person is legally accountable for any conduct he performs or causes to be performed in the name of the corporation or an unincorporated association or in its behalf to the same extent as if it were performed in his own name or behalf.

(b) Whenever a duty to act is imposed by law upon a corporation or an unincorporated association, any agent of the corporation or association having responsibility for the discharge of the duty is legally accountable for a reckless omission to perform the required act to the same extent as if the duty were imposed by law directly upon himself.

(c) When a person is convicted of an offense by reason of his legal accountability for the conduct of a corporation or an unincorporated association, he is subject to the sentence authorized by law when a natural person is convicted of an offense of the grade and the degree involved.

SECTION 2.08.   INTOXICATION

(1) Except as provided in Subsection (4) of this Section, intoxication of the actor is not a defense unless it negatives an element of the offense.

(2) When recklessness establishes an element of the offense, if the actor, due to self-induced intoxication, is unaware of a risk of which he would have been aware had he been sober, such unawareness is immaterial.

(3) Intoxication does not, in itself, constitute mental disease within the meaning of Section 4.01.

(4) Intoxication that (a) is not self-induced or (b) is pathological is an affirmative defense if by reason of such intoxication the actor at the time of his conduct lacks substantial capacity either to appreciate its criminality [wrongfulness] or to conform his conduct to the requirements of law.

(5) *Definitions.* In this Section unless a different meaning plainly is required:

(a) "intoxication" means a disturbance of mental or physical capacities resulting from the introduction of substances into the body;

(b) "self-induced intoxication" means intoxication caused by substances which the actor knowingly introduces into his body, the tendency of which to cause intoxication he knows or ought to know, unless he introduces them pursuant to medical advice or under such circumstances as would afford a defense to a charge of crime;

(c) "pathological intoxication" means intoxication grossly excessive in degree, given the amount of the intoxicant, to which the actor does not know he is susceptible.

SECTION 2.09. DURESS

(1) It is an affirmative defense that the actor engaged in the conduct charged to constitute an offense because he was coerced to do so by the use of, or a threat to use, unlawful force against his person or the person of another, that a person of reasonable firmness in his situation would have been unable to resist.

(2) The defense provided by this Section is unavailable if the actor recklessly placed himself in a situation in which it was probable that he would be subjected to duress. The defense is also unavailable if he was negligent in placing himself in such a situation, whenever negligence suffices to establish culpability for the offense charged.

(3) It is not a defense that a woman acted on the command of her husband, unless she acted under such coercion as would establish a defense under this Section. [The presumption that a woman acting in the presence of her husband is coerced is abolished.]

(4) When the conduct of the actor would otherwise be justifiable under Section 3.02, this Section does not preclude such defense.

SECTION 2.10. MILITARY ORDERS

It is an affirmative defense that the actor, in engaging in the conduct charged to constitute an offense, does no more than execute an order of his superior in the armed services which he does not know to be unlawful.

SECTION 2.11. CONSENT

(1) *In General.* The consent of the victim to conduct charged to constitute an offense or to the result thereof is a defense if such consent negatives an element of the offense or precludes the infliction of the harm or evil sought to be prevented by the law defining the offense.

(2) *Consent to Bodily Harm.* When conduct is charged to constitute an offense because it causes or threatens bodily harm, consent to such conduct or to the infliction of such harm is a defense if:

(a) the bodily injury consented to or threatened by the conduct consented to is not serious; or

(b) the conduct and the injury are reasonably foreseeable hazards of joint participation in a lawful athletic contest or competitive sport or other concerted activity not forbidden by law; or

(c) the consent establishes a justification for the conduct under Article 3 of the Code.

(3) *Ineffective Consent.* Unless otherwise provided by the Code or by the law defining the offense, assent does not constitute consent if:

(a) it is given by a person who is legally incompetent to authorize the conduct charged to constitute the offense; or

(b) it is given by a person who by reason of youth, mental disease or defect or intoxication is manifestly unable or known by the actor to be unable to make a reasonable judgment as to the nature or harmfulness of the conduct charged to constitute the offense; or

(c) it is given by a person whose improvident consent is sought to be prevented by the law defining the offense; or

(d) it is induced by force, duress or deception of a kind sought to be prevented by the law defining the offense.

SECTION 2.12.   DE MINIMIS INFRACTIONS

The Court shall dismiss a prosecution if, having regard to the nature of the conduct charged to constitute an offense and the nature of the attendant circumstances, it finds that the defendant's conduct:

(1) was within a customary license of tolerance, neither expressly negatived by the person whose interest was infringed nor inconsistent with the purpose of the law defining the offense; or

(2) did not actually cause or threaten the harm or evil sought to be prevented by the law defining the offense or did so only to an extent too trivial to warrant the condemnation of conviction; or

(3) presents such other extenuations that it cannot reasonably be regarded as envisaged by the legislature in forbidding the offense.

The Court shall not dismiss a prosecution under Subsection (3) of this Section without filing a written statement of its reasons.

SECTION 2.13.   ENTRAPMENT

(1) A public law enforcement official or a person acting in cooperation with such an official perpetrates an entrapment if for the purpose of obtaining evidence of the commission of an offense, he induces or encourages another person to engage in conduct constituting such offense by either:

(a) making knowingly false representations designed to induce the belief that such conduct is not prohibited; or

(b) employing methods of persuasion or inducement that create a substantial risk that such an offense will be committed by persons other than those who are ready to commit it.

(2) Except as provided in Subsection (3) of this Section, a person prosecuted for an offense shall be acquitted if he proves by a preponderance

of evidence that his conduct occurred in response to an entrapment. The issue of entrapment shall be tried by the Court in the absence of the jury.

(3) The defense afforded by this Section is unavailable when causing or threatening bodily injury is an element of the offense charged and the prosecution is based on conduct causing or threatening such injury to a person other than the person perpetrating the entrapment.

Article 3. General Principles of Justification

SECTION 3.01. JUSTIFICATION AN AFFIRMATIVE DEFENSE; CIVIL REMEDIES UNAFFECTED

(1) In any prosecution based on conduct that is justifiable under this Article, justification is an affirmative defense.

(2) The fact that conduct is justifiable under this Article does not abolish or impair any remedy for such conduct that is available in any civil action.

SECTION 3.02. JUSTIFICATION GENERALLY: CHOICE OF EVILS

(1) Conduct that the actor believes to be necessary to avoid a harm or evil to himself or to another is justifiable, provided that:

(a) the harm or evil sought to be avoided by such conduct is greater than that sought to be prevented by the law defining the offense charged; and

(b) neither the Code nor other law defining the offense provides exceptions or defenses dealing with the specific situation involved; and

(c) a legislative purpose to exclude the justification claimed does not otherwise plainly appear.

(2) When the actor was reckless or negligent in bringing about the situation requiring a choice of harms or evils or in appraising the necessity for his conduct, the justification afforded by this Section is unavailable in a prosecution for any offense for which recklessness or negligence, as the case may be, suffices to establish culpability.

SECTION 3.03. EXECUTION OF PUBLIC DUTY

(1) Except as provided in Subsection (2) of this Section, conduct is justifiable when it is required or authorized by:

(a) the law defining the duties or functions of a public officer or the assistance to be rendered to such officer in the performance of his duties; or

(b) the law governing the execution of legal process; or

(c) the judgment or order of a competent court or tribunal; or

(d) the law governing the armed services or the lawful conduct of war; or

(e) any other provision of law imposing a public duty.

(2) The other sections of this Article apply to:

(a) the use of force upon or toward the person of another for any of the purposes dealt with in such sections; and

(b) the use of deadly force for any purpose, unless the use of such force is otherwise expressly authorized by law or occurs in the lawful conduct of war.

(3) The justification afforded by Subsection (1) of this Section applies:

(a) when the actor believes his conduct to be required or authorized by the judgment or direction of a competent court or tribunal or in the lawful execution of legal process, notwithstanding lack of jurisdiction of the court or defect in the legal process; and

(b) when the actor believes his conduct to be required or authorized to assist a public officer in the performance of his duties, notwithstanding that the officer exceeded his legal authority.

SECTION 3.04.   USE OF FORCE IN SELF-PROTECTION

(1) *Use of Force Justifiable for Protection of the Person.* Subject to the provisions of this Section and of Section 3.09, the use of force upon or toward another person is justifiable when the actor believes that such force is immediately necessary for the purpose of protecting himself against the use of unlawful force by such other person on the present occasion.

(2) *Limitations on Justifying Necessity for Use of Force.*

(a) The use of force is not justifiable under this Section:

(i) to resist an arrest that the actor knows is being made by a peace officer, although the arrest is unlawful; or

(ii) to resist force used by the occupier or possessor of property or by another person on his behalf, where the actor knows that the person using the force is doing so under a claim of right to protect the property, except that this limitation shall not apply if:

(1) the actor is a public officer acting in the performance of his duties or a person lawfully assisting him therein or a person making or assisting in a lawful arrest; or

(2) the actor has been unlawfully dispossessed of the property and is making a re-entry or recaption justified by Section 3.06; or

(3) the actor believes that such force is necessary to protect himself against death or serious bodily harm.

(b) The use of deadly force is not justifiable under this Section unless the actor believes that such force is necessary to protect himself against death, serious bodily harm, kidnapping or sexual intercourse compelled by force or threat; nor is it justifiable if:

(i) the actor, with the purpose of causing death or serious bodily injury, provoked the use of force against himself in the same encounter; or

(ii) the actor knows that he can avoid the necessity of using such force with complete safety by retreating or by surrendering possession of a thing to a person asserting a claim of right thereto or by complying with a demand that he abstain from any action that he has no duty to take, except that:

> (1) the actor is not obliged to retreat from his dwelling or place of work, unless he was the initial aggressor or is assailed in his place of work by another person whose place of work the actor knows it to be; and

> (2) a public officer justified in using force in the performance of his duties or a person justified in using force in his assistance or a person justified in using force in making an arrest or preventing an escape is not obliged to desist from efforts to perform such duty, effect such arrest or prevent such escape because of resistance or threatened resistance by or on behalf of the person against whom such action is directed.

(c) Except as required by paragraphs (a) and (b) of this Subsection, a person employing protective force may estimate the necessity thereof under the circumstances as he believes them to be when the force is used, without retreating, surrendering possession, doing any other act which he has no legal duty to do or abstaining from any lawful action.

(3) *Use of Confinement as Protective Force.* The justification afforded by this Section extends to the use of confinement as protective force only if the actor takes all reasonable measures to terminate the confinement as soon as he knows that he safely can, unless the person confined has been arrested on a charge of crime.

SECTION 3.05. USE OF FORCE FOR THE PROTECTION OF OTHER PERSONS

(1) Subject to the provisions of this Section and of Section 3.09, the use of force upon or toward the person of another is justifiable to protect a third person when:

> (a) the actor would be justified under Section 3.04 in using such force to protect himself against the injury he believes to be threatened to the person whom he seeks to protect; and

> (b) under the circumstances as the actor believes them to be, the person whom he seeks to protect would be justified in using such protective force; and

> (c) the actor believes that his intervention is necessary for the protection of such other person.

(2) Notwithstanding Subsection (1) of this Section:

> (a) when the actor would be obliged under Section 3.04 to retreat, to surrender the possession of a thing or to comply with a demand before using force in self-protection, he is not obliged to do so before using force for the protection of another person, unless he knows that he can thereby secure the complete safety of such other person; and

> (b) when the person whom the actor seeks to protect would be obliged under Section 3.04 to retreat, to surrender the possession of a thing or to comply with a demand if he knew that he could obtain complete safety by so doing, the actor is obliged to try to cause him to do

so before using force in his protection if the actor knows that he can obtain complete safety in that way; and

(c) neither the actor nor the person whom he seeks to protect is obliged to retreat when in the other's dwelling or place of work to any greater extent than in his own.

SECTION 3.06. USE OF FORCE FOR THE PROTECTION OF PROPERTY

(1) *Use of Force Justifiable for Protection of Property.* Subject to the provisions of this Section and of Section 3.09, the use of force upon or toward the person of another is justifiable when the actor believes that such force is immediately necessary:

(a) to prevent or terminate an unlawful entry or other trespass upon land or a trespass against or the unlawful carrying away of tangible, movable property, provided that such land or movable property is, or is believed by the actor to be, in his possession or in the possession of another person for whose protection he acts; or

(b) to effect an entry or re-entry upon land or to retake tangible movable property, provided that the actor believes that he or the person by whose authority he acts or a person from whom he or such other person derives title was unlawfully dispossessed of such land or movable property and is entitled to possession, and provided, further, that:

(i) the force is used immediately or on fresh pursuit after such dispossession; or

(ii) the actor believes that the person against whom he uses force has no claim of right to the possession of the property and, in the case of land, the circumstances, as the actor believes them to be, are of such urgency that it would be an exceptional hardship to postpone the entry or re-entry until a court order is obtained.

(2) *Meaning of Possession.* For the purposes of Subsection (1) of this Section:

(a) a person who has parted with the custody of property to another who refuses to restore it to him is no longer in possession, unless the property is movable and was and still is located on land in his possession;

(b) a person who has been dispossessed of land does not regain possession thereof merely by setting foot thereon;

(c) a person who has a license to use or occupy real property is deemed to be in possession thereof except against the licensor acting under claim of right.

(3) *Limitations on Justifiable Use of Force.*

(a) *Request to Desist.* The use of force is justifiable under this Section only if the actor first requests the person against whom such force is used to desist from his interference with the property, unless the actor believes that:

(i) such request would be useless; or

(ii) it would be dangerous to himself or another person to make the request; or

(iii) substantial harm will be done to the physical condition of the property which is sought to be protected before the request can effectively be made.

(b) *Exclusion of Trespasser.* The use of force to prevent or terminate a trespass is not justifiable under this Section if the actor knows that the exclusion of the trespasser will expose him to substantial danger of serious bodily harm.

(c) *Resistance of Lawful Re-entry or Recaption.* The use of force to prevent an entry or re-entry upon land or the recaption of movable property is not justifiable under this Section, although the actor believes that such re-entry or recaption is unlawful, if:

(i) the re-entry or recaption is made by or on behalf of a person who was actually dispossessed of the property; and

(ii) it is otherwise justifiable under paragraph (1)(b) of this Section.

(d) *Use of Deadly Force.* The use of deadly force is not justifiable under this Section unless the actor believes that:

(i) the person against whom the force is used is attempting to dispossess him of his dwelling otherwise than under a claim of right to its possession; or

(ii) the person against whom the force is used is attempting to commit or consummate arson, burglary, robbery or other felonious theft or property destruction and either:

(1) has employed or threatened deadly force against or in the presence of the actor; or

(2) the use of force other than deadly force to prevent the commission or the consummation of the crime would expose the actor or another in his presence to substantial danger of serious bodily harm.

(4) *Use of Confinement as Protective Force.* The justification afforded by this Section extends to the use of confinement as protective force only if the actor takes all reasonable measures to terminate the confinement as soon as he knows that he can do so with safety to the property, unless the person confined has been arrested on a charge of crime.

(5) *Use of Device to Protect Property.* The justification afforded by this section extends to the use of a device for the purpose of protecting property only if:

(a) the device is not designed to cause or known to create a substantial risk of causing death or serious bodily injury; and

(b) the use of the particular device to protect the property from entry or trespass is reasonable under the circumstances, as the actor believes them to be; and

(c) the device is one customarily used for such a purpose or reasonable care is taken to make known to probable intruders the fact that it is used.

(6) *Use of Force to Pass Wrongful Obstructor.* The use of force to pass a person whom the actor believes to be purposely or knowingly and unjustifiably obstructing the actor from going to a place to which he may lawfully go is justifiable, provided that:

(a) the actor believes that the person against whom he uses force has no claim of right to obstruct the actor; and

(b) the actor is not being obstructed from entry or movement on land which he knows to be in the possession or custody of the person obstructing him, or in the possession or custody of another person by whose authority the obstructor acts, unless the circumstances, as the actor believes them to be, are of such urgency that it would not be reasonable to postpone the entry or movement on such land until a court order is obtained; and

(c) the force used is not greater than would be justifiable if the person obstructing the actor were using force against him to prevent his passage.

SECTION 3.07. USE OF FORCE IN LAW ENFORCEMENT

(1) *Use of Force Justifiable to Effect an Arrest.* Subject to the provisions of this Section and of Section 3.09, the use of force upon or toward the person of another is justifiable when the actor is making or assisting in making an arrest and the actor believes that such force is immediately necessary to effect a lawful arrest.

(2) *Limitations on the Use of Force.*

(a) The use of force is not justifiable under this Section unless:

(i) the actor makes known the purpose of the arrest or believes that it is otherwise known by or cannot reasonably be made known to the person to be arrested; and

(ii) when the arrest is made under a warrant, the warrant is valid or believed by the actor to be valid.

(b) The use of deadly force is not justifiable under this Section unless:

(i) the arrest is for a felony; and

(ii) the person effecting the arrest is authorized to act as a peace officer or is assisting a person whom he believes to be authorized to act as a peace officer; and

(iii) the actor believes that the force employed creates no substantial risk of injury to innocent persons; and

(iv) the actor believes that:

(1) the crime for which the arrest is made involved conduct including the use or threatened use of deadly force; or

(2) there is a substantial risk that the person to be arrested will cause death or serious bodily harm if his apprehension is delayed.

(3) *Use of Force to Prevent Escape From Custody.* The use of force to prevent the escape of an arrested person from custody is justifiable when the force could justifiably have been employed to effect the arrest under which the person is in custody, except that a guard or other person authorized to act as a peace officer is justified in using any force, including deadly force, that he believes to be immediately necessary to prevent the escape of a person from a jail, prison, or other institution for the detention of persons charged with or convicted of a crime.

(4) *Use of Force by Private Person Assisting an Unlawful Arrest.*

(a) A private person who is summoned by a peace officer to assist in effecting an unlawful arrest, is justified in using any force that he would be justified in using if the arrest were lawful, provided that he does not believe the arrest is unlawful.

(b) A private person who assists another private person in effecting an unlawful arrest, or who, not being summoned, assists a peace officer in effecting an unlawful arrest, is justified in using any force that he would be justified in using if the arrest were lawful, provided that (i) he believes the arrest is lawful, and (ii) the arrest would be lawful if the facts were as he believes them to be.

(5) *Use of Force to Prevent Suicide or the Commission of a Crime.*

(a) The use of force upon or toward the person of another is justifiable when the actor believes that such force is immediately necessary to prevent such other person from committing suicide, inflicting serious bodily injury upon himself, committing or consummating the commission of a crime involving or threatening bodily injury, damage to or loss of property or a breach of the peace, except that:

(i) any limitations imposed by the other provisions of this Article on the justifiable use of force in self-protection, for the protection of others, the protection of property, the effectuation of an arrest or the prevention of an escape from custody shall apply notwithstanding the criminality of the conduct against which such force is used; and

(ii) the use of deadly force is not in any event justifiable under this Subsection unless:

(1) the actor believes that there is a substantial risk that the person whom he seeks to prevent from committing a crime will cause death or serious bodily harm to another unless the commission or the consummation of the crime is prevented and that the use of such force presents no substantial risk of injury to innocent persons; or

(2) the actor believes that the use of such force is necessary to suppress a riot or mutiny after the rioters or mutineers have been ordered to disperse and warned, in any particular manner

that the law may require, that such force will be used if they do not obey.

(b) The justification afforded by this Subsection extends to the use of confinement as preventive force only if the actor takes all reasonable measures to terminate the confinement as soon as he knows that he safely can, unless the person confined has been arrested on a charge of crime.

SECTION 3.08. USE OF FORCE BY PERSONS WITH SPECIAL RESPONSIBILITY FOR CARE, DISCIPLINE OR SAFETY OF OTHERS

The use of force upon or toward the person of another is justifiable if:

(1) The actor is the parent or guardian or other person similarly responsible for the general care and supervision of a minor or a person acting at the request of such parent, guardian or other responsible person and:

(a) the force is used for the purpose of safeguarding or promoting the welfare of the minor, including the prevention or punishment of his misconduct; and

(b) the force used is not designed to cause or known to create a substantial risk of causing death, serious bodily injury, disfigurement, extreme pain or mental distress or gross degradation; or

(2) the actor is a teacher or a person otherwise entrusted with the care or supervision for a special purpose of a minor and:

(a) the actor believes that the force used is necessary to further such special purpose, including the maintenance of reasonable discipline in a school, class or other group, and that the use of such force is consistent with the welfare of the minor; and

(b) the degree of force, if it had been used by the parent or guardian of the minor, would not be unjustifiable under Subsection (1)(b) of this Section; or

(3) the actor is the guardian or other person similarly responsible for the general care and supervision of an incompetent person and:

(a) the force is used for the purpose of safeguarding or promoting the welfare of the incompetent person, including the prevention of his misconduct, or, when such incompetent person is in a hospital or other institution for his care and custody, for the maintenance of reasonable discipline in such institution; and

(b) the force used is not designed to cause or known to create a substantial risk of causing death, serious bodily harm, disfigurement, extreme or unnecessary pain, mental distress, or humiliation; or

(4) the actor is a doctor or other therapist or a person assisting him at his direction and:

(a) the force is used for the purpose of administering a recognized form of treatment which the actor believes to be adapted to promoting the physical or mental health of the patient; and

(b) the treatment is administered with the consent of the patient or, if the patient is a minor or an incompetent person, with the consent of his parent or guardian or other person legally competent to consent in his behalf, or the treatment is administered in an emergency when the actor believes that no one competent to consent can be consulted and that a reasonable person, wishing to safeguard the welfare of the patient, would consent; or

(5) the actor is a warden or other authorized official of a correctional institution and:

(a) he believes that the force used is necessary for the purpose of enforcing the lawful rules or procedures of the institution, unless his belief in the lawfulness of the rule or procedure sought to be enforced is erroneous and his error is due to ignorance or mistake as to the provisions of the Code, and other provision of the criminal law or the law governing the administration of the institution; and

(b) the nature or degree of force used is not forbidden by Article 303 or 304 of the Code; and

(c) if deadly force is used, its use is otherwise justifiable under this Article; or

(6) the actor is a person responsible for the safety of a vessel or an aircraft or a person acting at his direction and

(a) he believes that the force used is necessary to prevent interference with a lawful order, unless his belief in the lawfulness of the order is erroneous and his error is due to ignorance or mistake as to the law defining his authority; and

(b) if deadly force is used, its use is otherwise justifiable under this Article; or

(7) the actor is a person who is authorized or required by law to maintain order or decorum in a vehicle, train or other carrier or in a place where others are assembled, and:

(a) he believes that the force used is necessary for such purpose; and

(b) the force is not designed to cause or known to create a substantial risk of causing death, bodily harm, or extreme mental distress.

SECTION 3.09. MISTAKE OF LAW AS TO UNLAWFULNESS OF FORCE OR LEGALITY OF ARREST; RECKLESS OR NEGLIGENT USE OF OTHERWISE JUSTIFIABLE FORCE; RECKLESS OR NEGLIGENT INJURY OR RISK OF INJURY TO INNOCENT PERSONS

(1) The justification afforded by Sections 3.04 to 3.07, inclusive, is unavailable when:

(a) the actor's belief in the unlawfulness of the force or conduct against which he employs protective force or his belief in the lawfulness of an arrest which he endeavors to effect by force is erroneous; and

(b) his error is due to ignorance or mistake as to the provisions of the Code, any other provision of the criminal law or the law governing the legality of an arrest or search.

(2) When the actor believes that the use of force upon or toward the person of another is necessary for any of the purposes for which such belief would establish a justification under Sections 3.03 to 3.08 but the actor is reckless or negligent in having such belief or in acquiring or failing to acquire any knowledge or belief which is material to the justifiability of his use of force, the justification afforded by those Sections is unavailable in a prosecution for an offense for which recklessness or negligence, as the case may be, suffices to establish culpability.

(3) When the actor is justified under Sections 3.03 to 3.08 in using force upon or toward the person of another but he recklessly or negligently injures or creates a risk of injury to innocent persons, the justification afforded by those Sections is unavailable in a prosecution for such recklessness or negligence towards innocent persons.

SECTION 3.10. JUSTIFICATION IN PROPERTY CRIMES

Conduct involving the appropriation, seizure or destruction of, damage to, intrusion on or interference with property is justifiable under circumstances that would establish a defense of privilege in a civil action based thereon unless:

(1) the Code or the law defining the offense deals with the specific situation involved; or

(2) a legislative purpose to exclude the justification claimed otherwise plainly appears.

SECTION 3.11. DEFINITIONS

In this Article, unless a different meaning plainly is required:

(1) "unlawful force" means force, including confinement, which is employed without the consent of the person against whom it is directed and the employment of which constitutes an offense or actionable tort or would constitute such offense or tort except for a defense (such as the absence of intent, negligence, or mental capacity; duress; youth; or diplomatic status) not amounting to a privilege to use the force. Assent constitutes consent, within the meaning of this Section, whether or not it otherwise is legally effective, except assent to the infliction of death or serious bodily harm.

(2) "deadly force" means force which the actor uses with the purpose of causing or which he knows to create a substantial risk of causing death or serious bodily injury. Purposely firing a firearm in the direction of another person or at a vehicle in which another person is believed to be constitutes deadly force. A threat to cause death or serious bodily injury, by the production of a weapon or otherwise, so long as the actor's purpose is limited to creating an apprehension that he will use deadly force if necessary, does not constitute deadly force;

(3) "dwelling" means any building or structure, though movable or temporary, or a portion thereof, that is for the time being the actor's home or place of lodging.

Article 4. Responsibility

SECTION 4.01. MENTAL DISEASE OR DEFECT EXCLUDING RESPONSIBILITY

(1) A person is not responsible for criminal conduct if at the time of such conduct as a result of mental disease or defect he lacks substantial capacity either to appreciate the criminality [wrongfulness] of his conduct or to conform his conduct to the requirements of law.

(2) As used in this Article, the terms "mental disease or defect" do not include an abnormality manifested only by repeated criminal or otherwise antisocial conduct.

SECTION 4.02. EVIDENCE OF MENTAL DISEASE OR DEFECT ADMISSIBLE WHEN RELEVANT TO ELEMENT OF THE OFFENSE; [MENTAL DISEASE OR DEFECT IMPAIRING CAPACITY AS GROUND FOR MITIGATION OF PUNISHMENT IN CAPITAL CASES]

(1) Evidence that the defendant suffered from a mental disease or defect is admissible whenever it is relevant to prove that the defendant did or did not have a state of mind which is an element of the offense.

[(2) Whenever the jury or the Court is authorized to determine or to recommend whether or not the defendant shall be sentenced to death or imprisonment upon conviction, evidence that the capacity of the defendant to appreciate the criminality [wrongfulness] of his conduct or to conform his conduct to the requirements of law was impaired as a result of mental disease or defect is admissible in favor of sentence of imprisonment.]

SECTION 4.03. MENTAL DISEASE OR DEFECT EXCLUDING RESPONSIBILITY IS AFFIRMATIVE DEFENSE; REQUIREMENT OF NOTICE; FORM OF VERDICT AND JUDGMENT WHEN FINDING OF IRRESPONSIBILITY IS MADE

(1) Mental disease or defect excluding responsibility is an affirmative defense.

(2) Evidence of mental disease or defect excluding responsibility is not admissible unless the defendant, at the time of entering his plea of not guilty or within ten days thereafter or at such later time as the Court may for good cause permit, files a written notice of his purpose to rely on such defense.

(3) When the defendant is acquitted on the ground of mental disease or defect excluding responsibility, the verdict and the judgment shall so state.

SECTION 4.04. MENTAL DISEASE OR DEFECT EXCLUDING FITNESS TO PROCEED

No person who as a result of mental disease or defect lacks capacity to understand the proceedings against him or to assist in his defense shall be tried, convicted or sentenced for the commission of an offense so long as such incapacity endures.

SECTION 4.05. PSYCHIATRIC EXAMINATION OF DEFENDANT WITH RESPECT TO MENTAL DISEASE OR DEFECT

(1) Whenever the defendant has filed a notice of intention to rely on the defense of mental disease or defect excluding responsibility, or there is reason to doubt his fitness to proceed, or reason to believe that mental disease or defect of the defendant will otherwise become an issue in the cause, the Court shall appoint at least one qualified psychiatrist or shall request the Superintendent of the _____ Hospital to designate at least one qualified psychiatrist, which designation may be or include himself, to examine and report upon the mental condition of the defendant. The Court may order the defendant to be committed to a hospital or other suitable facility for the purpose of the examination for a period of not exceeding sixty days or such longer period as the Court determines to be necessary for the purpose and may direct that a qualified psychiatrist retained by the defendant be permitted to witness and participate in the examination.

(2) In such examination any method may be employed which is accepted by the medical profession for the examination of those alleged to be suffering from mental disease or defect.

(3) The report of the examination shall include the following: (a) a description of the nature of the examination; (b) a diagnosis of the mental condition of the defendant; (c) if the defendant suffers from a mental disease or defect, an opinion as to his capacity to understand the proceedings against him and to assist in his own defense; (d) when a notice of intention to rely on the defense of irresponsibility has been filed, an opinion as to the extent, if any, to which the capacity of the defendant to appreciate the criminality [wrongfulness] of his conduct or to conform his conduct to the requirements of law was impaired at the time of the criminal conduct charged; and (e) when directed by the Court, an opinion as to the capacity of the defendant to have a particular state of mind which is an element of the offense charged.

If the examination cannot be conducted by reason of the unwillingness of the defendant to participate therein, the report shall so state and shall include, if possible, an opinion as to whether such unwillingness of the defendant was the result of mental disease or defect.

The report of the examination shall be filed [in triplicate] with the clerk of the Court, who shall cause copies to be delivered to the district attorney and to counsel for the defendant.

SECTION 4.06. DETERMINATION OF FITNESS TO PROCEED; EFFECT OF FINDING OF UNFITNESS; PROCEEDINGS IF FITNESS IS REGAINED [; POST-COMMITMENT HEARING]

(1) When the defendant's fitness to proceed is drawn in question, the issue shall be determined by the Court. If neither the prosecuting attorney nor counsel for the defendant contests the finding of the report filed pursuant to Section 4.05, the Court may make the determination on the basis of such report. If the finding is contested, the Court shall hold a hearing on the issue. If the report is received in evidence upon such hearing, the party who contests the finding thereof shall have the right to

summon and to cross-examine the psychiatrists who joined in the report and to offer evidence upon the issue.

(2) If the Court determines that the defendant lacks fitness to proceed, the proceeding against him shall be suspended, except as provided in Subsection (3) [Subsections (3) and (4)] of this Section, and the Court shall commit him to the custody of the Commissioner of Mental Hygiene [Public Health or Correction] to be placed in an appropriate institution of the Department of Mental Hygiene [Public Health or Correction] for so long as such unfitness shall endure. When the Court, on its own motion or upon the application of the Commissioner of Mental Hygiene [Public Health or Correction] or the prosecuting attorney, determines, after a hearing if a hearing is requested, that the defendant has regained fitness to proceed, the proceeding shall be resumed. If, however, the Court is of the view that so much time has elapsed since the commitment of the defendant that it would be unjust to resume the criminal proceeding, the Court may dismiss the charge and may order the defendant to be discharged or, subject to the law governing the civil commitment of persons suffering from mental disease or defect, order the defendant to be committed to an appropriate institution of the Department of Mental Hygiene [Public Health].

(3) The fact that the defendant is unfit to proceed does not preclude any legal objection to the prosecution that is susceptible of fair determination prior to trial and without the personal participation of the defendant.

[Alternative: (3) At any time within ninety days after commitment as provided in Subsection (2) of this Section, or at any later time with permission of the Court granted for good cause, the defendant or his counsel or the Commissioner of Mental Hygiene [Public Health or Correction] may apply for a special post-commitment hearing. If the application is made by or on behalf of a defendant not represented by counsel, he shall be afforded a reasonable opportunity to obtain counsel, and if he lacks funds to do so, counsel shall be assigned by the Court. The application shall be granted only if counsel for the defendant satisfies the Court by affidavit or otherwise that as an attorney he has reasonable grounds for a good faith belief that his client has, on the facts and the law, a defense to the charge other than mental disease or defect excluding responsibility.

[(4) If the motion for a special post-commitment hearing is granted, the hearing shall be by the Court without a jury. No evidence shall be offered at the hearing by either party on the issue of mental disease or defect as a defense to, or in mitigation of, the crime charged. After hearing, the Court may in an appropriate case quash the indictment or other charge, or find it to be defective or insufficient, or determine that it is not proved beyond a reasonable doubt by the evidence, or otherwise terminate the proceedings on the evidence or the law. In any such case, unless all defects in the proceedings are promptly cured, the Court shall terminate the commitment ordered under Subsection (2) of this Section and order the defendant to be discharged or, subject to the law governing the civil commitment of persons suffering from mental disease or defect, order the defendant to be committed to an appropriate institution of the Department of Mental Hygiene [Public Health].]

SECTION 4.07. DETERMINATION OF IRRESPONSIBILITY ON BASIS OF REPORT; ACCESS TO DEFENDANT BY PSYCHIATRIST OF HIS OWN CHOICE; FORM OF EXPERT TESTIMONY WHEN ISSUE OF RESPONSIBILITY IS TRIED

(1) If the report filed pursuant to Section 4.05 finds that the defendant at the time of the criminal conduct charged suffered from a mental disease or defect which substantially impaired his capacity to appreciate the criminality [wrongfulness] of the conduct or to conform his conduct to the requirements of law, and the Court, after a hearing if a hearing is requested by the prosecuting attorney or the defendant, is satisfied that such impairment was sufficient to exclude responsibility, the Court on motion of the defendant shall enter judgement of acquittal on the ground of mental disease or defect excluding responsibility.

(2) When, notwithstanding the report filed pursuant to Section 4.05, the defendant wishes to be examined by a qualified psychiatrist or other expert of his own choice, such examiner shall be permitted to have reasonable access to the defendant for the purposes of such examination.

(3) Upon the trial, the psychiatrists who reported pursuant to Section 4.05 may be called as witnesses by the prosecution, the defendant or the Court. If the issue is being tried before a jury, the jury may be informed that the psychiatrists were designated by the Court or by the Superintendent of the _____ Hospital at the request of the Court, as the case may be. If called by the Court, the witness shall be subject to cross-examination by the prosecution and by the defendant. Both the prosecution and the defendant may summon any other qualified psychiatrist or other expert to testify, but no one who has not examined the defendant shall be competent to testify to an expert opinion with respect to the mental condition or responsibility of the defendant, as distinguished from the validity of the procedure followed by, or the general scientific propositions stated by, another witness.

(4) When a psychiatrist or other expert who has examined the defendant testifies concerning his mental condition, he shall be permitted to make a statement as to the nature of his examination, his diagnosis of the mental condition of the defendant at the time of the commission of the offense charged and his opinion as to the extent, if any, to which the capacity of the defendant to appreciate the criminality [wrongfulness] of his conduct or to conform his conduct to the requirements of law or to have a particular state of mind that is an element of the offense charged was impaired as a result of mental disease or defect at that time. He shall be permitted to make any explanation reasonably serving to clarify his diagnosis and opinion and may be cross-examined as to any matter bearing on his competency or credibility or the validity of his diagnosis or opinion.

SECTION 4.08. LEGAL EFFECT OF ACQUITTAL ON THE GROUND OF MENTAL DISEASE OR DEFECT EXCLUDING RESPONSIBILITY; COMMITMENT; RELEASE OR DISCHARGE

(1) When a defendant is acquitted on the ground of mental disease or defect excluding responsibility, the Court shall order him to be committed to

the custody of the Commissioner of Mental Hygiene [Public Health] to be placed in an appropriate institution for custody, care and treatment.

(2) If the Commissioner of Mental Hygiene [Public Health] is of the view that a person committed to his custody, pursuant to paragraph (1) of this Section, may be discharged or released on condition without danger to himself or to others, he shall make application for the discharge or release of such person in a report to the Court by which such person was committed and shall transmit a copy of such application and report to the prosecuting attorney of the county [parish] from which the defendant was committed. The Court shall thereupon appoint at least two qualified psychiatrists to examine such person and to report within sixty days, or such longer period as the Court determines to be necessary for the purpose, their opinion as to his mental condition. To facilitate such examination and the proceedings thereon, the Court may cause such person to be confined in any institution located near the place where the Court sits, which may hereafter be designated by the Commissioner of Mental Hygiene [Public Health] as suitable for the temporary detention of irresponsible persons.

(3) If the Court is satisfied by the report filed pursuant to paragraph (2) of this Section and such testimony of the reporting psychiatrists as the Court deems necessary that the committed person may be discharged or released on condition without danger to himself or others, the Court shall order his discharge or his release on such conditions as the Court determines to be necessary. If the Court is not so satisfied, it shall promptly order a hearing to determine whether such person may safely be discharged or released. Any such hearing shall be deemed a civil proceeding and the burden shall be upon the committed person to prove that he may safely be discharged or released. According to the determination of the Court upon the hearing, the committed person shall thereupon be discharged or released on such conditions as the Court determines to be necessary, or shall be recommitted to the custody of the Commissioner of Mental Hygiene [Public Health], subject to discharge or release only in accordance with the procedure prescribed above for a first hearing.

(4) If, within [five] years after the conditional release of a committed person, the Court shall determine, after hearing evidence, that the conditions of release have not been fulfilled and that for the safety of such person or for the safety of others his conditional release should be revoked, the Court shall forthwith order him to be recommitted to the Commissioner of Mental Hygiene [Public Health], subject to discharge or release only in accordance with the procedure prescribed above for a first hearing.

(5) A committed person may make application for his discharge or release to the Court by which he was committed, and the procedure to be followed upon such application shall be the same as that prescribed above in the case of an application by the Commissioner of Mental Hygiene [Public Health]. However, no such application by a committed person need be considered until he has been confined for a period of not less than [six months] from the date of the order of commitment, and if the determination of the Court be adverse to the application, such person shall not be permitted to file a further application until [one year] has elapsed from the date of any preceding hearing on an application for his release or discharge.

SECTION 4.09. [*Omitted*]

SECTION 4.10. IMMATURITY EXCLUDING CRIMINAL CONVICTION; TRANSFER OF
          PROCEEDINGS TO JUVENILE COURT

(1) A person shall not be tried for or convicted of an offense if:

(a) at the time of the conduct charged to constitute the offense he
was less than sixteen years of age[, in which case the Juvenile Court
shall have exclusive jurisdiction*]; or

(b) at the time of the conduct charged to constitute the offense he
was sixteen or seventeen years of age, unless:

(i) the Juvenile Court has no jurisdiction over him, or,

(ii) the Juvenile Court has entered an order waiving jurisdiction and consenting to the institution of criminal proceedings
against him.

(2) No court shall have jurisdiction to try or convict a person of an
offense if criminal proceedings against him are barred by Subsection (1) of
this Section. When it appears that a person charged with the commission of
an offense may be of such an age that criminal proceedings may be barred
under Subsection (1) of this Section, the Court shall hold a hearing thereon,
and the burden shall be on the prosecution to establish to the satisfaction of
the Court that the criminal proceeding is not barred upon such grounds. If
the Court determines that the proceeding is barred, custody of the person
charged shall be surrendered to the Juvenile Court, and the case, including
all papers and processes relating thereto, shall be transferred.

Article 5. Inchoate Crimes

SECTION 5.01. CRIMINAL ATTEMPT

(1) *Definition of Attempt.* A person is guilty of an attempt to commit a
crime if, acting with the kind of culpability otherwise required for commission of the crime, he:

(a) purposely engages in conduct that would constitute the crime if
the attendant circumstances were as he believes them to be; or

(b) when causing a particular result is an element of the crime, does
or omits to do anything with the purpose of causing or with the belief
that it will cause such result without further conduct on his part; or

(c) purposely does or omits to do anything which, under the circumstances as he believes them to be, is an act or omission constituting a
substantial step in a course of conduct planned to culminate in his
commission of the crime.

(2) *Conduct That May Be Held Substantial Step Under Subsection (1)(c).*
Conduct shall not be held to constitute a substantial step under Subsection
(1)(c) of this Section unless it is strongly corroborative of the actor's criminal
purpose. Without negativing the sufficiency of other conduct, the following,

* The bracketed words are unnecessary if   amended accordingly.
the Juvenile Court Act so provides or is

if strongly corroborative of the actor's criminal purpose, shall not be held insufficient as a matter of law:

(a) lying in wait, searching for or following the contemplated victim of the crime;

(b) enticing or seeking to entice the contemplated victim of the crime to go to the place contemplated for its commission;

(c) reconnoitering the place contemplated for the commission of the crime;

(d) unlawful entry of a structure, vehicle or enclosure in which it is contemplated that the crime will be committed;

(e) possession of materials to be employed in the commission of the crime, that are specially designed for such unlawful use or which can serve no lawful purpose of the actor under the circumstances;

(f) possession, collection or fabrication of materials to be employed in the commission of the crime, at or near the place contemplated for its commission, where such possession, collection or fabrication serves no lawful purpose of the actor under the circumstances;

(g) soliciting an innocent agent to engage in conduct constituting an element of the crime.

(3) *Conduct Designed to Aid Another in Commission of a Crime.* A person who engages in conduct designed to aid another to commit a crime that would establish his complicity under Section 2.06 if the crime were committed by such other person, is guilty of an attempt to commit the crime, although the crime is not committed or attempted by such other person.

(4) *Renunciation of Criminal Purpose.* When the actor's conduct would otherwise constitute an attempt under Subsection (1)(b) or (1)(c) of this Section, it is an affirmative defense that he abandoned his effort to commit the crime or otherwise prevented its commission, under circumstances manifesting a complete and voluntary renunciation of his criminal purpose. The establishment of such defense does not, however, affect the liability of an accomplice who did not join in such abandonment or prevention.

Within the meaning of this Article, renunciation of criminal purpose is not voluntary if it is motivated, in whole or in part, by circumstances, not present or apparent at the inception of the actor's course of conduct, that increase the probability of detection or apprehension or which make more difficult the accomplishment of the criminal purpose. Renunciation is not complete if it is motivated by a decision to postpone the criminal conduct until a more advantageous time or to transfer the criminal effort to another but similar objective or victim.

Section 5.02. Criminal Solicitation

(1) *Definition of Solicitation.* A person is guilty of solicitation to commit a crime if with the purpose of promoting or facilitating its commission he commands, encourages or requests another person to engage in specific conduct that would constitute such crime or an attempt to commit such crime or which would establish his complicity in its commission or attempted commission.

(2) *Uncommunicated Solicitation.* It is immaterial under Subsection (1) of this Section that the actor fails to communicate with the person he solicits to commit a crime if his conduct was designed to effect such communication.

(3) *Renunciation of Criminal Purpose.* It is an affirmative defense that the actor, after soliciting another person to commit a crime, persuaded him not to do so or otherwise prevented the commission of the crime, under circumstances manifesting a complete and voluntary renunciation of his criminal purpose.

SECTION 5.03. CRIMINAL CONSPIRACY

(1) *Definition of Conspiracy.* A person is guilty of conspiracy with another person or persons to commit a crime if with the purpose of promoting or facilitating its commission he:

(a) agrees with such other person or persons that they or one or more of them will engage in conduct that constitutes such crime or an attempt or solicitation to commit such crime; or

(b) agrees to aid such other person or persons in the planning or commission of such crime or of an attempt or solicitation to commit such crime.

(2) *Scope of Conspiratorial Relationship.* If a person guilty of conspiracy, as defined by Subsection (1) of this Section, knows that a person with whom he conspires to commit a crime has conspired with another person or persons to commit the same crime, he is guilty of conspiring with such other person or persons, whether or not he knows their identity, to commit such crime.

(3) *Conspiracy With Multiple Criminal Objectives.* If a person conspires to commit a number of crimes, he is guilty of only one conspiracy so long as such multiple crimes are the object of the same agreement or continuous conspiratorial relationship.

(4) *Joinder and Venue in Conspiracy Prosecutions.*

(a) Subject to the provisions of paragraph (b) of this Subsection, two or more persons charged with criminal conspiracy may be prosecuted jointly if:

(i) they are charged with conspiring with one another; or

(ii) the conspiracies alleged, whether they have the same or different parties, are so related that they constitute different aspects of a scheme of organized criminal conduct.

(b) In any joint prosecution under paragraph (a) of this Subsection:

(i) no defendant shall be charged with a conspiracy in any county [parish or district] other than one in which he entered into such conspiracy or in which an overt act pursuant to such conspiracy was done by him or by a person with whom he conspired; and

(ii) neither the liability of any defendant nor the admissibility against him of evidence of acts or declarations of another shall be enlarged by such joinder; and

(iii) the Court shall order a severance or take a special verdict as to any defendant who so requests, if it deems it necessary or appropriate to promote the fair determination of his guilt or innocence, and shall take any other proper measures to protect the fairness of the trial.

(5) *Overt Act.* No person may be convicted of conspiracy to commit a crime other than a felony of the first or second degree, unless an overt act in pursuance of such conspiracy is alleged and proved to have been done by him or by a person with whom he conspired.

(6) *Renunciation of Criminal Purpose.* It is an affirmative defense that the actor, after conspiring to commit a crime, thwarted the success of the conspiracy, under circumstances manifesting a complete and voluntary renunciation of his criminal purpose.

(7) *Duration of Conspiracy.* For purposes of Section 1.06(4) [relating to periods of limitation for bringing prosecutions—ed.]:

(a) conspiracy is a continuing course of conduct that terminates when the crime or crimes that are its object are committed or the agreement that they be committed is abandoned by the defendant and by those with whom he conspired; and

(b) such abandonment is presumed if neither the defendant nor anyone with whom he conspired does any overt act in pursuance of the conspiracy during the applicable period of limitation; and

(c) if an individual abandons the agreement, the conspiracy is terminated as to him only if and when he advises those with whom he conspired of his abandonment or he informs the law enforcement authorities of the existence of the conspiracy and of his participation therein.

SECTION 5.04.   INCAPACITY, IRRESPONSIBILITY OR IMMUNITY OF PARTY TO SOLICITATION OR CONSPIRACY

(1) Except as provided in Subsection (2) of this Section, it is immaterial to the liability of a person who solicits or conspires with another to commit a crime that:

(a) he or the person whom he solicits or with whom he conspires does not occupy a particular position or have a particular characteristic that is an element of such crime, if he believes that one of them does; or

(b) the person whom he solicits or with whom he conspires is irresponsible or has an immunity to prosecution or conviction for the commission of the crime.

(2) It is defense to a charge of solicitation or conspiracy to commit a crime that if the criminal object were achieved, the actor would not be guilty of a crime under the law defining the offense or as an accomplice under Section 2.06(5) or 2.06(6)(a) or (b).

SECTION 5.05.   GRADING OF CRIMINAL ATTEMPT, SOLICITATION AND CONSPIRACY; MITIGATION IN CASES OF LESSER DANGER; MULTIPLE CONVICTIONS BARRED

(1) *Grading.* Except as otherwise provided in this Section, attempt, solicitation and conspiracy are crimes of the same grade and degree as the

most serious offense that is attempted or solicited or is an object of the conspiracy. An attempt, solicitation or conspiracy to commit a [capital crime or a] felony of the first degree is a felony of the second degree.

(2) *Mitigation.* If the particular conduct charged to constitute a criminal attempt, solicitation or conspiracy is so inherently unlikely to result or culminate in the commission of a crime that neither such conduct nor the actor presents a public danger warranting the grading of such offense under this Section, the Court shall exercise its power under Section 6.12 to enter judgment and impose sentence for a crime of lower grade or degree or, in extreme cases, may dismiss the prosecution.

(3) *Multiple Convictions.* A person may not be convicted of more than one offense defined by this Article for conduct designed to commit or to culminate in the commission of the same crime.

SECTION 5.06. POSSESSING INSTRUMENTS OF CRIME; WEAPONS

(1) *Criminal Instruments Generally.* A person commits a misdemeanor if he possesses any instrument of crime with purpose to employ it criminally. "Instrument of crime" means:

   (a) anything specially made or specially adapted for criminal use; or

   (b) anything commonly used for criminal purposes and possessed by the actor under circumstances that do not negative unlawful purpose.

(2) *Presumption of Criminal Purpose From Possession of Weapon.* If a person possesses a firearm or other weapon on or about his person, in a vehicle occupied by him, or otherwise readily available for use, it is presumed that he had the purpose to employ it criminally, unless:

   (a) the weapon is possessed in the actor's home or place of business;

   (b) the actor is licensed or otherwise authorized by law to possess such weapon; or

   (c) the weapon is of a type commonly used in lawful sport.

"Weapon" means anything readily capable of lethal use and possessed under circumstances not manifestly appropriate for lawful uses it may have; the term includes a firearm that is not loaded or lacks a clip or other component to render it immediately operable, and components that can readily be assembled into a weapon.

(3) *Presumptions as to Possession of Criminal Instruments in Automobiles.* If a weapon or other instrument of crime is found in an automobile, it is presumed to be in the possession of the occupant if there is but one. If there is more than one occupant, it shall be presumed to be in the possession of all, except under the following circumstances:

   (a) it is found upon the person of one of the occupants;

   (b) the automobile is not a stolen one and the weapon or instrument is found out of view in a glove compartment, car trunk, or other enclosed customary depository, in which case it is presumed to be in the possession of the occupant or occupants who own or have authority to operate the automobile;

(c) in the case of a taxicab, a weapon or instrument found in the passenger's portion of the vehicle shall be presumed to be in the possession of all the passengers, if there are any, and, if not, in the possession of the driver.

SECTION 5.07. [*Omitted*]

Article 6. Authorized Disposition of Offenders

SECTION 6.01. DEGREES OF FELONIES

(1) Felonies defined by this Code are classified, for the purpose of sentence, into three degrees, as follows:

(a) felonies of the first degree;

(b) felonies of the second degree;

(c) felonies of the third degree.

A felony is of the first or second degree when it is so designated by the Code. A crime declared to be a felony, without specification of degree, is of the third degree.

(2) Notwithstanding any other provision of law, a felony defined by any statute of this State other than this Code shall constitute, for the purpose of sentence, a felony of the third degree.

SECTION 6.02. [*Omitted*]

SECTION 6.03. FINES

A person who has been convicted of an offense may be sentenced to pay a fine not exceeding:

(1) $10,0G0, when the conviction is of a felony of the first or second degree;

(2) $5,000, when the conviction is of a felony of the third degree;

(3) $1,000, when the conviction is of a misdemeanor;

(4) $500, when the conviction is of a petty misdemeanor or a violation;

(5) any higher amount equal to double the pecuniary gain derived from the offense by the offender;

(6) any higher amount specifically authorized by statute.

SECTION 6.04. PENALTIES AGAINST CORPORATIONS AND UNINCORPORATED ASSOCIATIONS; FORFEITURE OF CORPORATE CHARTER OR REVOCATION OF CERTIFICATE AUTHORIZING FOREIGN CORPORATION TO DO BUSINESS IN THE STATE

(1) The Court may suspend the sentence of a corporation or an unincorporated association that has been convicted of an offense or may sentence it to pay a fine authorized by Section 6.03.

(2)(a) The [prosecuting attorney] is authorized to institute civil proceedings in the appropriate court of general jurisdiction to forfeit the charter of a corporation organized under the laws of this State or to revoke the certificate authorizing a foreign corporation to conduct business in this State.

The Court may order the charter forfeited or the certificate revoked upon finding (i) that the board of directors or a high managerial agent acting in behalf of the corporation has, in conducting the corporation's affairs, purposely engaged in a persistent course of criminal conduct and (ii) that for the prevention of future criminal conduct of the same character, the public interest requires the charter of the corporation to be forfeited and the corporation to be dissolved or the certificate to be revoked.

(b) When a corporation is convicted of a crime or a high managerial agent of a corporation, as defined in Section 2.07, is convicted of a crime committed in the conduct of the affairs of the corporation, the Court, in sentencing the corporation or the agent, may direct the [prosecuting attorney] to institute proceedings authorized by paragraph (a) of this Subsection.

(c) The proceedings authorized by paragraph (a) of this Subsection shall be conducted in accordance with the procedures authorized by law for the involuntary dissolution of a corporation or the revocation of the certificate authorizing a foreign corporation to conduct business in this State. Such proceedings shall be deemed additional to any other proceedings authorized by law for the purpose of forfeiting the charter of a corporation or revoking the certificate of a foreign corporation.

SECTION 6.05. [*Omitted*]

SECTION 6.06. SENTENCE OF IMPRISONMENT FOR FELONY; ORDINARY TERMS

A person who has been convicted of a felony may be sentenced to imprisonment, as follows:

(1) in the case of a felony of the first degree, for a term the minimum of which shall be fixed by the Court at not less than one year nor more than ten years, and the maximum of which shall be life imprisonment;

(2) in the case of a felony of the second degree, for a term the minimum of which shall be fixed by the Court at not less than one year nor more than three years, and the maximum of which shall be ten years;

(3) in the case of a felony of the third degree, for a term the minimum of which shall be fixed by the Court at not less than one year nor more than two years, and the maximum of which shall be five years.

ALTERNATE SECTION 6.06. SENTENCE OF IMPRISONMENT FOR FELONY; ORDINARY TERMS

A person who has been convicted of a felony may be sentenced to imprisonment, as follows:

(1) in the case of a felony of the first degree, for a term the minimum of which shall be fixed by the Court at not less than one year nor more than ten years, and the maximum at not more than twenty years or at life imprisonment;

(2) in the case of a felony of the second degree, for a term the minimum of which shall be fixed by the Court at not less than one year nor more than three years, and the maximum at not more than ten years;

(3) in the case of a felony of the third degree, for a term the minimum of which shall be fixed by the Court at not less than one year nor more than two years, and the maximum at not more than five years.

No sentence shall be imposed under this Section of which the minimum is longer than one-half the maximum, or, when the maximum is life imprisonment, longer than ten years.

SECTION 6.07. [Omitted]

SECTION 6.08. SENTENCE OF IMPRISONMENT FOR MISDEMEANORS AND PETTY MISDEMEANORS; ORDINARY TERMS

A person who has been convicted of a misdemeanor or a petty misdemeanor may be sentenced to imprisonment for a definite term which shall be fixed by the Court and shall not exceed one year in the case of a misdemeanor or thirty days in the case of a petty misdemeanor.

SECTIONS 6.09.–6.11. [Omitted]

SECTION 6.12. REDUCTION OF CONVICTION BY COURT TO LESSER DEGREE OF FELONY OR TO MISDEMEANOR

If, when a person has been convicted of a felony, the Court, having regard to the nature and circumstances of the crime and to the history and character of the defendant, is of the view that it would be unduly harsh to sentence the offender in accordance with the Code, the Court may enter judgment of conviction for a lesser degree of felony or for a misdemeanor and impose sentence accordingly.

SECTION 6.13. [Omitted]

Article 7. Authority of Court in Sentencing [Omitted]

PART II. DEFINITION OF SPECIFIC CRIMES
OFFENSES INVOLVING DANGER TO THE PERSON
Article 210. Criminal Homicide

SECTION 210.0. DEFINITIONS

In Articles 210–213, unless a different meaning plainly is required:

(1) "human being" means a person who has been born and is alive;

(2) "bodily injury" means physical pain, illness or any impairment of physical condition;

(3) "serious bodily injury" means bodily injury which creates a substantial risk of death or which causes serious, permanent disfigurement, or protracted loss or impairment of the function of any bodily member or organ;

(4) "deadly weapon" means any firearm or other weapon, device, instrument, material or substance, whether animate or inanimate, which in the manner it is used or is intended to be used is known to be capable of producing death or serious bodily injury.

SECTION 210.1. CRIMINAL HOMICIDE

(1) A person is guilty of criminal homicide if he purposely, knowingly, recklessly or negligently causes the death of another human being.

(2) Criminal homicide is murder, manslaughter or negligent homicide.

SECTION 210.2. MURDER

(1) Except as provided in Section 210.3(1)(b), criminal homicide constitutes murder when:

(a) it is committed purposely or knowingly; or

(b) it is committed recklessly under circumstances manifesting extreme indifference to the value of human life. Such recklessness and indifference are presumed if the actor is engaged or is an accomplice in the commission of, or an attempt to commit, or flight after committing or attempting to commit robbery, rape or deviate sexual intercourse by force or threat of force, arson, burglary, kidnapping or felonious escape.

(2) Murder is a felony of the first degree [but a person convicted of murder may be sentenced to death, as provided in Section 210.6].

SECTION 210.3. MANSLAUGHTER

(1) Criminal homicide constitutes manslaughter when:

(a) it is committed recklessly; or

(b) a homicide which would otherwise be murder is committed under the influence of extreme mental or emotional disturbance for which there is reasonable explanation or excuse. The reasonableness of such explanation or excuse shall be determined from the viewpoint of a person in the actor's situation under the circumstances as he believes them to be.

(2) Manslaughter is a felony of the second degree.

SECTION 210.4. NEGLIGENT HOMICIDE

(1) Criminal homicide constitutes negligent homicide when it is committed negligently.

(2) Negligent homicide is a felony of the third degree.

SECTION 210.5. CAUSING OR AIDING SUICIDE

(1) *Causing Suicide as Criminal Homicide.* A person may be convicted of criminal homicide for causing another to commit suicide only if he purposely causes such suicide by force, duress or deception.

(2) *Aiding or Soliciting Suicide as an Independent Offense.* A person who purposely aids or solicits another to commit suicide is guilty of a felony of the second degree if his conduct causes such suicide or an attempted suicide, and otherwise of a misdemeanor.

[SECTION 210.6. SENTENCE OF DEATH FOR MURDER; FURTHER PROCEEDINGS TO DETERMINE SENTENCE*

(1) *Death Sentence Excluded.* When a defendant is found guilty of murder, the Court shall impose sentence for a felony of the first degree if it is satisfied that:

(a) none of the aggravating circumstances enumerated in Subsection (3) of this Section was established by the evidence at the trial or will be established if further proceedings are initiated under Subsection (2) of this Section; or

(b) substantial mitigating circumstances, established by the evidence at the trial, call for leniency; or

(c) the defendant, with the consent of the prosecuting attorney and the approval of the Court, pleaded guilty to murder as a felony of the first degree; or

(d) the defendant was under 18 years of age at the time of the commission of the crime; or

(e) the defendant's physical or mental condition calls for leniency; or

(f) although the evidence suffices to sustain the verdict, it does not foreclose all doubt respecting the defendant's guilt.

(2) *Determination by Court or by Court and Jury.* Unless the Court imposes sentence under Subsection (1) of this Section, it shall conduct a separate proceeding to determine whether the defendant should be sentenced for a felony of the first degree or sentenced to death. The proceeding shall be conducted before the Court alone if the defendant was convicted by a Court sitting without a jury or upon his plea of guilty or if the prosecuting attorney and the defendant waive a jury with respect to sentence. In other cases it shall be conducted before the Court sitting with the jury which determined the defendant's guilt or, if the Court for good cause shown discharges that jury, with a new jury empanelled for the purpose.

In the proceeding, evidence may be presented as to any matter that the Court deems relevant to sentence, including but not limited to the nature and circumstances of the crime, the defendant's character, background, history, mental and physical condition and any of the aggravating or mitigating circumstances enumerated in Subsections (3) and (4) of this Section. Any such evidence, not legally privileged, which the Court deems to have probative force, may be received, regardless of its admissibility under the exclusionary rules of evidence, provided that the defendant's counsel is accorded a fair opportunity to rebut such evidence. The prosecuting attorney and the defendant or his counsel shall be permitted to present argument for or against sentence of death.

The determination whether sentence of death shall be imposed shall be in the discretion of the Court, except that when the proceeding is conducted before the Court sitting with a jury, the Court shall not impose sentence of

---

* The Brackets indicate that the Institute took no position on the desirability of the death penalty.

death unless it submits to the jury the issue whether the defendant should be sentenced to death or to imprisonment and the jury returns a verdict that the sentence should be death. If the jury is unable to reach a unanimous verdict, the Court shall dismiss the jury and impose sentence for a felony of the first degree.

The Court, in exercising its discretion as to sentence, and the jury, in determining upon its verdict, shall take into account the aggravating and mitigating circumstances enumerated in Subsections (3) and (4) and any other facts that it deems relevant, but it shall not impose or recommend sentence of death unless it finds one of the aggravating circumstances enumerated in Subsection (3) and further finds that there are no mitigating circumstances sufficiently substantial to call for leniency. When the issue is submitted to the jury, the Court shall so instruct and also shall inform the jury of the nature of the sentence of imprisonment that may be imposed, including its implication with respect to possible release upon parole, if the jury verdict is against sentence of death.

Alternative formulation of Subsection (2):

(2) *Determination by Court.* Unless the Court imposes sentence under Subsection (1) of this Section, it shall conduct a separate proceeding to determine whether the defendant should be sentenced for a felony of the first degree or sentenced to death. In the proceeding, the Court, in accordance with Section 7.07 [relating to procedures on sentence], shall consider the report of the presentence investigation and, if a psychiatric examination has been ordered, the report of such examination. In addition, evidence may be presented as to any matter that the Court deems relevant to sentence, including but not limited to the nature and circumstances of the crime, the defendant's character, background, history, mental and physical condition and any of the aggravating or mitigating circumstances enumerated in Subsections (3) and (4) of this Section. Any such evidence, not legally privileged, which the Court deems to have probative force, may be received, regardless of its admissibility under the exclusionary rules of evidence, provided that the defendant's counsel is accorded a fair opportunity to rebut such evidence. The prosecuting attorney and the defendant or his counsel shall be permitted to present argument for or against sentence of death.

The determination whether sentence of death shall be imposed shall be in the discretion of the Court. In exercising such discretion, the Court shall take into account the aggravating and mitigating circumstances enumerated in Subsections (3) and (4) and any other facts that it deems relevant but shall not impose sentence of death unless it finds one of the aggravating circumstances enumerated in Subsection (3) and further finds that there are no mitigating circumstances sufficiently substantial to call for leniency.

(3) *Aggravating Circumstances.*

(a) The murder was committed by a convict under sentence of imprisonment.

(b) The defendant was previously convicted of another murder or of a felony involving the use or threat of violence to the person.

(c) At the time the murder was committed the defendant also committed another murder.

(d) The defendant knowingly created a great risk of death to many persons.

(e) The murder was committed while the defendant was engaged or was an accomplice in the commission of, or an attempt to commit, or flight after committing or attempting to commit robbery, rape or deviate sexual intercourse by force or threat of force, arson, burglary or kidnapping.

(f) The murder was committed for the purpose of avoiding or preventing a lawful arrest or effecting an escape from lawful custody.

(g) The murder was committed for pecuniary gain.

(h) The murder was especially heinous, atrocious or cruel, manifesting exceptional depravity.

(4) *Mitigating Circumstances.*

(a) The defendant has no significant history of prior criminal activity.

(b) The murder was committed while the defendant was under the influence of extreme mental or emotional disturbance.

(c) The victim was a participant in the defendant's homicidal conduct or consented to the homicidal act.

(d) The murder was committed under circumstances which the defendant believed to provide a moral justification or extenuation for his conduct.

(e) The defendant was an accomplice in a murder committed by another person and his participation in the homicidal act was relatively minor.

(f) The defendant acted under duress or under the domination of another person.

(g) At the time of the murder, the capacity of the defendant to appreciate the criminality [wrongfulness] of his conduct or to conform his conduct to the requirements of law was impaired as a result of mental disease or defect or intoxication.

(h) The youth of the defendant at the time of the crime.]

Article 211. Assault; Reckless Endangering; Threats

SECTION 211.0. DEFINITIONS

In this Article, the definitions given in Section 210.0 apply unless a different meaning plainly is required.

SECTION 211.1. ASSAULT

(1) *Simple Assault.* A person is guilty of assault if he:

(a) attempts to cause or purposely, knowingly or recklessly causes bodily injury to another; or

(b) negligently causes bodily injury to another with a deadly weapon; or

(c) attempts by physical menace to put another in fear of imminent serious bodily injury.

Simple assault is a misdemeanor unless committed in a fight or scuffle entered into by mutual consent, in which case it is a petty misdemeanor.

(2) *Aggravated Assault.* A person is guilty of aggravated assault if he:

(a) attempts to cause serious bodily injury to another, or causes such injury purposely, knowingly or recklessly under circumstances manifesting extreme indifference to the value of human life; or

(b) attempts to cause or purposely or knowingly causes bodily injury to another with a deadly weapon.

Aggravated assault under paragraph (a) is a felony of the second degree; aggravated assault under paragraph (b) is a felony of the third degree.

SECTION 211.2. RECKLESSLY ENDANGERING ANOTHER PERSON

A person commits a misdemeanor if he recklessly engages in conduct which places or may place another person in danger of death or serious bodily injury. Recklessness and danger shall be presumed where a person knowingly points a firearm at or in the direction of another, whether or not the actor believed the firearm to be loaded.

SECTION 211.3. TERRORISTIC THREATS

A person is guilty of a felony of the third degree if he threatens to commit any crime of violence with purpose to terrorize another or to cause evacuation of a building, place of assembly, or facility of public transportation, or otherwise to cause serious public inconvenience, or in reckless disregard of the risk of causing such terror or inconvenience.

Article 212. Kidnapping and Related Offenses; Coercion

SECTION 212.0. DEFINITIONS

In this Article, the definitions given in section 210.0 apply unless a different meaning plainly is required.

SECTION 212.1. KIDNAPPING

A person is guilty of kidnapping if he unlawfully removes another from his place of residence or business, or a substantial distance from the vicinity where he is found, or if he unlawfully confines another for a substantial period in a place of isolation, with any of the following purposes:

(a) to hold for ransom or reward, or as a shield or hostage; or

(b) to facilitate commission of any felony or flight thereafter; or

(c) to inflict bodily injury on or to terrorize the victim or another; or

(d) to interfere with the performance of any governmental or political function.

Kidnapping is a felony of the first degree unless the actor voluntarily releases the victim alive and in a safe place prior to trial, in which case it is a felony of the second degree. A removal or confinement is unlawful within the meaning of this Section if it is accomplished by force, threat or deception, or, in the case of a person who is under the age of 14 or incompetent, if it is accomplished without the consent of a parent, guardian or other person responsible for general supervision of his welfare.

SECTION 212.2. FELONIOUS RESTRAINT

A person commits a felony of the third degree if he knowingly:

(a) restrains another unlawfully in circumstances exposing him to risk of serious bodily injury; or

(b) holds another in a condition of involuntary servitude.

SECTION 212.3. FALSE IMPRISONMENT

A person commits a misdemeanor if he knowingly restrains another unlawfully so as to interfere substantially with his liberty.

SECTION 212.4. INTERFERENCE WITH CUSTODY

(1) *Custody of Children.* A person commits an offense if he knowingly or recklessly takes or entices any child under the age of 18 from the custody of its parent, guardian or other lawful custodian, when he has no privilege to do so. It is an affirmative defense that:

(a) the actor believed that his action was necessary to preserve the child from danger to its welfare; or

(b) the child, being at the time not less than 14 years old, was taken away at its own instigation without enticement and without purpose to commit a criminal offense with or against the child.

Proof that the child was below the critical age gives rise to a presumption that the actor knew the child's age or acted in reckless disregard thereof. The offense is a misdemeanor unless the actor, not being a parent or person in equivalent relation to the child, acted with knowledge that his conduct would cause serious alarm for the child's safety, or in reckless disregard of a likelihood of causing such alarm, in which case the offense is a felony of the third degree.

(2) *Custody of Committed Persons.* A person is guilty of a misdemeanor if he knowingly or recklessly takes or entices any committed person away from lawful custody when he is not privileged to do so. "Committed person" means, in addition to anyone committed under judicial warrant, any orphan, neglected or delinquent child, mentally defective or insane person, or other dependent or incompetent person entrusted to another's custody by or through a recognized social agency or otherwise by authority of law.

SECTION 212.5. CRIMINAL COERCION

(1) *Offense Defined.* A person is guilty of criminal coercion if, with purpose unlawfully to restrict another's freedom of action to his detriment, he threatens to:

(a) commit any criminal offense; or

(b) accuse anyone of a criminal offense; or

(c) expose any secret tending to subject any person to hatred, contempt or ridicule, or to impair his credit or business repute; or

(d) take or withhold action as an official, or cause an official to take or withhold action.

It is an affirmative defense to prosecution based on paragraphs (b), (c) or (d) that the actor believed the accusation or secret to be true or the proposed official action justified and that his purpose was limited to compelling the other to behave in a way reasonably related to the circumstances which were the subject of the accusation, exposure or proposed official action, as by desisting from further misbehavior, making good a wrong done, refraining from taking any action or responsibility for which the actor believes the other disqualified.

(2) *Grading*. Criminal coercion is a misdemeanor unless the threat is to commit a felony or the actor's purpose is felonious, in which cases the offense is a felony of the third degree.

Article 213. Sexual Offenses

SECTION 213.0. DEFINITIONS

In this Article, unless a different meaning plainly is required:

(1) the definitions given in Section 210.0 apply;

(2) "Sexual intercourse" includes intercourse per os or per anum, with some penetration however slight; emission is not required;

(3) "Deviate sexual intercourse" means sexual intercourse per os or per anum between human beings who are not husband and wife, and any form of sexual intercourse with an animal.

SECTION 213.1. RAPE AND RELATED OFFENSES

(1) *Rape*. A male who has sexual intercourse with a female not his wife is guilty of rape if:

(a) he compels her to submit by force or by threat of imminent death, serious bodily injury, extreme pain or kidnapping, to be inflicted on anyone; or

(b) he has substantially impaired her power to appraise or control her conduct by administering or employing without her knowledge drugs, intoxicants or other means for the purpose of preventing resistance; or

(c) the female is unconscious; or

(d) the female is less than 10 years old.

Rape is a felony of the second degree unless (i) in the course thereof the actor inflicts serious bodily injury upon anyone, or (ii) the victim was not a voluntary social companion of the actor upon the occasion of the crime and had not previously permitted him sexual liberties, in which cases the offense is a felony of the first degree.

(2) *Gross Sexual Imposition.* A male who has sexual intercourse with a female not his wife commits a felony of the third degree if:

(a) he compels her to submit by any threat that would prevent resistance by a woman of ordinary resolution; or

(b) he knows that she suffers from a mental disease or defect which renders her incapable of appraising the nature of her conduct; or

(c) he knows that she is unaware that a sexual act is being committed upon her or that she submits because she mistakenly supposes that he is her husband.

SECTION 213.2. DEVIATE SEXUAL INTERCOURSE BY FORCE OR IMPOSITION

(1) *By Force or Its Equivalent.* A person who engages in deviate sexual intercourse with another person, or who causes another to engage in deviate sexual intercourse, commits a felony of the second degree if:

(a) he compels the other person to participate by force or by threat of imminent death, serious bodily injury, extreme pain or kidnapping, to be inflicted on anyone; or

(b) he has substantially impaired the other person's power to appraise or control his conduct, by administering or employing without the knowledge of the other person drugs, intoxicants or other means for the purpose of preventing resistance; or

(c) the other person is unconscious; or

(d) the other person is less than 10 years old.

(2) *By Other Imposition.* A person who engages in deviate sexual intercourse with another person, or who causes another to engage in deviate sexual intercourse, commits a felony of the third degree if:

(a) he compels the other person to participate by any threat that would prevent resistance by a person of ordinary resolution; or

(b) he knows that the other person suffers from a mental disease or defect which renders him incapable of appraising the nature of his conduct; or

(c) he knows that the other person submits because he is unaware that a sexual act is being committed upon him.

SECTION 213.3. CORRUPTION OF MINORS AND SEDUCTION

(1) *Offense Defined.* A male who has sexual intercourse with a female not his wife, or any person who engages in deviate sexual intercourse or causes another to engage in deviate sexual intercourse, is guilty of an offense if:

(a) the other person is less than [16] years old and the actor is at least [four] years older than the other person; or

(b) the other person is less than 21 years old and the actor is his guardian or otherwise responsible for general supervision of his welfare; or

(c) the other person is in custody of law or detained in a hospital or other institution and the actor has supervisory or disciplinary authority over him; or

(d) the other person is a female who is induced to participate by a promise of marriage which the actor does not mean to perform.

(2) *Grading.* An offense under paragraph (a) of Subsection (1) is a felony of the third degree. Otherwise an offense under this section is a misdemeanor.

SECTION 213.4. SEXUAL ASSAULT

A person who has sexual contact with another not his spouse, or causes such other to have sexual conduct with him, is guilty of sexual assault, a misdemeanor, if:

(1) he knows that the contact is offensive to the other person; or

(2) he knows that the other person suffers from a mental disease or defect which renders him or her incapable of appraising the nature of his or her conduct; or

(3) he knows that the other person is unaware that a sexual act is being committed; or

(4) the other person is less than 10 years old; or

(5) he has substantially impaired the other person's power to appraise or control his or her conduct, by administering or employing without the other's knowledge drugs, intoxicants or other means for the purpose of preventing resistance; or

(6) the other person is less than [16] years old and the actor is at least [four] years older than the other person; or

(7) the other person is less than 21 years old and the actor is his guardian or otherwise responsible for general supervision of his welfare; or

(8) the other person is in custody of law or detained in a hospital or other institution and the actor has supervisory or disciplinary authority over him.

Sexual contact is any touching of the sexual or other intimate parts of the person for the purpose of arousing or gratifying sexual desire.

SECTION 213.5. INDECENT EXPOSURE

A person commits a misdemeanor if, for the purpose of arousing or gratifying sexual desire of himself or of any person other than his spouse, he exposes his genitals under circumstances in which he knows his conduct is likely to cause affront or alarm.

SECTION 213.6. PROVISIONS GENERALLY APPLICABLE TO ARTICLE 213

(1) *Mistake as to Age.* Whenever in this Article the criminality of conduct depends on a child's being below the age of 10, it is no defense that the actor did not know the child's age, or reasonably believed the child to be older than 10. When criminality depends on the child's being below a critical age other than 10, it is a defense for the actor to prove by a

preponderance of the evidence that he reasonably believed the child to be above the critical age.

(2) *Spouse Relationships.* Whenever in this Article the definition of an offense excludes conduct with a spouse, the exclusion shall be deemed to extend to persons living as man and wife, regardless of the legal status of their relationship. The exclusion shall be inoperative as respects spouses living apart under a decree of judicial separation. Where the definition of an offense excludes conduct with a spouse or conduct by a woman, this shall not preclude conviction of a spouse or woman as accomplice in a sexual act which he or she causes another person, not within the exclusion, to perform.

(3) *Sexually Promiscuous Complainants.* It is a defense to prosecution under Section 213.3, and paragraphs (6), (7) and (8) of Section 213.4 for the actor to prove by a preponderance of the evidence that the alleged victim had, prior to the time of the offense charged, engaged promiscuously in sexual relations with others.

(4) *Prompt Complaint.* No prosecution may be instituted or maintained under this Article unless the alleged offense was brought to the notice of public authority within [3] months of its occurrence or, where the alleged victim was less than [16] years old or otherwise incompetent to make complaint, within [3] months after a parent, guardian or other competent person specially interested in the victim learns of the offense.

(5) *Testimony of Complainants.* No person shall be convicted of any felony under this Article upon the uncorroborated testimony of the alleged victim. Corroboration may be circumstantial. In any prosecution before a jury for an offense under this Article, the jury shall be instructed to evaluate the testimony of a victim or complaining witness with special care in view of the emotional involvement of the witness and the difficulty of determining the truth with respect to alleged sexual activities carried out in private.

OFFENSES AGAINST PROPERTY

Article 220. Arson, Criminal Mischief, and Other Property Destruction

SECTION 220.1. ARSON AND RELATED OFFENSES

(1) *Arson.* A person is guilty of arson, a felony of the second degree, if he starts a fire or causes an explosion with the purpose of:

(a) destroying a building or occupied structure of another; or

(b) destroying or damaging any property, whether his own or another's, to collect insurance for such loss. It shall be an affirmative defense to prosecution under this paragraph that the actor's conduct did not recklessly endanger any building or occupied structure of another or place any other person in danger of death or bodily injury.

(2) *Reckless Burning or Exploding.* A person commits a felony of the third degree if he purposely starts a fire or causes an explosion, whether on his own property or another's, and thereby recklessly:

(a) places another person in danger of death or bodily injury; or

(b) place a building or occupied structure of another in danger of damage or destruction.

(3) *Failure to Control or Report Dangerous Fire.* A person who knows that a fire is endangering life or a substantial amount of property of another and fails to take reasonable measures to put out or control the fire, when he can do so without substantial risk to himself, or to give a prompt fire alarm, commits a misdemeanor if:

(a) he knows that he is under an official, contractual, or other legal duty to prevent or combat the fire; or

(b) the fire was started, albeit lawfully, by him or with his assent, or on property in his custody or control.

(4) *Definitions.* "Occupied structure" means any structure, vehicle or place adapted for overnight accommodation of persons, or for carrying on business therein, whether or not a person is actually present. Property is that of another, for the purposes of this section, if anyone other than the actor has a possessory or proprietary interest therein. If a building or structure is divided into separately occupied units, any unit not occupied by the actor is an occupied structure of another.

SECTION 220.2. CAUSING OR RISKING CATASTROPHE

(1) *Causing Catastrophe.* A person who causes a catastrophe by explosion, fire, flood, avalanche, collapse of building, release of poison gas, radioactive material or other harmful or destructive force or substance, or by any other means of causing potentially widespread injury or damage, commits a felony of the second degree if he does so purposely or knowingly, or a felony of the third degree if he does so recklessly.

(2) *Risking Catastrophe.* A person is guilty of a misdemeanor if he recklessly creates a risk of catastrophe in the employment of fire, explosives or other dangerous means listed in Subsection (1).

(3) *Failure to Prevent Catastrophe.* A person who knowingly or recklessly fails to take reasonable measures to prevent or mitigate a catastrophe commits a misdemeanor if:

(a) he knows that he is under an official, contractual or other legal duty to take such measures; or

(b) he did or assented to the act causing or threatening the catastrophe.

SECTION 220.3. CRIMINAL MISCHIEF

(1) *Offense Defined.* A person is guilty of criminal mischief if he:

(a) damages tangible property of another purposely, recklessly, or by negligence in the employment of fire, explosives, or other dangerous means listed in Section 220.2(1); or

(b) purposely or recklessly tampers with tangible property of another so as to endanger persons or property; or

(c) purposely or recklessly causes another to suffer pecuniary loss by deception or threat.

(2) *Grading.* Criminal mischief is a felony of the third degree if the actor purposely causes pecuniary loss in excess of $5,000 or a substantial

interruption or impairment of public communication, transportation, supply of water, gas or power, or other public service. It is a misdemeanor if the actor purposely causes pecuniary loss in excess of $100, or a petty misdemeanor if he purposely or recklessly causes pecuniary loss in excess of $25. Otherwise criminal mischief is a violation.

Article 221. Burglary and Other Criminal Intrusion

SECTION 221.0. DEFINITIONS

In this Article, unless a different meaning plainly is required:

(1) "occupied structure" means any structure, vehicle or place adapted for overnight accommodation of persons, or for carrying on business therein, whether or not a person is actually present.

(2) "night" means the period between thirty minutes past sunset and thirty minutes before sunrise.

SECTION 221.1. BURGLARY

(1) *Burglary Defined.* A person is guilty of burglary if he enters a building or occupied structure, or separately secured or occupied portion thereof, with purpose to commit a crime therein, unless the premises are at the time open to the public or the actor is licensed or privileged to enter. It is an affirmative defense to prosecution for burglary that the building or structure was abandoned.

(2) *Grading.* Burglary is a felony of the second degree if it is perpetrated in the dwelling of another at night, or if, in the course of committing the offense, the actor:

(a) purposely, knowingly or recklessly inflicts or attempts to inflict bodily injury on anyone; or

(b) is armed with explosives or a deadly weapon.

Otherwise, burglary is a felony of the third degree. An act shall be deemed "in the course of committing" an offense if it occurs in an attempt to commit the offense or in flight after the attempt or commission.

(3) *Multiple Convictions.* A person may not be convicted both for burglary and for the offense which it was his purpose to commit after the burglarious entry or for an attempt to commit that offense, unless the additional offense constitutes a felony of the first or second degree.

SECTION 221.2. CRIMINAL TRESPASS

(1) *Buildings and Occupied Structures.* A person commits an offense if, knowing that he is not licensed or privileged to do so, he enters or surreptitiously remains in any building or occupied structure, or separately secured or occupied portion thereof. An offense under this Subsection is a misdemeanor if it is committed in a dwelling at night. Otherwise it is a petty misdemeanor.

(2) *Defiant Trespasser.* A person commits an offense if, knowing that he is not licensed or privileged to do so, he enters or remains in any place as to which notice against trespass is given by:

(a) actual communication to the actor; or

(b) posting in a manner prescribed by law or reasonably likely to come to the attention of intruders; or

(c) fencing or other enclosure manifestly designed to exclude intruders.

An offense under this Subsection constitutes a petty misdemeanor if the offender defies an order to leave personally communicated to him by the owner of the premises or other authorized person. Otherwise it is a violation.

(3) *Defenses.* It is an affirmative defense to prosecution under this Section that:

(a) a building or occupied structure involved in an offense under Subsection (1) was abandoned; or

(b) the premises were at the time open to members of the public and the actor complied with all lawful conditions imposed on access to or remaining in the premises; or

(c) the actor reasonably believed that the owner of the premises, or other person empowered to license access thereto, would have licensed him to enter or remain.

Article 222. Robbery

SECTION 222.1. ROBBERY

(1) *Robbery Defined.* A person is guilty of robbery if, in the course of committing a theft, he:

(a) inflicts serious bodily injury upon another; or

(b) threatens another with or purposely puts him in fear of immediate serious bodily injury; or

(c) commits or threatens immediately to commit any felony of the first or second degree.

An act shall be deemed "in the course of committing a theft" if it occurs in an attempt to commit theft or in flight after the attempt or commission.

(2) *Grading.* Robbery is a felony of the second degree, except that it is a felony of the first degree if in the course of committing the theft the actor attempts to kill anyone, or purposely inflicts or attempts to inflict serious bodily injury.

Article 223. Theft and Related Offenses

SECTION 223.0. DEFINITIONS

In this Article, unless a different meaning plainly is required:

(1) "deprive" means: (a) to withhold property of another permanently or for so extended a period as to appropriate a major portion of its economic value, or with intent to restore only upon payment of reward or other compensation; or (b) to dispose of the property so as to make it unlikely that the owner will recover it.

(2) "financial institution" means a bank, insurance company, credit union, building and loan association, investment trust or other organization held out to the public as a place of deposit of funds or medium of savings or collective investment.

(3) "government" means the United States, any State, county, municipality, or other political unit, or any department, agency or subdivision of any of the foregoing, or any corporation or other association carrying out the functions of government.

(4) "movable property" means property the location of which can be changed, including things growing on, affixed to, or found in land, and documents although the rights represented thereby have no physical location. "Immovable property" is all other property.

(5) "obtain" means: (a) in relation to property, to bring about a transfer or purported transfer of a legal interest in the property, whether to the obtainer or another; or (b) in relation to labor or service, to secure performance thereof.

(6) "property" means anything of value, including real estate, tangible and intangible personal property, contract rights, choses-in-action and other interests in or claims to wealth, admission or transportation tickets, captured or domestic animals, food and drink, electric or other power.

(7) "property of another" includes property in which any person other than the actor has an interest which the actor is not privileged to infringe, regardless of the fact that the actor also has an interest in the property and regardless of the fact that the other person might be precluded from civil recovery because the property was used in an unlawful transaction or was subject to forfeiture as contraband. Property in possession of the actor shall not be deemed property of another who has only a security interest therein, even if legal title is in the creditor pursuant to a conditional sales contract or other security agreement.

SECTION 223.1. CONSOLIDATION OF THEFT OFFENSES; GRADING; PROVISIONS APPLICABLE TO THEFT GENERALLY

(1) *Consolidation of Theft Offenses.* Conduct denominated theft in this Article constitutes a single offense. An accusation of theft may be supported by evidence that it was committed in any manner that would be theft under this Article, notwithstanding the specification of a different manner in the indictment or information, subject only to the power of the Court to ensure fair trial by granting a continuance or other appropriate relief where the conduct of the defense would be prejudiced by lack of fair notice or by surprise.

(2) *Grading of Theft Offenses.*

(a) Theft constitutes a felony of the third degree if the amount involved exceeds $500, or if the property stolen is a firearm, automobile, airplane, motorcycle, motorboat or other motor-propelled vehicle, or in the case of theft by receiving stolen property, if the receiver is in the business of buying or selling stolen property.

(b) Theft not within the preceding paragraph constitutes a misdemeanor, except that if the property was not taken from the person or by threat, or in breach of a fiduciary obligation, and the actor proves by a preponderance of the evidence that the amount involved was less than $50, the offense constitutes a petty misdemeanor.

(c) The amount involved in a theft shall be deemed to be the highest value, by any reasonable standard, of the property or services which the actor stole or attempted to steal. Amounts involved in thefts committed pursuant to one scheme or course of conduct, whether from the same person or several persons, may be aggregated in determining the grade of the offense.

(3) *Claim of Right.* It is an affirmative defense to prosecution for theft that the actor:

(a) was unaware that the property or service was that of another; or

(b) acted under an honest claim of right to the property or service involved or that he had a right to acquire or dispose of it as he did; or

(c) took property exposed for sale, intending to purchase and pay for it promptly, or reasonably believing that the owner, if present, would have consented.

(4) *Theft from Spouse.* It is no defense that theft was from the actor's spouse, except that misappropriation of household and personal effects, or other property normally accessible to both spouses, is theft only if it occurs after the parties have ceased living together.

SECTION 223.2. THEFT BY UNLAWFUL TAKING OR DISPOSITION

(1) *Movable Property.* A person is guilty of theft if he unlawfully takes, or exercises unlawful control over, movable property of another with purpose to deprive him thereof.

(2) *Immovable property.* A person is guilty of theft if he unlawfully transfers immovable property of another or any interest therein with purpose to benefit himself or another not entitled thereto.

SECTION 223.3. THEFT BY DECEPTION

A person is guilty of theft if he purposely obtains property of another by deception. A person deceives if he purposely:

(1) creates or reinforces a false impression, including false impressions as to law, value, intention or other state of mind; but deception as to a person's intention to perform a promise shall not be inferred from the fact alone that he did not subsequently perform the promise; or

(2) prevents another from acquiring information which would affect his judgment of a transaction; or

(3) fails to correct a false impression which the deceiver previously created or reinforced, or which the deceiver knows to be influencing another to whom he stands in a fiduciary or confidential relationship; or

(4) fails to disclose a known lien, adverse claim or other legal impediment to the enjoyment of property which he transfers or encumbers in consideration for the property obtained, whether such impediment is or is not valid, or is or is not a matter of official record.

The term "deceive" does not, however, include falsity as to matters having no pecuniary significance, or puffing by statements unlikely to deceive ordinary persons in the group addressed.

SECTION 223.4. THEFT BY EXTORTION

A person is guilty of theft if he obtains property of another by threatening to:

(1) inflict bodily injury on anyone or commit any other criminal offense; or

(2) accuse anyone of a criminal offense; or

(3) expose any secret tending to subject any person to hatred, contempt or ridicule, or to impair his credit or business repute; or

(4) take or withhold action as an official, or cause an official to take or withhold action; or

(5) bring about or continue a strike, boycott or other collective unofficial action, if the property is not demanded or received for the benefit of the group in whose interest the actor purports to act; or

(6) testify or provide information or withhold testimony or information with respect to another's legal claim or defense; or

(7) inflict any other harm which would not benefit the actor.

It is an affirmative defense to prosecution based on paragraphs (2), (3) or (4) that the property obtained by threat of accusation, exposure, lawsuit or other invocation of official action was honestly claimed as restitution or indemnification for harm done in the circumstances to which such accusation, exposure, lawsuit or other official action relates, or as compensation for property or lawful services.

SECTION 223.5. THEFT OF PROPERTY LOST, MISLAID, OR DELIVERED BY MISTAKE

A person who comes into control of property of another that he knows to have been lost, mislaid, or delivered under a mistake as to the nature or amount of the property or the identity of the recipient is guilty of theft if, with purpose to deprive the owner thereof, he fails to take reasonable measures to restore the property to a person entitled to have it.

SECTION 223.6. RECEIVING STOLEN PROPERTY

(1) *Receiving.* A person is guilty of theft if he purposely receives, retains, or disposes of movable property of another knowing that it has been stolen, or believing that it has probably been stolen, unless the property is received, retained, or disposed with purpose to restore it to the owner. "Receiving" means acquiring possession, control or title, or lending on the security of the property.

(2) *Presumption of Knowledge.* The requisite knowledge or belief is presumed in the case of a dealer who:

(a) is found in possession or control of property stolen from two or more persons on separate occasions; or

(b) has received stolen property in another transaction within the year preceding the transaction charged; or

(c) being a dealer in property of the sort received, acquires it for a consideration which he knows is far below its reasonable value.

"Dealer" means a person in the business of buying or selling goods including a pawnbroker.

SECTION 223.7. THEFT OF SERVICES

(1) A person is guilty of theft if he purposely obtains services which he knows are available only for compensation, by deception or threat, or by false token or other means to avoid payment for the service. "Services" includes labor, professional services, transportation, telephone or other public service, accommodation in hotels, restaurants or elsewhere, admission to exhibitions, use of vehicles or other movable property. Where compensation for service is ordinarily paid immediately upon the rendering for such service, as is the case of hotels and restaurants, refusal to pay or absconding without payment or offer to pay gives rise to a presumption that the service was obtained by deception as to intention to pay.

(2) A person commits theft if, having control over the disposition of services of others, to which he is not entitled, he knowingly diverts such services to his own benefit or to the benefit of another not entitled thereto.

SECTION 223.8. [*Omitted*]

SECTION 223.9. UNAUTHORIZED USE OF AUTOMOBILES AND OTHER VEHICLES

A person commits a misdemeanor if he operates another's automobile, airplane, motorcycle, motorboat, or other motor propelled vehicle without consent of the owner. It is an affirmative defense to prosecution under this Section that the actor reasonably believed that the owner would have consented to the operation had he known of it.

Article 224. Forgery and Fraudulent Practices

SECTION 224.0. DEFINITIONS

In this Article, the definitions given in Section 223.0 apply unless a different meaning plainly is required.

SECTION 224.1. FORGERY

(1) *Definition.* A person is guilty of forgery if, with purpose to defraud or injure anyone, or with knowledge that he is facilitating a fraud or injury to be perpetrated by anyone, the actor:

(a) alters any writing of another without his authority; or

(b) makes, completes, executes, authenticates, issues or transfers any writing so that it purports to be the act of another who did not authorize that act, or to have been executed at a time or place or in a numbered sequence other than was in fact the case, or to be a copy of an original when no such original existed; or

(c) utters any writing which he knows to be forged in a manner specified in paragraphs (a) or (b).

"Writing" includes printing or any other method of recording information, money, coins, tokens, stamps, seals, credit cards, badges, trade-marks, and other symbols of value, right, privilege, or identification.

(2) *Grading.* Forgery is a felony of the second degree if the writing is or purports to be part of an issue of money, securities, postage or revenue stamps, or other instruments issued by the government, or part of an issue of stock, bonds or other instruments representing interests in or claims against any property or enterprise. Forgery is a felony of the third degree if the writing is or purports to be a will, deed, contract, release, commercial instrument, or other document evidencing, creating, transferring, altering, terminating, or otherwise affecting legal relations. Otherwise forgery is a misdemeanor.

SECTIONS 224.2.–224.4. [*Omitted*]

SECTION 224.5. BAD CHECKS

A person who issues or passes a check or similar sight order for the payment of money, knowing that it will not be honored by the drawee, commits a misdemeanor. For the purposes of this Section as well as in any prosecutions for theft committed by means of a bad check, an issuer is presumed to know that the check or order (other than a postdated check or order) would not be paid if:

(1) the issuer had no account with the drawee at the time the check or order was issued; or

(2) payment was refused by the drawee for lack of funds, upon presentation within 30 days after issue, and the issuer failed to make good within 10 days after receiving notice of that refusal.

SECTION 224.6. CREDIT CARDS

A person commits an offense if he uses a credit card for the purpose of obtaining property or serves with knowledge that:

(1) the card is stolen or forged;

(2) the card has been revoked or cancelled; or

(3) for any other reason his use of the card is unauthorized by the issuer.

It is an affirmative defense to prosecution under paragraph (3) if the actor proves by a preponderance of the evidence that he had the purpose and ability to meet all obligations to the issuer arising out of his use of the card. "Credit card" means a writing, or other evidence of an undertaking to pay for property or services delivered or rendered to or upon the order of a designated person or bearer. An offense under this Section is a felony of the third degree if the value of the property or services secured or sought to be secured by means of the credit card exceeds $500; otherwise it is a misdemeanor.

Sections 224.7.–224.14. [*Omitted*]

OFFENSES AGAINST THE FAMILY

Article 230. Offenses Against the Family

Section 230.1. Bigamy and Polygamy

(1) *Bigamy.* A married person is guilty of bigamy, a misdemeanor, if he contracts or purports to contract another marriage, unless at the time of the subsequent marriage:

(a) the actor believes that the prior spouse is dead; or

(b) the actor and the prior spouse have been living apart for five consecutive years throughout which the prior spouse was not known by the actor to be alive; or

(c) a Court has entered a judgment purporting to terminate or annul any prior disqualifying marriage, and the actor does not know that judgment to be invalid; or

(d) the actor reasonably believes that he is legally eligible to remarry.

(2) *Polygamy.* A person is guilty of polygamy, a felony of the third degree, if he marries or cohabits with more than one spouse at a time in purported exercise of the right of plural marriage. The offense is a continuing one until all cohabitation and claim of marriage with more than one spouse terminates. This section does not apply to parties to a polygamous marriage, lawful in the country of which they are residents or nationals, while they are in transit through or temporarily visiting this State.

(3) *Other Party to Bigamous or Polygamous Marriage.* A person is guilty of bigamy or polygamy, as the case may be, if he contracts or purports to contract marriage with another knowing that the other is thereby committing bigamy or polygamy.

Section 230.2. Incest

A person is guilty of incest, a felony of the third degree, if he knowingly marries or cohabits or has sexual intercourse with an ancestor or descendant, a brother or sister of the whole or half blood [or an uncle, aunt, nephew or niece of the whole blood]. "Cohabit" means to live together under the representation or appearance of being married. The relationships referred to herein include blood relationships without regard to legitimacy, and relationship of parent and child by adoption.

Section 230.3. [*Omitted*]

Section 230.4. Endangering Welfare of Children

A parent, guardian, or other person supervising the welfare of a child under 18 commits a misdemeanor if he knowingly endangers the child's welfare by violating a duty of care, protection or support.

SECTION 230.5. PERSISTENT NON-SUPPORT

A person commits a misdemeanor if he persistently fails to provide support which he can provide and which he knows he is legally obliged to provide to a spouse, child or other dependent.

OFFENSES AGAINST PUBLIC ADMINISTRATION

Article 240. Bribery and Corrupt Influence

SECTION 240.0. DEFINITIONS

In Articles 240–243, unless a different meaning plainly is required:

(1) "benefit" means gain or advantage, or anything regarded by the beneficiary as gain or advantage, including benefit to any other person or entity in whose welfare he is interested, but not an advantage promised generally to a group or class of voters as a consequence of public measures which a candidate engages to support or oppose;

(2) "government" includes any branch, subdivision or agency of the government of the State or any locality within it;

(3) "harm" means loss, disadvantage or injury, or anything so regarded by the person affected, including loss, disadvantage or injury to any other person or entity in whose welfare he is interested;

(4) "official proceeding" means a proceeding heard or which may be heard before any legislative, judicial, administrative or other governmental agency or official authorized to take evidence under oath, including any referee, hearing examiner, commissioner, notary or other person taking testimony or deposition in connection with any such proceeding;

(5) "party official" means a person who holds an elective or appointive post in a political party in the United States by virtue of which he directs or conducts, or participates in directing or conducting party affairs at any level of responsibility;

(6) "pecuniary benefit" is benefit in the form of money, property, commercial interests or anything else the primary significance of which is economic gain;

(7) "public servant" means any officer or employee of government, including legislators and judges, and any person participating as juror, advisor, consultant or otherwise, in performing a governmental function; but the term does not include witnesses;

(8) "administrative proceeding" means any proceeding, other than a judicial proceeding, the outcome of which is required to be based on a record or documentation prescribed by law, or in which law or regulation is particularized in application to individuals.

SECTION 240.1. BRIBERY IN OFFICIAL AND POLITICAL MATTERS

A person is guilty of bribery, a felony of the third degree, if he offers, confers or agrees to confer upon another, or solicits, accepts or agrees to accept from another:

(1) any pecuniary benefit as consideration for the recipient's decision, opinion, recommendation, vote or other exercise of discretion as a public servant, party official or voter; or

(2) any benefit as consideration for the recipient's decision, vote, recommendation or other exercise of official discretion in a judicial or administrative proceeding; or

(3) any benefit as consideration for a violation of a known legal duty as public servant or party official.

It is no defense to prosecution under this Section that a person whom the actor sought to influence was not qualified to act in the desired way whether because he had not yet assumed office, or lacked jurisdiction, or for any other reason.

SECTIONS 240.2.–240.7. [*Omitted*]

Article 241. Perjury and Other Falsification in Official Matters

SECTION 241.0. DEFINITIONS

In this Article, unless a different meaning plainly is required:

(1) the definitions give in Section 240.0 apply; and

(2) "statement" means any representation, but includes a representation of opinion, belief or other state of mind only if the representation clearly relates to state of mind apart from or in addition to any facts which are the subject of the representation.

SECTION 241.1. PERJURY

(1) *Offense Defined.* A person is guilty of perjury, a felony of the third degree, if in any official proceeding he makes a false statement under oath or equivalent affirmation, or swears or affirms the truth of a statement previously made, when the statement is material and he does not believe it to be true.

(2) *Materiality.* Falsification is material, regardless of the admissibility of the statement under rules of evidence, if it could have affected the course or outcome of the proceeding. It is no defense that the declarant mistakenly believed the falsification to be immaterial. Whether a falsification is material in a given factual situation is a question of law.

(3) *Irregularities No Defense.* It is not a defense to prosecution under this Section that the oath or affirmation was administered or taken in an irregular manner or that the declarant was not competent to make the statement. A document purporting to be made upon oath or affirmation at any time when the actor presents it as being so verified shall be deemed to have been duly sworn or affirmed.

(4) *Retraction.* No person shall be guilty of an offense under this Section if he retracted the falsification in the course of the proceeding in which it was made before it became manifest that the falsification was or would be exposed and before the falsification substantially affected the proceeding.

(5) *Inconsistent Statements.* When the defendant made inconsistent statements under oath or equivalent affirmation, both having been made within the period of the statute of limitations, the prosecution may proceed by setting forth the inconsistent statements in a single count alleging in the alternative that one or the other was false and not believed by the defendant. In such case it shall not be necessary for the prosecution to prove which statement was false but only that one or the other was false and not believed by the defendant to be true.

(6) *Corroboration.* No person shall be convicted of an offense under this Section where proof of falsity rests solely upon contradiction by testimony of a single person other than the defendant.

SECTIONS 241.2.–241.9. [*Omitted*]

Article 242. Obstructing Governmental Operations; Escapes

SECTIONS 242.0.–242.1. [*Omitted*]

SECTION 242.2. RESISTING ARREST OR OTHER LAW ENFORCEMENT

A person commits a misdemeanor if, for the purpose of preventing a public servant from effecting a lawful arrest or discharging any other duty, the person creates a substantial risk of bodily injury to the public servant or anyone else, or employs means justifying or requiring substantial force to overcome the resistance.

SECTION 242.3. HINDERING APPREHENSION OR PROSECUTION

A person commits an offense if, with purpose to hinder the apprehension, prosecution, conviction or punishment of another for crime, he:

(1) harbors or conceals the other; or

(2) provides or aids in providing a weapon, transportation, disguise or other means of avoiding apprehension or effecting escape; or

(3) conceals or destroys evidence of the crime, or tampers with a witness, informant, document or other source of information, regardless of its admissibility in evidence; or

(4) warns the other of impending discovery or apprehension, except that this paragraph does not apply to a warning given in connection with an effort to bring another into compliance with law; or

(5) volunteers false information to a law enforcement officer.

The offense is a felony of the third degree if the conduct which the actor knows has been charged or is liable to be charged against the person aided would constitute a felony of the first or second degree. Otherwise it is a misdemeanor.

SECTIONS 242.4.–242.5. [*Omitted*]

SECTION 242.6. ESCAPE

(1) *Escape.* A person commits an offense if he unlawfully removes himself from official detention or fails to return to official detention following temporary leave granted for a specific purpose or limited period. "Offi-

cial detention" means arrest, detention in any facility for custody of persons under charge or conviction of crime or alleged or found to be delinquent, detention for extradition or deportation, or any other detention for law enforcement purposes; but "official detention" does not include supervision of probation or parole, or constraint incidental to release on bail.

(2) *Permitting or Facilitating Escape.* A public servant concerned in detention commits an offense if he knowingly or recklessly permits an escape. Any person who knowingly causes or facilitates an escape commits an offense.

(3) *Effect of Legal Irregularity in Detention.* Irregularity in bringing about or maintaining detention, or lack of jurisdiction of the committing or detaining authority, shall not be a defense to prosecution under this Section if the escape is from a prison or other custodial facility or from detention pursuant to commitment by official proceedings. In the case of other detention, irregularity or lack of jurisdiction shall be a defense only if:

(a) the escape involved no substantial risk of harm to the person or property of anyone other than the detainee; or

(b) the detaining authority did not act in good faith under color of law.

(4) *Grading of Offenses.* An offense under this Section is a felony of the third degree where:

(a) the actor was under arrest for or detained on a charge of felony or following conviction of crime; or

(b) the actor employs force, threat, deadly weapon or other dangerous instrumentality to effect the escape; or

(c) a public servant concerned in detention of persons convicted of crime purposely facilitates or permits an escape from a detention facility.

Otherwise an offense under this section is a misdemeanor.

SECTIONS 242.7.–242.8. [*Omitted*]

Article 243. Abuse of Office [*Omitted*]

OFFENSES AGAINST PUBLIC ORDER AND DECENCY

Article 250. Riot, Disorderly Conduct, and Related Offenses

SECTION 250.1. Riot; Failure to Disperse

(1) *Riot.* A person is guilty of riot, a felony of the third degree, if he participates with [two] or more others in a course of disorderly conduct:

(a) with the purpose to commit or facilitate the commission of a felony or misdemeanor;

(b) with purpose to prevent or coerce official action; or

(c) when the actor or any other participant to the knowledge of the actor uses or plans to use a firearm or other deadly weapon.

(2) *Failure of Disorderly Persons to Disperse upon Official Order.* Where [three] or more persons are participating in a course of disorderly

conduct likely to cause substantial harm or serious inconvenience, annoyance or alarm, a peace officer or other public servant engaged in executing or enforcing the law may order the participants and others in the immediate vicinity to disperse. A person who refuses or knowingly fails to obey such order commits a misdemeanor.

SECTION 250.2. DISORDERLY CONDUCT

(1) *Offense Defined.* A person is guilty of disorderly conduct if, with purpose to cause public inconvenience, annoyance or alarm, or recklessly creating a risk thereof, he:

(a) engages in fighting or threatening, or in violent or tumultuous behavior; or

(b) makes unreasonable noise or offensively coarse utterance, gesture or display, or addresses abusive language to any person present; or

(c) creates a hazardous or physically offensive condition by any act which serves no legitimate purpose of the actor.

"Public" means affecting or likely to affect persons in a place to which the public or a substantial group has access; among the places included are highways, transport facilities, schools, prisons, apartment houses, places of business or amusement, or any neighborhood.

(2) *Grading.* An offense under this section is a petty misdemeanor if the actor's purpose is to cause substantial harm or serious inconvenience, or if he persists in disorderly conduct after reasonable warning or request to desist. Otherwise disorderly conduct is a violation.

SECTIONS 250.3.–250.4. [*Omitted*]

SECTION 250.5. PUBLIC DRUNKENNESS; DRUG INCAPACITATION

A person is guilty of an offense if he appears in any public place manifestly under the influence of alcohol, narcotics or other drug, not therapeutically administered, to the degree that he may endanger himself or other persons or property, or annoy persons in his vicinity. An offense under this Section constitutes a petty misdemeanor if the actor has been convicted hereunder twice before within a period of one year. Otherwise the offense constitutes a violation.

SECTION 250.6. LOITERING OR PROWLING

A person commits a violation if he loiters or prowls in a place, at a time, or in a manner not usual for law-abiding individuals under circumstances that warrant alarm for the safety of persons or property in the vicinity. Among the circumstances which may be considered in determining whether such alarm is warranted is the fact that the actor takes flight upon appearance of a peace officer, refuses to identify himself, or manifestly endeavors to conceal himself or any object. Unless flight by the actor or other circumstance makes it impracticable, a peace officer shall prior to any arrest for an offense under this Section afford the actor an opportunity to dispel any alarm which would otherwise be warranted, by requesting him to identify himself and explain his presence and conduct. No person shall be convicted of an offense under this Section if the peace officer did not comply with the preceding sentence, or if it appears at trial that the explanation given by the actor was true and, if believed by the peace officer at the time, would have dispelled the alarm.

SECTIONS 250.7.–250.12. [*Omitted*]

Article 251. Public Indecency

SECTION 251.1. OPEN LEWDNESS

A person commits a petty misdemeanor if he does any lewd act which he knows is likely to be observed by others who would be affronted or alarmed.

SECTION 251.2. PROSTITUTION AND RELATED OFFENSES

(1) *Prostitution.* A person is guilty of prostitution, a petty misdemeanor, if he or she:

(a) is an inmate of a house of prostitution or otherwise engages in sexual activity as a business; or

(b) loiters in or within view of any public place for the purpose of being hired to engage in sexual activity.

"Sexual activity" includes homosexual and other deviate sexual relations. A "house of prostitution" is any place where prostitution or promotion of prostitution is regularly carried on by one person under the control, management or supervision of another. An "inmate" is a person who engages in prostitution in or through the agency of a house of prostitution. "Public place" means any place to which the public or any substantial group thereof has access.

(2) *Promoting Prostitution.* A person who knowingly promotes prostitution of another commits a misdemeanor or felony as provided in Subsection (3). The following acts shall, without limitation of the foregoing, constitute promoting prostitution:

(a) owning, controlling, managing, supervising or otherwise keeping, alone or in association with others, a house of prostitution or a prostitution business; or

(b) procuring an inmate for a house of prostitution or a place in a house of prostitution for one who would be an inmate; or

(c) encouraging, inducing, or otherwise purposely causing another to become or remain a prostitute; or

(d) soliciting a person to patronize a prostitute; or

(e) procuring a prostitute for a patron; or

(f) transporting a person into or within this state with purpose to promote that person's engaging in prostitution, or procuring or paying for transportation with that purpose; or

(g) leasing or otherwise permitting a place controlled by the actor, alone or in association with others, to be regularly used for prostitution or the promotion of prostitution, or failure to make reasonable effort to abate such use by ejecting the tenant, notifying law enforcement authorities, or other legally available means; or

(h) soliciting, receiving, or agreeing to receive any benefit for doing or agreeing to do anything forbidden by this Subsection.

(3) *Grading of Offenses Under Subsection (2).* An offense under Subsection (2) constitutes a felony of the third degree if:

(a) the offense falls within paragraph (a), (b) or (c) of Subsection (2); or

(b) the actor compels another to engage in or promote prostitution; or

(c) the actor promotes prostitution of a child under 16, whether or not he is aware of the child's age; or

(d) the actor promotes prostitution of his wife, child, ward or any person for whose care, protection or support he is responsible.

Otherwise the offense is a misdemeanor.

(4) *Presumption From Living off Prostitutes.* A person, other than the prostitute or the prostitute's minor child or other legal dependent incapable of self-support, who is supported in whole or substantial part by the proceeds of prostitution is presumed to be knowingly promoting prostitution in violation of Subsection (2).

(5) *Patronizing Prostitutes.* A person commits a violation if he hires a prostitute to engage in sexual activity with him, or if he enters or remains in a house of prostitution for the purpose of engaging in sexual activity.

(6) *Evidence.* On the issue whether a place is a house of prostitution the following shall be admissible evidence: its general repute; the repute of the persons who reside in or frequent the place; the frequency, timing and duration of visits by non-residents. Testimony of a person against his spouse shall be admissible to prove offenses under this Section.

SECTION 251.3.–251.4. [*Omitted*]

PART III. TREATMENT AND CORRECTION [*Omitted*]
PART IV. ORGANIZATION OF CORRECTION [*Omitted*]

Index

†

0–314–03791–8

90000

9 780314 037916